From Beginning of Oral Language	**The Oral Tradition** Folktales Mythology Legends
1400s	**Early Books** Hornbooks Caxton's Printing Press—1476
1500s	**Chapbooks Introduced** "Jack the Giant Killer"
1600s	**The Puritan Influence** *Spiritual Milk for Boston Babes in either England, Drawn from the Breasts of Both Testaments for Their Souls' Nourishment* John Bunyan's *Pilgrim's Progress*
1693	**View of Childhood Changes** John Locke's *Some Thoughts Concerning Education*
1698	**First Fairy Tales Written for Children** Charles Perrault's *Tales of Mother Goose*
1719	**Great Adventure Stories** Daniel Defoe's *Robinson Crusoe* Jonathan Swift's *Gulliver's Travels* (1726)
1744	**Children's Literature: A True Beginning** John Newbery's *A Little Pretty Pocket Book* and *History of Little Goody Two Shoes*
1762	**Children Should Be Guided in Their Search for Knowledge** Jean Jacques Rousseau's *Emile*
1789	**Poetry About Children** William Blake's *Songs of Innocence*
Early 1800s	**The Romantic Movement in Europe** The Grimms' *German Popular Stories* including "Cinderella" and "Hansel and Gretel" Hans Christian Andersen's *Fairy Tales Told for Children*
1800s	**Illustrators Make Their Impact on Children's Books** Walter Crane's *The House That Jack Built* (1865) Randolph Caldecott's *The History of John Gilpin* (1878) Kate Greenaway's *Under the Window* (1878)
1860	**The Victorian Influence** Charlotte Yonge's *The Daisy Chain* and *The Clever Woman of the Family*

(continued on back endsheet)

THROUGH THE EYES OF A CHILD

An Introduction to Children's Literature

THROUGH THE EYES OF A CHILD

An Introduction to Children's Literature

Second Edition

DONNA E. NORTON

Texas A&M University

Merrill Publishing Company
A Bell & Howell Information Company
Columbus   Toronto   London   Melbourne

About the cover: Collage, a technique in which various materials are pasted to a picture surface, has been successfully introduced to children's literature by Jeannie Baker, Ezra Jack Keats, Leo Lionni, and other artists. Children respond readily to the imaginative use of materials and the rich texture apparent in the works of these illustrators. Inspired by collage in children's books, cover artist Cathy Watterson and a team of meticulous snippers and stitchers transformed the patterns and textures of everyday materials—fabric, tissue, lace, yarn, and wallpaper—into the fascinating world that literature offers to a child. This text discusses collage as an illustration technique and as an aid in promoting children's aesthetic development.

Published by Merrill Publishing Company
A Bell & Howell Information Company
Columbus, Ohio 43216

This book was set in Usherwood.

Administrative Editor: Jeff Johnston
Developmental Editor: Amy Marsh
Production Coordinator: Rebecca Bobb
Cover Designer: Cathy Watterson
Text Designers: Cynthia Brunk and Ann Mirels

Library of Congress Catalog Card Number: 86–62963
International Standard Book Number: 0–675–20725–8
Printed in the United States of America
1 2 3 4 5 6 7 8 9–92 91 90 89 88 87

FOLLOWING THE COM-pletion of her doctorate at the University of Wisconsin, Madison, Donna E. Norton joined the College of Education faculty at Texas A&M University where she teaches courses in children's literature, language arts, and reading. Dr. Norton is the 1981–1982 recipient of the Texas A&M Faculty Distinguished Achievement Award in Teaching. This award is given "in recognition and appreciation of ability, personality, and methods which have resulted in distinguished achievements in the teaching and the inspiration of students." She is listed in *Who's Who of American Women*.

Dr. Norton is the author of two books in addition to this volume: *The Effective Teaching of Language Arts*, 2d ed. and *Language Arts Activities for Children*, 2d ed. She is on the editorial board of several journals and is a frequent contributor to journals and presenter at professional conferences. The focus of her current research is multiethnic literature and comparative education. The multiethnic research includes a longitudinal study of multiethnic literature in classroom settings. This research is supported by grants from the Meadows Foundation and the Texas A&M Research Association. In conjunction with the research in comparative education, she developed a graduate course that enables students to study children's literature and reading instruction in England and Scotland.

Prior to her college teaching experience, Dr. Norton was an elementary teacher in River Falls, Wisconsin and in Madison, Wisconsin. She was a Language Arts/Reading Consultant for federally funded kindergarten through adult basic education programs. In this capacity she developed, provided inservice instruction, and evaluated kindergarten programs, summer reading and library programs, remedial reading programs, learning disability programs for middle school children, elementary and secondary literature programs for the gifted, and diagnostic and intervention programs for reading disabled adults. Dr. Norton's continuing concern for literature programs results in frequent consultations with educators from various disciplines, librarians, and school administrators and teachers.

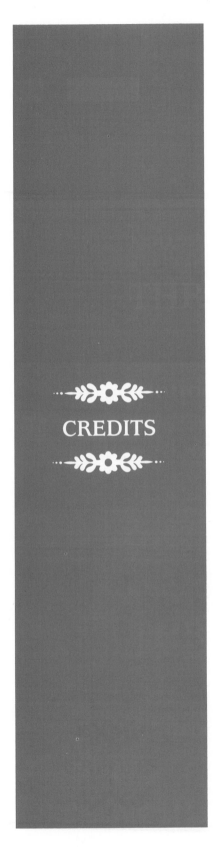

CREDITS

garet K. McElderry Book. (New York: Atheneum Publishers, 1976) Reprinted with the permission of Atheneum Publishers.

Page 344, from "Garbage Delight" in *Garbage Delight* by Dennis Lee. Text copyright © Dennis Lee, 1077. Reprinted by permission of Houghton Mifflin Company and Macmillan Co. of Canada Ltd.

Page 345, text of "Frosted-Window World" from *In One Door and Out the Other: A Book of Poems* by Aileen Fisher. (Thomas Y. Crowell) Copyright © 1969 by Aileen Fisher. By permission of Thomas Y. Crowell, Publishers.

Page 345, poem from Byrd Baylor, *The Desert Is Theirs*. Text copyright © 1975 by Byrd Baylor (New York: Charles Scribner's Sons). Reprinted with the permission of Charles Scribner's Sons.

Page 346, poem from Ann Atwood, *Fly with the Wind, Flow with the Water*. Copyright © 1979 by Ann Atwood (New York: Charles Scribner's Sons, 1979). Reprinted with the permission of Charles Scribner's Sons.

Page 346, text of "Change" from *River Winding: Poems by Charlotte Zolotow*. Copyright © 1970 by Charlotte Zolotow. By permission of Thomas Y. Crowell, Publishers.

Page 347, from *Moonsong Lullaby* by Jamake Highwater (New York: Lothrop, Lee & Shepard, 1981).

Page 347, poem from Myra Cohn Livingston, "I Haven't Learned to Whistle," from *O Sliver of Liver and Other Poems*. Copyright © 1979 by Myra Cohn Livingston. A Margaret K. McElderry Book. Reprinted with the permission of Atheneum Publishers.

Page 348, poem "Barefoot" from *Still More Small Poems* by Valerie Worth. Copyright © 1976, 1977, 1978 by Valerie Worth. Reprinted by permission of Farrar, Straus and Giroux, Inc.

Page 348, poem "The Spelling Test" reprinted by permission of Four Winds Press, a Division of Scholastic Inc., from *The Covered Bridge House and Other Poems* by Kaye Starbird. Copyright © 1979 by Kaye Starbird Jennison.

Page 348, poem "The Grasshopper" from *One at a Time* by David McCord. Copyright © 1952 by David McCord. By permission of Little, Brown and Company.

Page 349, poem "Dreams" from *The Dream Keeper* by Langston Hughes (New York: Knopf, 1932).

Page 350, poem "Teenagers" from *Waiting to Waltz: A Childhood* by Cynthia Rylant (Scarsdale, N.Y.: Bradbury, 1984).

Page 351, poem "The Furry Ones" from *Feathered Ones and Furry* by Aileen Fisher. Copyright © 1971 by Aileen Fisher. By permission of Thomas Y. Crowell, Publishers.

Page 352, poem "Teeny, Tiny Ghost" from Lilian Moore, *See My Lovely Poison Ivy*. Copyright © 1972, 1975 by Lilian Moore (New York: Atheneum, 1975). Reprinted with the permission of Atheneum Publishers.

Photos

All photos copyrighted by the individuals or companies listed.
Constance Brown, p. 252
Virginia Burroughs, p. 514
Tim Chapman, p. 548
Johan Elbers, p. 228
Janet Gagnon, p. 431
Jack Hamilton, p. 356
Michael Hayman/Corn's Photo Service, pp. 363, 553
Hilary Masters, p. 150
Tom McDonough, p. 414
Irma D. McNelia, p. 366
Dan O'Connor, p. 126
Charles Quinlan, pp. 181, 546
Ann E. Schullstrom, pp. 175, 256, 302, 314, 481, 610
Paul M. Shrock, p. 490
Strix Pix, pp. 308, 494, 613, 616
Thomas Victor, p. 294

Illustrations

Pages 27, 92, 113, 232, 280, 339, and 397 courtesy of Lilly Library, Indiana University, Bloomington, Indiana
Page 57, advertisement appeared in *Jo's Boys and How They Turned Out* by Louisa M. Alcott. From the collection of Julia Estadt
Page 145, from *The Original Mother Goose's Melody*, as first issued by John Newbery, of London, about A.D. 1760. Reproduced in facsimile from the edition as reprinted by Isaiah Thomas, of Worcester, Mass, about A.D. 1785. Reissued by Singing Tree Press, Detroit, 1969.
Page 456, illustration by Richard Westall. *Do you dispute me slave!* From Sir Walter Scott, *Ivanhoe*, Vol. 1. Edinburgh, 1820. Frontispiece. Rare Books and Manuscripts Division. The New York Public Library, Astor, Lenox and Tilden Foundations

Page 504, reproduced from *The Story of Mankind* by Hendrik Willem van Loon, by permission of Liveright Publishing Corporation. Copyright 1921, 1926 by Boni & Liveright, Inc. Copyright renewed 1948 by Helen C. van Loon. Copyright renewed 1954 by Liveright Publishing Corporation. Copyright 1936, 1938, 1951, 1967 by Liveright Publishing Corporation. Copyright © 1972 by Henry B. van Loon and Gerard W. van Loon
Page 610, Figure 12–1, courtesy OCLC, Inc., Dublin, Ohio

Development of Textbook Concept and Organization

Martha Barclay, Northern Iowa Area Community College; Delorys Blume, University of Central Florida; Robert O. Boord, University of Nevada, Las Vegas; N. Boraks, Virginia Commonwealth University; Maxine Burress, University of Wisconsin; Gertrude B. Camper, Roanoke College; Delila Caselli, Sioux Falls College; Virginia Chirbart, College of St. Benedict; Eileen Cunningham, St. Thomas Aquinas College; Douglas L. Decker, Virginia State University; Lois Elendine, Oklahoma Christian College; Marjorie L. Farmer, Pembroke State University; Kay E. Fisher, Simpson College; E. W. Freeman, LeMoyne-Owen College; Margaret Gunn, Delta State University; C. Hooker-Schrader, Longwood College; Louise M. Hulst, Dordt College; Betty Kingery, Westmar College; Eleanor W. Lofquist, Western Carolina University; Mary Maness, Bartlesville Wesleyan College; Charles Matthews, College of Charleston; Rita E. Meadows, Lakeland, Florida; D. D. Miller, University of Missouri—St. Louis; Dorothy Z. Mills, East Carolina University; Martha L. Morris, Indiana Central University; Joan S. Nist, Auburn University; Olga M. Santora, State University of New York; Ronnie Sheppard, Georgia College; Richard J. Sherry, Asbury College; Sidney W. Shnayer, California State University at Chico; Dorothy Spethmann, Dakota State College; John Stinson, Jr., Miami, Florida; Emilie P. Sullivan, University of Arkansas; Lola Jiles Sullivan, Florida International University; Marylin C. Teele, Loma Linda University; Barbara Townsend, Salisbury State College; Marion Turkish, William Paterson College; Linda Western, University of Wisconsin—Milwaukee; Marilyn Yoder, Grace College; Collette Zerba, Cardinal Stritch College.

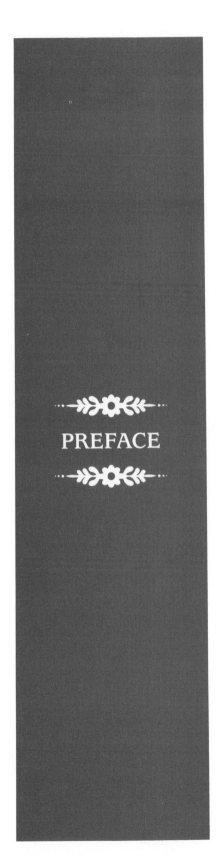

PREFACE

THIS TEXT IS INTENDED for any adult who is interested in evaluating, selecting, and sharing children's literature. Its focus and organization are designed for children's literature classes taught in the departments of English, Education, and Library Science. *Through the Eyes of a Child* is written in the hope that adults who work with children and literature will discover and share with children the enchantment in books and will help children develop a lifetime appreciation for literature and a respect for our literary heritage. It is my hope that my own love for literature and enthusiasm for books will be transmitted to the reader of this text.

NEW TO THE SECOND EDITION

A major concern in preparing this edition, as well as the first, was selecting from the thousands of books available. Between the two editions, I personally read over seven thousand books. The ones discussed in this second edition were chosen for their quality of literature and to create a balance between new books and those that have passed the test of time or are considered classics. As in the first edition, approximately twenty-five percent of the books included in each chapter were published within the two years preceding the publication of *Through the Eyes of a Child.* During the preparation of the second edition, each chapter was carefully screened for books that are no longer in print. The majority of these books have been replaced with selections that reflect current copyright dates. A few out-of-print books are included when they are the best examples for a specific discussion or when they are just too good to be ignored. Most of these books are still available in libraries.

Not only has the entire book been updated, but some chapters have also been reorganized to improve the clarity and exposition of topics. A number of important new topics are introduced, including non-English children's literature, research and children's literature, critics and literary criticism, children's responses to illustrations, lyric poetry, trends in realistic fiction, and information books about the human body. Other new material focuses on the ways in which children's books address such current topics as international terrorism and living in our nuclear age. Finally, the Instructor's Manual to accompany the text has been updated and expanded to included a full test bank.

HIGHLIGHTS

Two-Part Chapter Organization

This unique feature of the text, beginning in chapter five and extending through chapter twelve, places the characteristics, history, and titles of each genre next to the appropriate strategies for involving children in that genre. Thus, genre and involvement can be taught together, sequentially, or independently. The involvement strategies have been field tested at the university, elementary, and secondary school levels, and during inservice training for teachers and librarians.

Emphasis on Criteria for Book Evaluation and Selection

Each chapter builds a model for evaluating and selecting books based upon literary and artistic characteristics that readers can then use themselves. The importance of child development in this process is also stressed.

Issues

Each chapter identifies important issues that are related to the genre or content of the chapter and are designed to introduce teachers, librarians, and parents to current concerns. Most of these issue highlights are referenced to current periodicals and professional journals and are written to encourage readers' contemplation and further investigation. For this reason, they are presented as open-ended discussions.

Flashbacks

Also included in each chapter, these illustrated features highlight important people, works, and events in the history of children's literature. They are designed to provide a more complete understanding of the genre.

Through the Eyes of . . .

Beginning with chapter four, each chapter includes a personal statement by a well-known author or illustrator, providing a special glimpse into that person's "view" of the creation of children's books.

Annotated Bibliographies of Children's Literature

These extensive bibliographies include readability by grade level and interest by age range.

Text Teaching Aids

Each part of the two-part chapters concludes with suggested activities designed to either fos-

ter adult understanding of or children's appreciation for the genre. Special web diagrams are used to highlight the inter-relationships in literature, the many values of literature, and the multiple learning possibilities available. Webs are also used to illustrate the development of instructional activities and oral discussions about literature. The webbing process, according to my students, helps them clarify concepts, visualize relationships, and identify numerous values for sharing literature with children.

Chapter on Multiethnic Literature

This material was organized as a separate chapter to make it more accessible to librarians, teachers, and students of children's literature. Information about the criteria for selection, the choice of literature, and the development of literature-related activities resulted from longitudinal research that was partially supported by Texas A&M Research Association and the Meadows Foundation of Dallas, Texas.

Annual Update

Due to the many additions and changes in this field, I will prepare for adopters of *Through the Eyes of a Child* a list of the new children's books and award winners and the new professional publications, and a discussion of current issues or new developments in the field. This free update will be distributed by the publisher when requested by instructors who have adopted the text for their class.

ACKNOWLEDGMENTS

A massive project such as writing and publishing a children's literature text would not be possible without the enthusiasm, critical evaluation, suggestions, and hard work of many people. My appreciation is extended to my children's literature students, teachers, and librarians who discussed books with me, created enthusiasm for books, and shared books with children. The multiethnic literature chapter was enhanced by research supported by the Meadows Foundation; work by research associates Sue Mohrmann, Blanche Lawson, and Charmaine Bradley; field testing in the Bryan, Texas, schools; teachers and librarians across Texas who took part in the research; and support by curriculum coordinators Barbara Erwin and Dana Marable. The children's librarians at the Houston Public Library and the Houston Library archives deserve a special thank-you. They discussed reactions to books, searched for hard-to-locate literature, and allowed me to check out hundreds of books at one time. The writing of a text also requires typing expertise; the long hours of work performed by Loretta Johnson, Carolyn Kemp, and Cindy Warren made a finished manuscript possible.

The children's librarians at the Public Library of Columbus and Franklin County; Grandview, Ohio, Public Library; Bexley, Ohio, Public Library; and Westerville, Ohio, Public Library provided much assistance in locating numerous children's books.

I would like to thank the people at Merrill—Amy Marsh, developmental editor, who spent a great deal of time polishing and tying together many of the countless loose ends of this project; Rebecca Bobb, production editor, for her patience and persistence during the production phase of this revision; Cathy Watterson for the beautiful cover and chapter-opening artwork; Cindy Brunk and Ann Mirels for the attractive text design; Jo-Anne Weaver for the effective promotion coordination; Ken Montavon for the excellent advertising support; Jeff Johnston, executive editor; and Tim McEwen, chief executive editor.

My sincere appreciation is also extended to Patricia Clapp, Beverly Cleary, Tomie de Paola, Jean Fritz, Virginia Hamilton, Jamake Highwater, Madeleine L'Engle, Jack Prelutsky, Martin and Alice Provensen, and Jack Denton Scott for their contribution to this text. The insights, personal statements, and viewpoints of these authors and illustrators are especially rewarding in a textbook about children's literature.

I wish to thank Jane Madsen of Pennsylvania State University, Jerry Watson of the University of Iowa, John Senatore of the University of Southern Colorado, Shirley Kukenbill of the University of Texas, and Day Ann McClenathan of the State University of New York at Buffalo for their suggestions for improving the first edition of *Through the Eyes of a Child.* Their efforts have been invaluable in ensuring an accurate, timely, and lively text. My gratitude also goes to Sylvia Vardell of the University of Houston for her work on updating, revising, and expanding the Instructor's Resource Manual that accompanies the text.

Finally, I wish to dedicate this book to my husband, Verland, and my children, Saundra and Bradley, for their constant support, immense understanding, and insightful viewpoints.

Donna E. Norton

CONTENTS
IN
BRIEF

CONTENTS

12
NONFICTION: BIOGRAPHIES AND INFORMATIONAL BOOKS 562

SPECIAL FEATURES

THROUGH THE EYES OF A CHILD

An Introduction to Children's Literature

1

The Child and Children's Literature

VALUES OF LITERATURE FOR CHILDREN

PROMOTING CHILD DEVELOPMENT
THROUGH LITERATURE

LITERATURE ENTICES, MOTIVATES, AND instructs. It opens doors of discovery and provides endless hours of adventure and enjoyment. Children need not be tied to the whims of television programming or wait in line at the neighborhood theater in order to follow a rabbit down a hole into Wonderland, save a wild herd of mustangs from slaughter, fight in the Revolutionary War, grow up on a homestead in frontier America, learn about a new hobby that will provide many enjoyable hours, or model themselves after real-life people of accomplishment. These experiences are available at any time on the nearest bookshelf.

Adults have a responsibility in helping children become aware of the enchantment in books. As Bernice Cullinan (7) has suggested, "Books can play a significant role in the life of the young child, but the extent to which they do depends entirely upon adults. Adults are responsible for providing books and transmitting the literary heritage contained in nursery rhymes, traditional tales, and great novels" (p. 1).

As you read this book you will gain knowledge about literature so that you can share stimulating books and book-related experiences with children. This chapter introduces the various values of sharing literature with children in order to help

ISSUE

❈

The Publisher's Responsibility in a Pluralistic Society

ROBERT F. BAKER, writing from a publisher's viewpoint, presents literature students with a thoughtful overview of the multiple issues facing publishers of children's literature and other reading materials for children.[1] Most Americans, Baker asserts, believe that reading materials used with children should reflect the pluralistic, multicultural, multivalued mosaic of American life. While many people agree that a literature program should be nonracist and nonsexist, offer children insights into varied patterns of family life, allow children to experience literature of many kinds, and introduce them to a rich and diverse heritage, other important issues are related to the execution of these guidelines. Representative concerns mentioned by Baker include the following: (1) What is the range of skin colors that must appear in illustrations to avoid giving children the impression that all blacks look alike?

(2) How does one convey the range of occupational choices open to women? (3) How does one cope with mothers who are unhappy with the current portrait of the American family? (4) How should one determine what is excessive violence? (5) Should the Polynesian boy in *Call It Courage* be seen in his loincloth or should he be fully clothed? (6) How should one handle the demands for greater reliance on standard English? Additional sensitive issues identified by Baker for today's publishers include attitudes toward American values and ideals, theories of evolution and creation, viewpoints on business and labor, relationships between parents and children, treatments of religion, and political attitudes. Baker concludes that "in the final analysis, the publisher must make the final decision, weighing conflicting recommendations from a variety of well-meaning and well-informed sources."

[1]Baker, Robert F. "A Publisher Views the Development and Selection of Reading Programs." In *Indoctrinate or Educate?* edited by Thomas C. Hatcher and Lawrence G. Erickson, pp. 25–30. Newark, Del.: International Reading Association, 1979.

you search for books that can play a significant role in children's lives. It also focuses on the importance of considering children's stages of language, cognitive, personality, and social development when selecting children's literature and suggests books that exemplify children's needs during different stages of the maturing process.

VALUES OF LITERATURE FOR CHILDREN

Following a rabbit down a rabbit hole or walking through a wardrobe into a mythical kingdom sounds like a lot of fun. There is nothing wrong with admitting that one of the primary values of literature is pure pleasure, and there is nothing wrong with turning to a book to escape or to enjoy an adventure with new or old book friends. Time is enriched, not wasted, when children look at beautiful pictures and imagine themselves in new places. When children discover enjoyment in books, they develop favorable attitudes toward them that usually extend into a lifetime of appreciation. Doris Roettger (17) offers a strong rationale for allowing children many opportunities to read for enjoyment. In interviewing a large number of children, she asked them how school and reading could be made more enjoyable. The students recommended that (1) children be given a chance to read books each day, (2) teachers ask children about their interests and help them find books on those subjects, and (3) teachers tell children about books and give them time to talk about books with each other and with the teacher. This is good advice; librarians, teachers, parents, or anyone who works with children should heed it. All children should have opportunities to read or to listen to books being read each day.

While the primary value of literature may be pleasure, other benefits may be gained from books. They are the major means of transmitting our literary heritage from one generation to the next. Each new generation can enjoy the words of Lewis Carroll, Louisa May Alcott, Robert Louis Stevenson, and Mark Twain, and, through the work of storytellers such as the Brothers Grimm, can also experience the folktales originally transmitted through the oral tradition.

Literature plays a strong role in helping us understand and value our cultural heritage as well. Developing positive attitudes toward our own and other cultures is necessary for both social and personal development. Carefully selected literature can illustrate the contributions and values of the many cultures found in the child's world. This is especially critical in fostering an appreciation of the heritage of the ethnic minorities in American society. A positive self-concept is not possible unless we have respect for others as well as for ourselves; literature can contribute considerably toward this understanding.

The vicarious experiences of literature result in personal development as well as pleasure. Without literature, most children could not relive the European colonists' experiences as they cross the ocean and shape a new country in North America; they could not experience the loneliness and fear of a fight for survival on an isolated island; they could not travel to distant places in the galaxy. Historical fiction provides children with an opportunity to live in the past. Science fiction allows them to speculate about the "what ifs" of the future. Contemporary realistic fiction encourages them to experience relationships with the people and environment of today. Because children can learn from literature how other people handle their problems, sharing experiences with the characters in books can help children deal with similar problems, as well as understand other people's feelings.

Another value of literature is illustrated by a television interview with a high school sophomore who was a promising young scientist. When asked how he had become so knowledgeable, the boy replied, "I read a lot." For him, books had opened doors to new knowledge and expanded interests. Don't educators and parents want such doors opened for all children by the many books available? Informational books relay new knowledge about virtually every topic imaginable and at all levels of difficulty. Biographies and autobiographies tell about the people who gained this knowledge or made discoveries. Photographs and illustrations show the wonders of nature or depict the step-by-step process required to master a new hobby. Realistic stories from a specific time bring history to life. The cognitive development of even very young children may be stimulated through the use of concept books that illustrate colors, numbers, shapes, and sizes.

No discussion about the values of literature can be concluded without stressing the role literature plays in nurturing and expanding the imagination. Books take children into imaginative worlds that stimulate additional creative experiences as children tell or write their own stories and interact with each other during creative drama inspired by what they have read. Both well-written literature and the illustrations found in picture storybooks can stimulate children's aesthetic development. Children enjoy and evaluate these illustrations, and may explore artistic media by creating illustrations of their own.

Clearly, literature and literature-related activities nurture child development in myriad ways.

PROMOTING CHILD DEVELOPMENT THROUGH LITERATURE

Research in child development has identified recognizable stages in the language, cognitive, personality, and social development of children. All children do not progress through these stages at the same rate, but all children do pass through each stage as they mature. Researchers associate developmental stages with children of certain ages, but these connections are approximate, not absolute. Developmental characteristics apply to many, but not all, children in a particular age group. The general characteristics of children at each developmental stage provide clues for selecting appropriate literature. Certain books can benefit children during a particular stage of development, helping them progress to the next stage. Understanding the types and stages of child development is useful to anyone who works with children. Charts 1-1 through 1-4 list the characteristics of average children during each stage of language, cognitive, personality, and social development, respectively; summarize the educational implications of those characteristics; and suggest literature selections that can be used to further the development of children who demonstrate those characteristics.

Language Development

Preschool Children. During their first few years, children show dramatic changes in language ability. Most children learn language very rapidly. They usually speak their first words at about one year of age; at about eighteen months, they begin to put words together in two-word combinations called *telegraphic speech.* Speech during this stage of language development is made up mostly of nouns, verbs, and adjectives and usually contains no prepositions, articles, auxiliary verbs, or pronouns. When children say "pretty flower" or "all gone milk," they are using telegraphic speech. The number of different two-word combinations increases slowly, then shows a sudden upsurge around age two.

Martin Braine (5) began recording the speech of three eighteen-month-old children. He reported that the cumulative number of different two-word combinations for one child in successive months was 14, 24, 54, 89, 350, 1,400, 2,500+. This is a rapid expansion of speech in a very short time.

A longitudinal study conducted by Roger Brown (6) demonstrated how widely the rate of language development can vary from child to child. For example, one child successfully used six grammatical morphemes (the smallest meaning-bearing unit in a word) by the age of two years, three months; a second child did not master them until the age of three years, six months; and a third was four years old before reaching an equivalent stage in language development.

Speech usually becomes more complex by age three, when most children have added adverbs, pronouns, prepositions, and additional adjectives to their vocabularies. Children also enjoy playing with the sounds of words at this stage of language development. By age four, they produce grammatically correct sentences. This stage is a questioning one during which language is used to ask "why" and "how."

Literature and literature-related experiences can encourage language development in preschool children. Book experiences in the home, library, and/or nursery school can help children use language to discover their world, identify and name actions and objects, gain more complex speech, and enjoy the wonder of language. Many children first experience literature through picture books and Mother Goose rhymes. As these books are read to children or the pictures are discussed, children add new words to their vocabularies. Picture books help them give meaning to their expanding vocabularies. For example, children who are just learning to identify their hands and other parts of their bodies may find these parts in drawings of children. Parents of very young children may share Helen Oxenbury's excellent "Baby Board Books." *Dressing*, for example, includes a picture of a baby's clothing, followed by a picture of the child dressed in those items. The illustrations are sequentially developed to encourage talking about the steps in dressing. Other books in this series include titles such as *Friends; Playing; Family; I Can; I See;* and *I Hear.*

Young children also learn to identify actions in pictures, and enjoy recognizing and naming familiar actions such as those in Eve Rice's *Oh, Lewis!* In this picture book, Lewis is going shopping with his mother, but first he must find his mittens and have his jacket zipped, his boots buckled, and his hood tied. *Richard Scarry's The Best Word Book Ever* and *My First Word Book* appeal to young children and provide practice in naming common objects.

Many excellent books allow children to listen to the sounds of language and experiment with these sounds. For example, children may sing along with Sarah Hale's *Mary Had a Little Lamb,*

The loving environment captured by the illustrations and the accompanying nursery rhymes encourage language development. (From *Tortillitas Para Mama* selected and translated by Margot C. Griego, Betsy L. Bucks, Sharon S. Gilbert, and Laurel H. Kimball. Illustrated by Barbara Cooney. Copyright © 1981 by Margot Griego, Betsy Bucks, Sharon Gilbert, Laurel Kimball. Copyright © 1981 by Barbara Cooney. Reproduced by permission of Holt, Rinehart and Winston, Publishers.)

a popular picture book illustrating the old nursery song. Rhyming books are especially appealing to young children. Both the colorful pictures and the rhyming words in Barbara Emberley's *Drummer Hoff* fascinate them. They love to join in with the rhyming elements, "parriage"—"carriage," "farrell"—"barrel," and "bammer"—"rammer." Children may respond in both Spanish and English when they interact with the rhymes in *Tortillitas Para Mama* by Margot C. Griego et al.

Elementary-Age Children. Language development of course continues as children enter school and progress through the grades. Walter Loban (13) conducted the most extensive longitudinal study of language development in school-age children, examining the language development of the same group of over 200 children from age five to age eighteen. He found that children's power over language increases through successive control over different forms of language, including pronouns, verb tenses, and connectors such as *meanwhile* and *unless.*

Loban identified dramatic differences between children ranking high in language proficiency and those ranking low. The high group reached a level of oral proficiency in first grade that the low group did not attain until sixth grade and a level of written proficiency in fourth grade that the low group did not attain until tenth grade. Those who demonstrated high language proficiency excelled in the control of expressed ideas, showing unity and planning in both their speech and their writing. These students spoke freely, fluently, and easily, using a rich vocabulary and adjusting the pace of their words to their listeners. They were attentive and creative listeners themselves, far outranking the low group in listening ability. The oral communication of those with low language proficiency was characterized by rambling and unpurposeful dialogue demonstrating a meager vocabulary.

Children who were superior in oral language in kindergarten and first grade also excelled in reading and writing in sixth grade. They were more fluent in written language than were the low-ranked children, used more words per sentence, showed a richer written vocabulary, and were superior in using connectors and subordination to combine thoughts into complex forms of expression. Given the demonstrated connection between oral and written language skills, Loban concluded that teachers, librarians, and parents should give

CHART 1–1
Language Development

Characteristics	Implications	Literature Suggestions
Preschool: Ages two–three		
1 Very rapid language growth occurs. By the end of this period, children have vocabularies of about nine hundred words.	1 Provide many activities to stimulate language growth including picture books and Mother Goose rhymes.	Hayes, Sarah. *This is the Bear.* Wells, Rosemary. *Max's Birthday.*
2 They learn to identify and name actions in pictures.	2 Read books that contain clear, familiar action pictures; encourage children to identify actions.	Lindgren, Barbro. *Sam's Bath.* Oxenbury, Helen. *I Touch.* Rice, Eve. *Oh, Lewis!* Wells, Rosemary. *Max's Breakfast.*
3 They learn to identify large and small body parts.	3 Allow children to identify familiar body parts in picture books.	Berger, Terry, and Kandell, Alice. *Ben's ABC Day.* Oxenbury, Helen. *Dressing.*
Preschool: Ages three–four		
1 Vocabularies have increased to about fifteen hundred words. Children enjoy playing with sound and rhythm in language.	1 Include opportunities to listen to and say rhymes, poetry, and riddles.	Emberley, Barbara. *Drummer Hoff.* Griego, Margot, et al. *Tortillitas Para Mama.* Hale, Sarah Josepha. *Mary Had a Little Lamb.* Martin, Sarah Catherine. *The Comic Adventures of Mother Hubbard and Her Dog.* Yolen, Jane. *The Lullaby Songbook.*
2 They develop the ability to use past tense but may overgeneralize the *ed* and *s* markers.	2 Allow children to talk about what they did yesterday; discuss actions in books.	Hill, Eric, *Spot Goes to School.* Hill, Eric. *Spot's First Walk.*
3 Language is used as a tool to help children find out about their world.	3 Read picture storybooks to allow children to find out about and discuss pets, families, people, the environment.	Carle, Eric. *The Very Busy Spider.* Spier, Peter. *Bill's Service Station.* Spier, Peter. *Food Market.* Tafuri, Nancy. *Early Morning in the Barn.* Winter, Jeanette. *Come Out to Play.*
4 Speech becomes more complex, with more adjectives, adverbs, pronouns, and prepositions.	4 Expand the use of descriptive words through detailed picture books and picture storybooks. Allow children to tell stories and describe characters and their actions.	Crews, Donald. *Harbor.* Crews, Donald. *Freight Train.* Hill, Eric. *Spot Goes to the Beach.* Rinard, Judith E. *What Happens at the Zoo.*
Preschool: Ages four–five		
1 Language is more abstract; children produce gramatically correct sentences. Their vocabularies include approximately twenty-five hundred words.	1 Children enjoy books with slightly more complex plots. They can tell longer and more detailed stories, enjoy retelling folktales, and can tell stories using wordless books.	Cauley, Lorinda Bryan. *Boldilocks and the Three Bears.* Duff, Maggie. *Rum Pum Pum.* Goodall, John S. *Paddy Under Water.* Hutchinson, Veronica. *Henny Penny.* Magnus, Erica. *Old Lars.*
2 They understand the prepositions *over, under, in, out, in front of,* and *behind.*	2 Use concept books or other picture books in which these terms can be reinforced.	Bancheck, Linda. *Snake In, Snake Out.* Hutchins, Pat. *Rosie's Walk.* McMillan, Bruce. *Here a Chick, There a Chick.*

CHART 1–1 (cont.)
Language Development

Characteristics	Implications	Literature Suggestions
3 They enjoy asking many questions, especially those related to *why* and *how*.	3 Take advantage of this natural curiosity and find books to help answer their questions. Allow them to answer each others' questions.	Barton, Bryon. *Airport*. Cristini, Ermanno. *In the Pond*. Showers, Paul. *Look at Your Eyes*. Yabuuchi, Masayuki. *Whose Baby?*
Preschool—Kindergarten: Ages five–six		
1 Most children use complex sentences frequently and begin to use correct pronouns and verbs in present and past tense. They understand approximately six thousand words.	1 Give them many opportunities for oral language activities connected with literature.	Aardema, Verna. *Bringing the Rain to Kapiti Plain*. Aardema, Verna. *Why Mosquitoes Buzz in People's Ears: A West African Tale*. Bennett, Jill. *Tiny Tim: Verses for Children*. Grimm. *Hansel and Gretel*. Hutchins, Pat. *The Worst Monster*. Lee, Dennis. *Jelly Belly: Original Nursery Rhymes*.
2 Children enjoy taking part in dramatic play and producing dialogue about everyday functions such as home situations and grocery store experiences.	2 Read stories about the home and community. Allow children to act out their own stories.	Hurd, Edith Thacher. *I Dance in My Red Pajamas*. Kroll, Steven. *If I Could Be My Grandmother*. Seuss, Dr. *And to Think That I Saw It on Mulberry Street*. Spier, Peter. *Fire House: Hook and Ladder Company Number Twenty-Four*.
3 They are curious about the written appearance of their own language.	3 Write chart stories using the children's own words; have them dictate descriptions of pictures.	Briggs, Raymond. *The Snowman*. Krahn, Fernando. *Who's Seen the Scissors*. Willard, Nancy. *Night Story*.
Early Elementary: Ages six–eight		
1 Language development continues; many new words are added to their vocabularies.	1 Provide daily time for reading to children and allow for oral interaction.	Bryan, Ashley. *The Cat's Purr*. de Paola, Tomie. *Fin M'Coul: The Giant of Knockmany Hill*. Kellogg, Steven. *A Rose for Pinkerton*. Lewin, Hugh. *Jafta*. Ryder, Joanne. *Inside Turtle's Shell: And Other Poems of the Field*. Silverstein, Shel. *A Light in the Attic*.
2 Most children use complex sentences with adjectival clauses and conditional clauses beginning with *if*. The average oral sentence length is seven and one-half words.	2 Read stories that provide models for children's expanding language structure.	de Paola, Tomie. *The Legend of the Bluebonnet*. Hodges, Margaret. *Saint George and the Dragon*. Severo, Emöke de Papp. *The Good-Hearted Youngest Brother*. Skorpen, Liesel M. *His Mother's Dog*. Asian Cultural Centre for UNESCO. *Folktales from Asia for Children Everywhere*.
Middle Elementary: Ages eight–ten		
1 Children begin to relate concepts to general ideas. They use connectors such as *meanwhile* and *unless*.	1 Supply books as models. Let children use these terms during oral language activities.	Belpre, Pura, *The Rainbow-Colored Horse*. Hill, Donna. *Ms. Glee Was Waiting*.

CHART 1–1 (cont.)
Language Development

Characteristics		Implications		Literature Suggestions
2	The subordinating connector *although* is used correctly by 50 percent of children. Present participle active and perfect participle appear. The average number of words in sentence is nine.	2	Use written models and oral models to help children master these language skills. Literature discussions allow many opportunities for oral sentence expansion.	de Paola, Tomie. *The Quicksand Book.* Gilchrist, Theo. *Halfway up the Mountain.* Walter, Mildred. *Brother to the Wind.*
Upper Elementary: Ages ten–twelve				
1	Children use complex sentences with subordinate clauses of concession introduced by *nevertheless* and *in spite of.* Auxiliary verbs *might, could,* and *should* appear frequently.	1	Encourage oral language and written activities so children can use more complex sentence structures.	Corbett, W. J. *The Song of Pentecost.* Kennedy, Richard. *Amy's Eyes.* L'Engle, Madeleine, *A Swiftly Tilting Planet.* McKinley, Robin. *The Hero and the Crown.*

Sources: Bartel (2), Braga and Braga (4), Brown (6), Gage and Berliner (9), and Loban (13).

greater attention to developing children's oral language. Discussion should be a vital part of elementary school and library programs because it helps children organize ideas and illustrate complex generalizations.

Literature is a crucial resource in providing both a model for language and a stimulation for oral and written activities. This text will suggest a wealth of literature for use in the elementary grades: literature to be read aloud to children; literature to provide a model for expanding language proficiency; and literature to stimulate oral discussion, creative dramatics, creative writing, and listening enjoyment.

Literature provides stimulation for the dramatic play and creative dramatics that inspire children in the primary grades to express themselves verbally with much enjoyment. For example, in Maurice Sendak's *Where the Wild Things Are* Max gets into so much mischief when he is wearing his wolf suit that his mother sends him to his room without any supper. His vivid imagination turns the room into a forest inhabited by wild things. Max stays in the forest and becomes its king, but finally gets lonely and wants to return to the land where someone loves him. Children can relate to Max's experience and use it to stimulate their own wild experiences through cre-

ative drama. Marco, in Dr. Seuss's *And to Think That I Saw It on Mulberry Street*, is another boy who uses his imagination when he is in a normal environment. The setting is the street on which Marco walks home from school. The only thing Marco sees is a horse drawing a wagon, but this does not stifle his storytelling ability as he envisions what he would like to see on plain old Mulberry Street. Children enjoy using their imagination and turning the common occurrences of their own streets into creative experiences. Chapters five, six, and seven present books that involve children in such enchantment and also encourage language development.

Wordless picture books are excellent stimulators for oral and written language. Tomie de Paola's *Pancakes for Breakfast* presents a series of humorous incidents related to preparing pancakes. *Paddy Under Water*, by John Goodall, illustrates the adventures of a pig when he dons diving gear and visits a shipwreck. More complex wordless books may stimulate the oral language of older children. John Goodall's *The Story of an English Village* shows the changes that occur in a village from the fourteenth century to the twentieth century. Chapter five presents wordless picture books and stimulating activities that are useful with them.

Since the first edition of this textbook was published in 1983, teachers and professors of children's literature have requested a listing of non-English books that may be used by parents, teachers, and librarians. An increasing number of books meet the language needs of children who read, speak, or understand a language other than English. For example, as part of "In Celebration of the Child 1984," the Houston Public Library held an exhibit of children's literature that is representative of Hispanic cultures and is written in Spanish. The selections included Hispanic folktales, poetry, and religious literature that are excellent resources for encouraging language development and cultural enrichment.

Fun and interesting folktales written in Spanish and recommended by the Houston Public Library include Rosario Ferré's *Los Cuentos de Juan Bobo* (The Stories of Juan Bobo) from Puerto Rico; *Las Historias del Popol Vuh* (Stories from the Popol Vuy) from Guatemala; Carmen Lyra's *Los Cuentos de mi Tía Panchita* (The Stories of My Aunt Francisca) from Costa Rico, and Rogelio Sinan's *El Conejito, El Pato Patuleco y Otros: Narrativa Oral Panameña* (The Rabbit, Patuleco the Duck, and Others: Oral Narrative of Panama) from Panama.

Other recently published books in Spanish include both traditional literature and poetry. Younger children will enjoy reading or listening to Margo Glantz's Aztec myth, *La Guerra de los Hermanos* and Silvia Mistral's Christmas Eve legend, *La Cola de la Sirena*. Carmen Bravo-Villasante's *Al Corro de la Patata* is a collection of traditional folk rhymes, riddles, songs, and lullabies. Spanish poetry selections for children include works by respected poets from Argentina (María Elena Walsh's *Tutú Marambá*; Nicaragua (Rubén Darío's *Margarita* [Margarita]); Puerto Rico (Ester Feliciano Mendoza's *Ronda del Mar* [Poems of the Sea]); and Spain (José María Garrido Lopera's *Federico García Lorca y los Niños* [Federico García Lorca and the Children]).

Excellent sources for French-Canadian books for children include the yearly awards given by the Canadian Library Association (which presents awards for books written in English and in French) and recommended French-Canadian books compiled by the American Library Association.

Young preschool children's French-Canadian language development will be stimulated by Marie-Louise Gay's rhythmic text in *Un Léopard dans mon Placard* (A Leopard Inside My Cupboard). Wordgames provide the language stimulus in Darcia Labrosse's *Où est le Ver?* (Where Is the Worm?). Detailed illustrations in three picture books will stimulate early elementary children's descriptive vocabularies: Roger Paré's *Plaisirs de Chat* (Cat's Pleasures), Cécile Gagnon's *Surprises et Sortiliéges* (Surprises and Spells), and Ginette Anfousse's *Sophie, Pierrot et un Crapaud* (Sophie, Pierrot and a Toad) which includes a record that accompanies a lyrical text.

Middle elementary children will enjoy two humorous stories written in French. Puns provide the humor in Claude Dubé's animal story, *Cas Cocasses* (Funny Cases). Cartoon-type illustrations add to the fun in Robert Soulière's *Tony ou Vladimir* (Tony or Vladimir).

Folktales and science fiction can stimulate the interest and language development of upper elementary children. André Mareuil's *Récite du Saint-Laurent* (Saint Lawrence's Stories) includes folktales from Quebec. Science fiction selections include Denis Côté's *Hockeurs Cybernétiques* (Cybernetic Hockey Players) and Francine Loranger's *Chanson Pour un Ordinateur* (Computer's Song).

Although textbook space does not allow a complete listing of recommended books written in foreign languages, adults who share literature with children should be aware of the non-English books that are available. The children's literature periodicals *Booklist* and *Horn Book* print recommended lists of books printed in languages other than English. The American Library Association Committee on the Selection of Children's Books from Various Cultures compiles lists of recommended books. These lists should prove useful for any adult who is trying to meet the language, cultural, and literary needs of all children.

Cognitive Development

Factors related to helping children remember, anticipate, integrate perceptions, and develop concepts fill numerous textbooks and have been the subject of both research and conjecture. Jean Piaget (16) maintained that the order in which children's thinking matures is the same for all, although the pace varies from child to child. Early stimulation is also necessary if cognitive development is to occur. Children who grow up in isolated areas without a variety of experiences may be three to five years behind other children in developing the mental strategies that aid recall.

According to the child development authorities Mussen, Conger, and Kagan (14), the term *cognition* refers to the processes involved in "(1) perception—the detection, organization, and interpretation of information from both the outside world and the internal environment, (2) memory—the storage and retrieval of the perceived information, (3) reasoning—the use of knowledge to make inferences and draw conclusions, (4) reflection—the evaluation of the quality of ideas and solutions, and (5) insight—the recognition of new relationships between two or more segments of knowledge" (pp. 234–35). All these processes are essential for success in both school and adult life. Each is also closely related to understanding and enjoying literature. Without visual and auditory perception, literature could not be read or heard; without memory, there would be no way to see the relationships among literary works and to recognize new relationships as experiences are extended. Carefully selected literature and literature experiences are also an important means of stimulating cognitive development, by encouraging the oral exchange of ideas and the development of thought processes.

Dorothy Strickland (21) recommends that adults use literature to "capitalize on every opportunity to develop the child's ability to handle basic operations associated with thinking" (p. 55). She identifies eight cognitive skills that can be developed through the use of literature: observing, comparing, classifying, hypothesizing, organizing, summarizing, applying, and criticizing.

Observing. Colorful picture books are an excellent means of developing observational skills in both younger and older children. The humorous illustrations for Hilary Knight's *The Twelve Days of Christmas* contain pages crowded with animals, as a generous bear presents his true love with fiddling foxes, milking kittens, drumming rabbits, and dancing pigs. The final illustration showing the Christmas Fair stimulates considerable discussion. *Lentil*, by Robert McCloskey, contains excellent drawings of a midwestern town in the early 1900s: the town square, houses on the streets, the interior of the schoolhouse, the train depot, and a parade. Single lines of text accompany each picture, but the details of the pictures themselves illustrate the life-style and the emotions of the characters in the story. Older children enjoy searching for the art objects, literary characters, and present-day personalities in Mitsumasa Anno's detailed wordless book, *Anno's Italy*.

Comparing. Picture books and other literature selections provide many opportunities for comparing. Young children, for example, can compare the various attributes of the hats illustrated in Stan and Janice Berenstain's *Old Hat, New Hat*. The hats include ones that are heavy, light, loose,

Active animals and considerable detail provide a rich source for observation and discussion. (Reprinted with permission of Macmillan Publishing Co., Inc. from *The Twelve Days of Christmas* illustrated by Hilary Knight. Copyright © 1981 by Hilary Knight.)

tight, flat, tall, big, small, shiny, frilly, fancy, silly, and lumpy. These new hats can also be compared with the old hat, still considered the best one of all. Wordless books are also excellent for comparisons. *Changes, Changes*, by Pat Hutchins, opens with a picture of two doll figures who have built a house from blocks. The book continues to illustrate their adventures: when the house catches on fire, they change the structure of the blocks to form a fire truck; the fire truck puts out the fire but causes an overabundance of water; the dolls then change the blocks into a boat and sail safely to shore; on shore they build a truck and then a train; finally, they reach their preferred location and rebuild their house of blocks. Children could be asked to make comparisons and notice the changes in this book by examining the pictures, deciding what is being built and why, and then describing the changes that occur between pictures. Because there is one difference between the second house and the original, they can make a final comparison. Additional comparisons could be made as children build their own structures out of blocks and try to change the purpose of the structure by using only the original blocks.

Older children can also use pictures to compare. In *Tin Lizzie*, Peter Spier uses both words and illustrations to tell the story of a 1909 Model T touring car better known as a Tin Lizzie. The car is purchased new from a factory in Detroit and sent by rail to a small midwestern town. The Tin Lizzie progresses through several owners until it is finally found rusting in a modern-day farmyard. A businessman buys and restores the car to its original glory and then takes his family for rides through the city and countryside. This book shows the many changes that have taken place in the last seventy years, and children can make comparisons between the clothing, transportation, homes, towns, and streets shown in the different periods represented.

Different artists' renditions of the same story provide numerous opportunities for artistic comparisons. For example, there are several newly illustrated versions of Margery Williams's *The Velveteen Rabbit*, originally published in 1922, including those by Allen Atkinson, Michael Hague, and Ilse Plume. Versions of the popular folktale "Beauty and the Beast" include those illustrated in different styles by Warwick Hutton, Etienne Delessert, and Michael Hague. Students can consider the impact of color, line, design, and media on the interpretation of the text, as well as evaluate the accuracy of the illustrations.

Upper elementary children can make comparisons between the main characters, their struggles for survival, and their growing up in books such as Maia Wojciechowska's *Shadow of a Bull* and Elizabeth George Speare's *The Bronze Bow*.

Classifying. Children must be able to classify objects or ideas before they can see or understand the relationships among them. Various concept books use different levels of abstractness to introduce children to concepts such as color, shape, size, and usefulness. Eric Carle allows children to match blocks of color with the color shown in an illustration in his *My Very First Book of Colors*; illustrates the colorful story of a chameleon who wants to change his appearance in *The Mixed-Up Chameleon* and presents the eight basic colors, as well as simple addition and subtraction, in *Let's Paint a Rainbow*. Roger Duvoisin's *See What I Am* is a more difficult color concept book that introduces the primary colors and then mixes them to produce the secondary colors. The artist also shows how colors are used to make color illustrations in picture books.

Size concept books also vary in level of difficulty. Carle's *My Very First Book of Shapes*, encourages children to match black shapes with similar shapes in color. John Reiss's *Shapes* presents the shapes, their names, and their three-dimensional forms. Photographs in Tana Hoban's *Shapes, Shapes, Shapes* encourage children to search for circles, rectangles, and ovals.

Many other types of books can be used to develop children's classification skills. For example, after listening to the folktale "The Three Bears," children may classify the bears, porridge bowls, chairs, and beds according to their size, then identify which bear could best use a particular bowl, bed, or chair. (Flannelgraph characters and objects will make classification more concrete for young children.) Stories can be classified using categories such as animals, wild animals, pets; boy or girl as the main character; country or city setting. Characteristics of the story or characters can also be used for classification: realistic, unrealistic; likable, unlikable; happy, sad; funny, serious.

Hypothesizing. Helping children to hypothesize about the subject, plot, or characters in a story assists them in developing cognitive skills and also develops their interests, motivating them to read or listen to literature. For example, children could look at the cover illustration of Russell Hoban's *Nothing to Do* and guess what the book will be about. In this story, Father gives Walter a "something-to-do stone." Children can guess what Walter will do with the stone and decide what they would do if they had a similar stone.

Descriptive chapter titles and titles to subsections of books are excellent stimuli for verbal or written speculations by older children. For example, before reading or listening to Martha Brenner's *Fireworks Tonight!*, they can discuss what information they believe will be in each of the following sections: "Triumph and Tragedy on the Fourth," "Protective Regulation," "Mischief and Misuse," and "How Safe Are Fireworks?" After reading each section, they can review the accuracy of their predictions.

Organizing. Young children have difficulty understanding time concepts, sequence of time, and when things happen. Illustrated books about various aspects of time—from different hours of the day to the yearly cycle illustrated in Robert Welber's *Song of the Seasons*—familiarize children with the components and overall structure of this important part of their environment.

Plot development in literature itself requires and encourages children to learn forms of logical organization. After children have listened to or read a literature selection, they interpret this organization and improve their ability to put ideas into order when they retell a story or develop a creative drama. With their strong sequential plots and repetition of sequence and detail, folktales are especially appropriate for developing organizational skills. "The Little Red Hen" uses chronological order as the story progresses from the seed, to the planting, to the tilling, to the harvesting, to the baking, and finally to the eating. In "The Three Billy Goats Gruff," the goats cross the bridge and confront the troll in a size ordering that goes from small to medium to large. The Yiddish folktale "It Could Always Be Worse" tells the story of a man discontented with his small, crowded hut. He takes his rabbi's advice and brings a series of larger and larger animals into his hut. When he finally clears out the animals, he appreciates his house.

Cumulative folktales also reinforce the organization of the plot by repeating the sequence each time a new experience is added to the story. Paul Galdone uses this cumulative technique in the American folktale, *The Greedy Old Fat Man*. A pattern is established early in the story as the title character approaches a boy and girl with the threatening words, "I ate a hundred biscuits and drank a barrel of milk, and I'll eat you, too, if I can catch you!" (p. 3). Language and action are repeated as new victims are added to the list. By the time the greedy old man approaches a frisky squirrel, the sequence of the plot has become familiar: "I ate a hundred biscuits, I drank a barrel of milk, I ate a little boy, I ate a little girl, I ate a little dog, I ate a little cat, I ate a little fox, I ate some little rabbits, and I'll eat you, too, if I can catch you" (p. 22). The story ends in true folktale fashion as the squirrel outwits the greedy old fat man and the "victims" emerge unhurt.

"Why" tales also frequently depict a series of events to explain something. For example, Verna Aardema's *Why Mosquitoes Buzz in People's Ears: A West African Tale* describes the sequence of events that prevented the owl from waking the sun and bringing in a new day.

These kinds of folktales make excellent selections for flannelboard stories. When children retell the stories using the flannelgraphs or use the stories as the basis for creative drama, they develop and reinforce their organizational skills.

Summarizing. Summarizing skills can be developed with literature of any genre or level of difficulty. Children may summarize stories orally or in writing. Oral summaries may motivate other children to read the same book or story. After a recreational reading period in the classroom, library, or home, members of the group can retell the story, the part of the story they liked best, the most important information learned, the funniest part of the story, the most exciting part, and the actions of the most or least admired character.

Applying. Young children need many opportunities to apply the skills, concepts, information, or ideas they learn about in books. When they read concept books, for example, they should see and manipulate concrete examples, not merely look at pictures. Children who read Eric Carle's *My Very First Book of Numbers* or John Reiss's *Numbers* can count and group objects.

Information books also offer application opportunities. Numerous "how-to" books stimulate children's interest in hobbies, crafts, and sports.

CHART 1–2
Cognitive Development

Characteristics	Implications	Literature Suggestions
Preschool: Ages two–three		
1 Children learn new ways to organize and classify their worlds by putting together things that they perceive to be alike.	1 Provide opportunities for them to discuss and group things that are alike: color, shape, size, use. Use picture concept books with large, colorful pictures.	Hoban, Tana. *1, 2, 3.* Hoban, Tana. *What Is It?*
2 They begin to remember two or three items.	2 Exercise children's short-term memories by providing opportunities to recall information.	Alexander, Martha. *Out! Out! Out!* Duke, Kate. *Bedtime.* Maris, Ron. *Are You There, Bear?*
Preschool: Ages three–four		
1 Children develop an understanding of how things relate to each other: how parts go together to make a whole, and how they are arranged in space in relation to each other.	1 Give children opportunities to find the correct part of a picture to match another picture. Simple picture puzzles may be used.	Hoban, Tana. *Take Another Look.* Hutchins, Pat. *Changes, Changes.* Oxenbury, Helen. *I see.*
2 They begin to understand relationships and classify things according to certain attributes that they share, such as color, size, shape, and what they are used for. These classifications are perceptual.	2 Share concept books on color, size, shape, and use. Provide opportunities for children to group and classify objects and pictures.	Carle, Eric. *My Very First Book of Colors.* de Brunhoff, Laurent. *Babar's Book of Color.* Hoban, Tana. *Shapes, Shapes, Shapes.*
3 They begin to understand how objects relate to each other in terms of number and amount.	3 Give picture counting books to children. Allow them to count.	Bang, Molly. *Ten, Nine, Eight.* Carle, Eric. *My Very First Book of Numbers.* Tafuri, Nancy. *Who's Counting?*
4 Children begin to compare two things and tell which is bigger and which is smaller.	4 Share and discuss books that allow comparisons in size, such as a giant and boy, a big item and a small item, or a series of animals.	Campbell, Rod. *Dear Zoo.*
Preschool: Ages four–five		
1 Children remember to do three things told to them or retell a short story if the material is presented in a meaningful sequence.	1 Tell short, meaningful stories and allow children to retell them; flannelboard and picture stories help them organize the story. Give them practice in following three-step directions.	Galdone, Paul. *The Gingerbread Boy.* Galdone, Paul. *What's in Fox's Sack? An Old English Tale.* Ginsburg, mirra. *How the Sun Was Brought Back to the Sky.* Stevens, Janet. *The House That Jack Built.*
2 They increase their ability to group objects according to important characteristics but still base their rules on how things look to them.	2 Provide many opportunities to share concept books and activities designed to develop ideas of shape, color, size, feel, and use.	Carle, Eric. *My Very First Book of Shapes.* Hoban, Tana. *Circles, Triangles, and Squares.* Hoban, Tana. *Is It Red? Is It Yellow? Is It Blue?*

CHART 1–2 (cont.)
Cognitive Development

Characteristics	Implications	Literature Suggestions
3 They pretend to tell time but do not understand the concept. Things happen "now" or "before now."	3 Share books to help them understand sequence of time and when things happen, such as the seasons of the year, and what happens during different times of the day or different days of the week.	Rockwell, Anne. *First Comes Spring*.

Preschool—Kindergarten: Ages five–six

Characteristics	Implications	Literature Suggestions
1 Children learn to follow one type of classification (e.g., color, shape) though to completion without changing the main characteristic partway through the task.	1 Continue to share concept books and encourage activities that allow children to group and classify.	Emberley, Ed. *Ed Emberley's ABC*. Lobel, ARnold. *On Market Street*.
2 They count to ten and discriminate ten objects.	2 Reinforce developing counting skills with counting books and other counting activities.	Carle, Eric, *My Very First Book of Numbers*. Dubanevich, Arlene. *Pigs in Hiding*. Knight, Hilary. *Hilary Knight's The Twelve Days of Christmas*. Magee, Doug. *Trucks You Can Count On*.
3 They identify primary colors.	3 Reinforce color identification through the use of color concept books and by discussing colors found in other picture books.	Carle, Eric. *Let's Paint a Rainbow*. Hutchins, Pat. *Changes, Changes*.
4 They learn to distinguish between "a lot of" something or "a little of" something.	4 Provide opportunities for children to identify and discuss the differences between these concepts.	Gág, Wanda. *Millions of Cats*. Zemach, Margot. *It Could Always Be Worse*.
5 Children require trial and error before they can arrange things in order from smallest to biggest.	5 Share books that progress from smallest to largest. Have children retell stories using flannelboard characters drawn in appropriate sizes.	Galdone, Paul. *The Three Billy Goats Gruff*. Zemach, Margot, *It Could Always Be Worse*.
6 They still have vague concepts of time.	6 Share books to help them understand time sequence.	Clifton, Lucille. *Everett Anderson's Year*.

Early Elementary: Ages six–eight

Characteristics	Implications	Literature Suggestions
1 Children are learning to read; they enjoy reading easy books and demonstrating their new abilities.	1 Provide easy-to-read books geared to children's developing reading skills.	Griffith, Helen. *Alex and the Cat*. Lobel, Arnold. *Frog and Toad All Year*. Lobel, ARnold. *Uncle Elephant*. Marshall, Edward. *Four on the Shore*. Seuss, Dr. *The Cat in the Hat*.
2 They are learning to write and enjoy creating their own stories.	2 Allow children to write, illustrate, and share their own picture books. Wordless books can be used to suggest plot.	de Paola, Tomie. *The Hunter and the Animals: A Wordless Picture Book*. Van Allsburg, Chris. *The Mysteries of Harris Burdick*. Waber, Bernard. *The Snake: A Very Long Story*.

CHART 1–2 (cont.)
Cognitive Development

Characteristics	Implications	Literature Suggestions
3 The attention span is increasing and children enjoy longer stories than they did when they were five.	3 They enjoy listening to longer storybooks. They are starting to enjoy longer stories if the chapters can be completed each story time.	Goble, Paul. *Star Boy.* Grahame, Kenneth. *Wayfarers All: From the Wind in the Willows.* Hague, Kathleen. *The Man Who Kept House.* Van Allsburg, Chris. *The Polar Express.*
4 Children under seven still base their rules on immediate perception and learn through real situations.	4 Provide experiences which allow them to see, discuss, and verify information and relationships.	Bellville, Cheryl. *Rodeo.* Emberley, Ed. *Picture Pie: A Circle Drawing Book.* Reiss, John J. *Shapes.* Simon, Seymour. *Animal Fact/Animal Fable.* Simon, Seymour. *Meet the Computer.*
5 Sometime during this age they pass into the stage Piaget refers to as concrete operational.	5 Children have developed a new set of rules called groupings. They don't have to see all objects to group; they can understand relationships among categories.	Anno, Mitsumasa. *Anno's Counting Book.* Feelings, Muriel. *Moja Means One: Swahili Counting Book.*

Middle Elementary: Ages eight–ten

1 Reading skills improve rapidly, although there are wide variations in reading ability among children within the same age group.	1 Children enjoy independent reading. Provide books for appropriate reading levels. Allow them opportunities to share experiences with books with peers, parents, teachers, and other adults.	Blume, Judy. *Tales of a Fourth Grade Nothing.* Cleary, Beverly. *Ramona and Her Father.* Cleary, Beverly, *Ramona Quimby, Age 8.* Wilder, Laura Ingalls. *Little House in the Big Woods.*
2 The interest level of literature may still be above the reading level for many children.	2 Children need a daily time during which they can listen to a variety of books being read aloud.	Conly, Jane Leslie. *Racso and the Rats of NIMH.* Lewis, C. S. *The Lion, the Witch and the Wardrobe.* Martin, Eva. *Canadian Fairy Tales.* White, E. B. *Charlotte's Web.* White, E. B. *Stuart Little.*
3 Memory improves as they learn to attend to certain stimuli and to ignore others.	3 Help children set purposes for listening or reading before the actual literature experience.	Dallinger, Jane. *Grasshoppers.* Malnig, Anita. *Where the Waves Break: Life at the Edge of the Sea.* Nance, Joh. *Lobo of the Tasaday.* Selsam, Millicent. *Mushrooms.*

Upper Elementary: Ages ten–twelve

1 Children develop an understanding of the chronological ordering of past events.	1 Historic fiction and books showing historic changes helps them understand differing viewpoints and historical perspective.	Bess, Clayton. *Story for a Black Night.* British Museum of Natural History. *Man's Place in Evolution.* Forbes, Esther. *Johnny Tremain.* Meyer, Carolyn and Gallenkamp, Charles. *The Mysteries of the Ancient Maya.* Speare, Elizabeth. *The Sign of the Beaver.* Sutcliff, Rosemary. *Sun Horse, Moon Horse.* Voigt, Cynthia. *Building Blocks.*

CHART 1–2 (cont.)
Cognitive Development

Characteristics	Implications	Literature Suggestions
2 They apply logical rules, reasoning, and formal operations to abstract problems and propositions.	2 Use questioning and discussion strategies designed to develop higher level thought processes. Children enjoy more complex books.	Alexander, Lloyd. *Westmark*. *Beowulf*. Fritz, Jean. *Make Way for Sam Houston*. Hall, Lynn. *Danza!* Raskin, Ellen. *The Westing Game*.

Sources: Braga and Braga (4), Mussen, Conger, and Kagan (14); and Piaget and Inhelder (16).

For example, students can apply the information found in Barbara Isenberg and Marjorie Jaffe's *Albert the Running Bear's Exercise Book* when they try the exercises discussed and illustrated in the book. Children can use *Cactus in the Desert*, by Phyllis Busch, as they grow their own cactus gardens. Jim Arnosky's *Flies in the Water, Fish in the Air* provides information on fishing as a sport; and Sam Savitt's *Draw Horses with Sam Savitt* uses detailed directions and drawings to help children draw horses standing or in motion.

Criticizing. Neither adults nor children should be required or encouraged to accept everything they hear or read without criticism. Children should be given many opportunities to evaluate critically what they read or hear. Critical evaluation skills are developed when children sense the appropriateness, reliability, value, and authenticity of literature selections. Historical fiction selections are excellent for investigating and discussing the authenticity of the characters, settings, and plots.

Research indicates that the level and type of questioning strategies used with children affect their levels of thinking and their development of critical evaluative skills. Consequently, this text will present oral discussion skills, questioning

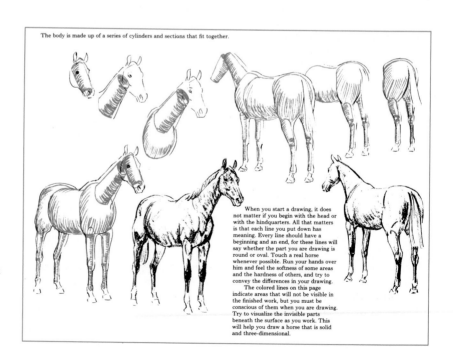

The body is made up of a series of cylinders and sections that fit together.

When you start a drawing, it does not matter if you begin with the head or with the hindquarters. All that matters is that each line you put down has meaning. Every line should have a beginning and an end, for these lines will say whether the part you are drawing is round or oval. Touch a real horse whenever possible. Run your hands over him and feel the softness of some areas and the hardness of others, and try to convey the differences in your drawing.

The colored lines on this page indicate areas that will not be visible in the finished work, but you must be conscious of them when you are drawing. Try to visualize the invisible parts beneath the surface as you work. This will help you draw a horse that is solid and three-dimensional.

The sequentially detailed illustrations encourage children to apply the artist's suggestions to their own drawings. (From *Draw Horses with Sam Savitt* by Sam Savitt. Copyright © 1981 by Sam Savitt. Reprinted by permission of the author and Viking Penguin Inc.)

strategies to stimulate critical evaluation, and ways of developing these skills by using specific books.

Personality Development

Children go through many stages of personality development as they gradually learn to express emotions acceptably, experience empathy toward others, and develop feelings of self-esteem. Young children have difficulty understanding and expressing their emotions. Infants cry whenever they are unhappy, angry, or uncomfortable. Slowly, with guidance, children learn to handle their emotions productively rather than disruptively. Expanded experiences, adult and sibling models, and personal success show them positive ways of dealing with emotions. Overcoming fears, developing trust, relinquishing the desire to have only their own way, and learning acceptable forms of interaction with both peers and adults inevitably involve traumatic experiences. Progressing through the stages of personality development is part of the maturing process, in which books can play a very important role.

Bibliotherapy is an interaction between reader and literature in which the ideas inherent in the reading materials can have a therapeutic effect upon the reader. Experts in child development frequently suggest bibliotherapy as a means of helping children through various times of stress. Joanne Bernstein's *Books to Help Children Cope with Separation and Loss* (3), provides an introduction to bibliotherapy and annotated bibliographies of books in various areas of childhood adjustment such as hospitalization, loss of a friend, and parents' divorce. Rhea Joyce Rubin's *Using Bibliotherapy* (19) and the *Bibliotherapy Source Book* (18) discuss the theoretical and practical aspects of designing a program for using books in therapy. Although most of the emotional problems young children experience are not as severe as coping with loss and separation, children must face numerous smaller crises that require personal adjustment.

Rosalind Engel (8) emphasizes the value of literature in helping children understand their feelings, identify with characters who experience similar feelings, and gain new insights into how others have coped with those same problems. According to Engel, "Image readiness begins at birth and involves all the actions and interactions between children and the members of their environment. Literature becomes an influence in the child's life as soon as others are willing to share it and the child responds" (p. 892).

Joan Glazer (10) identifies four ways in which literature contributes to children's emotional growth. First, it shows children that many of their feelings are also common to other children and that those feelings are both normal and natural. Second, it explores a feeling from several viewpoints, giving a fuller picture and providing the basis for naming that emotion. Third, actions of various characters show options for ways to deal with particular emotions. Fourth, literature makes clear that one person experiences many emotions, and that these sometimes conflict.

Fear and jealousy are emotions familiar to most children. Jealousy is a common reaction when a new baby comes into the home, for example. Books about new babies can help children express their fears and realize that their parents still love them, that it is not unusual to feel fearful about a new relationship. Ezra Jack Keats's *Peter's Chair* shows how one child handles these feelings when he not only gets an unwanted baby sister but also sees his own furniture painted pink for the new arrival. Overcoming feelings of jealousy can also be a theme in stories about animals. In Jenny Wagner's *John Brown, Rose and the Midnight Cat*, the dog fears that a cat coming into his home will disturb his very comfortable life with a nice widow. Books can help children anticipate and prepare themselves for strange situations that frighten them. Many children fear going to school for the first time or moving into a new school or neighborhood. Eric Carle's *Do You Want to Be My Friend?*, Miriam Cohen's *Will I Have a Friend?*, and Rosemary Wells's *Timothy Goes to School* present heroes who successfully cope with this problem. Harlow Rockwell has written and illustrated *My Doctor* and *My Dentist* to help answer young children's questions about the procedures and equipment used during physical checkups. Older children have many of their questions answered in James Howe's *The Hospital Book*. Barbara Greenberg's *The Bravest Babysitter* illustrates the common childhood fear of thunder and storms. This story reverses the normal situation: when the babysitter becomes frightened during a thunderstorm, the younger child tries to distract the fearful older one.

Illustrations of realistic situations provide a preview of a visit to a doctor. (From *The Checkup* by Helen Oxenbury. Copyright © 1983 by Helen Oxenbury. By permission of Dial Books for Young Readers, a Division of E. P. Dutton, Inc.)

Literature provides children with many examples of how to understand and cope with feelings of anger. Many children have days when absolutely nothing goes right. Books can act as a stimulus for discussing how children handled or could have handled similar situations. Young children, for example, can certainly identify with Judith Viorst's Alexander in *Alexander and the Terrible, Horrible, No Good, Very Bad Day* or with Patricia Giff's Ronald in *Today was a Terrible Day*. Edna Mitchell Preston and Rainey Bennett's *The Temper Tantrum Book* shows that even animals can have tantrums when they have experiences similar to those of young children. The animals explain what makes them angry. The book can prompt children to share what makes them angry and how they deal with this problem. Several books—including Jerrold Beim's *The Smallest Boy in the Class* and Robert Kraus's *The Littlest Rabbit*—show how fictional characters deal with the familiar problem of being teased by one's peers.

Literature can play a dramatic role in helping children develop positive and realistic self-concepts and feelings of self-esteem. Infants do not think of themselves as individuals. Between the ages of two and three, children slowly begin to realize that they have an identity separate from other members of the family. By age three, with the assistance of a warm, loving environment, most children have developed a set of feelings about themselves; they consider themselves "I." Egocentric feelings continue for several years, and children consider themselves the center of the universe. If the development of self-esteem is to progress positively, they need to know that their families, friends, and the larger society value them. Aliki Brandenberg's *The Two of Them*, for example, develops a strong relationship between a girl and her grandfather, which helps her accept his eventual death and be responsible for an orchard they both loved.

Illustrations and text develop understanding between a boy and his stepfather. (From *Like Jake and Me* by Mavis Jukes. Pictures by Lloyd Bloom. Illustrations copyright © 1984 by Lloyd Bloom. By permission of Alfred A. Knopf, Inc.)

All children must feel pride in their accomplishments and cultural heritage and must develop positive sex-role identifications. Those who have developed positive feelings of self-worth will be able to assume personal responsibility for their own successes and failures. Literature can help young children discover the capabilities they have and realize that acquiring some skills takes considerable time. For example, in Ezra Jack Keats's *Whistle for Willie*, Peter tries and tries to whistle. After considerable practice, he finally learns this skill. Books such as Jean Holzenthaler's *My Hands Can* and Ann and Paul Rand's *I Know a Lot of Things* help young children develop the realization that they can do many things. Positive attitudes toward one's heritage can be reinforced through reading and doing things that a child's cultural group favors and that show the many positive contributions of the people who belong to it. (This is especially important for ethnic minority groups, and chapter eleven discusses these implications.) If selected carefully, books provide excellent role models and illustrate that both males and females can function successfully in many different roles. (Chapter nine covers this topic in detail.)

Several excellent books for older children are based on the themes of overcoming problems and developing full maturity. In Scott O'Dell's *Island of the Blue Dolphins* a girl survives alone on an island off the coast of California. She is not rescued for eighteen years and must overcome loneliness, develop weapons that violate a taboo of her society, and create a life for herself. *Call It Courage*, by Armstrong Sperry, is another survival book, in which a boy must overcome his fear of the sea before he can return home.

Levels of reading achievement may influence feelings of self-worth. Alexander and Filler (1, pp. 6–7) reviewed research in the area of reading achievement and self-concept development and concluded that (1) low self-concepts may result when children feel that they are poor readers or are evaluated as poor readers by respected peers, parents, and/or teachers; (2) children who believe that others consider them unsuccessful readers may avoid reading entirely by refusing to make an effort or by deciding that they hate reading or find it boring; (3) if children believe that they are poor readers, they may in fact become poor readers; and (4) positive self-concepts lead children to further success in reading, while negative self-

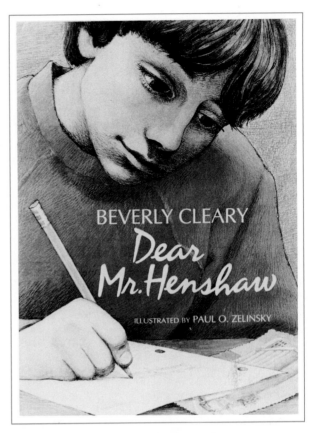

Writing to an author helps a boy accept his parents' divorce. (Jacket cover by Paul O. Zelinsky for *Dear Mr. Henshaw*, by Beverly Cleary. Copyright © 1983 by Beverly Cleary. By permission of William Morrow ad Company.)

concepts encourage even greater failure in the future.

Children's personality development is extremely important. If they do not understand themselves and believe that they are important, how can they value anyone else? Many literary selections and literature-related experiences developed throughout this text will reinforce positive personality development through experiences such as reading orally in a warm and secure environment, discussing and acting out various roles from literature, enhancing self-worth contributions, and simply enjoying a wide variety of literature.

CHART 1–3
Personality development

Characteristics	Implications	Literature Suggestions
Preschool: Ages two–three		
1 Children begin to think that they have their own identity separate from other members of the family.	1 Help children understand that they are people who have their own identity and their own worth.	Duke, Kate. *Clean-up Day.* Holzenthaler, Jean. *My Hands Can.* Stinson, Kathy. *Big or Little?*
2 They feel the need for security.	2 Holding a child during lap reading can add to a sense of security and enjoyment of books.	Carlstrom, Nancy. *Jesse Bear, What Will You Wear?* Lindgren, Barbro. *The Wild Baby.* Wells, Rosemary. *Max's Bedtime.*
Preschool: Ages three–four		
1 Children have developed a fairly steady self-concept; they identify themselves as "I" and have a set of feelings about themselves.	1 Children's self-concepts are affected by attitudes and behavior of those around them; they must feel that others care about them, accept them, and think they are worthy.	Jonas, Ann. *When You Were A Baby.* Krauss, Ruth. *The Carrot Seed.* Rand, Ann, and Rand, Paul. *I Know a Lot of Things.* Stinson, Kathy. *Red Is Best.* Williams, Barbara. *Someday, Said Mitchell.*
2 Children require warm and secure environments.	2 Share books with children in a warm atmosphere in classrooms, libraries, or at home.	Adoff, Arnold. *Black Is Warm Is Tan.* Dabcovich, Lydia. *Sleepy Bear.* Hill, Eric. *Spot's Birthday Party.* McPhail, David. *Dream Child.* Rice, Eve. *Benny Bakes a Cake.*
3 Children hide from unhappy situations by withdrawing, suggesting that problems don't exist, or by blaming someone else.	3 Special guidance should help children accept mistakes without decreasing their feelings of self-worth.	Sharmat, Marjorie. *A Big Fat Enormous Lie.*
4 They begin to become aware of their cultural heritage.	4 They need to be proud of who they are. Provide literature to stress cultural contributions and the contributions of the home and neighborhood.	Adoff, Arnold. *Black Is Warm Is Tan.*
Preschool: Ages four–five		
1 They continue to be egocentric; they talk in first person and consider themselves the center of the world.	1 Present literature in which they can identify with the character and the story.	Small, David. *Imogene's Antlers.* Vincent, Gabrielle. *Ernest and Celestine's Picnic.*
2 They improve in their ability to handle their own emotions in productive ways.	2 Help children identify other ways to handle problems. Use literature to help them see how others handle their emotions.	Galler, Helga. *Little Nerino.* Keats, Ezra Jack. *Peter's Chair.* Keats, Ezra Jack. *Regards to the Man in the Moon.* Viorst, Judith. *Alexander and the Terrible, Horrible, No Good, Very Bad Day.* Wagner, Jenny. *John Brown, Rose and the Midnight Cat.*

CHART 1–3 (cont.)
Personality development

Characteristics	Implications	Literature Suggestions
3 Fears of unknown situations may cause children to lose confidence and to lose control of their emotions.	3 Help children understand what is new to them and help them feel comfortable with their ability to handle unknown situations. Read about and discuss new situations.	Carle, Eric. *Do You Want to Be My Friend?* Rockwell, Harlow. *My Dentist.* Rogers, Fred. *Going to the Doctor.* Rogers, Fred. *Going to Day Care.*
4 They begin to respond to intrinsic motivation.	4 Children require good models for intrinsic motivation. Books are sources of models.	Bunting, Eve. *The Mother's Day Mice.* Williams, Barbara. *Chester Chipmunk's Thanksgiving.*
5 Children require warm and secure environments.	5 Continue reading to children in a loving atmosphere.	Buckley, Helen. *Grandmother and I.* Gammell, Stephen. *Wake Up, Bear . . . It's Christmas!* Larrick, Nancy. *When the Dark Comes Dancing: A Bedtime Poetry Book.*
Preschool—Kindergarten: Ages five–six		
1 Five-year-olds are usually outgoing, sociable, and friendly.	1 They enjoy stories showing similar characteristics in the main characters.	Flournoy, Valerie. *The Patchwork Quilt.* Hoffman, Phyllis, *Steffie and Me.* Marshall, James. *George and Martha One Fine Day.* Small, David. *Eulalie and the Hopping Head.*
2 Children are quite stable and adjusted in their emotional life; they are developing self-assurance and confidence in others.	2 These characteristics should be encouraged. Opportunities should allow children to expand self-assurance—it is closely related to self-worth.	Brandenberg, Aliki. *The Two of Them.* Lexau, Joan. *Benjie on His own.* Ormerod, Jan. *Sunshine.*
3 They require warmth and security in adult relationships even though self-assurance increases.	3 Continue to provide warm relationships through a close association during story time.	Brown, Margaret Wise. *The Runaway Bunny.* Hest, Amy. *The Crack-of-Dawn Walkers.* Murphy, Jill. *Peace at Last.* Zolotow, Charlotte. *My Grandson Lew.*
Early Elementary: Ages six–eight		
1 Six-year-olds are not as emotionally stable as five-year-olds; they show more tension, may strike out against a teacher or parent.	1 Help children discover acceptable ways to handle their tensions. Read stories to illustrate how other children handle their tensions.	Ehrlich, Amy. *Leo, Zack, and Emmie.* Jukes, Mavis. *Like Jake and Me.* Preston, Edna Mitchell. *The Temper Tantrum Book.*
2 Children seek independence from adults but continue to require warmth and security from the adults in their lives.	2 Provide opportunities for them to demonstrate independence; allow them to choose books and activities for sharing. Supply books in which characters develop independence.	Cleary, Beverly. *Ramona Quimby, Age 8.* Greene, Carol. *Hinny Winny Bunco.* Stanek, Muriel. *All Alone After School.* Wallace, Ian. *Chin Chiang and the Dragon's Dance.* Williams, Vera B. *Something Special for Me.*

CHART 1–3 (cont.)
Personality development

Characteristics	Implications	Literature Suggestions
Middle Elementary: Ages eight–ten		
1 The personality characteristic of cooperation is highly valued by fourth graders but declines in later grades.	1 Encourage literature activities that allow for cooperation; provide books stressing cooperation as the theme.	Baylor, Byrd. *The Best Town in the World.* Goffstein, M. B. *Family Scrapbook.*
2 Children have fewer fears about immediate and possible dangers but may have strong fears about remote or impossible situations, such as ghosts, lions, and witches.	2 Literature selections describing children's fears may be used for discussion and developing understanding of unrealistic fears.	Brittain, Bill. *The Wish Giver.* Johnston, Tony. *Four Scary Stories.*
Upper Elementary: Ages ten–twelve		
1 Many children have internalized their control; they believe that they are in control of what happens and assume more personal responsibility for successes and failures.	1 Reinforce responsibility, organizing, and making decisions. Provide books that illustrate the development of internalized control.	Cleary, Beverly. *Dear Mr. Henshaw.* Fox, Paula. *One-Eyed Cat.* MacLachlan, Patricia. *Sarah, Plain and Tall.* Shura, Mary Francis. *The Search for Grissi.*
2 Independence is a valued personality trait.	2 Supply literature to illustrate developing independence for both male and female characters.	O'Dell, Scott. *Island of the Blue Dolphins.* Park, Ruth. *Playing Beatie Bow.* Sperry, Armstrong. *Call It Courage.* Voigt, Cynthia. *Dicey's Song.* Voigt, Cynthia. *A Solitary Blue.*
3 Rapid changes in physical growth may cause some children to become self-conscious and self-critical; others may be preoccupied with their appearance.	3 Stories of other children who experience problems growing up may be especially appearing during this time.	Cleaver, Vera, and Cleaver, Bill. *Me Too.* Paterson, Katherine. *Come Sing, Jimmy Jo.*

Sources: Mussen, Conger, and Kagan (14); and Sarafino and Armstrong (20).

Social Development

According to child development authorities, the term *socialization* refers to the process by which children acquire behavior, beliefs, standards, and motives valued by their families and their cultural groups. Socialization is said to occur when children learn the ways of their groups so that they can function acceptably within them. They must learn to exert control over aggressive and hostile behavior if they are to have acceptable relationships with family members, friends, and the larger community. These acceptable relationships require that children develop an understanding of the feelings and viewpoints of others.

Quite obviously, socialization is a very important part of child development. Understanding the processes that influence social development is essential for anyone who works with children. Researchers have identified three processes that are most influential in the socialization of children. First, reward and punishment by parents and other adults reinforces socially acceptable attitudes and behavior and discourages socially unacceptable tendencies. For example, a child who refuses to share a toy with another child may be deprived of the toy, while appropriate sharing may be rewarded with a hug and a favorable comment. Second, observation of others teaches children the responses, behaviors, and beliefs considered appropriate within their culture. Children learn how to act and what to believe by imitating adults and peers. For example, a girl may learn about gender distinctions in our culture by observing and trying to copy her mother's role in the family. Children also observe what other members of the family fear and how members of their group react to people who belong to different racial or cultural groups. The third process, identification, may be the most important for socialization, since it requires emotional ties with the model. Children's thoughts, feelings, and actions become similar to those of people they believe are like them.

ISSUE

···❖···

Are Children's Picture Books Transmitting Images That Will Foster Children's Social Development?

THIS TEXTBOOK AND texts by Huck[1] and Cullinan[2] suggest that young children's literature appreciation and social development can be fostered through a careful selection of picture storybooks that encourage children to become sensitive to the feelings of others, to understand the various roles people play, and to understand different viewpoints and attitudes. Social science educator Joe Hurst, however, is very critical of the social images portrayed in many children's picture books.[3]

Hurst analyzed images found in Caldecott Medal winners published between 1958 and 1978 and in an equal number of non-award-winning picture books published during the same time period. In the area of participatory behavior Hurst concluded: "The picture books sampled provide a bland, passive view of life. Their illustrations, quoted dialogue, and author narratives present no role models of democratic participation or participatory behaviors. All the characters are portrayed in situations where few important decisions are made and where active participation is unnecessary" (p. 139).

Hurst's conclusions and recommendations are critical. His main concern is with decision making, active participation in the plots, and social issues. He recommends that children, teachers, and parents evaluate books relative to active, participatory role models and unprejudicial treatment of groups; that librarians order, display, and encourage children to read books related to active social participation; and that publishers make an effort to produce books that present a more realistic, active, unbiased view of America and the world. Hurst does not consider literary quality, integration of illustration and text, or enhancement of children's enjoyment in the literature he analyzed. These issues related to social development also need to be considered when educators and parents are choosing picture books to share with young children.

[1]Huck, Charlotte S. *Children's Literature in the Elementary School,* Third Edition, Updated. New York: Holt, Rinehart and Winston, 1979.

[2]Cullinan, Bernice E. "Books in the Life of the Young Child." In *Literature and Young Children,* edited by Bernice Cullinan and Carolyn Carmichael. Urbana, IL: National Council of Teachers of English, 1977.

[3]Hurst, Joe B. "Images in Children's Picture Books." *Social Education* (February 1981): 138–43.

Children's first relationships usually occur within the immediate family, then extend to a few friends in the neighborhood, to school, and finally to the broader world. Literature and literature-related activities can aid in the development of these relationships by encouraging children to become sensitive to the feelings of others. For example, Ann Herbert Scott's *Sam* is very unhappy when the members of his family are too busy to play with him. When they realize what is wrong, members of Sam's family remember to include him in their activities. The four-year-old in Eve Rice's *Benny Bakes a Cake* helps his mother in the kitchen, but faces disappointment when his dog eats the cake. Overcoming problems related to sibling rivalry is a frequent theme in children's books and is one that children can understand. In Charlotte Zolotow's *Big Brother*, a little sister is constantly teased by her older brother. In *Stevie*, by John Steptoe, Robert is upset when his mother takes care of a child from another family, but discovers that he actually misses Stevie when he leaves.

Many books for preschool and early primary children deal with various emotions related to friendship. Best friends may have strong attachments with each other, as shown in Miriam Cohen's *Best Friends* and Russell Hoban's *Best Friends for Frances*. In contrast, they may also experience problems, as Crosby Bonsall demonstrates in *It's Mine!—A Greedy Book*. In this book, best friends quarrel when one of them wants to play with the other's toys. Many emotions related to friendship are developed in Marjorie Sharmat's *Gladys Told Me to Meet Her Here*. When Irving's friend is late for a day at the zoo, he feels disappointment, worry, and finally anger.

Social development includes becoming aware of and understanding the different social roles people play. One of the greatest contributions made by literature and literature-related discussions is the realization that both boys and girls can achieve in a wide range of roles. Books that emphasize nonstereotyped sex roles and achievement are excellent models and stimuli for discussion. For example, Margery Facklam's *Wild Animals, Gentle Women* includes information on the lives and contributions of eleven women who have studied animal behavior. The author also shows how a student can prepare for this profession. An unusual book that tells the story of a role uncommon to women is Patricia Clapp's *I'm Deborah Sampson: A Soldier in the War of the Revolution*. Deborah disguises herself as a man in order to fight. Books are also being written that stress the nonstereotyping of emotions. Charlotte Zolotow's *William's Doll*, a book for young children, relates a young boy's experiences when he wants a doll. His brother and neighbor consider him a sissy; his father buys him masculine toys. His grandmother finally explains that it is perfectly all right for boys to have dolls.

Becoming aware of different views about the world is an important part of socialization, and literature is an excellent way of accomplishing this. Children may sympathize with the Native American girl who loves her family but longs for a free life among the wild horses in *The Girl Who Loved Wild Horses* by Paul Goble. They may also understand the slave's viewpoint and the consequences of prejudice when they read F. N. Monjo's *The Drinking Gourd*. Older children discover the consequences of prejudice when they read Mildred Taylor's *Let the Circle Be Unbroken* or Belinda Hurmence's *A Girl Called Boy*. Contemporary realistic fiction presents many different viewpoints on issues familiar to children today, including divorce (Judy Blume's *It's Not the End of the World*); religious nonconformity (Robbie Branscum's *The Saving of P.S.*); and environmental concerns (Mel Ellis's *The Wild Horse Killers* and Jean Craighead George's *Who Really Killed Cock Robin*). Chapters nine and eleven present these and other selections.

Moral Development. Acquiring moral standards is an important part of every child's social development. Preschool children start to develop concepts of right and wrong when they identify with their parents and with parental values, attitudes, and standards of conduct. The two-year-old knows certain acts are wrong. According to Piaget (16), children younger than seven or eight have rigid and inflexible ideas of right and wrong learned from their parents. Piaget suggests that between the ages of eight and eleven considerable changes occur in children's moral development. They start to develop a sense of equality and to take into account the situation in which the wrong action occurs. Children become more flexible and realize that there are exceptions to their original strict rules of behavior; at this time, the peer group begins to influence their conduct.

Lawrence Kohlberg (12) defines the stages or structure of children's and adults' moral judgment according to the choices made when two or

FLASHBACK

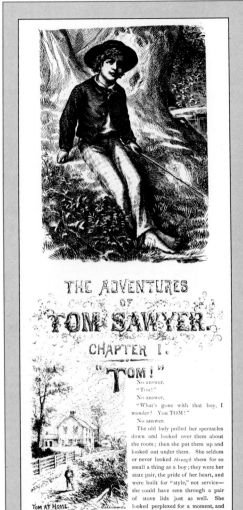

THE ADVENTURES OF TOM SAWYER, WRITTEN BY Mark Twain (Samuel Clemens) in the late nineteenth century, was one of the first adventure stories that was truly American in tone. In both *Tom Sawyer* and *The Adventures of Huckleberry Finn,* Twain captured the human, cultural, and geographical influences that affected a boy's life in a certain era of American history. Twain wrote from his own experiences living in the town of Hannibal, Missouri—an environment in which boys could explore the countryside, fish in a leisurely flowing stream, swim in the Mississippi River, and plan all types of mischief. *Tom Sawyer* portrays not only the free, adventurous life of childhood, but also Tom's discoveries about himself and those around him. There is the horror of a churchyard murder that Tom and his friend Huckleberry Finn accidentally witness. There is the racial bias some characters express. Twain's characters exemplify both the best and the worst of human qualities.

Twain's books became popular reading with children who wanted adventure stories about believable people in real locations. The popularity of the American adventure story set in a definite region may be seen in a partial list of much-loved books written by Twain's contemporaries: Kate Douglas Wiggin's *Rebecca of Sunnybrook Farm* takes place in rural Maine; Thomas Aldrich, in *The Story of a Bad Boy,* places his characters in a New England town; and Noah Brooks's *The Boy Emigrants* is set in the Great Plains.

more values conflict. Kohlberg considers the moral decisions that are made as well as the reasons why the decisions are chosen when he identifies the stages in moral development. At Stages 1 and 2, Kohlberg's "preconventional" level, the child responds to external, concrete consequences. During Stage-1 development the child chooses to be good or to obey rules in order to escape physical punishment. During Stage-2 development the child obeys or conforms in order to obtain rewards. Although Kohlberg's stages and children's ages cannot be equated because some people progress more rapidly through the sequence,

Stages 1 and 2 apparently dominate most children's behavior during the primary years.

At Stages 3 and 4, Kohlberg's "conventional" level, the child is concerned with meeting the external social expectations of family, group, or nation. During Stage-3 development the child desires social approval and consequently makes decisions according to the expectations of people who are important to the child. Stage 4 has a law-and-order orientation. The child conforms because of a high regard for social order and for patriotic duty. Although one stage builds on another and the transition between stages is grad-

CHART 1–4
Social development

Characteristics	Implications	Literature Suggestions
Preschool: Ages two–three		
1 Children learn to organize and represent their world; they imitate actions and behaviors they have observed.	1 Encourage children to role play so they can begin to take others' points of view and learn about behavior.	Carle, Eric. *The Mixed-up Chameleon.* Kraus, Robert. *The Littlest Rabbit.* Oxenbury, Helen. *Family.*
2 They transform things into make-believe: a yard-long ruler may be a horse.	2 Provide objects and books that suggest creative interpretations.	Ayal, Ora. *Ugbu.* Hutchins. Pat. *Changes, Changes.* Lionni, Leo. *Let's Make Rabbits.*
Preschool: Ages three–four		
1 They begin to realize that other people have feelings just as they do.	1 Encourage children to talk about how they felt when something similar happened to them; provide books that show feelings.	Alexander, Martha. *Nobody Asked Me If I Wanted a Baby Sister.* Keats, Ezra Jack. *Peter's Chair.*
2 Children enjoy playing together and develop strong attachments to other children.	2 Encourage growing social skills of sharing, taking turns, and playing cooperatively.	Cohen, Miriam. *Best Friends.* Hoban, Russell. *Best Friends for Frances.* Lindgren, Barbro. *Sam's Ball.*
3 They begin to enjoy participating in group activities and group games.	3 Let children be both leaders and followers during group activities after reading a book.	Bulla, Clyde. *Keep Running, Allen!* Oxenbury, Helen. *First Day at School.* Scott, Ann Herbert. *Sam.*
4 They begin to identify others' feelings by observing facial expressions.	4 Encourage them to become sensitive to their own and others' feelings by talking about feelings that accompany different facial expressions in books.	Berger, Terry. *I Have Feelings.* Bonsall, Crosby. *It's Mine!—A Greedy Book.* Hoban, Russell. *The Little Brute Family.* Lindgren, Barbro. *Sam's Lamp.*
Preschool: Ages four–five		
1 Children start to avoid aggression when angry and to look for a compromise. They are, however, frequently bossy, assertive, and prone to using alibis.	1 Praise children for talking out anger, help them to calm down and talk about the situation, direct them toward finding solutions. Choose books in which aggression is avoided.	Vincent, Gabrielle. *Smile, Ernest and Celestine.* Viorst, Judith. *I'll Fix Anthony.* Zolotow, Charlotte. *The Quarreling Book.*
2 They begin to understand consequences of good and bad and may engage in unacceptable behavior to elicit reactions.	2 Explain actions in their terms. Let children discuss alternative actions.	Beim, Jerrold. *The Smallest Boy in the Class.* Galdone, Paul. *The Little Red Hen.*
3 Children seldom play alone but begin to work by themselves.	3 Encourage persistence; let them work at something until it is completed to their satisfaction. This is crucial for problem solving and self-directed learning.	Burton, Virginia Lee. *Mike Mulligan and His Steam Shovel.* Carle, Eric. *The Very Busy Spider.*

CHART 1–4 (cont.)
Social development

Characteristics	Implications	Literature Suggestions
4 They increase their awareness of the different roles people play—nurse, police officer, grocery clerk, man, woman, etc.	4 Provide opportunities to meet different kinds of people through real life and books; encourage dramatic play around different roles.	Klein, Norma. *Girls Can Be Anything.* Oxenbury, Helen. *The Checkup.* Rockwell, Harlow. *My Doctor.* Zolotow, Charlotte. *William's Doll.*
5 They may exhibit unreasonable fears such as fear of the dark, thunder, animals, etc.	5 Help children overcome fears by sharing experiences of others who had fears but overcame them.	Greenberg, Barbara. *The Bravest Babysitter.*

Preschool—Kindergarten: Ages five–six

Characteristics	Implications	Literature Suggestions
1 Children like to help parents around the house; they are developing dependable behavior.	1 Allow children to be responsible for jobs that they can realistically complete. Read stories about children helping.	Rice, Eve. *Benny Bakes a Cake.* Rylant, Cynthia. *When I Was Young in the Mountains.* Williams, Vera B. *A Chair for My Mother.*
2 They protect younger brothers and sisters and other children.	2 Let them help and read to younger children, encourage them to become aware that they are growing into independent people. Share reasons why all people need security.	Howe, James. *There's a Monster Under My Bed.* Lisker, Sonia O. *Lost.*
3 They are proud of their accomplishments; they take pride in going to school and in their possessions.	3 Encourage a feeling of self-worth: praise accomplishments, encourage children to share school and home experiences, and allow them to talk about their possessions.	Fassler, Joan. *Howie Helps Himself.* Udry, Janice. *What Mary Jo Shared.*
4 They continue to show anxiety and unreasonable fear.	4 Help children overcome their fears and anxieties; stress that these are normal.	Sharmat, Marjorie. *The Best Valentine in the World.* Waber, Bernard. *Ira Sleeps Over.* Wells, Rosemary. *Timothy Goes to School.*
5 Children enjoy playing outside on their favorite toys: tricycles and sleds.	5 Provide opportunities for play, discussions about play, reading and drawing about outside play, and dictating stories about outside play.	Keats, Ezra Jack. *The Snowy Day.* McLeod, Emilie Warren. *The Bear's Bicycle.*
6 Children enjoy excursions to new and familiar places.	6 Plan trips to zoos, fire stations, etc. Read about these places, encourage children to tell about family trips.	Gretz, Susanna. *The Bears Who Went to the Seaside.*
7 They enjoy dressing up, role playing, and creative play.	7 Provide opportunities for them to dress up and play different roles. Read stories that can be used for creative play.	Cauley, Lorinda Bryan. *Goldilocks and the Three Bears.* Hadithi, Mwenye. *Greedy Zebra.* Ichikawa, Satomi. *Nora's Castle.*

CHART 1–4 (cont.)
Social development

Characteristics	Implications	Literature Suggestions
Early Elementary: Ages six–eight		
1 Children may defy parents when they are under pressure; they have difficulty getting along with younger siblings.	1 Encourage them to become more sensitive to family needs, to talk and read stories about situations, and direct them toward finding solutions.	Blume, Judy. The *One in the Middle is the Green Kangaroo.* Flournoy, Valerie. *The Patchwork Quilt.* Ness, Evaline. *Sam, Bangs, and Moonshine.* Sendak, Maurice. *Where the Wild Things Are.* Zolotow, Charlotte. *Big Brother.*
2 They want to play with other children but frequently insist on being first.	2 Encourage children both to lead and follow, read books in which children overcome similar problems.	Kellogg, Steven. *Best Friends.* Udry, Janice May. *Let's Be Enemies.*
3 Children respond to teachers' help or praise. They try to conform and please teachers.	3 Allow them to share work and receive praise. "Show and tell" is especially enjoyable for six- and seven-year-olds. Praise their reading and sharing of books.	Lobel, Arnold. *Frog and Toad All Year.* Schwartz, Alvin. *There Is a Carrot in My Ear and Other Noodle Tales.* Van Leeuwen, Jean. *More Tales of Oliver Pig.*
4 They enjoy sitting still and listening to stories read at school, at home, or in the library.	4 Provide frequent storytelling and story-reading times.	de Paola, Tomie. *The Clown of God.* Isele, Elizabeth. *The Frog Princess.* Rabe, Berniece. *The Balancing Girl.* Steptoe, John. *The Story of Jumping Mouse.* Turkle, Brinton. *Do Not Open.*
5 Children have definite inflexible ideas of right and wrong.	5 They identify with the values, attitudes, and standards of conduct their parents accept.	Friedman, Ina R. *How My Parents Learned to Eat.* Lobel, Arnold. *Grasshopper on the Road.* Williams, Jay. *The Reward Worth Having.*
6 They are curious about differences between boys and girls.	6 They ask questions about differences between boys and girls and where babies come from. Books help answer such questions.	Andry, Andrew, and Schepp, Steven. *How Babies Are Made* (plants and animals). Isenbart, Hans-Heinrich. *A Duckling Is Born.* Sheffield, Margaret, and Bewley, Sheila. *Where Do Babies Come From?* (human).
Middle Elementary: Ages eight–ten		
1 Concepts of right and wrong become more flexible; the situation in which the wrong action occurred is taken into consideration.	1 Experiences and books help them relate to different points of view; they begin to realize there are different attitudes, values, and standards from those their parents stress.	Branscum, Robbie. *The Saving of P.S.* Callen, Larry. *Who Kidnapped the Sheriff? Tales from Tickfaw.* Fritz, Jean. *The Double Life of Pocahontas.* Goble, Paul. *The Girl Who Loved Wild Horses.*
2 Children begin to be influenced by their peer groups.	2 Acceptance of the peer group becomes more important; this group can influence attitudes, values, and interests.	Allard, Harry. *Miss Nelson Is Missing.* Delton, Judy. *Kitty in the Middle.*

CHART 1–4 (cont.)
Social development

Characteristics	Implications	Literature Suggestions
3 Thinking is becoming socialized; they can understand other people's points of view. They feel that their reasoning and solutions to problems should agree with others.	3 Provide many opportunities for them to investigate differing points of view. Literature is an excellent source.	Byars, Betsy. *The Animal, the Vegetable, and John D. Jones.* Margolis, Richard J. *Secrets of a Small Brother.* Monjo, F. N. *The Drinking Gourd.* Sandin, Joan. *The Long Way to a New Land.*

Upper Elementary: Ages ten–twelve

Characteristics	Implications	Literature Suggestions
1 Children have developed racial attitudes; low-prejudiced children increase in perception of nonracial characteristics; high-prejudiced children increase in perception of racial characteristics.	1 Literature and instructional activities must develop multiethnic values and stress contributions of ethnic minorities.	Adoff, Arnold. *All the Colors of the Race.* Adoff, Arnold. *Malcolm X.* Highwater, Jamake. *Anpao—An American Indian Odyssey.* Paulsen, Gary. *Dogsong.* White, Florence. *Cesar Chavez: Man of Courage.*
2 They want to do jobs well instead of starting and exploring them; feelings of inferiority and inadequacy may result if they feel they cannot measure up to their own personal standards.	2 Encourage expansion of knowledge in high-interest areas; provide books in these areas; provide assistance and encouragement to allow them to finish jobs that meet expectations.	Cobb, Vicki, and Darling, Kathy. *Bet You Can't! Science Impossibilities to Fool You.* Simon, Seymour. *Your First Home Computer: Buying, It Using It, and Keeping It Working.*
3 They have a sense of justice and resist imperfections in the world.	3 Idealistic concerns increase interest in stories where people overcome injustice, improve some aspect of life, or raise questions about life.	Arnold, Caroline. *Saving the Peregrine Falcon.* Barry, Scott. *The Kingdom of Wolves.* Lasky, Kathryn. *The Night Journey.* Riskind, Mary. *Apple Is My Sign.* Rylant, Cynthia. *A Blue-Eyed Daisy.* Yates, Elizabeth. *Amos Fortune, Free Man.*
4 Peer groups exert strong influences on children; conformity to parents decreases and conformity to peers increases in social situations. May challenge parent.	4 If differences between peer and family values are too great, children may experience conflicts. Literature selections and discussions can help.	Brooks, Bruce. *The Moves Make the Man.* Byars, Betsy. *The Cybil War.* Greenberg, Jan. *The Iceberg and Its Shadow.*
5 Children have developed strong associations with gender-typed expectations: girls may fail in "masculine" tasks; boys in "feminine" tasks.	5 Provide books and discussions that avoid sex-stereotyped roles; emphasize that both sexes can succeed in many roles.	Clapp, Patricia. *I'm Deborah Sampson: A Soldier in the War of the Revolution.* Facklam, Margery. *Wild Animals, Gentle Women.* Fox, Mary. *Women Astronauts: Aboard the Shuttle.* Paige, David. *A Day in the Life of a Marine Biologist.* Tobias, Tobi. *Arthur Mitchell.* Yates, Elizabeth. *My Diary—My World.*

CHART 1–4 (cont.)
Social development

Characteristics	Implications	Literature Suggestions
6 Boys and girls accept the identiy of the opposite sex.	6 Girls more than boys begin to feel that marriage would be desirable; books that develop relationships with the opposite sex interest girls especially.	Benjamin, Carol Lea. *The Wicked Stepdog.* Cooper, Susan. *Seaward.* L'Engle, Madeleine. *A Ring of Endless Light.* Lunn, Janet. *The Root Cellar.*

Sources: Braga and Braga (4); Mussen, Conger, and Kagan (14); and Piaget and Inhelder (16).

ual, Stage-3 behaviors usually begin in the upper elementary grades and Stage-4 behaviors usually emerge in adolescence.

Stages 5 and 6 (which may be incorporated into a single stage) are at the "postconventional," autonomous, or principled level at which the person establishes his or her own definition of moral values. At Stage 5 the person responds to equal rights and consequently avoids violating the rights of others. At Stage 6 the individual con-

forms in order to avoid self-condemnation. Kohlberg estimates that only 25 percent of the population moves on in late adolescence or adulthood to this morality of equal rights, justice, and internal commitment to the principles of conscience.

Kohlberg has recently suggested that a Stage 7 in moral development is the highest level of ethical and religious thinking. He refers to this stage as one of qualitatively new insight and perspective, in which a person experiences wholeness—

ISSUE

···━➤➤❊❀❦━···

Challenges to Theories of Human Development

IS THERE A GENDER ISSUE in studies related to children's moral development? Is there a gender issue in studies related to children's language and communication development and to children's visual-spatial development? Was Piaget incorrect when he stated that children under the age of seven or eight do not have a grasp of cause-and-effect relationships? These are a few of the current developmental issues that are discussed in both the scientific and the popular press.

Several researchers are questioning Kohlberg's and Piaget's assertions about the social and moral development of children. Carol Gilligan contends that the developmental models of Kohlberg and Piaget "equate male development with child development"[1] and thereby ignore female development. Kohlberg, for example, based his hierarchy of moral development on a 20-year study of 84 males. Gilligan's research, which involved both female and male subjects, indicated that females and males develop different systems of values due to traditional gender roles that assign females the primary responsibility for taking care of others' needs. Females develop a "morality of responsibility" that stresses the importance of maintaining relationships and considering other people's feelings and points of view (roughly equivalent to Kohlberg's Stage 3). Males learn to place more value on competitive self-assertion and

[1] Gilligan, Carol. *In a Different Voice: Psychological Theory and Women's Development.* Cambridge, MA: Harvard University Press, 1982.

a union with nature, a deity, and the cosmos. Although Kohlberg recognizes Stage 7 as an aspiration rather than as a complete possibility, he maintains that Stage-7 behaviors support individuals through experiences of suffering, injustice, and death.

Children's literature contains numerous moments of crisis when characters make moral decisions and contemplate the reasons for their decisions. Although Kohlberg does not apply his stages of moral development to children's literature, both Donna Norton (15) and Cheryl Gosa (11) have developed such applications. Norton has used Kohlberg's stages of moral development as a research tool for evaluating the moral decisions of characters in biographical literature (see chapter 12). Gosa maintains that Kohlberg's stages are appropriate guidelines for categorizing and evaluating the moral decisions of characters in realistic fiction. If adults expect children to understand the decision-making process of characters in a story, Gosa asserts, they should be aware of the level of the decision that characters are making and consider whether or not children are at the stage when they can appreciate that decision. Otherwise, she contends, "fiction containing . . . high level decisions [will be] meaningless for early character development . . . and beyond the level of their readers" (11, p. 530).

Students of children's literature may find it valuable and thought-provoking to consider the stages of moral decisions represented by the characters in children's books when selecting literature for use with children. Chart 1-5 identifies Kohlberg's stages of moral development and lists decisions made by characters in books written for children from approximately age four through age twelve. As can be seen from the chart, the only book in this group that relies on Stage-6 decision-making processes is *Jacob Have I Loved*, which was also written for older readers. Stage-7 decisions were not found in the books. Decision-making processes may be used for discussions, as children consider the options open to the characters and how they might have responded in similar circumstances.

develop a "morality of rights" that considers rules more important than relationships (roughly equivalent to Kohlberg's Stages 5 and 6).

The implications of the gender differences between the Kohlberg and the Gilligan theories of moral development are highlighted by John West and Davele Bursor.[2] These educators argue that counselors or anyone else who works with children should understand gender differences in moral development and should be able to use these differences when counseling either girls or boys during the decision-making process.

Studies reported by Jo Durden-Smith and Diane Desimone[3] also question theories of language and cognitive development that are based primarily on male subjects. These authors report results from brain research that suggest sex-related differences between males and females. They outline brain research studies demonstrating female superiority in verbal skills, fine-motor coordination, and response to emotional content. These studies suggest that the left hemisphere and its abilities develop faster in girls than in boys. In contrast, males demonstrate superiority in visual-spatial skills and in mathematical and mechanical tasks. Consequently, some researchers conclude that the right hemisphere and its abilities develop faster in boys than in girls.

The ages of children in Piaget's pre-causal level are also being challenged. Maya Pines[4] reports on research by psychologists such as Rochel Gelman and Thomas Shultz showing that children as young as three or four have an understanding of cause and effect.

As might be expected, these studies, the interpretations of these studies, and the implications of these studies are highly controversial. Students of children's literature and child development may read the conflicting theories and discuss the implications.

[2] West, John D., and Bursor, Davele E. "Gilligan and Kohlberg: Gender Issue in Moral Development." *Humanistic Education and Development*. Vol. 22 (June 1984): 134–42.

[3] Durden-Smith, Jo, and Desimone, Diane. *Sex and the Brain*. New York: Arbor House, 1983.

[4] Pines, Maya. "Can a Rock Walk." *Psychology Today*. Vol. 17 (November 1983): 46–52.

CHART 1–5

Decision making in realistic fiction

	Kohlberg's Stages of Moral Development	Ages 4–7 *Send Wendell* by Genevieve Gray	Ages 6–8 *Benjie on His Own* by Joan M. Lexau	Ages 8–10 *Tales of a Fourth Grade Nothing* by Judy Blume	Ages 10+ *Jacob Have I Loved* by Katherine Paterson
1	**Pre-moral level** *Stage I*: Punishment and obedience orientation. Rules obeyed to avoid punishment.		Benjie obeys the big boys, he turns his pockets out to show them he has no money he is very frightened.	Three-year-old Fudge eats to avoid father's punishment. Nine-year-old Peter believes Fudge would behave if he was punished. Father allows Fudge to be in a commercial so firm does not lose account.	
	Stage II: Naive instrumental hedonism. The child conforms in order to obtain rewards.			Peter obeys his mother and tricks Fudge so they can go to lunch. Fudge stops complaining when he gets popcorn. Peter's puppy is a reward for his good behavior.	Louise takes off her dirty overalls rather than argue with her grandmother.
2	**Morality of conventional role conformity.** *Stage III*: Good-boy morality of maintaining good relations. The child conforms to avoid disapproval.	Six-year-old Wendell happily goes on errands because he loves Mama and likes to help her.	Benjie does not want his grandmother to walk him home after school but he "puts up with it." Benjie promises to be good while grandmother is in the hospital.	Peter does not want to share his room but knows there is no point in arguing with his mother. Peter says thank you for a gift he does not like.	
	Stage IV: Authority maintaining morality. The now says he is busy and suggests they send someone else.	Wendell's self-esteem increases as his uncle recognizes his worth. He now says he is busy and suggests they send someone else.			
3	**Morality of self-accepted principles.** *Stage V*: Morality of contract. A duty is defined in terms of contract, general avoidance of violation of the rights of others.		Benjie wants to ask grandmother to wait for him but does not because he knows it would worry her. Benjie laughs because he knows his grandmother is trying to cheer him up.		Louise expects her teacher to defend and explain her position. She is surprised and hurt when he does not. Louise does not talk back to her grandmother because such behavior is disrespectful to those who are older.
	Stage VI: Morality of individual principles of conscience. The child conforms to avoid self-condemnation.				Louise suggests that Christmas be cancelled because people are suffering and dying in World War II. Her classmates object; they do not understand her principles.

SUMMARY

Literature opens doors of discovery and adventure for children. It provides enjoyment, transmits our literary heritage, encourages understanding and valuing of our cultural heritage, provides vicarious experiences, transmits knowledge, nurtures and expands imagination, and stimulates four major types of child development: language, cognitive, personality, and social. Cognitive development includes observing, comparing, classifying, hypothesizing, organizing, summarizing, applying, and criticizing.

Child development occurs in recognizable stages. All children do not progress through these stages at the same rate, but all children develop in the same sequence of stages. Knowing the characteristics of children during these different stages can benefit parents, teachers, librarians, and other adults concerned with selecting appropriate literature and literature-related activities for children.

Throughout this text, the reader will discover numerous books that are beneficial to children during their different developmental stages, as well as suggestions about how to use appropriate literature in work with children.

Suggested Activities for Understanding the Child and Children's Literature

☐ Ask several children how school and reading literature could be made more enjoyable. Compare the responses you receive with those obtained by Doris Roettger (p. 5).

☐ Select several books such as Eve Rice's *Oh Lewis* that could encourage young children to identify familiar actions in books. Share these with a few preschool children and let them interact orally with the text.

☐ Listen to the language of several children who are the same age. Do you notice any differences in their language development? Are these differences similar to those identified by Walter Loban (p. 7)?

☐ Select several books that you believe would stimulate children's language development. Present the books and your rationale for choosing them to your literature class.

☐ With a group of your peers, compile an additional list of picture books that would be useful when developing one of the following cognitive skills: observing, comparing, hypothesizing, organizing, summarizing, applying, and criticizing. Share your findings with your class.

☐ Read several books in which young children must overcome problems such as jealousy, fear, or anger. Compare the ways the authors have allowed children to handle their problems. Do the feelings seem normal and natural? Is more than one aspect of a feeling developed? Are options shown for handling the emotion?

References

1 Alexander, J. Estill, and Filler, Ronald Claude. *Attitudes and Reading*. Newark, Del.: International Reading Association, 1976.

2 Bartel, Nettie. "Assessing and Remediating Problems in Language Development." In *Teaching Children with Learning and Behavior Problems*, edited by Donald Hammill and Nettie Bartel. Boston: Allyn & Bacon, 1975.

3 Bernstein, Joanne. *Books to Help Children Cope with Separation and Loss*. New York: Bowker, 1977.

4 Braga, Laurie, and Braga, Joseph. *Learning and Growing: A Guide to Child Development*. Englewood Cliffs, N.J.: Prentice-Hall, 1975.

5 Braine, Martin. "The Ontogeny of English Phrase Structure: The First Phase." In *Readings in Language Development*, edited by Lois Bloom. New York: John Wiley, 1978.

6 Brown, Roger. *A First Language/The Early Stages*. Cambridge, Mass.: Harvard University, 1973.

7 Cullinan, Bernice E. "Books in the Life of the Young Child." In *Literature and Young Children*, edited by Bernice Cullinan and Carolyn Carmichael. Urbana, Ill.: National Council of Teachers of English, 1977.

8 Engel, Rosalind. "Literature Develops Children's I's for Reading." *Language Arts* 53 (November/December, 1976): 892–98.

9 Gage, N. L., and Berliner, David C. *Educational Psychology*. Chicago: Rand McNally, 1979.

10 Glazer, Joan. *Children's Literature for Early Childhood*. Columbus, Ohio: Merrill, 1981.

11 Gosa, Cheryl. "Moral Development in Current Fiction for Children and Young Adults." *Language Arts* 54 (May 1977): 529–36.

12 Kohlberg, Lawrence. *Essays on Moral Development: The Philosophy of Moral Development*. New York: Harper & Row, 1981.

13 Loban, Walter. *Language Development: Kindergarten through Grade Twelve*. Urbana, Ill.: National Council of Teachers of English, 1976.

14 Mussen, Paul Henry; Conger, John Janeway; and Kagan, Jerome. *Child Development and Personality*. New York: Harper & Row, 1979.

15 Norton, Donna. "Moral Stages of Children's Biographical Literature: 1800s–1900s." *Vitae Scholasticae*. In Press, 1986.

16 Piaget, Jean, and Inhelder, B. *The Psychology of the Child*. New York: Basic Books, 1969.

17 Roettger, Doris. "Reading Attitudes and the Estes Scale." Paper presented at the Twenty-third Annual Convention of the International Reading Association, Houston, Texas, 1978.

18 Rubin, Rhea Joyce. *Bibliotherapy Source Book*. Phoenix, Arizona: Oryx Press, 1978.

19 Rubin, Rhea Joyce. *Using Bibliotherapy: A Guide to Theory and Practice*. Phoenix, Arizona: Oryx Press, 1978.

20 Sarafino, Edward P., and Armstrong, James W. *Child and Adolescent Development*. Glenview, Ill.: Scott, Foresman, 1980.

21 Strickland, Dorothy S. "Promoting Language and Concept Development." In *Literature and Young Children*, edited by Bernice Cullinan and Carolyn Carmichael. Urbana, Ill.: National Council of Teachers of English, 1977.

Additional References

Boegehold, Betty D. *Getting Ready to Read*. New York: Ballantine Books, 1984.

de Villiers, Peter, and de Villiers, Jill G. *Language Acquisition*. Boston: Harvard University Press, 1980.

Furth, Hans G. and Wachs, Harry. *Thinking Goes to School: Piaget's Theory in Practice*. New York: Oxford University Press, 1975.

Ginsburg, Herbert, and Opper, Sylvia. *Piaget's Theory of Intellectual Development: An Introduction*. Englewood Cliffs, N.J.: Prentice-Hall, 1969.

Greenfield, Patricia Marks. *Mind and Media: The Effects of Television, Video Games, and Computers*. Cambridge, Massachusetts: Harvard University Press, 1984.

Kagan, Jerome, and Brim, Orville G. *Constancy and Change in Human Development*. Boston: Harvard University Press, 1980.

Keil, Francis. *Semantic and Conceptual Development*. Boston: Harvard University Press, 1980.

Mussen, Paul H. *Handbook of Child Psychology*. New York: Wiley, 1983.

Shallcross, Doris J. and Sisk, Dorothy A. *The Growing Person: How to Encourage Healthy Emotional Development in Children*. Englewood Cliffs, N.J.: Prentice-Hall, 1982.

Singer, Dorothy G. and Revenson, Tracey A. *A Piaget Primer: How a Child Thinks*. New York: International Universities Press, 1978.

Wadsworth, Barry J. *Piaget's Theory of Cognitive and Affective Development*. 3rd ed. New York: Longman, 1984.

Winn, Marie. *The Plug-In Drug: Television, Children and the Family*. New York: Viking, 1985.

CHILDREN'S
LITERATURE

Aardema, Verna. *Bringing the Rain to Kapiti Plain*. Illustrated by Beatriz Vidal. Dial, 1981.
———, *Why Mosquitoes Buzz in People's Ears: A West African Tale*. Illustrated by Leo and Diane Dillon. Dial, 1975.
Adoff, Arnold. *All of the Colors of the Race*. Illustrated by John Steptoe. Lothrop, Lee & Shepard, 1982.
———. *Black Is Warm Is Tan*. Harper & Row, 1973.
———. *Malcolm X*. Crowell, 1970.
———, ed. *My Black Me: A Beginning Book of Black Poetry*. Dutton, 1974.
Ahlberg, Janet, and Ahlberg, Allen. *Peek-a-boo!* Viking, 1981.
Alexander, Lloyd. *Westmark*. Dutton, 1981.
Alexander, Martha. *Nobody Asked Me If I Wanted a Baby Sister*. Dial, 1971.
———. *Out! Out! Out!* Dial, 1968.
Allard, Harry. *Miss Nelson Is Missing*. Illustrated by James Marshall. Houghton Mifflin, 1977.
Andry, Andrew, and Schepp, Steven. *How Babies Are Made*. Time-Life, 1968.
Anno, Mitsumasa. *Anno's Britain*. Philomel, 1982.
———. *Anno's Counting Book*. Crowell, 1977.
———. *Anno's Italy*. Collins, 1980.
Arkhurst, Joyce Cooper. *The Adventures of Spider*. Illustrated by Jerry Pinkney. Little, Brown, 1964.
Arnold, Caroline. *Saving the Peregrine Falcon*. Photographs by Richard R. Hewett, Carolrhoda, 1985.
Arnosky, Jim. *Flies in the Water, Fish in the Air*. Lothrop, Lee & Shepard, 1986.
———. *Freshwater Fish and Fishing*. Four Winds, 1982.
Aruego, Jose. *Look What I Can Do*. Scribner's, 1971.
Asian Cultural Centre for UNESCO. *Folktales from Asia for Children Everywhere*. 1977, 1978, 1979.
Ayal, Ora. *Ugbu*. Harper & Row, 1979.
Banchek, Linda. *Snake In, Snake Out*. Crowell, 1978.
Bang, Molly. *Ten, Nine, Eight*. Greenwillow, 1983.
Barry, Scott. *The Kingdom of Wolves*. Putnam, 1979.
Barton, Byron. *Airport*. Crowell, 1982.
Baylor, Byrd. *The Best Town in the World*. Scribner's, 1983.

Most of these titles are annotated in the chapters in which they are discussed in depth.

Beim, Jerrold. *The Smallest Boy in the Class*. Morrow, 1949.
Bellville, Cheryl Walsh. *Rodeo*. Carolrhoda, 1985.
Belpre, Pura. *The Rainbow-Colored Horse*. Warne, 1978.
Benjamin, Carol Lea. *The Wicked Stepdog*. Crowell, 1982.
Bennett, Jill. *Tiny Tim: Verses for Children*. Illustrated by Helen Oxenbury. Delacorte, 1982.
Beowulf translated by Kevin Crossley-Holand. Illustrated by Charles Keeping. Oxford University Press, 1984.
Berenstain, Stan, and Berenstain, Janice. *Old Hat, New Hat*. Random House, 1970.
Berger, Terry. *I Have Feelings*. Human Science, 1971.
———, and Kandell, Alice. *Ben's ABC Day*. Lothrop, Lee & Shepard, 1982.
Bess, Clayton. *Story for a Black Night*. Houghton Mifflin, 1982.
Blume, Judy. *Are You There, God? It's Me, Margaret*. Bradbury, 1970.
———. *It's Not the End of the World*. Bradbury, 1972.
———. *The One in the Middle is the Green Kangaroo*. Bradbury, 1981.
———. *Tales of a Fourth Grade Nothing*. Dutton, 1972.
Bonsall, Crosby. *It's Mine—A Greedy Book*. Harper & Row, 1964.
Brandenberg, Aliki. *The Two of Them*. Morrow, 1979.
Branscum, Robbie. *The Saving of P.S.* Doubleday, 1977.
Brenner, Martha. *Fireworks Tonight!* Hastings House, 1983.
Briggs, Raymond. *The Snowman*. Random House, 1978.
British Museum of Natural History. *Man's Place in Evolution*. Cambridge, 1981.
Brooks, Bruce. *The Moves Make the Man*. Harper & Row, 1984.
Brown, Margaret Wise. *The Runaway Bunny*. Harper & Row, 1972.
Bryan, Ashley. *The Cat's Purr*. Atheneum, 1985.
Buckley, Helen E. *Grandmother and I*. Lothrop, Lee & Shepard, 1961.
Bulla, Clyde. *Keep Running, Allen!* Crowell, 1978.
Bunting, Eve. *The Mother's Day Mice*. Illustrated by Jan Brett. Clarion, 1986.
Burningham, John. *The Rabbit*. Crowell, 1975.
———. *The Snow*. Crowell, 1975.
Burton, Virginia Lee. *Mike Mulligan and His Steam Shovel*. Houghton, 1939.
Busch, Phyllis. *Cactus in the Desert*. Crowell, 1979.

Byars, Betsy. *The Animal, the Vegetable, and John D. Jones.* Illustrated by Ruth Sanderson. Delacorte, 1982.

————. *The Cybil War.* Viking, 1981.

Callen, Larry. *Who Kidnapped the Sheriff? Tales from Tickfaw.* Illustrated by Stephen Gammell. Little, Brown, 1985.

Campbell, Rod. *Dear Zoo.* Four Winds, 1982.

Carle, Eric. *The Very Busy Spider.* Putnam, 1985.

————. *Do You Want to Be My Friend?* Crowell, 1971.

————. *Let's Paint a Rainbow.* Philomel, 1982.

————. *The Mixed-up Chameleon.* Crowell, 1975.

————. *My Very First Book of Colors.* Crowell, 1974.

————. *My Very First Book of Numbers.* Crowell, 1974.

————. *My Very First Book of Shapes.* Crowell, 1974.

Carlstrom, Nancy. *Jesse Bear, What Will You Wear?* Illustrated by Bruce Degen. Macmillan. 1986.

Cauley, Lorinda Bryan. *Goldilocks and the Three Bears.* Putnam, 1981.

Chorao, Kay. *The Baby's Lap Book.* Dutton, 1977.

Chute, Marchette. *Rhymes about Us.* Dutton, 1974.

Clapp, Patricia. *I'm Deborah Sampson: A Soldier in the War of the Revolution.* Lothrop, Lee & Shepard, 1977.

Cleary, Beverly. *Dear Mr. Henshaw.* Illustrated by Paul O. Zelinsky. Morrow, 1983.

————. *Ramona and Her Father.* Illustrated by Alan Tiegreen. Morrow, 1977.

————. *Ramona Quimby, Age 8.* Morrow, 1981.

Cleaver, Vera, and Cleaver, Bill. *Me Too.* Lippincott, 1973.

Clifton, Lucille. *Everett Anderson's Year.* Holt, Rinehart & Winston, 1974.

Cobb, Vicki, and Darling, Kathy. *Bet You Can't! Science Impossibilities to Fool You.* Illustrated by Martha Weston. Lothrop, Lee & Shepard, 1980.

Cohen, Miriam. *Best Friends.* Macmillan, 1971.

————. *Will I Have a Friend?* Macmillan, 1971.

Conly, Jane Leslie. *Racso and the Rats of NIMH.* Harper & Row, 1986.

Cooper, Susan. *Seaward.* Atheneum, 1983.

Corbett, W.J. *The Song of Pentecost.* Illustrated by Martin Ursell. Dutton, 1983.

Crews, Donald. *Freight Train.* Greenwillow, 1978.

————. *Harbor.* Greenwillow, 1982.

Cristini, Ermanno and Puricelli, Luigi. *In the Pond.* Alphabet, 1984.

Dabcovich, Lydia. *Sleepy Bear.* Dutton, 1982.

Dallinger, Jane. *Grasshoppers.* Photographed by Uko Sato. Lerner, 1981.

de Brunhoff, Laurent. *Babar's Book of Color.* Random, 1984.

Delessert, Etienne. *Beauty and the Beast.* Creative Education, 1984.

Delton, Judy. *Kitty in the Middle.* Dell, 1980.

de Paola, Tomie. *The Legend of the Bluebonnet.* Putnam's, 1983.

————. *The Clown of God.* Harcourt Brace Jovanovich, 1978.

————. *Fin M'Coul: The Giant of Knockmany Hill.* Holiday, 1981.

————. *The Hunter and the Animals: A Wordless Picture Book.* Holiday, 1981.

————. *Pancakes for Breakfast.* Harcourt Brace Jovanovich, 1978.

————. *The Quicksand Book.* Holiday, 1977.

Dubanevich, Arlene. *Pigs in Hiding.* Four Winds, 1983.

Duff, Maggie. *Rum Pum Pum.* Macmillan, 1978.

Duke, Kate. *Bedtime.* Dutton, 1986.

————. *Clean-up Day.* Dutton, 1986.

Duvoisin, Roger. *See What I Am.* Lothrop, Lee & Shepard, 1974.

Ehrlich, Amy. *Leo, Zack and Emmie.* Dial, 1981.

Ellis, Mel. *The Wild Horse Killers.* Holt, Rinehart & Winston, 1976.

Emberley, Barbara. *Drummer Hoff.* Illustrated by Ed Emberley. Prentice-Hall, 1967.

Emberley, Ed. *Picture Pie: A Circle Drawing Book.* Little, Brown, 1984.

————. *Ed Emberley's ABC.* Little, Brown, 1978.

Facklam, Margery. *Wild Animals, Gentle Women.* Harcourt Brace Jovanovich, 1978.

Fassler, Joan. *Howie Helps Himself.* Illustrated by Joe Lasker. Whitman, 1975.

Feelings, Muriel. *Moja Means One: Swahili Counting Book.* Illustrated by Tom Feelings. Dial, 1971.

Flournoy, Valerie. *The Patchwork Quilt.* Illustrated by Jerry Pinkney. Dial, 1985.

Forbes, Esther. *Johnny Tremain.* Illustrated by Lynd Ward. Houghton Mifflin, 1943.

Fox, Mary. *Women Astronauts: Aboard the Shuttle.* Messner, 1984.

Fox, Paula. *One-Eyed Cat.* Bradbury, 1984.

Friedman, Ina R. *How My Parents Learned to Eat.* Illustrated by Allen Say. Houghton, 1984.

Fritz, Jean. *The Double Life of Pocahontas.* Illustrated by Ed Young. Putnam, 1983.

————. *Make Way for Sam Houston.* Illustrated by Elise Primavera. Putnam, 1986.

Gág, Wanda. *Millions of Cats.* Coward-McCann, 1928.

Galdone, Paul. *The Amazing Pig: An Old Hungarian Tale.* Houghton Mifflin, 1981.

————. *Cinderella.* McGraw-Hill, 1978.

————. *The Gingerbread Boy.* Seabury, 1975.

————. *The Little Red Hen.* Houghton Mifflin, 1973.

————. *Puss in Boots.* Houghton Mifflin, 1976.

————. *The Three Billy Goats Gruff.* Houghton Mifflin, 1973.

————. *What's in Fox's Sack? An Old English Tale.* Clarion, 1982.

Galler, Helga. *Little Nerino.* Neugebauer, 1982.

Gammell, Stephen. *Wake Up, Bear . . . It's Christmas!* Lothrop, Lee & Shepard, 1981.

George, Jean Craighead. *My Side of the Mountain.* Dutton, 1975.

Giff, Patricia. *Today Was a Terrible Day.* Viking, 1980.

Gilchrist, Theo. *Halfway up the Mountain.* Lippincott, 1978.

Ginsburg, Mirra. *How the Sun Was Brought Back to the Sky.* Macmillan, 1975.

Goble, Paul. *The Girl Who Loved Wild Horses.* Bradbury, 1978.

Goffstein, M.B. *Family Scrapbook.* Farrar, Straus & Giroux, 1978.

Goodall, John S. *Paddy under Water.* Atheneum, 1984.

————. *The Story of an English Village.* Atheneum, 1979.

Grahame, Kenneth. *Wayfarers All: From the Wind in the Willows.* Illustrated by Beverly Gooding. Scribner's, 1981.

Greenberg, Barbara. *The Bravest Babysitter.* Dial, 1977.

Greenberg, Jan. *The Iceberg and Its Shadow.* Farrar, Straus & Giroux, 1980.

Greene, Carol. *Hinny Winny Bunco.* Illustrated by Jeanette Winter. Harper & Row, 1982.

Gretz, Susanna. *The Bears Who Went to the Seaside.* Follett, 1973.

Griego, Margot C.; Bucks, Betsy L.; Gilbert, Sharon S.; and Kimball, Laurel H. *Tortillitas Para Mama.* Illustrated by Barbara Cooney. Holt, Rinehart & Winston, 1981.

Griffith, Helen. *Alex and the Cat.* Illustrated by Joseph Low. Greenwillow, 1982.

Grimm, Brothers. *Hansel and Gretel*. Retold by Rika Lesser. Illustrated by Paul O. Zelinsky. Dodd, 1984.

———. *The Bremen Town Musicians*. Retold and Illustrated by Ilse Plume. Doubleday, 1980.

Hadithi, Mwenye. *Greedy Zebra*. Illustrated by Adrienne Kennaway. Little, Brown, 1984.

Hague, Kathleen, and Hague, Michael. *The Man Who Kept House*. Harcourt Brace Jovanovich, 1981.

Hague, Michael. *Beauty and the Beast*. Holt, 1983.

Hale, Sarah Josepha. *Mary Had a Little Lamb*. Illustrated by Tomie de Paola. Holiday, 1984.

Hall, Lynn. *Danza!* Scribner's, 1981.

Hayes, Sarah. *This Is the Bear*. Illustrated by Helen Craig. Lippincott, 1986.

Hest, Amy. *The Crack-of-Dawn Walkers*. Illustrated by Amy Schwartz. Macmillan, 1984.

Highwater, Jamake. *Anpao—An American Indian Odyssey*. Harper & Row, 1980.

Hill, Donna. *Ms. Glee Was Waiting*. Atheneum, 1978.

Hill, Eric. *Spot's Birthday Party*. Putnam, 1981.

———. *Spot's First Walk*. Putnam, 1981.

———. *Spot Goes to the Beach*. Putnam's, 1985.

———. *Spot Goes to School*. Putnam's, 1984.

Hoban, Russell. *Best Friends for Frances*. Harper & Row, 1976.

———. *The Little Brute Family*. Macmillan, 1966.

———. *Nothing to Do*. Harper & Row, 1964.

Hoban, Tana. *Circles, Triangles, and Squares*. Macmillan, 1974.

———. *Is It Red? Is It Yellow? Is It Blue?* Greenwillow, 1978.

———. *Look Again!* Macmillan, 1971.

———. *1, 2, 3*. Greenwillow, 1984.

———. *Round & Round & Round*. Greenwillow, 1983.

———. *Shapes, Shapes, Shapes*. Greenwillow, 1986.

———. *Take Another Look*. Greenwillow, 1981.

———. *What Is It?* Greenwillow, 1984.

Hodges, Margaret. *Saint George and the Dragon*. Illustrated by Trina Schart Hyman. Little, Brown, 1984.

Hoffman, Phyllis. *Steffie and Me*. Harper & Row, 1970.

Holzenthaler, Jean. *My Hands Can*. Dutton, 1978.

Howe, James. *The Hospital Book*. Photos by Mal Warshaw. Crown, 1981.

———. *There's a Monster Under My Bed*. Atheneum, 1986.

Hurd, Edith Thacher. *I Dance in My Red Pajamas*. Illustrated by Emily Arnold McCully. Harper & Row, 1982.

Hurmence, Belinda. *A Girl Called Boy*. Clarion, 1982.

Hutchins, Pat. *The Very Worst Monster*. Greenwillow, 1985.

———. *Changes, Changes*. Macmillan, 1971.

———. *I Hunter*. Greenwillow, 1982.

———. *Rosie's Walk*. Macmillan, 1968.

Hutchinson, Veronica. *Henny Penny*. Little, Brown, 1976.

Hutton, Warwick. *Beauty and the Beast*. Atheneum, 1985.

Ichikawa, Satomi. *Nora's Castle*. Putnam, 1986.

Isele, Elizabeth. *The Frog Princess*. Illustrated by Michael Hague. Crowell, 1984.

Isenbart, Hans-Heinrich. *A Duckling Is Born*. Photographed by Othmar Baumli. Putnam, 1981.

Isenberg, Barbara, and Jaffe, Marjorie. *Albert the Running Bear's Exercise Book*. Illustrated by Diane de Groat. Clarion, 1984.

Johnston, Tony. *Four Scary Stories*. Putnam, 1978.

Jonas, Ann. *When You Were A Baby*. Greenwillow, 1982.

Jukes, Mavis. *Like Jake and Me*. Illustrated by Lloyd Bloom. Knopf, 1984.

Keats, Ezra Jack. *Peter's Chair*. Harper & Row, 1967.

———. *Regards to the Man in the Moon*. Four Winds, 1982.

———. *The Snowy Day*. Viking, 1962.

———. *Whistle for Willie*. Viking, 1964.

Kellogg, Steven. *Best Friends*. Dial, 1986.

———. *A Rose for Pinkerton*. Dial, 1981.

Kennedy, Richard. *Amy's Eyes*. Illustrated by Richard Egielski. Harper, 1985.

Kepes, Juliet. *Cock-a-Doodle-Doo*. Pantheon, 1978.

King-Smith, Dick. *Pigs Might Fly*. Illustrated by Mary Rayner. Viking, 1982.

Klein, Norma. *Girls Can Be Anything*. Dutton, 1975.

Knight, Hilary. *Hilary Knight's The Twelve Days of Christmas*. Macmillan, 1981.

Konigsburg, E. L. *Journey to an 800 Number*. Atheneum, 1982.

Krahn, Fernando. *Who's Seen the Scissors?* Dutton, 1975.

Kraus, Robert. *Leo the Late Bloomer*. Illustrated by Jose Aruego. Windmill, 1971.

———. *The Littlest Rabbit*. Scholastic, 1975.

Krauss, Ruth. *The Carrot Seed*. Harper & Row, 1945.

Kroll, Steven. *If I Could Be My Grandmother*. Pantheon, 1977.

Langstaff, John. *Oh, A-Hunting We Will Go*. Atheneum, 1974.

Larrick, Nancy. *When the Dark Comes Dancing: A Bedtime Poetry Book*. Putnam, 1983.

Lasky, Kathryn. *The Night Journey*. Warne, 1981.

Lee, Dennis. *Jelly Belly: Original Nursery Rhymes*. Harper, 1985.

L'Engle, Madeleine. *A Ring of Endless Light*. Farrar, Straus & Giroux, 1980.

———. *A Swiftly Tilting Planet*. Farrar, Straus & Giroux, 1978.

Lewin, Hugh. *Jafta*. Illustrated by Lisa Kopper. Carolrhoda, 1983.

Lewis, C.S. *The Lion, the Witch, and the Wardrobe*. Macmillan, 1951.

Lexau, Joan. *Benjie on His Own*. Dial, 1970.

Lindgren, Barbro. *The Wild Baby*. Illustrated by Eva Eriksson. Greenwillow, 1981.

———. *Sam's Ball*. Illustrated by Eva Eriksson. Morrow, 1983.

———. *Sam's Bath*. Illustrated by Eva Eriksson. Morrow, 1983.

———. *Sam's Lamp*. Illustrated by Eva Eriksson. Morrow, 1983.

Lionni, Leo. *Let's Make Rabbits*. Pantheon, 1982.

Lobel, Arnold. *Frog and Toad All Year*. Harper & Row, 1976.

———. *Grasshopper on the Road*. Harper & Row, 1978.

———. *On Market Street*. Illustrated by Anita Lobel. Greenwillow, 1981.

———. *Uncle Elephant*. Harper & Row, 1981.

Lowry, Lois. *Anastasia Again!* Houghton Mifflin, 1981.

Lunn, Janet. *The Root Cellar*. Scribner's, 1983.

MacLachlan, Patricia. *Mama One, Mama Two*. Illustrated by Ruth Lercher Bornstein. Harper & Row, 1982.

———. *Sarah, Plain and Tall*. Harper, 1985.

Magee, Doug. *Trucks You Can Count On*. Dodd, 1985.

Magnus, Erica. *Old Lars*. Carolrhoda, 1984.

Malnig, Anita. *Where the Waves Break: Life at the Edge of the Sea*. Photographs by Jeff Rotman. Carolrhoda, 1985.

Margolis, Richard J. *Secrets of a Small Brother*. Illustrated by Donald Carrick. Macmillan, 1984.

Maris, Ron. *Are You There, Bear?* Greenwillow, 1985.

Marshall, Edward. *Four on the Shore.* Illustrated by James Marshall. Dial, 1985.

Marshall, James. *George and Martha One Fine Day.* Houghton Mifflin, 1978.

Martin, Eva. Editor. *Canadian Fairy Tales.* Illustrated by Laszlo Gal. Douglas & McIntyre, 1984.

Martin, Sarah Catherine. *The Comic Adventures of Old Mother Hubbard and Her Dog.* Illustrated by Tomie de Paola. Harcourt Brace Jovanovich, 1981.

Mayer, Mercer. *The Great Cat Chase.* Four Winds, 1975.

McCloskey, Robert. *Lentil.* Viking, 1940.

———. *Time of Wonder.* Viking, 1957.

McKinley, Robin. *The Hero and the Crown.* Greenwillow, 1984.

McLeod, Emilie Warren. *The Bear's Bicycle.* Little, Brown, 1975.

McPhail, David. *The Dream Child.* Dutton, 1985.

Meyer, Carolyn, and Gallenkamp, Charles. *The Mystery of the Ancient Maya.* Atheneum, 1985.

Monjo, F.N. *The Drinking Gourd.* Harper & Row, 1969.

Moore, Clement Clarke. *The Night before Christmas.* Illustrated by Tomie de Paola. Holiday, 1980.

Murphy, Jill. *Peace at Last.* Dial, 1980.

Nance, John. *Lobo of the Tasaday.* Pantheon, 1982.

Ness, Evaline. *Sam, Bangs, & Moonshine.* Holt, Rinehart & Winston, 1966.

Oakley, Graham. *Hetty and Harriet.* Atheneum, 1982.

———. *The Church Mice in Action.* Atheneum, 1982.

O'Dell, Scott. *Island of the Blue Dolphins.* Houghton Mifflin, 1960.

Ormerod, Jan. *Sunshine.* Lothrop, Lee & Shepard, 1981.

Oxenbury, Helen. *First Day at School.* Dial, 1983.

———. *The Checkup.* Dial, 1983.

———. *Dressing.* Simon & Schuster, 1981.

———. *Family.* Simon & Schuster, 1981.

———. *Friends.* Simon & Schuster, 1981.

———. *I Can.* Random House, 1986.

———. *I See.* Random House, 1986.

———. *I Touch.* Random House, 1986.

———. *Playing.* Simon & Schuster, 1981.

———. *Working.* Simon & Schuster, 1981.

Paige, David. *A Day in the Life of a Marine Biologist.* Photographed by Roger Ruhlin. Troll Associates, 1981.

Park, Ruth. *Playing Beatie Bow.* Atheneum, 1982.

Paterson, Katherine. *Come Sing, Jimmy Jo.* Lodestar, 1985.

Paulsen, Gary. *Dogsong.* Bradbury, 1985.

Preston, Edna Mitchell, and Bennett, Rainey. *The Temper Tantrum Book.* Penguin, 1976.

Rabe, Berniece. *The Balancing Girl.* Illustrated by Lillian Hoban. Dutton, 1981.

Rand, Ann, and Rand, Paul. *I Know a Lot of Things.* Harcourt Brace Jovanovich, 1956.

Raskin, Ellen. *The Westing Game.* Dutton, 1978.

Reiss, John J. *Numbers.* Bradbury, 1971.

———. *Shapes.* Bradbury, 1974.

Rice, Eve. *Benny Bakes a Cake.* Greenwillow, 1981.

———. *Oh, Lewis!* Macmillan, 1974.

Rinard, Judith E. *What Happens at the Zoo.* National Geographic, 1984.

Riskind, Mary. *Apple Is My Sign.* Houghton Mifflin, 1981.

Rockwell, Anne. *First Comes Spring.* Harper, 1985.

Rockwell, Harlow. *My Dentist.* Greenwillow, 1975.

———. *My Doctor.* Macmillan, 1973.

Rogers, Fred. *Going to Day Care.* Photographed by Jim Judkis. Putnam, 1986.

———. *Going to the Doctor.* Photographed by Jim Judkis. Putnam, 1986.

Rose, Anne. *As Right As Right Can Be.* Dial, 1976.

Ryder, Joanne. *Inside Turtle's Shell: And Other Poems of the Field.* Illustrated by Susan Bonners. Macmillan, 1985.

Rylant, Cynthia. *A Blue-Eyed Daisy.* Bradbury, 1985.

———. *When I Was Young in the Mountains.* Illustrated by Diane Goode. Dutton, 1982.

Sandin, Joan. *The Long Way to a New Land.* Harper & Row, 1981.

Savitt, Sam. *Draw Horses with Sam Savitt.* Viking, 1981.

Scarry, Richard. *My First Book..* Random House, 1986.

———. *Richard Scarry's The Best Word Book Ever.* Western, 1963.

Schlee, Ann. *Ask Me No Questions.* Holt, Rinehart & Winston, 1982.

Schwartz, Alvin. *There Is a Carrot in My Ear and Other Noodle Tales.* Illustrated by Karen Ann Weinhaus. Harper & Row, 1982.

Scott, Ann Herbert. *Sam.* Illustrated by Symeon Shimin. McGraw-Hill, 1967.

Selsam, Millicent. *Mushrooms.* Photographed by Jerome Wexler. Morrow, 1986.

———. *Tyrannosaurus Rex.* Harper & Row, 1978.

Sendak, Maurice. *Where the Wild Things Are.* Harper & Row, 1963.

Seuss, Dr. *And to Think That I Saw It on Mulberry Street.* Vanguard, 1937.

———. *The Cat in the Hat.* Beginner, 1957.

Severo, Emöke de Papp. *The Good-Hearted Youngest Brother.* Illustrated by Diane Goode. Bradbury, 1981.

Sharmat, Marjorie. *The Best Valentine in the World.* Illustrated by Lilian Obligado. Holiday House, 1982.

———. *A Big Fat Enormous Lie.* Dutton, 1978.

Sheffield, Margaret, and Bewley, Sheila. *Where Do Babies Come From?* Knopf, 1973.

Showers, Paul. *Look at Your Eyes.* Crowell, 1962.

Shura, Mary Francis. *The Search for Grissi.* Illustrated by Ted Lewin. Dodd, 1985.

Silverstein, Shel. *A Light in the Attic.* Harper & Row, 1981.

Simon, Seymour. *Meet the Computer.* Illustrated by Barbara and Ed Emberly. Harper, 1985.

———. *Animal Fact/Animal Fable.* Crown, 1979.

———. *Your First Home Computer: Buying It, Using It, and Keeping It Working.* Illustrated by Roy Doty. Crown, 1985.

Skorpen, Liesel M. *His Mother's Dog.* Harper & Row, 1978.

Small, David. *Eulalie and the Hopping Head.* Macmillan, 1982.

———. *Imogene's Antlers.* Crown, 1985.

Speare, Elizabeth George. *The Sign of the Beaver.* Houghton Mifflin, 1982.

———. *The Bronze Bow.* Houghton Mifflin, 1961.

Sperry, Armstrong. *Call It Courage.* Macmillan, 1940.

Spier, Peter. *Bill's Service Station.* Doubleday, 1981.

———. *Food Market.* Doubleday, 1981.

———. *Fire House: Hook and Ladder Company Number Twenty-Four.* Doubleday, 1981.

———. *The Star-Spangled Banner.* Doubleday, 1973.

———. *Tin Lizzie.* Doubleday, 1975.

Stanek, Muriel. *All Alone After School.* Illustrated by Ruth Rosner. Whitman, 1985.

Steptoe, John. *The Story of Jumping Mouse.* Lothrop, 1984.

———. *Stevie.* Harper & Row, 1969.

Stevens, Janet. *The House That Jack Built.* Holiday House, 1985.

Stinson, Kathy. *Big or Little?* Illustrated by Robin Baird Lewis. Annick, 1983.

———. *Red Is Best.* Illustrated by Robin Baird Lewis. Annick, 1982.

Sutcliff, Rosemary. *Sun Horse, Moon Horse.* Illustrated by Shirley Felts. Dutton, 1978.

Tafuri, Nancy. *Early Morning in the Barn.* Greenwillow, 1983.

———. *Who's Counting?* Greenwillow, 1986.

Taylor, Mildred. *Let the Circle Be Unbroken.* Dial, 1981.

Tobias, Tobi. *Arthur Mitchell.* Illustrated by Carol Byard. Crowell, 1975.

Turkle, Brinton. *Do Not Open.* Dutton, 1981.

Udry, Janice May. *Let's Be Enemies.* Harper & Row, 1961.

———. *What Mary Jo Shared.* Whitman, 1966.

Van Allsburg, Chris. *The Mysteries of Harris Burdick.* Houghton Mifflin, 1984.

———. *The Polar Express.* Houghton Mifflin, 1985.

Van Leeuwen, Jean. *More Tales of Oliver Pig.* Dial, 1981.

Viorst, Judith. *Alexander and the Terrible, Horrible, No Good, Very Bad Day.* Illustrated by Ray Cruz. Atheneum, 1972.

———. *I'll Fix Anthony.* Harper & Row, 1969.

Voigt, Cynthia. *A Solitary Blue.* Atheneum, 1983.

———. *Building Blocks.* Atheneum, 1984.

———. *Dicey's Song.* Atheneum, 1982.

Waber, Bernard. *Ira Sleeps Over.* Houghton Mifflin, 1972.

———. *The Snake: A Very Long Story.* Houghton Mifflin, 1978.

Wagner, Jenny. *John Brown, Rose and the Midnight Cat.* Bradbury, 1978.

Wahl, Jan. *Jamie's Tiger.* Harcourt Brace Jovanovich, 1977.

Wallace, Ian. *Chin Chiang and the Dragon's Dance.* Atheneum, 1984.

Walter, Mildred Pitts. *Brother to the Sun.* Illustrated by Diane and Leo Dillon. Lothrop, 1985.

Wells, Rosemary. *Max's Bedtime.* Dial, 1985.

———. *Max's Birthday.* Dial, 1985.

———. *Max's Breakfast.* Dial, 1985.

———. *Timothy Goes to School.* Dial, 1981.

White, E.B. *Charlotte's Web.* Harper & Row, 1952.

———. *Stuart Little.* Harper & Row, 1945.

White, Florence M. *Cesar Chavez: Man of Courage.* Garrard, 1973.

Wilder, Laura Ingalls, *The First Four Years.* Illustrated by Garth Williams. Harper & Row, 1971.

———. *Little House in the Big Woods.* Harper & Row, 1932.

———. *These Happy Golden Years.* Harper & Row, 1943.

Willard, Nancy. *Night Story.* Illustrated by Ilse Plume. Harcourt Brace Jovanovich, 1986.

Williams, Barbara. *Chester Chipmunk's Thanksgiving.* Dutton, 1978.

———. *Someday, Said Mitchell.* Dutton, 1976.

Williams, Jay. *The Reward Worth Having.* Illustrated by Mercer Mayer. Four Winds, 1977.

Williams, Vera B. *Something Special for Me.* Greenwillow, 1983.

Winter, Jeanette. *Come Out to Play.* Knopf, 1986.

Wojciechowska, Maia. *Shadow of a Bull.* Illustrated by Alvin Smith. Atheneum, 1964.

Yabuuchi, Masayuki. *Whose Baby?* Philomel, 1985.

Yates, Elizabeth. *Amos Fortune, Free Man.* Aladdin, 1950.

———. *My Diary—My World.* Westminister, 1981.

Yolen, Jane. *The Lullaby Songbook.* Illustrated by Charles Mikolaycak. Harcourt Brace Jovanovich, 1986.

Zemach, Margot. *It Could Always Be Worse.* Farrar, Straus & Giroux, 1977.

Zolotow, Charlotte. *Big Brother.* Illustrated by Mary Chalmers. Harper & Row, 1966.

———. *My Grandson Lew.* Illustrated by William Pène du Bois. Harper & Row, 1974.

———. *The Quarreling Book.* Illustrated by Arnold Lobel. Harper & Row, 1963.

———. *William's Doll.* Illustrated by William Pène du Bois. Harper & Row, 1972.

FRENCH-CANADIAN REFERENCES

Anfouṡse, Ginette. *Sophie, Pierrot et un Crapaud.* LaCourte, 1983.

Côté, Denis. *Hockeurs Cybernétiques.* Illustrated by Gérard Dansereau. Paulines, 1983.

Dubé, Claude. *Cas Cocasses.* Illustrated by Normand Cousineau. Ville-Marie, 1983.

Gagnon, Cécile. *Surprises et Sortiliéges.* Illustrated by Christiane Beauregard. Pierre Tisseyre, 1984.

Gay, Marie-Louise. *Un Léopard dans mon Placard.* Ovale, 1984.

Labrosse, Darcia. *Où est le Ver?* Pierre Tisseyre, 1984.

Loranger, Francine. *Chanson pour un Ordinateur.* Illustrated by Laurent Bouchard. Fides, 1980.

Mareuil, André. *Récite du Saint-Laurent.* Illustrated by Anna Maria Balint. Paulines, 1984.

Paré, Roger. *Plaisirs de Chat.* Courte Echelle, 1983.

Soulière, Robert. *Tony ou Vladimir.* Illustrated by Philippe Béha. Pierre Tisseyre, 1984.

SPANISH REFERENCES

Bravo-Villasante, Carmen. *Al Corro de la Patala.* Editorial Escuela Española, Madrid (Bilingual Publications), 1984.

Darío, Rubén. *Los Motivos del Lobo.* Educa, 1984.

———. *Margarita.* Illustrated by Monika Doppert. Ekaré, 1980.

Feliciano Mendoza, Ester. *Ronda del Mar.* Instituto de Cultura Puertorriqueña, 1981.

Ferré, Rosario. *La Mona que le Pisaron la Cola.* Illustrated by Analida Burgos. Huracan, n.d.

———. *Los Cuentos de Juan Bobo.* Illustrated by José Rosa. Huracan, 1981.

Garrido Lopera, José María. *Federico García Lorca y los Niños.* Illustrated by José Ruiz Navarro. Everest, 1983.

———. *Juan Ramón Jiménez y los Niños.* Illustrated by José Ruiz Navarro. Everest, 1980.

Glantz, Margo. *La Guerra de los Hermanos.* Editorial Penélope, Mexico (Bilingual Publications), 1982.

González de León, Ulalume. *Las Tres Manzanas de Naranja.* Editorial Penélope, Mexico, 1982.

Las Historias del Popol Vuh. Educa, 1983.

Lyra, Carmen. *La Cucarachita Mandinga.* Illustrated by Ana María Dueñas. Educa, 1984.

———. *Los Cuentos de mi Tía Panchita.* Educa, 1984.

Mistral, Silvia. *La Cola de la Sirena.* Editorial Trillas, Mexico, 1983.

Sinan, Rogelio. *El Conejito, el Pato Patuleco y Otros: Narrativa Oral Panameña.* Illustrated by Jorge Korea. Educa, 1984.

Walsh, Maria Elena. *Tutú Marambá.* Editorial Sudamericana, Buenos Aires (Bilingual Publications), 1984.

2

History of Children's Literature

MANY PEOPLE ARE SURPRISED TO DIS-cover that childhood has not always been considered an important time of life. When students of children's literature look at the beautiful books published to meet children's needs, interests, and reading levels, many are amazed to learn that not too long ago books written specifically for children were not available.

Tracing the history of children's literature in Western culture highlights some fascinating milestones in the development of books for children. Changes in printing technology provided affordable books, but more important were changes in social attitudes toward children. When society looked upon children as little adults who must rapidly step into the roles of their parents, children had little time or need to read books relevant to a nonexistent childhood. When childhood began to be viewed as a special part of the human life cycle, literature written specifically for children became very important.

Within the context of human history as a whole, the history of children's literature is very short. Neither early tales told through the oral tradition nor early books were created specifically for children. When children's books were eventually written, they usually mirrored the dominant cultural values of their place and time. Thus a study of children's literature in Western Europe and North America from the fifteenth century through contemporary times reflects both changes in society as a whole and changes in social expectations of children and the family.

Literature researchers are beginning to view children's literature as a viable vehicle for studying social values and changing attitudes. Karen J. Winkler (47) maintains that the 1970s and 1980s have been characterized by an ever-increasing interest in the scholarly study of children's literature as an index to the social attitudes of a particular time. Robert Gordon Kelly's (23) "Mother Was a Lady: Self and Society in Selected American Children's Periodicals, 1865–1890" and Mary Lystad's (31) *From Dr. Mather to Dr. Seuss: Two Hundred Years of American Books for Children* are two examples of such research. The increasing number of doctoral dissertations that critically evaluate certain aspects of children's literature also suggests the current importance of children's literature as a research subject. For example, from the 1930s until 1970, approximately 200 dissertations covered topics related to children's literature. In contrast, the 1970s alone produced

nearly 800 such dissertations. Several of these studies suggest the interrelatedness of social, cultural, and economic factors and the story themes and values presented in children's literature of a certain period.

This chapter first considers some milestones in the development of children's literature, then focuses on changing views of children and the family reflected in early books for children and more contemporary stories. Chart 2–1 provides a brief overview of the historical milestones. Chart 2–2 lists important events in the history of children's book illustration. Chart 2–3 provides additional notable authors of children's literature. Charts 2–4, 2–5, and 2–6 provide overviews of literature as a reflector of prevalent attitudes about children and the family in different time periods.

MILESTONES IN THE HISTORY OF CHILDREN'S LITERATURE

The Oral Tradition

Long before the recorded history of humanity, family units and tribes shared their group traditions and values through stories told around the campfire. On every continent around the globe, ancient peoples developed folktales and mythologies that speculated about human beginnings, attempted to explain the origins of the universe and other natural phenomena, emphasized ethical truths, and transmitted group history from one generation to the next. When hunters returned from their adventures, they probably told about the perils of the hunt and about hostile encounters with other tribes. Heroic deeds were certainly told and retold until they became a part of a group's heritage. This oral tradition has existed since the first oral communication among human beings and goes back to the very roots of every civilization on earth. These tales were not told specifically to children, but children were surely present—listening, watching, learning, and remembering what they would later pass on to their own children.

The various native peoples of North America developed mythologies expressing their reverence for the rolling prairies, lush forests, ice floes, deserts, and blue lakes of their continent. In Latin and South America, storytellers of the Yucatan Peninsula and the Andes chronicled the rise of Maya, Aztec, and Inca empires, wars of expansion, and, eventually, the Spanish conquest of their homelands. Across Africa, highly respected storytellers developed a style that encouraged the audience to interact with the storyteller in relating tales of dramatic heroes, personified animals, and witty tricksters. In the extremely ancient cultures of Asia, from Mesopotamia to Japan, some early myths and folktales were eventually incorporated into the complex mythologies and philosophical tenets of Taoism, Confucianism, Hinduism, and Buddhism. In Europe, the earliest oral traditions of Celts, Franks, Saxons, Goths, Danes, and many other groups eventually influenced one another as a result of human migration, trade, and warfare; and the mythologies of ancient Greece and Rome became widely influential as the Roman Empire expanded over much of the continent.

The European oral tradition, according to Robert Leeson (26), reached its climax in the feudal era of the Middle Ages. What are often called *cas-* *tle tales* and *cottage tales* provided people with literature long before those tales were widely accessible in writing or in print. The ruling classes favored poetic epics about the reputed deeds of the lord of the manor or his ancestors. In the great halls of castles, minstrels or bards accompanied themselves on the lyre or the harp while singing tales about noble warriors such as Beowulf and King Arthur or ballads of chivalrous love in regal surroundings, such as found in the French version of Cinderella.

Around cottage fires or at country fairs, humbler people had different heroes. Storytellers shared folktales about people much like the peasants themselves, people who daily confronted servitude, inscrutable natural phenomena, and unknown spiritual forces. In these tales even the youngest or poorest person had the potential to use resourcefulness or kindness to go from rags to riches and live "happily ever after"

CHART 2–1
Historic milestones in children's literature

	Oral Tradition		
	"Beowulf"	1800s	The Romantic Movement in Europe
	"Jack the Giant Killer"		The Brothers Grimm
1400s	Early Books		Hans Christian Andersen
	Hornbooks	1800s	Illustrators Make Their Impact on Children's
	Caston's Printing Press—1476		Books
1500s	Chapbooks Introduced		Walter Crane
	"Jack the Giant Killer"		Randolph Caldecott
1600s	The Puritan Influence		Kate Greenaway
	Spiritual Milk for Boston Babes in either	1860	The Victorian Influence
	England, drawn from the Breasts of both		Charlotte Yonge's *The Daisy Chain* and *The*
	Testaments for their Souls' Nourishment		*Clever Woman of the Family*
	Pilgrim's Progress	1850-	Childhood Seen as an Adventure, Not a
1693	View of Childhood Changes	1900	Training Ground for Adulthood
	John Locke's *Some Thoughts Concerning*		Fantasy
	Education		Lewis Carroll's *Alice's Adventures in Won-*
1698	First Fairy Tales Written for Children		*derland*
	Charles Perrault's *Tales of Mother Goose*		Edward Lear's *A Book of Nonsense*
1719	Great Adventure Stories		Adventure
	Daniel Defoe's *Robinson Crusoe*		Robert Louis Stevenson's *Treasure Island*
	Jonathan Swift's *Gulliver's Travels*		Howard Pyle's *The Merry Adventures of*
1744	Children's Literature: A True Beginning		*Robin Hood*
	John Newbery's *A Little Pretty Pocket Book*		Jules Verne's *Twenty-Thousand Leagues un-*
	and *History of Little Goody Two Shoes*		*der the Sea*
1762	Children Should Be Guided in Their Search		Real People
	for Knowledge		Margaret Sidney's *The Five Little Peppers*
	Jean Jacques Rousseau's *Emile*		*and How They Grew*
1789	Poetry about Children		Louisa May Alcott's *Little Women*
	William Blake's *Songs of Innocence*		Johanna Spyri's *Heidi*

in great splendor. Often such achievement required outwitting or slaying wolves, dragons, malevolent supernatural beings, or great lords themselves.

By whatever name they were known—bards, minstrels, or devisers of tales—the storytellers of medieval Europe were entertainers: if they did not entertain, they lost their audiences or even their meals and lodging. Consequently, they learned to tell stories that had rapid plot development and easily identifiable characters. These storytellers also possessed considerable power. Sir Philip Sidney (39), a sixteenth century English poet, described storytellers as those with the power to keep children away from their play and old people away from their chimney corners. Whether woven from imagination or retold from legends and stories of old, a storyteller's tales could influence people who heard them. Thus if a minstrel's story offended or discredited a lord, the minstrel could be punished. By the end of the fourteenth century, feudal authority sought to control the tales being told and often jailed storytellers who angered either a ruler or the church.

Today many early European folktales, myths, and legends are considered ideal for sharing with children, but this was not the attitude of feudal Europe. Storytellers addressed audiences of all ages. A child was considered a small adult who should enter into adult life as quickly as possible, and stories primarily for young people were considered unnecessary. Consequently, the stories about giants, heroes, and simpletons that relieved the strain of adult life also entertained children. These favorite tales, which had been told and retold for hundreds of years, were eventually chosen for some of the first printed books in Europe.

Early Printed Books

Prior to the mid-1400s, the literary heritage of Europe consisted of the oral tradition and parchment manuscripts laboriously handwritten by monks and scribes. Manuscript books were rare and costly, prized possessions of the nobles and priests who were among the few Europeans able to read and write. To the extent that these books were meant for the young, they were usually designed to provide instruction in rhetoric, grammar, and music for privileged children who attended monastery schools. Children were rarely

The hornbook, which was used for instruction, usually contained the alphabet, numerals, and the Lord's Prayer. (Photo courtesy of The Horn Book, Inc.)

trusted with the books themselves, and usually wrote on slates as monks dictated their lessons.

A significant event occurred in the 1450s when the German Johann Gutenberg discovered a practical method for using movable metal type, making possible the mass production of books. William Caxton established England's first printing press in 1476 after learning the printing process in Germany. The use of printing presses led to the creation of hornbooks, printed sheets of text mounted on wood and covered with translucent animal horn, which were used to teach reading and numbers. The books, which were in the shape of a paddle, usually included the alphabet, a syllabary, numerals, and the Lord's Prayer. These tools for learning remained popular into the 1700s, when the battledore, a lesson book made of folded paper or cardboard, became more prevalent. Like hornbooks, battledores usually contained an alphabet, numerals, and proverbs or prayers.

When William Caxton opened his printing business in 1476, most of the books used with children were not written for their interest but adhered to the sentiment that young readers should read only what would improve their manners or instruct their minds. *Caxton's Book of Curtesye*, first printed in 1477 (13), contained directions for drawing readers away from vice and turning them toward a life of virtue. Verses guided readers toward personal cleanliness: comb your hair, clean your ears, clean your nose but don't pick it; polite social interactions: look people straight in the face when speaking; don't quarrel with dogs; suitable reverence in church: kneel before the cross, don't chatter; and correct table manners: don't blow on your food or undo your girdle at the table.

The majority of books Caxton published were not meant to be read by children, but three of his publications are now considered classics in children's literature. In 1481, he published the beast fable *Reynart the Foxe* (The History of Reynard the Fox), a satire of oppression and tyranny. This tale of a clever fox who could outwit all his adversaries became popular with both adults and children. Caxton's most important publication may be *The Book of the Subtyle Historyes and Fables of Esope* (The Fables of Aesop), which he translated from a manuscript by the French monk Machault in 1484. These fables about the weaknesses of people and animals were popular

with readers of various ages and are still enjoyed by children. F. J. Harvey Darton (9) maintains that Caxton's version of Aesop, "with infinitely little modernization, is the best text for children today" (p. 10). Caxton's publication in 1485 of Sir Thomas Malory's *Le Morte d'Arthur* (The Death of Arthur) preserved the legendary story of King Arthur and his knights, which has been published since in many versions suitable for young readers.

Caxton's translations, standardization of English, and literary style had a major impact upon English literature, according to Jane Bingham and Grayce Scholt (5). At least eight of Caxton's books are mentioned in the "Famous Prefaces" volume of *The Harvard Classics* (27). Cornelia Meigs et al. (34) also stress Caxton's importance in creating the first printed books in the English language, books that "were in outward form of a standard not easily equalled. The ample pages, the broad margins, the black-letter type which suggested manuscript, all contributed to their beauty and dignity, to their worthiness to be England's first widespread realization of her own literature" (p. 31).

Caxton's books were beautiful, but too expensive for the common people. Soon, however, peddlers (or "chapmen") were selling crudely printed chapbooks for pennies at markets and fairs, along with ribbons, patent medicines, and other wares. Customers could also go directly to the printer and select from large uncut sheets of as many as sixteen pages of text, which would then be bound into a hard-cover book. Some of the first chapbooks were based on ballads such as "The Two Children in the Wood," and traditional tales such as "Jack the Giant Killer." According to Lou J. McCulloch (32), the content of chapbooks fell into one of the following categories: religious instruction, interpretations of the supernatural, romantic legends, ballad tales, and historic narratives. John Ashton's (2) *Chap-Books of the Eighteenth Century* includes religious titles such as "The History of Joseph and his Brethren" and "The Unhappy Birth, Wicked Life, and Miserable Death of the Víle Traytor and Apostle Judas Iscariot"; traditional tales such as "Tom Thumb" and "A True Tale of Robin Hood"; and supernatural tales, such as "The Portsmouth Ghost."

Chapbooks were extremely popular in both England and the United States during the 1700s, but their popularity rapidly declined during the early 1800s. McCulloch (32) maintains that they were

This lesson book, or battledore, was made from folded paper or cardboard. (Courtesy of The Horn Book, Inc.)

From the 16th to the 19th century, peddlers sold inexpensive chapbooks in Europe and North America. (From *Chap-Books of the Eighteenth Century* by John Ashton. Published by Chatto and Windus, 1882. From the John G. White Collection, Cleveland Public Library.)

especially important as forerunners to many modern literary forms: children's books, western tales, and even comic books.

The Puritan Influence

Political upheaval, religious dissent, and censorship all affected English literature in the 1600s (5). As printing increased and literacy spread, the British monarchy realized the power of the press and in 1637 decreed that only London, Oxford, Cambridge, and York could have printing establishments.

The beliefs of the Puritans, dissenters from the established Church of England who were growing in strength and numbers in England and North America, also influenced literature of the period. Puritans considered the traditional tales about giants, fairies, and witches found in chapbooks to be impious and corrupting. They urged that children not be allowed to read such materials and instead be provided with literature to instruct them and reinforce their moral development. Puritans expected their offspring to be children of

God first and foremost, as Bernard J. Lonsdale and Helen K. Macintosh (30) describe: "Family worship, admonitions from elders, home instruction, strict attendance at school, and close attention to lessons all were aimed at perpetuating those ideals and values for which the parents themselves had sacrificed so much. To the elders, the important part of education was learning to read, write, and figure. Only literature that would instruct and warn was tolerated" (p. 161).

Awesome titles for books that stressed the importance of instructing children in moral concerns were common in Puritan times. In 1649, the grandfather of Cotton Mather (the Puritan who was so influential during the Salem witch-hunts in New England) wrote a book called *Spiritual Milk for Boston Babes in either England, Drawn from the Breasts of Both Testaments for Their Souls' Nourishment*. In 1671, the leading Puritan writer James Janeway published a series of stories about children who had led saintly lives until their deaths at an early age. His *A Token for Children, Being an Exact Account of the Conversion, Holy and Exemplary Lives, and Joyful Deaths of Several Young Children* was meant not for enjoyment, but to instruct Puritan children in moral development.

The most influential piece of literature written during this period was John Bunyan's *Pilgrim's Progress*, published in England in 1678. While moral improvement was this book's primary purpose, *Pilgrim's Progress* also contained bold action that appealed both to children and to older readers, some of whom adopted it for its entertainment, as well as religious, value. Bunyan's hero, Christian, experiences many perilous adventures as he journeys alone through the Slough of Despond and the Valley of Humiliation in his search for salvation. Characters such as Mr. Valiant-for-Truth, Ignorance, and Mrs. Timorous appear in settings such as the Valley of the Shadow of Death, the Delectable Mountains, and the Eternal City. Pilgrim acquires a companion, Faithful, who is executed in the town of Vanity Fair. Then another companion, Hopeful, helps him fight the giant Despair and finally reach his goal.

Pilgrim's Progress and the *Spiritual Milk for Boston Babes in either England* were required reading for colonial children in North America. Another important book in colonial homes was *The New England Primer*, a combination ABC and catechism designed to teach Puritan ideals. The ABCs were written in such a way that spiritual in-

The New England primer taught both Puritan ideals and the alphabet. (From *The New England Primer, Enlarged*, Boston, 1727 edition. From the Rare Books and Manuscript Division, The New York Public Library, Astor, Lenox, and Tilden Foundations.)

struction was the main theme. The primer appeared around 1690 and was printed in hundreds of editions until 1830. According to Cornelia Meigs et al. (34), the powerful influence of the primer lasted so long because in that era "the chance of life for young children was cruelly small" (p. 114), and spiritual preparation for an early death was thus imperative.

John Locke's Influence on Views of Childhood

In a social environment that viewed children as "small adults" and expected them to behave accordingly, few considered that children might have interests and educational needs of their own. The Puritans and other Calvinist Christians believed that everyone was born "predestined" to achieve either salvation or damnation and must

spend their lives attempting to prove their predestined worthiness to be saved. The English philosopher John Locke, however, envisioned the child's mind at birth as a *tabula rasa*, a blank page on which ideas were to be imprinted. In *Some Thoughts Concerning Education* (29), published in 1693, Locke stressed the interrelatedness of a healthy physical development and a healthy mental development, and advocated milder ways of teaching and bringing up children than had been previously recommended. According to John Rowe Townsend (43), Locke believed that children who could read should be provided with easy, pleasant books suited to their capacities—books that encouraged them to read and rewarded them for their reading efforts, but that did not fill their heads with useless "trumpery" or encourage vice. Locke found a grave shortage of books that could provide children with pleasure or reward, but did recommend *Aesop's Fables* and *Reynard the Fox* for the delight they offered children and the useful reflections they offered the adults in children's lives.

Locke's attitude was quite enlightened for his time and provided a glimmer of hope that children might be permitted to go through a period of childhood rather than immediately assume the same roles as their parents. While seventeenth-century European and North American culture contained few books appropriate for children, a realization dawned that children might benefit from books written to encourage their reading.

Charles Perrault's Tales of Mother Goose

An exciting development in children's literature occurred in seventeenth-century France. Charles Perrault, a gifted member of the Academie Française, published a book called *Contes de ma Mère l'Oye* (Tales of Mother Goose). The stories in this collection were not those normally referred to as Mother Goose rhymes today, but were well-known fairy tales such as "Cinderella," "Sleeping Beauty," "Puss in Boots," "Little Red Riding Hood," and "Blue Beard." Perrault did not create these tales, but retold stories from the French oral tradition that had entranced children and provided entertainment in the elegant salons of the Parisian aristocracy for generations. Perrault was one of the first writers to recognize that fairy tales have a special place in the world of children. Readers can thank Perrault or, as many scholars (36) now believe, his son Pierre Perrault d'Arman-cour, for collecting these tales that have been translated and retold by many different contemporary writers and illustrators of children's books. Here, at last, was the beginning of entertainment written for children rather than adopted by them because nothing else was available.

The Adventure Stories of Defoe and Swift

Two adventure books that appeared in the early eighteenth century were, like virtually all litera-

ture of the time, written for adults, but quickly embraced by children.

A political climate that rewarded dissenters by placing them into prison molded the author of the first great adventure story, *Robinson Crusoe*, published in 1719. Daniel Defoe was condemned to Newgate Prison after he wrote a fiery pamphlet responding to the political and religious controversies of his time. But Defoe wrote constantly even while in jail. He was motivated to write *Robinson Crusoe* when he read the personal accounts of a Scottish sailor, Alexander Selkirk, who had

Although not written for children, Daniel Defoe's adventure story became popular with eighteenth-century children. (Courtesy of Lilly Library, Indiana University, Bloomington, Indiana.)

been marooned on one of the Juan Fernandez Islands, located off the coast of Chile. This Scottish sailor had deserted ship after a disagreement with the captain and lived alone on the island for four years before he was discovered by another ship and brought back to England. Defoe was so captivated by Selkirk's experience that he wrote an adventure story to answer his questions about how a person might acquire food, clothing, and shelter if shipwrecked on an island.

The resulting tale appeared first in serial publication and then in a book. Children and adults enjoyed the exciting and suspenseful story. The book was so influential that thirty-one years after Defoe's death French philosopher Jean Jacques Rousseau, the founder of modern education, said that *Robinson Crusoe* would be the first book read by his son, Emile. According to Brian W. Alderson (1) *Robinson Crusoe* reflects an era in Western history when people had begun to believe in the natural goodness of human beings uninfluenced by corruption in the world around them. *Robinson Crusoe* became and remained so popular that it stimulated a whole group of books written about similar subjects, which came to be known as *Robinsonades*. The most popular Robinsonade was Johann Wyss's *The Swiss Family Robinson*.

The second major adventure story written during the early eighteenth century also dealt with the subject of shipwreck. Jonathan Swift's *Gulliver's Travels*, published in 1726, described Gulliver's realistic adventures with strange beings encountered in mysterious lands: tiny Lilliputians, giant Brobdingnagians, talking horses, and flying islands. Swift wrote *Gulliver's Travels* as a satire about the human race for adults. Children, however, thought of the story as an enjoyable adventure and adopted Gulliver as a hero.

These adventure stories must have seemed truly remarkable to children otherwise surrounded by literature written only to instruct or to moralize. The impact of these eighteenth-century writers is still felt today, as twentieth-century children enjoy versions of these first adventure stories.

Newbery's Books for Children

The 1740s are commonly regarded as the time when the idea of children's books began in Europe and North America (43). New ways of thought emerged as the middle class became larger and strengthened its social position. Be-

cause more people had the time, the money, and the education necessary for reading, books became more important. Middle-class life also began to center around the home and family rather than around the marketplace or the great houses of nobility. With this growing emphasis on family life began a realization that children should be children rather than small adults.

Into this social climate came John Newbery, an admirer of John Locke and an advocate of a milder way of educating children, who was also a writer and publisher. Newbery began publishing a line of books for children in 1744 with *A Little Pretty Pocket Book*. "Although his work reflected the didactic tone of the time," say Jane Bingham and Grayce Scholt (5), "his books were not intended to be textbooks. Their gilt-paper covers, attractive pages, engaging stories and verses— and sometimes toys which were offered with the books—provided 'diversion' for children of the English-speaking world" (p. 86). *A Little Pretty Pocket Book* included a letter from Jack the Giant Killer written both to instruct and to entertain children. Modern readers would not consider this early book for children very entertaining when compared with books written to amuse today's children, but it must have been revolutionary for its time. In 1765 Newbery published a more famous book, *History of Little Goody Two Shoes*, a fictitious story by Oliver Goldsmith.

Newbery's company, set up in London, became a success. His accomplishments are often attributed to his bustling energy, his interest in literature and writers, his love for children, and his taking note of children's tastes as measured by the popularity of their favorite chapbooks. Newbery's publications included *Nurse Truelove's New Year's Gift, Mother Goose, Tom Thumb's Folio*, and old favorites such as *Aesop's Fables, Robinson Crusoe*, and *Gulliver's Travels*. Because of Newbery's success, publishers realized that there was indeed a market for books written specifically for children. It is fitting that the coveted award given annually to the outstanding author of a children's literature selection bears Newbery's name.

Rousseau's Philosophy of Natural Development

While John Locke had advocated a milder and more rational approach to educating children, Jean Jacques Rousseau recommended a totally new approach. Locke believed that children should be led in their search for knowledge, but Rousseau believed that they should merely be accompanied. Rousseau maintained that children could and should develop naturally, with gentle guidance from wise adults who could supply necessary information. Margaret C. Gillespie (14) maintains that "at a time when the major emphasis was on sharpening the muscles of the mind and filling it to the brim with all the knowledge in the world it could absorb, Jean Jacques Rousseau's exhortations to 'retournez à la nature' had a strong impact on the complacency of educators" (p. 21).

In his *Emile*, published in 1762, Rousseau described the stages of children's growth, stressing the importance of experiences in harmony with children's natural development physically and mentally. Rousseau's stages progressed from early sensory motor development, through a concrete learning period, into a period where intellectual conceptualization was possible. As mentioned above, Rousseau believed that Daniel Defoe's *Robinson Crusoe* was the most important piece of literature emphasizing the necessity of humans using their own ideas to cope with their environment. Rousseau's impact on parents' attitudes toward children was "forceful and unmistakable," says Gillespie (14). "Now children were looked upon as 'little angels' who could do no wrong. They were permitted to be children rather than 'little adults'. They became the center of the educational scene rather than satellites around the curriculum" (p. 23).

William Blake's Poetry about Children

The English poet William Blake, who is credited with writing verses as if a child had written them, published his *Songs of Innocence* in 1789 and his *Songs of Experience* in 1794. F. J. Harvey Darton (9) characterizes Blake in the spiritual sense as "a child happy on a cloud, singing and desiring such songs as few but he could write" (p. 185). Blake's often quoted poem introducing *Songs of Innocence* provides the reader an opportunity to visualize this happy child. (The punctuation and spelling are from the engraved first edition cited in Darton, 1932.)

Introduction

Piping down the valleys wild
Piping songs of pleasant glee
On a cloud I saw a child.
And he laughing said to me.

Pipe a song about a Lamb:
So I piped with merry chear,
Piper pipe that song again—
So I piped, he wept to hear.

Drop thy pipe thy happy pipe
Sing thy songs of happy chear.
So I sung the same again
While he wept with joy to hear

Piper sit thee down and write
In a book that all may read—
So he vanish'd from my sight.
And I pluck'd a hollow reed

And I made a rural pen,
And I stain'd the water clear,
And I wrote my happy songs,
Every child may joy to hear

The Fairy Tales of Andersen and the Brothers Grimm

Sir Walter Scott's novels about the Middle Ages, enthusiasm for Gothic architecture, lyrical ballads, and Rousseau's philosophy of a return to nature all typified the Romantic Movement in late eighteenth-century Europe. This atmosphere encouraged an interest in folk literature.

In the early 1800s, two German scholars, Jakob and Wilhelm Grimm, became interested in collecting folktales that reflected the ancient German language and tradition. In researching their subject, the brothers listened to tales told by Dortchen and Gretchen Wild; the Wilds' maid, Marie; a farmer's wife called Frau Viehmännin; and other storytellers from throughout Germany. Although scholars disagree about how exactly the Brothers Grimm transcribed the tales they heard, Bettina Hürlimann (21) maintains that the brothers "did not just write down what they heard. Even for the first edition they did a lot of revising, comparing with other sources, and trying to find a simple language which was at the same time full of character. With time and with later editions it became clear that Jakob, the more scholarly, tried to keep the tales in the most simple, original form, more or less as they had heard them, and that Wilhelm, more of a poet, was for retelling them in a new form with regard to the children" (p. 71).

The Grimms' first edition of tales, published in 1812, contained eighty-five stories, including "Cinderella," "Hansel and Gretel," "Little Red Riding Hood," and "The Frog Prince." According to Hürlimann (21), the second edition, published in 1815, was designed more specifically for chil-

German Popular Stories, such as this 1826 edition, introduced the Grimms' folktales to English-speaking children. (Courtesy of Lilly Library, Indiana University, Bloomington, Indiana.)

dren, with illustrations and a minimum of scholarly comment on the tales it contained.

In 1823, the tales collected by the Brothers Grimm were translated into English and published under the title *German Popular Stories*. Since that time, hundreds of artists in many countries have illustrated tales such as "Snow White and the Seven Dwarfs," "Rumpelstiltskin," and "The Elves and the Shoemaker," which have become part of our literary heritage. (Chapter six discusses some editions of these tales that have been either translated or rewritten for children.)

Most of the published folktales and fairy tales discussed here thus far were written down by either Charles Perrault or the Brothers Grimm. The stories had been told in castles and cottages for many generations. Hans Christian Andersen, however, is generally credited with being the first

to create and publish an original fairy tale, using his own experiences to stimulate his writing. "The Ugly Duckling," "The Little Mermaid," and "The Red Shoes" are among Andersen's famous stories.

Andersen was born to a poor but happy family in Odense, Denmark. His cobbler father shared stories with him and even built a puppet theater for his son's enjoyment. Even when his father died and it seemed that he would have to learn a trade, Andersen retained his dream of becoming an actor. During these poverty-stricken years, he tried to forget his troubles by putting on puppet shows and telling stories to children. Because Andersen wanted to write stories and plays, he returned to school to improve his writing skills. While there, he suffered from cruel jokes about his looks; he was thin and had large feet and a large nose. (Doesn't this sound like a theme for one of his fairy tales?) In 1828, when Andersen was twenty-three, he began to write stories and poems. Five years later, he was recognized as a promising writer by the Danish government, whose financial support allowed him to travel and write about his experiences. When his *Life in Italy*, a rather scholarly work, was published, Andersen at last started to make money. His next book was far different: the first of his famous fairy tale books, it was written in the same colloquial language used to tell stories. When *Fairy Tales Told for Children* was published, a friend told Andersen that his *Life in Italy* would make him famous, but his fairy tales would make people remember him forever. Although Andersen did not believe his fairy tales were as good as his other books, he enjoyed writing them and produced a new fairy tale book each Christmas as a gift to children of all ages. When Andersen was sixty-two, he was invited back to Odense, the town in which he had known happiness, poverty, and then sadness. This time he was the honored guest at a celebration that lasted for an entire week.

Andersen's fairy stories are still popular; newly illustrated versions are published every year. These colorful picture-book versions, as well as tales in anthologies, are still enjoyed by children of many ages. (See chapter seven for a discussion of these modern fantasy books.)

Early Illustrators of Children's Books

The identity of the first picture book for children is debated. Eric Quayle (37) identifies *Kunst und Lehrbüchlein* (Book of Art and Instruction for Young People), published in 1580 by the German publisher Sigmund Feyerabend, as the "first book aimed at the unexplored juvenile market" (p. 11). The detailed, full-page woodcuts showing European life were the work of Jost Amman. Of particular interest are the pictures of a young scholar reading a hornbook, and of a child holding a doll.

Johann Amos Comenius, a Moravian teacher and former bishop of the Bohemian Brethren, is usually credited with writing the first non-alphabet picture book that strove to educate children. Bettina Hürlimann (21) describes Comenius as a great humanist who wanted children to observe God's creations—plants, stars, clouds, rain, sun, and geography—rather than memorize abstract knowledge. In order to achieve this goal, Comen-

ius took children out of the conventional classroom and into the natural world. He then wrote down their experiences in simple sentences using both Latin and the children's own language. He published these simple sentences and accompanying woodcuts in 1658 as *Orbis Pictus* (Painted World). Educational historian Ayers Bagley (3) identifies allegorical meanings in the illustrations and text, related to true understanding, right action, and correct speech as important contributors to the attainment of wisdom. Scholars disagree about whether Comenius drew the illustrations for *Orbis Pictus* himself or whether he instructed artists in their execution. Jane Bingham and Grayce Scholt (5) credit the woodcuts in the 1658 edition to Paul Kreutzberger and the wood engravings in the 1810 American edition to Alexander Anderson. Whoever the artist was, Hürlimann (21) emphasizes that "the pictures are in wonderful harmony with the text, and the book was to become for more than a century the most popular book with children of all classes" (p. 67).

Most book illustrations before the 1800s, especially those in the inexpensive chapbooks, were crude woodcuts. If color was used, it was usually hand applied by amateurs who filled in the colors according to a guide. Thomas Bewick is credited with being one of the earliest artists to illustrate books for children. His skillfully executed woodcuts graced *The New Lottery Book of Birds and*

A typical woodcut from *Orbis Pictus*, the first picture book for children. (A reprint of the *Orbis Pictus* has been published by Singing Tree Press, Gale Research Company, Detroit, Michigan.)

Beasts, published in 1771, and *A Pretty Book of Pictures for Little Masters and Misses; or Tommy Trip's History of Beasts and Birds*, published in 1779.

Three nineteenth-century English artists made an enormous impact on illustrations for children's books. According to Ruth Hill Viguers (11) in the introduction to Edward Ernest's *The Kate Greenaway Treasury*, the work of these artists "represents the best to be found in picture books for children in any era: the strength of design and richness of color and detail of Walter Crane's pictures; the eloquence, humor, vitality, and movement of Randolph Caldecott's art; and the tenderness, dignity, and grace of the very personal interpretation of Kate Greenaway's enchanted land of childhood" (p. 13).

Walter Crane's *The House That Jack Built*, published in 1865, was the first of his series of *toy books*, the name used for picture books published for young children. These books, engraved by Edmund Evans, are credited with marking the beginning of the modern era in color illustrations. From 1865 through 1898, Crane illustrated over forty books, including folktales such as *The Three Bears* and *Cinderella*, and alphabet books such as *The Farmyard Alphabet* and *The Absurd ABC*. Many of Crane's illustrations reflect his appreciation of Japanese color prints.

Randolph Caldecott's talent was discovered by the printer Edmund Evans. Caldecott's illustrations for *The History of John Gilpin*, printed by Evans in 1878, demonstrated his ability to depict robust characters, action, and humor. (The Caldecott Medal for children's book illustration, named for the artist, is embossed with the picture of Gilpin galloping through an English village.) Caldecott's lively and humorous figures jump fences, dance to the fiddler, and flirt with milkmaids in picture books such as *The Fox Jumps over the Parson's Gate, Come Lasses and Lads*, and *The Milkmaid*. Caldecott's picture books are now reissued by Frederick Warne.

Printer and engraver Edmund Evans also encouraged and supported the work of Kate Greenaway. Delighted by Greenaway's drawings and verses, Evans printed her first book, *Under the Window*, in 1878. It was so successful that 70,000 English editions and over 30,000 French and German editions were sold. Greenaway continued illustrating books that reflected happy days of childhood and the blossoming apple trees and primroses that had dotted the English country-

Randolph Caldecott's illustrations suggest action and vitality. (From *The Hey Diddle Diddle Picture Book* by Randolph Caldecott. Reproduced by permission of Frederick Warne & Co., Inc., Publishers.)

side of her youth. In a letter to her friend John Ruskin, Greenaway described her view of the world: "I go on liking things more and more, seeing them more and more beautiful. Don't you think it is a great possession to be able to get so much joy out of things that are always there to give it, and do not change? What a great pity my hands are not clever enough to do what my mind and eyes see, but there it is!" (11, p. 19). Other picture books illustrated by Greenaway include *Kate Greenaway's Birthday Book* (1880), *Mother Goose* (1881), *The Language of Flowers* (1884), and Robert Browning's *Pied Piper of Hamelin* (1880). Greenaway's name, like Caldecott's, has been given to an award honoring distinguished artistic accomplishment in the field of children's books. The Kate Greenaway Medal is given annually to the most distinguished British illustrator of children's books.

By the late 1800s when Crane, Caldecott, and Greenaway began drawing for children, European and North American attitudes toward children were also changing. According to Frederick Laws (25), these three artists "were under no public compulsion to be morally edifying or factually informative. Children were no longer supposed to be 'young persons' whose taste would be much the same whether they were five or fifteen. So long as they pleased children, artists were free; indeed, Crane wrote that 'in a sober and matter-of-fact age Toybooks afford perhaps the only outlet for unrestricted flights of fancy open to the modern illustrator who likes to revolt against the despotism of facts' " (p. 318).

CHART 2–2
Milestones in the history of children's illustration

1484	William Caxton, *Aesop's Fables,* contained over one hundred woodcuts.	1878	Randolph Caldecott, *The Diverting History of John Gilpin,* the first of sixteen picture books.
1658	Johann Amos Comenius, *Orbis Pictus* (Painted World), considered by many to be the first picture book for children.	1878	Kate Greenaway, *Under the Window.*
		1883	Howard Pyle, *Robin Hood.*
1771	Thomas Bewick, *The New Lottery Book of Birds and Beasts.*	1900	Arthur Rackham, illustrations for Grimms' *Fairy Tales.*
1784	Thomas and John Bewick, *The Select Fables of Aesop and Others.*	1901	Beatrix Potter, *The Tale of Peter Rabbit.*
		1924	E. H. Shepard, illustrations for A. A. Milne's *When We Were Very Young.*
1789	William Blake. *Songs of Innocence.*		
1823	George Cruikshank, translation of Grimms' *Fairy Tales.*	1933	Kurt Wiese, illustrations for Marjorie Flack's *The Story of Ping.*
1853	George Cruikshank, *Fairy Library.*	1933	E. H. Shepard, illustrations for Kenneth Grahame's *The Wind in the Willows.*
1865	John Tenniel, illustrations for Lewis Carroll's *Alice's Adventures in Wonderland.*	1937	Dr. Seuss, *And to Think That I Saw It on Mulberry Street.*
1865	Walter Crane, *The House That Jack Built,* the first of the toy books engraved by Evans.		

This brief discussion of illustrators does not mention all the artists who made contributions in the nineteenth century, but it does outline the relatively short history of children's book illustration. (Chapter four discusses many twentieth-century artists.) Chart 2–2 summarizes some milestones in the illustration of children's books from the fifteenth century into the early twentieth century.

The Victorian Influence

English-speaking people identify the reign of Great Britain's Queen Victoria, from 1837 to 1901, with a distinct social epoch, the "Victorian Age," although "Victorian" social influences certainly preceded and followed the queen's life. The rise of a highly competitive industrial technology, the growth of large cities and the decline of rural traditions, an emphasis on strictly controlled social behavior and Christian piety, and a romantic focus on home and family are some of the factors usually associated with the Victorian Age in Europe, North America, and elsewhere. The increasingly prosperous middle and upper classes began to view childhood, sentimentally, as an even more special stage in the human life cycle, while children of the working poor labored many hours a day in mines and factories.

Fred Raymond Erisman (10) has concluded that American children's literature of the late nineteenth and early twentieth centuries chiefly reflected upper-middle-class values, although it fell into two main categories: nonfiction was realistic, dealing with the social, technological, and biographical concerns of an urban society; fiction presented the ideal values of the well-to-do, implying that these were the typical American values. Robert Gordon Kelly's (24) research also reveals that American children's literature in the nineteenth century presented children with an ideal "concept of selfhood" for emulation, as well as indicating unresolved tensions about America's growing cities, a beginning emphasis on the responsibilities of a cultural elite, and changing ideas about childhood. According to Kelly (24), the "gentleman and lady" in children's literature "offered models for negotiating the difficult and precarious passage from childhood to adulthood as well as for moderating the economic competition . . . that was the most important social fact of American life" (p. 42). Children's literature encouraged the young to confront a dog-eat-dog world with courage, temperance, prudence, courtesy, self-reliance, and presence of mind. "So great was the emphasis on self-control," says Kelly (24, p. 41), "that one author warned that 'carelessness is worse than stealing.' "

Kelly identifies two typical story patterns in children's literature of the period. In the *ordeal,* a child loses the protection and influence of parents or other adults for a short time. Circumstances force the child to act decisively; the situ-

FLASHBACK

MRS. EWING'S STORIES.

"What's your name, boy?" — PAGE 247.

JAN OF THE WINDMILL.
A STORY OF THE PLAINS.

By Mrs. Ewing. Price, $1.00.

ROBERTS BROTHERS, Publishers,
BOSTON

JULIANA HORATIA EWING WAS ONE OF THE MOST prolific authors of the Victorian period. Many of her popular tales for children first appeared in English periodicals such as *The Monthly Packet* and *Aunt Judy's Magazine for Young People.* Her first book, *Melchior's Dream and Other Stories,* was published by the Society for the Promotion of Christian Knowledge in 1862. Among her other books were *Mrs. Overtheway's Remembrances* (1869), *Jan of the Windmill* (1876), *Brothers of Pity, and Other Tales* (1882), *Jackanapes* (1884), and *Daddy Darwin's Dovecot* (1884). The last two books were illustrated by Randolph Caldecott.

Literary critics considered Mrs. Ewing's writing to be among the best of the time. Their comments also reflected typically Victorian concerns and values. For example, a critic for the *Worcester Spy* described Mrs. Ewing as a genius whose writing touched the heart, excited tender and noble emotion, encouraged religious feeling, and deepened the scorn for the mean and the cowardly. This same critic recommended that children read Mrs. Ewing's stories because they nourished everything that was lovely in children's characters, Mrs. Ewing's "refining" and "ennobling" stories were popular for many years, remaining in print until the 1930s.

ations described often seem contrived to emphasize that sound character rather than sound reasoning is involved. The child demonstrates the expected behaviors, then returns to the safety of the family and is justly rewarded. The heroine of "Nellie in the Light House," published in an 1877 edition of *St. Nicholas* magazine, is the seven-year-old daughter of a lighthouse keeper. When her father goes to the mainland for supplies, the housekeeper is called away to nurse a neighbor, the housekeeper's husband collapses from a stroke, a storm causes high winds, and the beacon light is extinguished. Now alone, Nellie must overcome her fear and find a way to rekindle the beacon. She remembers a hymn her mother sang to her and rekindles the light, which then saves her father, caught in the storm.

In the second type of story, *change of heart,* a child who has not yet reached the ideal of self-discipline and sound moral character realizes the need for self-improvement. In "Charlie Balch's Metamorphosis," which appeared in an 1867 edition of the *Riverside Magazine for Young People,* the hero is a sullen and lazy boy who has withdrawn into himself after his mother's death. His father sends him to a boarding school where he joins a rough crowd of boys. Charlie realizes the errors of his ways during a sermon, and the rest of the story places him in situations that test his resolution for a change of heart. By the end of the story, Charlie has a cheerful disposition and better manners.

Charlotte Yonge was a prolific author of children's literature who wrote about the large families so common in Victorian times. Her own childhood had involved close ties with her brother and many cousins. Conversations among the people in her extended family later provided her with realistic settings and dialogue for her fiction. Yonge's stories also reflect the pronounced Christian ethic of the Victorian period. In Yonge's *The Daisy Chain*, for example, a husband and wife become missionaries in the Loyalty Islands. In typical Victorian fashion, Yonge's fiction portrays females as inferior to males. In *The Daisy Chain*, the hero's sister is advised not to compete with her brother at the university because a woman cannot equal a man scholastically. In *The Clever Woman of the Family*, published in 1865, the heroine thinks for herself, but whenever there is a disagreement between her ideas and a man's ideas, she must adhere to the superior wisdom of a brother, father, or husband.

Myra Stark (42) maintains that the Victorian Age was in the grip of an ideology that viewed women as either wives and mothers or failed wives or mothers. "Woman was the center of the age's cult of the family," Stark declares, "'The angel in the house,' tending to the domestic altar. She was viewed as man's inferior—less rational, weaker, needing his protection; but at the same time, she was exalted for her spirituality, her moral influence. Man was the active one, the doer; woman was the inspirer and the nurturer. The spheres of work in the world and in the home were rigidly divided between the sexes" (42, p. 4). Consequently, most Victorian literature for children directed middle- and upper-class girls and boys into the rigidly distinct roles expected of them as adults.

Some Victorian authors were sensitive to the realities of poor children's lives. In 1862, the English poet Elizabeth Barrett Browning wrote of these children's woes in her poem, "The Cry of the Children," describing the weeping of children in mines and factories while other children played. Another English author of the period, Charles Dickens, is famous for having aroused the Victorian conscience to the plight of unfortunate children, such as Dickens's fictional orphan in *Oliver Twist*.

Fantasy, Adventure, and Real People

As the world was changing, so, too, were views of childhood changing. Emphases in children's literature mirrored the new attitudes and world developments. Childhood was becoming, at least for

middle- and upper-class children, a more carefree and enjoyable period of life; this change was reflected in the increase in fantasy stories for children. As adventurers explored unknown areas of the world, their experiences inspired a new growth in adventure stories. And the character of specific families and localities was captured in the growing popularity of literature about ordinary people, places, and events in sometimes extraordinary circumstances. Each of these developments is discussed in the sections that follow.

Fantasy. By the mid-1800s, the puritanical resistance to fantasy in children's literature was on its way toward extinction in most segments of European and North American society. Children had been reading and enjoying the folktales of Perrault and the Brothers Grimm, and Andersen's stories had been translated into English. More and more educators and parents believed that literature should entertain children during their extended period of childhood rather than merely instruct them. Fantasy created a world, according to Raymond Chapman (8), where fears could be projected onto impossible creatures of the imagination while a child remained safe. Although growing to maturity seemed dangerous, the happiest people acquired new knowledge while retaining childlike qualities. Brian W. Alderson (1, p. 64) describes the creation of one of the landmarks in fantasy and nonsense.

One summer's day on the river at Oxford [England] a thirty-year-old lecturer in mathematics at Christ Church was taking the three daughters of his Dean, Edith, Lorina, and Alice, out for a row. His name was Charles Lutwidge Dodgson. The day was hot and the children wanted to have a story told them, a thing they had come to expect from Mr. Dodgson. So the young lecturer complied, his mind relaxing in the drowsy heat and his thoughts, which did not tire so easily, following paths of their own making.

The paths led directly down the rabbit hole and into adventures in Wonderland with the Cheshire Cat, the Queen of Hearts, and the Mad Hatter. The story told that afternoon in 1862 made such an impression on Alice that she pestered Dodgson to write it down. He wrote it for her, gave it to her as a gift, and, after it had been thoroughly enjoyed by many people, published it for others under the pseudonym Lewis Carroll.

According to Cornelia Meigs et al. (34), the revolutionary nature of Lewis Carroll's *Alice's Adven-*

tures in Wonderland and *Through the Looking Glass* when compared with earlier books written for children is due to "the fact that they were written purely to give pleasure to children. . . . Here . . . for the first time we find a story designed for children without a trace of a lesson or moral" (p. 194). (Chapter seven discusses the stories themselves.)

Edward Lear, the other great writer of fantasy for children in the nineteenth century, created absurd and delightful characters in the form of nonsense verses. Lear's *A Book of Nonsense* appeared in 1846, his *More Nonsense* in 1872. *Nonsense Songs, Botany and Alphabets*, published in 1871, contained Lear's "Nonsense Stories," "Non-

Edward Lear's illustrations heightened the humor of his limericks. (From *A Book of Nonsense* by Edward Lear. Published by Heinrich Hoffman, 1846. Courtesy of Lilly Library, Indiana University, Bloomington, Indiana.)

sense Geography," "Natural History," and "Nonsense Alphabets." *Laughable Lyrics* (1877) included the nonsense verses "The Quangle-Wangle's Hat," "The Dong with the Luminous Nose," and "The Youghy-Bonghy-Bo." (Chapter 8 discusses Lear's nonsense verses.)

Lear's work, like Carroll's, was popular with both young and adult readers. Both writers are often quoted and enjoyed today as much as they were when their works were created.

The illustrations and text for *Alice's Adventures in Wonderland* were designed to give pleasure, not to teach a lesson. (Illustration by John Tenniel. From *Alice's Adventures in Wonderland* by Lewis Carroll. Published by Macmillan and Co., 1865. Courtesy of Lilly Library, Indiana University, Bloomington, Indiana.)

Adventure. Europeans and North Americans were having many real-life adventures in the nineteenth century: explorers were seeking the North Pole, Florence Nightingale was pioneering for female independence as a director of nursing in the Crimean War, and a railroad was being constructed across the United States. If a person could not go to a remote region and overcome the perils lurking there, the next best adventure was the vicarious one offered through books.

Robert Louis Stevenson was the master of adventure stories written during this time. When

Treasure Island was published, it was considered the greatest adventure story for children since *Robinson Crusoe*, and Brian W. Alderson (1) agrees that Stevenson had the greatest influence on children's literature after Daniel Defoe.

Stevenson was born in Edinburgh, Scotland, the son of a lighthouse engineer. When he was a young boy, his father told him bedtime tales filled with "blood and thunder," and his nurse told him stories of body snatchers, ghosts, and martyrs. As an adult, he traveled to many lands, but he still loved the lochs, islands, and misty forests of his home. All these early experiences are evident in Stevenson's two most famous adventure stories, *Treasure Island* and *Kidnapped*.

Treasure Island had an interesting beginning. While trying to entertain his stepson, Stevenson drew a watercolor map of an island, then followed his drawing with the now famous story of pirates, buried treasure, and a young boy's adventures.

Both *Treasure Island* and *Kidnapped* have the ingredients of outstanding adventure literature: action, mystery, and pursuit and evasion in authentic historical settings. Stevenson believed that an adventure story should have a specific effect on its readers: it should absorb and delight them, fill their minds with a kaleidoscope of images, and satisfy their nameless longings. Stevenson believed that Robinson Crusoe discovering a footprint on his lonely beach, Achilles shouting against the Trojans, and Ulysses bending over his great bow were culminating moments that have been printed on the mind's eye forever (30). Children and adults should demand such moments in their literature, Stevenson believed—and achieved that quality himself in tales of "treasure and treachery . . . the comings and goings of . . . pirates, the ominous hints of the fearful events which are to come" (1, p. 257).

While Robert Lewis Stevenson wrote of pirates and buried treasure in the not-so-distant past, Howard Pyle took readers back to the Middle Ages to fight evil, overcome the king's injustice, and have a rollicking good time in the green depths of Sherwood Forest. Pyle's *The Merry Adventures of Robin Hood*, published in 1883, retold the old English ballad about Robin Hood, Little John, Friar Tuck, and the other merry men who robbed the rich to give to the poor and constantly thwarted the evil plans of the Sheriff of Nottingham. Here was swashbuckling entertainment that also provided children with a glimpse of an early period in European history. (See p. 241 in chapter six.)

The Industrial Revolution, the invention of the steam engine, and the prevalent feeling of new possibilities always just around the corner laid the groundwork for a new kind of adventure story in the last half of the nineteenth century. Jules Verne's science fiction adventure stories can certainly be classified as another benchmark in children's literature. Here was a writer who could envision submarines, guided missiles, and dirigibles long before such things were possible. His first science fiction book, *Five Weeks in a Balloon*, was published in France in 1863. His two most famous books, *Twenty-Thousand Leagues under the Sea*, published in 1869, and *Around the World in Eighty Days*, published in 1872, have also been immortalized in film. Consequently, the heroes of these books, Captain Nemo and Phileas Fogg, are well known both to readers and to movie fans. Verne was stimulated to write because he admired the work of an earlier author, Daniel Defoe, and Verne's *The Mysterious Island*, published in 1875, was written because of Verne's interest in *Robinson Crusoe*. The tribute accorded Verne's genius can be seen in the popularity of his works even today after his glorious inventions have become reality. Verne's detailed descriptions are so believable they seem as modern now as they did when they were published in the 1800s. The popularity of Verne's literature also caused other authors to write science fiction and expand this new genre.

Real People. During the later nineteenth and early twentieth centuries, a type of book that James H. Fraser (12) calls a *local-color story* came into its own. Realistic situations and people are the setting and subject of such stories, in which place, plot, and characters are tightly integrated. According to Fraser, "This integration, which reveals the complex involvement of human, cultural, and geographical influences, produces a rich literature—peculiarly rich for the student of American culture, and extraordinarily rich for the young persons fortunate enough to read it" (12, p. 55). The diversity of American geography and people are found in books like Edward Eggleston's *The Hoosier School Boy* (rural Indiana), Thomas Bailey Aldrich's *The Story of a Bad Boy* (a New England seafaring town), Kate Douglas Wiggin's *Rebecca of Sunnybrook Farm* (rural Maine), Mark Twain's *Huckleberry Finn* (a Mississippi

River town), and Frances Courtenay Baylor's *Juan and Juanita* (the Southwest). Fraser maintains that these local-color stories also transmit a conservative, traditional view of American life to the next generation because their characters are "carry-overs from an earlier age," an agrarian, preindustrial age, which the stories sentimentalize for their modern readers (12, p. 59).

The greatest American writer of realistic adventure in this period was Mark Twain (Samuel Clemens). While Robert Lewis Stevenson was writing about adventures on far-off islands, Twain was immortalizing life on the Mississippi River before the Civil War. Twain grew up in the river town of Hannibal, Missouri, where he lived many of the adventures about which he later wrote. He ex-

Mark Twain wrote adventures about life in the Mississippi River environment in which he himself had grown up. (From *Adventures of Huckleberry Finn* by Mark Twain. Published by Charles L. Webster and Co., 1885. Courtesy of Lilly Library, Indiana University, Bloomington, Indiana.)

plored the river, raided melon patches, and used a cave as a rendezvous to plan further adventures and mischief with his friends. These adventures made Tom Sawyer and Huckleberry Finn come alive for many adventure-loving children. Twain's heroes did not leave the continent, but they did run away from home, have exciting adventures on a nearby island, return in time to hear plans for their own funerals, and then attend those momentous occasions. Characters such as Injun Joe, Aunt Polly, Tom Sawyer, Becky Thatcher, and Huckleberry Finn still provide hours of reading pleasure for children and adults today.

Many American books in the Victorian era took the family as their subject, and series stories dealing with the everyday lives of large families became popular. Margaret Sidney, for example, wrote a series of books about the "five little Peppers." The first book, *The Five Little Peppers and How They Grew*, published in 1881, was followed by *The Five Little Peppers Midway* and *The Five Little Peppers Grown Up*.

Louisa May Alcott's account of family life in *Little Women*, published in 1868, is so real that readers feel they know each member of the March family intimately. This book showing the warm relationships and everyday struggles in a family of meager means is actually about Alcott's own family. In many ways, her life was quite different from the usual Victorian model, which accounts for the ways in which *Little Women* was ahead of its time. Alcott's father believed in educating his daughters; consequently, Alcott was first educated at home by her father and then went to the district school. Later she went to Boston to earn a living as a writer so that her family would not have to support her. She wrote constantly, publishing her early melodramatic stories in magazines. Alcott left Boston to nurse her sister during a terminal illness. (This incident became Beth's illness and subsequent death in *Little Women*.) During the Civil War, Alcott left home to nurse soldiers until poor health forced her to return to her family.

In 1867, a publisher asked Alcott to write a book for girls, and she decided to write about her own family. The resulting *Little Women* was an overwhelming success. Readers enjoyed the intimate details of a warm, loving, and very human family. The most popular character, Jo, shares many characteristics with Alcott herself, who believed in women's strength and capabilities. Jo is courageous, warm, and honest, but has a quick temper that often gets her into difficulty. She also leaves home to earn a living as a writer and help support her family. *Little Women* was so popular that in 1869 Alcott wrote a sequel, *Little Women, Part II*. She also wrote other favorites such as *An Old-Fashioned Girl*, *Little Men*, and *Eight Cousins*.

One very popular realistic story published in the nineteenth century had a setting foreign to most readers of its English translation. Mountains that climb into the sky, sheepherders, tinkling bells, rushing streams, flower-strewn meadows, a hut with a bed of fresh hay, and the freedom to wander in these delightful Swiss surroundings were found in Johanna Spyri's *Heidi*, published in Switzerland in 1880 and translated into English in 1884. Spyri based her book on her own childhood experiences in the Swiss Alps, which may help explain its realistic appeal, as described by Virginia Haviland (19): "In an era when so much children's literature was burdened with dead dialogue and moral content, the freshness of this story must have come as a breath of mountain air; today, Heidi holds her own with carefree heroines of any of the best modern children's books because she is real" (p. 79).

Actual experience in a foreign land was not the only basis an author had for providing a believable setting. Mary Mapes Dodge used research and imagination to provide credible background and characters in *Hans Brinker, or the Silver Skates, A Story of Holland*. Readers in The Netherlands accepted this story as authentic in 1865, even though Dodge had never visited their country.

Space does not allow a complete discussion of all the books written for children or written for adults and read by children in earlier eras of our history. Chart 2–3 lists some previously discussed books and other milestone books in children's literature that bring the world of children's books into the twentieth century.

ISSUE

❖

Are the Writings of Mark Twain Racist?

THE WRITINGS OF MARK Twain (Samuel Clemens), especially the *adventures of Huckleberry Finn*, are under protest in the 1980s because of Twain's depictions of black people. Those who suggest that the *Adventures of Huckleberry Finn* should be banned or rewritten point to the numerous uses of the word *nigger* and instances in which black Americans are stereotyped rather than presented as individual, well-rounded characters.

Twain might find this 1980s protest ironic; in the 1880s he was accused of going too far in advancing the cause of human equality and justice. Robert Scott Kellner,[1] a recognized Twain scholar, believes, however, that "a close examination of Twain's writing reveals an element of satire in his seemingly racist language, a satire directed at the reader who would choose to agree with the stereotyped image. Twain's language and imagery about the blacks in his stories work together as a mirror in which bigoted readers ultimately see themselves." Kellner stresses that, in the relationship between Huckleberry Finn and Jim, Twain makes clear that a black man is capable of earning a trust that withstands the pressures of an anti-black heritage—that he can give love and loyalty, strive for physical emancipation, and be a wise father figure for a misinformed boy.

As they read Twain's work, students of children's literature should consider whether it reflects a belief in the inequality of human beings or whether it suggests that people of all races share a common humanity.

[1] Kellner, Robert Scott. "Defending Mark Twain." *The Eagle.* Bryan-College Station, Texas, 11 April 1982, p. 1D.

CHART 2–3
Notable authors of children's literature

1477	William Caxton, *Caxton's Book of Curtesye*
1484	William Caxton, *The Fables of Aesop*
1485	William Caxton, *Le Morte d'Arthur*
1678	John Bunyan, *Pilgrm's Progress*
1698	Charles Perrault or Pierre Perrault d'Arman-cour, *Tales of Mother Goose*
1719	Daniel Defoe, *Robinson Crusoe*
1726	Jonathan Swift, *Gulliver's Travels*
1744	John Newbery, *A Little Pretty Pocket Book*
1789	William Blake, *Songs of Innocence*
1812	First volume of Grimm Brothers' fairy tales, *Kinder-und Hausmärchen*
	Johann Wyss, *Swiss Family Robinson*
1820	Sir Walter Scott, *Ivanhoe: A Romance*
1823	Clement G. Moore, *A Visit from St. Nicholas*
1826	James Fenimore Cooper, *The Last of the Mohicans*
1843	Charles Dickens, *A Christmas Carol*
1846	Edward Lear, *A Book of Nonsense*
	Hans Christian Andersen's fairy tales in English translations
1851	John Ruskin, *King of the Golden River*
1856	Charlotte Yonge, *The Daisy Chain*
1862	Christina Georgina Rossetti, *Goblin Market*
1863	Charles Kingsley, *The Water Babies*
1865	Lewis Carroll, *Alice's Adventures in Wonderland*
	Mary Elizabeth Mapes Dodge, *Hans Brinker, or the Silver Skates, a Story of Life in Holland*
1868	Louisa May Alcott, *Little Women*
1870	Thomas Bailey Aldrich, *The Story of a Bad Boy*
1871	George MacDonald, *At the Back of the North Wind*
1872	Jules Verne, *Around the World in Eighty Days*
1873	*St. Nicholas: Scribner's Illustrated Magazine for Girls and Boys,* edited by Mary Mapes Dodge
1876	Mark Twain, *The Adventures of Tom Sawyer*
1877	Anna Sewell, *Black Beauty*
1880	Margaret Sidney, *The Five Little Peppers and How They Grew*
1881	Joel Chandler Harris, *Uncle Remus; His Songs and Sayings: The Folklore of the Old Plantation*
1883	Howard Pyle, *Merry Adventures of Robin Hood of Great Renown, in Nottinghamshire*
	Robert Louis Stevenson, *Treasure Island*
1884	Johanna Spyri, *Heidi; Her Years of Wandering and Learning*
1885	Robert Louis Stevenson, *A Child's Garden of Verses*
1886	Frances Hodgson Burnett, *Little Lord Fauntleroy*
1889	Andrew Lang, *The Blue Fairy Book*
1892	Carlo Collodi, *The Adventures of Pinocchio*
	Arthur Conan Doyle, *The Adventures of Sherlock Holmes*

1894	Rudyard Kipling, *The Jungle Books*
1901	Beatrix Potter, *The Tale of Peter Rabbit*
1903	L. Leslie Brooke, *Johnny Crow's Garden*
	Kate Douglas Wiggin, *Rebecca of Sunnybrook Farm*
	J. M. Barrie, *Peter Pan; or The Boy Who Would Not Grow Up*
1904	Howard Garis, *The Bobbsey Twins; or Merry Days Indoors and Out* (There are over seventy books in the series.)
1908	Kenneth Grahame, *The Wind in the Willows*
1911	Frances Hodgson Burnett, *The Secret Garden*
1913	Eleanor H. Porter, *Pollyanna*
1918	O. Henry, *The Ransome of Red Chief*
1921	Hendrik Willem Van Loon, *The Story of Mankind* (One of the first informational books attempting to make learning exciting; first Newbery Medal, 1922)
1922	Margery Williams Bianco, *The Velveteen Rabbit*
1924	A. A. Milne, *When We Were Very Young*
1926	A. A. Milne, *Winnie-the-Pooh*
1928	Wanda Gág, *Millions of Cats*
	Carl Sandburg, *Abe Lincoln Grows Up*
1929	Rachel Field, *Hitty, Her First Hundred Years*
1932	Laura Ingalls Wilder, *Little House in the Big Woods*
	Laura E. Richards, *Tirra Lirra: Rhymes Old and New*
1933	Jean de Brunhoff, *The Story of Babar*
1937	Dr. Seuss, *And to Think That I Saw It on Mulberry Street*
	John Ronald Reuel Tolkien, *The Hobbit*
1939	James Daugherty, *Daniel Boone*
1940	Armstrong Sperry, *Call It Courage*
	Doris Gates, *Blue Willow*
1941	Lois Lenski, *Indian Captive, The Story of Mary Jemison*
	Robert McCloskey, *Make Way for Ducklings*
1942	Virginia Lee Burton, *The Little House*
1944	Robert Lawson, *Rabbit Hill*
1946	Esther Forbes, *Johnny Tremain*
1947	Marcia Brown, *Stone Soup*
1950	Beverly Cleary, *Henry Huggins*
1951	Olivia Coolidge, *Legends of the North*
1952	Lynd Ward, *The Biggest Bear*
	E. B. White, *Charlotte's Web*
	David McCord, *Far and Few*
1953	Mary Norton, *The Borrowers*
1954	Rosemary Sutcliff, *The Eagle of the Ninth*
1955	L. M. Boston, *The Children of Green Knowe*
1957	Else Holmelund Minarik, *Little Bear*
1958	Jean Fritz, *The Cabin Faced West*
	Elizabeth George Speare, *The Witch of Blackbird Pond*

CHART 2–3 (cont.)
Notable authors of children's literature

1959	Leo Lionni, *Little Blue and Little Yellow*		*Counting Book*
	Jean George, *My Side of the Mountain*		Robert Kraus, *Leon, the Late Bloomer*
1960	Michael Bond, *A Bear Called Paddington*	1972	Judith Viorst, *Alexander and the Terrible, Horrible, No Good, Very Bad Day*
	Scott O'Dell, *Island of the Blue Dolphins*		
1961	C. S. Lewis, *The Lion, the Witch, and the Wardrobe*	1973	Doris Smith, *A Taste of Blackberries*
		1974	Janet Hickman, *The Valley of the Shadow*
1962	Ronald Syme, *African Traveler, The Story of Mary Kingsley*	1975	Lawrence Yep, *Dragonwings*
		1976	Mildred Taylor, *Roll of Thunder Hear My Cry*
	Madeleine L'Engle, *A Wrinkle in Time*	1977	Jamake Highwater, *Anpao: An Indian Odyssey*
	Ezra Jack Keats, *The Snowy Day*		Patricia Clapp, *I'm Deborah Sampson: A Soldier in the War of the Revolution*
1964	Louise Fitzhugh, *Harriet the Spy*		
	Irene Hunt, *Across Five Aprils*		Katherine Paterson, *Bridge to Terabithia*
	Lloyd Alexander, *The Book of Three*		Margaret Musgrove, *Ashanti to Zulu: African Traditions*
1967	John Christopher, *The White Mountains*		
	E. L. Konigsburg, *Jennifer, Hecate, MacBeth, William McKinley and Me, Elizabeth*	1978	Tomie de Paola, *The Clown of God*
		1979	José Aruego and Ariane Dewey, *We Hide, You Seek*
	Virginia Hamilton, *Zeely*		
1969	John Steptoe, *Stevie*	1981	Nancy Willard, *A Visit to William Blake's Inn*
	William H. Armstrong, *Sounder*	1982	Nina Bawden, *Kept in the Dark*
	Theodore Taylor, *The Cay*		Laurence Pringle, *Water: The Next Great Resource Battle*
	Vera and Bill Cleaver, *Where the Lilies Bloom*		
	William Steig, *Sylvester and the Magic Pebble*		Cynthia Ryland, *When I Was Young in the Mountains*
1970	Betsy Byars, *Summer of the Swans*	1984	Paula Fox, *One-Eyed Cat*
	Judy Blume, *Are You There God? It's Me, Margaret*	1985	Rhoda Blumberg, *Commodore Perry in the Land of the Shogun*
1971	Arnold Lobel, *Frog and Toad Are Friends*		
	Muriel Feelings, *Moja Means One: Swahili*	1986	Jean Fritz, *Make Way for Sam Houston*

CHILDREN AND THE FAMILY IN CHILDREN'S LITERATURE

Attitudes toward children's place in the family have changed considerably over time. Before the Middle Ages, children were believed to be undeveloped adults who must be brought quickly into the adult world. They were not greatly valued, and infanticide was a regular practice. During the Middle Ages, poor children shared the poverty and hard work of their parents, while children from the upper class and nobility spent most of their childhood separated from their families, receiving instruction and training in the roles they would assume as adults. Not until relatively recently has childhood become the time for the close family interaction that we are familiar with today.

Books written for children or adopted by children over the last few centuries have usually reflected views of childhood and the family typical of their time. Researchers are increasingly viewing children's literature as an important source of information about these changing attitudes. In *Fifteen Centuries of Children's Literature: An Annotated Chronology of British and American Works in Historical Context*, Jane Bingham and Grayce Scholt (5) consider the historical background of children's books, including attitudes toward and treatment of children, discuss the development of children's books, and provide an annotated chronology of children's books. Robert Gordon Kelly (23), in *Mother Was a Lady: Self and Society in Selected American Children's Periodicals, 1865–1890*, considers the social values reflected in children's stories of the late nineteenth century. Mary Lystad (31) considers the sociology of children's books over two centuries in *From Dr. Mather to Dr. Seuss: Two Hundred Years of American Books for Children*.

Other researchers have analyzed children's literature over time: Jean Duncan Shaw (38) has studied themes in children's books published between 1850 and 1964; Alma Cross Homze (20) has analyzed the changing interpersonal relationships depicted in realistic fiction published between 1920 and 1960; and Mary Cadogan and Patricia Craig (6) have looked at the changing role of females in *You're a Brick, Angela! A New Look at Girls' Fiction from 1839 to 1975.* Studies of more recent historical periods include John Rowe Townsend's (43) analysis of the relationships between generations depicted in the literature of the 1950s and the 1960s and Carolyn Wilson Carmichael's (7) analysis of social values reflected in contemporary realistic fiction.

Unsurprisingly, a prominent theme in children's literature has been children's relationships within the family. Changing views about children and the family over time necessarily reflect other social attitudes as well. The time periods discussed here reflect the publication dates of a few popular American children's books in certain eras otherwise not so easily demarcated by precise years. Charts 2–4 through 2–6 present examples of social values, family life, and personal relationships and feelings expressed by children and other family members in these books of different eras. All these books are available today. The older books have been published in reproductions by Garland Publishing Company of New York and London.

The Child and the Family, 1856–1903

An emphatic sense of duty to God and parents, the rise of the public school and Sunday School movements, and the beginning of a belief that children are individuals in their own right are among the characteristics of the Victorian era identifiable in children's literature of the time. Much Victorian children's literature stresses the development of conscience, the merit of striving for perfection, and the male and female roles exemplified by family members. Illuminating examples of the social attitudes of this period may be drawn from Charlotte Yonge's *The Daisy Chain* (1856), Louisa May Alcott's *Little Women* (1868), Thomas Bailey Aldrich's *The Story of a Bad Boy* (1870), Margaret Sidney's *Five Little Peppers and How They Grew* (1880), and Kate Douglas Wiggin's *Rebecca of Sunnybrook Farm* (1903).

While these books have their differences, all of them stress the importance of accepting responsibility, whether for one's family, or for the poor and unfortunate, or for one's own self-improvement. For example, the older children in *The Daisy Chain* assume the task of raising the younger children when their mother dies; their greatest concerns are instilling Christian goodness in

May Alcott's illustrations for her sister Louisa May Alcott's *Little Women* reinforce the vision of a warm, loving Victorian family. (Illustration by May Alcott. From *Little Women or, Meg, Jo, Beth and Amy* by Louisa M. Alcott. Published by Roberts Brothers, 1868. Courtesy of Lilly Library, Indiana University, Bloomington, Indiana.)

their siblings and living up to their father's wishes. Likewise, the children in *Little Women* and *Five Little Peppers and How They Grew* feel responsible for their siblings and their mothers. Rebecca, in *Rebecca of Sunnybrook Farm*, feels this responsibility to such an extent that she completes four years of work at the academy in three years so that she can earn a living and help educate her siblings.

The characters in these books respect adult authority. Children strive to live up to their parents' ideals or want the acceptance and respect of their parents. The hero in *The Story of a Bad Boy* may not always ask or follow his grandfather's advice,

TWENTIETH-CENTURY, American publishers of children's books, like publishers in all historical periods, must respond to the issues of the times. Ann Durell identifies some of these changing issues in two articles published in the *The Horn Book.*[1, 2]

According to Durell, the 1950s was a time when publishing was fun because the rules were clear-cut. The taboos of the early 1900s were still in place: no lying or stealing unless suitably punished, no drinking, and no bad language. Racial prejudice was evidenced by the controversy that greeted Garth Williams's black and white couple in *The Rabbits' Wedding.* In the late 1950s, the library market took on new significance as Russia launched Sputnik and our educational system came under attack. Books were considered a means of improving education.

Durell categorizes the 1960s as a time of rapidly expanding school libraries in the United States. Title II of the Elementary and Secondary School Act mandated funds for the purchase of nontextbooks for schools. Both the sale of nonfiction and easy-to-read book titles and the expansion of school libraries increased rapidly. New issues were affecting the publishing trade, however, as the country was polarized by the Vietnam War and the new demands of the Great Society. The all-white world of children's books was challenged; editors started searching for black authors. For the most part, however, children's books did not reflect the social upheavals of the time.

The 1970s introduced literature that reflected the social upheavals. Reactions to two children's books in the early 1970s exemplify the changing times. When a white author won the Newbery Medal for writing about a black family *(Sounder),* protests intensified editors' search for authors and illustrators who represented ethnic minorities. Mickey's nudity in Maurice Sendak's *In the Night Kitchen* resulted in actions ranging from covering the nudity before the book was placed on the shelf to actual banning of the book. As the 1970s continued, concern about the sex roles portrayed in children's books increased; lists of taboos in children's books were reduced; and books reflected a more positive image of ethnic minorities. Durell emphasizes the paradox created by these changes and the new pressures exerted on publishers. On the one hand, the only criterion for allowing books to be published was the portrayal of a positive picture of females, minority groups, senior citizens, and handicapped. On the other hand, groups demanding conservative standards insisted on returning to the 1950s taboos. Consequently, censorship, but for different reasons, became an issue on both sides.

Many of these issues have not been resolved. Various viewpoints on them will be discussed in appropriate chapters throughout this book.

[1] Durell, Ann. "There Is No Happy Ending: Children's Book Publishing—Past, Present, and Future." *The Horn Book* 58 (Feb. 1982): 23–30.
[2] Durell, Ann. "There Is No Happy Ending: Children's Book Publishing—Past, Present, and Future." *The Horn Book* 58 (April 1982): 145–50.

but he admits that he deserves the terrible things that usually happen to him when he disobeys.

Respect for authority is underscored by the characteristic religious emphasis in these books. In *The Daisy Chain*, family members read the Bible together, discuss the meaning of the minister's sermons, debate the relative importance of the temptations in their lives, and organize a church and school for the poor. The Little Women receive strength from prayer and Bible reading. In *The Story of a Bad Boy*, Sundays are solemn days in which the family attends church, reads the scriptures, and eats food prepared the day before. The Five Little Peppers voice considerable admiration for the clergy and want to become "good." Rebecca of Sunnybrook Farm's aunt, like her father before her, is an influential member of her church.

Family life in these books reiterates the definite social roles assigned to males and females in the Victorian era. Females usually run the household and make decisions related to everyday life, but the husband and father is usually the undisputed head of the family. The author may even state this fact pointblank, so there is no misunderstanding on the part of the reader—as Louisa May Alcott does in *Little Women*:

To outsiders, the five energetic women seemed to rule the house, and so they did in many things; but the quiet scholar, sitting among his books, was still the head of the family, the household conscience, anchor, and comforter: to him the busy, anxious women always turned in troublous times, finding him, in the truest sense of those sacred words, husband and father.

Males and females attend separate schools in *The Story of a Bad Boy*, and only male characters attend the university in *The Daisy Chain* and *Little Women*. Education may also stress different objectives for males and females. Yonge's heroine in *The Daisy Chain* completes her brother's school assignments, but is not expected to understand mathematical concepts. Aldrich's hero wants training in "manly arts" such as boxing, riding, and rowing. In contrast, drawing, writing, and music are desired accomplishments for females in *Little Women*, piano lessons are sought by the oldest female Pepper, and writing is Rebecca's desire.

Considerable insights about the children and families in these books are gained by viewing the types of problems the heroes and heroines experience. Many of these problems involve attempts to abide by the period's standards of moral rectitude. Yonge's heroine strives to raise her family and help the poor. She works to keep the youngest baby an "unstained jewel" until the baby will return to her mother. She and her brother also face the problems associated with providing spiritual guidance to the poor. Many of Jo's problems in *Little Women* are related to controlling her "unfeminine" high energy and self-assertiveness; she looks to her pious mother for guidance in how to be "good."

Jo's only answer was to hold her mother close, and, in the silence which followed, the sincerest prayer she had ever prayed left her heart without words; for in that sad, yet happy hour, she had learned not only the bitterness of remorse and despair, but the sweetness of self-denial and self-control; and, led by her mother's hand, she had drawn nearer to the Friend who welcomes every child with a love stronger than that of any father, tenderer than that of any mother. (p. 103)

Rebecca of Sunnybrook Farm also confronts problems caused by the conflicts between her own high-spirited nature and adults' strict expectations about a young girl's behavior. She also experiences personal misgivings when her actions do not live up to her desire to be good. The advantages of these conflicts, however, are stated by Rebecca's English teacher at the academy: "Luckily she attends to her own development. . . . In a sense she is independent of everything and everybody; she follows her saint without being conscious of it." The problems Thomas Bailey Aldrich creates for his hero allow the "bad" boy to consider and strengthen his own moral code. Although he has several unhappy and even disastrous experiences, the hero does not dwell upon them, believing that they have caused him to become more manly and self-reliant.

Overcoming problems related to poverty and growing up without a father are major concerns of the Pepper children, but Margaret Sidney has their mother encourage them in this way: "You keep on a-tryin', and the Lord'll send some way; don't you go to botherin' your head about it now . . .—it'll come when it's time." The family's financial problems are finally solved when a wealthy old gentleman invites them to share his home.

CHART 2—4
Social values, family life, and personal relationships, 1856–1903

	BOOK, AUTHOR, DATE, SETTING				
	Charlotte Yonge. *The Daisy Chain*, 1856, 1868. Rural England. Middle class.	Louisa May Alcott, *Little Women*, 1868. New England city suburb; Large gardens, quiet streets.	Thomas Bailey Aldrich. *The Story of a Bad Boy*. 1870. New Orleans then to small New Hampshire town.	Margaret Sidney. *Five Little Peppers and How They Grew*. 1880. Poverty level. United States.	Kate Douglas Wiggin, *Rebecca of Sunnybrook Farm*. 1903. Small New England town.
SOCIAL VALUES					
Dignity of Human Beings	Concern for family members. Some poor described as uncivilized. Wanted to improve role of poor by building church.	More important to have personal dignity, self-respect, and peace than wealth. Concern for ill and poor.	In New Orleans Tom kicked a "negro boy" who was in his way. Tom believed Indians scalp children. In New Hampshire household, aunt and servant were friends. No social criticism mentioned.	Peppers were proud and believed they had a good life, although they were poor.	Prejudice stated by neighbor against being "dark complected." Aunt Miranda disowned her sister when she married against her wishes. Rebecca respected many people.
Acceptance of Responsibility	Duty to tend to poor. Founded and taught in school for poor. Each member accepted responsibility to younger siblings after mother's death.	Duty to poor; gave their Christmas breakfast to a poor family. Strong duty to family.	Main character did not dwell on unhappy events in story but believed in accepting reality.	Each member expressed responsibility for siblings and mother. Polly almost ruined her eyes sewing for mother when Polly had measles.	Rebecca worked hard to complete the academy in three years instead of four.
Belief in Equality of Opportunity	Boys had advanced education. Girls not expected to understand mathematical concepts. Girls trained to guide family. Poor children worked at early ages.	Girls were educated but not at the university. Males attended university.	Stressed Puritan ethic of diligence and common sense. Veneer of well being. Main character thought all adults had money when they wanted it.	Family said their ship would come in and hard times would be over.	Rebecca thought boys could do more exciting things than girls. Teacher stressed that girls could have a profession. Brother hoped to become a doctor.
Ambition	Charity, humility, devotion to good works. Development of Christian goodness.	Heroine, Jo, wanted to write. Other sisters: drawing, music. Work ethic stressed by son-in-law.	Males should learn "manly arts" and become self-reliant. Tom did not want to be lowest in his class. No single drive expressed by the main character.	Members wanted to help mother. Polly wanted to play the piano. Ann wanted their ship to come in. To be "good."	Rebecca wanted an education to help her family. To become a writer.
Obedience to Law, Patriotism	Respect stated for military profession.	Mother encouraged her husband to serve in the Union army. Mother devoted time to Soldiers Aid Society.	Generally, yes. Boys escaped from jail so father would not learn about their prank. Military experience held in high esteem.	No disrespect stated.	No disrespect stated.
Importance of Education and Knowledge	Both sexes read many books. Read Bible in Greek and English. Males attended university. Asked not to use slang.	Jo loved Aunt March's large library. They all read. Felt humiliated when punished at school. Father described as scholar. Jo asked not to use slang.	Gained enjoyment and escaped by reading. Attended boys' academy. Wanted to be promoted to higher position in class.	Polly wanted to learn. Wealthy cousins had tutor. Wealthy old gentleman promised to educate Polly.	Reading gave pleasure. Education could make it possible to improve position in life. Rebecca respected intelligence.

CHART 2—4 (cont.)

Social values, family life, and personal relationships, 1856–1903

	BOOK, AUTHOR, DATE, SETTING				
	Charlotte Yonge. *The Daisy Chain*, 1856, 1868. Rural England. Middle class.	Louisa May Alcott, *Little Women*, 1868. New England city suburb; Large gardens, quiet streets.	Thomas Bailey Aldrich. *The Story of a Bad Boy*. 1870. New Orleans then to small New Hampshire town.	Margaret Sidney. *Five Little Peppers and How They Grew*. 1880. Poverty level. United States.	Kate Douglas Wiggin, *Rebecca of Sunnybrook Farm*. 1903. Small New England town.
SOCIAL VALUES (cont.)					
Respect for Adult Authority	Children wanted to live up to their father's wishes and ideals. Asked mother's permission at home.	Children wanted their parents' acceptance. Looked up to a "noble" mother and turned to the "quiet scholar" who helped them during "troublesome times."	Respected adults but did not always ask permission. Tom did not mention something when he knew grandfather would disapprove.	Children always respected their widowed mother. Jasper wanted his father's respect.	Rebecca respected knowledge of English teacher and sought her advice.
FAMILY LIFE Description	Warm, close, and self-sufficient. Family center of heroine's existence. Cleanliness of home considered a virtue.	Warm, filled with laughter and singing. Children made their own fun; played "Pilgrim's Progress" and acted out plays. At 9:00, stopped worked and sang before going to bed.	Family and main character generally cheerful and affectionate. "Old Puritan austerity cropped but once a week." Main character interacted more with friends as they put on plays, formed a club, attended school, and played pranks.	Close, happy family who told stories and expressed love and concern for each other. Boys argued with new cousins.	Rebecca had a happy-go-lucky family led by father who had difficulty making money. Two aunts led a very conservative life.
Religion Stability	Stressed responsibility for raising good and holy children. Family read Bible and discussed meaning of Sunday services.	Father asked his wife to pray for the girls each evening. They turned to God to help them overcome troubles and temptations.	Nutter house had been in the family nearly one hundred years. Attic with its treasures was symbolic of the long residence of one family. Sundays were solemn. Attended church, read Bible, and ate cold meals.	Stable because of closeness but grew up under considerable pressure. Expressed great respect for minister.	Contrasts drawn between the two families. Rebecca's parents moved often. Aunts lived in the same home as their father.
Numbers in Family	Eleven children. Father. Mother (died early in story).	Four girls. Mother. Father (away in Army in Part 1).	One child living with grandfather in the north. Parents living in New Orleans.	Five children, widowed mother.	One of seven children. Father died, mother had difficulties.
Extended Family	Prim, middle-aged governess. Nurse. Servants.	Housekeeper.	Grandfather. Maiden aunt. Servant.	Wealthy old gentleman, his son, his daughter, and her children.	Two spinster sisters. Rebecca lived with them.
Relationships Within Family	Definite male and female roles. Children relied upon mother in the home. Father, head of household. Children respected each other.	Mother guided the heart. Father guided the soul. Father, head of family. Strong ties among sisters. Oldest sister's gentle advice influenced her sisters.	Grandfather understood the boy; he had once run away to sea. Grandfather showed pride when Tom won fight with a bully who harassed smaller boys.	Everyone pampered Phronsie, the pretty baby in the family. Phronsie and Polly brought changes in others' lives because of the influence of their personalities.	Aunt Jane was warmer and more understanding. Aunt Miranda was strict, head of household and respected traditional values.

CHART 2–4 (cont.)
Social values, family life, and personal relationships, 1856–1903

	BOOK, AUTHOR, DATE, SETTING				
	Charlotte Yonge, *The Daisy Chain,* 1856, 1868. Rural England. Middle class.	Louisa May Alcott, *Little Women,* 1868. New England city suburb; Large gardens, quiet streets.	Thomas Bailey Aldrich. *The Story of a Bad Boy,* 1870. New Orleans then to small New Hampshire town.	Margaret Sidney. *Five Little Peppers and How They Grew,* 1880. Poverty level. United States	Kate Douglas Wiggin, *Rebecca of Sunnybrook Farm,* 1903. Small New England town.
PERSONAL RELATIONSHIPS AND FEELINGS					
Independent Male or Female	Mother: at home, gentle power, strong authority. Father: skillful, clever, sensitive but showed vexation and sarcasm. Ethel: secretly kept up with brother's classical studies.	Jo: didn't want to grow up to be a lady. Jo: wanted to do something extraordinary. Jo: said her quick temper and restless spirit got her in trouble. Mother: managed household while husband was away.	Grandfather lived at ease on money invested in shipping. A maiden sister managed the household with her brother and servant. Tom had freedom to explore the countryside. Tom stressed male need to "learn to box, to ride, to pull an oar, and to swim."	Mother made family decisions but often had no idea about how they would manage. Boys got into more trouble than girls.	Rebecca was "plucky," "dauntless," and "intelligent." Aunt Miranda was strong-willed, managed their lives. Rebecca usually self-reliant.
Dependent Male or Female	Mother: reserved and shrinking from society. Males made major decisions. Girls clung to males.	Mother: worried about guiding children to meet husband's ideals. Children turned to parents for guidance. Beth: too bashful to attend school.	Girls attended separate school and were graduated by "a dragon of watchfulness." Pony's vanities compared to female "weaknesses."	Mother eventually accepted help from a wealthy gentleman who brought the family out of poverty. Polly, although plucky, often fainted.	Aunt Jane infrequently spoke out against Miranda. Aunts wanted dependent, obedient child.
Types of Problems	Concerned with not living up to parents' expectations and God's desire. Love of glory considered a temptation.	Overcoming problems that led to "sweetness of self-denial and self-control."	Problems allowed main character to consider his moral code. When he disobeyed something usually went wrong.	Concerned with being good. Problems connected with survival in poverty.	Tried to live up to the traditional behavioral ideals of a strict aunt and Rebecca's desire to be "respectably, decently good."
Friendships	Mainly with family members or people in own class.	Greatest among sisters. Neighbor boy.	A group of boys at the academy. The Centipede Club–all boys. Tom and older seaman. Aunt and female servant were friends.	Mainly each other in the family. A wealthy boy who rescued Phronsie and was impressed with the warm family. Phronsie and the wealthy gentleman whom she changed.	Rebecca was friendly. Liked many adults and children. They also liked her.

The Child and the Family, 1938–1960

The 1900s brought considerable change to American children's lives: many states passed child labor laws; John Dewey's influential theories encouraged a more child-centered educational philosophy; the quality and extent of public education improved; and religious training placed less emphasis on sinfulness and more emphasis on moral development and responsibility toward others. Children's literature reflected these changes, and children's book publishing expanded to meet the needs of an increasingly literate youthful population. Optimism was a keynote in the twentieth-century "Age of Progress," and, especially after World War II, "children's book editors saw a bright future ahead for the children of this country and the world" (33, p. 89).

This optimism is reflected in the views of children and the family depicted in American children's books of the late 1930s through the beginning of the 1960s. John Rowe Townsend's (43) conclusions about depictions of family life in children's literature of the 1950s apply to earlier literature as well: children live in stable communities where most children are happy and secure, the older generations are wise and respected, and the generations follow one another into traditional social roles in an orderly way.

The following books, written by award-winning authors, characterize the social values, the stability of family life, and the types of personal relationships depicted in children's literature of this period: Elizabeth Enright's *Thimble Summer* (1938), Eleanor Estes's *The Moffats* (1941), Sydney Taylor's *All-of-a-Kind Family* (1951), and Madeline L. Engle's *Meet the Austins* (1960).

The families in these books live in different locations around the United States and range from lower to upper-middle class, but the values they support are similar. The characters admire and emulate the traditional family model of breadwinning father, housewife mother, and their children, living together in one place for a number of years. Family members have happy and secure relationships with one another, complemented by mutual respect, warmth, and humor. The actions of the Moffats express confidence and trust in the family unit. The children in *All-of-a-Kind Family* cannot imagine what it would be like not to have a family. Vicky, in *Meet the Austins*, is pleased because her mother looks just the way she believes a mother should look.

Religious values are suggested in these stories by Sunday school attendance, preparing for the sabbath, or saying prayers before meals. Human dignity is stressed. The family in *Thimble Summer* brings an orphan boy into their home on trust without checking his background. The parents in *All-of-a-Kind Family* tell their children to accept people and not ask them about their personal lives. The Austin family feels empathy for others' problems, and the parents include their children in serious discussions.

Patriotism is strong in all books, and the law is respected. Education is considered important; children enjoy reading, go to school with the expectation that it will increase their understanding, and finish their homework before playing. Families prize even small collections of books. The work ethic is a powerful force in these families' lives. Children talk about saving their money to buy a farm, a mother takes in sewing to keep the family together, and a father works long hours, saving for the day when he can make life better

for his family. Children respect adult wisdom and authority. They enjoy listening to their elders tell about their experiences; they obey rules about minding their teachers and complying with parental desires.

Unsurprisingly, given their secure lives and confident adherence to established social standards, the children in these books have few emotional problems. They usually feel good about themselves and other family members. Their actions suggest dependence upon the family for emotional stability, but independence in their daily experiences, as they move without fear around the neighborhood, city, or countryside.

The Child and the Family, 1969–1980

Researchers who have analyzed children's literature over time have identified the 1960s and 1970s as a period in which traditional social, family, and personal values appeared to be changing. Alma Cross Homze (20) found that in the late 1950s adult characters in children's books were becoming less authoritarian and critical in their relationships with children, while children were becoming more outspoken, independent, and critical of adults. John Rowe Townsend (43) later concluded that children's literature of the 1960s had suggested an erosion of adult authority and a widening of the generation gap. Binnie Tate Wilkin (46) connects these trends in the children's literature of the 1960s and 1970s with changing "educational, social and political, and economic concerns" (p. 21), citing as examples the civil rights movements, protest marches, and assassinations of the period. "Almost all levels of society were challenged to respond to the activism," says Wilkin. "Book publishers responded with new materials reflecting dominant concerns. Distress about children's reading problems, federal responses to urban unrest, the youth movements, new openness about sexuality, religious protest, etc. were reflected in children's books" (46, p. 21).

In 1981, polls quoted by John F. Stacks (41) showed that about 20 percent of Americans still expressed belief in most of the tradional values of hard work, family loyalty, and sacrifice, while the majority of respondents embraced only some of those values, doubted that self-denial and moral rectitude were their own reward, and held tolerant views about abortion, premarital sex, remaining single, and not having children. Still,

Stacks concluded that people who believe in traditional values were becoming an increasingly vocal group that "could set to a significant degree the moral tone for the 1980s" (41, p. 18). Other research indicates that the American family has experienced far more continuity than change over the last fifty years. Norman Lobsenz (28) reports findings from the study *Middletown Families: 50 Years of Change and Continuity* showing that marriage is still viewed as important, al-

CHART 2–5
Social values, family life, and personal relationships, 1938–1960

	BOOK, AUTHOR, DATE, SETTING			
	Elizabeth Enright, *Thimble Summer*, 1938. Rural Wisconsin farm.	Eleanor Estes. *The Moffats*, 1941. Middle-sized New England city. Poor family.	Sidney Taylor, *All-Of-A-Kind Family*. 1951. New York, East Side (1912). Jewish family.	Madeleine L'Engle, *Meet the Austins*, 1960. Country home. Father M.D.
SOCIAL VALUES				
Dignity of Human Beings	An orphan boy was given love and respect of the family.	They trusted each other and strangers. They expected strangers to give them help when they were lost.	You accept people. "You don't ask them about their personal lives."	Family felt empathy toward others' problems. Children included in serious discussions.
Acceptance of Responsibility	Children accepted farm chores without complaining.	Older members responsible for younger brothers and sisters. Joe felt terrible when he lost coal money, and his mother would need to work late. He searched until he found it.	Child felt responsible for lost library book; her sisters offered their few pennies. They tried to avoid household chores. A promise was considered important.	Consideration for others was essential. One child could not disrupt the family.
Belief in Equality of Opportunity	Father believed his daughter could be the farmer in the family.	Family worked together. Males and females did many things together. Positive mood.	Father believed his work and savings would make it possible to have a better life.	Yes. Aunt Elena was a well-known concert pianist.
Ambition	Strong work ethic: Children talk about saving money to buy a farm.	Mother worked hard to keep family. Took in sewing. Traded sewing for free dancing lessons.	Father wanted more for his family than he could give them. Worked and saved for the day he could make their lives better.	Scientific experiments were considered important. Education was important.
Obedience to Law, Patriotism	Yes. No. Conflicts mentioned.	Nine-year-old always walked cautiously by police chief's house; never stood on his lawn.	Father did not want the U.S. flag placed on the floor.	Family rules were stressed.
Importance of Education and Knowledge	Reading important to the girls as a means of escape.	Five-year-old Rufus looked forward to school. "Go to school or be a dunce." All children had dancing lessons.	Great excitement because Friday was library day. Books were treasured.	Homework was to be finished before playing. Grandfather collected books.
Respect for Adult Authority	Children respected parents. Enjoyed listening to friends, great-grandmother tell stories about her life.	Girl worried about mimicking new superintendent of schools. Mother: "Do as the teacher says." Mother was voice of authority; they went to her to ask questions.	Children obediently followed parents. Called themselves "Mama's children."	"When daddy speaks that way we hop." Children did not want their parents to come home and find work not finished.
FAMILY LIFE				
Description	Very happy and secure family. Garnet had a nice mother and a nice family. Considerable trust of others.	Family was happy and secure in their relationships, although their rented house had a "for sale" sign on it. Mother didn't really share children's experiences but listened to them.	Happy secure family: a "gentle, soft" father; a loving, but strong mother. After five girls, father cried with happiness when boy was born.	Spontaneous family love. Mutual respect and understanding. Warmth and humor. Strong father who made them accept the consequences when they didn't do their homework.

though divorce is widely accepted; many wives and mothers have jobs, but still do most of the housework and childcare; and many married couples see more of their relatives than they do of their friends.

Comparison of children's literature written between the 1930s and early 1960s with children's literature written in the 1970s and early 1980s reveals both similarities and differences between the characterizations of the American family in

CHART 2–5 (cont.)
Social values, family life, and personal relationships, 1938–1960

	BOOK, AUTHOR, DATE, SETTING			
	Elizabeth Enright, *Thimble Summer*, 1938. Rural Wisconsin farm.	Eleanor Estes. *The Moffats*, 1941. Middle-sized New England city. Poor family.	Sidney Taylor, *All-Of-A-Kind Family*. 1951. New York, East Side (1912). Jewish family.	Madeleine L'Engle, *Meet the Austins*, 1960. Country home. Father M.D.
FAMILY LIFE (cont.)				
Religion Stability	Families had lived in the valley for generations. No strong religious emphasis.	Worked together for good of the family, even when Rufus had scarlet fever and they were quarantined. Went to Sunday school.	Very stable; could not imagine what it would be like not to have a family. Law of the Sabbath carefully observed.	Strong family ties. Sunday school and church important. Family prayed before meals and at other times in their day.
Numbers in Family	Three children. Mother. Father.	Four children. Widowed mother.	Six children. Father. Mother.	Four children. Father. Mother.
Extended Family	Brought an orphan boy to work on farm without checking I.D.		Mother's brother was a frequent visitor.	Orphaned ten-year-old daughter of a friend.
Relationships Within Family	Strong, trusting. Slight brother and sister friction.	Had fun together. Humorous experiences. Mother was supportive and loving. Not critical except about getting clothes dirty.	Mother planned games for children to make them enjoy dusting. Children were proud of their mother; wanted to introduce her to new librarian.	Children disagreed with each other but always made up. Father and mother talked over family problems with children.
PERSONAL RELATIONSHIPS AND FEELINGS				
Independent Male or Female	Independent female who loved her family. Hitchhiked to town without fear. Angry when brother suggested she do women's work.	Children could travel around town. Always found their way back.	Strong mother who took care of the family. Father owned his own business: a "junk shop." Children hid their candy from their mother.	Children were individual thinkers.
Dependent Male or Female		They relied upon each other and upon their mother to answer questions.	Children gave in to firm mother.	Vicky believed her older brother always knew what to say and could get her out of difficulties. Family depended on each other.
Types of Problems	No real problems.	Their house was for sale, and they accepted the possibility of moving. Some problems because of family illness or need for money. Problems overcome in humorous ways.	No major problems. Saved for lost library book, hid candy.	Maggy, an orphaned girl, was disturbed because she had never known love. Problems centered around helping her make adjustments.
Friendships	Next-door girl whose family had lived there for generations.	Family members. Neighbors. They made friends with strangers around town.	Very close to each other; no other children mentioned. Neighborhood peddlers and librarian were friends.	Children close friends. Uncle Douglas always understood them and knew how to make them feel good about themselves.

CHART 2—6
Social values, family life, and personal relationships, 1969–1980

	BOOK, AUTHOR, DATE, SETTING					
	Vera and Bill Cleaver, *Where the Lilies Bloom*, 1969. Smoky Mountains. Poor wildcrafters.	Zilpha Snyder, *The Changeling.* 1970. Upper-class white and lower-class white families.	Marilyn Sachs, *The Bears House*, 1971. Poor city neighborhood.	Norma Klein, *Mom, The Wolf Man, and Me.* 1972. Middle class.	Winifred Madison, *Call Me Danica*, 1977. Moved from Yugoslavia to Vancouver.	Betsy Byars, *The Night Swimmers*, 1980. Suburbs.

SOCIAL VALUES

Dignity of Human Beings	Father took pride in family name of Luther; wanted to instill pride in family. Wanted to keep family together and not accept charity.	Conflicts between individual rights and family values. Daughter's friend's family described as drifters.	Father deserted the family. Children felt a strong longing to stay together. Applied for welfare.	Daughter sometimes bragged about her illegitimacy to see people's reactions. A best friend did not ask about her father.	Father proud of his heritage: "Have pride in yourself. . . . Even if you are poor, don't be ashamed."	Children believed people "run you off" their property to make you feel so bad that you won't come back.
Acceptance of Responsibility	Fourteen-year-old promised her father she would keep family together. Kept her older sister from marrying their neighbor.	Martha's brother told the truth and saved her from trouble, although he got into trouble with the law.	Strong responsibility for each other. Oldest boy schemed to keep them together. Nine-year-old Fran Ellen had strong attachment for the baby.	Mother had a nontraditional schedule. They were not constrained by time and other more conventional family living styles. Mother responsible for care of daughter.	Daughter tried to help mother adjust to a new culture and develop confidence. Children tried to earn money for clothes.	Father let his daughter take over responsibility for the family. Father expressed feelings about burdens related to fatherhood: he would rather write lyrics.
Belief in Equality of Opportunity	Father stressed that you don't thank people who put you in bondage. You hate them or get out.	Heroine discovered appreciation for her own individuality and her special talents.	No. Fran Ellen was positive that she didn't have a chance of winning.	Mother was a professional photographer. Took her daughter on marches for women's rights and peace.	Mother: "Women get the worst of it." She believed in women's role. Mother: "Men don't like to see a woman chef—they think I should be washing dishes."	The children felt they could grow up and have their dreams. Didn't say how they would do it.
Ambition	Daughter wanted to overcome her ignorance and keep the family together.	Parents excelled in everything they did. Father: lawyer. Mother: charity worker. Expected daughter to share their traditional values and goals.	To survive together as a family.	Profession important to mother.	Danica studied hard. She wanted to become a doctor. Mother wanted her own restaurant.	Children wanted to do things that rich people did. Father wanted a hit recording. Retta wanted to grow up and be important.
Obedience to Law, Patriotism	Father disliked people in authority who might place him in bondage.	One family respected law. The other often ran from the law.	They were afraid of the law; it would separate their family and place them in a foster home.	Strong feelings against war.	Father expressed strong feelings about need to fight against an enemy who would take over his country.	Children waited until wealthier family had gone to bed and then swam in their pool. They knew they were trespassing.
Importance of Education and Knowledge	Daughter knew books would give her answers that she wanted.	Very important in Martha's family. Martha's brother and sister attended college.	Father considered Fletcher a sissy because he read books all the time. Mother defended Fletcher; he was something special.	Not stressed.	Studying came before work. Twelve-year-old Danica knew she would need to study very hard to reach her goal.	Not stressed.

	BOOK, AUTHOR, DATE, SETTING					
	Vera and Bill Cleaver, *Where the Lilies Bloom,* 1969. Smoky Mountains. Poor wildcrafters.	Zilpha Snyder, *The Changeling.* 1970. Upper-class white and lower-class white families.	Marilyn Sachs, *The Bears House,* 1971. Poor city neighborhood.	Norma Klein, *Mom, The Wolf Man, and Me.* 1972. Middle class.	Winifred Madison, *Call Me Danica,* 1977. Moved from Yugoslavia to Vancouver.	Betsy Byars, *The Night Swimmers,* 1980. Suburbs.
SOCIAL VALUES (cont.)						
Respect for Adult Authority	Children respected their father. Tried to do his wishes.	The girls from the two families were different. One respected authority more than the other.	Children expressed fear of adults in power.	Eleven-year-old had frank discussions with her mother. Some disagreement.	Children showed surprise when friends disobeyed parents or did things they knew their parents would not allow. Danica had strong guilt when "Never before had I lied to Mama or deceived her."	Children's father paid little attention to his children. The older sister tried to manage her brothers, not always successfully.
FAMILY LIFE						
Description	A proud independent family who learned to gather medicinal plants on slopes of Smokey Mountains.	One family with strong conventional values whose members, except for Martha, always succeeded. Martha felt out of place and concerned because she was different.	Father deserted them; mother was sick. The children argued and expressed fear of separation.	Mother and daughter had enjoyable relationship; they had fun together.	A proud loving family who stressed that real love is priceless and it is important to believe in oneself. They developed difficulty communicating when they faced new culture.	Father was a country singer who worked at night. Daughter was responsible for two boys. She considered herself a social director. She tried to manage their lives and boys rebelled. She was hurt because she felt unappreciated.
Religion Stability	Long-time mountain resident.	Martha's family was stable. Her friend's family moved often because of problems.	Unstable. Religion not mentioned.	Mother did not set household schedule. They enjoyed this freedom. They were Jewish but never talked about it.	They had lived in a small village for many years. Father's death changed stability. Church important in their lives. Mother: Marriage was the only way for two people to live together.	They had moved from old neighborhood and friends. Neighbors disapproved of a father who wore rhinestones and high-gloss boots and let his children "run loose at night like dogs." Religion not mentioned.
Numbers in Family	Four children. Father died early in the story.	Three children. Two parents. Friend's family: Eight children, two parents.	Five children. Sick mother. Father deserted.	One child. Mother.	Three children. Mother. Father died before they moved to Canada.	Three children. Father. Mother had died.
Relationships Within Family	Strong family ties.	Martha went outside of her family and created a world of imagination and friendship. Her own family didn't understand her.	Love between Fran Ellen and baby. Argued but tried to stay together. Mother ineffectual.	Daughter loved her unconventional life with her unmarried mother. Mother, daughter had frank discussions.	Strong love but at times difficulty confiding worries.	Father rarely interfered with or helped children. Retta learned her role model as a mother from T.V. Boys expected her to act like T.V. and grocery-store mothers.

CHART 2–6 (cont.)
Social values, family life, and personal relationships, 1969–1980

	BOOK, AUTHOR, DATE, SETTING					
	Vera and Bill Cleaver, *Where the Lilies Bloom,* 1969. Smoky Mountains. Poor wildcrafters.	Zilpha Snyder, *The Changeling.* 1970. Upper-class white and lower-class white families.	Marilyn Sachs, *The Bears House,* 1971. Poor city neighborhood.	Norma Klein, *Mom, The Wolf Man, and Me.* 1972. Middle class.	Winifred Madison, *Call Me Danica,* 1977. Moved from Yugoslavia to Vancouver.	Betsy Byars, *The Night Swimmers,* 1980. Suburbs.
FAMILY LIFE (cont.)						
Extended Family		Grandmother sometimes lived with family.		Mother's boyfriend lived with them on weekends.		
PERSONAL RELATIONSHIPS AND FEELINGS						
Independent Male or Female	Mary Call was very resourceful. Found a way to earn money wildcrafting.	Ivy Carson. Martha's friend, was creative and imaginative.	Children decided to look after themselves.	Mother had strong character. Daughter self-assured but worried about possible changes in their lives.	Father: Strong, independent. Danica had spirit, helped mother gain hope.	Retta planned exciting experiences like swimming at night in a private pool five blocks from house. She learned to cook from school cafeteria and watching T.V. commercials.
Dependent Male or Female	The children were dependent upon fourteen-year-old Mary who tried to hold family together.	Shy Martha was dependent upon her friend for enjoyable experiences. Martha cried easily.	Fran Ellen sucked her thumb. Worried about the baby. Escaped in her imagination to a dollhouse. Mother dependent.		Mother: Worried and dependent upon her husband. It was terrible for the children to see mother lose confidence.	Retta knew she had problems with the house and the boys. Didn't know what to do about them.
Types of Problems	After father died, they tried to survive as a family. Mary discovered that she needed other people.	Overcoming problems that allowed shy girl to appreciate her own indivi-dualtiy and special talents.	Tried to overcome problems related to parents' desertion and illness. Emotional problems: nine-year-old tried to solve her own problems.	Daughter feared how her life might change if her mother married.	Overcoming family problems after death of strong father. Overcoming problems adjusting to a new culture and gaining belief in oneself.	Tried to raise a motherless family when father worked at night and slept in daytime. Conflicts showed difficulty for a young girl trying to find her own place in the family.
Friendships	People could not trust friends when they had secrets.	Upper-middle-class girl and an unusual daughter of a drifter.	No friends at school; they teased Fran Ellen.	Daughter's best friend was a boy whose father was a rabbi. He never asked her questions about her father.	Danica made friends with the doctor: she walked his dogs. He encouraged her to strive for her dream.	One boy took pride in a male friend; he tried not to share friend with family.

the two periods. Many books still portray strong family ties and stress the importance of personal responsibility and human dignity, but the happy, stable unit of the earlier literature is often replaced by a family in turmoil as it adjusts to a new culture, faces the prospects of surviving without one or both parents, handles the disruption resulting from divorce, or deals with the extended family exemplified by grandparents or a foster home. Later literature also suggests that many acceptable family units do not conform to the traditional American model.

While many children's books could be selected for this discussion, the following books exemplify some of the diverse attitudes toward family and children in the period from 1969 to 1980: Vera and Bill Cleaver's *Where the Lilies Bloom* (1969), Zilpha Snyder's *The Changeling* (1970), Marilyn Sachs's *The Bears' House* (1971), Norma Klein's *Mom, the Wolf Man, and Me* (1972), Winifred Madison's *Call Me Danica* (1977), and Betsy Byars's *The Night Swimmers* (1980).

Family life varies considerably in these stories. The most traditional family values are expressed by the characters and actions in *Call Me Danica*, where the family demonstrates respect for religious and moral values by attending church, saying prayers, and stating that marriage is the only appropriate life-style for men and women. The greatest family instability is expressed in *The Bears' House*: the mother is emotionally and physically ill, the father has left, and the children fearfully argue about their actions. Religious values are not discussed in the book.

While children in the literature of the 1940s and 1950s had few personal and emotional problems, children in this time period may have considerable responsibility and may experience emotional problems as they try to survive. The strongest character in *Where the Lilies Bloom* attempts to hold the family together, but discovers that she needs people outside her immediate family. Snyder's heroine experiences conflicts between her individual needs and unique abilities and the needs of her family. The oldest boy in *The Bears' House* tries to organize his family, while his nine-year-old sister escapes into the imaginative world of a dollhouse family. The heroine of *Mom, the Wolfman, and Me* fears her life will change if her mother marries. The characters in *Call Me Danica* must overcome problems related to the death of a strong father, adjust to a new culture, and gain self-confidence. Characters in *The Night Swimmers* must look after themselves while their father works. The daughter in that book feels unappreciated, is jealous about a brother's attachment to a new friend, and realizes that the family needs help. Her personal problems increase because she is unsure of her place in the family.

Characters in the literature of this period may express concern about equal opportunities and question respect for the law, education, and adult authority. The children in *The Bears' House* are afraid to ask for assistance because they fear authorities would separate the family and place them in foster homes. This book illustrates a stereotypical attitude toward education: the father, before he leaves, calls the oldest boy a sissy because he likes to read books rather than take part in sports. The mother and daughter in *Call Me Danica* have difficulties because their ambitions are not seen as appropriate for women. In contrast, the mother in *Mom, the Wolf Man, and Me* is a successful photographer and allows her daughter to accompany her on women's rights and peace marches.

The two strongest stories related to the dignity of human beings and acceptance of responsibility are found in the books by Vera and Bill Cleaver and by Winifred Madison. The Cleavers' *Where the Lilies Bloom* is a story about the proud, independent mountain people who earn their living through wildcrafting (the gathering of wild plants for human use). The father, before he dies, asks his daughter to keep the family together without accepting charity and to instill in the children pride in having the name of Luther. In Madison's *Call Me Danica*, Danica's father tells the other members of the family to have pride in themselves and not be ashamed even if they are poor. The fathers in both books die, but they leave their families a heritage of pride and dignity. The families work together and eventually build new lives. An opposite condition is found in *The Bears' House*: the father deserts his children and sick wife. The children want to stay together so much that they apply for welfare and lie to the authorities about their parents. The father in *The Night Swimmers* works evenings, wants to write country music lyrics, and says that fatherhood is a burden. His daughter is responsible for her younger brothers.

Clearly, children's literature now presents a greater range and more realistic representations of family diversity.

EARLY RESEARCH INTO CHILDREN'S READING HABITS AND PREFERENCES

Since one of the earliest studies, "What Do Pupils Read?," was made in 1889 (15), children's reading habits and preferences have become an increasingly popular research topic. Between 1900 and 1920, approximately twenty reported studies analyzed children's reading interests, library withdrawals, and favorite books, as well as the literary characteristics of children's favorite books and other factors that influenced children's literature preferences. Between 1960 and 1974, however, according to an annotated bibliography by Dianne Monson and Bette Peltola (35), researchers made approximately 332 studies on equivalent topics.

Early studies of children's reading habits and preferences focused on questions still studied by researchers today. Research by Clara Vostrovsky (44) in 1899 and Franklin Smith (40) in 1907 identified how often children of certain ages used the library and how many books they read a year. In 1922, Florence Bamberger (4) studied the physical characteristics of books children preferred and found, among other things, that children in the 1920s, like children today, liked numerous brightly colored illustrations reflecting action and humor. In 1922 and 1923, Jenny Green (17, 18) made connections between the quantity and quality of a child's reading and the child's overall achievement in school. Studies by Clark Wissler (48) in 1898 and Arthur Jordan (22) in 1921 revealed that children preferred prose to poetry, although in 1925 William Scott Gray (16) asked to what extent these findings might have resulted from teachers' inappropriate choices of poetry and teaching methods. In 1915, H. J. Wightman (45) demonstrated the importance of adult enthusiasm for literature in positively influencing children's reading habits and literature preferences. Most students of children's literature today would agree with Wightman's conclusion that "interest and aspiration are contagious and are essential if the great majority of the public-school children ever form a love for reading" (45, p. 42). Contemporary research about these and other issues will be discussed throughout this book.

SUMMARY

Literature that is enjoyed by children and adults has its roots in the distant past when stories were told around campfires and cottage hearths, or in the great halls of castles. With the establishment of the printing press in 1476, mass production of books became possible. Many folktales became popular books. For many centuries children were considered small adults. The Puritans in the 1600s criticized the traditional stories about giants and fairies and stressed the publication of books that would instruct children in moral con-

cerns. These attitudes began to change in the eighteenth century as a result of the educational philosophies of John Locke and Jean Jacques Rousseau, who believed that children should have a period of childhood and books that catered to children's special needs. Charles Perrault's publication of *Tales of Mother Goose* in 1698 was a great milestone for children's literature. John Newbery, in 1744, is credited as being the writer whose books were a true beginning for children's literature. The research of the Brothers Grimm provided a collection of folktales that are still children's favorites. The Victorian period produced literature in which "gentleman and lady" characters offered models for negotiating the precarious passage from childhood to adulthood. The chapter concluded with an analysis of changing views of children and the family reflected in children's literature published in the Victorian era and the mid-to-late twentieth century and a brief review of early research into children's reading habits and preferences.

Suggested Activities for Understanding the History of Children's Literature

☐ Investigate the life and contributions of William Caxton. What circumstances led to his opening a printing business in 1476? Why were *Reynart the Fox, The Book of the Subtyle Historyes and Fables of Esope*, and *Le Morte d'Arthur* considered such important contributions to children's literature?

☐ Compare the literary quality of William Caxton's books with the literary quality of a reproduced chapbook. Why have chapbooks been identified as forerunners of children's books, western tales, and comic books?

☐ Trace the development of the hornbook from its introduction in the 1400s until it was superseded by the battledores in the 1700s. Consider any changes in these two types of lesson books and how they might have influenced the development of children's literature.

☐ Read John Bunyan's *Pilgrim's Progress*. Identify the characteristics that would make it acceptable Puritan reading. Compare these characteristics with the characteristics of books that would appeal to children.

☐ Choose a tale published by Charles Perrault in his *Tales of Mother Goose*, such as "Cinderella," "Sleeping Beauty," "Puss in Boots," "Little Red Riding Hood," "Blue Beard," or "Little Thumb." Compare the language and style of Perrault's early edition with the language and style in a twentieth century version of the same tale. What differences did you find? Why do you believe they were made?

☐ Select one of the "Robinsonades" published after the successful publication of Daniel Defoe's *Robinson Crusoe*. Compare the plot development, characterization, and setting with Defoe's text.

☐ Investigate the impact of John Newbery's publications on the history of children's literature. State why you do or do not believe that the Newbery Award should bear his name.

☐ Compare the backgrounds, possible motivations, and probable recording techniques of Jacob and Wilhelm Grimm with those of Charles Perrault. Can you identify any reasons for possible differences between or similarities in their tales?

☐ Choose one of the following great nineteenth-century English artists who made an impact on children's illustrations: Kate Greenaway, Walter Crane, or Randolph Caldecott. Read biographical information and look at examples of their illustrations. Share your information and reactions with your literature class.

☐ Read a Victorian novel such as Charlotte Yonge's *The Daisy Chain*. Identify how the book reflects Victorian values such as fortitude, temperance, prudence, justice, self-reliance, and strong family ties.

☐ Read Mark Twain's *Adventures of Tom Sawyer* or *Huckleberry Finn*. Consider the issue controversy about racism in Twain's work discussed on page 62. How would you evaluate Mark Twain's writing for the nineteenth century and for the twentieth century?

References

1 Alderson, Brian W., ed. and trans. *Three Centuries of Children's Books in Europe*. Cleveland: World, 1959.

2 Ashton, John. *Chap-Books of the Eighteenth Century*. London: Chatto and Windus, 1882.

3 Bagley, Ayers. *An Invitation to Wisdom and Schooling*. Society of Professors of Education Monograph Series, 1985.

4 Bamberger, Florence. *The Effect of the Physical Make-Up of a Book upon Children's Selection*. Johns Hopkins University Studies in Education, No. 4. Baltimore: Johns Hopkins Press, 1922.

5 Bingham, Jane, and Scholt, Grayce. *Fifteen Centuries of Children's Literature: An Annotated Chronology of British and American Works in Historical Context*. Westport, Conn.: Greenwood, 1980.

6 Cadogan, Mary, and Craig, Patricia. *You're a Brick, Angela! A New Look at Girls' Fiction from 1839 to 1975*. London: Gollancz, 1976.

7 Carmichael, Carolyn Wilson. "A Study of Selected Social Values As Reflected in Contemporary Realistic Fiction for Children," University Microfilm No. 71–31. East Lansing, Mich.: Michigan State University, 1971.

8 Chapman, Raymond. *The Victorian Debate: English Literature and Society 1832–1901*. New York: Basic Books, 1968.

9 Darton, F. J. Harvey. *Children's Books in England: Five Centuries of Social Life*. Cambridge: At the University Press, 1932, 1966.

10 Erisman, Fred Raymond. "There Was a Child Went Forth: A Study of St. Nicholas Magazine and Selected Children's Authors, 1890–1915," University Microfilm No. 66-12. Minneapolis: University of Minnesota, 1966.

11 Ernest, Edward. *The Kate Greenaway Treasury*. Cleveland: World, 1967.

12 Fraser, James H., ed. *Society and Children's Literature*. Boston: Godine, 1978.

13 Furnivall, Frederick J., ed. *Caxton's Book of Curtesye*. London: Oxford University Press, 1868.

14 Gillespie, Margaret C. *Literature for Children: History and Trends*. Dubuque, Iowa: Brown, 1970.

15 Gray, William Scott. *Reading: A Research Retrospective, 1881–1941*, edited by John T. Guthrie. Newark, Del.: International Reading Association, 1984.

16 Gray, William Scott. *Summary of Investigations Related to Reading: Supplementary Educational Monographs, No. 28*. Chicago: The University of Chicago, 1925.

17 Green, Jenny. "When Children Read for Fun," *School and Society* 16 (November 25, 1922): 614–16.

18 Green, Jenny. "When Children Read for Fun," *School and Society* 17 (April 7, 1923): 390–92.

19 Haviland, Virginia. *Children and Literature: View and Reviews*. Glenview, Ill.: Scott, Foresman, 1973.

20 Homze, Alma Cross. "Interpersonal Relationships in Children's Literature, 1920 to 1960," University

Microfilm No. 64-5366. University Park, Pa.: Pennsylvania State University, 1963.

21 Hürlimann, Bettina. "Fortunate Moments in Children's Books." In *The Arbuthnot Lectures, 1970–1979*, compiled by Zena Sutherland, pp. 61–80. Chicago: American Library Association, 1980.

22 Jordan, Arthur. *Children's Interests in Reading.* Teachers College Contributions to Education, No. 107. New York: Columbia University, 1921.

23 Kelly, Robert Gordon. "Mother Was a Lady: Self and Society in Selected American Children's Periodicals, 1865–1890," University Microfilm No. 71-5770. Iowa City, Iowa: University of Iowa, 1970.

24 Kelly, Robert Gordon. "Social Factors Shaping Some Nineteenth-Century Children's Periodical Fiction." In *Society and Children's Literature*, edited by James H. Fraser. Boston: Godine, 1978.

25 Laws, Frederick. "Randolph Caldecott." In *Only Connect: Readings on Children's Literature*, edited by Sheila Egoff, G. T. Stubbs, and L. F. Ashley. 2d ed. Toronto: Oxford University, 1980.

26 Leeson, Robert. *Children's Books and Class Society.* London: Writers and Readers, 1977.

27 Lenaghan, R. T., ed. *Caxton's Aesop.* Cambridge, Mass.: Harvard University, 1967.

28 Lobsenz, Norman. "News from the Home Front." *Family Weekly*, August 2, 1981, p. 9.

29 Locke, John. "Some Thoughts Concerning Education." In *English Philosophers*, edited by Charles W. Eliot. Harvard Classics, vol. 37. New York: Villier, 1910.

30 Lonsdale, Bernard J., and Macintosh, Helen K. *Children Experience Literature.* New York: Random House, 1973.

31 Lystad, Mary. *From Dr. Mather to Dr. Seuss: Two Hundred Years of American Books for Children.* Boston: G. K. Hall, 1980.

32 McCulloch, Lou J. *An Introduction to Children's Literature: Children's Books of the 19th Century.* Des Moines, Iowa: Wallace-Honestead, 1979.

33 McElderry, Margaret. "The Best Times, The Worst Times, Children's Book Publishing 1917–1974." *The Horn Book Magazine*, October 1974, pp. 85–94.

34 Meigs, Cornelia; Nesbitt, Elizabeth; Eaton, Anne Thaxter; and Hill, Ruth. *A Critical History of Children's Literature: A Survey of Children's Books in English.* New York: Macmillan, 1969.

35 Monson, Dianne, and Peltola, Bette. *Research in Children's Literature: An Annotated Bibliography.* Newark, Del.: International Reading Association, 1976.

36 Muir, Percy. *English Children's Books, 1600 to 1900.* New York: Praeger, 1954.

37 Quayle, Eric. *The Collector's Book of Children's Books.* New York: Clarkson N. Potter 1971.

38 Shaw, Jean Duncan. "An Historical Survey of Themes Recurrent in Selected Children's Books Published in America Since 1850," University Microfilm No. 67-11, 437. Philadelphia: Temple University, 1966.

39 Sidney, Sir Philip. *An Apologie for Poetrie.* London: 1595.

40 Smith, Franklin. "Pupils' Voluntary Reading," *Pedagogical Seminary* 14 (June, 1907): 208–22.

41 Stacks, John F. "Aftershocks of the 'Me' Decade." *Time*, August 3, 1981, p. 18.

42 Stark, Myra. *Florence Nightingale.* New York: Feminist Press, 1979.

43 Townsend, John Rowe. *Written for Children: An Outline of English-Language Children's Literature.* New York: Lippincott, 1975.

44 Vostrovsky, Clara. "A Study of Children's Reading Tastes," *Pedagogical Seminary* 6 (December, 1899): 523–35.

45 Wightman, H.J. "A Study of Reading Appreciation," *American School Board Journal* 50 (June, 1915): 42.

46 Wilkin, Binnie Tate. *Survival Themes in Fiction for Children and Young People.* Metuchen, N.J.: Scarecrow, 1978.

47 Winkler, Karen J. "Academe and Children's Literature: Will They Live Happily Ever After?" *Chronicle of Higher Education*, June 15, 1981.

48 Wissler, Clark. "The Interests of Children in the Reading Work of the Elementary Schools," *Pedagogical Seminary*. Vol. 5 (April, 1898):523–40.

Additional References

Andrews, Siri, ed. *The Hewins Lectures 1947–1962.* Boston: Horn Book, 1963.

Aries, Philippe. *Centuries of Childhood: A Social History of Family Life.* New York: Knopf, 1962.

Avery, Gillian. *Nineteenth Century Children: Heroes and Heroines in English Children's Stories, 1780–1900.* Ontario, Canada: Hodder, 1965.

Cable, Mary. *The Little Darlings: A History of Child Rearing in America.* New York: Scribner's, 1975.

Eames, Wilberforce. *Early New England Catechisms: A Bibliographical Account of Some Catechisms Published before the Year 1800, for Use in New England.* New York: Watts, 1964.

Egoff, Sheila; Stubbs, G. T.; and Ashley, L. F., eds. *Only Connect: Readings on Children's Literature.* 2d ed. Toronto: Oxford University, 1980.

Feaver, William. *When We Were Young: Two Centuries of Children's Book Illustration.* New York: Holt, Rinehart & Winston, 1977.

Gottlieb, Gerald, ed. *Early Children's Books and Their Illustrations.* Boston: Godine, 1975.

Haviland, Virginia. *The Travelogue Storybook of the Nineteenth Century.* Boston: Horn Book, 1950.

Hürlimann, Bettina. *Three Centuries of Children's Books in Europe.* Cleveland: World, 1968.

Kelly, R. Gordon. *Children's Periodicals of the United States.* Westport, Conn.: Greenwood, 1984.

Kingman, Lee, ed. *Newbery and Caldecott Medal Books: 1956–1965*. Boston: Horn Book, 1965.

——— *Newbery and Caldecott Medal Books: 1966–1975*. Boston: Horn Book, 1975.

LaBeau, Dennis, ed. *Children's Authors and Illustrators: An Index to Biographical Dictionaries*. Detroit: Gale, 1976.

MacLeod, Ann Scott. *A Moral Tale: Children's Fiction and American Culture, 1820–1860*. London: Archon, 1975.

Mahoney, Bertha E.; Latimer. Louise Payson; and Folmsbee, Beulah. *Illustrators of Children's Books 1744–1945*. Boston: Horn Book, 1947.

Miller, Bertha Mahony, and Field, Elinor Whitney, eds. *Newbery Medal Books: 1922–1955*. Boston: Horn Book, 1955.

———. *Caldecott Medal Books: 1938–1957*. Boston: Horn Book, 1957.

Neuburg, Victor E., ed. *The Penny Histories: A Study of Chapbooks for Young Readers over Two Centuries*. New York: Harcourt Brace Jovanovich, 1969.

Sutherland, Zena, comp. *The Arbuthnot Lectures, 1970–1979*. Chicago: American Library Association, 1980.

Temple, Nigel, ed. *Seen and Not Heard: A Garland of Fancies for Victorian Children*. New York: Dial, 1970.

Thomas, Alan G. *Great Books and Book Collectors*. New York: Putnam, 1975.

Thwaite, Mary F. *From Primer to Pleasure in Reading: An Introduction to the History of Children's Books in England from the Invention of Printing to 1914 with an Outline of Some Developments in Other Countries*. Boston: Horn Book, 1972.

Whalley, Joyce Irene. *Cobwebs to Catch Flies: Illustrated Books for the Nursery and Schoolroom, 1700–1900*. Berkeley: University of California, 1975.

3

Evaluating and Selecting Literature for Children

WHEN ONE CONSIDERS THE THOU-sands of books that have been published for children, selecting appropriate books to meet the needs of children seems an awesome task. Teachers and librarians must share the books they select with groups of children as well as with the individual child. Books need to be chosen to provide balance in the school library or public library. The objectives of a literature program also affect the evaluation and selection of children's books.

A literature program should have five objectives, according to Helen Huus (14). First, a literature program should help students realize that literature is for entertainment and can be enjoyed throughout their lives. Literature should cater to children's interests as well as create interest in new topics. Consequently, adults must know these interests and understand ways to stimulate new ones. Second, a literature program should acquaint children with their literary heritage. To accomplish this, literature that fosters the preservation of knowledge and allows its transmission to future generations must be provided. Adults must be familiar with fine literature from the past and share it with children. Third, a literature program should help students understand the formal elements of literature and lead them to prefer the best our literature has to offer. Children need to hear and read fine literature and appreciate that authors not only have something to say, but also say it extremely well. Adults must be able to identify the best in literature and share these books with children. Fourth, a literature program should help children grow up understanding themselves and the rest of humanity. When children identify with literary characters who confront and overcome problems like their own, they learn ways to cope with their own problems. Literature introduces children to people from other times and nations, encouraging children to see both themselves and their world in a new perspective. Fifth, a literature program should help children evaluate what they read, extending both their appreciation of literature and their imagination. Students need to learn how to compare, question, and evaluate the books they read.

If children are to gain enjoyment, knowledge of their heritage, a recognition and appreciation of what constitutes good literature, and an understanding of self and others, they need a balanced selection of literature. A literature program should include classics and contemporary stories, stories that are fanciful and realistic, prose as well as poetry, biographies, and books containing factual information. In order to provide this balance, adults need to know about many kinds of literature. This text will provide them with a wide knowledge of numerous types of books written for children.

This chapter focuses on evaluating books written for children by presenting and discussing the literary elements associated with plot development, characterization, setting, theme, style, and point of view. It also discusses children's literature interests, procedures for their evaluation, and characteristics of literature found in books chosen by children.

STANDARDS FOR EVALUATING BOOKS WRITTEN FOR CHILDREN

Many books written for children are simply not very good. Sheila Egoff (5) concludes that about 2.5 percent of children's books are excellent, about 35 percent are extremely poor, and the rest are mediocre. Ruth Kearney Carlson (2) points out how use of inferior books underestimates children, especially slow learners and poor readers, whom adults too often assume have no interest in stimulating ideas. Poor and mediocre books "have commonplace, dully written pages," they "seldom take strong stands for certain causes," and they "build laziness in young readers" (2, p. 18). If literature is to help develop children's potential, merit rather than mediocrity must be part of children's experience of literature. Both children and adults need opportunities to evaluate literature and a supporting context within which to help them make accurate judgments about a book's quality.

Literary criticism provides adults with guidelines for evaluating children's literature. Paul Heins (12) maintains that the critic must be acquainted with the best children's literature of the past and the present and thus be able to view a particular book from a larger perspective. In fact, he says, no real criticism can occur unless "judgments are being made in a context of literary knowledge and of literary standards" (12, p. 76). Concern with a book's place in a larger historical or aesthetic context and with its structure, technical subtlety, and overall literary integrity is not just dry analysis, but is part of "the joy of discovering the skill of the author" (11, p. 82).

Mary Kingsbury (16) builds a strong rationale for high-quality criticism that describes, compares, and judges literary texts: a critic must interpret a text accurately by understanding what the author is doing with language, contrast and compare a book with other books and with various book reviews, and then make his or her own judgments as objectively as possible. Kingsbury emphasizes the importance of both reading and writing literary criticism.

Northrop Frye, Sheridan Baker, and George Perkins (7) identify five focuses of all literary criticism, two or more of which are usually emphasized in evaluating a literary text. The relative importance of each of the following areas to a particular critic may depend on the critic's degree of concern with the work itself, the author, the subject matter, and/or the audience: "(1) the work in isolation, with primary focus on its form, as opposed to its content; (2) its relationship to its own time and place, including the writer; the social, economic, and intellectual milieu surrounding it; the method of its printing or other dissemination; and the assumptions of the audience that first received it; (3) its relationship to literary and social history before its time, as it repeats, extends, or departs from the traditions that preceded it; (4) its relationship to the future, as represented by those works and events that come after it, as it forms a part of the large body of literature, influencing the reading, writing, and thinking of later generations; (5) its relationship to some eternal concept of being, absolute standards of art, or immutable truths of existence" (7, p. 130).

Book reviews and longer critical analyses of books in the major literature journals provide valuable sources for librarians, teachers, parents, and other students of children's literature. As might be expected from Frye, Baker, and Perkins's five focus areas, these reviews emphasize different aspects of evaluation and criticism. Phyllis K. Kennemer (15) has identified three categories for classifying and evaluating the content of book reviews and longer book analyses: descriptive, analytical, and sociological. Descriptive statements report factual information about the story, plot, characters, theme, and illustrations. Analytical statements discuss, compare, and evaluate literary elements associated with characterization, plot, setting, theme, illustrations, and relationships with other books. Sociological statements emphasize a book's social context,

concerning themselves with characterizations of particular social groups, distinguishable ethnic characteristics, moral values, possible controversy, and potential popularity. Although a review may contain all three types of information, Kennemer concludes that the major sources of information on children's literature do emphasize one type of evaluation. For example, reviews in the *Bulletin of the Center for Children's Books* tend to be descriptive, but also mention literary elements. Reviews in *Booklist*, *The Horn Book*, *Kirkus Reviews*, and *The School Library Journal* chiefly analyze literary elements. *The School Library Journal* places the greatest emphasis on sociological analysis of any source Kennemer studied.

Reading and discussing excellent books, as well as analyzing book reviews and literary criticism, can increase one's ability to recognize and recommend excellent literature for children. Those of us who work with students of children's literature are rewarded when for the first time people see literature with a new awareness, discover the techniques an author uses to create a believable plot or memorable characterizations, and discover that they can provide a rationale for why a book is excellent, mediocre, or poor. Ideally, reading and discussing excellent literature helps every student of children's literature become a worthy critic, what Mary Kingsbury (16) defines as one "who offers us new perspectives on a text, who sees more in it than we saw, who motivates us to return to it for another reading" (p. 17).

LITERARY ELEMENTS

The major focus of this chapter is on literary elements. We will discover the ways in which authors of children's books use plot, characterization, setting, theme, style, and point of view to create memorable stories.

Plot

When asked to tell about a favorite story, children usually recount the story's plot, or plan of action. Children want a book to have a good plot: action, excitement, some suspense, and enough conflict to develop interest. A good plot also allows children to become involved in the action, feel the conflict developing, recognize the climax when it occurs, and respond to a satisfactory ending. Children's expectations and enjoyment of conflict vary according to their ages. Young children are satisfied with simple plots dealing with everyday happenings, but as children mature they expect and enjoy more complex plots. Following the plot of a story is like following a path winding through it, as the action develops naturally. If its plot is well developed, a book should be difficult to put down unfinished; if the plot is not well developed, the book will not sustain interest or will be so prematurely predictable that the story ends long before it should. The way the author develops this action assists children in their enjoyment of the story.

Developing Order of Events. Readers expect a story to have a good beginning that introduces the action and characters in an enticing way, a good middle section that develops the conflict, a recognizable climax, and an appropriate ending. If any element is missing, children consider a book unsatisfactory and a waste of time.

Authors have several approaches for presenting the events in a credible plot. In children's literature, events usually happen in chronological order. The author reveals the plot by presenting the first happening, followed by the second happening, and so forth, until the story is completed. Illustrations frequently reinforce the chronological order in picture storybooks for younger children. In *Sleepy Bear*, for example, Lydia Dabcovich follows a bear as he watches the birds fly away in the fall, finds a cave and sleeps through the snow, and finally rouses in the spring as the bees return.

One very strong and visible example of chronological order is found in cumulative folktales. Actions and characters are related to each other in sequential order, and each is mentioned again when action or a new character is introduced. Children who enjoy the cumulative style of the nursery rhyme "The House That Jack Built" will also enjoy a similar cumulative rhythm in Verna Aardema's *Bringing the Rain to Kapiti Plain: A Nandi Tale.* The American folktale "The Greedy Old Fat Man," retold and illustrated in book form by Paul Galdone, is an example of a text developed totally on the cumulative approach. As the greedy man encounters each prospective victim, he repeats his previous actions, until finally the man restates all of his previous encounters. This repetition is very effective with young children, as it encourages them to join in during the storytell-

Plot development in this story follows the main character as he progresses from a talented young juggler to an old man. (From *The Clown of God*, copyright © 1978 by Tomie de Paola. Reproduced by permission of Harcourt Brace Jovanovich, Inc.)

ing and allows them to anticipate the cumulative style of the folktale.

Cumulative, sequential action may also be developed in reverse, from last event to first, as in Verna Aardema's *Why Mosquitoes Buzz in People's Ears.*

The order of a story's events may follow the maturing process of the main character. In *The Clown of God*, Tomie de Paola introduces a small beggar boy who is happy because he has the wonderful gift of being able to juggle. His fortune changes as time passes, and he even juggles before royalty. Years go by and the juggler becomes old and unable to perform; he is rejected by the crowd and wearily heads home. His journey ends in church, where he performs his final juggling act. This magnificent performance results in his death, but also causes a miracle.

Authors of biographies frequently use chronological life events to develop plot. Jean Fritz, for example, traces the life of a famous Revolutionary War personage in *Traitor: The Case of Benedict Arnold*. Dates in the text help the reader follow the chronological order.

Books written for older readers sometimes use flashbacks in addition to chronological order. At the point when the reader has many questions about a character's background, or wonders why a character is acting in a certain way, the author may interrupt the order of the story and reveal information about a previous time or experience. Robert C. O'Brien uses flashbacks effectively in *Mrs. Frisby and the Rats of NIMH*. When both the reader and Mrs. Frisby are wondering why the rats were taken to the laboratory, how their intelligence was drastically increased, how they escaped from the laboratory, and how rat society was developed, the wise rat Nicodemus says, "To answer that I would have to tell you quite a long story about us, and NIMH, and Jonathan, and how we came here" (p. 97). After flashbacks answer the questions necessary for logical plot development, the story's chronological order continues. This technique is more complex than simple chronological order and is not usually used in the shorter plots written for young children.

Patricia MacLachlan, however, uses flashbacks to provide background information in a picture storybook for young children, *Mama One, Mama Two*. The plot begins as a young foster child has difficulty sleeping. The reasons for her separation from her mother, her love for her mother, and her hopes for the future are developed as she and her foster mother share a warm bedtime story. In this case, young children can understand the use of the flashback and identify with the flashback's contents.

Developing Conflict. Excitement in a story occurs when the main characters experience a struggle or overcome conflict. Conflict is the usual source of plots in literature. According to Rebecca J. Lukens (17), children's literature contains four kinds of conflict: person-against-person, person-against-society, person-against-nature, and person-against-self. Plots written for younger children usually develop only one kind of conflict, but many of the more complex plots in stories for older children use several conflicting situations.

Person against Person. One person-against-person conflict young children enjoy is the tale of that famous bunny, *Peter Rabbit*, by Beatrix Potter. In this story, Peter's disobedience and greed quickly bring him into conflict with the owner of the garden, Mr. McGregor, who has sworn to put Peter into a pie. Excitement and suspense develop as Peter and Mr. McGregor proceed through a series of life-and-death encounters: Mr. McGregor chases Peter with a rake, Peter becomes tangled in a gooseberry net, and Mr. McGregor tries to trap him inside a sieve. Knowledge of Peter's possible fate increases the suspense of these adventures. The excitement intensifies each time Peter narrowly misses being caught, and young readers' relief is great when Peter escapes for good. Children also sympathize with Peter when his disobedience results in a stomachache and a dose of camomile tea.

Conflicts between animals and humans, or animals and animals, or humans and humans are common in children's literature, including many popular folktales. Both Little Red Riding Hood and The Three Little Pigs confront a wicked wolf. Cinderella and Sleeping Beauty are among the fairytale heroines mistreated by stepmothers, and Hansel and Gretel are imprisoned by a witch. Giambattista Basile's *Petrosinella: A Neapolitan Rapunzel*, develops the conflict between a female ogre and a heroine who is imprisoned because the girl's mother craves parsley from the ogre's garden. The heroine in this tale does not wait for the prince to rescue her; instead she discovers the reason for her enchantment and makes it possible for the prince and herself to escape the ogre's power. Folktales from many lands develop plots in which animals come into conflict with one another and are either rewarded for courage, loyalty, or intelligence or punished for foolishness, wickedness, or ignorance. In Priscilla Jaquith's *Bo Rabbit Smart for True: Folktales from the Gullah*, one humorous conflict involves Bo Rabbit tricking a whale and an elephant into a pulling contest.

A humorous person-against-person conflict provides the story line in Beverly Cleary's *Ramona and Her Father*. Seven-year-old Ramona's life changes drastically when her father loses his job and her mother must work fulltime. Ramona's new time with her father is not as enjoyable as she had hoped it would be, however. Her father becomes tense and irritable as his period of unemployment lengthens. When his smoking in-

Illustrations and plot relate a humorous conflict between a seven-year-old and her father. (Illustration by Allan Tiegreen from *Ramona and Her Father* by Beverly Cleary. Copyright © 1975, 1977 by Beverly Cleary. By permission of William Morrow and Company.)

creases, Ramona decides that his life is in danger and devises a plan to save him. Her campaign includes hanging signs around the house and planting "no smoking" notes in the form of fake cigarettes in her father's pockets. Ramona and her father survive their experience and by the end of the story have returned to their normal, warm relationship.

Katherine Paterson develops a more complex person-against-person conflict for older children in *Jacob Have I Loved*. In this story one twin believes she is like the despised Esau in the Old Testament, while her sister is the adored favorite of the family. The unhappy heroine's descriptions of her early experiences with her sister, her growing independence as she works with her father, and her final discovery that she, not her sister, is the strong twin create an engrossing plot and memorable characters.

Person against Society.   Conflicts also develop when the main character's actions, desires, or values differ from those of the surrounding society. Deborah, the heroine in Patricia Clapp's *I'm Deborah Sampson: A Soldier in the War of the Revo-*

lution, is out of step with her time. She heads out to work for a farm family when her poverty-stricken mother can't take care of her. This experience causes Deborah to grow strong and determined. The American Revolution begins, and she sees the boys she has come to love leave home to fight for their country. Women are not allowed to join the army, so when her friend Robbie is killed, Deborah disguises herself as a boy and volunteers for service. The next three years find her hiding her identity and surviving in a masculine society. Throughout her experience, Deborah fears not death but discovery: "I was terrified! Not by the wound itself, not by the pain, but at the thought of a doctor's examination" (p.115).

Complex person-against-person conflict develops between twin sisters. (Jacket by Kinoko Craft from *Jacob Have I Loved* by Katherine Paterson [Thomas Y. Crowell Co.] Copyright © 1980 by Katherine Paterson.)

Numerous survival stories set in wartime develop person-against-society conflicts. In Uri Orlev's *The Island on Bird Street*, the conflict is between a Jewish boy and the society that forces him to live in fear, loneliness, and starvation rather than surrender.

Children's books often portray person-against-society conflicts that result from being "different" from the majority in terms of race, religion, or physical characteristics. Judy Blume's *Blubber* shows the cruelty to which a fat child is subjected by her peers. In Mary Stoltz's *Cider Days*, a Mexican girl in the United States must defend her heritage against racial bias. In Virginia Driving Hawk Sneve's *When Thunder Spoke*, a modern-day Sioux boy is torn between the old ways of his people and the new ways of the surrounding white society, which he often views with hostility because of its unjust treatment of Native Americans. In Brent Ashabranner's collection of biographies, *To Live in Two Worlds: American Indian Youth Today*, contemporary Native American youths describe the conflicts facing them as they try to adjust to the white society while retaining aspects of their own culture.

For the conflict between person and society in such books to be believable, the social setting and its values must be presented in accurate detail.

Person against Nature. Nature—not society or another person—is the antagonist in many memorable books for older children. When the author thoroughly describes the natural environment, the reader vicariously travels into a world ruled by nature's harsh law of survival. This is the case in Jean Craighead George's *Julie of the Wolves*. Miyax, a thirteen-year-old Eskimo girl also called by the English name Julie, is lost and without food on the North Slope of Alaska. She is introduced lying on her stomach, peering at a pack of wolves. The wolves are not her enemy, however. Her adversary is the vast cold tundra that stretches for hundreds of miles without human presence, a land so harsh that no berry bushes point to the south, no birds fly overhead so that she can follow, and continual summer daylight blots out the North Star that might guide her home: "No roads cross it; ponds and lakes freckle its immensity. Winds scream across it, and the view in every direction is exactly the same. Somewhere in this cosmos was Miyax; and the very life in her body, its spark and warmth, depended

upon these wolves for survival. And she was not so sure they would help" (p. 6). The constant wind, empty sky, and cold, deserted earth are ever present as Miyax crosses the Arctic searching for food, protecting herself from the elements, and making friends with the wolves who bring her food. The author encourages readers to visualize the power and beauty of this harsh landscape and to share the girl's sorrow over human destruction of this land, its animals, and the Eskimo way of life.

Another book that pits a young person against the elements of nature is Armstrong Sperry's *Call It Courage*. The hero's conflict with nature begins when the crashing, stormy sea—"a monster livid and hungry"—capsizes Mafatu's canoe during a hurricane, and his mother drowns: "Higher and higher it rose, until it seemed that it must scrape at the low-hanging clouds. Its crest heaved over with a vast sigh. The boy saw it coming. He tried to cry out. No sound issued from his throat. Suddenly the wave was upon him. Down it crashed. Chaos! Mafatu felt the paddle torn from his hands. Thunder in his ears. Water strangled him. Terror in his soul" (p. 24). This quote makes clear that there are two adversaries in the story: the hero is in conflict with nature and also in conflict with himself, as Mafatu battles to overcome his own terror and develop courage. The two adversaries are interwoven in the plot as Mafatu sails away from his island in order to prove that he is not a coward. Each time the boy wins a victory over nature he also comes closer to his main goal, victory over his own fear. Without that victory, he cannot be called by his rightful name Mafatu, "Stout Heart," nor can he have the respect of his father, his Polynesian people, and himself.

Person against Self. While few children face the extreme personal challenges described in *Call It Courage* and *Julie of the Wolves*, all children must overcome fears and personal problems while growing up. Person-against-self conflict is a popular plot device in children's literature.

Authors of contemporary realistic fiction often develop plots around children who face and overcome problems related to family disturbances. For example, the cause of the person-against-self conflict in Carol Lea Benjamin's *The Wicked Stepdog* is a girl's fear that she is losing her father's love. By describing the heroine's initial reactions to her new stepmother and her feelings about her father's actions, the author develops Louise's personal conflicts. The first-person narrative provides insights into Louise's changing attitudes as she overcomes feelings of fear and jealousy.

Lying is a problem that often gets children into difficulty. Sam, in *Sam, Bangs & Moonshine*, by Evaline Ness, does not mean to do any harm with her fibs, but they do cause her problems and almost cost her friend's life. Sam convinces her friend Thomas that she has a mermaid mother and a baby kangaroo. Thomas believes the story and goes out to Blue Rock to search for Sam's mother and the kangaroo. Unfortunately, the tide almost covers the rock before Thomas is rescued. When Sam realizes what she has done, her father asks her to tell herself the difference between real and "moonshine." She discovers that the mermaid mother, the baby kangaroo, and a dragon-drawn chariot are all "flummadiddle." Her father, her cat Bangs, and her friend Thomas are the real things. Sam overcomes her person-against-self conflict as she learns that there is good as well as bad moonshine.

In the modern fantasy, *The Hero and the Crown*, Robin McKinley develops two types of conflict. There is the conflict encountered as the heroine, Aerin, begins her quest and battles the forces of evil. Of equal importance, however, is her person-against-self conflict as she questions her

The illustrations suggest Sam's imaginary world of "moonshine." (From *Sam, Bangs & Moonshine:* written and illustrated by Evaline Ness. Copyright © 1966 by Evaline Ness. Reproduced by permission of Holt, Rinehart and Winston, Publishers.)

birthright, searches for answers to her heritage, and finally accepts who she is even though the terrible price is more than she imagined. The resolutions of the two conflicts are intertwined: acceptance of self and destruction of evil are both part of the climax and the conclusion of the book.

These plots tell credible stories without relying on contrivance or coincidence. They seem real to young readers because many of the same conflicts occur in children's own lives. Credibility is an important consideration in evaluating plot in children's books. Although authors of adult books often rely on considerable tension or sensational conflict to create interest, writers of children's books like to focus more on the characters and how they overcome problems.

Characterization

A believable, enjoyable story needs a strong plot and main characters who seem lifelike and who develop throughout the story. Characterization is one of the most powerful of literary elements when, according to Nancy Bond (1), "the writer uses imagination and human experience to create three-dimensional characters—characters with pasts, futures, parents, siblings, hopes, fears, sorrows, happiness. At the same time that the writer shows us individuals, he or she is showing us our common humanity, inviting identification and involvement" (p. 299).

The characters we remember fondly from our childhood reading usually have several sides to their characters; like real people they are not all good or all bad, and they change as they confront and overcome their problems. Laura, from various Laura Ingalls Wilder's "Little House" books, typifies what is often called a "round character" in literature. She is honest, trustworthy, and courageous, but can also be jealous, frightened, or angry. Her character is not only fully developed throughout the story, but also changes during its course. One child who enjoyed Wilder's books described Laura this way: "I would like Laura for my best friend. She would be fun to play with but she would also understand when I was hurt or angry. I could tell Laura my secrets without being afraid she would laugh at me or tell them to someone else." Any writer who can create such a friend for children is very skilled at developing characterization. How does an author develop such a memorable character? How can an author show the many sides of the character as well as demonstrate believable change as this character matures?

According to Charlotte S. Huck (13), the credibility of characters depends upon the writer's ability to reveal their full natures, strengths as well as weaknesses. Huck (13, p. 9) says that authors can achieve such three-dimensional characterization by (1) telling about characters through narration, (2) recording characters' conversations with others, (3) describing characters' thoughts, (4) revealing characters' thoughts about one another, and (5) showing characters in action.

In *Call It Courage*, Armstrong Sperry uses all these methods to reveal Mafatu's character and the changes that occur in him as he overcomes his fears. Sperry first tells the reader that Mafatu fears the sea, then, through narration, shows the young child clinging to his mother's back as a stormy sea and sharks try to end both their lives. Mafatu's memories of this experience, revealed in his thoughts and actions, make him "useless" in the eyes of his Polynesian tribe, as Sperry reveals through other characters' dialogue: "That is woman's work. Mafatu is afraid of the sea. He will never be a warrior" (p. 12). The laughter of the tribe follows, and Sperry then describes Mafatu's inner feelings: "Suddenly a fierce resentment stormed through him. He knew in that instant what he must do: he must prove his courage to himself, and to the others, or he could no longer live in their midst. He must face Moana, the Sea God—face him and conquer him" (p. 13). Sperry then portrays Mafatu's battle for courage through a combination of actions and thoughts: terror and elation follow one another repeatedly as Mafatu lands on a forbidden island used for human sacrifice, then dares to take a ceremonial spear even though doing so may mean death; confronts a hammerhead shark that circles his raft, then overcomes his fear and attacks the shark to save his dog. Mafatu celebrates a final victory when he kills the wild boar whose teeth symbolize courage. Mafatu's tremendous victory over fear is signified by his father's statement of pride: "Here is my son come home from the sea. Mafatu, Stout Heart. A brave name for a brave boy" (p. 115).

In *The Moves Make the Man*, Bruce Brooks develops characterization through basketball terminology. Brooks introduces this concept through the words of Jerome Foxworthy, a talented black student, who expresses these thoughts about his own character:

Moves were all I cared about last summer. I got them down, and I liked not just the fun of doing them, but having them too, like a little definition of Jerome. Reverse spin, triple jump, reverse dribble. . . . These are me. The moves make the man, the moves make me, I thought, until Mama noticed they were making me something else. (p. 44)

Brooks uses contrasting attitudes toward fake moves in basketball to reveal important differences between Jerome and Bix Rivers, a talented but disturbed white athlete.

This textbook discusses many memorable characters in children's literature. Some of these characters—such as the faithful spider Charlotte and a terrific pig named Wilbur, in E.B. White's *Charlotte's Web*—are old favorites who have been capturing children's imaginations for decades. Others—such as Max in Maurice Sendak's *Where the Wild Things Are* and Karana in Scott O'Dell's *Island of the Blue Dolphins*—are more recent arrivals in the world of children's books. Authors of picture story books, historical fiction, science fiction and fantasy, and contemporary realistic fiction have all created believable characters who are likely to be remembered long after the details of their stories have been forgotten.

Setting

A story's setting—its location in time and place—helps the reader share what a story's characters see, smell, hear, and touch, as well as making characters' values, actions, and conflicts more understandable. Whether a story takes place in the past, present, or future, its overall credibility may depend on how well plot, characterization, and setting support one another. Different types of literature—picture story books, fantasy, historical fiction, and contemporary realistic fiction—have their own requirements as far as setting is concerned, as discussed in later chapters. When a story is set in an identifiable historical period or geographical location, details should be accurate and both plot and characterization should be consistent with what actually occurred or could have occurred at that time and place.

In some books, setting is such an important part of the story that characters and plot cannot be developed without understanding time and

FLASHBACK

And a River went out of Eden.

GRAHAM ROBERTSON'S FRONTISPIECE FOR Kenneth Grahame's 1908 edition of *The Wind in the Willows* suggests an idyllic woodland setting for an animal fantasy. It also hints that all may not go well if the inhabitants leave this Eden.

Grahame's description of the river, the river bank, the changing seasons, the wild wood, and the wide world helps the reader visualize, and enter into, his story's location. Descriptions of wandering streams, whispering reeds and willows, and smells of marshlands also create a mood in which animal characters have the freedom to explore an enticing environment.

Other settings, however, are less desirable, settings that go beyond the river bank. In the wild wood, weasels, sloats, and foxes attack the peaceful inhabitants of the river bank. Beyond the wild wood is the wide world that may also entice some characters away from Eden into danger. Grahame creates the feeling, however, that that alien world does not really matter to the characters who enjoy living on the isolated river bank.

place. In other stories, however, the setting provides only a background. In fact, some settings are so well known that just a few words place the reader immediately into the expected location. "Once upon a time," for example, is a mythical

The appearance of a mythical white stag seems believable in this setting. (From *The White Stag*, written and illustrated by Kate Seredy. Copyright © 1937 by Kate Seredy. Copyright renewed 1965 by Kate Seredy. Reprinted by permission of Viking Penguin, Inc.)

time in days of yore when it was possible for magical spells to transform princes into beasts or to change pumpkins into glittering carriages. Thirty of the thirty-seven traditional fairy tales in Andrew Lang's *The Red Fairy Book* begin with "Once upon a time." Magical spells cannot happen everywhere; they usually occur in "a certain kingdom," "deep in the forest," in "the humble hut of a wise and good peasant," or "far, far away, in a warm and pleasant land." Children become so familiar with such phrases—and the imaginative visualizations of a setting that such phrases trigger in the reader's mind—that additional details and descriptions are not necessary.

Even when a setting is described quite briefly, however, it may serve several different purposes: creating a mood, providing an antagonist, establishing historical background, or supplying symbolic meanings.

Setting as Mood. Authors of children's literature and adult literature alike use settings to create moods that add credibility to a story's characters and plot. A reader would probably be a bit skeptical if a vampire appeared in a sunny American kitchen on a weekday morning while a family was preparing to leave for school and work. The same vampire would seem more believable in a moldy castle in Transylvania at midnight. The epic story of Attila the Hun, a famous invader of Eastern Europe in the fifth century AD, could be told as historical fiction, with a setting that emphasized accuracy of geographical and biographical detail. In *The White Stag*, however, Kate Seredy chose a more mythical approach to telling the story of how a migratory Asiatic people reached their new homeland in what became Hungary.

Gods, moonmaidens, and a supernatural animal are among this story's characters, and Seredy uses setting to create a mood in which such beings seem natural. The leader of the tribe stands before a sacrificial altar in a cold, rocky, and barren territory, waiting to hear the voice of the god Hadur, who will lead his starving people to the promised land. At this time, the white stag miraculously appears to guide the Huns in their travels—through "ghost hours" onto grassy hills covered with white birch trees, where they hear a brook tinkling like silver bells and a breeze that sounds like the flutes of minstrels. The reader expects magic in such a place, and is not disappointed to see "Moonmaidens, those strange changeling fairies who lived in white birch trees and were never seen in the daylight; Moonmaidens who, if caught by the gray-hour of dawn, could never go back to fairyland again; Moonmaidens, who brought good luck . . ." (p. 34).

The setting becomes less magically gentle when Attila is born. Attila's father has just challenged his god, and the result is terrifying: "Suddenly, without warning it [the storm] was upon them with lightning and thunder that roared and howled like an army of furious demons. Trees groaned and crashed to the ground to be picked up again and sucked into the spinning dark funnel of the whirlwind" (p. 64). This setting introduces Attila, the "Scourge of God," who in the future will lead his people home, with the help of the white stag.

Setting as Antagonist. Setting can be an antagonist in plots based on person-against-society or person-against-nature conflict. The descriptions of the Arctic in Jean Craighead George's *Julie of the Wolves* are essential; without them, the reader would have difficulty understanding the life-and-death peril facing Miyax. These descriptions make it possible to comprehend Miyax's love for the Arctic, her admiration of and dependence on the wolves, and her preference for the old Eskimo ways.

In *Witch of Blackbird Pond*, by Elizabeth George Speare, a Puritan colony in colonial New England is the story's setting, as well as the antagonist of newcomer Kit Taylor, whose colorful clothing and carefree ways immediately conflict with the standards of an austere society. Careful depiction of the colony's strict standards of dress and behavior helps the reader understand why the Puritans accuse Kit of being a witch.

Setting as Historical Background. Accuracy in setting is extremely important in historical fiction and in biography. Both the characters' actions and the conflict in the story may be influenced by the time period and the geographical location. Unless the author describes the setting carefully, children cannot comprehend unfamiliar historical periods or the stories that unfold in them. *A Gathering of Days*, by Joan W. Blos, is an example of historical fiction that carefully depicts the setting—in this case, a small New Hampshire farm in the 1830s. Blos brings rural nineteenth-century America to life through descriptions of little things such as home remedies, country pleasures, and country hardships. She describes in detail the preparation of a cold remedy, as the character goes to the pump for water, blows up the fire, heats a kettle of water over the flames, wrings out a flannel in hot water, sprinkles the flannel with turpentine, and places it on the patient's chest. She describes discipline and school life in the 1830s: disobedience can result in a thrashing; girls, because of their sex, are excused from all but the simplest arithmetic. The reader vicariously joins the characters in breaking out of the snow with a team of oxen, tapping the maple sugar trees, and collecting nuts. Of this last experience the narrator says, "O, I do think, as has been said, that if getting in the corn and potatoes are the prose of a farm child's life, then nutting's the poetry" (p. 131).

Make Way for Sam Houston by Jean Fritz is an example of biography in which the author places the biographical character into a carefully developed historical setting. Because this is a true story, Fritz describes two important historical settings. She depicts the settings associated with the nineteenth-century political hero as he moves from plantation Virginia to rural Tennessee to political Washington and finally to frontier Texas. Within these settings she develops the relationships between Sam Houston and the political figures of the time, such as Andrew Jackson, who influenced Sam's life. The historical period comes to life through Houston's descriptions of the everyday aspects of the environment and through dialogues between Houston and the real people who lived during that time.

The authors of historical fiction and biography must not only depict the story's time and location, but must also be aware of values, vocabulary, and other speech patterns consistent with the time and location. To do this, the author must be immersed in the past and do considerable research. Joan Blos researched her subject at the New York Public Library, libraries on the University of Michigan campus, and the town library of Holderness, New Hampshire. She also consulted town and county records in New Hampshire and discussed the story with professional historians. Jean Fritz referred to manuscripts and unpublished correspondence in the archives collections of the University of Texas and the Texas Baptist Historical Association.

Setting as Symbolism.   Settings often have symbolic meanings that underscore what is happening in the story. Symbolism is common in traditional folktales, where frightening adventures and magical transformations occur in the deep, dark woods, and splendid castles are the site of "happily ever after." Modern authors of fantasy and science fiction for children often borrow such symbolic settings from old folktales in order to establish a mood of strangeness and enchantment, but authors of realistic fiction also use subtly symbolic settings to accentuate plot or character development.

In one children's classic, *The Secret Garden*, by Frances Hodgson Burnett, a garden that has been locked behind a wall for ten years symbolizes a father's grief after the death of his wife, his son's illness, and the father and son's emotional estrangement from one another. The first positive change in the life of a lonely, unhappy girl occurs when she discovers the buried key to the garden and opens the vine-covered door: "It was the sweetest, most mysterious-looking place anyone could imagine. The high walls which shut it in were covered with the leafless stems of climbing roses which were so thick that they were matted together" (p. 76). Finding the garden, working in it, and watching its beauty return to life bring happiness to the girl, restore health to the sick

A boy and girl create a secret kingdom in which they can escape the problems of the real world. (Illustration by Donna Diamond from *Bridge to Terabithia* by Katherine Paterson. Copyright © 1977 by Katherine Paterson. A Newbery Medal winner. By permission of Thomas Y. Crowell, Publishers.)

boy, and reunite father and son. The good magic that causes emotional and physical healing in this secret kingdom is symbolized by tiny new shoots emerging from the soil and the rosy color that the garden's fresh air brings to the cheeks of two pale children.

In a more recent book, Katherine Paterson's *Bridge to Terabithia*, a secret kingdom in the woods symbolizes the "other world" shared by two young people who do not conform to the values of rural Virginia. The boy, Jess, would rather be an artist than follow the more masculine aspirations of his father, who accuses him of being a sissy. Schoolmates taunt the girl, Leslie, because she loves books and has no television. Jess and Leslie find that they have much in common, and create a domain of their own in which a beautiful setting symbolizes their growing sense of comradeship, belongingness, and self-love. Even the entrance to their secret country is symbolic: "It could be a magic country like Narnia, and the only way you can get in is by swinging across on this enchanted rope" (p. 39). They grab the old rope, swing across the creek, and enter their stronghold, where streams of light dance through the leaves of dogwood, oak, and evergreen, fears and enemies do not exist, and anything they want is possible. Paterson develops two credible settings as Jess and Leslie go from the world of school and home to the world that they make for themselves in Terabithia.

Theme

The theme of a story is the underlying idea that ties the plot, characterization, and setting together into a meaningful whole. When evaluating themes in children's books, one must consider what the author wanted to convey about life or society and whether that theme is worthwhile for children. Authors of children's books often directly state a book's theme, rather than imply it, as is common in books for adults. A memorable book has a theme—or several themes—that children can understand because of their own needs.

Historically Recurrent Literary Themes. Researchers have been fascinated by the effects of social, cultural, and economic factors on the themes found in literature of certain historical periods. Jean Duncan Shaw (22) has identified several themes that are pronounced in children's books published in the United States between 1850 and the 1960s: (1) search for values was a notable theme in the periods 1850–65, 1914–19, and 1936–70; (2) problems related to growing up were especially popular from 1865 to 1905, during the early 1930s, and after World War II; (3) books about travel and understanding people in other lands were most popular from 1918 until the Depression in the late 1920s; (4) lives of heroes dominated the children's literature of the pre–World War I years and remained strong through the late 1950s; (5) fantasy themes found in fairy tales reflected periods of economic prosperity, reaching peaks around 1910, in 1917–29, and from the 1950s into the 1960s; (6) the urge to acquire more knowledge about factual subjects was common around the early 1900s and during World War II. (See chapter nine for a discussion of themes in contemporary realistic fiction and chapter ten for a time line of themes in historical fiction.)

Adults and older children can acquire a better understanding of cultural values, social patterns, and economic realities in different times by identifying themes popular in children's books and investigating the history of different books' time periods. (Chapter two discussed this relationship between theme and historical period and provided examples.)

The Theme of Personal Development. Literature offers children an opportunity to identify with other people's experiences and thus better understand their own process of growing up. Consequently, the themes of many children's books deal with developing self-understanding. Gretchen Purtell Hayden (10) concluded that the following themes related to personal development were most predominant in children's books that had received the Newbery Medal: (1) difficulties in establishing good relationships between adults and children; (2) the need for morality to guide one's actions; (3) the importance of support from other people; (4) acceptance of self and others; (5) respect for authority; (6) the ability to handle problems; and (7) the necessity of cooperation.

Many of these themes are found in the books previously discussed in this chapter. The difficulty of establishing good relationships between adults and children is developed in a humorous way in Beverly Cleary's *Ramona and Her Father*. Cleary indicates that Ramona usually has a good relationship with her parents, but it rapidly deteriorates when her father loses his job and Ramona confronts new difficulties in getting along with adults who are worried and frustrated. Cleary describes Ramona's efforts to help her family and her own frustration when her actions do not work out as she hopes. For example, after the cat destroys a jack-o-lantern the family has made together, her father mistakenly thinks Ramona's sadness is due to the loss of the pumpkin: "Didn't grown-ups think children worried about anything but jack-o-lanterns? Didn't they know children worried about grown-ups?" (p. 85).

In Robert O'Brien's *Mrs. Frisby and the Rats of NIMH*, a group of superior rats search for a moral code to guide their actions. They have studied the human race and do not wish to make the same mistakes, but they soon realize how easy it is to slip into dishonest behavior. Using some equipment they find allows them to steal electricity, food, and water from human society, which then

Superior rats consider the morality of their actions in a complex plot. (Illustration by Zena Bernstein from *Mrs. Frisby and the Rats of NIMH* by Robert C. O'Brien. Copyright © 1971 by Robert C. O'Brien. [New York: Charles Scribner's Sons, 1971]. Reprinted with the permission of Atheneum Publishers.)

makes their lives seem too easy and pointless. Eventually, the rats choose a more difficult course of action, moving into an isolated valley and working to develop their own civilization.

One book that develops the importance of support from another human being is Theodore Taylor's *The Cay*. When Phillip and his mother leave Curaçao in order to find safety in the United States, their boat is torpedoed by a German submarine. Phillip, a white boy, and a black West Indian named Timothy become isolated first on a life raft and then on a tiny Caribbean island. Their need for each other is increased when Phillip becomes blind after a blow to the head and must, in spite of his racial prejudice, rely on Timothy for his survival. Phillip's superior attitudes gradually vanish as he becomes totally dependent on another person. When the two are finally rescued, Phillip treasures the way a wonderful friend has helped change his life for the better.

The Cay also stresses the theme of accepting self and others, as does Joan W. Blos's *A Gathering of Days*, in which Catherine experiences injustice for the first time when she and her friends secretly help a runaway slave. Catherine learns to respect authority as well when, after years of re-

sponsibility for her widowed father and little sister, she must trust and obey her new stepmother.

Many children's books deal in some way with the necessity of overcoming problems. Characters may overcome problems within themselves or in their relationships with others, or problems caused by society or nature. Memorable characters face their adversaries and, through a maturing process, learn to handle their own difficulties. Handling problems may be as dramatic and preplanned as Mafatu's search for courage in Armstrong Sperry's *Call It Courage* or may result from accident, as in Theodore Taylor's *The Cay*. In Evaline Ness's *Sam, Bangs & Moonshine*, Sam must overcome her tendency to lie. Katherine Paterson has Jess and Leslie cross *The Bridge to Terabithia* in order to overcome the difficulties of being nonconformists in the rest of their everyday lives.

The theme of cooperation is developed in Jean Craighead George's *Julie of the Wolves* when Miyax must make friends with frightening animals and a harsh environment in order to survive. Cooperation within the family and within the larger community is a theme throughout Laura Ingalls Wilder's "Little House" books about pioneers on the American frontier.

Style

Authors have a wide choice of words to select from and numerous ways to arrange words in order to create plots, settings, and characterizations. Many authors develop unique personal styles or styles suitable to particular stories by using words and sentences in creative ways. One effective way to evaluate style is to read a piece of literature aloud. The sound of a story should appeal to the senses and be appropriate to the story's contents. Language should bring characters to life, enhance plot development, and create mood.

The Girl Who Loved Wild Horses, by Paul Goble, was a Children's Choice selection for the year 1978 (see page 101). Children's reasons for choosing this book most often referred to the author's use of language. Goble chooses his words carefully, using precise verbs and similes to evoke a landscape of cliffs and canyons, beautiful wild horses, and the high-spirited Indian girl who loves them. One stallion's eyes are "cold stars," while his floating mane and tail are "wispy clouds." During a storm, the horses gallop "faster and faster, pursued by thunder and lightning. . . . like a brown flood across hills and through valleys" (p. 12 unnumbered).

Figurative language also enhances characterization, plot development, and setting in Jan Hudson's *Sweetgrass*, an historical novel about the Blackfeet, set on the Canadian prairies. Early in the story, for example, sweet berries symbolize a young girl's happiness and hopes: "Promises hung shimmering in the future like glowing berries above sandy soil as we gathered our bags for the walk home" (p. 12). Later, the same girl's acceptance of a disillusioning reality is symbolized by berries that are now bitter.

Authors may also select words and sentence structures with rhythms that evoke different moods in the story. Armstrong Sperry creates two quite different moods for Mafatu in *Call It Courage*. As Mafatu goes through the jungle, he is preoccupied and moves at a leisurely pace. Sperry uses long sentences to develop this mood: "His mind was not in this business at all: he was thinking about the rigging of his canoe, planning how he could strengthen it here, tighten it there" (p. 77). This dreamy preoccupation changes rapidly as Mafatu senses danger. Sperry's verbs become harsh and his sentences short and choppy as Mafatu's tension builds: "The boar charged. Over the ground it tore. Foam flew back from its tusks. The boy braced himself" (p. 78).

Many of the stories young children enjoy contain repetition of words, phrases, or sentences. Repetition is especially appealing because it encourages children to join in during the reading. It provides a pleasing rhythm in *When I Was Young in the Mountains*, by Cynthia Rylant. The author introduces her memories of Grandfather's kisses, Grandmother's cooking, and listening to frogs singing at dusk with "When I was young in the mountains," a phrase that adds an appropriate aura of loving nostalgia to the experiences she describes.

Authors use other literary devices, such as alliteration and rhyming, which are discussed in chapter five.

Point of View

Several people may describe a single incident in different terms. The feelings they experience, the details they choose to describe, and their judgments about what occurred may vary because of their backgrounds, values, and other perspec-

tives. Consequently, the same story may change drastically when told from another point of view. How would Peter Rabbit's story be different if Beatrix Potter had told it from the viewpoint of the mother rabbit? How would Armstrong Sperry's *Call It Courage* differ if told from the viewpoint of a Polynesian tribesman who loves the sea rather than from the viewpoint of a boy who fears it?

An author has several options when selecting point of view. A first-person point of view speaks through the "I" of one of the characters. If the author wishes to use a first-person narrative, the author must decide which character's actions and feelings should influence the plot development, characterization, and theme. An objective point of view lets actions speak for themselves. The author describes only the characters' actions, and the reader must infer the characters' thoughts and feelings. An omniscient point of view tells the story in the third person, with the author talking about "they, he, she." The author is not restricted to the knowledge, experience, and feelings of one person. Every feeling and thought of all characters can be revealed. When using a limited omniscient point of view the author concentrates on the experience of one character, but has the option to be all-knowing about other characters. (A limited omniscient point of view, focusing mainly on one character, may help the author clarify conflict and actions that would be less understandable if a first-person narrative were used.)

Although there is no preferred point of view for children's literature, an author's choice can affect how much children of certain ages believe and enjoy a story. Contemporary realistic fiction for children age eight and older often uses a first-person point of view or a limited omniscient point of view focusing on one child's experience. Older children often empathize with one character if they have had similar experiences. In *The Wicked Stepdog*, Carol Lea Benjamin introduces her first-person narrator through these thoughts: "I think most parents are pretty phony. Take my dad for example" (p. 1). The actions in the story are then interpreted through the viewpoint of that twelve-year-old character. Likewise, Beverly Cleary's popular "Ramona" stories are told from the viewpoint of a precocious seven- or eight-year-old child.

The consistency of point of view encourages readers to believe in a story's characters and plot development. Such belief is especially crucial in modern fantasy, where readers are introduced to imaginary worlds, unusual characters, and magical incidents. A writer may describe a setting as if it were being viewed by a character only a few inches tall. To be believable, however, the story cannot stray from the viewpoint of the tiny character. The character's actions, the responses of others toward the character, and the setting must be consistent. Chapter seven discusses the importance of point of view in modern fantasy.

Nonstereotypes

Stereotypes must be considered when evaluating literature for young children. Educators and other concerned adults have strongly criticized stereotypical views of both race and sex. Of particular concern are literary selections that inadequately represent minority groups and females or that represent them in an insensitive or demeaning way.

Teachers, librarians, and parents may confront a shortage of high-quality stories about members of racial and ethnic minority groups, of works by authors who write from a minority perspective, and of materials that depict the literary, cultural,

and historical influence of minorities. To remedy these deficiencies, adults must seek out and offer all children literature that lacks negative stereotypes and that presents an honest, authentic picture of different people and their cultural and historical contributions. When evaluating literature about minorities, for example, the following questions might be kept in mind: Are black, Native American, Hispanic, and other minority characters portrayed as distinct individuals, or are they grouped in one category under depersonalizing clichés? Does the author recognize and accurately portray the internal diversity of minority cultures? Is a minority culture respected or treated as inferior? Does the author accurately describe the values, behavior, and environment of characters who are members of minority groups? Are illustrations realistic and authentic? Because ethnic culture is so important in the United States, chapter eleven is devoted to multiethnic literature, discussing the value of multiethnic literature, images of ethnic groups found in literature of the past, criteria for evaluating multiethnic literature, and authors and their works. Chapter eleven also investigates approaches that adults can use to evaluate chil-

ISSUE

⋯❱❱✿❰❰⋯

Evaluation of Children's Literature: Literary Merit Versus Popularity Versus Social Significance

CHILDREN'S LITERATURE is evaluated not only by children who are its potential readers, but also by literary critics, teachers, librarians, parents, and publishers. Questions related to literary quality, social philosophy, and suitability of content are debated, along with a book's potential or proven ability to attract children's interest. The evaluation criteria used for book awards, criticism, and recommendations for book purchases frequently reflect the standards of diverse groups. The adult-selected award winners—exemplified by the Newbery Medal, Caldecott Medal, Notable Children's Books, and Boston Globe-Horn Book Award—suggest that the high-

est literary value should be a primary consideration when choosing books for children. In contrast, the various readers' choice awards, which are compiled from young readers' preferences, imply that children's interests and the popularity of books among children themselves should be an essential consideration. A third position, represented by groups such as the Council on Interracial Books for Children, suggests that books should be evaluated according to human values, with a book selection policy that stems from child development and psychology, cultural pluralism, and aesthetic standards.

The selection standards reflected by these three positions

dren's attitudes toward ethnic literature, develop an appreciation for multiethnic literature, create a multiethnic literature program, and improve the self-concepts of children from racial and ethnic minority groups. Understanding these approaches is essential because research indicates that if stereotypical attitudes are to change, reading positive multiethnic literature must be followed by discussions or other activities that allow interaction between children and adults.

Sexism in children's literature is a closely related issue that also requires adults to evaluate children's books with care. Much research supports Myra Sadker and David Sadker's (20) conclusion that "blatant quotes denigrating one sex, usually women, are relatively common in children's books, and it is not at all difficult to find statements that girls are dumb, silly, unable to keep secrets, and generally incompetent" (p. 232). Some children's books also stereotype males in ways that limit boys' options to express a wide range of feelings and interests. Sadker and Sadker maintain that if a book contains remarks that group all males or all females together and make insulting remarks about either sex as a whole, the book may be sexist. The entire book must be read before this decision can be reached, however, since isolated quotes should not be judged out of context. Chapter nine evaluates sexism in books.

THE RIGHT BOOK FOR THE INDIVIDUAL CHILD

Chapter one considered the different stages of children's development, as well as the role that literature can play in encouraging language growth, intellectual development, personality development, social development, and creative development. Because of these developmental stages, children have different personal and literary needs at different ages. Children in the same age group or at the same stage of development also have diverse interests and reading abilities that must be considered when selecting the right book for the individual.

Understanding why and what children read is necessary in order to help them select materials that stimulate their interests and enjoyment. John T. Guthrie (9) investigated several studies of why adults read, the results of which apply to children as well. Guthrie concluded that the two most im-

may or may not identify the same books as literature worthy of sharing with children. The merits of each type of evaluation are debated in professional literature, in college classrooms, and during professional conferences. Reviewers of children's books may emphasize one or more of these positions when they evaluate new books or compile lists of recommended books. It is helpful if readers can identify any particular bias of a reviewer so that they can interpret and use recommendations to meet their own individual needs.

Carolyn Bauer and LaVonne Sanborn[1] maintain that both literary quality and popularity are important. They suggest that books which have won both types of awards deserve considerable emphasis. Children do enjoy some books with literary value. From a list of 193 books that have won readers' choice awards, Bauer and Sanborn have identified 39 that were also literary merit award winners. Of these, *Mrs. Frisby and the Rats of NIMH, The Mouse and the Motorcycle, Old Yeller, Rascal,* and *The Trumpet of the Swan* have each won four readers' choice awards. Authors Beverly Cleary, George Selden, and E. B. White each have written two titles that have won awards for literary value and popularity.

Increased sensitivity to the human values expressed in books may result in debates about the merit of previously acclaimed literature. For example, Walter Edmonds's *The Matchlock Gun* won the Newbery Medal in 1942. The same book was criticized in the 1970s because of insensitive descriptions of Native Americans.

When evaluating literature and reading literature critiques, students of children's literature may consider each selection standard. How can the book be evaluated according to literary merit, popularity, and social significance?

[1] Bauer, Carolyn J., and Sanborn, LaVonne H. "The Best of Both Worlds: Children's Books Acclaimed by Adults and Young Readers." *Top of the News 38* (Fall 1981): 53–56.

portant reasons for reading were to obtain general knowledge and to gain relaxation and enjoyment. Jeanne S. Chall and Emily W. Marston (3) found that the most powerful determinants of adult reading are accessibility, readability, and interest. These factors also influence children's reading habits and preferences. If developing enjoyment through literature is a major objective of a reading program for children, many excellent books must be available to children, children's reading levels must be considered, and adults must know how to gain and use information about children's reading interests.

Accessibility

Literature must be readily accessible if children are to read at all. In order to know what books interest them, gain knowledge of their heritage, recognize and appreciate good literature, and understand themselves and others through literature, children must have opportunities to read and listen to many books. As suggested previously, a literature program for children should include a wide variety of high-quality literature, both old and new.

A survey by Susan Swanton (24) showed that gifted students owned more books and used public libraries more than did other students. Fifty-five percent of the gifted students Swanton surveyed identified the public library as their major source of reading material, as opposed to only 33 percent of the other students, most of whom identified the school library as their major source for books. Thirty-five percent of the gifted children owned more than 100 books. Only 19 percent of other students owned an equal number of books. Swanton concluded her findings with the following recommendations for cooperation between public libraries and schools:

1   Promote students' participation in summer reading programs that are sponsored by public libraries.
2   Inform parents about the value of reading aloud to children, giving children their own books, and parents as role models for developing readers.
3   Encourage school librarians to do book talks designed to entice children into reading.
4   Provide field trips to public libraries.
5   Advertise public library programs and services.

6   Make obtaining the first library card a special event.

The Child's Reading Ability

Readability is another major consideration in choosing literature for children, according to Jeanne S. Chall and Emily W. Marston (3). A book must conform to a child's reading level in order for a child to read independently. Children become frustrated when a book contains too many words they don't know. A child is able to read independently when able to pronounce about 98–100 percent of the words in a book and to answer 90–100 percent of comprehension questions asked about it. Reading abilities in any one age group or grade level range widely; adults working with children must provide, and be familiar with, an equally wide range of literature. Books listed in the annotated bibliographies at the end of chapters in this book are identified by grade-level of readability, although a book will not be readable to every child in the grade indicated. (See appendix E for a readability graph and directions for computing readability.)

Many children have reading levels lower than their interest levels. They need many opportunities to listen to, and otherwise interact with, fine literature. Chapter five presents comparisons between books designed to be read *by* young children and those designed to be read *to* young children.

The Child's Interests

Adults can learn more about children's interests by reviewing studies of children's interests and evaluating interest inventories. Attention should be given to information gained from each source.

For many years, researchers have investigated factors related to the leisure reading habits and interests of children at different age levels. A study by Vincent Greaney (8) identified some of these factors: (1) American and British studies indicate that the time and amount of leisure reading varies with age; children at the end of primary school read the most, after which a decline in leisure reading occurs among all but high-ability readers; (2) girls read more books than boys do, although boys read more nonfiction; (3) children from working-class homes do not read as much as those from higher socioeconomic backgrounds; and (4) the amount of leisure reading and the level of student achievement are directly related; good students read more and read higher-quality materials.

Several studies have investigated the literary interests of children at specific ages, grades, and ability levels. For example, Thomas William Dowan's (4) study of Florida school children concluded that in grades three through five boys are primarily interested in adventure, tall tales, historical nonfiction, how-to-do-it, sports, and science, while girls are primarily interested in animals, fairy tales, modern fantasy, children of the United States, and children from other lands. Similar results were found by Joan T. Feeley (6), who concluded that fourth- and fifth-grade boys like sports, excitement, and informational books, while fourth- and fifth-grade girls prefer social empathy, fantasy, and content dealing with their recreational interests.

Research indicates that children's reading interests are also influenced by their reading ability. Susan Swanton's (24) survey comparing gifted students with students of average ability reports that gifted children prefer mysteries (43 percent), fiction (41 percent), science fiction (29 percent), and fantasy (18 percent). In contrast, the top four choices for students of average ability were mysteries (47 percent), comedy/humor (27 percent), realistic fiction (23 percent), and adventure (18 percent). Gifted students indicated that they liked "science fiction and fantasy because of the challenge it presented, as well as its relationship to Dungeons and Dragons" (24, p. 100). Gifted students listed Judy Blume, Lloyd Alexander, J.R.R. Tolkien, and C.S. Lewis as favorite authors. Average students listed Judy Blume, Beverly Cleary, and Jack London.

While this information can provide some general ideas about what subjects and authors children of certain ages, sexes, and reading abilities prefer, adults should not develop stereotyped views about children's preferences. Without asking questions about interests, for example, there was no way to learn that a fourth grader was a Shakespeare buff, since research into children's interests does not indicate that a fourth-grade boy should like Shakespeare's plays. A first-grade girl's favorite subject was dinosaurs, which she could identify by name. Discovering this would have been impossible without an interview; research does not indicate that first-grade girls are interested in factual, scientific subjects. These two cases point to the need to discover children's interests before helping them select books that will entice and stimulate.

Informal conversation is one of the simplest ways to uncover children's interests. Ask a child to describe what he or she likes to do and read about. Some way of recording the information is usually needed when an adult is working with a number of children. Teachers and librarians can develop interest inventories in which students answer questions about their favorite hobbies, books, sports, television shows, and other interests. Adults can write down young children's answers. Older children can read the questionnaire themselves and write their own responses. Such an inventory might include some of the questions asked in Chart 3–1. (Changes would need to be made according to children's age levels, and additional information could be discovered if children told why they liked certain books.) After the interest inventory is made, its findings can serve as the basis for helping children select books and extend their enjoyment of literature.

THE CHILD AS CRITIC

Children are the ultimate critics of what they read, and adults should consider their preferences when evaluating and selecting books to share with them.

For the last few years, a joint project of the International Reading Association and the Children's Book Council has allowed approximately 10,000 children from around the United States to evaluate children's books published during a given year. Each year their reactions are recorded, and a research team uses this information to compile a list of "Children's Choices" in the following categories: beginning independent reading, younger children, middle grades, older readers, informational books, and poetry. This very useful annotated bibliography is published each year in the October issue of *The Reading Teacher*, or it may be obtained from the Children's Book Council, 67 Irving Place, New York, NY 10003.

A look at these lists of children's favorites also gives adults a better understanding of the characteristics of books that appeal to children. In order to identify characteristic elements found in the Children's Choices, Sam Leaton Sebesta (21) evaluated the books listed and tried to discover if their characteristics were different from those of books not chosen by children. His evaluation produced the following conclusions:

1 Plots of the Children's Choices are faster paced than those found in books not chosen as favorites.
2 Young children enjoy reading about nearly any topic if the information is presented in specific detail. The topic itself may be less important than interest studies have indicated; specifics rather than topics seem to underlie children's preferences.
3 Children like detailed descriptions of settings; they want to know exactly how the place looks and feels before the main action occurs.
4 One type of plot structure does not dominate Children's Choices. Some stories have a central focus with a carefully arranged cause-and-effect plot; others have plots that meander, with unconnected episodes.
5 Children do not like sad books.
6 Children seem to like some books that explicitly teach a lesson, even though critics usually frown on didactic literature.
7 Warmth was the most outstanding quality of books children preferred. Children enjoy books where the characters like each other,

---

1 Do you have a hobby? _____
   If you do, what is your hobby? _____
2 Do you have a pet? _____
   What kind of a pet do you have? _____
3 What is your favorite book that someone has read to you? _____
4 What kinds of books do you like to have read to you?
      real animals _____   picture books _____
      real children _____   information books _____
      science fiction _____   mysteries _____
      funny stories _____   fairy tales _____
      sports stories _____   poetry _____
      true stories _____   historical fiction _____
      fantasy animals _____   science books _____
      family stories _____   adventures _____
5 What is your favorite book that you have read by yourself? _____
6 What kinds of books do you like to read by yourself? (Similar to 4) _____
7 What sports do you like? _____
8 Who are your favorite sports stars? _____
9 What do you do when you get home from school? _____
10 What do you like to do on Saturday? _____
11 Do you like to collect things? _____
   What do you like to collect? _____
12 What are your favorite subjects in school? _____
13 Would you rather read a book by yourself or have someone read it to you?
   _____
14 Name a book you read this week. _____
15 Where would you like to go on vacation? _____
16 Do you go to the library? _____
   If you do, how often do you go? _____
   Do you have a library card? _____
17 Do you watch television? _____
18 If you do, what kinds of programs do you like?
      comedies _____   cartoons _____
      sports _____   westerns _____
      animal programs _____   music _____
      family stories _____   game shows _____
      educational TV _____   mysteries _____
      true stories _____   detective shows _____
      specials _____   science fiction _____
      news _____   other _____
19 Name your favorite television programs. _____
20 Who are your favorite characters on TV? _____
21 Name several subjects you would like to know more about. _____
   _____

CHART 3—1
An informal interest inventory

express their feelings in things they say and do, and sometimes act selflessly.

Sebesta believes this information should be used to help children select books and to stimulate reading and discussions. For example, children's attention can be drawn to the warmth, pace, or descriptions in a story in order to encourage their involvement with the story.

The various Children's Choices lists also suggest particular types of stories that appeal to young readers. The "beginning independent reading" category contains comical stories about more or less realistic family situations, humorous animal stories, stories that develop emotional experiences, action-filled fantasies, traditional stories, counting books, rhymes, and riddles. The "younger reader" category includes realistic stories about families, friends, school, and personal problems; animal stories; fantasies; fast-paced adventures; folktales; and humorous stories. Stories chosen by children in the middle grades include realistic stories about sibling rivalry, peer acceptance, fears, and not conforming to stereotypes; fantasies; suspense; and humorous stories. Popular informational books include factual and nonsensical advice about human health, factual information about animals, and biographical information about sports stars. Popular poetry includes collections by Judith Viorst, Shel Silverstein, and William Cole.

Children choose books from a wide variety of genres. Some are on highly recommended lists of children's books; others are not. Many educators and authorities on children's literature are concerned about the quality of books children read. According to Glenna Davis Sloan (23), children can make valid judgments about good books if they are taught to do so. Sloan believes that children can be trained to consider these questions: Did the story end the way you expected? Did the author prepare you for the ending? If so, how? If you could make up a different ending, how would you change the rest of the story?

If children are to improve their ability to make valid judgments about literature, they must experience good books and investigate and discuss what it is about a book that makes it memorable. Young children usually just enjoy and talk about books, but older ones can start to evaluate what they do and do not like about literature.

One sixth-grade teacher encouraged her students to make literary judgments and to develop a list of criteria for selecting good literature (19). The motivation for this literature study began when the students wondered what favorite books their parents might have read when they were in the same grade. To answer this question, the children interviewed their parents and other adults, asking them which books and characters were their favorites. They listed the books, characters, and number of people who recommended them on a large chart. Each student then read a book that a parent or another respected adult had enjoyed. (Many adults also reread these books.) Following their reading, the children discussed the book with the adult, considering what made or did not make the book memorable for them. At this time, the teacher introduced the concepts of plot, characterization, setting, theme, style, and format. The children searched the books they had read for examples of each element. Finally, they listed questions to ask themselves when evaluating a book:

Questions to Ask Myself When I Judge a Book

1 Is this a good story?
2 Is the story about something I think could really happen? Is the plot believable?
3 Did the main character overcome the problem, but not too easily?
4 Did the climax seem natural?
5 Did the characters seem real? Did I understand the characters' personalities and the reasons for their actions?
6 Did the characters in the story grow?
7 Did I find out about more than one side of the characters? Did the characters have both strengths and weaknesses?
8 Did the setting present what is actually known about that time or place?
9 Did the characters fit into the setting?
10 Did I feel that I was really in that time or place?
11 What did the author want to tell me in the story?
12 Was the theme worthwhile?
13 When I read the book aloud, did the characters sound like real people actually talking?
14 Did the rest of the language sound natural?

A review of these fourteen evaluative questions shows how closely they correspond to the criteria that should be used in evaluating the plot, characterization, setting, theme, and style found in literature.

Research cited above shows that children have preferences in the books they choose. Other research indicates that children also have preferences about how and when books should be read to them. Alicia Mendoza (18) reports the results of a survey of 520 elementary school children ranging in age from five to thirteen. The following recommendations, taken from Mendoza's longer report, highlight the importance of reading books to children and the preferences of children during those listening experiences: (1) Children throughout elementary grades enjoy having books read to them; consequently, parents and teachers should read to children frequently. (2) During conferences with parents, teachers should emphasize the importance of reading to children at home. (3) Role models are important; both parents should read to children. (4) Because children enjoy listening to stories in groups, teachers should encourage parents to make reading at home a group activity. (5) Parents and teachers should provide opportunities for children to read to other children. (6) Children should have opportunities to select the books read to them or read by them to others. (7) Children like information about a book before it is read to them; they should be told who the author is and be given a brief summary of plot, characters, and setting. (8) Children like and should be given an opportunity to discuss books and to read books after books are read aloud.

When children are encouraged to share, discuss, and evaluate books, and given opportunities to do so, they are able to expand their reading enjoyment and to select worthwhile stories and characters. Sharing and discussion can take place in the library, in a classroom, or in the home.

SUMMARY

A literature program should help students enjoy books, recognize and appreciate good literature, understand their heritage, and understand themselves and others. To develop these objectives, a balanced selection of literature is necessary: classic and contemporary stories, fanciful and realistic stories, prose and poetry, biographies, and informational books. Therefore, adults working with children must themselves acquire knowledge about many types of literature.

When selecting literature for children, adults should first consider the child who will be reading the book. Children have different personal and literary needs at various times. They also have diverse interests and reading abilities that must be considered when selecting the right book for each individual.

If literary merit and not mediocrity is to be a part of the literary experience, both children and adults need opportunities to read, discuss, and evaluate literature. The criteria usually used to evaluate children's literature emphasize the importance of literary elements such as plot, characterization, setting, theme, style, and point of view.

Plot is the story's plan of action; a good plot lets children share the action, feel the conflict, recognize the climax, and respond to a satisfactory ending. Children's expectations and enjoyment of conflict vary with their ages and what kinds of books they read. A good story has a beginning, a middle, and an end. Chronological order is the most common way to present events in children's literature. Plot develops when the main character overcomes conflict. There are four kinds of conflict in children's literature: person-against-person, person-against-society, person-against-nature, and person-against-self.

Characters should seem believable and should develop throughout the course of a story. Characterization is developed when the author tells about the characters, records their conversations, describes their thoughts, and shows the characters in action.

Setting is a story's location in time and place—past, present, or future. A setting should be plausible and, when identifiable locations and time periods are involved, geographically and historically accurate. Both plot and characterization should be consistent with the story's setting. Setting may be used to provide an instant background, create a mood, develop a conflict, suggest symbolism, or depict a complete historical background.

The theme is the underlying idea of the story that ties plot, characterization, and setting together into a meaningful whole. A story's theme should be worthwhile for children. Many themes found in children's books deal with developing self-understanding; establishing good relationships between adult and child; the need for a moral code to guide actions; the importance of support from other people; acceptance of self and others; respect for authority; the ability to handle problems; and the necessity of cooperation.

Style is the way an author arranges words to create plots, settings, and characterizations. Language should bring the characters to life, enhance plot development, and create the mood of the setting.

Point of view in literature is the viewpoint through which the author chooses to tell the story. The author may select a first-person point of view, an objective point of view, an omniscient point of view, or a limited omniscient point of view.

Suggested Activities for Understanding the Selection and Evaluation of Children's Literature

☐ Administer an interest inventory to children, tabulate the results, select several books that would appeal to their interests, and share the books with the children. What were their responses to the books?

☐ Compare the plots of several books written for younger children with plots in books written for older children. Compare the way events are ordered, the conflicts that are developed, the amount of suspense or tension, and the climax of the stories.

☐ Find examples of person-against-person, person-against-self, person-against-society, and person-against-nature conflicts in children's literature. Do some books develop more than one type of conflict? What makes the conflict believable? Share these examples with your class.

☐ Read one of Laura Ingalls Wilder's "Little House" books. Do you agree with the child who said she would like the character Laura for her best friend? How has the author developed Laura into a believable character? Give examples of techniques Wilder uses to reveal Laura's nature.

☐ Compare the main character in a fairy tale such as "Cinderella" or "Snow White" with the main character in a book such as Patricia Clapp's *I'm Deborah Sampson*, Scott O'Dell's *Island of the Blue Dolphins*, or Armstrong Sperry's *Call It Courage*. Describe each character. Does the character change in the course of the story? How does the author show that change?

☐ Find descriptions of settings that (1) are used to create a mood, (2) develop conflict, (3) are symbolic, and (4) describe an historical period. What is the importance of each setting? Close your eyes and try to picture the setting. If it is realistic, what did the author do to make it so? If it does not seem realistic, what is wrong? How would you improve it?

☐ Investigate themes found in children's literature published during the 1960s, 1970s, and 1980s. Which ones are most common? Can you draw any conclusions about the social, cultural, and economic influences of the times? Make a time line to summarize the results.

☐ Find several examples of writing in which the author's style has created a specific image. Read each selection to an audience. How does the audience respond to the author's use of style?

☐ Review the books in the most recent list of Children's Choices. What are some characteristics of books chosen by younger, middle elementary, and older readers?

References

1 Bond, Nancy. "Conflict in Children's Fiction." *The Horn Book* 60 (June 1984): 297–306.

2 Carlson, Ruth Kearney. "Book Selection for Children of a Modern World." In *Developing Active Readers: Ideas for Parents, Teachers, and Librarians*, edited by Dianne L. Monson and Day Ann K. McClenathan. Newark, Del.: International Reading Association, 1979, pp. 16–29.

3 Chall, Jeanne S., and Marston, Emily W. "The Reluctant Reader: Suggestions from Research and Practice." *Catholic Library World* 47 (February 1976): 274–75.

4 Dowan, Thomas William. "Personal Reading Interests as Expressed by Children in Grades Three, Four, and Five in Selected Florida Public Schools," University Microfilm no. 72–13,502. Tallahassee, Fla.: Florida State University, 1971.

5 Egoff, Sheila. "If That Don't Do No Good, That Won't Do No Harm: The Uses and Dangers of Mediocrity in Children's Reading." *Issues in Children's Book Selection: A School Library Journal/Library Journal Anthology.* New York: Bowker, 1973, pp. 4–5, 7.

6 Feeley, Joan T. "Interest Patterns and Media Preferences of Boys and Girls in Grades 4 and 5," Uni-

versity Microfilm no. 72–20,628. New York: New York University, 1972.

7 Frye, Northrop; Baker, Sheridan; and Perkins, George. *The Harper Handbook to Literature*. New York: Harper & Row, 1985.

8 Greaney, Vincent. "Factors Related to Amount and Type of Leisure Time Reading." *Reading Research Quarterly* 15 (1980): 337–57.

9 Guthrie, John T. "Why People (Say They) Read." *The Reading Teacher* 32 (March 1979): 752–55.

10 Hayden, Gretchen Purtell. "A Descriptive Study of the Treatment of Personal Development in Selected Children's Fiction Books Awarded the Newbery Medal," University Microfilm no. 70–19,060. Detroit: Wayne State University, 1969.

11 Heins, Paul. "Coming to Terms with Criticism." In *Crosscurrents of Criticism: Horn Book Essays 1968–1977*. Boston: The Horn Book, 1978, pp. 82–87.

12 Heins, Paul. "Out on a Limb with the Critics: Some Random Thoughts on the Present State of the Criticism of Children's Literature." In *Crosscurrents of Criticism: Horn Book Essays 1968–1977*. Boston: The Horn Book, 1978, pp. 72–81.

13 Huck, Charlotte S. *Children's Literature in the Elementary School*. New York: Holt, Rinehart & Winston, 1979.

14 Huus, Helen. "Teaching Literature at the Elementary School Level." *The Reading Teacher* 26 (May 1973): 795–801.

15 Kennemer, Phyllis K. "Reviews of Fiction Books: How They Differ." *Top of the News* 40 (Summer 1984): 419–421.

16 Kingsbury, Mary. "Perspectives on Criticism," *The Horn Book* 60 (February 1984): 17–23.

17 Lukens, Rebecca J. *A Critical Handbook of Children's Literature*. Glenview, Ill.: Scott, Foresman, 1981.

18 Mendoza, Alicia. "Reading to Children: Their Preferences," *The Reading Teacher* 38 (February 1985): 522–527.

19 Norton, Donna E. *The Effective Teaching of Language Arts* (2nd ed.). Columbus, Ohio: Merrill, 1985.

20 Sadker, Myra Pollack, and Sadker, David Miller. *Now Upon a Time, A Contemporary View of Children's Literature*. New York: Harper & Row, 1977.

21 Sebesta, Sam Leaton. "What Do Young People Think about the Literature They Read?" *Reading Newsletter*, no. 8. Rockleigh, N.J.: Allyn & Bacon, 1979.

22 Shaw, Jean Duncan. "An Historical Survey of Themes Recurrent in Selected Children's Books Published in America since 1850," University Microfilm no. 67–11. Philadelphia, Pa.: Temple University, 1966.

23 Sloan, Glenna Davis. *The Child as Critic: Teaching Literature in the Elementary School*. New York: Teachers College Press, 1975, p. 78.

24 Swanton, Susan. "Minds Alive: What and Why Gifted Students Read for Pleasure." *School Library Journal* 30 (March 1984): 99–102.

CHILDREN'S LITERATURE

Aardema, Verna. *Bringing the Rain to Kapiti Plain: A Nandi Tale.* Illustrated by Beatriz Vidal. Dial, 1981 (I:5–8). A cumulative tale from Kenya.

———. *Why Mosquitoes Buzz in People's Ears.* Illustrated by Leo and Diane Dillon. Dial, 1975 (I:5–9 R:6). A cumulative African folktale that tells the humorous reason for mosquitoes' buzzing.

Andersen, Hans Christian. *The Wild Swans.* Retold by Amy Ehrlich. Illustrated by Susan Jeffers. Dial, 1981 (I:7–12 R:7). Finely detailed illustrations develop a fantasy setting.

Ashabranner, Brent. *To Live in Two Worlds: American Indian Youth Today.* Photographed by Paul Conklin. Dodd Mead, 1984 (I:10+ R:7). Indian youth tell about their own lives.

Basile, Giambattista. *Petrosinella: A Neapolitan Rapunzel.* Illustrated by Diane Stanley. Warne, 1981 (I:7–10 R:6). An Italian version of "Rapunzel."

Benjamin, Carol Lea. *The Wicked Stepdog.* Crowell, 1982 (I:9–12 R:4). A twelve-year-old girl believes she has lost her father when he remarries.

Blos, Joan W. *A Gathering of Days.* Scribner's, 1979 (I:8–14 R:6). The fictional journal of a thirteen-year-old girl's life on a farm in New Hampshire in 1830.

Blume, Judy. *Blubber.* Bradbury, 1974 (I:10+ R:4). A girl becomes the victim in peer conflict.

Brooks, Bruce. *The Moves Make the Man.* Harper & Row, 1984 (I:10+ R:7). Basketball develops understanding between a black boy and a white boy.

Burnett, Frances Hodgson. *The Secret Garden.* Illustrated by Tasha Tudor. Lippincott, 1911, 1938, 1962 (I:8–12 R:7). A garden that hasn't been seen by anybody for ten years works its magic spell on a lonely girl, a sick boy, and an unhappy father.

Clapp, Patricia. *I'm Deborah Sampson: A Soldier in the War of the Revolution.* Lothrop, Lee & Shepard, 1977 (I:9+ R:6). Deborah disguises herself as a man and fights in the Revolutionary War.

———. *Witches' Children: A Story of Salem.* Lothrop, Lee & Shepard, 1982 (I:9+ R:6). A small group of girls creates witchcraft hysteria.

Cleary, Beverly. *Ramona and Her Father.* Illustrated by Alan Tiegreen. Morrow, 1977 (I:7–12 R:6). A warm and humorous story about Ramona, a second-grader, who tries to help her father through a trying period after he loses his job.

———. *Ramona Quimby, Age 8.* Illustrated by Alan Tiegreen. Morrow, 1981 (I:7–12 R:6). Humorous story about how a third-grader helps her family when her father returns to college.

Cooney, Barbara. *Chanticleer and the Fox.* A retelling of Geoffrey Chaucer's story. Crowell, 1958 (I:5–10 R:4). Chanticleer, the rooster with the most superior crow, and the sly fox trick one another.

Dabcovich, Lydia. *Sleepy Bear.* Dutton, 1982 (I:3–6 R:1). Illustrations and text follow a bear as he hibernates and wakes up in the spring.

de Paola, Tomie. *The Clown of God.* Harcourt Brace Jovanovich, 1978 (I:all R:4). A legend about a juggler who offers the gift of his talent and the miracle results.

Fritz, Jean. *The Cabin Faced West.* Illustrated by Feodor Rojankousky. Coward-McCann, 1958 (I:7–10 R:5). A young girl whose family has moved West dreams of going back home until she begins to see the frontier with new eyes.

———. *Make Way for Sam Houston.* Illustrated by Elise Primavera. Putnam's, 1986 (I:9+ R:6). The biography of a nineteenth-century hero.

———. *Traitor: The Case of Benedict Arnold.* Putnam, 1981 (I:8+ R:5). The life of the man who chose the British cause in the Revolutionary War.

Galdone, Paul. *The Greedy Old Fat Man.* Houghton Mifflin, 1983 (I:4–7 R:5). A cumulative American folktale.

George, Jean Craighead. *Julie of the Wolves.* Illustrated by John Schoenherr. Harper & Row, 1972 (I:10–13 R:7). An Eskimo girl lost on the North Slope of Alaska survives with the help of wolves.

Goble, Paul. *The Girl Who Loved Wild Horses.* Bradbury, 1978 (I:6–10 R:5). An American Indian girl loves wild horses, joins them in a flight during a storm, and finally goes to live with them.

Hudson, Jan. *Sweetgrass.* Tree Frog, 1984 (I:10+ R:4). A young Blackfeet girl grows up during the winter of the smallpox epidemic in 1837.

Jaquith, Priscilla. *Bo Rabbit Smart for True: Folktales From the Gullah.* Illustrated by Ed Young. Philomel, 1981 (I:all R:6). Four tales from the islands off the Georgia coast.

I = Interest by age range;
R = Readability by grade level.

Konigsburg, E.L. *Journey to an 800 Number*. Atheneum, 1982 (I:10 + R:6). A boy's lifestyle and ideas change drastically when he accompanies his father and a camel act.

Lang, Andrew. *The Red Fairy Book*. Illustrated by H.J. Ford and Lancelot Speed. McGraw-Hill, 1967 (I:all R:6). A recent edition of the classic fairytale book first published in 1890.

MacLachlan, Patricia. *Mama One, Mama Two*. Illustrated by Ruth Lercher Bornstein. Harper & Row, 1982 (I:5–7 R:2). A foster mother shares a story about a girl's real mother.

McKinley, Robin. *The Hero and the Crown*. Greenwillow, 1984 (I:10 + R7). Aerin faces the forces of evil during a quest.

Ness, Evaline. *Sam, Bangs & Moonshine*. Holt, Rinehart & Winston, 1966 (I:5–9 R:3). Sam's imagination almost costs a friend his life.

O'Brien, Robert C. *Mrs. Frisby and the Rats of NIMH*. Illustrated by Zena Bernstein. Atheneum, 1971 (I:8–12 R:4). Mrs. Frisby, a mouse, asks for help from a superior group of rats who are able to read.

O'Dell, Scott. *Island of the Blue Dolphins*. Houghton Mifflin, 1960 (I:10 + R:6). A girl survives alone on an island for eighteen years.

Orlev, Uri. *The Island on Bird Street*. Translated by Hillel Halkin. Houghton Mifflin, 1984 (I:10 + R:6). A twelve-year-old Jewish boy survives World War II in Warsaw.

Paterson, Katherine. *Bridge to Terabithia*. Illustrated by Donna Diamond. Crowell, 1977 (I:10–14 R:6). Terabithia is the special kingdom of a boy who wishes to be an artist and a girl different from the rest of her classmates.

————. *Jacob Have I Loved*. Crowell, 1980. (I:10 R:6). A girl overcomes the belief that her younger twin sister has stolen her birthright.

Potter, Beatrix. *A Treasury of Peter Rabbit and Other Stories*. Avenel, 1979 (I:2–7 R:5). Peter has an unhappy experience in Mr. McGregor's garden.

Raskin, Ellen. *The Westing Game*. Dutton, 1978 (I:10–14 R:5). Sixteen heirs are invited to solve the riddle surrounding the death of an eccentric millionaire.

Rylant, Cynthia. *When I Was Young in the Mountains*. Illustrated by Diane Goode. Dutton, 1982 (I:4–7 R:3). A young girl remembers special childhood experiences such as her grandmother's corn bread and going to the swimming hole.

Schlee, Ann. *Ask Me No Questions*. Holt, 1982 (I:10 + R:6). Two children discover the harsh reality of nineteenth-century England when they learn about hundreds of children who live in an asylum.

Seredy, Kate. *The White Stag*. Viking, 1937; Puffin, 1979 (I:10–14 R:7). Epic story of the Huns and Magyars as they migrate from Asia to Europe.

Sneve, Virginia Driving Hawk. *When Thunder Spoke*. Illustrated by Oren Lyons. Holiday, 1974 (I:8–12 R:4). A relic from the past influences a contemporary Sioux boy.

Speare, Elizabeth George. *The Witch of Blackbird Pond*. Houghton Mifflin, 1958 (I:9–14 R:4). Kit Tyler leaves her island home and rapidly comes into conflict with the Puritan way of life in colonial New England.

Sperry, Armstrong. *Call It Courage*. Macmillan, 1940 (I:9–13 R:6). A Polynesian boy travels alone in an outrigger canoe to overcome his fear of the sea.

Stoltz, Mary. *Cider Days*. Harper & Row, 1978 (I:8–12 R:6). A satisfying story about friendship between children who have different personalities and backgrounds.

Taylor, Mildred D. *Roll of Thunder, Hear My Cry*. Dial, 1976 (I:10 + R:6). A black Mississippi family in 1933 experiences humiliating and frightening situations, but retains its pride and independence.

Taylor, Theodore. *The Cay*. Doubleday, 1969 (I:8–12 R:6). A prejudiced young white boy and a black West Indian are shipwrecked on a barren Caribbean island.

Wilder, Laura Ingalls. *Little House in the Big Woods*. Harper, 1932 (I:8–12 R:6). The first book in a series about family life on the American frontier, told from a girl's viewpoint.

4

Artists and Their Illustrations

☐

VISUAL ELEMENTS: THE GRAMMAR OF
THE ARTIST

☐

ARTISTIC MEDIA

☐

ARTISTIC STYLE

☐

EVALUATING THE ILLUSTRATIONS IN
CHILDREN'S BOOKS

☐

OUTSTANDING ILLUSTRATORS OF
CHILDREN'S PICTURE BOOKS

MANY YOUNG CHILDREN MENTION THE illustrations when asked what attracted them to a book. The bright colors of an East African setting may entice them into an explorer's role as they search for camouflaged animals. Jagged lines and dark colors may excite them with the prospect of a dangerous adventure, while delicate lines and pastel colors may set them to dreaming about fairyland. The textures in illustrations may invite children to "feel" a bear's fur or an eagle's feathers. In these and many other ways, illustrations are an integral part of picture books for young children. Outstanding artists illustrate books for older children—such as Laura Ingalls Wilder's "Little House" series—but in such books the text can stand on its own. In picture books, however, the illustrations join the text in telling a story.

This chapter discusses the visual elements, media, and styles used by all illustrators of children's books, but focuses on the special requirements of picture-book illustration. It suggests criteria for evaluating illustrations in picture books, provides examples of high-quality books, and takes a closer look at several outstanding illustrators to see how they create memorable picture books.

VISUAL ELEMENTS: THE GRAMMAR OF THE ARTIST

Chapter three's discussion of literary elements and criteria for evaluating children's literature focused on the ways in which an author creates plot, characterization, setting, theme, and style using words. This chapter considers the ways in which an illustrator creates an appropriate visual representation of the techniques used by an author. The writer creates a compelling story by arranging words; the artist arranges visual elements to create a picture that will complement the writer's story. Edmund Burke Feldman (5) maintains that "a visual grammar based on artistic usage" (p. 218) consists of the elements of line, color, shape, and texture. When an artist organizes these elements into a unified whole, the artist has created a visual design that conveys meaning.

Line

Artists use line to suggest direction, motion, energy, and mood. Lines can be thin or wide, light or heavy, feathery or jagged, straight or curved.

According to Edmund Burke Feldman (5, p. 293), line is the most crucial visual element, for the following reasons:

1 Line is familiar to virtually everyone because of experience with drawing and writing.
2 Line is definite, assertive, intelligible (although its windings and patternings may be infinitely complex); it is precise and unambiguous; it commits the artist to a specific statement.
3 Line conveys meaning through its identification with natural phenomena.
4 Line leads the viewer's eye and involves the viewer in the line's "destiny."
5 Line permits us to do with our eyes what we did as children getting to know the world: handle objects and feel their contours. When handling an object we trace its outlines with our fingers. In our growth toward maturity, the outlines of things eventually become more important to us than their color, size, or texture as means of identifying them.

Feldman's discussion of the relationship between line and natural phenomena is especially interesting to people involved with children and with illustrations found in their literature. Experience with common natural phenomena may help children relate more meaningfully to works of art. Vertical lines, for example, look like trees in a windless landscape or like people who stand rather than move. Consequently, they suggest lack of movement. Horizontal lines, such as the surface of a placid lake or a flat horizon, suggest calm, sleep, stability, and an absence of strife. Most young children use a horizontal baseline in their drawings to convey the idea of the firm ground upon which they walk. Vertical lines and horizontal lines joined at right angles depict artificial elements that differ considerably from the natural world of irregular and approximate shapes. Two vertical lines connected by a horizontal line at the top give the feeling of a solid, safe place: a doorway, house, or building. In contrast, diagonal lines suggest loss of balance and uncontrolled motion—unless they form a triangle that rests on a horizontal base, which suggests safety. In both human design and nature, jagged lines have connotations of breakdown and destruction. Consequently, jagged lines suggest danger. Humans see curved lines as fluid because of their resemblance to the eddies, whirlpools, and concentric ripples in water. Because of

FLASHBACK

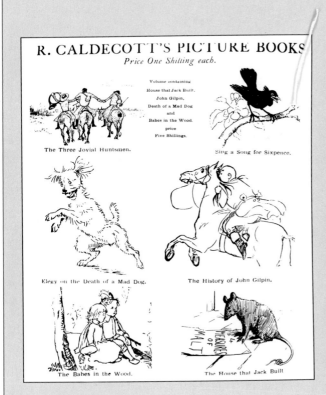

ILLUSTRATOR RANDOLPH CALDECOTT is credited with being the forefather of the modern picture book for children. Caldecott's illustrations made an enormous impact on children's book publishing in nineteenth-century England. His expert use of line created robust characters depicting humor, vitality, and action.

The books illustrated in this flashback are from a series of sixteen picture books, or "toy books," illustrated by Caldecott. William Cowper's *The History of John Gilpin* was published in 1878. The Caldecott Medal for excellence in illustrating children's books is embossed with a picture from this book. The remaining five books shown here were published between 1879 and 1900. Caldecott illustrated books by the top writers of his period, including Juliana Horatia Ewing *(Jackanapes)* and Washington Irving *(Old Christmas, Washington Irving's Sketch Book).* Caldecott's toy books, however, signaled the beginning of the high-quality picture books that would eventually be available for children.

this, circles and curved lines seem less definite and predictable than straight lines.

In *The Girl Who Loved Wild Horses*, Paul Goble uses line effectively to depict the natural setting and mood of a Native American folk tale, as well as to enhance plot development (see plate 10 in the color insert). Goble introduces the reader to the story's main character as she goes down to the river at sunrise to watch the wild horses. The illustration shows a calm, nonthreatening scene. The lines of the horses' legs are all vertical, since the horses are quietly drinking from the river. The calm is enhanced by their reflections in the water; not even a ripple breaks the tranquillity. On the next page, the girl rests in a meadow close to home. Goble illustrates the triangular shapes of teepees sitting securely on the ground. The text relates, however, that a rumble of thunder can be heard while the girl sleeps. The outlines of the clouds suggest this break in a peaceful afternoon: they are still rounded, but are also heavy, with protrusions jutting into the sky.

Movement in the story and in the illustrations becomes more pronounced as lightning flashes and the horses rear and snort in terror. Sharp lines of lightning extend from black, rolling clouds to the ground. Even the lines of the plants are diagonal, suggesting the power of the dangerous wind, as the horses gallop away in front of the storm. When night falls and the storm is over, the tired girl and horses stop to rest. Goble illustrates the hills with vertical lines connected by horizontal lines, suggesting the new feeling of safety and shelter under the moon and the stars.

In contrast to Paul Goble's depiction of familiar natural phenomena, the soft, delicate lines of Marcia Brown's illustrations for Charles Perrault's *Cinderella* create a mood and setting suggestive of a mythical kingdom that could only exist "once upon a time." The drawing of Cinderella's fairy godmother transforming her into a beautiful princess has an ethereal quality, as if the scene were floating on air. Because these illustrations seem to be almost as diaphanous and changeable as

The artist's use of delicate lines and colors suggests a magical setting for the story of Cinderella. (Illustration by Marcia Brown from *Cinderella*, by Charles Perrault. Copyright 1954 by Marcia Brown. Reprinted with the permission of Charles Scribner's Sons.)

clouds, the viewer is not surprised when a pumpkin turns into a coach and a rat becomes the driver of the coach. Even the illustrated architecture has this magical quality. Delicately curved windows, softly flowing draperies, and graceful pillars provide a fitting background for a favorite fairy tale.

Charles Keeping's illustrations for Alfred Noyes's ghost poem, *The Highwayman*, create quite a different mood. Stark black lines create ghostly, terrifying subjects and suggest the tale's sinister and disastrous consequences.

Color

A combination of line and color is perhaps the most common means artists use to convey mood and emotion in a picture book. Many human feelings about color are associated with natural phenomena. Reds, yellows, and oranges are most as-

sociated with fire, sun, and blood, and usually have "warm" or "hot" connotations: friendliness, high energy, anger. Blues, greens, and some violets are most associated with air, water, and plant life; their "coolness" or "coldness" can suggest moods and emotions ranging from tranquillity to melancholy.

One way to evaluate an illustrator's use of color is to consider how well the color language of the artist conveys or complements the mood, setting, characterization, and theme the writer develops in words. Marcia Brown's use of delicate line in her illustration of Charles Perrault's *Cinderella* is enhanced by her choice of colors. Soft pastels bring a shimmering radiance to the fairy-tale quality of the pictures. If she had chosen bright colors, the mood could have been destroyed. In contrast, Paul Goble uses bright colors and deep black, in addition to strong line, to illustrate a desert setting and the tension and movement of animals and forces of nature in *The Girl Who Loved Wild Horses*.

Color can depict the total mood of a story. In *Ox-Cart Man* Barbara Cooney visually translates Donald Hall's gentle story about a quieter time in American history by using soft pastels and muted hues of darker colors (see plate 14 in the color insert). Cooney portrays the hills of rural New England in the early 1800s as gentle curves of green, gray, and blue. The deep rusts, blues, and greens of the clothing look authentic for the time period. Cooney's color choices also show the passing of time. When the farmer begins his journey over hills and past villages, the whole countryside is aflame with the rusts and oranges of fall; by the time he reaches Portsmouth, the trees have only a few brown leaves. As he returns home, a soft, brown land awaits the first snowfall. The scene turns white in winter, then soft greens cover the hills before the trees explode with white and pink apple blossoms. Many readers of this book mention its feeling of tranquillity. One child said the pictures made her feel homesick; she had lived in an area that had hills, valleys, quiet farms, and visibly distinct seasons.

Warm, bright colors evoke the sun and heat of East Africa and the high energy of its wildlife in Jose Aruego and Ariane Dewey's *We Hide, You Seek* (see plate 17 in the color insert). The artists first researched animals living in Africa, then drew pictures that show the animals' spots, stripes, patterns, and colors in the natural environment, where animals camouflage themselves when they need to hide. Reddish-brown vines camouflage the giraffe's reddish-brown markings; tigers' spots make them hard to see against tree limbs; and yellow and green birds look just like leaves covered with sunlight. When the artists reveal the animals out of hiding, they use color to expose differences between the animals and their environment. The camouflages encourage children to search for the hidden animals before they turn the page to discover their locations. The mother of a two-year-old said that her son was so excited by this book he woke her up at midnight to read it again. This child appreciated color used as a puzzle for him to solve.

Maurice Sendak used alternating pages of color and black-and-white drawings in his illustrations for Janice Udry's *The Moon Jumpers*. Since the sun has set and cool night shadows surround the house, the sun is not important in this story and is shown in black and white. But the night has its own color scheme: the reader experiences deep green grass and a violet house bathed in the first glow from the pale yellow moon. A black-and-white giant looms toward the children who are jumping for the moon, but then it is only the shadow of the father walking across the grass.

Shape

Lines join and intersect to suggest the outlines of shapes, and areas of color meet to produce shapes. Organic shapes, irregular and curving, are common in nature and in handmade objects. Perfectly geometric shapes—exact, rigid, and often rectangular—usually have mechanical origins. As discussed earlier in relation to line, different shapes have different connotations to human beings. Illustrators may use organic, "free-form" shapes to convey anything from receptivity and imagination to frightening unpredictability; while geometric shapes in illustrations can connote complexity, stability, assertion, or severity (10).

Gerald McDermott, illustrator and author of *Arrow to the Sun*, uses traditional Native American patterns of line and color to create shapes that draw the reader into a desert world where humans, nature, and spiritual forces intertwine. Rich yellow, orange, and brown rectangles depict the pueblo home of the people. This building constructed by humans from natural materials is separated by a black void from the circular orange and yellow sun, which is the people's god.

The people worship this god in the kiva, a circular ceremonial chamber. A rectangular ray from the sun to the pueblo represents the spark of life that becomes the sun god's earthly son. He is illustrated as a black and yellow rectangle, while his mother's form has a more circular appearance. Black and yellow rectangles predominate in the illustrations until the son decides to search for his father and takes on the sun's power as

Geometric shapes and sunny colors give a powerful feeling to a Native American tale from the southwestern United States. (Illustration by Gerald McDermott from *Arrow to the Sun*. Copyright © 1974 by Gerald McDermott. Reprinted by permission of Viking Penguin, Inc.)

well as the rainbow of colors available to the sun. He returns to earth as an arrow, and his people, now illustrated in all the colors he has brought with him, celebrate with the dance of life.

A person's shape says much about a person's self-image. In *Crow Boy*, Taro Yashima uses line and color to create shapes that emphasize a small boy's growth from fright and alienation to self-confidence. Yashima first draws the boy as a small, huddled shape isolated from his classmates in white space. As an understanding teacher helps Crow Boy become more self-assured, his shape on the page becomes larger, more outreaching, and closer to the shapes of other characters. Yashima also stresses Crow Boy's transformation by outlining his new form with shades of white that suggest shimmering light.

Blair Lent uses shapes and colors inspired by Japanese art in his beautiful cut-cardboard illustrations for *The Wave*, by Margaret Hodges. Delicate geometric cuts convey the fragility of a village by the seashore, where the curving shapes of soft gold, gray, and brown waves at first roll gently across the page, in harmony with the human scene. Then the large, dark swirl of the tidal wave dominates the illustrations, and nature's unpredictable power demolishes human constructions. The final picture shows the tidy geometry of the rebuilt village and the sturdy rec-

tangular temple raised in honor of the wise farmer who had burned his crops to warn the people of the impending danger.

Ben Shahn's *The Shape of Content* (16) provides additional information on shape as an element in the graphic arts.

Texture

A child looking at an object for the first time usually wants to touch it to know exactly how it feels. Experience in touching rough bark, smooth skin, sharp thorns, and soft fur enables people to imagine how something feels without actually touching it. Book illustrators manipulate visual elements such as line, color, shape, and light and dark patterning to create textural imagery that satisfies our curiosity about how something feels.

Brian Wildsmith's *ABC* illustrates objects and animals in a way that visually communicates their texture. The short dark lines projecting from the outside of a nest look and "feel" like twigs, while a solid deep purple conveys the softness inside the nest. In another picture, short curling lines of white, green, and black evoke the texture of a yak's fur. Children touch this picture to see if it is real.

Owls with soft-textured feathers and big round eyes, peacocks ablaze with color, and roosters ready to fight are all found in Celestino Piatti's

The artist's use of contrasting color and line creates a feeling of texture. (From Celestino Piatti, *The Happy Owls*. Copyright © 1964 by Celestino Piatti (New York: Atheneum, 1964). Reprinted with the permission of Atheneum Publishers.)

Lines and color recreate the texture of a snowy owl of the far north. (Illustration by Leonard Baskin from *Under the North Star*, by Ted Hughes. Illustrations Copyright © 1981 by Leonard Baskin. Reprinted with permission of Viking Penguin, Inc.)

The Happy Owls. Piatti's forms are simple, and contrasts within the forms create a highly satisfactory visual design. The owls, for example, have fronts consisting of white feathers on a brown background, and wings and backs of brown, blue, and green feathers. In contrast, their eyes are large circular white orbs with red centers that stare directly at the viewer. Two thicknesses of black line assist in developing texture, form, and contrast. The owls' bodies and dominant eyes are outlined with wide black lines, while the lines in the feathers become finer and more delicate. Leonard Baskin's illustrations of northern birds and animals for Ted Hughes's *Under the North Star* convey the fluffiness of a snowy owl's camouflaging feathers, the powerful musculature be-

neath a grizzly bear's thick fur, and the crisp tension in the wings of an eagle poised for flight.

Organizing the Visual Elements: Design

Design, or composition, is the way in which an artist combines the visual elements of line, color, shape, and texture into a unified whole. When an illustration has overall unity, balance, and a sense of rhythm, viewers experience aesthetic pleasure; when an illustration's design is weak, viewers often feel that they are looking at an incomplete, incoherent, or boring picture.

Illustrators of children's books emphasize certain characters, develop main ideas, and provide background information. They also organize their illustrations so that the viewer can identify the most important element in a picture and follow a visual sequence within the picture. Artists show dominance in their work (5) by emphasizing size (the largest form is seen first); contrasting intense colors (an intense area of warm color dominates an intense area of cool color of the same size); placing the most important item in the center; using strong lines to provide a visual pathway for the eye; and emphasizing nonconformity (the viewer's eye travels to the exception or the item that is different). When evaluating illustrations in children's books, viewers should consider whether or not dominant images are consistent with the story's emphasis.

Tomie de Paola achieves balance through symmetry in his illustrations for *The Night before Christmas* (see plate 18 in the color insert). The strong vertical lines of the central fireplace are reinforced by hanging stockings, candles on the mantle, rows of trees in a picture over the mantle, and the legs of a chair and a table. To the left and the right of the fireplace, a person in a portrait looks toward the center of the illustration, where Santa stands on the hearth. For further emphasis, Santa's beard and the fur on his jacket are strikingly white against the rich reds and greens of the room.

Both authors and illustrators of children's books use repetition for emphasis. In illustrations, repetition can both create a sense of rhythm and provide a visual pathway for the eye. Virginia Lee Burton's illustrations are excellent examples of this technique. Burton's background in ballet and interest in the spatial concepts of dance may help account for her success in capturing rhythm and movement on paper (7). In

The Little House, for example, Burton shows the house sitting on a hill with trees on either side. A row of trees follows the curve of several hills behind the house. On each hill are progressively smaller trees, houses, people, and animals. Beyond the last curving line of trees, the text tells us, lies the city that will soon spread out and surround the Little House with traffic and skyscrapers.

Page design can provide a unifying quality throughout a picture book. Several artists develop visual continuity by framing text pages and/or illustrations. Trina Schart Hyman frames each text page in Margaret Hodge's *Saint George and the Dragon* with drawings of plants that are indigenous to the British Isles (see plate 12 in the color insert). Likewise, Hyman frames the text pages in Grimm's *Little Red Riding Hood* with complementary and unifying designs. Laszlo Gal borders each illustration in Eva Martin's *Canadian Fairy Tales* with lightly penciled sketches of objects chosen from the appropriate story. In *Hiawatha's Childhood*, derived from Henry Wadsworth Longfellow's famous poems, artist Errol Le

Repetition and line provide a visual pathway and suggest movement. (Illustration by Virginia Lee Burton from *The Little House*. Copyright 1942 by Virginia Lee Demetrios. Copyright renewed 1969 by George Demetrios. Reprinted by permission of Houghton Mifflin Company.)

The artist frames each illustration with sketches of objects found in the fairy tale. (© by Laszlo Gal 1984 from *Canadian Fairy Tales*, published by Douglas & McIntyre. In U.S., Dial Books, published as *Tales from the Far North*.)

Cain unifies the text by bordering each page with the tall birch trees shown in the cover illustration (see plate 6 in the color insert).

ARTISTIC MEDIA

The elements of line, color, shape, and texture are expressed through the materials and techniques the artist uses in illustrating a book. Ink, wood, paper, paint, and other media can create a wide variety of visual effects. Artist Harry Borgman (1) indicates a few of the possibilities in stating his own preferences: "If I want a bright, translucent wash tone, I would either use watercolor or dyes. For an opaque paint that is water resistant, I would use acrylics. If I want to draw a line that will dissolve a bit when water is washed over it, I would use a Pentel Sign pen" (p. 113). Borgman's remarks suggest the importance of an il-

Strong line and repetition in pen-and-ink drawings complement the story. (Illustration by Wanda Gág from *Millions of Cats*. Copyright 1928; renewed 1956, by Wanda Gág. Reprinted by permission of Coward, McCann & Geoghegan, Inc.)

lustrator choosing media and artistic techniques that are most appropriate for conveying the mood, setting, and characterization in a particular story.

Line and Wash

Many illustrations discussed in this chapter rely on lines drawn in ink to convey meaning and develop the mood of the story. For example, the crisp lines and repetition in Wanda Gág's pen-and-ink drawings help the reader visualize and believe in a world inhabited by *Millions of Cats*, each of which has special qualities appealing to an old man.

Ink is a versatile medium that may be applied with brush, sponge, cloth, or even the artist's fingers, as well as with pen. What often emerges, according to Norman Laliberté and Alex Mogelon (9) is "a terribly direct, strong, and uncompromising statement of the nature of our time and the talent of the artist. The very character of ink is challenging, demanding and a spur to experimentation and creativity. It is a bold form of expression, sparkling clean because it is so definite and positive" (p. 43).

In most cases, the author's words inspire the illustrator, but Tom Feelings's sensitive drawings of children inspired the accompanying poetry written by Nikki Grimes in *Something on My Mind*. Feelings's black-and-white drawings por-

tray the loneliness, fear, sorrow, and hope that children experience while growing up. The backgrounds in the illustrations are also superb: heavy black wrought-iron gates, lighter picket fences, an old Victorian house, and apartment-house steps all provide a believable setting and atmosphere for children's wishful thinking.

Artists also use varying qualities of pen-and-ink line to convey human emotions corresponding to characterizations in books. Ray Cruz's drawings for Judith Viorst's *Alexander and the Terrible, Horrible, No Good, Very Bad Day* communicate the very essence of a boy who experiences unhappy and frustrating emotions. The scowling expressions and hair on end convey the spirit of a boy who has lost his best friend and doesn't have any dessert in his lunch box.

Varying shades of water-thinned ink, sparely drawn figures, and textured paper suggest a traditional Japanese setting appropriate for Sumiko Yagawa's *The Crane Wife*. Illustrator Suekichi Akaba's traditional Japanese painting techniques complement the story of a transformed crane who rewards a poor farmer for his care, but returns to animal form when the young man becomes greedy and breaks his promise.

Watercolor, Acrylic, Pastel, and Oil

Watercolor can be applied in various ways—from thin, transparent washes to thick applications of

Opaque tempera over colored inks creates a three-dimensional effect. (From TATTIE'S RIVER JOURNEY by Shirley Rousseau Murphy, pictures by Tomie de Paola. Pictures copyright © 1983 by Tomie de Paola. Reproduced by permission of the publisher, Dial Books for Young Readers.)

pure pigment. The choice depends upon the effect the artist wishes to create. Boris Zvorykin uses gouache, a method of painting with opaque watercolors, to evoke the rich colors of traditional costume and a magical setting in *The Firebird and Other Russian Fairy Tales*, edited by Jacqueline Onassis (see plate 11 in the color insert).

Tomie de Paola's illustrations for Shirley Rousseau Murphy's *Tattie's River Journey* exemplify the effect of opaque tempera paint applied over colored inks. De Paola proceeded from a detailed pencil drawing, to an application of brown-black inks, to painting with colored inks, and finally to an application of opaque tempera. Some of the illustrations take on a three-dimensional quality as areas of colored ink show through the paint.

The effects of three color media—watercolors, pastels, and acrylics—are seen in Leo and Diane Dillon's illustrations for Margaret Musgrove's *Ashanti to Zulu: African Traditions*. Vibrantly colored jewelry and designs on artifacts contrast with the soft shades of the flowing garments. The river in the illustration that depicts the Lozi people is so transparent that the bottom of the boat shimmers through the water. In other pictures, the sky vibrates with heat from the sun, or jewel-like tones express the breathtaking beauty of exotic birds and plants.

Full-page oil paintings create a somber mood in Paul O. Zelinsky's illustrations for *Hansel and Gretel*, as told by the Brothers Grimm (see plate 20 in the color insert). Zelinsky's woods are a menacing place where evil is likely to exist.

Woodcuts

Woodcuts are among the oldest artistic media in both Western and Eastern culture. In the fifteenth century, the black-and-white woodcuts of the German artist Albrecht Dürer brought this medium to a new level of sophistication in Europe. As chapter two indicated, the first printed books, including the earliest books for children, were illustrated with black-and-white woodcuts. Later, Japanese artists pioneered in the creation of full-color woodcuts that inspired other artists in Europe and North America, such as the famous French artist Paul Gauguin.

To create a woodcut, an artist draws an image on a block of wood and cuts away the areas around the design. After rolling ink onto this raised surface, the artist presses the woodblock against paper, transferring the image from the block to the paper. Color prints require a different woodblock for each color in the picture. Woodcuts can be printed in many colors with varying degrees of transparency, and the grain and texture of the wood can add to the effect of the composition.

The bold lines and colors of woodcuts create a simplicity often desired by illustrators of folktales. Antonio Frasconi is a well-known woodcut artist who uses this medium effectively in books such as *The Snow and the Sun*, a South American folk rhyme. Strong lines create the image of cold wind blowing across the land, a feeling heightened by Frasconi's choice of colors: the power of

1. Maurice Sendak was inspired by the watercolors in William Blake's paintings in creating his illustrations for this book. Illustrations from *Outside Over There* by Maurice Sendak. Copyright © 1981 by Maurice Sendak. By permission of Harper & Row, Publishers, Inc.

2.

3.

Emeke was so happy and excited he almost forgot to thank Good Snake as he hurried back to his goats.

Good Snake called after him. "Be sure you find the bark and bamboo before the rains come."

Turtle laughed. "He, he, he. Beware! Things without wings don't fly."

The dark heavy clouds threatened to overflow. Emeke hurried toward his goats, wondering how he would find bark and bamboo before it rained. He touched the rock and remembered: *The rock will help you.*

4.

2. This engraving of *A Continuation of the Comic Adventures of Old Mother Hubbard and Her Dog* is an example of the illustrations found in early books for children. Reproduced by permission of the Department of Special Collections, Research Library, University of California, Los Angeles.

3. Informational books may dramatize content and present concepts through moveable pages. From *Leonardo da Vinci,* by Alice and Martin Provensen. Copyright © 1984 by Alice and Martin Provensen. Reprinted by permission of Viking Penguin Inc.

4. Contrasts between almost transparent colors and deeper shades enhance the mythical quality of a fantasy. Illustration by Leo and Diane Dillon from *Brother to the Wind* by Mildred Pitts Walter. Copyright © 1985 by Diane and Leo Dillon. By permission of Lothrop, Lee, & Shepard Books (a division of William Morrow & Company).

5. Finely detailed lines enhance the dreamlike quality of this fairy tale setting. Excerpted from *The Wild Swans*, retold by Amy Ehrlich, illustrated by Susan Jeffers. Illustrations copyright © by Susan Jeffers. Used by permission of The Dial Press.

When he heard the owls at midnight,
Hooting, laughing in the forest,
"What is that?" he cried in terror;
"What is that," he said, "Nokomis?"
And the good Nokomis answered:
"That is but the owl and owlet,
Talking in their native language,
Talking, scolding at each other."

6.

7.

8.

6. Birch trees frame the sides of each illustration and provide a continuity of both setting and design. From *Hiawatha's Childhood* by Henry Wadsworth Longfellow. Illustrations by Errol LeCain. Illustrations copyright © 1984 by Errol LeCain. Reprinted by permission of Farrar, Straus, & Giroux, Inc.

7. Vivid colors and simple shapes attract the reader's attention in this wordless picture book. Reprinted with permission of Macmillan Publishing Co., Inc. from *Changes, Changes* by Pat Hutchins. Copyright © 1971, Pat Hutchins.

8. Strong lines of the woodcuts and bold colors enhance the folklore quality of this cumulative tale. From the book *Drummer Hoff* by Barbara and Ed Emberley. Copyright © 1967 by Edward R. Emberley and Barbara Emberley. Published by Prentice-Hall Inc., Englewood Cliffs, N.J. 07632.

THE·PEACOCK'S·COMPLAINT
THE Peacock con-
-sidered it wrong
That he had not the nightingale's
song;
So to Juno he went,
She replied, "Be content
With thy having, & hold thy
fool's tongue!"
DO·NOT·QUARREL·WITH·NATURE·

9. Walter Crane's illustrated texts, characterized by subdued colors, strong design, and rich detail, are credited with marking the beginning of the modern era in color illustrations. From *The Baby's Own Aesop.* Reproduced by permission of the Department of Special Collections, Research Library, University of California, Los Angeles.

In an instant the herd was galloping away like the wind. She called to the horses to stop, but her voice was lost in the thunder. Nothing could stop them. She hugged her horse's neck with her fingers twisted into his mane. She clung on, afraid of falling under the drumming hooves.

10. Line and color combine to create a feeling of impending danger and terror. Notice the heavy black clouds with circular lines and jagged lightning. The diagonal lines of the horses' legs and manes complement the mood. Copyright © 1978 from the book *The Girl Who Loved Wild Horses* by Paul Goble. Reprinted with permission of Bradbury Press, Inc., Scarsdale, N.Y. 10583.

11. Reproductions of Boris Zvorykin's original gouache paintings (a method of painting with opaque watercolors) enrich this Russian folktale. An illustration from *The Firebird and Other Russian Fairy Tales*. Copyright © 1978 by Viking Penguin Inc. Reproduced by permission of Viking Penguin Inc.

12. Page design is enhanced by plain-colored borders on illustrated pages and drawings of plants and scenes bordering text pages. From *Saint George and the Dragon*. Retold by Margaret Hodges and illustrated by Trina Schart Hyman. Illustration copyright © 1984 by Trina Schart Hyman.

"Today we fish in the tub!"

14.

13. The artist's choice of rich colors and costuming detail capture a humorous royal environment. From *KING BIDGOOD'S IN THE BATHTUB*, text copyright © by Audrey Wood, illustrations copyright © 1985 by Don Wood. Reprinted by permission of Harcourt Brace Jovanovich, Inc.

14. Use of color and line draws the reader's attention to the farmer and the ox. From *The Ox-Cart Man* by Donald Hall, illustrated by Barbara Cooney. Illustrations copyright © 1979 by Barbara Cooney Porter. Reprinted by permission of Viking Penguin, Inc.

15. Bright, jeweled tones suggest magical abilities of an unusual fish in this German folktale. Illustration from *The Fisherman and His Wife* by the Brothers Grimm, translated by Elizabeth Shub, illustrated by Monika Laimgruber. Copyright © 1978 by Artemis Verlag. Reprinted by permission of Greenwillow Books (A Division of William Morrow & Company).

15.

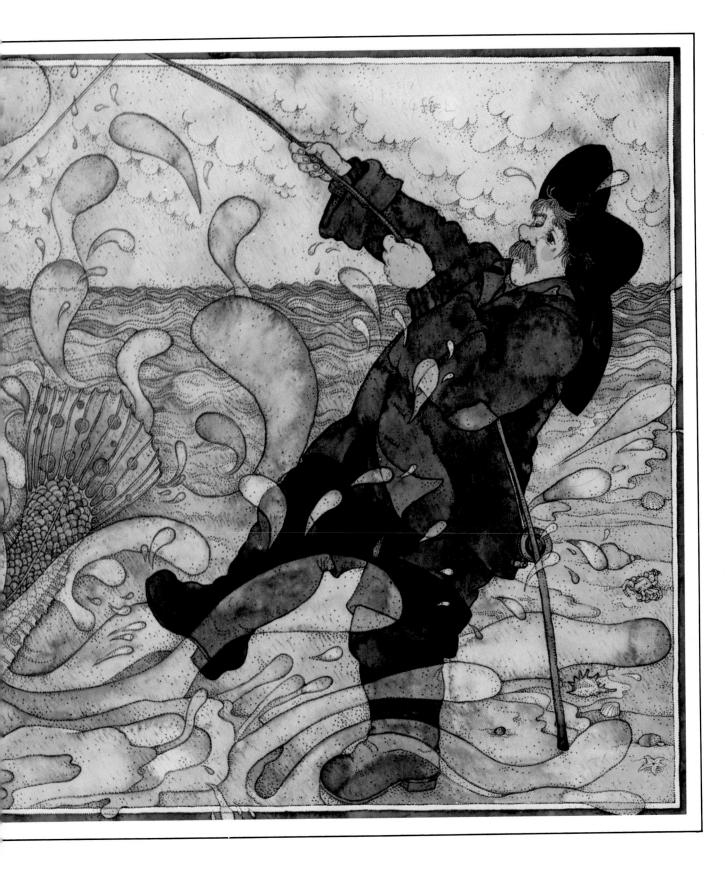

16.

16. The fragile beauty of a forest scene is shown in the artist's delicate use of line. Illustration from *The Nightingale* by Hans Christian Andersen, translated by Eva Le Gallienne, illustrated by Nancy Ekholm Burkert. Pictures copyright © 1965 by Nancy Ekholm Burkert. By permission of Harper & Row, Publishers, Inc.

17. Warm, vivid colors of red, yellow, orange are appropriate for an African setting. The color contrasts help readers locate the hidden animals. Illustration "Ready or not, here I come!" from *We Hide, You Seek* by Jose Aruego and Ariane Dewey. Copyright © 1979 by Jose Aruego and Ariane Dewey. Reprinted by permission of Greenwillow Books (A Division of William Morrow & Company).

18. de Paola achieves balance through symmetry. Notice the lines of the trees in the painting, the pictures on either side of the fireplace, and the fireplace decorations. Copyright © 1980 by Tomie de Paola. Reprinted from *The Night Before Christmas* by permission of Holiday House, Inc.

19. Use of color photographs taken during actual space explorations clarify the content of an informational book. From *Jupiter* by Seymour Simon. Published by William Morrow & Company, Inc., 1985. Photograph courtesy of NASA.

20. Dark, somber tones in full-page oil paintings create an appropriately menacing setting for a dramatic folktale. From *Hansel and Gretel*. Illustrated by Paul O. Zelinsky and retold by Rika Lesser. Illustrations copyright © 1984 by Paul O. Zelinsky.

Ready or not, here I come!

17.

19.

20.

the sun is shown in red; the snow and the wind are black and white. Woodcuts also bring a simple power to the Mother Goose characters found in Frasconi's *The House that Jack Built*. Gail Haley uses woodcuts to illustrate her version of an African folktale *A Story, a Story*, where the grain of the wood replicates the texture of native huts and communicates the earthy nature of a traditional setting.

Collage

Collage—a word derived from the French word *coller*, meaning "to paste" or "to stick"—is a recent addition to the world of book illustration. Pasting and sticking are exactly what artists do when using this technique. Any object or substance that can be attached to a surface can be used to develop a design. Artists may use cardboard, paper, cloth, glass, leather, metal, wood, leaves, flowers, or even butterflies. They may cut up and rearrange their own paintings or use paint and other media to add background. When photographically reproduced in a book, collages still communicate a feeling of texture.

Eric Carle, a popular artist of picture books for young children, develops his collages through a three-step process (8). He begins by applying acrylic paints to tissue paper. Next, he uses rubber cement to paste down the paper into the desired designs. Finally, he applies colored crayon to provide any needed accents. Carle is known for his striking, colorful storybooks. *The Very Hungry Caterpillar* won the American Institute of Graphic Art's award for 1970. Carle's painted collages add vibrant colors to *Twelve Tales from Aesop*. In addition to brightly colored collage illustrations, his most recent books include pop-ups or other features that encourage children to interact with the book. For example, readers work tabs that move a honeybee's wings, stinger, and tongue in *The Honeybee and the Robber*.

Another artist who illustrates primarily with collage is Ezra Jack Keats. In *Peter's Chair*, lace looks very realistic as it cascades from the inside of a cloth-covered bassinet. On the same page, pink wallpaper with large flowers provides the background for baby sister's room. Keats also combines paints and collage in his illustrations, a combination effectively used in *The Trip*. These illustrations have a three-dimensional quality appropriate for a story about a boy who builds his old neighborhood within a box and then visits it

in his imagination. Photographs are used in the collage illustrations in Keats's *Regards to the Man in the Moon*. These illustrations suggest the diversity that can be found in one medium.

Marcia Brown uses collage and paint to match the mood of Blaise Cendrars's *Shadow*. Brown's strong, dark images of the nighttime forest and her wispy ghosts strongly reinforce the spell cast by a storyteller in Cendrars's text.

A heavily textured look results when an artist uses leaves, wood, grasses, shells, and fur in collage illustrations. In *Grandmother* Jeannie Baker combines these and many other natural and artificial substances to create a story about a garden that is almost a jungle, a house full of treasures, and a grandmother and child who share many experiences.

Collage is discussed again on pages 185–186 to show how the collage medium and collage-illus-

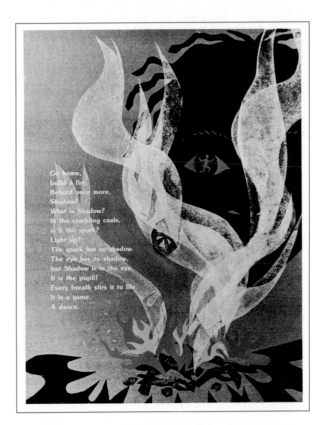

Collage and paint combine to create a shadowy, supernatural setting. (Illustration from *Shadow* by Marcia Brown. Illustrations © 1982 Marcia Brown. Reprinted with the permission of Charles Scribner's Sons.)

trated books can be used to stimulate children's interest in literature and art experiences.

ARTISTIC STYLE

Every artist has a personal style that distinguishes his or her artistic vision from that of other artists, serving as the "signature" of a distinct individual. Numerous individuals, however, gravitate toward similar ways of making visual statements through the use of line, color, shape, and texture. The many different styles of visual art identified by art critics and historians are a subject too complex for this text to discuss in detail. For our purposes, however, we may consider two very general categories of artistic style, the *representational* and the *abstract*.

Representational Art

Representational art, sometimes also called "realistic art," depicts subjects as they are commonly seen in everyday life. Representational artists do not necessarily attempt to create photographically exact images of their subjects, but instead create compositions that clearly refer to people, objects, or natural phenomena and that are not highly unrealistic. Many of the paintings and sculptures most familiar to us—Leonardo da Vinci's *Mona Lisa*, Auguste Rodin's *The Thinker*—are representational in style.

Since the first books for children were illustrated, the pictures in most children's books have been representational, as examples throughout this text show. Realistic imagery helps children identify with and learn more about things in their own environments, giving them a familiar base from which to expand their understanding of the world. In Susan Jeffers's line-and-wash illustrations for *Three Jovial Huntsmen*, for example, children can easily identify a leaf on the tip of a dog's tongue and two humans walking through the woods. At the same time, Jeffers's use of line encourages children to extend their visual perceptions in order to discover three deer hidden among the trees.

Lynd Ward's illustrations for *The Biggest Bear* are excellent examples of representational art creating the details of a realistic story. The reader can almost feel the rough shingles and unpainted siding on the buildings, and wheat looks ripe enough to harvest. When the bear cub runs in to claim the mash prepared for the chickens, sev-

Varying line qualities create a realistic woodland background and hide the animals. (Illustration by Susan Jeffers from *Three Jovial Huntsmen*. Copyright 1973. Reprinted with permission of Bradbury Press, Scarsdale, NY 10583.)

eral frightened chickens look as if they will fly off the page.

Author-illustrator Holling Clancy Holling combines imaginative fiction with factual information in beautifully illustrated books that take their themes from North American history and geography. Holling's detailed realistic illustrations draw older children into both new adventure and new learning. In *Paddle-to-the-Sea*, a Native American boy in the Canadian wilderness carves a wooden canoe and "paddle person," which he launches on a journey from Lake Superior to the Atlantic Ocean. *Seabird* is an ivory gull, carved by a young sailor on a whaling vessel, that accompanies several generations of one American family on their ocean voyages around the world. In each book, full-page realistic paintings in color encourage the reader to enter the story's different settings, while detailed black-and-white drawings on the text pages show, for example, how a sawmill turns logs into boards and how volcanoes in the ocean create islands.

Modern book illustrators, like most twentieth-century artists, have been profoundly influenced by stylistic innovations that have occurred over the last hundred years. Nineteenth-century French artist Claude Monet was among those who initiated a new approach to representational art known as *Impressionism* (originally a derogatory term applied by a disapproving contemporary critic). These artists departed from the tradition of representing the world in complex detail and instead focused on the play of light over objects in the natural environment. Usually working from outdoor subjects, they experimented with breaking up colors and shapes to create an *impression* of the scintillating, changeable quality of light at different moments (15, p. 294).

Thomas Locker's oil paintings for *Where the River Begins* reveal Impressionist influences on this modern artist. Locker's magnificent landscapes shimmer with sunlight emerging through mist, the moon illuminating rushing water, and the reflection of sunset on billowing clouds.

Expressionism, a later stylistic development in representational art, focused on using visual elements to express the artist's deepest inner feelings. Expressionist paintings by artists such as Vincent van Gogh and Edvard Munch reverberate with the rhythm of intense emotion expressed through emphatic color, texture, and movement of line. Such art begins to move away from the representational into the more abstractly symbolical. (Later twentieth-century artists such as Jackson Pollock developed a style known as *Abstract Expressionism*.)

Expressionistic influences are vividly evident in Toshi Maruki's illustrations for her book *Hiroshima No Pika* (The Flash of Hiroshima). Maruki's use of color and shape reinforces the emotional impact of horrific devastation, as mother and child experience the after effects of the atomic bomb. Swirling red flames pass over the forms of fleeing people and animals. Black clouds cover the forms of huddling masses and destroyed buildings. A more realistic rendering of this holocaust would probably be far less powerful.

Leonard Fisher's expressionistic paintings complement the mood of Myra Livingston's poems in *A Circle of Seasons*. Whites and pinks suggest apple blossoms and dogtooth violets. Greens and yellows symbolize the warming sun, the rain, and the wakening earth in spring. Hot sun reds, watery blues, and corn-ripened yellows seem appropriate for paintings accompanying summer

An oil painting reflecting Impressionist style depicts a shimmering landscape and a tranquil mood. (From WHERE THE RIVER BEGINS by Thomas Locker. Copyright © 1984 by Thomas Locker. Reproduced by permission of the publisher, Dial Books for Young Readers.)

poems, while the changing moods of autumn are suggested by oranges, reds, and shimmering frost against a dark blue sky. In winter paintings white squares against shades of blues and purples suggest ice crystals and snowflakes converging on a bleak winter world. The wintry mood is enhanced as hoarfrost, icicles, and frosted windowpanes gleam in silvery needle shapes against a dark blue background. The seasonal circle is completed when the text concludes with the first poem and painting.

Abstract Art

Some abstract art takes ordinary things as its subject, but emphasizes certain characteristics of a subject by changing or distorting the usual image. Pablo Picasso's abstract paintings, for example, reduce people and familiar objects to angular forms and shifting planes. The work of other modern artists has become so abstract—focusing on pure form and representing no actual person, place, or thing—that art experts describe it as *nonrepresentational*. For example, Piet Mondrian's famous geometrical compositions in oil show the artist attempting visual statements that are "objective, impersonal, and universal" in their implications (15, p. 39).

The elimination of representational images characteristic of abstract art (13, p. 208) is evident in Beverly Brodsky McDermott's illustrations for *The Golem*, a Jewish legend about a rabbi who uses a magic spell to create a man out of clay. "As I explored the mysteries of the Golem," says McDermott (11, Foreword), "an evolution took place. At first, he resembled something human. Then he was transformed. His textured body became a powerful presence lurking in dark corners, spilling out of my paintings. In the end he shatters into pieces of clay-color and returns to the earth. All that remains is the symbol of silence."

Both expressionist and abstract influences are apparent in Leo Lionni's illustrations. Lionni uses watercolor, textured collage, and thickly painted surfaces to recreate the feeling of a watery world in *Swimmy*. This is not a realistic world of easily discernible water plants and animals: seaweed has the texture of painted doilies, and fish are only suggestive outlines. Vivid colors and strong shapes predominate in Lionni's *Pezzettino*, the story of a small orange shape who is convinced that he is a piece of someone else. Pezzettino's

Muted colors and irregular shapes suggest an underwater kingdom. (Illustration by Leo Lionni from *Swimmy*, by Leo Lionni. Copyright © 1968 by Leo Lionni. Reprinted by permission of Pantheon Books, a division of Random House, Inc.)

search takes him to larger shapes composed of many smaller squares of solid color.

Janice Hartwick Dressel (4) presents arguments for and against using abstract art in children's books. She concludes that exposing children to such sophisticated, symbolical art may encourage children's higher levels of thinking and enhance their aesthetic response to all art.

EVALUATING THE ILLUSTRATIONS IN CHILDREN'S BOOKS

The collaborative process of creating a picture book for children makes special demands on an artist. Even when the illustrator and the author are the same person, "the artist" is a partner to "the writer" and must place his or her talents in the service of a certain story. Adults should consider the following criteria when evaluating the illustrations in picture books for children:

ISSUE

❖

Are Children's Book Illustrators Creating Books for Adults Rather Than for Children?

ERIC A. KIMMEL[1] CONtends that a noticeable trend in children's literature is "the appearance of a growing number of exotically illustrated, high-priced picture books that appear to be far too unusual or sophisticated to attract many children" (p. 41). In this category of picture books he identifies Wayne Anderson's *Ratsmagic;* Chris Van Allsburg's *The Garden of Abdul Gasazi* and *Jumanji;* Molly Bang's *The Grey Lady and the Strawberry Snatcher;* Graham Oakley's *Magical Changes;* David Macauley's *Unbuilding;* most of Harlin Guin's books; and Maurice Sendak's *Outside Over There.* Kimmel argues that books such as these are being written and illustrated to appeal to adult critics rather than to children. He speculates that children will ignore these books in favor of books by Ezra Jack Keats, Leo Lionni, and Tomie de Paola and books such as Virginia Lee Burton's *Mike Mulligan and His Steam Shovel,* Robert Mc-Closkey's *Blueberries for Sal,* and Maurice Sendak's *Where the Wild Things Are.*

Students of children's literature may look at these books, talk to librarians about children's preferences, and share the books with children. How do children of different ages respond to the pictures and the text? Does the way in which adults share illustrated books with children affect how children respond to them? What do children like about the pictures and the text? What do you like about the pictures and the text?

[1]Kimmel, Eric A. "Children's Literature without Children." *Children's Literature in Education* 13 (Spring 1982): 38-43.

1 The illustrator's use of visual elements—line, color, shape, texture—and of certain artistic media should complement the text's development of plot, characterization, setting, and theme.

2 The design of the illustrations—individually and throughout an entire book—should reinforce the text and convey a sense of balance and unity that stimulates the viewer's aesthetic appreciation.

3 The artistic style chosen by the illustrator should enhance the author's literary style.

4 The illustrations should help the reader anticipate the unfolding of a story's action and a story's climax.

5 The illustrations should portray convincing character delineation and development.

6 The illustrations should be accurate in historical, cultural, and/or geographical detail, consistent with the text.

OUTSTANDING ILLUSTRATORS OF CHILDREN'S PICTURE BOOKS

Thus far this chapter has mentioned many outstanding illustrators of picture books for children. A close look at several artists reveals the wide range of excellence in children's book illustration and the ways in which individuals fluent in artistic grammar create visual narratives that appeal to young children.

Nancy Ekholm Burkert

According to Michael Danoff (2), Nancy Ekholm Burkert "is an artist whose work is rooted in the particulars of nature. Her drawings capture the specifics of the natural world with awe-inspiring precision and clarity. For her, the natural world is as miraculous as any realm of fantasy. . . . In her eyes, currents of the metaphysical flow through the particulars of the physical world; the natural is one with the super-natural" (p. 1).

Burkert uses pen, brush, and colored inks to express her attunement with natural rhythms in a realistic style. Before illustrating *Snow White and the Seven Dwarfs*, a book-length version of the folktale told by the Brothers Grimm, Burkert visited Germany's Black Forest and read books about the Middle Ages. Consequently, Burkert's Snow White walks through a mysterious forest that the viewer can almost smell and feel, as sunlight filters down through the trees. The dwarfs' house is historically authentic in every detail: carved wood, pewter utensils, woven rugs, and a warm fireplace. (Burkert researched the details of this house at the Unterlinden Museum in Colmar, West Germany.) Realistic as these illustrations are, they also create a setting and mood in which magic spells and poisoned apples do not seem out of place.

Burkert's love of detailed line and delicate color creates a suitably magical mood and setting in her illustrations for Eva LeGalliene's translation of Hans Christian Andersen's *The Nightingale* (see plate 16 in the color insert). The text tells that the emperor lives in a beautiful palace, built of finest porcelain, but so fragile that one must move carefully so as not to disturb it. In Burkert's illustrations, soft pink and white blossoms covering the trees and mist rising gently from the sea are the background for the detailed drawings of the palace. Burkert creates a unity for the whole book by illustrating pages of text with blossoms, branches, and plants that gently curve around the margins.

Barbara Cooney

Barbara Cooney's illustrations for Donald Hall's *Ox-Cart Man* (discussed earlier; see plate 14 in the color insert) use gentle colors and rounded shapes to evoke the peaceful countryside of early nineteenth-century New England. In Cooney's illustrations for *Chanticleer and the Fox*, however, bold black lines create a strutting, vain rooster in the earlier portion of the book and a frightened, humble one as the story reaches its climax in the life-and-death struggle between Chanticleer and his enemy, the fox.

Cooney is skilled in using artistic techniques that best complement a particular text. Her illus-

THROUGH THE EYES OF AN ILLUSTRATOR

Illustrating and Books

TOMIE DE PAOLA, illustrator of over seventy books and winner of the Caldecott honor award, discusses early art experiences and the importance of doodling.

I AM A DOODLER. IN fact, I *love* to doodle. I always have. I keep pads of scratch paper and black and red fine-line markers by the telephones, at my drawing table, on my desk, in my carry-on bag when I fly; and when I was teaching, I never went to a meeting (faculty, committee, etc.) without my handy pad and markers.

Growing up, coloring books were absent from our house . . . at least, in my room. My tools were plain paper, pencils and my trusty crayolas. After all, I was going to be an artist when I grew up. And besides, my own drawings and doodles seemed to be far more interesting to me, and those around me, than the simple coloring book images. (My mother also admitted recently that plain paper was lots cheaper.)

I learned at an early age that there was a definite difference between out-in-out drawing and serious doodling. A drawing had more structure, more direction. A definite idea was usually the beginning of a drawing. For example, I might say, "I think I will do a drawing of a girl ice skating, wearing a fancy Ice Follies-type costume." (Yes, the Ice Follies were around way back then.) Then the problem would be to try to do a drawing that coincided with my original idea or vision.

Doodles were (and are) totally different. I would just put

trations for Margot Griego et al.'s *Tortillitas Para Mama* recreate the varied settings associated with Spanish nursery rhymes. Warm browns depict the interior of a Mexican home, cool blues warmed by the shining moon suggest a village by the water, and warm fuchsia pinks reflect the warmth of a mother and father sharing a quiet time with their baby.

Color also creates an appropriate mood in Cooney's illustrations for Delmore Schwartz's *"I Am Cherry Alive," the Little Girl Sang*. Shades of gold depict the pleasure and well-being of a little girl observing a tree covered with autumn leaves, while a "blue mood" is reflected in a mist-covered valley seen by the light of a pale moon.

Tomie de Paola

Tomie de Paola has illustrated, or written and illustrated, over seventy books, including traditional folktales from Italy, Scandinavia, and Mexico; informational books; and realistic fiction.

De Paola's illustrations for *The Clown of God* reveal the influence of two pre-Renaissance artists, Giotto and Fra Angelico, whose simplicity and strength of line de Paola admires: "I almost re-duce features to a symbol. And yet I think of my faces as good and warm. I try to show expression in very few lines" (6, p. 299). For *The Clown of God*, de Paola first penciled in the lines, then went over the sketches with raw sienna water-proof ink, a second brown pencil line, and brown ink. He completed the artwork with watercolors. Strong, simple lines are also very important in de Paola's *Songs of the Fog Maiden*. The addition of cool blues and greens creates a mood in which a fog maiden could easily move from her day garden to her night one and accomplish magic along the way.

De Paola also values his theater experience and makes use of it in his illustrations: "There are so many ways picture books are like theater-scenes, settings, characterization. A double page spread can be like a stage" (6, p. 300). De Paola's illustrations often have the symmetry of a stage setting, with actions that appear to take place in front of a backdrop. *Giorgio's Village*, for example, a pop-up book that recreates an Italian Renaissance village, is itself a stage-like setting in which windows open and tabs allow movement. Other books show the influence of films. In *Watch Out*

pencil to paper and see what happened. All sorts of interesting images would result. I might start out not really concentrating on my doodle but on what else I was doing at the time. Talking on the phone was a very good activity for doodling. Late at night under the covers with a flashlight and listening to the radio was another activity that produced more terrific doodles—some actually on sheets rather than on paper. The "state of the art" doodles of this early period though appeared as if by magic on my arithmetic papers. There would be columns of figures copied from the blackboard and before I knew it, the paper would be covered with pictures with no room for the answers. My teachers—well, at least, a few of them—were *not* amused. They warned me. I'd never learn to add, subtract, multiply, etc. They were right, but for me as an artist, the doodling proved to be a far more important activity. I was able to buy a calculator with a royalty check, and now, I have an accountant.

"Meeting doodles," especially faculty meeting doodles, proved to be among the most valuable for me. It was during a college faculty meeting that was about the same issues the previous dozen meetings had been about, that "Strega Nona" appeared on my pad. I didn't know who she was at that mo-ment, but a few months on my studio wall, and she soon let me know all about herself.

I've just opened a drawer and found some doodles that were done several years ago. (I stash doodles in different drawers so they can show up later and surprise me. My assistant saves all the phone-call doodles for me. My mother and an old friend both have doodles of mine in special drawers, waiting for the day they can cash in on them.)

The new found doodles are on the wall of my studio. There is a rather fetching sheep and two classy cats, dressed to kill. Who knows . . . someday . . . But remember! You read about them here first!

for the Chicken Feet in Your Soup, the action of the story and in the illustrations starts before the title page, which becomes both a part of the narrative and part of the illustrated action. In these and other ways, de Paola's large body of work demonstrates his belief that children should be exposed to many types of visual imagery.

Leo and Diane Dillon

Leo and Diane Dillon's strong interest in the folklore of traditional peoples is evident in their beautifully illustrated, award-winning books. Their work reflects careful research into the decorative motifs of various cultures and helps recreate and preserve traditional ways of life.

The text for Mildred Pitt Walter's *Brother to the Wind* is rich in folklore, symbols, and dreams. The Dillons use light and dark, soft pastels and deep colors, to show the contrast between a boy's mythical quest to fly and the earthbound unbelievers who are sure he will fail (see plate 4 in the color insert). In one illustration, the wind, which makes it possible for the boy to fly, is a transparent woman whose color and shape blend into the pale cloudy sky. Viewers are given the impression that only they and the boy, not the doubting villagers, can see the wind. The Dillons also use strong and soft shades of black and white to contrast myth and reality in the illustrations for Virginia Hamilton's *The People Could Fly: American Black Folk Tales*. Their illustrations for Verna Aardema's *Why Mosquitoes Buzz in People's Ears* recreate the mood and setting of a traditional African folktale. In every case, careful research precedes the Dillons' illustrations.

Roger Duvoisin

Drawings with strong black lines interspersed with pages highlighted in warm colors have proven successful for Roger Duvoisin, whose flair for design results from his varied art background. Duvoisin first specialized in mural painting and stage scenery, then began designing posters and illustrations. He became involved in textile design, and then entered the world of children's illustrations. Duvoisin has illustrated alphabet books, concept books, and picture storybooks. In *See What I Am*, he introduces children to the primary and secondary colors and shows how colors are used to make book illustrations.

Louise Fatio's *The Happy Lion* has become a favorite with children in part because of Duvoisin's expressive use of black-and-white line drawings to create an appealing lion with a long mane and a switching tail. Some of the illustrations in this book resemble staging for a play. A slightly opened door reveals the face of a curious, surprised lion. He peeks out and is framed by trees on either side as he walks down a path directly toward the reader. When the lion enters the town, Duvoisin helps pick up the pace of the story by showing more detail and motion in his drawings: women's purses stand in the air and groceries are flung around as frightened people run in diagonal lines away from the lion.

Susan Jeffers

Susan Jeffers emphasizes texture and motion of line to convey differences between reality and fantasy in her realistic, but magical illustrations. Her skilled use of line is especially apparent in her illustrations for Hans Christian Andersen's *The Wild Swans* (see plate 5 in the color insert). Strong dark lines depict forest, hillside, and stormy sea. More delicate, cross-hatched lines depict the sunshine and plants within the fragrant cedar grove. When a beautiful fairy enters the girl's dreams to guide her in freeing her brothers, Jeffers shows the contrast between the reality of the characters sleeping on the ground and the fairyland of the palace in the clouds. The girl herself is in warm greens and browns, while the fairy and the fairy castle are almost transparent blues and grays.

Jeffers uses variety of line to depict similar distinctions of nature and the mythical spirit world in her illustrations for Henry Wadsworth Longfellow's *Hiawatha*. Other books in which Jeffers develops mood and setting through detailed line drawings include Robert Frost's *Stopping by Woods on a Snowy Evening*, the Brothers Grimm's *Hansel and Gretel*, Eugene Field's *Wynken, Blynken and Nod*, and Charles Perrault's *Cinderella*, adapted by Amy Ehrlich.

Ezra Jack Keats

Ezra Jack Keats combines collage, paint, and empathy for children's needs and emotions in compositions that portray inner-city life. Sometimes this environment is peaceful, as in *The Snowy Day*, where Keats uses brilliantly white torn paper to convey the snow covering chimneys and rooftops as Peter looks out on a fresh white world. Later, shadowy blue footprints bring the text and the illustrations together as the reader is asked to look at Peter's footprints in the snow. Simple, rounded shapes depict snowbanks, and buildings are rectangles of color in the background. Peter's simple, red-clad figure stands out against the snowy background.

Keats evokes quite a different mood with collage and paint in *Goggles!* Here two children confront harsher realities, as they try to escape from bigger boys who want their possessions. The colors are dark, and the collages include thrown-away items that one might find in back alleys. Keats shows the frightening big boys as almost featureless black silhouettes. In one picture, a hole in a piece of wood frames the scene as the two small boys look through it and plan how to get home.

In other books—such as *Louie, The Trip*, and *Peter's Chair*—Keats's illustrations complement the loneliness, daydreams, or jealousy described in the text.

Robert Lawson

It is highly unusual for one person to win both the Caldecott Medal for excellence in children's book illustration and the Newbery Award for excellence in children's literature. Author-illustrator Robert Lawson was the first person to achieve this distinction. Lawson's philosophy about illustrating children's books suggests the reasons for his success. According to Annette H. Weston (17), Lawson believed that adults should not condescend to children in either word or picture. Rather than having limited tastes or understanding, Lawson felt, children are actually less limited than adults: "They are, for a pitifully few short years, honest and sincere, clear-eyed and open minded. To give them anything less than the utmost that we possess of frankness, honesty and sincerity is, to my mind, the lowest possible crime" (17, p. 257).

Lawson's illustrations are both witty and honest. He researched Spanish landscapes, architecture, bullfighting, and costumes before illustrating Munro Leaf's *The Story of Ferdinand*. His black-and-white line drawings strongly complement an amusing story about the problems connected with "being different," as a young bull prefers to smell flowers rather than prepare to fight in the bullring. At one point in the story, for example, Lawson uses powerful black lines to show Ferdinand finally acting like a fierce and en-

ergetic bull; but this occurs only because Ferdinand sits on a bee. Lawson's drawings ably convey the variety of human emotions in the story, whether they are experienced by human characters or by Ferdinand himself: the matador struts with pride, the picadores cringe in terror, and Ferdinand simply sits in the ring refusing to fight until he can return to his favorite tree and flowers.

Robert McCloskey

Robert McCloskey's illustrations present the real world of boys, girls, families, and animals. Detailed black-and-white drawings depict the settings in most of his books, although McCloskey also uses color to evoke the very essence of an island susceptible to forces of nature in *Time of Wonder*. In that book, McCloskey's watercolors first depict a serene world. When gentle rain approaches, the painting is so transparent that the first thing seen is a thin mist descending. Later, diagonal lines of raindrops break the surface of the peaceful water, and light fog surrounds two children as they experience the whispering sound of growing ferns. The island is not always serene, however. A hurricane bends the lines of the trees, as the illustrations themselves almost move on the page.

Black-and-white drawings illustrate McCloskey's delightful *Blueberries for Sal*. The child, whether stealing berries from a pail or mistakenly following a mother bear instead of her own mother, looks as if she could walk right off the page.

Clare Turlay Newberry

Recreating the many moods and motions of cats requires both a remarkable understanding of feline temperament and careful observation. Children often say that Clare Turlay Newberry must have watched cats for a long time in order to draw them so realistically and lovingly. The children are correct. In *Drawing a Cat* (14), Newberry explains that because cats do not stay in the same position for long, the artist must spend many hours observing and draw hundreds of sketches before successfully "capturing" cats as she does in her humorous books.

Newberry's cat illustrations—such as the totally believable *Widget*—suggest the feeling of fur. Widget's fur is fluffy when she is calm and contented, but stands on end in sharp spikes when

The artist's black-and-white illustrations create a moment of surprise for human and animal characters. (Illustrations by Robert McCloskey from *Blueberries for Sal*. Copyright 1948, © renewed 1976 by Robert McCloskey. Reprinted by permission of Viking Penguin Inc.)

danger in the form of a teddy bear or a dog named Pudge threatens her well-being. These effects result from painting with charcoal-gray watercolor on wet paper, then adding details with crayons after the paper is dry. While Newberry's illustrations are in grays, blacks, and browns, they forcefully demonstrate the text's characterization of the animals.

Alice and Martin Provensen

Color, symmetry, and effective use of space are noteworthy elements in the work of Alice and Martin Provensen. Recent illustrations by the Provensens, whose collaborative efforts include more than fifty books, reflect the world in earlier times or the world of fantasy. The Provensens create a feeling of flying through space in their book about the first flight across the English Channel, *The Glorious Flight across the Channel with Louis Bleriot, July 25, 1909*. Consecutive illustrations proceed from a close-up of the plane before it soars to a wide-angle view of the small plane surrounded by clouds and sky. The corresponding text reveals that Louis Bleriot is alone, lost in a world of swirling fog. The illustrators' use of space and color reinforces this mood of danger and exhilaration.

The impact of symmetry in design is felt in several of the Provensens' illustrations for Nancy Wil-

lard's *A Visit to William Blake's Inn: Poems for Innocent and Experienced Travelers*. In one illustration, for example, the Wonderful Car hovers over buildings that provide a visual center for the car; the steps of the flying vehicle lead the viewer's eye toward the passengers; and the two smaller sets of propeller blades balance the larger center blade.

Other books demonstrating the Provensens' skill in recreating historical periods include *Birds, Beasts and the Third Thing: Poems by D. H. Lawrence*; *A Peaceable Kingdom: The Shaker Abecedarius*; and *Leonardo da Vinci* (see plate 3 in the color insert).

Maurice Sendak

Time magazine has called Maurice Sendak "the Picasso of children's books." Sendak's artistic versatility in using color, line, and balance to create evocative moods and settings is evident in the many books he has illustrated or written and illustrated, including Janice Udry's *The Moon Jumpers*, previously discussed in this chapter. One of Sendak's primary aims in illustrating a text is to make "the pictures so organically akin to the text, so reflective of its atmosphere, that they look as if they could have been done in no other way. They should help create the special world of the story . . . creating the air for a writer" (12, p. 352).

This special relationship between text and illustration may be most apparent in Sendak's *Outside Over There* and *Where the Wild Things Are*. Sendak (3) has described the steps he took in creating the illustrations for *Outside Over There*, which he considers his best and most significant children's book (see plate 1 in the color insert). One of his first concerns was drawing ten-year-old Ida holding a baby. In order to produce realistic body postures, he made photographs of a child holding a baby. The baby kept slipping out of the child's arms, so that the clothes on both children drooped and became disheveled. These effects of body movements are replicated in the book's illustrations. Sendak referred to watercolors by the British poet and artist William Blake for inspiration in choosing colors that communicate the story's setting, mood, and characterization: "The colors belong to Ida. She is rural, of the time in the country when winter sunsets have that certain yellow you never see in other seasons. There's a description of women's clothing, watered silk, and that's what those skies are like—moist, sensuous, silken, almost transparent—the color I copied in the cape Ida wears and in other things showing up against soft mauve, blue, green, tan—all part of the story's feeling" (3, p. 46).

The illustrations for *Where the Wild Things Are* are totally integrated with the text and play a cru-

cial role in plot development and characterization, as well as setting. When Max is banished to his room for bad behavior, the room gradually becomes the kingdom of the wild things, with trees growing naturally out of the bedposts and the shag rug turning into grass. As the plot progresses, the illustrations cover more and more of the page; when Max becomes king of the wild things, six pages of illustrations are uninterrupted by text. Sendak's use of line creates a believably mischievous boy and humorous, but forceful wild things with terrible rolling eyes and horrible gnashing teeth.

Peter Spier

In Peter Spier's illustrations, carefully drawn lines recreate each stone in the London Bridge, express the movement and tension of a battle at sea, fill Noah's ark with animals, or present the changing American scene in authentic historical detail. Children find new details each time they look at Spier's *Noah's Ark*. Comparing an early drawing with a later one, for example, reveals that two snails are the last animals to board the ark and the last animals to leave. *The Fox Went Out on a Chilly Night* shows a country setting of farms, covered bridges, cemeteries, town squares, and colonial buildings. Spier illustrates the origins of

Symmetry of design directs the viewer's eye toward the distant garden. (Illustration by Chris Van Allsburg from *The Garden of Abdul Gasazi*. Copyright 1979 by Chris Van Allsburg. Reprinted by permission of Houghton Mifflin Company.)

our national anthem in *The Star-Spangled Banner*, with the drama and color of rockets glaring in the sky. All Spier's illustrations are based on considerable research and touring of historic sites.

Spier uses pen-and-ink and full-color wash illustrations in a series of "village" books designed in the shape of buildings such as supermarkets, schools, and fire stations. The detailed drawings in these books stimulate discussion as young children identify familiar objects and compare Spier's village with their own communities.

Chris Van Allsburg

Chris Van Allsburg's *The Garden of Abdul Gasazi*, *Jumanji*, and *The Mysteries of Harris Burdick* demonstrate the effectiveness of black and white illustrations. Both line and subtle shading focus attention along a visual pathway in the illustrations for *The Garden of Abdul Gasazi*. In one picture, the main character is framed by a central doorway. On either side of the doorway, a bright statue against dark leaves points down a black tunnel toward the circle of white representing the garden in which the story line develops. Use of such symmetry is one way artists create balance in their designs.

Van Allsburg's illustrations for *The Wreck of the Zephyr* are examples of the artist's use of line to create movement, and of his use of line and color to convey mood and emotion. As the story begins, rolling waves and billowing dark clouds suggest movement and the ominous forces of angry sea and sky. Later, the mood changes to fantasy, and the artist uses color to create a calm sea sparkling with light, a fantasy harbor town seen through shadows, soft clouds tinged with sunset, and a star-studded sky. Students may compare Van Allsburg's use of line and shading in his black and white illustrations with his use of line and color in *The Wreck of the Zephyr* and in *The Polar Express*.

SUMMARY

A high-quality picture book must be concerned with both art and writing. Both media bear the burden of narration. The illustrations should help create the mood and setting of the story, provide convincing character delineation, help the reader anticipate action, and be consistent with the text and accurate in historical, cultural, or geographical detail.

While the writer develops style by arranging words, the artist uses visual elements to create compositions designed to convey meaning and give pleasure. Lines, since they are used to suggest direction, motion, energy, and shapes, are the most crucial visual element used by artists.

Artists most often use a combination of line and color to convey mood and emotion in picture books. Different colors, associated with various natural phenomena, have different emotional connotations to human beings, which artists can use to elicit responses from the viewer that complement the text.

Shapes can also be used to express many different moods. Ranging from free form and imaginative to rigidly geometric and precise, shapes can suggest a variety of meanings to the viewer.

Illustrators may create a feeling of texture by manipulating shape, line, color, and light and dark patterning.

When artists organize visual elements into a unified picture, they create a design or composition. Artists can organize their illustrations to identify the most important element in a picture and to encourage the viewer to follow the visual sequence within it. Size, color intensity, central location, strong lines, and nonconformity can all be used for emphasis.

The elements of line, color, shape, and texture are influenced by the artistic media that artists choose to create illustrations. Woodcuts, collage, inks, watercolors, and other paints create different visual effects and moods.

Artistic styles may be viewed in terms of two general categories, the representational and the abstract. Representational art depicts everyday things in a way that is more or less realistic. Abstract art either depicts everyday things in a selectively exaggerated way or does not represent everyday things at all. Impressionism is a form of representational art that attempts to create the impression of light playing across the surface of objects and creating changeable images. Expressionism, another form of representational art, focuses on using emphatic line, color, shape, and texture to express an artist's deepest emotions.

The chapter concluded with a closer look at several outstanding illustrators of children's picture books.

Suggested Activities for Understanding Artists and Their Illustrations

☐ With some of your peers, select one of the following criteria for evaluating the illustrations and narrative portions of a picture book, find examples of books that clearly exemplify the criteria, and share them with the class: (a) The illustrations should help the reader anticipate both the action of the story and the climax (for example, Blair Lent's illustrations for Margaret Hodges's *The Wave* or Maurice Sendak's illustrations for *Where the Wild Things Are*). (b) The pictures should help create the basic mood of the story (Paul Goble's *The Girl Who Loved Wild Horses* or Marcia Brown's illustrations for Charles Perrault's *Cinderella*). (c) The illustrations should portray convincing character delineation and development (Taro Yashima's *Crow Boy*). (d) All pictures should be accurate and consistent with text (Barbara Cooney's illustrations for Donald Hall's *Ox-Cart Man*).

☐ Consider the ways in which lines are related to natural phenomena. Look carefully at the illustrations in several books. Are there examples in which vertical lines suggest lack of movement; horizontal lines suggest calmness or an absence of strife; vertical and horizontal lines connected at the top suggest stability and safety; diagonal lines suggest motion; and jagged lines symbolize danger?

☐ Compare the moods and settings suggested by the use of color in illustrations of Native American folk tales (for example, Gerald McDermott's *Arrow to the Sun* and Paul Goble's *The Girl Who Loved Wild Horses*) with the moods and settings suggested by the use of color in illustrations of fairy tales (Marcia Brown's *Puss in Boots* and Nancy Ekholm Burkert's illustrations for Eva LeGalliene's translation of Hans Christian Andersen's *The Nightingale*).

☐ Select a fairy tale such as "Cinderella" or "Snow White" that has been illustrated by several artists. Compare the artists' use of line, color, and shape to create the mood and setting of the story.

☐ Read the narrative portion of several picture storybooks. Evaluate whether or not dominant images in the illustrations complement the emphasis in the text. Choose an example that complements the text and one that does not; share the examples and your rationale for choosing them with the class.

☐ With a group of your peers, select one medium available to artists, such as woodcuts, collage, inks, watercolors, acrylics, pastels, and so forth. Investigate how different artists use the medium in picture book illustrations. Share your findings with the class.

☐ With some of your peers, investigate how artists use representational and abstract artistic styles. Consider the styles used by illustrators of several picture books. Does the style complement the intended mood of the text in each case? Share your findings with the class.

☐ Choose an outstanding illustrator of children's books. Find as many of the illustrator's works as you can. Search for the artist's use of the elements of art—line, color, shape, and texture—and the various media and styles used by the artist. Compare the books. Does the artist use a similar style in all works, or does this style change with the subject matter of the text? Compare earlier works with later ones. Are there any changes in the use of artistic elements, style, or media?

References

1 Borgman, Harry. *Art and Illustration Techniques*. New York: Watson-Guptill, 1979.

2 Danoff, Michael. Quoted in *The Art of Nancy Ekholm Burkert*, edited by David Larkin. New York: Harper & Row, 1977.

3 Davis, Joann. "Trade News: Sendak on Sendak." As told to Jean F. Mercier. *Publishers Weekly*, April 10, 1981, pp. 45–46.

4 Dressel, Janice Hartwick. "Abstraction in Illustration: Is It Appropriate for Children?" *Children's Literature in Education* 15 (Summer 1984): 103–112.

5 Feldman, Edmund Burke. *Varieties of Visual Experience*. New York: Abrams, 1972.

6 Hepler, Susan Ingrid. "Profile, Tomie de Paola: A Gift to Children." *Language Arts* 56 (March 1979): 269–301.

7 Kingman, Lee. "Virginia Lee Burton's Dynamic Sense of Design." *Horn Book* 46 (October 1970): 449–60.

8 Klingberg, Delores. "Profile—Eric Carle." *Language Arts* 54 (April 1977): 445–52.

9   Laliberté, Norman, and Mogelon, Alex. *The Reinhold Book of Art Ideas*. New York: Van Nostrand Reinhold, 1976.

10 MacCann, Donnarae, and Richard, Olga. *The Child's First Books: A Critical Study of Pictures and Texts*. New York: Wilson, 1973.

11 McDermott, Beverly Brodsky. *The Golem*. Philadelphia: Lippincott, 1976.

12 Moritz, Charles. *Current Biography Yearbook*. New York: Wilson, 1968.

13 Munro, Thomas. *Form and Style in the Arts: An Introduction to Aesthetic Morphology*. Cleveland: Case Western Reserve, 1970.

14 Newberry, Clare Turlay. *Drawing a Cat*. London: The Studio Limited, 1940.

15 Preble, Duane. *Art Forms*. New York: Harper & Row, 1978.

16 Shahn, Ben. *The Shape of Content*. Boston: Harvard University Press, 1957.

17 Weston, Annette H. "Robert Lawson: Author and Illustrator." *Elementary English* 47 (January 1970): 74–84.

Additional References

Bader, Barbara. *American Picture Books from Noah's Ark to the Beast Within*. New York: Macmillan, 1976.

Mahony, Bertha E.; Latimer, Louise Payson; and Folmsbee, Beulah. *Illustrations of Children's Books, 1744–1945*. Boston: Horn Book, 1947.

Townsend, John Rowe. *Written for Children*. New York: Lippincott, 1975.

CHILDREN'S LITERATURE

Aardema, Verna. *Why Mosquitoes Buzz in People's Ears*. Illustrated by Leo and Diane Dillon. Dial, 1975 (I:5–9 R:6) An African cumulative tale.

Andersen, Hans Christian. *The Nightingale*. Retold by Eva LeGalliene. Illustrated by Nancy Ekholm Burkert. Harper & Row, 1968 (I:6–12 R:8). The fairy tale beautifully illustrated.

———. *The Wild Swans*. Retold by Amy Ehrlich. Illustrated by Susan Jeffers. Dial, 1981 (I:7–12 R:7). Finely detailed illustrations develop a fantasy setting.

Anno, Mitsumasa. *Anno's Britain*. Philomel, 1982 (I:all). A wordless book illustrating a traveler's journey throughout Great Britain.

———. *Anno's Italy*. Collins, 1980 (I:all). A wordless book illustrating a traveler's journey throughout Italy.

Aruego, Jose, and Dewey, Ariane. *We Hide, You Seek*. Greenwillow, 1979 (I:2–6). Colors and lines create a camouflage book that allows children to look for hidden animals.

Baker, Jeannie. *Grandmother*. Deutsch, 1978 (I:5–8). Collages show a visit with Grandmother.

Baker, Olaf. *Where the Buffaloes Begin*. Illustrated by Stephen Gammell. Warne, 1981 (I:8+ R:7). Illustrations with soft, irregular shapes add power to a Native American legend.

Bemelmans, Ludwig. *Madeline*. Viking, 1939, 1977 (I:4–9 R:5). Madeline lives in Paris with eleven other little girls and has an appendectomy.

———. *Madeline in London*. Viking, 1961, 1977 (I:4–9 R:3). Madeline and eleven little girls visit London.

Brown, Marcia. *Once a Mouse*. Scribner's, 1961 (I:3–7 R:6). Woodcuts provide powerful illustrations for a fable from India.

———. *Puss in Boots*. Scribner's, 1952 (I:5–8 R:5). Fine lines suggest a magical setting.

Burton, Virginia Lee. *The Little House*. Houghton Mifflin, 1942 (I:3–7 R:3). Repetition creates a sense of rhythm in illustrations.

Carle, Eric. *Catch the Ball*. Philomel, 1982 (I:3–6). A string attached to a ball encourages children's vocabulary development.

———. *The Honeybee and the Robber: A Moving/Picture Book*. Philomel, 1981 (I:3–6). A brightly colored pop-up allows children to move the wings of a bee and a butterfly.

I = Interest by age range;
R = Readability by grade level.

———. *Let's Paint a Rainbow*. Philomel, 1982 (I:3–6). Rainbow colors help children learn eight basic colors.

———. *Twelve Tales From Aesop*. Philomel, 1980 (I:4–8). Painted collage illustrations enhance tales for young listeners.

———. *The Very Hungry Caterpillar*. Crowell, 1971 (I:2–7). A colorful collage picture book that presents the life cycle of the caterpillar who eats his way through the pages.

Cendrars, Blaise. *Shadow*. Illustrated by Marcia brown. Scribner's, 1982 (I:all). A highly illustrated version of an African poem.

Cooney, Barbara. *Chanticleer and the Fox*. Adapted from Geoffrey Chaucer. Crowell, 1958 (I:5–10 R:4). Chanticleer the rooster and a sly fox trick one another.

———. *The Little Juggler*. Adapted and illustrated by Cooney. Hastings, 1982 (I:all). An orphan offers his juggling talent as a Christmas gift to the Virgin Mary.

Crossley-Holland, Kevin, Adapter. *Beowulf*. Illustrated by Charles Keeping. Oxford, 1982 (I:10+ R:6). Strong lines depict the power of a heroic character.

Dana, Doris. *The Elephant and His Secret*. Illustrated by Antonio Frasconi. Atheneum, 1974 (I:3–7 R:4). The elephant takes the shadow of a mountain for his body in this tale told in both Spanish and English.

de Paola, Tomie. *Big Anthony and the Magic Ring*. Harcourt Brace Jovanovich, 1979 (I:5–9 R:3). Big Anthony uses Strega Nona's magic ring to turn himself into a handsome young man.

———. *Charlie Needs a Cloak*. Prentice-Hall, 1973 (I:3–6 R:4). A simple information book tells in a humorous way how a shepherd shears sheep, cards and spins wool, weaves and dyes the cloth, and then sews a cloak.

———. *The Clown of God*. Harcourt Brace Jovanovich, 1978 (I:all R:4). A legend about a juggler and a miracle.

———. *The Friendly Beasts: An Old English Christmas Carol*. Putnam, 1981 (I:3–8 R:2). The Christmas carol is illustrated in large colorful drawings.

———. *Giorgio's Village*. Putnam, 1982 (I:all). A pop-up book illustrating an Italian Renaissance village.

———. *Helga's Dowry: A Troll Love Story*. Harcourt Brace Jovanovich, 1977 (I:5–9 R:4). Helga leaves the world of trolls to earn a dowry.

———. *Songs of the Fog Maiden*. Holiday, 1979 (I:3–8 R:5). The fog maiden lives in a castle between the sun and the cold.

———. *Watch Out for the Chicken Feet in Your Soup*. Prentice-Hall, 1974 (I:3–7 R:2). Joey is embarrassed by his grandmother's old-fashioned ways until his friend shows great admiration for her.

———. *When Everyone Was Fast Asleep*. Holiday, 1976 (I:3–8 R:6). The fog maiden's cat brings two children out into an enchanted night.

Duvoisin, Roger. *See What I Am*. Lothrop, Lee, and Shepard, 1974 (I:5–9). Primary colors are introduced and then mixed to produce secondary colors.

Emberley, Barbara. *Drummer Hoff*. Illustrated by Ed Emberley. Prentice-Hall, 1967 (I:3–7 R:6). A cumulative rhyme depicting in woodcuts all the people associated with firing a cannon.

Fatio, Louise. *The Happy Lion*. Illustrated by Roger Duvoisin. McGraw-Hill, 1954 (I:3–7 R:7). A lion who lives in a zoo discovers that people aren't so friendly when he visits them in town.

Field, Eugene. *Wynken, Blynken and Nod*. Illustrated by Susan Jeffers. Dutton, 1982. The classic poem in a newly illustrated edition.

Frasconi, Antonio. *The House That Jack Built*. Crowell, 1958 (I:3–6). A cumulative folktale.

———. *The Snow and the Sun*. Harcourt Brace Jovanovich, 1961 (I:5–10 R:3). A South American folk rhyme written in Spanish and English.

Frost, Robert. *Stopping by Woods on a Snowy Evening*. Illustrated by Susan Jeffers. Dutton, 1978 (I:all). A highly illustrated version of the poem.

Gág, Wanda. *Millions of Cats*. Coward-McCann, 1928 (I:3–7 R:3). An old woman's desire for a pretty cat results in a fight among trillions of cats.

———. *Snow White and the Seven Dwarfs*. Coward-McCann, 1938 (I:5–9 R:6). The popular fairy tale.

———. *Tales from Grimm*. Coward-McCann, 1936 (I:6–9 R:4). Sixteen tales from Grimm including "Hansel and Gretel," "Rapunzel," and "The Frog Prince."

Goble, Paul. *The Girl Who Loved Wild Horses*. Bradbury, 1978 (I:6–10 R:5). An American Indian girl loves wild horses, joins them in a flight during a storm, and finally goes to live with them.

Griego, Margot C.; Bucks, Betsy L.; Gilbert, Sharon S.; and Kimball, Laurel H. *Tortillitas Para Mama*. Illustrated by Barbara Cooney. Holt, Rinehart and Winston, 1981 (I:3–7). Nursery rhymes in Spanish and English.

Grimes, Nikki. *Something on My Mind*. Illustrated by Tom Feelings. Dial, 1978 (I:all). Beautifully illustrated poems about the joys, fears, hopes, and sorrows of growing up.

Grimm, Brothers. *Hansel and Gretel*. Illustrated by Susan Jeffers. Dial, 1980 (I:5–9 R:6). Illustrations convey the dark mood of this classic folk tale.

———. *Hansel and Gretel*. Retold by Rika Lesser. Illustrated by Paul O. Zelinsky. Dodd, Mead, 1984 (I:all R:6) Another beautifully illustrated version of the folk tale.

———. *Little Red Riding Hood*. Illustrated by Trina Schart Hyman. Holiday House, 1983 (I:6–9 R:7) Richly bordered text pages add to the visual effect.

———. *Snow White and the Seven Dwarfs*. Illustrated by Nancy Ekholm Burkert. Farrar, Straus & Giroux, 1972 (I:7–12 R:6). Carefully researched illustrations complement this fairy tale.

Haley, Gail E. *A Story, a Story*. Atheneum, 1970 (I:6–10 R:6). An African tale about a spider man's bargain with Sky God.

Hall, Donald. *Ox-Cart Man*. Illustrations by Barbara Cooney. Viking, 1979 (I:3–8 R:5). Subtle illustrations complement a tale about a New England farmer in the early 1800s.

Hamilton, Virginia. *The People Could Fly: American Black Folktales*. Illustrated by Leo and Diane Dillon. Knopf, 1985 (I:9+ R:6) Black-and-white illustrations reinforce the folktale quality of the book.

Hodges, Margaret. *Saint George and the Dragon*. Illustrated by Trina Schart Hyman. Little, Brown, 1984 (I:9+ R:7) The classic tale beautifully illustrated.

———. *The Wave*. Illustrated by Blair Lent. Houghton Mifflin, 1964 (I:5–9 R:5). Woodcuts illustrate a Japanese folktale about a wise old man who saves his people from a tidal wave.

Holling, Holling Clancy. *Paddle-to-the-Sea*. Houghton Mifflin, 1941 (I:7–12 R:4). A Native American boy carves a canoe and places it where it will flow into Lake Superior.

———. *Seabird*. Houghton Mifflin, 1948 (I:7–12 R:4). A carved gull travels

with several generations of one family.

Hughes, Ted. *Under the North Star*. Illustrated by Leonard Baskin. Viking, 1981 (I:all). Poems about northern animals with realistic illustrations.

Jeffers, Susan. *Three Jovial Huntsmen*. Bradbury, 1973 (I:4–8). A highly illustrated version of the nursery rhyme.

Keats, Ezra Jack. *Dreams*. Macmillan, 1974 (I:3–8 R:3). Everyone dreams about Robert's handmade mouse.

———. *Goggles!* Macmillan, 1969 (I:5–9 R:3). Two boys escape from bullies.

———. *Louie*. Greenwillow, 1975 (I:3–8 R:2). Other children surprise Louie with a puppet.

———. *Peter's Chair*. Harper & Row, 1967 (I:3–8 R:2). Peter overcomes jealousy about a new baby sister.

———. *Regards to the Man in the Moon*. Scholastic Four Winds, 1981 (I:4–8 R:3). Two children build a spaceship out of junk and take an imaginary ride.

———. *The Snowy Day*. Viking, 1962 (I:2–6 R:2). Peter experiences a great snowfall.

———. *The Trip*. Greenwillow, 1978 (I:3–8 R:2). Louie is lonesome in a new neighborhood.

Krauss, Ruth. *A Hole Is to Dig*. Illustrated by Maurice Sendak. Harper & Row, 1952 (I:2–6 R:2). Illustrations of children depict children's definitions for such things as brothers, mud, and mountains.

Lawrence, D.H. *Birds, Beasts and the Third Thing: Poems by D. H. Lawrence*. Illustrated by Alice and Martin Provensen, Viking, 1982 (I:all). Illustrations depict English scenes from Lawrence's youth.

Lawson, Robert. *Ben and Me*. Little, Brown, 1939 (I:7–11 R:6). Amos Mouse tells the story of his friend Benjamin Franklin.

———. *Rabbit Hill*. Viking, 1944 (I:7–11 R:7). Will the new humans on the hill be friends or enemies to the animals that live there?

Leaf, Munro. *The Story of Ferdinand*. Illustrated by Robert Lawson. Viking, 1936 (I:4–10 R:6). Ferdinand proves that he'd rather smell the flowers than fight the matador.

Lear, Edward, and Nash, Ogden. *The Scroobious Pip*. Illustrated by Nancy Ekholm Burkert. Harper & Row, 1968. (I:all). A beautifully illustrated edition of the humorous poem.

LeGalliene, Eva. *The Nightingale*. A retelling of Hans Christian Anderson's tale. Illustrated by Nancy Ekholm Burkert. Harper & Row, 1965 (I:6–12 R:8). An Emperor learns that a live nightingale is preferable to a jeweled mechanical bird.

Lionni, Leo. *Alexander and the Wind-up Mouse*. Pantheon, 1969 (I:3–6 R:3). A real mouse envies a lovable wind-up mouse.

————. *A Color of His Own*. Random House, 1975 (I:2–7 R:5). An animal fable in which the chameleon looks for his own color.

————. *The Greentail Mouse*. Random House, 1973 (I:3–7 R:4). Field mice plan a Mardi Gras.

————. *Pezzettino*. Pantheon, 1975 (I:2–6 R:3). Pezzettino, or Little Piece, is so small that he believes he must be a piece of someone else.

————. *Swimmy*. Pantheon, 1963 (I:2–6 R:3). A little fish learns about the marvels of the sea.

Livingston, Myra Cohn. *A Circle of Seasons*. Illustrated by Leonard Everett Fisher. Holiday, 1982 (I:all). Poems about the four seasons.

Locker, Thomas. *Where the River Begins*. Dial, 1984 (I:all). Full-page paintings complement a search for the source of a river.

Longfellow, Henry Wadsworth. *Hiawatha*. Illustrated by Susan Jeffers. Dial, 1983 (I:all). The poem beautifully illustrated.

————. *Hiawatha's Childhood*. Illustrated by Errol LeCain. Farrar, Straus, Giroux, 1984 (I:all) Excerpts from Longfellow's longer poem.

McCloskey, Robert. *Blueberries for Sal*. Viking, 1948 (I:4–8 R:6). A little girl mistakes a bear for her mother.

————. *Lentil*. Viking, 1940 (I:4–9 R:7). Lentil saves a homecoming celebration.

————. *Make Way for Ducklings*. Viking, 1941 (I:4–8 R:4). A city park provides a safe home for the ducklings.

————. *One Morning in Maine*. Viking, 1952 (I:4–8 R:3). Sal and her family live on an island.

————. *Time of Wonder*. Viking, 1957 (I:5–8 R:4). A family confronts a hurricane on their island.

McDermott, Beverly Brodsky. *The Crystal Apple*. Viking, 1974 (I:4–9 R:4). A Russian folk tale brightly illustrated in an abstract style.

————. *The Golem*. Lippincott, 1976 (I:9–14 R:5). Illustrations capture the magic spell that creates the Golem from a lump of clay.

McDermott, Gerald. *Arrow to the Sun*. Viking, 1974 (I:3–9 R:2). Strong shapes and colors complement a Native American tale.

————. *Sun Flight*. Four Winds, 1980 (I:all R:6). Daedalus the master craftsman and his son construct wings and escape from Crete.

MacLachlan, Patricia. *The Sick Day*. Illustrations by William Pène Du Bois. Pantheon, 1979 (I:2–7 R:2). Father and Emily entertain each other when they get sick.

Martin, Eva. *Canadian Fairy Tales*. Illustrated by Laszlo Gal. Douglas & McIntyre, 1984 (I:7–16 R:4). Fairy tales illustrated in realistic detail.

Martin, Sarah Catherine. *The Comic Adventures of Old Mother Hubbard and Her Dog*. Illustrated by Tomie de Paola. Harcourt Brace Jovanovich, 1981 (I:3–7). A humorously illustrated edition of one nursery rhyme.

Maruki, Toshi. *Hiroshima No Pika*. Lothrop, Lee & Shepard, 1982 (I:8–12 R:4). A powerfully illustrated story about the horror of the atomic bomb.

Moore, Clement. *The Night Before Christmas*. Illustrated by Tomie de Paola. Holiday, 1980 (I:all). The popular poem brightly illustrated.

Mosel, Arlene. *Tikki Tikki Tembo*. Illustrated by Blair Lent. Holt, Rinehart & Winston, 1968 (I:5–9 R:7). A Chinese folktale explaining why Chinese children now have shorter names.

Murphy, Shirley Rousseau. *Tattie's River Journey*. Illustrated by Tomie de Paola. Dial, 1983 (I:5–8 R:5). A flood takes Tattie, her house and her animals to a new location.

Musgrove, Margaret. *Ashanti to Zulu: African Traditions* Illustrated by Leo and Diane Dillon. Dial, 1976 (I:7–12). Traditions of twenty-six African peoples in alphabetical order.

Newberry, Clare Turlay. *Marshmallow*. Harper & Row, 1942 (I:2–7 R:7). Oliver the cat has a new rabbit roommate.

————. *Widget*. Harper & Row, 1958. (I:2–7 R:6). Realistic drawings capture the image of a cat.

Noyes, Alfred. *The Highwayman*. Illustrated by Charles Keeping. Oxford, 1981 (I:10+). Strong black-and-white drawings complement the mood of the poem.

Onassis, Jacqueline, ed. *The Firebird and Other Russian Fairy Tales*. Illustrated by Boris Zvorykin. Viking, 1978 (I:8–14 R:3). Four Russian fairy tales retold in a beautifully illustrated edition.

Perrault, Charles. *Cinderella*. Adapted by Amy Ehrlich. Illustrated by Susan Jeffers. Dial, 1985 (I:5–8 R:4). Large, detailed illustrations accompany a simplified version of the fairy tale.

————. *Cinderella*. Illustrated by Marcia Brown. Harper & Row, 1954 (I:5–8 R:5). Fine lines suggest the mood of the fairy tale.

Piatti, Celestino. *The Happy Owls*. Atheneum, 1964 (I:3–7 R:4). The owls try to explain why they are happy; a group of fowls does not understand.

Provensen, Alice and Provensen, Martin. *The Glorious Flight Across the Channel with Louis Bleriot, July 25, 1909*. Viking, 1983 (I:all R:4). A highly illustrated account of the first flight across the English Channel.

————. *Leonardo da Vinci*. Viking, 1984 (I:all R:8). A pop-up book describing Leonardo da Vinci's accomplishments.

————. *A Peaceable Kingdom: The Shaker Abecedarius*. Viking, 1978 (I:all). A Shaker ABC, newly illustrated.

Ransome, Arthur. *The Fool of the World and the Flying Ship*. Illustrated by Uri Shulevitz. Farrar, Straus & Giroux, 1968 (I:6–10 R:6). Lines and warm colors focus attention in a Russian tale about a simple lad who overcomes enormous obstacles.

Schwartz, Delmore. *"I Am Cherry Alive," The Little Girl Sang*. Illustrated by Barbara Cooney. Harper & Row, 1979. An illustrated poem about a little girl who is celebrating being alive.

Sendak, Maurice. *In the Night Kitchen*. Harper & Row, 1970 (I:5–7). A young child dreams himself into a night world.

————. *Outside Over There*. Harper & Row, 1981 (I:5–8 R:5). Goblins steal a baby sister.

————. *Where the Wild Things Are*. Harper & Row, 1963 (I:4–8 R:6). Max is very mischievous and very imaginative.

Shannon, George. *Dance Away*. Illustrated by Jose Aruego and Ariane Dewey. Greenwillow, 1982 (I:2–6). Line and color complement the repetitive language as a rabbit outwits a hungry fox.

Simon, Seymour. *Jupiter*. Morrow, 1985 (I:all R:7). Photographs enhance this informational book.

Singer, Isaac B. *Zlateh the Goat*. Illustrated by Maurice Sendak. Harper &

Row, 1966 (I:6–10   R:6). A collection of Jewish folktales.

Spier, Peter. *Bill's Service Station*. Doubleday, 1981 (I:3–7). One of the "Village Book" series, cut in the shape of a building.

————. *The Erie Canal*. Doubleday, 1970 (I:all). An illustrated version of the folksong.

————. *Fire House: Hook and Ladder Company Number Twenty-Four*. Doubleday, 1981 (I:3–7). Detailed drawings of a fire house.

————. *Food Market*. Doubleday, 1981 (I:3–7). Detailed drawings depict a food market.

————. *The Fox Went Out on a Chilly Night*. Doubleday, 1961.(I:all). A highly illustrated version of the folksong.

————. *London Bridge Is Falling Down!* Doubleday, 1967 (I:5–12). The nursery rhyme is illustrated in detail.

————. *My School*. Doubleday, 1981 (I:3–7). Activities associated with a school.

————. *Noah's Ark*. Doubleday, 1977 (I:3–9). A detailed wordless book.

————. *The Pet Store*. Doubleday, 1981 (I:3–7). Detailed drawings of a pet store.

————. *The Star-Spangled Banner*. Doubleday, 1973. (I:8+). Our national anthem illustrated.

————. *Tin Lizzie*. Doubleday, 1975 (I:7–12   R:6). The history of an old car.

————. *The Toy Shop*. Doubleday, 1981 (I:3–7). Detailed drawings of a toy store.

Steptoe, John. *The Story of Jumping Mouse*. Lothrop, Lee & Shepard, 1984 (I:all   R:4).   Steptoe's illustrations convey the softness of a butterfly's wing and the sharpness of bristling cacti in this Great Plains Indian legend about a mouse who wanted to visit the far-off land.

Udry, Janice May. *The Moon Jumpers*. Illustrated by Maurice Sendak. Harper & Row, 1959 (I:3–9   R:2). Colors create a mood as children go out to play in the moonlight.

Van Allsburg, Chris. *The Garden of Abdul Gasazi*. Houghton Mifflin, 1979 (I:5–8   R:5). A boy has a magical experience in a magician's garden.

————. *Jumanji*. Houghton Mifflin, 1981 (I:5–8   R:6). An unusual game creates a jungle environment.

————. *The Mysteries of Harris Burdick*. Houghton Mifflin, 1984. (I:all). Pictures encourage children to solve mysteries.

————. *The Wreck of the Zephyr*. Houghton Mifflin, 1983 (I:5–8   R:6). A boy tries to become the greatest sailor in the world.

————. *The Polar Express*. Houghton Mifflin, 1985 (I:5–8   R:6). The glowing illustrations accompany an original Christmas story.

Viorst, Judith. *Alexander and the Terrible, Horrible, No Good, Very Bad Day*. Illustrated by Ray Cruz. Atheneum, 1972 (I:3–8   R:6). Nothing goes right for Alexander.

Wahl, Jan. *The Little Blind Goat*. Illustrated by Antonio Frasconi. Stemmer, 1981 (I:5–9   R:3). A blind goat is taught to overcome his handicap.

Walter, Mildred Pitts. *Brother to the Wind*. Illustrated by Diane and Leo Dillon. Lothrop, Lee & Shepard, 1985 (I:all   R:3). An original story set in Africa about a young boy who wishes to fly.

Ward, Lynd. *The Biggest Bear*. Houghton Mifflin, 1952 (I:5–8   R:4). A boy wants a bearskin to hang on his barn.

Wildsmith, Brian. *Brian Wildsmith's ABC*. Watts, 1963 (I:3–6). A word and a picture for each letter.

————. *Hunter and His Dog*. Oxford, 1979 (I:3–7   R:3). A hunting dog cares for wounded ducks.

Willard, Nancy. *A Visit to William Blake's Inn: Poems for Innocent and Experienced Travelers*. Illustrated by Alice and Martin Provensen. Harcourt Brace Jovanovich, 1981 (I:all). Poems describing a menagerie of guests.

Wood, Audrey. *King Bidgood's in the Bathtub*. Illustrated by Don Wood. Harcourt Brace Jovanovich, 1985 (I:6–9   R:1). The story of a humorous predicament.

Yagawa, Sumiko. *The Crane Wife*. Translated by Katherine Paterson. Illustrated by Suekichi Akaba. Morrow, 1981 (I:all   R:6). A traditional Japanese tale expressing the dangers of greed.

Yashima, Taro. *Crow Boy*. Viking, 1955 (I:4–8   R:4). A lonely outcast at school gains respect and self-confidence.

————. *Umbrella*. Viking, 1958 (I:3–7   R:7). Momo receives an umbrella for her third birthday and then waits impatiently for the rain to come.

Zolotow, Charlotte. *Mr. Rabbit and the Lovely Present*. Illustrated by Maurice Sendak. Harper & Row, 1962 (I:3–8   R:2). A little girl, with the help of a rabbit, searches for a gift for her mother's birthday.

5
Picture Books

A BOOK IS MORE THAN WORDS

INVOLVING CHILDREN IN PICTURE
BOOKS

A Book Is More Than Words

THE THOUGHT OF A CHILD, A LAP, AND A picture book arouses warm feelings in many adults, as they recall their own early experiences with books or a time when they shared books with a child. When a loving adult provides opportunities for a child to experience the enchantment found in picture books, both the child and the adult benefit.

The books included in the genre of picture books provide many values in addition to pleasure. The rhythm, rhyme, and repetition in nursery rhymes stimulate language development as well as auditory discrimination and attentive listening skills in young children. Alphabet books reinforce children's ability to identify letter/sound relationships and help expand children's vocabularies. Concept books enhance intellectual development by fostering children's understanding of abstract ideas. Wordless books encourage children to develop their observational skills, descriptive vocabularies, and ability to create a story characterized by logical sequence. Illustrations found in picture books stimulate sensitivity to art and beauty. The text of well-written picture storybooks encourages children's appreciation of literary style. All these values give picture books a very important role in children's development.

The first half of this chapter discusses criteria for evaluating and selecting picture books and provides detailed discussion and examples of the various types of picture books. The chapter concludes with a discussion of specific storybooks and the elements that make them memorable.

WHAT IS A PICTURE BOOK?

Most children's books are illustrated, but not all illustrated children's books are what we call *picture books*. As Esther Averill (1) has pointed out, the illustrations in many books are merely extensions of a more or less self-sufficient text. In a picture book, however, "the pictures play a livelier role, and are an integral part of the action of the book" (1, p. 307). Zena Sutherland and Betsy Hearne (9) stress that in picture books the illustrations are either as important as the text or more important than the text. Because children respond to stories told visually as well as verbally, some picture books are quite effective with no words at all. Many picture books, however, maintain a balance between the illustrations and the text, so that neither is completely effective without the other.

Thus the term *picture books* covers a wide variety of children's books, ranging from Mother Goose books and toy books for very young children to picture storybooks with plots that satisfy more experienced older children. Many of the picture books discussed in this chapter rely heavily upon illustrations to present content. In some, each scene or rhyme is illustrated. Other books with more complex verbal story lines are not as dependent upon pictures to develop their plots.

EVALUATING PICTURE BOOKS

Because the text and the illustrations in picture books rely upon and complement each other, adults must carefully consider the relationship between words and pictures when evaluating a picture book. Betsy Hearne (5) recommends that evaluators also "think complexity versus clutter, originality versus banality, loving versus cute, strong versus ponderous, and deepened versus decorated. Think of what you'd like to hang on the wall of your mind" (p. 577). The following questions can help adults select high-quality picture books for children.

1 Are the illustrations accurate, and do they correspond to the content of the story?
2 Do the illustrations complement the setting, plot, and mood of the story?
3 Do the illustrations enhance characterization?
4 Do both text and illustrations avoid stereotypes of race and sex?
5 Is the plot one that will appeal to children?
6 Is the theme worthwhile?
7 What is the purpose for sharing this book with children or recommending that they read it?
8 Is the author's style and language appropriate for children's interests and age levels?
9 Are the text, the illustrations, the format, and the typography in harmony?

Many picture books have another characteristic not shared by other children's books: the writer and the illustrator may be the same person. Well-known artists often create picture books. Chapter four concentrated upon artists and their media. This chapter places greater emphasis upon authors, or author-illustrators, and their literature.

Children's Responses to Picture Books

Educators, researchers, and authorities in children's literature are increasingly interested in children's responses to picture books and in the characteristics of picture books that appeal to children. Adults may consider children's own evaluations when selecting picture books to share with children.

Peggy Whalen-Levitt (11) emphasizes the role a child's age and experience play in determining a child's response to picture books. Very young children's first experiences with picture books are largely physical interactions, as they investigate the size, shape, texture, and moving parts of these unfamiliar objects in their expanding environments. They may stick a book into their mouths as a way of becoming acquainted with it or turn the pages even if the book is upside down. With adult guidance, children soon learn the specific purposes and pleasures associated with books. They begin to respond to the symbolic nature of books, focusing on the content of the pictures and connecting illustrated objects and concepts with the sounds and names adults give them. Children quickly begin to assume that a book will contain some kind of story, whether that story is an illustrated cow in a pasture or a "pattycake" rhyme to which they can move their own bodies. As their sense of time develops, children begin to see the connections among past, present, and future in a book's pictures and text and to expect that a story will have a beginning, middle, and end. Finally, after considerable time and experience with both books and everyday living, children adopt a critical stance in which they evaluate a book's text and illustrations in terms of their own views of reality and their own feelings and desires. Thus different types of books and book-related experiences are appropriate for children at different ages and stages of development.

Patricia Cianciolo (3) has identified four major factors that influence how a child perceives and evaluates the illustrations in picture books: a child's age and stage of cognitive and social development; the way in which an adult has (or has not) prepared a child for an experience with a picture book; the child's emotional state of readiness; and the number of times a child looks at the illustrations. Cianciolo's analysis of picture books listed in the Children's Choices also revealed that children prefer illustrations that depict here-and-now situations, fantasies of all kinds, and humorous exaggerations and slapstick; illustrations that are colorful and add more detail to the text's descriptions of characters, action, and setting; and illustrations in either a realistic or a cartoon-like style. Such preferences may help adults select picture books for children, but, Cianciolo stresses, adults can and should also use books and book-related activities to teach children "how to be more evaluative and discriminating in their selections" (3, p. 28).

MOTHER GOOSE BOOKS

Mother Goose rhymes are the earliest literature enjoyed by many young children; the rhymes, rhythms, and pleasing sound effects of these jingles appeal to young children who are experimenting with their own language patterns and, as discussed in chapter one, aid children's language development. A brief review of the basic characteristics of nursery rhymes indicates why children enjoy them, as well as why they encourage children's language development.

Appealing Characteristics of Mother Goose Rhymes

The *rhythm* in many nursery rhymes almost forces children to react to the verse. For example, they may clap their hands or jump up and down to the rhythm of this jingle:

> Handy dandy, Jack-a-Dandy
> Loves plum cake and sugar candy;
> He bought some at a grocer's shop
> And out he came, hop, hop, hop.

Rhyme is another aspect of many nursery verses that children enjoy. Rhyming words such as *dandy* and *candy, shop* and *hop,* invite them to join in and add the rhyming word or make up their own rhymes. Rhymes enhance the adventures of many favorite characters: "Little Miss Muffet sat on a tuffet"; "Jack and Jill went up the hill"; "Bobby Shafto's gone to sea, Silver buckles on his knee." Many of these verses rhyme at the end of each line; they also use internal rhyming elements: "Hickory, dickory, dock, the mouse ran up the clock"; "Rub, a dub, dub, three men in a tub." An easy way to test the influence of these rhyming verses is to ask older children to share one of their favorite Mother Goose rhymes. They can probably say several although they may not have heard or recited them for years.

Children also respond to the *repetition* of sounds in a phrase or line of a nursery rhyme. *Alliteration,* the repetition of an initial consonant in consecutive words, creates phrases that children enjoy repeating just to experience the marvelous feeling that results from the repetition of beginning sounds: "One misty, moisty, morning"; "Sing a song of sixpence"; "Diddle, diddle dumpling." Sentences that contain a great deal of alliteration become tongue twisters. Children love the challenge of this jingle:

> Peter Piper picked a peck of pickled
>   peppers.
> A peck of pickled peppers Peter Piper
>   picked.
> If Peter Piper picked a peck of
>   pickled peppers,
> Where's the peck of pickled peppers
>   Peter Piper picked?

Humor is another great appeal of Mother Goose verses for children.

> Hey, diddle, diddle!
> The cat and the fiddle,
> The cow jumped over the moon;
> The little dog laughed
> To see such sport,
> And the dish ran away with the spoon.

This verse is an example of *hyperbole,* the use of exaggeration for effect, which is common in Mother Goose rhymes. Children appreciate exaggerated, ridiculous situations, such as an old woman living in a shoe with so many children she doesn't know what to do, or a barber trying to shave a pig, or Simple Simon going fishing in his mother's pail.

> He went for water with a sieve,
> But soon it ran all through:
> And now poor Simple Simon
> Bids you all adieu.

Both good and bad little girls and boys live in Mother Goose land. In fact, the same children may be both good and bad. These characteristics have a strong appeal for young children, who are also good and bad at different times. Nursery rhymes often depict good children as going to bed when they should. Little Fred is one ideal child:

> When little Fred went to bed,
> He always said his prayers,
> He kissed mamma and then pappa,
> And straightway went upstairs.

FLASHBACK

ONE EARLY edition of Mother Goose rhymes, *The Original Mother Goose's Melody,* was first printed in London by John Newbery in 1760. (The first known English nursery rhyme book for children, *Tommy Thumb's Song Book for all little Masters and Misses,* was published in London in 1744.) Many experts believe that the poet and author Oliver Goldsmith collected the rhymes and prepared them for the press. Thomas Carnan, John Newbery's

Mother GOOSE's Melody. 37

*J*ACK and *Gill*
 Went up the Hill,
 To fetch a Pail of Water;
Jack fell down
And broke his Crown,
 And *Gill* came tumbling after.

Maxim.

The more you think of dying, the better you will live.

ARISTOTLE'S

38 Mother GOOSE's Melody.

ARISTOTLE'S STORY.
*T*HERE were two Birds fat on
 a Stone,
 Fa, la, la, la, lal, de;   [one,
One flew away, and then there was
 Fa, la, la, la, lal, de ;
The other flew after,
And then there was none,
 Fa, la, la, la, lal, de ;
And fo the poor Stone
 Was loft all alone,
 Fa, la, la, la, lal, de.

This may ferve as a Chapter of Confequence in the next new Book of Logick.

stepson, secured the copyright for the Newbery Mother Goose in 1780. The rhymes, which contained maxims or morals, were popular in both Great Britain and North America. Soon after the American Revolution, Isaiah Thomas of Worcester, Massachusetts, copied many of Newbery's books, including *The Original Mother Goose's Melody.* In the early 1800s the printers Munroe and Francis of Boston published a Mother Goose edition that closely resembled John Newbery's version.

Good children are also kind to animals:

> I like Little Pussy,
> Her coat is so warm,
> And if I don't hurt her
> She'll do me no harm;
> So I'll not pull her tail,
> Nor drive her away,
> But Pussy and I
> Very gently will play.

All children, however, are not so nice to animals:

> Ding, dong, bell,
> Pussy's in the well!
> Who put her in?
> Little Tommy Green.
> Who pulled her out?
> Little Johnny Stout.
> What a naughty boy was that,
> To try to drown poor pussy cat,

> Who never did him any harm.
> But killed the mice in his father's barn!

Animals themselves may also portray naughty behavior in nursery rhymes. The raven is certainly bad when he attacks a farmer and his daughter who are riding a mare:

> A raven cried croak! and they all tumbled down,
> Bumpety, bumpety, bump!
> The mare broke her knees, and the farmer his
>   crown,
> Lumpety, lumpety, lump!
> The mischievous raven flew laughing away,
> Bumpety, bumpety, bump!
> And vowed he would serve them the same the next
>   day,
> Lumpety, lumpety, lump!

While nursery rhymes may not explicitly state which behavior is good or bad, children have no difficulty identifying which is which and empathizing with the characters that display it.

Mother Goose Collections

The many different collections of Mother Goose rhymes contain more or less the same verses, but their formats, sizes, and illustrations are quite different. Some editions contain several hundred verses in large-book format, while others have fewer verses and are small enough for a young child to hold; some have illustrations reminiscent of eighteenth-century England, while others have modern illustrations. Many adult students in American university classes prefer the Mother Goose editions with settings in the England of the 1600s and 1700s—either reissues of the original early editions or editions first published in the twentieth century.

Two popular early editions, John Newbery's *The Original Mother Goose's Melody* and Kate Greenaway's *Mother Goose: Or, the Old Nursery Rhymes*, continue to be reissued. Newbery's edition may be of greater interest to adults than to children (the text contains a history of Mother Goose), although many older children enjoy looking at the early orthography in Newbery's edition and comparing the verses and illustrations with twentieth-century editions, which do not share Newbery's tendency to add a moral to the close of each nursery rhyme. In Newbery's edition, for example, "Ding dong bell, the cat is in the well," is followed by this maxim: "He that injures one threatens a Hundred" (p. 25). The edition illustrated by the well-known author-illustrator Kate Greenaway was first published in 1881. Greenaway's book is a small text suitable for sharing with one child. She illustrates the nursery rhymes with pictures of delicate children that appeal to the sentiments of most readers. (See page 55 for a discussion of Kate Greenaway's illustrations.)

Two collections assembled by Iona and Peter Opie provide older children and adults with an opportunity to examine early illustrated versions of Mother Goose. *A Nursery Companion* is a large, highly illustrated collection of nursery rhymes originally published in the early 1800s. The *Oxford Nursery Rhyme Book* contains 800 rhymes categorized according to contents. Black-and-white woodcuts, from both earlier editions and newly created works, illustrate this large volume. An informative preface and a list of sources for the illustrations increase the usefulness for those who wish to study early editions of nursery rhymes.

Girls and boys come out to play,
The moon it shines as bright as day;
Leave your supper, and leave your sleep,
And come to your playmates in the street;
Come with a whoop, come with a call,
Come with a good will, or come not at all;
Up the ladder and down the wall,
A halfpenny loaf will serve us all.

Nineteenth-century children and the English countryside highlight Kate Greenaway's illustrations for this early edition of Mother Goose. (From *Mother Goose: Or, the Old Nursery Rhymes*, by Kate Greenaway. Reproduced by permission of Frederick Warne & Company.)

Marguerite De Angeli's Book of Nursery and Mother Goose Rhymes is a twentieth-century edition with illustrations of appealing children in nineteenth-century English settings. In the foreword to her book, De Angeli describes how her illustrations were influenced by her English grandfather, who read nursery rhymes aloud to her when she was a child. De Angeli's illustrations show the flowering fields, blossoming hedgerows, stone walls, castles, and cobblestone streets of an earlier, rural England, with smiling, frolicking children reminiscent of Kate Greenaway's.

This large book contains 376 rhymes with several verses printed on each page.

Arnold Lobel's *Gregory Griggs and Other Nursery Rhyme People* contains rhymes about lesser-known characters such as Theophilus Thistle, the successful thistle sifter; Gregory Griggs, who had twenty-seven different wigs; Charley, Charley, who stole the barley; Michael Finnegan, who grew a long beard right on his chinnigan; and Terence McDiddler, the three-stringed fiddler. The language and strong rhyming patterns in these verses make the book appropriate for reading aloud. The humorous, nonsensical rhymes are enriched by Lobel's soft pastel illustrations; each rhyme is illustrated with a large picture, making it especially good for sharing with a group of children.

The placement of illustrations next to the matching nursery rhyme, the large-page format, and the humorous folk-art illustrations make *Tomie de Paola's Mother Goose* especially appealing to younger children. The series of pictures that accompany rhymes with multiple verses illustrate the sequential development in longer rhymes such as "Simple Simon." The plots of some of the rhymes are extended through the illustrations. For example, the illustrations accompanying "Jack and Jill" enhance the plot development by showing the actions on a marionette stage. Wallace Tripp's humorously illustrated *Granfa' Grig Had a Pig and Other Rhymes without Reason from Mother Goose* depicts many of the characters as animals. The series of pictures that illustrates some longer rhymes may also be used to stimulate oral language activities, especially those developing sequential order.

Picture Books That Illustrate One Mother Goose Rhyme or Tale

Children often want to know more about their favorite nursery rhyme characters. The humor and simple plots found in nursery rhymes lend themselves to expansion into picture storybook format. These picture storybook versions of Mother Goose rhymes may also stimulate creative interpretations as children think about what might happen if they expanded and illustrated the plots in other nursery rhymes.

Two illustrators have expanded "Old Mother Hubbard" into picture book format. Tomie de Paola's illustrations add a humorous touch to Sarah Catherine Martin's *The Comic Adventures of Old Mother Hubbard and Her Dog*. Old Mother Hubbard is dressed in a full skirt, bustle, high collar, and ribboned hat. Her dog is an orange, smartly trimmed poodle. The illustrations encourage additional interaction with the text as children identify other nursery rhyme characters drawn as a border on each page. Paul Galdone's *Old Mother Hubbard and Her Dog* is another highly illustrated version of this nursery rhyme. Children can compare dePaola's and Galdone's illustrations and those created by Robert Branston for an 1819 version of "The Comic Adventures of Old Mother Hubbard and Her Dog." The Branston version is in Iona and Peter Opie's *A Nursery Companion*.

Each verse of Sarah Josepha Hale's *Mary Had a Little Lamb* has several full-page color illustra-

Hey diddle, diddle,
The cat and the fiddle,
The cow jumped over the moon;
The little dog laughed
To see such sport,
And the dish ran away with the spoon.

Humorous illustrations and large-book format provide an appealing volume for young children. (Illustration reprinted by permission of G. P. Putnam's Sons from *Tomie de Paola's Mother Goose*. Copyright © 1985 by Tomie de Paola.)

The illustrator enhances the language of a cumulative tale by repeating the illustrations. (Illustrations copyright © 1985 by Janet Stevens. Reprinted from *The House That Jack Built* by permission of Holiday House.)

tions of nineteenth-century farm and school settings by Tomie dePaola.

Janet Stevens enhances the cumulative quality of *The House That Jack Built* by repeating the illustrations as well as the text. As the cumulative tale progresses, smaller versions of the brightly colored, humorous illustrations are repeated with each additional character.

Two expanded nursery rhyme stories have enough detail and accurate information to interest older readers as well as young children. Peter Spier's *London Bridge Is Falling Down* tells in pictures the story that accompanies the favorite nursery game song. Each line of the song is illustrated in detailed pictures that show forms of architecture, transportation, and dress typical of London in different eras. Of interest to older readers is an account of the history of London Bridge, beginning with the Romans building the first bridge in 43 B.C. and extending through the com-

pletion of the newest bridge in the 1970s. Spier's *To Market, to Market*, contains rhymes and pictures that depict farm and market life such as that found in the rhyme "To market, to market, to buy a fat pig." The final two pages of the book give a description and history of the town of New Castle, Delaware, and describe the numerous trips that Spier took through Delaware, Maryland, and Pennsylvania when sketching and collecting the details for the book. These concerns for accuracy and detail have resulted in a book that may be used to develop older children's oral discussion skills and develop historical perspectives.

"Mother Goose" in Other Lands

Traditional nursery rhymes and children's jingles are found in many different lands. The language and style may differ from the English Mother Goose, but the content of all nursery rhymes is amazingly alike. Nursery rhymes everywhere tell about good and bad children, wise and foolish people, animals, and nature. Unique characteristics in the rhymes of certain countries allow children to develop appreciation for the values and contributions of other cultures.

Verses in *The Prancing Pony: Nursery Rhymes from Japan*, collected by the Japanese educator Tasuku Harada in the early 1900s and translated by Charlotte B. De Forest, are illustrated with examples of the Japanese art of *kusa-e* (collage). Because rhyme and meter are literary devices not found in Japanese verse, De Forest "transmuted" the verses by adding both rhyme and meter to the originals in order to appeal to English-speaking children. Many of the verses are about flowers, cherry trees, birds, and animals, illustrating the Japanese love of nature.

The Prancing Pony

Your prancing, dancing pony—
　　Oh, please don't tie him here.
This cherry tree's in blossom—
　　Oh, dear, dear, dear!
He'll prance and dance and whinny,
　　He'll neigh and stamp and call,
And down the soft, pink blossoms
　　Will fall, fall, fall! (p. 31)

Keiko Hida, the illustrator of *The Prancing Pony* has used natural plant dyes to color the handmade textured rice paper used in the collages: browns are from cedar bark, red from madder roots, black from persimmon juice, yellow from the fruit of the cape jasmine, purple from the wood of the Judas tree, and indigo from the indigo plant. The resulting illustrations are simple geometric shapes, but they provide the feeling of running, flying, and prancing.

Robert Wyndham has translated Chinese nursery rhymes into an English version designed to appeal to English-speaking readers and listeners. *Chinese Mother Goose Rhymes* are about dragons, Buddhas, carriage chairs, the Milky Way, and lady bugs, which seem to fascinate children of many nationalities. Each of the sprightly rhymes is shown in English and in Chinese orthography, with a simple, colorful drawing to illustrate it. Turning games and nonsense words are well represented, as they are in English nursery rhymes.

Gee lee, gu lu, turn the cake,
Add some oil, the better to bake.
Gee lee, gu lu, now it's done;
Give a piece to everyone. (p. 40 unnumbered)

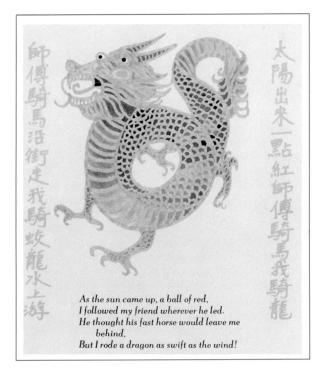

As the sun came up, a ball of red,
I followed my friend wherever he led.
He thought his fast horse would leave me behind,
But I rode a dragon as swift as the wind!

The Chinese orthography and illustrations suggest the oriental setting of the nursery rhymes. (From *Chinese Mother Goose Rhymes* by Robert Wyndham, with the permission of Philomel Books, a division of the Putnam Publishing Group. Copyright © 1968 by Robert Wyndham.)

N. M. Bodecker has translated and illustrated Danish nursery rhymes in *It's Raining, Said John Twaining*. Wooden shoes and royalty are common characters in the Danish verses. Like the English Mother Goose verses, Danish nursery rhymes use rhyming elements, tongue-twisting nonsense words, and riddles. The names of some characters in the rhymes, such as Skat Skratterat Skrat Skrirumskrat, appeal to young children's love of nonsense and alliterative sounds. Each rhyme in this book is illustrated with a colorful, full-page picture.

Margot C. Griego et al. have collected nursery rhymes and lullabies from Mexico and Spanish-speaking communities in the United States. *Tortillitas Para Mama* contains finger plays, counting rhymes, and clapping rhymes written in both Spanish and English.

Traditional nursery rhymes from many nations are an important contribution to our cultural heritage. They foster the self-esteem and language skills of children who are members of ethnic minorities in the United States and help all American children appreciate the values and contributions of cultures other than their own.

TOY BOOKS

An increasing number and variety of board books, pop-up books, flap books, cloth books, and plastic books entice young children into interacting with a story, developing their vocabularies, counting, identifying colors, and discussing book content with adults. These books are valuable additions to children's literature because they stimulate the language, cognitive, personal, and social development of preschool children. They also provide a happy experience with books that, ideally, extends into later childhood and adulthood.

Board books range in content from identifying baby's clothing to describing typical experiences at school or the doctor's office. Helen Oxenbury's board books are especially appropriate for younger children. Each page contains an easily identifiable picture of a baby's actions as he or she gets dressed, interacts with family members, or accomplishes a new skill. The five appealing books in this series are *Dressing*, *Family*, *Friends*, *Playing* and *Working*. Another series of board books that uses familiar items and one simple object per page is illustrated by Zokeisha. *Things I Like to Eat*, *Things I Like to Look At*, *Things I*

Creating Picture Books

ALICE and MARTIN PROVENSEN, whose work has won the New York Times Best Illustrative Children's Book award, the Brooklyn Museum's Art Books for Children Citation, and the Caldecott honor award, discuss the challenges of illustrating a new manuscript.

OUR WORK IS CONCENtrated on book illustration and starting each new book is still, after having worked together for thirty-seven years, an exhilarating experience. It is not surprising that there are so many husband and wife teams in the children's book field. Our marriages must surely have been enhanced by the enchantment of this shared experience. In addition to the actual illustration of a book, there is much craft, much measuring, calculation and minutae and many decisions in its making. It is a welcome thing to have a reliable, able, sympathetic (if sometimes critical), person working alongside.

Publishing a book is in many ways similar to producing a movie or a play. It is not done by one person. The illustrator's part in its production has most in common with the actor's performance. We approach each new book as a new role and have never developed a style or mannerisms that would suit every text.

A brilliant player, such as Alex Guiness, creates a new persona for each new part he plays, trying to find the inner and outer guise which will best express the texture of the character and the meaning of the play. Each new role presents him with a new challenge. For us, each new manuscript does the same.

The illustrator's task if one really is an *illustrator* (that is to say "illuminator") is to do the text full justice, trying as the actor does, to find the right line, the right tone and rhythm and the right spirit with which to bring a manuscript written or edited for children to the fulfillment of its intended purpose—a children's book.

Before we begin our search for what we hope will be this inevitable "rightness" in the finished illustrations, we try to choose a format (shape) for the book which will be suitable for the subject matter and the age group of its readers. Then, too, there is the length of the book (the number of pages), based not only on the length of the manuscript but also on the size of the type used, the number of lines on each page, the size and number of illustrations, all again relating to the age level of its audience and increasingly the cost of its production, to be considered.

At this stage we often have several and separate opinions about what the appearance of the finished book should be. We work toward the solution by making rough layouts and actually constructing crude dummies. It is now that the first rough sketches, by either of us, are drawn. We decide which scenes or characters are the most important, which will make the most vital pictures, which, in the case of a narrative manuscript, will forward the story line and in the case of diverse subject matter, as in a Mother Goose book, how the pages can be designed to unify the text visually.

It is always easy to find the wrong solutions. The right ones emerge through a process of experimentation, but once we have decided on a format, ordered the type set, agreed on what the spirit and appearance of the book should be, we try to set aside our individual egos and place our individual drawing styles and painting skills to the service of that image.

We have been given the opportunity to draw Bibles and books of nonsense, warriors and lions, mythological landscapes and modern city streets. We have illustrated alphabet books and music books, cookbooks and books of poetry and yet are always astonished and pleased to discover how much there is still to be done.

Like to Play With, and *Things I Like to Wear* enhance children's vocabulary development and identification of familiar objects. Three "Sam" board books written by Barbro Lindgren and illustrated by Eva Erikson encourage language development through identification of objects and discussion of actions as a young boy takes a bath, plays with friends, and experiences accidents at home. A humanized rabbit provides similar subjects for discussion and enjoyment in Rosemary Wells's *Max's Bath*, *Max's Bedtime*, *Max's Birthday*, and *Max's Breakfast*. Another book by Oxenbury, *I Hear*, identifies sounds within the environment. Kate Duke's board book *What Bounces?* encourages experimentation while her *The Playground* stimulates identification of playground equipment and discussion of actions.

Several board books develop concepts related to counting, the alphabet, and seasonal changes. For example, Rosemary Wells's *Max's Toys: A Counting Book* develops simple concepts related to numbers. Helen Craig's *The Mouse House ABC* introduces the alphabet through mice who are busy forming the letters from a variety of objects including wood, paint, and rope. Craig's *Mouse House Months* shows a tree as it goes through its seasonal changes.

Board books also develop understanding about children's expanding experiences and environment. Oxenbury's "Out-and-About Books" are excellent for slightly older children who are curious about and sometimes fearful of the world outside their homes. For example, *The Checkup* presents a humorous account of a child's visit to a doctor. All Oxenbury's books should stimulate discussion about activities that are important in most children's lives.

Lisa Bonforte's *Farm Animals*, Tony Chen's *Wild Animals*, and Michele Chopin Roosevelt's *Animals in the Woods* all illustrate common animals and discuss them in one or two simple sentences.

Peter Spier's various board books are shaped like the buildings they represent in interesting detail, including a service station, a toy shop, a firehouse, and a supermarket. Parents, librarians, and nursery school or kindergarten teachers may use these books to stimulate discussions and motivate children's interest in the environment.

Pop-up books may introduce children to beloved storybook characters, tell simple stories, or create fascinating three-dimensional settings. *The Peter Rabbit Pop-Up Book* is based on Beatrix Potter's classic story, and Margaret Wise Brown's *The Goodnight Moon Room: A Pop-Up Book* introduces settings from popular fiction. Jan Pienkowski's *Haunted House* uses pop-up and flap techniques to create the detailed setting of a house inhabited by ghostly characters.

Eric Carle's bright, colorful illustrations and pop-up techniques enhance a simple story line in *The Honeybee and the Robber: A Moving Picture Book*. The plot follows a honeybee as she encounters a bird, a fish, and a frog who all wish to eat her for breakfast. Children enjoy the action when they can make a bee move her wings, a bear cross his eyes, and a flower open its petals.

Flap books and other mechanical books encourage children's interaction with the text as they speculate about what is under a flap and then open it to discover whether they were correct. Eric Hill has written and illustrated an excellent series of flap books for preschool children. In *Where's Spot?*, for example, the plot revolves around a dog's full dinner bowl and discovering where the dog could be. Children join Spot's mother as they open a door or lift a covering in search of Spot. Each opening reveals a different animal. The lettering of Hill's books is large and clear against a white background, and the illustrations are both colorful and humorous. Young children return many times to rediscover what is behind each flap.

Robert Crowther has designed two mechanical books that help children develop concepts related to the alphabet and counting. *The Most Amazing Hide-and-Seek Alphabet Book* has clear capital and lower-case letters that conceal an object beginning with the letter. *The Most Amazing Hide-and-Seek Counting Book* uses pictures that rotate or lift to uncover objects for counting.

Cloth and plastic books help stimulate very young children's language development while helping them identify colors, sounds, and familiar everyday objects. In *I Can—Can You?*, Peggy Parish asks children to demonstrate their physical accomplishments, from touching their toes to putting away their toys.

The numerous toy books discussed here and listed in the bibliography indicate an apparent trend toward publishing more "reading" material for very young children. A visit to a book store or a search through publishers' catalogues will show students of children's literature even more available texts. *Booklist*, the journal for the American Library Association, regularly reviews toy books as part of its coverage of children's books.

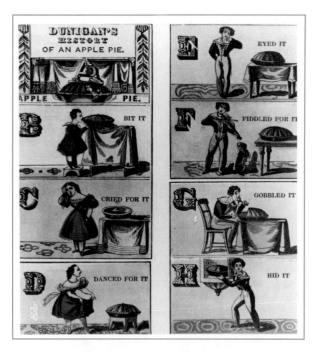

An early nursery rhyme traces the "History of an Apple Pie" throughout the alphabet. (From *One Hundred Nineteenth-Century Rhyming Alphabets in English*, by Ruth Baldwin. Carbondale, Ill: Southern Illinois University Press, 1972. From the John G. White Collection, Cleveland Public Library.)

ALPHABET BOOKS

Alphabet books have long been used to help young children identify familiar objects, as well as letters and sounds. The objects pictured in alphabet books should be easy for children to identify and should not have more than one commonly used name. For example, since young children often call a rabbit a bunny, *rabbit* might not be the best choice for illustrating the letter *r* in an alphabet book for very young children. If letter/sound identification is a major concern, the letters and corresponding illustrations should be easily identifiable. If young children use the book independently, the pages should not be cluttered with numerous objects that could confuse letter/sound identification.

When adults share alphabet books with older children, however, pages rich with detail and numerous objects may help children develop their observational and discussion skills. Children's ages and adults' educational objectives are basic considerations when evaluating any alphabet

book. Some alphabet books are most appropriate for young children, while others contain enough detail or historical insight to interest even the older child.

Early Alphabet Books

Like Mother Goose rhymes, alphabet books were among the first books published for children. Some early alphabet books have been reissued, and some new books are reminiscent of earlier texts. One very early ABC rhyme, "History of an Apple Pie," tells how "B bit it," "C cut it," and so forth, until the end of the alphabet and the pie. In 1886, Kate Greenaway illustrated the pie's alphabetical history in *A—Apple Pie*, and her original woodblock designs have been used in a reissue of this charming text.

Ruth Baldwin's *One Hundred Nineteenth-Century Rhyming Alphabets in English* contains a version of "History of an Apple Pie", as well as other early alphabets. The 296 pages of this large book are filled with colorful reproductions of nineteenth-century pictures and verses. Each rhyme is identified according to title, illustrator, publisher, and date of publication.

Alice and Martin Provensen have illustrated another early ABC in their *A Peaceable Kingdom: The Shaker Abecedarius*. The Shaker ABC was first published in the Shaker Manifesto of July 1882 under the title, "Animal Rhymes." According to Richard Barsam (2), it was written for the purpose of teaching reading. While Shaker teachers were strict disciplinarians, singing and dancing were part of children's school life. The rhyme and rhythm of these verses must have appealed to Shaker children, as they appeal to children today. The Provensens' charming illustrations show people engaged in typical Shaker occupations, wearing the dress of an earlier time in American history. Such historical alphabet books give contemporary children a valuable sense of life in the past, as they share a reading and learning experience that children in earlier eras also enjoyed.

Animal Themes in ABCs

The animal theme in the Shaker ABC is still very popular. Contemporary animal alphabet books range in complexity: some show one letter and a single animal for each entry; some have a single letter, a single animal, and a rhyming phrase; some have very descriptive phrases with each let-

Costumes and occupations in the illustrations show the Shaker influence on American children's literature. (From *A Peaceable Kingdom*, illustrated by Alice and Martin Provensen. Copyright © 1978 by Alice and Martin Provensen. Reprinted by permission of Viking/Penguin Inc.)

ter; and some develop an integrated story in alphabetical order.

Bert Kitchen's *Animal Alphabet* exemplifies books that at first glance seem deceptively simple. Each page in this large, handsome text contains a crisp black capital letter and an animal that climbs, hangs onto, sits upon, or peeks out from behind the letter. Even older readers may have difficulty guessing the animals' identities. Answers in the back of the book reveal jerboas, newts, and umbrella birds in addition to common frogs, lions, and elephants.

Ed Emberley's ABC is a more complex book that would be appropriate for slightly older children. It not only shows each letter, but also demonstrates, in a series of four pictures, how each letter is formed. This book is worthwhile to share with children as they learn to print letters and can motivate them to develop their own alphabet books.

This alphabet book is set to the language of a jump rope rhyme.(From *A, My Name Is Alice* by Jane Bayer. Pictures by Steven Kellogg. Pictures copyright © 1984 by Steven Kellogg. Reproduced by permission of the publisher, Dial Books for Young Readers.)

Two very colorful large-format alphabet books accompany each letter and illustration with a series of descriptive words or verses that repeat the letter. Leonard Baskin's illustrations in *Hosie's Alphabet* are lovely, full-page watercolors. The accompanying words are meant for young children to hear, not read. For example, an iguana illustrating the letter *I* is "an incredible scaly iguana," while a spider on the *S* page is "a gangling entangling spider." A jump rope rhyme forms the rhythmic background for Jane Bayer's *A, My Name Is Alice.* Illustrator Steven Kellogg interprets the rhyme for each letter through a picture of animals performing the humorous antics described in the verse.

Books for young children may use alphabetical order to develop a story line. Wanda Gág's *The ABC Bunny* is an older alphabet book still popular with young children, who follow the alphabetical adventures of the bunny after a falling apple wakes him up in his snug bed.

Other Alphabet Books

Anno's Alphabet: An Adventure in Imagination is a beautifully illustrated book by Mitsumasa

toys,

Detailed illustrations may enhance children's understanding of concepts and development of oral discussion skills. (From *On Market Street*, by Arnold Lobel. Copyright © 1981 by Anita Lobel. By permission of Greenwillow Books (A Division of William Morrow & Co.)

In this ABC book for younger children, the illustrator uses collage to depict each letter and accompanying objects. (Illustration from *ABC* by Elizabeth Cleaver. Copyright © 1985 Elizabeth Cleaver. Reprinted with the permission of Atheneum Publishers, Inc.)

Anno. The title is an excellent introduction to what is in store for observant readers. Large, simple objects suggest the beginning sound of each large letter, but Anno has also cleverly entangled numerous objects into the black-and-white border circling each page. For example, the *B* pages are bordered with bean stalks in which are entwined buttons, bees, bells, and birds. Children enjoy discovering these picture puzzles and searching for the hidden objects.

Brightly colored collages provide the visual focus in Elizabeth Cleaver's *ABC.* Letters and words that begin with each letter are printed on a white background. Each facing page contains a collage depicting the letter and the objects that begin with that letter. Poetry associated with individual letters provides the controlling element in Barbara Lalicki's *If There Were Dreams to Sell.*

A buying excursion in an old-fashioned market provides an enjoyable trip through the alphabet in Arnold Lobel's *On Market Street*, illustrated by Anita Lobel. The child buys gifts from the shop-keepers: apples, books, clocks, doughnuts . . . and finally zippers. The colorful illustrations help children develop concepts as they see and discuss the goods offered for sale.

Several alphabet books are designed to provide information to older students rather than to teach letter/sound relationships to younger ones. Two award-winning books present information about African life. Margaret Musgrove's *Ashanti to Zulu: African Traditions*, vividly illustrated by Leo and Diane Dillon, depicts the customs of twenty-six African peoples. *Jambo Means Hello: Swahili Alphabet Book*, by Muriel Feelings, introduces Swahili words and customs. These beautiful books can encourage children of all cultural backgrounds to learn more about African people.

COUNTING BOOKS

Counting books, like alphabet books, are often used for specific educational purposes. If an adult wishes to develop young children's concepts of one-to-one correspondence and their ability to count sequentially from one through ten, a counting book should contain easily identifiable numbers and corresponding objects. Effective number books for young children usually show one large number, the word for the number, and the appropriate number of objects—all on one page or on a double page. The actual number represented by an object or objects should be quite clear. For example, one star showing five points may be a poor choice for depicting the number five, since children may not understand that five, not one, is being depicted. Books that stimulate young children's manipulation of concrete objects are especially useful. For example, a counting book showing the number two and two blocks might encourage a child to count two real blocks.

One very simple counting book for young children, Eric Carle's wordless *My Very First Book of Numbers*, is designed so that children can easily match numbered squares with their corresponding illustrations.

Counting books for young children may stimulate language development and interaction with the text. In *Roll Over!* Mordicai Gerstein uses a nursery rhyme, fold-out flaps, and humorous il-

lustrations to involve children in counting the number of people in a bed. In Molly Bang's *Ten, Nine, Eight* a black father and child observe objects seen in the room and then say a rhythmic counting lullaby that proceeds backwards from ten to one until the drowsy child is ready for bed. In Nancy Tafuri's *Who's Counting?* children are encouraged to develop concepts related to the numbers one through nine.

Counting books for older children may develop the concept of numbers or of addition or subtraction, or may encourage children to search for many groups of the same number on a single page. Adults should consider children's abilities in order to select books of appropriate difficulty.

Mitsumasa Anno presents numbers one through ten and concepts of addition and subtraction in *Anno's Counting House*. On alternating double pages Anno shows the interiors and exteriors of two houses. In the old house ten people are preparing to move. Then there are only nine people in the old house and one in the new house. The process continues until the new house is furnished.

Count and See, by Tana Hoban, is a simple counting book with easy-to-identify number concepts that also extend to sets and higher numbers. The numbers, their corresponding written words, and a circle or circles illustrating the number appear in white on a black background. On the opposite page, a photograph illustrates the number with familiar things found in many children's environments: one fire hydrant, two children, . . . twenty watermelon seeds, . . . forty peanuts shown in groups of ten, . . . and one hundred peas shown in pods of ten each. The book could also be used for counting and grouping concrete items or making counting books that use the items shown in the pictures. (Counting and grouping aids cognitive development.)

In a slightly more complex book, Doug Magee uses photographs of a large tractor-trailer truck to introduce the parts of a truck and to reinforce counting. The photographer uses black and white photographs of truck parts in *Trucks You Can Count On* to illustrate numbers from one through ten. The wheels of the truck provide the concrete examples for counting to eighteen.

Hilary Knight's The Twelve Days of Christmas may also be used as a counting book. The humorous illustrations show the gifts given on each of the twelve days. Older children can count the accumulated objects on the final two-page

This unusual counting book depicts East African culture. (From *Moja Means One*, by Muriel Feelings. Illustrated by Tom Feelings. Illustrations Copyright © 1971 by Tom Feelings. Used by permission of Dial Press.)

spread. Are there twelve lords a-leaping, twenty-two ladies dancing, thirty fiddlers fiddling . . . and twelve partridges in pear trees?

Muriel Feelings's *Moja Means One: Swahili Counting Book* is the counting-book partner to her Swahili alphabet book, discussed above. Each double-page spread provides a numeral from one to ten, the Swahili word for the number, a detailed illustration (by Tom Feelings) that depicts animal or village life in Africa, and a sentence describing the contents of the illustration. This book may be more appropriate for stimulating interest in an African culture or providing information for older children than for presenting number concepts to younger children.

CONCEPT BOOKS

Many of the books recommended in chapter one for use in stimulating children's cognitive development are concept books. These books rely on well-chosen illustrations to help children grasp both relatively easy concepts—such as "red" and "circle"—and more abstract concepts that may be difficult for children to comprehend—"through," for example, or antonyms such as "fast" and

Real-life photographs clarify concepts related to shape. (From *Circles, Triangles, and Squares*, by Tana Hoban. Copyright 1974 by Tana Hoban. Reprinted with permission of Macmillan Publishing Company.)

"slow." Like counting books, concept books come in various degrees of difficulty; adults should consider both a child's level of understanding and a book's level of abstractness when selecting concept books.

Numerous books have been designed to help young children learn basic concepts such as color and shape. Eric Carle's *My Very First Book of Colors* is a simple, wordless book that asks a child to match a block of color with the picture of an object illustrated in that color. In Tana Hoban's *Circles, Triangles, and Squares*, large black-and-white photographs show common shapes that appear in everyday objects. In *Round & Round & Round*, Hoban uses large color photographs to show circular objects. Hoban's *Shapes, Shapes, Shapes* uses photographs to depict shapes such as circles, rectangles, and ovals. Hoban has used

photographs in several other excellent concept books, including *Big Ones, Little Ones*, in which mother and baby animals convey the meaning of "big" and "little"; and *Over, Under, Through and Other Spatial Concepts*, in which children are shown jumping "over" fire hydrants, walking "under" outstretched arms, and crawling "through" large pipes.

Authors have successfully tackled the challenge of explaining opposites and spatial concepts to children. In *Here a Chick, There a Chick*, Bruce McMillan uses photographs of captivating baby chicks to illustrate the meaning of terms such as "straight" and "crooked." In *Push-Pull, Empty-Full: A Book of Opposites*, Tanya Hoban uses photographs to develop the meanings of antonyms, such as "wet" (a puddle in the street) and "dry" (leaves in the street). Peter Spier's *Fast-*

ISSUE

❦

Picture Books and Controversy

SEVERAL BOOKS DIScussed in this chapter have stirred controversy and subsequently been removed from library shelves. Other books have had illustrations altered to meet specific standards. When Maurice Sendak's *In the Night Kitchen* was published in 1970, some parents, teachers, and librarians deplored the child's nudity. Several incidents occurred in which the nudity was covered with a drawn-on washcloth or the book was removed from the shelf. Garth Williams's *The Rabbit's Wedding* was criticized in the 1960s because the illustrations showed the marriage of a black rabbit and a white rabbit. In 1969 William Steig's *Sylvester and the Magic Pebble* was criticized for two reasons: some parents objected to police officers being portrayed as pigs; others objected to the portrayal of the mother doing housework while Sylvester and his father relaxed. *Changes, Changes,* by Pat Hutchins, was

criticized in the 1970s because the man has a more active role: he drives and decides what to make from the blocks, while the woman pulls the train whistle and hands him the blocks. One book not discussed in this chapter illustrates Americans' changing sensitivities toward certain social issues. Helen Bannerman's *Little Black Sambo* (1899) was popular for many years until the crudely drawn features of the characters and the story line were considered offensive and resulted in the book being taken off many library shelves.

As you evaluate picture books, consider which books might be controversial and the reasons for the controversy. Does controversiality change with the times? What subjects might have caused controversy in picture books published in the 1950s, 1960s, or 1970s? Are those subjects still controversial in the 1980s? Are any new areas of controversy developing today?

Several detailed illustrations show what "full" and "empty" mean. (From *Fast-Slow, High-Low: A Book of Opposites*, by Peter Spier. Copyright 1972 by Peter Spier. Reprinted by permission of Doubleday & Company.)

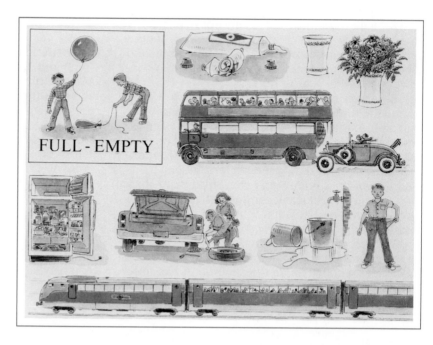

Slow, High-Low: A Book of Opposites is a more detailed and complex book showing, for example, many "empty" and "full" things such as balloons, toothpaste tubes, flower vases, buses, and refrigerators. Linda Banchek's *Snake In, Snake Out* presents spatial concepts in a humorous way, as an old woman tries to chase a friendly snake out of her house.

Donald Crews familiarizes children with different types of concepts in *Freight Train*. The train's cars are of different colors, and the train's movement across trestles, through cities, and into tunnels encourages children's understanding of concepts such as the opposites "darkness" and "daylight." Trains fascinate many young children, who eagerly learn concepts while enjoying the color, movement, and sound developed in this book. Anne Rockwell helps children understand seasonal changes and appropriate activities for each season in *First Comes Spring*. Nancy Tafuri encourages children's concept and language development by using large illustrations of animals in her almost wordless book *Early Morning in the Barn*. Masayuki Yabuuchi helps children identify terminology and understand relationships between baby animals and their appropriate parents in *Whose Baby?* Yabuuchi also encourages children to hypothesize about animal identity in *Whose Footprints?*

These and other concept books offer children pleasure as well as important learning experiences.

WORDLESS PICTURE BOOKS

In a new type of picture book, the illustrations tell the whole story without the addition of words. Children enjoy the opportunity to become authors and provide the missing text for wordless books—an excellent way of developing their oral and written language skills. Dorothy Strickland (8) maintains that "experiences with books that are thoughtfully planned to promote active verbal exchanges of ideas will have lasting positive effects upon both the communicative mode and the cognitive structure of the child" (p. 53). Wordless books stimulate creative thinking and enhance visual literacy abilities as children watch the pages for clues to the action. Wordless books are especially valuable because they allow children of different backgrounds and reading levels to enjoy the same book. The second part of this chapter suggests several ways of using wordless books to develop children's skills in discussion, oral interpretation, and creative writing.

Wordless books have various degrees of detail and plot complexity. Some contain considerable detail, while others do not. Some develop easily identifiable plots, while others can be interpreted in many different ways. Some are large, making them appropriate for sharing with a group, while others are small, easily held by one child or one adult with a child in the lap. Adults should consider all these characteristics when choosing wordless books for children of different ages, reading levels, and interests.

Pat Hutchins's *Changes, Changes* is a simple wordless book that appeals to children in preschool and kindergarten who enjoy building with blocks. The illustrations show two wooden dolls building a house of blocks, coping with a fire by turning the house into a fire truck, solving the problem of too much water by building a boat, reaching land by constructing a truck, and eventually rebuilding their home. The large and colorful pictures make actions easily identifiable. The book stimulates oral language, as well as problem solving and manipulation of the children's own blocks. In Jan Ormerod's *Sunshine* a child wakes up her parents and helps them prepare for their day. The action-filled color illustrations can stimulate oral discussions, creative dramatics, and writing.

Realistic humor is a popular theme of wordless books for young children. A series of wordless books by Mercer Mayer shows the humorous adventures of a boy, a dog, and a frog. *Frog Goes to Dinner*—the most detailed book in the series and, to many children, the funniest—illustrates the humorous disruptions that can occur if a frog hides in a boy's pocket and accompanies a family to a very fancy restaurant. Each of Mayer's books is small, just the right size for individual enjoyment or for sharing with an adult. The illustrations are expressive and contain sufficient detail to stimulate language development and enjoyment.

Several wordless books develop plots describing the antics of animals from the world of fantasy. Paula Winter's *Sir Andrew* revolves around a donkey who is so busy admiring himself he has an accident and causes accidents to others. John S. Goodall's *Paddy Under Water* follows Paddy Pork as he dives underwater and discovers a sunken ship. Emily Arnold McCully's *Picnic* follows a family of mice as they jubilantly go on a picnic, unhappily discover a small mouse is missing, and joyfully reunite the whole family. These illustrations contain enough plot development to stimulate the creation of narrative even by older children.

Some wordless books are exceptional because of their detail. John S. Goodall's *The Story of an English Village* illustrates the changes that occur in a village over several centuries. Older children can make comparisons between the time periods shown in the illustrations. Peter Spier's *Noah's Ark* is another excellent example of a detailed wordless picture book. The only words occur at the beginning of the book. The pictures show the building of the ark, the boarding of all the animals, the long wait, and the starting of life again as the land is plowed and cultivated. These pictures contain so much detail that a child can discover something new each time the book is read.

Several beautifully illustrated wordless books by Mitsumasa Anno also encourage oral discussion and storytelling by older children. The de-

The sequential organization and detail of the illustrations provide a story line that stimulates language development. (Illustration on unnumbered page 11 from *Picnic* by Emily Arnold McCully. Copyright © 1984 by Emily Arnold McCully. Reprinted by permission of Harper & Row, Publishers, Inc.)

tailed drawings in *Anno's Journey*, for example, are the result of the artist's travels through the countryside, villages, and larger towns of Europe. Anno adds to the enjoyment by suggesting that the reader look for certain details in the pictures, such as paintings and characters from children's literature. The pictures are detailed enough to keep even adults occupied. *Anno's Italy* and *Anno's Britain* follow a similar approach and encourage children to identify historical and literary characters. *Anno's Flea Market* captures the spirit of a busy market square in an old, walled city.

One enticing, almost wordless, book is Chris Van Allsburg's *The Mysteries of Harris Burdick*. A title and a one-line caption precede each picture. In the introduction to the book Van Allsburg asks readers to provide the missing stories. Teachers and librarians report that the illustrations contain enough elements of mystery and fantasy to motivate excellent oral and written stories.

Many wordless books are ideal for promoting oral language development. Others, however, are so obscure in story line that children may be frustrated when asked to tell the story. When choosing wordless books, an adult should consider the following questions:

1   Is there a sequentially organized plot that provides a framework for children who are just developing their own organizational skills?
2   Is the depth of detail appropriate for the children's age level? (Too much detail will overwhelm younger children, while not enough detail may bore older ones.)
3   Do the children have enough experiential background to understand and interpret the illustrations? Can they interpret the book during individual reading or would adult interaction be necessary?
4   Is the size of the book appropriate for the purpose? (Larger books are necessary for group sharing.)
5   Is the subject one that will appeal to the children?

The varied levels of complexity found in wordless books indicate that wordless books are appropriate for young children and for more advanced students. This same complexity, however, means that selection of materials will need careful consideration.

EASY-TO-READ BOOKS

Easy-to-read books are designed to be read by children with beginning reading skills. These beginner books serve as a transition between basal readers and library trade books. Like picture storybooks, these books contain many pictures designed to suggest the story line. Unlike picture storybooks, however, their vocabulary is controlled so that the young reader can manage independently. The process of controlling the vocabulary to fit the needs of beginning readers may result in contrived language; it is quite difficult to write stories that sound natural if all the words must be selected from the easiest level of readability.

Authors, teachers, and librarians use several different readability formulas in determining the approximate level of reading skill required to read a book. The Fry Readability Formula (4), for example, measures the reading level by finding the average number of sentences and syllables per 100 words. These averages are plotted on a graph that identifies the corresponding grade level for the book. (This technique is explained in appendix E.) Readability experts assume that easier books have short sentences and more monosyllabic words. As the reading level becomes higher, the sentences become longer and multisyllabic words become more numerous.

Comparing the readability of easy-to-read books and other picture storybooks illustrates the difference between the two types of books. A 100-word selection from one popular easy-to-read book, Dr. Seuss's *The Cat in the Hat*, showed sixteen sentences and 100 syllables for those 100 words. The sentences were very short and all words were of one syllable. Plotting these two findings on the Fry graph indicates a first-grade reading level. In contrast, a picture storybook also written for first-grade interests by Dr. Seuss, *And to Think That I Saw It on Mulberry Street*, has seven and one-half sentences and 126 syllables in a 100-word selection. This book's reading level is fifth grade. While both books appeal to children of about the same age, children themselves usually read the first book, while adults usually read the second to children.

Even though easy-to-read books may not meet all standards for literary quality, they do meet the needs of beginning readers. Because children need independent experiences with books that al-

Humorous illustrations enhance an unexpected experience in a favorite easy-to-read book. (From *The Cat in The Hat*, by Dr. Seuss. Copyright © 1957 by Dr. Seuss. Reprinted by permission of Random House, Inc.)

low them to reinforce their reading skills and develop pride in their accomplishments, adults should include easy-to-read books in every book collection for primary-age children. Easy-to-read books are also helpful to students who need successful experiences in remedial reading classes. Because of their controlled use of language and sentence structure, easy-to-read books are less appropriate for adults to read aloud to children, although children may enjoy reading them aloud to an appreciative adult.

Animal antics appeal to young children, and many favorite easy-to-read books have animals as the main characters. In Dr. Seuss's *The Cat in the Hat*, mentioned above, a cat amazes and entertains two children when he balances a fish bowl, a carton of milk, and a cake simultaneously. Seuss's humorous illustrations and rhyming dia-

logue appeal to children. The cat emphasizes this enjoyment:

> Look at me!
> Look at me!
> Look at me Now!
> It is fun to have fun
> But you have to know how. (p. 8)

Arnold Lobel has written and illustrated several enchanting easy-to-read books. The soft brown and green illustrations in Lobel's stories about Frog and Toad recreate the atmosphere of a woodland setting and show the friendship felt by these two characters. In *Frog and Toad Are Friends*, Frog tries to entice Toad out of his home in order to enjoy the new spring season. Children enjoy Toad's reactions when Frog knocks on the door:

> "Toad, Toad," shouted Frog,
> "wake up. It is spring!"

Soft woodland colors and animals with human characteristics combine in a memorable easy-to-read book. (From *Grasshopper on the Road*, written and illustrated by Arnold Lobel. Copyright © 1978 by Arnold Lobel. By permission of Harper & Row, Publishers, Inc.)

"Blah," said a voice
from inside the house.

In Lobel's *Grasshopper on the Road*, a curious insect decides to follow a winding country lane just to discover where it leads. Lobel develops more characterization than is found in many easy-to-read books by having the grasshopper encounter other rural inhabitants and then try to change their behavior patterns.

Helen V. Griffith develops a memorable animal character with feelings similar to those of her youthful readers in *Alex and the Cat*. When the dog is dissatisfied with himself, he attempts to be a cat, a wolf, and a rescuer of baby birds. After his adventures he concludes that he is better off being himself, a house pet. Other easy-to-read books with stories of animals that appeal to children include Syd Hoff's *Chester* and *Sammy the Seal* and Bernard Wiseman's *Morris Goes to School* and *Morris Has a Cold*.

Easy-to-read books are also designed to appeal to children's special interests—in mysteries, sports, science, history, or magic, for example. Crosby Bonsall's gang of boy private eyes solves several mysteries including *The Case of the Scaredy Cats* in which girls invade the boys' private-eye clubhouse and prove that they are just as good as boys. Short, scary stories are found in both Edward Marshall's *Four on the Shore* and Alvin Schwartz's *In a Dark, Dark Room*.

PICTURE STORYBOOKS

A common characteristic of many picture books discussed thus far is the use of illustrations, with only a brief narrative, to present all or most of the book's contents. This reliance on pictures is especially crucial in concept books, counting books, a majority of the alphabet books, and all wordless picture books. Many of these books do not have a continuous story line; instead, the illustrations are grouped according to a common theme or are in a specific order because of numerical or alphabetical sequence.

Picture storybooks, however, contain many illustrations but also develop a strong story line in the text. In a well-written picture storybook, the illustrations and narrative complement each other; children cannot deduce the whole story line merely by viewing the pictures.

When adults think about the enjoyable book experiences shared between adults and children during story hour or at bedtime, they usually remember the picture storybook. Childhood would be less exciting without friends like Mike Mulligan, Frances the badger, and Ferdinand the bull. What makes some picture books so memorable an experience for both children and adults? Strong plot, characterization, setting, humor, and style are part of the answer, but originality and imagination are also crucial elements in outstanding picture books.

Elements in Picture Storybooks

Originality and Imagination. The clever cat actually saves his friends the church mice from an invasion of rats, a boy gets his wishes from a charge card company whose machine goes mad, and a child's bedroom becomes the kingdom of all the wild things. Some adults never lose touch with the dreams, fears, and fantasies of their childhoods. As authors of picture storybooks for children, they are able to create imaginative new worlds in which the impossible becomes both real and believable.

In *The Church Mice Adrift*, Graham Oakley creates a cat named Sampson who develops a plan to save the church mice from invading rats. In another original tale, *The Wish Card Ran Out!*, James Stevenson gives his hero wishes by creating a spoof on credit cards. Charlie is unhappy when he does not get a baseball glove for his birthday, but then he finds a lost "International Wish" card issued by a big corporation that took over from wishing wells and fairy godmothers. A child's imagination structures the delightful story in Maurice Sendak's *Where the Wild Things Are*. Only in such fantasy can young children who have been disciplined turn their rooms into kingdoms inhabited by other wild things like themselves, then return home in safety before their suppers get cold.

Picture storybooks and their accompanying illustrations are filled with imaginative episodes such as these. They provide many hours of enjoyment during story hours and are excellent for stimulating children's imagination during creative play, storytelling, and creative writing.

Plot. The short attention spans of children who read or hear picture storybooks place special demands on plot development. The plots of picture storybooks are usually simple, clearly developed,

The illustrations support the irony in this humorous story. (From *The Church Mice in Action* by Graham Oakley. Copyright © 1982 Graham Oakley. Reprinted with the permission of Atheneum Publishers, Inc.)

And the plan's success depended on Sampson doing absolutely nothing. He did it perfectly.

and quite brief, involving few subplots or secondary characters. Such plots usually allow young children to become involved with the action, identify the problem, and solve it rapidly. For example, in the first three pages of Maurice Sendak's *Where the Wild Things Are* children know that Max is in so much trouble that he has been sent to bed without supper. Even though the thirty-seven words used thus far do not reveal what Max has done, the pictures explain his problems. Children see him standing on books, hammering nails into the wall, and chasing the dog with a fork. The plot is swiftly paced, and children rapidly join Max in his imaginary world as the room becomes wilder and wilder. Sendak introduces additional conflict and excitement when Max encounters the wild things and overcomes them with a magic trick. Children empathize with Max when he has played long enough, sends his new subjects off to bed, and returns home to his mother's love and his supper. The author uses only thirty-eight words to tell what happens between the time Max leaves the wild things and returns home. This book is an excellent example of the important relationship between illustrations and plot development; the illustrations become larger and larger as the drama increases

and then become smaller again as Max returns to his everyday life.

Other picture books deal with children's problems in more realistic plots. In *Like Jake and Me*, Mavis Jukes portrays the strained relationship between Alex and his big, powerful stepfather Jake, who refuses to allow Alex to help with various chores. When a large, hairy spider crawls into Jake's clothes, Alex discovers that even a powerful, ex-rodeo cowboy can be afraid, and Jake discovers that even a small boy can provide assistance.

Whether a plot is based on fantasy or realism, it usually involves a rapid introduction to the action, a fast pace, and a strong, emotionally satisfying climax. In *The Patchwork Quilt*, Valerie Flournoy develops a warm, emotionally satisfying plot that follows the construction of a family quilt. The quilt gradually draws the members of the family together as they remember past experiences associated with scraps of material, help Grandma sew, and marvel over the completed masterpiece that also reveals the family's life story.

Characterization. The characters in picture storybooks must have specific traits that make them appealing to young children and that meet the demands of the short format. Since a short story does not allow for the fully developed characters that older children and adults prefer, the characters in picture storybooks must experience situations and emotions immediately familiar and credible to the children. Maurice Sendak, for example, did not need to describe Max, the wild things, or the rumpus that takes place between them. His illustrations show these effectively.

Any child can understand the feelings of Judith Viorst's hero in *Alexander and the Terrible, Horrible, No Good, Very Bad Day*. Alexander wakes up with gum in his hair, does not get a prize in his cereal when everyone else does, receives reprimands from his teacher, loses his best friend, has a cavity filled at the dentist, gets in trouble for making a mess in his dad's office, had to eat lima beans for dinner, and is ignored by the cat, who goes to sleep with his brother. In this book, as in most picture storybooks, the illustrations supplement characterization in the text by showing the characters' actions and reactions to one another.

Many storybooks for children contain animal characters that act and speak like humans. Margaret Wise Brown's *The Runaway Bunny* uses a credible little bunny to demonstrate a child's need for independence and love. The dialogue between mother rabbit and baby bunny stresses the bunny's desire to experience some freedom by running away. Each time he suggests ways that he could run away, however, the mother rabbit counters with actions she would take to get him back. The love between the two animals is visible in both dialogue and pictures, and the bunny decides it would be better to stay with the mother who loves him.

In *Ernest and Celestine's Picnic* and in *Smile, Ernest and Celestine*, Gabrielle Vincent uses animal characters to portray easily identifiable emotions, such as excitement, dejection, resentment, jealousy, and acceptance. Young children can empathize with Celestine when, for example, a ram spoils her picnic, but her friend Ernest saves the day with some make-believe sunshine.

Setting. In picture storybooks, as in all literature, setting is used to establish a story's location in time and place, create a mood, clarify historical background if necessary, provide an antagonist, or emphasize symbolic meaning. Picture storybooks, however, strongly or sometimes totally rely on illustrations to serve these functions of a setting. Many books, such as Judith Viorst's *Alexander and the Terrible, Horrible, No Good, Very Bad Day*, Valery Flournoy's *The Patchwork Quilt*, and Vera Williams' *Something Special for Me* take place in the familiar contemporary world of television sets, blue jeans, and shopping centers. Other books take place in times, countries, or locations unfamiliar to the readers.

Ronald Himler's illustrations for Byrd Baylor's *The Best Town in the World* show how important illustrations are for illuminating time and place in picture storybooks. The brief poetic text alone cannot describe the details of a turn-of-the-century general store, the warmth created by a kerosene lamp, and the many activities associated with a picnic celebration in the days when a picnic was a major social event. Likewise, the early Yorkshire setting for James Herriot's *Moses the Kitten* would be almost incomprehensible to young children without Peter Barrett's illustrations. Even though Ian Wallace's *Chin Chiang and*

The illustration communicates the need for love between adults and children. (Illustrations by Clement Hurd from *The Runaway Bunny*, by Margaret Wise Brown. Copyright 1942 by Harper & Row, Publishers, Inc. Illustrations renewed © 1970 by Clement C. Hurd. By permission of Harper & Row, Publishers, Inc.)

the Dragon's Dance has a contemporary setting, children might have difficulty visualizing it without illustrations depicting the oriental section of Vancouver, British Columbia.

Toshi Maruki's dramatically expressive illustrations for *Hiroshima No Pika* (The Flash of Hiroshima) clarify the horrifying nature of the story's antagonist and mood, as seven-year-old Mii confronts the consequences of atomic warfare on August 6, 1945. The illustrator's choice of colors is especially dramatic. Swirling red flames pass over fleeing people and animals. Black clouds cover huddling masses and destroyed buildings. The illustrations suggest both the setting as antagonist and a destructive, frightening mood.

In *The Wreck of the Zephyr*, Chris Van Allsburg uses his illustrated settings to create a light mood, in a setting that subtly mixes reality and make believe. A boy who dreams of becoming the best sailor in the world experiences a calm sea sparkling with light and a star-studded night disturbed only by a magical ship flying through the sky.

The illustrations in all such worthy picture storybooks enhance the time, the place, the conflict, and the mood of the stories.

Humor. Selecting and sharing books that contribute to children's merriment is a major goal of any literature program. Research shows that humorous literature is particularly effective in attracting children to the pleasures of reading and writing. Many elements in picture storybooks can cause children to laugh out loud. An investigation by Sue Anne Martin (7) concluded that humor in books that had been awarded the Caldecott Medal had five general sources: (1) word play and nonsense, (2) surprise and the unexpected, (3) exaggeration, (4) the ridiculous and caricature, and (5) superiority.

Word Play and Nonsense. Theodor Geisel, better known as Dr. Seuss, is one of the most popular authors of children's books and an undisputed authority on word play and nonsense. Dr. Seuss's characters often make up totally new words and names to describe the animals found in their imaginations. In *If I Ran the Zoo*, Gerald McGrew's imaginary zoological garden contains an elephant-cat, a bird known as a Bustard, a beast called Flustard, and bugs identified as thwerlls and chugs. Of course, no one could find such animals in the usual jungles, so Gerald must search

for them in Motta-fa-Potta-fa-Pell, in the wilds of Nantasket, and on the Desert of Zind. Children enjoy not only the nonsense found in the rhyming text, but also the nonsensical illustrations of these strange animals.

Bill Peet's nonsense rhymes and nonsensical illustrations in *No Such Things* appeal to children. Peet uses both internal and end-of-line rhyming to create text such as the following:

"The blue-snouted Twumps feed entirely on weeds,
And along with the weeds they swallow the seeds.
Eating seeds causes weeds to sprout on their backs,
Till they look very much like walking haystacks." (p. 5)

Surprise and the Unexpected. Margot Zemach's *It Could Always Be Worse: A Yiddish Folktale* is an excellent example of the unexpected found in many picture storybooks. If a man lived in a small one-room hut with his wife and six children, and living conditions became so miserable that he went to the rabbi for advice, how might the rabbi respond to the problem? Children are certainly surprised when the rabbi suggests that the man bring his chickens, a rooster, and a goose into the hut. When conditions do not improve, the rabbi suggests adding the goat and the cow to the group. When life in the hut becomes so difficult that the rabbi suggests that the animals leave the hut immediately, the poor man discovers that the hut is actually quite roomy and peaceful.

Wilson Gage also uses irony to create surprise at the unexpected. In *Cully, Cully and the Bear*, a hunter discovers that the bear he's after is chasing him. The hunter decides that he does not need a bearskin and that, in fact, the ground is softer than any bearskin rug.

Exaggeration. Children's imaginations are often filled with exaggerated tales about what they can or would like to do. In James Stevenson's *Could Be Worse!*, however, the grandfather is the one who exaggerates. Grandpa does and says the same things day after day. Whenever anyone complains, Grandpa responds, "Could be worse." When he overhears his grandchildren commenting on his dull existence, he tells them what happened to him the previous evening: he was captured by a large bird and dropped in the mountains where he encountered the Abominable Snowman, then crossed a burning desert, escaped from a giant animal, landed in the ocean, and finally returned home on a paper airplane. After the grandchildren hear his story, they respond with his favorite expression, "Could be worse!" Stevenson uses similar exaggeration and characterization in *There's Nothing to Do.*

The Ridiculous and Caricature. The consequences of antlers suddenly appearing on a young girl's head provide the humor in *Imogene's Antlers*, in which author David Small caricatures the ridiculousness of some people's "what if" fears. To extend the humor, the story concludes with another "what-if": the antlers disappear, but an even more beautiful appendage replaces the antlers.

Human foolishness is caricatured in *The Three Wishes*, a folktale picture book by Paul Galdone. A woodcutter's problems begin when a fairy offers him three wishes. An accidental wish for a sausage causes such an argument with his wife that he wishes it were attached to her nose. He ponders the advisability of wishing for a barrel of gold, but finally relents and wishes for the sausage to be removed. Consequently, the only wealth the foolish woodcutter and his wife receive is the long sausage they share for supper.

Superiority. Some humorous picture storybooks gratify young children's desire to be superior to everyone else for a change or to easily overcome their problems. When a town simpleton surpasses not only his clever brothers but also the czar of the land, the result is an unusual tale of humorous superiority. Arthur Ransome's *The Fool of the World and the Flying Ship* is a Russian tale in which the good deeds performed by a simple lad allow him to obtain a flying ship, discover companions who have marvelous powers, overcome obstacles placed in his path by the czar, win the hand of the czar's daughter, and live happily ever after.

Style. Because a picture storybook contains so few words, its author must select those words very carefully. A storybook's style must also be designed to catch children's attention and stimulate their interest when an adult reads the story aloud. Adults can evaluate the effectiveness of a storybook's style by reading it orally to themselves or to a child.

One reason that folktales are so popular with children is their tendency to use repetition. When folktales were retold by word-of-mouth rather than in print, repetition made the story easier to remember. Today, repetition in both folktales and contemporary stories attracts children's attention and impresses a story's structure and content upon children's memories. Young children also enjoy repetition because it provides them an opportunity to join in with the dialogue.

In *The Witch's Hat*, Tony Johnston repeats both rhyming sounds and entire phrases. For example, "It was a magic pot, in case you forgot" is repeated after each incident with the enchanted hat. When an adult reads this book aloud, children quickly chime in with the repeated phrase.

Authors of picture storybooks also repeat single words in a sentence to create stronger impressions when books are read aloud. African folktales, for example, sometimes repeat a word several times. In Gail E. Haley's *A Story, A Story*, the Sky God describes Ananse, the tiny spider man, as "so small, so small, so small." Similar use of repetition conveys the impression of a dancing fairy, rain on a hornet's nest, and securing a man-eating leopard firmly by the feet. Verna Aardema uses this form of repetition to make a strong statement stronger in *Why Mosquitoes Buzz in People's Ears.* When a mother owl finds her dead baby, she is "so sad, so sad, so sad." The night that doesn't end is described as "long, long, long."

Young children enjoy listening to words that create vivid images. In the preface to *A Story, A Story*, Gail Haley says that many African words will be found in the book and asks readers to listen carefully so they can tell what the sounds of the words mean. Haley uses many unknown words to describe the movements of animals. A python slithers "wasawusu, wasawusu, wasawusu" down a rabbit hole; a rabbit bounds "krik, krik, krik" across an open space; and sticks go "purup, purup" as they are pulled out of the iguana's ears.

Careful choice of words also creates evocative moods in well-written picture storybooks. In *The Seeing Stick*, Jane Yolen creates a mood of wonder as Hwei Ming, the unhappy, blind daughter of a Chinese emperor, "sees" her father for the first time: "She reached out and her fingers ran eagerly through his hair and down his nose and cheek and rested curiously on a tear they found there. And that was strange, indeed, for had not the emperor given up crying over such things when he ascended the throne?" (p. 19 unnumbered).

Typical Characters and Situations in Outstanding Picture Storybooks

Children's picture storybooks include stories about people in disguise as animals, talking animals with human emotions, personified objects, humans in realistic situations, and humorous and inventive fantasies. This section discusses stories by some outstanding writers of books on these subjects.

People in Disguise as Animals. Many children's stories with animal characters are so closely associated with human life-styles, behavior patterns, and emotions that it is difficult to separate them from stories with human characters. If these stories were read without reference to the illustrations or to a specific type of animal, children might assume that the stories are about children and adults like themselves. These stories may be so popular with children because the children can easily identify with the character's emotions and the actions.

Russell Hoban's Frances the badger, for example, lives in a nice house with her two parents, loves bread and jam, and feels jealous when she gets a new baby sister. Children identify with Frances when, in *Bread and Jam for Frances*, she refuses to eat anything but her two favorite foods. Hoban has her parents, like good human parents, carefully guide Frances into her decision that eating only bread and jam is boring and that trying different foods is pleasant. In *A Baby Sister for Frances*, the young badger decides to run away from home when her mother becomes busy with the new baby. She packs a lunch to take with her on her journey, but goes only as far as the next room, from which she looks longingly at her parents and her sister. In this warm story, Hoban shows how Frances's need for her family helps her overcome her jealousy and decide to accept the new arrival. The warmth is expressed in Hoban's choice of language.

> Big sisters really have to stay
> At home, not travel far away,
> Because everybody misses them
> And wants to hug-and-kisses them.
> (p. 26 unnumbered)

In *Leo the Late Bloomer* Robert Kraus develops a credible character through realistic experiences shared by many children: Leo, a young tiger, can-

not read, write, draw, talk, or even eat neatly. One of Leo's parents worries, while the other suggests that Leo is merely a late bloomer. Kraus uses repetition to emphasize Leo's problem as the seasons go by: "But Leo still wasn't blooming." A satisfactory ending results in both text and illustrations as Leo finally discovers that he can do everything he couldn't do before, and a happy father and mother hear their happy child declare, "I made it!"

Fears and experiences resulting in temporary unhappiness are popular causes of conflict in stories about animals disguised as people. The young character in Jacqueline Martin's *Buzzy Bones and Uncle Ezra* fears the wind. In a satisfying ending, Martin allows her character to discover that wind, in the right circumstances, can also provide considerable pleasure. David McPhail uses a temporary unhappy experience to create a happy ending in *Fix-It*. A bear, who could easily be a young child, cries when the television does not work. After successive disappointments, her mother reads a book to try to calm the unhappy Emma. Emma discovers that reading is so much fun that she stays with the book rather than returning to the television.

Another animal who experiences very human problems is Rosemary Wells's Timothy in *Timothy Goes to School*. Timothy Raccoon has a hard time during his first week in school: he wears the wrong clothes and makes many mistakes in his work, while a classmate does everything right. The author develops a warm, satisfying ending as Timothy discovers a friend and has higher hopes for the future.

Talking Animals with Human Emotions. In other animal stories the animals live in traditional animal settings such as meadows, barnyards, jungles, and zoos. The animals in these stories display some animal traits, but they still talk like humans and have many human feelings and problems.

The main character in Munro Leaf's *The Story of Ferdinand* lives in a meadow with his mother and other cattle. Leaf develops contrasts between Ferdinand, who sits under his favorite cork tree smelling the flowers, and the bulls who run, jump, and butt their heads together practicing for the bullring. The story's theme is relevant to any human child: all individuals should be themselves, and being different is not wrong. Leaf allows Ferdinand to remain true to his individual nature. When he is taken to the bullring, he merely sits and smells the flowers.

Jean de Brunhoff uses a variety of emotional experiences to develop characters and plots in the various Babar books. Emotionally, Babar grows up, grieves when his mother dies, runs away to the city, returns to the jungle where he is crowned king, and raises a family. In Roger Duvoisin's *Petunia*, a goose becomes conceited when she finds a book and believes that merely carrying it around gives her wisdom. Petunia's advice creates an uproar in the barnyard when she maintains that firecrackers discovered in the meadow are candy and thus good to eat. Her true wisdom begins when she discovers that books have words and that she will need to learn to read if she really wants to be wise. Louise Fatio also takes her main character beyond the world he knows. *The Happy Lion* develops problems when he leaves his zoo cage to visit his good friends in town. To his wonderment, they respond with fright, screams, and running rather than with the "bonjour" he had expected.

Many young children like a combination of fast, slapstick adventure and an animal with easily identifiable human characteristics, such as Hans Rey's *Curious George*. The reader is introduced to this comedic monkey as he observes a large yellow hat lying on the jungle floor. His curiosity gets the better of him, he is captured by the man with the yellow hat, and his adventures begin. The text and illustrations develop one mishap after another, as George tries to fly, but falls into the ocean; grabs a bunch of balloons and is whisked away by the wind; and is finally rescued again by the man with the yellow hat. These rapid verbal and visual adventures bring delight to young children who are curious about the world around them and would like to try some of the same activities.

Other picture storybooks with animal characters satisfy children's desire for absurd situations, flights of fancy, and magical transformations. In William Steig's *Sylvester and the Magic Pebble*, for example, a young donkey accidentally changes himself into a rock and must figure out how to communicate with his grieving parents and return to his donkey form.

Personified Objects. The technique of giving human characteristics to inanimate objects is called *personification*. Children usually see nothing wrong with a house that thinks, a doll that feels, or a steam shovel that responds to emotions.

Virginia Lee Burton, a favorite writer for small children, is the highly skilled creator of things that have appealing personalities and believable emotions. In Burton's *Katy and the Big Snow*, an extraordinary red tractor named Katy responds to calls for help from the chief of police, the postmaster, the telephone company, the water department, the hospital, the fire chief, and the airport. "Sure," she says, and digs the town of Geoppolis out from a big snow two stories deep. When such real city departments believe in her, it is easy for the reader to believe in her also. In *Mike Mulligan and His Steam Shovel*, Mike's best friend is a large piece of machinery named Mary Anne, and a suspenseful story unfolds as the two friends try to dig the basement of Popperville's town hall in only one day. *The Little House* is a heroine who is strong and also needs love, as a growing city encroaches upon her and she becomes dilapidated and lonely. The house proceeds, like a real person, through a series of emotions until she is moved away from the city and happily settles down on her new foundation where "once again she was lived in and taken care of" (p. 39).

In Leo Lionni's *Alexander and the Wind-up Mouse*, a windup toy mouse and a real mouse become friends. Like many children who want to be something else and then decide they would rather be themselves, the real mouse is envious of the lovable windup mouse, and wishes to be transformed into a play mouse until he learns that the windup mouse is to be discarded. Then the real mouse uses his wish to transform his friend into a real mouse.

Themes related to self-discovery and the need for love are common in picture storybooks. These themes relate to children's personal and social development.

Humans in Realistic Situations. Young children enjoy stories about other children who share their concerns, problems, and pleasures. The numerous books written and illustrated by Ezra Jack Keats, for example, have plots, characters, and pictures that easily draw young children into other children's private worlds. One of Keats's very realistic heroes is *Louie*, a shy boy who usually does not talk to anyone. He responds to a puppet when the neighborhood children present a show, however, and a warm feeling results when the children give the puppet to him. In another book, Louie is very lonely when his family moves to a new neighborhood. He solves his problems in *The Trip* by building a model of his old neighborhood and going on an imaginative adventure with his old friends. In *Regards to the Man in the Moon*, other children tease Louie because his father is a junk dealer. His father's advice—that Louie build a spacecraft from junk—and his own imagination allow Louie and a friend to experience flight into outer space. When the other children hear of these adventures, they want to take part in them also.

While Keats's books usually have an inner-city setting, the settings created by another well-known children's author are usually the country or the coast of Maine. Robert McCloskey stresses warm family relationships in books such as *Blueberries for Sal*. This delightful story allows readers to share the berry-picking expeditions of a human mother and daughter and an adult bear and her cub. McCloskey develops drama when the youngsters get mixed up and start following the wrong parent, and provides a satisfying ending as both children are reunited with their mothers.

Loving relationships are popular themes in many picture storybooks for young children. In *The Crack-of-Dawn Walkers*, Amy Hest develops a loving relationship between grandfather and granddaughter by describing the pleasure that people enjoy during their early morning walks.

Vera Williams's *A Chair for My Mother* shows that even a young child can help her mother fulfill a dream. After a fire destroys the family's furniture, Williams's heroine earns money to help fill the large coin jar that represents her mother's and her grandmother's desire: a new, soft, comfortable chair. This goal is not easily reached, however; both mother and daughter must work together.

Mother and son share feelings about a dead grandfather in Charlotte Zolotow's *My Grandson Lew*. When six-year-old Lewis wakes up and informs his mother that he misses his grandfather, they remember together the grandfather's "eye hugs," scratchy beard, strong arms, and tobacco smell.

The growth of love and understanding between a young boy and a very old family member is the theme of Sharon Bell Mathis's *The Hundred Penny Box*. Michael develops an important relationship with his Great-great-aunt Dew, who moves into his home with an old box containing a penny for every year of her long life. This is one of many

picture storybooks, such as those of Ezra Jack Keats, that share with children of all backgrounds the warm relationships in nonwhite families (see chapter eleven). Arnold Adoff's *Black Is Brown Is Tan* tells the story of two children, their black mother and white father, and their loving grandmothers from both sides of the family.

Of course young children also confront problems in their families, including sex-role biases. In Charlotte Zolotow's *William's Doll*, a young boy wants a doll to hug, cradle, and play with. His brother calls him a creep, and his neighbor calls him a sissy. His father tries to interest him in "masculine" toys and brings him a basketball and an electric train. William enjoys both toys but still wants a doll. When his grandmother visits, he explains his wish to her, shows her he can shoot baskets, and tells her that his father does not want him to play with a doll. Grandmother under-

A realistic story shows that it is normal for a boy to want a doll. (Illustration by William Pène du Bois from *William's Doll*, by Charlotte Zolotow. Pictures copyright © 1972 by William Pène du Bois. By permission of Harper & Row.)

stands William's need, buys him a baby doll, and then kindly explains to William's upset father that William wants and needs a doll so that he can practice being a father just like his own father. Tomie de Paola deals with a similar situation in *Oliver Button Is a Sissy*. Such books can reassure children that there is nothing wrong with nonstereotypic behavior.

Picture storybooks increasingly present the real experiences of children with special educational needs or disabilities. These books tend to show that children with special needs are similar to other children. One appealing book is Jeanne Whitehouse Peterson's *I Have a Sister, My Sister Is Deaf*. The author tells in poetic form what it was like to grow up with a sister who plays the piano by feeling the rumble of the chords, climbs monkey bars, stalks deer by watching movements in the grass, lip-reads, and enjoys life. Bernard Wolf's *Anna's Silent World* takes the reader into the world of a happy deaf child as she learns to talk, read, join her classmates for stories and playground fun, and enjoy Saturday with her family and friends. Teachers report that this book helps sensitize children to the needs and feelings of the physically disabled.

Humorous and Inventive Fantasies. Dr. Seuss is one of the most popular authors of children's books. In his many outlandish stories he develops characters who are original, humorous, and talk in a style that children enjoy.

In *The 500 Hats of Bartholomew Cubbins*, both conflict and humor result when the king orders a peasant to remove his magical hat. Every time Bartholomew tries to remove one hat, another hat appears. When the number reaches 157 hats, the magicians cast a spell:

Dig a hole five furlongs deep,
Down to where the night snakes creep,
Mix and mold the mystic mud,
Malber, Balber, Tidder, Tudd. (p. 31 unnumbered)

As the hats begin to number in the hundreds, the king threatens Bartholomew with execution. Then hat number 500 is so beautiful the King offers to buy it for 500 gold pieces. With that offer, the spell is broken and a rich Bartholomew returns home.

In addition to being humorous and original, several of Seuss's characters must face moral issues. In *Horton Hatches the Egg*, Horton the elephant remains 100 percent faithful to his promise

A home becomes the site of an unexpected situation in this inventive fantasy. (From *Jumanji* by Chris Van Allsburg. Copyright © 1981 by Chris Van Allsburg. Reprinted by permission of Houghton Mifflin Company.)

to hatch a lazy bird's egg, in spite of leering by-standers and other unpleasant experiences. He gains his reward when the egg hatches and is an elphant-bird.

Chris Van Allsburg's *Jumanji* begins with a re-alistic scene involving two children who are asked to keep the house neat until their parents return with guests. Bored, the children make a mess with their toys and then go to the park, where they find instructions for a jungle adventure game that cannot be ended until one player reaches the golden city. When the children take the game home, they realize the consequences of the rules: a lion appears on the piano and chases one of them around the house. Other jungle ani-mals and jungle-related action enter the scene each time the children frantically throw the dice. Van Allsburg ends the story on a note of suspense and speculation. The children return the game, but two other children, who are notorious for never reading directions, pick up the game and run through the park.

John Burningham develops a humorously un-likely situation in *Avocado Baby*. At first the wea-kling baby of weakling parents refuses to eat. Then he eats an avocado and the parents are forced to put "Beware of the Baby" on the gate as the baby demonstrates his strength by carrying a piano upstairs, breaking his cot, and outmatching bullies.

Fantastic occurrences also form the plot of Trinka Noble's *The Day Jimmy's Boa Ate the Wash*. That a boy might have a pet boa constrictor is not too farfetched, but catastrophes occur when Jimmy takes his pet along on a class trip to a farm. Plot twists are resolved with Jimmy going home carrying a new pet pig under his arm and the farmer's wife happily knitting a sweater for the boa.

These picture storybooks can provide adults and children with many sharing experiences. The elements in outstanding picture books enhance children's enjoyment through their originality, imaginative plots, characterization, humor, and style.

SUMMARY

Picture books, in addition to providing pleasure for children, stimulate language and cognitive development, develop observational skills and descriptive vocabularies, increase sensitivity to art and beauty, and develop appreciation for lan-guage style. The appropriateness of a picture book depends upon the age of the children in-volved and whether the book is to be shared with one child or with a group.

When evaluating picture books, readers must consider whether or not the text and illustrations complement each other. The pictures should be an integral part of the book, both underscoring and supplementing what is described in the text. They should reflect the mood of the story and be accurate and authentic.

Literary elements found in Mother Goose books include rhythm, rhyme, repetition, and hyper-bole. The humor in the verses appeals to young children. Many different Mother Goose collections and picture storybook versions of single rhymes may be shared with children.

Toy books include board, pop-up, flap, cloth, and plastic books. They are designed to be shared with very young children and may en-courage children to interact with the text, develop vocabularies, count, identify colors, and discuss content with an adult.

Adults often share alphabet books with chil-dren in the expectation that children will learn to identify the letters and corresponding alphabet sounds. Alphabet books can also help develop children's observational and discussion skills.

Counting books range in complexity from those that show one large number and a drawing of the corresponding object to those that show numer-ous objects on one page or number concepts through 100. Counting and grouping objects aid children's cognitive development.

Concept books are written to stimulate chil-dren's cognitive development and to promote un-derstanding of difficult ideas as well as colors, shapes, opposites, spatial concepts, and size.

In wordless books, illustrations tell the whole story. These books are especially good for stimu-lating ideas and language, since they invite indi-vidual interpretations. Some wordless books de-velop easily identifiable plots, some have considerable detail, and others could have nu-merous interpretations.

Easy-to-read books are designed to be read by children with beginning reading skills; therefore authors use a controlled vocabulary. Children may increase their feelings of self-esteem and ac-complishment as they complete successful read-ing experiences.

Picture storybooks develop a definite story line. In a well-written picture storybook, the illustrations and narrative complement each other. Memorable storybooks contain elements of originality and imagination, plot, characterization, humor, and style. Many attractively illustrated picture storybooks with appealing story lines are found in traditional literature, discussed in chapter six.

☐ Choose a picture storybook that develops characterization through the illustrations. Try to depict this same characterization through narration. Compare the length of the two stories.

Suggested Activities for Adult Understanding of Picture Books

☐ Choose several different editions of Mother Goose that contain the same nursery rhymes. Compare the artists' interpretations of these characters—for example, the illustrations of Jack Sprat found in *Marguerite De Angeli's Book of Nursery and Mother Goose Rhymes*, Paul Galdone's *Jack Sprat, His Wife & His Cat*, Kate Greenaway's *Mother Goose*, and Wallace Tripp's *Granfa' Grig Had a Pig*.

☐ Select a common animal or object that often appears in children's books. Find several picture books that develop a story about that animal or object. Compare the ways the different artists depict the animals through the illustrations, and the ways the writers describe the animals and develop plots about them.

☐ Select several alphabet books appropriate for young children and for older children. Evaluate each group of books, then share the books, the rationale, and the evaluation with the class.

☐ Find examples of rhythm, rhyme, repetition of sounds, and hyperbole found in Mother Goose.

☐ Select several wordless books appropriate for stimulating young children's oral language development and several that are more appropriate for use with older children. Compare their details and plots.

☐ Begin a collection of nursery rhymes from other lands that illustrate the universal nature of children and the unique characteristics of people living in these countries.

☐ Find examples of humor in picture storybooks. Look for word play and nonsense, the unexpected, exaggeration, the ridiculous, and superiority.

References

1 Averill, Esther. "What Is a Picture Book?" In *Caldecott Medal Books: 1938–1957*, edited by Bertha Miller and Elinor Field. Boston: The Horn Book, Inc., 1957.

2 Barsam, Richard. *A Peaceable Kingdom*. New York: Viking, 1978.

3 Cianciolo, Patricia J. "A Look at the Illustrations in Children's Favorite Picture Books," In *Children's Choices: Teaching with Books Children Like*, edited by Nancy Roser and Margaret Frith. Newark, Del.: International Reading Association, 1983.

4 Fry, Edward. "Fry's Readability Graph: Clarifications, Validity, and Extension." *Journal of Reading* 21 (December 1977): 249.

5 Hearne, Betsy. "Picture Books: More Than a Story." *Booklist* Vol. 30 (December 1, 1983): 577–578.

6 MacCann, Donnarae, and Richard, Olga. *The Child's First Books: A Critical Study of Pictures and Texts*. New York: Wilson, 1973.

7 Martin, Sue Anne Gillespi. "The Caldecott Medal Award Books, 1938–1968: Their Literary and Oral Characteristics as They Relate to Storytelling," University Microfilm No. 72–16, 219. Detroit, Mich.: Wayne State University, 1969.

8 Strickland, Dorothy S. "Prompting Language and Concept Development." In *Literature and Young Children,* edited by Bernice Cullinan. Urbana, Ill.: National Conference of Teachers of English, 1977.

9 Sutherland, Zena, and Hearne, Betsy. "In Search of the Perfect Picture Book Definition," In *Jump Over the Moon: Selected Professional Readings*, edited by Pamela Barron and Jennifer Burley. New York: Holt, Rinehart and Winston, 1984.

10 Townsend, John Rowe. *Written for Children*. New York: Lippincott, 1975.

11 Whalen-Levitt, Peggy. "Making Picture Books Real: Reflections on a Child's-Eye View," In *The First Steps: Best of the Early CHLA Quarterly*, compiled by Patricia Dooley. Lafayette, Ind.: Purdue University, Children's Literature Association, 1984.

12 Wintle, Justin, and Fisher, Emma. *The Pied Pipers: Interviews with the Influential Creators of Children's Literature*. New York: Paddington, 1974.

Additional References

Cianciolo, Patricia, ed. *Picture Books for Children*. Chicago: American Library Association, 1973.

Coody, Betty. *Using Literature with Young Children*. Dubuque, Ia.: Brown, 1979.

Hopkins, Lee Bennett. *The Best of Book Bonanza*. New York: Holt, Rinehart & Winston, 1980.

Kingman, Lee, ed. *Newbery and Caldecott Medal Books, 1966–1975*. Boston: Horn Book, 1975.

Moore, Vardine. *Preschool Story Hour*. Metuchen, N.J.: Scarecrow. 1972.

Paulin, Mary Ann. *Creative Uses of Children's Literature*. Hamden, Conn.: Shoestring Press, 1982; paperback, 1985.

Peterson, Linda Kauffman, and Solt, Marilyn Leathers. *Newbery and Caldecott Medal and Honor Books: An Annotated Bibliography*. Boston, Mass.: G.K. Hall, 1982.

Roser, Nancy, and Margaret Fritz, eds. *Children's Choices: Teaching with Books Children Like*. Newark, Del.: International Reading Association, 1983.

Sartain, Harry W., ed. *Mobilizing Family Forces for Worldwide Reading Success*. Newark, Del.: International Reading Association, 1981.

Involving Children in Picture Books

IF READING PICTURE BOOKS IS TO BE A truly shared experience, adults must care enough to select books and prepare book-related activities that children will find stimulating and enjoyable. Picture-book experiences may involve nursery rhymes that stimulate oral language development and dramatization; alphabet, counting, and concept books that develop basic knowledge and discussion skills; wordless books that encourage children to find objects in pictures, make predictions, tell their own stories, or write creatively; picture storybooks ideal for reading aloud; illustrations that encourage aesthetic sensitivity; or picture books of all sorts that encourage children to join in with songs and movement. Whatever the book, if it is worth sharing, the sharing experience is worth thoughtful preparation. This section discusses a few of the many ways adults can use picture books to enhance children's personal development.

SHARING MOTHER GOOSE WITH CHILDREN

Mother Goose rhymes are a natural means of stimulating language development and listening appreciation in very young children. Linda Gibson Geller (5), who strongly endorses the use of nursey rhymes with young children, maintains that nursery rhymes popular with preschool children have one or more of the following characteristics: a simple story line; a simple story line that encourages finger play; a story in song with repeated chorus; a verse with nonsense words; a description of daily actions; and a choral reading in which children join in with the rhyming words.

Even two- and three-year-olds thoroughly enjoy and respond to the rhyme, rhythm, and nonsense found in nursery rhymes. Because passive listening may not encourage language development, adults must create experiences that motivate children to interact with the verses in enjoyable ways. Once children have heard the simpler Mother Goose rhymes several times, they usually know the rhymes from memory and can help an adult finish the verses by filling in the missing word or rhyming elements: "Jack and Jill, went up the ———, to fetch a pail of water, Jack fell down, and broke his ——, and Jill came tumbling after." In addition to providing enjoyment during a shared experience, this activity encourages auditory discrimination and attentive listening skills necessary for later successes in reading and language arts.

An adult may also insert an incorrect word into a rhyme familiar to children and have children correct the error. Children especially enjoy this exercise when the nursery rhyme book has large, colorful illustrations in which the children can point out what is wrong with the adult version. The adult could say, "Jack be nimble, Jack be quick, Jack jump over a pumpkin." or "Little Boy Blue come blow your horn/The pig's in the meadow, the chick's in the corn." Many children enjoy trying to trick the adult by making up their own incorrect versions.

Young children enjoy creative play and will spontaneously dramatize many of their favorite rhymes. Dramatization allows children to explore body movements, develop an awareness of their senses, expand their imaginations and language development, and experiment with characterization (15). One of the first adult-led creative drama activities recommended for beginning school-age children encourages development of a sense of movement and interpretation of a situation without the use of words. The adult can read or tell various nursery rhymes while children pretend to be each character in the rhyme and perform the action expressed in the verse. Enough time should be allowed following each line so that they can act out the part. Children especially enjoy acting out action rhymes such as "Little Miss Muffet," "Jack Be Nimble," and "The Cat and the Fiddle." After children have experiences with a number of multiple roles in the nursery rhymes, they can be led in the development of cooperative pantomimes. For example, "Little Miss Muffet" has two characters, a girl and a spider, while "The Cat and the Fiddle" has four. Children can form small groups and informally interact with others as they pantomime the action. A child or a group of children can also pantomime the action of a nursery rhyme character while another child or group guesses the identity of the character.

Geraldine Brain Siks (15) believes that nursery rhymes are an excellent way to introduce children to the concept that a drama has several parts—a beginning, a middle, and an end. (She recommends this as an introductory activity for both older and younger children.) The simple plots in many nursery rhymes make them ideal for this purpose. The rhyme "Humpty Dumpty" contains three definite actions that cannot be in-

Mother Goose rhymes stimulate language development and enjoyment when shared with an appreciative child.

terchanged and still retain a logical sequence: (1) beginning—"Humpty Dumpty sat on a wall"; (2) middle—"Humpty Dumpty had a great fall"; and (3) end—"All the King's horses and all the King's men couldn't put Humpty Dumpty together again." Children can listen to the rhyme, identify the actions, discuss the reasons for the order, and finally act out each part. The adult can encourage them to extend their parts by adding dialogue or characters that might be active in their creative extensions of beginning, middle, or ending incidents. Other nursery rhymes illustrating sequential plot development include "Jack and Jill," "Pat-a Cake, Pat-a Cake, Baker's Man," and "Rock-a-Bye Baby."

Nursery rhymes that children have memorized can be used for choral-speaking arrangements, even though the children may not have developed reading skills. Chapter eight suggests ways to stimulate oral language and appreciation through choral speaking.

Nursery rhymes can also be used with five-through eight-year-olds to stimulate creative dramatic skills through pantomime and role playing, to introduce children to the concept of plot development, to expand children's interpretive skills through choral speaking, and to encourage children's own storytelling.

Adults can encourage children to expand upon one of their favorite nursery rhymes, as do several delightful picture books devoted to one rhyme—such as Janet Stevens's *The House that Jack Built* and Sarah Martin's *The Comic Adventures of Old Mother Hubbard and Her Dog*. After sharing one of these books with children, the adult could ask them if there are any Mother Goose characters they would like to know more about. A discussion with first graders, for example, revealed that several children wanted to know what it would be like to live in a pumpkin. They talked about how they might decorate its interior, what they could do inside a pumpkin,

CHART 5—1
Mother Goose personages

Mother Goose Rhyme	Personages	Situations
There was an old woman who lived in a shoe.	Parliament James VI of Scotland and I of England	Geographic location of parliament. England had many people. This disliked monarch was not English, but Parliament told the people to get along as well as they could.
Old King Cole was a merry old soul.	Third century—King Cole	He was a brave and popular monarch.
Humpty Dumpty sat on a wall.	Richard III—1483	The "usurper" when he lay slain upon Bosworth Field.
I love sixpence, pretty little sixpence.	Henry VII—1493 Charles of France	Miserliness of Henry resulted in public jest. French ruler pacified Henry with £149,000 when Henry signed the treaty of Etaples.
Little Jack Horner sat in a corner eating his Christmas pie.	Jack Horner, an emissary of the Bishop of Glastonbury	Jack lived at Horner Hall and was taking twelve deeds to church-owned estates to Henry VIII. The deeds were hidden in a pie. On his way, he pulled out the deed to Mells Park estate and kept it.
Sing a song of sixpence, a pocket full of rye.	Henry VIII	Henry's humming over the confiscated revenues from the friars' rich grainfields.
Four and twenty blackbirds baked in a pie	The friars and monks	The title deeds to twenty-four estates owned by the church were put into a pie and delivered to Henry VIII.
When the pie was opened, The birds began to sing;	The friars and monks	The monks put their choicest treasures in chests and hid them in a lake.
Wasn't that a dainty dish To set before a king?	Henry VIII	Henry picked the deeds he wanted and bestowed others as payment.
The King was in the counting house Counting out his money	Henry VIII	Henry was counting his revenues.
The Queen was in the pantry Eating bread and honey;	Katherine of Aragon	She was eating the bread of England, spread with Spain's assurances that the King could not divorce her.
The maid was in the garden, Hanging out the clothes,	Anne Boleyn	Anne had dainty frocks from France and was smiling at the King in the garden of Whitehall Palace.
When down flew a blackbird, And snipped off her nose.	Anne Boleyn, Cardinal Wolsey, and the royal headsman.	Cardinal Wolsey broke Anne's engagement to Lord Percy. After marrying Henry VIII, the royal headsman executed Anne—1563.
To market, to market to buy a fat pig.	Henry VIII	Henry VIII declared himself head of the Church of England to obtain a divorce from Katherine of Aragon.
Needles and pins, needles and pins, When a man marries his trouble begins.	Katherine Howard and Henry VIII	After her marriage to Henry, she introduced pins from France to the English court. Ladies had to begin a separate allowance for this luxury.
Punch and Judy fought for a pie; Punch gave Judy a sad blow in the eye.	Punch—England Judy—France	England and France fought over Italy.
Little Boy Blue	Cardinal Wolsey	The cardinal was too busy with pleasant dreams about his fame to be aware of danger.

CHART 5–1
Mother Goose personages (cont.)

Mother Goose Rhyme	Personages	Situations
Hey diddle, diddle, The cat and the fiddle.	The cat—Queen Elizabeth 1 –1561	Queen Elizabeth played with her ministers as if they were mice. She liked to dance.
A frog he would a-wooing go,	Duke of Anjou and Queen Elizabeth I—1577	A satire about the wooing of forty-nine-year-old Elizabeth by the twenty-three-year-old French prince.
I saw a ship a sailing, A sailing on the sea,	Sir Francis Drake	Drake brought back potatoes and other foods that were introduced to England.
Mistress Mary, quite contrary. How does your garden grow?	Mary Queen of Scots and her royal maids	She wore flashing jewels and gowns from Paris.
Little Miss Muffet sat on a tuffet Eating her curds and whey; When along came a spider, and sat down beside her,	Mary Queen of Scots John Knox	At eighteen (1560), she was made monarch of Scotland. She laughed with her maids. John Knox denounced the frivolous Mary from the pulpit of St. Giles.
Little Bo-Peep has lost her sheep.	Mary Queen of Scots	Tells about Mary's problems as the clans rose and prepared for battle.
Jack Sprat could eat no fat, His wife could eat no lean.	Charles I Henrietta Maria of France	After their marriage, they each went their heedless ways and plundered England.
Yankee Doodle came to town, Riding on a pony; He stuck a feather in his hat, and called it macaroni.	Prince Rupert of the Palatinate, Royalist General of the Civil Wars—1653	Prince Rupert had a large following; he could lead men and showed great endurance. The feather signified that the wearer was one of his soldiers. Rupert could steal into an enemy's camp and take the horses.

and how neighbors might react to a pumpkin in the neighborhood. They dictated their story to the teacher and then divided it into separate sentences, each written and illustrated on tagboard by one child, then placed in the classroom library. This book was one of the most popular picture storybooks in the classroom. When more children created their own books, the children's librarian developed a library display of both commercially published Mother Goose books and books printed and illustrated by the children. Other Mother Goose rhymes that lend themselves to extended oral, written, or artistic versions include "Old Mother Hubbard," "Old King Cole," and "Simple Simon."

Even sixth-graders can benefit from activities related to Mother Goose rhymes. In one sixth-grade class, students were discussing their favorite early childhood stories and wondered whether Mother Goose had been a real person. This question led to library research, debate, and the creative writing of nursery rhymes about incidents and people in history and current events.

The children's search for the real Mother Goose led to conflicting answers. Some sources indicated that the original Mother Goose was Dame Goose of Boston. Another resource said that she was goose-footed Bertha, wife of Robert II of France. Still others referred to Charles Perrault's *Tales of Mother Goose*, published in 1697. And many others stated that there never was a Mother Goose. Following this research, members of the class chose the version they favored and debated the issue with one another.

Several of the children's sources indicated that some Mother Goose rhymes were based upon the lives of real people. The children found this idea fascinating, and they wondered who or what incident might have been the basis of "Little Miss Muffet," "Little Jack Horner" or "Humpty Dumpty." A search for possible personages and situations resulted in the information shown in Chart 5–1. (Please note that the authenticity of these connections between Mother Goose personages and real situations is not verifiable. The activity, however, proved fascinating to the students and increased their literary and historical awareness.)

Finally, the children wrote their own Mother Goose rhymes about people and situations in the news or in history, which acquainted them with unfamiliar ideas, beliefs, and customs of the past and present.

University students in children's literature classes have developed other stimulating ways of using Mother Goose with older children. For example, children have compared the illustrations in different editions of Mother Goose, discussed their personal responses to the illustrations, discovered more information about art media used by illustrators, demonstrated certain techniques to the group, and illustrated their own picture books to be shared with younger children.

SHARING ALPHABET BOOKS WITH CHILDREN

The most common way to share an alphabet book with children is to read it to them or have them identify objects in the pictures to reinforce their ability to identify letter/sound relationships. According to John Warren Stewig (18), however, alphabet books can and should also be used for developing children's visual literacy (the ability to look analytically at a picture and interpret it) and verbal literacy (the ability to talk clearly about one's observations, comparisons, and reactions). Stewig recommends a three-step sequence of activities using the illustrations in alphabet books: children can describe the object in a picture, compare two different objects, and say which picture they prefer and why. Since alphabet books have been illustrated and written at several levels of complexity, this activity could be used with children of all ages.

Stewig's recommended activities can be used, for example, with three ABC books, appropriate for young children, that contain different types of illustrations of butterflies: *Brian Wildsmith's ABC*, *Ed Emberley's ABC*, and Marcia Brown's *All Butterflies: An ABC*. During a discussion of these three books, the adult could use the following sequence in order to increase the children's visual and verbal literacy: (1) Ask the children to look at each picture and describe what the artist has drawn in the picture, what colors are used in the picture, how large the butterfly is, what the butterfly is doing, where the butterfly is in the picture, and so forth. (2) Ask the children to compare the illustrations of butterflies in the three

ABC books, focusing the discussion on similarities and differences in size, color, and setting and on which butterfly seems most real. (3) Have the children tell which picture they prefer and why.

It is very important to allow children to think about and articulate their own reasons for choosing a picture. This requires careful leadership by an adult, because the adult's opinion should not be used to sway children into forming one opinion. One child preferred the Wildsmith butterfly because it had beautiful purple and pink colors and resembled one he had painted that his mother had had framed. Another child preferred Marcia Brown's butterflies because when she looked at them, she felt as if she were walking in a beautiful meadow and watching the butterflies flying up ahead of her. A third child liked Emberley's butterfly because it was part of a humorous picture and she liked the idea of a butterfly sharing an experience with a bear and a bird. Each child had valid reasons for these preferences. To increase language skills further, children might pretend they were one of the butterflies and tell a story about what they would do if they were that butterfly. They could also paint butterfly pictures to increase aesthetic and visual skills.

USING PICTURE BOOKS THAT ENCOURAGE INTERACTION BETWEEN CHILD AND TEXT

Several books for young children encourage them to find hidden objects or to predict what is going to happen next. Young children love to play "I spy" and look for hidden objects in pictures. Actively involving children in a story experience stimulates their language development, cognitive development, and enjoyment.

Familiar folktale and nursery rhyme characters are hiding in the illustrations of Janet and Allen Ahlberg's *Each Peach Pear Plum: An I-Spy Story*. The two lines that precede each picture tell who is in the picture; the text also suggests a hidden figure. Children enjoy searching the pastel watercolor drawings for favorites such as Tom Thumb, Mother Hubbard, Cinderella, The Three Bears, Jack and Jill, and Robin Hood. Children, not an adult, should locate the hidden characters.

Another excellent book for interaction and discovery is *We Hide, You Seek*, by Jose Aruego and Ariane Dewey. Children would miss a great deal of potential enjoyment if an adult read the twenty-six words of the text without encouraging the children to find and identify the animals in the pictures, which tell the story of what happens when a group of African animals challenges a rhino to a game of hide and seek. The artists have camouflaged the animals so well that children must search for spotted leopards and giraffes hidden in the bush, reptiles and birds hidden in the desert, alligators and birds hidden in the swamp, zebras and lions camouflaged on the plains, and hippos and crocodiles hidden in the river.

Tana Hoban's *Take Another Look* encourages children to make predictions. This fascinating book allows the reader to peek through a hole and see a portion of the photograph found on the following page. Children can tell what they think the picture is, and why, before turning the page to see if their prediction was correct.

The effectiveness of such books depends in part on the adult's ability to stimulate children's active participation, whether they are reading or listening, sitting in the adult's lap or in a small group.

SHARING WORDLESS PICTURE BOOKS WITH CHILDREN

Wordless books are ideal for encouraging language growth, stimulating intellectual development, motivating creative writing, and evaluating a child's language skills. Adults should consider children's ages and the complexity of the plot or details when choosing wordless books. Some have considerable detail that stimulates observational skills and descriptive vocabularies; others are more appropriate for encouraging understanding and interpretation of sequential plot development.

Stimulating Cognitive and Language Development

Chapter one discussed the value of literature in promoting children's cognitive development. Several skills associated with the thinking process—observing, comparing, and organizing—can be developed through the use of wordless books. Children can describe what is happening in each picture and what details they observe, compare pictures or changes that occur as the result of the wordless plot, and organize their thoughts into a sequentially well-organized story. Describing, oral comparing, and storytelling also help them expand their vocabularies.

Children can describe the action in each detailed picture in Peter Spier's *Noah's Ark*, for example, as they follow the building of the ark, the loading of food, utensils, and animals, the problems that develop inside the ark, and the final landing and starting of life anew. One group of seven-year-olds—

1 identified animals they recognized in a double-page spread showing animals boarding the ark;
2 described the color, size, mode of traveling, and natural habitat of the animals;
3 identified humorous details in the illustrations;
4 identified Noah's problems and suggested possible causes and/or solutions;
5 speculated about Noah's feelings as he tried to rid the roof of too many birds, dealt with a reluctant donkey, and finally closed the doors of the ark;
6 thought of descriptive words for the animals, such as "slithering" snakes, "leaping" frogs, and "lazy brown" monkeys;
7 compared the position of the snails in the illustrations at the beginning of the book and at the end;
8 chose one picture each and told or wrote a detailed description of the picture.

Mercer Mayer's humorous wordless book *Frog Goes to Dinner* encourages before-and-after comparisons: people are enjoying a leisurely meal in one picture, for example, and in the next are experiencing the disruptions caused by Frog. A first-grader gave the following oral comparison when he discussed two pictures of the band: "The band was playing beautifully. They had their eyes closed and were enjoying the music. All of a sudden the frog jumped in the saxophone. Now the saxophone player tried to play but couldn't. His face puffed out and he looked funny. The other players jumped. The frog made the drum player fall into his drum. The horn player thought it was funny."

Mitsumasa Anno's wordless books help develop older children's observational skills. *Anno's Journey*, *Anno's Italy*, and *Anno's Britain* contain fascinating details that could be discovered during a visual trip through Europe. At the end of the books, there are lists of details that a reader should look for, such as characters from folktales or well-known paintings or people.

Sharing stories in the classroom or library allows children to discover the pleasure in books.

Motivating Writing

With their colorful illustrations, wordless books are ideal for motivating children to write or dictate captions, compose group stories, and write individual stories.

Dictation of Picture Captions. Many younger children enjoy having their parents or teachers write down their brief descriptions of the pictures in wordless books. First the children look at a book and discuss it. Then the adult writes down exactly what the child dictates about the picture. If reading readiness is also a goal, the adult should repeat each word as it is being written. When the captions are finished, the children and adult can read them in sequence while the children follow the illustrations and the printing. The adult can also mix the captions up and ask the children to put them in sequential order.

Wordless books that are simple enough for young children and also have a plot development that encourages children to dictate sequentially ordered sentences or picture captions include Fernando Krahn's *Who's Seen the Scissors?*; Martha Alexander's *Out! Out! Out!*; Pat Hutchins's *Changes, Changes*; and Mercer Mayer's various book adventures with Boy, Dog, and Frog.

Dictation of Group or Individual Stories. Educators in reading and language arts such as Roach Van Allen (1) and Russell Stauffer (17) recommend the use of language experiences that stimulate children's oral language and writing through exploring ideas and expressing feelings. These experiences in turn provide the content for group and individual stories composed by children and recorded by an adult. Many teachers introduce students to the "language experience" approach to literature through a group chart story. This activity is appropriate for any age group, but is most used as a reading-readiness or early-reading activity in kindergarten or first grade.

Usually an entire group (guided by the teacher) writes the chart story, following a shared motivational experience such as a field trip, an art project, a film, or listening to music or a story. Many of the wordless books discussed in this text provide excellent sources for the motivational activity.

If a wordless book is used to motivate the writing of a chart story, an adult first shares the book with the group. Following oral discussion, the children dictate the story, as an adult records it on posterboard, chalkboard or large sheets of newsprint, repeating each word aloud. (Some adults identify each child's contribution on the chart story by placing his or her name after the contribution.) It is essential that children be able to see each word as it is written. As the adult writes the chart story, children will see that sentences flow from top to bottom on the page, follow a left-to-right sequence, begin with capital letters, and end with periods. Following the completion of the chart story, the adult reads the whole story. Then, the children reread the story with the adult. Following this experience, some individual children may choose to read the whole story aloud while others choose to read only their own contributions.

Wordless books and their accompanying chart stories should be placed in an area easily accessible to children, so that they can enjoy reading the stories by themselves. Some teachers tape record the children's reading of the chart stories and then place the recording, the chart story, and the wordless book in a listening center. (For additional information on using the language experience method, see Russell Stauffer [17] and Roach Van Allen [1].)

The sequentially developed wordless books may also be used to teach children how to tell or write stories with stronger plots and sequential order. John Goodall's *The Adventures of Paddy Pork* contains more plot development than many wordless books. When the book was used with a group of fourth graders, the primary purpose was to encourage them to write a sequentially developed story. The teacher first shared the book orally with the children. They discussed the setting, characters in the story, and the probable events that occurred. The teacher encouraged the children to give their own interpretations of the pictures and then share their reasons for those interpretations. The children then wrote their own stories to accompany the pictures in the book. The stories may also be placed on tapes in a listening center, read to children in other classes, or added to the library.

Picnic, by Emily Arnold McCully, provides opportunities for children to write dialogue, describe settings, develop conflict and characterization, and discuss themes. University students report that Chris Van Allsburg's *The Mysteries of Harris Burdick* is one of the most enticing nearly wordless books for older elementary students. Children can speculate about each fantasy in Allsburg's book, write their own stories, and share the stories with other children who may have had different interpretations. Because there is no correct answer, children may choose to write more than one story about the same picture.

READING TO CHILDREN

The adult who reads to children accepts an opportunity and a responsibility for sharing a marvelous experience. Kay Vandergrift (19) states this dual role very well: "Through reading aloud, the reader re-creates for children not only their own world seen through other eyes but leads them also to worlds beyond the eye. Reading aloud is a way to let children enter, vicariously, into a larger world—both real and fanciful—in company with an adult who cares enough to take them on the literary journey" (p. 11).

The Values of Reading to Children

There is probably no better way to interest children in the world of books than to read to them. Listening to books read aloud is a way for children to learn that literature is a form of pleasure. Without parents, librarians, or other adults, a very young child would not experience nursery rhymes or stories such as Beatrix Potter's *Peter Rabbit* and younger elementary children would not experience the marvelous verses and stories of A.A. Milne or enter the joyous world of Dr. Seuss. For children just struggling to learn to read, a book may not be a source of happiness. In fact, books may actually arouse negative feelings in many children. Being read to helps them develop an appreciation for literature that they could not manage with their own reading ability.

The pleasure of the listening experience usually motivates children to ask for a book again or read it themselves. Very young children may ask for a book to be reread so many times that they memorize the content and then feel proud of being able to "read" their own book. When a teacher reads a particularly enjoyable selection to children in an elementary classroom, the children tend to check out all copies of that book in the class or school library. A study of fifth graders showed that when teachers read aloud to them for twenty to thirty minutes a day both the quantity and quality of the students' voluntary reading improved (16). Unfortunately, research also indicates that the amount of time a teacher spends reading stories usually decreases in the upper elementary grades, and is almost nonexistent in middle schools and high schools.

Another value of reading aloud is the improvement it often brings to related areas such as reading achievement and language and vocabulary development. A study by Dorothy Cohen (4) demonstrated that the vocabulary and reading scores of seven-year-olds who listened to books read aloud for twenty minutes each day improved significantly. Cohen's results are not surprising; listening to and discussing stories gives children opportunities to learn new meanings of familiar words, new synonyms for known words, and new words and concepts.

Reading aloud to children also improves their readiness for formal reading instruction. According to Mary Jett-Simpson (8), "Parents are the most important resource for developing readiness for formal reading instruction. Parents can establish an attitude toward reading by giving books an important place in their own daily lives as well as in the lives of their children" (p. 73). Jett-Simpson maintains that the most powerful sharing technique available is for a parent to set aside twenty to thirty minutes each evening to hold and read to a child.

In order to gain all of these benefits from reading, the adult must select appropriate literature, prepare the selection carefully, and read with enthusiasm and enjoyment.

Choosing the Books

Choosing the appropriate book for reading aloud depends, of course, upon the ages of the children, their interests, the need to balance the types of literature presented, the number of children who will share the listening experience, and the quality of the literature. A book selected for reading aloud should be worthy of the time spent by both reader and listeners. It should not be something picked up hurriedly to fill in time.

Style and illustrations are both considerations when choosing books to read aloud. The language in A.A. Milne's *Winnie the Pooh* and Dr. Seuss's *The 500 Hats of Bartholomew Cubbins* appeals to young listeners. Likewise, young children enjoy illustrations that are an integral part of the story. For example, illustrations in Robert McCloskey's *Lentil* help children visualize a midwestern town in the early 1900s, and the illustrations in Maurice Sendak's *Where the Wild Things Are* bring Max's exceptional adventure to life.

Other books, such as Tomie de Paola's *The Clown of God*, have such beautiful illustrations that they should be chosen to encourage aesthetic appreciation. Many books discussed in chapter four and in this chapter require that the illustrations be shared with children.

Children's ages, attention spans, and levels of reading ability are also important considerations when selecting stories to be read aloud. The books chosen should challenge children to improve their reading skills and increase their appreciation of outstanding literature. The numerous easy-to-read books should usually be left for children to read independently. Young children respond to short stories; in fact, the four- or five-year-old may benefit from several short story times a day rather than a twenty- or thirty-minute period. Books such as Pat Hutchins's *The Wind Blew* and Robert Kraus's *Leo the Late Bloomer* are short and have large, colorful pictures. *The Wind Blew* uses rhyming words to tell its story. *Leo the Late Bloomer* relates the problems of a young tiger who cannot talk, eat, or read correctly until, all at once, he finally blooms. As children enter kindergarten and advance into first grade, they begin to enjoy longer picture storybooks with more elaborate plots. Robert McCloskey's *Make Way for Ducklings* and the various Dr. Seuss books are favorites with beginning elementary school children. Books such as William Steig's *Caleb & Kate* and Graham Oakley's *The Church Mice Adrift* have enough plot development to appeal to second-grade children. By the time children reach third grade, they are ready for stories read a chapter at a time. (A reading period should not end in the middle of a chapter.) Third graders usually enjoy E. B. White's *The Trumpet of the Swan*, *Charlotte's Web*, and *Stuart Little*. Fourth and fifth graders often respond to books like Madeleine L'Engle's *A Wrinkle in Time* and C. S. Lewis's *The Lion, the Witch and the Wardrobe*. Armstrong Sperry's *Call It Courage* and Esther Forbes's *Johnny Tremain* often appeal to sixth- and seventh-grade students. (These books will be discussed in later chapters.)

Reading to children should not end in the elementary grades. Without enjoyable oral listening experiences many older children are not exposed to good literature because the literature is too difficult for them to read independently. Mary Kimmell and Elizabeth Segel (9) have compiled an annotated list of books that are appropriate for reading aloud to older children.

Preparing to Read Aloud

Many adults mistakenly believe that children's stories are so simple there is no need for an adult to read a selection before reading it to children. Ramon R. Ross (14) states his contrary view with considerable force: "If I were to lay down for you one single cardinal rule that must never be broken, it would be that you never, *never* read a story aloud to an audience unless you have first read it aloud to yourself" (p. 207). Many embarrassing situations, such as being unable to pronounce a word or selecting an inappropriate book, can be avoided if the adult first reads the story silently—in order to understand it, identify the sequence of events, recognize the mood, and identify any problems with vocabulary or concepts—and then reads it aloud in order to practice pronunciation, pacing, and voice characterization. Adults with little or no experience in reading to children can listen to themselves on a tape recorder. Adults should also decide how to introduce the story and what type of discussion or other activity, if any, might follow the reading.

The Reading Itself

What makes the story hour a time of magic or an insignificant part of the day? Research conducted by Linda Lamme (10) concludes that in addition to an enthusiastic reader and a carefully selected story, the following factors contribute to the quality of an adult's reading performance:

1 Child involvement, including reading parts of a selection with an adult, predicting what will happen next, or filling in missing words, is the most influential factor during oral reading.
2 Eye contact between the reader and the audience is essential.
3 Adults who read with expression are more effective than those who use a monotonous tone.
4 Good oral readers try to put variety into their voices; pitch should be neither too high nor too low, and volume should be neither too loud nor too soft.
5 Readers who point to meaningful words or pictures in the book as they read are better oral readers than those who merely read the story and show the pictures.
6 Adults who know the story and do not need to read the text verbatim are more effective during the presentation.

7 Readers who select picture books large enough for children to see and appealing enough to hold their interest or elicit their comments are most effective.
8 Grouping children so that all can see the pictures and hear the story is important.
9 Adults who highlight the words and language of the story by making the rhymes apparent, discussing unusual vocabulary words, and emphasizing any repetition are better readers.

Adults should consider all of these factors when preparing for an oral presentation and when actually reading a story to an audience of children. Properly prepared, the adult can take children on a much-appreciated literary journey.

USING PICTURE STORYBOOKS TO STIMULATE CHILDREN'S DEVELOPMENT

Child development authority Barbara Borusch (2) maintains that adults can use picture storybooks to stimulate children's language, cognitive, moral, and social development, as well as to motivate children's interest in other books.

Robert McCloskey's *Time of Wonder*, for example, describes a family's experiences on an island in Maine. The story's natural setting can encourage children to expand their vocabularies and to understand concepts such as porpoise, gull, barnacle, bay, island, and driftwood. McCloskey's vivid language and figures of speech can acquaint children with new ways of experiencing and describing what they see and hear in the world around them: rustling leaves, heavy stillness, slamming rain, and gentle wind soft as a lullaby. As choppy waves indicate the approaching storm, McCloskey gives children many opportunities to observe the sharp contrasts in nature. Adults sharing the book with children can help them apply these observational powers to their own everyday lives.

Discussing the similarities and differences between the island before the hurricane and after it, between islands in different parts of the world, and between the island in the book and the children's own environment also can enhance children's cognitive development. Children can be encouraged to observe storms in their own environment and describe the changes that result, using vocabulary that best conveys the color, sound, size, and time of such experiences.

Members of the family in *Time of Wonder* prepare for the hurricane and endure it together. Children who have read or heard the story can evaluate the responsibilities and the possible feelings of each family member and consider what they or their families might feel and do under similar circumstances.

One of the most valuable things about picture storybooks such as *Time of Wonder* is their potential to motivate children to seek out other reading experiences. In this case, children may want to read or listen to other fictional or informational books about the Maine coast, storms, weather, coastal regions, water recreation, treasures from the sea, and water birds and other wildlife.

DEVELOPING CHILDREN'S AESTHETIC SENSITIVITY

If the word *aesthetic* denotes the sensitivity to art and beauty, then looking at the beautiful illustrations in children's books must be an aesthetic experience for the viewer. Aesthetic sensitivity is important, according to H. S. Broudy (3), because "it is a primary source of experience on which all cognition, judgment, and action depend. It furnishes the raw material for concepts and ideals, for creating a world of possibility" (p. 636). Broudy believes that aesthetic experiences are so vital they should be considered a basic in children's education and that the best way to improve children's aesthetic sensitivity is to have them experiment with the various artistic media themselves.

Linda Leonard Lamme and Frances Kane (11) also maintain that children learn to appreciate the artistic media used in book illustrations when they are given the stimulation and time to become actively involved in making their own illustrations. Some artistic media are too complex for very young children, of course, but Lamme and Kane believe that collage is an ideal medium for stimulating children's creative interpretations of literature and developing their fine motor skills. In the process of making their own collages and reacting to the collages in book illustrations, children can also improve their vocabularies and oral discussion skills. Ezra Jack Keats, Leo Lionni, and Jeannie Baker are among the well-known illustrators of children's books who use collage. Adults can use the work of such artists first to enlighten themselves and then as a source of material for children to discuss and compare. (Jeannie Baker's collage illustrations for *Grandmother* are a fine source of inspiration for both adults and children because Baker uses many different textures to create large, colorful pictures.)

Based on their work with young children, Lamme and Kane recommend that adults use the following sequential procedures when introducing children to collage:

1 Encourage children to experiment with the collage technique by having them tear and cut shapes and pictures from plain paper or magazines and then paste the shapes onto another piece of paper.

2 Provide opportunities for children to experience different textures in the world around them and then use those textures in collages. Children could take a "texture exploration" walk, for example, during which they could feel and describe the textures of tree bark, leaves, grass, flowers, sidewalks, building materials, all types of fabrics, all types of paper, food, and so forth. After they have experienced and discussed various textures, have them collect items with different textural qualities, then use the items in charts and texture collages. Encourage the children to touch and carefully look at their collage experiments and discuss their reactions to different texture combinations.

3 Have the children create their own collages or series of collages using as many different tex-

tures as they wish. Then ask them to share these illustrations with one another, along with accompanying stories or descriptions.

4 Share with the children a picture book illustrated with collage. While reading the story and showing the children the pictures, ask the children to recognize the collage technique, discuss the feelings produced by each collage object and why they think the illustrator chose a certain material to represent it, and describe the texture they would feel if they could touch the original collage. Let them decide whether or not the collage illustrations make the story better.

Some picture book illustrations combine other artistic media with collage. Ezra Jack Keats's illustrations for *Maggie and the Pirate* are brightly colored combinations of collage and painting, while his *Regards to the Man in the Moon* uses bits of photography in the collages. Keats's *The Trip* even illustrates a young boy working with various colors and shapes of paper as he creates his own neighborhood within a box. This book could stimulate children's experimentation with both collage and painting.

Experimenting with simple cartoon techniques is another way that children can begin to develop their artistic skills and aesthetic sensitivities. Car-

toons are very popular with children, who greatly enjoy watching Charles Schultz's "Peanuts" characters on television or reading about them when Schultz's cartoon books are available in the library. Well-known cartoonists such as Syd Hoff (6, 7) have written books describing how they draw cartoons and illustrate picture storybooks for children—how they depict the different expressions on people's faces, show movement and various physical characteristics, and draw animals.

After experimenting with their own cartoons, children can look with new understanding and appreciation at picture storybooks illustrated by well-known cartoonists, such as Syd Hoff's easy-to-read book *Sammy the Seal*, James Stevenson's *Could Be Worse!*, and William Steig's *Caleb & Kate*. Children can discuss how well the cartoons complement the text and compare the effectiveness of cartoons and other types of book illustrations. They can write stories and illustrate them with cartoons. Children enjoy creating their own cartoon books or creating a newspaper format that combines the cartoons drawn by all the children in a group.

When children's ages and capabilities allow, experiments with more sophisticated artistic media, discussed in chapter four, can be used to enhance children's self-expression and aesthetic sensitivity.

ISSUE

How Much "Pizzazz" Is Necessary to Entice Children into a Library Reading Program?

SOME PEOPLE MAINTAIN that summer reading programs are more successful if libraries motivate reading by utilizing the techniques of the mass media and Madison Avenue, while others assert that success depends on using knowledge of child development to facilitate an interplay between children's inquiries, the librarian, and the library materials. Two librarians have argued these opposing points of view.

Mary Somerville builds a case for programs that begin "with a bang, not lag in the middle, and end with skyrockets".[1] She believes that programming must appeal to "media babies" who will not respond to a more traditional program and identifies the following ways of creating an effective summer reading program: pick a theme with dramatic possibilities, reinforce the theme in every aspect of the program, dramatize the theme with costumed actors, embody the theme in graphic figures, coordinate library materials with the theme, create a folder with pizzazz, offer prizes for program completion, in-

ACTIVITIES POSSIBLE WITH A PICTURE STORYBOOK

This chapter's recommendations for how to share picture books with children are only a few of the possible ways of creating stimulating and enjoyable experiences with books. The following list (13) shows the varied activities that teachers, librarians, and other adults have developed around Maurice Sendak's *Where the Wild Things Are*.

1 *Appreciative Listening:* Read the story to children; share the pictures and your enthusiasm.
2 *Oral Language*: After reading the book, discuss with children how they might also daydream like Max and make themselves heroes or heroines in a story. What kinds of activities would they dream about? Where would they go? What would they do? Ask children to pantomime their dreams.
3 *Oral Language and Art Interpretation:* Have children create masks depicting the wild things and perform a creative drama of the story and other adventures that Max might have during another visit to the fantasy land.
4 *Oral Language and Art Interpretation:* Have children create puppets of the Wild Things and depict their adventures through a puppet production.

5 *Art Interpretation:* At one time in his career Maurice Sendak constructed papier-mâché models of storybook characters. Have children select a favorite Sendak character and make a papier-mâché model.
6 *Art Interpretation:* Maurice Sendak once designed window displays for new books. Have a group of children design a bulletin board as if it were a window display advertising *Where the Wild Things Are*.
7 *Art Interpretation and Oral Language:* Ask children to design a colorful poster that could be used to convince other people to buy and read Sendak's book.
8 *Art Interpretation and Oral Language:* Have children create a travel poster or travel brochure that advertises Max's fantasy land or that illustrates a new fantasy land of their own. The poster should be designed to convince others that they would enjoy visiting the fantasy land.
9 *Appreciative Listening and Creative Writing:* Maurice Sendak enjoys listening to the music of Mozart, Beethoven, and Wagner while he works. Have children listen to a recording of one of these composers, describe what they visualize as they listen, and draw a series of pictures stimulated by the listening experience. Have them write a story that accompanies the pictures.

clude "razzle-dazzle" games, reduce clerical work, be a creative catalyst, and publicize the program.

Pete Giacoma is critical of the above programming. He believes that educators and researchers in the field of children's librarianship should consider children's psychology and cognitive development, rather than think of children as consumers whose attention is vied for according to rules established by advertisers.[2] Giacoma asks that developers of library programs consider the following questions: Will students who take part in the program remain enthusiastic readers? Will the students be library patrons when they reach adolescence and young adulthood? What is the quality of the relationship between the librarian as a professional librarian and the child? Giacoma concludes that the best library program correlates "thoughtfully designed professional quality offerings, freshened with creativity, and the personalities of commited librarians with the best innate desires of children to learn more details about this place—the world of ideas, facts, imaginings, words, visuals, and sounds to which they are still awakening" (p. 66).

[1] Somerville, Mary. "How to Knock the Stuffings Out of Your Summer Reading Program," *Top of the News* 37 (Spring 1981): 265–274.
[2] Giacoma, Pete. "The Stuffings and Nonsense of Summer Reading Programs: A Response." *Top of the News* 38 (Fall 1981): 64–67.

10 *Picture/Mood Interpretation:* Older children may also discover the relationship between illustration and text achieved by Sendak's book. Encourage them to look carefully at the illustrations while reading or listening to the text. Discuss the enlargement of illustrations as the plot advances. Use the following quote from an interview with Sendak (20, p. 23) to stimulate the discussion:

> One of the reasons why the picture book is so fascinating is that there are devices to make the form itself more interesting. In *Where the Wild Things Are* the device is really a matching of shapes. I used it to describe Max's moods pictorially: his anger, which is more or less normal in the beginning; its expansion into rage; then the explosion of fantasy as a release from that particular anger; and finally the collapse of that, when the fantasy goes and it's all over. The smell of food brings Max back to reality and he's a little boy again. A book is inert. What I try to do is animate it, and make it move emotionally.

After children have discussed the pictorial devices that Sendak uses to animate the text, encourage them to use illustrations to animate their own writing.

11 *Motivation and Enjoyment:* Create a Maurice Sendak reading center in the classroom or school library. Place in the center books written and illustrated by Sendak, books written by other authors and illustrated by Sendak, and any Sendak-motivated stories written and illustrated by children. Decorate the center with posters, papier-mâché characters, puppets, and other art work created by children. Encourage children to use the center.

While these activities are related to one book, they suggest the multiple experiences that could accompany many picture storybooks. Adults should always remember, however, that children's enjoyment of books and reading is the major goal. Books can be shared and savored without planning any accompanying activities.

SUMMARY

Sharing picture books with children provides adults and children with opportunities for enjoyable and rewarding experiences. If these experiences are worth sharing, they are also worthy of careful preparation. When selecting materials for the shared experiences, adults need to consider the nature of the picture book, the purpose of the activity, and the age, attention span, and interests of the children.

Mother Goose books can be used for language enrichment, dramatization, role playing, choral speaking, artistic interpretations, research projects, and creative writing. Investigating the origins of Mother Goose rhymes can inspire library research, oral discussion, and creative writing when the verses are used with older children.

Alphabet books that reinforce letter/sound relationships can be used as source material for developing visual and verbal literacy. Wordless books are ideal for encouraging language growth, stimulating intellectual development, and motivating creative writing.

Reading to children is one very enjoyable way of sharing picture books with children. Through these shared experiences, children learn that literature is pleasurable and are motivated to read books independently, expand their language competency, and develop reading-readiness skills.

Interaction with picture books can be designed to stimulate children's aesthetic sensitivity. Appreciation for the artistic media used in book illustrations is enhanced by having children become actively involved in making their own illustrations and encouraging them to experience and value the diverse art styles available in picture books.

Suggested Activities for Children's Appreciation of Picture Books

- [ ] Choose a nursery rhyme book appropriate for sharing with young children. Share the book with a child and encourage the child to interact with the rhymes by supplying missing words, making up rhyming games, or role-playing the characters found in the nursery rhymes.
- [ ] Choose several nursery rhymes that have a definite beginning, middle, and end. Use them with children to help them develop an understanding of plot development.
- [ ] Select several alphabet books that would be appropriate for encouraging visual and verbal literacy. Develop a series of questions that would encourage children to describe the

pictures, compare the pictures, and evaluate their personal preferences for the pictures. Share the alphabet books and questions with a group of children.

☐ Select a wordless book appropriate for use with younger children and one with enough detail to appeal to older children. Carefully plan an activity that encourages children's interaction with each book. Share the books with the two different age groups. Compare the responses received from each group.

☐ Select a picture storybook appropriate for reading aloud to children. Prepare the story for reading, and share the book with a group of children or a peer group.

☐ Compile a list of picture storybooks appropriate for sharing with five-, six-, seven-, and eight-year-old children.

☐ Choose an art medium used to illustrate children's books. Research the methods used by illustrators who use that medium. Develop a series of activities that allow children to experience and experiment with the medium, create their own illustrations, and discuss literature illustrations that use that medium.

☐ Compile a list of picture book illustrators and their illustrations that could be used to stimulate an understanding of collage, cartoons, and other artistic media.

☐ Choose a picture book that illustrates a nursery song, animal song or holiday song. Plan an interaction activity that encourages children to sing, accompany the song with rhythm instruments, play a singing game, or do a counting activity. Share the activity with a group of children or a peer group.

☐ Choose a children's picture storybook, other than Maurice Sendak's *Where the Wild Things Are*, and list the various activities that could be based on the book.

References

1   Allen, Roach Van. *Language Experiences in Communication*. Boston: Houghton Mifflin, 1976.

2   Borusch, Barbara. Personal correspondence with author, December 1, 1980.

3   Broudy, H. S. "How Basic Is Aesthetic Education? or Is It the Fourth R?" *Language Arts* 54 (September 1977): 631–37.

4   Cohen, Dorothy. "The Effect of Literature on Vocabulary and Reading Achievement." *Elementary English* 45 (February 1968): 209–13, 217.

5   Geller, Linda Gibson. *Wordplay and Language Learning for Children*. Urbana, Ill: National Council of Teachers of English, 1985.

6   Hoff, Syd. *How to Draw Cartoons*. New York: Scholastic, 1975.

7   Hoff, Syd. *Jokes to Enjoy, Draw, and Tell*. New York: Putnam, 1974.

8   Jett-Simpson, Mary. "Parents and Teachers Share Books with Young Children." In *Developing Active Readers: Ideas for Parents, Teachers and Librarians*, edited by Dianne L. Monson and Day Ann K. McClenathan. Newark, Del.: International Reading Association, 1979.

9   Kimmel, Mary and Segel, Elizabeth. *For Reading Out Loud*. New York: Dell, 1983.

10 Lamme, Linda Leonard. "Reading Aloud to Young Children." *Language Arts* 53 (November–December, 1976):886–88.

11 Lamme, Linda Leonard, and Kane, Frances. "Children, Books, and Collage." *Language Arts* 53 (November–December, 1976): 902–5.

12 Loban, Walter. *Language Development: Kindergarten through Grade Twelve*. Urbana, Ill.: National Council of Teachers of English, 1976.

13 Norton, Donna. *Language Arts Activities for Children*. Columbus, Ohio: Merrill, 1985.

14 Ross, Ramon R. *Storyteller*. 2d ed. Columbus, Ohio: Merrill, 1980.

15 Siks, Geraldine Brain. *Drama with Children*. New York: Harper & Row, 1977.

16 Sirota, Beverly S. "The Effect of a Planned Literature Program of Daily Oral Reading by the Teacher on the Voluntary Reading of Fifth Grade Children." University Microfilm No. 71–28, 560. New York: New York University, 1971.

17 Stauffer, Russell. *The Language-Experience Approach to the Teaching of Reading*. New York: Harper & Row, 1980.

18 Stewig, John Warren. "Alphabet Books: A Neglected Genre." *Language Arts* 55 (January 1978): 6–11.

19 Vandergrift, Kay. "Reading Aloud to Young Children." In *Using Literature with Young Children*, edited by Leland B. Jacobs. New York: Columbia University, Teachers College, 1974.

20 Wintle, Justin, and Fisher, Emma. *The Pied Pipers: Interviews with the Influential Creators of Children's Literature*. New York: Paddington, 1974.

CHILDREN'S LITERATURE

Mother Goose

Blegvad, Lenore. *This Little Pig-a-Wig and Other Rhymes about Pigs*. Atheneum, 1978 (I:3–6). Twenty-two nursery rhymes about pigs in a small book.

Bodecker, N. M. *It's Raining, Said John Twaining*. Atheneum, 1973 (I:4–7). Fourteen Danish nursery rhymes translated and illustrated.

De Angeli, Marguerite. *Marguerite De Angeli's Book of Nursery and Mother Goose Rhymes*. Doubleday, 1954 (I:4–7). A large book containing 376 nursery rhymes and illustrations with early English settings.

De Forest, Charlotte B. *The Prancing Pony: Nursery Rhymes from Japan*. Illustrations by Keiko Hida. Walker/Weatherhill, 1968 (I:5–10). Translations of traditional Japanese nursery rhymes collected by Tasuku Harada.

de Paola, Tomie. *Tomie de Paola's Mother Goose*. Putnam, 1985 (I:2–6). The large format and folk art make this a very appealing edition.

Frasconi, Antonio. *The House That Jack Built*. Harcourt Brace Jovanovich, 1958 (I:3–7). The popular nursery rhyme written in both English and French.

Galdone, Paul. *Old Mother Hubbard and Her Dog*. McGraw-Hill, 1961 (I:3–7). Humorous illustrations tell the complete story.

Greenaway, Kate. *Mother Goose: Or, the Old Nursery Rhymes*. Warne, 1881 (I:3–7). A small Mother Goose illustrated with charming Greenaway children.

Griego, Margot C.; Bucks, Betsy L.; Gilbert, Sharon S.; and Kimball, Laurel H. *Tortillitas Para Mama*. Illustrated by Barbara Cooney. Holt, Rinehart & Winston, 1981, (I:3–7). Nursery rhymes in Spanish and English.

Hale, Sara Josepha. *Mary Had a Little Lamb*. Illustrated by Tomie de Paola. Holiday, 1984 (I:3–7). A highly illustrated picture book version of the nursery rhyme.

Jeffers, Susan. *Three Jovial Huntsmen*. Bradbury, 1973 (I:4–7). Muted colors show hundreds of animals peeking out at three hunters who are unable to find them.

Lobel, Arnold. *Gregory Griggs and Other Nursery Rhyme People*. Greenwillow, 1978 (I:4–7). Thirty-four lesser known nursery rhymes about humorous predicaments.

I = Interest by age range;
R = Readability by grade level.

Marshall, James. *James Marshall's Mother Goose*. Farrar, Straus & Giroux, 1979 (I:3–7). Large humorous illustrations accompany each of the thirty-three nursery rhymes.

Martin, Sarah Catherine. *The Comic Adventures of Old Mother Hubbard and Her Dog*. Harcourt Brace Jovanovich, 1981 (I:3–7). A humorously illustrated edition of one nursery rhyme.

Miller, Mitchell. *One Misty Moisty Morning*. Farrar, Straus & Giroux, 1971 (I:3–7). A small collection of the more unusual nursery rhymes, illustrated with soft pencil drawings.

Newbery, John. *The Original Mother Goose's Melody*. (Reissue.) Detroit: Gale, 1969 (I: a11). One of the early Mother Goose collections.

Opie, Iona, and Opie, Peter. *A Nursery Companion*. Oxford, 1980 (I:all). A collection of twenty-seven early British nursery rhymes with the original colored illustrations.

———. *The Oxford Nursery Rhyme Book*. Illustrated by Joan Hassall. Oxford, 1955, 1984 (I:all). A collection of 800 rhymes and songs illustrated with black-and-white woodcuts.

Provensen, Alice, and Provensen, Martin. *The Mother Goose Book*. Random House, 1976 (I:all). A large collection of rhymes grouped according to topics.

Spier, Peter. *London Bridge Is Falling Down*. Doubleday, 1967 (I:all). Each line of the nursery rhyme and song is illustrated in detailed drawings.

———. *To Market, to Market*. Doubleday, 1967 (I:5–12). Drawings depicting New Castle, Delaware, as it might have appeared in 1826 are used to illustrate the nursery tale.

Stevens, Janet. *The House That Jack Built*. Holiday, 1985 (I:2–5). The cumulative nursery rhyme is developed into a humorously illustrated story.

Tarrant, Margaret. *Nursery Rhymes*. Crowell, 1978 (I:3–7). Forty-eight popular nursery rhymes illustrated with traditional drawings.

Tripp, Wallace. *Granfa' Grig Had a Pig and Other Rhymes without Reason from Mother Goose*. Little, Brown, 1976 (I:4–8). Humorous animal drawings illustrate 121 nursery rhymes in a large book format.

Tudor, Tasha. *Mother Goose*. Walck, 1972 (I:3–7). Seventy-seven popular Mother Goose rhymes illustrated in a small book format.

Wyndham, Robert. *Chinese Mother Goose Rhymes*. Illustrated by Ed Young. World, 1968; Philomel, 1982 (paperback) (I:4–7). Traditional Chinese rhymes translated into English.

Zuromskis, Diane. *The Farmer in the Dell*. Little, Brown, 1978 (I:3–6). Colorful eighteenth-century pictures illustrate the song.

Toy Books

Beisner, Monika. *A Folding Alphabet Book*. Farrar, Straus & Giroux, 1981 (I:4–6). A long folded book in which animals and other objects form the letters.

Bond, Michael. *Paddington's Pop-Up Book*. Illustrated by Igor Wood. Price, Stern, Sloan, 1977 (I:3–8). A humorous pop-up that introduces children to Paddington Bear.

Bonforte, Lisa. *Farm Animals*. Random House, 1981 (I:2–4). A board book illustrating and describing common farm animals.

Brown, Margaret Wise. *The Goodnight Moon Room: A Pop-Up Book*. Illustrated by Clement Hurd. Harper & Row, 1984 (I:2–4). A combination of flaps and pop-ups encourages children to interact with the text.

Campbell, Rod. *Dear Zoo*. Four Winds, 1982 (I:2–4). Illustrations encourage children to hypothesize about the contents of a crate.

Carle, Eric. *Catch the Ball*. Philomel, 1982 (I:3–6). A string attached to a ball encourages children's vocabulary development.

———. *The Honeybee and the Robber: A Moving Picture Book*. Philomel, 1981 (I:3–6). A brightly colored pop-up allows children to move the wings of a bee and a butterfly.

———. *Let's Paint a Rainbow*. Philomel, 1982 (I:3–6). A rainbow helps children learn the eight basic colors.

Chen, Tony. *Wild Animals*. Random House, 1981 (I:2–4). One or two sentences describe each illustration of a wild animal.

Craig, Helen. *The Mouse House ABC*. Random House, 1979 (I:3–6). A miniature foldout board book in which mice form the letters.

———. *Mouse House Months*. Random House, 1981 (I:3–6). A miniature foldout board book follows a tree through the seasons and shows a scene for each month.

Crowther, Robert. *The Most Amazing Hide-and-Seek Alphabet Book*. Viking, 1978 (I:3–6). A mechanical book with each letter concealing an object that begins with that letter.

———. *The Most Amazing Hide-and-Seek Counting Book*. Viking, 1981 (I:3–6). Colorful pages have pictures that pull, lift, or rotate to introduce counting.

de Paola, Tomie. *Giorgio's Village*. Putnam, 1982 (I:all). A pop-up of an Italian Renaissance village.

Duke, Kate. *Clean-up Day*. Dutton, 1986 (I: 1–3). A guinea pig helps in this board book.

———. *The Playground*. Dutton, 1986 (I: 1–3). Playground equipment is highlighted in this board book.

———. *What Bounces?* Dutton, 1986 (I:1–3). A guinea pig child experiments with things that bounce.

Goodall, John S. *Shrewbettina Goes to Work*. Atheneum, 1981 (I:4–6). Amusing plot in wordless pop-up.

Hill, Eric. *Spot's Birthday Party*. Putnam, 1982 (I:2–4). In a "lift the flap" book a dog plays hide-and-seek with the guests at his party.

———. *Spot's First Walk*. Putnam, 1981 (I:2–4). Readers discover what a dog sees on his walk when they lift each flap.

———. *Where's Spot?* Putnam, 1980 (I:2–4). Children may search for a missing dog under the flaps.

———. *Spot Goes to School*. Putnam, 1984 (I:2–4). A flap-book encourages readers to discover a dog's activities at school.

Johnson, John E. *The Sky is Blue, the Grass is Green*. Random House, 1980 (I:2–4). A cloth color-concept book.

Keussen, Gudren. *This Is How We Live in the Country*. Ars Edition, 1981 (I:3–5). A board book illustrating a European country setting.

———. *This Is How We Live in Town*. Ars Edition, 1981 (I:3–5). A board book illustrating a European urban setting.

Lindgren, Barbro. *Sam's Ball*. Illustrated by Eva Eriksson. Morrow, 1983 (I:2–4). A boy and a cat learn to play together.

———. *Sam's Bath*. Illustrated by Eva Eriksson, Morrow, 1983 (I:2–4). A boy puts many toys and his dog into the bathtub.

———. *Sam's Lamp*. Illustrated by Eva Eriksson. Morrow, 1983 (I:2–4). A boy falls when he tries to reach a lamp.

Oxenbury, Helen. *The Car Trip*. Dial/Dutton, 1983 (I:2–4). A young boy enjoys a car ride even though he gets sick from eating too much.

———. *The Checkup*. Dial/Dutton, 1983 (I:2–5). A young boy creates confusion when he visits the doctor.

———. *Dressing*. Wanderer Books, 1981 (I:1–3). A board book showing step-by-step dressing.

———. *Family*. Wanderer Books, 1981 (I:1–3). A board book shows baby with family.

———. *First Day of School*. Dial/Dutton, 1983 (I:2–5). A girl experiences her first day at nursery school.

———. *Friends*. Wanderer Books, 1981 (I:1–3). A board book illustrates baby and friends.

———. *I Can*. Random House, 1986 (I: 1–3). A board book illustrates simple actions.

———. *I Hear*. Random House, 1986 (I:1–3). This board book illustrates sounds in the environment.

———. *I See*. Random House, 1986 (I: 1–3). A child interacts with objects in the environment.

———. *I Touch*. Random House, 1986 (I: 1–3). A child touches objects.

———. *Playing*. Wanderer Books, 1981 (I:1–3). A board book shows baby playing.

———. *Working*. Wanderer Books, 1981 (I:1–3). A board book showing familiar work.

Parish, Peggy. *I Can—Can You?* Illustrated by Marylin Hafner. Greenwillow, 1980 (I:1–3). A plastic book demonstrating accomplishments.

Pienkowski, Jan. *Haunted House*. Dutton, 1979 (I:all). A spooky house comes to life behind flaps and in pop-ups.

Potter, Beatrix. *The Peter Rabbit Pop-Up Book*. Warne, 1983 (I:3–8). This pop-up version creates a detailed setting for young children.

Roosevelt, Michele Chopin. *Animals in the Woods*. Random House, 1981 (I:2–4). One or two sentences describe pictures of woodland animals.

Scarry, Richard. *Richard Scarry's Lowly Worm Word Book*. Random House, 1981 (I:1–3). A worm demonstrates familiar objects such as bath, body parts, and food.

Spier, Peter. *Bill's Service Station*. Doubleday, 1981 (I:3–7). One of the "Village Book" series, cut in the shape of a building.

———. *Fire House: Hook and Ladder Company Number Twenty-Four*. Doubleday, 1981 (I:3–7). Detailed drawings of a fire house.

———. *Food Market*. Doubleday, 1981 (I:3–7). Detailed drawings of a supermarket.

———. *My School*. Doubleday, 1981 (I:3–7). Activities associated with school.

————. *The Pet Store*. Doubleday, 1981 (I:3–7). Detailed drawings of a pet store.

————. *The Toy Shop*. Doubleday, 1981 (I:3–7). Detailed drawings of a toy store.

Wells, Rosemary. *Max's Bath*. Dial, 1985 (I:1–3). A young rabbit becomes stained when he takes juice and sherbet into the tub.

————. *Max's Bedtime*. Dial, 1985 (I:1–3). A young rabbit prepares for bed.

————. *Max's Birthday*. Dial, 1985 (I:1–3). A young rabbit enjoys his birthday.

————. *Max's Breakfast*. Dial, 1985 (I:1–3). A humorous book about a young rabbit's breakfast.

————. *Max's First Word*. Dial, 1979 (I:2–4). A board book for young children.

————. *Max's New Suit*. Dial, 1979 (I:2–4). A short board book story.

————. *Max's Ride*. Dial, 1979 (I:2–4). Humorous board book.

————. *Max's Toys: A Counting Book*. Dial, 1979 (I:2–4). A simple counting board book.

Zokeisha. *Things I Like to Eat*. Simon & Schuster, 1981 (I:1–3). One familiar food per page.

————. *Things I Like to Look At*. Simon & Schuster, 1981 (I:1–3). Pictures of familiar objects.

————. *Things I Like to Play With*. Simon & Schuster, 1981 (I:1–3). Colorful pictures of familiar toys.

————. *Things I Like To Wear*. Simon & Schuster, 1981 (I:1–3). Illustrations that help young children identify names of clothing.

Alphabet Books

Anno, Mitsumasa. *Anno's Alphabet: An Adventure in Imagination*. Crowell, 1975 (I:5–7). A wordless alphabet book that shows a single letter on one page and a single object beginning with that letter on the opposite page.

Azarian, Mary. *A Farmer's Alphabet*. Godine, 1981(I:5–8). Woodcuts present images of rural Vermont.

Baldwin, Ruth M. *One Hundred Nineteenth-Century Rhyming Alphabets in English*. Southern Illinois University, 1972 (I:all). A collection of older alphabets.

Baskin, Leonard. *Hosie's Alphabet*. Words by Hosea Tobias and Lisa Baskin. Viking, 1972 (I:6–8). Each double page has one letter of the alphabet, a short descriptive phrase, and a full-page picture of the object.

Bayer, Jane. *A, My Name is Alice*. Illustrated by Steven Kellogg. Dial, 1984 (I:3–7). Illustrations accompany the jump-rope rhyme.

Berger, Terry, and Kandell, Alice S. *Ben's ABC Day*. Lothrop, Lee & Shepard, 1982 (I:3–6). A child's familiar activities illustrate each letter.

Brown, Marcia. *All Butterflies: An ABC*. Scribner's, 1974 (I:3–7). Two-word phrases that also correspond with two letters of the alphabet are illustrated on each double page.

Cleaver, Elizabeth. *ABC*. Atheneum, 1985 (I: 3–7). A small book illustrates several items for each letter.

Craft, Kinuko. *Mother Goose ABC*. Platt & Munk, 1977 (I:4–8). Mother Goose rhymes are presented in alphabetical order.

Duvoisin, Roger. *A for the Ark*. Lothrop, Lee & Shepard, 1952 (I:6–8). A theme ABC illustrating the animals entering the ark.

Eichenberg, Fritz. *Ape in a Cape: An Alphabet of Odd Animals*. Harcourt Brace Jovanovich, 1952 (I:3–8). Each page presents one letter, a rhyming phrase about the illustration, and one large picture.

Emberley, Ed. *Ed Emberley's ABC*. Little, Brown, 1978 (I:5–8). An amusing alphabet that shows the formation of the letters and an animal representation for each letter.

Feelings, Muriel. *Jambo Means Hello: Swahili Alphabet Book*. Dial, 1974 (I:all). A beautiful book using the Swahili alphabet and drawings depicting the Swahili culture.

Gág, Wanda. *The ABC Bunny*. Coward-McCann, 1933 (I:3–6). A bunny has numerous adventures related to letters of the alphabet.

Greenaway, Kate. *A–Apple Pie*. Warne, 1886 (I:3–8). The old rhyme that was first referenced in 1671.

Hague, Kathleen. *Alphabears: An ABC Book*. Illustrated by Michael Hague. Holt, Rinehart, & Winston, 1984 (I:3–7). Illustrations of teddy bears depict letters.

Hoban, Tana. *A, B, See!* Greenwillow, 1982 (I:4–6). Photographs illustrate objects that begin with the uppercase letters.

Kitchen, Bert. *Animal Alphabet*. Dial, 1984 (I:all). Unusual animals accompany each letter of the alphabet.

Lalicki, Barbara. *If There Were Dreams to Sell*. Illustrated by Margot Tomes. Lothrop, Lee, & Shepard, 1984 (I:all). Poetry selections accompany each letter of the alphabet.

Lear, Edward. *An Edward Lear Alphabet*. Illustrated by Carol Newsom, Lothrop, Lee, & Shepard, 1983 (I:3–7). A newly illustrated version of Lear's famous nonsense rhyme.

Lobel, Arnold. *On Market Street*. Illustrated by Anita Lobel. Greenwillow, 1981 (I:4–7). Tradespeople show their wares from A to Z.

Mendoza, George. *Norman Rockwell's Americana ABC*. Dell, 1975 (I:all). Norman Rockwell paintings are used to illustrate each letter of the alphabet.

Milne, A. A. *Pooh's Alphabet Book*. Illustrations by E. H. Shepard. Dutton, 1975 (I:6–10). A small alphabet book using quotations and illustrations from the Pooh books.

Munari, Bruno. *Bruno Munari's ABC*. World, 1960 (I:3–6). Large letters and pictures are appropriate for sharing and discussing with younger children.

Musgrove, Margaret. *Ashanti to Zulu: African Traditions*. Illustrated by Leo and Diane Dillon. Dial, 1976 (I:7–12). Traditions and customs from twenty-six African tribes are presented in alphabetical order.

Nedobeck, Don. *Nedobeck's Alphabet Book*. Children's Press, 1981 (I:3–6). Illustrations and words depict the letters.

Newberry, Clare Turlay. *The Kitten's ABC*. Harper & Row, 1965 (I:3–6). Newberry's delightful kittens experience each letter of the alphabet.

Nicholson, William. *An Alphabet*. Wofsy, 1975 (I:all). A copy of an alphabet first published in 1897 illustrated with different occupations.

Niland, Deborah. *ABC of Monsters*. McGraw-Hill, 1978 (I:3–6). A small humorous alphabet that shows monsters doing funny things at a monster party.

Provensen, Alice, and Provensen, Martin. *A Peaceable Kingdom: The Shaker Abecedarius*. Viking, 1978 (I:all). A newly illustrated edition of alphabet animal rhymes first published in the Shaker Manifesto of July 1882.

Tudor, Tasha. *A Is for Annabelle*. Walck, 1954 (I:3–7). Verses and illustrations related to playing with a doll.

Wildsmith, Brian. *Brian Wildsmith's ABC*. Watts, 1962 (I:3–6). A word and a picture for each letter.

Counting Books

Anno, Mitsumasa. *Anno's Counting Book*. Crowell, 1977 (I:3–7). Large detailed drawings of landscapes illustrate each number.

———. *Anno's Counting House.* Philomel, 1982 (I:3–7). Cut-out windows show ten little people who demonstrate counting, adding, and subtracting.

Bang, Molly. *Ten, Nine, Eight.* Greenwillow, 1983 (I:3–6). A charming number game counts objects backwards.

Carle, Eric. *My Very First Book of Numbers.* Crowell, 1974 (I:3–6). A simple matching book in which the child matches black squares with an appropriate illustration.

———. *1, 2, 3, to the Zoo.* World, 1968 (I:3–7). Zoo animals with corresponding numbers.

———. *The Very Hungry Caterpillar.* Crowell, 1971 (I:2–7). A colorful collage book showing the life cycle of a caterpillar.

Feelings, Muriel. *Moja Means One: Swahili Counting Book.* Illustrations by Tom Feelings. Dial, 1971 (I:all). Numbers from one through ten are shown in numbers, written in Swahili and illustrated with scenes of Africa.

Gerstein, Mordicai. *Roll Over!* Crown, 1984 (I:3–6). A counting nursery rhyme with various animals.

Hoban, Tana. *Count and See.* Macmillan, 1972 (I:4–7). Photographs illustrate numbers.

Hutchins, Pat. *The Doorbell Rang.* Greenwillow, 1986 (I: 5–8). Math concepts develop as children divide cookies.

———. *I Hunter.* Greenwillow, 1982 (I:3–5). Camouflage encourages children to find and count the African animals.

Keats, Ezra Jack. *Over in the Meadow.* Scholastic, 1972 (I:5–8). The poem by Wadsworth is illustrated with animals that can be counted.

Knight, Hilary. *Hilary Knight's The Twelve Days of Christmas.* Macmillan, 1981 (I:all). A bear gives his friend the gifts listed in the English folk song.

Magee, Doug. *Trucks You Can Count On.* Dodd, 1985 (I:3–8). Counting involves the parts of a large tractor-trailer.

Milne, A. A. *Pooh's Counting Book.* Illustrated by E. H. Shepard. Dutton, 1982 (I:6–10). Numbers from one through ten are developed through quotes from various Pooh stories.

Nedobeck, Don. *Nedobeck's Numbers Books.* Children's Press, 1981 (I:3–6). Clearly illustrated objects show number concepts.

Reiss, John J. *Numbers.* Bradbury, 1971 (I:4–7). Objects illustrate number concepts with large numbers shown in sets of five or ten.

Tafuri, Nancy. *Who's Counting?* Greenwillow, 1986 (I:3–6). Viewers follow a dog through the development of the concepts one through nine.

Concept Books

Ahlberg, Janet, and Ahlberg, Allan. *The Baby's Catalogue.* Little, Brown, 1982 (I:2–6). Pictures and accompanying labels are categorized according to daily events and common objects.

Banchek, Linda. *Snake In, Snake Out.* Illustrated by Elaine Arnold. Crowell, 1978 (I:3–7). Eight words related to spatial concepts are presented through the story of an old woman and a snake.

Carle, Eric. *The Grouchy Ladybug.* Crowell, 1971 (I:4–7). A ladybug progresses through the day from six in the morning to six at night.

———. *The Mixed-up Chameleon.* Crowell, 1975 (I:2–6). A chameleon that wishes to be other animals takes on different colors.

———. *My Very First Book of Colors.* Crowell, 1974 (I:3–6). Nine colors shown in half-page blocks are matched with illustrations.

———. *My Very First Book of Shapes.* Crowell, 1974 (I:4–7). Children match black shapes with a similar shape represented in a colored illustration.

Crews, Donald. *Carousel.* Greenwillow, 1982 (I:4–8). Illustrations take reader on a carousel ride.

———. *Freight Train.* Greenwillow, 1978 (I:3–7). Colors, cars on a freight train, and concepts such as "through," "daylight," and "darkness" are developed.

———. *Harbor.* Greenwillow, 1982 (I:3–7). Children discover names of harbor ships as they go in and out of the harbor.

Dubanevich, Arlene. *Pigs in Hiding.* Four Winds, 1983 (I:3–6). An almost wordless book encourages children to search for the pigs.

Duvoisin, Roger. *See What I Am.* Lothrop, Lee & Shepard, 1974 (I:5–9 and older children interested in art). The primary colors are introduced and then mixed to produce the secondary colors.

Emberley, Ed. *Ed Emberley's Picture Pie: A Circle Drawing Book.* Little, Brown, 1984 (I:all). Colored illustrations show how to make pictures from circles and portions of circles.

Hoban, Tana. *Big Ones, Little Ones.* Greenwillow, 1976 (I:2–7). "Big" and "little" illustrated in photographs of mother and baby zoo animals.

———. *Circles, Triangles, and Squares.* Macmillan, 1974 (I:4–8). Shapes found in everyday objects.

———. *Dig, Drill, Dump, Fill.* Greenwillow, 1975 (I:5–10). Photographs presenting the world of heavy machinery.

———. *Over, Under & Through and Other Spatial Concepts.* Macmillan, 1973 (I:3–7). Photographs illustrate spatial concepts.

———. *Push–Pull, Empty–Full: A Book of Opposites.* Macmillan, 1972 (I:3–7). Photographs illustrate the meanings of antonyms.

———. *Round & Round & Round.* Greenwillow, 1983 (I:2–7). Colored photographs illustrate round objects found in the environment.

———. *Shapes, Shapes, Shapes.* Greenwillow, 1986 (I:3–8). Photographs illustrate various shapes in the environment.

———. *Take Another Look.* Greenwillow, 1981 (I:4–8). Viewers look at an object through a circular cutout, guess what it is, and turn the page to see if they were correct.

Kalan, Robert. *Blue Sea.* Illustrated by Donald Crews. Greenwillow, 1979 (I:3–7). Large illustrations of fish show size concepts.

McMillan, Bruce. *Here a Chick, There a Chick.* Lothrop, Lee & Shepard, 1983 (I: 3–6). Photographs illustrate opposites.

Rockwell, Anne. *First Comes Spring.* Crowell, 1985 (I: 3–6). Seasonal changes, activities, and appropriate clothing are shown through the life of a young bear.

Sattler, Helen. *Train Whistles.* Illustrated by Giulio Maestro. Lothrop, Lee & Shepard, 1985 (I: 3–9). Text and illustrations explain the meanings of signals used by train whistles.

Spier, Peter. *Crash! Bang! Boom!* Doubleday, 1972 (I:4–9). Detailed pictures show items that make various noises.

———. *Fast-Slow, High-Low: A Book of Opposites.* Doubleday, 1972 (I:5–10). Numerous detailed pictures illustrate opposites.

Tafuri, Nancy. *Early Morning in the Barn.* Greenwillow, 1983 (I:2–5). An almost wordless book illustrates the journey of three chicks as they explore the barnyard.

Yabuuchi, Masayuki. *Whose Footprints?* Philomel, 1985 (I:2–4). Pictures of animal footprints are followed by pictures of the animal that makes the print.

———. *Whose Baby?* Philomel, 1985 (I:2–4). Pictures of animal babies are followed by pictures of adult parents.

Wordless Books

Alexander, Martha. *Bobo's Dream*. Dial, 1970 (I:3–7). Bobo dreams that he becomes large and rescues his master's football from a group of bigger boys.

———. *Out! Out! Out!* Dial, 1968 (I:3–7). A little boy coaxes a bird out of a house by creating a trail of cereal.

Anno, Mitsumasa. *Anno's Britain*. Philomel, 1982 (I:all). The illustrations follow a traveler through Great Britain.

———. *Anno's Flea Market*. Bodley Head, 1984 (I:all). Hundreds of items in the flea market of an old city.

———. *Anno's Italy*. Collins, 1980 (I:all). Illustrations take the viewer on a trip through Italy.

———. *Anno's Journey*. Philomel, 1978 (I:6–12). Illustrations record the journey of the artist through the countryside, small towns, and cities of Europe.

———. *Topsy-Turvies—Pictures to Stretch the Imagination*. Walker/Weatherhill, 1970 (I:all). Children are instructed to decide what the little men are doing in the pictures.

Aruego, Jose. *Look What I Can Do*. Scribner's, 1971 (I:3–7). Two carabaos try to outdo each other and get into funny situations.

Briggs, Raymond. *The Snowman*. Random House, 1978 (I:3–7). A snowman comes to life and takes his young creator on a tour of strange lands.

Carle, Eric. *Do You Want to Be My Friend?* Crowell, 1971 (I:3–7). A mouse searches for a friend.

de Paola, Tomie. *The Hunter and the Animals: A Wordless Picture Book*. Holiday, 1981 (I:5–9). Forest animals convince the hunter to break his gun.

———. *Pancakes for Breakfast*. Harcourt Brace Jovanovich, 1978 (I:3–7). The procedures for making pancakes are shown in a humorous wordless book.

Goodall, John. *The Adventures of Paddy Pork*. Harcourt Brace Jovanovich, 1968 (I:5–9). A pig named Paddy leaves home and joins the circus.

———. *The Story of an English Village*. Atheneum, 1979 (I:all). The changes in an English village from the fourteenth century into the twentieth.

———. *Paddy Goes Traveling*. Atheneum, 1982 (I:5–9). Paddy Pork has an adventure on the beach.

———. *Paddy under Water*. Atheneum, 1984 (I:5–9). Paddy discovers a treasure chest.

Hutchins, Pat. *Changes, Changes*. Macmillan, 1971 (I:2–6). Two doll figures create different things out of blocks.

Keats, Ezra Jack. *Clementina's Cactus*. Viking, 1982 (I:all). An exploration of the desert.

Krahn, Fernando. *Who's Seen the Scissors?* Dutton, 1975 (I:4–8). A pair of scissors leaves a tailor shop and flies around town cutting various items.

McCully, Emily Arnold. *Picnic*. Harper & Row, 1984 (I:3–7). A young mouse is lost on the day of the family picnic.

Mayer, Mercer. *A Boy, a Dog and a Frog*. Dial, 1967 (I:5–9). A boy and a dog try unsuccessfully to catch a frog.

———. *A Boy, a Dog, a Frog, and a Friend*. Dial, 1971 (I:5–9). The frog's son accompanies the boy and the dog when they find a turtle. The turtle tricks them but then becomes a friend.

———. *Frog Goes to Dinner*. Dial, 1974 (I:6–9). Boy secretly puts Frog into his pocket and takes him along when the family goes to a fancy restaurant.

———. *Frog, Where Are You?* Dial, 1969 (I:5–9). Boy and Dog search for the missing Frog.

———. *The Great Cat Chase*. Four Winds, 1974 (I:5–7). A cat dressed up as a baby runs away and children try to catch him.

Mayer, Mercer, and Mayer, Marianna. *One Frog Too Many*. Dial, 1975 (I:5–9). Frog becomes jealous when Boy receives a new frog for his birthday.

Ormerod, Jan. *Sunshine*. Lothrop, Lee & Shepard, 1981 (I:4–8). A child wakes up and helps her parents leave the house on time.

Spier, Peter. *Noah's Ark*. Doubleday, 1977 (I:3–9). Detailed illustrations of Jacobris Revius's poem *The Flood*.

Van Allsburg, Chris. *The Mysteries of Harris Burdick*. Houghton Mifflin, 1984 (I:all). Mystery and fantasy pictures encourage readers to plot their own stories.

Winter, Paula. *Sir Andrew*. Crown, 1980 (I:5–9). A conceited donkey goes for a walk and breaks a leg.

Easy-to-Read Books

Benchley, Nathaniel. *Oscar Otter*. Illustrations by Arnold Lobel. Harper & Row, 1966 (I:5–9 R:2). Oscar gets lost and is chased by a fox, a wolf, and a moose.

———. *Small Wolf*. Illustrations by Joan Sandin. Harper & Row, 1972 (I:6–10 R:3). A Native American family moves west from Manhattan Island in order to avoid conflict with European colonists.

Bonsall, Crosby. *The Case of the Cat's Meow*. Harper & Row, 1965 (I:5–9 R:2). The Wizard Private Eyes try to solve the mystery of Mildred the missing cat.

———. *The Case of the Scaredy Cats*. Harper & Row, 1971 (I:5–9 R:1). Girls prove that girls are as good as boys.

Brenner, Barbara. *Wagon Wheels*. Illustrated by Don Bolognese. Harper & Row, 1978 (I:6–9 R:1). The true story of Ed Muldie and his family as they move from Kentucky to Kansas in 1878.

Bulla, Clyde Robert. *Daniel's Duck*. Illustrations by Joan Sandin. Harper & Row, 1979 (I:6–9 R:2). Daniel lives in the mountains of Tennessee and admires his neighbor's talent for carving.

Bunting, Eve. *The Big Red Barn*. Illustrated by Howard Knotts. Harcourt Brace Jovanovich, 1979 (I:6–9 R:2). Craig's grandpa teaches him to accept changes in his life.

Chenery, Janet. *The Toad Hunt*. Illustrations by Ben Shecter. Harper & Row, 1967 (I:5–9 R:2). An entertaining information book about toads and frogs.

Ehrlich, Amy. *Leo, Zack and Emmie*. Dial, 1981 (I:5–8 R:2). A girl affects the friendship of two boys.

Flower, Phyllis. *Barn Owl*. Illustrations by Cherryl Pape. Harper & Row, 1978 (I:5–8 R:1). A science book describing the barn owl's hunting methods.

Gage, Wilson. *Squash Pie*. Illustrated by Glen Rounds. Greenwillow, 1976 (I:5–8 R:3). A humorous story about a farmer who plants squash because he wants squash pie.

Gray, Genevieve. *How Far, Felipe?* Illustrated by Ann Grifalconi. Harper & Row, 1978 (I:6–9 R:2). A history book telling the story of Felipe and his donkey when they join Colonel Anzos's caravan in 1775 and travel to California.

Griffith, Helen V. *Alex and the Cat*. Illustrations by Joseph Low. Greenwillow, 1982 (I:5–8 R:1). A dog tries to realize his great dreams, but discovers that he is better off as a house pet.

Hoff, Syd. *Chester*. Harper & Row, 1961 (I:5–8 R:1). Chester is a wild horse who wants to belong to someone.

———. *Sammy the Seal*. Harper & Row, 1959 (I:5–8 R:1). Sammy lives in a zoo, but wants to see what it would be like on the outside.

Hopkins, Lee Bennett (ed.). *Surprises*. Illustrated by Megan Lloyd. Harper &

Row, 1984 (I:5–9). A collection of short poems selected for beginning readers.

Kessler, Leonard. *Kick, Pass, and Run*. Harper & Row, 1966 (I:5–8 R:1). Football explained in simple terms.

Leeuwen, Jean Van. *Tales of Oliver Pig*. Illustrated by Arnold Lobel. Dial, 1979 (I:5–7 R:2). Oliver the pig has five short adventures.

————. *More Tales of Oliver Pig*. Dial, 1981 (I:5–7 R:2). Further adventures of Oliver.

Lobel, Anita. *The Pancake*. Greenwillow, 1978 (I:5–8 R:3). The folktale of the pancake told in an easy-to-read version.

Lobel, Arnold. *Frog and Toad All Year*. Harper & Row, 1976 (I:5–8 R:1). Frog and Toad have some funny adventures throughout the various seasons of the year.

————. *Frog and Toad Are Friends*. Harper & Row, 1970 (I:5–8 R:1). Frog and Toad in five short stories.

————. *Frog and Toad Together*. Harper & Row, 1972 (I:5–8 R:1). Five short stories about the adventures of Frog and Toad.

————. *Grasshopper on the Road*. Harper & Row, 1978 (I:5–8 R:2). Grasshopper sets out on a trip and meets some insects who don't like to do something different every day.

————. *Owl at Home*. Harper & Row, 1975 (I:5–8 R:2). Five stories explore Owl's adventures.

————. *Uncle Elephant*. Harper & Row, 1981 (I:5–8 R:2). Uncle Elephant takes care of his nephew when the parents are lost at sea.

Marshall, Edward. *Four on the Shore*. Illustrated by James Marshall. Dial, 1985 (I:5–9 R:1). Four boys tell ghost stories.

Rice, Eve. *Once in a Wood. Ten Tales from Aesop*. Greenwillow, 1979 (I:6–9 R:2). Ten Aesop fables retold in an easy-to-read version.

Ryder, Joanne. *Fireflies*. Illustrations by Don Bolognese. Harper & Row, 1977 (I:6–9 R:1). The life cycle of a firefly in words and pictures.

Schwartz, Alvin. *In a Dark, Dark Room*. Illustrated by Dirk Zimmer. Harper & Row, 1984 (I:6–9 R:2). Seven scary stories.

Seuss, Dr. *The Cat in the Hat*. Random House, 1957 (I:4–7 R:1). A very unusual cat causes both amusement and mischief when he entertains two bored children on a rainy day.

————. *The Cat in the Hat Comes Back*. Random House, 1958 (I:4–7 R:1).

The cat returns and brings with him little cats A through Z.

Wiseman, Bernard. *Morris Goes to School*. Harper & Row, 1970 (I:5–8 R:1). Morris cannot count so he decides to go to school.

————. *Morris Has a Cold*. Dodd, Mead, 1978 (I:5–8 R:1). Boris Bear tries to help Morris Moose get rid of a cold.

Picture Storybooks

Aardema, Verna. *Why Mosquitoes Buzz in People's Ears*. Illustrated by Leo and Diane Dillon. Dial, 1975 (I:5–9 R:6). A cumulative African folk tale.

Adoff, Arnold. *Black Is Brown Is Tan*. Illustrated by Emily Arnold McCully. Harper & Row, 1973 (I:3–7). A happy family with a black mother and a white father share experiences.

Ahlberg, Janet, and Ahlberg, Allen. *Each Peach Pear Plum: An I-Spy Story*. Viking, 1978 (I:3–7). Two short lines on each page suggest what the reader should find in a picture.

————. *Peek-a-boo!* Viking, 1981 (I:2–6). A baby peeks through an opening on a page to discover the family's activities.

Aruego, Jose, and Dewey, Ariane. *We Hide, You Seek*. Greenwillow, 1979 (I:2–6). A rhino plays hide-and-seek with many camouflaged African animals.

Baker, Jeannie. *Grandmother*. Deutsch, 1979 (I:5–8). Collage illustrations show a visit with Grandmother.

Baylor, Byrd. *The Best Town in the World*. Illustrated by Ronald Himler. Scribner's, 1983 (I:all). The poetic text presents a nostalgic view of a small town.

Brandenberg, Aliki. *The Two of Them*. Greenwillow, 1979 (I:3–8 R:7). A girl and her grandfather develop a close relationship before he dies.

Brown, Marcia. *Shadow*. Scribner's, 1982 (I:all). A highly illustrated version of an African poem.

Brown, Margaret Wise. *Fox Eyes*. Illustrated by Garth Williams. Pantheon, 1977 (I:2–7 R:5). The red fox observes an opossum family and other animals.

————. *The Runaway Bunny*. Illustrated by Clement Hurd. Rev. ed. Harper & Row, 1972 (I:2–7 R:6). A beautiful children's story that emphasizes the need for both independence and love.

Bunting, Eve. *The Mother's Day Mice*. Illustrated by Jan Brett. Clarion, 1986 (I:3–6). Mice search the woods for perfect gifts.

Burningham, John. *Avocado Baby*. Crowell, 1982 (I:3–6 R:4). A weakling baby becomes strong after eating an avocado.

————. *The Snow*. Crowell, 1975 (I:2–5). A small boy plays outside with his mother.

Burton, Virginia Lee. *Katy and the Big Snow*. Houghton Mifflin, 1943, 1971 (I:2–6 R:4). Katy the strongest crawler tractor saves the town after a heavy snowfall.

————. *The Little House*. Houghton Mifflin, 1942 (I:3–7 R:3). A house is strong but needs love as it becomes dilapidated and lonely over the years.

————. *Mike Mulligan and His Steam Shovel*. Houghton Mifflin, 1939 (I:2–6 R:4). Mary Anne the steam shovel proves that she can dig in one day more than 100 men can dig in a week.

Carle, Eric. *The Secret Birthday Message*. Crowell, 1972 (I:3–7). Basic shapes shown in a birthday message.

Carlstrom, Nancy White. *Jesse Bear, What Will You Wear?* Illustrated by Bruce Degen. MacMillan, 1986 (I:3–6). A rhyming text follows a young bear's activities.

de Brunhoff, Jean. *The Story of Babar*. Random House, 1933, 1961 (I:3–9 R:4). The original story in which Babar eventually becomes king of the elephants.

————, and de Brunhoff, Laurent. *Babar's Anniversary Album: 6 Favorite Stories*. Random House, 1981 (I:3–9 R:4). Contains *The Story of Babar, The Travels of Babar, Babar the King, Babar's Birthday Surprise, Babar's Mystery*, and *Babar and the Wully-Wully*.

de Paola, Tomie. *The Clown of God*. Harcourt Brace Jovanovich, 1978 (I:all R:4). A legend about a juggler and a miracle.

————. *Nana Upstairs & Nana Downstairs*. Putnam, 1973 (I:3–7 R:6). Tommy has two beloved grandmothers: a great-grandmother upstairs and a grandmother downstairs.

————. *Oliver Button Is a Sissy*. Harcourt Brace Jovanovich, 1979 (I:5–8 R:2). Other boys call Oliver a sissy because he likes to dance, read books, and dress in costumes.

————. *The Quicksand Book*. Holiday, 1977 (I:5–9 R:4). A humorous story discussing the composition of quicksand and how to rescue someone who falls into quicksand.

————. *Strega Nona's Magic Lessons*. Harcourt Brace Jovanovich, 1982 (I:5–9 R:6). Disaster results when Big Anthony tries to use Strega Nona's magic.

DeWitt, Jamie. *Jamie's Turn*. Illustrated by Julie Brinckloe. Raintree, 1984 (I:6–9 R:3). A true story about a boy who saves his stepfather's life.

Duvoisin, Roger. *Petunia*. Knopf, 1950 (I:3–6 R:6). Petunia, the silly goose, learns that she has to do more than carry a book to gain wisdom.

Emberley, Barbara. *Drummer Hoff*. Illustrated by Ed Emberley. Prentice-Hall, 1967 (I:3–7 R:6). A cumulative rhyme depicting all the people associated with firing a cannon.

Fatio, Louise. *The Happy Lion*. Illustrated by Roger Duvoisin. McGraw-Hill, 1954 (I:3–7 R:7). A lion who lives in a zoo discovers people are not so friendly when he goes to town to visit them.

Flournoy, Valerie. *The Patchwork Quilt*. Illustrated by Jerry Pinkney. Dial, 1985 (I:5–8 R:4). The sewing of a family quilt develops close family memories.

Gág, Wanda. *Millions of Cats*. Coward-McCann, 1929 (I:3–7 R:3). The little old woman's desire for a pretty cat results in a fight between trillions of cats.

Gage, Wilson. *Cully, Cully and the Bear*. Illustrated by James Stevenson. Greenwillow, 1983 (I:4–6 R:2). A humorous tale in which a hunter goes after a bearskin to make his house more comfortable.

Galdone, Paul. *The Three Wishes*. McGraw-Hill,1967. (I:3–7 R:2). A humorous illustrated folktale about foolish actions.

Gammell, Stephen. *Wake Up Bear . . . It's Christmas!* Lothrop, Lee & Shepard 1981 (I:5–8 R:4). A Christmas story accompanied by humorous illustrations.

Gerstein, Mordicai, *The Room*. Harper & Row, 1984 (I:6–8 R:3). Text and illustrations follow the occupants of a room over many years.

Hader, Berta and Hader, Elmer. *The Big Snow*. Macmillan, 1948 (I:3–7 R:4). Wild animals prepare for winter and experience the big snow.

Haley, Gail E. *A Story, A Story*. Atheneum, 1970 (I:6–10 R:6). An African tale about how Ananse, the spider man, bargained with the Sky God.

Hays, Sarah. *This Is the Bear*. Illustrated by Helen Craig. Lippincott, 1986 (I:2–5). The writing style is similar to *This Is the House That Jack Built*.

Herriot, James. *Moses the Kitten*. Illustrated by Peter Barrett. St. Martin's, 1984 (I:all R:5). A young kitten finds a home on a Yorkshire farm.

Hest, Amy. *The Crack-of-Dawn Walkers*. Illustrated by Amy Schwartz. Macmillan, 1984 (I:5–8 R:3). A young girl develops a close relationship with her grandfather.

Hoban, Russell. *A Baby Sister for Frances*. Illustrated by Lillian Hoban. Harper & Row, 1964 (I:5–8 R:4). Frances the badger has a new baby sister, and things just aren't the same.

———. *A Bargain for Frances*. Illustrated by Lillian Hoban. Harper & Row, 1970 (I:4–8 R:2). This easy-to-read book tells the story of Frances and her friend Thelma.

———. *Best Friends for Frances*. Illustrated by Lillian Hoban. Harper & Row, 1969 (I:4–8 R:4). Frances discovers that her little sister is a lot of fun and can also be a best friend.

———. *Bread and Jam for Frances*. Illustrated by Lillian Hoban. Harper & Row, 1964 (I:4–8 R:4). Frances wants bread and jam, not eggs or anything else that is new.

———. *Nothing to Do*. Illustrations by Lillian Hoban. Harper & Row, 1964 (I:4–8 R:4). When Walter Possum complains that he has nothing to do, Father solves his problem.

Hughes, Shirley. *Alfie Gives a Hand*. Lothrop, Lee & Shepard, 1983 (I:3–6 R:4). When he helps a friend, Alfie discovers that he no longer needs his security blanket.

Hurd, Edith Thacher. *I Dance in My Red Pajamas*. Illustrated by Emily Arnold. McCully Harper, 1982 (I:3–7 R:3). The warm relationship between a girl and her visiting grandparents.

Hutchins, Pat. *Happy Birthday, Sam*. Greenwillow, 1978 (I:3–6 R:4). Grandpa's birthday present allows Sam to reach various items.

———. *The Wind Blew*. Macmillan, 1974 (I:3–6 R:4). A short, rhyming story that tells with colorful pictures what happened when the wind blew objects away from people.

Johnston, Tony. *The Witch's Hat*. Illustrated by Margot Tomes. Putnam's, 1984 (I:4–8 R:2). Repetitive language enhances a story about a hat that turns itself into various creatures.

Jonas, Ann. *When You Were a Baby*. Greenwillow, 1982 (I:2–5 R:2). The author reminds children about things they could not do as babies but can do as growing children.

Jukes, Mavis. *Like Jake and Me*. Illustrated by Lloyd Bloom, Knopf, 1984 (I:6–9 R:4). An incident with a spider brings a boy and his stepfather closer together.

Keats, Ezra Jack. *Dreams*. Macmillan, 1974 (I:3–8 R:3). Robert makes a mouse at school, and everyone else dreams his mouse saves Archie's cat from a dog.

———. *Goggles!* Macmillan, 1969 (I:5–9 R:3). Archie and Willie outwit bullies and reach home safely.

———. *A Letter to Amy*. Harper & Row, 1968 (I:3–8 R:3). Peter writes a birthday party invitation to his friend Amy.

———. *Louie*. Greenwillow, 1975. (I:3–8 R:2). Louie responds to a puppet in a play and later is given the puppet by the children who put on the show.

———. *Maggie and the Pirate*. Four Winds, 1979 (I:4–8 R:3). A "pirate" steals Maggie's pet cricket.

———. *Pet Show!* Macmillan, 1972 (I:4–8 R:2). Beautiful bright colors and collages illustrate a children's pet show.

———. *Peter's Chair*. Harper & Row, 1967 (I:3–8 R:2). Peter overcomes jealousy when his furniture is painted for his new baby sister.

———. *Regards to the Man in the Moon*. Four Winds, 1981 (I:4–8 R:3). Two children build a spaceship from junk and fuel it with their imaginations.

———. *The Trip*. Greenwillow, 1978 (I:3–8 R:2). Louie constructs a shoe box scene so he can visit his friends.

Kepes, Juliet. *Cock-a-Doodle-Doo*. Pantheon, 1978 (I:3–7). A tiger takes care of a baby chick and hopes it will make a good dinner.

Kellogg, Steven. *A Rose for Pinkerton*. Dial, 1981 (I:4–8 R:3). Humorous story about a girl who chooses a kitten as a friend for her great dane.

———. *Tallyho, Pinkerton!* Dial, 1982 (I:4–8 R:3). Rose the great dane and her owner go on a hilarious trip to the woods.

Kraus, Robert. *Leo the Late Bloomer*. Illustrated by Jose and Ariane Aruego. Windmill, 1971 (I:2–6 R:4). A large, colorful picture book tells the story of a young tiger who can't do anything right.

Leaf, Munro. *The Story of Ferdinand*. Illustrated by Robert Lawson. Viking, 1936 (I:4–10 R:6). A mild-mannered bull intended for the bullring manages instead to "be himself."

Lexau, Joan M. *Benjie on His Own*. Dial, 1970 (I:4–8). Benjie gets help for his grandmother and stays with neighbors while she is in the hospital.

Lindgren, Barbro. *The Wild Baby Goes to Sea*. Adapted from Swedish by Jack Prelutsky. Illustrated by Eva Eriksson. Greenwillow, 1983 (I:2–6). A story in rhyme tells about an imaginative child and a box.

Lionni, Leo. *Alexander and the Wind-up Mouse*. Pantheon, 1969 (I:3–6 R:3). A real mouse learns it's better to be real than to be a toy.

———. *The Biggest House in the World*. Pantheon, 1968 (I:3–6 R:7). A small snail decides it's better to be himself than to be the biggest in the world.

McCloskey, Robert. *Blueberries for Sal*. Viking, 1948 (I:4–8 R:6). A bear cub and a young girl get mixed up and start following the wrong mother.

———. *Lentil*. Viking, 1940 (I:4–9 R:7). Lentil saves the homecoming when Old Sneep tries to wreck the welcome.

———. *Make Way for Ducklings*. Viking, 1941 (I:4–8 R:4). A city park provides a safe home for the ducklings.

———. *One Morning in Maine*. Viking, 1952 (I:4–8 R:3). Sal and her family experience the joys of living on an island.

———. *Time of Wonder*. Viking, 1957 (I:5–8 R:4). A family explores an island in the spring, during a hurricane, and after the storm has passed.

McPhail, David. *Fix-It*. Dutton, 1984 (I:3–7 R:2). An emergency develops when the television does not function.

Marshall, James. *George and Martha One Fine Day*. Houghton Mifflin, 1978 (I:3–8). Two hippos have a thoroughly delightful day as they walk on a tightrope and visit an amusement park.

Martin, Jacqueline. *Buzzy Bones and Uncle Ezra*. Illustrated by Stella Ormai. Lothrop, Lee & Shepard, 1984 (I:3–8 R:6). A young mouse overcomes his fear of the wind.

Maruki, Toshi. *Hiroshima No Pika*. Lothrop, Lee & Shepard, 1982 (I:10+ R:4). A family experiences the atomic bomb on August 6, 1945.

Mathis, Sharon Bell. *The Hundred Penny Box*. Illustrated by Leo and Diane Dillon. Viking, 1975 (I:6–9 R:3). Young Michael becomes friends with his Great-great-aunt Dew and the old box in which she keeps a penny for every year of her life.

Mayer, Mercer. *There's A Nightmare in My Closet*. Dial, 1969 (I:3–7 R:3). A young boy decides to get rid of his nightmare by confronting the monster.

Ness, Evaline. *Sam, Bangs & Moonshine*. Holt, Rinehart, 1966 (I:5–9 R:3). Sam almost costs a friend his life.

Newberry, Clare. *Barkis*. Harper & Row, 1938 (I:3–8 R:6). A new birthday puppy at first causes problems because two children do not want to share him.

———. *Marshmallow*. Harper & Row, 1942 (I:2–7 R:7). Oliver the cat is introduced to a new roommate, a rabbit.

Noble, Trinka Hakes. *The Day Jimmy's Boa Ate the Wash*. Illustrated by Steven Kellogg. Dial, 1980 (I:5–8 R:4). Havoc results when a boy drops his pet boa constrictor in the hen house.

Oakley, Graham. *The Church Mice Adrift*. Atheneum, 1977 (I:5–10 R:6). The church cat saves the church mice from an invasion of rats.

———. *The Church Mice in Action*. Atheneum, 1982 (I:5–10 R:7). The church mice enter Sampson in a cat show.

———. *The Church Mice Spread Their Wings*. Atheneum, 1975 (I:5–10 R:6). Sampson and the mice discover that nature is not so placid.

———. *The Church Mouse*. Atheneum, 1972 (I:5–10 R:6). Arthur lives peacefully and enjoyably in a church.

———. *Hetty and Harriet*. Atheneum, 1982 (I:5–10 R:6). A discontented hen and her meek friend leave the security of their barnyard for a series of adventures.

Peet, Bill. *Cyrus the Unsinkable Sea Serpent*. Houghton Mifflin, 1975. (I:5–9 R:7). A not-so-fierce sea serpent rescues a sailing ship from squalls and pirates.

———. *The Gnats of Knotty Pine*. Houghton Mifflin, 1975 (I:5–9 R:6). Gnats save the forest animals during hunting season.

———. *How Droofus the Dragon Lost His Head*. Houghton Mifflin, 1971 (I:5–9 R:6). The tale of a good, kind dragon who befriends a poor family.

———. *No Such Things*. Houghton Mifflin, 1983 (I:4–8 R:6). Nonsense words and creatures combine to make humorous reading.

Peterson, Jeanne Whitehouse. *I Have a Sister, My Sister Is Deaf*. Illustrations by Deborah Ray. Harper & Row, 1977 (I:3–8 R:1). The author shares her enjoyable experiences with her deaf sister.

Provensen, Alice, and Provensen, Martin. *The Year at Maple Hill Farm*. Atheneum, 1978 (I:4–9 R:3). Large illustrations and text trace the seasons of the year.

Ransome, Arthur. *The Fool of the World and the Flying Ship*. Illustrated by Uri Shulevitz. Farrar Straus & Giroux, 1968 (I:6–10 R:6). A humble Russian lad manages to marry the czar's daughter.

Rayner, Mary. *Garth Pig and the Ice Cream Lady*. Atheneum, 1977 (I:5–9 R:4). A wolf uses an ice cream truck to capture a pig.

Rey, Hans. *Curious George*. Houghton Mifflin, 1941, 1969 (I:2–7 R:2). George begins his slapstick adventures when he leaves the jungle with the man who has a yellow hat.

Schatell, Brian. *Farmer Goff and His Turkey Sam*. Lippincott, 1982 (I:4–7 R:5). A prize-winning turkey who performs tricks runs away and wins a pie-eating contest.

Sendak, Maurice. *In the Night Kitchen*. Harper & Row, 1970 (I:5–7). A young child dreams that he is in the world of the night kitchen.

———. *Seven Little Monsters*. Harper & Row, 1977 (I:5–8). An illustrated account of the actions of Sendak's monsters.

———. *The Sign on Rosie's Door*. Harper & Row, 1960 (I:5–9 R:2). Rosie pretends she a singer and tries to stage a show.

———. *Where the Wild Things Are*. Harper & Row, 1963 (I:4–8 R:6). Max's vivid imagination turns his room into a forest inhabited by wild things.

Seuss, Dr. *And to Think That I Saw It on Mulberry Street*. Vanguard, 1937 (I:3–9 R:5). A young boy imagines all the fantastic things that could be on his street.

———. *Did I Ever Tell You How Lucky You Are?* Random House, 1973 (I:4–10 R:3). Many things are worse than sitting on a prickly cactus.

———. *Dr. Seuss's Sleep Book*. Random House, 1962 (I:4–10 R:5). Dr. Seuss gives the reader a humorous "Who's-Asleep-Score."

———. *The 500 Hats of Bartholomew Cubbins*. Vanguard, 1938 (I:4–9 R:4). Bartholomew has a bewitched hat that keeps reappearing as he tries to take off his hat before the King.

———. *Horton Hatches the Egg*. Random House, 1940, 1968 (I:3–9 R:4). Horton replaces lazy Mayzie on her nest and finally hatches an elephant bird.

———. *Hunches in Bunches*. Random House, 1982 (I:6-10 R:4). A young boy has problems deciding on his hunches.

————. *I Can Lick 30 Tigers Today!* Random House, 1969 (I:4–10 R:4). Contains several short stories.

————. *If I Ran the Zoo.* Random House, 1950 (I:4–10 R:3). A boy searches in odd places for some unusual animals.

Sharmat, Marjorie Weinman. *The Best Valentine in the World.* Illustrated by Lilian Obligado. Holiday House, 1982 (I:3–7 R:4). A fox believes his friend has forgotten to make him a valentine.

Skorpen, Liesel Moak. *His Mother's Dog.* Illustrated by M. E. Mullin. Harper & Row, 1978 (I:4–9 R:5). Jealousy results over a dog and a new baby.

Small, David. *Eulalie and the Hopping Head.* Macmillan, 1982 (I:4–7 R:5). A toad and her daughter find an abandoned doll in the woods.

————. *Imogene's Antlers.* Crown, 1985 (I:5–8 R:6). A humorous story about a young girl who wakes up wearing antlers.

Spier, Peter. *Bored—Nothing To Do!* Doubleday, 1978 (I:3–9). When two boys become bored, they build and fly their own airplane.

————. *The Legend of New Amsterdam.* Doubleday, 1979 (I:all). Illustrations and text about the city of New Amsterdam (New York) in the 1660s.

————. *Oh, Were They Ever Happy!* Doubleday, 1978 (I:4–9). Children surprise their parents when they paint the house.

————. *The Star-Spangled Banner.* Doubleday, 1973 (I:8+). The words of the national anthem illustrated in accurate details from history.

Steig, William. *The Amazing Bone.* Farrar, Straus & Giroux, 1976 (I:6–9 R:3). A pig and a talking bone escape from robbers and a hungry fox.

————. *Caleb & Kate.* Farrar, Straus & Giroux, 1977 (I:6–9 R:3). Caleb the carpenter goes to sleep in the woods and is changed into a dog by Yedida the witch.

————. *Farmer Palmer's Wagon Ride.* Farrar, Straus & Giroux, 1974 (I:6–9 R:5). The pig and his donkey have one misfortune after another.

————. *Sylvester and the Magic Pebble.* Simon & Schuster, 1969 (I:6–9 R:5). A magical pebble causes a donkey to turn into a rock.

Stevenson, James. *Could Be Worse!* Greenwillow, 1977 (I:5–9 R:3). Grandpa tells his grandchildren a whopper.

————. *Monty.* Greenwillow, 1979 (I:5–9). Three animals boss an alligator as he takes them across the river.

————. *The Sea View Hotel.* Greenwillow, 1978 (I:5–10 R:3). The story of a mouse at a resort with cartoon-like illustrations.

————. *There's Nothing to Do.* Greenwillow, 1986 (I:5–9 R:3). Humor and exaggeration characterize this story.

————. *The Wish Card Ran Out!* Greenwillow, 1981 (I:6–10 R:4). Cartoon illustrations enhance a humorous spoof on credit cards.

————. *We Can't Sleep.* Greenwillow, 1982 (I:4–8 R:4). Grandpa tells a story when Louie and Mary Anne cannot sleep.

Turkle, Brinton. *Do Not Open.* Elsevier-Dutton, 1981 (I:4–7 R:4). A monster pops out of a bottle marked "Do not open."

Ungerer, Tomi. *The Beast of Monsieur Racine.* Farrar, Straus & Giroux, 1971 (I:5–9 R:5). A strange beast steals prized pears and becomes a friend of Monsieur Racine.

Van Allsburg, Chris. *Jumanji.* Houghton Mifflin, 1981 (I:5–8 R:6). An unusual game creates a jungle environment.

————. *The Polar Express.* Houghton Mifflin, 1985 (I:5–8 R:6). A boy has an unusual adventure when he meets Santa Claus.

————. *The Wreck of the Zephyr.* Houghton Mifflin, 1983 (I:5–8 R:6). A boy tries to become the greatest sailor in the world.

Vincent, Gabrielle. *Ernest and Celestine's Picnic.* Greenwillow, 1982 (I:3–5 R:4). Ernest and Celestine have a picnic even though it is raining.

————. *Smile, Ernest and Celestine.* Greenwillow, 1982 (I:3–5 R:4). Celestine experiences jealousy when she finds Ernest's pictures.

Viorst, Judith. *Alexander and the Terrible, Horrible, No Good, Very Bad Day.* Illustrated by Ray Cruz. Atheneum, 1972 (I:3–8 R:6). A boy experiences a series of bad incidents.

Waber, Bernand. *The Snake: A Very Long Story.* Houghton Mifflin, 1978 (I:3–8). Collages of scenery and a traveling snake provide an around-the-world adventure.

Wagner, Jenny. *John Brown, Rose and the Midnight Cat.* Illustrated by Ron Brooks. Bradbury, 1978 (I:4–8). A dog fears that a cat will disturb his life in the home of a nice widow.

Wallace, Ian. *Chin Chiang and the Dragon's Dance.* Atheneum, 1984 (I:6–9 R:7). A young boy gains self-confidence and his grandfather's respect when he performs the Dragon's Dance.

Ward, Lynd. *The Biggest Bear.* Houghton Mifflin, 1952 (I:5–8 R:4). A boy searches for a bear because he wants a bearskin for the outside of his barn.

Wells, Rosemary. *A Lion for Lewis.* Dial, 1982 (I:3–7 R:4). Lewis, the youngest child, discovers a way to gain his big brother's and sister's attention.

————. *Timothy Goes to School.* Dial, 1981 (I:4–7 R:4). Timothy Raccoon goes through many trials during his first week in school.

Willard, Nancy. *Simple Pictures Are Best.* Illustrated by Tomie de Paola. Harcourt Brace Jovanovich, 1977 (I:5–9). Two characters frustrate a photographer when they keep adding items that they want included in a photograph for their wedding anniversary.

Williams, Barbara. *Chester Chipmunk's Thanksgiving.* Illustrated by Kay Charao. Dutton, 1978 (I:3–7). Chester wants to share Thanksgiving with his friends, but they are all busy.

————. *Someday, Said Mitchell.* Illustrated by Kay Charao. Dutton, 1976 (I:2–7). A small boy wants to provide his mother with various labor-saving devices.

Williams, Jay. *Everyone Knows What a Dragon Looks Like.* Illustrated by Mercer Mayer. Four Winds, 1976 (I:5–10). The Great Cloud Dragon saves a town.

————. *The Reward Worth Having.* Illustrated by Mercer Mayer. Four Winds, 1977 (I:5–10). Three soldiers of the king help an old man and get to choose their own rewards.

Williams, Vera. *Something Special for Me*. Greenwillow, 1983 (I:3–7 R:6). Rosa uses coins in a jar to buy a birthday present.

———. *A Chair for My Mother*. Greenwillow, 1982 (I:3–7 R:6). A young girl helps save money for a new chair.

Wolf, Bernard. *Anna's Silent World*. Lippincott, 1977 (I:5–10 R:6). A deaf girl's experiences in school and with friends.

Yolen, Jane. *The Seeing Stick*. Illustrated by Remy Charlip and Demetra Maraslis. Crowell, 1977 (I:5–8 R:6). In ancient China an old man helps a blind girl by carving pictures on a stick.

Zemach, Margot. *It Could Always Be Worse: A Yiddish Folk Tale*. Farrar, Straus & Giroux, 1976 (I:5–9 R:2). A rabbi advises a man who lives in a crowded hut.

Zolotow, Charlotte. *My Grandson Lew*. Illustrated by William Péne du Bois. Harper & Row, 1974 (I:5–8 R:2). Lewis and his mother share some beautiful memories about Lewis's grandfather who died four years before.

———. *The Quarreling Book*. Illustrated by Arnold Lobel. Harper & Row, 1963 (I:4–8). The day starts out all wrong when a father forgets to kiss his wife good-bye.

———. *William's Doll*. Illustrations by William Péne du Bois. Harper & Row, 1972 (I:4–8 R:4). William's desire for a doll results in various responses from his family.

6
Traditional Literature

☐

OF CASTLE AND COTTAGE

☐

INVOLVING CHILDREN IN TRADITIONAL
LITERATURE

Of Castle and Cottage

ENCHANTED SWANS WHO REGAIN HUMAN form because of a sister's devotion, a brave boy who climbs into the unknown world at the top of a beanstalk, witches, warriors, supernatural animals, royal personages divine and human—all are brought to life in the traditional literature. This literature contains something that appeals to all interests: humorous stories, magical stories, and adventure stories about brave men and women. The settings of these stories are as varied as the enchanted places in the human imagination and as the geography of our world, from scorching deserts to polar icecaps. Regardless of location or subject, these tales include some of the most beloved and memorable stories of everyone's childhood.

This chapter discusses the nature of our traditional literary heritage—its basic forms and themes, and what it has to offer children.

OUR TRADITIONAL LITERARY HERITAGE

The quest for our traditional literary heritage takes students of children's literature to a time before the beginning of recorded history and to all parts of the world. They find tales of religious significance that allowed ancient people to speculate about their beginnings; they find mythical heroes and heroines from all cultures who overcame supernatural adversaries to gain their rewards; and they find the brave deeds of real people that probably gratified the rulers of ancient tribes. Similarities in the types of tales and in the narrative motifs and content of traditional stories from varied peoples throughout the world constitute tangible evidence, according to folklorist Stith Thompson (19), that traditional tales are both universal and ancient.

Every social class has cultivated the art of traditional storytelling, which reflects the culture, natural environment, and social contacts of the storyteller and the audience. For example, storytellers who earned their living in medieval European castles related great deeds of the nobility. The English court heard about King Arthur, Queen Guinevere, and the Knights of the Round Table, and the French court heard stories of princely valor such as "The Song of Roland." In ancient China, stories for the ruling classes often portrayed a benevolent dragon, the symbol of imperial authority.

Commoners in medieval Europe lived lives quite different from those of the nobility, and their traditional stories differed accordingly. The stories peasants told one another reflected the harsh, unjust, and often cruel circumstances of their existence as virtual slaves to the nobles. Common themes in their folktales center on dreams of overcoming social inequality and attaining a better way of life: in many tales a poor lad outwits a nobleman, wins his daughter in marriage, and gains lifelong wealth. This theme is found in "The Flying Ship," a Russian tale; in "The Golden Goose," a German tale; and in "The Princess and the Glass Hill," a Norwegian tale. Other traditional stories, such as the English "Jack the Giant Killer," tell of overcoming horrible adversaries with cunning and bravery. The peasants in these stories are not always clever. Consequences of stupidity are emphasized, for example, in the Norwegian tale "The Husband Who Has to Mind the House" and in the Russian tale "The Falcon under the Hat." In place of the benevolent imperial dragon, the tales of early China's common people often involved a cruel and evil dragon whose power the heroine or hero overcame.

In early times, everyone in society, old and young, heard the same tales. The Puritans of seventeenth-century England and its colonies considered folktales about giants, witches, and enchantment to be immoral for everyone, but maintained that children in particular should hear and read only what instructed them and reinforced their moral development. Other social groups in Europe and North America felt differently, however. In 1698, the Frenchman Charles Perrault published a collection of folktales called *Tales of Mother Goose*, which included "Cinderella" and "Sleeping Beauty." Over one hundred years later, the Romantic Movement in Europe generated enthusiasm for exploring folklore to discover more about the roots of European languages and traditional cultures. In Germany, the Brothers Grimm carefully collected and transcribed oral tales from the storytellers themselves. These tales have been retold or adapted by many contemporary writers. Perrault and the Brothers Grimm thus brought new respect to traditional tales and ensured their availability for all

time. Their work influenced collectors in other countries, as well as writers of literature.

By the end of the nineteenth century, as discussed in chapter two, European and North American societies generally considered childhood a distinct, necessary, and valuable stage in the human life cycle. Improved technology created more leisure hours for the middle and upper classes and a need for literature to entertain children. Traditional literature became a valuable part of this childhood experience. Today, folk literature is considered an important part of every child's cultural heritage. It is difficult to imagine the early childhood and elementary school years of American children without "The Little Red Hen," "The Three Bears," and "Snow White and the Seven Dwarfs." Older children's literary experiences would not be complete without tales of Greek and Norse mythology.

TYPES OF TRADITIONAL LITERATURE

Traditional tales have been handed down from generation to generation by word of mouth. In contrast to a modern story, a traditional tale has no identifiable author. Instead, storytellers tell what they have received from previous tellers of tales. Folklorists and others interested in collecting and analyzing traditional literature do not always agree about how to categorize and define different types of traditional tales. This text discusses four types of traditional tales—folktales, fables, myths, and legends—drawing on definitions recommended by folklorist William Bascom (4).

Folktales

Folktales, according to Bascom, are "prose narratives which are regarded as fiction. They are not considered as dogma or history, they may or may not have happened, and they are not taken seriously" (4, p. 4). Because the tales are set in any time or any place, they seem almost timeless and placeless. Folktales usually tell the adventures of animal or human characters. They contain common narrative motifs—such as supernatural adversaries (ogres, witches, and giants), supernatural helpers, magic and marvels, tasks and quests—and common themes—such as reward of good and punishment of evil. (Not all themes and motifs are found within one tale.)

The subcategories of folktales include cumulative tales, humorous tales, beast tales, magic and wonder tales, *pourquoi* tales, and realistic tales.

Cumulative Tales. Tales that sequentially repeat the action, characters, or speeches in the story until a climax is reached are found among all cultures. Most cumulative tales give their main characters—whether animal, vegetable, human, or inanimate object—intelligence and reasoning ability. Adults often share these stories with very young children because the structure of a cumulative tale allows children to join in with the story as each new happening occurs. A runaway baked food is a popular, culturally diverse subject for cumulative tales; it is found not only in the German "Gingerbread Boy" but also in a Norwegian version, "The Pancake," an English version, "Johnny Cake," and a Russian version, "The Bun." In all these tales, the repetition builds until the story reaches a climax. Other familiar cumulative tales include the English "Henny Penny"; "The Fat Cat," a Danish tale; and "Why Mosquitoes Buzz in People's Ears," an African tale.

Humorous Tales. Folktales allow people to laugh at themselves as well as at others, an apparently universal pleasure. In tales such as the Russian "The Peasant's Pea Patch" the humor results from absurd situations or the stupidity of the character. Human foolishness resulting from unwise decisions provides the humor and a moral in the English folktale "Mr. and Mrs. Vinegar" and in the Norwegian tale "The Husband Who Has to Mind the House."

Beast Tales. Beast tales are among the most universal folktales, being found in all cultures. For example, the coyote is a popular animal in Native American tales, while the fox and wolf are found in many European tales. The rabbit and the bear are popular characters in the folktales of black culture in the United States. Beasts in folktales often talk and act quite like people. In some stories, such as "The Bremen Town Musicians," animal characters use their wits to frighten away robbers and claim wealth. In other tales, such as "The Three Billy Goats Gruff," animals may use first their wits and then their strength to overcome the enemy. Still other animals win through industrious actions such as those found in "The Little Red Hen." Tales about talking animals may show the cleverness of one animal and the stupidity of another character.

Magic and Wonder Tales. The majority of magic and wonder tales contain some element of magic.

The fairy godmother transforms the kind, lovely, mistreated girl into a beautiful princess ("Cinderella"); the good peasant boy earns a cloth that provides food ("The Lad Who Went to the Northwind"); a kindhearted simpleton attains a magical ship ("The Fool of the World and the Flying Ship"); or the evil witch transforms the handsome prince into a beast ("Beauty and the Beast"). Magic can be good or bad. When it is good, the person who benefits has usually had misfortune or is considered inferior by a parent or society. When it is bad, love and diligence usually overcome the magic—as in the German tale "The Six Swans" and the Norwegian tale "East of the Sun and West of the Moon."

Pourquoi Tales. *Pourquoi* tales—or "why" tales, in an English translation of the French word—answer a question, or explain how animals, plants, or humans were created and why they have certain characteristics. For example, why does an animal or a human act in a certain way? Kathleen Arnott's (1) *Animal Folk Tales around the World* contains several stories that are characteristic of this type of tale. "Why Siberian Birds Migrate in Winter," for example, tells why some birds migrate away from Siberia in the winter and why some birds stay behind and struggle to stay alive until spring. A West Indies folktale in this collection tells "Why You Find Spiders in Banana Bunches," and an American tale suggests "Why Rabbits Have Short Tails." Marcos Kurtycz's and Ana Garcia Kobeh's *Tigers and Opossums* presents six animal tales from Mexico that explain "Why the hummingbird is richly dressed," "Why the opossum has a hairless tail," and "Why the bat flies only at night," among other things. Children enjoy these tales and like to make up their own *pourquoi* stories about animal or human characteristics.

Realistic Tales. The majority of folktales include supernatural characters, magic, or other exaggerated incidents. A few tales, however, have realistic plots involving people who could have existed. One such tale, "Dick Whittington," tells about a boy who comes to London looking for streets paved with gold. He doesn't find golden streets, but he does find work with an honest merchant, and eventually wins his fortune. Some versions of this story suggest that at least parts of it are true; there was a Dick Whittington who was lord mayor of London.

Fables

Fables are brief tales in which animal characters that talk and act like humans indicate a moral lesson or satirize human conduct. For example, in the familiar "The Hare and the Tortoise" the hare taunts the tortoise about her slow movements and boasts about his own speed. The tortoise then challenges the hare to a race. The hare starts rapidly and is soon far ahead; but he becomes tired and, in his confidence, decides to nap. Meanwhile, the tortoise, keeping at her slow and steady pace, plods across the finish line. When the hare awakens, he discovers that the tortoise has reached the goal. The moral of this fable indicates that perseverance and determination may compensate for the lack of other attributes. (Both the early fables of Aesop and the modern picture storybook versions of fables are discussed in a later section.)

Myths

Myths, according to William Bascom (4), are "prose narratives which, in the society in which they are told, are considered to be truthful accounts of what happened in the remote past. They are accepted on faith; they are taught to be

CHART 6–1
Characteristics of folktale, myth, and legend

Form and Examples	Belief	Time	Place	Attitude	Principal Characters
Folktale	**Fiction**	**Anytime**	**Anyplace**	**Secular**	**Human or Nonhuman**
1. "Snow White and Seven Dwarfs" (European)	fiction	"once upon a time"	"in the great forest"	secular	human girl and dwarfs
2. "The Crane Wife" (Asian)	fiction	long ago	"in a faraway mountain village"	secular	human man, supernatural wife
3. "Why Mosquitoes Buzz in People's Ears" (African)	fiction	"one morning"	in a forest	secular	animals
Fable	**Fiction**	**Anytime**	**Anyplace**	**Secular/ Allegorical**	**Animal or Human**
1. "The Hare and the Frog" (Aesop)	fiction	"once upon a time"	on the shore of a lake	allegorical	animals
2. "The Tyrant who Became a Just Ruler" (Panchatantra—India)	fiction	"in olden times"	in a kingdom	allegorical	human king
Myth	**Considered Fact**	**Remote Past**	**Other World or Earlier World**	**Sacred**	**Nonhuman**
1. "The Warrior Goddess: Athena" (European)	considered fact	remote past	Olympus	deities	Greek goddess
2. "Zuñi Creation Myth" (Native American)	considered fact	before and during creation	sky, earth and lower world	deities	Creator Awonawilona, Sun Father, Earth Mother
Legend	**Considered Fact**	**Recent Past**	**World of Today**	**Secular or Sacred**	**Human**
1. "King Arthur Tales" (European)	considered fact	recent past	Britain	secular	king
2. "The White Archer" (Native American)	considered fact	recent past	Land of Eskimos	secular	Indian who wanted to avenge parents' death

believed; and they can be cited as authority in answer to ignorance, doubt, or disbelief. Myths are the embodiment of dogma; they are usually sacred; and they are often associated with theology and ritual" (4, p.4). Myths account for the origin of the world and humans, for everyday natural phenomena such as thunder and lightening, and for human emotions and experiences, such as love and death. The main characters in myths may be animals, deities, or humans, whose actions take place in an earlier world or in another world such as the underworld or the sky. Many ancient Greek myths, for example, explain the creation of the world, the creation of the gods and goddesses who ruled from Mount Olympus, and the reasons for natural phenomena. The myth about Demeter and Persephone, for example, explains seasonal changes.

Legends

Legends, says William Bascom (4), are "prose narratives which, like myths, are regarded as true by the narrator and his audience, but they are set in a period considered less remote, when the world was much as it is today. Legends are more often secular than sacred, and their principal characters are human" (p. 4). Many legends embroider the historical facts of human wars and migrations, brave deeds, and royalty. Legends from the British Isles tell about Robin Hood, the protector of the poor in the Middle Ages, who may have been an actual person. Legends from France tell about the miraculous visions of Joan of Arc, who led French armies into battle against the English. Legends from Africa describe how the prophet Amakosa saved the Juba people from extinction.

Distinguishing Different Types of Traditional Tales

Chart 6–1 (p. 205) summarizes and clarifies the differences among folktales, fables, myths, and legends, providing examples of each type of traditional literature.

VALUES OF TRADITIONAL LITERATURE FOR CHILDREN

Understanding and Identifying with Universal Human Struggles

Bruno Bettelheim (5) provides strong rationales for using traditional tales with children in *The*

Uses of Enchantment: The Meaning and Importance of Fairy Tales. Bettelheim claims, in his psychoanalytic approach to traditional tales, that nothing is as enriching to both children and adults as the traditional tale. To reinforce this claim, he argues that these tales allow children to learn about human progress and about possible solutions to human problems. Children can understand a problem because a tale states it briefly and pointedly. In addition, tales describe situations that subtly convey the advantages of moral behavior. Children learn that struggling against difficulties is unavoidable, but that if they directly confront unexpected and unjust hardships they can emerge victorious. Traditional tales present characters who are both good and bad. Children gain the conviction, according to Bettelheim, that crime does not pay. The simple, straightforward characters in traditional tales allow children to identify with the good and reject the bad. Children empathize with honorable characters and their struggles, learning that, while they too may experience difficulty or rejection, they too will be given help and guidance when needed.

Understanding the World

Traditional tales also help children improve their understanding of the world, as Ruth Kearney Carlson (7) outlines in eight respects.

First, according to Carlson, traditional tales help children better understand the nonscientific cultural traditions of early humanity. Greek and Roman myths, for example, tell how early Europeans tried to explain the mysteries of creation, human nature, and natural phenomena through the powers of gods, giants, and demons. These myths were taken so seriously that religions grew up around them. Such tales, in addition to providing lively entertainment, fill readers with admiration for the people who developed such answers for unanswerable questions.

Second, a study of traditional tales can show children the inter-relatedness of various types of stories and narrative motifs in cultures around the world. For example, the tale of a girl who loses her mother, acquires a jealous or evil stepmother, is mistreated (but remains gentle and kind), and finally receives rewards for her goodness is found in folk literature everywhere. Scholars have identified more than 900 versions of the Cinderella tale world-wide; four of these—French, German, English, and Vietnamese—are discussed later in this chapter. While these stories have different characters, settings, and types of enchantment, their underlying themes are the same.

Third, children learn about cultural diffusion as they observe how different versions of the same tale are dispersed throughout different parts of the world. Anyone who has tried to categorize traditional literature according to country of origin is amazed at the similarity found among tales. Classifying the geographic location of the tale is sometimes difficult if the author retelling it does not specify the translation's source. The similarities among these tales indicate the movement of people through migration and conquests that have occurred throughout history. They also emphasize that humans throughout the world have had similar needs and problems. Some folktales from different countries are almost identical. For example, the German tale "The Table, the Donkey and the Stick," is very similar to the Norwegian tale "the Lad Who Went to the North Wind." While researching animal tales, Kathleen Arnott (1) discovered that "almost every country has its traditional trickster, such as the fox in Palestine and the mouse-deer in Malaysia; its stupid, easily fooled creature, such as the bear in Lapland or the giraffe in West Africa; and its benevolent, goodnatured animal, such as the kangaroo in Australia" (introduction). The tales are very similar, although the animals and the settings are characteristic of the countries in which they are told.

Fourth, traditional tales can help children develop an appreciation for the culture and art of different countries. If the author who retells the tale retains authentic cultural detail, and if the illustrator carefully researches the culture before picturing its natural environment and customs, children gain appreciation for the social realities and cultural contributions of a country. Nancy Ekholm Burket's illustrations for Randall Jarrell's version of Grimm's *Snow White and Seven Dwarfs* reflect research in German history and culture. Paul O. Zelinsky studied seventeenth-century Dutch paintings before illustrating Rika Lesser's version of *Hansel and Gretel*. Suekichi Akaba used a traditional Japanese painting technique when illustrating Sumiko Yagawa's retelling of *The Crane Wife*.

Fifth, traditional tales provide factual information about different countries—information about geography, government, family patterns, food,

celebrations, likes and dislikes. For example, far from being an endangered species, wolves were numerous in medieval Europe and greatly feared by a largely rural population—as the German tale "Little Red Riding Hood" and the Hungarian tale "One Little Pig and Ten Wolves" demonstrate. In *Where the Buffalos Begin*, Olaf Baker shows the economic and spiritual importance of the buffalo to traditional Native Americans of the Great Plains. Contrasts in weather and geography are evident when children compare the warm lands of Arabian folktales with the icy settings of Norse mythology.

Sixth, traditional tales familiarize children with the many languages and dialects of cultures around the world. The names in traditional tales from different countries fascinate children. They enjoy hearing stories about Russian Maria Morevna, the beautiful Tsarevna; Vietnamese Tam, the girl who lived in the Land of Small Dragon; and Mazel and Shlimazel, who have a wager in the Yiddish folktale. Many tales include language or dialects characteristic of a country or time period. Howard Pyle's *The Story of King Arthur and His Knights* contains dialogue suggesting early English: "Sir Knight, I demand of thee why thou didst smite that shield. Now let me tell thee, because of thy boldness, I shall take away from thee thine own shield, and shall hang it upon yonder appletree, where thou beholdest all those other shields to be hanging" (p. 44). Reading this prose may be difficult even for older elementary children, but they do enjoy hearing it when an adult reads it to them.

Seventh, traditional tales encourage children to identify with the imaginations of people in times and places different from their own, and provide marvelous stimulation for creative drama, writing, and other forms of artistic expression. When children listen to traditional tales and then interact with their own imaginations, they gain respect for the people who created such wondrous tales.

Finally, traditional tales encourage children to realize that people from all over the world have inherent qualities of goodness, mercy, courage, and industry. In a Chinese tale, a loving brother rescues his sister from a dragon; in a German tale, a sister suffers six years of ordeals in order to bring her brothers back to human form. A Jewish folk character works hard to cultivate fig trees that may benefit his descendants but not himself; while the Norse Beowulf's strength of character defeats evil monsters.

Pure Pleasure

Traditional literature is extremely popular with children. In particular, folktales—with their fast-paced, dramatic plots and easily identifiable good and bad characters—are among the types of literature most appealing to young audiences.

F. André Favat (10) reviewed the relevant research and reached some interesting conclusions about interest in folktales among children of different ages:

1 Children between the ages of five and ten—or roughly from kindergarten through the fifth grade—are highly interested in folktales, whether they select books voluntarily or are presented with books and asked for their opinions.
2 This interest follows what might be called a *curve of reading preference*—that is, children's interest in folktales emerges at a prereading age and gradually rises to a peak between the approximate ages of six and eight. It then gradually declines.
3 Concurrent with this decline in interest in folktales emerges an interest in realistic stories.

Although folktales may appeal primarily to young children, children of various ages and interests do find them enjoyable. Animal tales such as "The Three Little Pigs," "The Little Red Hen," and "The Three Bears" have been illustrated in picture book format for young children, while some versions of fairy tales such as "Beauty and the Beast" are of interest to upper-elementary school children.

The preceding sections have suggested some reasons for the pleasure children derive from folk literature. Favat's research showed some possible reasons for children's interest in folktales. He maintains that the characteristics of folktales correspond with the characteristics Jean Piaget ascribed to children.

First, children believe that objects, actions, thoughts, and words can exercise magical influence over events in their own lives. Folktales are filled with such occurrences, as spells turn humans into animals, or vice versa, and humble pumpkins become gilded coaches.

Second, children believe that inanimate objects and animals have consciousness much like that of humans. The objects and animals in folktales that speak or act like poeple are consistent with children's beliefs.

Third, young children believe in punishment for wrongdoing and reward for good behavior. Folktales satisfy children's sense of justice: the good Goose Girl, for example, is rewarded by marrying the prince, and her deceitful maid is punished harshly.

Fourth, the relationship between heroes and heroines and their environments is much the same as the relationship between children and their own environments: children are the center of their universes: heroes and heroines are the centers of their folktale worlds. For example, when Sleeping Beauty sleeps for a hundred years, so does the whole castle.

FOLKTALES

Characteristics of Folktales

Because folktales differ from other types of literature, they have characteristics related to setting, plot development, characterization, style, and theme that may differ from other types of children's stories.

Setting. Setting in literature includes both time and place. The time in folktales is always the far-distant past, usually introduced by some version of "once upon a time." The first line of a folktale usually places the listener immediately into a time when anything might happen to peasants or nobility. A Russian tale, "The Firebird," begins "Long ago, in a distant kingdom, in a distant land, lived Tsar Vyslar Andronovich." Native American folktales may begin with some version of "when all was new, and the gods dwelt in the ancient places, long, long before the time of our ancients." A French tale is placed "on a day of days in the time of our fathers," while a German tale begins "in the olden days when wishing still helped one." These introductions inform the listener that enchantment and overcoming obstacles are both possible in the tales about to unfold.

Chapter three discussed the symbolic settings found in many folktales. These settings are not carefully described because there is no need for description. One knows immediately that magic can happen in "the great forest" of the Grimms' "Snow White and the Seven Dwarfs" or in "the great castle" of Madame de Beaumont's version of "Beauty and the Beast." The title of a Romanian tale, "The Land Where Time Stood Still," establishes the symbolic setting where the reader's or listener's imagination will accept and expect unusual occurrences.

The introduction that places the folktale in the far-distant past may also briefly sketch the location. A Chinese tale, "The Cinnamon Tree in the Moon," also suggests a nature setting "where not even a soft breeze stirs the heavens and one can see the shadows in the moon." After introducing such briefly described settings, the tales proceed immediately into identifying the characters and developing the conflict.

Characterization. Folktale characters are less completely developed than are characters in other types of stories. Just as oral storytellers lacked the time to describe a story's setting fully, they lacked the time to develop fully rounded characters. Thus folktale characters are essentially symbolic and "flat"—that is, they have a limited range of personal characteristics and do not change in the course of the story. A witch is always wicked, whether she is the builder of gingerbread houses in the German tale "Hansel and Gretel" or the fearsome Baba Yaga in the Russian "Maria Morevna." Other unchangeably evil characters include giants, ogres, trolls, and stepmothers. Characters easily typed as bad are accompanied by those who are always good. The young heroine is fair, kind, and loving. The youngest son is honorable, kind, and unselfish, even if he is considered foolish. Isaac Bashevis Singer's *Mazel and Shlimazel, or the Milk of the Lioness* demonstrates characteristic differences between good and bad characters: Mazel, the spirit of good luck, is young, tall, and slim, with pink cheeks and a jaunty stride; Shlimazel, the spirit of bad luck, is old, pale-faced, and angry-eyed, with a crooked red nose, a beard gray as a spider's web, and a slumping stride.

Folktales usually establish the main characters' natures early on, as Charles Perrault does in the first paragraph of "Cinderella: or The Little Glass Slipper":

There was once upon a time, a gentleman who married for his second wife the proudest and most haughty woman that ever was known. She had been a widow, and had by her former husband two daughters of her own humor, who were exactly like her in all things. He had also by a former wife a young daughter, but of an unparalleled goodness and sweetness of temper, which she took from her mother, who was the best creature in the world. *Histories or Tales of Past Times*, (p. 73)

Children easily identify the good and bad characters in folktales. This easy identification of heroes and heroines, as well as folktales' characteristically lively action, may account for the popularity of folktales with young children.

Plot Development. Conflict and action abound in folktales. The nature of the oral tradition made it imperative that listeners be brought quickly into the action and identify with the characters. Consequently, even in written versions, folktales immerse readers into the major conflict within their first few sentences. For example, the conflict in Paul Galdone's *The Little Red Hen* is between laziness and industriousness. The first sentence introduces the animals who live together in a little house. The second sentence introduces the conflict—that is, that the cat, dog, and mouse are lazy. The third sentence introduces the industrious hen. The remainder of the story develops the conflict between the lazy animals and the industrious fowl. The conflict is quickly resolved when the hen eats her own baking and doesn't share it with her lazy friends. Similarly, in "The Three Billy Goats Gruff," the goats want to get to the other side of the bridge in order to eat the grass in a pasture. The conflict comes rapidly when they discover a troll living under the bridge. The action increases as each goat approaches the bridge, confronts the troll, and convinces the troll to allow him to cross. This cannot go on indefinitely; with each crossing, the tension increases until the largest billy goat and the troll must settle their differences. The conflict quickly reaches a climax when the largest goat knocks the troll off the bridge and crosses to the other side. The goats eat happily forever after.

This conflict between characters representing good and characters representing evil is typical of most folktales. Even though the odds are uneven, the hero overcomes the giant in "Jack the Giant Killer," the girl and boy outsmart the witch in "Hansel and Gretel," the intelligent animal outwits the ogre in "Puss in Boots," and a brother saves his sister from a dragon in "The Golden Sheng."

Actions that recur in folktales have been the focus of several researchers. Vladimir Propp (17) analyzed one hundred Russian folktales and identified thirty-one recurring actions that account for the uniformity and repetitiveness of folktales. While all tales did not include all actions, Propp noted that the actions that did occur in a tale were in the same sequence as in other tales. More important, he discovered that similar patterns were apparent in non-Russian tales. Propp concluded that folktales' consistency of action does not result from the country of origin, but from the fact that tales remain true to the folk tradition.

F. André Favat (10) summarized Propp's findings and analyzed French and German tales according to their actions. The following list of recurring sequential actions that may be found in various combinations is adapted from Favat. In some tales, females are the primary actors; but most folktales, reflecting the values and social realities of their times and places of origin, assign these typical actions primarily to male characters.

1   One family member leaves home.
2   The hero or heroine is forbidden to do some action.
3   The hero or heroine violates a forbidden order.
4   The villain attempts to survey the situation.
5   The villain receives information about the victim.
6   The villain attempts to trick or deceive the victim in order to possess the victim or the victim's belongings.
7   The victim submits to deception and unwittingly helps the enemy.
8   The villain causes harm or injury to a member of a family.
9   One family member either lacks or desires to have something.
10 A misfortune or lack is made known; the hero or heroine is approached with a request or command; he or she is allowed to go or is sent on a mission.
11 The seeker agrees to, or decides upon, a counteraction.
12 The hero or heroine leaves home.
13 The hero or heroine is tested, interrogated, or attacked, which prepares the way for him or her to receive a magical agent or a helper.
14 The hero or heroine reacts to the actions of the future donor.
15 The hero or heroine acquires a magical agent.
16 The hero or heroine is transferred, delivered, or led to the whereabouts of an object.
17 The hero or heroine and the villain join in direct combat.
18 The hero or heroine is marked.
19 The villain is defeated.

20 The initial misfortune or lack is eliminated.
21 The hero or heroine returns.
22 The hero or heroine is pursued.
23 The hero or heroine is rescued from pursuit.
24 The hero or heroine, unrecognized, arrives home or in another country.
25 A false hero or heroine presents unfounded claims.
26 A difficult task is proposed to the hero or heroine.
27 The task is resolved.
28 The hero or heroine is recognized.
29 The false hero/heroine or the villain is exposed.
30 The hero or heroine is given a new appearance.
31 The villain is punished.
32 The hero or heroine is married and ascends the throne.

Many of the folktales discussed in this chapter contain these actions, or various combinations of these actions. All folktales have similar endings, just as they have similar beginnings and plot development; most tales end with some version of "and they lived happily ever after."

Style. Charles Perrault, the famed collector of French fairy tales in the seventeenth century, believed "that the best stories are those that imitate best the style and the simplicity of children's verses" (11, p. viii). Such a style permits few distracting details or unnecessary descriptions. This simplicity is especially apparent in the thoughts and dialogues of characters in folktales: they think and talk like people. For example, the dialogue in the Grimms' "The Golden Goose" sounds as if the listener were overhearing a conversation. The little old gray man welcomes the first son with: "Good morning. Do give me a piece of that cake you have got in your pocket, and let me have a draught of your wine—I am so hungry and thirsty." The clever, selfish son immediately answers: "If I give you my cake and wine I shall have none left for myself: you just go your own way." (Disaster rapidly follows this exchange.) When Dullhead,the youngest, simplest son, begs to go into the woods, his father's response reflects his opinion of his son's ability: "Both your brothers have injured themselves. You had better leave it alone; you know nothing about it." Dullhead begs very hard, and his father replies: "Very well, then—go. Perhaps when you have hurt yourself, you may learn to know better." This German folktale is filled with rapid exchanges as Dullhead is rewarded with the golden goose and moves humorously on toward his destiny with the king and the beautiful princess.

The language of folktales is often enriched through simple rhymes and verses. In "Jack and the Beanstalk," the giant chants:

> Fee, fi-fo-fum,
> I smell the blood of an Englishman,
> Be he alive, or be he dead,
> I'll have his bones to grind my bread.

The enchanted frog from the Grimms' "The Frog King" approaches the princess's door with these words:

> Princess! Youngest princess!
> Open the door for me!
> Dost thou not know what thou saidst to me
> Yesterday by the cool waters of the fountain?
> Princess, youngest princess!
> Open the door for me!

Likewise, the witch asks Hansel and Grethel:

> Nibble, nibble, gnaw,
> Who is nibbling at my little house?

As the story nears its end, another rhyme asks the duck for help:

> Little duck, little duck, dost thou see
> Hansel and Grethel are waiting for thee?
> There's never a plank or bridge in sight,
> Take us across on thy back so white.

The simple style, easily identifiable characters, and rapid plot development make folktales very appropriate for sharing orally with children. Storytelling techniques are suggested on pages 243–246.

Themes in Folktales

Folktales contain universal truths and reflect the traditional values of the times and societies in which they originated, many of which are still honored today. The characters, their actions, and their rewards and punishments develop themes related to the highest human hopes about moral and material achievement: good overcomes evil; justice triumphs; unselfish love conquers; intelligence wins out over physical strength; kindness, diligence, and hard work bring rewards. The tales also show what happens to those who do not meet the traditional standards: the jealous queen is punished, the wicked stepsisters are blinded by birds, the foolish king loses part of his fortune or

his daughter, the greedy man loses the source of his success or his well being.

The universality of these themes suggests that people everywhere have responded to similar ideals and beliefs. Consider, for example, the universality of two themes, the superiority of intelligence and the loss of rewards because of foolishness. The hero in the English "Jack the Giant Killer" outwits the much larger and less intelligent giant. Spider, in the African tale "A Story, A Story" outwits a series of animals and wins his wager with the being who controls stories. The hero in the Jewish "The Fable of the Fig Tree" is rewarded because he considers the long-range consequences of his actions. The heroine in the Chinese "The Clever Wife" uses her wits to bring the family power. In contrast, in an English tale, "Mr. and Mrs. Vinegar" lose their possessions because of foolish actions. In a German tale, "The Fisherman and His Wife," the couple returns to their humble position because of foolish choices and greed. The Russian characters in "The Falcon under the Hat" lose their possessions because of foolish actions. These themes are found in traditional literature around the world.

Motifs in Folktales

Kind or cruel supernatural beings, magical transformations of reality, and enchanted young people who must wait for true love to break the spells that confine them are all elements that take folktales out of the ordinary and encourage folk to remember and repeat the tales. Folklorists have identified hundreds of such elements, or *motifs*, found in folktales. Researchers use these motifs to analyze and identify the similarities in tales from various cultures. Some motifs are practically universal, suggesting similar thought processes in people living in different parts of the world. Other motifs help folklorists trace a tale's diffusion from one culture to another or identify tales that have a common source.

Some of the most common of the many motifs in folktales concern supernatural beings, extraordinary animals, and magical objects, powers, and transformations.

Supernatural Adversaries and Helpers. Supernatural beings in folktales are usually either adversaries or helpers. The wicked supernatural beings, such as ogres and witches, may find heroines or heroes, entice them into their cottages or castles, and make preparations to feast upon them. The encounter with the evil being may be the result of an unlucky chance meeting as in "Hansel and Gretel," or the main character may deliberately seek out the adversary, as in the Chinese tale "Li Chi Slays the Serpent." Luckily, the adversaries' intended victims usually outwit them. In addition to being evil, supernatural adversaries are usually rather stupid; consequently, they are overcome by characters who use wit and trickery to overcome them.

Supernatural helpers support many folklore heroes and heroines in their quests. Seven dwarfs help Snow White in her battle against her evil stepmother. A supernatural old man causes hardships to the selfish older brothers and rewards the generous younger brother in the Russian tale "The Fool of the World and the Flying Ship." This same motif is found in tales from western Asia, eastern Europe, and India.

Extraordinary Animals. Whether cunning or stupid, deceitful or upstanding, extraordinary animals are popular characters in the folktales of all cultures. In the English and French versions of "Little Red Riding Hood," the wolf plays the role of ogre, deceives a child, and is eliminated. In Japanese folklore, the fox has a malicious nature, can assume human shape, and has the power to bewitch humans. Tricky foxes and coyotes are important characters in Black American and Native American folktales as well.

Some extraordinary animals are loyal companions and helpers to deserving human characters. The cat in the French "Puss in Boots" outwits an ogre and provides riches for his human master. The German version of "Cinderella" collected by the Brothers Grimm contains no fairy godmothers; instead, white doves and other birds help Cinderella complete the impossible tasks her wicked stepmother requires.

Magical Objects, Powers, and Transformations. The possession of a magical object or power is a crucial factor in many folktales. When all seems lost, the hero may don the cloak of invisibility and follow "The Twelve Dancing Princesses" to solve a mystery and win his fortune, or the heroine's loving tears may fall into her true love's eyes, saving him from blindness, as in "Rapunzel." Folktale characters often obtain magical objects in an extraordinary manner, lose them or have them stolen, and eventually recover them.

This sequence occurs in the Norwegian "The Lad Who Went to the North Wind," in which a boy goes to the North Wind demanding the return of his meal, is given a magical object, loses it to a dishonest innkeeper, and must retrieve it. The dishonest innkeeper is eventually punished: in folktales, stealing a magical object often results in considerable problems for the thief.

Magical spells and transformations are also common in folktales around the world. The spell of a fairy godmother or a witch turns a pumpkin into a golden coach or puts a princess to sleep for a hundred years. One of the most common transformation motifs involves a prince being magically transformed into an animal ("The Frog Prince") or a beast-like monster ("Beauty and the Beast"). A gentle, unselfish youngest daughter usually breaks the enchantment when she falls in love with the animal or beast. In a Basque tale the beast is a huge serpent; a Magyar Hungarian tale has the prince transformed into a pig; and a Lithuanian tale tells of a prince who becomes a white wolf.

"The Crane Wife," a Japanese folktale, exemplifies the transformation from animal to human, as a poor farmer gains a wife when a wounded crane he cares for transforms herself into a lovely woman.

Many Native American tales include humans transformed into animals. "The Ring in the Prairie," a Shawnee Indian tale, includes transformations of humans and sky dwellers: a human hunter transforms himself into a mouse to capture a girl who descends from the sky; the sky dwellers secure part of an animal and are transformed into that specific animal. Many of the Native American transformation stories suggest a close relationship between humans and animals.

Multiple Motifs. Although a folktale may be remembered for one dramatic motif, most tales have multiple motifs. Consider the following motifs in "Jack and the Beanstalk": (1) a foolish bargain, (2) the hero acquires a magical object, (3) a plant with extraordinary powers, (4) the ogre repeats "fee-fi-fo-fum," (5) the hero is hidden by the ogre's wife, (6) the hero steals a magical object from the ogre, (7) the magical object possesses the power of speech, (8) the hero summons the ogre. Listing such common motifs provides folklorists with a means of analyzing folktales across cultures.

CHART 6–2
Common motifs in folktales from
different cultures

Common Motif	Culture	Folktale
Supernatural Adversaries		
Ogre	England	"Jack the Giant Killer"
Ogress	Italy	"Petrosinella"
Troll	Norway	"Three Billy Goats Gruff"
Giant	Germany	"The Valiant Little Tailor"
Dragon	China	"The Golden Sheng"
Witch	Africa	"Marandenboni"
Deceitful or Ferocious Beasts		
Wolf	Germany	"The Wolf and the Seven Little Kids"
Wolf	France	"Little Red Riding Hood"
Wolf	England	"The Three Little Pigs"
Wild hog, unicorn and lion	United States	"Jack and the Varmints"
Supernatural Helpers		
Fairies	France and Germany	"The Sleeping Beauty"
Fairy Godmother	Vietnam	"The Land of Small Dragon"
Jinni	Arabia	"The Woman of the Well"
Cat (fairy in disguise)	Italy	"The Cunning Cat"
Magical Objects		
Cloak of invisibility	Germany	"The Twelve Dancing Princesses"
Magical cloth	Norway	"The Lad Who Went to the North Wind"
Magical lamp	Arabia	"Aladdin and the Magic Lamp"
Magical mill	Norway	"Why the Sea Is Salt"
Magical Powers		
Granted wishes	Germany	"The Fisherman and His Wife"
Wish for a child	Russia	"The Snow Maiden"
Humans with extraordinary powers	Mexico	"The Riddle of the Drum"
Humans with extraordinary powers	Russia	"The Fool of the World and the Flying Ship"
Magical Transformations		
Prince to bear	Norway	"East of the Sun and West of the Moon"
Prince to beast	France	"Beauty and the Beast"
Bird to human	Japan	"The Crane Wife"
Human to animal	Native American	"The Ring in the Prairie"

Universality of Motifs. Chart 6–2 summarizes the discussion of motifs and demonstrates that folktales from many parts of the world contain the same motifs. The search for common motifs is an enlightening and rewarding activity for children as well as adults. Many of the values of sharing folktales with children are gained through comparative and cross-cultural study of traditional tales.

Folktales from the British Isles

English folktales about ogres, giants, and clever humans were among the first stories published as inexpensive chapbooks in the 1500s. Joseph Jacobs collected the tales and in 1890 published over eighty of them as *English Fairy Tales*. In 1892 Jacobs published a collection of Celtic fairy tales. These books, in reissue or in modern editions, are still available today. Their fast plots and rather unpromising heroes are popular with the children. For example, the various "Jack tales"—

including "Jack the Giant Killer" and "Jack and the Beanstalk"—develop plots around the villainous ogres or giants who terrorize a kingdom and the heroes who overcome their adversaries with trickery and cleverness rather than with magical powers.

Other villains in English folktales play adversarial roles similar to those of giants and ogres. For example, "Three Little Pigs" must outwit a wolf, and a young girl is frightened by "The Three Bears." In *What's in Fox's Sack? An Old English Tale*, retold and illustrated by Paul Goldone, the villain is a sly fox who manages to get a boy into his sack. A clever woman outsmarts the fox by placing a large bulldog inside the sack.

In Flora Annie Steel's English version of the Cinderella tale, *Tattercoats*, the heroine is mistreated not by a villainous stepmother and cruel stepsisters, but by her grandfather, who mourns his daughter's death in childbirth and rejects the child who survived, and by his cruel servants. (One variation of this tale does not require a

Paul Galdone's version of an English folktale compares the industrious with the lazy animals. (From *The Little Red Hen*, by Paul Galdone, published by Clarion Books, Ticknor & Fields: A Houghton Mifflin Company, New York. Copyright © 1973 by the author/illustrator.)

transformation in Tattercoats' looks and apparel; after she meets the prince in the forest, he discovers that she is a fine and beautiful person and invites her to attend the ball dressed just as she is.)

In addition to clearly defined good and bad characters, the repetitive language in many English folktales appeals to storytellers and listeners. In "The Three Little Pigs" the wolf threatens, "I'll huff and I'll puff and I'll blow your house in," and the pig replies, "Not by the hair on my chinny chin chin." "The Three Bears" repeats chairs, bowls of porridge, and beds, and the three bears' questions: "Who has been sitting in my chair? Who has been eating my porridge? Who has been sleeping in my bed?" Several versions of this folktale appeal to young children. Lorinda Bryan Cauley's *Goldilocks and the Three Bears* has compelling illustrations. Paul Galdone's *The Three Bears*, which may be used to develop size concepts, has large pictures that differentiate sizes of bears, bowls, beds, and chairs.

British folk literature is filled with humorous tales that stress human foolishness, making a point about human foibles. In the Scottish tale "Master above All Masters," found in David Buchan's *Scottish Tradition: A Collection of Scottish Folk Literature*, a wealthy tailor desires grander and longer names for himself, his family, and his possessions. One night the house catches on fire, and the manservant rushes up the stairs calling:

"Arise, Master above all Masters,
Put on thy Stuntifiers,
Waken Madame for the Dame
And Sir John the Greater,
For Old Killiecraffus
Has gone to the top of Montaigo,
And if you don't apply to the Well of Strathfountain
The whole Castle of Kilmundy
Will be burned in twa minutes" (p. 56)

By the time the servant finishes calling the long list of acquired names and titles, the house is ablaze, and only the people escape.

The consequences of greed, a universal motif found in folktales from many countries, are found in Susan Cooper's *The Silver Cow: A Welsh Tale*. In this tale the magic people, The Tylwyth Teg, send a marvelous cow out of the Bearded Lake as a reward for a young boy's music. The greed of the boy's father causes the cow and her offspring to return to the lake where they are turned into water lilies. In Gwyn Jones's "Where Arthur Sleeps," found in *Welsh Legends and Folk-Tales*, a greedy young man is thrown out of a cave filled with gold and silver and must return home with nothing.

An impossible task created by foolish boasting is one of the motifs in Harve Zemach's *Duffy and the Devil*, a Cornish tale resembling "Rumpelstiltskin." An inefficient maid named Duffy misleads her employer about her spinning ability and makes an agreement with the devil, who promises to do the knitting for three years. At the end of that time she must produce his name or go with him. When the time arrives, the squire goes hunting and overhears the festivities of the witches and the devil as the little man with the long tail sings this song:

Tomorrow! Tomorrow! Tomorrow's the day!
I'll take her! I'll take her! I'll take her away!
Let her weep, let her cry, let her beg, let her pray—
She'll never guess my name is . . . Tarraway! (p. 30
    unnumbered)

Thus Duffy learns the magic name and cheats the devil from claiming her soul. (The importance of a secret name is reflected in folktales from many cultures. In the English version of "Rumpelstiltskin" the name is Tim Tit Tot; a Scottish secret name is Whuppity Stoories; a tale from Nigeria is "The Hippopotamus called Isantim.")

Folktales from Ireland are filled with fairies, leprechauns and other little people. Many tales, such as "Connla and the Fairy Maiden," found in Joseph Jacob's *Irish Fairy Tales*, show the power of supernatural beings over humans. William Stobb's rendition of Jacobs's "Guleesh" shows that the fairy folk do not always outwit people. A young man races with the "sheehogues," tricks those fairy hosts out of a captured princess, and breaks a fairy spell so the princess can speak. This tale ends not with "and they lived happily ever after," but with an ending more characteristic of Irish folk literature:

There was neither cark nor care, sickness nor sorrow, mishap nor misfortune on them till the hour of their death, and may the same be with me, and with us all! (p. 32)

British folk literature contains fewer grand stories of mystical enchantment than do the French and the German. Peasants rather than royalty are usually the heroes and heroines in folktales of the British Isles. Consequently, the reader or listener can learn much about the problems, beliefs, values, and humor of common people in early British history. Themes in British folktales suggest that intelligence will win out over physical strength, that hard work and diligence will be rewarded, and that love and loyalty are basic values for everyone.

French Folktales

The majority of French folktales portray splendid royal castles rather than humble peasant cottages. Charles Perrault, a member of the Académie Française collected and transcribed many of these tales. In 1698, he published a collection of folktales called *Tales of Mother Goose* that in-cluded "Cinderilla" (original spelling), "Sleeping Beauty," "Puss in Boots," "Little Red Riding Hood," "Blue Beard," "Little Thumb," "Requet with the Tuft," and "Diamond and the Toads." These stories had entertained children and adults of the Parisian aristocracy and, consequently, are quite different from tales that stress wicked, dishonest kings being outwitted by simple peasants. A new edition of Perrault's tales, *The Glass Slipper: Charles Perrault's Tales of Time Past* includes eight tales highlighted by elegant illustrations that capture the formality of the early French court.

Many illustrators and translators of French fairy tales depict such royal settings. For example,

ISSUE

--- »≫❂≪« ---

Are "Cinderella" and Similar Traditional Tales Sexist?

PURITANS IN ENGLAND and the United States considered many of the traditional tales too violent to be shared with children. Today the tales are being attacked by groups who consider the actions of the beautiful, often helpless females, and the clever, handsome princes who rescue them to be sexist. Ethel Johnston Phelps is an author who believes the image of the good, obedient, meek, and submissive heroine is harmful and should be altered. She has published two books that depict brave and clever heroines: *Tatterhood and Other Tales*[1] and *The Maid of the North.*[2] *Time* magazine's review of these books concludes: "Though Phelps celebrates females who have brains and energy, her feminist lens at times distorts the drama beneath the surface of the folk tales" (3, p. 60). In defense of this criticism the *Time* writer provides two examples. In "The Twelve Huntsmen" Phelps has the prince collapse at the appropriate moment; in the original story the girl demonstrates this behavior. In "The Maid of the North" Phelps changes the dialogue from the original in which the maid fends off a suitor by describing the disadvantages of leaving home to join a stranger's household. In Phelps's version the maid expresses this viewpoint against marriage: "A wife is like a house dog tied with a rope. Why should I be a servant and wait upon a husband?"

Should these stories be rewritten to reflect changing attitudes of the times or will rewriting distort the value of the traditional tale? Are children harmed by the male and female stereotypes developed in traditional literature? If stories are tampered with, will children lose their identification with characters like themselves, who are often bewildered and feel like underdogs in traditional tales?

[1]Phelps, Ethel Johnston. *Tatterhood and Other Tales.* Feminist Press, 1978.
[2]Phelps, Ethel Johnston. *The Maid of the North.* Holt, Rinehart & Winston, 1981.
[3]"Sexes: Feminist Folk and Fairy Tales." *Time,* 20 July 1981, p. 60.

The tale of an enchanted beast emphasizes a regal setting. (From *Beauty and the Beast*, by Madame de Beaumont, translated and illustrated by Diane Goode. © 1978. Reprinted with permission of Bradbury Press, Inc.)

Marcia Brown's interpretation of Perrault's *Cinderella* is quite different from the German version of that tale. Cinderella has a fairy godmother who grants her wishes. A pumpkin is transformed into a gilded carriage, six mice become beautiful horses, a rat becomes a coachman with an elegant mustache, and lizards turn into footmen complete with fancy livery and lace. Cinderella is dressed in a beautiful gown embroidered with rubies, pearls, and diamonds. This version also has the magical hour of midnight when everything returns to normal. Perrault's *Cinderella* contains stepsisters who are rude and haughty, but they are not as cruel as in the German version. Cinderella even finds it possible to forgive them:

Now her stepsisters recognized her. Cinderella was the beautiful personage they had seen at the ball! They threw themselves at her feet and begged forgiveness for all their bad treatment of her. Cinderella asked them to rise, embraced them and told them she forgave them with all her heart. She begged them to love her always. (p. 27)

Cinderella not only forgives them, but also provides them with a home at the palace and marries them to the lords of the court. Brown's illustrations, drawn with fine lines and colored with pastels, depict a magical kingdom where life in the royal court is a marvelous existence.

The French version of "The Sleeping Beauty" suggests traditional French values: seven good fairies bestow the virtues of intelligence, beauty, kindness, generosity, gaiety, and grace on the infant princess. David Walker's version of *The Sleeping Beauty* shows this artist's background in theatrical set and costume design. His illustrations create the feeling of a stage setting, as fairies dance lightly across the great hall of the castle.

Diane Goode has translated and illustrated an edition of Madame de Beaumont's *Beauty and the Beast*. Meant originally for the wealthy classes in French society, de Beaumont's tale begins with the traditional "Once upon a time," but provides detailed descriptions tailored for an aristocratic audience. For example, Beauty enjoys reading, playing the harpsichord, and singing while she spins. When she enters the Beast's castle, he provides her with a library, a harpsichord, and music books. Goode's illustrations create a magical setting in which Beauty eventually loves the Beast for his virtue, although he lacks good looks and wit. Beauty's moral discrimination permits the Beast's transformation back into a handsome prince.

Warwick Hutton's shorter version of *Beauty and the Beast* focuses less on the wealthy classes. His Beauty is the youngest daughter of a merchant who has had bad luck. Unlike her ill-tempered and resentful older sisters, she looks on the bright side of their situation and tries to keep her family happy.

French folktales contain more enchantment than do tales from other countries. The motifs in these tales include fairy godmothers, fairies, remarkable beasts who help their young masters, unselfish girls who break enchantments, and deceitful beasts.

German Folktales

Mirror, mirror on the wall.
Who is the fairest of them all?

These words bring to mind one of the most popular childhood tales. German folktales—whether they are about enchanted princesses and friendly dwarfs, clever animals, or poor but honest peasants—are among the most enjoyed folktales in the world. Their accessibility to modern audiences is owed to the work of Wilhelm and Jacob Grimm, German professors who researched the roots of the German language through the traditional tales that had been told orally for generations. The Grimms asked village storytellers throughout Germany to tell them tales, then wrote the stories down and published them as *Kinder-und Hausmärchen*. The stories ultimately were translated into many languages and became popular in Europe, North America, and elsewhere.

A wolf is the villain in several German folktales young children enjoy. Wolves in these tales are cunning, dangerous, and receive just punishment. In Anne Rogers's version of the Grimms' *The Wolf and the Seven Little Kids*, the mother goat specifically warns her children about the deceitful wolf: "He may try to disguise himself, but you'll know him by his gruff voice and his black feet" (p. 1). After the wolf has tricked and eaten the kids, the mother goat cuts him open, saves her children, and places rocks inside the wolf. When awakened, the wolf feels terrible, loses his balance, and falls into the well.

Paul Galdone's version of *Little Red Riding Hood*, is particularly appropriate for younger children. Little Red Riding Hood is traveling through the woods to visit her grandmother. On the way, she stops to chat with the sly wolf, who then hurries ahead of her, gobbles up grandmother, and does the same thing to Little Red Riding Hood when she arrives. In this version, the huntsman rescues grandmother and Red Riding Hood from inside the wolf and places stones in the wolf's stomach. Trina Schart Hyman's version of this tale is more involved and appropriate for older children. In addition to the story, Hyman stresses the importance of a moral in the Grimms' folktales. The incident with the dangerous wolf teaches Red Riding Hood a lesson: "I will never wander off the forest path again, as long as I live. I should have kept my promise to my mother."

Not all animals in German folklore are as fearsome as the wolf. For example, "The Bremen Town Musicians," old animals about to be destroyed by their owners, have humorously appealing human qualities. In Hans Fischer's version of this tale, *The Traveling Musicians*, the donkey, hound, cat, and rooster set out to seek their fortunes as musicians. They give only one concert, but it is sufficient to frighten away a band of robbers whose house and treasures they can claim for themselves. Fischer's illustrations add to the humor of the text. Ilse Plume's softly colored illustrations for another version of this tale suggest the gentle nature of the animals and the story's setting in a sunlit forest.

Poor peasants and penniless soldiers are common heroes in German folklore. The peasant may not be cunning, but he is usually good. In "The Golden Goose," for example, the youngest son is even called Simpleton. When his selfish brothers leave home, their parents give them a fine rich cake and a bottle of wine, which they refuse to share with anyone. The despised Simpleton, however, is generous with the cinder cake and sour beer his parents give him. His kind heart is rewarded when he acquires a golden goose with magical powers that allow the lad to marry the princess. This tale contains many of the actions Vladimir Propp (17) discovered to be recurrent in folktales. In Warwick Hutton's version of "The Nose Tree," three poverty-stricken soldiers receive rewards of magical gifts when they share their campfire with a stranger, then lose their gifts to a tricky princess. The princess's thievery does not go unpunished, however. In a humorous ending, she tricks the soldiers out of an additional object, an apple that causes her nose to grow. Punishment of human greed is an important theme in German folktales.

Hansel and Gretel is the classic tale of an evil witch, a discontented and selfish mother, an ineffectual father, and two resourceful children. Rika Lesser's retelling, accompanied by Paul O. Zelinsky's illustrations, provides a rich source for this favorite tale (See plate 20 in the color insert).

Many of the best-loved German folktales are stories of princesses who sleep for a hundred years, have wicked stepmothers, and/or are enchanted by witches. One very lovely version of the Grimms' "Snow White" is translated by Randall Jarrell and illustrated by Nancy Ekholm Burkert. Burkert undertook considerable research in German museums and visited the Black Forest before creating her drawings for *Snow White and the Seven Dwarfs*, which thoroughly portrays every aspect of the mystical forest, the dwarfs' cottage, and the wicked stepmother's secret tower room.

Artist Errol LeCain has depicted the medieval beauty of two other fairy tales collected by the Brothers Grimm. *The Twelve Dancing Princesses* is the tale of twelve girls who mysteriously wear out their slippers every night. A poor soldier, who is given a cloak of invisibility after he helps an old woman, manages to follow the princesses and discover their secret, winning one of them as his bride. LeCain's *Thorn Rose, or the Sleeping Beauty* recreates the opulence of a magical kingdom in drawings of nobles, castles, good fairies who fly on beautifully plumed birds, and an evil fairy who flies on an orange dragon.

The German version of "Cinderella" in *The Complete Brothers' Grimm Fairy Tales* differs somewhat from the French rendering of this tale in both plot detail and mood. A bird in the hazel tree growing by her mother's grave, not a fairy godmother, gives Cinderella a dress made of gold and silver and a pair of satin slippers for the ball. When Cinderella is successfully united with the prince, no softness of heart leads her to forgive her cruel stepsisters. On her wedding day, the sisters join the bridal procession; but doves, perched peacefully on Cinderella's shoulders peck out the sisters' eyes.

Breaking enchantments through unselfish love is another common theme in German folklore. In the Grimms' "The Six Swans," the heroine can restore her brothers to human form only by sewing six shirts out of starwort. She cannot speak during the six years required for her task and suffers many ordeals before she is successful. The same theme and a similar plot are found in Elizabeth Crawford's translation of the Grimms' "The Seven Ravens."

Another lovely maiden who must go through considerable unhappiness before she is rescued by her prince is the Grimms' "Rapunzel." Giambattista Basile's Neapolitan version of this tale, *Petrosinella*, portrays a heroine more forceful than the German Rapunzel. The princess in the tower saves both herself and her prince when she discovers three acorns that are the cause of her enchantment.

Nonny Hogrogian's version of the Grimms' "The Devil With the Three Golden Hairs" exemplifies many of the characteristics of German folktales.

A poor, brave boy is rewarded; a wicked, greedy king is punished; a kind miller cares for the boy; a beautiful princess is rewarded; the devil's grandmother uses enchantment to help the boy; and the devil is outwitted. Other common folktale elements in this tale include a physical sign of luck, a quest, the importance of threes (three hairs, three questions), and magical transformations. The text concludes with a characteristic moral: "The youth, together with his bride, lived well and reigned well, for he who is not afraid can even take the hairs from the devil's head and conquer the kingdom."

German folktales are ideal candidates for storytelling. Their speedy openings, fast-paced plots, and high drama keep listeners entertained story after story. In these tales, adversaries include devils, witches, and wolves. The good-hearted youngest child is often rewarded, while selfishness, greed, and discontent are punished. The noble character frequently wins as a result of intervention by supernatural helpers, and magical objects and spells are recurring motifs.

This German tale shows the importance of a moral in traditional literature. (Illustration copyright © 1983 by Trina Schart Hyman. Reprinted from *Little Red Riding Hood* by permission of Holiday House.)

Norwegian Folktales

Pat Shaw Iverson (13) states that "if Norway were to show the world a single work of art which would most truly express the Norwegian character, perhaps the best choice would be the folktales, published for the first time more than a hundred years ago and later illustrated by Erik Werenskiold and Theodor Kittelsen" (p. 5). These folktales, collected by Norwegian scholars Peter Christian Asbjörnsen and Jörgen E. Moe, were published under the title *Norwegian Folk Tales* in 1845. Absjörnsen and Moe's interest in collecting the traditional tales of the Norwegian people was stimulated by reading the Grimms' *Kinder-und Hausmärchen*. They were also inspired by the "National Renaissance" then sweeping Europe, and folklore and folk music were excellent sources for studying early Norwegian traditions and history.

Claire Booss (6), a collector of the folktales of northern peoples, believes that climatic and geographic extremes created hardy, courageous, and independent people whose folktales reflect a strong sense of wonder, a fierce loyalty to ideals, and a great sense of humor. Booss also maintains that a sense of extremes inspires stories with the power to delight, haunt, and terrify.

It is interesting to compare Norwegian use of common folktale motifs with the use of supernatural adversaries and helpers, magical objects, and plots in folktales from other European cultures. Consider, for example, Mercer Mayer's version of "East of The Sun and West of the Moon." Motifs in this tale are similar to those in the French "Beauty and the Beast" and other tales of human enchantment and lost loves: an enchanted human demands a promise in return for a favor; the promise is at first honored; the maiden disenchants the human; he must leave because she does not honor her promise; she searches for him and finally saves him. The adversaries and helpers in this tale reflect a northern climate and culture. The human is enchanted by a troll princess who lives in a distant icy kingdom. The loving maiden receives help from, among others, Father Forest, who understands the body of earth and stone; Great Fish, who knows the blood of salt and water; and North Wind, who understands the mind of the earth, the moon, and the sun. The gifts each helper gives her allow her to overcome the trolls and

Humor is developed through exaggeration and ridiculous situations. (From *Old Lars*, by Erica Magnus. Copyright © 1984 by Erica Magnus Thomas. By permission of Carolrhoda Books, Inc.)

Many Norwegian tales are about humorous incidents. (From *Favorite Fairy Tales Told in Norway*, retold by Virginia Haviland. Illustrations Copyright © 1961 by Leonard Weisgard. By permission of Little, Brown and Company.)

golden goose who does not relinquish anyone who touches her, Tom forms a parade of unwilling followers: an old woman, an angry man who kicks at the woman, a smithy who waves a pair of tongs, and a cook who runs after them waving a ladle of porridge. At the sight of this ridiculous situation, the sad princess bursts into laughter. Tom wins the princess and half the kingdom. Compare this tale with the Grimms' "The Golden Goose."

This last tale suggests the humorous incidents common in Norwegian tales. Absurd situations also provide humor in Kathleen and Michael Hague's retelling of Asbjörnsen and Moe's "The Man Who Kept House." One comical experience after another occurs when a husband tries to prove that his wife's housework is easier than his farm work. After they exchange jobs, the baby tosses oatmeal onto the ceiling, the clean laundry

free the prince: a tinder box makes it possible to melt the ice encasing the youth, a shot from the bow and arrow causes the troll princess to turn to wood, and reflections in the fish scale cause the remaining trolls to turn to stone. Mayer's illustrations of snowy winters, creatures frozen in ice, icy mountains, and tree-covered landscapes also evoke a northern setting. Mayer's version of this tale differs from Claire Booss's version in *Scandinavian Folk & Fairy Tales*, in which a white bear offers a family riches if its youngest daughter is allowed to live in his castle.

Norwegian folktale collections provide many excellent stories for retelling. Several favorites are found in Virginia Haviland's *Favorite Fairy Tales Told in Norway*. Young children love to listen to, and dramatize the classic, "Three Billy Goats Gruff." Another favorite for storytelling and creative drama is "Taper Tom," whose hero is the characteristic youngest son who sits in a chimney corner amusing himself by grubbing in the ashes and splitting tapers for lights. His family laughs at his belief that he can win the princess's hand in marriage and half the kingdom by making the princess laugh. With the assistance of a magical

A gigantic rooster, or troll bird, is a ferocious adversary in this Norwegian folktale about trolls. (From *The Terrible-Troll Bird*, by Ingri and Edgar Parin D'Aulaire. Copyright © 1933, 1976 by Ingri and Edgar Parin D'Aulaire. Reprinted by permission of Doubleday & Company, Inc.)

is soiled, the goat gets into the house and creates chaos, and the husband almost hangs himself and the cow. Young children appreciate the fast-paced action and large, humorous illustrations in the Hagues' edition of this tale.

The humor in Erica Magnus's *Old Lars* results from another ridiculous situation. An old farmer hitches his horse to the sleigh, goes up to the mountains to gather wood, overloads the sleigh so the horse cannot pull the load, and empties the sleigh so the horse can return home. The old man is satisfied, however. He has accomplished enough work for one day.

Norwegian folktales help children appreciate Norwegian traditions, as well as providing children with much pleasure and excitement. Themes suggest the rewarding of unselfish love and the punishment of greed. The sharp humor, the trolls, and the poor boys who overcome adversity are all excellent subjects for storytelling.

Russian Folktales

Heroes and heroines who may be royalty or peasants; settings that reflect the deep snows of winter, the dark forest, the wooden huts of the peasants, or the gilded towers of the nobility's palaces; and villains who may be the long-nosed witch Baba Yaga or dishonest nobility or commoners are all found in Russian folktales. Two types of folktales are common in traditional Russian literature: short, merry tales characterized by rapid, humorous dialogue, with plots that often become absurd before things improve; and serious stories of enchantment and magic.

An example of a merry tale written in picture storybook format for young children is Guy Daniels's *The Peasant's Pea Patch*. The tale builds upon the absurd acts of a foolish person and suggests that the remedy for a problem may be worse than the problem. This peasant feeds honey and vodka to the cranes eating his peas, waits until they are asleep, ties them to his cart, and tries to drag them home. When the cranes awake, they take the peasant on a wild ride through the sky. The peasant attempts to solve his problem with another foolish act. He cuts the rope binding him to the cranes and plunges into a treacherous quagmire. When a strong duck lands on his head, he grabs the duck and is finally freed from the quagmire. His problems continue, however, in adventures with a bear and beehives before he limps home.

Humans in Russian folktales may be judged fools by their words or by their actions. Saying the wrong thing at the wrong time to the wrong person constitutes foolishness in Leo Tolstoy's *The Fool.*

Many Russian folktales are complex stories of quests, human longing, and human greed. *The Firebird and Other Russian Fairy Tales*, edited by Jacqueline Onassis and beautifully illustrated by Boris Zvorykin, contains four such folktales (see plate 11 in the color insert). The title story introduces the firebird, who has golden wings and eyes like oriental crystals. She plucks the golden apples from Tsar Vyslav's garden, beginning a quest by the Tsar's three sons to capture her.

Many of the characteristics of Russian folktales are found in Elizabeth Isele's retelling of "The Frog." The tale develops typical folktale characterizations: a ruler who requires a quest of his three sons, a youngest brother who receives the best prize, an enchanted princess who is wise, and supernatural helpers who give objects with magical powers or wise advice. Folktale elements include a quest, the importance of three, tasks to prove worth, magical transformations, punishment for lack of patience, magical objects, and rewards for kindness. The moral of the story suggests that lack of patience is punished, while kindness and perseverance are rewarded.

Other universal folktale themes found in Russian folktales include a desire for children, developed in a story about a childless couple who create "The Snow Maiden," and the beautiful child hated by her stepmother and stepsisters, developed in "Vassilissa the Fair," a Russian version of the Cinderella story. The latter tale and six others are collected in Aleksandr Nikolaevich Afanaséz's *Russian Folk Tales*, with illustrations by Ivan Bilibin, the late nineteenth-century Russian illustrator, depicting traditional costumes and early Russian settings.

Alexander Pushkin was one of the first Russian writers to transcribe the orally transmitted folktales of his century. Patricia Tracy Lowe has translated and retold several of these stories in picture storybook formats, including *The Tale of Czar Saltan, or the Prince and the Swan Princess* and *The Tale of The Golden Cockerel*, two tales reflecting the importance of keeping promises and the consequences of jealousy and greed. Another tale of good versus evil and the consequences of jealousy and greed is found in Yūzō Otsuka's *Suho and the White Horse: A Legend of Mongolia.*

The familiar themes of kindness rewarded and the motifs of magical powers and rather foolish, kindhearted peasants are found in Arthur Ransome's *The Fool of the World and the Flying Ship*. The czar has offered his daughter's hand in marriage to anyone who can build a flying ship. Kindness to an old man provides an aspiring peasant with the magical ship. Companions with extraordinary powers also aid the peasant in his quest. This tale implies that the czar does not want a peasant to marry his daughter.

In various tales, the Russian witch Baba Yaga may be an evil, child-eating villain or a respecter of human spirit who rewards courage. In Maida Silverman's rendition of "Anna and the Seven Swans," Baba Yaga has characteristics similar to the witch in the Brothers Grimm's "Hansel and Gretel." She steals children and intends to eat her human hostages. Quite a different Baba Yaga is portrayed in Elizabeth Isele's retelling of "The Frog Princess." The witch listens attentively to the prince's problem, respects him, and provides him with the information that makes a successful quest possible.

These and many other Russian folktales reflect a vast country containing numerous cultures. The themes suggest that talent, beauty, and kindness are appreciated and rewarded; and that people must pay the consequences for foolish actions, greed, broken promises, and jealousy. Humor suggests the universal need to laugh at oneself and others.

Jewish Folktales

Jewish folktales, according to Charlotte Huck (12), "have a poignancy, wit, and ironic humor that is not matched by any other folklore" (p. 194). An excellent example of this wit and humor is found in Margot Zemach's *It Could Always Be Worse*. This retelling of a Yiddish folktale relates the story of nine unhappy people who share a small one-room hut. The father desperately seeks the advice of the rabbi, who suggests that he bring a barnyard animal inside. A pattern of complaint and advice continues until most of the family's livestock is in the house. When the rabbi tells the father to clear the animals out of the hut, the whole family appreciates its large, peaceful home.

Isaac Bashevis Singer's *Mazel and Shlimazel, or the Milk of a Lioness* is longer and more complex. It pits Mazel, the spirit of good luck, against Shli-mazel, the spirit of bad luck. To test the strength of good luck versus bad, the two spirits decide that each of them will spend a year manipulating the life of Tam, a bungler who lives in the poorest hut in the village. As soon as Mazel stands behind Tam, he succeeds at everything he tries. He fixes the king's carriage wheel and is invited to court where he accomplishes impossible tasks; even Princess Nesika is in love with him. Just as Tam is about to complete his greatest challenge successfully, Mazel's year is over, and an old, bent man with spiders in his beard stands beside Tam. With one horrible slip of the tongue encouraged by Shlimazel, Tam is in disfavor and condemned to death. Shlimazel has won. But wait! Mazel presents Shlimazel with the wine of forgetfulness, which causes Shlimazel to forget poor Tam, rescues Tam from hanging, and helps Tam redeem himself with the king and marry the princess. Tam's success is more than good luck, however: "Tam had learned that good luck follows those who are diligent, honest, sincere and helpful to others. The man who has these qualities is indeed lucky forever" (p. 42).

Sincerity, unselfishness, and wisdom, are handsomely rewarded in Michael Gross's *The Fable of the Fig Tree*. In this warm Hebrew folktale, the king asks Elisha how he knows that he will live long enough to eat the figs of the tree he is planting. Elisha's answer pleases the king: "If the Lord desires it, I hope to do so. If not, my children will gather the fruit. My parents, and their parents before them, and all the generations of parents before them, planted trees for their children. Thus it is my duty to plant trees for my children" (p. 3 unnumbered). Elisha lives to reap a harvest, takes a basket of figs to the king, and is handsomely rewarded with a basket of gold pieces. An envious villager decides to claim an equal reward by taking both good and bad figs to the king; the king commands that the soldiers tie him to a post and allow passersby to throw the figs at him. The man's unsympathetic wife tells her husband that he should be thankful—that it would have been worse if he had given the king hazelnuts.

The Golem is Beverly Brodsky McDermott's retelling of a Jewish tale about human hopes for a better world and the realities of human limitations. The setting is the ghetto of Prague where the gates are fastened tightly, locking the Jews inside. Rabbi Lev has a dream that convinces him to mold a clay man to protect his people. Rabbi Lev and two others take sacred clay hidden under ancient prayer books and circle it, chanting secret names. As flames glow and water flows, a man takes form out of the clay. This man, the Golem, does not always act appropriately. When outsiders attack the ghetto, the Golem grows into a giant, crushes the mob, and scorches the earth. Lamenting over the imperfections in his creation, Rabbi Lev turns the Golem back into clay. McDermott's two years of research in developing this book included the study of Hebrew symbols and their corresponding magical qualities according to Cabalists (Jewish mystics). Both young children and older ones appreciate this tale's message that human attempts to play god are bound to reflect human imperfections. (Compare this version of the tale with the one by Isaac Bashevis Singer.)

Themes in Jewish folktales suggest that sincerity, unselfishness, and true wisdom are rewarded. The tales reflect human foibles as people face and overcome dissatisfaction and realize the dangers of excessive power.

Daylight flooded the attic and four men descended the narrow stairway.

This Jewish tale emphasizes the dangers of excessive power. (From *The Golem: A Jewish Legend*, written and illustrated by Beverly Brodsky McDermott. Copyright © 1976 by Beverly Brodsky McDermott. By permission of J. B. Lippincott, Publishers.)

Folktales from Asia

Asian folktales, like folktales everywhere, portray the feelings, struggles, and aspirations of the common people; depict the lives of the well-to-do; and reflect the moral values, superstitions, social customs, and humor of the times and societies in which they originated. Like medieval Europe, ancient Asia contained societies in which royalty and nobles led lives quite different from those of peasants and females had less freedom and social influence than males. Asian tales about the rich and the poor, the wise and the foolish, mythical quests, lovers, animals, and supernatural beings and powers contain themes and motifs common to all folklore, but also reflect the characteristic customs and beliefs of certain cultures.

Chinese Folktales.

"A teacher can open the door, but the pupil must go through it alone."
"The home that includes an old grandparent contains a precious jewel."

Such traditional Chinese sayings (20) suggest Chinese values and philosophical viewpoints expressed in Chinese folktales over the centuries. According to Louise and Yuan-hsi Kuo (14), Chinese tales often develop universal themes with roguish humor. Respect for ancestors, ethical standards, and conflict between nobility and commoners are popular topics in Chinese tales.

A dislike for imperial authority is evident in several Chinese equivalents to the "cottage" tales of medieval European peasants. In these tales the dragon, the symbol of imperial authority, is usually evil and is overcome by a peasant's wit. "The Golden Sheng," included in Louise and Yuan-hsi Kuo's *Chinese Folk Tales*, tells the story of a little girl captured by a malevolent flying dragon:

Your sister is suffering; your sister is suffering,
In the evil dragon's cave.
Tears cover her face;
Blood stains her back;
Her hand drills the rock.
Your sister is suffering; your sister is suffering. (p. 18)

A common folktale theme, reward for unselfish action, and a common folktale motif, a magical object, allow the girl's brother to rescue her and dispose of the beast. Enroute, the brother moves a dangerous boulder out of the path and is rewarded with a dazzling golden *sheng* that creates a melodious sound when blown into. The sound is so hypnotic that earthworms, lizards, and even dragons are forced to dance. While the dragon whirls, the brother and sister make their escape.

In "The Clever Wife," also in the Kuos' collection, a woman uses her wits to bring her family power in a China predominantly controlled by men. A man is terrified when a magistrate demands that he must weave a cloth as long as the road, brew enough wine to match the quantity of water in the ocean, and raise a pig as heavy as the mountain. His wife tells him to return to the magistrate with a ruler, a measuring bowl, and a kitchen scale, then inform the magistrate that he will finish the tasks as soon as the magistrate uses the ruler to measure the length of the road, the bowl to measure the volume of the ocean, and the scale to determine the weight of the mountain. The magistrate wonders how such a foolish-looking fellow could respond so cleverly. When the man admits it was his wife's idea, the magistrate says that the man received good counsel and that he will not bother the family again.

Numerous tales in Catherine Edwards Sadler's *Treasure Mountain: Folktales from Southern China* and in Neil Philip's *The Spring of Butterflies and Other Folktales of China's Minority Peoples*, reveal the consequences of kindness, humor and greed. Marilee Heyer's *The Weaver of a Dream: A Chinese Folktale* reveals characteristic rewarded behavior. Moss Roberts's large collection, *Chinese Fairy Tales and Fantasies*, is divided into tales about enchantment and magic, folly and greed, animals, women and wives, ghosts and souls, and judges and diplomats.

Japanese Folktales. Chinese culture influenced Japanese culture, and many Japanese tales are similar to the Chinese stories. Dragons, for example, are common in tales from both countries. The tiger, usually considered a symbol of power (16), is a legendary creature often found in Japanese tales. Davis Pratt and Elsa Kula's *Magic Animals of Japan* contains short stories about these and other animals—including the fox, either a symbol of abundance or a mischief maker able to transform himself, and the cat, a symbol of friendliness and prosperity.

Japanese folktales reflecting respected values and disliked human qualities include Patricia Newton's *The Five Sparrows: A Japanese Folktale*, the story of a woman who is richly rewarded after caring for an injured sparrow. A greedy neighbor in this tale is punished after she intentionally in-

Compassion is a highly regarded value in this Japanese folktale. (From *A Japanese Fairy Tale,* by Jane Hori Iké and Baruch Zimmerman. Pictures by Jane Hori Iké. Illustrations copyright © 1982 by Jane Iké. Reprinted by permission of Viking Penguin, Inc.)

jures three birds in order to demonstrate her caring qualities and gain rewards.

The unhappy consequences of greed and unwise counsel are common themes in Japanese folktales. Sumiko Yagawa's *The Crane Wife*, for example, contains the following motifs common to tales of transformed wives or husbands in other cultures: a reward for kindness (a poor farmer rescues a wounded crane which is transformed into a lovely wife); a prohibition set by the enchanted spouse (the wife asks her husband not to look upon her when she weaves cloth); the breaking of a promise and prohibition (the husband does watch the wife weaving) that forces the enchanted one to leave. Unlike many of the transformation tales discussed earlier, the loved one does not search for the disenchanted being. Instead, after the poor farmer accepts unwise advice, becomes greedy, and looks at his wife, he loses her and her helpful ability forever. Illustrator Suekichi Akaba's sparsely drawn figures and line and wash drawings on textured papers complement this traditional tale.

Another Japanese tale about a crane suggests the desirability of friendship between humans and supernatural creatures. Anne Laurin's *The Perfect Crane* tells about a lonely magician who develops a strong friendship with a crane he creates from rice paper.

Other Asian Folktales. The Asian Cultural Centre for UNESCO has published a series of five books called *Folk Tales from Asia for Children Everywhere* that contain stories from many Asian countries that children enjoy. For example, a story from Burma, "The Four Puppets," stresses the harm that wealth and power can bring if they are not tempered with wisdom and love. "The Carpenter's Son," a tale from Afghanistan, is similar to the Arabian story of Aladdin and his magic lamp.

Two Persian tales are the basis for Pamela Travers's *Two Pairs of Shoes*, in which worn slippers reflect the miserliness of one character and the humble roots of another.

A Vietnamese version of the Cinderella tale develops both motifs common in other versions and culturally related adaptations. Ann Nolan Clark's rendering of the tale in *In the Land of Small Dragon* includes these familiar motifs: the death of the mother, a cruel stepmother and stepsister, a persecuted heroine, magical assistance, a difficult task, meeting the prince, and proof of identity. Both the text and illustrations strongly reflect the Vietnamese origins of the story, however. For example, one of the father's two wives is the wicked adversary; the girl's tasks include working in the rice paddies and separating rice from husks; her fairy godmother gives her jeweled *hai* (slippers); and the prince is an emperor's son. The language, as shown by the following description of the maiden, makes it a good choice for sharing orally:

> Tam's face was a golden moon,
> Her eyes dark as a storm cloud,
> Her feet delicate flowers
> Stepping lightly on the wind.
> No envy lived in her heart,
> Nor bitterness in her tears. (p. 2)

Both Errol LeCain and Andrew Lang have published picture storybook versions of the Aladdin tale. It is one of several Arabian tales, collected in the original *The Thousand Nights and a Night*, supposedly told by Shahrazad to King Shahryar of Baghdad in her effort to keep from being beheaded.

Many folktales from India are included in a series of animal stories traditionally known as the *Panchatantra*. The original tales were moralistic and included tales about the reincarnations of the Buddha. English translations, however, usually delete the morals and the references to the Buddha. Consequently, the stories, some of which are included in Nancy DeRoin's *Jakata Tales*, have characteristics of folktales. Virginia Haviland's *Favorite Fairy Tales Told in India* is a fine source for other Indian folktales.

Eastern folktales contain such universal motifs as reward for unselfishness, assistance from magical objects, cruel adversaries, and punishment for dishonesty. The tales also emphasize the traditional values of the people: homage is paid to ancestors, knowledge and cleverness are rewarded, and greed and miserly behavior are punished.

African Folktales

African folktales are characterized by a highly developed oral tradition. Repetitive language and styles that encourage interaction with the storyteller make them excellent choices for sharing with children. Many of the stories are "why" tales that explain animal and human characteristics. Verna Aardema's *Why Mosquitoes Buzz in People's Ears* uses cumulative language to explain the buzz. *The Third Gift*, by Jan Carews, explains how the Jubas acquired work, beauty and imagination. Personified animals, often tricksters, are popular subjects. The hare, the tortoise, and Ananse the spider use wit and trickery to gain their objectives. Chapter eleven, "Multiethnic Literature," discusses other tales that reflect traditional values of African peoples.

North American Folktales

Many North American folktales have roots in the cultures of other parts of the world or have been influenced by written literature and characters created by professional writers. Consequently, identifying tales that began in a specifically North American oral tradition is difficult and in some cases impossible.

Folklorists identify four types of folktales found in North America: Native American (and Native Canadian) tales that were handed down over centuries of tribal storytelling; folktales of black

Americans that reflect African and European themes but that were changed as slaves faced difficulties in a new land; variants of European folktales, containing traditional themes, motifs, and characters, changed to meet the needs of a robust, rural North America; and boisterous, boastful tall tales that originated on this continent.

Native American Folktales.

Native American tales are usually considered the only traditional tales that are truly indigenous to the United States. Any study of the traditional literature of native peoples in North America reveals that there is not one group of folktales; instead, the tales differ from region to region and tribe to tribe, although most Native American folktales have things in common. Many of the tales are nature stories that reveal why or how animals obtained specific characteristics. For example, Margaret Hodges's *The Fire Bringer* retells the Native American story about how coyotes received their markings and how a certain tribe obtained fire. Likewise, William Toye's *The Loon's Necklace* explains how the loon received its characteristic markings. Animal trickster tales are popular in Native American culture, as elsewhere. The tricksters are often ravens, rabbits, or coyotes that have powers of magical transformation. Heroes and heroines may also use transformation in undertaking their quests. In *Arrow to the Sun: A Pueblo Indian Tale*, for example, a boy becomes an arrow as he searches for his father, the sun-god.

The importance of the folktale as a means of passing on tribal beliefs is revealed in Olaf Baker's *Where the Buffaloes Begin*. A young Native American of the Great Plains learns from a tribal storyteller about a sacred spot where the buffaloes rise out of a lake. After he finds the lake and waits quietly in the night, he hears the words of the storyteller singing in his mind:

Do you hear the noise that never ceases?
It is the Buffaloes fighting far below.
They are fighting to get out upon the prairie.
They are born below the Water but are fighting for the Air.
In the great lake in the Southland where the Buffaloes begin! (p. 20)

The diversity of Native American cultures, customs and folktales is illustrated in Jamake Highwater's *Anpao: An Indian Odyssey*. Highwater's book emphasizes the importance of traditional tales in transmitting Native American culture. Chapter eleven, "Multiethnic Literature," discusses these tales and others.

Black American Folktales.

Many black American folktales reflect both an African origin and an adaptation to a new environment and the harsh reality of slavery. For example, a rabbit trickster, who triumphs over more powerful animals is popular in African folklore. He is also one of the most popular characters in tales collected from black people on southern plantations. This character's popularity with black Americans was probably related to their experience of slavery, in which cunning, wit, and deception were often the only weapons available against oppression. (The tortoise and Ananse, the spider, play similar trickster roles.)

The trickster Br'er Rabbit is a famous figure in black American folktales collected by Joel Chandler Harris in nineteenth-century Georgia and published as *Uncle Remus and His Friends* (1892); and *Told by Uncle Remus* (1905). In 1981, Priscilla Jaquith published similar tales collected from black people living on the Sea Islands off the coasts of Georgia and South Carolina. The tales in *Bo Rabbit Smart for True: Folktales from the Gullah* are excellent examples of the infusion of later culture, language, and environment into tales from other places and earlier times. African words, such as *cooter* for "tortoise," combine with Elizabethan English and dialect from the provinces of Great Britain, such as *bittles* for "victuals." In the African tradition, the stories repeat key words to increase their significance: "Alligator, Miz Alligator and all the little alligators slither into the field, KAPUK, kapuk, kapuk, kapuk, kapuk, kapuk, kapuk, kapuk." These stories about a small, clever rabbit who outsmarts other animals such as whales and elephants are fun and exciting to young children.

The stories in Jaquith's and Harris's collections have motifs in common with one another and with other black American tales about a trickster rabbit found in West Virginia. Though not as powerful as his adversaries, the rabbit is more intelligent, and manages to outwit them. Some of these stories, such as Jaquith's version of "Alligator's Sunday Suit," contain a serious moral often found in black American folklore: "Don't go looking for trouble, else you might find it."

THROUGH THE EYES OF AN AUTHOR

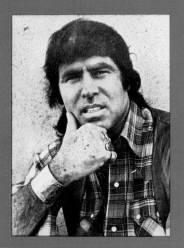

Traditional Native American Tales

Expert in traditional Native American literature and culture and collector of traditional tales, JAMAKE HIGHWATER, author of *Anpao: An American Indian Odyssey*, discusses his own feelings and beliefs.

IN A VERY REAL SENSE, I am the brother of the fox. My whole life revolves around my kinship with four-legged things. I am rooted in the natural world. I'm two people joined into one body. The contradiction doesn't bother me. But people always assume the one they're talking to is the only one there is. That bothers me. There is a little of the legendary Anpao in me, but also a little of John Gardner. I stand in both those worlds, not between them. I'm very much a twentieth century person, and yet I'm traditional Northern Plains Indian.

I've always had an enormous regard for the intellect. Still, I like to go home to my people, who are in touch with the beginning of things. At home, people are carpenters; some are poets, painters, and teachers; some work on construction jobs. They are people who perceive the importance of small things that are easily missed by those of us who move much too quickly.

I came to terms with the solemn aspects of life very early. I was always among Indians, for we traveled the powwow circuit. I was always listening to some older person telling stories. They are nameless to me now, and countless, because there were so many. I was introduced to the Indian world as children in my tribe were in the 1870s when we were a nomadic people. I was rootless, yet connected to a vital tradition. The elders talked to me and gave me a sense of the meaning of my existence.

I talk and think as a poet, but I don't want to perpetuate the romantic notion of the Indian as watching chipmunks his entire life, waiting to see which side of the tree the moss grows on. For the Indian, art is not reserved for a leisure class, as it is in Anglo society. It is part of our fundamental way of thinking. We are an aesthetic people. Most primal people are. We represent a constant chord that's been resounding ever since man began. While those Cro-Magnon people in the caves of southern France (at least according to Western mentality) should have been out worrying about the great likelihood that they wouldn't survive, they were building scaffolds fifty or sixty feet high and with tiny oil lamps were painting the ceilings of their caves with marvelous magical images. These images were an implicit and important part of their lives. For us, this aesthetic reality is a continuous process. The kiva murals of the Hopi and the Mimbres pottery rival the finest accomplishments of Western art. This idea of life as art is part of being Indian. It's not quaint or curious or charming. It's fundamental, like plowing a field. There's great beauty in plowing a field.

I think Indians have become a metaphor for a larger idea. We are building bridges toward cultures. Some people in white society are also building bridges toward us, and they sometimes join together. That means that it's possible for everyone to find the Indian in himself. It's a kind of sensibility that I'm talking about.

Drawn from an interview with Jane B. Katz, 1980.

Variants of European Tales. The traditional literatures of the United States and Canada contain many variants of traditional European folktales. European settlers from England, France, and elsewhere brought their oral traditions with them and then adapted the stories to reflect a new environment. Consequently, many North American folktales involve familiar European themes, motifs, and characters in settings that portray the unknown wilderness and harsh winters confronted by early colonizers of North America. The only indigenous Canadian traditional literature is the folktales of Native Canadian and Inuit peoples.

Eva Martin's *Canadian Fairy Tales* contains twelve French-Canadian and English-Canadian variations on traditional European tales. A series of "Ti-Jean" tales contains several familiar themes and motifs: the lazy fellow kills one thousand flies with one blow, uses his wits to capture a unicorn and steal a giant's seven league boots, and eventually marries the princess. In the Canadian variant of "Beauty and the Beast," the enchanted beast is female and the prince stays in her castle.

The best-known North American variants of European tales belong to the "Jack" cycle, in which a seemingly nonheroic person overcomes severe obstacles and outwits adversaries. The American "Jack and the Varmits," for example, is similar to the English "The Brave Little Tailor." In keeping with the European tradition, the American Jack is rewarded by a king. Instead of a giant, Jack must overcome a wild hog, a unicorn, and a lion. The influences of rural America are found in both the setting and language. The lion, who was killing cattle, horses, and humans, came over the mountains from Tennessee. Both the king and Jack speak in frontier dialect.

Tall Tales. Boastful frontier humor is also found in North American tall tales that reflect settlers' hardships as they face severe climatic changes, unknown lands, and other people whose lives reflect strange, often unappreciated cultures.

Exaggerated claims in tall tales—such as those found in Walter Blair's *Tall Tale America: A Legendary History of Our Humorous Heroes*—may declare that the American soil is so rich that fast-growing vines damage the pumpkins by dragging them on the ground; that frontier people are so powerful they can lasso and subdue a cyclone; that the leader of the river boaters can outshoot, outfight, outrun, and outbrag everyone in the world. The North American heroes and heroines who faced extremes in weather, conquered humans and beasts, and subdued the wilderness are not the godlike heroes and heroines of European mythology. Instead, their lives reflect the primitive virtues of brute force, animal cunning, and courage. The characters and situations in tall tales reflect frontier idealism: people are free to travel, live self-sufficient lives, and are extremely resourceful. American tall tales contain several types of heroes, both fictional and based on real people. Hard-working, persevering characters—such as Johnny Appleseed, who considered it his mission to plant apple trees across the country—demonstrate duty and endurance. Boisterous, bragging roughnecks—such as Davy Crockett, Calamity Jane, and Paul Bunyan—perform otherwise impossible feats, outshooting a thousand enemies or conquering mighty rivers and immense forests. Other characters—such as that "steel-driving man" John Henry—reflect a country changing from a rural and agricultural way of life to one that is urban and mechanized.

Comparing Folktales

The folktales discussed in this section have many similarities in plot, characterization, and style. They also reflect cultural differences. Chart 6–3 summarizes some of these similarities and differences by comparing tales from several cultures. Students of children's literature may analyze other tales from each culture to identify common characteristics.

FABLES

Legend credits the origin of the fable in Western culture to a Greek slave named Aesop who lived in the sixth century B.C. Aesop's nimble wit supposedly got his master out of numerous difficulties. "Aesop" may not have been one person, however, and several experts attribute these early European fables to various sources. Fables are found worldwide; the traditional literatures of China and India, for example, contain fables similar to Aesop's. Whatever their origins, fables are excellent examples of stories handed down over centuries of oral and written literary tradition.

Characteristics of Fables

The fable, according to R. T. Lenaghan (15) in his introduction to *Caxton's Aesop*, has the following

CHART 6–3
Comparisons of folktales from different cultures

Culture and Examples	Protagonist— Main Character	Portrayal of Hero/Heroine	Characteristics of Other Characters	Setting	Intended Audience	Dominant Plot Situation	Qualities Admired	Conclusion Indication of Characters' Fate
British "Jack the Giant Killer"	Simple peasant lad.	Simple peasant lad who is brave and outwits villains.	Evil giants. Weak king who cannot solve problem.	Rural mountain cave.	Common people.	Hero sets out to rid kingdom of giants.	Intelligence, bravery.	Happy ending. Villains slain. Hero rewarded with knighthood.
French "Sleeping Beauty"	Adolescent girl who is also a princess (about fifteen).	Prince "pursued on by love and honor"; "valiant."	Wicked fairy who gives gift of death. Father who cannot protect his daughter. (He was away when the girl fell asleep.)	Castle. Prince goes through series of rooms similar to Versailles.	Nobility.	Threatened girl is rescued by a prince.	Values admired at court: beauty, wit of an angel, grace, dancing, and singing.	Happy ending. Prince and Princess are married.
German "Hansel and Gretel"	Boy and girl, woodcutter's children.	Hansel cares for his sister, but Gretel outwits witch.	Stepmother who wants to leave the children in the woods. Weak father who cannot care for his children. Wicked witch.	The forest.	Common people.	Abandoned children outwit a wicked witch.	Outwitted witch.	Wicked witch punished by burning to death. Stepmother dead. Children rewarded with jewels. Happy ending.
Norwegian "The Lad Who Went to the North Wind"	Simple peasant lad.	Simple, but honest, peasant lad who finally realizes he has been tricked.	Powerful north wind. Scolding mother. Dishonest, greedy innkeeper.	Rural, far north.	Common people.	Hero sets out to retrieve lost object.	Honesty, kindness.	Dishonest innkeeper beaten. Boy rewarded with magical objects. Happy ending.
Russian "The Fool of the World and the Flying Ship"	Simple young peasant.	Foolish, kind-hearted young peasant.	Dishonorable Czar who tries to trick hero. Four companions with great powers.	Rural countryside. Czar's palace.	Common people.	Simple boy sets out on a quest; he is aided by acquiring magical ship and companions.	Kindness, honesty.	Unhappy Czar gains an unwanted son-in-law. Peasant marries royalty. Happy ending.
Jewish "Mazel and Schlimazel"	Poor peasant.	Ne'er-do-well bungler before good luck intercedes.	Spirit of good luck is happy and attractive. Spirit of bad luck is slumped and angry.	King's court and countryside.	Common people.	Simple boy, accompanied by good luck then bad luck, sets out on a series of quests.	Dilligence, honesty, sincerity, helpfulness.	Bad luck forgets about his victim. Good luck stays with him. Hero marries the princess, and eventually becomes wisest of prince consorts. Happy ending.
Chinese "The Golden Sheng"	Poor adolescent girl stolen by dragon.	Boy who grew up very rapidly.	Evil, cruel dragon.	Rural.	Common people.	A young boy goes on a quest to save his sister from a dragon.	Helpfulness, dilligence, loyalty.	Dragon whirls himself to death. Brother and sister return to mother where they use remains of the dragon to help their work. Happy ending.
African "How Spider Got a Thin Waist"	Tricky and greedy spider.	Greedy spider who does not work but plays in the sun.	Hard-working villagers.	Forest and village.	Common people.	Hero tries to get food without working.	Greed is punished.	Greedy spider gains a thin waist.
Native American "The Fire Bringer"	Young Paiute Indian boy.	Boy who is concerned about his people.	Intelligent coyote, swift runners.	Mesa and mountain.	Common people.	Boy and coyote set out to get fire for the Paiutes.	Intelligence, swiftness, bravery.	Boy and coyote honored.

characteristics: "(1) it is fiction in the sense that it did not really happen; (2) it is literary entertainment; (3) it is poetic fiction with double or allegorical significance; and (4) it is a moral tale, usually with animal characters" (p. 12). The main characters in fables are usually animals that talk and behave like humans and possess other human traits. Fables are short, usually having no more than two or three characters who perform simple, straightforward actions that result in a single climax. They contain a human lesson expressed through the foibles of personified animals.

These characteristics apparently appealed to traditional storytellers around the world. In fifteenth-century England, fables were among the first texts William Caxton printed on his newly

created printing press. R. T. Lenaghan (15) credits the fable's popularity at that time to its generic ambiguity: it could be used as an entertaining story, a teaching device, or a sermon. It could also reach people of various degrees of intelligence, be bluntly assertive or cleverly ironic, be didactic or skeptical. Readers could emphasize whatever function of the fable they chose.

The fable's continuing popularity led Randolph Caldecott to create his own edition of Aesop in the nineteenth century. *The Caldecott Aesop*, first published in 1883 and reissued in 1978, provides modern readers with an opportunity to enjoy fables accompanied by the hand-colored drawings of a great illustrator of children's books. Caldecott's illustrations first show the animals in a fable, then people replacing the animals.

They had not gone very far before they met a farmer.

He burst out laughing when he saw them. "How silly you are," he cried. "Fancy carrying a donkey! Why *he* should be carrying *you*, not *you* carrying *him*."

"The Miller, the Boy and the Donkey" is an example of a single fable that has been told in picture-book format. (From *The Miller, the Boy and the Donkey*, by Brian Wildsmith, published by Oxford University Press © Wildsmith 1969.)

FLASHBACK

¶ Here begynneth the book
of the subtyl historyes and Fables
of Esope whiche were translated
out of Frensshe in to Englysshe
by william Caxton

At Westmynstre In the yere of oure Lorde
.m. cccc.lxxxiij

THE BOOK OF THE *Subtyl Historyes and Fables of Esope,* published in the fifteenth century, is considered one of William Caxton's most important contributions to European literature. These fables, or cautionary animal tales with morals, have been popular with readers for centuries. In the seventeenth century, John Locke recommended fables as ideal reading for children. Many artists since the 1400s have chosen to illustrate the fables. They are still popular today.

Contemporary Editions of Fables

Fables are popular subjects for modern storytellers and illustrators. Young children like the talking animals and the often humorous climaxes. Brian Wildsmith has used several fables originally translated by Jean de La Fontaine in picture storybook format. *The Lion and the Rat* vividly depicts the fable of the rat who returns a lion's kindness by gnawing holes in a net that entraps the lion. Each sentence in this book for young children is illustrated with a large, colorful two-page drawing. The illustrations fully develop the animals' personified characteristics, and children can see that patience and hard work can bring success when size, strength, and anger cannot. Wildsmith has also illustrated each line in La Fontaine's translation of *"The Miller, the Boy and the Donkey,"* a humorous fable about a miller who foolishly follows everyone's advice when he takes his donkey to market. (It is interesting to compare this version with others; the donkey does not drown in Wildsmith's picture storybook as he does in the original Aesop fable.)

Other recent book-length versions of certain fables expand a fable into a longer, more detailed narrative story. In *The Tortoise and the Hare* Janet Stevens expands the story line of the fable by including the exercises Tortoise undertakes to prepare for the race and the actions of Tortoise's friends as they try to deter Hare. In *The Town Mouse and the Country Mouse* Lorinda Bryan Cauley's illustrations and text provide details associated with the different life styles of the two main characters.

Numerous collections of Aesop's fables have also been compiled and illustrated for slightly older children. It is interesting to compare these various editions to see how the fables have been interpreted and illustrated. Anne Terry White's edition of Aesop contains forty fables. She introduces them by saying that Aesop made his animals behave like humans to make a point without hurting the feelings of the great and powerful leaders who could be cruel to a slave. When Aesop told a story about an animal, White says, his listeners understood his true meaning. White's fables (complemented by Helen Siegle's woodcuts) are in a simple narrative form, with descriptions and dialogue among the talking beasts that are easily accessible to contemporary children. For example, in "The Lion and the Mouse" White describes the capture of the mouse in this way:

"Bang! The Lion clapped his paw to his face and felt something caught. It was furry. Lazily he opened his eyes. He lifted up one side of his huge paw just a little bit to see what was under it and was amazed to find a Mouse. (p. 5)

White gives a moral to each fable in this collection. The moral of "The Lion and the Mouse" is simply stated:

"Little friends may prove to be great friends."

Ennis Rees uses rhyming verse to retell Aesop's fables in *Lions and Lobsters and Foxes and Frogs*. Here, for example, is the lion capturing the mouse in "The Lion and the Mouse":

> He seized the mouse in his paw
> And was going to eat him,
> But stopped when he looked down and saw
> That the mouse would entreat him.

Contemporary versions of fables differ in illustrator's style as in author's style. Heidi Holder's *Aesop's Fables* contains detailed, elegant paintings surrounded by equally detailed borders. Michael Hague's *Aesop's Fables* is illustrated with full-page paintings in more somber, earthy tones.

Interesting comparisons can also be made between contemporary versions of Aesop and versions published in earlier centuries. The language, spelling, and illustrations in these various editions differ widely. Some were intended for adults, other specifically for children. Older children can learn more about their literary heritage by comparing and discussing various versions of these ancient stories.

Detailed drawings, with a castle in the background, create an elegant setting for a fable. (From *Aesop's Fables*, by Heidi Holder. Copyright © 1981 by Heidi Holder. Reproduced by permission of Viking Penguin Inc.)

MYTHS

Every ancient culture made up stories that answered questions about the creation of the earth, the origins of people, and the reasons for natural phenomena. The Greeks called these explanations *mythos*, which means "tales" or "stories." Although today people sometimes use the word *myth* to describe any story they consider to be untrue, in literary terms a myth is a story containing fanciful or supernatural incidents intended to explain nature or tell about the gods and demons of early peoples (2). In the distant past, as in some traditional cultures today, these stories were taken as fact made sacred by religious belief. The supernatural characters in the myths were considered divine. They controlled forces of nature on earth and ruled the sun, moon, stars, and planets. Many of them had their own temples, where people worshipped them with prayer and sacrifice to win their favor.

Myths live on in contemporary literature and provide an understanding of the rich cultural heritage we have acquired from ancient civilizations all over the world. Greek, Roman, and Norse mythology have been most influential in Western culture. Many terms used in those mythologies are also found in modern language, such as our names for the planets and for the days of the week. Children find these stories exciting and become interested in this rich literary heritage.

Jane Yolen (21) identifies several ways in which myths are valuable to children. Myths provide children with knowledge about ancestral cultures, a way of looking at another culture from the inside out. Myths are models for belief; they are serious statements about existence and provide a framework for understanding a people and everything they did or thought. Myths are tools for self-understanding and expanded self-expression; they offer new dimensions for imagination and suggest ways that children can gain insights from their daydreams. Myths also provide a means of introducing children to the use of literary allusions: An author describing something as being "as swift as Diana" or "as mighty as Zeus" is alluding to characteristics of the gods.

Greek and Roman Mythology

The best-known myths in Western culture are probably those that originated in ancient Greece. When the Romans conquered Greece, they adopted many Greek myths, applying them to their own equivalent deities. In order to understand these stories, Helen Sewell (18), says that one must be acquainted with ancient Greek ideas about the structure of the universe. The Greeks believed that the universe had been created out of unorganized matter called *chaos*, a swirling and transparent vapor. Form and shape resulted in *order* and *cosmos*. The Greeks believed that the first things formed out of chaos were the gods: *Gaia* (meaning "earth"; *Terra* is the Roman name) and *Ouranos* (meaning "sky"; *Uranus* is the Roman name) (2). From the offspring of female Gaia and male Ouranos emerged the remaining Greek gods and goddesses, who lived on Mount Olympus (an actual mountain in Greece) and frequently came down from those lofty heights into the human world.

The Greeks believed that the earth was flat and circular, with their own country being the center. Around the earth flowed the River Ocean. The Dawn, the Sun, and the Moon were supposed to rise out of the eastern ocean, driven by gods, giving light to gods and mortals. The majority of the stars also rose out of, and sank into, this ocean. The Greeks believed that the northern part of the earth beyond the mountains was inhabited by a race of people called *Hyperboreans*. In these mountains were the caverns from which came the piercing north winds that sometimes chilled Greece. On the south lived the Ethiopians, whom the gods favored; on the west lay the Elysian Plain, where mortals favored by the gods were transported to enjoy immortality. (Roman myths drew essentially the same picture.)

Although this mythology and the previously discussed folktales contain similar motifs and themes, the myths include Bascom's requirements for setting, time, attitude, and principal characters. Consider these points in Edna Barth's version of the myth *Cupid and Psyche* and the Norse folktale "East of the Sun and West of the Moon."

"Cupid and Psyche"	"East of the Sun and West of the Moon"
Setting	
Olympus, Greece An earlier world	Any kingdom
Time	
In a remote past when gods and goddesses dwelled on earth	Once upon a time

Attitude

Sacred, worship of deity required or punishment resulted	Secular

Principal Characters

Venus, goddess of love, and her son Cupid, and a mortal girl	Transformed human boy and human girl
Mortal who becomes immortal	Troll princess

The plot development in the two tales is similar: a young girl breaks a promise, her loved one leaves, she searches for him, and she must overcome obstacles or perform tasks before they are reunited. The principal characters differ in important characteristics, however. Psyche, a beautiful mortal princess, is the object of a goddess's anger and jealousy. She later falls in love with a god, performs tasks stipulated by the goddess, and requires intervention from the most divine ruler, Jupiter. Edna Barth (3) sees a strong religious significance in the "Cupid and Psyche" myth. The myth, she reminds us, originally represented the progress of the human soul as it travels toward perfection. Symbolized by Psyche, the soul originated in heaven where all is love, symbolized by Cupid. The soul is then condemned for a period of time to wander the earth and undergo hardship and misery. If the soul proves worthy, it will be returned to heaven and reunited with love.

Circumstances surrounding the creation of the gods and goddesses, their places within the Olympian family, the consequences resulting from their varied personality traits, and their accomplishments create exciting tales and enjoyable reading for children. Chart 6–4 contains examples of Greek and Roman gods and goddesses, their realms of influence and their accomplishments, and examples of texts that include myths about these deities.

Selecting Versions of Greek and Roman Myths.

Contemporary versions of Greek and Roman myths vary widely in terms of authors' style, complexities of text, and illustrations. Adults must consider these factors when choosing myths to share with children of various ages and interests. Eight- or nine-year-olds, for example, enjoy Edna Barth's *Cupid and Psyche*. Barth's rendition of this myth is appropriate for children who enjoy folktales such as "Beauty and the Beast" and "East of the Sun and West of the Moon." Younger children also enjoy Gerald McDermott's book-length version of the Daedalus myth, *Sun Flight*. McDermott's text for this myth about a mortal punished for attempting to rival the gods is based on his animated film that won the Zellerbach Award for Films as Art at the San Francisco International Film Festival. Bold colors depict the setting on Crete as father and son fashion their wings. The final flight sequences of the story are told through the illustrations, as McDermott changes Icarus's colors from the blues and greens of his initial flight, to orange and red as he nears the sun, to reds and browns as he falls in flames, and

Compare this Greek myth with the Norwegian folktale "East of the Sun and West of the Moon." (From *Cupid and Psyche*, by Edna Barth, published by Clarion Books, Tickner & Freeds: A Houghton Mifflin Company, New York. Copyright © 1976 by the illustrator, Ursula Arndt.)

CHART 6–4

Greek and Roman gods and goddesses

Name	Ruler	Accomplishments	Examples of Texts
Zeus (Jupiter)	Ruler of Mount Olympus King of deities and humans	Used lightning to gain control of the universe	Gates's *Lord of the Sky: Zeus*
Hera (Juno)	Queen of deities and humans Goddess of marriage and child-birth	Protected married women	Bulfinch's *A Book of Myths*
Athena (Minerva)	Goddess of wisdom, war, and handicrafts	Established rule of law Gave olive tree to mankind Protected cities	Gates's *The Warrior Goddess: Athena*
Apollo (Apollo)	God of Sun Patron of truth, music, medicine, and archery	Established the oracle (prophets who gave advice)	Gates's *The Golden God: Apollo* Bulfinch's *A Book of Myths*
Artemis (Diana)	Goddess of moon and the hunt Guardian of animals, nature, and women	Mighty archer and hunter	Bulfinch's *A Book of Myths*
Aphrodite (Venus)	Goddess of love and beauty	Flowers sprang up where she walked Had power to beguile gods Gave birth to Fear and Terror	Gates's *Two Queens of Heaven: Aphrodite and Demeter*
Demeter (Ceres)	Goddess of crops	Giver of grain and fruit Caused famine when Hades took her daughter to the underworld	Coolidge's *Greek Myths* Gates's *Two Queens of Heaven: Aphrodite and Demeter*
Hermes (Mercury)	Divine messenger of the gods Protector of flocks, cattle, and mischief makers	Trickster who was named god of commerce, orators, and writers	Gates's *The Golden God: Apollo*
Poseidon (Neptune)	God of the sea and earthquakes	Gave horses to humans Answered voyager's prayers	*D'Aulaires' Book of Greek Myths*
Dionysus (Bacchus)	God of wine, fertility, the joyous life, and hospitality	Gave Greece the gift of wine	Bulfinch's *A Book of Myths* Coolidge's *Greek Myths*
Ares (Mars)	God of war	Symbol of evils and suffering caused by war	*D'Aulaires' Book of Greek Myths*
Hephaestus (Vulcan)	God of fire and artisans	From his forges came Pandora, the first mortal woman Created mechanical objects	*D'Aulaires' Book of Greek Myths*
Eros (Cupid)	God of love (some of Venus)		Barth's *Cupid and Psyche* Richardson's *The Adventures of Eros and Psyche*

NOTE: *Roman names in parentheses.*

to greens as he is engulfed by the waves. Penelope Farmer's version of this myth, *Daedalus and Icarus*, is also appropriate for younger children.

Many older children enjoy longer, more developed versions of the myths. Adults may wish to compare Ian Serraillier's version of the Daedalus myth with McDermott's and Farmer's versions. Serraillier's *A Fall from the Sky* includes the rea-

sons for Daedalus's jealousy, his trial, and his attempts to escape judgment. The intervention of the goddess Athena and the symbolization of the partridge are also included in this more complex version. Enthusiastic readers of Greek mythology enjoy comparing these three versions.

Elizabeth Silverthorne's *I, Heracles* is written from the hero's viewpoint. Silverthorne introduces him by having him speak to the reader and explain why he is so strong:

I hope you won't think I'm bragging when I tell you about some of the things I've done. I really do have superhuman strength, you know, but I don't take any credit for it. My mother is Alcmena—she's an earthly princess—and my father is Zeus—he is the ruler of all the other gods on Mount Olympus. Naturally that makes me half man and half god, and that accounts for my strength. (p.11)

Many children enjoy this first-person style and state that Heracles seems like a very real hero.

Doris Gates develops stories with fast-paced plots and language that suggests word pictures. Her style reads well and is an excellent choice for sharing orally. For example, her description of the goddess's creation in *The Warrior Goddess: Athena* seems appropriate for a warrior:

She sprang from the head of Zeus, father of gods. Born without a mother, she was fully grown and fully armed. Her right hand gripped a spear, while her left steadied a shield on her forearm. The awful aegis, a breast ornament bordered with serpents, hung from her neck, and from her helmeted head to her sandaled feet she was cloaked in radiance, like the flash of weaponry. So the great goddess Athena came to join the

family of gods on high Olympus, and, of all Zeus's children, she was his favorite. (p. 11)

Older children can contrast this description with Gates's description of the creation of the goddess of love and beauty in *Two Queens of Heaven: Aphrodite and Demeter*:

There appeared a gathering of foam on the water. It resembled the white spindrift that trails behind a great wave as it breaks. But this form did not trail. It formed itself into a raft rising and falling with the sea. Suddenly a woman's figure appeared atop the raft balancing on slender feet. She was young and beautiful beyond anything in human form the sun had ever shone on. (pp. 9–10)

Versions of myths told by Olivia Coolidge, Charles Kingsley, and Padraic Colum are also good choices for older children.

Norse Mythology

A far different group of gods and heroes existed in Norse mythology's universe of ice, glaciers, and cold mountains. The harsh conditions of the far North helped form the Norse people and their legends. According to Kevin Crossley-Holland (9), the recurring strains in Norse mythology include

Highly illustrated versions of myths, such as this story about the goddess Ceres and her daughter Proserpina, provide introductions to mythology for young readers. (From *Daughter of Earth: A Roman Myth*, retold and illustrated by Gerald McDermott. Copyright © 1985 by Gerald McDermott. Used by permission of Delacorte Press.)

a strong sense of fate that governs the lives of both gods and humans; a heroic bond between characters that is characterized by physical and-moral courage, loyalty, and a willingness to take vengeance; a belief in omens; an ironic wit; a restless spirit of adventure; and a keen sense of wonder in the natural world and a close identification with nature. Unsurprisingly, Norse mythology tells that a frost giant was the first being created on earth.

Norse mythology influenced subsequent oral and written literature in northern Europe. Shakespeare was influenced by an old Norse tale when he wrote Hamlet; J. R. R. Tolkien, a professor of Anglo-Saxon literature at Oxford University, relied on his knowledge of the northern sagas when he wrote *The Hobbit* and *The Lord of the Rings*.

The tales of the northern gods and goddesses were collected during the twelfth and thirteenth centuries from the earlier oral tradition. These original tales formed two volumes, the *Elder* and

"The Hammer of Thor" is an excellent choice for storytelling. (From *Legends of the North*, by Olivia Coolidge. Copyright © 1951 and © renewed 1979 by Olivia E. Coolidge. Reprinted by permission of Houghton Mifflin Co.)

the *Younger Edda*. These texts are now the sources for most of our knowledge about Norse mythology. According to Olivia Coolidge (8), Norse mythology maintains that the earth began when a frost giant, Ymer, came out of the swirling mists. The shifting particles formed a great cow whose milk nourished Ymer. As time went by, sons and daughters were also created out of the mists. Gods took form when the cow began to lick the great ice blocks that filled the mists. As she licked, a huge god appeared. When he stood up, his descendants were formed from his warm breath. These gods knew that the frost giants were evil and vowed to destroy them. A mighty battle resulted between the gods and the frost giants, with the gods finally overpowering the giants. Ymer was destroyed, and the remaining giants fled into the outer regions and created a land of mists and mountains. The mightiest of the gods, Odin, looked at the dead frost giant, Ymer, and suggested that the gods use his body to make a land where they could live. They formed Ymer's body into the round, flat earth, and on its center they built mountains that would contain their home, Asgard. Ymer's skull was used to form the great arch of heaven; the blood was the ocean, a barrier between the earth and giantland. The gods stole sparks from the fiery regions to light the stars, and built chariots in which they placed sun and moon spirits who would ride over the earth.

Pedraic Colum portrays the strong moral code of Odin in his version of "The Building of the Wall," found in *The Children of Odin*. Even though a protective wall is built around Asgard, Odin grieves: "But Odin, the Father of the Gods, as he sat upon his throne was sad in his heart, sad that the Gods had got their wall built by a trick, that oaths had been broken, and that a blow had been struck in injustice in Asgard" (p. 12).

Olivia E. Coolidge's *Legends of the North* is an excellent source of stories about these Norse gods and goddesses who lived on earth in the mighty citadel of Asgard and the heroes and heroines who lived under their power. In "The Apples of Idun," one learns that the divine beings often walked on earth because the mighty Odin believed they should know their realm intimately, in stone, flower, and leaf.

In Coolidge's text Thor, the god of war, strides around with red hair bristling and fierce eyes ablaze. Sometimes he rides in his chariot drawn by red-eyed goats, as shaggy and fierce as their master. One humorous selection from this book that children enjoy is "The Hammer of Thor," in which Thor searches loudly for his missing hammer. Children probably feel close to Thor as he responds in exasperation when Freyja, the goddess of beauty, asks him where he put it. He shouts, "If I knew where I put it, I should not be looking for it now" (p. 35). Thor discovers that the giant Thyrm has stolen the hammer and wants Freyja as ransom. When the goddess vehemently refuses to become the giant's bride, the suggestion is made that Thor dress up as a bride and go to giantland to retrieve his own hammer. After considerable argument, the huge god dresses in gown and veil to cover his fierce eyes and bristling beard, and, accompanied by the impish Loki, leaves for giantland. Mighty Thor remains quiet as the wedding feast progresses, and it is fast-witted Loki who answers the giant's questions and calms his suspicions. Finally, Thor is able to touch his hammer as the wedding ceremony begins. This is what he has been waiting for; he regains his hammer, overpowers the giant, removes his skirts, and leaves for home. Thor's courage, loyalty, and willingness to take vengeance are all recurring strains found in this mythology. The humor and action in this tale make it excellent for storytelling.

Other enjoyable Norse tales suitable for sharing with children include Ingri and Edgar Parin D'Aulaire's *Norse Gods and Giants* and Kevin Crossley-Holland's *The Faber Book of Northern Legends*.

LEGENDS

The great legends in traditional literature are closely related to mythology. Many of these legends have been transmitted over the centuries in the form of *epics*, long narrative poems about the deeds of traditional or historical human heroes and heroines of high station. Two of the better-known Greek epics are the *Iliad* and the *Odyssey*. The *Iliad* is an account of the Trojan War. The *Odyssey* reports the journey of Odysseus (Ulysses in Latin) as he defeats the cyclops, overcomes the song of the sirens, and manages to survive ten long years of hazardous adventures. Gods, goddesses, and other supernatural beings play important roles in such epics; but the focus is on human characters.

"Beowulf," the story of a human warrior, is usually considered the outstanding example of Norse epic poetry. Beowulf's struggle against evil

has three main episodes: (1) Beowulf fights and kills the monster Grendel. (2) Beowulf dives to the depths of a pool and attacks Grendel's mother, She. (3) Beowulf fights the dragon Firedrake, and is mortally wounded. Versions of this epic are available in both narrative and poetic form. One version, which the author Robert Nye calls a *new telling*, is written in narrative form for younger readers. Beowulf is strong, but he is also good—loyal, courageous, and willing to take vengeance. His characterization epitomizes the heroic code found in Norse myths. A combination of heroic deeds and honorable characteristics make it possible for his good name to live after him. Nye's *Beowulf*, for example, describes the hero as having real strength that "lay in the balance of his person—which is perhaps another way of saying that he was strong because he was good, and good because he had the strength to accept things in him which were bad" (p. 25). His good is so powerful that it is felt by the evil monsters and is instrumental in their defeat.

Fate, a strong code of honor, and a willingness to avenge wrong are emphasized in Kevin Crossley-Holland's version of *Beowulf*. The importance of fate is developed as Beowulf considers the outcome of his forthcoming struggle with the monster, Grendel: "Who knows? Fate goes always as it must" (p. 11) and "If a man is brave enough and not doomed to die, fate often spares him to fight another day" (p. 13). The importance of fate is reemphasized after Beowulf's victory as King Hrothgar declares: "Beowulf, bravest of men, fate's darling! Your friends are fortunate, your enemies not to be envied" (p. 34).

A strong code of honor is developed when Beowulf refuses to use a sword or a shield because the monster fights without weapons. Honor and vengeance are combined as Beowulf cries that he will avenge the Danes, the people who gave refuge to his father. Honor and vengeance are also part of the monster's code, and Beowulf is pleased when he discovers: "There is honor amongst monsters as there is honor amongst men. Grendel's mother came to the hall to avenge the death of her son" (p. 25). Crossley-Holland's conclusion emphasizes Beowulf's heroic characteristics: "They said that of all kings on earth, he was the kindest, the most gentle, the most just to his people, the most eager for fame" (p. 46).

Many of the heroes and heroines in epic legends reflect a strong sense of goodness as they overcome various worldly evils. The line between legend and myth is often vague, however. The early legends usually enlarged upon the lives of religious figures such as martyrs and saints. In more recent times, legends developed around the lives and accomplishments of royal figures and folk heroes and heroines. The following comparison shows the similarities and differences between myth and legend:

Myth: "The Birth of Athena"	Legend: "Tales of King Arthur"
Belief	
Told as factual	Told as factual (British
Belief in gods	chieftain of fifth-sixth century)
Setting	
Mount Olympus, Greece	British Isles
An earlier world	
Time	
In the remote past when gods and goddesses dwelled on earth	Time of kings and knights
	A recognizable world
Attitude	
Sacred, goddess sprang from head of Zeus, father of gods	Sacred, quest for Holy Grail
	Secular, established Round Table and leader of knights
Principal Character	
Nonhuman, assists heroes and heroines in quests	Human king
	Does not have supernatural powers

We consider the tales of King Arthur to be legends rather than myths because they are stories primarily about humans rather than primarily about supernatural beings and because historical tradition maintains that King Arthur once actually existed in fairly recent times. Tales of this legendary British king were so popular in early England that Sir Thomas Malory's *Morte d'Arthur* was one of the first books published in England. Another early version of the tale is Howard Pyle's *The Story of King Arthur and His Knights*. The first section of Pyle's version, "The Book of King Arthur," reveals how Arthur removes the sacred sword from a stone signifying that he is rightful King of England, claims his birthright, weds Guinevere, and establishes the Round Table. The

second section, "The Book of Three Worthies," tells about Merlin the magician, Sir Pellias, and Sir Gawaine. The original version of this book, with Pyle's illustrations, has been reissued. Other editions of Arthurian legends include Rosemary Sutcliff's *The Sword and the Circle: King Arthur and the Knights of the Round Table*, *The Light Beyond the Forest*, and *The Road to Camlann: The Death of King Arthur*.

Selina Hasting's *Sir Gawain and the Loathly Lady* retells one of the Arthurian legends in a picture-book format. Characteristically, the tale includes a challenge, a quest, and enchantment, and a promise demanded by the code of chivalry. Juan Wijngaard's illustrations capture both the evil menace of the black knight and the ancient splender of Arthur's court.

Ruth Robbins's *Taliesin and King Arthur* is a charming, beautifully illustrated picture book

A legendary setting is depicted in this tale about early England. (From *Taliesin and King Arthur*, by Ruth Robbins. Copyright © 1970 by Ruth Robbins for text and illustrations. Reprinted by permission of the publisher, Houghton Mifflin Company.)

that relates the legend of a young bard who pleases King Arthur with his songs and his ability to tell of deeds to come and rites long buried. It describes the Yule festival and the Grand Meeting of the Bards.

Another legendary figure in English culture is Robin Hood, the hero of Sherwood Forest. Stories about Robin Hood were told orally for centuries and were mentioned in manuscripts as early as 1360. Legend suggests that he was born Robert Fitzooth, Earl of Huntingdon, in Nottinghamshire, England, in 1160. According to the tales he was a great archer. He and his band of outlaws poached the king's deer, robbed the rich, and gave money to the poor.

Stories of Robin Hood are very popular with children. Movies and television plays have been produced about his adventures. Howard Pyle's *The Merry Adventures of Robin Hood* and the shorter version, *Some Merry Adventures of Robin Hood*, provide children with visions of what it would be like to live "in merry England in the time of old" and to interact with Little John, Maid Marian, Friar Tuck, the Sheriff of Nottingham, and King Richard of the Lion's Heart. Children enjoy comparing the various editions and describing the strengths and weaknesses of each. For this purpose, even the Walt Disney movie that presents Robin Hood as a fox, Little John as a bear, and Prince John as a lion makes an interesting comparison and adds to a lively discussion, especially about characterization.

The hero in Margaret Hodges's adaptation of the English legend, *Saint George and the Dragon* (see color plate 12), exemplifies the characteristics found in legendary heroes: he is noble, courageous, and willing to avenge a wrong. Other contemporary versions of European legends include Nina Bawden's *William Tell*, and Kate Seredy's *The White Stag*, which tells the story of how the Hun-Magyar tribes migrated into Eastern Europe and created Hungary.

The Hawaiian Islands provide the setting for Marcia Brown's *Backbone of the King: The Story of Pakáa and His Son Ku*. The characters exemplify the characteristics of other legendary heroes. Bravery, honor, and willingness to avenge a wrong are developed in this tale of a chief, a trusted supervisor to the king, who is unjustly wronged and then brought back to honor through the brave actions of his son.

These legends help children understand the conditions of the times that created the need for brave and honorable men and women. They are tales of adventure that stress the noblest actions of humans, as well as those less noble, in which justice reigns over injustice. Children can feel the magnitude of the oral tradition as they listen to these tales; reading aloud is the best way to introduce them to children. Chapter 11, "Multiethnic Literature," discusses more of the stirring legends of non-European cultures.

SUMMARY

Traditional literature includes stories handed down orally over the centuries. Two milestones in traditional literature were Charles Perrault's book of French folktales, and the Brothers Grimm's collections of German traditional tales.

Folklorists usually identify four types of traditional literature: folktales, fables, myths, and legends. Cumulative tales, humorous tales, beast tales, magic or wonder tales, *pourquoi* tales, and realistic tales can be categorized as types of folktales.

Traditional tales allow children to learn about problems of human beings and possible solutions. In addition, traditional tales develop children's understanding of the world through exposure to the traditions and universal struggles and emotions of people everywhere. The strongest value of traditional tales for children may be the enjoyment gained by hearing and reading them.

Suggested Activities for Adult Understanding of Traditional Literature

☐ Read the stories included in Charles Perrault's *Tales of Mother Goose* and some tales collected by the Brothers Grimm. Note the similarities and differences you discover in the characterizations, settings, and actions. Describe the people for whom you believe the stories were originally told.

☐ Choose a professional group that has been interested in researching and interpreting traditional literature (such as, early Christian scholars, folklorists, psychologists, anthropologists). Investigate their interpretations of several folktales.

☐ Read an example of a cumulative tale, a humorous tale, a beast tale, a magic or wonder tale, a *pourquoi* tale, and a realistic tale.

Compare their characterizations, settings, styles, and themes.

☐ Choose a common theme found in folktales, such as that in "Cinderella" or trickster stories. Find examples of the same story in folktales from several countries. What are the similarities and differences? How do the stories develop cultural characteristics?

☐ Choose an animal often found in traditional literature. Read stories that include that animal, choosing stories from cultures throughout the world. Is the animal revered or despised? How would you account for this?

☐ Select a country and several traditional tales from that country. Choose stories for which the illustrators conducted extensive research before completing the drawings. Share the discoveries about the fine arts of the country with the class.

☐ Find examples of settings, plot developments, or characterizations found in literature from different countries. Discuss any similarities and differences with the class.

☐ Choose three folktales from different countries. Compare the actions developed in the three tales using the list on page 210.

☐ Choose several examples of folktales that are not compared in Chart 6–3. Following a similar format, analyze the tales.

☐ Read a fable in *Caxton's Aesop* and in *The Caldecott Aesop*. Compare it with the same fable written in a modern version. Are there any differences in writing style, language, spelling, and illustrations between the earlier and later versions? If there are, what do you believe is the reason for the differences? Share the two versions with a child. How does the child respond to each version?

☐ Select numerous folktales from one country. Investigate the information you can learn about the culture, people, and country with your peers. Share your findings with the class.

☐ Compare the versions of creation and the characteristics of gods and goddesses in Greek and Norse mythology. Why do you believe any differences exist?

☐ Choose a folktale, fable, myth, and legend. Develop a chart similar to Chart 6–1 that compares the four types of stories.

References

1   Arnott, Kathleen. *Animal Folk Tales around the World*. New York: Walck, 1970.

2   Asimov, Isaac. *Words from the Myths*. Boston: Houghton Mifflin, 1961.

3   Barth, Edna. *Cupid and Psyche*. Boston: Houghton Mifflin, 1976.

4   Bascom, William. "The Forms of Folklore: Prose Narratives." *Journal of American Folklore* 78 (Jan–Mar. 1965):3–20.

5   Bettelheim, Bruno. *The Uses of Enchantment: The Meaning and Importance of Fairy Tales*. New York: Knopf, 1976.

6   Booss, Claire. *Scandinavian Folk & Fairy Tales*. New York: Avenel Books, 1984.

7   Carlson, Ruth Kearney. "World Understanding through the Folktale." In *Folklore and Folk Tales around the World*, edited by Ruth Kearney Carlson. Newark, Del.: International Reading Association, 1972.

8   Coolidge, Olivia E. *Legends of the North*. Boston: Houghton Mifflin, 1951.

9   Crossley-Holland, Kevin. *The Faber Book of Northern Legends*. Boston: Faber & Faber, 1983.

10 Favat, F. André. *Child and Tale: The Origins of Interest*. Urbana, Ill.: National Council of Teachers of English, 1977.

11 Hearn, Michael Patrick. Preface to *Histories or Tales of Past Times*, by Charles Perrault. New York: Garland, 1977.

12 Huck, Charlotte S. *Children's Literature in the Elementary School*. New York: Holt, Rinehart & Winston, 1979.

13 Iverson, Pat Shaw, trans. *Norwegian Folk Tales*. New York: Viking, 1960.

14 Kuo, Louise, and Kuo, Yuan-hsi. *Chinese Folk Tales*. Millbrae, Calif.: Celestial Arts, 1976.

15 Lenaghan, R.T., ed. *Caxton's Aesop*. Cambridge: Harvard University, 1967.

16 Pratt, Davis, and Kula, Elsa. *Magic Animals of Japan*. Berkeley, Calif.: Parnassus, 1967.

17 Propp, Vladimir. *Morphology of the Folktale*. Translated by Laurence Scott. Austin, Tex.: University of Texas, 1968.

18 Sewell, Helen. *A Book of Myths, Selections from Bulfinch's Age of Fable*. New York: Macmillan, 1942.

19 Thompson, Stith. *The Folktale*. New York: The Dryden Press, 1946.

20 Wyndham, Robert. *Tales the People Tell in China*. New York: Messner, 1971.

21 Yolen, Jane. "How Basic Is Shazam?" *Language Arts* 54 (September 1977): 645–51.

Involving Children in Traditional Literature

□

STORYTELLING

□

**COMPARING FOLKTALES FROM
DIFFERENT COUNTRIES**

□

**INVESTIGATING FOLKTALES FROM
A SINGLE COUNTRY**

□

**CREATIVE DRAMATICS AND
FOLKLORE**

□

**USING TRADITIONAL LITERATURE
TO MOTIVATE CREATIVE WRITING**

□

**INTERPRETING TRADITIONAL
IMAGES IN ART**

Traditional tales are among children's most memorable experiences with literature. With their well-defined plots, easily identifiable characters, rapid action, and satisfactory endings, the tales lend themselves to many enjoyable experiences in the classroom, library, home, or around the campfire. This section explores ways to recapture the oral tradition through storytelling, comparing folktales from different countries, creative dramatics, creative writing, and art interpretations.

STORYTELLING

Learning the ancient art of oral storytelling is well worth the effort, in the pleasure it affords both the teller and the audience. John Warren Stewig (13), lists three important reasons to include storytelling in childhood experiences. First, storytelling helps children understand the oral tradition of literature. In the past, children were initiated into their literary heritage through storytelling. Unhappily, this experience does not often occur today. Second, storytelling allows the adult an opportunity to better bring children into the literary experience. Free from dependence on a book, the storyteller can use gestures and actions to involve children in the story. Third, when an adult tells a story, children understand that it is a worthy activity and are stimulated to try telling stories themselves.

Choosing the Story

The most important factor in choosing a story is to select one that is really enjoyable. The narrator should enjoy spending time preparing the story and retelling it with conviction and enthusiasm.

Storytelling demands an appreciative audience. The storyteller must be aware of children's interests, ages, and experience. Young children have short attention spans, so story length must be considered when selecting a tale. Children's ages will also influence the subject matter of the tale. Young children like stories about familiar subjects such as animals, children, or home life. They respond to the repetitive language in cumulative tales and enjoy joining in when stories such as "Henny Penny" reach their climax. Simple folktales such as "The Three Bears," "The Three Little Pigs," and "The Three Billy Goats Gruff" are excellent stories to share with young children. Children from roughly ages seven through ten enjoy folktales with longer plots, such as those collected by the Brothers Grimm; "Rapunzel" and "Rumpelstiltskin" are favorites. Other favorites include Jewish folktales such as "It Could Always Be Worse." Older children enjoy adventure tales, myths, and legends.

Folktales have several characteristics that make them appropriate for storytelling: strong beginnings that bring listeners rapidly into the fast-paced action; several strong characters with whom listeners easily identify; strong climaxes that are familiar to children; and satisfactory endings. All these characteristics are worthwhile criteria for selecting tales.

Storytellers should also consider the mood they wish to create, whether humorous and light-hearted or more serious and scary. If, for example, the adult wants to choose an appropriate story for Halloween, then mood is very important. Even the site for storytelling affects mood and story selection. One group of people sitting on high rocks overlooking Lake Superior asked a storyteller for a tale. The wind was causing the waves to crash with a mighty roar onto the rocks below, and when the group looked out over the lake, they could see only a wide stretch of water, with no humans in sight. The view to the north was one of thick forests, ferns, and distant waterfalls. The Norse myth, "The Hammer of Thor," from Olivia E. Coolidge's *Legends of the North* seemed ideal for this setting.

Preparing the Story for Telling

Storytelling does not require memorization, but it does require preparation. Certain steps will help the storyteller prepare for this enjoyable experience. Ramon Royal Ross (11) recommends the following sequence of steps:

1 Read the story aloud several times. Try to get a feeling for its rhythm and style, so that when it is retold the interpretation will be faithful to the original.
2 Think of the major actions of the story and try to find where one action or bit ends and another begins. These bits give an outline to follow in telling the story.

3 Develop a sense of the characters in the story. Envision the characters—the clothes they wear, their shapes and sizes, unusual features, personality traits, how they speak, their mannerisms, and the like.
4 Think through the setting of the story. The storyteller should be able to draw a map showing where the story took place.
5 Look for phrases to incorporate in the story when it is told. Read the story again. What phrases and language patterns should be used to tell the story?
6 Begin telling parts of the story aloud, testing different ways to say the same words. The intonation should agree with the meaning the teller hopes to convey.
7 Plan gestures that add to the story. Once gestures have been decided, they may be practiced in front of a mirror.
8 Prepare an introduction and a conclusion for the story. Give background information, share information about hearing the story for the first time, or share an object related to the story.
9 Finally, practice the entire story. Time the telling at each practice. Record the story on audio tape. Play it back and listen for voice qualities to be cultivated and others to be discarded. Practice in front of a mirror, noting posture, gestures, and general impression.

Sharing the Story with an Audience

Because a storyteller has spent considerable time in preparation, the story should be presented effectively. This presentation is enhanced by creating an interest in the story, setting a mood, creating an environment where children can see and hear the storyteller, and presenting the story with effective eye contact and voice control.

Book jackets, giant books, miniature books, travel posters, art objects, puppets, or music may be used to stimulate children's interest in the story. The librarian or teacher who regularly tells stories to large groups of children can use any of these methods so that children will look forward to the story hour. Colorful book jackets from folktales or myths not only entice children, but also help set the mood for the storytelling. For example, a display might be developed around the book jacket for Elizabeth Isele's *The Frog Princess*. In addition to the book jacket illustrated by Michael Hague, the display could include a toy frog, a piece of linen, a container of flour, a toy duck, a toy hare, a small wooden chest, an egg, and a needle. Accompanying questions might include the following: How could a frog make it possible for a prince to become the ruler of the country? How could a piece of linen and a container of flour allow a princess to prove her worth? What would you do if you had to find a needle that was inside an egg, that was inside a duck, that was inside a hare, that was inside a chest?

Stories about giants lend themselves very well to displays of large books. One librarian drew huge figures of giants and beanstalks on large sheets of tagboard. The sheets were placed together to form a gigantic book that stimulated interest in "Jack and the Beanstalk." Likewise, drawings of a huge hammer stimulated interest about Thor when the librarian had prepared a Norse myth for telling. The giant books worked very well in these cases; the children speculated about the size or strength of anyone who could read such a large book. Miniature books stimulated children's interest before another story hour when "Tom Thumb" was the story. The storyteller used other tiny objects, many formed out of clay, that would be appropriate for a little person.

If the story has an identifiable location, travel posters can stimulate interest and provide background information. They are especially appealing when used with folktales from other countries. Travel posters about Greece and Italy have been used with Greek and Roman mythology. Travel posters showing Norwegian fiords and mountains can accompany Norse myths, while posters showing pictures of the Black Forest and old European castles are appropriate for "Snow White and the Seven Dwarfs" and "Sleeping Beauty."

Objects from the story or from the country that is the story's setting can also increase children's interest. Dolls, plates, figurines, stuffed animals, and numerous other everyday objects and curios can add to the story hour.

After interest is high. the storyteller can concentrate on setting the mood for story time. Many storytellers use story-hour symbols. For example, if a small lamp is the symbol for story hour, children know that when the lamp is lit, it is time to listen. Music can also be a symbol; a certain record, music box tune, piano introduction, or guitar selection can introduce story hour. These techniques are usually effective, since children learn to associate them with an enjoyable listening experience.

The story has been prepared, and the storyteller has considered how it will be introduced. Now it can be told to a group of children. Donna E. Norton (9, p. 335) has the following suggestions for telling the story:

1 Find a place in the room where all children can see and hear the presentation.
2 Either stand in front of the group or sit with them.
3 Select an appropriate introduction: use a prop, tell something about the author, discuss a related event, or ask a question.
4 Maintain eye contact with the children. This engages them more fully in the story.
5 Use appropriate voice rate and volume for effect.
6 While telling the story, use a short step or shift in footing to indicate a change in scene or character or to heighten the suspense. A seated storyteller can lean forward or away from the children.
7 After telling the story, pause to give the audience a chance to soak in everything said.

Using Feltboards to Share Folktales

Storytelling does not require any props. In fact, some of the best storytellers use nothing except their voices and gestures to recapture the plots and characters found in traditional tales. Most storytellers, however, enjoy adding variety to their repertoire. Children also enjoy experimenting with different approaches to storytelling; the flannelboard or feltboard lends itself to storytelling by both adults and children.

A feltboard is a rectangular-shaped lightweight board covered with felt, flannel cloth, or lightweight indoor-outdoor carpeting. This board acts as the backdrop for figures cut from felt, pellon, or other material backed with Velcro. Felt or pellon figures will cling directly to the feltboard, while any object, even leather, wood, or foam rubber will adhere to the felt if first backed with a small square or strip of Velcro. Other materials such as yarn or cotton balls will also cling to the feltboard and may be used to add interest and texture to the story.

Stories that lend themselves to feltboard interpretations have only a few major characters, plots that depend upon oral telling rather than upon

physical action, and settings that do not demand exceptional detail. All these characteristics are similar to those already stipulated for the simple folktales that young children enjoy. Very pleasing types of stories to retell on the feltboard are the folktales "Three Billy Goats Gruff," "The Three Bears," "The Gingerbread Boy," and "Henny Penny." Paul Anderson (1) maintains that "the best stories for use on a flannel board are those that follow a repetitive refrain, those that have one major plot with no subplots, those that contain the kind of action that can be illustrated by figures on the board and can be told with a reasonable number of figures" (p. 8). Anderson believes that stories involving magic are particularly appropriate for use with feltboard: a frog can change into a prince, and a "Cinderella" covered with rags and soot can become a princess in a beautiful gown.

Consider the Norwegian folktale "The Three Billy Goats Gruff." First, use simple cut-outs or objects to represent the characters. The three goats range in size from a small goat to a great big goat with curved horns. The ugly old troll has big eyes and a long, long nose. The setting can be easily shown: a bridge crossing a stream, and green grass on the other side of the bridge. The action can be illustrated effectively. Each goat can go "Trip, trap! Trip, trap! over the bridge."

The troll can challenge each goat with, "Who's that tripping over my bridge?" The climax is also easily illustrated: the big billy goat knocks the troll off the bridge and continues to cross to the other side. The plot develops sequentially from small billy goat, to medium-size billy goat, and finally to great big billy goat.

The English folktale "The Donkey, the Table, and the Stick" is another story that makes an effective feltboard production. Children enjoy seeing the magic donkey produce gold coins when his ear is pulled and they laugh over the poor lad's exasperation as nothing happens when he pulls and pulls the common donkey's ear. They are enthusiastic about the table that can produce turkey, sausages, and other good things. They laugh when the storyteller tries to get the ordinary table to produce food. Finally, they are overjoyed when the magic stick beats the evil innkeeper. Feltboard characters can show these actions effectively.

Cumulative tales are excellent for feltboard presentations. As the storyteller introduces each new character, he or she places it on the feltboard. Children join the dialogue as "The Fat Cat," for example, encounters first the gruel, then the pot, the old woman, Skahottentot, Skilinkenlot, five birds, seven dancing girls, the lady with the pink parasol, the parson, and the woodsman.

Through these presentations, children learn about sequential order and also improve their language skills. Children's literature students who use feltboard stories with children often find that the children either ask if they can retell the stories or make up their own feltboard stories to share. If adults provide feltboards and materials, children will naturally enjoy telling stories in this manner.

Whether the story is told to one child or to a group, storytelling is well worth the effort of preparation and presentation. Watching children as they respond to a magical environment and then make their own first efforts as storytellers proves that storytelling should be included in every child's experience.

COMPARING FOLKTALES FROM DIFFERENT COUNTRIES

Understanding how various types of traditional stories are related, becoming aware of cultural diffusion, and learning about different countries are values gained from reading traditional literature. One way to help children gain these values is by comparing folktales from different countries. Two different approaches provide valuable experiences.

Comparing Different Versions of the Same Folktale

Many older children are fascinated to discover that some tales appear in almost every culture. The names may vary, magical objects may differ, and settings may change, but the basic elements of the story remain the same. Four different versions of the Cinderella story were discussed earlier in this chapter, but over nine hundred versions of the Cinderella story have been found throughout the world. Mary Ann Nelson (8) claims that there are over five hundred European versions. Jane M. Bingham and Grayce Scholt (2) and Elinor P. Ross (10) suggest that older children should investigate the motifs in these tales. Questions such as the following can be compiled with the children's assistance to guide their search and discovery:

Questions to Ask about the Cinderella Tales

1 What caused Cinderella to have a lowly position in the family?
2 What shows that Cinderella has a lowly position in the household?
3 How is she related to other household members?
4 What happens to keep Cinderella away from the ball?
5 How does she receive her wishes or transformation?
6 Where does Cinderella meet the prince?
7 What is the test signifying the rightful Cinderella?
8 What happens to the stepsisters?

Sources for comparisons include the Cinderella versions listed in this book: Mary Ann Nelson's (8) anthology, Bingham and Scholt's (2) synopses of twelve variants of the Cinderella story, and folklore collections from around the world. Chart 6–5 represents some key variants found in Cinderella tales from different countries.

After children have read, listened to, and discussed many Cinderella tales, their investigations may agree with conclusions found in Bingham and Scholt's research. These investigators (2) compared twelve Cinderella tales and concluded the following:

1 The menial position of the heroine is usually shown by describing the impossible tasks she is asked to do. These tasks reflect the culture of the story.
2 Supernatural powers aid the heroine. Many powers relate to the dead mother: she returns in the form of an animal, or a tree appears over her grave.
3 The magical clothes of the transformed heroine are usually elegant and appropriate for the culture: gold and silver, or Indian dress of leather and beads.
4 The hero and heroine usually meet in places that are important to the culture: a ball, a theater, a church, or a wigwam.
5 The male figure has an elevated position in society. He is of noble birth in the majority of the tales, but the Chinese tale describes him as a scholar.
6 Seven of the twelve tales include cruel stepmothers. The heroine has to contend with cruel stepsisters or sisters.
7 Eight tales have some form of shoe test for identifying Cinderella. A Japanese version requires the heroine to compose a song; a Native American version asks the heroine to identify what the chief's sledstrings and bowstrings are made of.

CHART 6-5
Variations found in Cinderella stories from different countries

Origin	Cause of Lowly Position	Outward Signs of Lowly Position	Cinderella's Relationship to Household	How She Receives Wishes	What Happens to Keep Her from Social Occasion	Where She Meets the Prince	What Happens to Stepsisters	Test of Rightful Cinderella
French Perrault, "Cinderella"	Mother died. Father remarried.	Sitting in ashes. Vilest household tasks.	Stepdaughter to cruel woman. Unkind stepsisters.	Wishes to fairy godmother.	(Ball) No gown. Family won't let her go.	Castle ball. Beautifully dressed.	Forgiven. Live in palace. Marry lords.	Glass slipper.
German Grimm, "Cinderella"	Mother died. Father remarried.	Wears clogs, old dress. Sleeps in cinders. Heavy work.	Stepdaughter to cruel woman. Cruel stepsisters.	Wishes to bird on tree on mother's grave.	(Ball) Must separate lentils.	Castle ball. Beautifully dressed.	Blinded by birds.	Gold slipper.
English "Tattercoats"	Mother died at her birth. Grandfather blames her.	Ragbag clothes. Scraps for food.	Despised granddaughter. Hated by servants.	Gooseherd plays pipe.	(Ball) Grandfather refuses.	In forest. Dressed in rags.	Grandfather weeps. Hair grows into stones.	None.
Vietnamese "In the Land of Small Dragon"	Mother died. Father's number two wife hates her.	Collects wood. Cares for rice paddies.	Stepdaughter to hateful woman. Hated by half-sisters.	Fairy. Bones of fish.	(Festival) Must separate rice from husks.	Festival.	Not told.	Jeweled slipper (hai).
Chinese "Beauty and Pock Face"	Mother turned into cow.	Straightens hemp. Hard work.	Stepdaughter to cruel woman. Cruel stepsister.	From bones of mother in earthenware pot.	(Theater) Straighten hemp. Separate sesame seeds.	Scholar picks up shoe from road.	Roasted in oil.	Walks on eggs. Climbs ladder of knives. Jumps into oil.
Micmac—Native American "Little Burnt Face"	Mother died.	Burned face, Ragged garments.	Despised by two jealous sisters.	The Great Chief's sister changes her.	She must make her own dress.	Wigwam by the lake.	Sent back to wigwam in disgrace.	Describe the Great Chief.

8 In five of the twelve tales, the wicked stepmother or stepsisters meet violent ends.

9 All the tales reflect the societies that produced them. Native American tales refer to wigwams, moccasins, and bowstrings; Japanese stories refer to kimonos, rice, and oni.

Other tales are also suitable for comparisons. P. T. Travers (14) has included five versions of the Sleeping Beauty tale and one of her own translations in *About the Sleeping Beauty*. This collection contains her own version, which has Arabian roots; "Dornroschen or Briar-Rose," from the Grimms' *Household Tales*; "La Belle au Bois Dormant, or The Sleeping Beauty in the Wood," from Charles Perrault; "Sole, Luna, e Talia or Sun, Moon, and Talia," from the Italian *The Pentamerone of Giambattista Basile*; "The Queen of Tubber Tintye," from *Myths and Folklore of Ireland;* and "The Petrified Mansion," from *Bengal Fairy Tales*. "Little Red Riding Hood" and "The Lad Who Went to the North Wind" also have many variants. Linda Western's "A Comparative Study of Literature through Folk Tale Variants" (15) is another source of different versions of tales.

A search for variant versions of a tale is an enjoyable experience that encourages children to develop an understanding of the impact of cultural diffusion on literature. They also realize that each culture has placed the tale in a context that reflects the society of the storyteller and the audience.

INVESTIGATING FOLKTALES FROM A SINGLE COUNTRY

Children can learn a great deal about a country and its people by investigating a number of traditional tales from that country. This investigation also increases children's understanding of the multicultural heritage of their own country and develops their understanding of, and positive attitudes toward, cultures other than their own.

This fact was made clear when a group of fifth-grade children was studying folktales to learn more about the people of a country. They were reading and discussing Russian folktales at a time that relationships between the Soviet Union and the United States were strained. As they read these tales, especially the merry ones with their rapid, humorous dialogues and absurd plots, the children decided that the common people who could invent and enjoy those stories must be similar to themselves. They realized that they were laughing at the same type of story that could also bring humor to children in the Soviet Union. During this investigation and sharing of folktales, the children gained increased respect for many cultures. Children commented, for example, that Jewish folktales often stress the unselfish desire for a better world or reward sincerity and wisdom. They were also impressed by the fact that the Chinese "Cinderella" married a scholar and not a nobleman. They learned, through the folktales, to respect the ancient values of the people who created them.

A successful folktale study of one country was conducted in a fifth-grade classroom. The web shown in Figure 6–1 illustrates the related motivation, stimulating activities, and folktales that stressed personal values, disagreeable human qualities, symbols, and supernatural beings. The children first listened to, read, and discussed folktales from China. Objects displayed throughout the room stimulated their interest. A large red paper dragon met the children as they entered the room. Other objects included joss sticks (incense), lanterns, Chinese flutes, a tea service, fans, statues of mythical beasts, lacquered boxes and plates, silk, samples of Chinese writing, a blue willow plate, jade, and pictures of art work, temples, pagodas, people, and animals. Many Chinese folktales were displayed on the library table. In the background, a recording of Chinese music was playing. The chalkboard contained a message, written in Chinese figures, welcoming the children to China. The students looked at the displays, listened to the music, tried to decipher the message, and discussed what they saw and heard. They located China on a map and on a globe. Then they listed questions they had about China—questions about the people, country, values, art, music, food, houses, animals, and climate.

The teacher read aloud some of the foreword to Louise and Yuan-hsi Kuo's *Chinese Folk Tales* (5). She asked the students to close their eyes and imagine the scene, to listen carefully, and then to tell when this scene took place. Did it happen in modern times or many centuries ago?

But suddenly the room echoes with an ear-splitting clash of cymbals and the sonorous boom of a drum and in the street below our window prances a splendid lion. The sound of cymbals and the beat of drums have been heard incessantly since early morning and are merely a prelude to a major part to come: a procession with gay silk banners flying, votive offerings of barbe-

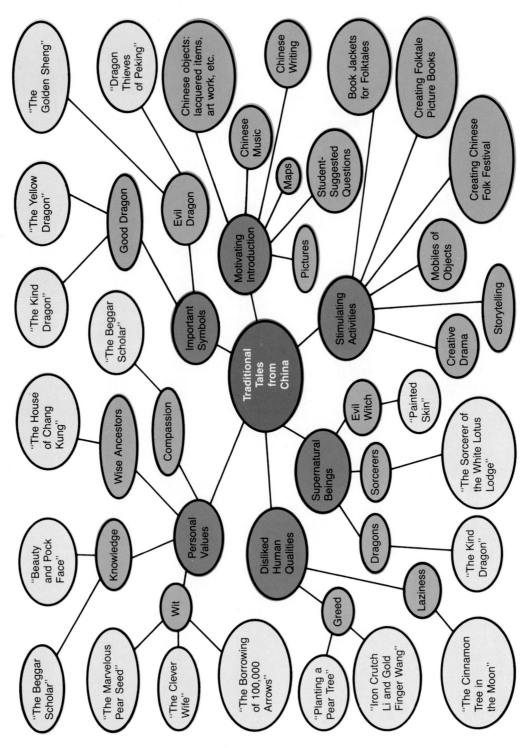

FIGURE 6–1

cued pigs . . . golden brown and saffron, cartloads heaped with fruit, red-colored eggs and other delicacies, giant joss sticks, candles and lanterns. A magnificent dragon, gyrating and performing with vigor and intensity to the rapid beat of a drum, will bring the procession to a climax. Throngs crowd the doorways, line the path, as excited onlookers join the ranks to mingle with those on their way to the temple . . . journey's end. This is the day of days . . . the grand finale of five days of celebration in homage to T'ien Ho, the Heavenly Goddess of the Sea . . . she who will bestow blessings on all who worship her, and protect them for the entire year. (p. 7)

After listening to the selection, the children speculated about the time period and gave their reasons for choosing either ancient or modern times. Many children were quite surprised to hear that the event was a festival held in modern Hong Kong. This discussion led into reading Chinese folktales in order to learn more about the Chinese people and a heritage that could still influence modern-day people.

Next, the teacher shared several of her favorite Chinese folktales with the children. They included the humorous "The Clever Woman" and "The Borrowing of 100,000 Arrows." She also provided brief introductions to other tales. These introductions were told to stimulate students' interest in reading the tales. Children then chose tales to read independently. As they read, they also considered their questions about China. Consequently, when they discovered information about the culture and the people, they jotted this information down so that it could be shared with the class.

After considerable information had been collected, the children discussed ways of verifying whether or not the information was accurate. They compared the information with library reference materials and magazines such as *National Geographic*. They also invited to the classroom several visitors who were either Chinese or had visited China.

The students used their knowledge about the people, culture, and literature of China in their own art, creative drama, and writing. They drew travel posters, book jackets for folktales, and illustrations for folktales and made mobiles of folkliterature objects. One artistic activity was to create picture storybooks from single folktales. Children chose a favorite tale not already in picture-book format, illustrated it with drawings, and bound the pages together. Because many of the published picture books contained information about the origin of the tale, they included similar information on the inside of their own front covers. Published book jackets often tell about the illustrator and the research that was done to provide authentic pictures. The students' books also contained this information. They told about themselves and how they prepared for their drawing assignment, and described the medium they used for their illustrations. They shared these books with each other and other classes and proudly displayed them in the library.

The class chose some stories for creative drama. The class was divided into groups according to favorite folktales. Each group then chose a method for sharing the story with the rest of the class. Some groups recreated the stories as plays, others chose puppetry, and one group used pantomime with a narrator reading the lines.

The children invited their parents to attend a Chinese folktale festival. They shared their art projects, picture storybooks, new information, and creative dramas with an appreciative audience.

This initial unit about one country led to an interest in folktales from other countries. The children next read folktales from Japan and other Asian countries. They discovered the similarities among many of these tales, especially in the symbolic animals found in both Chinese and Japanese folktales. They went on to detect Chinese influence on non-Asian writers when they read the beautiful version of Hans Christian Andersen's *The Nightingale*, illustrated by Nancy Ekholm Burkert.

The discovery of similar mythical animals led to another interesting search through folklore. The teacher read Winifred Miller's article "Dragons—Fact or Fantasy?" (7) and the children discovered that both Chinese and Japanese folktales had good and evil dragons; good dragons, a representation of Han nobility, were found in folktales told to ruling classes; and folktales about the common people referred to the dragon as evil. With the teacher's guidance, the students accomplished many of the activities suggested by Miller's article.

Folktales lend themselves well to many activities, and the teacher and librarian will find many ways to increase world understanding through literature. Chapter eleven presents a unit that includes African, Native American, Mexican American, and Asian folktales.

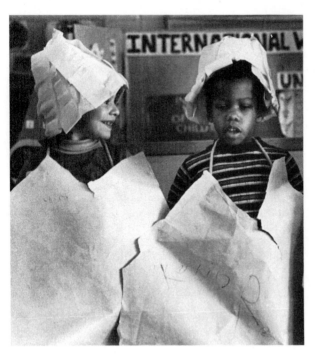

Folklore may encourage children to act out their favorite stories.

CREATIVE DRAMATICS AND FOLKLORE

Folklore is a natural source of materials for storytelling and also stimulates creative drama. Elizabeth Cook (3) maintains that the most exciting ways of retelling traditional tales are through drama, either in movement alone or in movement accompanied by words. Children can mime many sequences as the adult reads to them, children can act out individual parts, or groups of children can recreate their own versions of the tales.

Pantomime

Pantomime is creative drama in which an actor plays a part with gestures and actions without using words. Pantomime, according to Geraldine Siks (12), should be part of a planned drama curriculum in which children learn to relax and concentrate, experiment with body movement, use their senses, stimulate their imaginations, develop language and speech, and understand and use characterization. Children's first pantomime experiences usually include activities in which they learn to relax and experiment with different ways to move their bodies. After they have an idea about what their bodies can express, pantomiming folktales can help them interpret various actions and emotions.

Familiar folktales young children enjoy are excellent for pantomime. For example, children pretend to be each character in Paul Galdone's *The Three Bears* as an adult reads the story aloud. Children can pretend to be as small as the little wee bear, average size for the middle-sized bear, and huge for the great big bear. As bears, they can prepare their porridge, sit in their chairs, lie in their beds, and walk in the woods. Then, as Goldilocks, they can show curiosity as they peep into the window and then through the keyhole and cautiously enter the bears' home. They can react to porridge that is too hot, too cold, and just right. They can show discomfort as they try to climb into the great big chair, sink into the too soft chair, and then rock comfortably in the little chair until they surprisingly crash to the floor. They can show similar reactions to the three beds. As bears, they can return to the house, demonstrate outrage over the famous lines, "Somebody has been tasting my porridge," "Somebody has been sitting in my chair," and "Somebody has been lying in my bed." Finally, they can return to the character of Goldilocks as she awakens, sees the bears, and dashes into the woods. This experience allows children to demonstrate emotions and develop believable characterization through body movement.

Other folktales that young children like to pantomime are "The Three Little Pigs," "The Three Billy Goats Gruff," and "The Little Red Hen."

When children start to enjoy longer folktales, there are many sources of materials for pantomime. They can put on their cloaks of invisibility and tiptoe behind "The Twelve Dancing Princesses" as the princesses descend the winding stairs. They can stop in fright as they accidentally step on the long dress of a princess. They can walk in wonderment through the silver forest, gold forest, and diamond forest. As prince and princess, they can dance gracefully through the night and then sleepily climb the winding stairs.

Because many magical tales show vivid contrasts between good and evil characters, children can form pairs and play opposing or complementary roles. *Cinderella* has scenes between good and evil characters: Cinderella and her stepmother, or Cinderella and her stepsisters. There are also scenes between evil characters and evil forces: the stepmother and stepsisters plot to leave Cinderella at home, force her to work, or try to fit their feet inside the slipper. They can pantomime the opposing characters of good and bad luck in Isaac Bashevis Singer's Jewish tale *Mazel and Shlimazel, or the Milk of the Lioness.*

All opposing forces are not between good and evil. Children also enjoy and learn when the opposing forces are cleverness and foolishness. They can portray these roles of clever soldier and foolish woman in the Russian tale, "The Falcon under the Hat." There are the same opposing forces as the woman's son, Fedka, searches for a greater fool than his mother, who has lost her money to the soldier. The following scenes suggest the pantomime possibilities for this tale, using Guy Daniels' *The Falcon under the Hat: Russian Merry Tales and Fairy Tales*:

1   Fedka makes "a kow-tow—a low, humble bow—to the sow" (p. 16) in his effort to convince the baroness that the sow is to become his sister-in-law.
2   The foolish baroness responds in amusement; she orders her fur coat placed on the sow, the carriage hitched to the horses, and then watches, in laughter, as Fedka rides out of the yard with her prized belongings.
3   The baron returns home, jumps on his horse, and pursues Fedka.
4   Fedka hides the carriage and is sitting alongside the road guarding his hat when the baron approaches.
5   The baron asks Fedka about the carriage; Fedka convinces him that he could find the carriage if he could leave the valuable falcon that is under his hat. The baron offers to sit with the hat so that Fedka can find and return the carriage; he pays Fedka three hundred rubles in case the falcon escapes.
6   Fedka jumps on the baron's horse, leaves him guarding the empty hat, rides off to retrieve the carriage, and returns home. (He has found several people who are more foolish than his mother.)

After children have pantomimed these characters, they like to add words and extend this folktale into a humorous play. Many other folktales discussed in this chapter have excellent scenes that describe humorous confrontations between characters.

Scenes from Greek and Norse mythology are excellent pantomime subjects for older children.

Children can enact Psyche's search for Cupid; Jason's search for the golden fleece; Persephone descending into the underground world of Hades; Apollo's sun chariot trailing across the sky; and Thor frantically searching for his missing hammer, dressing as a bride, and retrieving his hammer from the giant Thrym. Quite different movements and expressions are necessary to depict gods, goddesses, heroes, and heroines found in Greek and Norse mythology. Acting out the scenes through pantomime helps children understand the qualities of these traditional folklore characters and appreciate the language found in the myths.

Creative Interpretations

As children pantomime stories such as "The Three Bears" or "The Falcon under the Hat," they usually want to add words and create their own plays. It is a natural extension of pantomime to add "Somebody has been sitting in my chair" or to create a dialogue in which the hero tries to convince the baroness that she should loan him her pig. Pantomiming provides a foundation for other creative activities; it allows children to experience the movement and emotion of the story and characters before they try to work with dialogue. Stories used to stimulate pantomime can also be used for creative interpretations requiring words. Folklore meets Barbara M. McIntyre's (6) criteria for stories that are appropriate for dramatization. They should (1) have ideas worth sharing, (2) involve conflict, (3) include action in the development of the plot, (4) contain characters who seem real, and (5) have situations in which interesting dialogue can be developed. The folktales discussed in this chapter qualify in all of these areas.

Folklore can be used to stimulate creative dramatizations in two ways. The stories themselves can be recreated, or the stories can serve as stimulators to help children create new interpretations. Usually children first act out stories that are close to the original in plot and characterization. As they become more secure, they also enjoy making up new stories or creating additional ones about a character. Whatever the purpose for using the folktales, however, the adult needs to guide children's dramatizations in a sequence of steps, as one third-grade teacher did when using "The Golden Goose," by the Brothers Grimm:

1   *Stimulate children's interest in the story.* The teacher placed a yellow toy goose, a dry crust of bread, and a bottle of sour liquid in front of the class. She then asked the children if they thought they could acquire a fortune and a beautiful princess if they had the objects. She let them try to think of ways they might accomplish this miracle. The children decided that a little magic might help.

2   *Present the story so that children will have a foundation to draw upon in creating their dramatization.* The teacher next told the story of "The Golden Goose," using the toy goose, the stale bread, and the sour liquid to assist her. This time, however, as the stale bread was transformed, she had a pastry to take its place, and as the sour liquid was changed, she had a jug of sweet grape juice to exchange.

3   *Guide the children's planning and presentation of their creative dramatization.* The teacher encouraged the class to talk about their favorite characters in the story. She then asked them to improvise the actions of each character in various scenes in the story—the despised and mistreated Dummling (or Simpleton, depending upon the version used), his parents, and his brothers; Dummling sharing his food with the old man, cutting down the trees, discovering the golden goose; and so forth. The class discussed which actions they would like to include in the play and what sequence of events they would use. They decided to use the goose, the bread, the liquid, the pastry, and the grape juice as props. After the children were satisfied with the sequence and who should play each role (at least for the first time), they acted out the story with encouragement from the teacher when necessary. They did not try to memorize lines but improvised the general mood. They put on their production several times so the children could play various roles and take turns being the audience.

4   *Help the children evaluate their performance.* The teacher encouraged the children to discuss the good things about their play: Why did they feel sorry for Dummling? How did the older brothers show that they thought they were brighter than Dummling? What did they do so that the children did not feel sorry for their bad luck? What did the old

man do to let them know he was very old? Why did they laugh at Dummling? The children made many positive comments about their play. Then they talked about how they could improve the presentation.

A Christmas Festival or Winter Holiday Celebration

Gallant knights show off their skills in tests of archery and outdoor games; the great hall is decorated with mistletoe; the Yule log is on the fire; plum puddings, wild boar, and roasted venison cover the banquet tables; and minstrels and storytellers prepare to enchant the holiday merrymakers. Books say this is how the Christmas season was celebrated in the days of King Arthur. Books also say that in the 1800s groups of Cornish young people traveled from house to house performing the play *Duffy and the Devil.* Children in a fifth-grade class combined these two English holiday traditions to develop their own Christmas festival. (This can be called a Winter Holiday Celebration without referring to Christmas.)

To prepare for the festival, the fifth-graders chose English folktales and parts of heroic tales that could be told to a gathering of people. Readings from King Arthur and Robin Hood were included along with "The Marriage of Sir Gawain," and the folktales "Jack the Giant Killer," "Mr. and Mrs. Vinegar," and "The Donkey, the Table, and the Stick."

They developed Harve Zemach's *Duffy and the Devil* into a creative dramatization to add to the traditional Christmas setting. To assist the children in developing the play, the teacher used steps similar to those described earlier for "The Golden Goose." After the teacher shared the story with the class, the children talked about their favorite parts and characters. They improvised the actions of Squire Lovel of Trovel unhappily observing his old housekeeper Jone; the old woman chasing Duffy with a broom; Duffy convincing Squire Lovel that she is a marvelous housekeeper; and numerous other scenes from the story. Then they discussed the actions and scenes they would like to include in their dramatization. The group decided to retain the flavor of the early English language in the story. While they did not completely memorize their parts, they did use words such as *bufflehead, clouts, whillygogs,* and *whizamagees.* Next they chose players, practiced the sequence, and discussed what they liked about the play and how it could be improved.

On the day of the festival, the room was decorated like an Old English hall at Christmas. Every class member had some part: introducing a ballad or folktale and giving a little information about it, reading a heroic tale, telling a folktale, or being in the play *Duffy and the Devil*. Both guests and children thoroughly enjoyed their Christmas festival. All agreed that the oral tradition was alive in that fifth-grade class.

The Way of Danger: The Drama of Theseus

During a study of Greek mythology, one university student developed a creative dramatization around the adventures of the Greek hero Theseus. With a group of fifth-grade students, she read Ian Serraillier's *The Way of Danger: The Story of Theseus* and other myths about Theseus. The students located the settings for Theseus's adventures and plotted his travels on a map.

Next, with teacher guidance, the group outlined the life of Theseus into the major scenes they wished to portray and then dramatized their story. The following outline resulted from their planning:

The Life of Theseus

I. Theseus as a boy
   A. Aethra and Aegeus (his mother and father)
   B. Theseus and Aethra (his mother)
   C. Theseus and Pittheus (his grandfather)
II. Theseus journeys to Athens
   A. He meets the Club-bearer
   B. He meets the Foot-washer
   C. He meets the Stretcher
III. Theseus meets his father, the king
   A. He encounters Madea, the witch
   B. He is remembered by his father
IV. Theseus and the Minotaur
   A. He travels to Crete
   B. He encounters Minos, the wicked king
   C. Ariadne saves him from Minotaur
   D. He returns to Athens

Additional Ways to Use Traditional Literature for Creative Dramatics

Mythology and other traditional stories are filled with tales that lend themselves to creative interpretations. The following are a few ideas that children's literature students, classroom teachers, and librarians have performed successfully:

1 Following the reading of King Midas, a group of children performed the story. Later, they divided into groups and chose another object besides gold as an obsession. They each performed the King Midas story as if everything the king touched turned to objects such as ice cream, chocolate, or money.

2 An adult read the Greek myth about Meleager to students, omitting the part where the queen burns the fire that kills Meleager. The teacher guided the children in developing a court trial for the purpose of identifying Meleager's killer, including a judge, defense lawyers, prosecution lawyers, witnesses, suspects, and jury. The class conducted a trial, and the lawyers elicited stories from each witness and suspect. Each player developed a story according to the facts presented in the literature. Jury members discussed their opinions, provided rationales, and then voted on who they believed was the guilty person. After the court trial, the adult shared the story's real ending with the group.

3 After reading myths about Poseidon, ancient Greek god of the sea, children became interested in his challenge to Athena, the warlike goddess of wisdom and patron of the city of Athens. Poseidon wanted to rule Athens. The gods, however, decided that the city should be awarded to the one who could produce the gift most useful to mortals. Athena gave mortals the olive tree and thereby won the contest. Students accomplished several creative activities that were motivated by this myth. They debated about which gift was the most useful, Poseidon's or Athena's; they developed short plays showing the desirability of each; they created other challenges and acted out the results.

The high drama found in the plots and characters of traditional literature can lend themselves very well to any number of such creative dramatizations.

USING TRADITIONAL LITERATURE TO MOTIVATE CREATIVE WRITING

The exciting or humorous adventures of characters in traditional tales can motivate children's creative writing. (See page 365 for a description of the steps necessary to develop creative writing with literature.)

The heroes and heroines of Greek mythology are popular with ten-, eleven-, and twelve-year-old children, for example. One teacher used children's enthusiasm for Elizabeth Silverthorne's *I, Heracles* to encourage them to write about other interesting characters in the Greek myths. Silverthorne's story is written in the first person, thus allowing Heracles to tell his own story, interpret his own feelings, and describe his own relationships with others. After the teacher shared the story with children (they had already read other myths), she encouraged each of them to pretend to be a character from Greek mythology and write a self-description and story of exploits. Some quite interesting and well-expressed "autobiographies" resulted from this activity. Other effective creative writing assignments motivated by mythology have included asking students to pretend they are Zeus and to write a story about how they would rule Mount Olympus, and asking students to pretend they have done a favor for a god or goddess and been rewarded. In this last assignment, children were supposed to consider what they would ask for as a reward, write a story about themselves performing the favor, and include information about the favor they asked for and the consequences, if any, of their wish.

Many folktales, fables, and legends can motivate similar creative writing experiences. *Pour-quoi* ("why") tales often answer questions about why animals act or look a certain way. A third-grade teacher shared Edward Dolch's *"Why" Stories from Different Countries* (4) with her children. They talked about stories such as "How the Rabbit Lost His Tail," "Why the Bear Has a Little Tail," and "Why the Stork Has No Tail" and speculated about other ways that one of these animals might have lost its tail. Then the children wrote their own stories about why a rabbit, a bear, or a stork might have a short tail. They also wrote their own versions of *pourquoi* stories such as "Why the Chicken Cannot Fly," "Why the Horse Has a Mane," and "Why the Rabbit Hops."

INTERPRETING TRADITIONAL IMAGES IN ART

Traditional tales, especially those that have not been written in simplified language, are filled with passages that evoke visual images. The tales can inspire young artists, like illustrators of picture books, to recreate the birth of the Greek goddess Aphrodite out of the foaming, shimmering sea; depict the sacred lake where a Native American boy waits for the buffalo to appear; or por-

Children enjoy making a gingerbread house after listening to "Hansel and Gretel."

tray the cave of an evil flying dragon, where a Chinese girl is held captive.

Allowing children to experience the artistic moods of traditional literature through paints, chalk, or crayons is another way to help them extend their enjoyment. For example, an adult could use the Norse tale "The Valkyrie," from Olivia E. Coolidge's *Legends of the North*, to stimulate children to draw or paint a picture in shades of the hottest colors: What are the dancing flames that attract Sigurd to venture toward the glowing horizon? What is the circling pillar of smoke? Have robbers burned a citadel? Has a dragon breathed fire on the farmlands of a great king? These questions can introduce children to an artistic experience in which they interpret Sigurd's adventures. As an adult reads a passage such as the following, children can close their eyes and try to visualize color and mood, then express the images in color on paper:

By dawn Sigurd could hear the hissing of the fire. Greyfell picked his way with care over the hot faces of the rock, which were bathed in a bright red light. The flames made a ring of flickering points, now sinking, now flaring, now parting, now shooting out over the sides of the mountain as though caught in a sudden wind. (p. 105)

Gail E. Haley's *The Green Man*, a legend about a man who lives in the woods and cares for animals could inspire numerous forest scenes. One teacher read the legend to her third graders, encouraged them to discuss the tapestry-like illustrations, and asked them to consider possible reasons for changes in the man's behavior. Next she quoted Haley's concluding comments about the Green Man: "Legend tells us that there will be a Lord of the Forest 'for as long as the Greenwood stands.' It is certainly easy to believe that the Green Man is there—hidden among the leaves watching to make sure that all is well" (p. 29). Finally, she asked the children to pretend to be the Green Man and illustrate the greenwood as they believed it should appear. During another art period, she asked them to illustrate two pictures, one that would make them happy if they were the Green Man, and another that would make them sad.

Folktales, fables, myths, and legends contain scenes, characters, and story lines that are excellent stimuli for children's artistic self-expression. The tales allow children's imaginations to expand and encourage them to create an imaginary world in chalk, paint, or other media.

SUMMARY

The oral tradition may be recaptured through the use of many activities in the classroom, library, or home. Storytelling is one of the most enjoyable and rewarding ways to share traditional literature. It helps children understand the oral tradition, allows the adult an opportunity to involve children in storytelling, and stimulates children to try storytelling themselves. The storyteller should enjoy the stories. The stories should be appropriate for the interests, ages, and experience of the children and have considerable action, strong beginnings, strong characters, and contain satisfactory endings. Storytelling does not require memorization, but developing an effective storytelling experience does require preparation. The storyteller must read the story aloud, think of the major actions, develop a sense of the characters, think through the setting, and look for phrases that might be incorporated into the story. Storytelling can also be enhanced by stimulating interest in the story, setting a mood for the story, creating an appropriate environment, and presenting the story with effective eye contact and voice control.

Children learn to understand the relatedness of traditional story types, become aware of cultural diffusion, and learn about different countries when they read traditional literature. Activities that let children compare different versions of the same folktale and investigate many folktales from one country allow them to develop these values.

Drama is a most exciting way to share traditional tales. Tales may be shared through movement alone (pantomime) or in movement accompanied by words (creative dramatics). Materials for pantomime range from simple folktales to mythology. In addition to pantomiming whole stories, children can pantomime contrasting forces of good and evil or cleverness and foolishness. Folklore can be used to stimulate creative dramatizations in two ways: the stories themselves can be recreated, or the stories can act as stimulants to help children create new interpretations. Children do require guidance in their interpretations. Guidance includes stimulating their interest in the story, presenting the story, guiding their planning for the creative interpretation, directing their creative dramatization, and helping them evaluate their presentations.

Adults can also use traditional literature to motivate children's creative writing. The chapter concluded with suggestions for using the visual images found in traditional literature to encourage artistic interpretations.

Suggested Activities for Children's Appreciation of Traditional Literature

☐ Choose a folktale of interest, prepare the story for telling, and share the story with either one child or a group of children.

☐ Select a cumulative tale such as "The Gingerbread Boy" or a simple folktale such as "The Three Bears" and prepare it as a feltboard story. Share the story with either one child or a group.

☐ Select a folktale that has many versions from diverse cultures. For example, "Sleeping Beauty" is found in many cultures. What questions should children ask when they investigate the tales? Develop a chart similar to the one in the text for "Cinderella." What are the key similarities and differences? How do the tales reflect the culture? Draw a list of conclusions that could be made from the folktales.

☐ With a peer group, select a country to investigate. Develop a list of appropriate traditional tales and a list of related examples of art, music, and so forth, and design some activities that would help children develop an understanding of the country.

☐ Choose a folktale that has rapid action appropriate for pantomiming. Lead a peer group or a group of children through the pantomime.

☐ Lead a peer group or a group of children through the four steps described in this chapter for developing creative interpretations: stimulating interest, presenting the story, guiding the planning and presentation of the creative dramatization, and helping the group to evaluate their presentation.

☐ Compile a file of creative writing ideas that could be motivated by traditional literature.

☐ Select a story from traditional literature that evokes visual images. Share the selection with a child, and encourage the child to interpret the story using paints, chalk, or crayons.

☐ Compile a file of folktales that contain vivid word pictures; describe how these tales could be used to help children interpret the mood of the tale through art.

References

1 Anderson, Paul S. *Story Telling with the Flannel Board*. Minneapolis: Denison, 1971.

2 Bingham, Jane M., and Scholt, Grayce. "The Great Glass Slipper Search: Using Folk Tales with Older Children." *Elementary English* 51 (October 1974): 990–98.

3 Cook, Elizabeth. *The Ordinary and the Fabulous: An Introduction to Myths, Legends, and Fairy Tales*. 2d ed. Cambridge: At the University Press, 1976.

4 Dolch, Edward. *"Why" Stories from Different Countries*. New Canaan, Conn.: Garrard, 1958.

5 Kuo, Louise, and Kuo, Yuan-hsi. *Chinese Folk Tales*. Millbrae, Calif.: Celestial Arts, 1976.

6 McIntyre, Barbara M. *Creative Drama in the Elementary School*. Itasca, Ill.: Peacock, 1974.

7 Miller, Winifred. "Dragons—Fact or Fantasy?" *Elementary English* 52 (April 1975): 582–85.

8 Nelson, Mary Ann. *A Comparative Anthology of Children's Literature*. New York: Holt, Rinehart & Winston, 1972.

9 Norton, Donna E. *The Effective Teaching of Language Arts*. Columbus, Ohio: Merrill, 1985.

10 Ross, Elinor P. "Comparison of Folk Tale Variants." *Language Arts* 56 (April 1979): 422–26.

11 Ross, Ramon Royal. *Storyteller*. 2d ed. Columbus, Ohio: Merrill, 1980.

12 Siks, Geraldine. *Drama with Children*. New York: Harper & Row, 1977.

13 Stewig, John Warren. "Storyteller: Endangered Species?" *Language Arts* 55 (March 1978): 339–45.

14 Travers, P. T. *About the Sleeping Beauty*. Illustrated by Charles Keeping. New York: McGraw-Hill, 1975.

15 Western, Linda. "A Comparative Study of Literature through Folk Tale Variants." *Language Arts* 57 (April 1980): 395–402.

CHILDREN'S LITERATURE

FOLKTALES

African—Black Literature

See page 556, chapter eleven.

American—Native American

See page 559, chapter eleven.

Asian

Asian Cultural Centre for UNESCO. *Folk Tales from Asia for Children Everywhere*, Book Three. Weatherhill, 1976 (I:8–12 R:6). Stories from Afghanistan, Burma, Indonesia, Iran, Japan, Pakistan, Singapore, Sri Lanka, and Vietnam.

———. *Folk Tales from Asia for Children Everywhere*, Book Four. Weatherhill, 1976 (I:8–12 R:6). Folktales from Bangladesh, Cambodia, India, Korea, Laos, Malaysia, Nepal, Philippines, and Thailand.

———. *Folk Tales from Asia for Children Everywhere*, Book Five. Weatherhill, 1977 (I:8–12 R:6). Stories from India, Philippines, Pakistan, Japan, Malaysia, Burma, and Iran.

Clark, Ann Nolan. *In the Land of Small Dragon*. Illustrated by Tony Chen. Viking, 1979 (I:7–12 R:7). A Vietnamese variation of "Cinderella."

DeRoin, Nancy, ed. *Jataka Tales*. Illustrated by Ellen Lanyon. Houghton Mifflin, 1975 (I:7–9 R:5). Animal tales from India attributed to Buddha.

Haviland, Virginia. *Favorite Fairy Tales Told in India*. Illustrated by Blair Lent. Little, Brown, 1973 (I:8–10 R:5). A collection of characteristic tales.

———. *Favorite Fairy Tales Told in Japan*. Illustrated by George Suyeoka. Little, Brown, 1967 (I:8–10 R:5). A collection of Japanese folktales.

Heyer, Marilee. *The Weaver of a Dream: A Chinese Folktale*. Viking, 1986 (I:8+ R:5). A retelling of "The Chuang Brocade."

Iké, Jane, and Zimmerman, Baruch. *A Japanese Fairy Tale*. Warne, 1982 (I:5–8 R:5). A man takes the disfiguration of his future wife.

Kuo, Louise, and Kuo, Yuan-hsi. *Chinese Folk Tales*. Celestial Arts, 1976 (I:8–12 R:6). Folklore from the rulers and the minority tribes of China.

Lang, Andrew. *Aladdin and the Wonderful Lamp*. Illustrated by Errol LeCain. Viking, 1981 (I:7–9 R:6). Deep color and ornamentation appropriately illustrate a tale from *The Arabian Nights*.

Laurin, Anne. *The Perfect Crane*. Illustrated by Charles Mikolaycak. Harper & Row, 1981 (I:5–9 R:6). A Japanese tale about the friendship between a magician and the crane he creates from rice paper.

Lee, Jeanne M. *Legend of the Milky Way*. Holt, 1982 (I:6–9 R:5). A heavenly princess and her earthly husband are transformed into stars.

Louie, Ai-Lang. *Yeh Shen: A Cinderella Story From China*. Illustrated by Ed Young. Philomel, 1982 (I:7–9 R:6). This ancient Chinese tale has many similarities with versions from other cultures.

Mosel, Arlene. *The Funny Little Woman*. Illustrated by Blair Lent. Dutton, 1972 (I:5–8 R:5). A little woman pursues a rice dumpling and is captured by wicked people.

Newton, Patricia Montgomery. *The Five Sparrows: A Japanese Folktale*. Atheneum, 1982 (I:5–8 R:6). Kindness is rewarded and greed is punished.

Philip, Neil, ed. *The Spring of Butterflies and Other Folktales of China's Minority Peoples*. Translated by He Liyi. Illustrated by Pan Aiqing and Li Zhao. Lothrop, Lee and Shepard, 1986 (I:9+ R:6). Tales from northwestern China.

Pratt, Davis, and Kula, Elsa. *Magic Animals of Japan*. Parnassus, 1967 (I:8–12 R:7). Tales of the fabled creatures of Japan.

Roberts, Moss. *Chinese Fairy Tales and Fantasies*. Pantheon, 1979 (I:10 R:6). A collection of tales about enchantment, greed, animals, women, ghosts, and judges.

Sadler, Catherine Edwards. *Treasure Mountain: Folktales from Southern China*. Illustrated by Cheng Mung Yun. Atheneum, 1982 (I:8 R:6). Six folktales depict customs and beliefs.

Travers, Pamela. *Two Pairs of Shoes*. Illustrated by Leo and Diane Dillon. Viking, 1980 (I:9–12 R:6). Two Persian tales reflect men's characters through their responses to their shoes.

Wyndham, Robert. *Tales the People Tell in China*. Illustrated by Jay Yang. Messner, 1971 (I:8–12 R:6). Myths, legends, and folktales from China.

Yagawa, Sumiko. *The Crane Wife*. Illustrated by Suekichi Akaba. Morrow, 1981 (I:7–10 R:6). A wife sacrifices herself for her husband and must return to her animal form when he breaks his promise.

I = Interest by age range;
R = Readability by grade level.

British (United Kingdom)

Buchan, David, ed. *Scottish Tradition: A Collection of Scottish Folk Literature.* Routledge & Kegan Paul, 1984 (I:9+ R:5). A large adult collection that provides selections for oral sharing.

Cauley, Lorinda Bryan. *The Cock, the Mouse, and the Little Red Hen.* Putnam, 1982 (I:3–6 R:4). The repetitive language appeals to young children.

———. *Goldilocks and the Three Bears.* Putnam, 1981 (I:3–7 R:4). Large colorful illustrations appeal to children.

Cooper, Susan, Retold By. *The Silver Cow: A Welsh Tale.* Illustrated by Warwick Hutton, Atheneum, 1983 (I:5–8 R:5). A cow and her offspring return to the lake because of a farmer's greed.

de Paola, Tomie. *The Friendly Beasts: An Old English Christmas Carol.* Putnam, 1981 (I:3–9). The Bethlehem setting is depicted in this folk song.

Galdone, Paul. *The Little Red Hen.* Seabury, 1973 (I:3–7 R:3). The industrious hen won't share her cake with lazy friends.

———. *The Three Bears.* Seabury, 1972 (I:3–7 R:5). The traditional tale illustrated with large, humorous pictures.

———. *The Three Sillies.* Houghton Mifflin, 1981 (I:3–7 R:2). Colorful, humorous illustrations add to this tale about a man's search for three people sillier than his future in-laws.

———. *What's in Fox's Sack? An Old English Tale.* Clarion, 1982 (I:3–7 R:2). A fox is outsmarted by a woman who puts a bulldog in his bag.

Garner, Alan. *Alan Garner's Book of British Fairy Tales.* Illustrated by Derek Collard. Delacorte, 1985 (I:9–12 R:6). Twenty-one tales, including some that are not familiar.

Godden, Rumer. *The Dragon of Og.* Illustrated by Pauline Baynes. Viking, 1981 (I:9–12 R:6). Scottish tale about the new lord who refuses to give the dragon bullocks from his herd.

Jacobs, Joseph. *Ardizzone's English Fairy Tales.* Illustrated by Edward Ardizzone, Deutsch, 1980 (I:9+ R:7). Twelve stories illustrated with black-and-white drawings.

———. *Celtic Fairy Tales.* Illustrated by John D. Batten, Dover 1892, reissue 1968 (I:9+ R:6). A selection of Celtic, Irish, and Gaelic tales.

———. *English Fairy Tales.* Illustrated by John D. Batten, Muller, 1890, reissue 1942, 1979 (I:8–12 R:4). A collection of sixty English folktales.

———. *Guleesh.* Illustrated by William Stobbs. Follett, 1972 (I:7–12 R:5). An Irish folktale about the sheehogues, the fairy hosts of Ireland, and a boy who joins them when they capture the king's daughter.

———. *Irish Fairy Tales.* Illustrated by John D. Batten. Castle, 1984 (I:9 R:6). Twenty-six tales from Celtic Ireland.

Jones, Gwyn. *Welsh Legends and Folk-Tales.* Oxford, 1955, Puffin, 1982 (I:9+ R:7). A collection of over thirty Welsh tales.

Kellogg, Steven. *Chicken Little.* Morrow, 1985 (I:5–8 R:5). A humorous, modern version of the tale, with cars, trucks, and helicopters.

Steel, Flora Annie. *Tattercoats.* Illustrated by Diane Goode. Bradbury, 1976 (I:7–10 R:7). The gooseherd plays the role of the fairy godmother in this English version of "Cinderella."

Zemach, Harve. *Duffy and the Devil.* Illustrated by Margot Zemach. Farrar, Straus & Giroux, 1973 (I:8–12 R:6). A Cornish tale that resembles "Rumplestiltskin," but the maid makes an agreement with the devil.

French

de Beaumont, Madame. *Beauty and the Beast.* Translated and illustrated by Diane Goode. Bradbury, 1978 (I:8–14 R:7). Lovely illustrations accompany the tale of a girl who is willing to sacrifice her own life for the love of her father.

Hutton, Warwick, Retold By. *Beauty and the Beast.* Atheneum, 1985 (I:9 R:6). Love breaks an evil spell.

Perrault, Charles. *Cinderella.* Illustrated by Marcia Brown. Scribner's, 1954 (I:5–8 R:5). Fine lines suggest the mood of the fairy tale.

———. *Favorite Fairy Tales.* Edited by Jennifer Mulherin. Grosset, 1983 (I:all). An eighteenth century version with original illustrations.

———. *The Glass Slipper: Charles Perrault's Tales of Time Past.* Translated by John Bierhorst. Illustrated by Mitchell Miller. Four Winds, 1981 (I:9–12 R:6). A new translation of *Histoires ou contes du temps passé.*

———. *Histories or Tales of Past Times.* Garland, 1977 (I:10+ R:6). Reprint of the 1729 edition printed in London.

———. *Puss in Boots.* Illustrated by Marcia Brown. Scribner's, 1952 (I:5–8 R:5). A faithful cat helps his master.

———. *The Sleeping Beauty.* Translated and illustrated by David Walker. Crowell, 1976 (I:8–14 R:6). Beautifully illustrated book that resembles the stage setting for an opera or ballet.

———. *Tom Thumb.* Retold and Illustrated by Lidia Postma. Schocken, 1983 (I:6–9 R:6). Detailed illustrations accompany the classic tale.

German

deRegniers, Beatrice Schenk. *Red Riding Hood.* Illustrated by Edward Gorey. Atheneum, 1972 (I:4–8 R:2). A verse format of the story based on the Brothers Grimm version.

Galdone, Paul. *Hansel and Gretel.* McGraw-Hill, 1982 (I:5–7 R:3). A folktale appropriate for younger children.

———. *Little Red Riding Hood.* McGraw-Hill, 1974 (I:4–8 R:4). Large, colorful pictures retell the Grimms' folktale.

Grimm, Brothers. *The Bremen Town Musicians.* Retold and illustrated by Ilse Plume. Doubleday, 1980 (I:5–8 R:5). Soft, colored illustrations show animals going through the forest.

———. *Cinderella.* Illustrated by Nonny Hogrogian. Greenwillow, 1981 (I:6–12 R:6). An attractive version of the German tale.

———. *The Complete Brothers Grimm Fairy Tales.* Edited by Lily Owens, Avenel, 1981 (I:all R:7). Tales that were previously published in *Grimm's Household Tales.*

———. *The Devil with the Three Golden Hairs.* Retold and Illustrated by Nonny Hogrogian. Knopf, 1983 (I:5–9 R:7). A boy completes a quest to earn the King's daughter for his bride.

———. *Favorite Tales from Grimm.* Retold and illustrated by Mercer Mayer. Four Winds, 1982 (I:7–10 R:6). Twenty illustrated stories.

———. *The Fox and the Cat: Animal Tales from Grimm.* Translated by Kevin Crossley-Holland and Susan Varley. Illustrated by Susan Varley. Lothrop, Lee and Shepard, 1986 (I:9+R:6). An anthology of animal folktales.

———. *Hansel and Gretel.* Illustrated by Anthony Browne. Watts, 1982 (I:9–12 R:5). Illustrations showing a contemporary setting should be interesting for a comparative study.

———. *Hansel and Gretel.* Illustrated by Susan Jeffers. Dial, 1980 (I:5–9 R:6). Illustrations with strong line and a magnificent gingerbread house should appeal to readers.

———. *Hansel and Gretel.* Retold by Rika Lesser. Illustrated by Paul O. Zelinsky, Dodd, 1984 (I:all R:6). Full-page illustrations depict the dark forests of an earlier time.

———. *Hansel and Gretel.* Translated by

Anthea Bell. Illustrated by Otto S. Svend, Larousse, 1983 (I:6–9 R:7). An English translation of the folktale published in Denmark.

———. *Little Red Cap*. Illustrated by Lisbeth Zwerger, Translated by Elizabeth Crawford. Morrow, 1983 (I:4–7 R:4). The folktale about a deceitful wolf.

———. *Little Red Riding Hood*. Retold and Illustrated by Trina Schart Hyman, Holiday, 1983 (I:6–9 R:7). Richly detailed page borders add to this attractive version.

———. *The Musicians of Bremen*. Translated by Anne Rogers. Illustrated by Otto S. Svend. Larousse, 1974 (I:4–8 R:6). An old dog, donkey, cat, and rooster decide to become musicians.

———. *The Nose Tree*. Retold and illustrated by Warwick Hutton. Atheneum, 1981 (I:5–9 R:6). Trickery and humorous illustrations are good for the story hour.

———. *Rapunzel: From the Brothers Grimm*. Retold by Barbara Rogasky. Illustrated by Trina Hyman, Holiday, 1982 (I:6–9 R:6). The forest setting seems right for a girl imprisoned in a high tower.

———. *Rare Treasures from Grimm: Fifteen Little-Known Tales*. Translated by Ralph Manheim. Illustrated by Erik Blegvad. Doubleday, 1981 (I:9–12 R:6). Each tale is illustrated by a full-page painting.

———. *The Seven Ravens*. Translated by Elizabeth Crawford. Illustrated by Lisbeth Zwerger. Morrow, 1981 (I:6–9 R:6). A girl frees her brothers from an enchantment.

———. *The Six Swans*. Illustrated by Adrie Hospes. McGraw-Hill, 1973 (I:7–12 R:5). A sister saves six brothers enchanted by their evil stepmother.

———. *The Sleeping Beauty*. Illustrated by Warwick Hutton. Atheneum, 1979 (I:7–12 R:6). Watercolors illustrate the story of magic and enchantment.

———. *Snow White and the Seven Dwarfs*. Translated by Randal Jarrell. Illustrated by Nancy Ekholm Burkert. Farrar, Straus & Giroux, 1972 (I:7–12 R:6). The illustrations were carefully researched by the artist and reflect the Black Forest and German heritage.

———. *Thorn Rose, or the Sleeping Beauty*. Illustrated by Errol LeCain. Bradbury, 1977 (I:7–12 R:7). Lovely illustrations depict the opulence of a magical kingdom.

———. *Tom Thumb*. Translated by Anthea Bell. Illustrated by Otto S. Svend. Larousse, 1976 (I:5–9 R:6). The small boy who is no bigger than your thumb runs away from two strangers and two thieves.

———. *The Twelve Dancing Princesses*. Illustrated by Errol LeCain. Viking, 1978 (I:7–12 R:7). Twelve princesses mysteriously dance holes in their shoes every night.

———. *The Twelve Dancing Princesses and Other Tales from Grimm*. Illustrated by Lidia Postma. Dial, 1986 (I:9–12 R:5). An anthology of German tales.

———. *Wanda Gág's The Six Swans*. Translated by Wanda Gág. Illustrated by Margot Tomes. Coward-McCann, 1982 (I:5–9 R:4). A newly illustrated edition of Gág's translation from *More Tales from Grimm*.

———. *The Wolf and the Seven Little Kids*. Translated by Anne Rogers. Illustrated by Otto S. Svend. Larousse, 1977 (I:4–8 R:4). Seven little goats have a conflict with the wolf when their mother leaves the house.

Hispanic Literature
See page 558, chapter eleven.

Jewish
Gross, Michael. *The Fable of the Fig Tree*. Illustrated by Mila Lazarevich. Walck, 1975 (I:6–10 R:7). An old man plants a tree even if he can't benefit from the fruit.

McDermott, Beverly Brodsky. *The Golem*. Lippincott, 1976 (I:8+ R:5). Rabbi Lev creates a man out of a lump of clay, but the Golem does not protect the Jewish people the way the rabbi envisions.

Singer, Isaac Bashevis. *The Golem*. Illustrated by Uri Shulevitz. Farrar, Straus & Giroux, 1982 (I:8+ R:5). Another version of this Jewish folktale.

———. *Mazel and Shlimazel, or the Milk of the Lioness*. Illustrated by Margot Zemach. Farrar, Straus & Giroux, 1967 (I:8–12 R:4). Mazel, the spirit of good luck, and Shlimazel, the spirit of bad luck, have a contest.

Zemach, Margot. *It Could Always Be Worse*. Farrar, Straus & Giroux, 1977 (I:5–9 R:2). A poor hut seems small when all the animals are removed.

Norwegian
Asbjörnsen, Peter Christian, and Moe, Jorgen E. *The Man Who Kept House*. Retold by Kathleen and Michael Hague. Illustrated by Michael Hague. Harcourt Brace Jovanovich, 1981 (I:5–9 R:6). Humorous illustrations show the husband's problems when he takes over his wife's chores.

———. *Norwegian Folk Tales*. Illustrated by Erik Werenskiold and Theodor Kittelsen. Viking, 1960 (I:6–10 R:3). A collection of thirty-five Norwegian folktales.

———. *The Three Billy Goats Gruff*. Illustrated by Marcia Brown. Harcourt Brace Jovanovich, 1957 (I:3–7 R:5). Goats prance across pages of this favorite tale for telling.

Booss, Claire, ed. *Scandinavian Folk & Fairy Tales*. Avenel, 1984. A large adult collection of tales from Norway, Sweden, Denmark, Finland, and Iceland that will provide sources for storytelling.

Galdone, Paul. *The Three Billy Goats Gruff*. Seabury, 1973 (I:5–8 R:5). A picture storybook about the three billy goats who defeat the troll who lives under the bridge.

Hague, Kathleen, and Hague, Michael. *East of the Sun and West of the Moon*. Harcourt Brace Jovanovich, 1980. (I:7–9 R:5). A maiden lives in the castle of an enchanted white bear.

Haviland, Virginia. *Favorite Fairy Tales Told in Norway*. Illustrated by Leonard Weisgard. Little, Brown, 1961 (I:6–10 R:4). This collection includes "The Princess on the Glass Hill," "Why the Sea Is Salt," "The Three Billy Goats Gruff," "Taper Tom," "Why the Bear is Stumpy-Tailed," "The Lad and the North Wind," and "Boots and the Troll."

Magnus, Erica, Adapted By. *Old Lars*. Carolrhoda Books, 1984 (I:4–7 R:3). A humorous Norwegian folktale about an old man who goes up the mountain to load wood.

Mayer, Mercer. *East of the Sun and West of the Moon*. Four Winds, 1980 (I:8–10 R:4). A beautifully illustrated version of the Asbjörsen and Moe tale.

Russian
Afanasév, Aleksandr Nikolaevich. *Russian Folk Tales*. Translated by Robert Chandler. Illustrated by Ivan I. Bilibin. Random House, 1980 (I:8–12 R:7). Seven memorable tales collected by the nineteenth-century folklorist.

Bain, R. Nisbet, ed. *Cossack Fairy Tales and Folktales*. E. W. Mitchell. CORE Collection, 1976 (I:9+ R:7). Twenty-seven western Ukrainian folktales are reprinted from a 1894 edition.

Daniels, Guy. *The Falcon under the Hat: Russian Merry Tales and Fairy Tales*. Illustrated by Feodor Rojan-kovsky. Funk & Wagnalls, 1969 (I:7–12 R:4). A collection of short humorous stories and fairy tales translated from Russian folk literature.

————. *The Peasant's Pea Patch*. Illustrated by Robert Quackenbush. Delacorte, 1971 (I:5–9 R:4). A merry Russian tale about a poor peasant who tries to protect his pea patch.

Isele, Elizabeth, Retold By. *The Frog Princess*. Illustrated by Michael Hague. Crowell, 1984 (I:6–10 R:4). A czar's son marries the enchanted Vasilisa the Wise.

Mikolaycak, Charles, Retold By. *Babushka*. Holiday, 1984 (I:6–9 R:7). An old woman leaves gifts as she searches for the Christ Child.

Otsuka, Yūzō. *Suho and the White Horse: A Legend of Mongolia*. Adapted from Ann Herring's translation. Illustrated by Suekichi Akaba. Viking, 1981 (I:5–8 R:6). In a tale about good versus evil, a herdsman's horse is killed because of a nobleman's greed.

Pushkin, Alexander. *The Tale of Czar Saltan or the Prince and the Swan Princess*. Translated by Patricia Tracy Lowe. Illustrated by I. Bilibin. Crowell, 1975 (I:8–12 R:6). The czar marries the youngest daughter, but her sisters trick her into exile.

————. *The Tale of the Golden Cockerel*. Translated by Patricia Tracy Lowe. Illustrated by I. Bilibin. Crowell, 1975 (I:8–12 R:6). A czar fails to keep his promise to a sorcerer.

Ransome, Arthur. *The Fool of the World and the Flying Ship*. Illustrated by Uri Shulevitz. Farrar, Straus & Giroux, 1968 (I:6–10 R:6). A simple lad overcomes obstacles to wed the czar's daughter.

Silverman, Maida, Retold By. *Anna and the Seven Swans*. Illustrated by David Small, Morrow, 1984 (I:6–9 R:6). Anna searches for her brother who was taken by Baba Yaga.

Tolstoy, Leo. *The Fool*. Translated by Anthea Bell. Illustrated by Lapointe. Schocken, 1981 (I:5–8). A story in rhyme tells about a foolish man who says the wrong things to the wrong people.

Zvorykin, Boris, illustrator. *The Firebird and Other Russian Fairy Tales*. Edited by Jacqueline Onassis. Viking, 1978 (I:8–14 R:3). "The Firebird," "Maria Morevna," "The Snow Maiden," and "Vassilissa The Fair" are retold in a beautifully illustrated edition.

Other Folktales

Basile, Giambattista. *Petrosinella*. Adapted from the translation by John Edward Taylor. Illustrated by Diane Stanley. Warne, 1981 (I:7–10 R:6). An Italian version of "Rapunzel."

Blair, Walter. *Tall Tale America: A Legendary History of Our Humorous Heroes*. Illustrated by Glen Rounds. Coward-McCann, 1944 (I:8–12 R:5). A collection of exaggerated tales.

Chase, Richard, Collected By. *The Jack Tales*. Illustrated by Berkeley Williams, Jr. Houghton Mifflin, 1943 (I:all R:5). A collection of tales from the Southern Appalachians.

Galdone, Paul. *The Amazing Pig: An Old Hungarian Tale*. Houghton Mifflin, 1981 (I:5–8 R:3). A humorous tale about a king who promises his daughter in marriage to any man who tells him something he cannot believe.

Ginsburg, Mirra. *Two Greedy Bears*. Illustrated by Jose Aruego and Ariane Dewey. Macmillan, 1976 (I:3–6 R:4). In a Hungarian tale, two greedy bears fight over cheese; a fox solves the problem by eating the cheese.

Haviland, Virginia. *Favorite Fairy Tales Told in Italy*. Illustrated by Evaline Ness. Little, Brown, 1967 (I:6–10 R:4). A fine source of Italian folktales.

Kellogg, Steven, Retold By. *Paul Bunyan*. Morrow, 1984 (I:6–9 R:7). A highly illustrated version of the tall tale.

Martin, Eva, Retold By. *Canadian Fairy Tales*. Illustrated by Laszlo Gal, Douglas & McIntyre, 1984 (I:7–10 R:4). Twelve traditional tales reflect the Canadian influence on the French, Irish, and British oral tradition.

Severo, Emoke de Papp, trans. *The Goodhearted Youngest Brother*. Illustrated by Diane Goode. Bradbury, 1981 (I:5–8 R:6). A Hungarian tale reveals how a kindhearted youngest brother releases three beautiful princesses from enchantment.

FABLES

Aesop. *Aesop's Fables*. Illustrated by Heidi Holder. Viking, 1981 (I:9–12 R:7). Nine fables illustrated with full-color paintings.

————. *Aesop's Fables*. Retold by Anne Terry White. Illustrated by Helen Siegle. Random House, 1964 (I:6–10 R:3). Forty of Aesop's fables told in story format.

————. *Aesop's Fables*. Selected and Illustrated by Michael Hague. Holt, Rinehart and Winston, 1985 (I:9–12 R:7). Thirteen fables illustrated with full-page paintings.

————. *Lions and Lobsters and Foxes and Frogs*. Retold by Ennis Rees. Illustrated by Edward Gorey. Young Scott, 1971 (I:8–10 R:7). Seventeen Aesop fables told in verse.

Caldecott, Randolph. *The Caldecott Aesop: A Facsimile of the 1883 Edition*. Doubleday, 1978 (I:all R:7). A reproduction of the earlier Aesop's fable written and illustrated by Caldecott.

Cauley, Lorinda Bryan, Retold By. *The Town Mouse and the Country Mouse*. Putnam's, 1984 (I:6–8 R:5). A picture story book version of the fable.

La Fontaine, Jean de. *The Lion and the Rat*. Illustrated by Brian Wildsmith. Watts, 1963 (I:6–8). A highly illustrated version of the fable.

————. *The Miller, the Boy and the Donkey*. Illustrated by Brian Wildsmith. Watts, 1969; Oxford, 1981 (I:6–8). An illustrated version of the fable.

Stevens, Janet, Adapted By. *The Tortoise and the Hare*. Holiday House, 1984 (I:6–8 R:3). A picture storybook version of an Aesop fable.

MYTHOLOGY

Greek and Roman Myths

Barth, Edna. *Cupid and Psyche*. Illustrated by Ati Forberg. Seabury, 1976 (I:7–12 R:6). Princess Psyche is loved by Cupid but hated by Venus, the goddess of love.

Bulfinch, Thomas. *A Book of Myths*. Illustrated by Helen Sewell. Macmillan, 1942, 1964 (I:10+ R:6). A collection of Greek myths written in short-story format.

————. *Myths of Greece & Rome*. Penguin, 1981 (paperback) (I:10 R:8). A good source for the myths.

Colum, Padraic. *The Golden Fleece and the Heroes Who Lived Before Achilles*. Illustrated by Willy Pogany. Macmillan, 1921, 1949, 1962 (I:9+ R:6). Jason and the Greek heroes search for the golden fleece.

Coolidge, Olivia. *Greek Myths*. Illustrated by Edouard Sandoz. Houghton Mifflin, 1949 (I:10+ R:7). An excellent collection of myths.

D'Aulaire, Ingri, and D'Aulaire, Edgar Parin. *D'Aulaires' Book of Greek Myths*. Doubleday, 1962 (paperback, 1980) (I:8+ R:6). A collection of tales about gods, goddesses, and heroes.

Evslin, Bernard. *Hercules*. Illustrated by Jos A. Smith, Morrow, 1984 (I:9 R:6). The tales of a great hero.

Farmer, Penelope. *Daedalus and Icarus*. Illustrated by Chris Connor. Harcourt, Brace Jovanovich, 1971 (I:8+ R:6). Daedalus attempts to rival the gods.

Fisher, Leonard Everett. *The Olympians: Great Gods and Goddesses of Ancient Greece*. Holiday, 1984 (I:8 R:3). Brief biographies accompany large illustrations.

Gates, Doris. *The Golden God: Apollo*. Illustrated by Constantinos CoConis. Viking, 1973 (I:9+ R:6). Story of Apollo and his associations with other gods and goddesses.

———. *Lord of the Sky: Zeus*. Illustrated by Robert Handville. Viking, 1972 (I:10+ R:7). The myths centering around Zeus.

———. *Two Queens of Heaven: Aphrodite and Demeter*. Illustrated by Trina Schart Hyman. Viking, 1974 (I:9+ R:5). A group of myths telling the exploits of Aphrodite and Demeter.

———. *The Warrior Goddess: Athena*. Illustrated by Don Bolognese. Viking, 1972 (I:9+ R:6). Exploits of the goddess Athena, Zeus's daughter.

Kingsley, Charles. *The Heroes*. Mayflower, 1980 (I:8+ R:6). Tales of Greek heroes.

McDermott, Gerald. *Daughter of Earth: A Roman Myth*. Delacorte, 1984 (I:8–12). A highly illustrated version of Pluto's kidnapping of Proserpina.

———. *Sun Flight*. Four Winds, 1980 (I:all R:6). Daedalus the master craftsperson and his son construct wings in an attempt to escape from Crete.

Richardson, I. M. *Demeter and Persephone, The Seasons of Time*. Illustrated by Robert Baxter. Troll, 1983 (I:9 R:6). The Greek myth about Hades, Persephone, and Demeter.

———. *The Adventures of Hercules*. Illustrated by Robert Baxter, Troll, 1983 (I:9 R:6). The Roman hero performs twelve labors.

———. *Prometheus and the Story of Fire*. Illustrated by Robert Baxter, Troll, 1983 (I:9 R:6). Greek myth tells how Prometheus gave mortals fire.

Serraillier, Ian. *A Fall from the Sky*. Illustrated by William Stobbs. Walck, 1966 (I:10+ R:6). Daedalus is punished by the loss of his son.

———. *The Way of Danger: The Story of Theseus*. Illustrated by William Stobbs. Walck, 1963 (I:10+ R:5). The son of the king of Athens kills the Minotaur and rescues Theseus from the underworld.

Silverthorne, Elizabeth. *I, Heracles*. Abingdon, 1978 (I:8–12 R:5). The hero tells of his twelve labors.

Norse Myths and Epics

Colum, Padraic. *The Children of Odin*. Illustrated by Willy Pogany. Macmillan, 1920, reissued in 1984 (I:9+ R:6). Thirty-five tales.

Coolidge, Olivia E. *Legends of the North*. Illustrated by Edouard Sandoz. Houghton Mifflin, 1951 (I:9–14 R:6). The northern legends and the tales from the sagas.

Crossley-Holland, Kevin, Retold By. *Beowulf*. Illustrated by Charles Keeping. Oxford, 1982 (I:9+ R:4). A highly illustrated narrative version of the epic.

———, Ed. *The Faber Book of Northern Legends*. Illustrated by Alan Howard. Faber & Faber, 1983 (I:9+ R:6). A collection of Norse myths, Germanic heroic legends, and Icelandic sagas.

D'Aulaire, Ingri, and D'Aulaire, Edgar Parin. *Norse Gods and Giants*. Doubleday, 1967 (I:8–12 R:6). A collection of Norse tales, including explanations about creation, tales of Thor, Odin, and Loki.

Nye, Robert. *Beowulf*. Illustrated by Alan E. Cober. Wang, 1968 (I:9+ R:5). Beowulf overcomes the monster Grendel and other evils by using both strength and cunning.

LEGENDS

Bawden, Nina. *William Tell*. Illustrated by Pascale Allamand. Lothrop, Lee & Shepard, 1981 (I:6–9 R:5). Tale of the fourteenth-century Swiss patriot who inspired his people to fight for their freedom.

Brown, Marcia. *Backbone of the King: Story of Pakáa and His Son Ku*. University of Hawaii Press, 1966 (I:10+ R:5). A boy helps his father regain his noble position.

Haley, Gail E. *The Green Man*. Scribner's, 1980 (I:7–10 R:6). Paintings resembling tapestries accompany the legend about a man who lived in the woods and cared for the animals.

Hastings, Selina. *Sir Gawain and the Green Knight*. Illustrated by Juan Wijngaard. Lothrop, Lee & Shepard, 1981 (I:9–12 R:4). One of King Arthur's knights is challenged by a giant adversary.

———. *Sir Gawain and the Loathly Lady*. Illustrated by Juan Winjngaard. Lothrop, 1985 (I:10+ R:6). An elaborately illustrated version of one of the Arthurian tales.

Hodges, Margaret, Adapted By. *Saint George and the Dragon*. Illustrated by Trina Schart Hyman. Little, Brown, 1984 (I:all R:7). An English legend adapted from Edmund Spenser's *Faerie Queene*.

Miles, Bernard. *Robin Hood: His Life and Legend*. Illustrated by Victor G. Ambrus. Hamlyn, 1979 (I:8–12 R:7). A highly illustrated version of the English legend.

Pyle, Howard. *The Merry Adventures of Robin Hood*. 1883. Reprint. Scribner's, 1946 (I:10–14 R:8). The original, longer version of Robin Hood's adventures.

———. *Some Merry Adventures of Robin Hood*. Scribner's, 1954 (I:8–12 R:7). Twelve stories selected from the original version of Robin Hood.

———. *The Story of the Champions of the Round Table*. Scribner's, 1905, reissued (I:12+ R:8). Contains four books including "Story of Lancelot" and "Book of Sir Tristram."

———. *The Story of King Arthur and His Knights*. Scribner's, 1903, reissued (I:12+ R:8). A reissue of the classic.

———. *The Story of King Arthur and His Knights*. Scribner's, 1933 (I:12+ R:8). The story of how Arthur becomes king of England, establishes the Round Table, and performs heroic deeds.

Riordan, James. *Tales of King Arthur*. Illustrated by Victor G. Ambrus. Rand McNally, 1982 (I:9–12 R:6). New illustrations for a classic legend about the English hero.

Robbins, Ruth. *Taliesin and King Arthur*. Parnassus, 1970 (I:8–14 R:6). A Welsh poet sings of his own past and wins the honor of being greatest bard of all.

Seredy, Kate. *The White Stag*. Viking, 1937, 1965 (I:10–14 R:7). Story of the Hun Magyar migration into what became Hungary.

Sutcliff, Rosemary. *The Light Beyond the Forest*. Dutton, 1981 (I:10+ R:7). The quest for the Holy Grail.

———. *The Road to Camlann: The Death of King Arthur*. Illustrated by Shirley Felts. Dutton, 1982 (I:10+ R:7). Mordred attempts to destroy the kingdom by exposing Queen Guinevere and Sir Lancelot.

———. *The Sword and the Circle: King Arthur and the Knights of the Round Table*. Dutton, 1981 (I:10+ R:7). Includes thirteen stories associated with King Arthur.

7
Modern Fantasy

☐
TIME, SPACE, AND PLACE
☐
INVOLVING CHILDREN IN MODERN
FANTASY

Time, Space, and Place

☐
EVALUATING MODERN FANTASY

☐
BRIDGES BETWEEN TRADITIONAL AND MODERN FANTASY

☐
ARTICULATE ANIMALS

☐
TOYS

☐
PREPOSTEROUS CHARACTERS AND SITUATIONS

☐
STRANGE AND CURIOUS WORLDS

☐
LITTLE PEOPLE

☐
SPIRITS FRIENDLY AND FRIGHTENING

☐
TIME WARPS

☐
SCIENCE FICTION

In the time of swords and periwigs and full-skirted coats with flowered lappets—when gentlemen wore ruffles, and gold-laced waistcoats of paduasoy and taffeta—there lived a tailor in Gloucester.

With these rhythmical words from *The Tailor of Gloucester* (p. 11), one of the most popular authors of modern fantasy takes her readers into a time and a setting where the impossible becomes convincingly possible. When children escape into Beatrix Potter's world, they enter the intriguing sphere of fantasy.

Authors create modern fantasy by altering one or more characteristics of our world of everyday reality. They may create entirely new worlds, as exemplified by J. R. R. Tolkien's "Middle Earth" in *The Hobbit*, or they may give their characters extraordinary experiences in the real world, as Margaret J. Anderson does in *In the Keep of Time*. Realistic characters may go down a rabbit hole and enter another domain, as in Lewis Carroll's *Alice's Adventures in Wonderland*, or nonrealistic characters, such as Mary Norton's little people in *The Borrowers*, may exist in an otherwise realistic setting. In one way or another, however, an author of fantasy breaks through the familiar web of the actual and permits the reader to enter imaginative realms of possibility. More than one fourth of the sixty-three books listed by the Children's Literature Association in *Touchstones: A List of Distinguished Children's Books* (4) are modern fantasy.

This chapter discusses various types of modern fantasy for children, stressing the ways in which modern authors of fantasy literature follow in the footsteps of the anonymous storytellers who created and transmitted the traditional fantasies of oral literature. It suggests criteria for evaluating modern fantasy and recommends numerous outstanding fantasy stories that children enjoy.

EVALUATING MODERN FANTASY

Like all authors of fiction, authors of high-quality modern fantasy use basic literary elements to create stories that are interesting, engrossing, and believable to the reader. Adults evaluating modern fantasy for children should use the criteria recommended in chapter three, while considering the special uses of literary elements the fantasy genre requires.

Suspending Disbelief: Point of View

"If fantasy is to be successful," says Rebecca J. Lukens (12), "we must willingly suspend disbelief. If the story's characters, conflict, and theme seem believable to us, we find it plausible and even natural to know the thoughts and feelings of animal characters or tiny people. In fact, the story may be so good that we wish it were true. . . .This persuasion that the writer wishes to bring about—persuasion that 'what if' is really 'it's true'—is most successful when the writer is consistent about point of view" (p. 108).

The point of view of a story is determined by the author's choice of the person telling it. A story could be told quite differently from the perspective of a child, a mother, a wicked witch, an animal or supernatural beast, or an objective observer. Authors of fantasy must decide which point of view would best facilitate a believable telling of a story, then sustain that point of view consistently in order to persuade the reader to keep suspending disbelief in the fantastic elements of the story.

The Borrowers, by Mary Norton, seems believable because most of this story about "little people" is told from the viewpoint of Arrietty, who is only six inches tall. The little people's family sitting room seems authentic because the reader sees through Arrietty's eyes, the postage-stamp-sized portraits on the walls, a work of art created by a pillbox supporting a chess piece, and a couch made from a human's padded trinket box. Even the reaction to a miniature book that is Arrietty's diary is dealt with through the physical capabilities of a miniature person: "Arrietty braced her muscles and heaved the book off her knees, and stood upright on the floor" (p. 20). The reader is ready to believe the story because the author describes sights, feelings, and physical reactions as if a six-inch-tall person were actually living through the experience. In *The Tale of Peter Rabbit*, Beatrix Potter, creates believable situations (17) by telling the story from both Peter Rabbit's point of view and the first-person point of view of the storyteller, who occasionally interjects comments such as "I am sorry to say that Peter was not very well during the evening." In this case, the authoritative, realistic voice of the storyteller reassures the reader that the fantastic events being described are normal and understandable.

Perry Nodelman (15) emphasizes the need for an author to consider both the storyteller and the implied audience when creating a credible fantasy. "Only by ignoring the fact that it is fantastic," says Nodelman, "by pretending to be a true story about a real world shared by characters in the story, the storyteller, and the people who hear the story, can a fantasy establish its credibility and work its magic on those who actually hear it" (p. 16).

Suspending Disbelief: Characterization

Of course the character from whose point of view the story is told must be believable also, for the reader to suspend disbelief. Merely giving a character unusual powers or placing a character in a fanciful world does not create a believable character. Whether an author humanizes animals and inaminate objects, gives supernatural beings human traits, or places realistic human characters into fantastic situations, the characters in a fantasy story must be both internally coherent and accessible to the reader.

Language is one way that authors of fantasy can make characters believable. In *The Hobbit* and *The Lord of the Rings*, for example, J.R.R. Tolkien creates distinct languages for different groups of characters. Ruth Noel (14), in her evaluation of Tolkien's use of language, concludes that the musical flow of Elvish words and names implies that the Elves are noble people who love beauty and music. In contrast, the guttural Dwarfish, which sounds less familiar to English-speaking readers, indicates that the Dwarfs themselves are different from humans and Elves. Likewise, the croaked curses of the Orcs establish them as a coarse, cruel, unimaginative people, and the prolonged chants of the Ents demonstrate their peaceful life in the forest.

Characters may also seem believable when they are placed in a realistic context before they enter the world of fantasy. In "The Chronicles of Narnia," C.S. Lewis develops normal human characters who visit a realistic English home and enter into childhood games familiar to most children. When these realistic characters confront the fantastic and believe it, the reader believes it too. Likewise, Margaret Anderson's characters in *In the Keep of Time* have a strong foundation in reality before they enter their time warp fantasies, encouraging readers' belief.

When the author develops a logical framework, and develops characters' actions that are consistent within this framework, there is an internal consistency within the story. This consistency is important in characterization, as it is in point of view. If, for example, animals supposedly live and behave like animals, they should *consistently* do so, unless the author has carefully developed when they change, why they change, and how they change. When readers are able to believe in the characters, they also suspend disbelief in the characters' fantastic experiences.

Creating a World: Setting

The magical settings of traditional tales let children know that anything will be possible in the stories that take place in such environments. Writers of modern fantasy may also create totally new and magical worlds in which unusual circumstances are believable, or they may combine reality and fantasy as characters or stories go back and forth between two worlds. In either case, if the story is to be credible, the author must develop the setting so completely that readers can see, hear, and feel it.

The settings for Mary Norton's "Borrowers" books, described through the eyes of little people, are an integral part of each story. The inside of a cottage drain becomes both an escape route and an antagonist in *The Borrowers Afloat*. Readers experience a new world as they vicariously join the Borrowers inside the drain: "There were other openings as they went along, drains that branched into darkness and ran away uphill. Where these joined the main drain a curious collection of flotsam and jetsam piled up over which they had to drag the soap lid . . . the air from that point onwards, smelled far less strongly of tea leaves" (p. 105). The setting in the drain changes from a fairly calm escape route to one filled with drumming noises and fright as a bath drain opens. Norton now describes a setting that becomes the antagonist: "A millrace of hot scented water swilled through her clothes, piling against her at one moment, falling away the next. Sometimes it bounced above her shoulders, drenching her face and hair; at others it swirled steadily about her waist and tugged at her legs and feet" (p. 110). Norton provides so much detail in her description of this setting that readers can see the contents of the inside of the drain as

if they too were only six inches tall, can smell the soap and tea leaves deposited in the drain, and can hear the changing sounds of water echoing through the drainage system or gushing down in thundering torrents.

Other authors must create convincing new worlds as characters go from realistic to fantasy settings. Alice, in *Alice's Adventures in Wonderland*, by Lewis Caroll, begins her adventures on a realistically peaceful river bank in nineteenth-century England, then travels down a rabbit hole into a unique world quite different from her normal one, which Carroll describes in great detail from her viewpoint. Twelve-year-old Rose, in Janet Lunn's *The Root Cellar*, goes down into a root

Detailed descriptions of the same setting in two different centuries provide an authentic background to this story. (Illustration by Ruth Sanderson from *The Root Cellar*, by Janet Lunn. Copyright © 1981 Charles Scribner's Sons. Reprinted with the permission of Charles Scribner's Sons.)

cellar on an old dilapidated farm, in twentieth-century Canada. When she leaves the root cellar, she enters a nineteenth-century world in which the farm is once again prosperous. The people in that earlier time are engrossed by the approaching American Civil War. Believable descriptions of the same setting in two different centuries are important to the story. Lunn develops an authentic Civil War setting by describing the sights, sounds, feelings, and concerns that the main character experiences as she travels throughout the northeastern United States to find a boy who had not returned from the war. Authors whose characters travel in time warps must create believable, authentic settings for two time periods. These historical settings are integral parts of books such as Lunn's *The Root Cellar.*

Universality: Themes

Memorable modern fantasies develop themes related to universal values, desires, struggles, and emotions. Ned Hedges (9) concluded that classic fantasies for children tend to affirm specific human values and condemn specific human weaknesses.

The constant battle between good and evil, the need for faith and perseverance in the face of obstacles, the importance of personal and social responsibility, and the power of love and friendship are important themes in works of modern fantasy ranging from George MacDonald's Victorian story *At the Back of the North Wind* to Madeleine L'Engle's contemporary books of science fiction. Children easily identify with such themes, especially when an author develops them within the framework of consistently believable setting, characterization, and point of view.

Criteria for Selecting Modern Fantasy

Adults should consider the following questions when selecting modern fantasy to share with children:

1 Does the author encourage the reader to suspend disbelief by developing a point of view that is consistent in every detail, including sights, feelings, and physical reactions?
2 If the author develops several time periods, are the settings authentic and an integral part of the story?
3 Does the author pay careful attention to the details in the setting? Do these details reflect the story's point of view?
4 Does the author use an appropriate language, or create a believable language, consistent with characterization in the story?
5 How does the author's use of characterization allow children to suspend disbelief? Do characters begin in a real world before they travel to the world of fantasy? Does a believable character accept a fanciful world, characters, or happenings? Is every action consistent with the framework developed by the author?
6 Is the theme worthwhile for children?

Many books of modern fantasy admirably satisfy these criteria and provide great enjoyment to children and adults alike.

BRIDGES BETWEEN TRADITIONAL AND MODERN FANTASY

In many ways, modern fantasy stories are direct descendants of the folktales, fables, myths, and legends of the oral tradition. Tales about talking animals, wise and foolish humans, supernatural beings, heroic adventurers, and magical realms are as popular with children and adults today as they were hundreds of years ago. Many authors of modern fantasy discussed in this chapter have drawn upon themes, motifs, settings, and characterizations common in traditional literature. Of course in the distant past people believed that the content of some fairy tales, myths, and legends had a basis in fact, while most readers of modern fantasy must willingly suspend their disbelief in extraordinary beings and events. Still, as writers hope to entice their readers into out-of-the-ordinary experiences, authors of modern fantasy play a role similar to that of storytellers of old who enchanted live audiences with tales that had been orally transmitted over generations.

The "bridges" between traditional fantasy and modern fantasy are evident in many contemporary tales of wonder, but they are especially strong in literary folktales, allegories, and tales about mythical quests and conflicts.

Literary Folktales

Some authors of fantasy in the past hundred years or so have deliberately attempted to replicate the "Once upon a time" of traditional folktales, with their dark forests, castles, princesses and princes, humble people of noble worth, and "happily ever afters." The traditional theme of goodness rewarded and evil punished is common in literary folktales, as are motifs involving magic. Dorothy De Wit (6) compares, for example, the magic of smallness in the traditional tale "Tom Thumb" with that in Hans Christian Andersen's literary folktale "Thumbelina" and the magic sleep in the folktale "Snow White and the Seven Dwarfs" with that in Washington Irving's *Rip Van Winkle*.

Hans Christian Andersen. Charles Perrault is usually credited with publishing the first children's book of fairy tales, but Hans Christian Andersen is credited with writing, a century later, the first fairy tale for children. While Perrault wrote down stories from the oral tradition, Andersen created new stories for theater audiences and readers. Zena Sutherland, Dianne L. Monson, and

Now one day the old lady fell ill, and it was said she was near death. She needed care and nursing all the time, and there was no one more closely related to her than Karen. But there was a great ball in the town, and Karen had been invited. She looked at the old lady, who was sure to die in any case, she looked at the red shoes, and she thought it would be no sin. So she put the red shoes on, and there was no harm in that – but then she went to the ball and began to dance, as she ought not to have done.

Characteristics of traditional tales are found in this story about a girl who is punished for her pride. (From *The Red Shoes*, by Hans Christian Andersen. Illustrated by Chihiro Iwasaki. Illustrations copyright © 1983 by Chihiro Iwasaki. By permission of Picture Book Studio USA.)

May Hill Arbuthnot (18) point out that although Andersen's first stories for children were "elaborations of familiar folk and fairy tales, . . . he soon began to allow his imagination full rein in the invention of plot, the shaping of character, and the illumination of human condition. These later creations, solely from Andersen's fertile imagination, are called literary fairy tales, to distinguish them from the fairy tales of unknown origin, those created by common folk. Andersen's work served as inspiration for other writers" (p. 215).

Andersen's "The Wild Swans" is a literary fairy tale quite similar to the Grimms' traditional tale "The Six Swans." Both stories involve enchantment by an evil stepmother and the courage and endurance of a young girl who is willing to suffer in order to free her brothers.

Experts in children's literature believe that some of Andersen's other literary fairy tales are based on his own life. For example, Andersen's unpleasant experiences in school, where the teacher poked fun at a poor boy's lack of knowledge, large size, and looks, may have inspired his story "The Ugly Duckling." Lorinda Bryan Cauley's illustrations for a book-length version of this story show the transformation of the Ugly Duckling into the most beautiful swan in the garden lake. Cauley's realistic and humorous pictures portray the duckling's agony in the barnyard, where every animal seems to focus contempt upon him. Children can follow, in pictures and text, the sorrow felt by the duckling and then his realization that he is not something to be pitied. They can observe his head emerging from under his wing, not in conceit, but in wonder, as he senses his transformation.

Nancy Ekholm Burkert has beautifully illustrated two of Andersen's stories that reflect the beauty of natural life versus the heartbreak associated with longing for mechanical perfection or metallic glitter. *The Nightingale* tells of a Chinese emperor who turned from the voice of a faithful nightingale to a jeweled, mechanical bird. He learns, however, that only the real, unjeweled bird's song can bring comfort and truth. *The Fir Tree* is the story of a little fir tree who learns only after he is taken from the forest the significance of what he has lost.

Illustrator Susan Jeffers and author Amy Ehrlich have combined their talents to create three beautiful versions of Andersen's tales. Jeffers's finely detailed drawings suggest a fantasy setting

ISSUE

Does the Work of Hans Christian Andersen Merit the Popularity and Acclaim It Has Received?

CRITICS DISAGREE about the literary merit of the 158 fairy tales written by Hans Christian Andersen and translated into 82 languages. Speaking from a favorable viewpoint, Alan Moray Williams describes the tales as combining "the freshness of vision and the innocence of childhood with the gentle irony and knowledge of human psychology that only hard experience can produce. They are racy with the homely speech of the Danish common people and warm with the beauty of the countryside" (1, p. 236). While Williams does not believe that all of the tales are equally good, he concludes that "most are little masterpieces" (p. 237).

In contrast, Roger Sale finds little literary merit in the majority of Andersen's tales. Sale describes Andersen's work in these terms: "He aims satiric shafts, he points his morals and adorns his tales. Of all the major reputations among authors of children's literature, Andersen's is much the hardest to understand or justify . . . . What is wrong with his work is, almost without exception, what is wrong with all inferior children's literature" (2, p. 64). Sale is especially critical of "The Little Mermaid" and "Thumbelina," which he considers inferior because he believes that Andersen was trying to justify his own personal feelings through the actions of the characters. Sale prefers Andersen's more impersonal stories, such as "The Snow Queen."

The reader and listener must decide whether Andersen's tales are magical gems that children never quite forget or are inferior products of a writer's personal war with the world around him, in which the writer uses his unhappiness as an exploitable resource.

[1]Williams, Alan Moray. "Hans Christian Andersen." In *Only Connect: Writings on Children's Literature*, ed. Sheila Egoff, G. T. Stubbs, and L. F. Ashley. New York: Oxford University Press, 1980.

[2]Sale, Roger. *Fairy Tales and After: From Snow White to E. B. White*. Cambridge, Mass.: Harvard University Press, 1978.

in *Thumbelina* and *The Wild Swans*. Her illustrations for and Amy Ehrlich's retelling of *The Snow Queen* may be contrasted with another version of the same tale retold by Naomi Lewis and illustrated by Errol LeCain.

Michael Hague, Kay Nielson, and Edward Ardizzone are among those who have illustrated collections of Andersen's tales for adults to read aloud to children or for children to read independently. *Michael Hague's Favorite Hans Christian Andersen Fairy Tales* includes nine stories written in larger print. More extensive collections include *Ardizzone's Hans Andersen* and *Hans Andersen: His Classic Fairy Tales*, illustrated by Michael Foreman.

Jane Yolen. Jane Yolen has used the format of the classic folktale to weave original stories about the power of kindness, the conquest of fear, and the madness of pride. Her settings, language, and characters are similar to those in the best traditional tales. The five tales in *The Girl Who Cried Flowers* take place in magical realms such as "on the far side of yesterday," "far to the North, where the world is lighted only by the softly flickering snow," and ancient Greece. The main characters also have a folktale quality. "Silent Bianca," for example, is a strange and beautiful girl with a face as pale as snow and hair as white as a moonbeam; she is not only beautiful, but also wise. She does not speak as others do, however; her sentences must be plucked out of the air and her fragile words warmed by the hearth fire before they can be heard. A king who seeks a wife both beautiful and wise hears of Bianca and sends his unhappy counselors, who want a girl of noble birth, to bring her to his castle. The king creates an obstacle to measure the wisdom of both Silent Bianca and his arguing counselors. Silent Bianca proves her wisdom, tricks the king's guards, and marries the king. They live happily ever after, with the king spending many hours by the hearthstone listening to the counsel of his wise and loving queen.

Among Yolen's other books of short stories written to resemble traditional tales is *The Dream Weaver* in which a blind gypsy storyteller weaves gossamer tales to fit a particular character. As each person approaches the Dream Weaver, she takes the thread from her basket, strings the warp, and spins her tale.

Yolen uses the noble quest theme and the legendary characters of traditional literature to create a humorous story in *The Acorn Quest*. This gentle spoof on King Arthur and the Knights of the Round Table has animal characters who somewhat resemble their traditional human counterparts: King Earthor, Sir Runsalot, and Wizard Squirrelin. The characters frequently quarrel and have difficulty focusing on the problem of probable famine. The plot develops around their quest for a golden acorn at the edge of the world. On the journey they confront a traditional enemy, a dragon, and the human enemy, greed.

Religious and Ethical Allegory

Religious themes provide a strong link between traditional and modern fantasy. According to Bruno Bettelheim (2), "Most fairy tales originated in periods when religion was a most important part of life; thus, they deal, directly or by inference, with religious themes" (p. 13). Many traditional tales from around the world reflect the religions that were prominent in their times and places of origin: Islam, Buddhism, Judaism, to name but a few. Some European folktales, such as the German "Our Lady's Child," directly refer to the Roman Catholic beliefs of the Middle Ages. In this tale recorded by the Brothers Grimm, a young girl becomes mute when she disobeys the Virgin Mary and then lies about what she has

done. After suffering severe ordeals, she desires only to confess her sin, and the Virgin Mary rewards her confession by renewing her power of speech and granting her happiness. Other European folktales and legends develop less explicit religious themes by using the prolonged metaphors of allegory: characters representing "goodness" or "wisdom" must confront and overcome characters representing "badness" or "foolishness."

In our more secular age, as Bettelheim (2) points out, "these religious themes no longer arouse universal and personally meaningful associations" in the majority of people, as they once did; but modern authors of fantasy still create religious and ethical allegories. Some authors actually replicate the heroic humans, witches, personified animals, and magical settings of traditional literature. Others use characters and settings consistent with their own times. Readers may respond to these stories on different levels, since they are both religious allegories and tales of enchantment and high adventure.

George MacDonald. The strongly moralistic atmosphere of Victorian England and training as a Congregational minister influenced a writer who used allegorical fantasy to portray and condemn the flaws in his society. George MacDonald's *At the Back of the North Wind*, first published in 1871 and reissued in 1966, is the story of Diamond, the son of a poor coach driver, who lives two lives: the harsh existence of impoverished working-class Londoners; and a dreamlike existence in which he travels with the North Wind, who takes him to a land of perpetual flowers and gentle breezes, where no one is cold or sick or hungry.

MacDonald uses the North Wind, a beautiful woman with long flowing hair, to express much of his own philosophy. "Good people see good things; bad people, bad things" (p. 37), she tells Diamond, whom MacDonald describes as a good boy, "God's baby." When Diamond questions her reality, she says, "I think . . . that if I were only a dream, you would not have been able to love me so. You love me when you are not with me, don't you?" (p. 363). Diamond clings to the back of the North Wind, with her streaming hair enfolding him, and they fly to a sweet land where it is always May. Diamond returns home from that visit but the end of the story further suggests the

The flowing lines of the North Wind seem to enfold little Diamond. (Illustration by E. H. Shepard from *At the Back of the North Wind*, by George MacDonald. Children's Illustrated Classics series. Reprinted with permission of J M Dent & Sons, Ltd.)

allegorical implications of MacDonald's tale of a poor boy's escape from cruel realities:

I walked up the winding stair, and entered his room. A lovely figure, as white and almost as clear as alabaster, was lying on the bed. I saw at once how it was. They thought he was dead. I knew that he had gone to the back of the North Wind. (p. 378)

C. S. Lewis. A professor of medieval and renaissance literature at Cambridge University, C. S. Lewis used his interest in theology and his knowledge about medieval allegory, classical legend, and Norse mythology to create a highly acclaimed and popular fantasy saga. "The Chronicles of Narnia" (winner of the Carnegie Medal for best children's books), beginning with *The Lion, the Witch and the Wardrobe* and ending seven

books later with *The Last Battle*, develop a marvelous adventure story interwoven with Christian allegory. Children can enjoy the series for its high drama alone, or they can read it for its allegorical significance.

While *The Lion, the Witch and the Wardrobe* is the first book in the series, *The Magician's Nephew* informs readers how the saga began and how the passage between the magical world of Narnia and Earth was made possible. The tree grown from the magical Narnia apple has blown over and its wood used to build a large wardrobe. This is the same wardrobe through which the daughters of Eve and the sons of Adam (*The Lion, the Witch and the Wardrobe*) enter into the kingdom, meet the wicked White Witch, and help the great lord-lion Aslan defeat the powers of evil. In *The Lion, the Witch and the Wardrobe*, Aslan gives his life to save Edmund, who has betrayed them all. Aslan, however, rises from the dead and tells the startled, bereaved children that the deeper magic before the dawn of time has won. "It means that though the witch knew the Deep Magic, there is a magic deeper still which she did not know. Her knowledge goes back only to the dawn of Time. But if she could have looked a little further back, into the stillness and the darkness before Time dawned, she would have read there a different incantation. She would have known that when a willing victim who has committed no treachery was killed in a traitor's stead, the Table would crack and Death itself would start working backward" (pp. 132–33). From Aslan, the children learn that after they have once been crowned, they will remain kings and queens of Narnia forever.

After this initial adventure, the remaining books in the chronicle tell other fantastic tales of adventure and overcoming evil. The final Christian allegory is contained in the last book of the series, *The Last Battle*. Here the children are reunited with Aslan after their death on earth and discover "for them it was only the beginning of the real story. All their life in this world and all their adventures in Narnia had only been the cover and the title page: now at last they were beginning Chapter One of the Great Story which no one on earth has read: in which every chapter is better than the one before."

The stories in the "Chronicles of Narnia" are filled with adventures and characters that appeal to children. There are magical spells, centaurs, dwarfs, unicorns, ogres, witches, and minotaurs. Throughout the stories, characters strive for high ideals and recognize the importance of faith.

Mythical Quests and Conflicts

Quests for lost or stolen objects of power, descents into darkness to overcome evil, and settings where lightning splinters the world and sets the stage for the battle between two opposing forces are found both in traditional myths and legends and in modern fantasy. Some authors of modern fantasy borrow magical settings and characters from traditional tales of heroism, while others create new worlds of enchantment in which the age-old battle between the powers of good and the powers of evil continues. These modern stories may contain some threads of the allegory that characterized many traditional tales—such as the English legends about King Arthur, his Knights of the Round Table, and the quest for the Holy Grail. Most modern fantasies about mythical quests and conflicts, however, emphasize high adventure, as their characters ac-

quire new knowledge and learn honorable uses of personal power.

J. R. R. Tolkien. Destiny, supernatural immortals, evil dragons, and rings of power are all found in J. R. R. Tolkien's popular stories. His writings, according to Ruth S. Noel (14), "form a continuation of the mythic tradition into modern literature . . . . In no other literary work has such careful balance of mythic tradition and individual imagination been maintained" (pp. 6–7). This balance between myth and imagination is not accidental in Tolkien's writing. Tolkien studied mythology for most of his life; he was a linguistic scholar and professor of Anglo-Saxon literature at Oxford University. His chief interest was the literary and linguistic tradition of the English West Midlands, especially as revealed in *Beowulf* and *Sir Gawain and the Green Knight.* Tolkien respected the quality in myths that allows evil to be unexpectedly averted and great good to succeed. He masterfully develops this battle between good and evil in *The Hobbit* and in *The Lord of the Rings,* its more complex sequel.

ISSUE

❖❖❖❖

Children's Reading Choices: *The Hobbit* Versus *Halloween II*

THE RESULTS OF A NAtional survey of children's reading choices published in *Booklist*[1] present librarians, teachers, and parents with concerns, thought-provoking messages, some reasons for satisfaction, and several reasons for dissatisfaction. Of the fifty most popular titles, eleven are modern fantasy, thirty-one are realistic fiction, two are poetry, three are picture storybooks, two are historical fiction, and one is traditional literature. The top ten books include two selections from modern fantasy: E. B. White's *Charlotte's Web* and Roald Dahl's *Charlie and the Chocolate Factory.* Other choices in the top fifty discussed in this chapter include J.R.R. Tolkien's *The Hobbit,* Madeleine L'Engle's *A Wrinkle in Time,* Beverly Cleary's *The Mouse and the Motorcycle,* C. S. Lewis's *The Lion, the Witch, and the Wardrobe,* Roald Dahl's *James and the Giant Peach,* among others.

Although these books are found on almost all recommended lists, comments made by librarians and teachers who took part in the survey should cause us to reflect upon children's choices, the quality of the library and classroom literature program, and the need to lead children into high-quality literature. The author of the article, Barbara Elleman, compares this Chosen by Children list with the 1982 juvenile bestseller list issued by Dalton Bookstores. Only three titles appeared on both lists. The Dalton list included Disney and Sesame Street spin-offs, Straw-

According to Tolkien (19), these stories were at first a philological game in which he invented languages: "The stories were made rather to provide a world for the languages than the reverse. I should have preferred to write in 'Elvish'" (p. 242). This creation of languages with their own alphabets and rules helps make Tolkien's characters believable.

Careful attention to detail and vivid descriptions of setting in Middle Earth also add credibility to Tolkien's stories. For example, he introduces the reluctant hobbit, Bilbo Baggins, to the challenge and promise of joining a quest to regain the dwarfs' treasures by using a dwarfs' chant:

> Far over the misty mountains cold
> To dungeons deep and caverns old
> We must away ere break of day
> To find our long-forgotten gold. (p. 37)

As Bilbo, the wizard Gandalf, and the twelve dwarfs proceed over the mountains toward the lair of the evil dragon Smaug, Tolkien describes a place where lightning splinters the peaks and rocks shiver. When Bilbo descends into the mountain dungeons to confront Smaug, Tolkien's setting befits the climax of a heroic quest: red light, wisps of vapor, and rumbling noises gradually replace the subterranean darkness and quiet. Ahead, in the bottom-most cellar, lies a huge red-golden dragon surrounded by precious gold and jewels.

As in traditional tales, the quest is successful, the dragon is slain, and the goblins are overthrown. The hero retains his decency, his honor, and his pledge always to help his friends.

The ring found during the hobbit's quest becomes the basis of the plot in the "Ring" trilogy: *The Lord of the Rings*, *Fellowship of the Ring*, and *The Return of the King*. In his foreword to *Fellowship of the Ring*, Tolkien says that he had no intention of writing a story with an inner meaning or message. The story is not meant to be allegorical. "As the story grew it put down roots (into the past) and threw out unexpected branches; but its main theme was settled from the outset by the inevitable choice of the Ring as the link between it and The Hobbit" (19, p. 6). Many junior-high

---

berry Shortcake, and Smurfs. Elleman concluded that children purchases the Dalton books without the guidance of teachers and librarians.

Consider the following points made in the article and conclusions reached by participants in the survey. Are these points reasons for satisfaction or dissatisfaction with the classroom and library literature program?

1 The authors on the Chosen by Children list are generally respected authors; several have won awards for literary merit.
2 Libraries that promote children's book interests contain authors such as Tolkien and L'Engle; it appears that children can be led to good literature.
3 Children's choices may reflect only what is being read at the time in the classroom and not actual preferences.
4 Many spin-offs from television shows and films such as *King Kong* and "Battlestar Galactica" are favorites with children.
5 Several librarians noted junior-high students' preference for adult horror novels such as *Halloween II*.
6 Popularity does not always mean high-quality literature.
7 Certain categories of literature are missing from the Chosen by Children list, including nonfiction, most classics, and fairy tales (except "Cinderella").

As you consider the implications of each of the above statements, also consider the implications of this comment by one of the adults who took part in the survey:

> This survey dramatized for me the tremendous power a teacher has to raise and broaden tastes and cultural value among her students. Thirty minutes a week in the library can supplement, enrich, and stimulate a good classroom program; it cannot adequately nourish a poor one. Children who are required to read challenging books (yet encouraged to select them according to their own tastes) learn the joys of literature. Those who aren't led (or pushed) through that door may never open it on their own. (p. 508)

[1]Elleman, Barbara. "Chosen By Children." *Booklist* 79 (Dec. 1, 1982): 507–9.

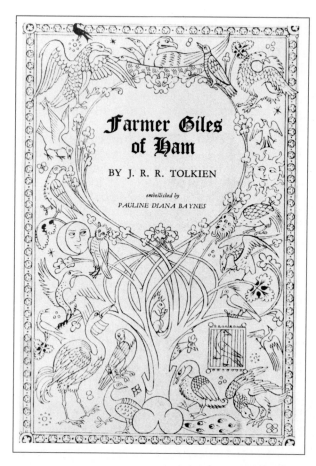

The mythological text and the illustrations are strongly interrelated in J. R. R. Tolkien's books. (From *Farmer Giles of Ham*, by J.R.R. Tolkien. Copyright © 1976 by George Allen & Unwin (Publishers) Ltd. Reprinted by permission of Houghton Mifflin Company.)

and high-school students, college students, and other adults have been brought back into the world of mythology through Tolkien's books.

Lloyd Alexander. The stories that unfold in Lloyd Alexander's mythical land of Prydain reflect Alexander's vivid recollections of Wales, favorite childhood stories, and knowledge of Welsh legends. When Alexander researched the Mabinogion, a collection of traditional Welsh legends, he discovered the characters of Gwydion Son of Don, Arawn Death-Lord of Annuvin, Dallben the enchanter, and Hen Wen the oracular pig. In Alexander's outstanding "Prydain Chronicles" these characters become involved in exciting adventures of good versus evil.

Alexander's books take place in a time when "Fair Folk" lived with humans, a time of enchanters and enchantments, a time before the passages between the world of enchantment and the world of humans were closed. In the first "Prydain Chronicle," *The Book of Three*, Alexander introduces the forces of good and evil and an assistant pig-keeper, Taran, who dreams of discovering his parentage and becoming a hero. (Alexander tells the reader that all people are assistant pig-keepers at heart because their capabilities seldom match their aspirations and they are often unprepared for what is to happen.) The forces of good include the enchanter Dallben, who reads the prophecy written in *The Book of Three*, the Sons of Don and their leader Prince Gwydion, who in ancient times voyaged from the Summer Country to stand as guardians against the evil Annuvin; and the Princess Eilonwy, descendant of enchanters. They are aided by Hen Wen, an oracular pig who can foretell the future by pointing out ancient symbols carved on letter sticks. The forces of evil are led by a warlord who wants to capture Hen Wen because she knows his secret name. This name is powerful because "once you have the courage to look upon evil, seeing it for what it is and naming it by its true nature, it is powerless against you, and you can destroy it" (p. 209).

Throughout his "Prydain" series—*The Black Cauldron*, *The Castle of Llyr*, *Taran Wanderer*, and *The High King*—Alexander develops strong, believable characters with whom upper-elementary and older children can identify, as the world of fantasy becomes relevant to the world of reality. The characters gain credibility through Alexander's history of the people and their long struggle against the forces of evil. Alexander encourages the reader to believe in the tangible objects of power because the characters place so much faith in the legend of the sword, the prophecies written in *The Book of Three*, and the fearsome black cauldron.

Alexander's literary style also strengthens the credibility of the fantasy and enhances plot development and characterization in his other fantasy adventure stories, such as *Westmark*, *The Kestrel*, and *The Beggar Queen*. In *The Beggar Queen*, for example, Alexander carefully builds a foundation for the action that follows; he develops strong person-versus-person, person-versus-self, and person-versus-society conflicts; he uses ghosts from the past to introduce the various con-

A detailed map helps make the
land of Prydain more credible to
the reader. (From *The High King*,
by Lloyd Alexander. Map by Evaline Ness. Copyright © 1968 by
Lloyd Alexander. Copyright © 1968
by Holt, Rinehart and Winston. Reproduced by permission of Holt,
Rinehart and Winston, Publishers.)

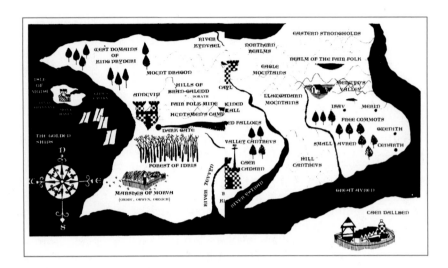

flicts and factions; he describes people's characteristics through animal symbolism; and he concludes each chapter on a point of tension and
excitement with a foreshadowing of the conflict to
come.

Ursula K. LeGuin. Somewhere in the land of fantasy lies Earthsea, an archipelago of imaginary islands where wizards cast their spells and people
live in fear of fire-blowing winged dragons. Responsible wizards attempt to retain a balance between the forces of good and the evil force that
seek dominance.

Ursula LeGuin convinces the reader to suspend
disbelief through her detailed descriptions of
Earthsea, its inhabitants, and the culture of the
islands, permeated with magic. LeGuin's series of
Earthsea books convincingly develops a strong
theme about the responsibilities attached to great
power by tracing the life of Sparrowhawk from
the time he is an apprentice wizard until he is
finally the most powerful wizard in the land.

In the first book in the series, *A Wizard of
Earthsea*, the young boy has powers strong
enough to save his village, but also a pride and
impatience that places him in grave danger. A
master wizard cautions Sparrowhawk about
wanting to learn and use powers of enchantment
he is not yet mature enough to understand:

Have you never thought how danger must surround
power as shadow does light. This sorcery is not a game
we play for pleasure or for praise. Think of this: that
every act of our Art is said and is done either for good,
or for evil. Before you speak or do you must know the
price that is to pay! (p. 35)

Sparrowhawk, renamed Ged, does not understand the warning. This conflict with another apprentice leads to a duel of sorcery skills, in which
Ged calls up a dead spirit and accidentally un-
leashes an evil being onto the world. LeGuin's description of the rent in the darkness, the blazing
brightness, the hideous black shadow, and Ged's
reaction to the beast help convince the reader
that evil really was released. This belief in unleashed evil is important because the remainder
of the book follows Ged as he hunts the shadow-
beast across the islands to the farthest waters of
Earthsea and develops an understanding that he
is reponsible for his own actions.

Older and more experienced, Ged understands
the power of darkness and light in the *Tombs of
Atuan* and *The Farthest Shore*. LeGuin develops a
character who has meaning for people living in
any time or place. Ged must overcome both personal problems and outside conflicts before he
reaches responsible maturity, understanding the
consequences of his actions and the difficulty of
attaining true freedom:

Freedom is a heavy load, a great and strange burden
for the spirit to undertake. It is not easy. It is not a gift
given, but a choice made, and the choice may be a
hard one. The road goes upward towards the light; but
the laden traveler may never reach the end of it."
(*Tombs of Atuan*, p. 157)

Alan Garner. Alan Garner was the most influential writer of fantasy in Great Britain of the 1960s,
according to John Rowe Townsend (20). Garner's
books are full of magic: the old magic of sun,
moon, and blood that survives from crueler

times; the high magic of thoughts and spells that checks the old magic, and that serves as a potent but uncertain weapon against the old evil. Garner's stories transcend time barriers by allowing present-day children to discover objects that contain ancient spells influential in old legends. The ancient masters of good and evil then emerge either to pursue or to safeguard the children.

Garner creates a believable fantasy in *The Weirdstone of Brisingamen* by first placing two realistic characters into a realistic English country setting. Garner achieves credibility through the reactions of the children as they discover the powers in a tangible object, a tear-shaped piece of crystal that has been handed down over many generations. The plot then revolves around this lost "weirdstone" that is sought by both the forces of good and the forces of evil. The children, aided by two dwarfs, set out to return the stone to the good wizard who is its guardian. Along the way, however, they encounter evil characters—a shape-changing witch, giant troll women, and a wolf who chased them through underground tunnels and across the countryside. The final confrontation reveals the power of the weirdstone.

The children meet the characters of legend and fantasy again in *The Moon of Gomrath*. Now they possess the magical "Mark of Fahla" that the evil powers of the underworld want. They are saved, however, by the intervention of the good wizard and his faithful followers.

Robin McKinley. Magical objects are the focus of quests in Robin McKinley's *The Blue Sword* and *The Hero and the Crown*. McKinley makes *The Blue Sword* believable by carefully depicting a realistic colony called Daria and realistic characters—colonial officials of Her Majesty's Government, career army officers—who are unlikely to be influenced by the extraordinary. Fantasy elements enter the story when Harry is kidnapped by the leader of the Hillfolk and taken to the kingdom of Demar. From Harry's point of view, McKinley reveals a people who have the ability to speak in the old tongue, the language of the gods. In *The Hero and the Crown*, which McKinley describes as a "prequel" to *The Blue Sword*, the power of a magical object is revealed through the sword that brings power from its original owner, Lady Aerin, who was the savior of her people. There is a strong feeling of destiny as the heroine sets forth to regain the objects of power and restore the power to her kingdom. As in many tra-

ditional epics, Aerin's quest results in increasingly difficult tests. She proceeds from slaying small dragons to finally overcoming an evil magician. McKinley strongly emphasizes responsibility, as Aerin discovers that, even though the price is high, her destiny and her responsibility to her people require this quest.

Susan Cooper. Students of children's literature may identify the influence of English, Celtic, and Welsh legends and myths in Susan Cooper's series of modern fantasies. Her books about the guardians of Light combatting the forces of Darkness contain references to the legend in which King Arthur does not die but lies resting in a place from which he will arise when the need is greatest. According to Celtic tradition, the words on Arthur's tomb mean "Here lies Arthur, King once and King to be." Richard Cavendish (3) reports that the Welsh version of the legend places Arthur's resting place in a cave in Snowdonia. A similar cave is important in Cooper's *The Grey King*, and Arthur and his knights rise again in *Silver on the Tree* to assist in the final battle against evil. The wizard, Merlin, Arthur's legendary confidant, plays a crucial role throughout Cooper's series. Merlin, introduced as Merriman Lyon, has the legendary magician's ability to suspend the laws of nature and to travel into the past as well as the future. Throughout the series Merriman retains Merlin's role of representing a profound wisdom from an ancient past that leads the powers of good against the powers of evil.

Other legendary objects, places, and occurrences are found throughout the series. For example, the power of a seventh son of a seventh son dominates the characters on heroic quests. Arthur's sword, his ship, and even his dog's name are important in Cooper's books.

Quests for the objects of power form the thread of continuity in Cooper's stories. In *Over Sea, Under Stone* three children visit Cornwall and find an old map disclosing a hidden treasure that could hinder the forces of Darkness. With the help of the good Old Ones, the children find the Grail, but they lose the manuscript that is the key to the chalice's inscriptions.

In *The Dark Is Rising*, the responsibility for continuing the quest falls upon eleven-year-old Will Stanton. While born in twentieth-century England, Will has a special responsibility as the seventh son of a seventh son and the last born of the Old Ones whose powers can be used against the

A quest and a battle between good and evil character-ize Cooper's high fantasy. (Illustration by Joseph A. Smith from *Seaward* by Susan Cooper. [A Margaret K. McElderry Book.] Illustration copyright © 1983 Joseph A. Smith. Reprinted with the permission of Atheneum Publishers, Inc.)

powers of Darkness. Early in his quest, his impatience and ignorance cause him to help the forces of Darkness. He swears he will never again use the power unless he has a reason and knows the consequences. His knowledge increases until he finally understands the magnitude of his powers, and is able to use them successfully in this book and others in the series:

Will realized once more, helplessly, that to be an Old One was to be old before the proper time, for the fear he began to feel now was worse than the blind terror he had known in his attic bed, worse than the fear the Dark had put into him in the great hall. This time, his fear was adult, made of experience and imagination and care for others, and it was the worst of all. (p. 127)

Greenwitch, the third book of the series, continues the quest for the Grail and the missing manuscript. *The Grey King* and *Silver on the Tree* complete the series.

Cooper encourages readers to suspend disbelief in her fantasies by developing a strong foundation in the reality of the twentieth century. When her realistic contemporary characters travel into earlier centuries, her readers follow them willingly into mythical worlds and share their quests for greater knowledge. There is a tie, however, between the past and present. For example, in *The Dark is Rising*, Will goes back into the past to recover the Sign of Fire. When he has fulfilled his quest, there is a great crashing roar, a rumbling, a growling, and he is back in the present, where thunder is creating earsplitting sounds. The action is believable, and the reader feels that the old ways are actually awakening, their powers alive again.

ARTICULATE ANIMALS

Concerned rabbit parents worry about what will happen to their family when new human folks move into the house on the hill, a mongoose saves his young owner from a deadly cobra, and a mole and a water rat spend an idyllic season floating down an enchanting river. Humanized animals who talk like people but still retain some animal qualities are among the most popular modern fantasy characters. Authors such as Beatrix Potter and Kenneth Grahame have been able to create animal characters who display a careful balance between animal and human characteristics. This balance is not accidental; many successful authors in this category of modern fantasy write from close observations of animal life that result in understanding and loving animals.

Young children are drawn to the strong feelings of loyalty the animals express as they help each other out of dangerous predicaments, stay with friends when they might choose other actions, or protect their human owners while risking their own lives. The memorable animal characters, like all memorable characters in literature, show a wide range of recognizable traits. Children often see themselves in the actions of their animal friends.

FLASHBACK

BEATRIX POTTER'S ILLUSTRATIONS FOR THIS 1902 edition of *The Tale of Peter Rabbit* demonstrate her ability to create animal characters with needs and feelings similar to those of young children. Her detailed drawings reflect her knowledge of animals and the English countryside. *The Tale of Peter Rabbit* was the first in a series of books Potter wrote and illustrated. Potter's other well-known books include *The Tailor of Gloucester* (1902), *The Tale of Squirrel Nutkin* (1903), *The Tale of Benjamin Bunny* (1904), and *The Tale of Mrs. Tittlemouse* (1910).

Beatrix Potter. "Once upon a time there were four little Rabbits, and their names were—Flopsy, Mopsy, Cotton-tail, and Peter" (p. 3). Children of all ages can identify this sentence as the beginning of an enjoyable story, *The Tale of Peter Rabbit*. Potter, who wrote so knowledgeably about small animals, spent many holidays in the country observing nature, collecting natural objects, and making detailed drawings. Potter had small pets, including a rabbit, mice, and a hedgehog, who later became very real in her illustrated books for children. As an adult she purchased a farm that offered further stimulation for her stories about articulate animals.

Potter's first book, *The Tale of Peter Rabbit*, began as a letter sent to a sick child. When she later submitted the story to a publisher, it was rejected. She did not let this rejection dissuade her and had the book printed independently. When young readers accepted Peter Rabbit with great enthusiasm, the publisher asked if he might print the book.

Potter's characters may seem real to children because they show many characteristics that children themselves demonstrate. Peter Rabbit, for example, wants to go to the garden so badly that he disobeys his mother. Happiness, found in a vast store of vegetables, changes rapidly to fright as he encounters the enemy, Mr. McGregor. Children can sympathize with his fright as he tries unsuccessfully to flee. They can also respond to a satisfying ending as Peter narrowly escapes and

reaches the security of his mother's love. Children know that such behavior cannot go unpunished. Peter must take a dose of camomile tea to compensate for a stomach ache, while his sisters feast on milk and blackberries.

Potter's illustrations, drawn in careful detail, complement the story and suggest the many moods of the main character. Peter appears secretive as he stealthily approaches and squeezes under the garden gate, ecstatic as he munches carrots, and hopeless as he reaches the door in the wall and discovers that he is too fat to squeeze under it. In this illustration, his ears hang dejectedly, a tear trickles down his cheek, one front paw is clenched in fright against his mouth, and his back paws are huddled together. These illustrated moods, are so realistic that children feel a close relationship with Peter.

The Tale of Peter Rabbit is found in a reissue of the 1902 Warne publication, as well as the 1979 edition of *A Treasury of Peter Rabbit and Other Stories*.

Michael Bond. Paddington Bear is another animal character whose warmth and appeal are related to the author's ability to encourage children to see themselves in the actions of the animal. Unlike Beatrix Potter's Peter Rabbit, who lives in an animal world, Michael Bond's Paddington lives with an English family after they discover the homeless bear in Paddington Station. The family and neighborhood's acceptance of the bear creates a credible and humorous series of stories beginning with *A Bear Called Paddington*. Bond's characterization of Paddington may seem real to children because Paddington displays many childlike characteristics. He gets himself into trouble, and he tries to hide his errors from people who would be disappointed in or disapprove of his actions. He is hard to communicate with when he is in one of his difficult moods, and, like a human child, he is often torn between excitement and perplexity. The excitement of preparing the itinerary for a trip in *Paddington Abroad* is balanced by Paddington's trouble in spelling hard words, his difficulty understanding why the bank does not return the same money he put in his savings account, and his inability to read his prepared map. Children in the early elementary grades greatly enjoy these humorous episodes. (Note how closely Paddington's characteristics correspond to characteristics of young children discussed in chapter one.)

Rudyard Kipling. While the majority of articulate animal stories familiar to Americans occur in the woods and farmlands of Europe and the United States, one series has the jungles of India as a setting. Rudyard Kipling's early life spent in Bombay, India, had a great influence on his later writing. He spent much time in the company of Indian *ayahs* (nurses) who told him the native tales about the jungle animals. His own young children were the first to hear his most famous stories about the man-cub Mowgli and his brothers, Akela the wolf, Baloo the bear, and Bagheera the panther, published in *The Jungle Book* in 1894.

The story "Mowgli's Brothers" is one of Kipling's most popular. Kipling develops animal characters as diverse as the man-eating tiger Shere Khan, who claims the young Mowgli as his own, and Mother Wolf, who demonstrates her maternal instincts as she protects the man-cub and encourages him to join her own cubs. The law of the jungle is a strong element in the story, as the animals sit in council and decide Mowgli's fate. This story has the strong flavor of a traditional tale. The suspense rises until old Baloo the bear finally speaks for the man-cub. As in traditional tales about articulate animals, powerful feelings of loyalty grow as Mowgli saves the life of his old friend Akela, the wolf.

The characters, plot, and language of "Rikki-Tikki-Tavi" make it an excellent choice for oral

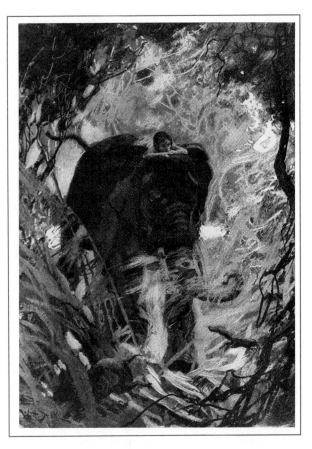

Kipling's young children were the first to hear his stories of articulate animals and a boy raised by the jungle animals. Illustration by W. H. Drake. (From *The Jungle Book* by Rudyard Kipling. Published by Macmillan and Co., 1894. Courtesy of Lilly Library, Indiana University, Bloomington, Indiana.)

storytelling. The wicked cobras Nag and Nagaina live in the garden of a small boy and his parents. They plan a battle against those humans and the heroic mongoose, Rikki-Tikki, a hunter with eyeballs of flame, and the sworn enemy of all snakes. In keeping with the oral tradition, the action develops rapidly as the boy's loyal mongoose kills Nag, and then faces his most deadly peril, a female cobra avenging her mate and protecting her unborn babies. Kipling's language is excellent for the oral recitation. As the tension mounts, Rikki-Tikki asks:

What price for a snake's egg? For a young cobra? For a young king-cobra? For the last—the very last of the brood? The ants are eating all the others down by the melon-bed. (p. 117)

A happy-ever-after ending has Rikki-Tikki defeating his enemy and remaining on guard so there will not be another threat in the garden.

Humorous incidents and language that is most effective when shared orally are characteristics of Kipling's *Just So Stories*. Young children enjoy the language in favorite tales such as "The Elephant's Child," the story of an adventurous young animal who lives near the banks of the "great, gray-green, greasy Limpopo River."

Kenneth Grahame. Like Rudyard Kipling, Kenneth Grahame first told his stories to his own young children. The animals in *The Wind in the Willows*, however, are much farther along the road toward "humanization" than are Mowgli's friends in the jungle (20).

Grahame creates characters who prefer the idyllic life and consider work a bore, who long for wild adventures, who demonstrate human frailties through their actions, and who are loyal to friends. The idyllic life is exemplified in the experiences of Mole and Water-Rat as they explore their river world. Grahame introduces his readers to Mole as the scent of spring is penetrating Mole's dark home with a spirit of longing and discontent. Lured out of his hole, Mole observes the busy animals around him, and muses that the best part of a holiday is not resting but seeing other animals busy at work. Through detailed description, Grahame communicates this perpetual vacationer's delight and carefree joy to the reader:

He thought his happiness was complete when, as he meandered aimlessly along, suddenly he stood by the edge of a full-fed river. Never in his life had he seen a river before—this sleek, sinuous, full-bodied animal, chasing and chuckling, gripping things with a gurgle and leaving them with a laugh, to fling itself on fresh playmates that shook themselves free, and were caught and held again. All was a-shake and a-shiver—glints and gleams and sparks, rustle and swirl, chatter and bubble. The Mole was bewitched, entranced, fascinated. (p. 6)

Grahame creates credibility for the adventures of his most eccentric character, Toad of Toad Hall, by taking him away from the peaceful surroundings of his ancestral home. In the Wide World, where presumably such adventures could happen, he wrecks cars, is imprisoned, and escapes in a washerwoman's clothing basket. While he is gone, the less desirable animals who live in the Wild Wood, the stoats and the weasels, take over his home. When he returns, Toad's friends—brave Badger, gallant Water-Rat, and loyal Mole—help him recapture Toad Hall and tame the Wild Wood. Grahame suggests that a subdued and altered Toad, accompanied by his friends, recaptures his life of contentment along the river, at the edge of the Wild Wood, but far away from the Wide World beyond.

Grahame's writing style, as illustrated by the quote above, creates strong characterization and visual images of the setting. Many children find the text difficult to read, however, so it may be preferable for adults to read this story to children.

Young children may become acquainted with the various characters in this book through picture storybooks that are excerpts from chapters in *The Wind in the Willows*. Beverley Gooding has illustrated *The Open Road* and *Wayfarers All: From the Wind in the Willows*, and Adrienne Adams has illustrated *Wind in the Willows: The River Bank*, all suitable for young readers.

Russell E. Erickson. Students of children's literature may find it interesting to compare the settings, characterizations, and plot developments in Russell E. Erickson's various books about Warton the toad, written for young readers, with those of Kenneth Grahame. When the first book in Erickson's series, *A Toad for Tuesday*, was published, the critic for *Booklist* characterized it as a small-scale *Wind in the Willows*.

First, the settings in the books are similar. Warton lives in a secure environment, under a stump in the deep woods. Outside this environment are places, such as the bog, that are filled with danger, unsavory characters, and possibilities for high adventure, if one wants to take the risk.

Second, Erickson's and Grahame's books develop similar characters, although Erickson's characterizations are less in-depth and complex than Grahame's. Warton the toad is a loyal friend who is willing to leave his environment either to help a friend or to fulfill his curiosity. His brother Morton is a timid and wary creature who prefers his culinary chores and his placid environment. The wildcat is a ferocious predator who never ceases his attack on the peaceful creatures.

Third, like Grahame, Erickson develops credibility for his characters' adventures by taking his characters out of their secure environments. In *Warton and Morton*, Warton convinces his timid brother to leave home in search of culinary delights. During their search they encounter feuding muskrats and a dangerous flood. In *Warton and the Traders*, Warton leaves his peaceful forest to search for his missing aunt in the dangerous bog, which is inhabited by a wildcat who eats the little creatures of the woodland, snakes who slither through murky waters, and bats who flutter through dark skies. In true heroic fashion, Warton develops a scheme that saves the bog from the fierce wildcat and helps his aunt care for a wounded fawn. In *Warton and the Castaways* the toads are swept away in a flood and survive a racoon's pursuit. Friendship is a strong theme in all of Erickson's books.

Robert Lawson. This winner of the Newbery Award, the Caldecott Medal, and the Lewis Carroll Shelf Award has created a believable world in which animals retain their individualized characters. Unlike the river world of Mole in *The Wind in the Willows*, Robert Lawson's animal kingdom is influenced by the peculiarities of humans. Like other distinguished authors of articulate animal stories, Lawson spent time closely observing animals (22). In 1936, he built a house in Connecticut called Rabbit Hill. He says that he had wanted to write a story about the animals who ate everything he planted, the deer who trampled his garden, the skunks who upset his garbage pail, and the foxes who killed his chickens. Instead, when he started to write, he found himself growing fond of Little Georgie, a young rabbit, and the other animals on the hill.

The resulting book, *Rabbit Hill*, presents the impact of humans on animals from the animals' point of view. This consistent point of view allows Lawson to create believable characters, as the animals on the hill wait expectantly after they learn that new Folks are coming. They wonder if this change will bring about a renewal of older and pleasanter days when the fields were planted, a garden cultivated, and the lawns manicured. But Mother Rabbit fears that the Folks will be lovers of shotguns, traps, poison gases, and worst of all, boys.

Lawson centers much of his book around the exploits of the exuberant rabbit Little Georgie, who retains his curiosity and love for a good chase even when his father warns him that misbehavior and parental indulgence can have swift and fatal consequences. The animals believe that all will be well when the new owners put up a sign, saying "Please drive carefully on account of small animals." Then Little Georgie has a dreadful experience with a car on the black road, and the Folks from the hill take the limp rabbit into the house. Gloom settles over the animals. Is Georgie alive, and, if so, why does he not appear? What terrible experiences are the Folks planning for Little Georgie? The animals learn that the new Folks are considerate and caring. The story has a satisfactory ending when the animals pay tribute to their new Folks on the hill.

George Selden. Like Robert Lawson, George Selden loves the Connecticut countryside and creates animals with strong and believable individualities. His *The Cricket in Times Square*, however, has an urban setting, the subway station at Times Square. Two animal characters, Tucker Mouse and Harry Cat, are city dwellers. The other animal, Chester Cricket, arrives accidentally, having jumped into a picnic basket in Connecticut and been trapped until he arrived in New York.

Seldon tells their story from the animals' point of view and develops additional credibility by retaining some of each animal's natural characteristics: the city-wise Tucker Mouse lives in a cluttered drainpipe because he enjoys scrounging and does not consider neatness very important; Chester Cricket is a natural musician and prefers playing when the spirit moves him rather than when people want to hear him. The plot of the story develops around Chester's remarkable ability to play any music he hears and the need for returning kindness to the poor owner of the newsstand in the subway. Selden concludes his story with a natural longing that might be felt by anyone taken from his native environment. Chester becomes homesick for autumn in Connecticut and leaves the city to return home. When Tucker asks him how he'll know that he has reached home, Chester reassures him, "Oh, I'll know! . . . I'll smell the trees and I'll feel the air and I'll know" (p. 154).

This is a touching story of friendship, of longing for one's home, and of the love and understanding that can be felt even between a child and a tiny insect. Additional stories about these animals are found in Selden's *Tucker's Countryside*, *Harry Cat's Pet Puppy*, and *Chester Cricket's Pigeon Ride*. (This latter book has a large format and illustrations designed to appeal to young children.)

E. B. White. *Charlotte's Web* has been identified by Roger Sale (16) as "the classic American children's book of the last thirty years" (p. 258), while Rebecca Lukens (12) uses the book as a touchstone, the story around which she develops her critical standards for literature. Therefore this book provides a fitting example for an extended illustration of the techniques an author of fantasy may use to encourage readers to suspend disbelief.

E. B. White introduces his characters within the reality of an authentically described working farm. His human characters have no unusual powers. They do not treat animals like people, and White does not give animals human characteristics. The harsh reality is that the farmer must keep only animals that can show a profit. In this setting, Mr. Arable moves toward the hoghouse, with ax in hand, to kill the runt in a newly born litter of six pigs. His daughter, Fern, pleads with her father to let her raise the pig. As Wilbur grows, the profitability of the farm again influences Wilbur's fate. Mr. Arable is not willing to provide for Wilbur's growing appetite. Fern again saves Wilbur, but without a hint of fantasy: she sells him to Uncle Holmer Zuckerman, who lives within easy visiting distance.

Wilbur's new home also begins on a firm foundation of reality as White describes the barn in which Wilbur will live and the afternoons when Fern visits Wilbur. On an afternoon when Fern does not arrive, White changes the story from reality to fantasy: Wilbur discovers that he can talk. As he realizes this, his barnyard neighbors begin to talk to him. From this point on, White carefully develops the animal characters into distinct individuals consistent in speech, actions, and appearance.

Wilbur, feels lonely, friendless, and dejected, and often complains. He is a character who must be helped by others' actions. When he discovers that he is being fattened to become smoked bacon and ham, he acts nonheroically: he bursts into tears, screams that he wants to live, and cries for someone to save him. Fern does not rescue him this time. Instead, White answers Wilbur's needs by giving him a barnyard friend, Charlotte A. Cavatica, a beautiful gray spider. Charlotte has quiet manners, and is intelligent and loyal. She reassures Wilbur during their quiet talks, spins the webs that save Wilbur's life, and accompanies him on his trip to the fair. The character of Templeton, the barnyard rat, is convincingly revealed

through his actions. He creeps furtively in his search for garbage, talks sneeringly to the barnyard animals, and eats until he gorges himself. White underscores this characterization by describing Templeton as having no morals or decency.

Through the reactions of the farm families, White allows readers to suspend disbelief about the possibility of a spider spinning a web containing words. When the local residents react in "joyful admiration" and notify their local newspaper (the *Weekly Chronicle*), White's readers tend to believe this could really have happened.

Readers can accept even the final, natural death of Charlotte, because life and friendship continue through Charlotte's offspring. Wilbur understands this as he welcomes three of Charlotte's daughters to his home:

Welcome to the barn cellar. You have chosen a hallowed doorway from which to string your webs. I think it is only fair to tell you that I was devoted to your mother. I owe my very life to her. She was brilliant, beautiful, and loyal to the end. I shall always treasure her memory. To you, her daughters, I pledge my friendship, forever and ever. (p. 182)

Additional Articulate Animals. Readers may wish to compare E. B. White's *Charlotte's Web* with Dick King-Smith's believable characters and plot in *Pigs Might Fly*. Like Wilbur, Daggie Dogfoot is the runt of the litter. Unlike Wilbur, Daggie Dogfoot is physically disabled.

Robert O'Brien's *Mrs. Frisby and the Rats of NIMH* is an excellent example of an author's use of consistent point of view, interesting theme, and believable characters, plot, and setting in modern fantasy. (See chapter three for a discussion of O'Brien's book.) This consistency continues in Jane Leslie Conly's sequel, *Racso and the Rats of NIMH*, in which the author, who is the daughter of O'Brien, extends the story. Now the intelligent rat colony must save their Thorn Valley home from the threat of a dam and the accompanying tourism.

W. J. Corbett's *The Song of Pentecost* is an example of an articulate animal book that may be read at two levels: as an exciting adventure story about mice who must move away from the encroaching human environment or die, and as an allegory of human experience.

Beverly Cleary develops humorous animal stories for young children through imaginative and unusual plots. *Ralph and the Motorcycle* and

Cleary's other books about a mouse named Ralph are good introductions to modern fantasy.

TOYS

When children play with dolls or have conversations with their stuffed animals and other toys, they demonstrate their belief in the human characteristics they give their playthings. When an author tells a story from a toy's point of view, young readers are encouraged to draw upon their own imaginative experiences with toys, suspend disbelief, and feel what it must be like to be loved by children, to live in a beautiful dollhouse, or to be replaced by newer toys.

Rumer Godden. Every child who loves dolls knows that a doll is only a thing unless a child loves it. This is also Rumer Godden's philosophy. She writes books about the dolls who live in her own Observatory House and has her dolls carry on a correspondence with another old family of dolls (5).

By telling *The Dolls' House* from the viewpoint of a doll, Godden creates a believable story about a group of small dolls who long to leave a shoebox and live in their own house. "It is an anxious, sometimes a dangerous thing to be a doll," Godden tells her readers. "Dolls cannot choose; they can only be chosen; they cannot 'do'; they can only be done by; children who do not understand this often do wrong things, and then the dolls are hurt and abused and lost; and when this happens, dolls cannot speak, nor do anything except be hurt and abused and lost. If you have any dolls, you should remember that" (p. 13).

Godden creates dolls who have a range of human characteristics. For example, Mr. and Mrs. Plantagenet are quite ordinary dolls with extraordinary hearts; Tottie is an antique Dutch doll with a warm, friendly character; and Marchpane is an elegant nineteenth-century china doll with a vile disposition. These characteristics play an important role as the dolls express their desire for a new home. When an elegant dollhouse arrives, Marchpane declares that the house is rightfully hers and that the rest of the dolls are her servants. Godden describes the dolls' increasing unhappiness until a tragedy opens the eyes of the two children and the story ends on a note suggesting that justice is related to one's conduct.

Margery Williams. *The Velveteen Rabbit* is told from the viewpoint of a stuffed toy that lives in a nursery and learns to know his owner. Conversations between the stuffed rabbit and an old toy horse are especially effective, allowing Margery Williams to share her feelings about the reality of toys with the reader. When the rabbit asks the wise, old Skin Horse what it means to be real, the Skin Horse informs him that "Real isn't how you are made . . . . It's a thing that happens to you. When a child loves you for a long, long time, not just to play with, but REALLY loves you, then you become Real" (p. 17). The horse tells the rabbit that becoming real usually happens after a toy's hair has been loved off, its eyes have dropped out, and its joints have loosened. Then, even if the toy is shabby, it does not mind because it has become real to the child who loves it.

The plot of the story develops around the growing companionship between the boy and the toy.

Companionship and love between a boy and a toy seem believable in this fantasy. (From *The Velveteen Rabbit*, by Margery Williams. Illustrated by Michael Hague. Illustrations copyright © 1983 by Michael Hague. Reprinted by permission of Henry Holt and Company, publishers.)

Children's reactions to this story suggest how meaningful the toy-child relationship is to young children. Teachers and librarians describe young children's concern when the rabbit is placed in the rubbish pile because he spent many hours in bed with the boy when he had scarlet fever. When the nursery fairy appears and turns the toy into a real rabbit, however, children often say that this is the right reward for a toy who has given so much love. These reactions suggest the credibility of a story written from a toy's point of view.

Comparisons may be made between versions of this book illustrated by William Nicholson (the original edition), Michael Green, Ilse Plume, Allen Atkinson, and Michael Hague.

A. A. Milne. Winnie-the-Pooh, according to his creator A. A. Milne (13), does not like to be called a teddy bear because a teddy bear is just a toy; whereas Pooh is alive. The original Pooh was a present to Milne's son, Christopher Robin, on his first birthday. The boy and Pooh became inseparable, playing together on the nursery floor, hunting wild animals among the chairs that became African jungles, and having lengthy conversations over tea. Christopher Robin's nursery contained other "real" animals, including Piglet, Eeyore, Kanga, and Roo. When Milne wrote his stories about Christopher Robin's adventures with all these animals, he was not only thinking about his own son, but also remembering himself as a boy.

Winnie-the-Pooh and *The House at Pooh Corner* are filled with stories about Pooh because Pooh likes to hear stories about himself: "He's that sort of Bear." Milne develops credibility for the actions in his stories by taking Pooh and the others out of the nursery and into the hundred-acre wood, where an inquisitive bear can have many adventures. Several stories relate experiences that suggest Pooh's reality: he climbs trees looking for honey and eats Rabbit's honey when he pays a visit. The text and illustrations leave no doubt that Pooh is a toy, however. No real bear would be so clumsy as to fall from branch to branch or become stuck in Rabbit's doorway. Children may feel a close relationship with Christopher Robin because every time Pooh gets into difficulty the human child must rescue "silly old bear."

Carlo Collodi. The adventures of a wooden marionette who is disobedient, prefers the joys of play time to the rigors of school, and finally learns his lesson and wins his opportunity to become a real boy are similar to the experiences of Carlo Collodi, his creator. The Italian author of *Pinocchio* described himself as "the most irresponsible, the most disobedient, and impudent boy in the whole school" (5, p. 74). His story reflects a lesson Collodi learned in school: "I persuaded myself that if one is impudent and disobedient in school he loses the good will of the teachers and the friendship of the scholars. I too became a good boy. I began to respect the others and they in turn respected me" (p. 76).

Pinocchio's insistence on doing only what he wants leads to a series of adventures: he sells his spelling book instead of attending school, he becomes involved with a devious fox and cat, he goes to a land of perpetual play time, and he is transformed into a donkey. After Pinocchio learns some bitter lessons, he searches for his creator, Geppetto, who works to restore his health. Now Pinocchio begins to practice his reading and writing, and eventually becomes a real person. Through the words of the blue fairy, Collodi explains why Pinocchio is being rewarded:

Because of your kind heart I forgive you for all your misdeeds. Boys who help other people so willingly and lovingly deserve praise, even if they are not models in other ways. Always listen to good counsel and you will be happy. (p. 193)

The influence of traditional folktales and fables is evident in Collodi's use of animals with human traits to teach a lesson and of magical transformations that punish and reward Pinocchio on his path to self-improvement (10).

PREPOSTEROUS CHARACTERS AND SITUATIONS

Children love exaggeration, ridiculous situations, and tongue-twisting language. Stories that appeal to a reader's sense of humor usually include repetition, plays on words, and clever and original figures of speech, according to Mary Cordella Berding (1), who concludes that the best way to describe a humorous character is through vivid and graphic descriptions of dress, features, or actions.

Carl Sandburg. Readers might expect some unusual characters to be the residents of Rootabaga Country, where the largest city is a village called Liver and Onions. They are usually not disap-

ISSUE

❖

Should A Literary Classic Be Rewritten to Conform to Society's Changing View of Childhood?

IS PINOCCHIO AN EGOTIS-tical and self-centered puppet who cannot, as yet, anticipate the consequences of his actions? Or is Pinocchio a lovable mischiefmaker who is inherently obedient, totally innocent, and thoroughly well-intentioned? Is Geppetto a parent who displays anger, rage, and frustration when his child is disobedient and displays love and sacrifice when the child is in need? Or is Geppetto a parent who displays only love, support, and self-sacrifice? Richard Wunderlich and Thomas J. Morrissey raise issues related to changing the characters and incidents in Carlo Collodi's *The Adventures of Pinochio* to meet the changing social definition of childhood.[1]

These researchers traced the changing characterizations and incidents found in various editions of *Pinocchio* since it was first published in 1883. For example, Collodi's Pinocchio was originally a complex figure; he was egotistical, self-centered, intractable, impudent, and rude. In the 1900s, abridged and condensed editions weakened or changed his

nature by omitting episodes or cutting them. By the 1930s, Pinocchio's mischief became a series of disconnected pranks that made Pinocchio lovable. Likewise, the incident in which Pinocchio and Geppetto are swallowed by a large fish has changed with time. In the original they were swallowed by a shark or dogfish. Later, this fearsome creature became a sea monster, a whale, and "Monstro the Whale" (Walt Disney).

Wunderlich and Morrissey conclude that "changes in *Pinocchio* manifest changes in the social definition of childhood. And thus a literary classic, written in terms of one perception, has been tragically rejected and rewritten to conform to another" (p. 211).

Students of children's literature may read the different versions of *Pinocchio* and consider the inappropriateness or appropriateness of changes that have been made since the original publication. Are similar changes found in other children's literature classics? If changes are apparent, how do the changes influence characterization, plot development, and theme?

[1]Wunderlich, Richard and Morrissey, Thomas J. "The Desecration of Pinocchio in the United States." *The Horn Book* (April 1982): 205–212.

---

pointed when they hear Carl Sandburg's *Rootabaga Stories*. Told originally to the author's own children, these stories do lose part of their humor if they are read rather than heard. The alliteration and nonsensical names are hard for children to read themselves, but they are fun to listen to.

Sandburg begins his ridiculous situation by describing how to get to Rootabaga Country by train: riders must sell everything they own, put "spot-cash money" into a ragbag, then go to the railroad station and ask for a ticket to the place where the railroad tracks run into the sky and never come back. They will know they have arrived when the train begins running on zigzag tracks, when they have traveled through the country of Over and Under where no one gets out of the way of anyone else, and when they look out the train windows and see pigs wearing bibs.

The residents of Rootabaga Country have tongue-twisting names such as Ax Me No Questions, Rags Habakuk, Miney Mo, and Henry Hag-glyhoagly and become involved in tongue-twist-ing situations. For example, when Blixie Bimber puts a charm around her neck, she falls in love with the first man she meets with one *x* in his name (Silas Baxby), then with a man with two *x*'s (Fritz Axanbax), and finally with a man with three *x*'s (James Sixbixdix).

Sandburg's characters often talk in alliteration, repeating an initial sound in consecutive words. When the neighbors see a family selling their possessions, for example, they speculate that the family might be going "to Kansas, to Kokomo, to Canada, to Kankakee, to Kamchatka, to the Chat-tahoochee" (p. 6). These stories are brief enough to share with children during a short story time, but the uncommon names and the language re-quire preparation by the storyteller or oral reader.

Astrid Lindgren. Swedish author Astrid Lind-gren creates an unusual and vivacious character, who wears pigtails and stockings of different col-ors, in *Pippi Longstocking*. Lindgren relies on con-siderable exaggeration to develop a character who is supposedly the strongest girl in the world. She demonstrates her ability when she lifts her horse onto the porch of her house and when, in *Pippi in the South Seas*, she saves her playmate Tommy from a shark attack.

Pippi's unconventional behavior and carefree existence appeal to many children. She is a child who lives in a home, all by herself. She sleeps on a bed with her feet where her head should be and decides to attend school because she doesn't want to miss Christmas and Easter vacation.

Pippi's adventures continue in *Pippi in the South Seas* and in *Pippi on the Run* illustrated with large color photographs.

Other Preposterous Stories. Floating through the air inside a huge peach propelled by five hundred and two seagulls provides a getaway for an unhappy child in Roald Dahl's, *James and the Giant Peach*. Children thoroughly enjoy the fresh-ness and originality of this story. Other enjoyably preposterous journeys occur when a housepain-ter is granted an unusual wish in *Mr. Popper's Penguins*, by Richard and Florence Atwater; when an eccentric inventor restores an old car in Ian Fleming's *Chitty Chitty Bang Bang*; and when a bed takes flight in Mary Norton's *Bed-Knob and Broomstick*. Pamela L. Travers's preposterous nanny, Mary Poppins, goes on new adventures in-

fluenced by traditional myths, legends, and fairy tales in *Mary Poppins in Cherry Tree Lane*.

STRANGE AND CURIOUS WORLDS

While on their way to Carl Sandburg's Rottabaga Country, young readers may also find themselves falling down rabbit holes or flying off into even stranger and more curious worlds of modern fan-tasy.

Lewis Carroll. A remarkable realm unfolds when one falls down a rabbit hole, follows an under-ground passage, and enters a tiny door into a land of cool fountains, bright flowers, and most unusual inhabitants. The guide into this world is also rather unusual: an articulate white rabbit who wears a waistcoat complete with pocket watch.

Perhaps even more remarkable is the fact that this world of fantasy was created by a man who was dreadfully shy with adults, had a tendency to stammer, and displayed prim and precise habits. Charles Lutwidge Dodgson, better known as Lewis Carroll, was a mathematics lecturer at Ox-ford University during the sedate Victorian period of English history. Warren Weaver (21) describes the life of this Victorian don: "Dodgson's adult life symbolized—indeed, really caricatured—the re-straints of Victorian society. But he was essen-tially a wild and free spirit, and he had to burst out of these bonds. The chief outlet was fan-tasy—the fantasy which children accept with such simplicity, with such intelligence and charm" (p. 16). Dodgson may have been shy with adults, but he showed a very different personality with children. He kept himself supplied with games to amuse them, made friends with them easily, and enjoyed telling them stories.

A story told on a warm July afternoon to three young daughters of the dean of Dodgson's Col-lege at Oxford made Lewis Carroll almost immor-tal. As the children—Alice, Edith, and Lorina Lid-dell—rested on the riverbank, they asked Dodgson for a story. The result was the remark-able tale that later became *Alice's Adventures in Wonderland*. Even the first line of the story is reminiscent of a warm, leisurely afternoon:

Alice was beginning to get very tired of sitting by her sister on the bank and having nothing to do: Once or twice she had peeped into the book her sister was reading, but it had no pictures or conversations in it,

"And what is the use of a book" thought Alice, "without pictures or conversations?" (p. 9)

From that point on, however, the day enters another realm of experience, as Alice sees a strange white rabbit muttering to himself and follows him down, down, down into Wonderland, where the unusual is the ordinary way of life. Drinking mysterious substances changes one's size; strange animals conduct a race with no beginning and no finish that everyone wins; a hookah-smoking caterpillar gives advice; the Dormouse, the March Hare, and the Mad Hatter have a very odd tea party; the Cheshire Cat fades in and out of sight; and the King and Queen of Hearts conduct a ridiculous trial.

These strange adventures have a broad appeal to children everywhere because, according to Warren Weaver (21), "something of the essence of childhood is contained in this remarkable book—the innocent fun, the natural acceptance of marvels, combined with a healthy and at times slightly saucy curiosity about them, the element of confusion concerning the strange way in which the adult world behaves, the complete and natural companionship with animals, and an intertwined mixture of the rational and the irrational. For all of these, whatever the accidents of geography, are part and parcel of childhood" (p. 6).

Throughout the book, Alice expresses a natural acceptance of the unusual. When she finds a bottle labeled "Drink Me," she does so without hesitation. When the White Rabbit sends her to look for his missing gloves, she thinks to herself that it is queer to be a messenger for a rabbit, but she goes without question. During her adventures in this strange land she does, however, question her own identity. When the Caterpillar opens their conversation by asking, "Who are you?" Alice replies, "I—I hardly know, Sir, just at present—at least I know who I was when I got up this morning, but I think I must have been changed several times since then . . . . I can't explain myself. I'm afraid, Sir, because I'm not myself, you see" (p. 23).

Lewis Carroll's language is appealing to children, especially if an adult reads the story to them; but the children do have difficulty reading the stories for themselves, and some of the word plays are difficult for them to understand. Carroll's version of the story for young children, *The Nursery "Alice"*, is written as though the author were telling the tale directly to children:

A tea party with unusual guests adds to Alice-in-Wonderland's confusion. (From *The Nursery "Alice"*, by Lewis Carroll. Illustrated by John Tenniel. Published by Macmillan Publishing Co., 1890, 1979.)

This is a little bit of the beautiful garden I told you about. You see Alice had managed at last to get quite small, so that she could go through the little door. I suppose she was about as tall as a mouse, if it stood on its hindlegs; so of course this was a very tiny rose-tree: and these are very tiny gardeners. (p. 41)

Carroll is noted for his nonsense words as well as for his nonsensical situations. He claimed that even he could not explain the meanings of some words. Myra Cohn Livingston (11) quotes a letter in which Carroll explains at least some words in his popular poem "Jabberwocky":

I am afraid I can't explain "vorpal blade" for you—nor yet "tulgey wood:" but I did make an explanation once for "uffish thought"—It seems to suggest a state of mind when the voice is gruffish, the manner roughish, and the temper huffish. Then again, as to "burble"; if you take the three verbs, "<u>b</u>leat," "m<u>ur</u>mur" and "war<u>ble</u>," and select the bits I have underlined, it certainly makes "burble": though I am afraid I can't distinctly remember having made it that way.

The appeal of Carroll's nonsensical characters and fantasy, both to himself and to children, may be explained in a quote from a letter he wrote in 1891:

In some ways, you know, people that don't exist are much nicer than people that do. For instance, people that don't exist are never cross: and they never contradict you: and they never tread on your toes! Oh, they're ever so much nicer than people that do exist!

James Barrie. *Peter Pan*, the classic flight of James Barrie's imagination into Never Land, was first presented as a play in 1904. Barrie begins his fantasy in the realm of reality, describing the children of Mr. and Mrs. Darling in their nursery as their parents prepare to leave for a party. When the parents leave the house, the world of fantasy immediately enters it in the form of Peter Pan and Tinker Bell, who are looking for Peter's lost shadow. Thus begins an adventure in which the Darling children fly, with the help of fairy dust, to Never Land, that kingdom which is "second to the right and then straight on till morning" (p. 31). In Never Land they meet the lost boys, children who have fallen out of their baby carriages when adults were not looking, and discover that there are no girls in Never Land because girls are too clever to fall out of their baby carriages. Along with Peter Pan, who ran away from home because he didn't want to grow up, the children have a series of adventures in Mermaids' Lagoon, with the fairy Tinker Bell, and against their arch-enemy Captain Hook and his pirates. The children finally decide to return home and accept the responsibility of growing up.

Barrie's description of Mermaids' Lagoon encourages readers to visualize this fantasy land:

If you shut your eyes and are a lucky one, you may see at times a shapeless pool of lovely pale colours suspended in the darkness; then if you squeeze your eyes tighter, the pool begins to take shape, and the colours become so vivid that with another squeeze they must go on fire. But just before they go on fire you see the lagoon. This is the nearest you ever get to it on the mainland, just one heavenly moment; if there could be two moments you might see the surf and hear the mermaids singing. (p. 111)

Barrie's settings and characters seem real. They may seem especially real to children who do not wish to grow up. The reader who does not want to take on the responsibility of adulthood may sympathize with the adult Wendy who longs to accompany Peter Pan but cannot. The book closes on a touch of nostalgia, as Peter Pan returns to claim each new generation of children who are happy and innocent.

LITTLE PEOPLE

Traditional folktales and fairy tales describe the kingdoms of small trolls, gnomes, and fairies; Hans Christian Andersen wrote about tiny Thumbelina, who sleeps in a walnut shell; and J. R. R.

Tolkien created a believable world for the hobbit. Contemporary authors of fantasy also satisfy children's fascination with people who are a lot like them, only much smaller.

Carol Kendall. In *The Gammage Cup*, Carol Kendall creates a new world, the Land between the Mountains, in which little people in the valley of the Watercress River live in twelve serene towns with names like Little Dripping, Great Dripping, and Slipper-on-the-Water. Kendall gives credibility to this setting by tracing its history, carefully describing its buildings, and creating inhabitants who have lived in the valley for centuries.

The valley has two types of residents. The Periods display smug conformity in their clothing, their insistence on neat houses, and their similar attitudes and values. In contrast, the five Minnipins—whom the Periods refer to as "Oh Them"—insist upon being different. Gummy roams the hills rather than have a suitable job; Curley Green paints pictures and wears a scarlet cloak; Walter the Earl digs for ancient treasure; Muggles refuses to keep her house organized; and Mingy questions the rulers' authority. The conflict between the two sides reaches a climax when the five Minnipins refuse to conform to one standard and decide that they would rather outlaw themselves, leave their homes, and become exiles in the mountains than conform to the Periods' wishes.

Kendall allows nonconformity to save the valley; the Minnipins discover the ancient enemy, the Mushrooms or Hairless Ones, who have tunneled a way into the valley through an old gold mine. These five exiles also rally the villagers and lead the Minnipins in a glorious victory over the enemy. At this point the exiles return to their homes as heroes.

Kendall uses similar techniques to encourage readers to suspend disbelief in *The Firelings*. She creates folklore expressed in myths and tall tales, and a history engraved on Story Stones; she describes the Firelings' government; and she portrays a convincing setting on the slope of Belcher, a volcano that serves as the focus of a plot about sacrifice and escape.

It is interesting to compare the themes, characterizations, and detailed histories and settings in Kendall's two books about little people.

Mary Norton. The little people in Mary Norton's stories do not live in an isolated kingdom of their own, but are found in "houses which are old and quiet and deep in the country—and where the human beings live to a routine. Routine is their safeguard. They must know which rooms are to be used and when. They do not stay long where there are careless people, or unruly children, or certain household pets" (p. 9). In *The Borrowers* Norton persuades readers to suspend disbelief by developing a foundation firmly planted in reality. She describes the old country house in detail, including a clock that has not been moved for over eighty years. Realistic humans living in the house see and believe in the little people.

Norton makes her stories more believable by describing the setting and the fearsome normal-sized people through the eyes of the Clock family, who are only six inches tall. The Clocks' size forces them to lead a precarious life by borrowing their food and furnishings from the human occupants of the house. Norton further encourages readers to suspend disbelief through the effort made to catch the little people. *The Borrowers* reaches an exciting climax as the housekeeper vows to have the Borrowers exterminated by all available means; the rat-catcher arrives complete with dogs, rabbit snares, sacks, spade, gun, and pickax. When a human boy takes an ax and desperately tries to dislodge the grating from the brick wall, so that the little people can escape, the reader has no doubt that those extraordinary beings are waiting in the shadows for his aid. *The Borrowers Afloat*, *The Borrowers Aloft*, and *The Borrowers Avenged* continue the Clocks' adventures in the world of fields and hedgerows. Sights, sounds, smells, and experiences seem original and authentic as the reader looks at the world from this unusual perspective.

SPIRITS FRIENDLY AND FRIGHTENING

Most children love a good ghost story or a tale about beings from the spirit realm, whether frightening or friendly. Authors who write about this subject may develop elements from folklore and the historic past.

Lucy Boston. The winner of the Lewis Carroll Shelf Award for *The Children of Green Knowe*, Lucy Boston uses her own historic manor house at Hemingford Grey near Cambridge, England, as the setting for her stories. The house and the way of life past generations experienced in it provided Boston ideas for a series of stories written about an old manor house and the friendly presences who return there from generations past.

The first book of the series, *The Children of Green Knowe*, introduces the house, its owner Mrs. Oldknowe, her great-grandson Tolly, and the children who have previously lived in the house. Boston describes the house through the eyes of Tolly, a lonely, shy boy who comes to live in this old house with furnishings similar to those found in a castle. The past becomes alive for Tolly as children who have lived in the house in generations past come back to play with each other and bring vitality to the house and gardens. Readers are not surprised by these actions because Great-grandmother Oldknowe expects the children to return and enjoys having them visit. Boston allows readers to learn more about the people in the past through the stories Mrs. Oldknowe tells Tolly.

Other books in this series include *The Treasure of Green Knowe*, *The River at Green Knowe*, *A Stranger at Green Knowe*, and *An Enemy at Green Knowe*. In all the stories, ancestors return because someone wanted to keep their memories alive.

Other Stories about Spirits. In Joan Phipson's *The Watcher in the Garden*, a garden has a benevolent power of its own that provides refuge from destructive spirits, protects itself and an old blind man who owns and loves it, and attracts and heals an emotionally disturbed teenage girl. The garden croons over her, encourages her to lose her unhappy identity, and smooths away the stress of living, changing her life. The author develops the growing importance of the garden as a sanctuary: "She felt herself being pulled back again. The garden had begun to grow as an idea in her mind, too, as an alternative world that she could inhabit when her day-to-day existence became too hard to bear" (p. 27). As Kitty becomes more involved with the garden and protecting the blind man from outside forces, she begins to believe in the power of the garden.

Many fantasy tales contain presences less benevolent than those found in Boston's and Phipson's books. Demonic forces, incantations, and vanishing humans provide the suspense in John Bellairs's *The Spell of the Sorcerer's Skull*. William Hooks's *Mean Jake and the Devils* tells the story of a contest of wits between Three Devils—Big Daddy Devil, D.J. or Devil Junior, and Baby Deviline—and Mean Jake, who is forced to wander the swamps because he is not allowed to enter either heaven or hell. The witty dialogue creates more humor than fright during this contest.

A contest of wills between an elderly woman and an otherworld creature is developed in Patricia Wrightson's *A Little Fear*. The conflict develops when the Njimbin, an otherworld creature who can influence nature, challenges old Mrs. Tucker by trying to force her from her cottage in rural Australia. Wrightson develops a strong female character who finally outwits the ancient being.

Older children who enjoy stories about ghosts and goblins like the humorous pranks of K. M. Briggs's *Hobberdy Dick*, the suspense and humor of Mollie Hunter's *The Wicked One*, and Peter Fleischman's three short tales of the supernatural in *Graven Images*. Fleischman's tales are successful because they build upon suspenseful turns of events, human folly, and comic mishaps.

TIME WARPS

Children who read stories based on time warp themes discover that there are more things in this world than progress and theories about the future. Time warp stories encourage children to consider what might have happened in their own towns or geographic locations hundreds of years ago, as well as what the future might hold for others who will stand on that same spot in centuries to come. Symbols and tangible objects from the past unite past, present, and future, as believable characters travel to a distant past or see a future yet to materialize. Unlike many of the modern fantasies that bridge the world between old and new fantasy, these time warp stories focus on human development rather than the forces of good and evil. The problems are solved by the characters not by supernatural powers.

Margaret J. Anderson. History is not just royalty, palaces, and famous people. Margaret J. Anderson's fantasies take twentieth-century children back in time to experience the hopes and struggles of ordinary people in the past.

Anderson's *In the Keep of Time, In the Circle of Time,* and *The Mists of Time* take place in Scotland, where the fantasy builds on a strong foundation of reality. In each book, tangible objects have an aura of permanence that seems to transcend time. In *In the Keep of Time*, the ancient Smailholm Tower, a border keep built in ancient

times when Scotland was at war with England, allows children access to past and future. In *The Circle of Time*, the same tower and The Stones of Arden, an ancient circle comprising twelve-foot-high stones, create the opportunity for a journey in time. Each story contains some occurrence that allows the change to take place: a child is touched by a person from another time; a key glows when the moment is right for the children to walk through a door and enter another time period; and mists encircle the stones in a dense fog when the children are brought into the future. The trilogy concludes in *The Mists of Time,* set in the twenty-second century.

Anderson's characters and settings are believable in the past, present, and future, and help readers understand the changes that take place over time. The power of love, understanding, and friendship among people, even across the years, is a strong theme in Anderson's stories.

Andre Norton. Interests in history, legend, science, and helping children overcome present-day problems are evident in Andre Norton's popular fantasies, which include both time warps and science fiction.

Norton uses time warp stories effectively to help her characters conquer personal problems in their modern lives: they go back in time and successfully overcome a problem, an experience that gives them the courage to face a crisis in their own times. Strong values from the past help those modern children shape their destinies.

Norton creates credibility by establishing a strong foundation in modern reality before allowing her characters to enter a time warp. In *Red Hart Magic*, two unrelated children, Chris and Nan, resent their parents' marriage, and the problem increases when the parents travel on business and leave the children with an aunt. The children are unhappy with each other and with schoolmates who try to bully them. Then Chris finds a perfect miniature of an old English inn in a Salvation Army store. When he brings it home, he and Nan discover that they have shared a most unusual dream. Did they dream it, or did they actually go back to the inn during the time of Henry VIII? Did they save a priest from discovery and imprisonment? They "dream" their way back to the inn three times during different periods in English history. These experiences develop the children's confidence, and they use values developed in their experience to help them solve contemporary problems. Their greatest accomplishment is deciding that attempts to make a real family are worthwhile.

In *Lavender Green Magic* a father is missing in Vietnam, and three children must live with unknown grandparents and attend a school where they are the only black children in their classes. A dream pillow embroidered with two mysterious patterns and an overgrown maze planted in 1683 transport the children back into colonial America, where they solve the mystery of an ancient curse, discover that good is stronger than evil, find a way to save their grandparents' home, and resolve their own discontent. Norton's stories tie the past with the present because they stress overcoming personal problems.

David Wiseman. Educator and historian David Wiseman combines his knowledge of Cornwall in England and the burial ground at the mining parish of Gwennap to create a time warp story with a fast plot, memorable characters, and authentic setting. In *Jeremy Visick* Wiseman develops credibility by placing the story in a contemporary setting, where a lively, naughty, likable, and moody twelve-year-old boy is drawn to an old cemetery and a tombstone inscribed with the words: "And to Jeremy Visick, aged twelve years, whose body still lies in Wheal Maid" (p. 14). Wiseman ties the plot into Cornish mining history during Matthew's discussions with a neighbor who describes the old mines and the disasters that took place over one hundred years ago and during a history assignment that requires students to investigate the Cornish family whose men were killed in the accident. Detailed descriptions of Matthew's interactions with the earlier family, the mine shaft as it would have appeared, the terror created by the accident, and Matthew's frantic search for an escape route from the nineteenth-century accident create a credible and exciting time warp story.

In *Thimbles* an interest in family history provides the framework that allows a young girl to move across time from the present to 1819. Two thimbles she finds in her grandmother's trunk are the tangible objects that link the past and the present. When she finds herself back in the earlier time, she is using one of the thimbles to finish a cap of liberty for a protest march demanding the right to vote. Wiseman's detailed historical settings and recreation of the issues of the times create a believable time warp fantasy. Wiseman, like many other authors of time warp

fantasies, uses the past to help contemporary characters in their personal and social development, as they achieve a positive relationship with people of the past and see the continuity in their own lives.

Additional Time Warp Stories. Detailed descriptions of the same farm and countryside in the twentieth century and during the American Civil War create a believable setting in Janet Lunn's time warp fantasy *The Root Cellar*, as an unhappy orphan confronts problems in both the present and the past that encourage her personal development. Time warp experiences help children overcome problems related to growing up and

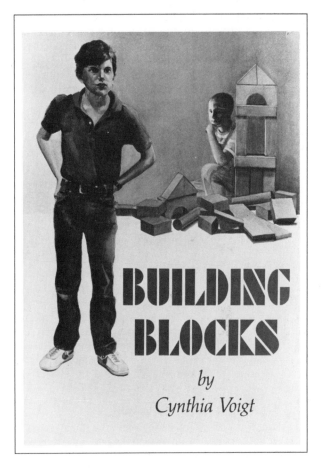

A time warp experience develops understanding between a boy and his father. (Illustration by Eileen McKeating from *Building Blocks* by Cynthia Voigt. Illustrations copyright © 1984 Eileen McKeating. Reprinted with the permission of Atheneum Publishers, Inc.)

family relationships in Ruth Park's *Playing Beatie Bow* and Cynthia Voigt's *Building Blocks*.

SCIENCE FICTION

Writers of science fiction rely on hypothesized scientific advancements and imagined technology of the future to create their plots. In order to achieve credibility, they provide detailed descriptions of these "scientific facts," portray characters who believe in the advanced technology or the results of advanced technology, and create a world where science interacts with every area of society. Like other modern fantasies, science fiction stories also rely on an internal consistency among setting, characters, and plot to encourage readers' suspension of disbelief.

Science fiction written for young children often emphasizes the adventure associated with traveling to distant galaxies or encountering unusual aliens. Stories for older readers often hypothesize about the future of humanity and stress problem solving in future societies.

Critics do not agree on the identity of the first science fiction novel. Margaret P. Esmonde (7) identifies Mary Godwin Shelley's *Frankenstein*, published in 1817, as the earliest science fiction story because the protagonist is a scientist, not a wizard, and the central theme relates to the proper use of knowledge and the moral responsibility of the scientist for his discovery. Roland J. Green (8) traces the emergence of the popularity of science fiction from the mid-1800s through the present-day explosion of interest. Jules Verne published the first major science fiction novel, *Five Weeks in a Balloon*, in 1863; he focused that book and later famous books enjoyed by older children and adults, such as *Twenty-Thousand Leagues Under the Sea*, on technology and inventions, without attempting to develop a society around them. Later in the nineteenth century, H. G. Wells began writing science fiction novels, such as *War of the Worlds*, that had a strong influence on the genre. His writings, according to Green, differed from those of Jules Verne in that they included the systematic "extrapolation of social trends to create a detailed picture of a future society, revolutionary inventions, interplanetary warfare, and time travel" (p. 46).

After World War I, as technological advances continued at an even faster pace, science fiction writing was influenced by the growth of maga-

LONG AGO WHEN I WAS just learning to read, and the world was (as usual) tottering on the brink of war, I discovered that if I wanted to look for the truth of what was happening around me, and if I wanted to know what made the people tick who made the events I couldn't control, the place to look for that truth was in story. Facts simply told me what things were. Story told me what they were about, and sometimes even what they meant. It never occurred to me then, when I was little, nor does it now, that story is more appropriate for children than for adults. It is still, for me, the vehicle of truth.

As for writing stories for children, whether it's fantasy or "slice-of-life" stories, most peo-ple are adults by the time they get published. And most of us adults who are professional writers are writing for our-selves, out of our own needs, our own search for truth. If we aren't, we're writing down to children, and that is serving neither children, nor truth.

I'm sometimes asked, by both children and their elders, why I've written approximately half of my books for children, and I reply honestly that I've never written a book for children in my life, nor would I ever insult a child by doing so. The world is even more con-fused now than it was when I first discovered story as medium for meaning, and story is still, for me, the best way to make sense out of what is happening, to see "cosmos in

zines such as *Amazing Stories*. John W. Campbell, Jr.'s editorship of *Astounding Science Fiction*, beginning in 1938, was highly influential: Campbell insisted that the authors of stories he published develop strong characterization, plausible science and technology, and logical speculation about future societies. He encouraged talented science fiction writers such as Robert A. Heinlein and Isaac Asimov.

In the 1960s, an increasing number of authors began to write science fiction stories. These were more suited to older children and young adults than to young children because the plots often relied on a developed sense of time, place, and space. Science fiction became a topic of interest for university and high school courses. The media were extremely influential during this period: the movie *2001: A Space Odyssey* and the television program "Star Trek" created a devoted science fiction audience and suggested the imaginative potential of science fiction subjects. In the 1970s and 1980s, audiences flocked to pictures such as *Star Wars* and *E.T.* Young people today read and reread the paperback versions of these movies. Many writers are creating high-quality science fiction for young people.

Madeleine L'Engle. Do we all need each other? Is every atom in the universe dependent on every other? Questions like these confront Madeleine L'Engle's characters as they travel the cosmos, face the problems of being different, fight to overcome evil, understand the need for all things to mature, and discover the power of love.

It is interesting to note L'Engle's thoughts about herself as she wrote *A Wrinkle in Time:* "I was trying to discover a theology by which I could live, because I had learned that I cannot live in a universe where there's no hope of anything, no hope of there being somebody to whom I could say, 'Help'!" (23, p. 254). In *A Wrinkle in Time* L'Engle creates characters who are "different" from people around them, but who have high intelligence and strong bonds of love and loyalty to one another. Meg Murry and Charles Wallace are the children of eminent scientists. Meg worries about the way the people in their town make fun of her brother as backward and strange. Her father consoles her by telling her that her brother is doing things in his own way and time. And, in fact, Charles Wallace has very special powers: he can probe the minds of his mother and sister, and he is also extremely bright.

---

chaos" (as Leonard Bernstein said). It is still the best way to keep hope alive, rather than giving in to suicidal pessimism.

Books of fantasy and science fiction, in particular, are books in which the writer can express a vision, in most cases a vision of hope. A writer of fantasy usually looks at the seeming meaninglessness in what is happening on this planet, and says, "No, I won't accept that. There has got to be some meaning, some shape and pattern in all of this," and then looks to story for the discovery of that shape and pattern.

In my own fantasies I am very excited by some of the new sciences; in a *A Wrinkle in Time* it is Einstein's theories of relativity, and Planck's Quantum theory; tesseract is a real word, and the theory of tessering is not as far fetched as at first it might seem. If anyone had asked my grandfather if we'd ever break the sound barrier, he'd have said, "Of course not." People are now saying "Of course not" about the light barrier, but, just as we've broken the sound barrier, so, one day, we'll break the light barrier, and then we'll be freed from the restrictions of time. We will be able to tesser.

In *A Wind in the Door,* I turn from the macrocosm to the microcosm, the world of the cellular biologist, Yes, indeed, there are mitochondria, and they live within us; they have their own DNA, and we are their host planet. And they are as much smaller than we are as galaxies are larger than we are. How can we—child or adult—understand this except in story?

Concepts which are too difficult for adults are open to children, who are not yet afraid of new ideas, who don't mind having the boat rocked, or new doors opened, or mixing metaphors! That is one very solid reason my science fiction/ fantasy books are marketed for children; only children are open enough to understand them. Let's never underestimate the capacity of the child for a wide and glorious imagination, an ability to accept what is going on in our troubled world, and the courage to endure it with courage, and respond to it with a realistic hope.

L'Engle's development of those characters provides a realistic foundation for the science fiction fantasy that follows, when the children discover that their scientist father is fighting the "dark thing"—a thing so evil it could overshadow a planet, block out the stars, and create fear beyond the possibility of comfort. The children travel in the fifth dimension to a far-distant planet where their father has been imprisoned by the evil power of "It." L'Engle states that this villain is a naked brain because "the brain tends to be vicious when it's not informed by the heart" (23, p. 254). The heart proves more powerful than the

The power of love is a strong theme in this science fiction story. (From *A Wind in the Door*, by Madeleine L'Engle. Farrar, Straus & Giroux, 1973. Copyright © by Leo and Diane Dillon. Reprinted by permission of Leo and Diane Dillon.)

evil It in this story: Meg's ability to love deeply saves her father and Charles.

The battle against evil continues in *A Wind in the Door*, in which Charles appears to be dying, and in *A Swiftly Tilting Planet* readers discover the climactic purpose of Charles's special abilities. L'Engle creates a realistic foundation for the science fiction when fifteen-year-old Charles and his father construct a model of a *tesseract*, a square squared and then squared again that is considered the dimension of time. Because they can construct it, the reader feels that it must be true. Another credible character adds realism to the story: the phone rings, and the president of the United States asks for help. Elements of traditional fantasy enter this science fiction story in the form of an ancient rune designed to call the elements of light and hold back evil and a unicorn that aids Charles in his perilous journey.

In all her books, L'Engle emphasizes the mystery and beauty of the cosmos and the necessity of maintaining the natural balance in the created order of the universe.

Anne McCaffrey. Pern is the third planet of Rukbat, a golden G-type star in the Sagittarian Sector. When a wildly erratic bright red star approaches Pern, spore life, which proliferates at an incredible rate on the red star's surface, spins into space and falls in thin threads onto Pern's hospitable earth. The spore life is not hospitable to life on Pern, however; it destroys all living matter. In order to counteract this menace, the colonists in Anne McCaffrey's *Dragonsong* enlist a life form indigenous to the planet. These creatures, called *dragons*, have two remarkable characteristics: they can travel instantly from place to place by teleportation, and they can emit flaming gas when they chew phosphine-bearing rock. When guided by the dragonriders, they can destroy the spore before it reaches the planet.

In this setting a young girl fights for her dream to become a harpist. Because her father believes that such a desire is disgraceful for a female and forbids her to play her music, Menolly runs away and makes friends with the dragons. After a series of adventures in both *Dragonsong* and *Dragonsinger*, Menolly learns that she need no longer hide her skill or fear her ambitions:

The last vestige of anxiety lifted from Menolly's mind. As a journeyman in blue, she had rank and status enough to fear no one and nothing. No need to run or hide. She'd a place to fill and a craft that was unique to her. She'd come a long, long way in a sevenday. (*Dragonsinger*, p. 264)

Monica Hughes. The role of free choice, the importance of truth, and the consequences of intolerance and superstition are themes in Monica Hughes's science fiction trilogy. Beginning in *The Keeper of the Isis Light*, Hughes creates Isis, a harsh planet that holds a lighthouse designed to guide colonists from Earth. The planet's only inhabitants are Olwen, the orphaned daughter of the original lighthouse keepers, and Guardian, an indestructible robot. Over the years, Guardian has made adaptations in Olwen's body to allow her to survive Isis's ultraviolet light and thin air. Strong conflict develops as Guardian tries to protect Olwen from the reactions and the prejudices of new settlers who are unable to accept her because of these adaptations. Hughes explores both the need to be accepted by others of one's own kind and the intolerance of humans to people who do not conform to accepted standards of "normal." In a strong conclusion, Olwen discovers that she is not willing to pay the price necessary for acceptance.

The Guardian of Isis is set several decades into the future. Hughes explores the consequences of living in a community where science and invention are considered harmful and where taboos and superstitions rule people's lives. The wisdom of Olwen and Guardian helps a young, questioning inhabitant realize that "it is the damage of today that we must repair, and then slowly build a better way of living. But not by looking back" (p. 122).

The final book in Hughes's trilogy, *The Isis Pedlar*, explores what could happen if an unscrupulous trickster lands on a planet where naive people are in an agricultural phase of social development. The people who have feared technology and invention and who have developed strong taboos and superstitions are very susceptible to the lies and greed created by the pedlar. In the end, however, the wisest of the people discover that "our destiny is our own and we'll work it out without interference" (p. 113). The themes in Hughes's books are popular themes in much of science fiction.

John Christopher. The future world John Christopher envisions in *The White Mountains* is quite different from the world hoped for by people today. In Christopher's future, people have lost their free will, and machines called Tripods have taken over. These machines maintain control through a capping ceremony that places a steel plate on the skull, making the wearer docile and obedient. Fourteen-year-old Will Parker, who is angered by the prospect of an inescapable voice inside his head, discovers that a colony of free people lives in the White Mountains far to the south. Will makes his escape with two other young people, but the Tripods follow them. Throughout Will's adventures, Christopher emphasizes the importance of free will, as Will discovers that freedom and hope are the most important luxuries in life.

In *The City of Gold and Lead* and *The Pool of Fire* the free humans plan their battle against the Tripods and then defeat them. Yet quarreling factions defeat Will's attempts to plan for new unity among the victorious humans. Christopher's stories are exciting, but also sober reminders of what could happen if humanity allows itself to lose the battle for free will.

SUMMARY

Modern fantasy takes children into imaginative worlds where animals and dolls can talk, where wizards cast their spells, and where alien beings live in far-distant galaxies. Modern fantasy must meet the standards of all fine literature and must also develop a point of view to encourage the reader to suspend disbelief; it must create settings that allow the reader to see, hear, and feel the environment; and it must present believable characters. The themes developed by writers of modern fantasy include some very important human values.

Fantasy that bridges the worlds between old and new literature has many elements of traditional literature. The fantasies of C. S. Lewis, J. R. R. Tolkien, and Lloyd Alexander contain elements of mythology. Modern fairy tales by Hans Christian Andersen, Joan Aiken, and Jane Yolen are similar in motif and subject to traditional tales.

Memorable stories about articulate animals depict animals who talk like people but still retain some animal qualities. Literature by Beatrix Potter, Kenneth Grahame, E. B. White, and Robert Lawson suggests an understanding of, and a liking for, animals. Stories about dolls and toys suggest the imaginative world of a living nursery.

Authors of literature considered classics for children, such as Lewis Carroll and James Barrie, have created strange worlds found at the base of a rabbit hole or at the end of a journey through space propelled merely by trust and pixie dust.

Modern fantasy writers also transport children through time warps to experience life through the eyes of realistic people living in the past or to help modern children solve their contemporary problems by effectively solving problems in the past. Science fiction writers may transport readers into new galaxies or futuristic worlds on earth. Honorable characters may battle forces of evil by searching for that one moment when a decision could make a difference, or they may rebel against a society controlled by machines. The importance of retaining free will is an important theme in many futuristic science fiction stories.

Suggested Activities for Adult Understanding of Modern Fantasy

☐ Read Hans Christian Andersen's "The Wild Swans." Compare the plot, characterization, and setting with the Grimms' "The Six Swans." What are the similarities and differences?

☐ Choose a book written from the point of view of someone who is different from a normal person. What techniques does the author use to encourage readers to suspend disbelief and consider the possibility that the story could happen?

☐ Discuss C. S. Lewis's "The Chronicles of Narnia" with another adult who has read the books and with a child who has read them. What are the differences, if any, in the two people's interpretations?

☐ After reading J. R. R. Tolkien's *The Hobbit* or *The Lord of the Rings*, identify common elements and symbols in Tolkien's work and mythology. Consider the use of fate, subterranean descents, denial of death, mortals and immortals, supernatural beings, and the power granted to objects.

☐ Authors who write about believable articulate animals balance reality and fantasy by allowing the animals to talk but still retain some animal characteristics. Choose an animal character such as Beatrix Potter's Peter Rabbit, Little Georgie from Robert Lawson's *Rabbit Hill*, or Mole from Kenneth Grahame's *The*

Wind in the Willows. What human and animal characteristics can you identify? Has the author developed a credible character? Why or why not?

☐ This text discussed Susan Cooper's use of English, Celtic, and Welsh legend and mythology in her fantasies. After reading Pat O'Shea's *The Hounds of the Morrigan,* investigate and identify elements from Irish legend and mythology.

References

1 Berding, Sister Mary Cordelia. "Humor as a Factor in Children's Literature." University Microfilm No. 65–12,889. Cincinnati: University of Cincinnati, 1965.

2 Bettelheim, Bruno. *The Uses of Enchantment: The Meaning and Importance of Fairy Tales*. New York: Knopf, 1976.

3 Cavendish, Richard, ed. *Legends of the World*. New York: Schocken Books, 1982.

4 Children's Literature Association. *Touchstones: A List of Distinguished Children's Books*. Lafayette, Ind.: Purdue University; Children's Literature Association, 1985.

5 Commire, Anne. *Something about the Author: Facts and Pictures about Contemporary Authors and Illustrators of Books for Young People*. Detroit: Gale, 1971.

6 De Wit, Dorothy. *Children's Faces Looking Up: Program Building for the Storyteller*. Chicago: American Library Association, 1979.

7 Esmonde, Margaret P. "Children's Science Fiction" in *The First Steps: Best of the Early ChLA Quarterly*, compiled by Patricia Dooley. Lafayette, Ind.: Purdue University; Children's Literature Association, 1984.

8 Green, Roland J. "Modern Science Fiction and Fantasy: A Frame of Reference." *Illinois School Journal* 57 (Fall 1977): 45–53.

9 Hedges, Ned Samuel. "The Fable and the Fabulous: The Use of Traditional Forms in Children's Literature." University Microfilm No. 68–18,020. Lincoln: University of Nebraska, 1968.

10 Heins, Paul. "A Second Look: The Adventures of Pinocchio." *The Horn Book* April 1982: 200–204.

11 Livingston, Myra Cohn. *Poems of Lewis Carroll*. New York: Crowell, 1973.

12 Lukens, Rebecca J. *A Critical Handbook of Children's Literature*. Glenview, Ill.: Scott, Foresman, 1976.

13 Milne, A. A. *The Christopher Robin Story Book*. New York: Dutton, 1966.

14 Noel, Ruth S. *The Mythology of Middle Earth*. Boston: Houghton Mifflin, 1977.

15 Nodelman, Perry. "Some Presumptuous Generalizations about Fantasy." In *The First Steps: Best of the Early ChLA Quarterly*, compiled by Patricia Dooley. Purdue University: Children's Literature Association, 1984, pp. 15–16.

16 Sale, Roger. *Fairy Tales and After: From Snow White to E. B. White.* Cambridge, Mass.: Harvard University, 1978.

17 Shohet, Richard Matther. "Functions of Voice in Children's Literature." University Microfilm No. 72–297. Cambridge, Mass.: Harvard University, 1971.

18 Sutherland, Zena; Monson, Dianne L.; and Arbuthnot, May Hill. *Children and Books.* Glenview, Ill.: Scott, Foresman, 1981.

19 Tolkien, J. R. R. *Fellowship of the Ring.* Boston: Houghton Mifflin, 1965.

20 Townsend, John Rowe. *Written for Children.* New York: Lippincott, 1975.

21 Weaver, Warren. *Alice in Many Tongues.* Madison, Wis.: University of Wisconsin, 1964.

22 Weston, Annette H. "Robert Lawson: Author and Illustrator." *Elementary English* 47 (January 1970): 74–84.

23 Wintle, Justin, and Fisher, Emma. *The Pied Pipers: Interviews with the Influential Creators of Children's Literature.* New York: Paddington Press, 1974.

Additional References

Antczak, Janice. *Science Fiction: The Mythos of a New Romance.*: Neal/Schuman, 1985.

Barron, Neil, ed. *Anatomy of Wonder: Science Fiction*, 2nd ed. New York: Bowker, 1981.

Boyer, Robert H., and Zahorski, Kenneth J., eds. *Fantasists on Fantasy: A Collection of Critical Reflections.* New York: Avon, 1984.

Franklin, H. Bruce. *Robert A Heinlein: America As Science Fiction.* New York: Oxford University Press, 1980.

Wehmeyer, Lillian Biermann. *Images in a Crystal Ball: World Futures in Novels for Young People.* Littleton, Colo.: Libraries Unlimited, 1981.

Involving Children in Modern Fantasy

ADULTS CAN EXTEND THE MAGICAL EXperiences children gain through modern fantasy by providing varied opportunities for children to interact with the settings, characters, and plots of the stories.

Modern fantasy can encourage children's personal development when children are encouraged to understand elements in fantasy, interpret modern fantasy through puppetry and through art, develop a fantasy interest center, and make connections between science and science fiction and between social studies and science fiction.

HELPING CHILDREN RECOGNIZE, UNDERSTAND, AND ENJOY ELEMENTS IN FANTASY

Challenging the intellect, revealing insights into the world of reality, stimulating and nurturing the imagination, and nurturing the affective domain are values that make fantasy a worthy genre of literature for all children. The definition of modern fantasy, however, suggests that many children may have difficulty comprehending the stories. Unlike realistic fiction, which mirrors a more or less real world, modern fantasy presents an altered picture of the real world. Authors often enrich their fantasies with allegory, irony, figurative language, and folklore elements.

These elements may increase gifted children's appreciation of the stories, but may cause confusion for less able readers. Susan Swanton's (18) survey of the literary choices of gifted and other students supports this contention. While almost half the gifted students' preferred books were classified as modern fantasy (29 percent science fiction, 18 percent other fantasy), none of other students' top choices were similarly classified. Gifted students indicated that they liked "science fiction and fantasy because of the challenge it presented" (p. 100).

This difference in the reading preferences of different students is unfortunate; modern fantasy should be available and can be pleasurable to all readers. Picture books, with detailed illustrations and simple plots, may help children understand the more complex elements found in modern fantasy. They can stimulate discussion, illumi-

CHART 7–1

Elements	Modern Fantasy	Picture Books
Allegory	Lewis's "Chronicles of Narnia" Corbett's *The Song of Pentecost*	Holder's *Aesop's Fables* Lobel's *Fables*
Irony	Brittain's *The Wish Giver*	Oakley's *The Church Mice in Action* Gage's *Cully, Cully and the Bear*
Figurative Language	Brittain's *The Wish Giver* Showell's *Cecelia and the Blue Mountain Boy*	Lewin's *Jafta* and *Jafta's Mother*
Folklore Elements: Power in Tangible Objects A Quest	Lunn's *The Root Cellar* Cooper's *Seaward* McKinely's *The Hero and the Crown*	Marshak's *The Month Brothers* Severo's *The Good-Hearted Youngest Brother* Hodges's *Saint George and the Dragon*
Magical Powers	McKinley's *The Blue Sword*	Grimm's *The Devil with the Three Golden Hairs*
Transformations	Alcock's *The Stone Walkers* Cooper's *Seaward*	Andersen's *The Wild Swans* Williams's *The Velveteen Rabbit*
Punishment for Misused Ability	Brittain's *The Wish Giver*	Van Allsburg's *The Wreck of the Zephyr*

nate meanings, and form bridges between illusion and understanding. Chart 7–1 identifies elements in modern fantasy, modern fantasy selections, and picture books that develop and illustrate the same literary element. (The picture books include both modern fantasy and traditional tales.)

To stimulate greater discussion, children may read and discuss the picture books in each category before reading and discussing the fantasy. After children recognize and understand the literary elements in the picture books, they may identify similar elements in the fantasy selections. For example, illustrated fables with double or allegorical meanings, moral implications, and animal characters who talk, behave like humans, and possess human traits provide excellent examples of allegory. For example, this discussion

could help older children answer the following questions after reading W. J. Corbett's *The Song of Pentecost*: What does the title mean? Why is the leader of the mice named Pentecost? What allegorical implications are found in the author's development of characterizations, settings, problems, resolutions of problems, and morals?

Each of the other picture books in Chart 7–1 illustrates an important element in fantasy. For example, Hugh Lewin's highly illustrated *Jafta* and *Jafta's Mother* are excellent sources for showing figurative language that is related to the environment. Lewin describes and illustrates Jafta's feelings by comparing them to the feelings and actions of animals in Jafta's African environment. The double-spread illustrations show both the boy and the particular animal demonstrating actions such as skipping like a spider, stamping like an elephant, and grumbling like a warthog. Bill Brittain, in the modern fantasy *The Wish Giver*, also uses figurative language to suggest character traits and to enhance the small town, rural setting.

PUPPETRY INTERPRETATIONS OF MODERN FANTASY

Young Hans Christian Andersen's favorite toys were a puppet theater and puppets. Eva Moore's *The Fairy Tale Life of Hans Christian Andersen* (10) describes the five-year-old Hans watching his father put on puppet plays, the eight-year-old Hans creating his own plays and sewing clothes for the puppets, and the seventeen-year-old Hans putting on puppet shows for the children of Copenhagen. Throughout Moore's book, readers sense how important puppets and the interaction between puppet and fantasy were to Andersen's

A simple stage and puppets may increase children's enjoyment of literature.

development. Children today can develop that sense of wonder as they watch puppetry productions or create their own puppets and stage their own productions.

People throughout history have enjoyed this interaction between puppet and puppeteer. Puppets were found in Egyptian tombs; they were part of rituals in ancient Greece and Japan; and Punch and Judy shows in England were very popular. Any viewer of television who watches the "Muppets," "Sesame Street," or "Mr. Rogers" can attest to the current popularity of puppets. Muppet characters such as Miss Piggy and Kermit the Frog have even been interviewed on newscasts.

Children often enjoy learning about the history of puppets. Older children can explore informational books on puppetry, or adults can share pictures and illustrations with them. Sources that adults will find useful include Bill Baird's *The Art of the Puppet* (1), which contains colored photographs and information on the history of puppetry; Jeune Scott-Kemball's *Javanese Shadow Puppets* (14), which has photographs of the British Museum's collection of puppets; Rene Simmen's *The World of Puppets* (16), which presents a history of puppets; and George Speaight's *Punch and Judy: A History* (17), which includes the history of one type of puppetry production. These books provide historical information and may also stimulate children's interest in puppetry.

Choosing Stories That Stimulate Puppetry

Geraldine Siks (15) develops a strong case for nurturing children's imagination through the use of puppets. She says that "a well-planned puppetry project, by its very nature, can serve as an introduction to all the arts, not as separate entities, but as an integrated whole" (p. 177). Siks believes that puppetry projects should start with existing stories that provide the foundation of plot and character upon which the puppet play can be developed. She envisions a logical progression of simple stories, beginning with nursery rhymes, progressing to folktales and fairy tales and modern fantasy, moving on to contemporary stories, and ending with children creating original scripts.

The characteristics of stories or scenes from stories appropriate for puppetry productions are similar to those of many traditional tales and shorter modern fantasies or scenes from modern fantasies. Nancy E. Briggs and Joseph A. Wagner

(2) have identified the following characteristics of stories that are appropriate inspirations for puppetry:

1 A story's structure should be clear and understandable.
2 Stories should contain action that can be shown through the movements and voices of puppet characters. (Facial expressions are not possible with puppets.)
3 The story's pace should be rapid.
4 Stories selected should be those that children will want to repeat; they should be well liked and easily understood.
5 Characters should present challenging, imaginative subjects for puppet construction, but should not be impossible to construct.
6 The size of the puppet stage usually determines how many characters can be accommodated; consequently, the story should require that no more characters appear at one time than the stage can accommodate. (Three to five puppeteers are usually all that will fit comfortably behind a stage without the stage collapsing or the players getting in each other's way.)

In addition, if sets are to be added to the puppet theater, the story should require only a few simple ones. There is always a danger in puppetry that children will become so engrossed in making the puppets and the sets that there is no time or emphasis placed upon the actual objective of the puppet production.

Children who have had considerable experience with children's literature and listening to stories told or read by adults often have many ideas about stories to use in puppet presentations. Adults sometimes find it helpful to share some appropriate stories with children and then let them select the story or stories they would like to share with an appreciative audience of their peers.

Besides many of the traditional stories discussed in chapter six, children and adults will find many modern fantasy stories or particular scenes appropriate and enjoyable for puppetry productions. Young elementary students enjoy creating the Beatrix Potter stories as puppet productions. The interactions and adventures of Mother Rabbit, Flopsy, Mopsy, Cottontail, Peter, and Mr. McGregor make a satisfying puppet play that lets a number of children take different roles. Children have had whole Beatrix Potter festivals;

one group put on *The Tale of Peter Rabbit*, while another portrayed the adventures of Benjamin Bunny as he and Peter go back to the garden to retrieve Peter's coat and run into the cat, and a third depicted the confrontation between Nutkin, the squirrel, and Old Brown, the owl. Stories from *Winnie-the-Pooh* are also enjoyable for puppetry. Because there are a number of Pooh stories, children can use their puppets during the creation of several different plots.

Hans Christian Andersen's fantasies—such as "The Emperor's New Clothes," "The Princess and the Pea," and "The Tinderbox"—are enjoyable sources for lower and middle elementary puppeteers. The humorous characters and situations in Carl Sandburg's *Rootabaga Stories* are fun to create as puppets and sets, as well as to present as puppet plays. Children find that characters such as Jason Squiff with his popcorn hat, popcorn mittens, and popcorn shoes, and Rags Habakuk with a blue rat on each shoulder encourage their imaginations to soar and create new situations for these characters.

Middle and upper elementary students have recreated many scenes from L. Frank Baum's *The Wizard of Oz*, showing Dorothy and Toto whirling through the air and landing in Oz, Dorothy's saving the Scarecrow, the meeting with the Tin Woodman and the Cowardly Lion, the journey through the deadly poppy field, their arrival in the Emerald City, their interview with the wizard, and the exciting encounters with the Wicked Witch of the West.

Jane Yolen's fantasy stories found in *The Hundredth Dove and Other Tales* have also stimulated puppetry presentations. One group of upper elementary students created their own fantasy after reading Yolen's *Dream Weaver*; they pretended to be dream weavers and created puppet plays from the magical threads of their imaginations.

Adults and children can find more ideas for appropriate puppetry stories by reading various books on puppetry plays. For example, Lewis Mahlmann and David Cadwalader Jones's *Puppet Plays for Young Players* (7) contains adaptations of twelve plays, including "The Princess and the Pea," "Pinocchio," "The Tinderbox," "Alice's Adventures in Wonderland," and "The Wizard of Oz," as well as several traditional fairy tales. These authors have adapted eighteen additional stories in *Puppet Plays from Favorite Stories* (8). This collection contains both traditional and modern fantasy selections.

Creating the Puppets

The four major types of puppets are hand puppets, rod puppets, shadow puppets, and marionettes. The professional puppeteer or college student who is investigating puppetry may use a wide variety of marionettes and other complex puppets. Young children will have better results creating and working simple puppets. Hand puppets are usually considered ideal for the beginning puppeteer because they are the easiest to construct and control.

Hand puppets range from stockings or paper sacks placed over the hand to puppets with heads constructed from papier-mâché. A paper-bag puppet is very easy and quick to construct. To make this puppet, children can draw features directly on the bag, allowing the mouth opening to fall on the fold of the bag, or they can cut features from construction paper and glue them onto the bag. Objects such as buttons, yarn, felt, and pipe cleaners can add features to paper-bag puppets.

Paper plates also provide material for easily constructed puppets that can be manipulated by the child's hand. Children fold the paper plate in half and add features to it. This folding allows the child to manipulate the puppet's speaking action. Ears can be added to the plate and pipe cleaners glued onto the plate for whiskers.

Boxes of various sizes may be turned into hand puppets. To form the base of a puppet, cut a box on the sides and fold it, then add features to the box to create the desired character.

Puppets with papier-mâché heads can be given features that look real. The heads can be formed by using a plastic foam ball, a crumpled newspaper ball, or an inflated balloon as a base. Before the papier-mâché is added to the base, place a cardboard tube from paper toweling into the center of the neck. This tube should be wide enough to hold one or two fingers. Then cut newspaper or toweling into small pieces or strips, dip them into thinned wallpaper paste or glue, and apply them over the form until the desired features have been formed. After the head has dried, features can be painted onto the head and hair can be added. A simple garment can then be cut and sewn or glued together to fit over the hand.

Very simple puppets can be constructed by cutting characters from construction paper or cardboard and attaching figures to sticks. The child maneuvers the puppet by grasping the lower end of the rod and moving it across the stage.

Children can actually become human puppets by constructing cardboard shapes or designing box shapes large enough to cover their bodies and represent characters from modern fantasies.

Sometimes stories suggest objects that can be turned into puppets. One group of children created puppets for Carl Sandburg's "The Wedding Procession of the Rag Doll and the Broom Handle and Who Was in It." One child turned a broom into a puppet who was ready for a wedding. He added facial features to a broom, attached a coat hanger just below the face, and placed a shirt and jacket over the coat hanger. The bottom of the broom handle became the stick by which the puppet was maneuvered. A fireplace shovel, tablespoons, dishpans, frying pans, and striped bibs were also turned into puppets. After the children made their puppets and recreated the wedding procession, they created other situations in which their characters played major roles.

Children As Puppeteers

Preparing for a puppet presentation when literature is the stimulus is similar to preparing for other types of creative dramatizations. George Merten (9) recommends that the story be read several times until the players feel they know it thoroughly. He suggests that the children develop a mental image of the characters, their personalities, and some of their quirks. They should consider the necessary relationships among characters if they are going to portray the plot and characters to an audience. Next, the group should improvise each segment while the adult considers where and when the scene takes place, who is in the scene, what happens in the scene, how the scene moves forward, and the scene's objective. George Latshaw (5) believes the players should go through a three-step improvisation in which they pantomime the scene, then repeat the same scene but add sounds that express the characters' feelings (yawns, giggles, gasps), and finally improvise using dialogue. The final puppet play should be believable to both actors and audience.

Children usually enjoy giving a puppet production several times so that several children can play different parts or all the children who made a certain puppet character can play that particular part. Many stories discussed earlier have several different scenes so that many children can become involved in the production both as players and audience.

Teachers, librarians, and other adults who work with children find that children will turn many favorite stories into puppet productions if they are given an opportunity to create puppets and even a simple stage on which to perform. Many productions will be very informal, with one or two children putting on a play for their own enjoyment. Whether the production is two children behind a living room sofa or a group of fifth graders staging a more elaborate story for classmates or parents, a magical quality usually transforms the children into storybook characters.

Paper Bag Puppet: the Owl from *Winnie-the-Pooh*

Box Puppet: Tin Man from *The Wizard of Oz*

cut

fold

Rod Puppet: a Winged Monkey belonging to the Wicked Witch

Paper Plate Puppet: Peter Rabbit

Papier-mâché Head Puppet: the Wicked Witch of the West from *The Wizard of Oz*

Human Puppet: the Cowardly Lion from *The Wizard of Oz*

Puppets Made from Objects

Fire Shovel Guest

Spoon-Licker Guest

Broom Handle Bridegroom

ART INTERPRETATIONS OF MODERN FANTASY

Strange and curious worlds, imaginary kingdoms, animal fantasy, and preposterous situations found in modern fantasy all lend themselves to artistic interpretations. Betty Coody (3) says that "creative art-literature experiences occur in the classroom when boys and girls are moved by a good story well told or read, when art materials are made available, and when time and space are allowed for experimenting with the materials" (p. 92). (A word of caution: art should allow children to expand their enjoyment of a story through self-expression; it should not be used as a forced activity following the reading of every story.)

Modern fantasy selections that can stimulate artistic interpretations range from books that interest preschool children through books appropriate for upper elementary and middle school children. A wide variety of art media may be explored in relation to modern fantasy selections, as well as to other literary genres.

Murals and Friezes

Mural and frieze interpretations of literature encourage children to work in a group in order to create a large picture. A mural is usually made by designing and creating a picture on a long piece of paper that may be placed on the floor or on long tables so that children can work together on it. A frieze is similar to a mural, but it consists of a long narrow border or band of paper that stretches across a wall or around a room.

A group of children usually plans the content of the mural and decide the responsibilities of each individual. Drawings on the mural may be created with paints, chalk, or crayons. Objects cut out of construction paper can be added on top of the background paintings. The finished mural may be placed on a large bulletin board or may cover whole sections of a wall or hallway. Murals can depict one setting suggested by a book or can be divided into segments to illustrate different parts of a story.

Stories with vivid descriptions of settings are enjoyable sources of mural subjects for young children. Beatrix Potter's *The Tale of Squirrel Nutkin* contains a description of the island in the middle of the lake where the squirrels go to gather nuts. Children have created murals showing a large lake surrounded by a woods, with a tree-covered island in the center. The largest tree is the hollow oak tree, the old brown owl's home. Because the story takes place in the autumn, children can create trees and bushes covered with shades of red, gold, and orange. On the lake, they can paint squirrels sailing toward the island on rafts. One group of children gathered real acorns, autumn leaves, and twigs to add to the mural. Other stories that suggest scenic murals include scenes in the hundred-acre wood in A. A. Milne's *Winnie-the-Pooh;* the river world of Mole, the Wild Wood, and Toad's home at Toad Hall in Kenneth Grahame's *The Wind in the Willows;* and the barn and/or barnyard world of E. B. White's *Charlotte's Web.*

Children have also drawn in large mural format to show the travels of various characters in stories. They have illustrated Little Georgie's journey as he travels across the countryside in search of Uncle Analdas's home in chapters three and four of Robert Lawson's *Rabbit Hill.* Little Georgie travels to the Twin Bridges, walks briskly down the Hill, moves quietly past the home of the Dogs of the Fat-Man-at-the-Crossroads, runs happily across the High Ridge, leaps over Deadman's Brook, and eventually finds Uncle Analdas's disorderly burrow.

An illustration of an actual frieze of richly carved people and animals that decorated Greek architecture often interests children and helps them create their own friezes depicting the important characters and events in a story.

After reading Carl Sandburg's *Rootabaga Stories,* one group of children wanted to create a humorous frieze. They showed the train and its occupants traveling toward Rootabaga Country through the land of Over and Under, the country of balloon pickers, and the country of circus clowns; the tracks running in zigzags in the land where pigs wear bibs; and the final destination of the village of Liver and Onions.

The characters and their adventures found in J. R. R. Tolkien's *The Hobbit* and Lloyd Alexander's "Prydain Chronicles" are other fine inspirations for friezes by older children.

Collage, Montage, and Mosaic

Three types of art involve gluing other materials onto a flat surface in order to create an artistic interpretation. All three are also enjoyable ways to interpret literature. A *collage* is made by pasting different shapes and textures of materials onto the surface to create a picture. (See pages

185–86 for detailed suggestions for introducing children to collage through picture storybooks.) Many materials—including newspapers, lace paper doilies, velvet, burlap, felt, satin, yarn, tinfoil, rope, buttons, toothpicks, twigs, bark, corrugated paper, tissue paper, and paints—should be collected so that children have many things to choose from that will give the desired effect when they are creating collages.

Young children like working with texture and then feeling the results of the different materials on their collages. Beatrix Potter's *The Tale of Peter Rabbit and Other Stories* is an enjoyable source of ideas and inspiration for collage interpretations. Some young children created Peter by cutting a jacket out of material and shoes out of construction paper, then adding a cotton-ball tail and string whiskers. They portrayed him in a gooseberry net made from string or nylon netting and had him peering forlornly at a scarecrow complete with brass-buttoned jacket, hanging shoes, and three-dimensional lettuce plants. Russell Erickson's various Warton the toad books, Roald Dahl's *James and the Giant Peach*, and Jane Yolen's *The Girl Who Cried Flowers* are other excellent inspirations for collage.

A *montage* is a composite picture created by bringing together into a single composition a number of different pictures or parts of pictures and arranging them to form a blended whole. Children can create a montage by cutting pictures from magazines or other sources and then mounting them on a surface so that the surfaces overlap. The pictures and the way they are arranged may suggest a feeling, a theme, a mood, or a concept. They may be quite abstract in nature or may rely on concrete symbols to develop a concept. This may be the first time that some children experience an art form that is not necessarily realistic. Through montage, they find that they can select and rearrange pictures and parts of pictures until the result expresses their feelings.

E. B. White's *Charlotte's Web* is one story that has stimulated the creation of montage. Throughout the book, Templeton the rat is portrayed as an animal who "had a habit of picking up unusual objects around the farm and storing them in his home" (p. 45). He collected delectable food scraps: part of a ham sandwich, a chunk of Swiss cheese, and a wormy apple core. Children have developed a montage that suggests the essence of the material objects Templeton prizes. After reading Ian Fleming's *Chitty Chitty Bang Bang*, children have created a montage of antique cars and a candy factory. Older children have created more complex themes. They have used the montage process to suggest the battle between good and evil in J. R. R. Tolkien's *The Hobbit* and *The Lord of the Rings* and Lloyd Alexander's "Prydain Chronicles." They have created montages of symbols representing past, present, and future inspired by the time warp fantasies of Margaret J. Anderson and others. They have used montage to create worlds of friendly ghosts, such as those found in Lucy Boston's *The Children of Green Knowe*, and of less benevolent spirits, such as Mollie Hunter's *The Wicked One*.

A *mosaic* results from gluing small objects of different colors onto a surface so that they create an overall design or picture. Children can select a favorite character from literature; draw the character on a surface of heavy paper, cardboard, or wood; select appropriate small objects to fill in the lines—such as seeds, stones, or small bits of paper; place glue inside the shape; and then attach the objects to the surface. They may fill in the background with color or drawings if they wish. Favorite characters for this activity include Margery Williams's *The Velveteen Rabbit*, A. A. Milne's characters in *Winnie-the-Pooh*, and Lewis Carroll's characters in *Alice's Adventures in Wonderland*.

Papier-Mâché

Children enjoy creating sculptures of their favorite animal or human characters in the books they read. Papier-mâché characters are created by covering a lightweight structural form with strips of newspaper or paper toweling that have been dipped into thinned wallpaper paste. Children can make the structural form by inflating a balloon of appropriate size, wadding and taping newspaper into the desired shape, selecting a plastic container that resembles the desired shape, forming the shape from clay, or developing a wire or wire-mesh construction. All these techniques are described in step-by-step detail in Whitman's *A Whitman Creative Art Book, Papier-Mâché* (19).

The statues in the queen's courtyard in C. S. Lewis's *The Lion, the Witch and the Wardrobe* are interesting subjects for papier-mâché treatments, as are Rudyard Kipling's Mowgli, Rikki-Tikki-Tavi, and other characters in *The Jungle Books* and animal characters in *Just So Stories*. Children's fa-

Children are creating settings for dioramas out of boxes and paint.

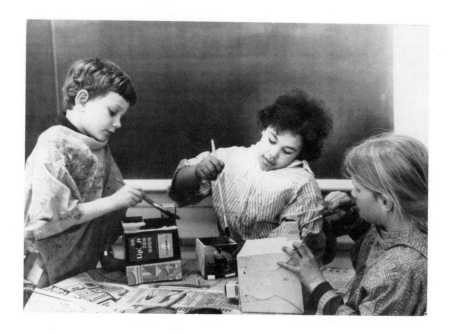

vorite articulate animals provide lively subjects for papier-mâché.

Shadowboxes

Many stories lend themselves to miniature recreations of settings inside a box or framed on a shelf. Stories about small people or dolls, such as Mary Norton's *The Borrowers* or Rumer Godden's *The Dolls' House* are obvious sources of inspiration for such shadowboxes or dioramas. Children of many ages, and adults as well, are often fascinated by miniatures. Children enjoy collecting small items around their own homes, such as spools, thimbles, bottle caps, and boxes and then turning them into furniture for Norton's Clock family. After reading *The Dolls' House*, children may wish to learn more about the elegant dollhouse described in the book and then choose and recreate a favorite room from the house. Books such as Barbara Farlie and Charlotte L. Clarke's *All about Doll Houses* (4) illustrate many kinds of dollhouses, period rooms, furniture, and accessory projects. Children can see, for example, how beads from a broken necklace can be turned into a lamp and how a round bottle top can be turned into a teapot.

Robert O'Brien's *Mrs. Frisby and the Rats of NIMH* can inspire children to recreate the inside of the laboratory, the rats' new colony in Thorn Valley, and other scenes. The strange and curious world of Lewis Carroll's *Alice's Adventures in Wonderland* provides many exciting scenes for dioramas, such as Alice's tea party with the Mad Hatter. James Barrie's Never Land in *Peter Pan* provides other rewarding subjects for dioramas, including the Darling children's nursery and Captain Hook's ship.

These scenes are merely suggestive of the many interpretations that children can attempt in using literature to stimulate art work. For many children, art interpretation allows them to interact with their favorite characters in a new way. As suggested earlier, however, they do not need to interpret all their reading with art projects. For young children, art should be an enjoyable extension of their story, not a general assignment to draw their favorite part. Classrooms and homes that provide a rich background of art materials will encourage children to create many interpretations of their favorite storybook settings and characters.

DEVELOPING A FANTASY INTEREST CENTER: A MODERN FANTASY WEB

University students in children's literature classes can use the webbing process suggested by Donna Norton (12) to identify related topics around a central theme or subject, identify children's books related to the topic, and then develop stimulating activities that encourage children to interact with the characters and situations in these books. One group chose this technique to help formulate and develop a children's literature interest center for the middle elementary grades around the central subject, "Imagine That."

After choosing their central, unifying subject, the university students identified six major categories of modern fantasy that would be appropriate for their "Imagine That" theme. Next, they identified children's modern fantasy selections that would be suitable for each category. In order to satisfy the interests and reading needs of different students, they identified books that were on several different reading levels or that, like *Pinocchio*, had been published in various versions with different levels of reading difficulty. Following their search of the literature, they completed a literature web identifying the books they would use (see Figure 7–1).

With these books in hand and the web developed, the group divided its responsibilities. Each student wrote motivational paragraphs for an introduction to the books that might captivate children's interests and encourage them to read the books. Next, the students developed four or five different activities to encourage children to interact with the book through art interpretations, creative dramatics, oral discussions, or creative writings. They shared their paragraphs and activities in order to receive feedback from each group member. They placed the motivational paragraphs and directions for the suggested activities on large cards and put them into an attractive fantasy-land interest center complete with books, necessary materials, and room to display the completed activities. Because several students were student teaching at the time, they placed the interest center in their classrooms and shared it with children. Examples of motivational paragraphs and book-related activities developed around three of the six categories in the literature web of interest are shown in Figure 7–2.

The students who developed and used this literature interest center with children found that other children in the class wanted to read books because of the interest and the activities that were generated. Some activities were teacher-led or teacher-motivated; others the children could do independently.

STRATEGIES FOR INVOLVING CHILDREN WITH SCIENCE FICTION

Science fiction stories have inspired children to become scientists and writers. Scientist Carl Sagan (13) of the popular "Cosmos" television series, credits the science fiction stories of H. G. Wells with stimulating the boyhood dreams of flying to the moon and Mars that eventually led him to become an astronomer. Robert Goddard, the inventor of modern rocketry, read Wells's *War of the Worlds*, while stories about the space traveler Buck Rogers influenced George Lucas, the creator of the movies *Star Wars* and *The Empire Strikes Back*.

Science fiction provides pure enjoyment but it can also be used to stimulate interaction between science fiction and science or social studies.

Interaction between Science and Science Fiction

Many science fiction books are based on scientific principles and can be used as springboards for discussions involving critical and creative thinking and the reinforcement of scientific facts. Children's research skills can become sharper as they verify the scientific information in the fantasies. Children's appreciation and evaluation of settings in science fiction are also enhanced as they discuss the various books. (Interaction between science and science fiction is a highly motivating subject for gifted and talented students.)

Several children's literature students and upper-elementary and middle-school teachers have developed activities that stress the interaction between the science curriculum and the reading of science fiction. One group of adults was stimulated by the suggestions of Dorothy Zjawin (20), who recommended different ways to encourage the interaction between science and science fiction. The class divided into small groups, each of which chose the study of astronomy, the human body, inventions, or changes in nature, including environmental problems, weather, ecosystems, or time. Next, the groups identified science fiction books that could be shared orally with children or displayed in the library for children to read independently. Then the groups investigated the science curriculum and discovered science-related materials, scientific principles, and topics in current science magazines that could stimulate upper-elementary students' interests. Finally, they

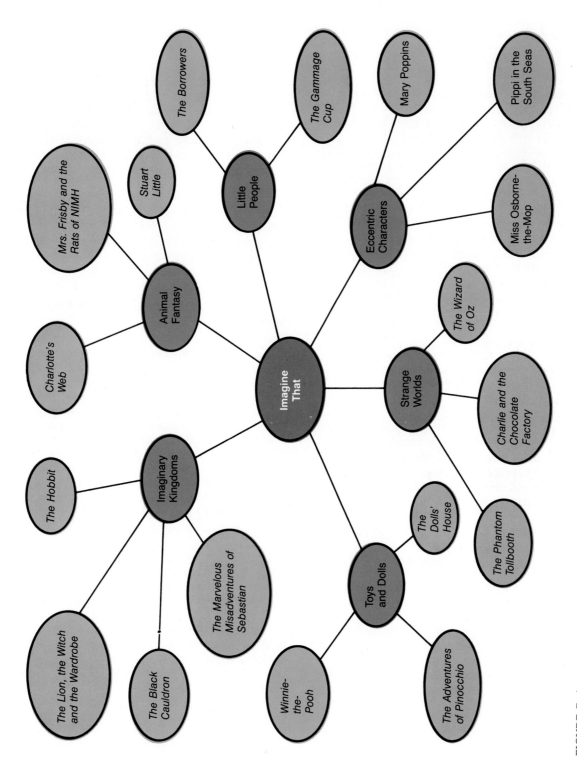

FIGURE 7–1

IMAGINARY KINGDOMS

> *The Lion, the Witch and the Wardrobe* by C. S. Lewis.
>
> It's true! A wardrobe leads to another land called Narnia, a land where it always snows but it's never Christmas. Peter, Susan, Edmund, and Lucy discover Narnia and must help break the wicked Snow Queen's spell. The centaurs, beavers, unicorns, and talking horses depend on the Pevensie children and on Aslan, the noble lion.

EXAMPLES OF ACTIVITIES

> Pretend you are Edmund's shadow. You are right there with him in all his adventures. You hear what he says and you know how he feels. Write a character sketch about Edmund from the viewpoint of his shadow. Include the things he does and why you, his shadow, think he does them. How and why does Edmund change? How do you feel about being his shadow? What would you say if you could talk?

> With a group of classmates who have read this book, act out "what happened about the statues" for the rest of the class. Refer to chapter sixteen for this exciting adventure.

> Choose your favorite part in *The Lion, the Witch and the Wardrobe* (about three pages). Practice reading it; when you are ready, record your selection. Following your recording, tell why this was your favorite part in the book. After everyone is finished, we will all listen to the tapes of *The Lion, the Witch and the Wardrobe*.

> Create and construct a box movie using ten scenes in proper sequence from *The Lion, the Witch and the Wardrobe*. Write an accompanying script to narrate the movie. Present your movie to the class.

ANIMAL FANTASY

> *Mrs. Frisby and the Rats of NIMH* by Robert O'Brien
>
> "You must go, Mrs. Frisby," said the owl, "to the rats under the rosebush. They are not, I think like other rats."
>
> The rats under the rosebush are *not* like other rats. Mrs. Frisby, a mouse, did go to the rats for help, and she did discover their secret. Mrs. Frisby found rats that could read, use machines, and plan a self-supporting rat society. She also found rats that were in great danger. Could tiny Mrs. Frisby help them? Read the book and find out for yourself.

EXAMPLES OF ACTIVITIES

> The publisher is searching high and low—it doesn't know what to do. The public is going wild and wants a sequel to *Mrs. Frisby and the Rats of NIMH*. Please help this publisher. Write to the publisher, and tell the editor why you should write *Mrs. Frisby and the Rats of NIMH, Part II*. In your letter tell what you would include in your story. (Compare your ideas with Jane Leslie Conly's *Racso and the Rats of NIMH*.)

> *Choose a friend who has read Charlotte's Web.* Pretend that you are Nicodemus and your friend is Charlotte. Have a conversation in which you tell each other what it is like to live the life of a rat or a spider. Tell about your best friends, your adventures, and the advantages and disadvantages of being the kind of creature you are. During your conversation, tell each other why you think humans dislike spiders and rats.

> Pretend that you are a mouse or a rat. Somehow you have found your way into Ms. *(teacher's name)*'s classroom. You have never seen anything like it. Write about your adventures as you journey through the classroom and meet the people or objects in the room.

STRANGE WORLDS

> *The Phantom Tollbooth* by Norton Juster
>
> Inside the mysterious package that Milo found in his room was what looked like a genuine turnpike tollbooth. But Milo was in for an even bigger surprise when he drove his small electric car through the tollbooth gate. Suddenly, he found himself in The Lands Beyond, the enchanted home of some of the craziest creatures ever imagined. As Milo traveled through this confusing world, he was joined by an ill-mannered little Humbug and a ticking watchfob named Tock. The three characters found themselves drawn into a chain of adventures that led them closer and closer to the forbidden Mountains of Ignorance and black-hearted demons that awaited them there.

EXAMPLES OF ACTIVITIES

> Pretend that you are Milo: you just can't believe that you have found The Lands Beyond. You don't want to forget this crazy world that is so different from the one that you know. There must be a way to record your adventures. You decide to keep a diary. Write seven entries in your diary telling about different adventures in the enchanted and confusing world of The Lands Beyond. In your final entry, include any important lessons that you have learned. Bind your entries together and design a cover for your diary.

> Choose a friend who has also read *The Phantom Tollbooth* and together prepare a debate to present to the class. One of you is a faithful citizen of Dictionopolis and the other is from Digitopolis. Each of you must try to convince the class that your kingdom is better. Tell the class about the advantages of living where you live and the disadvantages of living in the other place. Defend your own kingdom so that your classmates will choose to live there.

FIGURE 7–2
Motivational paragraphs and activities

shared their activities with children. The following are examples of books, discussion topics, and related activities that proved rewarding:

Astronomy and Science Fiction

Science Fiction to Be Shared with Children

1 Cameron, Eleanor. *The Wonderful Flight to the Mushroom Planet*. Two boys, with the help of a friend, construct a spaceship and travel to a strange planet.
2 Engdahl, Sylvia Louise. *This Star Shall Abide*. A boy learns the secrets of his planetary civilization.
3 Marzollo, Jean, and Marzollo, Claudio. *Jed's Junior Space Patrol: A Science Fiction Easy-to-Read*. This intergalactic adventure includes robots and telepathic creatures.

(See chapter twelve for nonfiction books about planets and space flights.)

Discussion Topics and Other Related Activities

1 Children discussed the possibility of living in a space colony. How would colonists control their environment? How would they communicate with other colonies? How would they travel between colonies? During the discussions, the adult encouraged children to let their imaginations soar; they also had to consider scientific principles and the ways authors of science fiction stories had solved these problems. (They discussed films and television programs as well.)
2 Because many science fiction stories take place on other planets, children considered the possibilities of discovering a new planet. Children and teachers shared excerpts from the magazine *Science 81* (March 1981), about astronomers' search for a possible tenth planet in our solar system, out beyond distant Pluto "at least five billion miles from the sun, or 50 times further away than Earth" (p. 6). They considered the possible characteristics of such a planet and any life forms that might be there, then wrote their own science fiction stories describing astronomers searching for the new planet, astronauts traveling to the new planet, or space colonists living on the new planet.
3 The above discussion on astronomers searching for new planets led to a discussion about

NASA's proposed 430-foot-long orbiting space telescope, described in the April 1981 issue of *Science 81*. Children considered what they might discover if they could "peer seven times further into space than ever before, perhaps to the edge of the universe itself" (p. 10).
4 The latest discoveries about the characteristics of other planets and the sun, as discovered by Voyagers 1 and 2 explorations of the solar system and orbiting telescope, stimulated discussions about science fiction and about how these characteristics would affect possible life on the planet or the development of space colonies. Two articles in the January/February 1981 issue of *Science 81*, Bruce Murray's "After Saturn, What?" and J. Kelly Beatty's "No Small Rapture," and an article in *Omni*, Mike Edelhart's "New Sun" (April 1980), provided background information for the teachers, as well as illustrations to be shared with children. For example, teachers used the following quote from Bruce Murray to start a discussion about the environment on Mars: "Robots launched by the United States have changed the imaginary, Earthlike Mars of Percival Lowell into the detailed scientific reality of ancient volcanic mountains, vast chasms, and water-cut channels much larger than any similar features on Earth" (*Science 81*, January/February 1981, p. 24). Children considered additional characteristics of Mars and compared them with the environments developed in science fiction.

How Could Changes in Natural Events or Environments Affect the Future of Earth or Another Planet?

Science Fiction to Be Shared with Children

1 Doyle, Arthur Conan. *The Lost World*. People on earth discover a lost land in which prehistoric animals still live.
2 Hamilton, Virginia. *Dustland*. The air in a future earth time supports only dust and mutant animals and humans.
3 McCaffrey, Anne. *Dragonsong*, *Dragonsinger* and *Dragonquest*. Colonists on Perm create a life form to destroy the spore life that invades the planet and has the ability to destroy all living matter.

4 Snyder, Zilpha Keatley. *Below the Root*. A thirteen-year-old survivor of a society that has experienced devastating destruction sets out to discover a civilization that supposedly lives underground.

Discussion Topics and Other Related Activities

1 Students discussed what could happen on earth if prehistoric animals were discovered and then began to multiply rapidly. They considered competition for food, eating habits of various prehistoric animals, conditions necessary for rapid reproduction, and what might happen to plants, smaller animals, and human life. They also considered what could happen if species that are now considered endangered were to multiply rapidly. What changes in the environment might account for the reversal? What would be the consequences for other life?

2 Several science fiction books develop plots around consequences of changes in the earth because of pollution and overpopulation. Children developed discussions and writings around this quote by Joan Stephenson Graf in *Science 81* (March 81): "Global 2000, a presidential report on the future, predicts that between 600,000 and one million plant and animal species will become extinct in 20 years as a result of the expansion of human populations and the exploitation of natural resources. The loss of species, and the biological diversity they represent, is unrecoverable, and the consequences of these losses are impossible to predict" (p. 102).

Another source of scientific facts about endangered plant life and probable consequences is Elizabeth Stark's article "You Can't See the Forests or the Trees" in *Science 81* (April 1981). A teacher used this topic to stimulate discussions, beginning with the following quote: "The world's tropics will be bald and barren. With the forest canopy gone, surface temperatures will swing wildly, atmospheric concentrations of carbon dioxide will rise precipitously, and one million species will die. The aftermath of a nuclear war? Not quite. According to a grim report released by the U.S. Interagency Task Force on Tropical Forests, this is what much of the world's forests will look like in less than 50 years if dev-

astation of woodlands continues . . . . What remains of our diminishing tropical woodlands will be gone within 70 years if deforestation in the Third World continues at its present rate" (p. 78).

3 Children considered various environmental problems on earth today or problems that could develop due to litter from disabled space ships or other space-traveling vehicles such as Voyager I. Through discussions, they tried to predict and provide various solutions to these problems.

The Influence of Inventions, Machines, and Computers

Science Fiction to Be Shared with Children

1 Christopher, John. *The White Mountains*. A futuristic mechanized society forms the setting for the story.

2 Hamilton, Virginia. *The Gathering*. A computer programmed by survivors helps rehabilitate a wasteland.

3 Hughes, Monica. *Devil on My Back.*. A rigid class system is imposed on society by the computer.

4 Watson, Simon. *No Man's Land*. A mechanized world causes a boy to rebel.

Discussion Topics and Other Related Activities

1 Children considered changes that had occurred in the world over the last one hundred years due to inventions such as airplanes, automobiles, calculators, computers, and even light bulbs. They speculated about a world without these inventions and a world in which any of these inventions could become too powerful.

2 Children made their own inventions, drew and created models of them, described the purposes and advantages of their inventions, shared them with other children, and speculated what might happen if their inventions became too powerful.

3 Robots such as R2D2 and C3PO in *Star Wars* also fascinate children. They designed their own robot models, described capabilities of the robots, and contemplated what other worlds or earth might be like if robots were plentiful or if they became more powerful than their human inventors.

For these children, there is a close relationship between science fiction and astronomy.

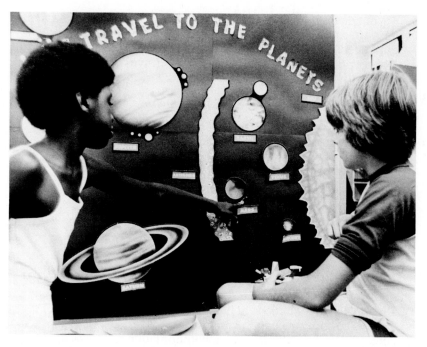

Interaction between Social Studies and Science Fiction

Science fiction relates not only to scientific principles and technology, but to the possible impact of technological changes such as mechanization, space travel, and life on other planets upon people and societies. Because science fiction is of high interest to many upper-elementary students, science fiction and related activities can meet the following four motivational requirements for social studies recommended by John P. Lunstrum and Bob L. Taylor (6):

1   Use materials and approaches that are responsive to and built on student interests.
2   Design and/or use strategies that demonstrate the relevance of the reading task in social studies, focusing on the study and discussion of controversy and the clarification of values.
3   Help students who have negative attitudes toward reading in the social studies and little confidence in their ability to experience success in this area.
4   Encourage students to use language activities, such as role-playing games and listening more effectively. Arouse curiosity about the communication process, of which reading is an integral part, and develop interpersonal communication skills. (p. 21)

Alan Myers's (11) recommendations for using science fiction in social studies classrooms cor-

respond with many of these motivational requirements. Myers says that science fiction has an important position in social studies classes because "broad themes like the nature of government, the merits of different types of social organization, racial hatred, poverty, and exploitation in unfamiliar contexts" (p. 183) can stimulate the debating of issues without being hindered by children's stereotypes. Myers also suggests that through science fiction children acquire a sense of the relationship between cause and effect; in so doing, they can begin to grasp the sweep of history that is so important to any study of social studies.

Many science fiction books lend themselves to the development of debates on issues related to society and social studies. Classroom teachers have successfully used the following issues and books to motivate children to consider different viewpoints during social studies classes.

Issue: People who differ from those around them are often misunderstood, feared, and even hated. This treatment is inconsistent with the prevalent belief that fellowship and love are essential if society is to survive.

1   Hughes, Monica. *The Keeper of the Isis Light.* Settlers from earth do not accept the physical adaptations made by another human being who has learned to survive on the harsh planet of Isis.

2 Key, Alexander. *Escape to Witch Mountain.* Two children from another planet have strange powers. As they search for their identities, they must outwit sinister forces who would like to use their powers.

3 L'Engle, Madeleine. *A Wrinkle in Time.* People fear and whisper about Charles Wallace because he is different from the other children in the town; he can communicate without speaking.

Issue: Should society allow its members to have free will? What could happen if people do not strive to retain freedom of choice?

1 Christopher, John. *The White Mountains.* People in the twenty-first century are controlled by machines called Tripods. When human members of the society reach the age of fourteen, steel plates are inserted into their skulls so they can be controlled by the state.

2 Christopher, John. *The City of Gold and Lead.* Will tries to discover the secrets of the Tripod culture by spying inside the major Tripod city.

3 Christopher, John. *The Pool of Fire.* People try to set up a new government after defeating the Tripods; dissident groups, however, cannot agree on a unified approach.

4 Hughes, Monica. *The Guardian of Isis* and *The Isis Pedlar.* The role of free choice is explored within a society that fears science and invention.

Other social studies activities that have resulted from children discussing science fiction include planning future cities. Because authors of science fiction stories often describe futuristic cities either on earth or on other inhabited planets, children enjoy the challenge of creating their own model cities. They can consider what their city would look like and how it would function if they could build it any way that they wished. One sixth-grade class designed such a city by combining research into known design possibilities and the children's imaginations. The children investigated energy-efficient buildings, transportation systems, sanitation systems, and suburban/urban growth before building their own model city. They chose high-rise office and apartment buildings for their efficient use of urban space, but designed the buildings for energy efficiency and beauty. Their suburban homes were partially or totally below ground and had energy-efficient solar collectors. Shopping centers made use of below- and above-ground space, with light shafts

bringing in light for plants and people. The children's transportation system included clean, electric mass transit; computerized road systems for private cars to ensure a safe, steady stream of traffic; and moving sidewalks. Their sanitation system used a three-phase treatment process that produced drinkable water, and garbage was incinerated by the power plant to provide recycled power. The children also included museums, recreational facilities, parks, trees, and an arboretum in their city. They considered the issues of controlling growth, how many people would provide an ideal number for their city, and satisfying their city's future energy needs.

Children have also thought about the impact on their own lives and society if an alien people landed on earth or if space exploration discovered life forms on other planets. Through role playing, they have imagined that first meeting, how they might communicate, and how humans and aliens could function together without destroying either culture. Because television programs such as "Star Trek" often deal with the issue of interfering with another culture, children have also considered the possibility of earth being invaded or colonized by aliens who are far superior intellectually to people on earth, or the reverse situation in which space exploration could discover human life forms who have not progressed as far as earth's civilization.

Children have discussed the impact of various environments on space travelers who are trying to colonize diverse environments. Children have constructed whole new environments in their classrooms. They have designed settings that include atmosphere, plants, animals, and land characteristics, created new languages, developed communication systems, and suggested fine arts possibilities.

ACTIVITIES POSSIBLE WITH ONE BOOK OF MODERN FANTASY

Teachers and librarians can develop numerous activities around one book of modern fantasy that children enjoy. Madeleine L'Engle's *A Wrinkle in Time*, for example, is a popular science fiction story with characters, settings, and themes that stimulate discussion, artwork, and creative dramatization. Many outstanding books can serve as the basis for such activities. Suggestions related to L'Engle's book may be used as guidelines for activities focused on other books.

Oral Discussion

Discussing L'Engle's text with children can help them focus on characterization, setting, plot development, theme, and style. The following questions and suggestions are listed in a chronological order linked to the material in the book, as indicated by page or chapter references. If adults wish to focus on characterization, setting, plot, theme, or style at one time, they may group these questions accordingly. Some questions require that children consider information presented at different points in the text and then integrate this information into an answer that requires synthesis. An adult leading the discussion may wish to interject the appropriate text passages as children consider their answers. As the discussion develops, the adult should listen to the children's responses and, if appropriate, encourage divergent thinking. (Divergent questions encourage more than one "correct" answer, as children verbalize different interpretations of a story. These questions often require them to consider their own experiences and reactions when they interact with the text.)

Suggestions for Oral Discussion

1 *Characterization.* What did Meg's father mean when he told Meg not to worry about Charles Wallace because "he does things in his own way and in his own time"? Was father right? What exceptional behavior did Charles Wallace display? Why was Charles Wallace considered strange and backward by the villagers? Why didn't he want the people in the village to know his real capabilities? (chapter 2)

2 *Plot development, Setting.* Tesseract is mentioned in several places in the book. Lead a discussion in which the children present ideas about what they think is meant by the word:

p. 21   Mrs. Whatsit informs Mrs. Murry that there is such a thing as a tesseract.

p. 23   Mrs. Murry tells the children that she and their father used to have a joke about a concept called tesseract.

p. 76   The term *tesseract* is described as traveling in the fifth dimension—going beyond the fourth dimension to the fifth dimension. The five dimensions are described as first, line; second, a flat square; third, a cube; fourth, time; and fifth, the square of time, a tesseract in which people can travel through space without going the long way around.

3 *Setting, Style: Emotional Response to Language.* Throughout the book, L'Engle makes associations between smells and emotions. Discuss some of these associations: Mrs. Whatsit's statement that she found Charles Wallace's house by the smell; and then her reaction in which she describes how lovely and warm the house is inside (p. 17); or the delicate fragrance that Meg smells when the gentle beast with tentacles relieves her of her pain (p. 175). Encourage children to express their own associations between smells and emotions.

4 *Theme.* Mrs. Who told Meg that if she wanted to help her father she would need to stake her life on the truth. Mrs. Whatsit agreed and told the children that their father was staking his life on the truth. What did Mrs. Who and Mrs. Whatsit mean by their remarks (p. 92)? How had Mrs. Whatsit staked her life in the battle against evil (p. 92)?

5 *Characterization, Author's Style, Theme.* Throughout the book, L'Engle has developed descriptions and associations around "It." Discuss these associations and meanings:

p. 72   "It" is described as a dark thing that blotted out the stars, brought a chill of fear, and was the evil their father was fighting.

p. 88   It is described as evil; It is the powers of darkness. It is being fought against throughout the universe. The great people of earth who have fought against It include Jesus, Leonardo da Vinci, Michelangelo, Madame Curie, Albert Einstein, and Albert Schweitzer. Discuss how these people fought against darkness and encourage children to identify other people who fought or are fighting against darkness.

p. 108   It makes its home in Camazotz, the most oriented city on the planet, the location of the Central Intelligence Center.

p. 118   The man was frightened about the prospect of being sent to it for reprocessing.

p. 141   It sometimes calls Itself "The Happiest Sadist."

p. 158   It is a huge brain.

p. 170   Meg felt iciness because she had gone through the dark thing.

6   *Characterization, Plot Development.* Mrs. Whatsit gave each child a talisman in which she strengthened their greatest ability: for Calvin, it was the ability to communicate with all kinds of people; for Meg, it was her faults; and for Charles Wallace, it was the resilience of his childhood (p. 100). How did the children use these abilities throughout the story in their fight against It and in their endeavors to free Mr. Murry? Which ability is most important? Why?

7   *Characterization, Theme, Setting.* Why did L'Engle introduce the children to Camazotz by showing the children skipping and bouncing in rhythm, identical houses, and women who opened their doors simultaneously (p. 103)? Why was the woman so frightened about an Aberration? What eventually happened to the Aberration? What is the significance of these actions?

8   *Characterization, Theme.* Compare the people living in Camazotz with Meg, Charles Wallace, and Calvin. How does one account for these differences (p. 118)? Could the people living in a city on earth become like the people in Camazotz? Why or why not? Why did the man at Central Intelligence Center tell the children not to fight It so that life would be easier for them? What would happen if everyone took the man's suggestion (p. 121)? What are the consequences of allowing someone to accept all the pain, the responsibility, and the burdens of thought and decision? Would this be good or bad? Give a reason for your answer.

9   *Plot development.* What was Meg's reason for saying the periodic table of elements when she was standing before It (p. 161)?

10   *Characterization, Plot Development, Theme.* What characteristics did Meg have that made her the only one who would be able to go back to Camazotz and try to save Charles from the power of It (p. 195)? What was the only weapon that Meg had that It did not possess (p. 203)? How did Meg use this weapon to free Charles Wallace? Do any people ever use this weapon? Has anyone here ever used this weapon? Is it a weapon for good or for bad?

Artwork

Art activities accompanying *A Wrinkle in Time* can stimulate children's interpretations of setting and characterization. Ideally, children can again demonstrate their divergent thinking as they interpret the author's language and descriptions.

Suggestions for Art Interpretations

1   *Characterization, Descriptive Language.* Mrs. Whatsit goes through several different transformations in the course of the book. Encourage children to illustrate these transformations. Suggestions include Mrs. Whatsit's appearance as a plump, tramplike character in her blue and green paisley scarf, red and yellow flowered print, red and black bandanna, sparse grayish hair, rough overcoat, shocking pink stole, and black rubber boots (pp. 16–17). Next, the children see her transformed from this rather comical character into a beautiful winged creature with "wings made of rainbows, of light upon water, of poetry" (p. 64). The reader also discovers that Mrs. Whatsit had been a star who gave her life in the battle against It (p. 92).

2   *Setting.* The medium is able to show the children visions through her globe. Ask the children to pretend to be sitting before a magical globe and draw either the series of visions that the children see or the visions people would like to see if they could ask the globe to show them anything.

3   *Setting.* Meg, Mr. Murry, and Calvin travel to a strange planet inhabited by creatures with four arms and five tentacles attached to each hand. The planet also has a different appearance from Earth or Uriel. Ask the children to create a shadowbox showing the inhabitants and their planet.

Creative Dramatization

Creative drama allows children to interact with the characters in the story, interpret aspects of plot development, and express their reactions to the author's style.

Suggestions for Creative Dramatizations

1 *Characterization.* Have children role-play Mrs. Whatsit's first visit to Charles Wallace's home and Meg's and Mrs. Murry's reactions to her.

2 *Setting, Author's Style.* Chapter 4 has been used by upper elementary classes to create a Reader's Theater presentation. Children have accompanied their oral readings with music that depicts the mood of the action and setting as Meg describes the light disappearing (p. 56); the sensations of moving with the earth (p. 58); leaving the silver glint of autumn behind and arriving in a golden field filled with light, multicolored flowers, singing birds, and an air of peace and joy (pp. 59–61); the transformation of Mrs. Whatsit into a beautiful winged creature with a voice as warm as a woodwind, with the clarity of a trumpet, and the mystery of an English horn; and ascending into the atmosphere to observe the moon and then seeing the dark ominous shadow that brought a chill of fear—the dark thing that their father was fighting.

3 *Author's Style.* Have children pantomime the passages of pages 56 and 57 when Meg experiences the black thing, complete with darkness, the feeling of the body being gone, her legs and arms tingling, traveling through space, and reuniting with Charles and Calvin on Uriel.

4 *Theme, Characterization.* Have children debate the argument between Meg and It, talking through Charles Wallace, found on page 160. Have them consider the question, and encourage one side to take It's view—like and equal are the same thing; people will be happy if they are alike—while the other side argues Meg's point—like and equal are two different things; people cannot be happy if they are the same.

5 *Characterization, Extending Plot.* Have children pretend that the story continues and role-play the scene in the kitchen after Mr. Murry, Charles Wallace, Meg, and Calvin return home. What would they say to Mrs. Murry and the two boys? What would Mrs. Murry and the boys say to them?

Many other science fiction books encourage creative thinking and imagination. If the stories can inspire other children as they did Carl Sagan, they can open new universes and dimensions for children who discover this form of literature.

SUMMARY

Modern fantasy, from the marvelous tales of Hans Christian Andersen, to the make-believe land of Lewis Carroll, to the space adventures of Madeleine L'Engle, provides opportunities for many enjoyable experiences in the classroom, home, and library. Modern fantasies, like traditional tales, should be included in children's story hours.

Puppetry can be an exciting way to encourage children to interact with the characters in a story. Puppetry nurtures imagination through the integration of literature, drama, music, art, and dance. The strange and curious worlds, imaginary kingdoms, animal fantasies, and preposterous situations found in modern fantasy lend themselves to motivating artistic interpretations, such as murals and friezes, collage, montage, mosaic, papier-mâché, and dioramas. Classrooms and homes that provide a rich background of art materials will help children create many interpretations of their favorite storybook settings and characters.

This chapter described a children's literature interest center, developed around the theme "Imagine That." The interest center included examples of motivational paragraphs and book-related activities around the categories Imaginary Kingdoms, Animal Fantasy, and Strange Worlds.

Science fiction is a source of literature that may be read for pleasure and escape; the stories may also be used to stimulate interaction between science and science fiction or social studies and science fiction.

Suggested Activities for Children's Appreciation of Modern Fantasy

☐ Develop a story-hour program that includes several short stories, a major story, and connecting materials appropriate for sharing with a designated age group of children. Decide on a unifying theme around a modern fantasy topic. Combine modern fantasy and traditional literature.

☐ Using the criteria for selecting effective stories for puppetry recommended on page 303, compile a list of stories or scenes from longer stories that might be appropriate for children's puppetry productions. After sharing the stories with children, encourage them to select one they would like to develop as a puppetry presentation. Help them decide on the types of puppets they will create, and interact with them as they pantomime the story, express the characters' feelings, and add dialogue to their production.

☐ With a peer group, investigate one of the methods for artistic interpretation discussed in this chapter—mural, frieze, collage, montage, mosaic, papier-mâché, or diorama. Demonstrate the use of the method to the rest of the class.

☐ Share a modern fantasy selection that lends itself to artistic interpretations. Interact with a child or a group of children as they interpret the story through a mural, frieze, collage, montage, mosaic, papier-mâché, or diorama. How did various children decide to interpret the story? Did they interact with setting, characters, or plot? Did they account for all three aspects of the story? Did they develop an abstract feeling or mood, or did they create concrete images? Encourage the children to tell about their artistic interpretations.

☐ With a peer group, develop a modern fantasy web of interest around children's literature. For example, webs could be developed around such topics as "Travels in Time, Space, and Imagination" or "Animals As People." Identify books that would be appropriate for the topic. Develop an introduction for each book to stimulate interest in the book. Suggest activities to encourage children to interact with the stories in a variety of ways.

☐ Search the science curriculum for topics that could be related to science fiction. Identify appropriate children's science fiction that shows relationships with one of the topics. Develop an oral discussion lesson to share with children. In the lesson, suggest discussion questions and issues that could be used to stimulate creative and critical thinking; relate the science content to the science fiction story.

☐ Choose a science fiction book and develop an in-depth plan for sharing the book with children. Include in the plan discussion questions, activities that relate to science or social

studies, creative dramatizations, artistic interpretations, and creative writing suggestions.

References

1 Baird, Bill. *The Art of the Puppet.* New York: Macmillan, 1965.

2 Briggs, Nancy E., and Wagner, Joseph A. *Children's Literature through Storytelling and Drama.* Dubuque, Iowa: Brown, 1979.

3 Coody, Betty. *Using Literature with Young Children.* Dubuque, Iowa: Brown, 1979.

4 Farlie, Barbara L., and Clarke, Charlotte L. *All about Doll Houses.* New York: Bobbs-Merrill, 1975.

5 Latshaw, George. *Puppetry, the Ultimate Disguise.* New York: Rosen, 1978.

6 Lunstrum, John P., and Taylor, Bob L. *Teaching Reading in the Social Studies.* Newark, Del.: International Reading Association, 1978.

7 Mahlmann, Lewis, and Jones, David Cadwalader. *Puppet Plays for Young Players.* Boston: Plays, 1974.

8 Mahlmann, Lewis, and Jones, David Cadwalader. *Puppet Plays from Favorite Stories.* Boston: Plays, 1977.

9 Merten, George. *Plays for Puppet Performance.* Boston: Plays, 1979.

10 Moore, Eva. *The Fairy Tale Life of Hans Christian Andersen.* Illustrated by Trina Schart Hyman, New York: Scholastic, 1969.

11 Myers, Alan. "Science Fiction in the Classroom." *Children's Literature in Education* 9 (Winter 1978): 182–87.

12 Norton, Donna E. "A Web of Interest." *Language Arts* 54 (November 1977): 928–32.

13 Sagan, Carl. *Cosmos,* Public Broadcasting System, October 26, 1980.

14 Scott-Kemball, Jeune. *Javanese Shadow Puppets.* London: British Museum, 1970.

15 Siks, Geraldine. *Drama with Children.* New York: Harper & Row, 1977.

16 Simmen, Rene. *The World of Puppets.* Photographed by Leonardo Bezola. New York: Crowell, 1975.

17 Speaight, George. *Punch and Judy: A History.* Boston: Plays, 1970.

18 Swanton, Susan. "Minds Alive: What and Why Gifted Students Read for Pleasure," *School Library Journal.* Vol. 30 (March 1984): 99–102.

19 *A Whitman Creative Art Book, Papier-Mâché.* Racine. Wis.: Whitman, 1967.

20 Zjawin, Dorothy. "Close Encounters of the Classroom Kind." *Instructor* 87 (April 1978): 54–57.

CHILDREN'S LITERATURE

Aiken, Joan. *The Wolves of Willoughby Chase*. Illustrated by Pat Marriott. Doubleday, 1963 (I:7–10 R:5). An English country house is the setting for a Victorian melodrama.

Alcock, Vivien. *The Stone Walkers*. Delacorte, 1981 (I:9+ R:5). Statues come to life in a British fantasy.

Alexander, Lloyd. *The Beggar Queen*. Dutton, 1984 (I:10+ R:7). The climax to the Westmark trilogy.

————. *The Black Cauldron*. Holt, Rinehart & Winston, 1965 (I:10+ R:7). Taran and his companions seek to find and destroy the evil cauldron.

————. *The Book of Three*. Holt, Rinehart & Winston, 1964 (I:10+ R:5). The first of the Prydain Chronicles.

————. *The Castle of Llyr*. Holt, Rinehart & Winston, 1966 (I:10+ R:5). The adventure increases when Princess Eilonwy is abducted by the forces of evil.

————. *The Cat Who Wished to Be a Man*. Dutton, 1973 (I:8–10 R:4). The high wizard owns a cat who asks to be changed into a man.

————. *The First Two Lives of Lukas-Kasha*. Dutton, 1978 (I:8–10 R:3). Lukas, a carpenter's apprentice, is conjured into a strange land where he is known as the king.

————. *The High King*. Holt, Rinehart & Winston, 1968 (I:10+ R:5). The final book in the Prydain Chronicles.

————. *The Kestrel*. Dutton, 1982 (I:10+ R:7). The characters in Westmark face war and corruption.

————. *The Marvelous Misadventures of Sebastian*. Dutton, 1970 (I:10+ R:6). A young musician living in the eighteenth century has a series of adventures.

————. *Taran Wanderer*. Holt, Rinehart & Winston, 1967. (I:10+ R:5) The fourth book of the Prydain Chronicles.

————. *The Town Cats and Other Tales*. Illustrated by Laszlo Kubinyi. Dutton, 1977 (I:8–12 R:6). Eight tales about cats who succeed in outwitting humans.

————. *Westmark*. Dutton, 1981 (I:10+ R:7). Moral dilemmas and high adventure combine to give a story of good versus evil.

————. *The Wizard in the Tree*. Illustrated by Laszlo Kubinyi. Dutton, 1975 (I:10+ R:6). Mallory, a kitchen maid, encounters Arbican, a wizard, and her life is changed forever.

I = Interest by age range;
R = Readability by grade level.

Allard, Harry. *Bumps in the Night*. Illustrated by James Marshall. Doubleday, 1979 (I:5–8 R:3). In a book for young children, Dudley Stork is frightened when he hears bumps at night.

Andersen, Hans Christian. *Ardizzone's Hans Andersen*. Translated by Stephen Corrin. Illustrated by Edward Ardizzone. Atheneum, 1979 (I:8–12 R:5). A collection of fourteen fairy tales.

————. *The Emperor's New Clothes*. Retold by Anne Rockwell. Translated by H. W. Dulcken. Illustrated by Anne Rockwell. Harper & Row, 1982 (I:6–9 R:6). Everyone except a child is afraid to tell the emperor the truth about his clothes.

————. *The Fir Tree*. Illustrated by Nancy Ekholm Burkert. Harper & Row, 1970 (I:7–10 R:6). The little tree yearns for a different life and realizes too late that he should have enjoyed the beautiful forest.

————. *Hans Andersen: His Classic Fairy Tales*. Translated by Erik Haugaard. Illustrated by Michael Foreman. Doubleday, 1974 (I:7–10 R:7). A collection of eighteen Andersen tales.

————. *Michael Hague's Favorite Hans Christian Andersen Fairy Tales*. Illustrated by Michael Hague. Holt, Rinehart & Winston, 1981 (I:5–8 R:7). A collection of nine stories printed in fairly large type.

————. *The Nightingale*. Translated by Eva Le Gallienne. Illustrated by Nancy Ekholm Burkert. Harper & Row, 1965 (I:all R:7). The emperor learns to value the real nightingale more than the jeweled mechanical bird.

————. *The Red Shoes*. Translated by Anthea Bell, Illustrated by Chihiro Iwasaki. Neugebauer, 1983 (I:6–10 R:5). A girl must dance as punishment for her pride.

————. *The Snow Queen*. Retold by Amy Ehrlich. Illustrated by Susan Jeffers. Dial, 1982 (I:6–9 R:6). Detailed line drawings suggest a wintry world.

————. *The Snow Queen*. Adapted by Naomi Lewis. Illustrated by Errol LeCain. Viking, 1979 (I:6–9 R:6). An icy Snow Queen is shown against a dark blue background.

————. *The Steadfast Tin Soldier*. Illustrated by Thomas DiGrazia. Prentice-Hall, 1981 (I:6–8 R:6). The toy soldier falls in love with a paper ballerina.

————. *The Swineherd*. Translated by Anthea Bell. Illustrated by Lisbeth Zwerger. Morrow, 1982 (I:8–10 R:6).

A princess does not merit the love of a prince.

————. *Thumbelina*. Retold by Amy Ehrlich. Illustrated by Susan Jeffers. Dial, 1979 (I:6–8 R:6). A beautifully illustrated version of the tale about a girl who is only one inch tall.

————. *The Ugly Duckling*. Retold and illustrated by Lorinda Bryan Cauley. Harcourt Brace Jovanovich, 1979 (I:6–8 R:2). The ostracized duckling turns into a beautiful swan.

————. *The Wild Swans*. Retold by Amy Ehrlich. Illustrated by Susan Jeffers. Dial, 1981 (I:7–12 R:7). Finely detailed illustrations develop a fantasy setting.

Anderson, Margaret J. *In the Circle of Time*. Knopf, 1979 (I:9+ R:5). Two children find themselves in twenty-second-century Scotland.

————. *In the Keep of Time*. Knopf, 1977 (I:9+ R:6). Children step first into the past of the Middle Ages and then into the twenty-second century.

————. *The Mists of Time*. Knopf, 1984 (I:9+ R:5). A story set in 22nd-century Scotland concludes the trilogy.

Atwater, Richard, and Atwater, Florence. *Mr. Popper's Penguins*. Illustrated by Robert Lawson. Little, Brown, 1938 (I:7–11 R:7). Excitement develops when Captain Cook, an Antarctic penguin, is sent to a quiet, dreaming house painter who longs for adventure.

Barrie, James. *Peter Pan*. Illustrated by Nora S. Unwin. Scribner's, 1911, 1929, 1950 (I:8–10 R:6). Wendy, Michael, and John accompany Peter Pan to Never Land.

Baum, L. Frank. *The Wizard of Oz*. Illustrated by W. W. Denslow. Reilly, 1956 (I:8–11 R:6). Many illustrations of the original 1900 edition.

————. *The Wizard of Oz*. Illustrated by Michael Hague. Holt, Rinehart & Winston, 1982 (I:8–11 R:6). A newly illustrated version of Oz.

Bellairs, John. *The Spell of the Sorcerer's Skull*. Dial, 1984 (I:8–12 R:4). A professor disappears and a boy fights evil forces.

Bethancourt, T. Ernesto. *The Mortal Instruments*. Holiday, 1977 (I:10+ R:6). A computer takes control of a boy.

Bond, Michael. *A Bear Called Paddington*. Illustrated by Peggy Fortnum. Houghton Mifflin, 1960 (I:6–9 R:4). Begins a series of adventures after a bear joins a human family.

————. *Paddington Abroad*. Illustrated by Peggy Fortnum. Houghton Mifflin, 1972. (I:6–9 R:4) Paddington plans the family vacation.

————. *Paddington at Large*. Illustrated by Peggy Fortnum. Houghton Mifflin, 1963. (I:6–9 R:4). Paddington has another series of humorous adventures.

————. *Paddington Helps Out*. Illustrated by Peggy Fortnum. Houghton Mifflin, 1961 (I:6–9 R:4). The bear's actions provide humorous episodes.

————. *Paddington Marches On*. Illustrated by Peggy Fortnum. Houghton Mifflin, 1965 (I:6–9 R:4). Continued episodes in bear's life.

————. *Paddington Takes the Air*. Illustrated by Peggy Fortnum. Houghton Mifflin, 1971 (I:6–9 R:4). More about Paddington.

————. *Paddington On Screen*. Illustrated by Barry Macey. Houghton Mifflin, 1982 (I:6–9 R:4). Part of the series of bear stories.

Bond, Nancy. *A String in the Harp*. Atheneum, 1976 (I:10+ R:8). The key to a harp allows Peter to experience events in Taliesin's life.

Boston, Lucy M. *The Children of Green Knowe*. Illustrated by Peter Boston. Harcourt Brace Jovanovich, 1955 (I:8–12 R:6). An old English house, a great-grandmother, and children who lived in the house during past generations make life happy again for a lonely boy.

————. *An Enemy at Green Knowe*. Illustrated by Peter Boston. Harcourt Brace Jovanovich, 1964 (I:8–12 R:6). A psychology researcher and an evil spirit threaten the existence of Green Knowe.

————. *The Guardians of the House*. Illustrated by Peter Boston. Atheneum, 1975 (I:8–12 R:6). Three carvings in an old house cause a boy to have a series of adventures.

————. *The River at Green Knowe*. Illustrated by Peter Boston. Harcourt Brace Jovanovich, 1959 (I:8–12 R:6). Ancestors from the past visit Green Knowe again.

————. *A Stranger at Green Knowe*. Illustrated by Peter Boston. Harcourt Brace Jovanovich, 1961 (I:8–12 R:6). An escaped gorilla seeks sanctuary at Green Knowe.

————. *The Treasure of Green Knowe*. Illustrated by Peter Boston. Harcourt Brace Jovanovich, 1958 (I:8–12 R:6). Tolly finds a treasure hidden in his great-grandmother's house.

Briggs, K. M. *Hobberdy Dick*. Greenwillow, 1977 (I:10+ R:6). An old English manor house in the seventeenth century is the home of hobgoblin Hobberdy Dick.

Brittain, Bill. *The Devil's Donkey*. Illustrated by Andrew Glass. Harper & Row, 1981 (I:9–12 R:5). A boy is changed into a donkey when he comes under the spell of Old Magda.

————. *The Wish Giver*. Illustrated by Andrew Glass. Harper & Row, 1983 (I:8–12 R:5). Three children have surprising experiences when their wishes are granted.

Cameron, Eleanor. *The Wonderful Flight to the Mushroom Planet*. Illustrated by Robert Henneberger. Little, Brown, 1954 (I:8–10 R:4). Two boys construct and fly a spaceship.

Carroll, Lewis. *Alice's Adventures in Wonderland*. Illustrated by S. Michelle Wiggins. Ariel/Knopf, 1983 (I:8+ R:6). Double-page illustrations accompany the classic.

————. *Alice's Adventures in Wonderland*. Illustrated by Justin Todd. Crown, 1984 (I:8+ R:6). Photographs of Alice Liddell provided models for Todd's depiction of Alice.

————. *Alice's Adventures in Wonderland*. Illustrated by John Tenniel. Macmillan, 1866; Knopf, 1984 (I:8+ R:6) A facsimile edition.

————. *Through the Looking-Glass, and What Alice Found There*. Illustrated by John Tenniel. Macmillan, 1872; Knopf, 1984 (I:8+ R:6). A facsimile edition.

————. *Alice's Adventures in Wonderland*. Illustrated by John Tenniel. Macmillan, 1865, 1963 (I:all R:6). The classic tale of an adventure that begins as Alice falls down the rabbit hole.

————. *Alice's Adventures in Wonderland, Through the Looking Glass, and the Hunting of the Snark*. Illustrated by Sir John Tenniel. Chatto, Bodley Head & Jonathan Cape, 1982 (I:all). A reissue of the classic stories celebrates Carroll's 150th anniversary.

————. *The Nursery "Alice."* Illustrated by John Tenniel. Macmillan, 1890, 1979 (I:6–10 R:5). A version of Alice's Adventures in Wonderland prepared by Lewis Carroll for young children.

Chambers, Aidan, ed. *Ghost after Ghost*. Illustrated by Bert Kitchen. Kestrel, 1982 (I:9+ R:6). A collection of nine ghost stories.

Christopher, John. *The City of Gold and Lead*. Macmillan, 1967 (I:10+ R:6). In this science fiction story, Will wins an athletic contest so he may go to the city of the Tripods.

———. *The Pool of Fire*. Macmillan, 1968 (I:10+ R:6). The Tripods are finally defeated, but Will's plans for world unity are hindered by quarreling factions among the people.

———. *The White Mountains*. Macmillan, 1967 (I:10+ R:6). A boy questions the Tripods' control over humans.

Cleary, Beverly. *The Mouse and the Motorcycle*. Illustrated by Louis Darling. Morrow, 1965 (I:7–11 R:3). Ralph makes friends with a boy who owns a toy motorcycle.

———. *Ralph S. Mouse*. Illustrated by Paul O. Zelinsky. Morrow, 1982 (I:7–11 R:3). Ralph finds himself in school.

———. *Runaway Ralph*. Illustrated by Louis Darling. Morrow, 1970 (I:7–11 R:3). Ralph is an unusual mouse who rides a motorcycle and doesn't like his life in an old hotel.

Cohen, Daniel. *The Restless Dead: Ghostly Tales from around the World*. Dodd, Mead, 1984 (I:9+ R:7). A collection of eleven ghost stories.

Collodi, Carlo. *The Adventures of Pinocchio: Tale of a Puppet*. Translated by M. L. Rosenthal, Illustrated by Troy Howell. Lothrop, Lee & Shepard, 1983 (I:9+ R:7). A newly translated version of the classic.

———. *The Adventures of Pinocchio*. Illustrated by Naiad Einsel. Macmillan, 1892, 1963 (I:7–12 R:7). The adventures of a disobedient marionette who eventually learns to be a real boy.

———. *The Adventures of Pinocchio*. Retold by Neil Morris. Illustrated by Frank Baber. Rand McNally, 1982 (I:7–12 R:7). A recent version of the classic story.

Conley, Jane Leslie. *Racso and the Rats of NIMH*. Illustrated by Leonard Lubin. Harper & Row, 1986 (I:8–12 R:4). A sequel to *Mrs Frisby and the Rats of NIMH*.

Cooper, Susan. *The Dark Is Rising*. Illustrated by Alan E. Cober, Atheneum, 1973 (I:10+ R:8). The last of the Old Ones goes on a quest to overcome the forces of evil.

———. *Greenwitch*. Atheneum, 1974 (I:10+R:8). The quest continues for the key to the inscriptions on the grail.

———. *The Grey King*. Atheneum, 1975 (I:10+ R:8). Will Stanton sets out on a dangerous quest to regain the golden harp.

———. *Over Sea, under Stone*. Illustrated by Margery Gill, Harcourt Brace Jovanovich, 1965 (I:10+ R:8). Three children go on a quest for "The Grail."

———. *Seaward*. Atheneum, 1983 (I:10+ R:5). A boy and a girl face perils as they travel from the real world into a complex world filled with good and evil.

———. *Silver on the Tree*. Atheneum, 1977, 1980 (I:10+ R:8). The final battle between the forces of good and evil takes place.

Corbett, W.J. *The Song of Pentecost*. Illustrated by Martin Ursell. Dutton, 1983 (I:9+ R:6). The Pentecost mouse leads his followers to safety in an allegorical tale.

Dahl, Roald. *James and the Giant Peach*. Illustrated by Nancy Ekholm Burkert. Knopf, 1961 (I:7–11 R:7). A boy's unhappiness changes when a peach grows large enough for him to enter.

Dillon, Barbara. *What's Happened to Harry*. Illustrated by Chris Conover. Morrow, 1982 (I:9–12 R:5). Hepzibah the Hateful lures Harry into her kitchen on Halloween and transforms him into a poodle.

Doyle, Arthur Conan. *The Lost World*. Random House, 1959 (I:10+ R:7). Prehistoric animals live in a hidden land.

Engdahl, Sylvia Louise. *This Star Shall Abide*. Illustrated by Richard Cuffari. Atheneum, 1972 (I:10+ R:6). A boy in the future learns about his planet.

Erickson, Russell E. *A Toad for Tuesday*. Illustrated by Lawrence DiFiori. Lothrop, Lee & Shepard, 1974 (I:6–9 R:4). An owl captures Warton, but Warton becomes his friend rather than his dinner.

———. *Warton and Morton*. Illustrated by Lawrence DiFiori. Lothrop, Lee & Shepard, 1976 (I:6–9 R:4). Two toads are separated in the swamp.

———. *Warton and the Castaways*. Illustrated by Lawrence DiFiori. Lothrop, Lee & Shepard, 1982 (I:6–9 R:4). The toads survive a flood.

———. *Warton and the Traders*. Illustrated by Lawrence DiFiori. Lothrop, Lee & Shepard, 1979 (I:6–9 R:4). A toad has an adventure when he leaves his secure woodland home.

Fleischman, Paul. *Graven Images*. Illustrated by Andrew Glass. Harper & Row, 1982 (I:10+ R:6). Three stories of the supernatural.

Fleming, Ian. *Chitty Chitty Bang Bang*. Illustrated by John Burmingham. Random House, 1964 (I:7–11 R:6). A restored car has remarkable properties.

Garner, Alan. *Elidor*. Walck, 1967 (I:10+ R:7). Four children explore an old church in England and are drawn into a world in the grip of an evil power.

———. *The Moon of Gomarth*. Philomel, 1979 (I:10+ R:5). A wizard saves the children from the powers of the underworld.

———. *The Owl Service*. Walck, 1968 (I:10+ R:5). The discovery of an old set of dishes decorated with an owl pattern marks the beginning of some strange events.

———. *The Weirdstone of Brisingamen*. Walck, 1969 (I:10+ R:5). Two modern English children discover the truth about an ancient legend as they battle witches, troll women, and wolves.

Godden, Rumer. *The Dolls' House*. Illustrated by Tasha Tudor. Viking, 1947, 1962 (I:6–10 R:2). Three dolls want a home of their own.

———. *The Mousewife*. Illustrated by Heidi Holder. Viking, 1982 (I:7–10 R:3). A mousewife wishes for adventure, and a turtledove longs for freedom.

Grahame, Kenneth. *The Open Road*. Illustrated by Beverley Gooding. Scribner's, 1979 (I:7–10 R:7). Based on a chapter from *The Wind in the Willows*.

———. *Wayfarers All: From the Wind in the Willows*. Illustrated by Beverley Gooding. Scribner's, 1981 (I:7–10 R:7). A picture book version of one of the original chapters.

———. *The Wind in the Willows*. Illustrated by E. H. Shepard. Scribner's, 1908, 1940 (I:7–12 R:7). Mole, Water-Rat, and Toad of Toad Hall have a series of adventures along the river, on the open road, and in the wild wood.

Hamilton, Virginia. *Dustland*. Greenwillow, 1980 (I:10+ R:7). The psychic unit travels into a future time when earth supports only dust and mutant forms of animal and human life.

———. *The Gathering*. Greenwillow, 1981 (I:10+ R:7). The psychic group of friends go into a domed city of the future.

———. *Justice and Her Brothers*. Greenwillow, 1978 (I:10+ R:7). Justice and her brothers have psychic powers.

———. *The Magical Adventures of Pretty Pearl*. Harper & Row, 1983 (I:10+ R:5). Pretty Pearl comes to earth to help former slaves journey from Georgia to Ohio.

Hooks, William H. *Mean Jake and the Devils*. Illustrated by Dirk Zimmer. Dial, 1981 (I:9–12 R:6). Three stories about how Mean Jake outwits Big Daddy Devil, Devil Junior, and Baby Deviline.

Howe, James. *The Celery Stalks at Midnight*. Illustrated by Leslie Morrill. Atheneum, 1983 (I:8–10 R:5). This animal fantasy is a sequel to *Bunnicula* and *Howliday Inn*.

Hughes, Monica. *Devil on My Back*. Atheneum, 1985 (I:9+ R:6). A person-vs.-society conflict in science fiction.

———. *The Guardian of Isis*. Atheneum, 1984 (I:9+ R:8). A sequel to *The Keeper of the Isis Light*.

———. *The Isis Pedlar*. Atheneum, 1983 (I:9+ R:8). The final story in the science fiction trilogy.

———. *The Keeper of the Isis Light*. Atheneum, 1984 (I:9+ R:8). The first book in a trilogy set on a distant planet.

———. *Ring-Rise Ring-Set*. Watts, 1982 (I:9+ R:6). A science fiction novel portraying life after a great climatic change.

Hunter, Mollie. *The Wicked One*. Harper & Row, 1977 (I:10+ R:7). A hot-tempered Scotsman and a Grollican have an adventure filled with suspense and humor.

Juster, Norton. *The Phantom Tollbooth*. Illustrated by Jules Feiffer. Random House, 1961 (I:9+ R:8). Milo enters a tollbooth and finds himself in the Kingdom of Wisdom.

Kendall, Carol. *The Firelings*. Atheneum, 1982 (I:10+ R:6). A world of little people live on the edge of a volcano.

———. *The Gammage Cup*. Illustrated by Erik Blegvad. Harcourt Brace Jovanovich, 1959 (I:8–12 R:4). The peaceful existence of a land inhabited by little people is challenged by five nonconformists and an outside enemy.

Key, Alexander. *Escape to Witch Mountain*. Illustrated by Leon B. Wisdom, Jr. Westminster, 1968 (I:8–12 R:6). Two children search for others like themselves after a sinister man tries to use their powers.

———. *The Forgotten Door*. Westminster, 1965 (I:8–12 R:6). A boy from another planet is not understood by people.

King-Smith, Dick. *The Mouse Butcher*. Illustrated by Margot Apple. Viking, 1982 (I:9–12 R:6). An animal fantasy explores what happens when cats are isolated on an island.

———. *Pigs Might Fly*. Illustrated by Mary Rayner. Viking, 1982 (I:9–12 R:6). The runt of the litter helps his fellow pigs in their time of need.

Kipling, Rudyard. *The Elephant's Child*. Illustrated by Lorinda Bryan Cauley. Harcourt Brace Jovanovich, 1983 (I:5–7 R:7). A highly illustrated version of one of the "Just So Stories."

———. *The Jungle Book*. Doubleday, 1964 (originally 1894,) (I:8–12 R:7). A collection of jungle stories including "Mowgli's Brothers," "Tiger-Tiger!" "Rikki-Tikki-Tavi," and "Toomai of the Elephants."

———. *Just So Stories*. Doubleday, 1902, 1907, 1952 (I:5–7 R:5). A collection enjoyed by young children.

———. *Just So Stories*. Illustrated by Victor G. Ambrus. Rand McNally, 1982 (I:5–7 R:5). The classic stories newly illustrated.

Langton, Jane. *The Astonishing Stereoscope*. Illustrated by Erik Blegvad. Harper & Row, 1971 (I:10+ R:7). Edward and Eleanor discover that they can enter the world of pictures inside the stereoscope.

Lawson, Robert. *Ben and Me*. Little, Brown, 1939 (I:7–11 R:6). The autobiography of Benjamin Franklin's friend, Amos Mouse.

———. *Rabbit Hill*. Viking, 1944 (I:7–11 R:7). The animals on the hill are waiting expectantly for the new folks.

L'Engle, Madeleine. *A Swiftly Tilting Planet*. Farrar, Straus & Giroux, 1978 (I:10+ R:7). Charles Wallace travels a perilous journey through time to keep a mad dictator from destroying the world.

———. *A Wind in the Door*. Farrar, Straus & Giroux, 1973 (I:10+ R:7). Strange beings come to enlist the children's aid in the galactic fight against evil.

———. *A Wrinkle in Time*. Farrar, Straus & Giroux, 1962 (I:10+ R:5). A search for Meg and Charles's father takes them across the galaxy into combat with an evil darkness that is threatening the cosmos.

LeGuin, Ursula K. *The Farthest Shore*. Illustrated by Gail Garraty. Atheneum, 1972 (I:10+ R:6). Ged, the Archmage of Roke, is placed in final combat against an evil wizard.

———. *Tombs of Atuan*. Illustrated by Gail Garraty. Atheneum, 1971, 1980 (I:10+ R:5). Ged, the wizard, comes to the Tombs of Atuan seeking the missing half of the Ring of Erreth-Akbe.

———. *A Wizard of Earthsea*. Illustrated by Ruth Robbins. Parnassus, 1968 (I:10+ R:6). Young Sparrowhawk shows great powers of enchantment.

Lewis, C. S. *The Last Battle*. Illustrated by Pauline Baynes. Macmillan, 1956. The final book in the "Chronicles of Narnia" sees Aslan lead his people into paradise.

———. *The Lion, the Witch and the Wardrobe*. Illustrated by Pauline Baynes. Macmillan, 1950 (I:9+ R:7). Four children enter the magical kingdom of Narnia through a wardrobe.

———. *The Magician's Nephew*. Illustrated by Pauline Baynes. Macmillan, 1955 (I:9+ R:7). This sixth book in the chronicles explains how Aslan created Narnia.

———. *Prince Caspian, the Return to Narnia*. Illustrated by Pauline Baynes. Macmillan, 1951 (I:9+ R:7). The prince leads his army of talking beasts against the Telmarines.

———. *The Silver Chair*. Illustrated by Pauline Baynes. Macmillan. 1953 (I:9+ R:7). The children complete Aslan's mission.

———. *The Voyage of the Dawn Treader*. Illustrated by Pauline Baynes. Macmillan, 1952 (I:9+ R:7). Lucy and Edmund are reunited with King Caspian of Narnia.

Lewis, Naomi, ed. *The Silent Playmate: A Collection of Doll Stories*. Illustrated by Harold Jones. Macmillan, 1981 (I:7–9 R:6). An anthology of fantasies, folktales, poems, and realistic stories about dolls.

Lindgren, Astrid. *Pippi in the South Seas*. Illustrated by Louis S. Glanzman, Viking. 1959 (I:7–11 R:5). Pippi continues her hilarious adventures on a South Seas island.

———. *Pippi Longstocking*. Illustrated by Louis S. Glanzman. Viking, 1950 (I:7–11 R:5). Pippi does some very unusual things such as scrubbing the floor with brushes tied onto her feet.

———. *Pippi on the Run*. Photographs by Bo-Erik Gyberg. Viking, 1971, 1976 (I:6–10 R:3). Large color photographs accompany the story of Pippi, the strongest girl in the world.

Lunn, Janet. *The Root Cellar*. Scribner's, 1983 (I:10+ R:4). A girl has a time warp experience that sends her back to Canada in the 1860s.

McCaffrey, Anne. *Dragonquest*. Ballantine, 1981 (I:10+ R:6). Continued adventures on a distant planet.

———. *Dragonsinger*. Atheneum, 1977 (I:10+ R:6). Menolly studies under the masterharper of the planet Pern.

———. *Dragonsong*. Atheneum, 1976 (I:10+ R:6). The planet Pern must be protected from the spores that can destroy all living matter.

MacDonald, George. *At the Back of the North Wind*. Illustrated by Arthur Hughes. Dutton, 1871 and 1966 (I:10+ R:6). In an allegorical story a poor boy travels to "Back of the North Wind."

————. *The Princess and the Goblin*. Illustrated by Nora S. Unwin. Macmillan, 1872, 1951 (I:10+ R:9). Princess Irene discovers her fairy godmother spinning magical thread.

MacDonald, Reby Edmond. *The Ghosts of Austwick Manor*. Atheneum, 1982 (I:9–12 R:6). An old dollhouse allows two sisters to go back in time and discover a family curse.

McKinley, Robin. *The Blue Sword*. Greenwillow, 1982 (I:10+ R:7). A girl discovers her mysterious powers and her heritage.

————. *The Hero and the Crown*. Greenwillow, 1984 (I:10+ R:7). Aerin faces the forces of evil during her quest for the crown.

Mahy, Margaret. *The Changeover*. Atheneum, 1984 (I:10+ R:7). A girl discovers her supernatural powers and saves her brother.

Marzollo, Jean and Marzollo, Claudio. *Jed's Junior Space Patrol: A Science Fiction Easy-to-Read*. Illustrated by David S. Rose. Dial, 1982 (I:6–8 R:1). Robots and telepathic animals add to the space adventure.

Milne, A. A. *The Christopher Robin Story Book*. Illustrated by Ernest H. Shepard. Dutton, 1966 (I:6–10 R:3). A collection of stories and poems from four Milne books.

————. *The House at Pooh Corner*. Illustrated by Ernest H. Shepard. Dutton, 1928, 1956 (I:6–10 R:3). Pooh builds a house.

————. *Winnie-The-Pooh*. Illustrated by Ernest H. Shepard. Dutton, 1926, 1954 (I:6–10 R:5). Pooh has adventures with his nursery friends and Christopher Robin.

Norton, Andre. *Lavender Green Magic*. Illustrated by Judith Gwyn Brown. Crowell, 1974 (I:9–12 R:6). A magic dream pillow and a maze planted in the 1600s lead three children back to a time when people believed in witches.

————. *Red Hart Magic*. Illustrated by Donna Diamond. Crowell, 1976 (I:9–12 R:4). A miniature inn permits time travel.

Norton, Mary. *Bed-Knob and Broomstick*. Illustrated by Erik Blegvad. Harcourt Brace Jovanovich, 1943, 1971 (I:7–11 R:6). An old brass bed becomes a flying machine.

————. *The Borrowers*. Illustrated by Beth and Joe Krush. Harcourt Brace Jovanovich, 1952, 1953 (I:7–11 R:3). Three little people survive by borrowing items from the human household above.

————. *The Borrowers Afield*. Illustrated by Beth and Joe Krush. Harcourt Brace Jovanovich, 1955 (I:7–11 R:4). The Clock family leave their home under the floorboards and escape into the fields.

————. *The Borrowers Afloat*. Harcourt Brace Jovanovich, 1959 (I:7–11 R:4). Fantasy about little people.

————. *The Borrowers Aloft*. Harcourt Brace Jovanovich, 1961 (I:7–11 R:4). Additional tales about small people in a normal world.

————. *The Borrowers Avenged*. Illustrated by Beth and Joe Krush. Harcourt Brace Jovanovich, 1982 (I:7–11 R:4). A new book in the Borrowers series.

O'Brien, Robert C. *Mrs. Frisby and the Rats of NIMH*. Illustrated by Zena Bernstein. Atheneum, 1971 (I:8–12 R:4). A group of superior rats escape from a laboratory.

O'Shea, Pat. *The Hounds of the Morrigan*. Holiday, 1986 (I:10+ R:6). Irish traditional literature influences this modern fantasy.

Park, Ruth. *Playing Beatie Bow*. Atheneum, 1982 (I:10+ R:6). A girl from Sydney, Australia, travels in time back to the 1870s.

Phipson, Joan. *The Watcher in the Garden*. Atheneum, 1982 (I:10 R:7). A garden has a strange influence on an older man, a girl, and a disruptive boy.

Potter, Beatrix. *The Tailor of Gloucester, From the Original Manuscript*. Warne, 1969, 1978 (I:5–9 R:8). Text is illustrated with Potter's original drawings.

————. *The Tale of Peter Rabbit*. Warne, 1902. The original tale of the mischievous rabbit.

————. *A Treasury of Peter Rabbit and Other Stories*. Avenel, 1979 (I:3–7 R:6). A collection of favorite stories, including "Peter Rabbit," "Benjamin Bunny," "Squirrel Nutkin," "Two Bad Mice," and "Jeremy Fisher."

Rodgers, Mary. *Summer Switch*. Harper & Row, 1982 (I:8–12 R:6). A father and son switch identity in this humorous fantasy.

Rodowsky, Colby F. *The Gathering Room*. Farrar, Straus & Giroux, 1981 (I:10+ R:7). Spirits of people buried in the cemetery are friends of a nine-year-old boy.

Sandburg, Carl. *Rootabaga Stories*. Illustrated by Maud and Miska Petersham. Harcourt Brace Jovanovich, 1922, 1950 (I:8–11 R:7). A series of short nonsense stories.

Selden, George. *Chester Cricket's Pigeon Ride*. Illustrated by Garth Williams.

Farrar, Straus & Giroux, 1981 (I:6–9 R:4). Chester goes on a night tour of Manhattan because he misses his country home.

————. *The Cricket in Times Square*. Illustrated by Garth Williams. Farrar, Straus & Giroux, 1960 (I:7–11 R:3). Chester the cricket accidentally finds himself in a subway station below Times Square.

————. *Harry Cat's Pet Puppy*. Farrar, Straus & Giroux, 1975 (I:7–11 R:3). Harry experiences problems after he adopts a dog.

————. *Tucker's Countryside*. Farrar, Straus & Giroux, 1969 (I:7–11 R:3). The friends come to Connecticut to help Chester save the meadow.

Showell, Elen Harvey. *Cecelia and the Blue Mountain Boy*. Illustrated by Margot Tomes, Lothrop, Lee & Shepard, 1983 (I:8–12 R:5). A girl discovers music on a remote Appalachian mountain.

Sleator, William. *Interstellar Pig*. Dutton, 1984 (I:10 R:8). A game becomes a real experience in a science fiction story.

Snyder, Zilpha Keatley. *Below the Root*. Illustrated by Alton Raible. Atheneum, 1975. (I:9–12 R:6). A girl searches for a civilization underground.

Tolkien, J. R. R. *Farmer Giles of Ham*. Illustrated by Pauline Baynes. Houghton Mifflin, 1978 (I:7–10 R:6). Farmer Giles becomes a hero when he accidentally fires his blunderbuss into a giant's face.

————. *Fellowship of the Ring*. Houghton Mifflin, 1967 (I:12+ R:8) Part of the trilogy enjoyed by older readers.

————. *The Hobbit*. Houghton Mifflin, 1938 (I:9–12 R:6). Bilbo Baggins, a hobbit, joins forces with thirteen dwarfs in their quest to overthrow the evil dragon.

————. *The Lord of the Rings*. Houghton Mifflin, 1974 (I:12+ R:8). Part of the trilogy enjoyed by older readers.

————. *The Return of the King*. Houghton Mifflin, 1967 (I:12+ R:8). Part of the trilogy enjoyed by older readers.

Travers, Pamela L. *Mary Poppins*. Illustrated by Mary Shepard. Harcourt Brace Jovanovich, 1934, 1962 (I:7–11 R:7). An unusual nanny arrives with the east wind and changes the life of the Banks family.

————. *Mary Poppins in Cherry Tree Lane*. Illustrations by Mary Shepard. Delacorte, 1982 (I:7–11 R:7). The nanny returns to give the Banks children a magical happening in the park on Midsummer Eve.

Voigt, Cynthia. *Building Blocks*. Atheneum, 1984 (I:9 R:7). A time warp experience helps a boy understand his father.

Watson, Simon, *No Man's Land*. Greenwillow, 1976 (I:10+ R:6). Mechanization in the twenty-first century causes a boy to rebel.

Wetterer, Margaret K. *The Giant's Apprentice*. Illustrated by Elise Primavera. Atheneum, 1982 (I:9–12 R:5). A blacksmith's apprentice is rescued from an evil giant.

White, E. B. *Charlotte's Web*. Illustrated by Garth Williams. Harper & Row, 1952 (I:7–11 R:3). Charlotte, with the help of Templeton the rat, saves Wilbur's life and creates a legend.

———. *Stuart Little*. Illustrated by Garth Williams. Harper & Row, 1945 (I:7–11 R:6). Mrs. Little's second son is quite different from the rest of the family; he is a mouse.

Williams, Margery. *The Velveteen Rabbit*. Illustrated by Allen Atkinson, Knopf, 1984 (I:6–9 R:5). Another newly illustrated version of the 1922 classic.

———. *The Velveteen Rabbit*. Illustrated by Michael Hague. Holt, Rinehart & Winston, 1983 (I:6–9 R:5). Drawings emphasize the boy.

———. *The Velveteen Rabbit*. Illustrated by Ilse Plume. David R. Godine, 1982 (I:6–9 R:5). New illustrations for a classic tale.

———. *The Velveteen Rabbit: Or, How Toys Become Real*. Illustrated by Michael Green. Running Press, 1982 (I:6–9 R:5). Drawings in brown tones create a newly illustrated version of the story.

———. *The Velveteen Rabbit: Or How Toys Become Real*. Doubleday, 1958. Illustrated by William Nicholson. (I:6–9 R:5). A toy rabbit is given life after his faithful service to a child.

Wiseman, David. *Jeremy Visick*. Houghton Mifflin, 1981 (I:10+ R:4). A contemporary Cornish boy goes back in time to discover the location of a boy lost in a mine accident.

———. *Thimbles*. Houghton Mifflin, 1982 (I:10+ R:4). Two thimbles in an old family trunk provide the ties between the present and 1819 when a girl goes back in time.

Wrightson, Patricia. *A Little Fear*. Hutchinson, 1983 (I:9 R:6). An old woman outwits the Njimbin, a creature from Australian folklore.

Yolen, Jane. *Dragon's Blood*. Delacorte, 1982 (I:10+ R:7). On the planet Austar IV a boy raises a dragon to be a fighter.

———. *The Acorn Quest*. Illustrated by Susanna Natti. Crowell, 1981 (I:7–10 R:6). The quest is for a golden acorn that could end the famine for the animals.

———. *Dream Weaver*. Illustrated by Michael Hague. Collins, 1979 (I:8–12 R:5). Seven tales spun by a blind gypsy dream weaver tell of love, death, and loyalty.

———. *The Girl Who Cried Flowers*. Illustrated by David Palladini. Crowell, 1974 (I:7–10 R:6). Five original fairy tales about giants, miraculous abilities, and wisdom overcoming adversity.

———. *The Hundredth Dove and Other Tales*. Illustrated by David Palladini. Crowell, 1977 (I:7–10 R:6). Seven original fairy tales.

———. *Neptune Rising: Songs and Tales of the Undersea Folks*. Illustrated by David Weisner. Philomel, 1982 (I:7–10 R:6). A collection of stories about undersea beings.

———. *The Robot and Rebecca and the Missing Owser*. Illustrated by Lady McCrady. Knopf, 1981 (I:8–10 R:5). The year is 2121 and Rebecca's three-legged pet is missing.

8

Poetry

□
RHYTHMIC PATTERNS OF LANGUAGE
□
INVOLVING CHILDREN IN POETRY

Rhythmic Patterns of Language

Rainbow Writing

Nasturtiums with
their orange cries
flare like trumpets;
their music dies.

Golden harps
of butterflies;
the strings are mute
in autumn skies.

Vermillion chords,
then silent gray;
the last notes of
the song of day.

Rainbow colors
fade from sight,
come back to me
when I write.

Eve Merriam
Rainbow Writing, p. 3

Poetry, according to Eve Merriam (20), is "Rainbow Writing" because it colors the human mind with the vast spectrum of human experience. Just as the rainbow inspires an awe of nature, so too may a poem inspire an awe for words and the expression of feelings. Cecil Day-Lewis (7) agrees. He compares the effect of poetry on words to the effect of sand on pennies: in a miraculous way, poetry brightens words that may have appeared dull or ordinary. Poetry adds a new dimension to the imagination. It often has a musical quality that attracts children and appeals to their emotions. The poet's choice of words can suggest new images and create delightful word plays. When a poet can see and feel from a child's point of view, poetry can provide children with hours of enjoyment.

Many poems allow children to see or feel with fresh insights. The first section of this chapter discusses the values of poetry, the characteristics of poems children prefer, the criteria for selecting poetry, and the elements and forms of poetry. It concludes with a discussion of children's poets and the poems they write to create this magical world of the rainbow for their youthful readers.

THE VALUES OF POETRY FOR CHILDREN

Edwin Muir (23) believes that poets and children have much in common. When "most lucky," says Muir, poets are like children new to the world, experiencing things around them "as if for the first time, in their original radiance or darkness" (p. 269). Children can share feelings, experiences, and vision with poets. Poetry also brings them new understanding of the world. It encourages children to play with words, interpret the world in a new way, and realize the images that are possible when words are chosen carefully. Through poetry, children may discover the power imprisoned in words, a power that the poet can release (8).

Jean Le Pere, during a stimulating address to the International Reading Association (15), identified six reasons for sharing poetry with children. First, poetry provides pure enjoyment. Young children begin to discover the enjoyment in poetry by hearing and sharing nonsense poems, Mother Goose rhymes, and tongue twisters. They grow into poetry through story poems such as those written by A. A. Milne. They gradually discover the many exciting forms available to the poet. Second, poetry provides children with knowledge about concepts in the world around them: size, numbers, colors, and time. Third, because choice of precise and varied words plays such an important role in poetic expression, poetry encourages children to appreciate language and expand their vocabularies. Horses not only run, they clop; kittens jump, but they also pounce; and the moon may be not only bright, but also a silver sickle. Fourth, poetry helps children identify with people and situations. With Robert Louis Stevenson they go up in a swing; with Robert Frost they share a snowy evening in the woods; and with Karama Fufuka they brag that "My Daddy Is a Cool Dude." Fifth, poetry expresses moods familiar to children and helps children understand and accept their feelings. Other children empathize with the child in Charlotte Zolotow's "Nobody Loves Me." Sometimes it seems as if nobody loves the speaker, and sometimes it seems as if everybody loves him—feelings common to all children. Finally, poetry grants children insights into themselves and others, developing their sensitivity to universal needs and feelings. Through poems written by other children, as well as by adults, children discover that others have experiences similar to their own and express feelings poetically.

WHAT IS POETRY?

What is this literary form that increases enjoyment, develops appreciation for language, and helps children gain insights about themselves? Poetry is an elusive subject not easily defined; it is not based on fact or easily measured or classified. There is not one accepted definition of poetry. Consider, for example, the following definitions of poetry suggested by poetry critics, poets, and children. Critic Patrick Groff (13) maintains that poetry for children is writing that, in addition to using the mechanics of poetry, transcends literal meaning. He explains: "The use of original combinations of words is probably the easiest, the best, and the most obvious way to write poetry that transcends the literal and goes beyond a complete or obvious meaning. Consequently, in poetry a word has much more meaning than a word in prose. In the former the emphasis is connotative rather than denotative. Words possess suggested significance apart from their explicit and recognized meanings. It is the guessing element that requires the reader to go below the surface of words, to plumb their literal meanings. Figurative language most often provides the guessing element" (p. 185).

An emotional and physical reaction defined poetry for poet Emily Dickinson who related poetry to a feeling: if she read a book that made "her body so cold no fire could warm" her, she knew it was poetry; if she felt physically as if the top of her head were taken off, she also knew it was poetry.

Judson Jerome (14) contends that poetry is words performed. He stresses that the meaning of the words cannot be separated from their sounds. Just as a visual shape is important to the sculptor or the painter, so the tonal shape is important to the poet. Jerome compares the work of the poet to the composition of a musician; in both forms, the total quality is essential.

Poet Harry Behn (3) reports a thought-provoking example of what children think poetry is or is not. When he asked children to tell him what poetry should be, one boy replied, "Anything that recites nicely without people. . . . People are stories. A poem is something else. Something way out. Way out in the woods. Like Robert Frost waiting in a snowstorm with promises to keep"

(p. 159). Other answers suggested the range of children's definitions of poetry: "A poem should be about animals, what you feel, springtime, something funny, anything you see and hear, anything you can imagine. Anything. Even a story!" (p. 159). While these definitions differ, they do reveal that children have very personal reactions to poetry.

Overall, these various definitions of poetry highlight the importance of an original combination of words, a distinctive sound, and an emotional impact. A visual element is also significant in poetry. Some poems are like paintings; they must be seen to be appreciated. Poets may make a statement or increase the impact of their words by carefully arranging the words on the page. Lines are grouped into stanzas, open spaces may emphasize words, an important word may be capitalized, or the arrangement of the whole poem may suggest the subject matter.

Such essential elements of poetry must be savored to be enjoyed. Like a painting or a sculpture, poetry cannot be experienced rapidly. It must be read slowly, even reread several times, for the reader or listener to become immersed in its sounds and imagery. In other words, children must have time to see, hear, and feel the world of the poet.

CHARACTERISTICS OF POEMS CHILDREN PREFER

Harry Behn's (3) interview with children suggests that they differ in their definitions of poetry and in their likes and dislikes. Adults should consider children's individual interests when choosing poetry for them. Samuel French Morse (22) believes that children can honestly judge what speaks to their imaginations and that their judgment must be respected.

THROUGH THE EYES OF A POET

Poetry Doesn't Have to Be Boring!

Creator of strange beasts and fanciful worlds of humorous incidents, JACK PRELUTSKY shares his views on making poetry exciting.

ONCE THERE WAS A teacher who had charge of thirty-three open and eager young minds. One Monday morning, the teacher opened her curriculum book, which indicated that she should recite a poem to her students. She did, and it came out something like this:

> Blah blah the flower,
> blah blah the tree,
> blah blah the shower,
> blah blah the bee.

When she had finished her recitation she said, "Please open your geography books to page one-hundred-thirty-seven."

On Tuesday morning, the teacher (a wonderful person who happened to be rather fond of poetry) decided, on her own initiative, to read another poem to her class. This poem, which was somewhat longer than the first, came out something like this:

> blah blah blah blah blah blah hill,
> blah blah blah blah blah blah still,
> blah blah blah blah blah blah mill,
> blah blah blah blah daffodil.

Then she said, "Please open your history books to page sixty-two."

She went on like this for the entire week, and by Friday, the children (who knew what was coming when she opened her book of verse) began making peculiar faces and shifting restlessly in their seats. The staunchest aesthetes in the group had begun to lose interest in flowers, bees, and hills, etc. Many of the children were harboring strange feelings about poetry. They began saying things about poetry to themselves and to each other. Here are some of the things they said:

Even though children's interests and experiences vary widely, students of children's literature will discover valuable information in the research that has investigated children's poetry choices. Several researchers have identified poems that children enjoy and analyzed the subjects and elements in these poems. Carol Fisher and Margaret Natarella (9) examined children's poetry preferences in the first through the third grade. They found that children preferred narrative poems and limericks, poems about strange and fantastic events, traditional poems, and poems that rhymed and/or used alliteration and onomatopoeia to create sound patterns. Ethel Bridge (4) investigated children's poetry preferences in the middle grades and concluded that both girls and boys like poems related to their own experiences and interests, humorous poems, and poems with elements of rhythm and rhyme. Because children's interests vary so widely, she

concluded, poetry selections are difficult to categorize according to grade level.

Ann Terry (25) investigated the poetry preferences of children in the fourth, fifth, and sixth grades. She also analyzed poetic elements in the poems the children preferred. She concluded that:

1 Children's enthusiasm for poetry declines as children advance in the elementary grades.
2 Children respond more favorably to contemporary poems than to traditional ones.
3 Children prefer poems dealing with familiar and enjoyable experiences.
4 Children enjoy poems that tell a story or have a strong element of humor.
5 Children prefer poems that feature rhythm and rhyme.
6 Among the least popular poems are those that rely too heavily on complex imagery or subtly implied emotion.

"Poetry is boring."
"Poetry is dumb."
"Poetry doesn't make any sense."
"Poetry is about things that don't interest me."
"I hate poetry."

Once there was another teacher with a class of thirty-three young students. She was also a wonderful person with a fondness for poetry. One Sunday evening, she opened her curriculum book and saw that a unit of poetry was scheduled for the next day's lesson. "Hmmmmmm," she mused. "Now what poem shall I share with them tomorrow?" After giving it some careful thought, she settled on a poem about a silly monster, which the poet had apparently created out of whole cloth, and which she thought might stimulate her pupils' imaginations. "Hmmmmmm," she mused again. "Now how can I make

this poem even more interesting?" She deliberated a bit more and, in the course of memorizing the poem, came up with several ideas. The next morning, this is what happened:

"Children," she said. "Today is a special day. It is the first day of silly monster week, and to honor the occasion, I am going to share a silly monster poem with you." She held up a small tin can, and continued. "The monster lives in this can, but I am not going to show it to you yet, because I would like you to imagine what it looks like while I'm reciting the poem."

She then recited the poem, and upon reaching the last word in the last line, suddenly unleashed an expanding snake from the can. The children reacted with squeals of mock terror and real delight. Then they asked her to recite the poem

again, which she did. Afterward, she had them draw pictures of the silly monster. No two interpretations were alike.

The drawings were photographed and later presented in an assembly as a slide show, with the children reciting the poem in chorus. She shared a number of other poems during "silly monster week," always showing her honest enthusiasm and finding imaginative methods of presentation. She used masks, musical instruments, dance, sound-effects recordings, and clay sculpture. The children grew so involved that she soon was able to recite poems with no props at all. At the end of the week, these are some of the things her students said about poetry:

"Poetry is exciting."
"Poetry is fun."
"Poetry is interesting."
"Poetry makes you think."
"I love poetry."

7 The majority of teachers in the fourth, fifth, and sixth grades pay little attention to poetry, seldom read it to children, and do not encourage them to write their own poems.

When Terry analyzed the forms of poetry children preferred or disliked, she concluded that narrative poems and limericks were among the most preferred, while haiku and free verse were among the least popular. As for poetic elements, Terry found that the most preferred poems contained pronounced rhythm and rhyme, or otherwise emphasized sound. In contrast, complex imagery and figurative language were elements in the least liked poems. Her content analysis showed that the most popular poems were humorous, even nonsensical, with most about familiar experiences or animals.

Both Bridge and Terry stress that adults should provide children with many experiences that include a wide range of poetry. Terry also recommends that books on poetry be made accessible to children, that listening centers include tapes and records of poetry, and that a rich poetry environment be used to stimulate children's interest in writing their own poetry.

One reason for the narrow range of poems children enjoy may be that adults infrequently share poetry with them. The enjoyment of poetry, like the enjoyment of other types of literature, can be increased by an enthusiastic adult who reads poetry to children. Because Terry's research indicates that teachers of older children seldom use poetry with them, enthusiasm for poetry must first be stimulated among adults themselves, if parents, teachers, and librarians are to share poetry with children.

The need for and the advantages of longer interactions with poetry are exemplified in an analysis of poetry included in the International Reading Association's Children's Choices. Sam Sebesta (24) reports that "serious poetry, blank and free verse, and extended imagery—all qualities that children disapproved of in other preference studies—are present on the lists of Children's Choices" (p. 67). For example, children liked serious traditional poems such as Robert Frost's "Stopping by Woods on a Snowy Evening" and the poems in Arnold Adoff's *My Black Me: A Beginning Book of Black Poetry*. They liked the personified desert in Byrd Baylor's *The Desert Is Theirs*. They chose Arnold Adoff's free verse *Tornado!*, and the imagistic poems about everyday things in

Valerie Worth's *More Small Poems*, and Myra Cohn Livingston's *The Way Things Are and Other Poems*. In addition, Sebesta found that the number of poetry books included in children's literary preferences implied a greater affection for poetry than was previously found in many other studies.

Sebesta's conclusions about the reasons for the discrepancies between the previous studies and the Children's Choices provide valuable insights for anyone responsible for selecting and sharing poetry. First, unlike many of the research studies that present poetry in a brief fashion, the poetry on the Children's Choices is available in the classroom and is shared with children over a two- to six-week period. Second, unlike most of the studies that present poetry orally, the poetry on the Children's Choices includes books that emphasize the visual impact of poetry. The selections frequently develop unique arrangements on the page, and the illustrations arouse the readers' interests and feelings. Third, recent developments in teaching poetry emphasize both the study of poetry's structure and readers' responses to poetry. This merger of the two approaches may expand the range of poetry that children enjoy.

CRITERIA FOR SELECTING POETRY FOR CHILDREN

The research discussed above indicates some of the form and content characteristics of poetry that children prefer. The following list of criteria for selecting poetry for children is compiled from recommendations by Leonard Clark (5), Patrick Groff (13), Harry Behn (3), Samuel Morse (22), Myra Cohn Livingston (16), and Kinereth Gensler and Nina Nyhart (12):

1 Poems with exciting meters and rhythms are most likely to appeal to young children.
2 Poems for young children should emphasize the sound of language and encourage play with words.
3 Sharply cut visual images and words used in a fresh, novel manner allow children to expand their imaginations and see or hear the world in a new way.
4 Poems for young children should tell simple stories and introduce stirring scenes of action.
5 Poems selected should not have been written down to children's supposed level.

6 The most effective poems are presented with a careful incompleteness of information so that children have room to interpret, to feel, and to put themselves into the poems. The degree to which the reader is provoked to find the part that is missing or not understood is another measure of a poem's worth. Does the poem encourage children to extend comparisons, images, and findings?

7 The subject matter should delight children, say something to them, titillate their egos, strike happy recollections, tickle their funny bones, or encourage them to explore.

8 Poems should be good enough to stand up under repeated readings.

ELEMENTS OF POETRY

The poet uses everyday language in different ways to encourage readers to see familiar things in a new light, to draw on their senses, and to fantasize with the imaginative quality of their minds. The poet also uses certain devices to create a medley of sounds, suggest a visual interpretation, and communicate a message to others or himself. The above criteria for selecting poetry for children refer to the importance of poetic elements such as rhythm, rhyme and other sound patterns, repetition, figurative language, and shape in the creation of poetry.

Rhythm

The word *rhythm*, is derived from the Greek *rhythmos*, "to flow." In poetry this flowing quality refers to the whole movement of words in the poem. Sound, stress, pitch, and number and pattern of syllables all direct and control the ideas and feelings expressed in a poem. Many poems have a definite, repetitive cadence, or meter, with certain lines containing a certain number of pronounced "beats." For example, limericks (discussed on p. 339) have a strict rhythmic structure easily recognizable even when one is hearing them in a foreign language. Free verse, however, usually has a rather casual, irregular rhythm not so different from that of everyday speech.

Poets use rhythm for four specific purposes. First, rhythm can increase enjoyment in hearing language. Young children usually enjoy the repetitive cadences of nursery rhymes, chants, and nonsensical verse. Rhythm encourages children to join in orally, experiment with the language, and move to the flow of language. Second, rhythm can highlight and emphasize specific words. Poets often use stress to suggest the importance of words. Third, rhythm can create a dramatic effect. An irregular meter or repeatedly stressed words may immediately attract a listener's or reader's attention. Fourth, rhythm can suggest the mood of a poem. For example, a rapid rhythm can suggest excitement and involvement, while a slow, leisurely rhythm can suggest a lazy, contemplative mood. David McCord uses rhythm to suggest the sounds a stick might make if a child dragged it along a fence. Rhythm in this poem highlights and emphasizes specific words, attracts and holds attention, and suggests a certain mood.

The Pickety Fence

The pickety fence
The pickety fence
Give it a lick it's
The pickety fence
Give it a lick it's
A clickety fence
Give it a lick it's
A lickety fence
Give it a lick
Give it a lick
Give it a lick
With a rickety stick
Pickety
Pickety
Pickety
Pick

David McCord
*Far and Few: Rhymes of the
Never Was and Always Is*, p. 7

Rhythm is often used to give the listener or reader the feeling of being involved with the poem's action. Kinereth Gensler and Nina Nyhart (12), who have used poetry to stimulate children's feeling of involvement, suggest that the rhythm of a poem works particularly well when it reinforces the poem's content. Consider, for example, Robert Louis Stevenson's "From a Railway Carriage." The rhythm suggests the dash and rattle of a train as it crosses the country. One can easily imagine oneself peering out the window as the scenery rushes by.

From a Railway Carriage

Faster than fairies, faster than witches,
Bridges and houses, hedges and ditches;
And charging along like troops in a battle,

All through the meadows the horses and
   cattle:
All of the sights of the hill and the plain
Fly as thick as driving rain;
And ever again, in the wink of an eye,
Painted stations whistle by.

Here is a child who clambers and scrambles,
All by himself and gathering brambles;
Here is a tramp who stands and gazes;
And here is the green for stringing the daisies!
Here is a cart run away in the road
Lumping along with man and load;
And here is a mill and there is a river:
Each a glimpse and gone forever!

Robert Louis Stevenson
A Child's Garden of Verses, 1883

Rhyme and Other Sound Patterns

Sound is an important part of the pleasure of poetry. One of the ways a poet can emphasize sound is through rhyming words. Many beloved traditional poems for children—such as Edward Lear's "The Owl and the Pussy-Cat"—use careful rhyme schemes. The twenty-five most preferred poems in Ann Terry's (25) study of children's poetry preferences contain a rhyming pattern. Rhyming words may occur at the ends of lines and within lines. Poets of nonsense verse may even create their own words to achieve a humorous, rhyming effect. Consider, for example, Zilpha Keatley Snyder's use of rhyme in "Poem to Mud." The end rhymes—*ooze–slooze, crud–flood,* and *thickier–stickier,*—suggest visual and sound characteristics of mud. The internal rhymes—*fed–spread, slickier–stickier–thickier*—create a tongue-twisting quality.

Poem to Mud

Poem to mud—
Poem to ooze—
Patted in pies, or coating the shoes.
Poem to slooze—
Poem to crud—
Fed by a leak, or spread by a flood.
Wherever, whenever, whyever it goes,
Stirred by your finger, or strained by your toes,
There's nothing sloopier, slipperier, floppier,
There's nothing slickier, stickier, thickier,
There's nothing quickier to make grown-ups sickier,
Trulier coolier,
Than wonderful mud.

Zilpha Keatley Snyder
Today Is Saturday, pp. 18–19

Poets also use *alliteration*, the repetition of initial consonants or groups of consonants, to create sound patterns. In "The Tutor," Carolyn Wells uses repetition of the beginning consonant *t* to create a humorous poem about a teacher trying to teach "two young tooters to toot." "The Tutor" is one of the poems selected by Isabel Wilner for *The Poetry Troupe*, a collection of over two hundred poems that children have selected for reading aloud. Mary Ann Hoberman's four-line poem, "Gazelle" also in Wilner's collection, contains fifteen words beginning with *g*. If a poem contains a great deal of alliteration, a tongue twister results.

Assonance, the repetition of vowel sounds, is another means of creating interesting and unusual sound patterns. Jack Prelutsky uses the frequent repetition of the long *e* sound in the following poem:

Don't Ever Seize a Weasel by the Tail

You should never squeeze a weasel
for you might displease the weasel,
and don't ever seize the weasel by the tail.

Let his tail blow in the breeze;
if you pull it, he will sneeze,
for the weasel's constitution tends to be a little frail.

Yes the weasel wheezes easily;
the weasel freezes easily;
the weasel's tan complexion rather suddenly turns
   pale.

So don't displease or tease a weasel,
squeeze or freeze or wheeze a weasel
and don't ever seize a weasel by the tail.

Jack Prelutsky
A Gopher in the Garden and Other Animal Poems, p. 19

The sounds of some words suggest the meaning they are trying to convey. The term *onomatopoeia* refers to words that imitate the actions or things with which they are associated. Words such as *plop, jounce,* and *beat* may suggest to children the loud sound of rain hitting the concrete in Aileen Fisher's "Rain." Young children who like to experiment with language may develop their own nonsense words that suggest to them a certain sound or meaning. In Kinereth Gensler and Nina Nyhart's (12) *The Poetry Connection*, two poems written by second graders incorporate onomatopoeic language. One boy uses consecutive letter *d*s to suggest that rain sounds like a machine gun. A girl uses repetitive words—*lip–lap* and *slip–slap*—to suggest the sound of a waterfall.

Repetition

Poets frequently use repetition to enrich or emphasize words, phrases, lines, or even whole verses in a poem. David McCord uses considerable repetition of whole lines in "The Pickety Fence," and Lewis Carroll uses repetition to accent his feelings about—

Beautiful Soup

Beautiful Soup, so rich and green,
Waiting in a hot tureen!
Who for such dainties would not stoop?
Soup of the evening, beautiful Soup!
Soup of the evening, beautiful Soup!
 Beau—ootiful Soo—oop!
 Beau—ootiful Soo—oop!
Soo—oop of the e—e—evening,
 Beautiful, beautiful Soup!

Beautiful Soup! Who cares for fish,
Game, or any other dish?
Who would not give all else for two
Pennyworth only of beautiful Soup?
 Beau—ootiful Soo—oop!
 Beau—ootiful Soo—oop!
Soo—op of the e—e—evening,
 Beautiful, beauti—FUL SOUP!

Lewis Carroll
Alice's Adventures in Wonderland, 1865

"Beautiful Soup" is another favorite for oral reading; children find they can recreate that marvelous sound of rich, hot soup being taken from the spoon and placed carefully or noisily into their mouths.

Lullabies shared with young children are often enhanced by repetition. Christina G. Rossetti's "Lullaby" uses repetition to suggest a musical quality.

Lullaby

Lullaby, oh, lullaby!
Flowers are closed and lambs are sleeping;
Lullaby, oh, lullaby!
Stars are up, the moon is peeping;
Lullaby, oh, lullaby!
While the birds are silence keeping,
 (Lullaby, oh, lullaby!)
Sleep, my baby, fall a-sleeping,
 Lullaby, oh, lullaby!

Christina Rossetti
Sing-Song, 1872

The cumulative illustrations reinforce the repetitive lines of the poetry. (Illustration by Anita Lobel from *A Rose in My Garden* by Arnold Lobel. Illustration copyright © 1984 by Anita Lobel. By permission of Greenwillow Books, a division of William Morrow and Company, Inc.)

Imagery

Imagery is a primary element in poetry. It encourages children to see, hear, feel, taste, smell, and touch the world created by the poet. We have already seen how rhythm, sound patterns, and repetition cause the reader to experience what a poet is describing. Poets also use figurative language (language with nonliteral meanings) to clarify, add vividness, and encourage readers to experience things in new ways. Several types of figurative language are used in poetry. This discussion will focus on metaphor, simile, personification, and hyperbole.

Metaphors are implied comparisons between two things that have something in common but are essentially different. Metaphors highlight certain qualities in things to make the reader see them in a new way. In the introduction to *Flashlight and Other Poems,* Judith Thurman uses metaphor when she asserts that a "poem is a flashlight, too: the flashlight of surprise. Pointed at a skinned knee or at an oil slick, at pretending to sleep or at kisses, at balloons, or snow, or at the soft, scary nuzzle of a mare, a poem lets us feel and know each in a fresh, sudden and strong light" (26, Introduction). Thurman demonstrates her command of metaphor when she compares the Milky Way to thick white breath in cold air, or clay to a clown without bones, or, in "Spill," a flock of flying sparrows to loose change spilling out of a pocket:

Spill

the wind scatters
a flock of sparrows—
a handful of small change
spilled suddenly
from the cloud's pocket

Judith Thurman
*Flashlight and Other
Poems*, p. 16

While metaphors are implied comparisons, *similes* are direct comparisions between two things that have something in common but are essentially different. The comparisons made by similes are considered direct because the word *like* or *as* is usually included in the comparison. A thirteen-year-old Russian child uses simile to capture the mystery and allure of moonlight on the ocean. Notice the use of the word *like* in the first line. What are the commonalities between a silver sickle and a new moon?

The Path on the Sea

The moon this night is like a silver sickle
Mowing a field of stars.
It has spread a golden runner
Over the rippling waves.
With its winking shimmer
This magic carpet lures me
To fly to the moon on it.

Inna Miller in
The Moon is like a Silver Sickle,
Miriam Morton, ed., p. 28

Such insightful comparisons can develop what Judson Jerome (14) has described as meaning that transcends words. Poetic imagery can open children's minds to a new world of imagination and allow them to ascend to a different level of consciousness.

Personification allows the poet to give human emotions and characteristics to inanimate objects, abstract ideas, and nonhuman living things.

For example, in Olive Dove's "Snowing" (found in Paddy Bechely's anthology *Drumming in the Sky: Poems from 'Stories and Rhymes'*), the effects of a snowstorm are personified as readers glimpse cherry trees that have "white arms upstretched" and "scratchy claw marks." Personification is an important element in Byrd Baylor's poetry about Native Americans and Native American legends. In *Moon Song*, Baylor personifies the moon as a mother who gives birth to Coyote Child, wraps him in her magic, caresses him with pale white mist, shines on him with love. Kaye Starbird uses personification in the following poem to encourage readers to visualize a wind with human characteristics.

The Wind

In spring, the wind's a sneaky wind,
A tricky wind,
A freaky wind,
A wind that hides around the bends
And doesn't die, but just pretends;
So if you stroll into a street
Out of a quiet lane,
All of a sudden you can meet
A smallish hurricane.

And as the grown-ups gasp and cough
Or grumble when their hats blow off,
And housewives clutch their grocery sacks
While all their hairdos come unpinned . . .
We kids—each time the wind attacks—
Just stretch our arms and turn our backs,
And then we giggle and relax
And lean against the wind.

Kaye Starbird
The Covered Bridge House and Other Poems, p.11

Hyperbole is the use of exaggeration to create a specific effect. John Ciardi's humorous "Mummy Slept Late and Daddy Fixed Breakfast" suggests that a waffle is so tough it cannot be dented by a hacksaw or a torch.

Mummy Slept Late and Daddy Fixed Breakfast

Daddy fixed the breakfast.
He made us each a waffle.
It looked like gravel pudding.
It tasted something awful.

"Ha, ha," he said, "I'll try again.
This time I'll get it right." But what I got was in between
Bituminous and anthracite.

"A little too well done? Oh well,
I'll have to start all over."
That time what landed on my plate
Looked like a manhole cover.

I tried to cut it with a fork:
The fork gave off a spark.
I tried a knife and twisted it
into a question mark.

I tried it with a hack-saw.
I tried it with a torch.
It didn't even make a dent.
It didn't even scorch.

The next time Dad gets breakfast
When Mommy's sleeping late,
I think I'll skip the waffles.
I'd sooner eat the plate!

John Ciardi
You Read to Me, I'll Read to You, p. 18

Shape

Poets may place their words on the page in a way designed to enhance the poem's meaning and to create a greater visual impact. Word division, line division, punctuation, and capitalization can all add special emphasis to a poem's content, as when Lewis Carroll writes about "Beau—ootiful Soo—oop!" (see page 335). The shape of the poem may represent the thing or the physical experience the poem describes. In Regina Sauro's "I Like to Swing," the poem becomes wider and wider toward the bottom as the sweep of the swing becomes wider and wider. In "Seals," by William Jay Smith (anthologized in Stephen Dunning, Edward Lueders, and Hugh Smith's excellent *Reflections on a Gift of Watermelon Pickle . . . and Other Modern Verse*), the poem forms the curving shape of a supple seal, reinforced by an accompanying photograph of a seal. Such poems are examples of the concrete poetry discussed later in this chapter (see page 340). Children enjoy discovering that shape may be related to the meaning of the poem and experimenting with shape in their own poetry writing.

FORMS OF POETRY

Some children do not believe they are reading a poem unless the lines rhyme. While adults should not spend time with young children analyzing the form of a poem, children should realize that poetry has many different forms and that, as poet Amy Lowell (17) once remarked, "every form is proper to poetry" (p.7). Children should be encouraged to write their own poetry; when they write poetry, they enjoy experimenting with different forms. For such experiments, however, they need to be immersed in poetry and led through many enjoyable experiences with poems. This section takes a brief look at various forms of poetry including lyric, narrative, ballad, limerick, concrete, free verse, and haiku.

Lyric Poetry

A lyric poem—according to Northrop Frye, Sheridan Baker, and George Perkins (10)—is "a poem, brief and discontinuous, emphasizing sound and picture imagery rather than narrative or dramatic movement. Lyrical poetry began in ancient Greece in connection with music, as poetry sung, for the most part, to the accompaniment of a lyre" (p. 268). The epic poems of the Greeks were narratives emphasizing heroic deeds. The lyric poem—now, as in the past—emphasizes musical, pictorial, and emotional qualities. The musical roots of lyric poetry are indicated by the fact that the lines or verses of a song are now termed *lyrics.*

Poet Jose Garcia Villa's (6) definition of poetry emphasizes the importance of a lyrical quality. According to Villa, a poem must be magical, musical, and fly like a bird. Many of the poems discussed in this chapter have such a lyrical quality.

Children's early experiences with poetry may be through Mother Goose rhymes sung to music and through traditional lullabies sung at bedtime. Consider the melody associated with the words in the following traditional lullaby:

Hush, Little Baby

Hush, little baby, don't say a word,
Mama's going to buy you a mocking bird.
And if that mocking bird don't sing,
Mama's going to buy you a diamond ring.
And if that diamond ring turns to brass,
Mama's going to buy you a looking glass.
And if that looking glass gets broke,
Mama's going to buy you a billy goat.
And if that billy goat won't pull,
Mama's going to buy you a cart and bull.
And if that cart and bull turn over,
Mama's going to buy you a dog named
  Rover.
And if that dog named Rover won't bark,
Mama's going to buy you a horse and cart.
And if that horse and cart fall down,
You'll still be the sweetest little baby in town.

Traditional poem

Later, children's favorite storybook characters may make up verses and sing their poems—as does A.A. Milne's Winnie-the-Pooh, for example.

Many poets write poems that have a singing quality. Jack Prelutsky's anthology *The Random House Book of Poetry for Children* contains, for example, Lois Lenski's "Sing a Song of People," which recreates the tempo of people traveling through the city; John Ciardi's "The Myra Song," which captures the personality of a gay little girl who enjoys singing, skipping, chattering, and playing; and William Blake's "Introduction to 'Songs of Innocence,'" with its piper of "happy songs/Every child may joy to hear."

Narrative Poetry

Poets may be expert storytellers. When a poem tells a story, it is narrative poetry. Story poems, with their rapid action and typically chronological order, have long been favorites of children. They are an excellent means of increasing children's interest in, and appreciation of, poetry.

Robert Browning's "The Pied Piper of Hamelin," first published in 1882, contains many of the characteristics that make narrative poems appealing to children. The actions of the villainous rats, for example, are easy to visualize:

> Rats!
> They fought the dogs, and filled the
>   cats,
>   And bit the babies in the cradles,
> And ate the cheeses out of the vats,
>   And licked the soup from the cook's
>   own ladles,
> Split open the kegs of salted sprats,
> Made nests inside men's Sunday
>   hats,
> And even spoiled the women's chats
>   By drowning their speaking
>   With shrieking and squeaking
> In fifty different sharps and flats.

The plot develops rapidly as the townspeople approach the mayor and the town council demanding action. Into this setting comes the hero:

> And in did come the strangest figure!
> His queer long coat from heel to head
> Was half of yellow and half of red;
> And he himself was tall and thin,
> With sharp blue eyes, each like a pin,
> And light, loose hair, yet swarthy
>   skin,
> No tuft on cheek nor beard on chin,
> But lips where smiles went out and
>   in—
> There was no guessing his kith and
>   kin!

> And nobody could enough admire
> The tall man and his quaint attire:

With rapidity, the council offers the stranger a thousand gilders to rid the town of its rats, and the piper places the pipe to his lips. The tempo of the poem now resembles the scurrying of rats:

> And out of the house the rats came
>   tumbling.
> Great rats, small rats, lean rats,
>   brawny rats,
> Brown rats, black rats, gray rats, tawny rats,
> Grave old plodders, gay young friskers,
>   Fathers, mothers, uncles, cousins,
> Cocking tails and pricking whiskers,
>   Families by tens and dozens,
> Brothers, sisters, husbands, wives—
> Followed the piper for their lives.
> From street to street he piped advancing,
> And step for step they followed dancing,

>   Robert Browning
>   *The Pied Piper of Hamelin*, 1882

After the efficient disposal of the rats comes the confrontation when the mayor refuses to pay the thousand gilders. In retribution the piper puts the pipe to his lips and blows three notes. Now the poem's tempo resembles the clapping of hands and the skipping of feet as every child in the town merrily follows the piper through the wondrous portal into the mountain.

Other narrative poems long popular with children include Clement Moore's "A Visit from St. Nicholas" (now better known as "The Night Before Christmas"), which has been produced as books illustrated by Tomie de Paola and by Tasha Tudor; Lewis Carroll's delightful "The Walrus and the Carpenter," in which some young oysters go for a walk on the beach with one hungry animal and one hungry human; and Henry Wadsworth Longfellow's romantic dramas from early American history, "The Song of Hiawatha" and "Paul Revere's Ride." Many contemporary poets—including John Ciardi, Jack Prelutsky, and Beatrice Curtis Brown—also write narrative poems about nonsensical or realistic topics.

Ballads

The ballad is a form of narrative folk song developed in Europe during the Middle Ages. Minstrels and bards (*bard* is the Welsh word for poet) sang these tales of legend or history, often accompa-

FLASHBACK

THERE WAS AN OLD MAN OF THE WEST, WHO NEVER COULD GET ANY REST: SO THEY SET HIM TO SPIN, ON HIS NOSE AND HIS CHIN, WHICH CURED THAT OLD MAN OF THE WEST.

AN ARTIST who painted birds and reptiles, Edward Lear also entertained children with his absurd poetry and accompanying drawings. These poems entertained without providing instruction. Illustrations and verses in *A Book of Nonsense,* published in 1846, popularized the limerick. Other early nonsense collections of Lear's verses included *More Nonsense* (1872), *Laughable Lyrics* (1877), *Nonsense Botany* (1888), and *Gueery Leary Nonsense* (1911).

nying themselves on stringed instruments. Modern poets have used the ballad form for poems they intend to be read rather than sung, but traditional ballads are part of the oral literary heritage of European culture, passed on by word of mouth. Action, usually heroic or tragic, is the focus of traditional ballads such as "Tom Dooley" and "Barbara Allen." "The meter is simple," says Cecil Day-Lewis (7), "because the ballads were composed by simple people, and often members of the audience liked to make up additional stanzas. It is a fast-moving meter because a ballad generally had quite a long story to tell, and it was necessary to keep it on the go so that listeners shouldn't get bored" (p.57). Day-Lewis compares ballads to movies because both are highly dramatic, relying on fast-paced incidents and dialogue.

Salt-Sea Verse, compiled by Charles Causley, contains a number of sea ballads. Among the most famous is Samuel Taylor Coleridge's "The Rime of the Ancient Mariner." Gene Kemp's anthology *Ducks and Dragons: Poems for Children* contains a variety of English, Scottish, and American ballads that children may enjoy reading or hearing read aloud.

Limericks

The short, witty poems called limericks are very popular with children. Four of the best-liked poems in Ann Terry's (25) study of children's poetry preferences were limericks. All limericks have the same basic structure and rhythm: they are five-line poems in which the first, second, and fifth lines rhyme and have three pronounced beats each, and the third and fourth lines rhyme and have two pronounced beats each. The limerick form was popularized by Edward Lear in the nineteenth century. The following is an example of humorous verse from Lear's *A Book of Nonsense.*

> There was an Old Man with a beard,
> Who said, "It is just as I feared!—
>   Two Owls and a Hen,
>   Four Larks and a Wren
> Have all built their nests in my beard."
>
> Edward Lear
> *A Book of Nonsense,* 1846

Children enjoy the visual imagery this poem creates. They can see and laugh at the predicament of a man having all those fowl nesting in his beard. They also enjoy reciting the definite rhythm and rhyme found in the limerick. David McCord (18), who has written numerous contemporary limericks himself, says that for a limerick to be successful it must have perfect rhyming and flawless rhythm. McCord's amusing limericks in his *One at a Time: Collected Poems for the Young* illustrate the author's ability to play with words and the sounds of language. They may also stimulate children to experiment with language by writing their own limericks. Other contemporary poets who write limericks include N.M. Bodecker, author of *A Person from Britain Whose Head Was the Shape of a Mitten and Other Limericks*.

Concrete Poems

Concrete means something that can be seen or touched, something physically real. When a poet emphasizes the meaning and experience of the poem by shaping it into the form of a picture, concrete poetry results. Robert Froman's poem "Dead Tree," from *Seeing Things: A Book of Poems*, is lettered in the shape of a dead tree trunk.

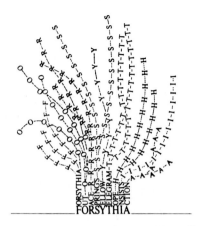

Mary Ellen Solt, ed.
Concrete Poetry: A World View

Mary Ellen Solt was inspired to create both a poem and a picture about the promise of spring in a forsythia bush. Children should turn this poem on its side to read the thoughts of the author.

Children find that concrete poetry is exciting to look at. Observing concrete objects and writing their own picture poems about them also stretches children's imaginations.

Free Verse

Free verse is characterized by little or no rhyme and a rhythm similar to everyday speech. Skateboards are very popular with children, who experience the movement in this poem by Lillian Morrison even though it has little rhyme and no repetitive meter:

The Sidewalk Racer
or
On the Skateboard

Skimming
an asphalt sea
I swerve, I curve, I
sway; I speed to whirring
sound an inch above the
ground; I'm the sailor
and the sail; I'm the
driver and the wheel
I'm the one and only
single engine
human auto
mobile.

Lillian Morrison
*The Sidewalk Racer and Other Poems
of Sports and Motion*, p.12

YOU LIVED A LONG TIME TREE. NOW YOU STAND AWHILE, BARE AND ALONE A MONUMENT TO YOUR PAST, UNTIL YOU ARE READY TO FALL AND BECOME FOOD FOR YOUR FUTURE.

Robert Froman
Seeing Things: A Book of Poems, p. 9

Haiku

Haiku is a very old form of Japanese poetry with specific characteristics: the poem has three lines; the first line has five syllables, the second line has seven, and the final line has five. According to Ann Atwood (1, introduction), a modern writer of haiku, the seventeen syllables of a haiku are a valuable discipline as well as a limitation, resulting ideally in a poem that is "both simple and profound, constructive and expansive, meticulously descriptive yet wholly suggestive." Such poems must be savored, not read hurriedly. Poets of haiku link themselves with nature and the cycle of the seasons.

The following example of Atwood's haiku accompanies a photograph of a beach scene in which a stream of water is placing its mark upon the land:

> A blank page of sand—
> at the water's cutting edge
> the pattern shaping.
>
> Ann Atwood
> *Haiku: The Mood of Earth,*
> p. 4 unnumbered

Haiku by the great Japanese poet Issa, among other geniuses of this art, illustrate how this ancient form of verse has been used to express feelings, experiences, and vision in just the right words. Poems by Issa and important information about his life are included in Richard Lewis's *Of This World: A Poet's Life in Poetry.* Ann Atwood's haiku are collected in her *Haiku: The Mood of the Earth* and other books.

POETS AND THEIR POEMS

Adults who share poetry with children have many classic and contemporary poems from which to select engrossing new experiences for the young. Poets who write for children use subject matter of interest to children—feelings, visions, and dreams as relevant a hundred years ago as today, or situations and environments typical of the later twentieth century. Looking through the books of poetry written for children allows the reader to identify ideas and contents popular with authors of children's poetry: humorous poems; nature poems; poems that encourage children to identify with characters, situations, and locations; poems that suggest moods and feelings; animal poems; and poems about ghosts, dragons, and magic. Although these categories sometimes overlap and some poets write about many different topics, many children's poets focus on certain subjects and types of poetry.

Nursery Rhymes, Nonsense, and Humor: Poems for Starting Out Right

Nursery rhymes are among the best-known literature in America and are the first form of poetry most children experience (see chapter five). According to Nicholas Tucker (27), nursery rhymes are appropriate to share with young children because they are based on easily memorized rhymes and rhythms that help young children master speech. The rhymes encourage children to respond orally as they join in with the rhyme, answer a question formulated by the rhyme, or provide a missing word suggested by the rhyme. Tongue twisters and alliteration expand children's delight in the sounds of language and teach them that words can be manipulated in a playful way. Tucker maintains that characters found in nursery rhymes have important links with children's imaginative life and with antiquity. Children also find a common bond with other children when they share the same nursery rhyme.

Research has shown that children particularly like poetry that tickles their funny bones. Jean Le Pere (15) and Cornelia Meigs (19) believe that nonsense rhymes are the logical successors to Mother Goose rhymes as a means of introducing children to poetry in an enjoyable way. According to Meigs the nonsense poems of great poets such as Edward Lear and Lewis Carroll are ideal: they suggest spontaneous fun through emphatic, regular rhythms, heightened by alliteration. Nonsense verses convey an absurd meaning or even no meaning at all. Humorous poetry, while closely related to nonsense poetry, deals with amusing or comical happenings that might actually befall a person or an animal. Numerous contemporary poets also write nonsensical or humorous verse that entices children into the fun and life-enriching world of poetry.

Edward Lear. Edward Lear, introduced earlier as the popularizer of the limerick form, had many loyal friends among the leaders and creative artists of Great Britain in the nineteenth century. He was welcomed into their homes and became an "Adopty Duncle" to their children. These were the children for whom he wrote and illustrated the nonsense verses collected in *A Book of Nonsense* and *Nonsense Songs and Stories*: limericks, narrative poems, tongue twisters, and alphabet rhymes.

Lear's nonsense poems can be found in many anthologies and have also been illustrated in single editions by several well-known illustrators. *Hilary Knight's The Owl and the Pussy-Cat* is an excellent choice for young children. The highly illustrated text begins with a fantasy situation and presents the poem as a story told by Professor Comfort. A careful search of the illustrations reveals numerous references to Lear's works and interests. *The Pelican Chorus & The Quangle-Wangle's Hat* and *The Courtship of the Yonghy-Bonghy-Bó and the New Vestments* are illustrated by Kevin Maddison in full-page watercolors. *The Scroobious Pip*, illustrated by Nancy Ekholm Burkert, is a longer, more complex poem that was discovered after Lear's death and completed by Ogden Nash. Older children and adults enjoy this poem and the beautiful illustrations as they speculate about the nature of the Scroobious Pip.

Lewis Carroll. Carroll's works are historical milestones of children's literature (see pages 58–59) and are included in chapter seven's discussion of modern fantasy. His nonsense verses are found in *Alice's Adventures in Wonderland* and *Through the Looking Glass*.

One of Carroll's most famous poems is "Jabberwocky," from *Through the Looking Glass*, which introduces those marvelous nonsense words *brillig*, *slithy toves*, and *borogoves*. This poem has been published as a lovely book illustrated by Jane Breskin Zalben. A large collection of Carroll's poems, along with illustrations by John Tenniel, Harry Furniss, Henry Holiday, Arthur B. Frost, and Carroll himself, can be found in Myra Cohn Livingston's compilation of *Poems of Lewis Carroll*. This book also provides considerable information about the poet, who was also a mathematician named Charles Lutwidge Dodgson.

Laura E. Richards. Contemporary children may be surprised to discover that another well-known author of nonsense poetry is the daughter of Julia Ward Howe, who wrote a beautiful but somber poem, "The Battle Hymn of the Republic." Like Lear and Carroll, Richards has shared marvelous words and sounds with children. There are *wizzy wizzy woggums*, *ditty dotty doggums*, and *diddy doddy dorglums*. There are *Rummy-jums*, *Viddi-pocks*, and *Orang-Outang-Tangs*. Her collection *Tirra Lirra, Rhymes Old and New* contains many rhymes that emphasize the sound of language and encourage children to play with words. One of her best-loved nonsense poems follows.

Eletelephony

Once there was an elephant,
Who tried to use the telephant—
No! No! I mean an elephone
Who tried to use the telephone—
(Dear me! I am not certain quite
That even now I've got it right.)

Howe'er it was, he got his trunk
Entangled in the telephunk;
The more he tried to get it free,
The louder buzzed the telephee—
(I fear I'd better drop the song
Of elephop and telephong!)

Laura E. Richards
*Tirra Lirra, Rhymes
Old and New*, p. 31

Shel Silverstein. One of the most popular children's poets, Silverstein writes a lot of nonsense and humorous poetry. Librarians report that Silverstein's *Where the Sidewalk Ends* and *A Light in the Attic* are in considerable demand by young readers. Improbable characters and situations in *A Light in the Attic* include a Quick-Digesting Gink, Sour Ann, and a polar bear in the Frigidaire. Silverstein covers slightly more realistic topics in poems like "The Boa Constrictor," from *Where the Sidewalk Ends*, in which the narrator describes the experience of being swallowed by a boa constrictor. Children enjoy dramatizing this popular action poem.

Consider Silverstein's use of rhythm, rhyme, sound patterns, and repetition in "Ickle Me, Pickle Me, Tickle Me Too."

Ickle Me, Pickle Me, Tickle Me Too

Ickle Me, Pickle Me, Tickle Me too
Went for a ride in a flying shoe.
"Hooray!"
"What fun!"
"It's time we flew!"
Said Ickle Me, Pickle Me, Tickle Me too.

Ickle was captain, and Pickle was crew
And Tickle served coffee and mulligan stew
As higher
And higher
And higher they flew,
Ickle Me, Pickle Me, Tickle Me too.

Ickle Me, Pickle Me, Tickle Me too,
Over the sun and beyond the blue.
"Hold on!"
"Stay in!"
"I hope we do!"
Cried Ickle Me, Pickle Me, Tickle Me too.

Ickle Me, Pickle Me, Tickle Me too
Never returned to the world they knew,
And nobody
Knows what's
Happened to
Dear Ickle Me, Pickle Me, Tickle Me too.

Shel Silverstein
In *Where the Sidewalk Ends*, pp.16–17

Jack Prelutsky. The world created by Prelutsky's nonsense and humorous poetry for children could be described as "the kingdom of immortal zanies." Within the pages of *The Queen of Eene*, children will find preposterous characters such as peculiar "Mister Gaffe," "Poor Old Penelope," "Herbert Glerbertt," and the "Four Foolish Ladies," Hattie, Harriet, Hope, and Hortense. *Rolling Harvey down the Hill* describes the humorous experiences of a boy and his four friends. In *The Sheriff of Rottenshot* eccentric characters include Philbert Phlurk, Eddie the spaghetti nut, and a saucy little ocelot. *The Baby Uggs Are Hatching* contains poems about oddly named creatures such as sneepies and slitchs. Another unusual individual is "Pumberly Pott's Unpredictable Niece," described in the following poem.

Pumberly Pott's Unpredictable Niece

Pumberly Pott's unpredictable niece
declared with her usual zeal
that she would devour by piece after piece,
her uncle's new automobile.

She set to her task very early one morn
by consuming the whole carburetor;
then she swallowed the windshield, the headlights
  and horn,
and the steering wheel just a bit later.

She chomped on the doors, on the handles and locks,
on the valves and the pistons and rings;
on the air pump and fuel pump and spark plugs and
  shocks,
on the brakes and the axles and springs.

When her uncle arrived she was chewing a hash
made of leftover hoses and wires
(she'd just finished eating the clutch and the dash
and the steel-belted radial tires).

"Oh what have you done to my auto," he cried.
You strange unpredictable lass"

"The thing wouldn't work, Uncle Pott," she replied,
and he wept, "It was just out of gas."

Jack Prelutsky
The Queen of Eene, pp. 10–11

William Jay Smith. Smith's *Mr. Smith & Other Nonsense* and *Laughing Time* contain many funny and entrancing poems, including limericks similar to those of Edward Lear. Smith's poem about escape to a strange land illustrates the spirit of fun that makes his poetry appealing to children:

The Land of Ho-Ho-Hum

When you want to go wherever you please,
Just sit down in an old valise,
  And fasten the strap
  Around your lap,
And fly off over the apple trees.

And fly for days and days and days
Over rivers, brooks, and bays
  Until you come
  To Ho-Ho-Hum
Where the Lion roars, and the Donkey
  brays.

Where the unicorn's tied to a golden chain,
And Umbrella Flowers drink the rain.
  After that,
  Put on your hat,
Then sit down and fly home again.

William Jay Smith
Laughing Time, p. 8

Mr. Smith & Other Nonsense ends with an autobiographical poem, "Mr. Smith," in which the reader learns that Mr. Smith has a gentle disposition and a smooth chin, likes people in arts and sciences, collects hats, has never been to Majorca, and abhors boiled cabbage.

John Ciardi. Two books by a poet who has been both a professor of English and a columnist for *Saturday Review World* are written with a simple vocabulary to appeal to children with beginning reading skills: Ciardi's *I Met a Man* and *You Read to Me, I'll Read to You*. In the second book the author tells the reader, "All the poems printed in black, you read to me," and "All the poems printed in blue, I'll read to you." This collection contains the popular "Mummy Slept Late and Daddy Fixed Breakfast," presented on pages 336–37. Other popular poems in this book tell about characters such as "Change McTang McQuarter Cat" and "Arvin Marvin Lillisbee Fitch."

Some of Ciardi's poems are better understood by older children; they often contain satirical observations about human behavior or problems of society. Many of these more sophisticated poems are included in *Fast and Slow*. For example, "And They Lived Happily Ever After for a While" tells what happens when two people who live in the Garbage Mountains are married and then build an oxygen tent in order to survive. The humorous poems in Ciardi's *Doodle Soup* also tend to be caustic.

N. M. Bodecker. Poems that suggest children should wash their hands with number-one dirt, shampoo their hair with molasses, and rinse off in cider are welcomed by young readers. Bodecker uses word play in "Bickering" to create humorous verse enjoyed by older children.

> *Bickering*
> The folks in Little Bickering
> they argue quite a lot.
> Is tutoring in bickering
> required for a tot?
> Are figs the best for figuring?
> Is pepper ice cream hot?
> Are wicks the best for wickering
> a wicker chair or cot?
> They find this endless dickering
> and nonsense and nit pickering
> uncommonly invigor'ing
> I find it downright sickering!
> You do agree!
>
> N. M. Bodecker
> *Hurry, Hurry Mary Dear*, p. 13

In *Hurry, Hurry Mary Dear*, the title poem depicts a harassed woman who is told to pick apples, dill pickles, chop trees, dig turnips, split peas, churn butter, smoke hams, stack wood, take down screens and put up storm windows, close shutters, stoke fires, mend mittens, knit sweaters, and brew tea. This might not be so bad, but the man who is giving the orders sits in a rocking chair all the time. Finally, Mary has enough: she places the teapot carefully on the demanding gentleman's head. Of equal enjoyment are the verses and illustrations in Bodecker's *Let's Marry Said the Cherry*, which includes poems about "The Lark in Sark," "The Geese in Greece," and "The Snail at Yale."

Other Poets and Anthologies of Humorous Verse. The idiosyncrasies of *Jonathan Bing* create a humorous book of verse by Beatrice Curtis Brown. In these poems, Jonathan Bing visits the king, displays his manners, does arithmetic, reads a book, dances, catches tea, and finally moves away. All of poor old Jonathan's actions, however, are a little different from what might be expected.

Dennis Lee shares a banquet of nonsense verse with the reader in *Garbage Delight*. The last verse of the title poem suggests what readers are in for if they want to join the feast:

> With a nip and a nibble
> A drip and a dribble
> A dollop, a walloping bite:
> If you want to see grins
> All the way to my shins
> Then give me some Garbage Delight,
>   Right now!
> Please pass me the Garbage Delight.
>
> Dennis Lee
> *Garbage Delight*, pp. 38–39

Role reversals provide the humorous content in Arnold Adoff's cumulative poem *The Cabbages Are Chasing the Rabbits*. The poem proceeds as the vegetables chase the rabbits and the rabbits chase the dogs.

An early love of William Blake's *Songs of Innocence* and *Songs of Experience* inspired Nancy Willard's *A Visit to William Blake's Inn: Poems for Innocent and Experienced Travelers*. The nonsense and lyric poems in the book, evocatively illustrated by Alice and Martin Provensen, present the odd assortment of guests and workers at the inn, including a rabbit that makes the bed and two dragons that bake the bread.

William Cole has compiled several anthologies of humorous verse, including limericks, two-line poems, and longer poems: *Oh, That's Ridiculous!*, *Oh, What Nonsense!*, and *Poem Stew*. Jill Bennett's collection of poems, *Tiny Tim: Verses for Children*, includes a variety of jingles and other humorous poems. Bryan Holme's *A Present of Laughter: Wit and Nonsense in Pictures and Verse* is a large collection of English nonsense verse.

Nature Poems

Poets, like children, have marveled at the opening of the first crocus, seen new visions in a snowflake, or stopped to watch a stream of crystal-clear water tumbling from a mountain top. They have understood that people should feel a reverence and respect for nature, which entails a special way of hearing as well as a special way of looking.

Aileen Fisher. Fisher's poetry communicates excitement and wonder of discovering nature. Fisher's vision is fresh, full of the magic possible when a person really looks at the natural world. She creates images that are real to children and that may encourage them to extend these images to other observations. In her poems about winter, evergreens after a snowfall wear woolly wraps, snow fills the garden chairs with teddy bears, and footsteps go so quietly the observer thinks they are asleep. Fisher's "Frosted-Window World" allows children to visit winter's house by going inside a frosted windowpane:

> *Frosted-Window World*
>
> The strangest thing,
> the strangest thing
> came true for me today:
> I left myself beneath the quilt
> and softly slipped away.
>
> And do you know
> the place I went
> as shyly as a mouse,
> as curious as a cottontail,
> as watchful as a grouse?
> Inside the frosted windowpane
> (it's rather puzzling to explain)
> to visit Winter's house!
>
> How bright it was.
> How light it was.
> How white it was all over,
> with twists and turns
> through frosted ferns
> and crusted weeds and clover,
> through frost-grass
> reaching up to my knees,
> and frost-flowers
> thick on all the trees.
>
> The brightest sights,
> the whitest sights
> kept opening all around,
> for everything
> was flaked with frost,
> the plants, the rocks,
> the ground,
> and everything was breathless-still
> beneath the crusty rime—
> there wasn't any clock to tick
> or any bell to chime.
> Inside the frosted windowpane
> (it's rather puzzling to explain)
> there wasn't any Time.

> How clear it was.
> How queer it was.
> How near it was to heaven!
> Till someone came
> and called my name
> and said, "It's after seven!"
> And heaven vanished like an elf
> and I whisked back, inside myself.
>
> Aileen Fisher
> *In One Door and Out the Other:*
> *A Book of Poems*, pp. 59–60

Byrd Baylor. The closeness felt between the land and the creatures who live upon it is strikingly presented in Baylor's poetry. She tells readers that they must learn *The Other Way to Listen* if they are to be fortunate enough to hear corn singing, wildflower seeds bursting open, or a rock murmuring to a lizard. Nature will not talk to people if people feel superior, the old man in the poem teaches the child. A person must respect every aspect of nature, humble as well as grand, but must begin with the small things: one ant, one horned toad, one tree. In several of Baylor's books, Peter Parnall's sensitive illustrations are attuned both to nature and to Baylor's words.

The poems in *Desert Voices* are written from the viewpoints of various inhabitants of the desert, animal and human. In *The Desert Is Theirs*, a poem about Native Americans, the poetry and accompanying illustrations develop the theme that the land is meant to be shared; it belongs not only to people, but also to spiders, scorpions, birds, coyotes, and lizards. This beautifully illustrated poem tells how Earthmaker created the desert, Spider People sewed the sky and earth together, and Elder Brother taught the people to live in the sun and touch the power of the earth. The reader discovers that the Papagos know how to share the earth:

> Papagos try
> not to anger
> their animal brothers.
>
> They don't
> step on
> a snake's track
> in the sand.
>
> They don't disturb
> a fox's bones.
> They don't shove
> a horned toad
> out of the path.

Flowing lines in the illustrations create the mood for poems about the desert. From Byrd Baylor, *The Desert Is Theirs*. Text copyright © 1975 by Byrd Baylor; Illustrations copyright © 1975 by Peter Parnall. Reprinted with the permission of Charles Scribner's Sons.)

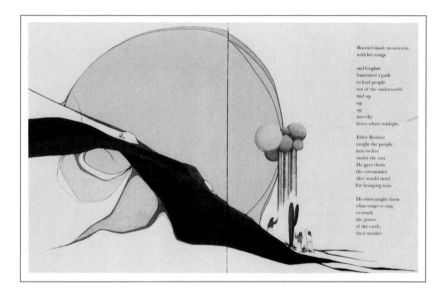

They know
the land belongs
to spider and ant
the same as it does
to people.

They never say,
"This is my land
to do with as I please."
They say,
"We share . . .
we only share."

Byrd Baylor
The Desert is Theirs, p. 15 unnumbered

Ann Atwood. A love of nature and an appreciation of cultures other than our own is evident in Atwood's several books of poetry and color photographs. Her poems, many of them haiku, seem to capture the essence of a rippling brook or a fog-shrouded mountain, and demonstrate that she herself practices the "unhurried art of gazing" she so values in Eastern culture (2, introduction).

The poem that introduces her book *Fly with the Wind, Flow with the Water* expresses the sensitivities characteristic of all Atwood's nature poetry:

This is a book about things
that soar and swing
  and leap and run
  and tumble and swirl
    and flutter and float . . .
It is a book about things that move:
  clouds and creatures
  trees and grasses

and of course it is about YOU—
running and jumping and wonderfully belonging
    with everything
  that flies with the wind
  and flows with the water

Ann Atwood
Fly with the Wind, pp. 1–2 unnumbered

Other Nature Poets and Anthologies. Charlotte Zolotow's poetry is about childhood experiences and nature. Two different editions of Zolotow's *River Winding* provide an interesting basis for comparing the effects of illustrations. Children may enjoy evaluating the illustrations by Regina Shekerjian (1970 edition) and by Kazue Mizumura (1978 edition). The poem "Change" demonstrates how Zolotow is able to bring nature and children's experiences together in poetry:

Change

The summer
still hangs
heavy and sweet
with sunlight
as it did last year.

The autumn
still comes
showering gold and crimson
as it did last year.

The winter
still stings
clean and cold and white
as it did last year.

The spring
still comes
like a whisper in the dark night.

It is only I
who have changed.

Charlotte Zolotow
River Winding, p. 5 (1978 ed.)

Unusual nature photographs by John Earl were the inspiration for a collection of poems selected by Lee Bennett Hopkins: *To Look at Any Thing*. The photographs are stimulating for children, who try to discover animals or pictures in the fantastic shapes that can be found in close-up photographs of gnarled driftwood, moss-draped branches, and ice-covered rocks. This kind of observation can stimulate children to write poetry of their own. *Moments*, another collection of nature poems selected by Hopkins, contains poems about the four seasons of the year.

The ancient stories of Native Americans provide the inspiration for Jamake Highwater's *Moonsong Lullaby*. Notice the images in the following excerpt from the longer poem.

Listen carefully, child.
The singing is everywhere.
The dark trees,
the clouded sky,
the mountains,
the grasslands all echo
the Moon's mellow music
until the last long whisper
that brings the dawn.

Jamake Highwater
Moonsong Lullaby, unnumbered

Poems protesting the treatment given the land and suggesting the need for living in harmony with nature are found in Aline Amon's anthology *The Earth Is Sore: Native Americans on Nature*. Nature also provides the focus for many of the selections included in John Bierhorst's *The Sacred Path: Spells, Prayers & Power Songs of the American Indians*.

Identifying with Characters, Situations, and Locations

Poems about experiences that are familiar to children make up one very large category of poetry for children. These familiar experiences may be related to friends or family, may tell about everyday occurrences, or may provide insights into children's environment.

Myra Cohn Livingston. Whether she is writing about whispers tickling children's ears or the celebration of holidays such as Christmas and Martin Luther King Day, Livingston's verses create images and suggest experiences to which children can relate. One child felt his mouth puckering as he read Livingston's poem about learning to whistle.

I Haven't Learned to Whistle

I haven't learned to whistle.
I've tried—
But if there's anything like a whistle in me,
It stops
Inside.

Dad whistles.
My brother whistles
And almost everyone I know.

I've tried to put my lips together with wrinkles,
To push my tongue against my teeth
And make a whistle
Come
Out
Slow—

But what happens is nothing but a feeble gasping
Sound
Like a sort of sickly bird.

(Everybody says they never heard
A whistle like *that*
And to tell the truth
Neither did I.)

But Dad says, tonight, when he comes home,
He'll show me again how
To put my lips together with wrinkles,
To push my tongue against my teeth,
To blow my breath out and really make a
    whistle.
And I'll *try!*

Myra Cohn Livingston
O Sliver of Liver, p. 12

Additional poems by Myra Cohn Livingston may be found in *The Way Things Are: And Other Poems* and *Celebrations*.

Valerie Worth. Small common things in the world of children can, according to the poems written by Worth, contain magical qualities. Experiences described poetically in *More Small Poems* include looking at a moth's wing through a magnifying glass, observing a kitten with a stiffly arched back, and seeing and hearing fireworks that spill their colors through the night sky. Additional common objects, seen with uncommon insights, are the subjects for Worth's *Still More Small Poems*: grandmother's door with the fancy glass pattern, a kite riding in the air, and rags that are no longer faithful pajamas but crumpled cloth used to wash windows. Something as simple as taking off one's shoes becomes a sensual experience in the following poem.

Barefoot

After that tight
Choke of sock
And blunt
Weight of shoe,

The foot can feel
Clover's green
Skin
Growing,

And the fine
Invisible
Teeth
Of gentle grass,

And the cool
Breath
Of the earth
Beneath.

Valerie Worth
Still More Small Poems, p. 13

Kaye Starbird. Children's honest reactions to experiences such as Mother wanting to jump out of her skin, a friend keeping them waiting once too often, and an obnoxious girl at summer camp are found in Starbird's *The Covered Bridge House and Other Poems*. The poem about the summer camp experience, "Watch Out," describes the exasperation of one girl at Camp Blue Sky when another girl pulls a series of pranks. Starbird's poetry can also be a lesson to teachers, as when she suggests what should not be done when teaching spelling:

The Spelling Test

One morning in a spelling test
The teacher said to Hugh:
"I have a word for you to spell
The word is 'kangaroo.' "
But Hugh was puzzled by the word
Which wasn't one he knew,
So, when he wrote it on the board,
He printed "hannagrue."

"No, No! Go take your seat again,"
The teacher said to Hugh,
"And take along this copy card.
The card says 'kangaroo,'
Then get your pencil out," she said,

"And get your notebook, too.
And write the word a hundred times
And tell me when you're through."

So Hugh did just exactly what
The teacher told him to,
And, when he handed in his work,
The teacher said to Hugh:
"I hope you know your spelling now."
And Hugh said, "Yes, I do,"
Then—walking bravely to the board—
He printed "kannagrue."

Kaye Starbird
The Covered Bridge House and Other Poems, p. 17

David McCord. The poetic genius of McCord was illustrated earlier through his poem, "The Pickety Fence." His work has won him numerous honors, including the Sarah Josepha Hale Medal, a Guggenheim Fellowship, and, in 1977, the first national award for excellence in children's poetry awarded by the National Council of Teachers of English. Clifton Fadiman (18, coverleaf) has said that "David McCord stands among the finest of living writers of children's verse. He is both an acrobat of language and an authentic explorer of the child's inner world."

One at a Time: Collected Poems for the Young contains over two hundred of McCord's poems: favorite chants, such as "Song of the Train," alphabet verses, riddles, poetic conversations, and numerous other poems about animals, children's experiences, nature, and nonsense. The last section of the book, "Write Me Another Verse," attempts to show the reader how to write different poetry forms, including the ballad, the tercet, the villanelle, the clerihew, the cinquain, and the haiku. Earlier in the book, McCord gives directions for writing the couplet (two-line verse), the quatrain (four-line verse), the limerick (five-line verse), and the triolet (eight-line verse).

McCord's skill in using shape to enhance the meaning of a poem is illustrated in the following:

The Grasshopper

Down
a
deep
well
a
grasshopper
fell.

By kicking about
He thought to get out.
  He might have known better,

For that got him wetter.
To kick round and round
Is the way to get drowned,
  And drowning is what
  I should tell you he got.

But
the
well
had
a
rope
that
dangled
some
hope.
And sure as molasses
On one of his passes
  He found the rope handy
  And up he went, *and he*

it
up
and
it
up
and
it
up
and
it
up
went

And hopped away proper
As any grasshopper.

> David McCord
> *One at a Time: Collected Poems*
> *for the Young*, pp. 28–30

Other Poets Who Identify With Characters, Situations, and Locations. *My Daddy Is a Cool Dude*, by Karama Fufuka, presents the experiences of a child who lives in an urban black community. Children can identify with Fufuka's descriptions of good times and bad: celebration of family holidays, the pride felt in a new baby, wanting a bicycle but needing new shoes, listening to the neighbors fighting, or watching the ambulance taking away Jerry Lee's big brother who "o-deed." Fufuka (11) says about her writing, "In writing these poems I have gone back to my childhood and relived the experiences of those years of growing and learning. I have tried to deal here with both the positive and negative aspects of life which constitute reality for a child in the urban black community today. I have tried to do so with the honesty of a child and I hope that

adult readers of my poems will work to change those negative images for the sake of the children who will inherit our tomorrows" (p. 9).

Both realistic and fanciful experiences related to growing up contribute the subjects for X.J. Kennedy's poems in *The Forgetful Wishing Well: Poems for Young People*. Developing an understanding of poetry provides motivation for the selection of poems in Kennedy's anthology *Knock at a Star: A Child's Introduction to Poetry*. The poems in the text are organized to help readers understand elements in and types of poetry.

The excitement of skateboarding, running in the women's 400-meter race, and riding the surf is found in Lillian Morrison's *The Sidewalk Racer and Other Poems of Sports and Motion*. Morrison (21) says that she enjoys writing this kind of poetry because she loves rhythms, "the body movement implicit in poetry, explicit in sports. I have always believed that the attempt to achieve excellence in either of these fields is both noble and exciting. And there are emotions connected with sports, sometimes a kind of transcendence and beauty one wants to catch. One turns naturally to poetry to express these things" (p. 63). (See page 340 for Morrison's "The Sidewalk Racer.")

Moods and Feelings

Children can learn through poets' descriptions of everyday life, dreams, and nostalgia that others experience many moods and feelings like their own.

Langston Hughes. Although Hughes is not considered primarily a children's poet, his poetry explores human feelings, asks difficult questions, and expresses hopes and desires that are meaningful to readers of any age. Some of his poems—such as "Merry-Go-Round"—can be used to help children understand and identify with the feelings and experiences of black people in earlier eras of American history. In another poem, Hughes provides vivid descriptions of what life would be like without dreams:

Dreams

Hold fast to dreams
For if dreams die
Life is a broken-winged bird
That cannot fly.
Hold fast to dreams
For when dreams go

The illustrations enhance the mood of the various holidays. (Illustration copyright © 1985 by Leonard Everett Fisher. Reprinted from *Celebrations* by Myra Cohn Livingston by permission of Holiday House.)

Life is a barren field
Frozen with snow.

Langston Hughes
The Dream Keeper, 1932, 1960

The photograph that accompanies "Dreams" in the anthology *Reflections on a Gift of Watermelon Pickle . . . and Other Modern Verse*, edited by Dunning, Lueders, and Smith, shows a solitary dried weed surrounded by a barren field covered with ice crystals. When this poem was shared with a group of fifth graders, one of the students reminded the class that dreams did not need to die, but, like the weed, could be reborn in the spring.

Cynthia Rylant.   Moods and feelings related to growing up form the unifying theme in Rylant's *Waiting to Waltz: A Childhood*. Rylant's poems

paint a word picture of a young girl feeling pride in her small town, pondering the relationships within the town, and revealing the experiences that are influencing her own maturation. In "Teenagers," for example, Rylant explores the longings of a child who is "too big" for some things and not big enough for others.

Teenagers

Watching the teenagers
in Beaver
using hairspray and
lipstick.
Kissing at ballgames.
Going steady.
And wanting it fast,
wanting it now.
Because all my pretend
had to be hidden.
All my games
secret.
Wanting to be a wide-open child
but too big,
too big.
No more.
Waiting to shave
and wear nylons
and waltz.
Forgetting when
I was last time
a child.
Never knowing
when it
ended.

Cynthia Rylant
Waiting to Waltz: A Childhood, p. 44

Other Poets and Anthologies That Develop Moods and Feelings.   Arnold Adoff's *All the Colors of the Race* contains poems written from the viewpoint of a girl who has black and white parentage. The poems reflect her thoughts and moods as she contemplates her heritage and other experiences in her life. *On Our Way* is Lee Bennett Hopkins's anthology of poetry about the pride and love that are a part of being black, with relevant photographs of today's world by David Parks.

The moods associated with the various interactions between two brothers form the themes in Richard J. Margolis's *Secrets of a Small Brother*. These poems reveal a range of feelings, including jealousy, anger, love, and compassion.

A dream-like mood is captured in the illustrations for a lullaby. (From *The Dream Child* by David McPhail. Copyright © 1985 by David McPhail. By permission of E. P. Dutton, Inc.)

A bedtime fantasy forms the setting for the adventures in David McPhail's *The Dream Child*. McPhail's selection of incidents in the world of Dream Child and Tame Bear creates a happy and safely adventurous dream-like mood. Adventures that could be frightening or disruptive end with discord transformed into harmony. Other moods and feelings related to nighttime, bedtime, and happy dreams are the focus of Nancy Larrick's colorfully illustrated anthology *When the Dark Comes Dancing: A Bedtime Poetry Book* and Kay Chorao's anthology *The Baby's Bedtime Book*, in which a full-page painting accompanies each selection. Fantastic events in a dream world create a happy, imaginative setting in Nancy Willard's *Night Story*.

Animals in Poetry

Animals, whether they are teddy bears, cuddly puppies, purring kittens, or the preposterous beasts of imagination, hold a special place in the hearts of both children and adults. Therefore, it is not surprising that many poets have written about animals. In *Feathered Ones and Furry*, Aileen Fisher shares with children her love for all types of animals, including the furry:

The Furry Ones

I like
the furry ones—
the waggy ones
the purry ones
the hoppy ones
that hurry,

The glossy ones
the saucy ones
the sleepy ones
the leapy ones
the mousy ones
that scurry,

The snuggly ones
the huggly ones
the never, never
ugly ones . . .
all soft
and warm
and furry.

Aileen Fisher
Feathered Ones and Furry, p. viii

Other books of animal poems by one author include David Kherdian's *Country Cat, City Cat*, which describes the lives of two quite different kinds of cats, and X.J. Kennedy's *Did Adam Name* the Vinegarroon?, an alphabetical collection of twenty-six poems about common and uncommon beasts, some mythical and some extinct.

Anthologies of animal poems include Lee Bennett Hopkins's *My Mane Catches the Wind: Poems about Horses*, which describes the birth of a colt and the beauty of a stallion, among other poems that will appeal to horse lovers. Animals and other experiences associated with the circus are the subject of poems in Hopkins's *Circus! Circus!*

Ghostly Poems

Halloween, lonely dark staircases, and empty old houses are settings for the poems in Lilian Moore's *See My Lovely Poison Ivy*. Some of the poems are frightening; others, such as the following, are not.

Teeny Tiny Ghost

A teeny, tiny ghost
no bigger than a mouse,
at most,
lived in a great big house.

It's hard to haunt
a great big house
when you're a teeny tiny ghost
no bigger than a mouse,
at most.

He did what he could do.

So every dark and stormy night—
the kind that shakes a house with
   fright—
if you stood still and listened right,
you'd hear a
teeny
tiny

BOO!

Lilian Moore
See My Lovely Poison Ivy, p. 38

Other vivid poems about ghoulies, ghosties, and graveyards are found in Daisy Wallace's collection, *Ghost Poems*, illustrated by Tomie de Paola. Alfred Noyes's classic poem *The Highwayman* provides a ghostly conclusion to a tale of love, horror, and unselfish motives. Charles Keeping's black and white illustrations reinforce the drama in this poem for older readers. Prior to death, the characters are sketched in black. Following death, the horseman becomes a predominantly white figure riding through ghostly trees, approaching the old inn door, and finding the

landlord's daughter who is now herself a ghostly figure. The world of spirits and eerie images is also evoked by Blaise Cendrars's words and Marcia Brown's illustrations in *Shadow*. Cendrars's carefully chosen words suggest a shadow that prowls, mingles, watches, spies, and sprawls in silence. Brown's collages reinforce this ghostly world.

SUMMARY

Poetry allows children to experience the world with new understanding and share feelings, experiences, and visions with the poet. Reading and sharing poetry is a valuable experience for children because poetry both provides pure enjoyment and serves several educational purposes: (1) helping children gain knowledge about concepts in the world around them, (2) developing children's appreciation for language, (3) encouraging children to identify with characters and situations, (4) providing children with kindred spirits who share their feelings and moods, and (5) inspiring children with insights into themselves and others.

Writers of poetry rely on several elements when they create poetry. While not all these elements are found in all poetry, the following elements were discussed in this chapter: rhythm, rhyme and other sound patterns, repetition, imagery, and shape. The numerous forms of poetry include lyric, narrative, ballad, limerick, concrete, free verse, and haiku.

Research studies about children and poetry have indicated that children's enthusiasm about poetry declines as they advance in the elementary grades; that teachers of older students seldom read poetry to them or encourage the children to write poems; that children particularly enjoy or prefer contemporary poems about familiar experiences, poems that tell a story or are humorous, and poems that have strong rhyme and rhythm; and that children dislike poems with complex imagery.

Several types of poems are especially suitable for fostering children's love of poetry: humorous poems; nature poems; poems identifying with characters, situations, and locations; poems about moods and feelings; animal poems; and poems dealing with ghostly realms. Some people focus on one of these categories, although many others write poems of various types.

Suggested Activities Designed for Adult Understanding of Poetry

☐ Read a poem that relies heavily on rhyming elements. Find the location of the rhyming words (at the end of the line, at the beginning of the line, within the line). Read the poem orally. What feelings do the rhyming elements suggest?

☐ Look through an anthology of poetry and find some poems that rely on sound patterns to create excitement. Prepare for oral presentation a poem that relies on alliteration (the repetition of initial consonant sounds) or assonance (the repetition of vowel sounds). Share the poem orally with a peer group.

☐ Locate several poems that develop literal imagery and several poems that suggest figurative imagery. Is there a difference in the interest level of the two types of imagery? Share the poems with a child. Does the child respond in the same way to these types?

☐ Compile a list of similes and metaphors found in a poem. What image is the poet trying to suggest? Does the simile or metaphor paint a more effective or more easily visualized word picture than a realistic word would produce?

☐ Compare the subject matter of limericks written by Edward Lear with the subject matter of limericks written by contemporary poets such as N. M. Bodecker or William Jay Smith. How are they similar? How do they differ?

☐ Read several collections of haiku. Based on your reading, tell what Ann Atwood (1) meant when she said that haiku is "begun by the writer and completed by the reader."

☐ Select and read several poems by one poet of humorous verse—such as Edward Lear, Lewis Carroll, Laura E. Richards, Jack Prelutsky, William Jay Smith, John Ciardi, or N. M. Bodecker. What poetic elements does the poet use? What subjects does the poet write about?

☐ Compare the content and style of a poet who wrote humorous verse in the nineteenth century (such as Lewis Carroll or Edward Lear) with a contemporary author of humorous verse (such as Jack Prelutsky or N. M. Bodecker). What are the similarities and differences between the writers in the two time periods?

References

1 Atwood, Ann. *Haiku: The Mood of Earth*. New York: Scribner's, 1971.

2 Atwood, Ann. *Haiku-Vision: In Poetry and Photography*. New York: Scribner's, 1977.

3 Behn, Harry. *Chrysalis, Concerning Children and Poetry*. New York: Harcourt Brace Jovanovich, 1968.

4 Bridge, Ethel Brooks. "Using Children's Choices of and Reactions to Poetry As Determinants in Enriching Literary Experience in the Middle Grades." Philadelphia: Temple University, 1966. University Microfilm No. 67–6246.

5 Clark, Leonard. "Poetry for the Youngest." In *Horn Book Reflections*, edited by Elinor Whitney Field. Boston: Horn Book, 1969.

6 Cowen, John E. "Conversations with Poet Jose Garcia Villa on Teaching Poetry to Children." In *Teaching Reading Through the Arts*, edited by John E. Cowen. Newark, Del.: International Reading Association, 1983, pp. 78–87.

7 Day-Lewis, Cecil. *Poetry for You*. New York: Oxford, 1947.

8 Drew, Elizabeth. *Discovering Poetry*. New York: Norton, 1933.

9 Fisher, Carol, and Natarella, Margaret. "Young Children's Preferences in Poetry: A National Survey of First, Second, and Third Graders." *Research in the Teaching of English* 16 (December 1982): 339–354.

10 Frye, Northrop; Baker, Sheridan; and Perkins, George. *The Harper Handbook to Literature*. New York: Harper & Row, Publishers, 1985.

11 Fufuka, Karama. *My Daddy Is a Cool Dude*. New York: Dial, 1975.

12 Gensler, Kinereth and Nyhart, Nina. *The Poetry Connection: An Anthology of Contemporary Poems with Ideas to Stimulate Children's Writing*. New York: Teachers & Writers, 1978.

13 Groff, Patrick. "Where Are We Going with Poetry for Children?" In *Horn Book Reflections*, edited by Elinor Whitney Field. Boston: Horn Book, 1969.

14 Jerome, Judson. *Poetry: Premeditated Art*. Boston: Houghton Mifflin, 1968.

15 Le Pere, Jean. "For Every Occasion: Poetry in the Reading Program." Albuquerque, N. Mex.: Eighth Southwest Regional Conference, International Reading Association, 1980.

16 Livingston, Myra Cohn. "Not the Rose . . ." In *Horn Book Reflections*, edited by Elinor Whitney Field. Boston: Horn Book, 1969.

17 Lowell, Amy. *Poetry and Poets*. New York: Biblo, 1971.

18 McCord, David. *One at a Time*. Boston: Little, Brown, 1977.

19 Meigs, Cornelia, and Nesbitt, Elizabeth. *A Critical History of Children's Literature*. New York: Macmillan, 1969.

20 Merriam, Eve. *Rainbow Writing*. New York: Atheneum, 1976.

21 Morrison, Lillian. *The Sidewalk Racer and Other Poems of Sports and Motion*. New York: Lothrop, Lee & Shepard, 1977.

22 Morse, Samuel French. "Speaking of the Imagination." In *Horn Book Reflections*, edited by Elinor Whitney Field. Boston: Horn Book, 1969.

23 Muir, Edwin. "A Child's World Is As a Poet." In *Children and Literature: Views and Reviews*, edited by Virginia Haviland. Glenview, Ill.: Scott, Foresman, 1973.

24 Sebesta, Sam. "Choosing Poetry." In *Children's Choices*, edited by Nancy Roser and Margaret Frith. Newark, Del.: International Reading Association, 1983.

25 Terry, Ann. *Children's Poetry Preferences: A National Survey of Upper Elementary Grades*. Urbana, Ill.: National Council of Teachers of English, 1974.

26 Thurman, Judith. *Flashlight and Other Poems*. New York: Atheneum, 1976.

27 Tucker, Nicholas. "Why Nursery Rhymes?" In *Children and Literature: Views and Reviews*, edited by Virginia Haviland. Glenview, Ill.: Scott, Foresman, 1973.

KNOWLEDGE ABOUT CONCEPTS, APPRE-
ciation for language, empathy with characters and situations, insights about oneself and others, self-expression, and pure enjoyment are all values of poetry for children.
Unfortunately, research has supported Jon E.
Shapiro's (15) assertion that "poetry has often
been the most neglected component of the language arts curriculum" (p. 91). Over 75 percent
of the middle-elementary teachers in Ann Terry's
(17) study of children's poetry preferences read
poetry to their children less than once a month.
This finding may also relate to the fact that the
children in Terry's study reported a decreased interest in poetry as they progressed through the
elementary grades.

Shapiro (15) maintains that adults' own lack of
interest in poetry causes them to neglect it in the
classroom. The only way for adults to overcome
this aversion and to feel comfortable when sharing poetry with children is to read poetry written
by many fine authors and thus discover a new or
revitalized delight in poetry.

John Gough (4) argues that the anthology format of many poetry collections discourages children's enjoyment. Individual poems are presented in isolation, rather than in a continuity
that sustains children's interests. Gough believes
that appreciation of poetry should be carefully
developed and nurtured through a logical sequence: nursery rhymes and songs; rhymed stories, such as Dr. Seuss's *The Cat in the Hat;* narrative poems that are highly, but carefully,
illustrated; stories, such as A. A. Milne's *Winnie-
the-Pooh*, in which characters, adventures, and
poems are strongly interrelated; narrative poems
that give contextual support to the poetry; and
then a coherent, related sequence of poems by
one poet, in which the poems encourage readers
to understand the personality of the poet and to
appreciate the poems.

University students in this author's classes often say that their aversion to poetry stems from
the way it was presented in their elementary,
middle school, and high school classrooms. They
fondly remember the rhymes and jingles shared
in kindergarten and first grade. But those pleasant associations are undercut by later memories

Involving Children in Poetry

☐

MOVING TO POETRY

☐

**POETRY AND CREATIVE
DRAMATIZATIONS**

☐

POETRY AND CHORAL SPEAKING

☐

POETRY AND MUSIC

☐

WRITING POETRY

of forced memorization of poems and thinking exercises in which everyone had to agree with the teacher's analysis of the poem. One student recalled her feelings of terror every Friday when she had to recite a memorized poem in front of the class, and then had points deducted from her presentation for each error she made.

Other university students, however, describe more positive memories of poetry in their elementary classrooms: teachers who spontaneously shared a wide variety of poetry with their classes; teachers who encouraged students to write poems and share them with an appreciative audience; teachers who had their students experiment with choral readings of poetry, sometimes accompanied by rhythm instruments. One student remembered a teacher who always had a poem to reflect the mood of a gentle rain, a smiling jack-o-lantern, or a mischievous child. Another remembered going outside on a warm spring day, looking at the butterflies and wildflowers in a meadow, listening to the world around her, sharing her feelings with the class, and then writing a poem to express the promise of that beautiful day. Yet another remembered a

librarian who always included poetry in story-hour presentations.

After university students explore the various ways of sharing poetry with children, many of them sadly conclude that something was left out of their education. This section considers some ways that adults may encourage children to enjoy and experience poetry by moving to poetry, using poetry as the basis for creative dramatizations, developing choral speaking, combining music and poetry, and writing poetry themselves.

MOVING TO POETRY

The rhythm, sound, characters, and things in many poems encourage physical responses from children. An observer of children in a playground is likely to see two children swinging a rope while a third child jumps to the rhythm and the actions described in a chant such as the following:

Teddy bear, teddy bear, turn around.
Teddy bear, teddy bear, touch the ground.
Teddy bear, teddy bear, close your eyes.
Teddy bear, teddy bear, be surprised.
Teddy bear, teddy bear, climb up the stairs.
Teddy bear, teddy bear, say your prayers.
Teddy bear, teddy bear, turn out the light.
Teddy bear, teddy bear, say good night.

In a similar way, children may be inspired to move when an adult slowly reads a poem aloud. Valerie Worth's *More Small Poems*, provides children with the opportunity to become a "Kitten," arching their backs, dancing sideways, tearing across the floor, crouching against imagined threats, and pouncing with claws ready; or "Fireworks" exploding in the air, billowing into bright color, and spilling back down toward earth in waterfalls. They can be spectacular in a much quieter way as a "Soap Bubble" that bends into different shapes, rises shimmering into the air, then pops and disappears. Worth's *Still More Small Poems* encourages children to experience the free flight of a "Kite" as the wind tears it from a hand and sends it soaring; to become a "Mushroom" pushing up through the soil; or to go "Barefoot," as their feet emerge from choking socks and they feel the cool clover and gentle blades of grass between their toes.

Children enjoy moving as if they are rockets or airplanes. Leland B. Jacobs's anthology, *Poetry for Space Enthusiasts*, includes several excellent poems that encourage movement. B. J. Lee's "Into

Children respond to the rhythm in a jumping-rope chant.

ISSUE

---◆◆◆◆◆---

Analyzing Poetry: Help or Hindrance?

WILL CHILDREN ENjoy and understand poetry more if they analyze the meaning and meter, identify figurative language, and define terminology and poetic devices? The activities suggested in basal readers that include poetry and in literature anthologies designed to be shared with children frequently suggest the importance of such analysis. Teachers or librarians may ask children to read or listen to a poem for the specific purpose of identifying the author's meaning and theme, locating the similes and metaphors, or identifying the rhyming schemes. Adults encourage such activities in the belief that analyzing poetic devices improves children's understanding, enjoyment, and writing of poetry.

Louise M. Rosenblatt takes a contrasting viewpoint.[1] She maintains that reading poetry should be an aesthetic experience in which children focus upon cognitive and affective elements such as sensations, images, feelings, and ideas that allow them to have a "lived-through" experience. She believes that focusing children's attention on analysis is detrimental when children have not yet had many opportunities to experience poetry on their own terms. Adults should first encourage children to savor what they visualize, feel, think, and enjoy while hearing or reading poetry.

[1] Rosenblatt, Louise M. "What Facts Does This Poem Teach You?" *Language Arts* 57 (April 1980): 386–94.

Space" takes them from the launching pad, into the countdown, through the blast-off, and into a spinning capsule orbiting the earth and reaching into space. With Alice E. London's "Space Pilot," they zoom past the moon, circle the planets, and bring their rocket back to earth.

Poetry anthologies, especially if they group poems according to theme, provide numerous opportunities for moving to poetry. For example, Jack Prelutsky's anthology *The Random House Book of Poetry for Children* allows children to become Stanley Kunitz's "The Waltzer in the House" and William Jay Smith's "Seal."

POETRY AND CREATIVE DRAMATIZATIONS

One of the values of poetry for children noted earlier by Jean Le Pere (9) was encouragement to identify with characters and situations. Ann Terry (17) discovered that narrative poems were among children's favorite poems. Creative dramatizations enhance children's enjoyment of the situations found in poetry (6).

Clement C. Moore's narrative poem "A Visit from St. Nicholas" (now familiarly known as "The Night Before Christmas") suggests several scenes that can be dramatized: children can prepare for the Christmas celebration by trimming the tree and decorating the room; they can imagine the sugarplum dreams and act them out; they can reenact the father's response to hearing the clatter of hoofs; they can be reindeer pulling the loaded sleigh or St. Nicholas as he comes down the chimney, fills the stockings, and then bounds up the chimney and drives out of sight. This poem has many other dramatic possibilities. Children have created the dialogue for an imaginary meeting between the father or the children and St. Nicholas. What would they say to each other? How would they act? If the children could ask St. Nicholas questions, what would they ask? If St. Nicholas could ask questions, what would he want to know? Children have imagined themselves as St. Nicholas going into many homes on Christmas Eve. What was the most unusual experience they had? They have imagined themselves going back to St. Nick's workshop at the

North Pole. What kind of a welcome would they receive?

Adults have used the nonsensical situations found in Jack Prelutsky's poems in *The Queen of Eene* to stimulate humorous dramatizations. One group, for example, dramatized the conversation and actions of the "Four Foolish Ladies," Hattie, Harriet, Hope, and Hortense, as they roped a rhinoceros and took him to tea. Then the group imagined and acted out other predicaments that could have been created by the actions of the foolish ladies. "Gretchen in the Kitchen," stimulates spooky witch scenes at Halloween. The quarts of curdled mud, salted spiders, ogre's backbone, and dragon's blood provide a setting appealing to children who are preparing to be spooks, witches, and black cats.

Other poems can be used to stimulate creative dramatizations:

1   "The Pied Piper of Hamelin," by Robert Browning, located in numerous sources, including Iona and Peter Opie's *The Oxford Book of Children's Verse.*
    The piper lures the rats to their deaths and then entices the children to follow him to a strange land after the mayor refuses to pay for services rendered.
2   *Night Story* by Nancy Willard. A small boy has a series of adventures in dreamland.
3   "Hurry, Hurry Mary Dear," from N. M. Bodecker's book of the same title.
    A harassed woman follows the directions of a demanding man until she has finally had enough.
4   *Jonathan Bing*, by Beatrice Curtis Brown.
    Jonathan tries to visit the king and do other tasks; each time his actions are inappropriate.
5   "The Adventure of Chris," by David McCord, found in *One At A Time: Collected Poems for the Young.*
    A toad and a boy have a discussion about arithmetic, spelling, and what not to miss on earth.
6   *A Visit to William Blake's Inn: Poems for Innocent and Experienced Travelers* by Nancy Willard.
    The characters and the incidents can stimulate many dramatizations, such as visiting with the man in the marmalade hat who arrives with a bucket and mop or riding in Blake's Celestial Limousine.

POETRY AND CHORAL SPEAKING

Choral speaking, the interpretation of poetry or other literature by two or more voices speaking as one, is a group activity allowing children to experience, enjoy, and increase their interest in rhymes, jingles, and other types of poetry. During a choral-speaking or choral-reading experience, children discover that speaking voices can be combined as effectively as singing voices in a choir. Young children who cannot read can join in during repeated lines or can take part in rhymes and verses they know from memory; older children can select anything suitable within their reading ability. Choral speaking is useful in a variety of situations: library programs, classrooms, and extracurricular organizations.

Increasing children's enjoyment of poetry and other literature, not developing a perfect performance, is the main purpose for using choral speaking with elementary children. Adults should allow children to enjoy the experience and experiment with various ways of interpreting poetry. Donna Norton (11) has suggested several guidelines for encouraging children to interact in choral arrangements:

1   When selecting materials for children who cannot read, choose poems or rhymes that are simple enough to memorize.
2   Choose material of interest to children. Young children like nonsense and active words; consequently, humorous poems are enjoyable first experiences and encourage children to have fun with poetry.
3   Select poems or nursery rhymes that use refrains, especially for young children. Refrains are easy for nonreaders to memorize and will result in rapid participation from each group member.
4   Let children help select and interpret the poetry. Have them experiment with the rhythm and tempo of the poem, improvise the scenes of the selection, and try different voice combinations and various choral arrangements before they decide on the best structural arrangements.
5   Let children listen to each other as they try different interpretations within groups.

Barbara McIntyre (10) maintains that adults should also understand the different phases through which children should be guided in their choral interpretations of poetry. First, because young children delight in the rhythm of nursery rhymes, they should be encouraged to explore the rhythm in poetry. They can skip to the rhythm of "Jack and Jill," clap to the rhythm of "Hickory Dickory Dock," and sway to the rhythm of "Little Boy Blue." They can sense fast or slow, happy or sad rhythms through their bodies. They can explore the rhythm and tempo as they "hoppity, hoppity, hop" to A. A. Milne's poem "Hoppity" (found in *When We Were Very Young*).

Second , children should be encouraged to experiment with the color and quality of voices available in the choral-speaking choir. McIntyre (10) says that children do not need to know the meaning of *inflection* (the rise and fall within a phrase), *pitch levels* (the change between one phrase and another), *emphasis* (the pointing out of the most important word), and *intensity* (the loudness and softness of the voices), but adults must understand these terms so they can recommend exciting materials that allow children to try different ways of interpreting a poem.

Third, children should be encouraged to understand and experiment with different types of choral arrangements, such as refrain, line-a-child or line-a-group, antiphonal or dialogue, cumulative, and unison arrangements.

Refrain Arrangement

In this type of arrangement, an adult or a child reads or recites the body of a poem, and the other children respond in unison when a refrain or chorus is repeated. Poems such as Maurice Sendak's *Pierre: A Cautionary Tale*, Lewis Carroll's "Beautiful Soup," and Jack Prelutsky's "The Yak" have lines that seem to invite group participation. A nursery rhyme that encourages young children to participate is "A Jolly Old Pig."

Leader:	A jolly old pig once lived in a sty, And three little piggies she had, And she waddled about saying
Group:	"Grumph! grumph! grumph!"
Leader:	While the little ones said
Group:	"Wee! Wee!"
Leader:	And she waddled about saying
Group:	"Grumph! grumph! grumph!"
Leader:	While the little ones said
Group:	"Wee! Wee!"

Line-a-Child or Line-a-Group Arrangement

To develop this arrangement, one child or a group of children reads the first line, another child or group reads the next line, a third child or group reads the next line, and so forth. This arrangement continues with a different child or different group of children reading each line until the poem is finished. Enjoyable poems for line-a-child arrangements include Zilpha Keatley Snyder's "Poem to Mud," Laura E. Richard's "Eletelephony," and Jack Prelutsky's "Pumberly Pott's Unpredictable Niece." A familiar nursery rhyme can be used to introduce this arrangement:

Child 1 or Group 1:	One, two, buckle my shoe;
Child 2 or Group 2:	Three, four, shut the door;
Child 3 or Group 3:	Five, six, pick up sticks;
Child 4 or Group 4:	Seven, eight, lay them straight;
Child 5 or Group 5:	Nine, ten, a good fat hen.

Antiphonal or Dialogue Arrangement

This arrangement highlights alternate speaking voices. Boys' voices may be balanced against girls' voices, or high voices may be balanced against low voices. Poems such as "Eskimo Chant" found in *The New Wind Has Wings: Poems from Canada* compiled by Mary Alice Downie and Barbara Robertson encourage children to respond in either joyful or fearful voices. Poems with a question-and-answer format or other dialogue between two people are obvious choices for antiphonal arrangements. Poems such as Kaye Starbird's "The Spelling Test" and the nursery rhyme "Pussy-Cat, Pussy-Cat" are enjoyable dialogue arrangements. Paul Fleischman's *I Am Phoenix: Poems for Two Voices* includes poems about birds that are appropriate for choral arrangements. Children enjoy chorally reading the lyrics from folk songs. The words of "Yankee Doodle," for example, can be used with one group of children reading each verse and another group responding with the chorus. The words from the folk song, "A Hole in the Bucket," present a dialogue between Liza and Henry:

| Boys: | There's a hole in the bucket, dear Liza, dear Liza, There's a hole in the bucket, dear Liza, There's a hole. |
| Girls: | Well, fix it, dear Henry, dear Henry, dear Henry. Well, fix it, dear Henry, dear Henry, go fix it. |

Boys: With what shall I fix it, dear Liza, dear Liza?
        With what shall I fix it, dear Liza, with what?

Girls: With a straw, dear Henry, dear Henry, dear Henry.
        With a straw, dear Henry, dear Henry, with a straw.

Boys: But the straw is too long, dear Liza, dear Liza.
        But the straw is too long, dear Liza, too long.

Girls: Then cut it, dear Henry, dear Henry, dear Henry.
        Then cut it, dear Henry, dear Henry, then cut it.

Boys: Well, how shall I cut it, dear Liza, dear Liza?
        Well, how shall I cut it, dear Liza, well, how?

Girls: With a knife, dear Henry, dear Henry, dear Henry.
        With a knife, dear Henry, dear Henry, with a knife.

Boys: But the knife is too dull, dear Liza, dear Liza.
        But the knife is too dull, dear Liza, too dull.

Girls: Then sharpen it, dear Henry, dear Henry, dear Henry.
        Then sharpen it, dear Henry, dear Henry, then sharpen it.

Boys: With what shall I sharpen it, dear Liza, dear Liza?
        With what shall I sharpen it, dear Liza, with what?

Girls: With a whetstone, dear Henry, dear Henry, dear Henry.
        With a whetstone, dear Henry, dear Henry, with a whetstone.

Boys: But the whetstone's too dry, dear Liza, dear Liza.
        But the whetstone's too dry, dear Liza, too dry.

Girls: Then wet it, dear Henry, dear Henry, dear Henry.
        Then wet it, dear Henry, dear Henry, then wet it.

Boys: With what shall I wet it, dear Liza, dear Liza?
        With what shall I wet it, dear Liza, with what?

Girls: With water, dear Henry, dear Henry, dear Henry.
        With water, dear Henry, dear Henry, with water.

Boys: Well, how shall I carry it, dear Liza, dear Liza?
        Well, how shall I carry it, dear Liza, how?

Girls: In a bucket, dear Henry, dear Henry, dear Henry.
        In a bucket, dear Henry, dear Henry, in a bucket.

Boys: But there's a hole in the bucket, dear Liza, dear Liza.
        There's a hole in the bucket, dear Liza, a hole.

Cumulative Arrangement

A crescendo arrangement may be used effectively to interpret a poem that builds up to a climax. The first group reads the first line or verse; the first and second groups read the second line or verse; the first, second, and third groups read the third line or verse; and so forth, until the poem reaches its climax. Then all the groups read together. Edward Lear's "The Owl and the Pussy-Cat" may be read in a cumulative arrangement by six groups; John Ciardi's "Mummy Slept Late and Daddy Fixed Breakfast" is also fun for six groups to develop into a climax, as Daddy's waffles become impossible to eat. Other poems appropriate for cumulative reading include Arnold Adoff's *The Cabbages Are Chasing the Rabbits* and Arnold Lobel's *The Rose in My Garden*. The nursery rhymes "There Was a Crooked Man" and "This Is the House That Jack Built" are also enjoyable.

Group 1:	This is the house that Jack built.
Group 1,2:	This is the malt That lay in the house that Jack built.
Group 1,2,3:	This is the rat that ate the malt, That lay in the house that Jack built.
Group 1,2,3, 4:	This is the cat, That killed the rat, that ate the malt, That lay in the house that Jack built.
Group 1,2,3, 4,5:	This is the dog, That worries the cat, That killed the rat, that ate the malt, That lived in the house that Jack built.
Group 1,2,3, 4,5,6:	This is the cow with the crumpled horn, That tossed the dog, that worried the cat, That killed the rat, that ate the malt, That lay in the house that Jack built.
Group 1,2,3, 4,5,6,7:	This is the maiden all forlorn. That milked the cow with the crumpled horn, That tossed the dog, that worried the cat, That ate the rat, that ate the malt, That lay in the house that Jack built.
Group 1,2,3, 4,5,6,7,8:	This is the man all tattered and torn, That kissed the maiden all forlorn, That milked the cow with the crumpled horn, That tossed the dog, that worried the cat, That killed the rat, that ate the malt, That lay in the house that Jack built.
Group 1,2,3, 4,5,6,7,8,9:	This is the priest all shaven and shorn, That married the man all tattered and torn, That kissed the maiden all forlorn, That milked the cow with the crumpled horn, That tossed the dog, that worried the cat,

Group 1,2,3,
4,5,6,7,8,9,
10:

That killed the rat, that ate the malt,
That lay in the house that Jack built.
This is the cock that crowed in the morn,
That waked the priest all shaven and
    shorn,
That married the man all tattered and
    torn,
That kissed the maiden all forlorn,
That milked the cow with the crumpled
    horn,
That tossed the dog, that worried the
    cat,
That killed the rat, that ate the malt,
That lay in the house that Jack built.

Group 1,2,3,
4,5,6,7,8,9,
10,11:

This is the farmer that sowed the corn,
That kept the cock that crowed in the
    morn,
That waked the priest all shaven and
    shorn,
That married the man all tattered and
    torn,
That kissed the maiden all forlorn,
That milked the cow with the crumpled
    horn,
That tossed the dog, that worried the
    cat,
That killed the rat, that ate the malt,
That lay in the house that Jack built.

A reverse arrangement may be developed in which all groups begin together; with each subsequent line or verse, a group drops out until only one group remains. William Cole's "I'm Mad at You," from *I'm Mad at You*, works well for this interpretation because the child in the poem starts out in great anger but by the end has let off enough "steam" to feel "like peaches and cream."

Unison Arrangement

In this arrangement, the entire group or class reads or speaks a poem together. This arrangement is often the most difficult to perform, because it may tend to create a singsong effect. For this reason, shorter poems such as Myra Cohn Livingston's "O Sliver of Liver," Lillian Morrison's "The Sidewalk Racer" or "On the Skateboard," and Judith Thurman's "Campfire" are appropriate.

Additional Suggestions for Choral Speaking

Fran Tanner (16) recommends that older children experiment with the effects of grouping their voices according to resonance: light, medium, and dark voices. Through experimentation, chil-

dren discover that light voices may effectively interpret happy, whimsical, or delicate parts; medium voices may add to descriptive and narrative parts; and dark voices may interpret robust, tragic, and heavier material. Tanner recommends the following classic poem for such an experiment:

The Brook

(light)	I slip,
(medium)	I slide,
(dark)	I gloom.
(medium)	I glance.
	Among my skimming swallows;
(light)	I make the netted sunbeams dance
	Against my sandy shallows.
(dark)	I murmur under moon and stars
	In brambly wildernesses;
(medium)	I linger by my shingly bars,
(light)	I loiter round my cresses;
(medium)	And out again I curve and flow
	To join the brimming river,
(dark)	For men may come
(dark and medium)	and men may go,
(all)	But I go on forever.

Alfred, Lord Tennyson

The poems in a single poetry collection may be read, discussed, and developed into various choral-speaking arrangements. For example, this activity could accompany Nancy Larrick's anthology, *When the Dark Comes Dancing: A Bedtime Poetry Book*. The poems might be presented in the following ways: Martin Brennan's "Benue Lullaby," refrain; Margaret Wise Brown's "Little Donkey Close Your Eyes," line-a-group; Arthur Guiterman's "Nocturne," antiphonal between lighter voices and heavier voices; Felice Holman's "Night Sounds," antiphonal between male and female voices; Sabine Baring-Gould's "Now the Day Is Over," reverse cumulative; Vachel Lindsay's "The Moon's the North Wind's Cooky," reverse cumulative followed by cumulative; Myra Cohn Livingston's "The Night," unison; and Eve Merriam's "Lullaby," unison.

Librarians, teachers, and other adults who want to use thematic poetry and choral-speaking arrangements throughout the year will find it helpful to compile a file of poems that highlight the different months and seasons. One student in a literature class encouraged her fourth-grade students to experiment with many choral arrangements throughout the year and made a file of the poems and the choral arrangements they enjoyed. She and her students chose their poems from Hazel Fellman's *The Best Loved Poems of the American People*, Helen Ferris's *Favorite Poems* *Old and New*, Rosalind Hughes's *Let's Enjoy Poetry*, Isabel Wilner's *The Poetry Troupe*, and Irving Wolfe's *Music through the Years*. Chart 8.1 lists the poems and choral arrangements this teacher chose to use with each of the months.

CHART 8–1
The months in poetry and choral speaking

	Poem	Author	Month	Choral Arrangement
1.	"The Months of the Year"	Sara Coleridge	September	Line-a-Group; each group reads two lines associated with the twelve months.
2.	"September"	Edwina Falls	September	Unison.
3.	"Father William"	Lewis Carroll	September (fun anytime)	Dialogue—two groups; young man and Father Williams.
4.	"Witch, Witch"	Rose Fyleman	October Halloween	Antiphonal—Adult or group reads questions; second group answers.
5.	"Old Roger"	Anonymous	October Halloween	Refrain.
6.	"Harvest"	M. M. Hutchinson	November Thanksgiving	Cumulative.
7.	"Over the River"	Anonymous	November Thanksgiving	Line-a-Group; six groups.
8.	"In the Week When Christmas Comes"	Eleanor Farijeon	December Christmas	Line-a-Group; six groups.
9.	"Long, Long Ago"	Anonymous	December Christmas	Refrain.
10.	"A Visit from St. Nicholas"	Clement C. Moore	December Christmas	Antiphonal.
11.	"Whispers"	Myra Cohn Livingston	January (snow)	Unison.
12.	"When a Ring's Around the Moon"	Mary Jane Carr	January	Cumulative.
13.	"Dark-Eyed Lad Columbus"	Nancy Byrd Turner	February	Line-a-Group.
14.	"This Land Is Your Land"	Woody Guthrie	February	Refrain.
15.	"March, March Come with Your Broom"	Annette Wynne	March spring	Refrain.
16.	"Faith, I Wish I Were a Leprechaun"	Margaret Ritter	March St. Patrick's Day	Refrain.
17.	"The Umbrella Brigade"	Laura E. Richards	April showers	Line-a-Group.
18.	"Mister Rabbit"	Anonymous	April Easter	Dialogue; Rabbit and Friend.
19.	"Smart"	Shel Silverstein	May (just for fun)	Cumulative.
20.	"Whale"	Mary Ann Hoberman	June (oceanography)	Refrain.
21.	"The Green Grass Growing All Around"	Folk Rhyme	June	Cumulative.

Music encourages the additional
enjoyment of poetry.

POETRY AND MUSIC

The rhythms of poetry and music naturally complement each other. Rhythm instruments, including sticks, bells, tambourines, and blocks, allow children to emphasize the rhythm of a poem and interpret its mood. A group of six-year-olds, for example, thoroughly enjoyed accompanying David McCord's "The Pickety Fence" (from *Far and Few: Rhymes of the Never Was and Always Is*) with their rhythm band sticks. They experimented with the sticks until they sounded just like a picket fence being struck by a child with a stick. They recorded the poem and its accompaniment, and were pleased with the sound interpretation.

Many old ballads and chants have been passed down through the generations in the form of folk songs. They may be listened to, read in choral arrangements, sung, or accompanied by movement, improvisations, and rhythm instruments.

Ruth Crawford Seeger's *American Folk Songs for Children—In Home, School, and Nursery School* (14) presents words, music, and suggestions for interpreting the rhythm and lyrics. The suggestions are a result of using the materials extensively with young children. The following are taken from Seeger's (14, pp. 35–38) recommendations for sharing songs with young children.

1   Sing the song first at its natural speed; allow children to experience the impression of the song as a whole rather than analyzing the song.
2   The songs should not drag. Most were originally sung at a lively speed and with a strong metrical accent.
3   The adult who is sharing the songs with young children should sit directly with the children when presenting and singing the songs.

4   Children should be allowed to listen, then interpret the songs at their own leisure.

5   Many folk songs make excellent rhythm band music.

6   Repeat a song many times, especially when using the songs for rhythmic activities.

7   Include both action songs and listening songs when planning the activities for a session. The changing needs and moods of the children should be considered when making the selections.

8   Do not hurry when moving from one song or activity to another; children frequently derive pleasure from savoring a favorite song or interpreting a song in several different ways. Very young children may need several repetitions before they feel confident enough to join into the activity.

9   Have confidence; be ready with a few "link" songs that draw the children together if there is a need to bring younger children back into the group.

10 Listen to the children; wait, watch, and be ready for them to interpret the words or music. Keep your eyes and attention on the children, not on an instrument or printed page. Be sensitive to signals from the children, even small movements, that give you clues about what the children need or want to do next.

Some old ballads found in poetry or folk song books have been written and illustrated as picture books. John Langstaff has made a book of the English ballad "The Golden Vanity"—which begins, "There was a gallant ship, and a gallant ship was she." He has also recorded the song. Children enjoy singing these words, as well as reading the words to a musical accompaniment. Langstaff presented his music to children at a recent Children's Literature of the Sea Conference (8). He provided them with background information about sea chanties; he told them that sea chanties were sung by sailors and by early colonists who brought them to America; he described how "The Golden Vanity" had been sung by people in England and Scotland for over three hundred years; then he enthusiastically encouraged the children to accompany him as he sang several songs, including "The Golden Vanity." When they sang the sea chanty, "Fire Down Below," he encouraged them to use their voices to suggest the rhythmical movement of gathering water in a bucket and then throwing the water on the fire:

> Fire! Fire! Fire down below,
> It's fetch a bucket of water, girls,
> There's fire down below.

Some of Lewis Carroll's nonsense poetry has been set to music by Don Harper in *Songs from Alice*. The music is included in the text so the words can be sung or an accompaniment played to choral renditions. Colorful, humorous illustrations make this an enjoyable book to share with children.

Folk Songs in Sequence

Ruth Seeger (14) suggests that ballads and other folk chants and songs be grouped in order to immerse children in a total experience with a subject. For example, children who are fascinated by trains can experience a sequence progressing from the laying of the tracks through meeting someone at the station. This sequence might include the following railroad-related activities, as the teacher reads or the children sing the songs (the music to the songs is found in Seeger's *American Folk Songs for Children—In Home, School, and Nursery School* and other folk song collections).

A Railroad Experience

1   *"This Old Hammer"*: Tracks were laid across America by railroad gangs hitting their hammers to the beat of work songs. While the teacher reads or they sing the words to the song—"This old hammer shine like silver,/ Shine like gold, boys,/Shine like gold"—the children can pretend to be hammering the tracks in place to the rhythm of the words or music.

2   *"John Henry"*: Children can pretend to pick up their twelve-pound hammers and compete with the steam drill to the rhythm of this tribute to a famous "steel driving man."

3   *"The Train Is A-Coming"*: Children can pretend to be engines, passenger cars, coalcars, flatcars, boxcars, and a caboose as they move to the words "The train is a-coming, oh yes."

The words can be changed so that each child is identified, through repetitive verses, as part of the train.

Jamie is the engine, oh yes,
Jamie is the engine, oh yes,
Jamie is the engine, Jamie is the engine,
Jamie is the engine, oh yes.
Through
Mary is the caboose, oh yes,
Mary is the caboose, oh yes,
Mary is the caboose, Mary is the caboose,
Mary is the caboose, oh, yes.

Similarly, children can become the different workers on the train, as each child selects an occupation and then improvises words to suggest the part:

Betsy is the engineer, oh yes,
Betsy is the engineer, oh yes,
Betsy is the engineer, Betsy is the engineer,
Betsy is the engineer, oh, yes.

4 *The Little Black Train*: Children can continue their train movement as they keep their "wheels a-moving and rattling through the land," around curves and up long hills "a-whistling and a-blowing, and straining every nerve."

5 *When the Train Comes Along*: To dramatize this song, part of the group can be the train arriving and the remainder can go to the station to meet the train.

WRITING POETRY

Donald Graves's (5) research into the development of children's writing process suggests that adults should work with children during the writing process rather than after material is completed. Beatrice Furner (3) recommends a similar approach, but also stresses the need for the oral exchange of ideas before children write. Children need a motivational phase before they write, an opportunity to clarify ideas, a transcribing period, and an opportunity to share their poems. An adult sharing poetry-writing experiences with children can use the following sequence, adapted from research by Donna Norton (11).

An Instructional Sequence for
Creative Poetry Writing

I. Motivation
A. Using ongoing activities
B. Everyday experiences
C. A new, adult-introduced experience

II. Oral Exchange of Ideas
A. Questions and answers extending stimulation activity
B. Brainstorming ideas, vocabulary, etc.
C. Clarifying ideas
III. Transcribing Period
A. Individual dictation of poems to an adult
B. Individual writing
C. Teacher interaction to help clarification and idea development
D. Adult assistance when required
E. Revision and editing through small-group interaction and teacher interaction
IV. Sharing Poetry
A. Reading the poetry to a group
B. Audience development
C. Making permanent collections
D. Extending poetry, if desired, to choral reading, art, etc.
V. Post Transcribing
A. Keeping writing folders
B. Writing conferences
C. Teaching conventions of writing through the writing process

Motivation for Poetry Writing

The three categories of motivational activities outlined above suggest numerous topics that can be used to stimulate the writing of poetry. Many ongoing activities already occurring in the classroom, in the library, or in an extracurricular organization are natural sources of topics for self-expression through poetry. For example, while teaching a social studies unit a second-grade teacher showed a film about farm life, encouraging children to observe the characteristics and actions of farm animals and then write about them in poetic form. A Girl Scout leader encouraged her children to describe and write about their feelings following a soccer game. A librarian asked children to write their own color poems after they had heard Mary O'Neill's poems about colors in *Hailstones and Halibut Bones*.

Gerald Duffy (2) has identified the frequent sharing of poetry as a very effective way to motivate children to write poetry. University students have used both poetry written by adult authors and poetry written by other children as a way of stimulating children to write their own poems. For example, they have used Kenneth Koch's

The oral exchange of ideas helps children expand and clarify their ideas before writing poetry.

Wishes, Lies, and Dreams (7), reading the poems under a certain topic category to children and then using suggestions developed by Koch to encourage children to write their own poems. Several of these categories include everyday experiences that are common to children and allow them to think of these experiences in new ways. A third-grade teacher encouraged his students to consider all the wishes they might make if they had the opportunity and then asked them to write a poem expressing those wishes. The following is an example of a third grader wishing for her fondest dreams:

> I wish I had a puppy,
>   not a dog, a puppy
>   not a cat, a puppy
>   not a kitten, a puppy
> I wish I was rich
>   not poor, but rich
>   not a little bit of money, a lot
>   so I'm really rich
> I wish I had a Genie
>   not a pony, a Genie
>   not a pig, a Genie
>   not a pig or a pony
>   a Genie
> I wish I could
> have anything
>   know anything
>   be anything
>   see anything
>   and do anything
>   I wish

> Eight-year-old

Many adults encourage children to write poetry by introducing them to new experiences that allow them to nurture their awareness and their observational powers. They may go for a walk in a flower-strewn park or meadow, listen to the noises around them, smell spring in the air, touch the trees and flowers, describe their sensations with new feelings, and then write a poem about their experience. This poem resulted from a sixth grader's visual experiences in the out-of-doors:

> *Woodland*
>
> Cool crisp air calls me
> Late September afternoon
> Crimson, gold, green, rust
> Falling leaves whisper softly
> Come look, what's new in the woods?
>
> Eleven-year-old

Even the sun shining through a window can be used to inspire a poem:

> *The Sunshine*
>
> The sunshine entered the morning
> And birds began to sing.
> The sunshine entered the clouds
> And a rainbow appeared.
> The sunshine entered the
>   afternoon
> And made the evening clear.
> Your smile entered the room
> And sunshine entered my heart.
>
> Eleven-year-old

Other experiences that adults have found to be successful stimuli for poetry include listening to music, becoming involved in art projects, closely observing and touching objects, considering the various uses for unique objects, and looking at and discussing pictures. One girl described very well how music affected her:

> *A Song*
>
> Something I want to say
> But haven't got the words
> To say what I feel
> The music makes it easy
> The music sets me free.
>
> Nine-year-old

A sixth-grade teacher found music to be especially stimulating for her students. She says, "We spent several sessions writing to music such as *Icarus* by Winter Consort and *Night on Bald Mountain* by Mussorgsky. The children let their imaginations soar, they visualized the images created by the music, and wrote their impressions. They especially enjoyed sharing their impressions with each other" (personal communication to author).

Another class of older students studied the possible relationships between art and poetry. They first viewed and discussed the art chosen from the Metropolitan Museum of Art to illustrate the poems in Kenneth Koch and Kate Farrell's anthology *Talking to the Sun*, sharing their feelings about the art, the poetry, and the appropriateness or inappropriateness of the matches between the art and poetry. Then they chose their own selections from great works of art and wrote poems depicting the moods and feelings aroused in them, the settings, or the characters in the paintings. The focus for this activity was enhancing the viewer's and writer's enjoyment, not creating literal interpretations of the art works.

Oral Exchange of Ideas

During an oral exchange of ideas, an adult encourages children to think aloud about the subject. Through brainstorming, for example, children may gain many ideas from each other and experience objects and ideas in a new way. Susan Nugent Reed (13) describes how a poet-in-the-schools, Bill Wertheim, encouraged discussion before writing:

The figure of a skeleton in one of the classrooms evolved into a lesson about death. Wertheim wrote, "The discussion went from Halloween to skeletons, to fear of skeletons, to monsters, to dying: loss of something and/or someone we love. How it feels to die, how it feels to lose someone you care about." He indicated that the topic first was discussed aloud, then later on paper. For those children who preferred an alternative topic, he suggested writing about coming back to life. Wertheim said it was the most touching lesson he had ever taught and that some children cried. This led to a discussion about crying, trust, and kindness. He took this opportunity to express the idea that "crying is OK, even for boys." He said that the children were kind and supportive of one another. (p. 110)

During an outside observational session, children might look at clouds and share their impressions, describe the way the light filters through the leaves, or close their eyes and describe the sounds they hear.

The librarian who encouraged children to write color poems after listening to Mary O'Neill's poems in *Hailstones and Halibut Bones* asked children to observe colors all around them. They searched for objects that reminded them of the colors and talked about their moods as reflected by colors. For example, brainstorming the color white produced some of these associations: snowflakes, winter silence, puffy clouds, a wedding veil, the flash of winning, a frost-covered window, quivering vanilla pudding, heaps of popcorn, a plastered wall, apple blossoms, pale lilac blossoms, sails skimming across the lake, a forgotten memory, fog rising from the marsh, a polar bear, and a gift wrapped in tissue paper. After this experience, children began to look at common objects and feelings with new awareness.

Transcribing Period

Adults often help young children write by taking dictation. Children tell an adult their thoughts while the adult writes them down. Parents indicate that even very young children enjoy seeing their creative jingles, rhymes, and poems in print. Many poems written by young children are very spontaneous. Children enjoy playing with language and feeling the tantalizing tickle of new words falling off their tongues. One university student told how meaningful it was that her mother had kept a notebook of her early experiences writing poetry. Another university student, who had had several poems published, felt that his early spontaneous poetry, written down by his mother, had stimulated his desire to become a professional writer. Parents who have been successful in this type of dictation have been very careful with their children and have not forced dictation upon a child or criticized any thoughts or feelings expressed. The experience has been a warm, trusting relationship in which children discover that their thoughts can be written down and saved for sharing with themselves and others.

When children have mastered the mechanics of writing, they usually write their own poems. The adult working with them still interacts with them, however, as they progress with their writing. The adult can encourage them to reread their poems aloud orally, ask questions to help clarify a problem or an idea, or answer questions pertaining to spelling and punctuation.

Sharing Poetry

The ideal way to share poetry is to read it to an appreciative audience. Consequently, many adults encourage children to share their creations

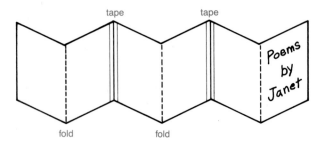

with others. Attractive bulletin boards of children's poems may also stimulate children to read each others' poems and write more poems.

Children enjoy making permanent collections of their poems. One teacher had each child develop an accordion-pleated poem book. To construct their books, the children folded large sheets of heavy drawing paper in half, connected several sheets with tape, and printed their poems and an accompanying illustration on each page.

Other classes have made their own books by constructing covers in various appropriate shapes, cutting paper to match the shapes, and

binding the cover and pages together. A group of second graders placed Halloween poems inside a jack-o-lantern book, fourth graders wrote city poems inside a book resembling a skyscraper, and third graders placed humorous mythical animal poems inside a book resembling a Dr. Seuss beast.

Although it is not necessary to extend writing of poetry to any other activity, children often enjoy using their own poetry for choral-reading arrangements, art interpretations, or dramatizations.

Writing Various Forms of Poetry

Many children enjoy experimenting with writing different types of poems such as limericks, cinquains, and diamantes. Limericks, for example, were among the poetry most enjoyed by children in Ann Terry's (17) study of children's poetry preferences. David McCord's *One at a Time: Collected Poems for the Young* describes the content and form of limericks and provides examples that can be shared with children. The nonsense limericks of Edward Lear, N. M. Bodecker, and William Jay Smith may be used to stimulate these five-line poems that follow this form: lines 1, 2, and 5 rhyme and have a three-beat rhythm; lines 3 and 4 rhyme and have a two-beat rhythm. Brainstorming words that rhyme helps children when they are completing their rhyming lines.

After reading and listening to a number of limericks, a sixth grader wrote about and illustrated the following predicament:

> There once was a girl named Mandy
> Whose hair was dreadfully sandy
> She never did wash it
> Instead she did frost it
> The icing made Mandy smell dandy
>
> Eleven-year-old

Cinquains are another form of poetry having specific structural requirements. These poems help children realize that descriptive words are important when expressing a feeling in poetry and that rhyming words are not necessary. A cinquain uses the following structure:

Line 1:   One word for the title.
Line 2:   Two words that describe the title.
Line 3:   Three words that express action related to the title.
Line 4:   Four words that express a feeling about the title.

Line 5: One word that either repeats the title or expresses a word closely related to the title.

Brainstorming descriptive words and action words will add to children's enjoyment when they write and share their own cinquains. The following cinquains were written by middle school children:

Tree

Huge,   woody
Expanding,   reproducing,   entertaining
Leaves   are   colorfully   crisp
Oak

Eleven-year-old

Lasagna

Hot,   delectable
Steaming,   bubbling,   oozing
Always   great   on   Fridays
Paisans

Eleven-year-old

A diamante is a diamond-shaped poem. Poems written in the diamante format progress from one noun to a final noun that contrasts with the first noun. Because this form is more complex than the cinquain, adults should describe each line and draw a diagram of the diamante to assist children in seeing the relationships among the lines. The diamante has the following structure:

Line 1: One noun.
Line 2: Two adjectives that describe the noun.
Line 3: Three words that express action related to the noun.
Line 4: Four nouns or a phrase that expresses a transition in thought between the first noun and the final contrasting noun.
Line 5: Three words that express action related to the contrasting noun.
Line 6: Two adjectives that describe the contrasting noun.
Line 7: One contrasting noun.

Diagramming this type of poem as follows is also helpful:

noun

describing   describing
action   action   action
transition   nouns   or   phrase
action   action   action
describing   describing
noun

Children find it helpful to brainstorm suggestions for contrasting nouns that could form the framework for the ideas developed in a diamante. One teacher brainstormed with upper elementary students and developed the following contrasts:

sun—moon	summer—winter
tears—smiles	war—peace
day—night	sky—ground
young—old	love—hate
life—death	angel—devil
happy—sad	darkness—light
friends—enemies	boredom—excitement
man—woman	dreams—reality

Next, the group wrote its own poetry. The following poems are examples created by this experience:

Light

Beautiful, bright
Seeing, glistening, refreshing
Light is sometimes blinding
Groping, cautioning, frightening
Evil, insecure
Dark

Ten-year-old

Friends

Happiness, security
Understanding, caring, laughing
Reaching out your hand
Hating, hurting, fighting
Silence, tension
Enemies

Ten-year-old

SUMMARY

Poetry should be a vital part of children's lives, but it has been slighted in many elementary school curricula. Poetry can become an enjoyable experience for children if adults consider children's interests, share poems often and with enthusiasm, encourage children to experience (not dissect) poetry, and relate poems to children's experiences.

The rhythms and sounds found in many poems encourage physical responses from children. Young children respond to chants and rhymes; other poems encourage them to interpret subjects through bodily movements. Children can also experience poetry through creative dramatizations; narrative poems, nonsensical humorous situations, and holiday themes all lend themselves to creative dramatizations.

Another means of stimulating children's interest in poetry is through choral-speaking arrangements: refrain, line-a-child, antiphonal or dialogue, cumulative, and unison. Music is also a means of encouraging children to experience poetry. Rhythm band instruments can complement the rhythm of a poem; old ballads and chants may be used to encourage the interpretation of music and poetry.

Poets-in-the-school programs encourage children to write and enjoy poetry. Poetry writing may also be encouraged by providing stimulating experiences that follow an instructional sequence: a motivational phase, an oral exchange of ideas, a composing period, and a sharing time. Many children also enjoy writing limericks, cinquains, and diamantes. Published poetry is an effective stimulus for all these experiences.

Suggested Activities for Children's Appreciation of Poetry

☐ Develop a card file of poetry that would be appropriate to use with children. Type the poems on cards using a primary-type typewriter. On the back of each card list several suggestions for sharing the poem with children. Put the cards into a logical categorization.

☐ Ask children to tell their favorite jumping-rope chants. Collect as many of these chants as possible. Share any new chants with children. Ask them why they like and remember such chants.

☐ Select a series of poems that encourages physical response from children. Share the poems with a group of children or a peer group. Include poems that encourage children to soar through the air, mimic the movements of an animal, or become something other than themselves.

☐ Select a poem or a series of poems that encourages creative dramatizations. Plan the steps needed to encourage children to interpret the poetry.

☐ Select poems that could be interpreted through choral-speaking arrangements: refrain, line-a-group, antiphonal or dialogue,

cumulative, and unison. Share the poems with a group of children or a peer group.

☐ Using Seeger's recommendations for sharing songs with children, found on pages 363–64, select several songs for an appropriate age group. Share the songs with children or a peer group. Evaluate the group's response to them.

☐ Following the instructional sequence for creative poetry writing suggested on page 365, develop a lesson plan designed to stimulate children's writing of poetry.

References

1 Baskin, Barbara Holland; Harris, Karen H.; and Salley, Coleen C. "Making the Poetry Connection." *The Reading Teacher* 30 (December 1976): 259–65.

2 Duffy, Gerald G. "Crucial Elements in the Teaching of Poetry Writing." In *The Language Arts in the Middle School*, edited by Martha L. King, Robert Emans, and Patricia J. Cianciolo. Urbana, Ill.: National Council of Teachers of English, 1973.

3 Furner, Beatrice A. "Creative Writing through Creative Dramatics." *Language Arts* 50 (March 1973): 405–8.

4 Gough, John. "Poems in a Context: Breaking the Anthology Trap." *Children's Literature in Education* 15 (Winter 1984): 204–210.

5 Graves, Donald H. "Research Update—Language Arts Textbooks: A Writing Process Evaluation." *Language Arts* 53 (September 1976): 645–51.

6 Heinig, Ruth Beall, and Stillwell, Lyda. *Creative Dramatics for the Classroom Teacher.* Englewood Cliffs, N.J.: Prentice-Hall, 1974.

7 Koch, Kenneth. *Wishes, Lies, and Dreams.* New York: Vintage Books/Chelsea House, 1970.

8 Langstaff, John. "Sea Chanties." College Station, Tex.: Children's Literature of the Sea Conference, 1981.

9 Le Pere, Jean. "For Every Occasion: Poetry in the Reading Program." Albuquerque, N. Mex.: Eighth Southwest Regional Conference, International Reading Association, 1980.

10 McIntyre, Barbara M. *Creative Drama in the Elementary School.* Itasca, Ill.: F. E. Peacock, 1974.

11 Norton, Donna. *The Effective Teaching of Language Arts.* Columbus, Ohio: Merrill, 1985.

12 Peck, Pauline C. "Poetry: A Turn on to Reading." In *Using Literature and Poetry Affectively*, edited by Jon E. Shapiro. Newark, Del.: International Reading Association, 1979.

13 Reed, Susan Nugent. "Career Idea: Meet the Poet at His Craft." In *Using Literature and Poetry Affec-*

tively, edited by Jon E. Shapiro. Newark, Del.: International Reading Association, 1979.

14 Seeger, Ruth Crawford. *American Folksongs for Children—In Home, School, and Nursery School.* New York: Doubleday, 1948.

15 Shapiro, Jon E. *Using Literature and Poetry Affectively.* Newark, Del.: International Reading Association, 1979.

16 Tanner, Fran. *Creative Communication: Projects in Acting, Speaking, Oral Reading.* Pocatello, Idaho: Clark, 1979.

17 Terry, Ann. *Children's Poetry Preferences: A National Survey of the Upper Elementary Grades.* Urbana, Ill.: National Council of Teachers of English, 1974.

CHILDREN'S LITERATURE

Adoff, Arnold. *All the Colors of the Race*. Illustrated by John Steptoe. Lothrop, Lee & Shepard, 1982. A girl from a mixed racial parentage reflects on tolerance.

————. *Birds: Poems*. Illustrated by Troy Howell. Lippincott, 1982. Thirty poems about birds.

————. *The Cabbages Are Chasing the Rabbits*. Illustrated by Janet Stevens. Harcourt Brace Jovanovich, 1985. A cumulative poem developed on the idea of role reversals.

————. *Eats Poems*. Illustrated by Susan Russo. Lothrop, Lee & Shepard, 1979. Poems that celebrate a love affair with food.

————. *My Black Me: A Beginning Book of Black Poetry*. Dutton, 1974. A collection of black poetry.

————. *Outside/Inside Poems*. Illustrated by John Steptoe. Lothrop, Lee & Shepard, 1981. Poems that emphasize a boy's hopes and wishes.

Amon, Aline (comp.). *The Earth Is Sore: Native Americans on Nature*. Illustrated by Aline Amon. Atheneum, 1981. Native American poems reflect the need to live in harmony with nature.

Atwood, Ann. *Fly with the Wind, Flow with the Water*. Scribner's, 1979. Haiku poems about things in nature that swing, soar, leap, run, tumble, swirl, flutter, and float are accompanied by color photographs.

————. *Haiku: The Mood of Earth*. Scribner's, 1971. Beautiful photographs accompany haiku nature poems.

————. *Haiku-Vision: In Poetry and Photography*. Scribner's, 1977. Nature photographs are accompanied by haiku.

Baylor, Byrd. *The Desert Is Theirs*. Illustrated by Peter Parnall. Scribner's, 1975. A poem that stresses the love the Papago Indians have for their desert home.

————. *Moon Song*. Illustrated by Ronald Himler. Scribner's, 1982. A Pima Indian legend, in poetic text, tells how Coyote was born and survived.

————. *The Other Way to Listen*. Illustrated by Peter Parnall. Scribner's, 1978. You have to be patient to hear cactuses blooming and rocks murmuring, but it's worth it.

Baylor, Byrd, and Parnall, Peter. *Desert Voices*. Scribner's, 1981. Ten creatures from the desert give their viewpoints on their surroundings.

Bechely, Paddy (comp.). *Drumming in the Sky: Poems from 'Stories and Rhymes.'* Illustrated by Priscilla Lamont. British Broadcasting, 1981. Poems selected from the BBC Radio series.

Bennett, Jill (comp.). *Days Are Where We Live and Other Poems*. Illustrated by Maureen Roffey. Lothrop, Lee & Shepard, 1982. Poems for very young children cover subjects such as playing, eating, and walking.

————. *Tiny Tim: Verses for Children*. Illustrated by Helen Oxenbury. Delacorte, 1982. A variety of poems, including jingles and humorous poems.

Bierhorst, John (ed.). *The Sacred Path: Spells, Prayers & Power Songs of the American Indians*. Morrow, 1983. A collection from sources across North America.

Blegvad, Lenore (comp.). *The Parrot in the Garret: And Other Rhymes About Dwellings*. Illustrated by Erik Blegvad. Atheneum, 1982. Twenty-five rhymes that stress dwellings and their inhabitants.

Bodecker, N. M. *Hurry, Hurry Mary Dear*. Atheneum, 1976. A collection of forty-three humorous poems accompanied by pen sketches.

————. *Let's Marry Said the Cherry*. Atheneum, 1974. A collection of nonsense poems relying heavily upon word play.

————. *A Person from Britain Whose Head Was the Shape of a Mitten and Other Limericks*. Dent, 1980. A collection of absurd limericks.

Brown, Beatrice Curtis. *Jonathan Bing*. Illustrated by Judith Gwyn Brown. Lothrop, Lee & Shepard, 1968. Idiosyncrasies and humorous situations create a series of poems about a man who has difficulty performing normal social functions.

Browning, Robert. *The Pied Piper of Hamelin*. Illustrated by Kate Greenaway. Warne Classic, 1888. A reissue of the original poem with delightful illustrations of children by Greenaway.

Carroll, Lewis. *The Hunting of the Snark*. Illustrated by Helen Oxenbury. Watts, 1970. Large, colorful illustrations accompany Carroll's poem.

————. *Jabberwocky*. Illustrated by Jane Breskin Zalben. Warne, 1977. A picture interpretation of Carroll's poem in watercolors.

————. *Poems of Lewis Carroll*. Selected by Myra Cohn Livingston. Crowell, 1973. A collection of poems from *Alice's Adventures in Wonderland* and *Through the Looking-Glass*.

————. *Songs from Alice*. Music by Don Harper. Illustrated by Charles Folkard. New York: Holiday House, 1979. Carroll's nonsense poems set to music and humorously illustrated.

Causley, Charles (comp.). *Salt-Sea Verse*. Illustrated by Antony Maitland. Kestrel, Puffin, 1981. An anthology of poems about the sea.

Cendrars, Blaise. *Shadow*. Translated and illustrated by Marcia Brown. Scribner's, 1982. An eerie poem about the world of spirits.

Chorao, Kay. *The Baby's Bedtime Book*. Dutton, 1984. A collection of lullabies.

Ciardi, John. *Doodle Soup*. Illustrated by Merle Nacht. Houghton Mifflin, 1985. A collection of humorous poems.

———. *Fast and Slow*. Illustrated by Becky Gaver. Houghton Mifflin, 1975. Thirty-four humorous and nonsense poems.

———. *I Met a Man*. Illustrated by Robert Osborn. Houghton Mifflin, 1961. A controlled vocabulary creates poetry for beginning readers.

———. *You Read to Me, I'll Read to You*. Illustrated by Edward Gorey. Lippincott, 1962. Poems for a child to read, followed by poems for an adult to read.

Cole, William. *I'm Mad at You!* Illustrated by George MacClain. Collins, 1978. A collection of poems expressing angry thoughts.

——— (comp.). *Oh, That's Ridiculous!* Illustrated by Tomi Ungerer. Viking, 1972. Nonsense poetry collected from poets noted for their humorous poetry.

———. *Oh, What Nonsense!* Illustrated by Tomi Ungerer. Viking, 1966. Another collection of humorous poetry.

——— (comp.). *Poem Stew*. Illustrated by Karen Ann Weinhaus. Lippincott, 1981. A collection of humorous poems related to food.

Downie, Mary Alice and Robertson, Barbara (comp.). *The New Wind Has Wings: Poems from Canada*. Illustrated by Elizabeth Cleaver. Oxford University Press, 1984. A collection of poems.

Dunning, Stephen; Lueders, Edward; and Smith, Hugh (comp.). *Reflections on a Gift of Watermelon Pickle . . . and Other Modern Verse*. Lothrop, Lee & Shepard, 1967. An anthology of 114 poems accompanied by photographs.

Fellman, Hazel (ed.). *The Best Loved Poems of the American People*. Doubleday, 1936. An anthology.

Ferris, Helen (ed.). *Favorite Poems Old and New*. Doubleday, 1957. An anthology.

Field, Eugene. *Wynken, Blynken and Nod*. Illustrated by Susan Jeffers. Dutton, 1982. The classic poem in a newly illustrated edition.

Fisher, Aileen. *Feathered Ones and Furry*. Illustrated by Eric Carle. Crowell, 1971. Fifty-five poems about furry animals and feathery birds.

———. *In One Door and Out the Other: A Book of Poems* Illustrated by Lillian Hoban. Crowell, 1969. A collection of poems about childhood experiences.

Fleischman, Paul. *I Am Phoenix: Poems for Two Voices*. Illustrated by Ken Nutt. Harper & Row, 1985. Poems about birds, designed to be read by two readers.

Froman, Robert. *Seeing Things: A Book of Poems*. Crowell, 1974. Several concrete poems are in this collection.

Frost, Robert. *Stopping by Woods on a Snowy Evening*. Illustrated by Susan Jeffers. Dutton, 1978. Large pictures illustrate Frost's poem.

Fufuka, Karama. *My Daddy Is a Cool Dude*. Illustrated by Mahiri Fufuka. Dial, 1975. Twenty-seven poems about life in an urban black community as seen through the experience of a child.

Harrison, Michael, and Stuart-Clark, Christopher (comp.). *The New Dragon Book of Verse*. Oxford, 1983. An anthology of classic and contemporary poetry categorized according to subject.

Highwater, Jamake. *Moonsong Lullaby*. Photographed by Marcia Keegan. Lothrop, Lee & Shepard, 1981. A poem inspired by ancient Native American stories.

Holman, Felice. *The Song in My Head*. Illustrated by Jim Spanfeller. Scribner, 1985. A collection of whimsical poetry.

Holme, Bryan (comp.). *A Present of Laughter: Wit & Nonsense in Pictures & Verse*. Viking, 1982. An anthology of English nonsense verse.

Hopkins, Lee Bennett (ed.). *Circus! Circus!* Illustrated by John O'Brien. Knopf, 1982. Circus poems by poets such as Jack Prelutsky and Beatrice Schenk de Regniers.

——— (ed.). *Moments*. Illustrated by Michael Hague. Harcourt Brace Jovanovich, 1980. Fifty poems about the four seasons.

——— (ed.). *My Mane Catches the Wind: Poems about Horses*. Illustrated by Sam Savitt. Harcourt Brace Jovanovich, 1979. A collection of twenty-two poems about horses written by different poets.

——— (ed.). *On Our Way*. Photographs by David Parks. Knopf, 1974. A collection of twenty-two poems by black authors.

——— (comp.). *Surprises*. Illustrated by Megan Lloyd. Harper & Row, 1984. A collection of easy-to-read poems.

——— (comp.). *To Look at Any Thing*. Photographs by John Earl. Harcourt Brace Jovanovich, 1978. Unusual nature photographs are accompanied by appropriate poems.

Hughes, Langston. *The Dream Keeper*. Knopf, 1932. Copyright 1960 by L. Hughes. A collection of poems by the black poet.

———. *Selected Poems of Langston Hughes*. Knopf, 1942, 1959. Many poems relate to Hughes's black heritage.

Hughes, Ted. *Under the North Star*. Illustrated by Leonard Baskin. Viking, 1981. Poems about northern animals.

Jacobs, Leland B. (ed.). *Poetry for Space Enthusiasts*. Illustrated by Frank Aloise. Garrard, 1971. An anthology of poems about space travel.

Janeczko, Paul B. *Postcard Poems: A Collection of Poetry for Sharing*. Bradbury, 1979. One hundred poems, each brief enough to write on a postcard and share with a friend.

Kemp, Gene (comp.). *Ducks and Dragons: Poems for Children*. Illustrated by Carolyn Dinan. Farber & Farber, 1980; Puffin, 1983. An anthology of poems about seasons, reality, animals, fantasy, fear, and old songs.

Kennedy, X.J. *Did Adam Name the Vinegarroon?* Illustrated by Heidi Johanna Selig. Godine, 1982. Poems about unusual animals.

———. *The Forgetful Wishing Well: Poems for Young People*. Illustrated by Monica Incisa. Atheneum, 1985. A collection of poems about meaningful experiences.

———. *The Phantom Ice Cream Man*. Illustrated by David McPaihl. Atheneum, 1979. Poems about strange beasts, including a muddle-headed messer and a giant sloth who gobbles locomotives.

Kennedy, X.J. and Kennedy, Dorothy M. (comps.). *Knock at a Star: A Child's Introduction to Poetry*. Illustrated by Karen Ann Weinhaus. Little, Brown, 1982. The anthology is organized to help children understand poetry.

Kherdian, David. *Country Cat, City Cat*. Illustrated by Nonny Hogrogian. Four Winds, 1978. Poems about cats and birds against a background of changing seasons.

Koch, Kenneth and Farrell, Kate (comps.). *Talking to the Sun*. Metropolitan Museum of Art/Holt, Rinehart

& Winston, 1985. Reproductions from the Metropolitan Museum illustrate this anthology.

Lalicki, Barbara (comp.). *If There Were Dreams to Sell*. Illustrated by Margot Tomes. Lothrop, Lee & Shepard, 1984. The poems follow an alphabetical format.

Langstaff, John. *The Golden Vanity*. Illustrated by David Gentleman. Harcourt Brace Jovanovich, 1972. The old English ballad about a "gallant ship."

Larrick, Nancy. (comp.) *Piper, Pipe That Song Again*. Illustrated by Kelly Oechsli. Random House, 1965. An anthology of poetry.

———— (comp.). *When the Dark Comes Dancing: A Bedtime Poetry Book*. Illustrations by John Wallner. Philomel, 1982. Poetry to be read aloud at bedtime.

Lawrence. D. H. *Birds, Beasts and the Third Thing*. Selected and Illustrated by Alice and Martin Provensen. Viking, 1982. Twenty-three poems focus on Lawrence's "Delight of Being Alone."

Lear, Edward. *A Book of Bosh*. Compiled by Brian Alderson. Penguin, 1982. A collection of Lear's poetry.

————. *The Complete Nonsense Book*. Dodd, Mead, 1946. Includes *A Book of Nonsense*, originally published in 1846, and *Nonsense Songs and Stories*, originally published in 1871.

————. *The Courtship of the Yonghy-Bonghy-Bó and the New Vestments*. Illustrated by Kevin Maddison. Viking, 1980. New illustrations for poems first published in *Laughable Lyrics*, 1877.

————. *Hilary Knight's The Owl and the Pussy-Cat*. Illustrated by Hilary Knight. Macmillan, 1983. Knight creates a fantasy around Lear's poem.

————. *The Nonsense Books of Edward Lear*. New American Library, 1964. Nonsense poems are still enjoyed by children.

————. *Nonsense Omnibus*. Warne, 1943. Original illustrations and verses from four of Lear's collections.

————. *The Pelican Chorus & the Quangle-Wangle's Hat*. Illustrated by Kevin W. Maddison. Viking, 1981. Two of Lear's poems are illustrated in full-page watercolors.

Lear, Edward, and Nash, Ogden. *The Scroobius Pip*. Illustrated by Nancy Ekholm Burkert. Harper & Row, 1968. A beautifully illustrated picture book about the wondrous animal that is neither fish nor fowl, insect nor beast.

Lee, Dennis. *Garbage Delight*. Illustrated by Frank Newfeld. Houghton Mifflin, 1978. A banquet of nonsense poems.

Lewis, Richard. *Of This World: A Poet's Life in Poetry*. Photographs by Helen Buttfield. New York: Dial, 1968. Poems by the Japanese poet Issa and information about his life.

————. *The Wind and the Rain*. Photographs by Helen Buttfield. Simon & Schuster, 1968. A collection of nature poems written by children.

Livingston, Myra Cohn. *Celebrations*. Illustrated by Leonard Fisher. Holiday, 1985. A collection of sixteen poems about holidays.

————. *A Circle of Seasons*. Illustrated by Leonard Everett Fisher. Holiday, 1982. Poems about the four seasons.

————. *How Pleasant to Know Mr. Lear!* Illustrated by Edward Lear. Holiday, 1982. Includes Lear's poems, art and biographical information.

————. *O Sliver of Liver*. Illustrated by Iris Van Rynbach. Atheneum, 1979. A variety of poems, including cinquains, haiku, and poems about nature, holidays, daily life, human relationships, and emotions.

————. *Sea Songs*. Illustrated by Leonard Fisher. Holiday, 1986. A collection of poems about the sea.

————. *Sky Song*. Illustrated by Leonard Fisher. Holiday, 1983. Poems about the sky.

————. *The Way Things Are and Other Poems*. Atheneum, 1974. Poems about everyday things.

———— (comp.). *Christmas Poems*. Illustrated by Trina Schart Hyman. Holiday, 1984. An anthology of eighteen Christmas poems.

———— (comp.). *Thanksgiving Poems*. Illustrated by Stephen Gammell. Holiday House, 1985. Contemporary and traditional holiday poems.

———— (ed). *Why Am I Grown So Cold? Poems of the Unknowable*. Atheneum, 1982. Poems about ghosts and monsters.

Lobel, Arnold. *The Rose in My Garden*. Illustrated by Anita Lobel. Greenwillow, 1984. A cumulative poem traces the flowers in the garden.

————. *Whiskers and Rhymes*. Greenwillow, 1985. Rhyming poems for young children.

Longfellow, Henry Wadsworth. *Hiawatha*. Illustrated by Susan Jeffers. Dutton, 1983. Hiawatha's boyhood is illustrated in detailed artwork.

————. *Hiawatha's Childhood*. Illustrated by Errol LeCain. Farrar, Straus & Giroux, 1984. Winner of the 1985 Greenaway Medal provides a mystical setting.

————. *Paul Revere's Ride*. Illustrated by Paul Galdone. Crowell, 1963. The classic poem illustrated for younger children.

Loveday, John (comp.). *Over the Bridge: An Anthology of New Poems*. Illustrated by Michael Foreman. Kestrel, Penguin, 1981. An anthology of poetry by British poets.

Margolis, Richard J. *Secrets of a Small Brother*. Illustrated by Donald Carrick. Macmillan, 1984. The poems are written from a younger brother's perspective.

McCord, David. *Away and Ago: Rhymes of the Never Was and Always Is*. Illustrated by Leslie Morrill. Little, Brown, 1974. Poems about familiar places, objects, and experiences.

————. *Far and Few: Rhymes of the Never Was and Always Is*. Illustrated by Henry B. Kane. Little, Brown, 1952. Includes the popular nonsense poems found in "Five Chants."

————. *One at a Time: Collected Poems for the Young*. Illustrated by Henry B. Kane. Little, Brown, 1977. A large collection of poems on many subjects.

McPhail, David. *The Dream Child*. Dutton, 1985. The poetic text follows a child's imaginative journey.

Merriam, Eve. *Rainbow Writing*. Atheneum, 1976. Poetry designed to color our minds with the vast spectrum of human experience.

————. *A Word or Two with You: New Rhymes for Young Readers*. Illustrated by John Nez. Atheneum, 1981. Seventeen poems that emphasize rhyming and word play.

Milne, A. A. *When We Were Very Young*. Illustrated by Ernest H. Shepard. Dutton, 1961. Delightful poems about Winnie-the-Pooh and the hundred-acre wood.

————. *Winnie-the-Pooh*. Illustrated by Ernest H. Shepard. Dutton, 1954. The classic story, with poems, about Christopher Robin's friend the bear.

————. *The World of Christopher Robin*. Illustrated by E. H. Shepard. Dutton, 1958. Poems about a boy and his toy animal friends.

Moore, Clement. *The Night Before Christmas*. Illustrated by Tomie de Paola. Holiday, 1980. Large, brightly colored illustrations in picture book format.

————. *The Night Before Christmas*. Illustrated by Tasha Tudor, Rand McNally, 1975. Large illustrations of popular Christmas poem.

Moore, Lilian. *See My Lovely Poison Ivy*. Illustrated by Diane Dawson. Atheneum, 1975. Poems about witches, ghosts, goblins, bats, and monsters.

————. *Something New Begins*. Atheneum, 1982. Fifteen new poems as well as selections from her previous poems.

———— (ed.). *Go with the Poem*. Mc-Graw-Hill, 1979. A collection of ninety poems written by outstanding twentieth-century poets.

Morrison, Lillian. *The Sidewalk Racer and Other Poems of Sports and Motion*. Lothrop, Lee & Shepard, 1977. Poems about sports, including surfing, tennis, boxing, football, skateboarding, and baseball.

Morton, Miriam (ed.). *The Moon is Like a Silver Sickle: A Celebration of Poetry by Russian Children*. Illustrated by Eros Keith. Simon & Schuster, 1972. A collection of ninety-two poems written by Russian children.

Noyes, Alfred. *The Highwayman*. Illustrated by Charles Keeping. Oxford, 1981. Story poem about a highwayman who risked his life every evening to visit the innkeeper's daughter.

———— . *The Highwayman*. Illustrated by Gilbert Riswold. Prentice-Hall, 1969. The story poem illustrated.

O'Neill, Mary. *Hailstones and Halibut Bones*. Illustrated by Leonard Weisgard. Doubleday, 1961. Poems that describe the basic colors.

Opie, Iona, and Opie, Peter (comps.). *The Oxford Book of Children's Verse*. Oxford, 1984. This anthology includes poems from the medieval period through the twentieth century.

Pomerantz, Charlotte. *If I Had A Paka: Poems in Eleven Languages*. Illustrated by Nancy Tafuri. Greenwillow, 1982. Poems that rely on foreign words.

Prelutsky, Jack. *The Baby Uggs Are Hatching*. Illustrated by James Stevenson. Greenwillow, 1982. Humorous poems about Grebles, Sneepies, and Slitchs.

———— . *A Gopher in the Garden and Other Animal Poems*. Illustrated by Robert Leydenfrost. Macmillan, 1966, 1967. Humorous poems about animals.

———— . *The Headless Horseman Rides Tonight*. Illustrated by Arnold Lobel. Greenwillow, 1980. Twelve scary poems about giants, banshees, poltergeists, and zombies.

———— . *The Queen of Eene*. Illustrated by Victoria Chess. Greenwillow, 1978. Fourteen humorous poems, each illustrated with a funny illustration.

———— . *Rolling Harvey Down the Hill*. Illustrated by Victoria Chess. Greenwillow, 1980. Humorous poems about the adventures of five boys.

———— . *The Sheriff of Rottenshot*. Illustrated by Victoria Chess. Greenwillow, 1982. Humorous poems use a strong rhyming pattern.

———— (comp.). *The Random House Book of Poetry for Children*. Illustrated by Arnold Lobel. Random House, 1983. An anthology of over 500 poems divided according to themes.

Richards, Laura E. *Tirra Lirra, Rhymes Old and New*. Illustrated by Marguerite Davis. Little, Brown, 1955. Over one hundred humorous poems including "Eletelephony" and "Bobbily Boo and Wollypotump."

Rossetti, Christina. *Goblin Market*. Illustrated and adapted by Ellen Raskin. Dutton, 1970. A picture book version of the poem originally published in 1862.

Rylant, Cynthia. *Waiting to Waltz: A Childhood*. Illustrated by Stephan Gammell, Bradbury, 1984. A collection of poems about growing up in a small Appalachian town.

Sandburg, Carl. *Rainbows Are Made*. Edited by Lee Bennett Hopkins. Illustrated by Fritz Eichenberg. Harcourt Brace Jovanovich, 1982. A collection of seventy poems.

Seeger, Ruth Crawford. *American Folksongs for Children—In Home, School, and Nursery School*. Illustrated by Barbara Cooney, Doubleday, 1948. Words and music to numerous folksongs, plus suggestions for using them with young children.

Sendak, Maurice. *Pierre: A Cautionary Tale*. Harper & Row, 1962. A boy learns that he should sometimes care.

Seuss, Dr. *The Cat in the Hat*. Random House, 1957. An illustrated humorous poem.

Silverstein, Shel. *A Light in the Attic*. Harper & Row, 1981. Humorous poems about situations such as the polar bear in the Frigidaire.

———— . *Where the Sidewalk Ends*. Harper & Row, 1974. A collection of humorous poems.

Skofield, James. *Nightdances*. Illustrated by Karen Gundersheimer. Harper & Row, 1981. A boy and his parents go outside on a moonlit night.

Smith, William Jay. *Laughing Time*. Illustrated by Juliet Kepes. Little, Brown, 1955. Humorous poems about animals and people.

———— . *Mr. Smith & Other Nonsense*. Illustrated by Don Bologne. Delacorte, 1968. Nonsense verses about things big and little, imaginary dialogues, and nonsense birds.

Snyder, Zilpha Keatley. *Today is Saturday*. Illustrated by John Arms. Atheneum, 1969.

Starbird, Kaye. *The Covered Bridge House and Other Poems*. Illustrated by Jim Arnosky. Four Winds, 1979. Thirty poems about childhood experiences such as jumping rope, hopping after falling on a sky slope, and wondering why no one can get rags from ragweed.

Thurman, Judith. *Flashlight and Other Poems*. Illustrated by Reina Rubel. Atheneum, 1976. Poems describing familiar things such as balloons, closets, and going barefoot.

Viorst, Judith. *If I Were in Charge of the World and Other Worries: Poems for Children and their Parents*. Illustrated by Lynne Cherry. Atheneum, 1981. Poems about everyday situations that frustrate.

Wallace, Daisy. *Fairy Poems*. Illustrated by Trina Schart Hyman. Holiday House, 1980. A collection of poems about leprechauns and fairies.

———— . *Ghost Poems*. Illustrated by Tomie de Paola. Holiday, 1979. A collection of seventeen poems about ghosts.

Willard, Nancy. *Night Story*. Illustrated by Ilse Plume. Harcourt, Brace, Jovanovich, 1986. A small boy has an adventure in dreamland.

———— . *A Visit to William Blake's Inn: Poems for Innocent and Experienced Travelers*. Illustrated by Alice and Martin Provensen. Harcourt Brace Jovanovich, 1981. Poems describing a menagerie of guests.

Wilner, Isabel (ed.). *The Poetry Troup*. Scribner's, 1977. An anthology of over two hundred poems selected for reading aloud.

Worth, Valerie. *More Small Poems*. Illustrated by Natalie Babbitt. Farrar, Straus & Giroux, 1976. Ordinary objects such as acorns, soap bubbles, and Christmas lights are subjects of short poems.

———— . *Still More Small Poems*. Illustrated by Natalie Babbitt. Farrar, Straus & Giroux, 1978. Twenty-five poems about ordinary objects such as doors, rocks, slugs, and mushrooms.

Yolen, Jane (ed.). *The Lullaby Songbook*. Illustrated by Charles Mikolaycak. Harcourt Brace Jovanovich, 1986. A collection of lullabies from various cultures.

Zolotow, Charlotte. *River Winding*. Illustrated by Kazue Mizumura. Crowell, 1978. Poems for young children that paint images of things seen and remembered.

———— . *River Winding*. Illustrated by Regina Shekerjian. Abelard-Schuman, 1970. The same poems as in the above edition, but illustrated by a different artist.

9

Contemporary Realistic Fiction

□

WINDOW ON THE WORLD

□

INVOLVING CHILDREN IN REALISTIC
FICTION

Window on the World

NEW TERMINOLOGY ENTERS THE DIScussion of children's books as students of children's literature leave the realm of Mother Goose, most picture storybooks, traditional literature, and modern fantasy. Terms such as *relevant books*, *extreme realism*, *problem novel*, and *everyday occurrences* are found in critiques and discussions of contemporary realistic fiction. While some books in this genre are among the books most popular with older children, they are also among the books some adults find most controversial. Interest groups, educators, and parents criticize and debate the value of some realistic stories for children. Many adults are concerned about issues such as censorship, sexism, violence, alienation from society, racism, and promiscuity.

This chapter discusses what contemporary realistic fiction is, how it is different from stories in other genres, how realistic fiction has changed, why it should be shared with children, the criteria for evaluating realistic fiction, and issues related to realistic fiction.

WHAT IS CONTEMPORARY REALISTIC FICTION?

The term *contemporary realistic fiction* implies that everything in a realistic story—including characters, setting, and plot—is consistent with the lives of real people in our contemporary world. The word *realistic* does not mean that the story is true, however; it means only that the story could have happened.

Use of the words *realistic* and *fiction* together is confusing to some children, who have trouble distinguishing contemporary realistic fiction from modern fantasy or from stories that really happened. Certainly authors of modern fantasy attempt to make their stories "realistic," in the sense that they try to create believable characters, settings, and plots; make their stories as internally consistent as possible; and often ground their stories in familiar reality before introducing elements of fantasy. Contemporary realistic fiction, however, requires that characters and settings seem as real as the contemporary world we know, and that plots focus on familiar, everyday

CHART 9–1

Differences between modern fantasy and contemporary realistic fiction

	Modern Fantasy	Contemporary Realistic Fiction
Characters:	Personified toys, little people, supernatural beings, real people who have imaginary experiences, animals who behave like people	Characters who must act like real people Animals who should always behave like animals
Setting:	Past, present, or future Imaginary world May travel through time and space	Contemporary world as we know it
Plot Development:	Conflict may be against supernatural powers Problems may be solved through magical powers	Conflict develops as characters cope with problems such as growing up, survival, family problems, and inner city tensions Antagonists may be self, other family members, society, or nature
Creating Believable Stories:	Authors must encourage readers to suspend disbelief	Authors may rely on "relevant subjects," everyday occurrences, or extreme realism

problems, pleasures, and personal relationships. The supernatural has no part in such stories, except occasionally in the beliefs of realistic human characters.

Two popular animal stories demonstrate the differences between modern fantasy and contemporary realistic fiction that are summarized in Chart 9–1. In Beatrix Potter's fantasy, *The Tale of Peter Rabbit*, Peter talks, thinks, acts, and dresses like an inquisitive, sometimes greedy, sometimes frightened human child, who needs his mother's love and care. While the story's garden setting is realistic, Peter's home is furnished with human furniture. Conflict in this fantasy develops because Peter demonstrates such believable childlike desires. In contrast, the three animals in Sheila Burnford's *The Incredible Journey* retain their animal characteristics as they struggle for survival in a realistically depicted Canadian wilderness: a trained hunting dog leads his companions across the wilderness; an English bulldog, who is a cherished family pet, seeks people to give him food; and the Siamese cat retains her feline independence. Conflict in this realistic story develops as the animals become lost and face problems while trying to return to their home. Burnford does not give them human thoughts, values, or other human characteristics. The setting and the characters are not only believable;

they are also completely realistic by the standard of what we know and expect in our everyday world.

VALUES OF REALISTIC FICTION FOR CHILDREN

One of the greatest values of realistic fiction for children is that many realistic stories allow children to identify with characters of their own age who have similar interests and problems. Children like to read about people they can understand. Thus their favorite authors are those who express a clear understanding of children. For example, one girl said about Judy Blume's *Are You There God? It's Me, Margaret*, "I've read this book five times; I could be Margaret."

Realistic fiction can help children discover that their problems and desires are not unique and that they are not alone in experiencing certain feelings and situations. Children who are unhappy about their physical appearance may identify with Constance Greene's *The Unmaking of Rabbit*, for example, or shy children may discover a comrade in Elizabeth Billington's *Part-Time Boy*. These young characters face and overcome their problems while remaining true to themselves.

Realistic fiction also extends children's horizons by broadening their interests, allowing them to experience new adventures, and showing them different ways to view and deal with conflicts in their own lives. They can vicariously live a survival adventure and mature in the process as they read Scott O'Dell's *Island of the Blue Dolphins*, for example, or experience the death of a father in Vera and Bill Cleaver's *Where the Lilies Bloom*.

Reading about children who are facing emotional problems can help children discharge repressed emotions and cope with fear, anger, or grief (3). For example, books about divorce or abuse may help children cope with a traumatic period in their lives. In Beverly Cleary's *Dear Mr. Henshaw*, readers may discover that parents as well as children are hurt by divorce. Children may realize the consequences of wife and child abuse by reading Betsy Byars's *Cracker Jackson*. (*A word of caution*: realistic fiction should *not* be used to replace professional help in situations that may warrant such intervention. Children experiencing severe depression, anger, or grief may require professional help.) Many of the books discussed in this chapter can stimulate discussion and help children share their feelings and solve their problems. (Using realistic fiction to stimulate discussion, role playing, and other problem solving is discussed in the second part of this chapter.)

Of course, realistic fiction also provides children with pleasure and escape. Realistic animal stories, sports stories, mysteries, and humorous stories are enjoyable getaways for young people.

HOW REALISTIC FICTION HAS CHANGED

Synonyms for *realistic* include other adjectives such as *lifelike*, *genuine*, and *authentic*. Of course what people consider "lifelike" depends upon the social context; what seems realistic to us might seem quite fantastic to people in different societies or in earlier eras of our own history. Chapter two, "History of Children's Literature," indicated the degree to which changing concepts of childhood and family life in European and North American societies have influenced children's literature. (See Charts 2-4–2-6 in Chapter two.)

In the Victorian era of the late nineteenth and early twentieth century, realistic fiction emphasized traditional family roles and ties in warm, close, and stable family units that lived in one place for generations; strict roles for males and females, stressing higher education and careers

for males and wifehood and motherhood for females; respect for law and adult authority; strong religious commitment; duty to educate, Christianize, or care for the poor; and problems related to overcoming sinfulness and becoming good.

Realistic fiction continued to emphasize many of these values well into the second half of the twentieth century, although the literature began to depict both female and male children gaining more independence. The characters in realistic children's fiction were usually white, middle-class, and members of stable families consisting of a father, a mother, and their children. Nontraditional families and family disturbances were virtually unrepresented in this literature.

Beginning roughly in the 1960s, however, the content of contemporary realistic fiction has become more diverse—no doubt reflecting the increasingly diverse and complex social life in the United States and elsewhere. Realistic stories for children depict some unhappy and unstable families, single-parent families, and families in which both parents work outside the home; career ambitions are not as confined to traditional gender roles as they were in the past; children often have considerable responsibility and independence; fear of or disrespect for law and authority is more common; education and religion receive less stress; ethnic and racial minorities are more in evidence; and, in general, people's economic, emotional, and social problems receive more emphasis.

John Rowe Townsend (30) is among the researchers who have pointed out the striking contrasts between children's realistic fiction of the 1950s and of the late 1960s. The 1950s were one of the quietest decades in children's literature: in keeping with traditional values, children were pictured as part of a stable community in which grandparents were wise, parents were staunch and respected, and childhood was happy and secure. In contrast, children's literature of the late 1960s implied an erosion of adult authority and an apparent widening of the generation gap; it was no longer considered self-evident that parents knew best and that children could be guided into accepting the established codes and behavior. In a study of themes found in contemporary realistic fiction published in the late 1970s, Jane M. Madsen and Elaine B. Wickersham (21) found that popular themes for young children dealt with overcoming fear and responsibility and that stories about problems related to adoption, divorce, disabilities, and minority social status were more common than in the past. Contemporary realistic fiction for older children now often depicts children overcoming family and personal problems as they confront quarreling or divorcing parents, deserting or noncaring parents, cruel foster families, conflicts between personal ambitions and parental desires, and the death of loved ones. Discovery of self and development of maturity as children face and overcome their fears are other popular themes in stories written for older children. These books often stress the importance of self-esteem and being true to one's self.

"New Realism" and the "Problem Novel"

New realism is the term Shelton L. Root (25) applies to certain segments of contemporary realistic fiction, which he describes as "that fiction for young readers which addresses itself to personal problems and social issues heretofore considered taboo for fictional treatment by the general public, as enunciated by its traditional spokesmen: librarians, teachers, ministers, and others. The new realism is often graphic in its language and always explicit in its treatment" (p. 19).

Some literary critics question the merit of at least portions of this "new realism." Sheila Egoff (11), for example, applauds distinguished realistic novels of the last two decades that have strong literary qualities, including logical flow of narrative, delicate complexity of characterization, insights that convey the conduct of life as characters move from childhood to adolescence and to adulthood, and a quality that touches both the imagination and the emotions. She criticizes what she terms the "problem novel," however. In an outstanding realistic novel, says Egoff, conflict is integral to the plot and characterization; its resolution has wide implications growing out of the personal vision and/or experience of the writer. In contrast, she maintains, conflict in a "problem novel" stems from the writer's social standards more than from the writer's personal feelings and emotions. The author's intentions may be good; but, in an effort to make a point or argue a social position, the author creates a "cardboard" story, rather then one that really comes alive. The conflict is specific rather than universal, and narrow rather than far-reaching in its implications. Egoff identifies other typical characteristics of the "problem novel":

1. Concern with externals, with how things look rather than how things are. The author begins with a problem, rather than with a plot or characters.
2. The protagonist is burdened with anxieties and grievances that grow out of alienation from the adult world.
3. The protagonist often achieves temporary relief from these anxieties through an association with an unconventional adult from outside the family.
4. The narrative is usually in the first person, and its confessional tone is self-centered.
5. The vocabulary is limited, and observation is restricted by the pretense that an ordinary child is the narrator.
6. Sentences and paragraphs are short, language is flat, without nuance, and the language may be emotionally numb.
7. Inclusion of expletives seems obligatory.
8. Sex is discussed openly.
9. The setting is usually urban.

Jack Forman (12) adds that, in contrast to the fully developed characterizations in books of literary quality, many topical novels "are peopled with characters who are more mouthpieces of a particular point of view than fully developed protagonists" (p. 470). Beverly Cleary (8) further articulates the difference between stories that focus on problems and stories that focus on people: "I'm more interested in writing about people than problems. *Dear Mr. Henshaw* [the winner of the 1984 Newbery Medal] is about a boy that had a problem, not a problem that had a boy. I don't search for a new problem" (p. 1F).

Educators and critics of children's literature in the mid-1980s disagree, however, about how prominent "new realism" and "problem novels" actually are in contemporary realistic fiction for children. Critics such as Bertha M. Cheatham (6) maintain that novels "mirroring real-life situations and tackling controversial subjects (drugs, sex, suicide) are increasing in numbers" (p. 25), while critics such as Marilyn F. Apseloff (1) see "a definite swing away from the serious 'new realism' which dominated the lists half a decade ago" (p. 32) in the United States, Europe, and Japan. Apseloff notes an apparently increasing demand for adventure stories, humorous stories, and realistic fiction of high literary quality.

Nancy Vasilakis (31) maintains that in the late 1960s taboos began "falling like dominoes. . . .

No subject was too lurid, no language too explicit, and no outlook too bleak"; but by the mid-1980s "librarians were questioning the existence of too many books that are poorly written, dishonest, and manipulative, simply because they are destined to be popular" (p. 768). Vasilakis concludes that controversial books are no longer automatic bestsellers. Instead, "the fear of censorship, concern over declining standards, and the economic recession of the early eighties forced publishers and librarians alike, after the first few tremors, to hunker down and become more discriminating in their choices of what to publish and what to buy" (p. 769). Today's students of children's literature are living in an interesting era of book publishing for children and have the opportunity to analyze new books of contemporary realistic fiction and contemplate the different directions that authors may choose to pursue.

CONTROVERSIAL ISSUES RELATED TO REALISTIC FICTION

The degree to which realistic fiction should reflect the reality of the times leads to controversy as writers create characters who face problems relating to sexism, sexuality, violence, and drugs. There is no simple solution; what one group considers controversial, another does not. Realistic fiction has resulted in more controversy and calls for censorship than any other genre; educators must be aware of some concerns in this area of literature.

Sexism

Psychological oppression in the form of sex role socialization clearly conveys to girls from the earliest ages that their nature is to be submissive, servile, and repressed, and their role is to be servant, admirer, sex object and martyr. . . . The psychological consequences of goal depression in young women . . . are all too common. In addition, both men and women have come to realize the effect on men of this type of sex role stereotyping, the crippling pressure to compete, to achieve, to produce, to stifle emotion, sensitivity and gentleness, all taking their toll in psychic and physical traumas.

This position statement by the Association of Women Psychologists (2) stresses the dangers to both females and males when they are expected to live up to the traditional roles created by society and reflected in literature. The controversial

issue of sexism in children's literature involves not only the exclusion of females from children's books but the stereotyped roles in which children's books often depict females. Female characters are often shown as homemakers or as employees in "feminine" occupations; they often have characteristics that suggest they are passive, docile, fearful, and dependent. Children's books do not necessarily depict the roles of homemakers and of employees in traditionally female occupations in a condescending or demeaning light, but the implication that these are the *only* roles open to females has a harmful effect on the girls and boys who read these stories.

People concerned with sexism have evaluated the roles of males and females in children's literature and in the elementary classrooms. These evaluations are usually harshly critical of the negative forces of sex-role stereotyping. Ramona Frasher (13), for example, reviewed research on sexism and sex-role stereotyping in children's literature and identified some current trends. In Newbery Award-winning books published prior to the 1970s, male main characters outnumbered female main characters by about three to one. In addition, negative comments about females and stereotyping were common. Frasher's analysis of Newbery Award winners published between 1971 and 1980 showed the ratio of male characters to female characters was about equal. In addition, female characters tended to be portrayed with more positive and varied personality characteristics and exhibited a greater variety of behaviors. Even though these changes reflect a heightened sensitivity to feminist concerns, Frasher's article identifies three areas still of major concern: (1) changes are found predominantly in books written for children in middle and late childhood years; (2) the rush to respond to criticism resulted in too many examples of poor or marginal literature; (3) until more authors are able to write with ease about both sexes engaged in a broad scope of activities and exhibiting a range of characteristics, children's literature will remain stereotyped. Frasher's conclusion emphasizes the need for critical evaluation in this area: "The number of books accessible to children is immense; it will take many years of publishing quality nonsexist literature to insure that a random selection is as likely to be nonstereotyped as it is to be stereotyped" (p. 77).

Educators, psychologists, and other concerned adults also criticize the sexism and sex-role stereotyping in realistic picture books. Aileen Pace Nilsen (22) analyzed the role of females in 80 Caldecott Medal winners and honor books. She chose picture books because illustrated books are "the ones influencing children at the time they are in the process of developing their own sexual identity. Children decide very early in life what roles are appropriate to male and female" (p. 919). Of the books that were realistic (as compared with fantasy), she found fewer stories having girls as the leading characters. She also compared the number of girl- and boy-centered stories over a twenty-year period; the percentage of girl-centered stories had decreased from a high of 46 percent in 1951–55 to a low of 26 percent in 1966–70. Nilsen does not recommend that children not read these books, but she does suggest that they be provided with equally interesting books that have female main characters. She also recommends that artists become aware of the stereotypes they can perpetuate in illustrating books. She points out that in Ezra Jack Keats's *Goggles*, Peter's sister sits on the sidewalk beside a baby and draws pictures while the boys' excitement rages around her. Likewise, in *A Tree Is Nice*, the boys are pictured in the upper branches of the trees, while the girls are pictured sitting in the lowest branches, waving to boys climbing trees, or sprinkling plants with a watering can.

Many female protagonists in books for older children behave in ways quite different from the heroines of traditional literature. They reflect the fairly recent realization that females are also *heroes*, with considerable intellectual, emotional, and physical potential that is demonstrated in their actions. Some of the most memorable girl characters—including Karana in Scott O'Dell's *Island of the Blue Dolphins*, Queenie in Robert Burch's *Queenie Peavy* (who insisted that she would grow up to be a doctor, not a nurse), Harriet in Louise Fitzhugh's *Harriet the Spy*, and even Jo in Louisa May Alcott's Victorian novel, *Little Women*—are believable and exciting because they are individuals who do not follow stereotypic behavior patterns.

These nontraditional behaviors can, of course, also result in controversy; women's roles and women's rights are political issues with advocates who express strong opinions on both sides. One of the areas that illustrates women's changing roles is the portrayal of the minor characters in a story. Mothers may be sports writers, as in Ellen Conford's *The Revenge of the Incredible Dr. Rancid and His Youthful Assistant, Jeffrey*, photographers who travel on assignments and join peace marches accompanied by their daughters, as in Norma Klein's *Mom, the Wolf Man and Me*, and book illustrators who travel on consulting contracts, as in Lois Lowry's *Anastasia on Her Own*. Recent books suggest that the stereotyped roles of males and females may be changing, as increasingly varied occupations and behavior patterns are found in the books. Teachers, librarians, and parents should be aware, however, that not all people look on these changes favorably.

Sexuality

Today is a time of increasing sophistication and frankness about sexuality; television programs and movies portray sexual relationships that would not have been shown to earlier generations of adults, let alone children. Premarital and extramarital sex, concerns about sexual development, homosexual experiences, and sex eduation are controversial topics in children's literature.

Several books written for older children describe nontraditional living situations in which a child's mother lives with a male friend. In Stuart Buchan's *When We Lived with Pete*, Tommy and his mother live with a man who is not ready to get married. In Norma Klein's more controversial *Mom, the Wolf Man and Me*, Theodore spends weekends with Brett's mother, which leads eleven-year-old Brett to ask her mother if she is having sexual relations with him. This results in a frank discussion about sexual intercourse. As might be expected, this book has met with varying reactions. John M. Kean and Carl Personke (19) point out that numerous children today are living in one-parent households and that such children should have the opportunity to read about "a warm home environment that differs from the usual pattern" (p. 334). In contrast, several librarians and literature professors at one reading conference (27) reported receiving many negative comments from parents and college students about the sexual discussions and the unconventional life-style described in Klein's book.

Books describing children's concerns about their developing sexuality may also be controversial. For example, Judy Blume's popular *Are You There God? It's Me, Margaret* has been reviewed favorably as a book that realistically conveys preadolescent girls' worries over menstruation and body changes. Yet in 1981 this book was one of several taken from library shelves and burned because of some adults' view that it had a negative influence on children. In that same year, the national television news showed angry adults criticizing the morality of the book, as well as many others, and the resulting flames of protest.

The results of a recent censorship survey may surprise many students of children's literature. Ken Donelson (9) reports that Judy Blume, with five titles and thirty-three protests, is the second most widely protested author. (John Steinbeck, with seven titles and forty-five protests, is the most widely protested author.) In addition to *Are You There God? It's Me, Margaret*, Blume's *Then Again, Maybe I Won't; Deenie; Forever; It's Not the End of the World*, and *Blubber* have been strongly criticized or censored because of their sexual content and/or strong language.

Other Controversial Issues

Television, movies, and books have all been accused of portraying too much violence. Children's cartoons are often criticized for their excessive violence. Children's books become the object of controversy when they portray what some people define as inappropriate behavior, or when they describe excessive violence. Many realistic books containing violence have inner-city settings. For example, Frank Bonham's *Durango Street* describes the hero's bid for survival in a world of grim gang violence and drugs, where he could be used for "bayonet practice." Drugs also play a significant role in Walter Dean Myers's *It Ain't All for Nothin'!* Some people believe that children should read about the reality of drugs in the world around them, while others believe that their minds should not be contaminated by the mention of drugs.

Profanity and other language objectionable to some people are also controversial. What is considered objectionable has changed over the years, however. Mary Q. Steele (28) describes her own experiences with writing: in the 1950s, editors deleted "hecks" and "darns" from manuscripts written for children; now a more permissive climate encourages authors to write relevant dialogue. Ken Donelson's (9) survey on censorship reports that a committee unsuccessfully challenged the placement of Katherine Paterson's *The Great Gilly Hopkins* in an elementary library because the author used supposedly objectionable language.

ISSUE

···❯❯❮❮···

Freedom to Read Versus Censorship of Literature

THE LAST TEN YEARS, ACcording to James Davis, have produced an increase in the number of organized group efforts to censor children's literature and school textbooks.[1] These groups believe that books which they suspect are capable of subverting children's religious, social, or political beliefs should be censored and that teachers should not be allowed to use such materials in the classroom. Newsletters from organized groups suggest the harmful effects of sharing certain books or books by certain authors with children; many adults maintain that children are more influenced or damaged by "objectionable" materials than are adults[2]; school boards ban books because of ideas some people find objectionable; and lawyers and legislators debate the rights of schools to use certain books or to teach specific content. Tom Williams, a minister and spokesperson for those who believe library books should adhere to a local community standard, recommends that books should be scrutinized and selected according to a community standard determined by public referendum or by a library board elected directly by the people.[3]

In contrast to this view of censorship, Leanne Katz, coordinator for the National Coalition against Censorship, maintains that librarians should follow principles of diversity

Such controversy usually arises because adults are concerned that young children may use profanity.

Other issues that can become controversial in children's books include viewpoints on war and peace, religion, death, and racial matters. (Chapter eleven discusses critics' concerns about books related to Black Americans, Hispanics, Native Americans, and Asian Americans.)

Guidelines for Selecting Controversial Fiction for Children

The question of how "realistic" realistic fiction should be is answered very differently by various groups. Historically, schools and the literature read by children have often been under the pressures of censorship, as different groups tried to impose their values on all children. While modern censors might laugh at the literary concerns of the Puritans, there is still concern over appropriate subjects for children's literature. When children's books explore sexuality, violence, moral problems, racism, and religious beliefs, they are likely to be thought objectionable by those who believe that children should not be ex-

posed to such ideas. Teachers and librarians need to be knowledgeable about their communities, the subjects that may prove controversial, and the merits of controversial books they would like to share with children. John M. Kean and Carl Personke (19) say that "even though educators attempt to avoid controversy by selecting only 'safe' books that they believe won't offend anyone, someone is likely to be offended. . . . Everybody has a value position that he considers important and that he thinks the schools ought to perpetuate for his children and for other people's children. When educators have an empathetic understanding of the community, they will be better able to work with parents—helping parents to view the wide range of books that are appropriate for children, rather than telling them which are the 'right' materials" (p. 340).

Day Ann K. McClenathan (20) suggests that wholesale avoidance of books containing controversial topics, in addition to encouraging overt censorship, is inappropriate because (1) a book about a relevant sociological or psychological problem can give young people opportunities to grow in their thinking processes and to extend their experiences; (2) problems in books can pro-

and respect for individual decision making that encourage access to a wide variety of ideas. In Katz's view, banning books is a "dictatorship over our minds and a dangerous opening to religious, political, artistic and intellectual repression" (4, p. 2). To counter increased efforts for censorship, professional educational journals and professional organizations are responding with articles such as William Palmer's "What Reading Teachers Can Do before the Censors Come,"[5] and

documents such as the American Library Association's *Bill of Rights,*[6] which stresses that the freedom to read is guaranteed by the United States Constitution. Palmer defends the right to read without censorship and suggests the following four-stage approach for educators who may need to defend their use of literature: (1) prepare a rationale for the study of literature, (2) develop community support for freedom to read, (3) prepare a written statement on book and material selection,

and (4) have a written policy to handle censorship efforts.

The issue of censorship will in all likelihood continue through the 1980s, as concerned adults on both sides of the question argue whether literature and educators should indoctrinate children into the mores and morals of a community or encourage children to expand their ideas and understandings through exposure to and discussion of a variety of books and ideas.

[1]Davis, James E. *Dealing with Censorship,* Urbana, Ill.: National Council of Teachers of English, 1978.

[2]Woods, L. B. "For Sex: See Librarian." *Library Journal,* 1 September 1978, pp. 1561–67.

[3]"Should Librarians Have the Final Say in Selecting Books for the Public Library." *Family Weekly,* 10 January 1982, p. 2.

[4]Ibid.

[5]Palmer, William S. "What Reading Teachers Can Do before the Censors Come." *Journal of Reading* 25 (January 1982): 310–14.

[6]American Library Association. "The Freedom to Read." *Bill of Rights.* Chicago, Ill.: American Library Association, 1972.

ISSUE

Are Violence and Inhumanity Appropriate Character Traits Signifying the Transition from Childhood to Adulthood?

BOOKS SUCH AS FRED Gipson's *Old Yeller* and Armstrong Sperry's *Call It Courage* have been criticized because they include acts of killing which symbolize the male initiation into manhood. Critics who have labeled such plots as belonging to "the cult to kill" suggest that young men are being conditioned to believe they must perform violent actions or be strong enough to kill even a loved pet if they are to achieve manhood. Some consider this masculine stereotype harmful and detrimental to healthy social development. The struggle and strain to live up to such an image is believed to place considerable pressures on males and to suggest that any other behavior is unmanly.

In contrast, other writers suggest that eliminating such acts of violence in children's literature would ignore our literary past and the archetypes found in myth and epic literature. This viewpoint stresses that children should not be isolated from their literary past even though violence may play a key role in the lives of traditional heroes. In addition, eliminating acts of violence from historical fiction would force writers to ignore the harsher realities of life on the frontier and in wilderness areas or the ritualistic rites of passage that are part of many tribal cultures.

Writers of children's literature texts often suggest that each act of violence in a book must be interpreted according to the total plot of the story and the changes that occur in the character, the character's self-concept, and the character's view of the world.

vide some children with opportunities for identification and allow others an opportunity to empathize with their peers; (3) problems in books invite decisions, elicit opinions, and afford opportunities to take positions on issues.

Given these controversial issues, and the need for books that are relevant to the interests, concerns, and problems of today's children, adults should consider some guidelines when choosing realistic fiction for children. Day Ann K. McClenathan (20) provides a useful guide for selecting books that might be considered controversial.

1   Know exactly what the problem is and consequently what might be considered controversial. This means you have to really read the book. You can't rely on the opinion of someone else or even on a good review. It's necessary that you, as a member of a school and a community, be able to appraise specific content in light of the mores of that particular milieu. What might offend in one community

would go unnoticed or unchallenged in another.

2   Ascertain the author's point of view and weigh the power of positive influence against exposure to a theme some people perceive negatively. For example, if an author writes about the drug culture, but events in the story clearly point up harmful effects of drug use, then reluctance to use the book may result in a missed opportunity for healthy shaping of attitudes.

3   Apply literary criteria to the selection of library books in such a way that vulnerability to the arguments of would-be censors is at least partially reduced by the obvious overall quality of book choices. Occasionally, teachers and librarians select books of inferior quality because they deal with topics having a high interest for middle grade or older children. This sometimes happens with books involving experimentations with sex. The information in such books may be harmless (or

even useful), but the book may fall short of accepted literary criteria. If the book is then targeted because it offends community groups, it will be difficult to defend, and having it in your school collection will suggest that considerations other than literary quality determine choices. In addition to generally accepted literary criteria, you will want to examine books that attempt to counter stereotypes for what can be thought of as the overcorrection syndrome. Sometimes, in a passion to change images, authors will work too hard on the issue itself with the result that plot and characterization suffer.

4 Know and be able to explain your purpose in using a particular book. Have answers ready to the following questions:
   a. Will the topic be understood by the group with which I intend to use the book?
   b. What are some of the merits of this particular book that have influenced me to use it, rather than another book of comparable literary, sociological, or psychological importance?
   c. Is the book an acceptable model in terms of writing style and use of language?
   d. Are my objectives in using this book educationally defensible (for example, presentation and/or clarification of information, extension of experiences, refinement of attitudes, promotion of reading habits)?
5 In order to clarify and maintain your own sincere objectivity, review and be prepared to discuss both sides of the censorship question. (pp. 33–35)

USE OF LITERARY ELEMENTS

Contemporary realistic fiction should meet the basic literary criteria discussed in chapter three. A believable conflict that could really occur in our contemporary world should be integral to the plot, characterization, setting, and theme. An author should thoroughly develop internal or external conflicts and characterizations so that readers can understand the characters' responses. In this next section, consider how several authors develop credible stories through their depiction of conflict and plot development, characterization, and style.

Plot Development

The conflicts at the center of plots in contemporary realistic fiction may arise from external forces, as characters try to overcome problems related to families, peers, or the society around them, or they may arise as the characters try to overcome problems related to inner conflicts. Internal conflicts often result from conflict with external forces. Consequently, person-versus-self conflicts are common in contemporary realistic fiction. As in traditional literature, conflict in contemporary realistic fiction may involve protagonists in some sort of quest (16). Caron Lee Cohen (7) identifies four major components in the development of person-against-self conflicts: problem, struggle, realization, and achievement of peace or truth. "The point at which the struggle wanes and the inner strength emerges seems to be the point of self-realization," says Cohen (p. 28). "That point leads immediately to the final sense of peace or truth that is the resolution of the quest. The best books are those which move readers and cause them to identify with the character's struggle."

Of course, if readers are to understand the conflict and empathize with characters' responses, the characters themselves must be convincingly developed, with the pressures they experience and the motives they act upon made very clear. According to Hazel Rochman (24), the age of protagonists in realistic fiction for older children is not so important as the author's convincing depiction of common hopes, fears, and important choices.

As an example of credible conflict, consider how Paula Fox develops a person-versus-self conflict in *One-Eyed Cat*. The author sets the stage for the forthcoming conflict by describing an incident in which Uncle Hilary gives Ned a loaded Daisy air rifle for his eleventh birthday. Ned's father, the Reverend Wallace, forbids his son to use the gun until he is at least fourteen. Instead of hiding the gun, Ned's father takes it to the attic where it can easily be found. The conflicting relationship of trust is developed as Ned considers, "The painful thing was that, though Ned didn't always trust his father, his father trusted him, and that seemed to him unfair, although he couldn't explain why it was so" (p. 40).

Ned cannot resist the temptation of the gun, and fires it, shooting a wild stray cat. The person-versus-self conflict deepens as the author vividly describes Ned's fear and accompanying guilt when he sees the "gap, the dried blood, the little worm of mucus in the corner next to the cat's nose where the eye had been" (p. 70). The author's choice of metaphor explains Ned's emotional response as "the gun was like a splinter in his mind" (p. 90). Ned's quest becomes to save the wild cat from sickness and starvation during the approaching winter, and also becomes a quest to overcome his sense of guilt and remorse and to tell the truth about what has happened.

Fox's novel follows Cohen's (7) four major components. The problem results because Ned betrays his parent's trust; the struggle continues as Ned feels increasingly guilty because of his lies as he tries to save the wounded animal; the point of self-realization begins when Ned feels relief as he confesses his guilt to a critically ill older neighbor; and peace and truth finally result on a moonlit night when Ned confesses his actions to his mother after they see a one-eyed cat and kittens emerging from the woods. In a satisfying conclusion, Ned and his mother exchange revealing confessions. This book may be so successful because the conflict appeals to more than one age or ability group. Most readers can empathize with the desire to accomplish a forbidden action and the terror of possible consequences. More mature readers can appreciate the psychological portrayal of a boy as he successfully accomplishes a hurdle in the maturation process.

Characterization

The characterization of Ned in Fox's *One-Eyed Cat* is an integral part of the conflict. For example, by describing Ned's actions, by clarifying his response to his parents and to the wounded cat, and by revealing his thoughts during his traumatic experiences, Fox develops Ned's character traits. Readers know Ned intimately. They understand his hopes, his fears, his past, his present, and his relationships with his parents.

Complex characterizations that lead to self-discovery and to developing personal relationships are also important in Cynthia Voigt's books about the Tillerman family. In *Homecoming*, Voigt focuses on the children's experiences after their emotionally ill mother deserts them. In the sequel, *Dicey's Song*, Voigt focuses on the characterization of four children and their grandmother: a young girl who is trying to hold her family together, a learning-disabled girl who has a gift for

music, a gifted boy who tries to hide his giftedness because he does not want to be different, a younger brother who strikes out in anger, and a grandmother whom the townspeople consider eccentric. In *A Solitary Blue*, Voigt focuses on Jeff Greene, a friend of Dicey Tillerman, as he faces his mother's desertion and his father's inability to interact on a personal basis. Finally, in *The Runner*, Voigt goes back to an earlier time in the life of Grandmother Tillerman, a time filled with frustration as Bullet Tillerman (Dicey's uncle), a high school running champion, battles his father and himself. In all Voigt's books, as in Fox's *One-Eyed Cat*, readers discover that the protagonists are believable people with many-sided personalities

Symbolism enhances characterization as a girl makes discoveries about herself. (Illustration by James Shefcik from *Dicey's Song* by Cynthia Voigt is used by permission of Atheneum Publishers. Illustrations copyright © 1982 James Shefcik.)

like their own. Readers come to know these characters intimately, sharing their hopes, fears, pasts, and presents.

Throughout her books Voigt effectively uses symbolism to reveal characterization and to clarify important character development. The author's use of symbolism associated with the blue heron is especially meaningful in *A Solitary Blue*. Consider the implications for Jeff's characterization in the following examples. When Jeff has a low self-esteem he views the heron as a creature that "occupied its own insignificant corner of the landscape in a timeless, long-legged solitude" (p. 45). Later, when Jeff feels angry, broken, and bruised due to his mother's behavior, he again views the heron; " 'Just leave me alone', the heron seemed to be saying. Jeff rowed away, down the quiet creek. The bird did not watch him go" (p. 91). Finally, when Jeff discovers that he is a worthwhile person, he realizes that the solitary heron reminds him of his best friend, Dicey Tillerman. When Dicey laughingly states that she was thinking that the bird reminded her of Jeff, Jeff is flattered by the comparison. Now Jeff knows that he, like the heron, is a "rare bird" with staying power and a gentle spirit.

The synthesis of symbolism and character traits is equally important in *Dicey's Song*. For example, a careful tracing of musical selections, including the title, shows that the author uses music to reflect characterization and to illustrate changes in personal development. Likewise, a dilapidated boat and a tree provide important symbolic meanings. In *The Runner*, Voigt uses Bullet's reactions toward being boxed in and his attitudes toward running to develop characterization.

More mature readers enjoy the development of and the interactions with the characters in all three books. *A Solitary Blue* provides an opportunity for readers to analyze the heroine of *Dicey's Song* from another perspective, that of Jeff Greene. Likewise, *The Runner* provides an opportunity for readers to understand the angry children described later by Grandmother Tillerman and to understand some of the reasons for Grandmother Tillerman's responses when she interacts with her grandchildren.

Authors' Style

An effective literary style greatly enhances plot and characterization in realistic fiction. Vivid descriptions, believable dialogue, symbolism, precise figures of speech, and other stylistic techniques subtly provide the reader with in-depth understanding of characters and situations. In *Dicey's Song*, for example, Cynthia Voigt develops a synthesis of symbolism and character traits; allusions to familiar music are one of Voigt's symbolic means of emphasizing changes in the character's personal development.

An author's style of writing can develop descriptions that appeal to the senses, that awaken readers to the emotional impact of a situation, and that suggest the mood of the story of the situation. These moods in contemporary realistic fiction range from terror to humor. Consider, for example, how Tormod Haugen uses short, choppy sentences and descriptive words to create the image of *The Night Birds,* the birds that Jake believes live in his closet and that symbolize a seven-year-old boy' s conflicts and inner terrors:

The night birds. He remembered the first time they were there. But in a way they'd been there as long as he could remember. Suddenly one night he'd woken up. Something had woken him. Then he heard them. Buzzing in the air from all sides. He saw them too. Like black shadows, even blacker than the night. They popped out of the dark and just were there. Big, flapping wings with feathers that made a rushing sound. Red, staring eyes. As if they had fire in them. And beaks that were open, big and dangerous. They wanted to peck at him. Closer and closer, thousands of them. The night was full of birds. The darkness was nothing but birds. His room was bursting with birds. They wanted to get him. He screamed and got under the quilt. The first birds struck the bed with their claws and tried to pull off his quilt. He heard the birds scream, loud and shrill. Louder than he could (p. 34).

Other authors use language to create humorous moods. Humor is an important element in Beverly Keller's *No Beasts! No Children!* In a tale about family adjustment following divorce, Keller develops humor through irony and the descriptions of preposterous situations. First, there is the irony of the divorce itself. The children's father is a marriage counselor who is trying to find himself. Second, there are preposterous situations caused by three mischievous children, three huge dogs, an extremely strict housekeeper who dislikes animals, a landlord who dislikes both dogs and children, and a mule with white stripes.

In *Anastasia on Her Own*, Lois Lowry does not rely on the descriptions of preposterous situations to develop humor. Instead, she highlights the humor in a realistic contemporary situation:

Housekeeping and taking care of a younger brother provide numerous humorous experiences. (Jacket painting copyright © 1985 by Diane de Groat from *Anastasia on Her Own* by Lois Lowry. Reprinted by permission of Houghton Mifflin Company.)

two busy professional parents trying to manage a household and raise two children, and an enthusiastic, determined young protagonist who believes that housekeeping can be easy if the family can only develop and closely follow a nonsexist household schedule. An unexpected consulting contract temporarily removes Anastasia's mother from the household and allows Anastasia an opportunity to test her theories.

Lowry develops humor by contrasting Anastasia's dream world with the world of reality; by describing the consequences when a naive, but determined, young girl approaches household tasks that are beyond her ability; and by describing the consequences of unexpected interruptions. Chapter one, for example, contains Anastasia's full-page schedule, which details hourly tasks from 7:00 A.M. to 8:00 P.M. In contrast, the eighth schedule in the book reads simply:

Housekeeping Schedule
  Aftermath
  Clean up. For hours and hours and hours.
  Cry (p. 122)

There is the humor in contrasts between young Anastasia's fantasy dreams of her first date and the actuality of thirteen-year-old Steve Harvey: "She had envisioned someone tall and handsome—someone who looked a lot like Lawrence Olivier in Wuthering Heights—maybe wearing a tuxedo and holding a corsage in his hand" (p. 113). Instead, Steve wears a sweatshirt bearing

the words PSYCHOTIC STATE, discusses chicken pox scabs, stuffs peanuts into his mouth, talks with his mouth full, and tells her that her first attempt at adult entertaining was horrible.

Well-written stories of this sort, with convincingly developed plots and characterizations, make many books of contemporary realistic fiction highly popular with children.

CRITERIA FOR EVALUATING REALISTIC FICTION

In addition to the basic literary criteria, high-quality contemporary realistic fiction should satisfy the following requirements, as suggested by Root (25), and by previous discussions in this chapter:

1 The content should be honestly presented; sensationalizing and capitalizing on the novelty of the subject should be avoided.
2 A story should expose personal and social values central to our culture, while at the same time revealing how the overt expression of those values may have changed.
3 The story should allow the reader to draw personal conclusions from the evidence; the author should respect the reader's intelligence.
4 The author should recognize that today's young readers are in the process of growing toward adult sophistication.

5 The language and syntax should help reveal the background and nature of characters and situations.

6 The author should write in a hopeful tone; a story should communicate in an honest way that there is hope in this world.

7 Children's literature should reflect a sensitivity to the needs and rights of girls and boys without preference, bias, or negative stereotypes. Males should be allowed to show emotions, females should be able to demonstrate courage and ambition. Girls and boys should not be denied access to certain occupations because of their sex. Children should sense that they can be successful in many occupations.

8 If violence is included in the story, does the author treat the subject appropriately? Does the author give the necessary facts? Are both sides of the conflict portrayed fully, fairly, and honestly? Is the writing developed with feeling and emotion? Does the author help children develop a perspective about the subject?

9 A story should satisfy children's basic needs and provide them with increased insights into their own problems and social relationships.

10 A story should provide children with enjoyment.

The literary techniques authors use to develop credible realistic fiction are discussed in the following sections of the text; children's personality and social development will also be emphasized to assist adults in recommending or choosing specific books for children.

FAMILY LIFE

The family stories of the late 1930s through the early 1960s depict some of the strongest, warmest family relationships in contemporary realistic fiction for children. (See the analysis of family life on pages 70–73.) Today's children still enjoy the warmth and humor represented by the families in Elizabeth Enright's *Thimble Summer*, Eleanor Estes's *The Moffats*, Sydney Taylor's *All-of-a-Kind Family*, and Madeleine L'Engle's *Meet the Austins*. The characters' actions suggest that security is gained by family members working together, that each member has responsibility to other members, that consideration for others is desirable,

and that family unity and loyalty can overcome hard times and peer conflicts.

Since the early 1960s, many changes have taken place in realistic fiction's characterization of the American family. Authors writing in the 1970s and 1980s have often focused on the need to overcome family disturbances, as children and adults adjust to new social realities. Death of one or both parents, foster families, single-parent families, children of unmarried females, the disruptions caused by divorce and remarriage, and child abuse are some of the issues related to children and their families that now appear in contemporary realistic fiction for children.

This literature may help children realize that many types of family units other than the tradi-

Sydney Taylor creates family stories that show warmth, humor, and strong family relationships. (Cover illustration by Gail Owens. From *Ella of All-of-a-Kind Family*, by Sydney Taylor. Copyright © 1978 by Sydney Taylor. Illustrations copyright © 1978 by Gail Owens. Reprinted by permission of the publisher, E.P. Dutton.)

tional one are common and legitimate in our society today. Children may also see that problems often can be solved if family members work together. Even when depicting the most disturbing of relationships, authors of realistic fiction may show a family's strong need for unity and desire to keep at least some of its members together.

Authors of realistic stories about family disturbances use several literary techniques to create credible plots and characters. Often they focus on painful and potentially destructive situations and feelings that are common in society today. These situations are usually familiar to readers who may have experienced similar situations, who may have known someone who had such experiences, or who may fear that they will have similar experiences. Authors often tell these stories from the perspective of the child or children involved. First-person or limited omniscient point of view from a child's perspective can be very successful in depicting child characters' emotional and behavioral reactions as they first discover a problem, experience a wide range of personal difficulties and emotions as they try to change or understand the situation, and finally arrive at an acceptance of the situation. Characterization may portray the vulnerability of the characters, create sympathy for them, and describe how they handle the jolting disruptions and personal discoveries that affect their lives. Symbolism and allusion may emphasize a conflict and characterization. Authors often use characters' reactions to change, trouble, and new discoveries to trace the characters' development of better relationships with others or positive personal growth. Some authors, however—such as those trying to make a point about child abuse—use specific situations or discoveries to allow children to escape from all reality. A family member may be the antagonist in these realistic stories about family life, or the antagonist may be an outside force, such as death of a parent, divorce, or moving to a new location. To relieve the impact of painful situations, authors may add humor to characterization or plot development. Humor can make a situation bearable, create sympathy for a character, or clarify the nature of a confrontation.

Divorce and Remarriage

In Peggy Mann's *My Dad Lives in a Downtown Hotel*, Joey experiences a series of strong emotional reactions to his parents' divorce. First he believes

the separation is his fault. Mann develops the strength of these feelings through Joey's actions: he makes out a list of promises he will keep if his father returns and delivers them to his father. When his promises have no effect on the situation, Joey's emotional reactions change; he goes through a period of hating his father and feeling very confused. Mann suggests that Joey accepts the change in his family life when he can enjoy being with his father during their Sunday visits.

In *Dear Mr. Henshaw*, Beverly Cleary effectively uses letters and diary entries written by her sixth-grade hero, Leigh Botts, to develop believable characterization and plot and to show changes in Leigh as he begins to accept the actuality of his parent's divorce. As a classroom assignment, Leigh sends his favorite author a list of ten questions. Mr. Henshaw answers Leigh's questions, but also sends Leigh a list of ten questions that he wants Leigh to answer about himself. At first Leigh refuses to answer the questions. Then his mother insists that because Mr. Henshaw answered Leigh's questions Leigh must answer Mr. Henshaw's questions. The answers to the questions allow Cleary an opportunity to provide important background information and to reveal Leigh's personal feelings about himself, his family, and his parents' divorce. Eventually Leigh begins to write a diary—both because Mr. Henshaw suggests it and because Leigh's mother refuses to fix the television. By midpoint in the book, the diary entries begin to change and Leigh realizes changes in his own character:

I don't have to pretend to write to Mr. Henshaw anymore. I have learned to say what I think on a piece of paper. And I don't hate my father either. I can't hate him. Maybe things would be easier if I could. (p. 73)

The entries seem believable because Cleary includes both humorous and painful experiences that are important in Leigh's life.

In *The Animal, The Vegetable, and John D. Jones*, author Betsy Byars focuses on three children's reactions to painful changes in the family. Clara and Deanie's father asks the widow he loves and her son to share a summer vacation with him and his daughters. The two sisters, who had been experiencing sibling rivalry, now confront an outside antagonist in the person of a boy named John D. Byars describes him as a worthy opponent: he is bright, sophisticated, conceited, and writing a book of advice for his inferiors, who, incidentally, are all other children. John D. is also vulnerable, however, and perhaps sensitive; his book is about functioning in a hostile world. Byars describes a series of incidents that emphasize the parents' dilemma, imply their inability to handle the situation, and create sympathy for the characters. Whenever the adults plan a happy excursion something goes wrong: at a cookout the only edible hamburger falls in the sand; during a visit to an amusement park Clara escapes her family only to become sick after riding the Space Cyclone and then seeing John D. with a huge sundae. Although Byars's descriptions of these situations are humorous, the story contains some hostile undercurrents. Byars uses a near tragedy to focus the attention of all the characters on the importance of others. Their reactions indicate that they have learned a great deal about interpersonal relationships.

In Carol Lea Benjamin's *The Wicked Stepdog*, twelve-year-old Lou is afraid of losing her father's love when he presents her with a new stepmother and a new "stepdog." Benjamin's first-person narrative from Lou's viewpoint emphasizes Lou's sometimes painful and sometimes humorous reactions to her changed family. Lou's changing responses to her stepmother's golden retriever symbolize her gradual acceptance of new circumstances. At first she hates to walk the dog, but by the end of the story, when she meets a boy who also walks a dog, stepdog-walking has become one of Lou's favorite pasttimes.

Single-Parent Families

Single-parent families have always existed, but recent realistic fiction for children portrays such families more often, and sometimes more candidly, than did most realistic fiction in the past. In contemporary novels for children, some of these families are doing quite well, while others face serious problems due to the lack of a mother's or a father's emotional and economic support.

A family's struggle to survive without one parent is a popular plot in contemporary realistic fiction. Authors may suggest that the experience strengthens the children in the family or that the experience causes so many difficulties that the children find coping impossible. In Vera and Bill Cleaver's *Where the Lilies Bloom*, a fourteen-year-old girl experiences conflict between her desire to keep a promise she made her dying father and

her developing realization that she must break that promise in order to ensure her family's survival. Although Mary Call's father dies quite early in the plot, the Cleavers characterize him plausibly as a person who lives by a strong moral and family code. He demands that his daughter take pride in the family name, instill that pride in her brothers and sisters, and hold the family together without accepting charity. Later, this promise becomes a crucial element of the plot and in Mary Call's character development. The authors develop a believable and interesting conflict as Mary Call tries to do as her father demanded, but gradually realizes that she must accept help if she is to gain the knowledge she needs and improve her family's welfare. This story lacks sentimentality; Mary Call recognizes her father's weaknesses and eventually realizes that his judgment about his oldest daughter and the despised neighbor, Kaiser Pease, was in error. The authors lighten the almost insurmountable odds against survival by adding touches of humor. This is especially true in the sequel, *Trial Valley*, as a more mature Mary Call copes with both family problems and expectant suitors. (Students of children's literature may find it interesting to compare the characteristics of this contemporary female protagonist with the Victorian female protagonist in Charlotte Yonge's *The Daisy Chain*, discussed in chapter two.)

In Marilyn Sachs's *The Bears' House*, detailed portrayal of a harsh reality is crucial to give the plot and the protagonist's responses full credibility. Five children live in a crowded apartment; their mother is emotionally disturbed, and their father deserts the family. The children's distrust of the adult world is expressed through their fear of being placed in foster homes and their need to lie to their social worker. Sachs contrasts the harsh reality of nine-year-old Fran Ellen's life with the beautiful make-believe place of her fantasies. When she sits in front of the dollhouse in her fourth-grade classroom, she can visit the Bear family and sit on Pappa Bear's lap when she feels unhappy. The conclusion of the story illustrates that contemporary realistic fiction may not have a "happy ever after" ending: Fran Ellen withdraws into her make-believe world, where she has found her own way to survive in frightening and bewildering circumstances.

In *The Night Swimmers*, Betsy Byars uses a painful and possibly destructive situation to highlight a young girl's personal and social develop-

A child leaves her own harsh reality for a make-believe dollhouse
world. (From *The Bears' House*, by
Marilyn Sachs. Copyright © 1971
by Marilyn Sachs. Reprinted by
permission of Doubleday & Company, Inc.)

ment and her acceptance of difficult discoveries.
Retta's mother has died. She and her younger
brothers are being reared by their father, who
works nights and is more concerned about developing his career as a singer/composer than about
attending to his children. Byars chronicles Retta's
personal growth by describing her feelings after
her mother's death, the moment when she understands her father's career goals (in reaction to her
mother's death he composed a hit song, but did
not pay attention to the children), her changing
feelings as she tries to be a mother to her two
younger brothers, and her final realization that
she must accept her father as he is, not as she
would like him to be. Byars uses humor to highlight some of these situations and to focus on the
painful moments: Retta discovers how a mother
should act by observing mothers in the supermarket; she gains cooking skills by watching television commercials. Retta's and her younger
brother Roy's reactions to their own final discoveries may be the most poignant moments in the
book. Roy discovers that the Bowlwater Plant is
not the enormous and wondrous vegetation of his
imagination, but is a smelly and ugly chemical
factory. Retta realizes that their father is so ob-
sessed with stardom that he cannot relate to his

children in the way Retta would like. Roy expresses their discoveries effectively when he
compares swallowing a hard truth about life with
Popeye swallowing his spinach: both experiences
make you stronger.

In *Mom, the Wolf Man and Me*, Norma Klein
creates a close and somewhat offbeat relationship
between a girl and her mother, a professional
photographer. Eleven-year-old Brett accepts the
fact that her mother and father never married,
enjoys her unconventional life, accompanies her
mother on peace marches, and has frank discussions with her. (Some parents react negatively to
the frank discussions about premarital sex in this
book.) Only when her mother meets the Wolf
Man and considers marriage does Brett experience fear and confusion. She is afraid her happy
life will change and unsuccessfully tries to convince her mother and the Wolf Man that they
should not marry. Hila Colman creates a different
mother-daughter relationship in *Tell Me No Lies*.
When twelve-year-old Angela learns that her
mother was unmarried when Angela was born,
Angela hates her mother for lying and runs away
to find her father. Colman uses this experience to
create an atmosphere in which the girl can understand and forgive her mother. When she finds

her father, she discovers he is not like her dreams; in fact, he cannot accept her as his daughter. This turning point in the novel allows Angela to return home with new understanding. Both of these stories depict changes from the realistic fiction of the 1950s. The family structures, life-styles, expressed values, and types of problems reflect contemporary concerns and issues.

Child Abuse and Foster Homes

The adult world, as reflected in children's literature, may cause children unhappy and cruel experiences rather than provide happy and secure environments for children's development. The American Library Association's recent bibliography of literature related to child abuse includes thirty-nine titles that reflect chronic child abuse relating to violence, sexual harassment, or neglect. According to Betsy Hearne (15), "Some of the books are grim, but most offer the hope or outright assertion that children can break out of tormenting situations through determined, independent actions. Sharing these books with children encourages exactly the kind of awareness that might help a victim of child abuse or help a friend help out" (p. 1261).

Marion Dane Bauer explores the sinister side of foster care in *Foster Child*. Twelve-year-old Renny is placed in a foster home when her great-grandmother becomes too ill to care for her. Her foster father, Pop Beck, expresses sexual interest in the girls staying at his farm. Readers realize the danger in this situation when Renny and her friend run away and try to live in the great-grandmother's empty house. In Marilyn Sachs's *A December Tale*, five-year-old Henry and ten-year-old Myra are rejected by their father and must move from foster home to foster home. In response to systematic beatings and a foster mother who steals the money intended for their care, Henry retreats into offensive language and antisocial behavior, while Myra finds escape in fantasies about her hero, Joan of Arc. Sachs describes in detail the brutality the children face and their emotional responses.

More hopeful treatments of foster care and child abuse appear in Patricia MacLachlan's *Mama One, Mama Two*, a picture storybook depicting the warm, loving relationship between a foster mother and her foster child, and in Betsy Byars's *Cracker Jackson*, in which an eleven-year-old boy manages to convince adults that his former babysitter and her daughter are being abused by their husband and father. As in her other books, Byars uses humor and compassion to lighten the fear in the situation.

Depending upon their own backgrounds, some children may have difficulty relating to the harsh facts presented in books such as those by Bauer and Sachs. One child who read Sach's *A December Tale* could not believe that a teacher, a rela-

Humor and compassion lighten the tone in a story about child abuse. (From *Cracker Jackson*, by Betsy Byars. Jacket illustration by Diane de Groat. Text copyright © Betsy Byars, 1985. Jacket illustration copyright © Viking Penguin Inc., 1985. Reprinted by permission of Viking Penguin Inc.)

tive, or a friend would not come to the children's rescue. As you read *A December Tale*, Bauer's *Foster Child*, MacLachlan's *Mama One, Mama Two*, and Byars's *Cracker Jackson*, consider each author's possible purpose; how each author developed setting, characterization, and theme; and the possible responses of young readers.

GROWING UP

Children face numerous challenges as they venture further from the family environment and begin the often difficult process of growing up (see chapter one). Forming and maintaining relationships with peers is one important task. Children may also need to overcome emotional problems in order to develop or recover self-esteem and identify their roles in their widening world. As they grow older, they may feel self-conscious about their changing bodies and developing sexuality. They must confront other facts of life as well, including the need for survival and the inevitability of death. Books that explore children's concerns can stimulate discussion with children facing these same concerns. Such books also let children know that they are not alone, that other children experience and overcome the same problems.

Peer Relationships

Children, like adults, need the shared understanding, pleasure, challenge, sense of equality, and security that friendship with peers provides. Peer relationships involve many of the joys and sorrows with which children become familiar in family life, but they also expand children's understanding of other people and the world around them in ways that familiar family ties cannot. Contemporary realistic fiction portrays children forming friendships with peers who are much like themselves in certain ways and with peers who may at first seem strange. Many books discussed throughout this chapter explore the meaning of real friendship and suggest that best friends should support, rather than hurt, each other. These stories may help children overcome the disappointment that results when a friend moves or may stimulate a discussion about the meaning of friendship.

Authors often develop conflict in stories about interpersonal relationships by using person-against-self and/or person-against-person con-

flicts. In credible person-against-self conflicts, authors enable readers to understand and identify why the character has an inner conflict, how the character handles this conflict, and what causes the conflict to be resolved. The resolution should not be contrived; it should appear as a natural outcome of the story. Contrived endings result when authors try too rapidly and too conveniently to create happy endings for serious and hurtful situations. In credible person-against-person conflicts, authors develop both a believable protagonist and a believable opposing force that serves as the antagonist. Readers need to understand why conflict occurs between the two forces. Do differences in values, personalities, or character traits cause conflict? An author's development of characterization should reflect such differences and encourage readers to understand why the characters act and react as they do. The conflicts authors identify and the ways characters overcome these conflicts usually communicate a unifying theme about interpersonal relationships. The most successful themes develop naturally, as readers glimpse truths about friendship and life in general from the actions of the characters. The least successful themes are created solely for didactic purposes.

A person-against-self conflict and carefully developed characterization create a credible plot in E. L. Konigsburg's *Jennifer, Hecate, Macbeth, William McKinley, and Me, Elizabeth*. Konigsburg encourages readers to understand Elizabeth's inner conflict and need for a friend by emphasizing her shyness: she is a new girl in school, she goes to school alone, and she is afraid she will cry when she walks into her classroom. Elizabeth's shyness and need for a friend are reemphasized through her responses when she meets Jennifer, a very imaginative girl. At first Elizabeth complies with Jennifer's demands and suggestions even when she does not want to do what her new friend asks of her. Later, as she gains confidence in herself, Elizabeth becomes assertive. Her inner conflict is resolved when the friends no longer need the support of the game in which they pretend to be witch and assistant witch. Now they can be just good friends and act as equals.

Mary Stolz develops a person-against-society conflict as well as a person-against-self conflict in *Cider Days*. The person-against-self conflict develops as Polly faces loneliness after her best friend moves and then learns to respect the courage of a new friend. The person-against-society conflict

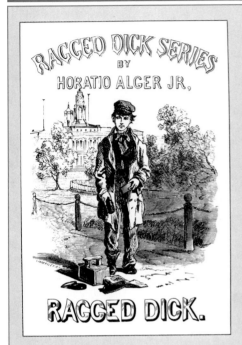

THE RAGGED DICK SERIES, PUBLISHED IN 1868, told of the sad plight of children who tried to survive in a city without family or friends. They often worked long hours in factories or on farms. Many died. Horatio Alger, Jr., wrote the series in the hope that readers would be sympathetic to the cause of poor children and the Children's Aid Society. Since 1854, the society had been finding homes for these abandoned children.

Horatio Alger's *Frank's Campaign* (1864) was the first of a series of books in which poor American youths went from rags to riches. Other books by Alger that have a similar theme include *Fame and Fortune* (1868), *Sink or Swim* (1870), *Strong and Steady* (1871), *Brave and Bold* (1874), *Risen from the Ranks* (1874), and *From Farm Boy to Senator; Being the History of the Boyhood and Manhood of Daniel Webster* (1882).

develops when Polly tries to make friends with a new neighbor, a Mexican girl named Consuela. Stoltz encourages readers to glimpse conflicts caused by racial bias by describing several class-mates' reactions to Consuela and her responses to them.

In *The Robbers* Nina Bawden creates effective characterization and emphasizes important aspects of plot development by contrasting the life-styles of two children—one who has lived in the security of his grandmother's apartment in a cas-tle and one who is knowledgeable in the ways of the London streets. When nine-year-old Philip moves to London, life is difficult because his schoolmates tease him about his princely man-ners and physically attack him. His outlook changes, however, when he becomes friends with Darcy, whose crippled father has been a canal worker. As the two become close friends, Philip discovers that all people do not live in his secure, protected world. Older students may enjoy com-paring this book by an English author with books on friendship by American authors. They will dis-cover that the English characters reflect greater concern for class distinctions and express feelings of inevitability because of class.

Physical Changes

In order to develop credible problems, authors who write about physical maturity often describe an embarrassing physical characteristic and ex-plore the way the character, friends, and family members respond to the characteristic and the character. The stories may depict both person-against-self and person-against-person conflicts. Person-against-person conflicts may include peer victimization of the main character, with the story being told from the viewpoint of either the victim-ized child or a child who is part of the peer group. In the latter case the author may develop the consequences of peer victimization by having the peer group turn against the main character. Some problems have simplistic or humorous res-olutions; other resolutions are complex and ex-press the extreme sensitivity of children as they experience changes in their bodies and increased self-consciousness about their appearance as they grow up.

Constance C. Greene uses two different ap-proaches to develop and resolve the conflicts in *The Ears of Louis* and *The Unmaking of Rabbit*. In *The Ears of Louis*, a boy responds to the jeers of

"Elephant Boy," "Dumbo," and "Stay out of the wind or you will sail to Alaska" by taping his ears to the sides of his head and wearing a football helmet to try to reduce their size. Because he has a supportive next-door neighbor and a best friend who believes ears are a sign of character, Louis's emotional problems are not severe. Greene resolves Louis's problem with an overly simplistic solution: when the older boys learn that he can play football, his peers are impressed by his popularity and no longer tease him. In *The Unmaking of Rabbit*, however, the solution cannot be as simple because Greene creates more conflict for Paul, an eleven-year-old boy who lives with his grandmother. His peers tease him about his father who deserted him and his mother who visits him infrequently. They also taunt him about his big ears, pink nose, and a tendency to stutter. Although Paul has a loving and supportive grandmother, he longs for a close relationship with friends. The author reveals Paul's true character when he has the opportunity to gain the friends he desires. This is a difficult decision, however, because the overtures are from a gang of boys who want him to help them break the law. The author convinces readers that Paul has made an important discovery about himself and suggests his appropriate handling of an important moral issue when he decides that a clear conscience is worth more than friends. The resolution of this story's conflict is more interesting, emotionally satisfying, and true to life than the resolution of Louis's conflict because Paul faced so many more conflicts.

Self-consciousness about small size causes self-esteem problems for eleven-year-old Jeffrey in Ellen Conford's *The Revenge of the Incredible Dr. Rancid and His Youthful Assistant, Jeffrey*. Jeffrey believes that in real life the little guy is always physically whipped: "One of those harsh realities of life you have to face when you're built like me, you're going to spend most of your free time wishing you were built like Clint Eastwood, and the rest of your free time being scared of guys who are" (p. 5). To make matters worse, his mother is the first female sports editor in the county and his father is very self-confident. The bully in Jeffrey's life is a sixth grader twice his size. The author reveals a great deal about Jeffrey's true character when the bully picks on his only friend and Jeffrey steps in to resolve the problem.

In *Are You There God? It's Me, Margaret*, Judy Blume explores a young girl's developing sexuality. Eleven-year-old Margaret has many questions about the physical changes occurring in her body, including breast development and the onset of menstruation. This topic is also found in Norma Klein's *Tomboy*. Unlike Margaret, ten-year-old Toe does not look forward to bodily changes. While Margaret feared she might be the last girl in her group to menstruate, Toe fears that she is the first. She believes that if her friends discover her secret they will not allow her to join the Tomboy Club; she does not believe a girl mature enough to have a baby can be a tomboy. Toe discovers that the physical changes she fears are also happening to her best friend, and the two girls decide to abandon the club. These books discuss a topic that is very serious to girls approaching physical maturity.

Emotional Changes

Books that develop plots around emotional maturity—and physical maturity as well—differ in several important ways from the realistic fiction of the past. Several authors, for example, imply that the character's own parents are ineffective in helping the child cope with emotional changes and problems, are unavailable, or are unable to understand the child. Current realistic fiction often suggests that a person outside the family, an understanding grandparent or a knowledgeable friend, is the most important influence on a child's discovery of self—in contrast to literature of the past in which strong parents and caring brothers and sisters provide necessary support. Current books, unlike many family stories in the past, also suggest that children have numerous problems as they struggle to grow toward emotional maturity.

Books discussed throughout this chapter reflect the wide range of emotional issues that children confront while growing up. For example, in Lois Lowry's *Anastasia Krupnik*, a ten-year-old girl begins to overcome her desire to be the center of attention and her jealousy when she is able to place her family's new baby on her list of loves instead of her list of hates.

Shyness is another common symptom of children's emotional problems and need for emotional adjustment. Maria Gripe's *Elvis and His Secret* is one of several stories that portray painfully

Fears related to growing up provide strong person-versus-self conflict. (From *COME SING, JIMMY JO*, by Katherine Paterson. Jacket illustration copyright © by Deborah Chabrian. Copyright © 1985 by Katherine Paterson. Reproduced by permission of the publisher, Dial Books for Young Readers.)

shy children who interact unsuccessfully with their families and try to make people understand their needs. Gripe's shy Elvis feels ignored by his parents. His mother prefers being surrounded by the sound of television or chattering on the telephone. In contrast, his grandfather and older friend encourage him, understand him, and reassure him, through their actions, that they feel he is special—because he is Elvis.

Painful shyness causes person-against-self conflict, and the demands of a gifted but often selfish family create person-against-person conflicts for a gifted eleven-year-old boy in Katherine Paterson's *Come Sing, Jimmy Jo*. Paterson explores a young singer's fears and personality development after he reluctantly joins his Appalachian family's musical group and moves away from the protection of his beloved grandmother. Changes in attitudes toward his gift and in personality development are effectively developed as the author describes Jamie's changing responses to the audiences. Jamie proceeds from being a frightened boy who feels sick when he plays in front of people; to a bewildered boy who believes that his father, but not his mother, will protect him from the aggressive fans; to an entertainer who accepts his gift and discovers pleasure in sharing music. Readers can identify with Paterson's character because his fears about growing up and unexpected changes are universal.

Survival

Physical and emotional survival is a fundamental challenge for all humans. Confrontation with dangers in nature, society, or self require and, ideally, develop strength of character in young people and adults. The strong personalities in survival literature are especially popular with older children who enjoy adventure stories.

Authors of survival literature use several literary techniques to create credible plots and characters. Person-against-nature, person-against-society, and person-against-self conflicts are often the stimuli for complex and exciting plots. Authors may develop a forceful natural or social setting as a story's antagonist, clarifier of conflict, or means of developing a desired mood. Style is also important in survival literature. Careful selection of words, imagery, and rhythm patterns can heighten the emotional impact and credibility of adventures outside most readers' realms of experience. Authors of survival literature usually rely on a consistent point of view—often first-person or limited omniscient—to encourage the reader to identify with and believe in the protagonist's experience.

Surviving in Nature. In Jean Craighead George's *My Side of the Mountain*, Sam Gribley leaves his home in New York City to live off the land in the

Catskill Mountains. George tells part of the story in the form of Sam's diary, which adds a sense of authenticity to the story and creates the feeling that the reader is sharing an autobiographical account of Sam's experiences. Detailed descriptions of Sam preparing and storing food, tanning and sewing a deerhide suit, and carving and firing the interior of his home in a hemlock tree are told in a matter-of-fact manner and resemble the writing of someone who is keeping a log of his experiences and observations. The detailed descriptions of wild edible plants and other important survival techniques also suggest to readers that Sam prepared carefully for his experiment in surviving in the wild.

George creates other exciting survival-in-nature stories in *Julie of the Wolves*, as a thirteen-year-old girl lost in the Arctic tundra develops a friendship with wolves (see chapter three), and in *River Rats, Inc.*, in which two boys rafting on the turbulent Colorado River become lost in the Grand Canyon and must improvise food and shelter.

The consistent first-person point of view used by Scott O'Dell in *Island of the Blue Dolphins* creates a plausible setting, plot, and main character. When Karana, a young Indian girl who survives years alone on a Pacific Island, tells readers, "I will tell you about my island," readers visualize the important features from her viewpoint and believe the description. When she says "I was afraid," the fear seems real; later, her discovery of her brother's body justifies her fear. This first-person viewpoint increases the reader's belief in her personal struggles as she is torn between two forces. Will she adhere to the tribal law that prohibits women from making weapons? Or will she construct the weapons that will probably mean the difference between her life or death? Her inner turmoil heightens the suspense, as suggested by the following quote:

Would the four winds blow in from the four directions of the world and smother me as I made the weapons? Or would the earth tremble, as many said, and bury me beneath its falling rocks? Or, as others said, would the sea rise over the island in a terrible flood? Would the weapons break in my hands at the moment when my life was in danger, which is what my father had said? (p. 54)

Other major decisions are also more meaningful because they are told through Karana's point of view. When she decides to take a tribal canoe and sail in the direction her people sailed, read-

ers believe her turmoil as the canoe begins to leak and she must again make a difficult decision: should she go back and face loneliness or go on and face probable disaster? Karana decides to return to her island and make it as much of a home as she can. O'Dell now emphasizes the small details of days filled with improving shelter, finding food, and hiding supplies against the possibility of her Aleut enemies returning to the island. Karana's need for companionship is shown when she cannot kill the leader of the wild dogs after wounding him; she takes him to her shelter, cares for him, and names him Rontu. Returned to health, Rontu becomes her constant companion and defender. After Rontu's death, Karana tames another dog who eventually sails with her to the mainland when her long years on the island are finally over.

A strong male character who survives an experience with his feared enemy, the sea, and discovers courage on an island is found in Armstrong Sperry's *Call It Courage* (see chapter 3).

Surviving Inner-City Reality. Dangerous, polluted, and economically deprived inner cities are the environment in which many American children face the challenges of growing up. Several authors of realistic fiction portray the problems of overcoming poverty, gang violence, and living without the security of a strong, supportive family. It is easy to rely on sensationalism for plot development in such stories, and numerous authors do. Authors such as Virginia Hamilton, Walter Dean Myers, and Ezra Jack Keats (see chapter five) create inner-city stories with literary merit.

One of the strongest inner-city stories is Virginia Hamilton's *The Planet of Junior Brown*. Hamilton's memorable characters enliven a complex story about friendship, loyalty, and learning to live together. The three main characters, all outcasts, live on the fringe of the busy New York City that closes around them. Junior Brown is a talented pianist who should be recognized for his skill, but the fact that he weighs almost three hundred pounds causes people to leave him alone. Consequently, he feels ugly and is afraid of being trapped in small spaces. Buddy Clark is a very intelligent street boy who has lived on his own since the age of nine. The third outcast is Mr. Pool, a former teacher, who is now the school's custodian. He feels that tough black children who know the city streets should be given an opportunity to learn, but the rigid school regime caused him to lose heart, give up his teaching job, and return to the school basement. In this basement, however, Mr. Pool has a secret room where he can create a new world and teach Junior Brown and Buddy Clark.

Hamilton uses the symbolism associated with the word *planet* to develop each character's place in the story. Junior Brown's planet is an artistic creation that hangs suspended from metal rods and spherical tracks attached to the ceiling of the hidden room. While the children in the rooms above go through their normal day, the three outcasts build their solar system, create their planets, and learn about science and each other.

Buddy Clark's planet is not a work of art and science; it is the frightening inner-city reality of homeless boys, hunger, and survival. On his planet, this strong character first learns about personal survival from an experienced street survivor called a "planet leader," then becomes a leader with a planet and inhabitants of his own to train and supervise. Buddy spends part of his time in one world, as the protector and companion of Junior Brown, and the rest of his time in another world, where he takes care of children and works to feed and clothe them. Hamilton develops a strong theme as Buddy Clark takes the other outcasts to his own planet in the basement of a deserted house and shares with them his own views of life:

"We are together," Buddy told them, "because we have to learn to live for each other. . . . If you stay here, you each have a voice in what you will do here. But the highest law for us is to live for one another. I can teach you how to do that." (p. 210)

Walter Dean Myers's *It Ain't All for Nothin'* also depicts two different worlds. One is the secure world of twelve-year-old Tippy's religious, caring grandmother; the other is the violent world of crime and his father's neglect. Tippy begins to live more in the second world when his grandmother becomes crippled by arthritis and can no longer care for herself or her grandson. The boy is frightened and angered by his father's use of drugs and his keeping stolen goods and guns in the apartment. In his need to forget, Tippy begins to drink. Life becomes frightening; his father is involved in a robbery, during which one of his friends is wounded. Myers emphasizes Tippy's inner conflicts between the world of his grandmother and the world of his father when Tippy debates his own actions. Myers suggests hope for Tippy when the boy makes the hard decision to tell an older friend about the problems in his father's apartment, informs the police, and decides that his life will not be like his father's.

Surviving in a Dangerous World. A new type of survival literature is emerging in both American and British children's literature: realistic fiction that mirrors international headlines about new dangers that have arisen in our modern age. In the person-against-society conflicts of this survival literature, the protagonists are usually innocent children and the antagonists are terrorist groups, oppressive military governments, mass violence, and nuclear accidents.

In Susan Lowry Rardin's *Captives in a Foreign Land*, six children are kidnapped while accompanying their parents to a conference in Rome and are transported to a remote Middle Eastern desert. Rardin explains that she wrote the book in order to explore how American young people would respond to a totally unfamiliar situation in which the usual American support systems were nonexistent. The children's interactions with their kidnappers reveal the kidnappers' reasons for their actions and their attitudes toward Americans. The survival plot develops and the characters change as the children realize that they must plan and execute their own liberation.

Rosemary Harris's *Zed* is a more complex story. Eight years after Thomas was held hostage by terrorists, his teacher asks him to write his remembrances. Harris focuses on an eight-year-old boy's changing perceptions of both victims and terrorists as they are confined together for four days in a London office. In addition to experiencing irrevocable changes in himself, Thomas witnesses courage, cowardice, cruelty, and kindness in both his own family members and members of the terrorist group.

James Watson's *Talking in Whispers*, a 1983 British Carnegie Honor book for older children, is a frightening survival story in which the main character is hunted by the security forces of a South American military government that denies basic human rights. The antagonists in Louise Moeri's *Downwind* are both an accident at a nuclear power plant and the human fear and violence that result as people try to flee. Moeri's theme stresses the dangers of nuclear power and the need to make important decisions if the world is to be saved.

Dealing with Death

Part of growing up is realizing and gradually accepting the fact of death. An increasing number of realistic fiction stories develop themes related to the acceptance of death and the overcoming of emotional problems following the death of a loved one. As might be expected, different authors treat the subject differently, depending on the developmental level of their intended readers. Differences in cause of conflict, characterization, resolution of conflict, depth of emotional involvement, and themes are apparent in books of realistic fiction about death. Consider how several authors develop these areas in books written for younger readers, preadolescents, and teenagers. For comparative purposes, consider Charlotte Graeber's *Mustard* and Eve Bunting's *The Empty Window* written for younger readers; Constance C. Greene's *Beat the Turtle Drum* and Peggy Mann's *There Are Two Kinds of Terrible* written for ten- to twelve-year-olds; and Judy Blume's *Tiger Eyes* and Richard Peck's *Remembering The Good Times* written for readers in their early teens; and Robert Cormier's *The Bumblebee Flies Anyway* written for teenagers and young adults.

In Charlotte Graeber's *Mustard*, a book for young children, members of a family share the sorrow following a fourteen-year-old cat's heart attack and their decision to let the veterinarian help the cat die in peace. Graeber focuses on the importance of the pet to a young boy and encourages readers to understand this relationship to the cat by describing his disbelief in the cat's ailments and his reactions after the pet dies. When Alex and his father go to the pet shelter to donate some of Mustard's things, Alex declines the offer of a kitten because he does not have room at the moment for anything but memories of Mustard. In another year he may be ready for a pet, he says. This resolution encourages readers to understand that healing takes time, memories are worth retaining, and family members can help each other in times of sadness.

Eve Bunting's picture storybook *The Empty Window* explores a boy's feelings of fear, guilt, and sadness as he faces the death of his best friend. C. G. realizes he has been afraid to see his dying friend when he recognizes that the time spent in capturing a wild parrot who lived in the tree outside his friend's window was an excuse for not visiting him. Joe teaches C. G. something about the meaning of life when he thanks him for

A boy faces the realization of his friend's illness. (Illustration by Judy Clifford from *The Empty Window*, by Eve Bunting. Reprinted by permission of Frederick Warne and Co., Inc.)

the parrot but asks him to release it because "once the parrots were free and then someone caught them and caged them, but they go free again. That's why I like them" (unnumbered). Bunting also makes an important point about people who may be critically ill. C.G. realizes that although Joe is dying he has not changed. They can still sit and talk as they did before.

Two examples of stories written for ten-through twelve-year-olds have more fully developed characters and deal with the more difficult emotions related to adjusting to the death of a family member. Constance C. Greene's *Beat the Turtle Drum* develops the basis for a girl's reactions to her sister's accidental death by describing the warm relationship between ten-year-old Joss and her twelve-year-old sister and best friend Kate. Kate believes that her parents prefer her younger sister. After Joss dies as a result of a fall from a tree, Kate faces both the sorrow of losing a friend and the inner conflict resulting from her belief that her sister was the favorite. Greene encourages readers to glimpse Kate's inner turmoil when she finally admits her feelings to an understanding relative, who responds:

I bet Joss would've felt the same way. If it'd been you, she might've said the same thing. And both of you would've been wrong. I think when a child dies, it's the saddest thing that could ever happen. And the next saddest is the way the brothers and sisters feel. They feel guilty, because they fought or were jealous or lots of things. And here they are, alive, and the other one is dead. And there's nothing they can do. It'll take time, Kate. (p. 105)

Kate gradually understands that resolution of her grief and conflicting emotions will take more than a moment, but that she will receive pleasure from her memories of Joss.

In *There Are Two Kinds of Terrible*, Peggy Mann compares a boy's emotions when he breaks his arm and when his mother dies of cancer. Robbie can recover from the first kind of terrible, but the second kind is irreversible. Still, his mother's death actually brings him closer to his distant father, who is suffering intense grief too.

The believable characters in Richard Peck's *Remembering the Good Times* help readers in their teens identify with this story about the suicide of a best friend. Peck first carefully develops the distinct personalities of two boys and a girl in their junior-high years. Kate is involved with people and believes in herself; Buck does not know which group he belongs with; and Trav is angry, unsure of himself, and afraid of the future. Peck develops the main person-versus-self conflict by describing Trav's increasing fears as he discusses current events, as he reacts to evidence that he is expected to grow up to be like his very successful parents, and as he becomes angry when he feels that he is not being prepared for the realities of life. The author develops a strong relationship among the three friends. After Trav's suicide, Kate admonishes herself because she did not notice the little things that should have warned them about Trav's approaching suicide. The author explores various responses to Trav's death, as high school administrators blame parents, parents blame the school, a knowledgeable older friend states the community's real responsibility, and Kate and Buck discover that they can remember the good times of their friendship.

The cause of the conflict in Blume's story for older readers, *Tiger Eyes*, is both the sudden, vi-

olent death of a parent and a society that creates such violence. The author develops a person-against-self conflict as a teenage girl, Davey, tries to adjust emotionally and physically to the death of her father, who was a robbery victim. Blume also develops a person-against-society conflict as the characters respond to and reflect about a society in which there is violent death, vandalism, excessive teen-age tension, and powerful weapons. The author's characterization encourages readers to understand Davey's turmoil. Blume shows Davey's emotional ties with her father; her physical reactions when she faces peers (she faints at school but cannot tell the nurse her problem); her need for a quiet place to reflect; her interactions with a man dying from cancer and an uncle who will not allow her to take chances but designs weapons at Los Alamos; and her interactions with two friends who are also facing inner conflicts. The resolution of the conflicts requires considerable time, but Davey can finally face what happened, tell new friends how her father died, and consider her own future.

The setting in *The Bumblebee Flies Anyway*, Robert Cormier's psychological novel for teenagers and young adults, is a terminal care facility in which a sixteen-year-old boy realizes that his treatment is only experimental and that he is actually dying. Peck uses symbolism to convey Barney's feelings about being a terminally ill guinea pig: "the complex" is a facility for experimental medicine; "the Handyman" is a doctor who treats the patients and creates illusions; "the merchandise" is special medicines, chemicals, and drugs that are calculated to produce expected responses; and "the bumblebee" is a sportscar in a junkyard that at first appears to be shining and new, but that is actually only a cardboard mockup of reality.

All these stories about death deal with irreversible problems that are very difficult to experience. Consequently, individual children's responses to the books may be very personal. An eight-year-old said he felt better after reading *The Empty Window*. He had a friend who was very ill; he was pleased that someone else felt like he did. An eleven-year-old, however, began to read *Two Kinds of Terrible* and then could not finish it. She said she did not want to read a book that reminded her that her mother might die. Several responses by fourteen-year-olds to *Tiger Eyes* demonstrate how very personal reactions to realistic fiction can be. One reader said, "This is not a good book to read in class. You need to be by yourself so you can cry if you want to." Another child said, "It's great. You get into the story and forget everything. I was afraid Davey was going to kill herself, but I thought, Judy Blume wouldn't kill her main character." A third reader said that the story was sad but its moral was happy: "Take a chance on your talents; planning someone's life for them doesn't make them happy; it's always better to face the truth rather than run from it; life is a great adventure; you can't go back in time. So pick up the pieces and move ahead; and some changes happen down inside of you and only you know about them." These responses indicate that a fourteen-year-old grasped many of the complex themes Blume wove into her novel. It is also interesting to note that the themes the reader identified are positive rather than negative glimpses of life.

PEOPLE AS INDIVIDUALS, NOT STEREOTYPES

Stereotypical views of males and females, the disabled, and the elderly are becoming less prevalent in children's literature. Chapter eleven, "Multiethnic Literature," discusses contemporary realistic fiction that portrays racial and ethnic minorities in unstereotyped ways.

Males and Females

Publishers are becoming sensitive to the need for literature that does not portray either sex in stereotypic roles. For example, since 1981 the Houghton Mifflin Publishing Company's (18) guidelines for eliminating sex stereotypes in materials it publishes have included the following:

1   Published materials should present a balance of both sexes, including female and male protagonists, female and male contributors to society, and females and males in a variety of jobs. Stories should suggest that both females and males can prepare for and succeed in a variety of occupations.
2   Literature should recognize that males and females share the same basic emotions, personality traits, and capabilities. Both sexes should be included in portrayals of active pastimes and in solitary pursuits.
3   Sensitivity, taste, and nonstereotypic images should be employed when using humor to characterize the sexes.

4   Literature should present a broad range of historical references to women, including contributions of well-known and less well-known women.
5   Where appropriate, literature should include reference to legal, economic, and social issues related to women.
6   Historical books should include coverage of the roles and activities of women in past centuries.

As the roles of females in our society shift away from the stereotypes of the past, female characters in children's literature reflect these changes. Contemporary realistic fiction contains more girls who are distinct individuals; they may be brave, they may be tomboys, and they may be unorthodox. Mothers in realistic fiction are also taking on different roles. Often they work outside the home; they may even have jobs more demanding than those of their husbands. Whatever roles females in recent realistic fiction play, they are characters quite different from female characters in earlier children's literature, even literature of the fairly recent past.

Consider, for example, the popular contemporary character Ramona, created by Beverly Cleary. Stories of her exploits span the years from the early 1950s into the 1980s. In *Henry and Beezus*, published in 1952, readers discover that the girls, Beezus and Ramona, are considered worthy playmates even by an active boy such as Henry Huggins. These thoughts at least imply that active pastimes are not usually considered appropriate for girls; girls may not even be considered creative playmates. In later books, however, Ramona comes into her own. In *Ramona the Pest* (1968) she is not the stereotypic quiet girl; instead, she is the "worst rester" in kindergarten. By the time *Ramona and Her Father* was published in the late 1970s, the roles in her family have changed: her father loses his job and stays home, while her mother returns to work on a fulltime basis. Ramona now humorously tries to help her father through this change in his life. *Ramona and Her Mother* explores a working mother's life as viewed by her seven-year-old daughter. By 1981 *Ramona Quimby, Age 8* is "helping" her family while her father returns to college. The "Ramona" books are popular with children who enjoy reading about the exploits of this spunky, humorous girl.

Louise Fitzhugh's hero in *Harriet the Spy* is an eleven-year-old girl whom other characters describe as exceptional, intelligent, and curious. Harriet's actions support these descriptions as she hides in her secret places, observes her neighbors and classmates, and writes down her observations. The extent of this popular character's resourcefulness and self-confidence is revealed when her classmates find her notebook and organize "The Spy Catcher Club." Now Harriet uses all her considerable creativity to devise a plan that will convince her friends to forgive her. Harriet is far from the fainting female of most traditional literature and Victorian fiction, who must be rescued from her failures by the males in the story. She is even able to return to her real loves, spying and writing. More tales about Harriet are found in *The Long Secret* and *Sport*.

The exuberant, precocious protagonist in Vera and Bill Cleaver's *Lady Ellen Grae* does not accept the feminine role her father and society expect of her. The Cleavers describe first Ellen Grae's unrestricted life with her artist father and then her reactions when he wants her to leave her beloved Thicket, Florida, live with her aunt in Seattle, and learn to be a "lady." At this point Ellen strongly presents her personal philosophy:

I've found, that most things are simply a matter of mental reconciliation, because the mind is elastic—it stretches and can be pulled this way and that. The trick is not to flinch from it. If you do you're a goner before you get started. Mentally, I've reconciled myself to a thousand things: school, being a girl, collard greens, baths . . . But Seattle? Oh, no. No, sir. I, Ellen Grae Derryberry, do not reconcile to things like Seattle. I like it here and here I intend to stay until it's time for me to hop into my grave. (p. 19)

Although the Cleavers develop a plot that allows Ellen Grae to return to her father, she also discovers that there are many things that she doesn't know. Because she doesn't like to be ignorant about anything, she decides that she will learn about them on her own. The Cleavers at least imply that Ellen may discover many dimensions of womanhood and not just the confining one she has pictured.

E. L. Konigsburg's *From the Mixed-Up Files of Mrs. Basil E. Frankweiler* is another book of realistic fiction in which a female protagonist belies the traditional stereotypes about passive femininity. Claudia Kincaid leads her brother in running away from home and hiding out in the Metropolitan Museum of Art. When the two children are given one hour to search the files and discover the answer to a mystery involving a statue of an angel, Claudia tells her impatient brother that five minutes of planning are worth fifteen minutes of haphazard looking. Her techniques prove successful, and they discover the answer to the statue's authenticity.

Stereotyped views of males are also changing in our society and in children's literature. In Katherine Paterson's *Bridge to Terabithia*, for example, a boy hates football, aspires to be an artist, and feels pressured by his father's traditionally masculine expectations of him. Although the father is afraid that Jess is becoming a "sissy," Jess finds support for being his true self in a strong friendship with the story's other protagonist, a girl named Leslie who is also a nonconformist in their rural community. One outstanding book of realistic fiction from the mid-1960s portrays the wider options for males that are becoming more prevalent in children's literature today. In Maia Wojciechowska's *Shadow of a Bull*, the son of a famous and supposedly fearless bullfighter learns that a male doesn't have to prove his manliness through acts of physical daring or violence. Manolo's village expects him to follow in his dead father's footsteps. As the men of the village begin training him in the art of bullfighting, Manolo believes he is a coward because he has no interest in being a bullfighter. Manolo eventually learns that in order to be truly brave he must be true to himself and not attempt to satisfy others' expectations. The author effectively reveals the resolution of Manolo's person-versus-self conflict when Manolo tells the waiting crowd in the bullring that he prefers to study medicine rather than become a bullfighter.

The Physically Different or Disabled

Most children and adults dislike to stand out in a crowd because of their appearance or physical capabilities. They may also feel discomfort when they see someone who does not conform to the customary standards of how a person should look or who is physically disabled. Children's realistic fiction is becoming increasingly sensitive to the importance of overcoming cruel or condescending stereotypes and of portraying all people as the complete individuals they truly are.

In *Blubber*, Judy Blume shows how peer cruelty to the physically different can have negative consequences for all concerned, as classmates torment a girl they consider grossly overweight. A strong peer leader manipulates her friends into composing a list entitled "How to Have Fun with Blubber" and forces the girl herself to make self-demeaning statements such as "I am Blubber, the smelly whale of class 206" (p. 72). The main character realizes the crushing impact of what she has done when she tries to stop the cruelty and her classmates then turn on her.

In *Please Don't Tease Me. . .,* Jane M. Madsen and Diane Bockoras relate the true story of a child whose body is swollen from eukocytoclastic angiitis. The authors' theme of needing understanding and friendship may be so compelling because Bockoras is telling her own story.

Authors who develop realistic plots around credible characters who have physical disabilities often describe details related to a character's disability, the feelings and experiences of the disabled person, and the feelings and experiences of family members and others who interact with the character. Accurate, honest, and sensitive books provide physically disabled children with characters and situations close to their own experience. Well-written books also help other children empathize with and gain understanding of the physically disabled. While adults should evaluate these books by literary standards, they should also evaluate them by their sensitivity. Mary Sage (26) recommends the following criteria when evaluating books concerning the disabled:

1 The author should deal with the physical, practical, and emotional manifestations of the disabling condition accurately but not didactically.
2 Other characters in the story should behave realistically as they relate to the disabled individual.
3 The story should provide honest and workable advice to the disabled character about his or her condition and potential for the future.

The resolution of conflict can be a special concern in realistic fiction dealing with physical disabilities. Does the author concoct a happy ending because he or she believes all children's stories should have happy endings, or does the resolution of conflict evolve naturally and honestly? Through fiction that honestly deals with handicaps, readers can empathize with children who

are courageously overcoming their problems and with their families who are facing new challenges. Writers of such literature often express the hope that their stories will encourage positive attitudes toward the physically disabled. As mainstreaming brings more disabled children into regular classrooms, this goal becomes more important for both children and adults.

Stories set in different historical periods often reflect changing attitudes about physical disabilities and provide a basis for discussion with children. Julia Cunningham's story of a mute boy in *Burnish Me Bright* takes place in a French village of the past. The boy encounters prejudice, misunderstanding, fear, and even hostility. Monsieur Hilaire, a retired performer who befriends the boy and brings him into his world of pantomime, clarifies the reasons behind society's prejudice:

These people you have known are no worse than the others that walk the world but they share with the others a common enemy, and the enemy is anyone who is different. They fear the boy who can't speak, the woman who lives by herself and believes in the curative power of herbs, the man who reads books instead of going to the café at night, the person like me who has lived in the distant differences of the theater. They are not willing to try to understand, so they react against them and occasionally do them injury.(p. 18)

In Larry Callen's *Sorrow's Song*, nondisabled people have quite different reactions to a modern-day girl who is mute. Sorrow's best friend, a boy named Pinch, sees her this way: "She is so smart, I don't even like to think about it. She knows words I never heard of. But Sorrow can't use words the way most people can. Sorrow can't talk" (p. 5). Her teacher defends Sorrow and challenges a man who thinks her condition is tragic: "Sorrow Nix is more normal than the two of us. Don't you do anything that will make her feel otherwise" (p. 56). Pinch's mother considers Sorrow someone special and compares her to a weeping willow, which she considers a very friendly tree. The author, however, does not imply that Sorrow is always happy. Callen draws parallels between Sorrow's special needs and the needs of an injured whooping crane. When the crane flies away to live its own life, there is a strong feeling that Sorrow has won her own conflict. The author develops a strong theme about individual abilities and not judging people by outward appearances.

In *From Anna*, Jean Little develops a credible perspective on visual impairment by describing a girl's frightening experiences when letters are blurred, look the same, or even appear to jiggle across the page. Jean Little explores the conflicting emotions of a child with cerebral palsy in *Mine for Keeps*, and Eleanor Spence sensitively portrays the experience of a boy with a hearing loss in *The Nothing Place*. Comparisons between experiences of deaf children and reactions toward deafness in different periods in history may be made using Mary Riskind's *Apple Is My Sign* and Veronica Robinson's *David in Silence*. Riskind's setting is a school for the deaf in the early 1900s, a time when hearing aids were unavailable. The characterizations and conflicts in Robinson's contemporary book are based on her work as a librarian in a school for the deaf. Robinson explores the problems of a child born deaf when he moves into a new town and tries to make friends with children who fear him because he is different. Robinson develops the theme that a person can win the respect of others by proving his own worth as a person.

The physically disabled include those whose mental capacities are not up to the social norm. Authors who write plausible books about the relationships between mentally disabled children and their normal siblings often portray the conflicting emotions of normal characters who experience both protective feelings and feelings of anger toward the disabled child. In Betsy Byars's *The Summer of the Swans*, Sara is a normal teenager who is discontented with her looks, sometimes miserable for no apparent reason, and often frustrated with her mentally retarded brother as she loves and cares for him. The author encourages readers to understand and empathize with Charlie's gentle nature as he is fascinated by the swans who glide silently across the lake and with his confusion and terror when he follows the swans and becomes lost. During a frantic search for Charlie, Sara forgets her personal miseries. When the siblings are reunited, Sara discovers that she feels better about herself and life in general than she had before.

Vera and Bill Cleaver's *Me Too* portrays the protective relationship of a twelve-year-old girl with her mentally retarded twin. Jean Little's *Take Wing* uses the story of a mentally disabled seven-year-old to make a strong case for schooling the educably mentally retarded and for their prospects for self-sufficiency when they are helped by special teachers who understand their needs. Reading such stories may help other children understand the emotions of families who have mentally disabled children and the emotions of the children themselves when they face the often frightening and perplexing world around them.

The Elderly

When children's literature students evaluate the characterization of elderly people in children's books they often discover stereotypes. Denise C. Storey (29) describes a study in which fifth grade children analyzed the elderly characters found in books from their classroom library. The children concluded that (1) some elderly people lead boring, lonely lives where nothing changes; (2) grandparents in books look older than their own grandparents; (3) the elderly do not work, have fun, or do anything exciting; (4) young people are mean to elderly people; (5) book characters do not want to listen or talk to the elderly; (6) some elderly people are characterized as being mean, crabby, overly tidy, fussy, and unfair; (7) the elderly like to remember the good old days or dream of better times; and (8) there are few happy books about the elderly.

Some authors of contemporary realistic fiction are exploring the problems related to ageism with greater sensitivity than expressed in books of the past. When evaluating books dealing with ageism, adults should select books that show elderly people in a wide variety of roles. Close experiences between grandparents and grandchildren are common in books for young children, such as Tomie de Paola's *Nana Upstairs & Nana Downstairs* and Sharon Bell Mathis's *The Hundred Penny Box*. Books for older children often stress the worthwhile contributions that are still being made by the elderly, the warm relationships that can develop between grandparents and grandchildren, and the desire of elderly people to stay out of nursing homes. Some books are very serious; others develop serious themes through a humorous story.

Eleanor Clymer's *The Get-Away Car* should appeal to children because it includes humor, mystery, and adventure. The author's characterization depicts a resourceful, energetic woman who is granddaughter Maggie's idea of a perfect grandmother because she lives by the motto "Fun first, work later." Other children in their tenement support Grandma's philosophy and join in the outings and fun. All goes well until Maggie's Aunt Rubey decides that Grandma is not capable of taking care of a young girl; her solution is to put Grandma into a home for the elderly and have Maggie move in with Aunt Rubey. While Aunt Rubey is trying to change their lives, Grandma and the children decide to borrow a car and run away to Cousin Esther's home in upstate New York. Along the way, they have many adventures. The story has a satisfying ending as the children solve the mystery of the old black car, a way is found for Cousin Esther to restore her formerly beautiful home, and Grandma convinces everyone that she is capable of looking after her granddaughter.

Kidnapping Mr. Tubbs is a more complex book in which author Don Schellie explores the feel-

Humor and mystery add to a story about a young person and an elderly person. (From *The Get-Away Car*, by Eleanor Clymer. Copyright © 1978 by Eleanor Clymer. Reprinted by permission of the publisher, E. P. Dutton.)

ings of the young and the elderly and develops a theme related to the human dignity, self-worth, and contributions made by people of all ages. Mr. Tubbs, a nearly one-hundred-year-old cowboy, lives in a nursing home and has neither freedom nor a relative who cares for him. His friends are a teen-age volunteer and A. J., the grandson of the man who shares his room. The young people "snatch" Mr. Tubbs out of the rest home to satisfy his wish to visit the ranch in northern Arizona where he worked as a cowboy, the place that gave him happy memories and remembered friends. The author uses discoveries during this trip to reveal lessons learned by young and old. Mr. Tubbs discovers that many places he remembers have changed for the worse, and A. J. realizes that he has always avoided becoming involved with the elderly because he fears they will die like his early childhood friend. A.J. expresses one of the story's major themes when he tries to convince Mr. Tubbs that he is not worthless, but very much needed by his young friend.

Other outstanding books about the elderly and the young people who love and respect them include Betsy Byars's *The House of Wings* and Vera and Bill Cleaver's *Queen of Hearts*. These books, with their diverse, nonstereotyped depictions of elderly people, provide discussion materials that encourage older children to explore the role of elderly people in literature and their own feelings about the elderly.

ANIMAL STORIES, MYSTERIES, SPORTS STORIES, AND HUMOR

Animals

The animals in contemporary realistic fiction are quite different from the animals in traditional literature and modern fantasy who talk and act like people or have other magical powers. The animal stories in realistic fiction have a strong sense of reality and sometimes tragedy. Realistic animal stories place specific demands upon authors. When evaluating realistic animal stories for children, adults should consider the following questions:

1   Does the author portray animals objectively, without giving them human thoughts or motives?
2   Does the behavior of the animal characters agree with information provided by knowl-

edgeable observers of animals and authorities on animal behavior?

3 Does the story encourage children to respond to the needs of animals or the needs of people to love animals without being too sentimental or melodramatic?

Authors who write credible animal stories often depict warm relationships between children and pets. The conflict in such stories usually occurs when something happens to disrupt the security of the pet's life. The antagonist may be a physical change in the animal, an environment different from the pet's secure home, or a human character whose treatment of the animal is cruel or even life threatening. Detailed descriptions of the animal's physical changes, the setting that becomes an antagonist, or the cruel human character may encourage children to understand the vulnerability of animals to such forces.

Credible stories about wild animals usually reflect considerable research about animal behavior and natural habitats. Conflict may arise when animals face natural enemies, when humans take them from natural surroundings and place them in domestic environments, or when humans hunt or trap them.

Some authors use animal-against-society or animal-against-person conflicts to develop strong themes advocating protection of animals. Other themes stress the human development made possible by human interaction with animals. Many authors stress the positive consequences of loyalty and devotion between humans and animals.

Consider, for example, the various techniques used by Theodore Taylor in *The Trouble with Tuck*. Taylor first develops a believably close relationship between Helen and her golden Labrador. Helen's love for Tuck and her family's devotion to the dog are strengthened as Taylor describes two incidents in which Tuck saves Helen from harm or possible death. The reactions of family members when the veterinarian declares that Tuck is going blind and cannot be helped reinforce their devotion to the dog and make plausible their acceptance of Helen's resolution of the problem: she calls a trainer for seeing eye dogs and makes an appointment for her parents without telling the trainer that the blind individual is a dog. Although the trainer's initial reaction is negative, the family is finally offered an older seeing eye dog whose master has died. Now the

Photographs depict the changes in a dog's life as he goes from family pet to a working dog in the Klondike. (From *The Call of the Wild*, text by Jack London, photographs by Seymour Linden. Photographs copyright © 1977 by Seymour Linden. Published by Harmony Books [A Division of Crown Publishers, Inc.]. Used by permission of Seymour Linden.)

author describes Helen's trials and frustrations as she tries to train Tuck to follow the seeing eye dog. After weeks of disappointment, she is rewarded when Tuck accepts and follows the older dog. This story, based on a true incident, emphasizes determination, loyalty, and human self-confidence that may develop because of animal and human interaction.

A classic book with a notable dog as the main character is Jack London's *Call of the Wild*, first published in 1903. This story depicts life in the Klondike during the Alaskan gold rush. London develops a credible story of transformation as Buck progresses from a docile pet to a rugged work dog and finally to an animal who is inescapably drawn by the wild cries of the wolf pack. London develops these remarkable changes in Buck by providing details of his life before and after he is stolen from his home in California and brought, raging and roaring, to face the primitive law of the Klondike. Buck changes as he reacts to a beating and the fierce fangs of fighting dogs, but retains his spirit; while crossing the country-side in a dogsled harness, his long-suppressed instincts come alive. This is also the story of strong bonds between dog and human. After a succession of sometimes cruel owners, Buck is purchased by kind John Thornton. Buck apparently feels an adoration for John that causes him continually to return from his wilderness treks until the terrible day when he returns to camp to find that John has been killed. Only then are the bonds between man and dog broken, allowing Buck to roam with the wolf pack:

His cunning was wolf cunning, and wild cunning; his intelligence shepherd intelligence and St. Bernard intelligence; and all this, plus an experience gained in the fiercest of schools, made him as formidable creature as any that roamed the wild. (p. 114)

Other well-known books about dogs that have been popular in the last few decades include Jim Kjelgaard's *Big Red*, in which a mountain boy raises a dog that wins a prize in a big-city dog show; Fred Gipson's *Old Yeller*, the story of a boy and his dog in the Texas hill country of the 1860s; and Sheila Burnford's *The Incredible Journey*, an outstanding realistic story about a Labrador retriever, an English bull terrier, and a Siamese cat that travel 250 miles through the Canadian wilderness in search of their human family. A more recent realistic story, Helen Griffiths's *Running Wild*, portrays the problems that result when domesticated pets are allowed to live in the wilds, as abandoned puppies become a pack of mature dogs that kill livestock and terrorize farmers in a mountainous region of Spain.

Horse stories also have qualities that make them a marvelous experience for children. The horses and their owners, or would-be owners, usually have loyal and devoted relationships. Often the little horse, who may have been laughed at or scorned, becomes the winner of a race and begins a famous line of horses. Sadness in many of these stories results when both horse and owner must overcome severe obstacles and even mistreatment.

Two outstanding authors of horse stories are Marguerite Henry and Walter Farley. Henry's stories reflect research and knowledge about horses and their trainers, and several of them report the history of a breed of horses. One memorable story narrates the ancestry of Man o' War, the greatest racehorse of his time. In *King of the Wind*, the reader travels back 200 years to the royal stables of a sultan of Morocco, where Agba, a young horse tender, has a dream of glory for a golden Arabian stallion with a high white chest. The story travels from Morocco to France as the Sultan sends six of his best horses to King Louis XV, who rejects the horses that have become thin from their voyage. Agba and the once beautiful Sham are handed over to several degrading and even cruel masters before the English Earl of Godolphin discovers their plight and takes them home with him. In England Agba's dream and promise to the horse come true. Three of the golden Arabian's offspring win various important races. When the great Arabian horse, renamed The Godolphin Arabian, stands before royalty, Agba's thoughts flash back to the promise he made in Morocco:

"My name is Agba. Ba means father. I will be a father to you, Sham, and when I am grown I will ride you before the multitudes. And they will bow before you, and you will be the king of the Wind. I promise it." He had kept his word! (p. 169)

Other enjoyable books by Marguerite Henry include *Justin Morgan Had a Horse*, the story of the Morgan horse; *Black Gold*, the story of a racehorse and the jockey who brings her to winning form; *Misty of Chincoteague*, the story of the small, wild descendants of the Spanish horses shipwrecked off the Virginia coast; and *San Domingo: The Medicine Hat Stallion*, a story of a Nebraska frontier boy and his affection for an unusual horse. All Henry's stories reflect an understanding of horses and the people who feel loving attachments to them.

A beautiful black stallion and his descendents are the chief characters in a series of books written by Walter Farley. The first, *The Black Stallion*, introduces a beautiful wild horse being loaded, unwillingly, onto a large ship. On this same ship is Alec Ramsay, who understands and loves horses. The two are brought together as the ship sinks, and the black horse pulls Alec through the waves to a small deserted island. Friendship de-

A highly illustrated version of the horse story features photographs from the movie. (Photograph furnished by United Artists from the film *The Black Stallion*. Copyright United Artists. Reprinted with permission.)

velops as the two help each other survive, and Alec discovers the joy of racing on the back of the amazing horse. After they are rescued, Alec's friend realizes what a remarkable horse he has; they secretly train the horse for a race between the two fastest horses in the United States. In an exciting climax, the unknown mystery horse wins the race. This story has also been written as a picture storybook illustrated with color photographs from the movie of the same name. Questions about the black stallion's heritage are answered in Farley's *The Black Stallion Returns*. Many other stories in Farley's series focus on the great horse and his notable and courageous descendants.

Helen Griffiths relies on a detailed setting and background information on horses and bullfighting to develop a plausible story in *The Dancing Horses*, set in post–Civil War Spain. The need for taking responsibility for the animals in one's care is emphasized in Lynn Hall's *Danza!*, whose human protagonist is a Puerto Rican boy.

Several of the books already discussed stress the vulnerability of animals to changes in their environments or to humans who interfere with their way of life. In *The Wheel on the School*,

Meindert DeJong explores the impact of negative environmental change and positive human intervention on birds. DeJong introduces several issues related to storks through the questions and investigations of six school children and their teacher in a Dutch fishing village. After they ask "Why didn't the storks come to Shora?" they explore the various reasons for the missing storks: the roofs are too steep, there are no trees, there are too many storms, and there is too much salt spray. A plausible situation develops because the children take the problem seriously and work hard to rectify it. Their honest concern suggests to the reader the possibility that this is a vital matter that should be of interest to others. The author also suggests that every effort counts; the children must overcome many obstacles, but a stork family finally accepts the wheel on the schoolhouse roof.

Jean Craighead George explores the problems that result when wild creatures are tamed in *The Cry of the Crow*. Mandy Tressel's family in the piney woods of the Florida Everglades kills crows to save their strawberry crop. Mandy, however, secretly feeds and tames a young crow, the only survivor of her younger brother's gun blast. As Mandy raises the crow, Nina Terrance, she discovers that the crow can imitate some human speech. When wild crows try to lure Nina away from her human friend, Mandy, knowing that she should encourage the bird to return to the wild, asks her mother's advice. George develops the girl's inner conflicts when she ignores her mother's warnings and decides to keep the bird. The author explores the controversy related to taming wild creatures through the neighbors' mixed reactions to the crow; some threaten to poison her, some are intrigued by her speech, and others want to put her in a cage as a tourist attraction. The return home of Mandy's young brother brings the conflict to a climax. When he repeats the same words he said as he killed the crow family, the crow attacks his face. The author suggests Mandy's feelings as she is torn between her love for her pet and her brother: "I'll never feed her again. Mommy was right. She'd be gone now, far, far away, if I hadn't been selfish and dumb. . . . If she hurts you, I'll never forgive myself" (p. 142). When Nina again attacks the boy, Mandy makes the difficult decision that the crow must be killed; the two children realize that they are both responsible for Nina's death.

Mysteries

Footsteps on a foggy night, disappearing people, mysterious strangers, and unusual occurrences woven together into an exciting, fast-paced plot create mystery stories that appeal to older children. One eleven-year-old girl, an avid reader of mysteries, listed the following four characteristics that make a mystery exciting for her: (1) it should have an exciting plot that holds your interest, (2) it should contain suspense, (3) the mystery should have enough clues so that the reader can follow the action, and (4) the clues should be written in such a way that readers can try to discover "who done it." In answer to the question, "What has caused your interest in mysteries?" she replied that she had read Donald J. Sobol's *Encyclopedia Brown* in third grade and enjoyed trying to follow the clues. She said that her favorite suspense story was Virginia Hamilton's *The House of Dies Drear*, a tale about the Underground Railroad discussed in chapter eleven.

The best-known mysteries for young readers are probably contained in Donald J. Sobol's *Ency-*

clopedia Brown series. In each of the books ten-year-old Leroy Brown helps his father, the police chief of Idvalle, solve crimes by figuring out the clues. For example, in *Encyclopedia Brown Tracks Them Down*, Leroy solves the case of the missing ambassador by reviewing the gifts presented to him at a birthday party. In another case in that book, he solves the riddle of the flower can and discovers the identity of the boy who stole a 1861 Confederate coin worth $5,000 by tricking the culprit with a homonym. *Encyclopedia Brown Sets the Pace* contains ten more cases in which young readers can identify the thief or even try to solve the problem of a bully who picks on smaller children. Sobol provides readers with the solutions and the reasoning behind them.

A mystery associated with a possible killing provides the suspense and the conflict in Robbie Branscum's *The Adventures of Johnny May*. In addition to the mystery, a person-against-self conflict develops as a young girl believes she has witnessed a killing. The possible killer is Homer, a gentle, friendly man who would not even kill a deer or hurt an animal. The possible victim is a hateful, bitter man. Johnny May's personal conflict increases when she does not report her suspicions. With the aid of three friends, Johnny May searches for clues that will both prove Homer's innocence and relieve Johnny May's conscience.

Powers of observation play an important role in the mysteries of Robert Newman, two of which are set in the London of Sherlock Holmes's time. *The Case of the Baker Street Irregular* and *The Case of the Vanishing Corpse* include suspense, sinister characters who must be outwitted, and several mysteries that at first seem not to be related but actually are.

Ellen Raskin's several books challenge readers to join often preposterous characters in working out puzzle clues. These clues may be word puzzles, a series of obscurely written messages, or even observations gained through reading. *The Mysterious Disappearance of Leon (I Mean Noel)* is a humorous word puzzle, a game about names, liberally sprinkled with clues. As the story of Leon and Little Dumpling, the heirs to Mrs. Carillon's Pomato Soup fortune, proceeds, Raskin informs the reader that there is a very important clue in a particular section or that the reader should use a bookmark to mark the location of Leon's fourteen messages because they contain very important clues. Noel's final words, for example, as he bobs up and down in the water cause Little Dumpling years of searching. What is meant by "Noel glub C blub all . . . I glub new . . ."? In *Figgs & Phantoms* the clue Raskin provides is "the bald spot." This clue eventually helps Mona Figg discover if she has or has not actually visited Capri, the Figg family's idea of a perfect heaven. Raskin's *The Westing Game* includes many clues that must be worked through before the teams of players solve the mystery.

Zilpha Keatley Snyder's mysteries involve kidnapping, complex games, or mysterious secret environments: in *The Famous Stanley Kidnapping Case* masked strangers kidnap five unusual children who accompany their parents to Italy; in *The Egypt Game* six children create an ancient Egyptian world in an abandoned storage yard and solve a murder mystery. Numerous clues and mounting tension create a fast-moving plot in Barbara Corcoran's *You're Allegro Dead*, in which two twelve-year-old girls encounter a mysterious intruder and a kidnapping instead of the summer camp activities they expected.

These mysteries provide escape and enjoyable reading through their plots and suspense. They allow children to become involved in the solutions through clues and character descriptions. They also suggest that children themselves—if they are observant, creative, and imaginative—can solve mysteries.

Sports

Sports stories rate highly with children who are sports enthusiasts. Some quite reluctant readers will finish a book about their favorite sport or sports hero. The majority of these stories are about boys, however, and few authors yet write about girls who enjoy participating in sports. Many stories deal with the high ideals of fair play, the values of sports, overcoming conflicts between fathers and sons, and overcoming fears connected with a sport. Unfortunately, many of the stories are didactic and have familiar plot lines and stock characters.

Authors who write about baseball often imply that the sport has therapeutic values. Often the emphasis in these books is on the role baseball can play in helping children overcome problems at home, develop new friendships, face physical disabilities, or feel accomplishment. Matt Chris-

topher's *The Fox Steals Home*, for example, tells the story of troubled Bobby Canfield as he faces his parents' divorce and the prospect of his father's taking a job far from home. His father and his grandfather have coached him and nicknamed him "Fox." His proudest moment comes when he steals home and demonstrates to his father what a good player he has become.

Likewise, Barbara Cohen's main character in *Thank You, Jackie Robinson*, finds that a mutual interest in baseball allows him to develop a special friendship. This friendship with an older man is especially important; Sam's father is dead, his mother manages an inn, and his sister has no interest in baseball. In *Hang Tough, Paul Mather*, Alfred Slote writes about a leukemia victim whose greatest interest is baseball. He must face the knowledge that he has a short time to live and that his parents are trying to prevent him from playing to protect him. An understanding doctor helps him play his last season with dignity and courage.

Football is both the major interest and the cause of conflict between father and son in Matt Christopher's *Football Fugitive*. Larry Shope loves football and longs for his father to leave his law practice long enough to watch him play. Larry and his father become closer when Mr. Shope provides legal assistance for a professional football star. Christopher's *Face-Off* describes Scott Harrison's love for hockey and the fear of being struck in the face that keeps him from playing his best, to his teammates' disgust. Christopher's *The Twenty-One-Mile Swim* describes a marathon swim that results when the son of Hungarian immigrants is teased about his small size and his inadequate swimming skills. Christopher's *Dirt Bike Racer* focuses on boys and their minibikes.

Frank Bonham's *The Rascals from Haskell's Gym* is another one of the few sports stories with female heroes. Sissy Benedict is a gymnast who becomes involved in the competition between the Butterflies Gymnastics Club and their arch rivals, Haskell's Raskells. Another story about girls in sports is K. M. Peyton's *The Team*, in which Ruth Hollis joins an English Pony Club team, prepares her horse for competition, and enters cross-country races. This book will be enjoyable for young riders who have experienced the same thrill during a competitive race.

The section on biographies in chapter twelve discusses other sports stories.

Humor

Humorous stories, whether involving figures of fantasy or realistic people living in our contemporary world, are among children's favorites. Authors who write about humorous situations that could happen to real people (these situations and characters may stretch probability) allow children to understand that life can be highly entertaining and not always serious. Writers may encourage readers to laugh at themselves and at numerous human foibles. Humorous situations and characterization may highlight real problems and make reading about them palatable.

Authors of humorous realistic fiction use many of the sources of humor discussed in chapter five—word play, surprise and the unexpected, exaggeration, and ridiculous situations. For example, authors may use a play on words or ideas to create a humorous situation or clarify a charac-

ter's feelings. Consider Betsy Byars's *The Cybil War*, an entertaining story about a fifth-grade boy who has a crush on a girl. The "war" develops as Cybil Ackerman responds in various ways to Simon's advances, which are intentionally misinterpreted by his best friend. Beverly Cleary uses a twist on the words of a familiar television commercial to create a funny incident in *Ramona Quimby, Age 8*. When Ramona gives her book report she presents it in the style of a television commercial. Her statement, "I can't believe I read the whole thing," causes a hilarious reaction among her classmates. In *The One in the Middle is the Green Kangaroo* Judy Blume uses a humorous analogy to clarify the middle child's feelings: "He felt like the peanut butter part of a sandwich squeezed between Mike and Ellen" (p. 7).

Exaggeration provides humor in Helen Cresswell's various books in "The Bagthorpe Saga." The series, including *Ordinary Jack*, *Absolute*

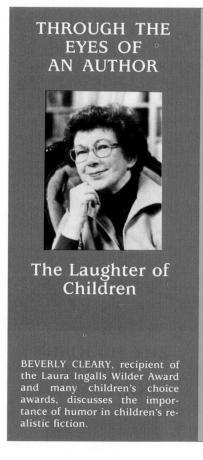

THROUGH THE EYES OF AN AUTHOR

The Laughter of Children

BEVERLY CLEARY, recipient of the Laura Ingalls Wilder Award and many children's choice awards, discusses the importance of humor in children's realistic fiction.

ALTHOUGH FOR OVER thirty years I have been absorbed in stories that spring from the humor of everyday life, I try not to think about humor while writing, because of the sound advice given me by my first editor Elisabeth Hamilton, whom I met after writing *Henry Huggins & Ellen Tebbits*. In discussing writing for children, I happened to mention humor. Elisabeth, a forceful woman, interrupted. "Darlin'," she said, "don't *ever* analyze it. Just do it." I have followed her advice. While I am writing, if I find myself thinking about humor and what makes a story humorous, I am through for the day; and that chapter usually goes into the wastebasket, for spontaneity has drained out of my work. Although introspection is valuable to every writer, I find that analyzing my own work is harmful because it

makes writing self-conscious rather than intuitive. When I am not writing, however, I find myself mulling over the subject of humor, my kind of humor, and why so many children find it funny.

As a child I would have agreed that humor is "what makes you laugh." I could not find enough laughter in life or in books, so the stories I write are the stories I wanted to read as a child in Portland, Oregon—humorous stories about the problems which are small to adults but which loom so large in the lives of children, the sort of problems children can solve themselves. I agree with James Thurber's statement: "Humor is the best that lies closest to the familiar, to that part of the familiar which is humiliating, distressing, even tragic. . . . There is always a laugh in the utterly familiar."

Zero, *Bagthorpes Unlimited*, *Bagthorpes v. the World*, and *Bagthorpes Abroad* presents the talented and eccentric Bagthorpes, who feel that life is a hilarious challenge. For example, when Uncle Parker wins a Caribbean cruise as a prize in a slogan-writing contest, the competitive Bagthorpes begin to enter every contest imaginable; the result is chaos as the prizes start arriving. In *Bagthorpes Unlimited*, the family attempts immortality by creating the great Bagthorpe daisy chain, a chain of daisies 4,750 feet long containing 22,000 daisies that they hope will place them in the *Guinness Book of World Records*. The fame they earn is not, however, what Mr. Bagthorpe had envisioned; instead of being interviewed as a serious writer for a story in the *Sunday Times*, he is photographed on his front lawn surrounded by daisies and enthusiastic chain weavers. In *Bagthorpes v. the World*, Mr. Bagthorpe is still feeling the trauma of having his one chance at national

acclaim whisked away from him. The author suggests his frame of mind: "It needed only the slightest nudge, he felt, to topple the balance of his mind and send it plummeting into full-scale schizophrenia or paranoia" (p. 18). The nudge that creates chaos in this episode is the arrival of a bank statement showing that he is overdrawn at the bank by "billions." In addition to plots filled with humorous exaggerated incidents, "The Bagthorpe Saga" recreates a family overflowing with loyalty and happiness. Children enjoy reading about a family that includes an eccentric grandmother, a precocious and unpredictable cousin, and assorted aunts and uncles. One fourth grader expressed her hope that Helen Cresswell would write more books about the Bagthorpes because her books made children laugh.

Judy Blume uses a surprising and unexpected situation in *Tales of a Fourth Grade Nothing*, in which the humorous conflict between two broth-

---

My first book *Henry Huggins*, a group of short stories about the sort of children I had known as a child, was written with a light heart from memories of Portland. As I wrote I discovered I had a collaborator, the child within myself—a rather odd, serious little girl, prone to colds, who sat in a child's rocking chair with her feet over the hot air outlet of the furnace, reading for hours, seeking laughter in the pages of books while her mother warned her she would ruin her eyes. That little girl, who has remained with me, prevents me from writing down to children, from poking fun at my characters, and from writing an adult reminiscence about childhood instead of a book to be enjoyed by children. And yet I do not write solely for that child; I am also writing for my adult self. We are collaborators who must agree. The feeling of being two ages at one time is delightful, one that surely must be a source of great pleasure to all writers of books enjoyed by children.

By the time I had published five books, several things had happened which forced me to think about children and humor: I had children of my own, twins—a boy and a girl; reviews said my books were hilarious or genuinely funny; a textbook of children's literature said my books were to be read "purely for amusement"; and enough children had written to me to give me some insight into their thoughts about my books.

One phrase began to stand out in these letters from children. Letter after letter told me my books were "funny and sad." Until these letters arrived, I had not thought of *Henry Huggins* as sad. The words, at that time never used by adults in reference to my books, began to haunt me. Funny and sad, or even funny and tragic, describes my view of life. To borrow another phrase from James Thurber, I had chosen "reality twisted to the right into humor rather than to the left into tragedy"—for that is my nature. I feel that comedy is as illuminating as tragedy—more so for younger readers who may be frightened or discouraged by tragedy in realistic fiction.

ers is brought to a climax when the younger boy swallows the older brother's pet turtle. An unexpected situation provides humor in Lois Lowry's *Anastasia On Her Own* when a naive cook, trying to prepare a gourmet dinner, asks for and receives cooking advice from a stranger who is calling to sell tap dancing lessons. In Sheila Greenwald's *Give Us a Great Big Smile, Rosy Cole*, several ridiculous situations develop when an author/photographer who is writing successful information books that chronicle his nieces' accomplishments now turns to Rosy, who has no accomplishments except her definite inability to play the violin. Greenwald's book is characteristic of many realistic humorous stories about people. Although most of the incidents are humorous, the actions of the characters reflect and highlight human foibles. The main characters learn something about themselves as they experience situations that may be more humorous to the reader than to them.

SUMMARY

Popular themes in contemporary realistic fiction include wrestling with fear and responsibility, overcoming family and personal problems in the face of illegitimacy, quarreling or divorcing parents, and conflicts between children's ambitions and their parents' desires. Overcoming problems created by the death of a loved one, problems created by deserting or noncaring parents, and emotions created by handicapped siblings are also found in realistic fiction. Discovery of self and developing maturity are popular themes in stories for older children.

Realistic fiction is especially enjoyable for many children because the stories are written about young people who are the same age, share the same interests, or have the same concerns. Realistic fiction also can help children understand human problems and how people similar to themselves have coped with them. It provides the enjoyment of escape as children read exciting mystery and adventure stories.

Realistic fiction has resulted in more controversy and more calls for censorship than any other type of children's literature. Controversial issues include sexism, sexuality, violence, drugs, profanity and objectionable language, viewpoints on war and peace, religion, death, and racial matters.

Suggested Activities for Adult Understanding of Realistic Fiction

☐ Sexism in literature, including the harmful sex-role socialization resulting from female- and male-role stereotyping, is a major concern of many educators and psychologists. In a school, public, or university library, choose a random sampling of children's literature selections. If these books were the only sources of information available about male and female roles, what information would be acquired from the books and their illustrations? Is this information accurate?

☐ Read a study that analyzes realistic fiction such as Gloria Toby Blatt's "Violence in Children's Literature: A Content Analysis of a Select Sampling of Children's Literature and a Study of Children's Responses to Literary Episodes Depicting Violence." (4); Carolyn Wilson Carmichael's "A Study of Selected Social Values as Reflected in Contemporary Realistic Fiction for Children" (5); Ann E. Hall's "Contemporary Realism in American Children's Books" (14); Alma Cross Homeze's "Interpersonal Relationships in Children's Literature from 1920 to 1960" (17); or Judith Ann Noble's "The Home, the Church, and the School as Portrayed in American Realistic Fiction for Children 1965–1969" (23). Read a sampling of the most current literature. How does this literature compare with the earlier findings?

☐ Compile an annotated bibliography of books that show both girls and boys in nontraditional sex roles. What is the strength or weakness of each book?

☐ Compare the professional roles of fathers and mothers in literature published in the 1970s and 1980s with the professional roles of fathers and mothers in literature published in earlier periods. Do the later books illustrate the changing family roles of both males and females? Is there conflict in the story if roles are reversed? How is this conflict handled?

☐ Interview children's librarians in public or school libraries. Ask them to state the guidelines used by the library when selecting books that might be considered controversial for children. What are the issues, if any, that they feel are relevant in the community? Can they identify any books that have caused controversy in the libraries? If there are such books, how did they handle the controversy?

☐ Many realistic fiction stories deal with the problems children must face and overcome when they experience separation from a friend, a neighborhood, a parent, or the ultimate separation caused by death. Choose one area, read several books that explore these problems, and recommend the ones that could be shared with younger children and those that might be more appropriate for older children. Explain the decision. Annotated bibliographies such as those found in Joanne E. Bernstein's *Books to Help Children Cope with Separation and Loss* (3) could be helpful in the search.

☐ Read a survival story such as Jean Craighead George's *My Side of the Mountain* or Scott O'Dell's *Island of the Blue Dolphins*. What writing style or technique does the author use that allows the reader to understand the awesome power of natural enemies?

☐ Compare the characteristics of a specific type of animal in a modern fantasy story with the characteristics of the same type of animal in a realistic animal adventure story.

References

1 Apseloff, Marilyn F. "New Trends in Children's Books from Europe and Japan." *School Library Journal* 32 (Nov. 1985): 30–32.

2 Association of Women Psychologists. "Statement Resolutions and Motions." Miami, Fla.: American Psychological Association Convention, September 1970.

3 Bernstein, Joanne E. *Books to Help Children Cope with Separation and Loss*. New York: Bowker, 1977.

4 Blatt, Gloria Toby. "Violence in Children's Literature: A Content Analysis of a Select Sampling of Children's Literature and a Study of Children's Responses to Literary Episodes Depicting Violence," University Microfilm No. 72–29,931. East Lansing, Mich.: Michigan State University, 1972.

5 Carmichael, Carolyn Wilson. "A Study of Selected Social Values as Reflected in Contemporary Realistic Fiction for Children," University Microfilm No. 71–31, 1972. East Lansing, Mich.: Michigan State University, 1971.

6 Cheatham, Bertha M. "News of '85: SLJ's Annual Roundup." *School Library Journal* 32 (Dec. 1985): 19–27.

7 Cohen, Caron Lee. "The Quest in Children's Literature." *School Library Journal* 31 (Aug. 1985): 28–29.

8 Connell, Christopher. "Middle-Class Housewife Writes High-Class Children's Tales." Bryan-College Station *Eagle*, March 28, 1984, p. 1F.

9 Donelson, Ken. "Almost 13 Years of Book Protests—Now What?" *School Library Journal* 31 (March 1985): 93–98.

10 Dresang, Eliza. "A Newbery Song for Gifted Readers." *School Library Journal* 30 (Nov. 1983): 33–37.

11 Egoff, Sheila. "The Problem Novel." In *Only Connect: Readings on Children's Literature*, edited by Sheila Egoff, G. T. Stubbs, and L. F. Ashley. Toronto: Oxford University, 1980.

12 Forman, Jack. "Young Adult Books: Politics—The Last Taboo." *Horn Book* 61 (July/Aug. 1985): 469–471.

13 Frasher, Ramona. "A Feminist Look at Literature for Children: Ten Years Later." In *Sex Stereotypes and Reading: Research and Strategies*. edited by E. Marcia Sheridan. Newark: International Reading Association; 1982.

14 Hall, Ann E. "Contemporary Realism in American Children's Books." *Choice* (November 1977): 1171–78.

15 Hearne, Betsy. "Contemporary Issues—Child Abuse." *Booklist* 81 (May 1, 1985): 1261–1262.

16 Henke, James T. "Dicey, Odysseus, and Hansel and Gretel: The Lost Children of Voigt's *Homecoming*." *Children's Literature in Education* 16 (Spring 1985): 45–52.

17 Homeze, Alma Cross. "Interpersonal Relationships in Children's Literature from 1920 to 1960," University Microfilm No. 64-5366. University Park, Pa.: Pennsylvania State University, 1963.

18 Houghton Mifflin Company. *Eliminating Stereotypes, School Division Guidelines*. Boston: Houghton Mifflin, 1981.

19 Kean, John M., and Personke, Carl. *The Language Arts: Teaching and Learning in the Elementary School*. New York: St. Martin's, 1976.

20 McClenathan, Day Ann K. "Realism in Books for Young People. Some Thoughts on Management of Controversy." In *Developing Active Readers: Ideas for Parents, Teachers, and Librarians*, edited by Dianne L. Monson and Day Ann K. McClenathan. Newark, Del.: International Reading Association, 1979.

21 Madsen, Jane M., and Wickersham, Elaine B. "A Look at Young Children's Realistic Fiction." *The Reading Teacher* 34 (December 1980): 273–79.

22 Nilsen, Aileen Pace. "Women in Children's Literature." *College English* 32 (May 1971): 918–26.

23 Noble, Judith Ann. "The Home, the Church, and the School as Portrayed in American Realistic Fiction for Children 1965–1969," University Microfilm No. 31, 271. East Lansing, Mich.: Michigan State University, 1971.

24 Rochman, Hazel. "Young Adult Books: Childhood Terror." *Horn Book* 61 (Sept./Oct. 1985): 598–602.

25 Root, Shelton L. "The New Realism—Some Personal Reflections." *Language Arts* 54 (January 1977): 19–24.

26 Sage, Mary. "A Study of the Handicapped in Children's Literature." In *Children's Literature, Selected Essays and Bibliographies*, edited by Anne S. MacLeod. College Park, Md.: Univ. of Maryland College of Library and Informational Services, 1977.

27 Sam Houston Area Reading Conference, Sam Houston State University, February, 1981.

28 Steele, Mary Q. "Realism, Truth, and Honesty." *Horn Book Magazine* 46 (February 1971): 17–27.

29 Storey, Denise C. "Fifth Graders Meet Elderly Book Characters," *Language Arts* 56 (April 1979): 408–12.

30 Townsend, John Rowe. *Written for Children: An Outline of English-Language Children's Literature*. New York: Lippincott, 1974.

31 Vasilakis, Nancy. "Young Adult Books: An Eighties Perspective." *Horn Book* 61 (Nov./Dec. 1985): 768–769.

IF REALISTIC FICTION IS TO MEET children's needs by offering them opportunities to identify with others, extend their horizons, and gain personal insights, then adults who work with children must be aware of a wide range of realistic fiction and activities that encourage children in this growth.

It is not necessary, or even advisable, to attach literature-related activities to all realistic fiction that children read, but some activities are very appropriate for this genre. This section considers how realistic fiction may be used to stimulate role-playing experiences that strengthen children's understanding of the world around them and offers suggestions for handling real problems. It also takes an in-depth look at the development of children's-literature units that stress themes of island survival and survival in mountains, canyons, and tundra. In addition to activities and discussions that stress the setting's influence upon the conflicts in the stories, this unit relates literature to the science curriculum through activities that increase children's understanding of geography and botany. This section also stresses how literature can be used to develop an appreciation for the contributions of females and an understanding of the various roles both males and females can play in life. The section concludes with questioning strategies that can accompany realistic fiction or any other genre of literature.

USING REALISTIC FICTION DURING ROLE PLAYING AND BIBLIOTHERAPY

Role playing is an oral creative dramatics activity in which children consider a problem or the possible actions of people and then act out the situations as they believe they might actually unfold in real life. Laurie and Joseph Braga (5) give several reasons for encouraging role playing with children. First, they stress that role playing helps young children develop an understanding of the world around them. Through playing roles of various people—such as teachers, doctors, and police officers—they learn about their world, acquire important social skills, and become acquainted with the important contributions

Involving Children in Realistic Fiction

☐

USING REALISTIC FICTION DURING ROLE PLAYING AND BIBLIOTHERAPY

☐

USING CHILDREN'S INTEREST IN SURVIVAL TO MOTIVATE READING AND INTERACTION WITH LITERATURE

☐

USING WEBBING IN GUIDED DISCUSSIONS ABOUT REALISTIC FICTION

☐

DEVELOPING AN APPRECIATION FOR INDIVIDUALS: IMPROVING SELF-ESTEEM AND UNDERSTANDING

☐

DEVELOPING QUESTIONING STRATEGIES WITH REALISTIC FICTION

many people make to our society. Second, the Bragas suggest that role playing enhances children's understanding of various ways to handle problems when children focus on common problematic situations, play the roles of the people concerned, switch roles to develop understanding of other points of view, and talk about what happened, why it happened, and what they think should be done. The Bragas believe that adults can learn a great deal about children as they listen to children's responses during role-playing activities and follow-up discussions.

Literature can be the stimulus for involving children in activities that satisfy both these purposes of role playing. Realistic picture books about doctors, dentists, and other neighborhood helpers can be used to encourage young children to act out the roles of adults with whom they come in contact. Such role playing can decrease their fears by allowing children to experience a role before facing a real situation. Books about families encourage children to role play interactions between different members of a family, nuclear or extended.

The plots in realistic fiction provide many opportunities for children to role play problem situations. Zena Sutherland and May Hill Arbuthnot (17) recommend that literature selected for stimulating, thought-provoking problem situations should (1) contain characters who are well developed and have clearly defined problem situations; (2) have plots that contain logical stopping places so that children can role play the endings; (3) include problems, such as universal fears and concerns, that allow children to identify with the situations; and (4) present problems that help students develop their own personal value systems.

Adults who use literature in role playing may either choose stories in which a problem is developed to a certain point and then have children role play the unfinished situation, or have children role play various solutions to problems after they have read or listened to the whole story.

Fannie and George Shaftel (16) recommend certain steps in guiding older children in a literature related, role-playing experience. First, the adult introduces and reads the problem story to the children. During the introduction, the adult helps the children think about the situation and how it might be solved. Second, the adult encourages the children to describe the characters in the story; then the children choose parts for the

first role-playing situation. Third, the adult discusses the responsibility of the audience, suggests observations that children could make, and encourages them to consider the reasonableness of the solution. Fourth, players discuss what they will do during the role-playing activity. Fifth, the children role play the problem situation, with each participant playing the role of the character he or she has chosen to represent. Sixth, when the role playing is over, the adult leads the audience and the characters in discussing the actions, consequences, and possible alternative behaviors of the characters. Seventh, children re-enact the role-playing situation using new actions and solutions suggested during the discussion. Eighth, the adult again leads a discussion focused upon the different solutions to the problem. Finally, the children assess the possible outcomes of each portrayal and draw conclusions about the best way or ways to handle the problem.

The books of realistic fiction discussed in this chapter offer considerable stimulus for role-playing problem situations. Because the books are categorized according to their content, adults may refer to this chapter when searching for specific types of situations connected with family life, peer friendships, overcoming stereotypes, and so forth. The following books also contain problem situations that adults have used to stimulate children's role-playing experiences:

Family Life

1   **Responsibility toward family members and friends:** *The Moffats*, by Eleanor Estes.
    Rufus's friend Hughie feels unhappy during the first day of school. In fact, Hughie runs away, causing Rufus to follow him and persuade him to return.
    Ask children to pretend they are Rufus and Hughie. If they were Rufus, what arguments would they use to persuade Hughie to stay in school or return to school?

2   **Responsibility toward family members:** *Meet the Austins*, by Madeleine L'Engle.
    The Austin parents include their children in many important family discussions and stress the importance of sharing family responsibilities.
    Ask children to pretend that they are family members and role play what they believe is meant by responsibility toward the family. The conflicts between Maggy and various

Austin family members are also useful for role playing.

Family Disturbances

1 **Problems related to accepting parents' divorce and discovering oneself**: *Dear Mr. Henshaw* by Beverly Cleary.
Ask the children to pretend that they are either Leigh Botts or Mr. Henshaw. It is March 31, five months after the two people started their correspondence. The two characters are taking part in a conversation. What information did they learn about each other? How did the writing experience affect either of their lives? How would Leigh Botts change the answers to any of the questions that he answered in his letters dated between November 20 and November 27? What advice would they give to each other?
2 **Problems connected with surviving without a parent**: *Mama*, by Lee Bennett Hopkins.
Ask children how they could convince Mama that they love her for herself and not for the stolen gifts she brings them.

Interpersonal Relationships

1 **The loss of a friend and the meaning of friendship**: *A Secret Friend*, by Marilyn Sachs. Encourage children to empathize with Jessica as she tries to regain Wendy's friendship. What would they do and say in that situation?
2 **Being accepted by others**: *Take Wing*, by Jean Little.
Many scenes in this book illustrate relationships between a mentally disabled child and his parents, siblings, and peers.
Please Don't Tease Me . . . by Jane M. Madsen and Diane Bockoras.
The authors present discussion questions that might be used to highlight this true story about feelings.
3 **Relationships with the elderly**: *How Does It Feel to Be Old?*, by Norma Farber.
Ask children to think about all of the good and bad things suggested in the book that relate to growing old. Have them role play a situation revolving around each person who might have a conversation with grandmother about the positive side of becoming older.

Physical Maturity

1 **Overcoming problems related to physical characteristics**: *The Ears of Louis* or *The Un-making of Rabbit*, by Constance C. Greene.
Encourage children to empathize with Louis's or Paul's feelings about their big ears. How would they react to taunts of "Elephant Boy" or teasing about a pink nose? Ask them to role play scenes between Louis and his best friend, Louis and his friendly neighbor, Louis and his classmates, and Louis and the older boys who want him to join them for a football game.
2 **Overcoming problems related to physical characteristics**: *Blubber*, by Judy Blume.
This book contains many episodes of insensitivity between children and the girl who is overweight.

These stories allow children to empathize with characters who have problems that many children in elementary school experience. Through role playing, children may discover ways to handle problems and increase their sensitivity to the problems of others.

In recent years, librarians and educators have recommended reading and interacting with particular books as a way for individuals to gain insights into their own problems. *Bibliotherapy*, according to the *Dictionary of Education* (8), means the "use of books to influence the total development, a process of interaction between the reader and literature which is used for personality assessment, adjustment, growth, clinical and mental hygiene purposes; a concept that ideas inherent in selecting reading material can have a therapeutic effect upon the mental or physical ills of the reader" (p. 58). By this definition, everyone can be helped through reading; bibliotherapy is a process in which every literate person participates at some time. Joanne Bernstein (3) has described bibliotherapy as "the self-examination and insights that are gained from reading, no matter what the source. The source can be fiction or nonfiction; the reading can be directed (in settings ranging from reading guidance to formal therapy), self directed, or accidental. The reader might begin reading when actively looking for insights or the insights might come unexpectedly. In any case, the insight is utilized to create a richer and healthier life" (p. 21).

Bernstein (3) suggests that adults can use books to help children gain insights into their own lives and to help them identify with others if adults (1) know how and when to introduce the materials, (2) are sufficiently familiar with the materials, and (3) know each child's particular need. Bernstein stresses that if books are being used to help children cope with their problems, adults should not force the books upon them; instead, adults should provide a selection of materials from which children can choose and then be patient until children are ready to use them. After a child has read a book, an adult should be available for discussion or, more important, for listening. During a discussion, children can talk about the actions and feelings of the characters in the story, suggest areas in which they agree and disagree with the characters, consider the consequences of the character's actions, and talk about other ways that a problem might be approached. At other times, an adult should not intrude with any formalized discussion, but should be available as someone ready to listen with empathy.

Many books provide additional resources for university students who are interested in bibliotherapy. Bernstein's (3) book contains a bibliography of adult references pertaining to bibliotherapy and an extensive annotated bibliography of children's books that deal with accepting a new sibling; going to a new school; getting used to a new neighborhood; coping with death, divorce, desertion, serious illness, and displacement due to war; and dealing with foster care, stepparents, and adoption.

Analyzing Children's Responses to Literature

Use of realistic fiction and other types of books for role playing and bibliotherapy may be more effective if adults have a general understanding of children's responses to literature. Louise Rosenblatt (14) states that a literature selection "should not be thought of as an object, an entity, but rather as an active process lived through during the relationship between a reader and a text" (p. 12). The reader brings to the reading or listening task past experiences, present interests, and expectations that influence the reading process. Consequently, two different readers often read and interpret the same piece of literature in different ways. Arthur Applebee (1) emphasizes that the stories children hear lead them to make expectations about what a story should be and about what new stories will be like.

Studies of children's oral or written responses to literature may analyze the types of comments made by children when they retell a selection or

CHART 9–2
Classifying children's comments about books

Type of Response	Examples
Descriptive	Retelling the story, naming the characters, listing the media used in illustration.
Analytic	Pointing to the uses of language, structure, point-of-view, in the work.
Classificatory	Placing the work in its literary historical context.
Personal	Describing the reader's reactions to the work and the emotions and memories that have been evoked.
Interpretive	Making inferences about the work and its parts, relating the work to some way of viewing phenomena (e.g., psychology).
Evaluative	Judging the work's merit on personal, formal, or moral criteria.

talk about a story. Alan C. Purves and Dianne L. Monson (12), in a review of children's responses to literature, identify characteristic responses of children in different grades. For example, children up to the third grade tend to respond to and retell literal aspects of a story. In addition to literal responses, fourth- and fifth-grade students tend to elaborate on their responses by placing themselves in the roles of the characters, comparing themselves to the characters, and talking about their personal reactions and evaluations. By sixth grade, students began to emphasize and interpret characterizations. In seventh and eighth grades, the numbers of interpretations increase and the evaluations frequently emphasize meaning and understanding. Eighth-grade students begin to look for hidden or deeper meanings in the stories.

Adults who work with children and literature can learn a great deal about children's responses to literature by analyzing what children choose to say or write about when they discuss literature. Purves and Monson (12) recommend a classification system for adults to use when they analyze children's comments about literature. See chart 9–2.

USING CHILDREN'S INTEREST IN SURVIVAL TO MOTIVATE READING AND INTERACTION WITH LITERATURE

Many realistic fiction adventure stories portray the physical survival and increased emotional maturity of the main characters. The plots and strong characterizations in this type of realistic fiction encourage children to live these adventures vicariously. The physical characteristics described in the stories show children how to develop an understanding of the importance of setting when it causes major conflicts in the story. University students have used children's interest in physical and emotional survival to develop stimulating literature-related activities to share with children.

Two very interesting instructional activities developed by university students and then shared with classrooms of children centered around the survival theme. One group developed an in-depth literature unit around "Physical and Emotional Survival on Islands." Another group chose "Physical and Emotional Survival on Mountains, in Canyons, and on Arctic Tundra." Each group organized its units by using the webbing process.

Island Survival

The university students who chose the island survival theme identified the following books that focus on an individual's or a small group's ability to survive physically and grow in maturity because of their experiences:

Island of the Blue Dolphins, by Scott O'Dell
Call It Courage, by Armstrong Sperry
The Cay, by Theodore Taylor
The Swiss Family Robinson, by Johann David Wyss

The group read the books and identified the central themes and the main areas that challenge the character's physical survival: characteristics of the natural environment, including climatic conditions of the islands caused by their geographical locations, and survival needs related to other human needs. This central theme and six subtopics associated with survival were identified in the first phase of the "Survival on Islands" web (see Figure 9–1). During the next phase, the group identified subjects related to each subtopic on the web. The group developed the extended web shown in Figure 9–2.

After finishing the web, the group planned learning activities that encouraged children to develop an understanding of the importance of setting, to realize that setting may cause major conflicts, and to increase their understanding of each identified physical survival topic. The university students also identified many topics listed on their webs that were related to the upper-elementary science curriculum. They realized that they could use interesting literature selections to increase children's understanding of scientific principles. They developed activities to stimulate oral language, written language, and artistic interpretations of the plots and characters. The following examples are taken from the physical survival activities developed around Scott O'Dell's *Island of*

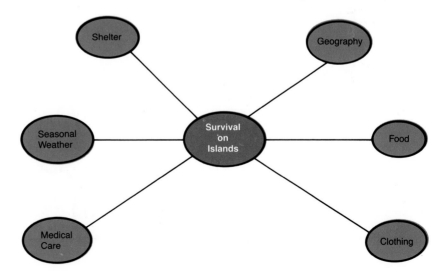

FIGURE 9–1

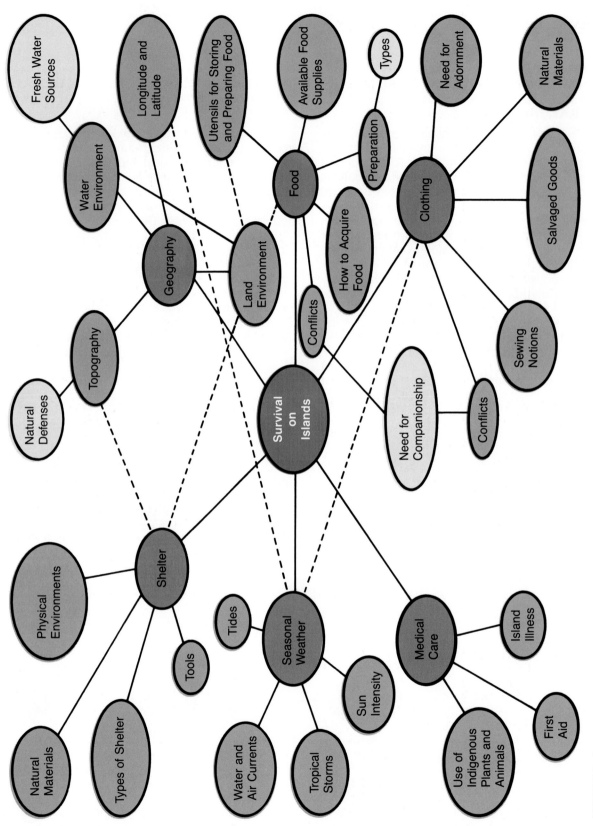

FIGURE 9–2

the Blue Dolphins. Several activities are included for each main subtopic in the web to allow the reader to visualize the types of physical survival activities that are possible in the classroom. Many of these activities are also appropriate for discussion in the library.

Physical Survival Activities Developed
Around Scott O'Dell's
Island of the Blue Dolphins

I   Seasonal Weather
  A. Karana's life revolves around the seasons; she calculates time and the jobs she must do according to the seasons. Lead a discussion with the children that helps them identify the seasons on the island, the characteristics of the seasons, and the reasons for Karana's total involvement in the seasons. O'Dell's text provides many clues to seasonal weather: the flowers are plentiful in the spring because of heavy winter rains; in the spring, the birds leave the island and fly to the north; Karana gathers food for the winter; storms with winds and high waves are described.
  B. On a large mural draw the Island of the Blue Dolphins, depicting the different seasons and weather conditions described in the book.
  C. Pretend to be Karana and write a dairy: include five entries from each season on the island. In the entries, describe seasonal weather and activities during that season.

II. Medical Care
  A. Use of Indigenous Plants and Animals: In the wilderness, accidents or illnesses are dangerous; there are no doctors or drugstores. Read page 96 to find out what Karana used on Rontu's wound. Find this plant (coral bush) in a reference book and consider why it would help Rontu's wound.
  B. First Aid and Use of Indigenous Plants and Animals: Pretend that you and your family are isolated on an island in the Pacific. Consider the minor illnesses or accidents that could easily occur while on the island. For example, sunburn is common in warm climates. Other problems might include poisonous stings, broken legs, stomach upsets, head-

aches, and wounds. Research some plants, herbs, and other first aid resources that might be found on the island. Make an illustrated island survival book for medical care; include drawings of plants, their medical properties, and sketches of first aid measures. After this is finished, lead a discussion in which the children consider Karana's personal medical needs and how she handled her problems.

III. Clothing
  A. Natural Materials: Karana and her people lived on an island where the only sources of clothing were natural materials, plant and animal, found on the island or in the sea. What garments did Karana make for herself? What natural materials did she use? Divide into groups and investigate the procedures Karana would need to use and the time that would be involved in making a skirt from yucca fibers, a belt or a pair of sandals from sealskin, an otter cape, or a skirt of cormorant skins. (Even the needle and thread were made from natural sources.) If possible, try making a garment from natural materials. After the natural materials and the procedures are described, lead a discussion to help children develop an understanding of the importance of obtaining clothing in an isolated area and the influence the need to obtain clothing has on the characters' actions. Encourage them to consider how their own lives are different because of the ease of acquiring clothing or the materials for clothing. Children can identify the natural materials available in their environment if they were required, like Karana, to make their clothing from original natural sources.
  B. Natural Materials and the Need for Adornment: Karana and the women of her island wanted flowers and jewelry that would improve their appearance. Ask the group to consider why Karana found satisfaction in making a flower wreath for her hair and for Rontu's neck. Have them investigate the types of flowers that Karana might have used to make her wreath. If possible, ask the

children to make their own flower wreaths using flowers in their own locality. Karana was also fond of jewelry. Ask the group to consider the implications of Karana's spending five nights to make a circlet of abalone shells as a present for the Aleut girl, Tutok. Allow children to examine jewelry made from seashells. If possible, have them make their own jewelry from seashells. This can also be an opportunity for investigating the types of seashells that might be available on Karana's island.

IV. Food

A. Available Food Supplies: Make a list of the foods Karana ate in the story. References are made to the scarlet apples that grow on cactus bushes (tunas) and foods from the sea such as abalones and scallops. Research the possible sources that might be available on a Pacific island. Investigate several cookbooks and make an Island of the Blue Dolphins Cookbook using the foods and seasonings Karana might find.

B. Utensils for Storing and Preparing Food: How did Karana fix her food? Where did she store the food to preserve it and protect it from animals? Karana had to make all of the utensils and storage containers for her food and water. Draw or make a list of five things Karana had to make in order to cook or store her food. Tell or show how she made these utensils or storage containers. Why was it important that Karana create each item? What could have happened if she had not created ways to store food? What impact did preparing and storing food have on her use of time and the plot of the story?

C. How to Acquire Food: Women in Karana's village were forbidden to make weapons. What is the significance for Karana when, in spite of her fear, she makes weapons to protect herself and to obtain food? Why did she think of destructive winds when she considered the advisability of making weapons? Draw several weapons that Karana created, explain how she made them, and identify the natural resources she used.

D. How to Acquire Food and Available Food Supplies: Rontu and Karana encounter and later hunt a devilfish. From the description on pages 103–4 and 118–24 try to determine another name for a devilfish. Use reference books and pay close attention to the details. Why did Karana spend her whole winter crafting a special kind of spear to hunt the devilfish?

E. Conflicts between Food or Clothing Sources and Need for Companionship: A conflict arises for Karana when she begins to make friends with some animals on the island. What is the significance of her statement on page 156 that she would never kill another otter, seal, cormorant, or wild dog? Encourage children to debate this issue as it could relate to their own lives. (Another topic for debate is the destruction of animals such as the sea otter. Karana decided to stop killing the otters even for a cape and would not tell the white men where the otters were located. Ask children to investigate the controversy connected with killing or saving the sea otter and then, taking a pro or con position, debate the issue.)

V. Geography

A. Topography: Based on Karana's description of the Island of the Blue Dolphins in chapter two and other parts of the book, make a map of the island. The map should include a scale and symbols. To make the scale, the equivalent length of a league must be determined. In her descriptions of where the sun rises and sets, Karana has given the north, south, east, and west directions. Place these symbols on the map. Chart the wind directions on the map. (The island is two leagues long and one league wide. A league is equivalent to about three miles. The island looks like a dolphin lying on its side. The tail points toward sunrise, which would be east, and the nose points toward sunset, which would be west.)

B. Physical Environment, Longitude and Latitude: The Island of the Blue Dolphins is real. On a large map or atlas that shows the California coastline try to find San Nicolas, which is located about seventy-five miles southwest of Los Angeles. Identify the longitude and latitude of the island. What is the effect of this longitude and latitude upon the island? Compare a description of San Nicolas in a reference book with the description of the island. Are there any similarities or differences? If someone were marooned on an island, what longitude and latitude would that person choose in order to have a natural environment most advantageous to survival? Write a short story describing the setting and how one would survive on the island.

C. Topography, Physical Environment: Several geographical terms are used in *Island of the Blue Dolphins*. Below is a list of some of these terms. To develop an understanding of the geography of the island, define each term as used in the story, find pictures illustrating each term, and draw examples of the terms as they looked on Karana's island. Try to see each one through Karana's eyes. What was the significance of each feature for Karana's survival?

mesa   cliffs   ravine
harbor   canyon spring
cove

VI. Shelter
A. Types of Shelters, Natural Materials, Physical Environments: In her struggles for survival, Karana constructed both a fenced-in house (pp. 74–76) and a cave dwelling (p. 89). Reread the descriptions of each house and consider Karana's needs when she constructed these shelters. What was the advantage of each type of shelter? How did each shelter relate to the natural materials found upon the island, the physical environment of the island, and the tools that Karana had available for her use? Why did the need for shelter play such an important part in the development of the story and in the use of Karana's time and energy? Choose one of her island shelters and build a model of the shelter. Look at our

own environment. If people were isolated in their physical environments without the houses and other buildings they have now, what type of natural shelter would they construct? Write a short story describing the decision-making processes people use as they think about the type of shelter they will construct. In this story consider the need for protection against weather changes, natural predators that might harm them or take their food supplies, topography of the land that could be used to their advantage, the proximity of the shelter to life-sustaining food and water supplies, and the availability of building materials and tools needed for construction. Build a model of this shelter.

Students developed similar activities around each island survival book. Discussions and activities stressed the importance of setting in the developing conflict and the effects upon the growth of the characters as they overcame problems connected with setting or loneliness. Students also made comparisons between the various characters, their settings, and the physical and emotional strategies that led to survival. In a final activity, the students set the classroom up as an island. Students divided into groups according to shelter, food, clothing, geography, medical care, and seasonal weather. They chose and developed an activity that represented their area of interest during Island Day. They constructed shelters in which the various interest centers were located. Students shared tool making and cooking experiences. Art and science experiences were used to depict weather, geography, clothing, food, and shelter. A special demonstration showed possible medical care needed for island survival. While learning about the impact of setting upon characters in survival literature, the students also discovered much about their own environments and how they might conquer their own worlds.

Survival in Mountains, Canyons, and Tundra

Three books by Jean Craighead George have stimulated interesting discovery activities related to survival in the mountains of the northeastern United States, in a canyon in the southwestern United States, and on the Arctic tundra: *My Side of the Mountain*, *River Rats, Inc.*, and *Julie of the Wolves*. The stories also stress emotional and personal maturation and physical survival.

After developing a web similar to the one developed for island survival, upper-elementary students compared the three different settings according to their geographical locations, topography, longitude and latitude, and physical environments; their natural food supplies; the clothing they required; any medical care required and how characters in the books solved this problem; seasonal changes in weather that influenced the characters' actions; and the types of shelters the characters made out of natural materials. Students compared the actions of the main characters in each story and identified different ways that the characters responded to personal and environmental problems. One class developed a large chart (see Chart 9–3) that helped them define these differences.

The description of edible foods and their growing locations found in *My Side of the Mountain* and *River Rats, Inc.* relate to topics studied in the science curriculum. To highlight these relationships, students reviewed the types and environmental implications of vegetation that grew along the water and in the desert regions described in *River Rats, Inc.* They identified the edible plants that characters found in each location and the procedures characters used to prepare and store the foods. For example, page 70 in *River Rats, Inc.* lists the following water-loving plants that created either a beautiful "Inner Kingdom" or, equally important, nourishing foods: cottonwoods, watercress, cattails, monkey flowers, maidenhair fern, wild garlic, and Indian vine.

In *My Side of the Mountain*, they identified the larger trees that covered the slopes of a northeastern mountain: hemlock, oak, walnut, and hickory. They located references to plants that

	Catskill Mountains	Southwest Canyon	Arctic Tundra
Geography			
topography			
longitude and latitude			
physical environment			
fresh water sources			
Food			
available supplies			
how to acquire food			
how to create utensils			
food preparation			
Clothing			
requirements related to environment			
natural materials			
sewing notions			
Medical Care			
major concerns			
first aid			
use of indigenous plants and animals			
Seasonal Weather			
sun intensity			
seasonal storms			
air currents			
Shelter			
requirements due to weather			
requirements due to topography			
natural materials			
types of shelter tools			

CHART 9–3

grew next to springs decorated with "flowers, ferns, moss, weeds—everything that loved water" (p. 30). Then they followed a character's search for edible food, the steps in preparing the food, and methods of storing the food. Some plant foods included hickory nuts and salt from hickory limbs (p. 23), apples (p. 24), walnuts, cattails, arrowleaf (p. 24), bulbs of dogtooth violets (pp. 27–28), dandelion greens (p. 28), strawberries (p. 35), wild garlic, jack-in-the-pulpit roots (p. 45), daisies, inner bark from the poplar tree, acorns (p. 62), sassafras roots (p. 66), pennyroyal, winterberry leaves (p. 67), arrowleaf bulbs, cattail tubers, bulrush roots, and wild onions (p. 81).

Referring to Laurence Pringle's *Wild Foods: A Beginner's Guide to Identifying, Harvesting and Preparing Safe and Tasty Plants from the Outdoors* (11) and Euell Gibbons's *Stalking the Wild Asparagus* (7), students investigated the wild plants mentioned in *My Side of the Mountain*, read suggestions for identifying and preparing them, compared these suggestions with the way the book's main character identified and prepared them, and identified which plants might be found near their own homes. (Warnings were also stressed; many wild plants are dangerous to eat. Therefore the teacher recommended that children not eat any plant unless they were accompanied by someone who knew exactly which plants were safe and which were dangerous.)

Because cattails were mentioned in both books and were available near the school, the students gathered them and tried grinding them into flour. They also followed Laurence Pringle's suggestions for boiling cattail rhizomes and using them as a potato substitute. This experience increased their empathy for the characters in the book, who had to work hard to survive on natural foods.

Children related this research into natural foods and their preparation to the climatic conditions, geographical locations, and amount of water available for plants in both *River Rats, Inc.* and *My Side of the Mountain*.

USING WEBBING IN GUIDED DISCUSSIONS ABOUT REALISTIC FICTION

The webbing, or semantic mapping, techniques used in the survival activities discussed above may also be used to show the plot, conflict, setting, characterization, and theme of realistic fiction, and other literature, in a visual way that encourages oral discussions. My own current research (10) with fifth through eighth grade students shows that webbing is one of the most effective ways to help students understand important characteristics of a story. It also helps students increase their appreciation of literature and improve their reading and writing competencies. Prior to the webbing experience, the teacher introduces the literary elements of setting, characterization, plot development, conflict, and theme by reading and discussing folktales with the children. Then the teacher draws simple webs that include each of these components, while leading discussions that help students identify the important characteristics that are being placed on the web.

This use of webbing can be applied, for example, to Byrd Baylor's *Hawk, I'm Your Brother*, a contemporary realistic story about a Native American boy's dreams of flying like a hawk. (Chapter 11 discusses using this book to develop an understanding of author's point of view.) First, the teacher introduces the story. As part of the introduction, the teacher draws the beginning of the web on the board, placing *Hawk, I'm Your Brother* in the center circle and extending the terms *setting*, *characterization*, *conflicts*, *plot development*, and *themes* from that center. Next, the teacher reads the story to the students as they listen for the various categories. After the story is completed, the teacher leads a discussion in which the students fill in the various categories on the web. As the teacher completes the web on the board, the students copy the web onto their own papers. If necessary, the teacher rereads parts of the story as the students consider what information should be placed on the web. Some of the webs become quite large and may cover several chalkboards. In another class period following the development of the web, students write their own stories about the book. They use the information on the web to help them construct their stories. Figure 9–3 provides an example of a less complex web that sixth-grade students developed.

Other types of charting are also effective when leading discussions about books. Mary G. Flender (6) provides examples of charts that depict book covers, plot discussions, character attributes, themes, stylistic details, and connections between books.

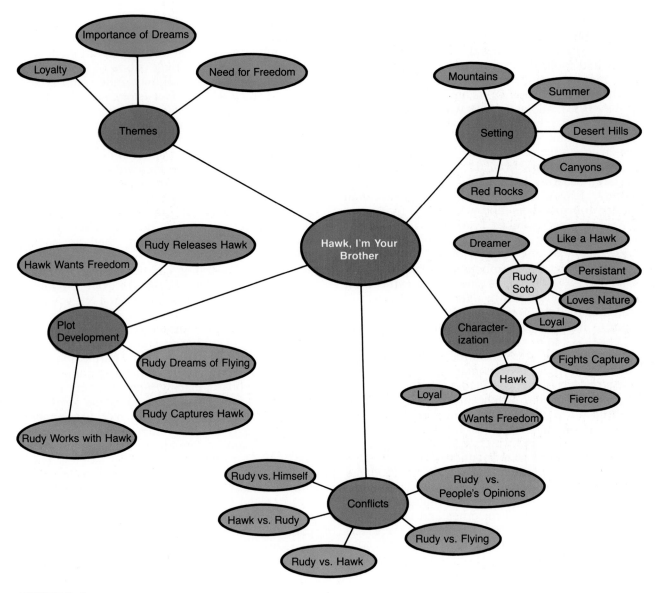

FIGURE 9–3
A literary discussion web

DEVELOPING AN APPRECIATION FOR INDIVIDUALS: IMPROVING SELF-ESTEEM AND UNDERSTANDING

Researchers and writers in educational publications have found that, until quite recently, children's textbooks lacked sufficient portrayals of positive female roles. Myra Pollack Sadker and David Miller Sadker (15) say that "a growing body of research. . .attests to loss of female potential as girls go through school, and many writers have analyzed the way sex stereotyping occurs in classrooms across the country—from sexist teaching patterns to segregated activities. One key way that girls learn to undervalue themselves is through the books they read. When children open elementary school texts, they read most often about the activities and adventures of boys"

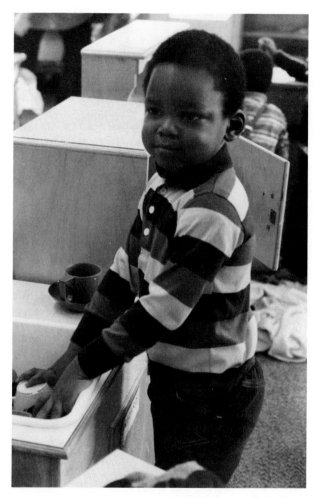

Nonstereotypic realistic fiction can help children overcome sex stereotypes.

(p. 231). The research discussed on pages 382–83 attests to the stereotyping of males and females found in children's literature.

Children's literature students have identified literature suggesting that females and males do not necessarily act in stereotypic ways. Books that illustrate nonstereotypic behavioral patterns can help teachers, librarians, and parents who wish to combat stereotypes. Many of the books of realistic fiction discussed in the first half of this chapter are excellent sources that illustrate a wide range of behavioral patterns. The following books are categorized according to the specific stereotypic behaviors they refute:

1   Both girls and boys can overcome great struggles in nature and survive:

Female: Scott O'Dell's *Island of the Blue Dolphins*
Male: Armstrong Sperry's *Call It Courage*

2   Both young girls and young boys can be brave and intelligent:

Female: Beverly Cleary's *Ramona The Brave*
Male: Eleanor Schick's *Joey on His Own*

3   Girls can be independent and take care of their younger siblings or pets:

Female: E. L. Konigsburg's *From the Mixed-Up Files of Mrs. Basil E. Frankweiler*
Female: Theodore Taylor's *The Trouble with Tuck*

4   Both girls and boys can be intelligent and curious:

Female: Louise Fitzhugh's *Harriet the Spy*
Male: Donald J. Sobol's *Encyclopedia Brown Sets the Pace*

5   Boys can express feelings of fear. Facing death is not the only way to demonstrate courage:

Male: Maia Wojciechowska's *Shadow of a Bull*

6   Boys can be shy or gentle:

Male: Maria Gripe's *Elvis and His Secret*

These books have led to interesting discussions and comparisons, as children have learned that both boys and girls can demonstrate a wide range of acceptable behaviors—or have read stories that verified what their own experience had already taught them about the full range of feelings and behaviors available to girls and boys.

DEVELOPING QUESTIONING STRATEGIES WITH REALISTIC FICTION

Not all literature selections should be accompanied by questioning. Nevertheless, librarians and teachers responsible for encouraging children to think about and react to literature in a variety of ways find it helpful to have a framework for designing questions that assist children in focusing upon certain aspects of a story and questions that require higher-level thought processes.

Teachers and librarians who wish to develop such questioning strategies will find assistance in taxonomies of reading comprehension, such as those developed by Benjamin Bloom (4) or Thomas C. Barrett (2). The questions that follow are examples of the types that can be developed around realistic fiction. Barrett, for example, identifies four levels of reading comprehension:

literal recognition or recall, inference, evaluation, and appreciation. Questions related to these levels can be developed in relation to realistic fiction, such as Katherine Paterson's *Jacob Have I Loved*, which is used in the extended examples below. Paterson's book is appropriate for the upper-elementary and middle-school grades. These questions are only a guide suggesting the types of questions that might be developed around any book. A librarian or teacher might choose to focus upon only a few of these questions. The number of questions are included simply to illustrate a variety of examples from each subsection of the taxonomy, not to suggest that every question must be discussed.

Questions That Encourage Literal Recognition

Literal recognition requires children to identify information provided in the literature. Teachers may require children to recall the information from memory after reading or listening to a story or to locate information while reading a literature selection. Literal-level questions such as the following often use words such as *who, what, where,* and *when*:

1 *Recall of details*:
   Where does the story *Jacob Have I Loved* take place?
   When does the story take place?
   Who are the characters in the story?
2 *Recall of sequence of events*:
   What was the sequence of events that led Louise to believe that Caroline was the favored child in the family?
   What was the sequence of events that caused Louise to move from an island to a mountain community?
3 *Recall of comparisons*:
   Compare the author's physical description of Louise and Caroline. Compare the way Louise thought the family treated her with the way she thought they treated her twin sister, Caroline.
4 *Recall of character traits*:
   Describe Louise's response to the story about the birth of the twins, Louise and Caroline.
   Why did the people living on the island consider Wallace a coward?
   How does Grandma respond to Caroline, to Louise, to Captain Wallace, to her son, and to her daughter-in-law?

Questions That Stimulate Inference

When children infer an answer to a question, they go beyond the information the author provides and hypothesize about such things as details, main ideas, sequence of events that might have led to an occurrence, and cause-and-effect relationships. Inference is usually considered a higher-level thought process; the answers are not specifically stated within the text. Examples of inferential questions include the following:

1 *Inferring supporting details*:
   At the end of *Jacob Have I Loved*, Joseph Wojtkiewicz says "God in heaven's been raising you for this valley from the day you were born." What do you believe he meant by this statement?
2 *Inferring main idea*:
   What do you believe is the theme of the book? What message do you think the author was trying to express to the reader?
3 *Inferring comparisons*:
   Think about the Captain Wallace, who is such a part of Louise's story. Compare that character with the one who left the island when he was a young man. How do you believe they are alike and how do you believe they are different?
4 *Inferring cause-and-effect relationships*:
   If you identified any changes in Captain Wallace, what do you believe might have caused them?
   Why do you believe Louise dreamed about Caroline's death?
   Why do you believe she felt wild exultation and then terrible guilt after these dreams?
5 *Inferring character traits*:
   What do you believe caused Louise to change her mind about wanting Hiram Wallace to be an islander who escaped rather than a Nazi spy? What is Louise saying about herself when she emphasizes the word *escaped*?
   Why do you believe Louise became so upset whenever she was called "Wheeze"?
   Why do you think Louise was so upset when Call invited Caroline to join Call and Louise during their visit to the captain?
   At the end of the book, after Louise has delivered twins to a mountain family, she becomes very anxious over the healthier twin. Why do you think she gave this advice, "You should hold him. Hold him as much as you can. Or let his mother hold him" (p. 215)? What does

this reaction say about Louise's own character and the changes in character that took place in her lifetime?

6 *Inferring outcomes*:

There were several places in the book when the action and outcome of the story might have changed if characters had acted in different ways. (Students can read or listen to the book up to a certain point and predict what the outcome will be.)

At the end of chapter four, a mysterious man leaves the boat and walks alone toward an abandoned house. Who do you think he is? How do you think this man will influence the story?

At the end of chapter twelve, Caroline finds and uses Louise's hidden hand lotion. What do you think will happen after Louise angrily breaks the bottle and runs out of the house?

At the close of chapter fourteen, the captain has offered to send Caroline to Baltimore to continue her musical education. How do you think Caroline, her parents, and Louise will react to this suggestion?

At the end of chapter seventeen, Louise and the captain are discussing what she plans to do with her life. Louise responds that she wants to become a doctor but cannot leave her family. Knowing Louise and her family, how do you think the story will end?

Questions That Encourage Evaluation

Evaluative questions require children to make judgments about the content of the literature by comparing it with external criteria such as what authorities on a subject say or internal criteria such as the reader's own experience or knowledge. The following are examples of evaluative questions:

1 *Judgment of adequacy or validity*:

Do you agree that Louise in *Jacob Have I Loved* would not have been accepted as a student in a medical college? Why or why not? This story took place in the 1940s; would the author have been able to include the same scene between a woman and a university advisor if the story had taken place in the 1980s? Why or why not?

2 *Judgment of appropriateness*:

What do you think the author meant by the reference to the quote, "Jacob have I loved, but Esau have I hated." How does this biblical

line relate to the book? Do you think it is a good title for the book? Why or why not?

3 *Judgment of worth, desirability, or acceptability*:

Was Louise right in her judgment that her parents always favored Caroline? What caused her to reach her final decision? Do you believe Louise made the right decision when she left the island? Why or why not?

Questions That Stimulate Appreciation

Appreciation of literature requires a heightening of sensitivity to the techniques authors use in order to create an emotional impact on their readers. Questions can encourage children to respond emotionally to the plot, identify with the characters, react to an author's use of language, and react to an author's ability to create a visual image through the choice of words in the text. The following are examples of questions that stimulate appreciation:

1 *Emotional response to plot or theme*:

How did you respond to the plot of *Jacob Have I Loved*? Did the author hold your interest? If so, how?

Do you believe the theme of the story was worthwhile? Why or why not? Pretend you are either recommending this book for someone else to read or recommending that this book not be read; what would you tell that person?

2 *Identification with characters and incidents*:

Have you ever felt, or known anyone who felt, like thirteen-year-old Louise or her twin sister, Caroline? What caused you or the person to feel that way?

How would you have reacted if you were thirteen-year-old Louise? How would you have reacted if you were Caroline?

Pretend to be a grown-up Louise in chapter eighteen talking with your mother about leaving the island. What emotions do you think your mother would feel when you respond, "I'm not going to rot here like Grandma" (p. 200)? How would you feel when she told you, "I chose to leave my own people and build a life for myself somewhere else. I certainly wouldn't deny you that same choice. But . . . oh, Louise, we will miss you, your father and I" (p. 201)?

3 *Imagery*:

How did the author encourage you to see the relationship between the island setting and the mountain-locked valley? Close your eyes and try to picture each setting. How are they alike? How are they different?

Pretend that you are Louise telling Joseph Wojtkiewicz about your island (p. 208). Describe the island so he and his daughters can see a land that is both similar to, and different from, their own valley.

These examples are not organized according to any sequence for presentation to children, but they do exemplify the range of questions that are considered when the teacher's focus is on strengthening children's reading comprehension abilities.

Oral Questioning Strategies That Focus, Extend, Clarify, and Raise Comprehension

Research suggests an effective order for presenting comprehension questions to children. Adults find the research reported by Robert Ruddell (13) helpful when designing questions that encourage children to focus upon certain aspects of literature. Strategies that encourage children to *focus* their attention, *extend* their answer, *clarify* a response, and *raise* the level of response have been proven, according to Ruddell, to be the most significant vehicles for effectively developing children's comprehension. These strategies, combined with questions developed around a taxonomy, provide a useful guide for adults who wish to increase their ability to lead oral discussions that encourage children to respond on several levels of reading comprehension. The following definitions of each strategy and examples are developed around the literal, inferential, evaluative, and appreciative questions from *Jacob Have I Loved*:

1   *Focusing*: Focusing questions allow children to center their attention upon a purpose for listening to or reading a story. They provide the mental set for the oral discussion that follows and often bring attention to the factual information in a story that must be understood before children can answer an inference question, provide an evaluation of what has been read, or respond emotionally to the theme, characters, and plot.
Literal recall of character traits: Louise's mother and grandmother often tell about the

birth of the twins. Describe Louise's response to this story.

2   *Extending*: If the focus question has not provided the desired answer or included sufficient information, the adult should ask an extending question so that children can provide additional information on the subject. The subject and comprehension level of the extending question are the same as those of the focusing question. Questions such as "Is there anything else you can tell about the subject?" or "Who has another idea about ———?" allow an adult to probe further.
Literal recall of character traits: Who could give another idea about Caroline's refusing to breathe, the midwife trying to get her to breathe, and how happy everyone was when Caroline let out her first cry?

3   *Clarifying*: A clarifying question encourages children to explain or rephrase previous information if the answer is unclear or if they have misinterpreted the question. An adult may ask children to return to a previous comment in order to explain or rephrase their answer. Sometimes it is necessary to go to a lower level of comprehension in order to clarify a statement. Questions such as "Do you mean that ———?" or "Could you explain in more detail what happened to ———?" encourage children to rethink or clarify a point.
Literal recall of character traits: Explain in more detail Louise's emotions when she hears about the attention paid to Caroline while she lies in a basket.

4   *Raising*: A raising strategy allows an adult to obtain additional information on the same subject but at a higher level of comprehension. The adult can ask questions that shift the focus from a factual to an inferential level of comprehension or from a factual or inferential level to an evaluative or appreciative level.
Raising from literal recall of character traits to inferring character traits: At the end of this book, after Louise has delivered twins to a mountain family, she becomes very anxious about the healthier twin. Why do you think she advised, "You should hold him. Hold him as much as you can. Or let his mother hold him" (p. 215)? What does this reaction to the baby tell about Louise's character and the

changes in her character that took place in her lifetime?

Raising to appreciative comprehension, identification with characters and incidents: Have you ever felt or known anyone who felt like thirteen-year-old Louise when she listened to the story about her birth and thought, "I felt cold all over, as though I was the newborn infant a second time, cast aside and forgotten"? (p. 15) How would you have reacted if you were Louise and heard this story repeatedly? What experience do you think could make you feel "cold all over" if you were Caroline and heard this story?

SUMMARY

Activities suggested in this chapter stress the expansion of children's reactions to realistic fiction through role playing, bibliotherapy, units around survival literature, activities designed to overcome stereotypes about males and females, and questioning strategies.

The plots in realistic fiction provide many opportunities to role play problem situations, allowing children to learn more about their world and how they might solve problems. Adults may use literature to provide a stimulus for role playing either by reading to a certain point and having children role play the unfinished situation, or by having children role play various solutions to problems after reading or listening to the whole story. Realistic fiction is also a means of allowing individuals to gain insights into their own problems through bibliotherapy.

The plots found in survival literature suggest both the physical survival and increased emotional maturity of the main characters. The stories also stress the importance of a setting that may create the major conflicts in the stories. An island survival unit and a unit around survival in mountains, canyons, and tundra suggest the importance of setting and how it may also be used to reinforce the science curriculum.

Researchers recommend that adults counteract stereotypic behavior and occupations found in some basal readers and children's literature by initiating corrective action, reviewing stories, and providing a balanced portrayal of the contributions and roles of both females and males. Children's literature provides one source of material for creating this balance.

The chapter concluded with examples of questioning strategies developed around a comprehensive taxonomy.

Suggested Activities for Children's Appreciation of Realistic Fiction

☐ Using the criteria for selecting appropriate literature for role playing, develop a file of stories that have problem situations appropriate for elementary school children. Include stories that can be used by reading to a certain point and allowing children to role play possible solutions, as well as stories that are more appropriate for role playing after an entire story has been read. Choose a role-playing situation and lead a role-playing activity with either a group of children or a peer group.

☐ Listen to several children tell you about a book they have read. Analyze the children's responses using Chart 9–2, "Classifying Children's Comments about Books."

☐ Choose a survival book listed on the "Survival on Islands" web. Develop instructional activities for the book that correspond with the web. Suggested books include *Call It Courage*, *The Cay*, *The Swiss Family Robinson*, *My Side of the Mountain*, *River Rats, Inc.*, or *Julie of the Wolves*.

☐ Review the stories in a basal reader, and evaluate their content according to stereotypic roles for either males or females. Assume that some corrective action might be required if a balanced portrayal of contributions of males and females is to occur, and identify several children's literature selections that could be used to balance a viewpoint. How could the literature be used in an instructional setting?

☐ Identify a list of children's literature sources that show many behavioral patterns for boys and girls, men and women.

☐ Develop a bibliography of books that illustrate nonstereotypic behavioral patterns in boys and girls. Write a short summary to describe the behavioral patterns that are shown in each book.

☐ Choose a realistic fiction book other than *Jacob Have I Loved*. Develop questioning strategies that follow a taxonomy of comprehension such as that developed by Thomas C. Barrett or Benjamin Bloom.

References

1 Applebee, Arthur S. "Children and Stories: Learning the Rules of the Game." *Language Arts* 56 (Sept. 1979).

2 Barrett, Thomas C. "Taxonomy of Reading Comprehension." In *Reading 360 Monograph*. Lexington, Mass.: Ginn, 1972.

3 Bernstein, Joanne. *Books to Help Children Cope with Separation and Loss*. New York: Bowker, 1977.

4 Bloom, Benjamin. *Taxonomy of Educational Objectives*. New York: Longmans, 1956.

5 Braga, Laurie, and Braga, Joseph. *Learning and Growing: A Guide to Child Development*. Englewood Cliffs, N. J.: Prentice-Hall, 1975.

6 Flender, Mary G. "Charting Book Discussions: A Method of Presenting Literature in the Elementary Grades." *Children's Literature in Education* 16 (Summer 1985): 84–92.

7 Gibbons, Euell. *Stalking the Wild Asparagus*. New York: McKay, 1962, 1970.

8 Good, Carter. *Dictionary of Education*. New York: McGraw-Hill, 1969, 1973.

9 Moody, Mildred, and Limper, Hilda. *Bibliotherapy: Methods and Materials*. Chicago: American Library Association, 1971.

10 Norton, Donna E. "The Expansion and Evaluation of a Multiethnic Reading/Language Arts Program Designed for 5th, 6th, 7th, and 8th Grade Children," Meadows Foundation Grant, No. 55614, A Three Year Longitudinal Study. Texas A&M University, 1984–1987.

11 Pringle, Laurence. *Wild Foods: A Beginner's Guide to Identifying, Harvesting and Preparing Safe and Tasty Plants from the Outdoors*. Illustrated by Paul Breeden. New York: Four Winds, 1978.

12 Purves, Alan C., and Monson, Dianne L. *Experiencing Children's Literature*. Glenview, Ill.: Scott, Foresman, 1984.

13 Ruddell, Robert B. "Developing Comprehension Abilities: Implications from Research for an Instructional Framework." In *What Research Has to Say about Reading Instruction*, edited by S. J. Samuels. Newark, Del.: International Reading Association, 1978.

14 Rosenblatt, Louise. *The Reader, The Text, and the Poem: The Transactional Theory of the Literary Work*. Carbondale, Ill.: Southern Illinois University Press, 1978.

15 Sadker, Myra Pollack, and Sadker, David Miller. *Now upon a Time: A Contemporary View of Children's Literature*. New York: Harper & Row, 1977.

16 Shaftel, Fannie R., and Shaftel, George. *Role-Playing for Social Values: Decision-Making in the Social Studies*. Englewood Cliffs, N. J.: Prentice-Hall, 1967.

17 Sutherland, Zena, and Arbuthnot, May Hill. *Children and Books*. Glenview, Ill.: Scott, Foresman, 1981.

CHILDREN'S LITERATURE

Amdur, Nikki. *One of Us*. Illustrated by Ruth Sanderson. Dial, 1981. (I:9–12+ R:5). A blind boy and caring for a rabbit help a girl adjust to a new school.

Bauer, Marion Dane. *Foster Child*. Seabury, 1977 (I:12+ R:6). A foster child suffers child abuse.

Bawden, Nina. *Kept in the Dark*. Lothrop, Lee & Shepard, 1982 (I:10+ R:7). A psychological thriller results when a previously unknown relative returns.

———. *The Peppermint Pig*. Lippincott, 1975 (I:9–12 R:6). A family moves to rural Norfolk, England.

———. *The Robbers*. Lothrop, Lee & Shepard, 1979 (I:8–12 R:5). Philip leaves the security of his grandmother's rural castle home to live with his remarried father in London.

Baylor, Byrd. *Hawk, I'm Your Brother*. Illustrated by Peter Parnall. Scribner's 1976 (I:all). Rudy Soto would like to glide through the air like a hawk.

Benjamin, Carol Lea. *The Wicked Stepdog*. Crowell, 1982 (I:9–12 R:4). A twelve-year-old girl fears she is losing her father's love when he remarries.

Billington, Elizabeth. *Part-Time Boy*. Illustrated by Dianede Groat. Warne, 1979 (I:8–12 R:5). A director of a natural science center helps a ten-year-old accept himself.

Blume, Judy. *Are You There God? It's Me, Margaret*. Bradbury, 1970 (I:10+ R:6). Eleven-year-old Margaret wonders about the changes that are occurring in her body.

———. *Blubber*. Bradbury, 1974 (I:10+ R:4). The children in the fifth grade start a campaign against a heavier girl in the class.

———. *The One in the Middle is the Green Kangaroo*. Illustrated by Amy Aitken. Bradbury, 1981 (I:6–9 R:2). A middle child gains self-esteem when he gets a part in a play.

———. *Otherwise Known as Sheila the Great*. Dutton, 1972 (I:9–12 R:6). Ten-year-old Sheila experiences an exciting summer.

———. *Tales of a Fourth Grade Nothing*. Illustrated by Roy Doty. Dutton, 1972 (I:7–12 R:4). Peter's problem is his two-year-old brother, Fudge.

———. *Tiger Eyes*. Bradbury, 1981. (I:12+ R:7). A fifteen-year-old girl faces violence and fear.

Bonham, Frank. *Durango Street*. Dutton, 1965 (I:12+ R:5). Gang violence is realistically portrayed as two inner-city gangs cut out their territories.

———. *The Rascals from Haskell's Gym*. Dutton, 1977 (I:10+ R:6). Two gymnastic teams compete in this story about girls' sports.

Branscum, Robbie. *The Adventures of Johnny May*. Illustrated by Deborah Howland. Harper, 1984 (I:8–12 R:6). A girl solves a mystery and provides Christmas for her grandparents.

Bridgers, Sue Ellen. *All Together Now*. Knopf, 1979 (I:11+ R:7). When a twelve-year-old spends the summer with her grandparents, she finds a new circle of friends.

Brooks, Bruce. *The Moves Make the Man*. Harper, 1984 (I:10+ R:7). Basketball develops understanding between a black and a white boy.

Buchan, Stuart. *When We Lived with Pete*. Scribner's, 1978. (I:12+ R:6). Tommy Bridge makes the final move that gives him the family he wants.

Bunting, Eve. *The Empty Window*. Illustrated by Judy Clifford. Warne, 1980 (I:7–10 R:3). A boy captures a wild parrot to give to his best friend who has only a short time to live.

Burch, Robert. *Queenie Peavy*. Illustrated by Jerry Lazare, Viking, 1966 (I:10+ R:6). A strong female character longs for the day when her father will return from jail, but then discovers his true nature.

Burnford, Sheila. *The Incredible Journey*. Illustrated by Carl Burger. Little, Brown, 1960, 1961 (I:8+ R:8). Three animals travel through 250 miles of Canadian wilderness.

Byars, Betsy. *After the Goat Man*. Illustrated by Ronald Himler, Viking, 1974 (I:9–12 R:7). An overweight boy meets a man who is trying to protect his home from an advancing interstate highway.

———. *The Animal, The Vegetable, and John D. Jones*. Illustrated by Ruth Sanderson. Delacorte, 1982 (I:9–12 R:5). Three children come into conflict when their single parents share a vacation.

———. *Cracker Jackson*. Viking, 1985 (I:10+ R:6). An eleven-year-old boy tries to save his former baby sitter from abuse by her husband.

———. *The Cybil War*. Illustrated by Gail Owens, Viking, 1981 (I:9–12 R:6). Two fourth graders battle for a girl's affections.

———. *The 18th Emergency*. Illustrated by Robert Grossman. Viking, 1973 (I:8–12 R:3). Problems arise from insulting the biggest boy in school.

I = Interest by age range;
R = Readability by grade level.

———. *Good-bye, Chicken Little*. Harper & Row, 1979 (I:10+ R:7). Jimmy feels guilty because he thinks he didn't try hard enough to keep his uncle from walking across thin ice.

———. *The House of Wings*. Illustrated by Daniel Schwartz. Viking, 1972 (I:8–12 R:3). A transformation takes place as Sammy, with the help of a blind crane, learns to love his grandfather.

———. *The Night Swimmers*. Illustrated by Troy Howell. Delacorte, 1980 (I:8–12 R:5). An older sister tries to care for her brothers while her father works nights.

———. *The Summer of the Swans*. Illustrated by Ted CoConis. Viking, 1970 (I:8–12 R:4). A mentally disabled boy goes out alone in search of the wild swans.

Callen, Larry. *Sorrow's Song*. Illustrated by Marvin Friedman. Little, Brown, 1979 (I:8–10 R:3). A young girl who cannot talk takes care of a wounded whooping crane.

Cameron, Eleanor. *Julia's Magic*. Illustrated by Gail Owens, Dutton, 1984 (I:9–12 R:5). Julia causes difficulty when she breaks a perfume bottle.

———. *That Julia Redfern*. Illustrated by Gail Owens. Dutton, 1982 (I:9–12 R:5). A book about Julia is based on experiences when she is younger.

Carrick, Carol. *The Accident*. Illustrated by Donald Carrick. Seabury, 1976 (I:5–8 R:4). Christopher experiences a series of emotions after his dog is killed.

Christopher, Matt. *Dirt Bike Racer*. Illustrated by Barry Bomzer. Little, Brown, 1979 (I:10+ R:4). Twelve-year-old Ron Baker restores a minibike.

———. *Face-Off*. Illustrated by Harvey Kidder. Little, Brown, 1972 (I:8–12 R:4). Scott Harrison must overcome a tremendous fear about a hockey player.

———. *Football Fugitive*. Illustrated by Larry Johnson. Little, Brown, 1976 (I:9–12 R:6). Larry wishes his father would take an interest in football.

———. *The Fox Steals Home*. Illustrated by Larry Johnson. Little, Brown, 1978 (I:8–12 R:6). Baseball helps a boy overcome his worries about his parents' divorce.

———. *The Twenty-One-Mile Swim*. Little, Brown, 1979 (I:10+ R:5). A boy of small stature decides that he will swim the twenty-one miles across the lake.

Cleary, Beverly. *Dear Mr. Henshaw*. Illustrated by Paul O. Zelinsky, Morrow, 1983 (I:9–12 R:5). Corresponding with an author helps a boy overcome problems related to his parents' divorce.

———. *Henry and Beezus*. Illustrated by Louis Darling. Morrow, 1952 (I:7–10 R:6). Henry and the girl he finds least obnoxious have a humorously good time.

———. *Mitch and Amy*. Illustrated by George Porter. Morrow, 1967 (I:7–10 R:6). A humorous story about everyday experiences.

———. *Ramona and Her Father*. Illustrated by Alan Tiegreen. Morrow, 1977 (I:7–10 R:6). Ramona tries to help her father through a trying period after he has lost his job.

———. *Ramona and Her Mother*. Illustrated by Alan Tiegreen. Morrow, 1979 (I:7–10 R:6). Ramona's mother goes to work.

———. *Ramona the Brave*. Illustrated by Alan Tiegreen. Morrow, 1975 (I:7–10 R:6). Ramona has many difficulties until she finally wins a truce with the first-grade teacher.

———. *Ramona the Pest*. Illustrated by Louis Darling. Morrow, 1968 (I:7–10 R:4). Ramona enters kindergarten and spreads exasperation into a wider sphere.

———. *Ramona Quimby, Age 8*. Illustrated by Alan Tiegreen. Morrow, 1981 (I:7–10 R:6). Ramona faces new challenges when her father returns to college.

Cleaver, Vera, and Cleaver, Bill. *I Would Rather Be a Turnip*. Lippincott, 1971 (I:11+ R:6). Changes occur in twelve-year-old Annie's life when her illegitimate nephew comes to live with her family.

———. *Lady Ellen Grae*. Illustrated by Ellen Raskin. Lippincott, 1968 (I:8–12 R:6). An eleven-year-old tomboy goes to Seattle so she can learn to be a lady.

———. *A Little Destiny*. Lothrop, Lee & Shepard, 1979 (I:12+ R:6). When Lucy decides to avenge her father's death, she discovers that her destiny is a matter of her own choosing.

———. *Me Too*. Lippincott, 1973 (I:10–14 R:7). Lydia tries to educate her mentally disabled sister so that she will not be different.

———. *Queen of Hearts*. Lippincott, 1978 (I:11+ R:6). Twelve-year-old Wilma makes discoveries about herself and her grandmother.

———. *Trial Valley*. Lippincott, 1977 (I:11+ R:5). In a sequel to *Where the Lilies Bloom*, Mary Call struggles to keep the family together.

———. *Where the Lilies Bloom*. Illustrated by Jim Spanfeller. Lippincott, 1969 (I:11+ R:5). Four children hide their father's death so they can remain together.

Clymer, Eleanor. *The Get-Away Car*. Dutton, 1978 (I:8–12 R:3). A humorous story about a resourceful grandmother who solves her granddaughter's and her own problems.

Cohen, Barbara. *Thank You, Jackie Robinson*. Illustrated by Richard Cuffari. Lothrop, Lee & Shepard, 1974 (I:10+ R:6). Sam and a sixty-year-old black man become best friends because of their interest in baseball.

Colman, Hila. *Tell Me No Lies*. Crown, 1978 (I:10+ R:5). Twelve-year-old Angela reacts to her illegitimacy with anger and resentment.

Conford, Ellen. *The Revenge of the Incredible Dr. Rancid and His Youthful Assistant, Jeffrey*. Little, Brown, 1980 (I:10+ R:4). A small, skinny boy discovers a way to become a superhero and overcome the class bully.

Corcoran, Barbara. *You're Allegro Dead*. Atheneum, 1981 (I:10+ R:5). Twelve-year-old friends encounter a mystery at a summer camp.

Cormier, Robert. *The Bumblebee Flies Anyway*. Pantheon, 1983 (I:14+ R:6). A sixteen-year-old boy faces illness in a terminal care facility.

Creswell, Helen. *Absolute Zero: Being the Second Part of the Bagthorpe Saga*. Macmillan, 1978 (I:8–12 R:6). The Bagthorpes began competing in their efforts to win contests.

———. *Bagthorpes Abroad*. Macmillan, 1984 (I:8–10 R:6). The family vacations in a dilapidated, maybe ghostly, house in Wales.

———. *Bagthorpes Unlimited*. Macmillan, 1978 (I:8–12 R:6). The Bagthorpes try to set a new world record.

———. *Bagthorpes v. the World: Being the Fourth Part of the Bagthorpe Saga*. Macmillan, 1979 (I:8–12 R:6). An overdraft notice from the bank sends the Bagthorpes into a chaotic survival campaign.

———. *Ordinary Jack*. Macmillan, 1977 (I:8–12 R:6). The first book in the series about the humorous Bagthorpes.

Cunningham, Julia. *Burnish Me Bright*. Illustrated by Don Freeman. Pantheon, 1970 (I:8–12 R:8). A mute boy in a French village is taught to pantomime by a retired actor and then is persecuted by the villagers.

———. *Come to the Edge*. Pantheon, 1977 (I:12+ R:7). A psychological story about a fourteen-year-old boy who must discover the will to love.

———. *Dorp Dead*. Illustrated by James Spanfeller. Pantheon, 1965 (I:11+

R:7). A complicated psychological novel about an eleven-year-old orphan who faces evil.

———. *The Silent Voice*. Dutton, 1981 (I:10+ R:8). A teenage mute boy is helped by a group of Parisian performers and a famous mime.

DeJong, Meindert. *Shadrach*. Illustrated by Maurice Sendak. Harper & Row, 1953 (I:8–10 R:4). A boy in the Netherlands tries to sneak away from his protective mother and grandmother.

———. *The Wheel on the School*. Illustrated by Maurice Sendak. Harper & Row, 1954 (I:10+ R:6). The children of Shora, Netherlands, make a home for storks.

Desbarats, Peter. *Gabrielle and Selena*. Illustrated by Nancy Grossman. Harcourt Brace Jovanovich, 1968 (I:5–8 R:4). A story of interracial friendship.

Dicks, Terrance. *The Baker Street Irregulars in the Case of the Crooked Kids*. Elsevier/Nelson, 1981 (I:10+ R:6). The youthful detectives capture a ring of juvenile thieves.

———. *The Baker Street Irregulars in the Case of the Ghost Grabbers*. Elsevier/Nelson, 1981 (I:10+ R:6). A haunted house provides the setting.

———. *The Baker Street Irregulars in the Case of the Blackmail Boys*. Elsevier/Nelson, 1981 (I:10+ R:6). A group of London youngsters outwit criminals.

———. *The Baker Street Irregulars in the Case of the Cinema Swindle*. Elsevier/Nelson, 1981 (I:10+ R:6). A boy uses techniques developed by Sherlock Holmes to solve a mystery.

———. *The Baker Street Irregulars in the Case of the Cop Catchers*. Dutton, 1982 (I:10+ R:6). The amateur detectives solve the case of the disappearance of a police sergeant.

Domke, Todd. *Grounded*. Knopf, 1982 (I:9–12 R:5). A sixth grader involves his classmates in a play so he can earn money to build a glider.

Dubellar, Thea. *Maria*. Translated by Anthea Bell. Illustrated by Mance Post. Morrow, 1982 (I:9–12 R:5). A girl retains her sense of self even though she experiences many family problems.

Enright, Elizabeth. *Thimble Summer*. Holt, Rinehart & Winston, 1938, 1966 (I:7–12 R:5). Nine-year-old Garnet spends the summer on her Wisconsin farm.

Estes, Eleanor. *The Moffats*. Illustrated by Louis Slobodkin. Harcourt Brace Jovanovich, 1941 (I:7–10 R:4). The happy Moffat children experience a series of adventures.

Farber, Norma. *How Does It Feel to Be Old?* Illustrated by Trina Schart Hyman. Dutton, 1979 (I:5–8 R:2). A grandmother tells her granddaughter about the good and bad experiences related to growing old.

Farley, Walter. *The Black Stallion*. Illustrated by Keith Ward. Random House, 1944 (I:8+ R:3). The black stallion saves Alec's life.

———. *The Black Stallion Picture Book*. Photographs furnished by United Artists. Random House, 1979 (I:6–8 R:2). A picture storybook version of *The Black Stallion*.

———. *The Black Stallion Returns*. Random House, 1945, 1973 (I:8+ R:3). Alec learns the history of the horse and finds himself in the center of a blood feud and an important race.

Fassler, Joan. *Howie Helps Himself*. Illustrated by Joe Lasker. Whitman, 1974 (I:4–8 R:2). A child with cerebral palsy tries very hard to move his wheelchair by himself.

Fitzhugh, Louise. *Harriet the Spy*. Harper & Row, 1964 (I:8–12 R:3). Eleven-year-old Harriet keeps a notebook of observations about people.

———. *The Long Secret*. Harper & Row, 1965 (I:8–12 R:3). A sequel to the above book.

———. *Sport*. Delacorte, 1979 (I:8–12 R:3). When eleven-year-old Sport inherits $20 million, his mother appears and tries to get the money.

Fox, Paula. *The Moonlight Man*. Bradbury, 1986 (I:12+ R:5). A girl makes discoveries about herself and her father after her parents' divorce.

———. *One-Eyed Cat*. Bradbury, 1984 (I:10+ R:5). An eleven-year-old boy shoots a cat and then must face his guilt.

George, Jean Craighead. *The Cry of the Crow*. Harper & Row, 1980 (I:10+ R:5). Mandy must make a choice when her pet crow attacks her brother.

———. *Julie of the Wolves*. Illustrated by John Schoenherr. Harper & Row, 1972 (I:10+ R:7). An Eskimo girl lost on the North Slope of Alaska survives with the help of wolves.

———. *My Side of the Mountain*. Dutton, 1959 (I:10+ R:6). Sam Gribley creates a home inside of a rotted out tree.

———. *River Rats, Inc*. Dutton, 1979 (I:10+ R:7). Two boys must survive with the help of a wild boy, a canyon, and the desert beyond.

Gerson, Corinne. *Son for a Day*. Illustrated by Velma Ilsley. Atheneum, 1980 (I:7–11 R:4). A humorous story

about a boy who joins divorced fathers who bring their children to the zoo.

Gipson, Fred. *Curly and the Wild Boar*. Illustrated by Ronald Himler. Harper & Row, 1979 (I:10+ R:7). Curly is determined to kill the wild boar that smashed his prize melon.

———. *Old Yeller*. Illustrated by Carl Burger. Harper & Row, 1956 (I:10+ R:6). Old Yeller is bitten by a rabid wolf as he saves the lives of those he loves.

Graeber, Charlotte. *Mustard*. Illustrated by Donna Diamond. Macmillan, 1982 (I:7–10 R:4). A boy faces the death of his beloved fourteen-year-old cat.

Greenberg, Jan. *The Iceberg and Its Shadow*. Farrar, Straus & Giroux, 1980 (I:9–14 R:6). A story of peer manipulation and victimization similar to Judy Blume's *Blubber*.

Greene, Constance. *Al(exandra) the Great*. Viking, 1982 (I:8–12 R:3). A girl's vacation plans are changed when her mother gets pneumonia.

———. *Beat the Turtle Drum*. Illustrated by Donna Diamond. Viking, 1976 (I:10+ R:7). After an accident the family must cope with Joss's death.

———. *The Ears of Louis*. Illustrated by Nola Langner. Viking, 1974 (I:8–12 R:3). Louis tries many solutions to his big ears before he discovers that he has many desirable characteristics and skills.

———. *The Unmaking of Rabbit*. Viking, 1972 (I:10+ R:5). Eleven-year-old Paul is teased about his big ears and his stuttering.

Greenwald, Sheila. *Give Us a Great Big Smile, Rosy Cole*. Little, Brown, 1981 (I:8–10 R:4). Rosy's uncle decides he will base a book on his niece and her violin.

Griffiths, Helen. *The Dancing Horses*. Holiday, 1982 (I:10+ R:6). A poor boy struggles to realize his dreams in post–Civil War Spain.

———. *Running-Wild*. Illustrated by Victor Ambrus. Holiday. 1977 (I:10+ R:6). A boy discovers the tragic results when two dogs grow wild in the forest.

Gripe, Maria. *Elvis and His Secret*. Illustrated by Harald Gripe. Delacorte, 1972, 1976 (I:9–12 R:5). A shy six-year-old has difficulty communicating with his parents.

Haas, Jessie. *Keeping Barney*. Greenwillow, 1982 (I:9–12 R:5). A girl gets a chance to care for a horse and tries to win his devotion.

Hall, Lynn. *Danza!* Scribner's 1981 (I:10–14 R:5). A boy's care for a horse helps his own personal development in a story set in Puerto Rico.

Hamilton, Virginia. *The Planet of Junior Brown*. Macmillan, 1971 (I:12+ R:6). Three outcasts from society create their own world in a secret basement room.

Harris, Rosemary. *Zed*. Farber & Farber, 1982 (I:12+ R:7). An eight-year-old boy is held by terrorists in London.

Haugen, Tormod. *The Night Birds*. Translated from the Norwegian by Sheila La Farge. Delacorte, 1982 (I:10+ R:3). A seven-year-old boy faces real and imagined terrors.

Hautzig, Esther. *A Gift for Mama*. Illustrated by Donna Diamond. Viking, 1981 (I:8–10 R:4). Sarah mends clothing to earn money for a Mother's Day gift.

Henry, Marguerite. *Black Gold*. Illustrated by Wesley Dennis. Rand McNally, 1957 (I:8–12 R:6). The history of a great racing horse named Black Gold and the trainer and jockey who loved him.

———. *Justin Morgan Had a Horse*. Illustrated by Wesley Dennis. Rand McNally, 1954 (I:8–12 R:6). The story of how Little Bub inherited the name of his owner Justin Morgan.

———. *King of the Wind*. Illustrated by Wesley Dennis. Rand McNally, 1948, 1976 (I:8–12 R:6). The story of the great Godolphin Arabian who was the ancestor of Man o' War.

———. *Misty of Chincoteague*. Illustrated by Wesley Dennis. Rand McNally, 1947, 1963 (I:8–12 R:6). Misty is the descendant of the Spanish horses that swam to Assateague Island after a shipwreck.

———. *San Domingo: The Medicine Hat Stallion*. Illustrated by Robert Lougheed. Rand McNally, 1972 (I:9–14 R:4). A boy's greatest joy is his foal with the markings believed sacred by the Indians.

Hopkins, Lee Bennett. *Mama*. Knopf, 1977 (I:7–10 R:6). A boy worries about his mother and tries to change her.

Houston, James. *Long Claws: An Arctic Adventure*. Atheneum, 1981 (I:8–10 R:6). Two Eskimo children go across the tundra in order to bring food to their starving family.

Hunt, Irene. *Up a Road Slowly*. Follett, 1966 (I:11+ R:7). The story of a girl's life and the influence of an aunt with whom she stays after her mother dies.

Keller, Beverly. *No Beasts! No Children!* Lothrop, Lee & Shepard, 1983 (I:8–

12 R:4). A father, his children, and their pets cope by themselves.

Kjelgaard, Jim. *Big Red*. Illustrated by Bob Kuhn. Holiday, 1945, 1956 (I:10+ R:7). Danny trains a champion Irish setter.

Klein, Norma. *Mom, the Wolf Man and Me*. Pantheon, 1972 (I:12+ R:6). Eleven-year-old Brett loves her life with her lively unwed mother.

———. *Tomboy*. Four Winds, 1978 (I:9–12 R:4). Ten-year-old Antonia doesn't want to grow up and experience the changes that naturally happen to a girl.

Konigsburg, E. L. *About the B'nai Bagels*. Atheneum, 1969 (I:8–12 R:7). Mark Setzer has special problems with his little league baseball team: his mother is the manager, and his brother is the coach.

———. *From the Mixed-Up Files of Mrs. Basil Frankweiler*. Atheneum, 1967 (I:9–12 R:7). Eleven-year-old Claudia and her younger brother run away to the Metropolitan Museum of Art.

———. *(George)*. Atheneum, 1970, 1980 (I:10+ R:7). A story about a multiple personality and how the differences were resolved.

———. *Jennifer, Hecate, Macbeth, William McKinley, and Me, Elizabeth*. Atheneum, 1967, 1976 (I:8–12 R:4). Elizabeth becomes an apprentice witch in this story of interracial friendships.

———. *Journey to an 800 Number*. Atheneum, 1982 (I:10+ R:7). A boy learns to appreciate his father when he spends the summer with him.

———. *Throwing Shadows*. Atheneum, 1979 (I:11+ R:7). A collection of five short stories about people making discoveries about themselves.

L'Engle, Madeleine. *Meet the Austins*. Vanguard, 1960 (I:10+ R:6). The six Austins have a family filled with spontaneous love, understanding, and personal discipline.

Lexau, Joan M. *Benjie on His Own*. Illustrated by Don Bolognese. Dial, 1970 (I:5–8 R:4). Benjie makes it home from school and helps his grandmother.

Little, Jean. *From Anna*. Illustrated by Joan Sandin. Harper & Row, 1972 (I:8–12 R:5). Nine-year-old Anna lives in a world blurred by poor eyesight until she is placed in a special class.

———. *Mine for Keeps*. Illustrated by Lewis Parker. Little, Brown, 1962 (I:8–12 R:4). A girl crippled by cerebral palsy leaves the security of a home for the physically disabled and returns to her own family.

———. *Take Wing*. Illustrated by Jerry Lazare. Little, Brown, 1968 (I:8–12 R:4). A boy cannot learn to read and is slow in learning to take care of himself.

London, Jack. *Call of the Wild*. Photographs by Seymour Linden. Harmony, 1977 (orig. 1903) (I:10+ R:5). The classic story of a brave dog and the Klondike gold rush.

Lowry, Lois. *Anastasia Again!* Illustrated by Diane deGroat. Houghton Mifflin, 1981. (I:8–12 R:6). Anastasia must adjust to living in the suburbs.

———. *Anastasia at Your Service*. Illustrated by Diane deGroat. Houghton Mifflin, 1982 (I:8–12 R:6). An older Anastasia becomes a household servant rather than a companion to a rich woman.

———. *Anastasia Krupnik*. Houghton Mifflin, 1979 (I:8–12 R:6). Ten-year-old Anastasia forms a hate list and a love list and discovers that eventually all of the items are on one list.

———. *Anastasia on Her Own*. Houghton Mifflin, 1985 (I:8–12 R:4). A humorous tale in which Anastasia takes over housekeeping when her mother leaves for a consulting job.

———. *The One Hundredth Thing About Caroline*. Houghton Mifflin, 1983 (I:8–12 R:3). An eleven-year old retaliates when she thinks she is to become the victim of murder.

McDonnell, Christine. *Don't Be Mad, Ivy*. Illustrated by Diane deGroat. Dial, 1981 (I:6–9 R:3). A young girl overcomes everyday problems connected with home and school.

McGraw, Eloise Jarvis. *The Money Room*. Atheneum, 1981 (I:10+ R:6). The mystery of possible hidden money adds to a tale of family survival after the father's death.

MacLachlan, Patricia. *Mama One, Mama Two*. Illustrated by Ruth Lercher Bornstein. Harper & Row, 1982 (I:4–8 R:3). A child has a happy foster home experience.

Madsen, Jane M. and Bockoras, Diane. *Please Don't Tease Me . . .* Illustrated by Kathleen T. Brinko. Judson, 1983 (I:6–9 R:6). A physically disabled girl asks for understanding.

Mann, Peggy. *My Dad Lives in a Downtown Hotel*. Illustrated by Richard Cuffari. Doubleday, 1973 (I:7–10 R:4). A boy experiences many emotions as he discovers that his parents are divorcing.

———. *There Are Two Kinds of Terrible*. Doubleday, 1977 (I:10+ R:5). A boy must face his mother's death.

Masterman-Smith, Virginia. *The Great Egyptian Heist*. Four Winds, 1982 (I:10+ R:5). Mystery surrounds diamonds found in an Egyptian coffin.

Mauser, Pat Rhoads. *A Bundle of Sticks*. Illustrated by Gail Owens. Atheneum, 1982 (I:9–12 R:5). An eleven-year-old is humiliated by a bully and takes self-defense lessons.

Moeri, Louise. *Downwind*. Dutton, 1984 (I:10+ R:7). A 12-year-old boy and his family escape a possible radiation leak at a nuclear power plant.

Myers, Walter Dean. *It Ain't All for Nothin'*. Viking, 1978 (I:10+ R:4). A boy's life changes drastically when he enters his father's world of crime and neglect.

Neville, Emily. *It's Like This, Cat*. Illustrated by Emil Weiss. Harper & Row, 1963 (I:8–12 R:6). David Mitchell has two best friends, an older boy and a stray tomcat.

Newman, Robert. *The Case of the Baker Street Irregular*. Atheneum, 1978 (I:10+ R:6). Kidnappings, bombings, and the mystery of the identity of Andrew's mother bring Andrew and Sherlock Holmes together.

———. *The Case of the Vanishing Corpse*. Atheneum, 1980 (I:10+ R:6). A series of incidents bring Andrew into contact with Constable Wyatt.

O'Dell, Scott. *Island of the Blue Dolphins*. Houghton Mifflin, 1960 (I:10+ R:6). Twelve-year-old Karana survives alone for eighteen years before a ship takes her to the California mainland.

Park, Barbara. *Don't Make Me Smile*. Knopf, 1981 (I:9–12 R:5). A ten-year-old boy reacts to his parents' divorce.

Paterson, Katherine. *Bridge to Terabithia*. Illustrated by Donna Diamond. Crowell, 1977 (I:10–14 R:6). Two nonconformists create their own magical realm.

———. *Come Sing, Jimmy Jo*. Dutton, 1985 (I:10+ R:4). An eleven-year-old boy makes self-discoveries through his musical gift.

———. *The Great Gilly Hopkins*. Crowell, 1978 (I:10+ R:6). A rebellious girl tries to adjust to abandonment and foster homes.

———. *Jacob Have I Loved*. Crowell, 1980 (I:10+ R:7). A twin feels that her sister has deprived her of parental affection and schooling.

Paulsen, Gary. *Dancing Carl*. Bradbury, 1983 (I:10+ R:4). Two boys learn to respect a war veteran who had a traumatic experience.

Peck, Richard. *Remembering the Good Times*. Delacorte, 1985 (I:12+ R:4).

A strong friendship develops among three students until one takes his own life.

Peyton, K.M. *The Team*. Crowell, 1976 (I:10+ R:5) A girl joins a pony club.

Phipson, Joan. *Hit and Run*. Atheneum, 1985 (I:10+ R:6). A survival story set in Australia.

———. *A Tide Flowing*. Atheneum, 1981 (I:10+ R:5). The friendship of a quadriplegic helps a young man cope with his mother's death and his father's rejection.

Rabe, Berniece. *The Balancing Girl*. Illustrations by Lillian Hoban. Dutton, 1981 (I:7–9 R:4). A physically disabled girl proves she is a capable person.

Rardin, Susan Lowry. *Captives in a Foreign Land*. Houghton, 1984 (I:10+ R:6). Six American children are held hostage.

Raskin, Ellen. *Figgs & Phantoms*. Dutton, 1974 (I:10+ R:5). An unusual family is constantly searching for Capri, their idea of heaven.

———. *The Mysterious Disappearance of Leon (I Mean Noel)*. Dutton, 1971 (I:10+ R:5). A word puzzle is used to solve the mystery of the disappearing Leon.

———. *The Westing Game*. Dutton, 1978 (I:10+ R:5). Sixteen heirs are invited to solve a riddle.

Rinkoff, Barbara. *The Watchers*. Knopf, 1972 (I:10+ R:6). Chris thought he could learn a lot about people by observing them from a distance.

Riskind, Mary. *Apple Is My Sign*. Houghton Mifflin, 1981 (I:9–12 R:5). A deaf boy goes to a school for the deaf in the early 1900s.

Robertson, Keith. *In Search of a Sandhill Crane*. Illustrated by Richard Cuffari. Viking, 1973 (I:10+ R:7). Link Keller searches the Michigan wilderness in order to photograph sandhill cranes.

Robinson, Veronica. *David in Silence*. Illustrated by Victor Ambrus. Lippincott, 1966 (I:8–12 R:7). A boy who was born deaf has difficulty making friends in a new town.

Roy, Ron. *Where's Buddy?* Illustrated by Troy Howell. Houghton Mifflin, 1982 (I:9–12 R:5). A diabetic boy becomes lost when his older brother does not look after him.

Sachs, Marilyn. *The Bears' House*. Illustrated by Louis Glanzman. Doubleday, 1971 (I:8–11 R:6). An unhappy fourth grader tries to cope with a sick mother and a deserted father.

———. *A December Tale*. Doubleday, 1976 (I:12+ R:7). The brutal world of child abuse is the topic of this book.

———. *A Secret Friend*. Doubleday, 1978 (I:8–12 R:4). Two best friends break their relationship after many years.

Schellie, Don. *Kidnapping Mr. Tubbs*. Four Winds, 1978 (I:12+ R:7). Two young people help an old cowboy who lives in a nursing home visit the ranch that had been so important to him.

Schick, Eleanor. *Joey on His Own*. Dial, 1982 (I:5–7 R:2). A young boy's pride increases when he goes to the grocery store by himself.

Shreve, Susan. *Family Secrets: Five Very Important Stories*. Illustrated by Richard Cuffari. Knopf, 1979 (I:8–10 R:7). A collection of five stories about five different family problems.

Slote, Alfred. *Hang Tough, Paul Mather*. Lippincott, 1973 (I:9–12 R:3). Baseball helps Paul Mather face his life when he discovers that he has an incurable blood disease.

Smith, Doris Buchanan. *Kelly's Creek*. Illustrated by Alan Tiegreen. Crowell, 1975 (I:7–10 R:4). A boy with a learning disability discovers that he has special skills.

Snyder, Zilpha Keatley. *The Changeling*. Illustrated by Alton Raible. Atheneum, 1970 (I:10+ R:7). Martha tells about her friendship with a girl who is very different from her own family.

———. *The Egypt Game*. Illustrated by Alton Raible. Atheneum, 1967 (I:10+ R:6). A group of sixth-grade children recreate the land of Ancient Egypt.

———. *The Famous Stanley Kidnapping Case*. Atheneum, 1979 (I:10+ R:7). Kidnappers hold the children for ransom in a deserted basement.

Sobol, Donald J. *Encyclopedia Brown Sets the Pace*. Illustrated by Ib Ohlsson. Scholastic/Four Winds, 1982 (I:7–10 R:5). A new series of cases to solve.

———. *Encyclopedia Brown Tracks Them Down*. Illustrated by Leonard Shortall. Crowell, 1971 (I:7–10 R:3). Clues and solutions make it possible for children to solve the mysteries.

Spence, Eleanor. *The Nothing Place*. Illustrated by Geraldine Spence. Harper & Row, 1973 (I:10+ R:6). Twelve-year-old Glen loses part of his hearing after an illness.

Sperry, Armstrong. *Call It Courage*. Macmillan, 1940 (I:9–13 R:6). A Polynesian boy travels alone in an outrigger canoe.

Stolz, Mary. *Cider Days*. Harper & Row, 1978 (I:8–12 R:6). A satisfying story about friendship between children who have different personalities and backgrounds.

————. *Ferris Wheel*. Harper & Row, 1977 (I:8–12 R:6). Polly Lewis is unhappy when her best friend moves away.

————. *What Time of Night Is It?* Harper & Row, 1981 (I:10+ R:6). Three children face problems when their mother leaves home.

Taylor, Sydney. *All-of-a-Kind Family*. Illustrated by Helen John. Follett, 1951 (I:7–10 R:4). Five girls live with their parents on New York's East Side in 1912.

————. *Ella of All-of-a-Kind Family*. Illustrated by Gail Owens. Dutton, 1978 (I:10+ R:5). Ella is now grown-up and must decide whether or not she wants a singing career.

Taylor, Theodore. *The Cay*. Doubleday, 1969 (I:10+ R:6). A blind American boy is stranded on a Caribbean Cay with a West Indian.

————. *The Trouble With Tuck*. Doubleday, 1981 (I:6–9 R:5). Based on a true incident, the story follows a girl as she trains a blind Labrador to follow a guide dog.

Vogel, Ilse Margaret. *My Summer Brother*. Harper & Row, 1981 (I:9–12 R:4). A nine-year-old expresses feelings about mother-daughter rivalry and her first crush.

Voigt, Cynthia. *Dicey's Song*. Atheneum, 1982 (I:10+ R:5). Dicey brings her brothers and sister to their grandmother's house after their mother abandons them.

————. *Homecoming*. Atheneum, 1981 (I:10+ R:5). The children survive as they try to reach their grandmother.

————. *A Solitary Blue*. Atheneum, 1983 (I:10+ R:6). A boy develops a loving relationship with his father after he faces his mother's desertion.

————. *The Runner*. Atheneum, 1985 (I:10+ R:5). Another book about the Tillerman family goes back in time to Bullet's high school experiences.

Watson, James. *Talking in Whispers*. Victor Gollancz, 1983 (I:12+ R:7). In a political thriller, a boy survives against an oppressive military government.

Wiss, John David. *The Swiss Family Robinson*. Illustrated by Lynd Ward. Grosset & Dunlap, 1949 (I:10+ R:6). A classic story of a family shipwrecked.

Wojciechowska, Maia. *Shadow of a Bull*. Illustrated by Alvin Smith. Atheneum, 1964 (I:10+ R:5). Manolo discovers that true bravery is not always in the bullring.

10

Historical Fiction

□

THE PEOPLE AND THE PAST COME ALIVE

□

INVOLVING CHILDREN IN HISTORICAL
FICTION

The People and the Past Come Alive

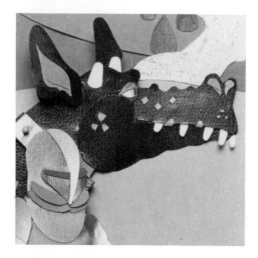

THE THREAD OF PEOPLE'S LIVES WEAVES through the past, the present, and into the future. Many Americans have a deep desire to trace their roots—here in this hemisphere or back to Europe, Asia, or Africa. What did their ancestors experience? Why did their ancestors travel to North America? What were their ancestors' personal feelings and beliefs? What was life like for the settlers who pioneered the American frontier and for the native North Americans who greeted them? Did people of the past have the same concerns as people of the present? Can their experiences suggest solutions for today's problems?

Through the pages of historical fiction, the past becomes alive. It is not just dates, accomplishments, and battles; it is people, famous and unknown, who lived during certain times and who, through their actions and beliefs, influenced the course of history. This chapter discusses the values of historical fiction for children, the criteria for evaluating historical fiction, some specific demands on the authors of historical fiction, and examples of historical fiction written about different time periods. Books of historical fiction are linked to a short discussion of events in the time period they reflect, in the hope that this chronological framework will give the reader a better understanding of the sweep of history as portrayed in these books.

VALUES OF HISTORICAL FICTION FOR CHILDREN

Children cannot actually cross the ocean on the *Mayflower* and see a new world for the first time, or experience the arrival of the first Europeans on their native shores, or feel the consequences of persecution during World War II. They can imagine all these experiences, however, through the pages of historical fiction. With Patricia Clapp's *Constance: A Story of Early Plymouth*, they can imagine they are standing on the swaying deck of the *Mayflower* and seeing their new home. While reading Scott O'Dell's *The Feathered Serpent*, they can imagine they are inhabitants of Montezuma's palace who are witnessing the emperor's tragic encounter with the Spanish conquistador Hernando Cortés. With a twelve-year-old girl in Els Pelgrom's *The Winter When Time Was Frozen*, they can imagine they are given sanctuary in the home of a Dutch farm family during World War II.

As children relive the past through vicarious experiences, they are also reading for enjoyment. Tales based on authentic historical settings or episodes are alive with adventures that appeal to many children. They may follow the adventures of a young girl living on the Wisconsin frontier in Carol Ryrie Brink's *Caddie Woodlawn*. They may read to discover if a girl can successfully hide her identity and pretend to be a man in Patricia Clapp's *I'm Deborah Sampson: A Soldier in the War of the Revolution*. They may follow the adventures of Jeff Bussey in Harold Keith's *Rifles for Watie* as he tries to find information behind enemy lines during the Civil War.

Children who read historical fiction gain an understanding of their own heritage. The considerable research that precedes the writing of an authentic historical story enables the author to incorporate information about the period naturally into the story. Children gain knowledge about the people, values, beliefs, hardships, and physical surroundings common to a period. They discover the events that preceded their own century and made the present day possible. Through historical fiction, children can begin to visualize the sweep of history.

As characters in historical fiction from many different time periods face and overcome their problems, readers may discover important universal truths, identify feelings and behaviors that encourage them to consider alternative ways to handle their own problems, empathize with viewpoints that may be different from their own, and realize that history consists of many people who have learned to work together.

The journal of the National Council for the Social Studies, *Social Education* (8), maintains that an emphasis on human relations is a primary criterion for selecting notable books. Through historical fiction, children can discover that in all times people have depended upon one another and that throughout history human beings have had similar needs. They learn that when human relationships deteriorate tragedy usually results. Historical fiction allows children to judge these relationships and realize that their own present and future are linked to the actions of humans in the past. Outstanding books of historical fiction

for children satisfy what Joan W. Blos (1, p. 375) believes is a primary role of literature, "tying together the past, the present, and the promise of the future" in a way that "confirms human bonds."

CRITERIA FOR EVALUATING HISTORICAL FICTION

When evaluating historical fiction for children, adults must be certain that a story adheres to the criteria for excellent literature discussed in chapter three. Historical fiction must also satisfy special requirements in terms of setting, characterization, plot development, and theme.

Setting

Because historical fiction must be authentic in every respect, the careful development of setting for a certain time period is essential. A setting this important to a story is called an *integral setting*. Rebecca Lukens (6) says that an integral setting must be described in details so clear that the reader understands how the story is related to a time and place. This is of particular concern in historical fiction written for children, because children cannot visualize historical periods from memory. The writer must provide images of the setting through vivid descriptions that do not overpower plot and characterization.

When writing lengthy books for older children, authors have more time to develop integral settings in which the actions and characters are influenced by both time and place. The setting in historical fiction may guide readers into the plot, encourage them to feel the excitement of a time period, and create visual images that encourage them to accept the character's experiences.

Chapter three discussed the role of setting as an antagonist. The setting plays the role of antagonist in many stories about exploration and pioneering; for example, In Harold Keith's *The Obstinate Land*, a family must overcome drought, hail, and bitter cold. Each new setback strengthens the main character and brings the family and neighbors closer together in their fight to survive. In Honore Morrow's *On to Oregon!*, sleet storms, rugged mountains, swift streams, and natural predators act as antagonists. The description leaves little doubt that the children are confronting a beautiful but awesome adversary. The setting may also be the antagonist in a story set in a city. In *Anna, Grandpa, and the Big Storm*, Carla Stevens develops the 1888 blizzard in New York City into an antagonist.

Authors of historical fiction sometimes contrast settings in order to develop the conflict and suggest how the settings influence the characters. This technique is used in both Ann Petry's *Tituba of Salem Village* and Elizabeth George Speare's *The Witch of Blackbird Pond*. Both authors have taken protagonists from the warm, colorful Caribbean and placed them in the bleak, somber surroundings of a Puritan village. Time and place then influence how the other characters react to these protagonists and how these characters respond to their new environments.

Some settings in historical fiction create happy, nostalgic moods. In Cynthia Rylant's picture storybook *When I Was Young in the Mountains*, the

The illustrations reflect a happy setting in an Appalachian mountain community. (From *When I Was Young in the Mountains*, by Cynthia Rylant, illustrated by Diane Goode. Illustrations © 1982 by Diane Goode. Reprinted by permission of the publisher, E. P. Dutton, Inc.)

illustrations and the text allow readers to glimpse a girl's happy years of growing up in the Appalachian mountains of Virginia. This peaceful setting is a world of swimming holes, country stores, and family evenings on the porch. The illustrations help integrate the details of the time period into the story.

Esther Forbes integrates many details of colonial life into the setting of her story for older readers, *Johnny Tremain*. The sights, sounds, and smells of revolutionary Boston are woven into the characters' daily routines. The reader knows that Johnny sleeps in a loft, wears leather breeches and a coarse shirt, likes the bustling wharf, and is proud of his work in the silversmith's shop. Forbes also used historical research when creating an authentic setting for her Pulitzer Prize-winning fictional biography *Paul Revere and the World He Lived In*. In *Winding Valley Farm: Annie's Story*, Anne Pellowski, combines Polish customs and descriptions of rural farming practices to create the feeling of an ethnic community during the early 1900s.

Characterization

The actions, beliefs, and values of characters in historical fiction must be realistic for the time period. Authors of historical novels admit that it is sometimes difficult not to give their historical characters contemporary actions and values. Geoffrey Trease (11), author of several historical novels, encountered this problem when he wanted a girl in a story about the Roman Empire to meet a boy and form a friendship. His research showed that Roman citizens kept their daughters in seclusion and would never have allowed them to associate with a noncitizen's child. He admits that he had to search a long time for a twist in the plot that would resolve this dilemma. Trease believes that "history has all the raw material the novelist needs" (11, p. 27). Consequently, if authors know their job, they will not need to alter facts. At the same time, Trease believes that the concerns of characters in historical fiction should be relevant to contemporary readers, and carefully selects historical periods, people, and events that have modern-day significance.

Choosing the main and supporting characters can cause additional problems. Hester Burton (3) says that she never uses a famous person as the pivotal character in her stories and never develops dialogue for a famous person unless she has documentary evidence that the character actually carried on such a conversation or would have held those specific sentiments. She feels that creating a historical situation that includes a fictional character is legitimate, but does not believe in leading a famous person on a fictional adventure. Many authors of historical fiction apparently agree with Burton. Numerous books use fictional characters in historical settings. In Esther Forbes's *Johnny Tremain*, for example, a fictional silversmith's apprentice is the pivotal character, while Paul Revere and Samuel Adams are background characters.

Authors develop characterization through dialogue, thoughts, actions, and descriptions. While all these need to appear authentic, the speech of the characters and the language characteristic of a period can cause problems for writers of historical fiction. For example, Harold Keith wanted one of his characters in *The Obstinate Land* to speak with a dialect: "Mattie Cooper's Arkansas dialect was hard to pin down until I had the good fortune to discover old files of the magazine *Dialect Notes*, containing several studies by Dr. J. W. Carr, associate professor of English and Modern Languages at the University of Arkansas, 1901–06" (4, author's notes). This study provided Keith with the words and the pronunciation necessary to develop a character whose speech was realistic for the time and the location. Authors of children's historical fiction must be careful, however, not to use so many colorful terms from a period that the story is difficult for a young reader to comprehend.

Literature critic Rebecca Lukens (6) stresses the importance of believable characters in helping readers understand the differences and similarities between people in different times and places. Readers must believe that the characters in historical fiction are human beings like themselves.

Plot

Credible plots in historical fiction emerge from authentically developed time periods. The experiences, the conflicts, and the characters' resolutions of conflicts must reflect the times—whether the antagonist is another person, society, nature, or internal dilemmas faced by the protagonist. Conflict in historical fiction often develops when characters leave their own secure or known environments and move into more alien ones. Au-

thors may highlight the problems, the culture, or diverse values of a time period by exploring the conflicts developed because of a character's inner turmoil or societal pressures.

In Ann Schlee's *Ask Me No Questions* the protagonist's person-against-self conflict develops after she moves from London to avoid a cholera epidemic in 1848. While living with her aunt and uncle, Laura uncovers a neighbor's sinister activities. Although he is supposedly training children acquired from the workhouses, Laura discovers that the children are starving and ill. The author develops a person-against-self conflict as Laura faces her own moral dilemmas. Should she help the children even if she must steal food from her own relatives and then lie about her actions? The dilemmas in this story based on a true incident seem believable because of Schlee's believable descriptions of Laura's discoveries—for example, children eating pig slops in her aunt's barn. The author's descriptions of Laura's formidable aunt, with her strong Victorian attitudes toward children, illuminate reasons for Laura's conflict.

Scott O'Dell develops a credible person-against-self conflict in *The Captive* by developing and describing the moral dilemmas a young Jesuit seminarian faces when he leaves his Spanish homeland in the early 1500s and accompanies an expedition to the Americas. O'Dell describes the Jesuit's faith and his desire to bring Christianity to the native Maya of New Spain, his turmoil when he discovers the real motives behind the Spaniards' actions, his refusal to betray the native people, his pondering over his inability to change them and his justification for his own grasping for power by impersonating a Mayan god. The various characterizations help readers understand both good and bad human motives. O'Dell's detailed descriptions of the incidents that cause the main character's moral dilemmas and the character's responses to these dilemmas create credible conflict for the time period.

William H. Hooks' *Circle of Fire* explores the moral dilemmas created by prejudice. Hooks's story takes place in North Carolina in the 1930s, as a white boy and his two black friends try to prevent a Ku Klux Klan attack on Irish gypsies. Hooks develops additional believable personal conflict when the eleven-year-old boy discovers that his father, whom he loves and respects, is probably involved in the Klan.

Each of these stories also develops plausible person-against-society conflicts. The conflict in

Ask Me No Questions is credible because Ann Schlee convincingly develops Victorian attitudes about children that on the one hand are sentimental and protective and on the other hand allow poor children to work hard and go hungry. The conflict in *The Captive* develops because of human greed and the Spaniards' socially supported prejudice against non-Europeans, which O'Dell compellingly portrays. Likewise, the conflict in *Circle of Fire* develops because of social prejudice.

Authors who develop credible person-against-society conflicts must describe the values and beliefs of the time period, or the attitudes of a segment of the population, in such way that readers understand the nature of the antagonist. In Kathryn Lasky's *The Night Journey*, deadly anti-Semitism is the antagonist that forces a Jewish family to plan and execute a dangerous flight from czarist Russia. The plot seems more credible because a modern-day family in this book believes that these memories would be so painful the great-grandmother should not be encouraged to remember her own experiences.

Well-developed person-against-self and person-against-society conflicts help readers understand the values expressed during a time period and the problems, moral dilemmas, and social issues faced by the people. Authors often use these conflicts and their resolutions to develop themes in historical fiction.

Theme

Themes in historical fiction, as in any literature, should be worthwhile, as relevant in today's society as they were in the historical periods being represented. Many books of historical fiction have universal themes that have been relevant throughout human history.

The search for freedom, for example, is a theme in literature of all time periods, from Rosemary Sutcliff's stories about tribal Britons confronting the invading Vikings and Roman armies in *Blood Feud* and *Frontier Wolf*, to Elizabeth Yates' story about an African slave in colonial Boston, *Amos Fortune, Free Man*.

Love of the land and the independence it provides are powerful themes in books about the westward expansion of European settlers in North America and about the Native American peoples they displace. Europeans leave relatives and established communities to face unknown dangers and acquire homesteads. Native Americans first attempt to share their beloved natural environment with the new arrivals, then find themselves being pushed out of their homes. Children in both groups inherit their parents' dreams and fight to retain their land.

Themes of loyalty and honor are also common in stories about all time periods. People are loyal to friends and family members, following them on difficult quests and avenging their deaths or dishonor; they are loyal to their principles and defend them. Many books of historical fiction for children stress the cruelty and futility of war, even when adherence to moral principles may have helped cause the conflict. Novels about war in various historical periods often develop the age-hold theme of overcoming injustice, but may also show the ways in which people on both sides of a conflict have much in common. Nonviolent beliefs of people such as the Quakers are the bases of themes in some historical novels.

These themes are relevant to human understanding, whether the stories in which they are developed take place in ancient Rome or in contemporary America.

Important Questions

The following questions summarize the criteria that adults should consider (in addition to considerations of literary quality raised in chapter three) when evaluating historical fiction for children:

1   Is the setting authentic in every detail?
2   Are details integrated into the story so that they do not overwhelm the reader or detract from the story?
3   If the setting is the antagonist, are the relationships between characters and setting clearly developed?
4   Do the characters' actions express values and beliefs that are realistic for the time period?
5   Is the language authentic for the period without relying on so many colorful terms or dialects that the story is difficult to understand?
6   Do the characters' experiences, conflicts, and resolutions of conflicts reflect what is known about the time period?
7   Is the theme worthwhile?

THE DEMANDS OF HISTORICAL AUTHENTICITY

The need for authentic historical detail places special demands on authors of historical fiction. Some authors actually lived through the experiences they write about or knew someone who lived through them. Other authors write about historical periods far removed from their personal experiences. To gather their data, they must rely on sources of information far different from the person who remembers vividly the people and the minute details of a historical period.

Laura Ingalls Wilder, the author of the "Little House" books, lived in the big woods of Wisconsin, traveled by covered wagon through Kansas, lived in a sod house in Minnesota, and shared her life with Pa, Ma, Mary, and Carrie when they finally settled in South Dakota. Wilder's books sound as if they were written immediately after an incident occurred, but Wilder actually wrote the stories describing her life from 1870 through 1889 much later, between 1926 and 1943. Authors who write about their own past experiences need to have both keen powers of observation and excellent memories in order to share the details of their lives with others.

Predominantly happy experiences in the past may be easy to remember. For authors who write about painful experiences in their own lives, however, the doors of memory may be more difficult to open. Johanna Reiss found herself remembering things she had preferred to forget when she began writing the story of her experiences as a Jewish child hidden by Dutch gentiles during the Holocaust and World War II. According to the publishers of *The Upstairs Room*, Reiss (9) "did not set out to write a book about her experiences during the Second World War; she simply wanted to record them for her two daughters, who are now about the age she was when she went to stay with the Oastervelds" (p. 197). When she started to write, Reiss began remembering experiences that she had never talked about with anyone because they were too painful. To reinforce her memory, she took her children back to Usselo, Holland, where she visited the Dutch family who had protected her and looked again at the upstairs room and the closet in which she had hidden from the Nazis.

Authors such as Carol Ryrie Brink write about relatives' experiences. In *Caddie Woodlawn*, Brink recreates the story of her grandmother and her grandmother's family. In her author's note to the book (2), Brink tells how she lived with her grandmother and loved to listen to her tell stories about her pioneer childhood:

It was many years later that I remembered those stories of Caddie's childhood, and I said to myself, "If I

loved them so much perhaps other children would like them too." Caddie was still alive when I was writing, and I sent letters to her, asking about the details that I did not remember clearly. She was pleased when the book was done. "There is only one thing that I do not understand," she said. "You never knew my mother and father and my brothers—how could you write about them exactly as they were?" "But, Gram," I said, "You told me." (p. 283)

Of course modern-day authors have no first-hand experience of some earlier times and cannot even talk to someone who lived during certain historical periods, so they must use other resources in researching their chosen time periods. Hester Burton (3), a well-known writer of historical fiction with British settings, says:

Ideally I should be so knowledgeable that I have no need to turn to a book of reference once I have actually started writing the book. I should be able to see clearly in my mind's eye the houses in which my characters live, the clothes they wear, and the cars and carriages and ships in which they travel. I should know what food they eat, what songs they sing when they are happy, and what are the sights and smells they are likely to meet when they walk down the street. I must understand their religion, their political hopes, their trades and—what is most important—the relationships between different members of a family common to their particular generation. (p. 299)

To acquire this much knowledge about a time period demands considerable research. Some authors have chosen to research and write about one period; others have written books covering many different time periods. Rosemary Sutcliff has written several outstanding books of historical fiction, and John Townsend (10) says that in the area of serious historical novels Sutcliff stands above the rest. Sutcliff reveals her thorough knowledge of certain historical periods in both the stories themselves and her introductions to them. In her introduction to *Song for a Dark Queen*, for example, she outlines the historical events that influence the incidents in the book, describes how her plot arose out of reading certain scholarly works about the culture of the period, then lists the sources that provided her with background information for the story.

Kathryn Lasky reveals the influence of extensive research in her author's note for *Beyond the Divide*. Lasky says she based the book in part on Theodora Kroeber's biography of the last Yahi Indian, *Ishi: The Last of His Tribe* and in part on J. Goldsborough Bruff's journal that describes his own experiences during the gold rush. Lasky describes her own discoveries about the West: "Mrs. Kroeber's story was the first true western tale I had ever read. This was not the West of television, nor was the gold rush the one written about in my school books. The bad guys were worse than I had ever imagined, and the greed for gold was pernicious and deadly to the human spirit. People did not just rob, they killed, and on occasion massacred. The conditions of survival were the most arduous imaginable, but there was one emigrant whose spirit was left miraculously intact" (5, p. 253). These discoveries, characterizations, settings, and themes are apparent in her historical novel.

Reading about any of the well-known authors of historical fiction whose books are noted for authentic backgrounds reveals that authors first spend hundreds of hours researching county courthouse records and old letters, newspapers, and history books; conducting personal interviews; and visiting museums and historical locations. Authors must then write stories that develop believable settings, characters, and plots without sounding like history textbooks. In doing so, they must carefully consider the many conflicting points of view that may surround particular events. Writing excellent historical fiction is a very demanding task.

A CHRONOLOGY OF HISTORICAL FICTION

Students of children's literature and other adults who share historical fiction with children must understand at least some of a time period's history in order to evaluate stories reflecting that period and to share them effectively with children. Following a three-year study, Donna Norton (7) found that university students' understanding, evaluation, and utilization of historical fiction improved if students in children's literature courses discussed books of historical fiction in a chronological order reflecting the historical settings of the books, briefly identified the actual historical happenings in each time period, identified major themes in literature written about a specific period (although of course some books have multiple themes), discussed the implications of recurring themes, identified how authors develop believable plots for a time period, and discussed the modern significance of the literature. In order to assist in the study of historical fiction, this chapter discusses books of historical fiction in an order similar to the one used during Norton's

study. Ideally, this framework will assist readers of historical fiction as they discuss the literature in children's literature classes, extend the time line to other periods, and undertake individual studies of historical fiction for children. Chart 10–1 presents a simple chronology of Western and North American history and the main themes developed in books with settings in each period.

Ancient Times through the Middle Ages

Western culture began over 5,000 years ago in the ancient Sumerian and Egyptian societies of the Middle Eastern "Cradle of Civilization." Absolute rulers directed vast numbers of slaves in constructing temples and pyramids in honor of themselves and their gods. In 332 B.C. Alexander the Great conquered most of the Middle East. Two hundred years later, the great military might of the Romans was creating an empire that eventually surrounded the Mediterranean Sea and covered most of Europe for hundreds of years. As the Roman Empire became larger, encompassing many different cultures and geographical areas, Roman rule became harsher and harsher.

In pre-Roman times, various Celtic peoples, including Britons and Gaels, inhabited the British Isles. These people lived in tribes ruled by chiefs and often warred with one another over land and people. In 55 B.C. Julius Caesar failed in an attempt to add present-day England and Scotland to the Roman Empire. One hundred years later, Emperor Claudius succeeded in annexing Britain. Roman legions were left behind to subdue the people and keep peace among the tribes.

This Roman dominance lasted throughout Europe until about A.D. 410, when fierce tribes of Teutonic peoples from northern Europe invaded and sacked Rome, beginning the long medieval period in European history that has sometimes been called the "Dark Ages." In their great ships, Vikings from Norway led by people such as Eric the Red raided the coasts of Europe and demonstrated their remarkable seafaring skills by exploring Greenland and Iceland; in about A.D. 1000 Norse explorers under Leif Ericson's command crossed the Atlantic Ocean and stayed briefly in a place in North America they called "Vinland." Teutonic Saxons and Angles from the continent invaded and settled Britain. The once unified Roman Empire dissolved into many small domains ruled by competing feudal lords and the warrior nobility that served them in on-going battles. The lords lived in fortified castles surrounded by cottages and fields in which enslaved peasants produced food and wealth for them. Constant warfare and rampant disease, such as the plague, or "Black Death," ravaged the developing towns of England, France, and elsewhere. The strong Christian beliefs of the Middle Ages led to the construction of magnificent cathedrals and to crusades in which Christian warriors attempted to capture Jerusalem for the Roman Catholic Church, which still survived in splendor and power after the fall of Rome.

Authors who write historical fiction about the ancient world and medieval times in Europe often tell their stories from the viewpoint of slaves or other people subjugated by the powerful. Other authors represent the perspectives of the mighty, such as Romans and Vikings, and show the ways in which all people have certain desires and fears in common and confront similar problems. Through these various perspectives, authors of historical fiction for children encourage young readers to imagine and empathize with the personal and social conflicts of people in the distant past. Strong themes emerge as the charac-

3000 B.C.	Ancient Times through the Middle Ages
	Loyalty to family, friends, and country
	The consequences of ignorance, prejudice, and hatred
	Hatred, not people, is the greatest enemy
	The power of love
	The search for freedom and riches
	Courage
	Physical disabilities do not limit a person's humanity
	People can overcome their handicaps
A.D. 1492	Change in the Old World and Discovery of the New
	The search for freedom, riches, and land
	The consequences of greed
	The tragedy of war
	Personal conscience and moral dilemmas
	People need to work together
1692	The Impact of Salem
	The consequences of ignorance and prejudice
	Moral obligations to defend what is right
	People seek freedom from persecution
1776	The American Revolution
	Freedom is worth fighting for
	Strong beliefs require strong commitments
1780	Early Expansion of the United States
	Love of the land
	Perseverence in the face of hardship
	The consequences of hatred and prejudice
	Friendship, faith, moral obligation, and strong family bonds
1861	The Civil War Years
	The tragedy of war
	The search for freedom
	Strong family ties
	Personal conscience
	Prejudice and hatred as destructive forces
1860s	The Western Frontier
	Love for the land
	People need each other
	The importance of courage and hope
	Conflict of cultures
1900	The Early Twentieth Century
	The struggle for survival
	Prejudice and discrimination as destructive forces
	Strong family ties
1939	World War II
	Hatred and prejudice as destructive forces
	Freedom is worth fighting for
	Moral obligation and personal conscience

CHART 10–1
Eras and themes in historical fiction

ters fight for their beliefs and personal freedoms, follow their dreams, struggle with moral dilemmas, and/or overcome prejudices or self-doubts that could destroy them.

In *The Bronze Bow*, Elizabeth George Speare focuses upon Israel during Roman rule. She portrays the harshness of the Roman conquerors by telling the story through the eyes of a boy who longs to avenge the death of his parents. (His father was crucified by Roman soldiers, and his mother died from grief and exposure.) Daniel bar Jamin's bitterness intensifies when he joins a guerrilla band and nurtures his hatred of the Romans. His own person-against-self conflict comes to a turning point when he almost sacrifices his sister because of his hatred. The author encourages readers to understand Daniel's real enemy. When Daniel talks to Jesus, both Daniel and the reader realize that hatred, not Romans, is the enemy. In fact, the only thing stronger than hatred is love. The author shows the magnitude of Daniel's change when at the close of the story he invites a Roman soldier into his home.

Rosemary Sutcliff uses a real British mystery twenty centuries old as the basis for her historical novel *Sun Horse, Moon Horse*. The magical Uffington White Horse has raced across the Berkshire Downs in England for over two thousand years. What force, in approximately 100 B.C., motivated the carving of this beautiful animal into the hillside? Who was the sculptor who could create an earthen horse alive with movement and power? Sutcliff's novel about the Iceni, a tribe of early Britons before the Roman invasion, presents her version of how this horse, still visible today, came to be carved into the high downs.

Sutcliff's theme, "the search for freedom," is developed through a comparison of the peaceful existence of the Iceni before their capture to the time of their subjugation by another tribe covetous of the Iceni's land and horses. An Iceni boy's strong desire for freedom for his people, combined with his artistic talent, gives the tribe their chance for liberation. The boy agrees to complete the carving of the conquering tribe's sun-horse symbol if, after he has completed the carving, his people can go free. He does not only carve the symbol of his enemies, however; he also carves the moon horse, symbol of his own tribe. His final actions express the depth of his tribal loyalty, desire for his tribe's freedom, and belief in the symbolism of the moon horse: upon completion of the moon-horse carving, he asks that his own life

be sacrificed upon the horse to give it necessary life and strength. Sutcliff reaffirms the tribe's own loyalty to and admiration for the boy through the feelings expressed by the new leader:

Heart-brother . . . wait for me in the Land of Apple Trees. Whether it be tomorrow, or when I am Lord of many spears in the north, and too old to sit a horse or lift a sword, wait for me until I come. And do not be forgetting me, for I will not forget you. (p. 106)

The Iceni tribe's futile effort to stem the tide of Roman conquest is the subject of Sutcliff's *Song for a Dark Queen*. The year is A.D. 62, over 150 years after the Iceni left the Berkshire Downs in search of new horse runs. The leading character is a queen rather than a male chieftain. (The

A horse symbol expresses a tribe of early Britons' desire for freedom. (From *Sun Horse, Moon Horse*, by Rosemary Sutcliff. Text © 1977 by Rosemary Sutcliff. Decorations copyright © 1977 by The Bodley Head. Reprinted by permission of the publisher, E. P. Dutton.)

Iceni leadership did not go from father to son, but down the "moonside," from mother to daughters). Through descriptions of the queen's early training and her reactions when her tribe is conquered by the Romans, Sutcliff shows the reader the basis for the Iceni's belief in their strong female leader. She has been trained from early childhood to lead men in battle, and she heads a revolt that almost succeeds in overpowering Roman rule and defending ancient tribal culture. Her efforts fail, however. The Romans overpower the Iceni and place them firmly under Roman dominance. Sutcliff emphasizes her theme about the importance of freedom to the Iceni by describing how the queen decides to sacrifice her own life rather than be a captive.

In books about the Roman legions, such as *Frontier Wolf* and *Lantern Bearers*, Sutcliff develops believable characters whose desires and actions express such timeless themes as loyalty, honor, desire for freedom, and self-sacrifice.

Authors who write about the Viking period develop both honorable heroes who strive for human freedom, and evil men who kill and enslave. Vivid descriptions are important for these characterizations. Sutcliff's description of the approaching Vikings is especially effective in *Blood Feud* because it is told from the viewpoint of Jestyn, an English boy who believes terrible stories about the Vikings:

The men who stood there glancing me over were the true Viking kind that I had heard of in stories and been told to pray God I might never see in life. Men with grey ring-mail strengthening their leather byrnies, iron-bound war-caps, long straight swords. One had a silver arm-ring, one had studs of coral in the clasp of his belt, one wore a rough wolf-skin cloak. (p. 14)

Sutcliff's vivid descriptions help the reader understand Jestyn's reactions to being purchased for six gold pieces and a wolf skin and to wearing the hated thrall ring of a slave. When Jestyn concludes that his master is a good man, readers are encouraged to believe in his worth. The remainder of the book stresses the themes of honor toward parents and loyalty between friends as the Viking and his now-loyal friend search for the murderer of the Viking's father.

The settings in historical fiction about the Vikings often stress the sea's importance. The sea is not usually an antagonist in these stories, since it enables Vikings to gain riches and expand their world. In Erik Christian Haugaard's *Hakon of Rogen's Saga*, the sea is the road that leads everywhere, the reality from which a young Viking boy's dreams are made. Haugaard develops a fast-paced plot as the enemies of Hakon's father attack, and Hakon is left to the mercies of an uncle who wishes to steal his birthright. Fleeing for his life, Hakon hides in a secret cave, where he ponders his feelings about courage, strength, and freedom. He realizes that if he can be alone without fear no one can call him weak, even if he is not yet strong enough to wield a sword. The actions of a few loyal comrades and of a freed slave help him recapture Rogen, his island home, and his birthright. The author emphasizes through Hakon's thoughts and actions that freedom is the greatest birthright that anyone can have. When Hakon assumes rule of the island, his people swear loyalty to him, and he declares, "I swear that on Rogen shall rule only justice. That no man shall fear his tongue nor his thought, but each man shall live in peace" (p. 113).

While the Vikings were roaming the seas, knights in armor all across Europe were challenging one another over land and power, and humble people were working in the fields of nobles or serving the mighty in the great halls of castles. In *The Door in the Wall*, Marguerite DeAngeli uses an English castle and its surroundings as the setting for her story about ten-year-old Robin, who is expected to train for knighthood. The plot has an unusual twist when Robin is stricken with a mysterious ailment that paralyzes his legs. The door in the title of the story now becomes symbolic as a monk gives unhappy Robin difficult advice: "Thou hast only to follow the wall far enough and there will be a door in it" (p. 16). This symbol is very important in the story, as DeAngeli develops the plot by tracing Robin's search for his own door and the preparation necessary to find it. The monk helps Robin by guiding his learning, encouraging him to carve and to read, and expressing the belief that Robin's hands and mind, if not his legs, must be taught because they represent other doors in the wall. Robin worries that as a disabled person who walks with crutches he will be useless as a knight. His father's friend, Sir Peter, reassures him by saying that if a person cannot serve in one way, another means of serving will present itself. Sir Peter is proven correct when Welsh forces attack the castle. Robin proves his worth to himself and the castle by escaping the enemy sentry and obtaining help from the neighboring castle. DeAngeli encourages readers to understand the importance of accepting people for what they are, rather than rejecting

FLASHBACK

T HE HISTORICAL NOVEL BECAME POPULAR IN THE
1800s with the publication of stories by Sir Walter
Scott and Charlotte Yonge. Scott's story of medieval
English life, *Ivanhoe* (1820), was often used as a school
assignment for older children. Other popular books by Scott
included *The Lady of the Lake* (1810), *Waverly: Or, 'Tis Sixty
Years Since* (1814), *Rob Roy* (1818), and *Tales of the Crusaders*
(1825). Yonge's historical books included *The Little Duke*
(1854), *Richard the Fearless* (1856), and *The Lances of
Lynwood* (1855). Her series of "Cameos from History" (1850s–
1890s), published in *The Monthly Packet,* offered vicarious
adventure, relaxation, and a sense of history to Victorian
children.

them because of a physical disability, when Robin's father congratulates him: "The courage you
have shown, the craftsmanship proven by the
harp, and the spirit in your singing all make so
bright a light that I cannot see whether or not
your legs are misshapen" (p. 120). Many children
enjoy this beautiful story about a child who finds
a door in his wall. One girl said that it was her
favorite book because she liked the way Robin
overcame his problem and was happy with his
life. The theme is especially appropriate for
teaching positive attitudes about the physically
disabled.

More severe problems related to living with a
disabling condition in medieval Europe appear in
Gloria Skurzynski's *Manwolf.* The author builds a
plot around the symptoms of a rare skin disease—hair grows on skin exposed to the sun, and
scarring creates an animal appearance—and a
superstitious people's prejudice against and fear
of anyone who has this disease. The belief in
werewolves and the personal tragedy that results
from such a belief are shown by the attacks on a
young boy and by his mother's attempts to protect him. The lifelong battle against prejudice is

suggested by the mask the father wears to hide
his own features from the superstitious people.

The following themes are expressed in historical fiction about ancient and medieval times. Students of children's literature may wish to consider how and why these themes relate to specific
happenings in the time periods. Are any of these
themes significant in our modern-day world?

1　Loyalty to family, friends, and country is one
of the noblest human traits.
2　Human ignorance, prejudice, and hatred can
have destructive consequences for all concerned.
3　Hatred, not people, is the greatest enemy of
humankind.
4　Love is stronger than hatred and prevails
through times of great trouble.
5　Humans will always search for freedom and
riches.
6　Courage is more important than physical
strength.
7　A physical disability does not reduce a person's humanity.
8　People can overcome their handicaps.

Change in the Old World and Discovery of the New

By the fifteenth century, Europe had entered the Renaissance, a time of cultural "rebirth" and great social change. Large cities were bustling with trade, as middle-class merchants attained more social prominence. New forms of Protestant Christianity were arising out of medieval Catholicism and challenging the religious and political power of the established church. In Germany, Johann Gutenberg was inventing the printing press, which William Caxton soon used to publish the first printed books in England. Great artists such as Michelangelo and William Shakespeare began to raise the visual arts and literature to new heights of creative glory, inspired by the rediscovery of ancient Greek and Roman culture. Ordinary people were expecting and demanding greater economic, political, and religious freedom. Explorers were sailing off to prove their belief that the world was round and then to acquire great riches in the New World they discovered in the Western Hemisphere.

Christopher Columbus's arrival on a Caribbean island in 1492 was soon followed by Spanish explorers' conquest of ancient Maya and Aztec cultures in Central America. By the late sixteenth and the early seventeenth century, colonies were springing up along the Atlantic coast of North America, as people followed their lust for wealth and adventure or their desire for freedom from the religious persecution and political conflicts that were occurring in England and elsewhere.

Strong person-against-self conflicts, settings that depict Mayan and Aztec cultures, and themes that illustrate the human consequences of greed are found in Scott O'Dell's historical novels based on the Spanish conquest of Mexico in the early 1500s. O'Dell's *The Captive*, *The Feathered Serpent*, and *The Amethyst Ring* focus not so much on events of the time period as on the moral dilemmas a young priest faces in the New World.

A young, idealistic Jesuit seminarian, Julián Escobar, leaves his secure home in Spain and joins an expedition to Central America, inspired by the prospect of saving the souls of native peoples in "New Spain." During the long voyage across the Atlantic, he begins to realize that the Spanish grandee leading the expedition actually intends to exploit and enslave the Mayas and the Aztecs, rather than simply convert them to Christianity.

Later he questions whether he has the spirit or the patience to spread the Christian faith within cultures so different from his own. O'Dell explores changes in Julián by stressing the changing conflicts in Julián's life: Should he take on the role of the Mayas' mythical Kukulcán in order to save his own life and make his views palatable to people with their own ancient beliefs? Should he advise attacking a neighboring city before his own Mayan city is attacked? How should he respond to the Mayan rites of sun worship? Why did God permit both good and evil?

Julián's defense of his inability to change the Mayas and of his own eventual grasping for power demonstrate changes in his character and how he resolves his moral dilemma. In *The Feathered Serpent*, for example, he thinks back to Augustine's teachings and concludes that evil exists because God wills it. Therefore, idol worship and human sacrifice are beyond his control. Julián does admit, however, that this argument may only be a defense of his own actions.

O'Dell's descriptions of Mayan and Aztec cities and temples and other aspects of their cultures encourage readers to understand that an advanced civilization inhabited the Americas long before European exploration and settlement. Readers may also ponder the right of one culture to destroy another culture whose citizens worship different gods and possess riches desired by a foreign power.

In 1620 the *Mayflower* brought the first group of settlers to New England. The Pilgrims made no easy conquest of the wilderness. Their sponsors in England did not provide enough supplies, their first winter was filled with sickness and starvation, and the new settlers were apprehensive about the native peoples who lived beyond their settlement.

Authors who write about the settlement of Plymouth colony often focus upon the reasons for leaving England and the hardships faced by the Pilgrims. In *Constance: A Story of Early Plymouth*, for example, Patricia Clapp tells the story of the early settlement of New England from the viewpoint of a fourteen-year-old girl. Because she did not want to leave her cherished London, Constance's first view of the new world from the deck of the *Mayflower* is an unpleasant one. Clapp encourages readers to understand the various viewpoints of the Pilgrims by contrasting Constance's view of a bleak and unfriendly land with the excitement and anticipation expressed by her fa-

THROUGH THE EYES OF AN AUTHOR

Making the Past Come Alive

Graduate of Columbia University's School of Journalism and author of books set in an earlier America. PATRICIA CLAPP discusses the importance of experiencing with and reacting to the protagonists in historical fiction.

AS THE WRITER OF HIStorical novels, the most rewarding comment I can receive from a young reader is "I felt as if I was there!" Then I know that the book has achieved what I worked for, an immediacy and realism that make the past as alive to the reader as the present in which he lives.

I can only create that immediacy and realism by being there myself. I don't mean checking out the location by visiting the place, although I do that too, whenever I can. I mean feeling the emotions, smelling the air, tasting the food, wearing the clothes— being there. That probably explains why most of my books are written in the first person. I become Constance Hopkins, or Elizabeth Blackwell, or Deborah Sampson, or Mary Warren, and write the story as I live it.

This is not to say that months of research don't precede every book. They do, and I love every minute of them. But what I absorb must become a natural part of the narrative, not paragraphs of exposition which most young people skip over as quickly as possible. For example, there is no need to describe the pastry of the 1780s by giving the recipe for Maid of Honor Tarts when Deborah Sampson makes them. It is enough to mention the succulent ingredients, the sugar and butter, the ground almonds and sherry wine, the currant preserves spread in the bottoms of the patty pans. The reader knows as well as Deborah and I how delicious they will taste.

The same holds true with physical responses. I must be there, experiencing and reacting with my protagonist. When Deborah sits alone by a campfire, weeping as she tries to pry a British musket ball from her shoulder with her army jackknife, we suffer together because we are one. When Mary Warren is caught in the thick web of 17th century superstition she struggles with terrified helplessness, and I struggle with her. When Constance Hopkins seeks escape from the confusion in her heart by walking deep into the Plymouth woods and hacking fiercely at small branches to be used for kindling, kicking them into a pile, feeling her hair caught and tumbled by encroaching twigs, I feel the same sting of cold pine-scented air on my face and the same quick rushing of blood as the axe bites into the wood.

It is an exciting way to live: to move back to whatever era interests me, to live there and then, to know the people and their problems and triumphs. My world is wide and timeless. There is a brief but difficult transition when I cover my typewriter, push my chair back, and return to what some people refer to as "the real world," but there is always the knowledge that I can, at will, retreat into some long-ago time. When a young person tells me "I felt as if I was really there," I know I have taken him traveling with me.

ther, William Bradford, John Alden, and Miles Standish. Clapp's vivid descriptions of Constance's first encounter with Samoset, a Native American, her feelings of resentment about doing "womanly" tasks, and her grief when she sees friends struggle and die during the first long winter encourage readers to understand the many facets of Constance's character. Clapp demonstrates the changes in Constance's feelings toward America when, six years after her first disappointing view of New England, she and her new husband decide to begin their life together in the new world. Through her story, readers understand that people will accept hardships to acquire political and religious freedom. They also discover the importance of working together for survival.

Arnold Lobel's *On the Day Peter Stuyvesant Sailed into Town,* a picture storybook for young children, humorously brings the colonial setting of New Amsterdam to life. When Stuyvesant arrived on the shores of present-day New York in 1647, he found a town near collapse. The streets were reverting to weeds and were littered with garbage, animals ran freely, houses were falling into disrepair, and the walls of the fort were crumbling. Stuyvesant considered this abominable and quickly told the settlers to improve their town. He was so successful that within the next ten years the town had doubled in size and became as neat as any Dutch community in Europe. The pictures in this book help children visualize the setting of sailing ships, colonial dress and homes, and Dutch windmills.

While early colonists in North America were struggling to survive, ominous clouds were gathering over England. Conflict between the Catholic King Charles I and the staunchly Protestant Parliament led to war in 1642. Authors who place their settings in England during this time frequently develop themes related to the tragedy of war. The character development often explores the influences that shape a person's growing awareness of the reality of war.

One of the strongest leaders to emerge during the English Civil War was Oliver Cromwell, an ordinary man but a great military organizer. In Erik Christian Haugaard's historical fiction set during this period, a young boy in the book *A Messenger for Parliament* and then in *Cromwell's Boy* discovers the tragic reality of war. After eleven-year old Oliver's mother dies, he follows his ne'er-do-well

father into war. Haugaard effectively encourages readers to understand Oliver's changing feelings as he talks to other boys about the glory of war and describes it in terms of a game. When the boys joke about taking swords and money from dead soldiers, Oliver begins to see warfare in a new light:

Till now I had not thought that the taking of a sword or a dagger on the battlefield would mean robbing the dead. Though I had seen the sacking of Worcester, war seemed to me still a game. Jack's words made me feel the fear I had not felt before. It came creeping like the shadows of twilight. (p. 64)

Oliver matures rapidly in this harsh time. He is finally given the responsibility of getting a message through to Cromwell. After long days of walking and danger, he reaches Cromwell's home and delivers the message. Cromwell is pleased with young Oliver's bravery and tells him that with allies such as Oliver on it side, Parliament has nothing to fear. Oliver has made a true friend, and Cromwell asks him to be his personal messenger. In *Cromwell's Boy*, Oliver is a much older thirteen. He rides a horse well, does not divulge secrets, and looks inconspicuous. His ability to serve Cromwell extends beyond messages, as he goes into the dangerous stronghold of the king's army as a spy. Haugaard suggests the lessons that Oliver has learned and develops an important theme by using a flashback in which Oliver remembers his youthful experiences:

In my youth there was little time for dreams. Life challenged me early. The leisure to reflect was not my lot; tomorrow was ever knocking on the door of today with new demands. It made me resourceful and sharpened my wit, but the purpose of life must be more than just to survive. You must be able—at least for short moments—to hold your precious soul in your hands and to contemplate that gift with love and understanding. (p. 1)

Consider the following themes developed in historical fiction about the age of cultural and social change in Europe and about early European settlement of the Western Hemisphere. Why and how are they related to specific happenings in the time periods? Are there other periods in history in which these themes have relevance? Do they have relevance for us today?

1 Human greed is a strong motivational force and can have destructive consequences.
2 Moral dilemmas must be faced and resolved.

3 Humans will face severe hardships to acquire the political and/or religious freedom they desire.

4 People must work together if they are to survive.

5 Overcoming problems can strengthen character.

6 War creates human tragedy.

7 Life is more than physical survival.

8 Land is important; people will endure numerous hardships to acquire land for personal reasons or for the glory of their country.

The Impact of Salem

Belief in witchcraft was a common superstition in medieval Europe. Thousands of religious and political nonconformists, independent thinkers and artists, mentally ill persons, and other unusual people seen as a threat to the established social order—such as Joan of Arc—were accused of witchcraft and burned at the stake. Belief in witchcraft continued even in the relatively more enlightened sixteenth and seventeenth centuries and crossed the Atlantic with the first settlers of North America.

In the New England colonies of the late 1600s, strict Puritan religious beliefs governed every aspect of social life. Any kind of nonconformity was viewed as the work of the devil. The famous witch-hunt of 1692 in Salem, Massachusetts, began when a doctor stated that the hysterical behavior of several teenage girls was due to the "evil eye." Within six months, twenty persons had been sentenced to death and one hundred and fifty had been sent to prison. Boston minister Cotton Mather was one of those who preached the power of the devil and the need to purge the world of witchcraft. People charged with witchcraft were pardoned in 1693 when Sir William Phipps, royal governor of the Massachusetts Bay Colony, said that the witch-hunt proceedings were too violent and not based upon fact. Belief in witchcraft faded in the 1700s as new scientific knowledge began to explain previously frightening phenomena.

The conflict in stories set in this short period of American history is usually person-against-society. Authors often take their characters out of an environment in which society is not an antagonist and place them in a hostile environment where their usual behavior patterns create suspicion. For example, is a person a witch because he or she brews tea from herbs to give to the ill? Does spinning thread faster and better prove a person is a witch? Does speaking to a cat indicate witchcraft? These are the charges that face the protagonist in Ann Petry's *Tituba of Salem Village*.

Contrasts in setting suggest the drama that follows. Petry describes two slaves living in comparative freedom by a sparkling sea on the coral-encrusted coastline of Barbados. The setting changes rapidly from their tropical home to a dark ship that is taking the slaves to New England. Tituba and her husband lose their fairly permissive owner in Barbados and in his place acquire a solemn, dark-clothed minister from Boston. Even their first meeting is ominous: Tituba backs away from a tall, thin shadow that blots out the sun and covers her body. The change in setting is complete as Petry describes the minister's house in Salem. Rotten eggs on the doorstep of the gloomy, neglected building greet Reverend Parris, his family, and the two slaves to their new home. Soon people in the town are muttering threats, teenage girls are becoming hysterical, and townspeople are testifying that Tituba can transform herself into a wolf or travel without her body. Tituba's crime is not witchcraft, but simply that she is not only a strange black person in a predominantly white community, but also more capable and intelligent than many of the people around her. This book develops insights into the consequences of inhumanity, regardless of time or place. The reader is encouraged to see and feel the danger in mass accusations and how people can be afraid to defend what they know is right. (Compare Petry's characterization and plot development with Patricia Clapp's *Witches' Children: A Story of Salem*, which relates the Salem experience through the eyes of a bound girl.)

Tituba was noticed and suspected because she was a talented slave, but others who were different were also objects of this cruel obsession. The free white protagonist in Elizabeth George Speare's *The Witch of Blackbird Pond* also comes from Barbados, but Kit's life is quite different from Tituba's. Contrasts between the people in Kit's early childhood environment and the people in New England encourage readers to anticipate the building conflict. On Barbados Kit was raised by a loving grandfather who encouraged her to read history, poetry, and plays. After his death Kit travels to New England to live with her aunt. Several experiences on the ship suggest that her former life-style may not be appropriate for her new world. For example, when she tries to discuss Shakespeare with a fellow passenger, he is shocked because a girl should not read such things: "The proper use of reading is to improve our sinful nature, and to fill our minds with God's holy word" (p. 28). An even harsher response occurs after she jumps into a harbor and swims to rescue a child's doll. (The Puritans believe that only guilty people are able to stay afloat.) When Kit's actions in the Puritan village remain consistent with her earlier behavior, she raises the suspicions of the townspeople: she wears colorful clothes she brought from Barbados; she teaches children to read by writing frivolous verses such as "Timothy Cook, jumped over the brook;" she has children act out stories from the Bible; and she becomes friendly with Hannah Tupper, a Quaker, whom the villagers believe is a witch. When sickness breaks out in the town, the people believe they are bewitched and blame Hannah. Kit risks her life to warn her friend, and they escape before Hannah's cottage is burned by angry men. Kit's action incurs the wrath of the settlement, and she is arrested for witchcraft. The charges brought against her are similar to those brought against Tituba. Unlike Tituba, Kit has friends and family who stand by her and assist in her acquittal. She learns that it is important to choose your friends and then stand by them.

The protagonists in Petry's and Speare's books are heroes of courage, high spirit, and honor in trying circumstances. Both remain true to their beliefs, even when faced with hostility and superstition, and are examples of voices that cry out against the injustices around them. Because of their actions, a few people realize the consequences of blind fear and hatred.

Consider the following themes developed in historical fiction about the Salem witch-hunts. What are the consequences of inhumanity and persecution developed in other time periods? What historical events coincide with such persecution?

1 Prejudiced persecution of others is a frightening and destructive social phenomenon.
2 People seek freedom from persecution.
3 Moral obligations require some people to defend others' rights.

The American Revolution

The inhabitants of the thirteen American colonies founded by the British came from different countries and had differing sympathies and practices.

They did, however, have several strong antagonisms in common: they shared a fear of the native peoples of North America; they went through a period when they shared a dread of French conquest; and they came to conflict with their ruler, the British crown. Although British subjects, the colonists had no elected representatives in the British Parliament that made decisions affecting their lives. For example, the colonists were allowed to buy tea, a popular beverage, only from the British East Indian Company, and Parliament levied a heavy tax on that tea. By the mid-eighteenth century, an accumulation of such injustices was uniting colonists from New Hampshire to Georgia in opposition to their common oppressor across the Atlantic.

A series of demands made by the British government hastened the uniting of the colonies. In 1765, Britain tried to raise money by passing the Stamp Act, which placed a tax on all paper used in the colonies and declared all unstamped documents to be legally void. Then the British demanded that British soldiers in the colonies be quartered by the colonists themselves. When in 1773 several British ships bearing tea arrived in Boston Harbor, the Bostonians would not accept the shipment. They refused to pay taxes without the right to vote for those who would represent them. Colonists disguised as Indians boarded the ships and dumped the tea into the harbor. The British Parliament responded by closing Boston Harbor, blocking it from trade. Many colonists' sympathies were now in accord with the goal of independence from Great Britain. Samuel Adams and others like him rallied the colonists in support of this cause. The Declaration of Independence and the long years of the Revolutionary War soon followed—an exciting time in American history.

We are all familiar with the famous leaders of this period, but as Elizabeth Yates (12) points out, many other Americans whose names we do not know played dynamic roles in creating a new nation:

Those who lived in small towns and villages and on distant farms, who thought and talked about events and made their feelings known: men who left their stock and crops and marched off to fight because they were convinced of the rightness of the stand that had been made, women who took over the work of the farms along with the care of their homes and families. Their names made no news. They did no particular acts of heroism, except as the living of each day was heroic in itself. Hard work they knew well, and hardship they could endure. Giving their lives or living their lives, they were as much the foundation of the new nation as were those whose names have long been known. (p. 6)

While famous people are found in the backgrounds of much historical fiction about the American Revolution that has been written for children, everyday people are the heroes of most of these books. In general, two types of stories are written about the revolutionary period: tales about those who defend the homefront while others go off to war and tales about males and females who become actively involved in the war itself.

The best-known children's story about this period is Esther Forbes's *Johnny Tremain*. Forbes creates a superbly authentic setting. Paul Revere and Samuel Adams play important parts in the story, but a silversmith's apprentice named Johnny and other unknown boys like him are the heroes. Through Johnny's observations, actions, and thoughts, Forbes emphasizes the issues of the times, the values of the people, and the feelings about freedom. Johnny discovers the political thinking of the time when he hears a minister preach sermons filled with anger against taxation without representation, delivers messages for the secret anti-British Boston Observers, and rides for the Boston Committee of Correspondence. Forbes's writing style creates believable action and dialogue, as in this excerpt from a speech calling the rebels to action:

Friends! Brethren! Countrymen! That worst of Plagues, the detested tea shipped for this Port by the East Indian Company, is now arrived in the Harbour: the hour of destruction, of manly opposition to the machinations of Tyranny, stares you in the Face; Every Friend to his Country, to Himself, and to Posterity, is now called upon to meet. (p. 107)

Johnny is one of the "Indians" who throw the despised tea into Boston Harbor. He experiences the anger and resulting unity when British troops close the harbor. He is there when British troops and colonial rebels clash at Concord. Unhappily, he is also there when his best friend dies. He makes the discovery that a sixteen-year-old is considered a boy in times of peace but a man in times of war. As a man, he has the right to risk his life for what he believes.

An unusual hero in the Revolutionary War, based on a real person, is the female soldier in Patricia Clapp's *I'm Deborah Sampson: A Soldier in the War of the Revolution*. Deborah sees her adopted brothers go off to war, where one of them dies. She believes so strongly in the need to fight that she disguises herself as a man, joins a regiment of soldiers, travels with them across the countryside, and is wounded. Her greatest fear when she is wounded is that her identity will be discovered. Deborah is a strong, memorable character who vividly lives in the pages of Clapp's story. (See page 88 for a discussion of conflict in this novel.)

Most school children know about Paul Revere's ride, but Gail E. Haley has chosen a not-so-famous ride to share with younger readers. *Jack Jouett's Ride* takes place in 1781 and tells a tale of daring equal to Paul Revere's. This time, a young rider discovers that British troops are riding toward Charlottesville, Virginia, to capture Thomas Jefferson, Patrick Henry, and other leaders of the Revolution. Jack saddles his horse, moves out into the night, and rides across meadows and thickets to spread the alarm. This picture storybook, with its vivid illustrations and simple language, appeals to young children and helps them grasp in the flavor of historic events.

Consider the themes and the historical facts from this period. Why do you think the following

Detailed illustrations of the setting help younger readers visualize the days of the American Revolution. (From *Jack Jouett's Ride*, by Gail E. Haley. Reprinted by permission of Viking Penguin, Inc.)

themes are developed in the literature? How and why are these themes similar to or different from themes in stories about other wartime periods?

1   Freedom is worth fighting for.
2   Strong beliefs require strong commitments.

Early Expansion of the United States

As more and more settlers came to America, the need for additional land became evident. Many settlers headed away from the Atlantic coastline into the rolling, tree-covered hills to the west, north, and south. These settlers had something in common: they sought freedom and land and had considerable courage. Some settlers developed friendly relationships with Native American* peoples; others experienced hostilities. It was not uncommon for settlers to be captured by Indians and taken into their tribes, sold as slaves, or held for ransom. Many abductions, however, were in retaliation for settlers' attacks against the native inhabitants of the wilderness.

Stories about early pioneer expansion are popular with children who enjoy vivid characters and rapid action. The young characters may be popular with children because they often show extraordinary courage and prove they can be equal to adults. Many of the stories depict strong family bonds. They may focus on everyday experiences or on tense drama. Authors create vivid descriptions of the new land that encourage readers to understand why a family is willing to give up a secure environment to live on a raw and dangerous frontier. Person-against-nature conflicts often appear in these stories. Person-against-self conflicts occur as characters face moral dilemmas such as racial prejudice.

Alice Dalgliesh's *The Courage of Sarah Noble* is an excellent story for young children. (Sarah, according to the author, did exist.) Dalgliesh encourages readers to visualize the courage that even an eight-year-old can demonstrate when she accompanies her father to their new land in Connecticut. On their journey through the wilderness Sarah often remembers her mother's words: "Keep up your courage, Sarah Noble!" (p. 2). She says them when the wolves howl in the forest, when she is surrounded by strange Indian chil-

Survival and friendship are important in this story set in the 1700s. (From *The Sign of the Beaver*, by Elizabeth George Speare. Copyright © 1983 by Elizabeth George Speare. By permission of Dell Publishing Company.)

dren, and when her father leaves her with friendly Indians so that he can travel back to Massachusetts. This is a story of friendship and faith as well as courage. The need to help others is one of its main themes: Sarah and her father help each other and develop strong ties with an Indian family, which invites Sarah to stay with them, makes her deerskin moccasins, and treats her like a daughter.

Themes of friendship and faith, moral obligation, working together, and love for land are all found in Elizabeth George Speare's *The Sign of the Beaver*. The Maine wilderness in the 1700s can be either an antagonist or a friend. Matt, the thirteen-year-old main character, faces a life-and-death struggle when his father leaves him alone to guard their frontier cabin through the winter. Without food or a gun, Matt confronts a harsh natural environment, fear of the local Indians,

---

*This book primarily uses the term *Native Americans* to denote the people historically referred to as *American Indians*. The term *Indian* is sometimes used interchangeably with *Native Americans* and in some contexts is used to name certain tribes of Native Americans.

and the possibility that he may never see his parents again. A Penobscot boy, in spite of his people's own conflicts about the way white settlers are changing their land, befriends Matt and teaches him how to survive.

The frontier of human understanding rather than the frontier of physical expansion is the setting for Carol Carrick's *Stay Away from Simon!* Attitudes toward and fears about a mentally retarded boy provide the conflict in this story set on Martha's Vineyard in the 1830s. The author creates believable fear and misunderstanding as two children, Lucy and Josiah, risk getting lost in a snow storm rather than walk on the road with Simon. The author encourages readers to understand how ridiculous these fears are by developing Simon as a caring individual who leads the children to safety.

Joan W. Blos's *A Gathering of Days: A New England Girl's Journal, 1830–32* is the fictional journal of a thirteen-year-old girl on a New Hampshire farm. Blos says that she tried to develop three types of truthfulness: "the social truthfulness of the situation, the psychological truthfulness of the characters, and the literary truthfulness of the manner of telling" (1, p. 371). Consequently, the characters are similar to those who, drawn by unknown artists, stare from New England portraits. Likewise, the tone of the story is similar to *Leavitt's Almanac*, written for farmers, with the form and style found in journal writings of that period.

Both Elizabeth George Speare's *Calico Captive* and Lois Lenski's *Indian Captive: The Story of Mary Jemison* are stories about white girls captured by native tribespeople. Both girls face difficult conflicts and harsh circumstances, but their experiences eventually cause them to question their former prejudices. Speare's Miriam learns more about the Indians from Pierre, a *coureur des bois*. Mary Jemison, after much inner turmoil, finally decides that the Seneca are her people:

At that moment she saw Old Shagbark looking at her, his brown eyes overflowing with kindness and understanding. He knew how hard it was for her to decide. . . .She saw the Englishman, too. His lips were smiling, but his eyes of cold gray were hard. Even if she were able to put all her thoughts into words, she knew he would never, never understand. Better to live with those who understood her because they loved her so much, than with one who could never think with her, in sympathy, about anything. . . .Squirrel Woman's scowling face and even Gray Wolf's wicked one no

longer held any terrors, because she understood them. (p. 268)

The previous two books express the viewpoints of white people who had difficult experiences in the early days of an expanding America. Other books, written from Native American viewpoints, describe the harmful influences of an expanding white population. In *Sweetgrass*, a winner of the Canadian Library Association's Book of the Year Award, Jan Hudson focuses on a young Blackfeet girl's struggle for maturity as she faces a life-and-death battle in 1837. The weapons in this battle are not guns and arrows, but smallpox, the "white man's sickness," and resulting hunger and death. Hudson employs figurative language involving signs and omens to develop believable characters, plot, and themes related to moral obligations, responsibility toward others, and retaining one's dreams. For example, the main character considers the importance of her name. She believes it is appropriate because Sweetgrass is "ordinary to look at but it's fragrant as the spring" (p. 12). Later, her Grandmother tells her that Sweetgrass has the power of memories. As Sweetgrass considers her own future, readers discover that she is joyfully approaching womanhood, "I felt mightier than a brave . . . . I felt I was holding the future like summer berries in my hands" (p. 26). Instead of allowing the signs and omens to control her life, Sweetgrass searches for ways to use them to overcome old taboos and help herself and her family in a time of great trouble: "I would make father do what I wanted. I would find the signs, the power to control my own days. I would make by life be what I wanted" (p. 15).

The themes in books of historical fiction about the early expansion of the United States vary considerably, depending on the perspective developed by the various authors and the age level of the readers. Consider the following themes. Why do you think they were chosen by authors who write stories about this period? How do they compare to themes found in different time periods? Are the themes significant today?

1 Friendship and faith are important human characteristics.
2 People long for their own land and the freedom ownership implies.
3 People will withstand considerable hardships to retain their dreams.

ISSUE

···❖···

Unbalanced Viewpoints in Historical Fiction

THE REPORTING OF HIStory may change depending upon the viewpoint of the author. This is equally true in the writing of historical fiction. Too many frontier books are told from the white settlers' perspective rather than from the perspective of Native Americans. In this context, some fear that children will not realize the hardships experienced or the contributions made by Native Americans. Stories told from the white settlers' perspective emphasize kidnappings of white children, wagon trains attacked by warring Indian tribes, settlements attacked and burned, settlers rescued by soldiers, and frontier heroes who created their reputations as Indian fighters. Some critics believe that historical fiction about settlement of North America should include more stories told from the Native American perspective. These stories might include Indian children who were kidnapped by white settlers or place a greater emphasis upon the reasons for the kidnapping of the white children; portray the numerous peaceful tribes who lived in harmony with settlers; and emphasize the diversity of the many Native American cultures.

Students of children's literature may consider issues related to the viewpoints of authors and the consequences of unbalanced narratives of other time periods; for example, early explorers, Roman invasion of Britain, religious freedom and settlement of America, the Revolutionary War, the Civil War, and World War II.

4 Strong family bonds help physical and spiritual survival.
5 Prejudice and hatred are destructive forces.
6 The greatest strength comes from within.
7 Moral obligations require personal commitment.

The Civil War Years

In the early centuries of American history, white slave traders brought hundreds of thousands of black Africans to this continent in chains and sold them on auction blocks as field workers, house servants, and skilled craftspeople. Many people in both the North and the South believed that slavery was immoral. Although they had not been able to pass laws against it, they were able to assist slaves in their flight toward Canada and freedom. Helping runaway slaves was a dangerous undertaking, especially after the passage of the Fugitive Slave Act in 1850 made it a crime. Handbills offering rewards for the return of certain slaves added to the danger by urging "slave-catchers" to hunt for any suspected runaways. Because of the dangers and the need for secrecy, an illicit network of people dedicated to assisting fugitive slaves linked North and South. Free people led the fugitives from one safe hiding place to another on each part of their journey along the Underground Railroad to Canada.

Conflicts between northern and southern interests that had emerged during the Constitutional Convention increased in the 1850s and led to the outbreak of the Civil War in 1861. The United States was torn apart. Allegiances were drawn, not only between states, but also within families. In some cases, relatives were on opposite sides of the conflict and faced one another on the battlefields of Bull Run and Gettysburg.

Strong human drama emerges from this historical period. Some authors focus upon slavery and the experiences of slaves during captivity or as fugitives seeking freedom. Other authors focus on the impact of the Civil War on young soldiers or on the people who remained at home. Person-against-society and person-against-self conflicts are common in historical fiction covering this period, as some characters confront prejudice and hatred and others wrestle with their consciences and discover the human tragedy associated with slavery and war. Authors who create credible plots must consider not only historical events but also the conflicting social attitudes of the times. The themes developed in this literature reflect strong human values, as writers express the need for personal freedom, ponder the right of one person to own another, consider the tragedies of war, and question the killing of one human by another.

The attitudes expressed toward blacks create special problems for authors who write about slavery. How accurately should historical fiction reflect attitudes and circumstances of the times? Should authors use terms of the period that are considered insensitive and offensive today? James Collier and Christopher Collier, for example, in their authors' note to *Jump Ship to Freedom*, consider the use of the word *nigger*. Although today the word is considered offensive, would avoiding it in a novel about slavery distort history? The Colliers chose to use the term as a way of illustrating their main character's change in attitude as he develops self-respect and self-confidence and of highlighting the social attitudes of the other characters in the book. In *Jump Skip to Freedom*, those who use the word *nigger* express racial bias toward blacks, and those who do not are concerned with the rights and self-respect of all humans. Consider for example, how the slave Daniel uses the word. At first he refers to himself as a nigger. He considers himself unintelligent, inferior to whites, and unable to think of himself as a person. He allows other people's opinions to reinforce these beliefs. Self-realization develops slowly as Daniel discovers that he can develop and carry out a plan to recover his father's confiscated funds and free himself, associate with people who consider him capable and slavery immoral, meet his moral obligations to his mother, and fight for his rights. After he makes these personal discoveries, he refuses to call himself nigger.

A slave ship in which human cargo are chained together in cramped quarters provides the setting for Paula Fox's *The Slave Dancer*. The story is told from the point of view of a thirteen-year-old white boy from New Orleans who is kidnapped by slave traders to play his fife on their ship. When the ship reaches Africa, Jessie learns about the trade in human "Black Gold" and discovers that, in their greed for trade goods, African chiefs sell their own people and people kidnapped from other tribes. For four long nights, longboats bring their cargoes to the slave ship: men and women who are half-conscious from the pressure of bodies and bruised by ankle shackles. The detailed setting and descriptions of the conditions on the ship seem believable: Jessie describes the holds as pits of misery, is horrified by the low regard for human life, and is shocked when prisoners who die are thrown overboard. Jessie learns the reason for having him aboard when slaves are dragged on deck and forced to dance; a dead or weak slave cannot be sold for profit, and the slave traders believe that dancing keeps their bodies strong.

This book has stirred considerable controversy. Some have criticized the fact that the slaves in the book are not treated like human beings or even given names. Many college students, however, say that while reading *The Slave Dancer* they realized for the first time the true inhumanity of slavery. Fox reveals the impact of the experience on Jessie by flashing ahead in time to Jessie's memories:

At the first note of a tune or a song, I would see once again as though they'd never ceased their dancing in my mind, black men and women and children lifting their tormented limbs in time to a reedy martial air, the dust rising from their joyless thumping, the sound of the fife finally drowned beneath the clanging of their chains. (p.176)

A book written for young children explains the purposes of the Underground Railroad. F. N. Monjo's *The Drinking Gourd* tells of a family that is part of the Underground Railroad and their role in helping a fugitive slave family escape. Even though this is an "easy-to-read" book, it illustrates the importance of one family's contributions, with dialogue between father and sons disclosing the purpose of the Railroad. Young readers also experience excitement and danger as Tommy accompanies his father and an escaping black family on the next part of their journey.

The impact of the Civil War years on free whites in the United States is the subject of several novels in which idealistic young men come

Fugitive slaves travel the Underground Railroad to freedom. (Illustration (pp. 34–35) from *The Drinking Gourd*, by F.N. Monjo. Pictures by Fred Brenner. An I CAN READ History Book. Pictures copyright © 1970 by Fred Brenner. Reprinted by permission of Harper & Row, Publishers, Inc.)

to realize that war is not simply a glamorous time of brass bands and heroic battles led by banner-carrying leaders. Stories about fighting soldiers often show men realizing the true horrors of war. Janet Hickman's *Zoar Blue* depicts the emotional effects of war when the younger members of the Separatists, a nonviolent religious group in Zoar, Ohio, defy their elders and enlist in the Union Army. Hickman encourages children to understand the person-against-society and person-against-self conflicts these young men experience as they struggle to maintain personal values out of step with the times. They feel loyalty to their country and are moved by Abraham Lincoln's call for troops, but the teachings of their church stress that people of conscience do not fight each other. Outsiders not of their faith taunt them about playing tunes on a piano while "braver" men play tunes on cannons. When the young men finally join the army, they continue to feel conflict about killing other people. They long for the simplicity and stability of their home community in the days before they had to face such dilemmas:

He had learned the Principles too well, perhaps. A Separatist could not murder any enemy, much less, one supposed, a countryman. How was it possible to follow the Principles and be a soldier too? There was no way to make sense between the war and such arguments. He had tried. (p.54)

Hickman gives further depth to the story by developing the perspective of the nonfighting residents of Zoar—their physical sacrifices and their grief for their sons—and by showing the changes in the soldiers after they return home.

One of the finest books to depict the wartime hardships and conflicts of family members who remain at home is Irene Hunt's *Across Five Aprils*. The beginning conflict is effectively introduced as members of a family in southern Illinois debate the issues related to the Civil War and choose their allegiances: Matt Creighton, the head of the family, argues that a strong union must be maintained; the majority of his sons agree with him, but one son argues that people in the South should be able to live without government interference. Hunt develops a strong personal conflict as Jethro, the youngest son, is emotionally torn between two beloved brothers, one who joins the Union Army and another who fights for the Confederacy. The consequences of hatred are illustrated when young toughs burn the Creightons' barn and put oil into their well because of the family's divided allegiances. The author allows readers to glimpse a different view of people when neighbors guard the farm, help put in the crops, and rebuild the barn. This is a touching story of a heroic family overcoming their problems at home and awaiting news of fighting sons. In spite of disagreement, the Creightons maintain strong family ties. When the son fighting for the South learns that one of his brothers was killed at Pittsburg Landing, he sends a message to his mother that he was not in that battle and did not fire the bullet that killed his brother. This story helps children understand the real tragedy of the Civil War: brothers fought against brothers and neighbors against neighbors.

Consider the following themes developed by authors who write about slavery and the Civil War period. Why are so many of the themes related to overcoming great personal and social conflicts? How do these themes relate to events and values of the times? Are they appropriate for the time period? What other time periods, if any, reflect

JANET HICKMAN
ZOAR BLUE

Strong personal values conflict with social values in this Civil War story. (From *Zoar Blue*, by Janet Hickman. Copyright © 1978, Janet Hickman. Reprinted with permission of Macmillan Publishing Co.)

similar themes and what do they have in common with the Civil War period? Are any of these themes significant in contemporary life and literature?

1 War creates human tragedy.
2 Moral obligations must be met even if one's life or freedom is in jeopardy.
3 Moral sense does not depend on skin color, but on what is inside a person.
4 People should take pride in themselves and their accomplishments.
5 Prejudice and hatred are destructive forces.
6 Humans search for freedom.
7 Personal conscience may not allow humans to kill others.
8 Strong family ties help people persevere.

The Western Frontier

The American frontier was extending further and further west in the 1800s. White Americans were giving up their settled towns and farms in the East to make their fortunes in unknown territories. Former slaves saw the frontier as a place to make a new start in freedom, and Asian immigrants to the West Coast moved inland to work on the railroads that were beginning to span the Great Plains. The Homestead Act of 1862 promised free land to settlers willing to stake their claims and develop the land. Stories of rich earth in fertile valleys caused families to break away from their roots and travel several thousand miles over prairies and mountains to reach Oregon. Others dreamed of rich prairie land that did not need to be cleared of rocks or timber, and covered wagons carried many of them into the Oklahoma Territory. Whether the pioneers stopped in the Midwest or went along the Oregon Trail, the journey was perilous. They fought nature as they battled blizzards, dust storms, mountain crossings, and swollen rivers. They fought people as they met unfriendly Native Americans, outlaws, and cattle ranchers who did not want them to farm. Some demonstrated noble human qualities as they helped each other search for new land and made friends with the Native Americans they encountered. Others demonstrated greed and prejudice in their interactions with other pioneers and Native Americans. Native peoples themselves were experiencing a time of considerable trauma as outsiders invaded their ancient territories, staking claims to land that had once been without ownership or boundaries and killing the buffalo and other wild animals on which the people relied for subsistence. The American government had begun its campaign to relocate Native Americans onto reservations that were minuscule in size and resources compared to the rich stretches of prairie and mountain that had long been native people's domain.

This period of American history—with its high hopes, dangers, triumphs, and tragic conflicts—still captures the imagination of Americans. Stories about pioneer America are very popular with children, as exemplified by the continuing interest in books such as Laura Ingalls Wilder's "Little House" series. Historical fiction for children includes three general types of stories about this period: adventure stories in which the characters cross the prairies and mountains; stories about family life on pioneer homesteads; and stories about interactions between Native Americans and pioneers or Native Americans and military forces. Authors who write about crossing the continent explore people's reasons for moving and their strong feelings for the land. Self-discovery may occur in young characters as they begin to understand their parents' motivations and values. Detailed descriptions of settings allow readers to understand the awesome continent as both inspiration and antagonist. Stories set on homesteads often develop warm family relationships as families seek to achieve their dreams. Like earlier stories about Native Americans and colonial settlers, these Native American and pioneer stories include tales of captive children and stories that depict white people's harsh treatment of Native Americans as a traditional way of life is forcibly altered.

Moving West. Barbara Brenner's *Wagon Wheels* is an enjoyable book for young readers. Based on fact, it tells about a black pioneer family that leaves Kentucky after the Civil War and moves to Kansas to receive land under the Homestead Act. The family develops a friendly relationship with members of an Indian tribe without whose help they would have starved. Young children enjoy the story because it shows that pioneer children were courageous: three boys survive a prairie fire and travel over one hundred miles to join their father. This is one of the few books written about blacks as a part of the frontier experience.

Honore Morrow tells the story of earlier pioneers to the far West in *On to Oregon!*, a book for older children. Morrow's novel about pioneers from Missouri in the 1840s is more than an adventure story about a family crossing the continent; it is also a psychological story about the challenge of surviving in harsh circumstances. After his parents die on the trail, thirteen-year-old John Sager becomes head of the family and leads his brothers and sisters on to Oregon over a thousand miles of treacherous mountains, canyons, and rivers. The people in the wagon train do not want responsibility for the Sager children and plan to send them back East. The author shows the strength of the father's dream by describing John's actions as he refuses to forfeit his father's dream; he works out a scheme so that the people think he and his siblings will be traveling with Kit Carson. The children secretly pack their goods on

oxen and head out on the lonely trail. Now the awesome natural environment becomes the chief antagonist against which the children must struggle before reaching a warm, gentle valley in the Oregon of their dreams. Morrow encourages readers to understand the importance of reading about the contributions of people who made westward expansion possible. Consider, for example, the possible impact of the author's closing statements:

You and I will never hear that magic call of the West, "Catch up! Catch up!" We never shall see the Rockies framed in the opening of our prairie schooner and tingle with the knowledge that if we and our fellow immigrants can reach the valleys in the blue beyond the mountains and there plow enough acreage, that acreage will belong forever to America. (p. 235)

Kathryn Lasky's *Beyond the Divide*, a story of survival set in the ruggedness of the far West just before the Civil War, develops strong themes related to both the destructive nature of greed and prejudice and the constructive power of dreams, hope, and moral obligations. Louise Moeri effectively develops similar themes in *Save Queen of Sheba*, as twelve-year-old King David and his young sister Queen of Sheba (named after biblical characters) survive a Sioux raid and set out alone across the prairie in hope of finding the wagons that separated from their portion of the wagon train. The author effectively demonstrates the strength of King David's feeling of reponsiblity by developing his varied emotional responses during several emotionally and physically draining experiences. For another view of the western trails, young children enjoy Sibyl Hancock's *Old Blue*, based on a true incident involving a boy who went on a cattle drive in 1878. The hero of the story is actually an intelligent steer who can find the right direction even in a storm.

Pioneer Family Life. Many stories about pioneer life depict the power of the family working to conquer outside dangers and build a home filled with love and decency. One author in particular has enabled children to vicariously experience family life on the frontier. Laura Ingalls Wilder, through her "Little House" books, recreated the world of her own frontier family from 1870 through 1889. The "Little House" books have sold in the millions and received literary acclaim. A popular television series introduced the Ingalls family to millions of new friends.

The first book, *Little House in the Big Woods*, takes place in a deep forest in Wisconsin. Unlike those in many other pioneer stories, this setting is not antagonistic. Although the woods are filled with bears and other wild animals, the danger never really enters the log cabin in the clearing. Any potential dangers are implied through Pa's stories about his adventures in the big woods, told in the close family environment inside the cabin. Other descriptions of family activities also suggest that the environment, while creating hard work for the pioneer family, is not awesome or dangerous: they clear the land, plant and harvest the crops, gather sap from the sugar bush, and hitch up the wagon and drive through the woods to Grandpa's house. Wilder focuses upon individual members of the family and their interactions with one another. Pa's actions, for example, imply that he is a warm, loving father. After working all day he has time to play the fiddle, play mad dog with the children, and tell them stories. Likewise, Ma takes care of their physical needs but also helps them create paper dolls. The impact of what it means to live in the relative isolation of the frontier where a family must be self-sufficient is also implied through the children's actions and thoughts: they feel secure when the attic is hung with smoked hams and filled with pumpkins; they are excited when they get new mittens and a cloth doll for Christmas; and they are astonished when they visit a town for the first time and see a store filled with marvelous treasures.

In the rest of the "Little House" books, Laura and her family leave the big woods of Wisconsin to live in the prairie states: Kansas, Minnesota, and South Dakota. They go to a one-room school, build a fish trap, have a grasshopper invasion, worry when Pa must walk three hundred miles to find a job, and live through a blizzard. Wilder's description of the winter in *Little Town on the Prairie* encourages modern-day children to share the experience:

All winter long, they had been crowded in the little kitchen, cold and hungry and working hard in the dark and the cold to twist enough hay to keep the fire going and to grind wheat in the coffee mill for the day's bread. All that long, long winter, the only hope had been that sometime winter must end, sometime blizzards must stop, the sun would shine warm again. (p. 3)

When Laura gets her first job in the little town of De Smet, South Dakota, she earns twenty-five cents a day and her dinner for sewing shirts. Unselfishly, she saves this money to help send her sister Mary to a college for the blind in Vinton, Iowa. The series ends with stories about Laura's experiences as a school teacher, her marriage to Almanzo Wilder, and their early years together on a prairie homestead. One reason children like these books so much is the feeling of closeness they have with Laura.

Carol Ryrie Brink's *Caddie Woodlawn* presents another loving frontier family. The time and setting are similar to the first "Little House" book: the last half of the nineteenth century in Wisconsin. In fact, the real Caddie, Brink's grandmother, lived approximately thirty miles north of where Laura Ingalls Wilder was born. Caddie is a warm-hearted, brave, rambunctious girl who loves to play in the woods and along the river with her brothers. She is also a friend of Native Americans in the area. In one dramatic situation, Caddie jumps on a horse and rides through the night woods to warn her friend, Indian John, about some settlers' plot to attack John's people. Caddie's experiences differ from present-day ones, but her worries about growing up are similar to those of any girl, no matter when she lives. With Caddie, children know that everything will be alright: "When she awoke she knew that she need not be afraid of growing up. It was not just sewing and weaving and wearing stays. It was a responsibility, but, as Father spoke of it, it was a beautiful and precious one, and Caddie was ready to go and meet it" (p. 251).

Patricia MacLachlan's *Sarah, Plain and Tall* is a more recently published book about pioneer family life. In this book for younger readers, MacLachlan develops the strong need for a loving mother and a happy family life and introduces the children's need for singing in the home by contrasting the singing that took place before the mother's death with the quiet, sad atmosphere that dominates life after the mother's death. The father's needs are revealed through his actons when he places an advertisement for a wife in an eastern newspaper, in response to which "plain and tall" Sarah enters the family's life. The children's need for a mother and a happy home is reflected in their desire for singing, in their re-reading of Sarah's letters until the letters are worn out, in their desire to be perfect for Sarah, in their frightened reactions when Sarah misses the sea, in their trying to bring characteristics of the sea into their prairie farm, and in their com-

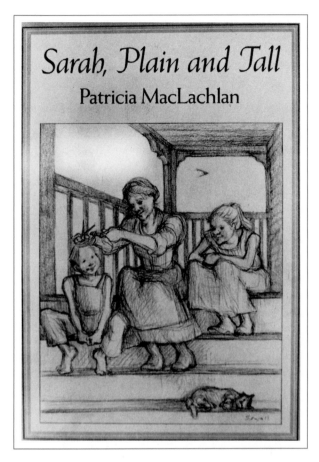

The need for warm family relationships provides a focus for this frontier story. (Jacket art by Marsha Sewall from *Sarah, Plain and Tall*, by Patricia MacLachlan. Jacket art copyright © 1985 by Marcia Sewall. Reprinted by permission of Harper & Row, Publishers, Inc.)

plete happiness when they realize that Sarah will stay on the prairie. MacLachlan's characterization of Sarah reveals a strong, loving, independent pioneer woman who discovers that her love for her new family is stronger than her feelings of loneliness for the sea. Like Wilder's and Brink's, MacLachlan's characters may seem so real because she drew them from her own family history.

Harold Keith combined personal experiences, interviews with two grandfathers who had lived on the Oklahoma frontier, and research into newspaper files and historical journals in writing *The Obstinate Land*. In 1893 Fritz Romberg and his family leave south Texas to homestead on for-

merly Cherokee land on the Oklahoma prairie. The family's dream is to own a farm without being obligated to anyone. The author encourages the reader to see the land for the first time through the reactions of three people. Their contrasting feelings about the land are consistent with Keith's characterizations; Father is excited because it's a land without timber, stumps, or rocks that's "shouting to be farmed" (p. 2). Fritz, the thirteen-year-old, is "exhilarated by the lonely magnificence of the country, and the sense of freedom it inspired" (p. 2). The mother, Freda, looks at the land with sadness: "You can look a long way and see nothing" (p. 3). She has torn up her roots, left her relatives, left her small daughter in a distant cemetery, and traveled to an unknown land.

Keith develops an effective plot in this book because he relies upon both authentic conflicts of the time period and conflicts with the natural environment of Oklahoma. The Romberg family has trouble with a family of "sooners" (people who illegally crossed the boundaries before the land was open to homesteaders) that claims the land that the Rombergs desire and with a neighboring cattle rancher who tries through legal and illegal means to drive them off the land. Nature becomes a fearsome antagonist during a series of disasters: a hard winter that contributes to the death of Fritz's father and several years of crop failures due to hail, grasshoppers, and drought. Every time the Rombergs consider moving, however, they think of their original dream and decide to stay. This tenacity is reflected in Fritz's final feeling of self-worth:

Fritz was proud of having been able to endure against the stiff challenge thrown out by the land and the elements. He had hung on tenaciously and won. The more he sacrificed and the harder he had worked, the more he came to appreciate himself. The struggle had broadened his character and made him a man. (p. 209)

Other outstanding books about pioneer family life include Scott O'Dell's *Carlota*, the story of the strong and independent daughter of a Spanish landholder in early California, and Ann Nolan Clark's *Year Walk*, in which a Spanish Basque boy develops self-understanding on an western sheep ranch (see chapter eleven for discussions of these books).

Pioneers and Native Americans. The West Texas frontier of the 1860s provides the setting for Patricia Beatty's *Wait for Me, Watch for Me, Eula Bee*. The story centers on the capture of two farm children by Comanche and Kiowa Indians, the subsequent escape of the older boy, the changing loyalties of the very young girl as she learns to love her Comanche foster parent, and her rescue by her brother. Beatty's descriptions of camp life, food, travel, and behavior create a vivid picture of the period. Her author's notes list the sources for her information on Comanche and Kiowa tribes and their treatment of captives. While the author's descriptions and characterizations depict the Comanche as leading a harsh life built on raiding and warfare, they also depict how much the Comanche value children. The developing love between the little girl and her Comanche foster parent exemplifies a warm, loving relationship. Sadness in this book stems from the tragic results of two cultures that have little understanding of each other.

A true story from the 1850s is the basis for Evelyn Sibley Lampman's *White Captives*. White men in the Southwest came upon some Tonto Apache women and children who were berry picking, killed the women, and took two girls as slaves. One of the captured girls escaped and took the news back to the Apache, who sent out a raiding party to avenge the women's deaths. They killed most members of the Oatman family, who were traveling alone, but, like the white men, took two girls of the family captive. Lampman's retelling of this story contains considerable information about the Native American viewpoint and way of life. The girls were slaves for two different tribes, the nomadic Apache, who were hunters, and the Mohave, who were farmers. Lampman effectively brings Native American spiritual beliefs into the story through Mohave religious beliefs and ceremonies, such as rituals that preceded the planting of crops. The Oatman girls, like most white settlers, are shocked to discover that Native Americans have moral principles and spiritual beliefs, similar to their own. The Mohave belief in a great flood and the finding of sanctuary at the top of a sacred mountain is similar to the Biblical story of Noah. Lampman informs readers that after the older girl's rescue (her sister died in captivity) she told her story to a minister named Stratton. His book, *Captivity of the Oatman Girls, Being an Interesting Narrative of Life among the Apache and Mohave Indians*, published in 1857, sold over 25,000 copies. "In a small way," says Lampman, "the book probably

did as much to turn public sentiment against the Indians as *Uncle Tom's Cabin* did against . . . slavery" (p. 177). *White Captives*, written over one hundred years later, presents a fairer view of hardworking Native Americans and the reasons behind their hostility toward white settlers.

A tragic period in Navaho history, 1863–1865, is the setting for Scott O'Dell's *Sing Down the Moon*. The story of the three-hundred-mile forced march that culminates in the Navahos being held prisoner at Fort Sumner, New Mexico, is told through the viewpoint of a Navaho girl, Bright Morning. O'Dell effectively uses both descriptions of physical settings and characterizations to depict a human tragedy. The Navahos are forced to leave their home, the beautiful Canyon de Chelly, with its fruit trees, green grass, sheep, and cool water, for the harsh wind-swept reality of the landscape around Fort Sumner. The greatest tragedy does not result from the loss of their home, however, but from the loss of their spiritual hope. Still, Bright Morning does not give up her dream of returning to her beautiful canyon, and O'Dell creates a thought-provoking, bittersweet ending. Bright Morning and her husband escape from the U. S. Army and return to her hidden valley. It is as she remembers it: the blossoms are on the trees, a sheep and a lamb are grazing on the green land and the tools she hid from the soldiers are waiting. But a menacing shadow looms over their happiness: readers cannot forget that the Navaho family is hiding from the soldiers they saw on the horizon.

Many authors who write about the pioneer period stress the quest for and love of land and the conflict between different cultures. Consider the following themes developed in historical fiction about pioneer America. How do the themes correspond with historical events? What other periods have similar themes? What are the similarities between times with similar themes?

1 Humans have moral obligations that must be met.
2 People have strong dreams of owning land.
3 Families can survive if they work together.
4 People need each other and may work together for their mutual good.
5 Battles can be won through legal means rather than through unlawful actions.
6 Hatred and prejudice are destructive forces.
7 Without spiritual hope, humans may lose their will to live.

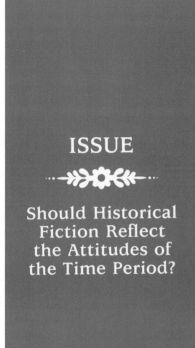

ISSUE

--->>❀<<---

Should Historical
Fiction Reflect
the Attitudes of
the Time Period?

THE SEARCH FOR AU-thenticity in setting, character development, attitudes, and actions for a historical time period, and a sensitivity toward racial perspectives create dilemmas for authors, publishers, and reviewers of historical fiction for children. Should historical fiction reflect the attitudes and circumstances of the times? Or should historical fiction reflect the changing attitudes toward people of all races? These issues become especially critical when historical fiction is reviewed by literary critics and various interest groups. *Sounder,* by William H. Armstrong, is an example of historical fiction that has been both acclaimed for literary merit and criticized for its portrayal of a black family. Literary acclaim is exemplified in the awarding of the Newbery Medal in 1970.

However, *Sounder* has been denounced by some critics because they believe it emasculates the black man and destroys the black family by showing it as spiritless and submissive rather than actively fighting injustice. In contrast, other critics maintain that the book authentically depicts the poverty, ignorance, and attitudes of the times; consequently, the family members acted in the only way possible. A similar debate centers around the depiction of black characters in Paula Fox's 1973 Newbery Medal winner *The Slave Dancer.* Students of children's literature should consider this issue and the implications for writers, publishers, and selectors of literature when they read historical fiction that depicts Black Americans, Asian Americans, and Hispanic Americans.

The Early Twentieth Century

Recent books of historical fiction with settings in the early 1900s often depict social conflicts and the Great Depression, which began in 1929. These stories stress both physical and spiritual survival as people strive to maintain pride and independence. Strong person-against-society and person-against-self conflicts develop as people experience or express racial prejudice and face financial hardships.

Felice Holman's *The Wild Children* is set in Russia in 1917–1921, the time following the Bolshevik Revolution. The main characters are children who are left homeless because their parents are either dead or imprisoned. The antagonist is a society that fears political freedom. Holman's vivid descriptions of children's living conditions and their fear of authority create a believable antagonist. The children's struggle for survival and their need for each other emphasize that love and

loyalty help people endure and survive castastrophic experiences.

Mildred D. Taylor's *Roll of Thunder, Hear My Cry* explores both the subtle and the explicit racial prejudice many white Americans expressed toward black Americans in the early twentieth century. Consider, for example, the subtle discrimination developed by the author: Cassie and her brother, who live in rural Mississippi, excitedly await their new schoolbooks, only to receive badly worn, dirty castoffs from the white elementary school. When Cassie's brother looks at the inside cover of his book, he sees that on its twelfth date of issue to him, it is described as being in very poor condition and the race of the student is listed as "nigra." The children's warm family life gives them the strength to confront such discrimination. First, they refuse the books. Then they create a minor accident for the bus driver who consistently and intentionally splashes the black children's clothes with dirty water as he drives the white children to their separate school. (There is no bus service for the black school.) After the children secretly deepen one of the puddles in the road, the bus breaks an axle and its riders must walk. Other expressions of racism portrayed in this book are far less subtle, however, and include the family's experiences with night riders and cross burnings. Now, understandably, the family feels fear as well as humiliation and indignation. In a sequel to this book, *Let the Circle Be Unbroken*, Taylor helps the reader see how white and black people's estrangement from and suspicion of each other results from ingrained social prejudices.

The family in *Roll of Thunder, Hear My Cry* owns its own land; the mother has graduated from a teacher's college, and the children consistently attend school. The family experiences injustice, but a loving environment helps protect and strengthen them. The experiences in William H. Armstrong's *Sounder* are harsher and filled with tragedy. An early twentieth-century family of black sharecroppers lives in one of numerous ramshackled cabins scattered across the vast fields of the white landlord. When the poverty-stricken father steals a ham to feed his hungry family, he is handcuffed, chained, and taken to jail. The futility of protest is suggested as Sounder, the family's faithful coon dog, tries to save the father and is wounded by the white sheriff's shotgun. Comparisons between the two incidents are developed as both the father and Sounder are gone: the father to jail and then to a succession of chain gangs, and Sounder to the woods to heal his wounds. A strong bond between man and dog is inferred as Sounder returns, a crippled remnant of his former self. He does not bark until the father returns home, himself crippled by a dynamite blast in the prison quarry. The two old friends are physically and emotionally tired and have only a short life together. The final vision of the two friends is one of remembered strength as the son, grown to manhood, recalls his father and the faithful dog as they were before the tragic happenings:

The pine trees would look down forever on a lantern burning out of oil but not going out. A harvest moon would cast shadows forever of a man walking upright, his dog, bouncing after him. And the quiet of the night would fill and echo again with the deep voice of Sounder, the great coon dog. (p. 116)

Critics of *Sounder* believe that, because the dog is the only character in the book with a name, the book implies that the characters need not be respected as human beings. Critics also object to the black family being characterized as submissive and spiritless. Others argue that the family should be nameless because the tragedy depicted in the story was one shared by many poor black sharecroppers during that period. In this latter view, tragedy is seen as a strong bond between all people who experience injustice. Readers may consider both viewpoints and form their own evaluations of *Sounder*.

In *Circle of Fire*, William H. Hooks also explores the consequences of hatred and prejudice. The setting is North Carolina in the 1930s; the conflict is between the Ku Klux Klan and a group of Irish gypsies. The author creates a believable person-against-society conflict by telling the story through the viewpoint of an eleven-year-old boy who befriends the gypsies. Readers may wish to consider an assertion Hooks makes in his end note: "The Ku Klux Klan grows and expands, reaching even into the alien territory of the North. *Circle of Fire*, set in the 1930s, is about the turbulent drama that occurred when someone dared step outside that 'rightful place.' These same events could happen today" (p. 147).

The consequences of social injustice and the conflict between classes shape the plot development in Harry Kullman's *The Battle Horse*. In this story set in 1930s Stockholm, the characters find that they must re-examine their own motives as a consequence of a game in which the knights are the rich preppies and the horses are the poor public school children. The author concludes on a strong theme for social equality: "One day we horses will travel over the Seven Seas like Gulliver and we won't carry the rich and powerful on our backs any more. We'll take control of our lives and everybody will have the same opportunities and the same rights in our kingdom, the Kingdom of the Horses, and there won't be any words for lying or deceit, no words for violence or war, no words for rich or poor" (p.183).

Franklin D. Roosevelt's fireside chats, a father who mends his shoes with folded paper, and a twelve-year-old's dreams of having her own suitcase contribute to Constance C. Greene's convincing portrayal of the Depression era in *Dotty's Suitcase*. Greene depicts the pressures of hard times by describing how the family of Dotty's friend must move to find work, the experiences of a man who loses both wealth and family because of the crash of the stock market in 1929, and the worries of children and adults about the cost of food. Dotty longs to escape from the Depression by obtaining a suitcase and traveling with money she hopes to acquire. Her true character is exposed when she finds the money and the suitcase and gives the money to her friend's family. Dotty discovers that she is rich compared to her friend: she has enough to eat, her father has a job, and she has a radio.

The importance of personal dreams to uphold the human spirit, the detrimental and strengthening consequences of physical and personal hardships, and the sustaining power of love are themes Crystal Thrasher develops in *A Taste of Daylight*. Thrasher encourages readers to understand the magnitude of the Depression by portraying the problems a country family faces after they move to the city. Contrasts between rural and urban survival problems, descriptions of physical scars that are related to manual labor, and responses of characters that enhance family survival create a believable story.

The themes developed in historical fiction set in the early twentieth century highlight both negative and positive human attitudes and values. Consider the following themes found in the literature. How do the themes relate to the historical events? Are these themes found during any other time period in historical fiction?

1   Humans will strive for the survival of physical body and human spirit.
2   Prejudice and discrimination are destructive forces.
3   There is a bond between people who experience injustice.
4   Monetary wealth does not create a rich life.

World War II

In 1933, Adolf Hitler took power in Germany, and Germany resigned from the League of Nations. In 1935, Hitler reintroduced conscription of German soldiers and recommended rearmament, contrary to the Treaty of Versailles. Along with a rapid increase in military power came an obsessive hatred of the Jewish people. In March 1938, Hitler's war machine began moving across Europe. Austria was occupied, and the imprisonment of Jews began. World War II became a reality when

the Germans invaded Poland on September 1, 1939.

The 1940s saw the invasion of Norway, Belgium, and Holland; the defeat of the French army; and the heroic evacuation of British soldiers from Dunkirk. These years, from the start of the invasions through the defeat of Hitler's forces in 1945, have inspired many tales of both sorrow and heroism.

Authors who write children's historical fiction with a World War II setting often focus on Jewish experiences in hiding and in concentration camps, Japanese Americans' experiences in internment centers in the United States, or the perseverance of people in occupied lands. Because some of these stories are written by people who lived similar experiences, they tend to be emotional. The authors often create vivid conflicts by describing characters' fears and the nature of the setting and antagonists. Authors may explore the human consequences of war and/or prejudice by having characters ponder why their lives are in turmoil, by describing characters reactions to their situations and to one another, and by revealing what happens to the characters or their families as a result of war. As might be expected, the themes of these stories include the consequences of hatred and prejudice, the search for religious and personal freedom, and the role of personal conscience and obligations toward others.

The Holocaust. The Nazis' terrible crimes against Jewish people are familiar to adults and children alike. Stories about the Holocaust help children sense the bewilderment and terror of a time when innocent people were the subject of irrational hatred and persecution.

Johanna Reiss tells a fictional version of her own story in *The Upstairs Room*. The author allows readers to glimpse varying consequences of prejudice and hatred as the young girl hears news of the war and asks why Hitler hates her people; she is barred from restaurants and the public school; and she learns that many Jewish people are being taken to forced labor camps. Reiss depicts the obligations of one human to another when a Dutch family offers, in spite of great danger, to hide Johanna and her sister on their farm. The farmer builds a secret space in an upstairs closet to provide a hiding place for the two girls. At first Johanna does not understand why she and her sister must hide, but gradually she realizes their serious predicament as word of the Holocaust spreads.

Reiss's style and first-person point of view create several scenes that show the breathless fear of the children as they hide in the cramped closet:

Footsteps. Loud Ones. Boots. Coming up the stairs. Wooden shoes. Coming behind. Sini put her arms around me and pushed my head against her shoulder. Loud voices. Ugly ones. Furniture being moved. And Opoe's protesting voice. The closet door was thrown open. Hands fumbled on the shelves. Sini was trembling. She tightened her arms around me. I no longer breathed through my nose. Breathing through my mouth made less noise. (p. 149)

Both the girls and the family protecting them are brave during this unsuccessful search by Nazi troops. The story ends happily, as Canadian troops liberate the town and at last Johanna and her sister may leave their room. This is a powerful story of the experiences of common people during German occupation. (Some adults have criticized this book because of realistic dialogue in which members of the farm family use swear words.)

Trust in and loyalty toward a parent are strong motivational forces in Uri Orlev's story of survival set in the Jewish ghetto of Warsaw, Poland. *The Island on Bird Street* chronicles Alex's experiences as he, while waiting hopefully for his father's return, turns a bombed-out building into a refuge. Surrounded by houses emptied of food, Alex feels that his refuge is similar to the desert island in his favorite book, *Robinson Crusoe*. Orlev develops two purposes for the setting: the symbolism of a lonely "island" on which Alex, like Robinson Crusoe, must learn how to survive, and the terrifying historical background of the Holocaust, in which Alex witnesses the capture of his Jewish family and friends, experiences fear and loneliness, and nurses a resistance fighter's wounds. The book concludes on a strong note of hope as Alex's father returns, finds his son where he promised to wait, and takes him to the forest to be with the partisans who are resisting the Nazis.

In *When Hitler Stole Pink Rabbit*, Judith Kerr uses personal experiences to provide details about a Jewish family that flees Germany just before the Nazis can arrest the father. Another family makes its escape in Sonia Levitin's *Journey to America*. In both these books, the families show

Symbolic and historical settings are integral to a story set in the Warsaw ghetto. (Jacket illustration copyright © 1984 by Jean Titherington from *The Island on Bird Street* by Uri Orlev. Reprinted by permission of Houghton Mifflin Company.)

considerable courage in times of great danger. Although they must leave wealth, possessions, and friends behind, they feel that everything will be all right if they can be together.

Other books about the impact of the Holocaust include Aranka Siegal's *Upon the Head of the Goat: A Childhood in Hungary 1939–1944*, which chronicles a nine-year-old girl's experiences from the time she hears about Hitler until her family boards a cattle train to Auschwitz, and Benjamin Tene's *In the Shade of the Chestnut Tree*, whose subject is the Warsaw Ghetto. After reading these stories, children often are concerned about the implications of not acting when other people are unjustly accused of crimes.

Internment of Japanese Americans. The Jewish people weren't the only ones to live through persecution and fear during World War II. Many children are surprised to read stories about the American treatment of Japanese Americans during World War II. Two books by Yoshiko Uchida tell about a Japanese American family's experiences after the bombing of Pearl Harbor. (Although the stories are fictional, they are based on what happened to Uchida and her family.) In *Journey to Topaz*, the police take away Yuki's father, a businessman in Berkeley, California, and send Yuki, her mother, and her older brother to a permanent internment center in Utah, called Topaz. Uchida creates vivid pictures of the internment camp by describing, for example, latrines without doors, the lines of people waiting to use them, and the wind blowing across the desert into the barracks. The fear of the interned people and their wardens climaxes when the grandfather of Yuki's best friend goes searching for arrowheads and is shot by a guard who believes he is trying to escape. Family members experience conflicting feelings when Yuki's brother, wishing to prove his loyalty to America, joins an army unit composed of Japanese Americans. Yuki's story continues in *Journey Home*, in which the family returns to Berkeley only to discover distrust, difficulty finding work, and anti-Japanese violence. The family feels hope and strength more than bitterness, however. Yuki discovers that coming home is having everyone she cares about around her.

Other Wartime Stories. Some other World War II stories create adventurous plots. For example, Marie McSwigan's *Snow Treasure* is based on a true incident in 1940 in which $9 million in Norwegian gold bullion (thirteen tons) is slipped past Nazi sentries and shipped to Baltimore. The unusual twist is that children on sleds were able to get the bullion past the Nazi troops to a boat hidden in a fiord. Children enjoy this story because it demonstrates how important even the work of young children can be when they all work together to preserve their country.

Marian Bauer explores the far-reaching effects of war on human emotions in *Rain of Fire*. After World War II, twelve-year-old Steve first feels great pride in his veteran brother, Matthew; but when Matthew doesn't live up to Steve's heroic expectations, Steve's feelings slowly change to confusion and hostility. Only after a near tragedy does Matthew share with Steve his experiences in Hiroshima, Japan, helping Steve to understand his brother's reluctance to talk about war. The author develops the turning point in Steve's feelings as Steve tries to convince Matthew that he must share those experiences so that tragedies like Hiroshima cannot happen again.

The themes in children's historical fiction with settings during World War II resemble themes found during other times of great peril. Consider the following themes. How do they relate to historical events? What are characteristics of other historical periods that have similar themes?

1 Humans will seek freedom from religious and political persecution.

Children demonstrate that they can be courageous even during times of peril. (From *Snow Treasure*, by Marie McSwigan. Copyright 1942 by E. P. Dutton & Co., Inc. Renewal © 1970 by Kathryn McSwigan Laughlin.)

2 Prejudice and hatred are destructive forces.
3 Moral obligation and personal conscience are strong human forces.
4 Freedom is worth fighting for.
5 Family love and loyalty help people endure catastrophic experiences.

SUMMARY

Historical fiction provides a means for children to live vicariously in the past. While they are learning about the experiences of others, they are also reading for enjoyment and gaining understanding of their heritage. Through historical fiction, children can discover that all people are dependent upon one another regardless of the time in which they live. They also discover that people have had similar human needs throughout history; historical fiction allows them to judge human relationships and realize that their own present and future are linked to people and events of times past.

Adults should evaluate historical fiction according to the criteria used for any fine literature, but there are several specific demands placed on its authors. Setting is integral to historical fiction and must be authentic in every respect. Settings often function as antagonists, as is common in pioneer stories. The actions, beliefs, and values of the characters must be realistic for the period. The plots must be credible for the time period. The experiences, conflicts, and characters' resolution of conflicts must reflect the times. The themes in historical fiction should be worthwhile and relevant both in today's society and in the historical setting. These themes often stress humans' search for freedom, love for land, loyalty and honor, and the cruelty and futility of war. Considerable research is necessary before an author can write credible historical fiction.

Books of historical fiction and their characteristic themes were discussed in a chronological order reflecting the historical eras in which the stories take place.

Suggested Activities for Adult Understanding of Historical Fiction

☐ Find an example of historical fiction written for beginning readers and another written for older readers. Compare the settings. Can they both be described as *integral settings*? If the book written for younger children does not provide as many details as the one for older children, has the author used any other medium to relate these details to the reader? For example, compare Arnold Lobel's setting in *On the Day Peter Stuyvesant Sailed into Town* with Esther Forbes's setting in *Johnny Tremain*.

☐ Locate a story such as Honore Morrow's *On to Oregon!* in which the setting takes on the role of antagonist. How has the author developed the realization that the setting is the antagonist? How do the characters overcome these obstacles of nature? What happens to the characters as they face and overcome the antagonist?

☐ Writers of historical fiction often place famous persons into the backgrounds of their stories, while the pivotal character is usually fictional. Read a story such as Erik Christian Haugaard's *Cromwell's Boy* and compare the roles of the little-known eleven-year-old Oliver Cutter with the well-known Oliver Cromwell. Why did the author choose a little-known person as the main character?

☐ Writing an excellent historical fiction novel requires considerable research by the author. Choose several authors of historical fiction and investigate the sources they used.

☐ Read the acceptance speech of an author of historical fiction for children who has been awarded the Newbery Medal (1). What were the author's reasons for choosing to write about that period in history? Does the author discuss the sources used?

☐ Using Chart 10-1, "Eras and Themes in Historical Fiction," make a list of historical literature that develops each theme during a selected time period.

References

1 Blos, Joan W. "Newbery Medal Acceptance." *The Horn Book* 56 (August 1980): 369–73, 374–77.
2 Brink, Carol Ryrie. *Caddie Woodlawn*. Illustrated by Trina Schart Hyman. New York: Macmillan, 1935, 1973.
3 Burton, Hester. "The Writing of Historical Novels." In *Children and Literature: Views and Reviews*, edited by Virginia Haviland, pp. 299–304. Glenview, Ill.: Scott, Foresman, 1973.

4   Keith, Harold. *The Obstinate Land*. New York: Crowell, 1977.

5   Lasky, Kathryn. *Beyond the Divide*. New York: Macmillan, 1983.

6   Lukens, Rebecca J. *A Critical Handbook of Children's Literature*. Glenview, Ill.: Scott, Foresman, 1976.

7   Norton, Donna E. "A Three-Year Study Developing and Evaluating Children's Literature Units in Children's Literature Courses." A paper presented at the College Reading Association, National Conference, Baltimore, Maryland, October, 1980.

8   "Notable Children's Trade Books in the Field of Social Studies." *Social Education* 42 (April 1978): 318–21.

9   Reiss, Johanna. *The Upstairs Room*. New York: Crowell, 1972.

10 Townsend, John Rowe. *Written for Children*. New York: Lippincott, 1974.

11 Trease, Geoffrey. "The Historical Story: Is It Relevant Today?" *The Horn Book* (February 1977): 21–28.

12 Yates, Elizabeth. *We, The People*. Illustrated by Nora Unwin. Hanover, N.H.: Regional Center for Educational Training,1974.

Involving Children in Historical Fiction

☐

COLONIAL TIMES THROUGH THE REVOLUTIONARY WAR

☐

PIONEER AMERICA

☐

AMERICAN HISTORY IN FOLK SONGS

THE EXCITEMENT OF PLOT AND CHARAC-terization and the authenticity of much historical fiction make it a natural source of enjoyment and learning for children. Anne Troy (13) says that for children "history is one of the areas where fiction seems to be preferable and many times nearly replaces textbooks" (p. 473). Historical fiction helps children acquire the idea that history is people rather than merely a series of events, says Troy. Children can learn to love and respect history when they vicariously share the experiences of a character with whom they identify. Surrounding themselves with the flavor and spirit of an historical period, they also visualize how real people are affected by the times in which they live.

Troy suggests adults can bring history to life by guiding children toward individual reading selections, reading historical fiction aloud to students, encouraging dramatic presentations of short scenes from favorite books, and using literature in pleasant ways to develop attitudes, feelings, and general concepts about history. She warns that this should be done with great care, without pressure or preaching, so that literature does not become "too much of a teaching-learning medium which could turn children off to all literature for fun" (p. 474).

A writer of historical fiction, Geoffrey Trease (12), makes a strong case for using the genre to add new meaning and excitement to social studies:

So even in the context of social studies, the historical story has an important part to play, and it would be wasteful not to utilize all that the writer has so painstakingly researched and made available to children in an attractive form. (p. 28)

Thus historical fiction allows children to learn about the continuity of events, understand human relationships, and immerse themselves in the settings characteristic of specific times.

Another author of historical fiction, Alberta Wilson Constant (11), stresses the desirability of allowing children to be immersed in a book:

One of the best things that you can do for children is to teach them how to escape into a book. Let them be for a while somebody else. Let them stand with their feet on the cobblestones of Paris with Jean Valjean and hear the pursuing steps of police inspector Javert; let them walk into the jungle of Mowgli and hear the cry of their hero the panther and the long howl of the mother wolf. Show them how to mount the winged horse Pegasus and let him carry them away. He will bring them back safely. They'll be better, and they'll be stronger for the journey. (p. 23)

Constant believes that it is equally important for children to be immersed in the American past, as they feel the joy and challenge of new frontiers, the pride of human self-sufficiency, and the fun of being a pioneer child.

Joan Aiken (1) emphasizes that writers must develop within children an awareness of the past, an appreciation for the past, and a feeling of indebtedness toward the past. Aiken believes that as children begin to value and appreciate the contributions of people before their own times, they should realize that they also have obligations to make contributions to future generations.

COLONIAL TIMES THROUGH THE REVOLUTIONARY WAR

Celebrations throughout the United States commemorated the bicentennial of our country in 1976. The bicentennial stimulated interest in searching for our roots and learning more about the early colonial days and the Revolutionary War. Carol Gay (6), says that the important task of sharing a sense of the colonial past with children, can be effectively approached through the following activities: (1) sharing with children the same stories that Colonial children read, (2) encouraging children to take a penetrating look at a historical figure, and (3) inviting students to compare the values and problems of colonial times with those of contemporary times. While these activities would be meaningful for any time period, this section will consider some ways to accomplish each of these goals with historical fiction related to colonial days.

Sharing Books Read by Colonial Children

What books were available to children in the North American colonies of the 1600s and 1700s? What books did they read at school and at home? One of the books most commonly referred to in colonial literature and used in colonial education was the hornbook. (Reproductions are available

A boy learns about colonial children by reading a book read by children in the 1600s.

through The Hornbook, Inc., Boston, Massachusetts.) As discussed in chapter two, the original hornbooks were thin pieces of three-by-five inch wood onto which tacks attached a printed paper covered with a transparent sheet of yellowish horn. The hornbook contained the alphabet, vowel-consonant and consonant-vowel combinations, the Lord's Prayer, and sometimes Arabic numerals. It was designed to teach a colonial child to read and spell.

Another book mentioned often in the literature of colonial times is the *New-England Primer* (4). (This primer came out in many editions over the years and is available in a reissued text.) The chapbooks popular in England were also found in the colonies. Some of these had didactic messages; others contained entertaining traditional tales such as "Tom Thumb," "Reynard the Fox," "Jack the Giant Killer," and "Robin Hood." These stories are available today. A very influential book written during the seventeenth century was John Bunyan's *Pilgrim's Progress*. Both children and adults enjoyed following Christian on his perilous journey as he searched for salvation. Other popular books of colonial times that contemporary children may enjoy include *Babes in the Woods* (reissued in Frederick Warne's edition of Randolph Caldecott's *Picture Book No. 1*), John Newbery's *The History of Little Goody Two Shoes*, and Daniel Defoe's *Robinson Crusoe*. Reading from these books or listening to stories read from them allows children to develop a close relationship with characters from the past. It is exciting to discover that today they laugh at, or are excited by, the same plots and characters that fascinated children over two hundred years ago.

Taking a Penetrating Look at a Historical Figure

Older elementary and middle-school children can learn about the process of scholarly research used by historical novelists or biographers when they recreate a day in the life of famous American colonists or Native Americans of the period, such as Benjamin Franklin, Pocahontas, George Washington, Betsy Ross, Abigail Adams, or Paul Revere. While many books of historical fiction discussed earlier develop fictional stories about unknown people, many others also refer to famous people and leaders. For example, Esther Forbes's *Johnny Tremain* includes frequent mention of well-known figures during the American Revolution. Children can do research on these historical figures because considerable information about them is available.

The first step is to identify a figure about whom there is sufficient source material. With the person selected, the class can break into smaller research groups, each to work on a different period in the person's life. Next, the children should accumulate as many reference materials as possible. In addition to biographies, information about the person's home, any speeches or writing by the person, reproductions of the front page of a newspaper that might have been available at that time, and a copy of the *Farmer's Almanac* listing the weather conditions for the period would all be valuable resources. Each group should develop a composite picture of what the historical figure did during the chosen period; this should include the person's possible thoughts, writings, actions, associations, concerns, and so on.

Carol Gay (6) says that children should gain two values from this activity: they should experience such a close intimate look at a day from the

past that the person and the place will come alive for them, and they should gain an awareness about how research uncovers the past. This understanding of the human qualities of the past is important to children; through such understanding they become aware of "those human qualities that persevere through each century and bind the past and the present together" (p. 15).

Comparing the Values and Problems of Colonial Times with Those of Other Historical Periods

Historical fiction set in colonial times presents two types of human problems and their associated values. Stories related to the early colonial period stress a search for religious and political freedom, as the colonists fight the tyranny of a hated government and brave the frequent miseries associated with starting over in a new land. The colonists face danger, disease, and even starvation in order to fulfill their dream of freedom and new land. In some books, such as Patricia Clapp's *Constance: A Story of Early Plymouth*, people must make personal adjustments as they first long to return to a beloved home, then battle the role mandated by their society, and finally discover love for their new land. Much historical fiction set in the Revolutionary War period also stresses the battle for freedom, as well as stressing the tragedy of war, and showing the personal and emotional problems associated with people who follow their consciences during wartime.

Some books that develop similar problems and values have settings in different time periods. Students may discuss these problems and values, then compare and relate them to current experiences. A few examples of historical fiction that may be used to stimulate such discussion are listed below:

Humans have a need for political and religious freedom. They will go through many hardships in search of freedom.
Colonial Times: Patricia Clapp's *Constance: A Story of Early Plymouth*; Elizabeth George Speare's *The Witch of Blackbird Pond*
Czarist Russia: Kathryn Lasky's *The Night Journey*
World War II: Dale Fife's *Destination Unknown*; Aranka Siegal's *Upon the Head of the Goat: A Childhood in Hungary 1939–1944*; Yoshiko Uchida's *Journey Home*

Sometimes people must fight or risk freedom to save what they believe in.

Colonial Times: Esther Forbes's *Johnny Tremain*; Patricia Clapp's *I'm Deborah Sampson: A Soldier in the Revolution*

Post-Revolutionary Times: James and Christopher Collier's *Jump Ship to Freedom*

Civil War: Irene Hunt's *Across Five Aprils*

World War II: Marie McSwigan's *Snow Treasure*

War and hatred are destructive forces.

Colonial Times: Patricia Clapp's *I'm Deborah Sampson: A Soldier of the Revolution*.

English Civil War: Erik Christian Haugaard's *Cromwell's Boy*

Civil War: Janet Hickman's *Zoar Blue*

World War II: Johanna Reiss's *The Upstairs Room*; Uri Orlev's *The Island on Bird Street*

When children see and discuss the relationships among values that have been held across historical periods, they begin to realize that these same values are also important today.

Using Creative Dramatizations to Stimulate Interest in Colonial America

Many exciting dramas unfold in the pages of historical fiction written about the colonial period, especially about Revolutionary War days. Jone Wright and Elizabeth Allen (20) describe a creative dramatization in which a group of sixth graders reenacted Paul Revere's ride. The children added an interesting dimension to this activity with comparative dramatizations: one group dramatized Henry Wadsworth Longfellow's poem "Paul Revere's Ride," while the second dramatized the ride as told by Jean Fritz in *And Then What Happened, Paul Revere?* (chapter twelve) and Louis Wolfe in *Let's Go with Paul Revere* (19). The second group also verified additional facts about Revere's ride by reading a magazine article (2). After the group members read and discussed their sources, they pantomimed various actions and planned the scenes they wanted to include:

Poetry Group

1 Paul talking to his friends about hanging the signal lights.
2 Paul rowing alone across the river.
3 Paul waiting on the opposite shore for the signal to be hung.
4 Paul galloping alone through the countryside: 12:00 P.M., Medford; 1:00 A.M., Lexington; 2:00 A.M., Concord.
5 Paul galloping on through the night.

Authentic Sources Group

1 Patriots giving the signal.
2 Patriots rowing Revere across the river.
3 Paul Revere warning patriots at Cambridge and Concord.
4 British soldiers capturing and releasing Paul Revere.

After the two dramatizations, the children discussed the differences between the two presentations and drew some interesting conclusions about the romanticizing of history and the researching of historical data.

"The worst of Plagues, the detested tea shipped for this Port by the East Indian Company, is now arrived in the Harbour" (p. 107). With words like these in Esther Forbes's *Johnny Tremain* the colonists were told that they must rally to the cry for freedom if they wanted to repeal the hated taxation-without-representation laws. This scene is another natural subject for creative dramatizations. The following scenes depicting the Boston Tea Party could be dramatized:

Boston Tea Party from Johnny Tremain, by Esther Forbes

1 Samuel Adams asking the printer to duplicate the placard announcing the tea shipment.
2 Johnny Tremain going from house to house, using the secret code, notifying the Observers that there would be a secret meeting.
3 The meeting of the Observers and a decision being reached about the tea.
4 The meeting in front of Old South Church, with Josiah Quincy talking to the crowd and Samuel Adams giving the message that the tea would be dumped.
5 The colonists throwing the tea into Boston Harbor.

The Impact of Salem

Incidents of unreasonable fears and unjustified persecutions appear throughout history. The historical fiction books written about the late 1600s provide stimulating sources for oral discussion, creative dramatizations, clarification of values, writing, understanding setting and characterization, and comparing literary works that develop similar themes. Ann Petry's *Tituba of Salem Village* is about an enslaved black woman and Elizabeth George Speare's *The Witch of Blackbird Pond* is about a free teenaged white girl; both experience the impact of witch-hunts and unjustified persecution. These stories are excellent for discussion and comparison. The teacher of a sixth-grade class mapped the following discussion and learning possibilities for using these two books with her students:

Dramatization: Tituba

Dramatize the family approaching the gloomy house in Salem Village and meeting Goody Good.

Recreate the scene in which the children bring in the fortune-telling cards and try to convince Tituba to read their fortunes.

Dramatize the court scene, including the witnesses against Tituba and the appearance of Samuel Conklin who comes to her defense.

Interview Tituba, her husband, the minister, Betsy, Abigail, and Samuel Conklin. How does each describe the experiences leading up to the trial? How do they feel about the results of the trial? Are they pleased when Tituba is free?

Dramatization: Kit

Dramatize Kit's first meeting with her relatives.

Recreate the Dame's school and Kit providing instruction for her six students.

Role play the conversations between Kit and the Quaker woman, Hannah Tupper, who lives in the meadow.

Dramatize the scenes during which Kit is accused of witchcraft, is taken as a prisoner to the shed, stands trial for witchcraft, and is freed because Prudence demonstrates her reading skills.

Developing Characterization: Tituba

How did each of these people see Tituba and feel about her?

Her former owner in Barbados

The minister

The minister's wife

Betsy and Abigail

Dr. Griggs

The residents of Salem Village

Samuel Conklin

Tituba

Developing Characterization: Kit

How did each of these people see Kit and feel about her?

Kit's grandfather

Matthew Wood

Aunt Rachel

Reverend Gershom Bulkeley

William Ashby

Judith and Mercy

Goodwife Cruff

Hannah Tupper

Nat Eaton

Kit

Importance of Setting: Both Books

Compare the jewellike setting of Barbados with Tituba's description of the house in Salem and Kit's description of the colorless Puritan village.

Why do you believe both authors chose to take their heroines from tropical islands to very different locations?

What might have happened in each story if Kit and Tituba had remained in Barbados?

Values Clarification: Tituba

Why did Tituba's former owner decide to sell her two dear companions? Do you believe her reason was good? Why or why not?

Why do you believe Abigail encouraged the other girls to try to put Betsy into a trance?

What special skills did Tituba have that made her different from the people in Salem Village? Why would the people hate and fear her?

Why do you believe the minister did not come to her defense or pay her jail fees?

Why was Samuel Conklin the only one to come to Tituba's defense? How did he demonstrate his faith in her?

Values Clarification: Kit

Why did Kit's grandfather want her to read and discuss plays? Why do you think the Puritans reacted so differently to her desire to read such material?

Why do you believe Kit enjoyed going to the meadow and visiting Hannah Tupper? Why were the villagers afraid of both the meadow and Hannah Tupper?

What makes Hannah Tupper different from the villagers? Why would the people fear her?

What made Kit Tyler different from the villagers? Why would people fear her?

What was the difference between the way Goodwife Cruff felt about her daughter Prudence and the way Kit felt about Prudence? Who was right?

How would Prudence's life have been different if Kit had not helped her? Why do you think Kit helped Prudence? Why do you think Kit didn't speak out in court about Prudence, even if her answer might have helped her own case?

Why do you believe Kit's friend, "dear dependable William," did not come to her defense at the trial? Why did Nat Eaton risk his own liberty to testify for her?

Personal Response: Tituba

How would you have felt if you had been Tituba and had been forced to leave your homeland? What would your reaction have been to your new family and the people of the village?

Have you ever known anyone or read about anyone who was feared or disliked because that person was different from others? Has this ever happened to you? When? Who helped you when you needed help?

Personal Reponse: Kit

If you had been Kit, would you have risked your safety to help both Hannah Tupper and Prudence Cruff? Why or why not?

Have you ever felt like Kit? When?

Which story did you like better? Why?

Were you satisfied with the ending of each story? Why or why not? If you could change either story, how would you change it?

Do you believe a story about such personal persecution could be written about a person today? What would be the cause of the persecution? How might the person solve his or her problem?

Writing: Both Books

Pretend that you are either Tituba or Kit. Choose a period of time from the story and write your experiences in a journal format.

Pretend to be someone living in Salem Village who has relatives in England. Write a letter to these relatives telling them about what has been happening in Salem.

Pretend to be a twentieth-century writer developing a script for a television "You Are There" program. Write the script for a reenactment of the trial of either Tituba or Kit.

Related Literature

Books of historical fiction with settings from other time periods that also develop themes of fear and unjustified persecution:

Suspicion toward, and persecution of Navaho Indians: Scott O'Dell's *Sing Down the Moon*.

Suspicion toward, and persecution of, Jewish people during World War II: Johanna Reiss's *The Upstairs Room*, Esther Hautzig's *The Endless Steppe: A Girl in Exile*; Judith Kerr's *When Hitler Stole Pink Rabbit*; Sonia Levitin's *Journey to America*; Aranka Siegal's *Upon the Head of the Goat: A Chilhood in Hungary 1939–1944*; Uri Orlev's *The Island on Bird Street*.

Suspicion toward, and persecution of gypsies: William Hooks's *Circle of Fire*.

PIONEER AMERICA

Most children are fascinated with that time in American history when courageous adults and children were struggling across the country on foot, on horseback, or in covered wagons. They like to hear about children who rode on canal barges, floated on rafts down the Ohio, or traveled on steamboats down the Mississippi. They also enjoy vicariously experiencing the frontier years after the covered wagons had been unloaded and families began their new lives in a sod house or a log cabin.

Teachers of social studies find this period exciting. They use the fiction of the pioneer period to help children develop closer ties with the past, understand the relationships between past and present values, understand the physical environment of the time, and discover the links between the pioneer past and the present. Ways of developing these understandings range from sharing an individual story with children to developing total units that encourage children to identify with the period through music, art, stories, games, foods, values, home remedies, and the research of historic characters.

Introducing Pioneer America to Children

In order to immerse children in the physical environment of the time and to stimulate their curiosity, an adult can show them objects that were important, for both survival and pleasure, to a pioneer family: quilts, tools (hammer, nails, spade, hoe, grindstone), tallow candles, lengths of cotton cloth, wooden buckets, iron pots, skillets, earthenware jugs, tin lanterns, dried herbs, food (a barrel of flour; yeast; dried beans, peas, and corn; salt; sugar; dried apples; a slab of bacon), seed corn, cornhusk dolls, a treasured china-head doll, a yoke, a churn, a spinning wheel, a fiddle, a log cabin (made from Lincoln Logs), and pictures of pioneers. These objects should be accompanied by displays of historical fiction such as those discussed earlier in this chapter, books that pioneer children might have read, and books about pioneer art, music, and crafts.

One teacher introduced some third-grade students to the pioneer period by dressing in pioneer style, greeting the students at the classroom door, and taking them on a classroom tour. By enthusiastically presenting artifacts, the teacher excited the children and made them want to know more.

Values from the Past

Children can learn about the past and relate it to the present when they identify the values held and problems overcome by people living in pioneer America. Children can compare these values and problems and the solutions of problems, as depicted in historical fiction, with those of today. The pioneer period is filled with stories that stress love of the land; the need for positive relationships among family members, neighbors, pioneers, and Native Americans; the struggle for survival; and the need for bravery. The following experiences encourage children to clarify their own values as well as those of others:

Love of the Land

1   Pioneers were drawn to the West because of the opportunity to own rich farmland. Some people left their homes in the East when their land no longer produced good crops. Others traveled to the West because they wanted more room or fewer neighbors. Still others acquired the free land provided under the Homestead Act. After children have read one of the books that place this strong emphasis on the land (such as Honore Morrow's *On to Oregon!;* Barbara Brenner's *Wagon Wheels;* and Harold Keith's *The Obstinate Land*), ask them to identify these pioneers' reasons for moving and any conflicts that family members felt when they were deciding whether or not to move.

At this point, role playing could help clarify the attitudes of pioneer family members. Ask the students to imagine that the year is 1866. The Civil War just ended the year before. They are living on a small New England farm. They are sitting with their immediate family and their visiting aunt and uncle at the evening meal. Their aunt begins excitedly talking about an article in the paper telling how lots of people are going west to claim free land provided under the Homestead Act of 1862. Their aunt and uncle are ready to sell their farm, pack a few belongings, and travel to the West in a covered wagon. The aunt wants her brother's family to join them. Suggest that the students role play the reactions of the different family characters and decide whether or not they should go. Based on common characteristics found in historical fiction stories, the characters might express these concerns:

Mother: She knows that her husband wants to own a better farm, but her family lives in the East and she doesn't want to leave them. In addition, she has lost one child who is buried on the old farm. She is also concerned about living on the frontier away from a church, a school, and the protection of close neighbors.
Father: He is unhappy with his rocky farm and the poor production it has provided. He has dreamed of a farm with rich soil that could produce better crops and support his family.
Twelve-Year-Old Daughter: She is filled with the excitement of a new adventure. She wants to see new lands and Indians. In addition, she

is not displeased with the prospect of leaving school for a while.

Seven-Year-Old Son: The farmhouse is the only home he has ever known; his best friend and his relatives live in the surrounding countryside. He'd love to see some Indians and he wants to please his father but he doesn't know what to expect in a land that far from home.

The students could consider each person's arguments and decide if they would have moved to a new land. They can continue by talking about what they would take with them if they decided to homestead. Finally, the discussion can be drawn into the present time. Do people still have a strong loyalty to the land? Do they want to own their own land? Encourage children to provide reasons for their arguments.

2 The desire for unspoiled land as well as adventure can be placed into a modern framework by having students pretend their families are moving to a wilderness area in Alaska. Why would they want to move? Why would they not want to move? What problems do they think they would encounter before moving? How would they solve them? What problems would they encounter in the Alaskan wilderness? How would they solve them? Finally, do they believe these problems and their solutions are similar to those experienced by pioneers?

Human Relations

1 Many stories about pioneer days present different ways of dealing with Indians and diverse attitudes toward them. The only solution many books give is a battle between the Indians and whites. In contrast, Alice Dalgliesh's *The Courage of Sarah Noble* presents a family who settles on land for which the native people have been given a fair price, with the provision that they retain their right to fish in the river. Sarah's parents believe that all people must be treated fairly. Encourage children to discuss the reasons for various actions, the beliefs of the pioneers, and the consequences.

2 After children have read the "Massacre" and "Ambassador to the Enemy," chapters in Carol Ryrie Brink's *Caddie Woodlawn*, ask them to discuss the decision made by the settlers to attack the Indians because they thought the Indians were going to attack them. Why did

the settlers reach their decision? Was it accurate? Why or why not? Then, ask the students to place themselves in Caddie's role. If they were Caddie, would they have warned the Indians? Why or why not? What might have been the results if Caddie had not made her evening ride? Finally, bring the discussion to contemporary times. Ask the students if there are times when people today might decide to act out of fright rather than out of knowledge? What events would they consider important enough to risk their own safety?

3 Books about pioneers also include many stories about people's need to help others. Neighbors and family members help each other and provide moral support during times of crisis. The "Little House" series, by Laura Ingalls Wilder, contains many incidents of family support and working with neighbors. Fritz and his neighbor in Harold Keith's *The Obstinate Land* help each other till the soil, plant crops, guard fields against the dangers of marauding cattle, and share the necessities of survival. Encourage children to discuss the values of positive human relationships during both pioneer and contemporary times.

The Pioneer Environment

Pioneer stories are rich in descriptions of the homes, crafts, store goods, food, transportation, books, and pleasures of the pioneers.

Amusements of the Pioneer Family

Allowing children to take part in the same experiences that entertained pioneer children is a good way to help them feel closer to their counterparts in the past. For example, Laura Ingalls Wilder's *Little House in the Big Woods* describes these happy moments that can be recreated with children:

1 For a special birthday treat, Pa played and sang "Pop Goes the Weasel" for Laura. Some of her happiest memories were related to Pa's fiddle. Other songs mentioned in the book are "Rock of Ages" (the fiddle could not play weekday songs on Sunday) and "Yankee Doodle."

2 The family traveled through the woods to a square dance at Grandpa's house. At the dance, the fiddler played and the square-dance caller called the squares for "Buffalo Gals," "The Irish Washerwoman," and "The Arkansas Traveler."

3 After the day's work was finished, Ma would sometimes cut paper dolls for the girls out of stiff white paper and make dresses, hats, ribbons, and laces out of colored paper.

4 In the winter evenings, Laura and Mary begged Pa to tell them stories. He told them about "Grandpa and the Panther," "Pa and the Bear in the Way," "Pa and the Voice in the Woods," and "Grandpa's Sled and the Pig." Enough details are included in these stories so that they can be retold to children.

A School Day with the Pioneer Family

A day in school for pioneer children (if a school was available) was quite different from a contemporary school day. Historical fiction and other sources provide enough information about school, books read, and parables memorized to interest children and recreate a school day that emphasizes spelling, reading, and arithmetic.

Modern children may be surprised that Ma in Laura Ingalls Wilder's *On the Banks of Plum Creek* considered three books on the subjects of spelling, reading, and arithmetic among her "best things" and gave them solemnly to the girls with the advice that they care for them and study faithfully. Likewise, Fritz in Harold Keith's *The Obstinate Land* sold his most prized possession to pay for the schooling of his brother and sister. In addition, these children had to ride sixteen miles on one pony every day in order to get to and from school.

1 A number of early textbooks and other stories have been reissued in their original form and can be shared with children. For example, children can read the rhyming alphabet; practice their letters; and learn to read words of one, two, three, four, and five syllables from the *New England Primer* (4).

2 Pioneer children also read and wrote maxims to practice their handwriting or as punishment for bad behavior. Joan W. Blos's *A Gathering of Days: A New England Girl's Journal, 1830–32* tells of this experience in the 1830s and lists some maxims that were written, such as—

> Speak the truth and lie not.
> To thine own self be true.
> Give to them that want.

ISSUE

·····❋❋❀❋❋·····

Does Watching Television Influence the Reading of Literature?

BOTH EDUCATORS AND parents express mixed reactions about children's television habits. The positive viewpoint stresses the many films, plays, and stories that can deepen children's understanding of a variety of literature and introduce them to new ideas, background information, and literary forms. Television shows such as "Little House on the Prairie" are cited for their ability to provide historical backgrounds and stimulate children to read Laura Ingalls Wilder's books. On the other hand, many people claim that children watch so much television that their reading decreases and their reading achievement declines. Critics of television viewing by children may also be concerned with related topics such as television and aggression, child development, child psychology, and sociology.

To illustrate the spectrum of materials that have been written on the subject, Diane Erbeck compiled an annotated bibliography of articles that discuss the positive and/or negative aspects of television viewing.[1] The balanced presentation of articles suggests that the issues related to television viewing have not been resolved. Does television discourage or encourage reading of literature? Does watching television promote passivity? Can literature in book form compete with the visual stimulation found in the adoption of a story for television?

3 Additional methods of instruction are described in other stories. Carol Ryrie Brink's *Caddie Woodlawn* describes an 1860 method for memorizing the multiplication tables; the children sang them to the tune of "Yankee Doodle." Recreating a typical school day during which children read from the primer, recite and copy parables, have a spelling bee, and sing their multiplication tables would help them visualize the pioneer child's life and develop an understanding that education was considered important in earlier times.

A Day in the General Store

The country store was also very different from the contemporary department store or large shopping mall. It fascinated children, however, just as department stores create excitement in today's children. Laura Ingalls Wilder's first experience in a general store is described in *Little House in the Big Woods*. This store included bright materials, kegs of nails, kegs of shot, barrels of candy, cooking utensils, plowshares, knives, shoes, and dishes. In fact it had just about everything.

1 A source of information about the kinds of materials that might be available to a pioneer family in the late 1800s is a reissue of an early Sears, Roebuck and Company catalogue (10). Through these pages, children can acquire an understanding of the merchandise available and the fashions of the day. They can use the information found in these sources either to recreate a child-sized general store in one corner of the room or create miniature stores in boxes.

Pioneer Chores

Wash on Monday
Iron on Tuesday
Mend on Wednesday
Churn on Thursday
Clean on Friday
Bake on Saturday
Rest on Sunday

1 While people may not keep this kind of a work schedule today, the daily activities of the pioneer family associated with the house and other outside responsibilities are of interest to

Results reported from a television-related school project sponsored by the Home and School in Ridgewood, New Jersey,[2] suggest some of the problems connected with television. A group of parents and teachers felt that students wasted too much of their time watching television. Children in the fourth, fifth, and sixth grades agreed to turn off their televisions for one week and keep a diary of their reactions and activites. School officials reported astonishment at the reactions of the families: "The Hawes experiment was supported almost unanimously by the students. But school officials, accustomed for years to parental railing about the perils of television for youthful viewers, were stunned to find that many mothers and fathers balked at being without television" (p. 1). Reports of the activities carried on by students did not indicate that there was a considerable increase in either reading of literature or school achievement.

A point of view often stressed by educators is that television can have positive effects on children if there is planned interaction with others to counter passivity. Iris Tiedt[3] suggests that a film based on literature adds visual interpretation to a book, stimulates interest in reading the book, stimulates oral discussion, and extends children's imaginations. Television viewing can be positively used by having children study how a literature presentation differs in film and in print and discuss and critically evaluate what they see or hear. While there seems to be no clear research evidence about the effects of television on children's reading and appreciation of literature, it may be the quality of the television programs and the quality of the interaction that is essential if television is not to have a detrimental influence on literature reading.

[1]Erbeck, Diane M. "Television and Children: A Pro/Con Reading List." *Top of the News* 37 (Fall 1980): 47–53.

[2]Mayer, Jane. "Some Cried a Lot, But Youths Survived Week without TV." *The Wall Street Journal,* 6 January 1982, pp. 1, 21.

[3]Tiedt, Iris. "Input, Media Special." *Language Arts 53* (February 1976): 119.

The pioneer setting in historical fiction seems real when children reenact chores.

children. Preparing food is mentioned in many stories. Because pioneer families could not go to the local store for supplies, they needed to prepare their own. Churning butter is one activity that children enjoy doing. A simple recipe for butter that children can make easily is given below:

½ pint whipping cream
¼ teaspoon salt
Pint jar with tight cover

Pour the ½ pint of whipping cream into the pint jar. Seal the cover tightly onto the jar. Shake the jar until the cream turns to butter. Remove the lid, pour off the liquid, and work out any excess liquid. Add salt and stir it into the butter. Remove butter from jar and shape it.

According to Laura in *Little House in the Big Woods*, Ma was not always satisfied with white butter. Children may wish to experiment with the technique Ma used to add a yellow color to the butter. She rubbed a carrot over a pan that had nail holes punched across the bottom. She placed the soft, grated carrot into a pan of milk, then warmed the mixture and poured it into a cloth bag. When she squeezed the bag, bright yellow milk ran from the cloth and was added to the cream in the churn (p. 30).

2 Because pioneer families had no refrigerators or freezers, they had to find other ways to preserve their foods. If they lived in the North, they used nature's icebox in the winter. In Joan W. Blos's *A Gathering of Days: A New England Girl's Journal, 1830–32*, children read about chopping off a frozen wedge of soup and heating it in the kettle. Other stories describe the feeling of well-being when the pantry, shed, attic, and cellar were filled with food. In contrast, people experienced great concern when only seed corn remained between the family and starvation. Children

learn about different ways the pioneers preserved fruits and vegetables by reading Eliot Wigginton's *The Foxfire Book* (18). Children enjoy drying their own apples and then having them for a special snack.

The people in pioneer fiction become alive for children who cannot actually live on a prairie homestead. Children can sing the same songs pioneer children sang, dance to the music of a pioneer fiddle, listen to the pioneer storyteller, imagine they attend a pioneer school, imagine they go to the general store, and do the chores of the homestead.

Significance of American Trails in Westward Expansion

Deep ruts across a sea of prairie grass, markers along a river crossing, and scars created by oxen hooves sliding down the rock side of a canyon were the pioneer equivalent of modern interstate highways. Like highways, these trails were important for moving passengers and commerce across the country; without them, the West could not have been opened for expansion. It is hard to imagine a thousand men, women, and children, with two hundred covered wagons, following such rough trails across prairies, deserts, and mountains to reach California or Oregon.

Children can discover additional information about the trails referred to in books of historical fiction by reading Bruce Grant's *Famous American Trails* (8). They can discuss the purpose for the trails (such as cattle drives, wagon trails, fast movement of mail), the locations of the trails, the physical hardships found along the trails, forts built along the trails, and distances covered by the trails. They can draw a large map of the United States, place on it the major westward trails, and then trace, using different colored pencils, the routes taken by pioneers in various books of historical fiction. The following books provide enough descriptions of locations to be of value in this activity:

Alice Dalgliesh, *The Courage of Sarah Noble*: Westfield, Massachusetts, to New Milford, Connecticut, by foot and horse backpack, 1707.

Honore Morrow, *On to Oregon!*: Missouri to Oregon by covered wagon, horse, and foot, 1844.

Evelyn Sibley Lampman, *White Captives*: Illinois to Santa Fe Pass, by wagon train; divided as some went to Salt Lake City, Utah, and others traveled south to Socorro on the Rio Grande, 1851.

Laura Ingalls Wilder, "Little House" books: Pepin, Wisconsin, to Kansas, to Minnesota, and to Dakota Territory near De Smet by covered wagon, 1870s.

Research Skills

Many historical fiction books describe the sources used by the authors to develop the setting and the authenticity of a period. Encouraging children to choose a specific time period and location and then discover as much as possible about the people and their times will help them develop respect for research skills and gain new insights into the period.

In one class, children researched their own small city during the late 1800s. The group investigated documents at the historical society; searched old newspapers; found old family albums, journals, and letters; searched documents at the courthouse; interviewed people whose relatives had lived in the town during that time; read references to discover information about fashions, transportation, and food; and located buildings that would have existed during that time. After they had gathered this information, they pretended that they were living a hundred years earlier and wrote stories about themselves; the stories contained only authentic background information.

Additional Activities Related to Pioneer American Literature

1 Have the children pretend that they are newspaper reporters sent from an eastern paper to discover what living on the frontier is really like. Encourage them to write news stories that will be sent back to the newspaper. In addition, have them pretend that they can take tintype pictures to accompany their stories; have them draw pictures of the scenes they would like to photograph.

2 Many pioneers moved to the West because they received encouraging letters from friends and relatives. Have children write letters to friends or relatives telling the Easterners why they should or should not sell all their property and move to ———.

3 Several books of historical fiction, such as Joan W. Blos's *A Gathering of Days: A New England Girl's Journal, 1830–32* are written in journal format. Have children select a character from a historical fiction story and write

several journal entries for a specific period in the story.

4   Many scenes from historical fiction about the pioneer period can be dramatized. The experiences of Alice Dalgliesh's Sarah Noble in playing and living with the Indian family when her father leaves her to return for his wife are interesting scenes to dramatize.

A Culminating Activity Related to Pioneer America

Children enjoy sharing their knowledge about pioneer days with parents or other children. A class can plan a pioneer day in which children display pioneer objects, food, arts and crafts; demonstrate songs or dances learned; and share information gained, creative writing completed, and art projects made during their study of pioneer life and historical fiction.

AMERICAN HISTORY IN FOLK SONGS

Folk songs, like historical fiction, present a panorama of American history, creating a picture of the common people during different periods. The books discussed in this chapter often refer to characters listening to, singing, or playing music. Several songs have already been suggested as a means of making the pioneer period come alive for today's children.

One very exciting historical unit used with children combined folk music, historical fiction, and social studies. Singing or square dancing to the music of the times allowed the children to share a memorable, enjoyable experience that was similar to that of the characters in the books they were reading. The words of the songs helped convey the essence of certain periods. Chart 10–2 lists folk songs from different historical periods.

The folk songs in the chart, and information about the historical struggles of the times, can be found in the following books: C. A. Browne's *The Story of Our National Ballads* (3), Edith Fowke and Joe Glazer's *Songs of Work and Protest* (5), Tom Glazer's *A New Treasury of Folk Songs* (7), and Carl Sandburg's *The American Songbag* (9).

The teacher who developed this historical song and literature unit with fourth-grade children used the following time periods: Revolutionary War, early expansion, Civil War, and pioneer America. He collected many books at different levels of reading ability: some he shared orally

CHART 10–2
Folk songs

1754 and 1776	"Yankee Doodle"—symbolic of the struggle for freedom.
1796–1800	"Jefferson and Liberty"—Jefferson pledged to repeal the Sedition Act.
Early 1800s	"Blow Ye Wings in the Morning"—whaling industry along the eastern seaboard.
1825–1913	"Low Bridge Everybody Down"—mule drivers on the Erie Canal.
1841–1847	"Patsy Works on the Railroad"—Irish workers completing railroad in eastern United States.
1850s	"Sweet Betsy from Pike"—taking a covered wagon to California.
1850s	"Go Down Moses"—freedom song of the black slaves.
1850s	"Oh, Freedom"—freedom song of the black slaves.
1859	"John Brown's Body"—attack on garrison at Harper's Ferry to capture arms and liberate slaves.
1861	"The Battle Hymn of the Republic"—Julia Ward Howe watched the campfires of the Union Army.
1872	"John Henry"—a steel-driving man drilling the Big Bend Tunnel on the Chesapeake and Ohio Railroad.
1888	"Drill, Ye Tarriers, Drill"—dynamiters blasting their way through the mountains as the railroads crossed the continent.
1870–90	"The Old Chisholm Trail"—herding cattle from San Antonio, Texas northward.
1897	"Hallelujah, I'm a Bum"—hoboing on the open road.
Early 1900s	"Sixteen Tons"—coal mining song.

with the group; others the children read themselves.

Literature that he identified for the Revolutionary War period included the following: Patricia Clapp's *I'm Deborah Sampson: A Soldier in the War of the Revolution*; Esther Forbes's *Johnny Tremain*; and Leonard Wibberley's *John Treegate's Musket* (14), *Peter Treegate's War* (15), *Sea Captain from Salem* (16), and *Treegate's Raiders* (17).

Books of historical fiction related to the early expansion period included Honore Morrow's *On to Oregon!* and Joan Blos's *A Gathering of Days: A New England Girl's Journal, 1830–32*.

Books related to the Civil War period included Harold Keith's *Rifles for Watie*, Janet Hickman's *Zoar Blue*, and Irene Hunt's *Across Five Aprils*.

Books about pioneer America included Carol Ryrie Brink's *Caddie Woodlawn*, all of Laura Ingalls Wilder's "Little House" series, and Harold Keith's *The Obstinate Land*.

In addition to books of historical fiction, the teacher used biographies of famous people from the time period (see chapter twelve) and other informational books about the period from the Revolutionary War through the days of pioneer America. The students involved themselves in history; they sang the songs of the people, acted out scenes from the stories, made artifacts such as cornhusk dolls, wrote creative stories, and investigated the historical periods.

One day the children sat in a circle on the floor and sang folk songs from the Civil War period. After they sang each song, some children shared their experiences. They pretended to be slaves, seeking freedom by way of the Underground Railroad; Separatists in Ohio deciding if they should or should not fight in the Civil War; and different members of the Creighton family, who were now home from the war, sharing their experiences from Irene Hunter's *Across Five Aprils*. Both the teacher and the children thoroughly enjoyed the experience and gained considerable information about their American heritage and about literature reflecting this heritage. When evaluating their experience, the children indicated that they had never had such an enjoyable time learning social studies. The characters of the past actually lived for these children, as they discovered the pleasures that may be gained from reading.

figure, comparing the values and problems depicted in colonial times with those of contemporary times, and taking part in creative dramatizations in order to stimulate interest in colonial America.

Pioneer America is an especially exciting period for many elementary children. Historical fiction helps children develop closer ties with the past, understand the relationships between pioneer values and present values, and understand the physical environment of pioneer times. Adults can help children develop these understandings by sharing individual stories with children or developing total pioneer America units. Children can involve themselves in the time period through music, art, games, foods, drama, home remedies, living conditions, and researching western expansion trails.

Students can personally discover the research skills that are necessary to write credible historical fiction about pioneers by investigating sources available to them in their hometowns. They can write journal entries and creative stories about time periods that they can investigate.

Folk songs depicting a specific historical period can also increase children's appreciation of historical fiction and the people of the past. Sharing songs that were sung by the common people of a time allows children another means to experience history vicariously. The vivid music and exciting plots of historical stories help to emphasize that reading and sharing literature can be very enjoyable.

SUMMARY

Children can learn to appreciate and respect history when they share vicarious experiences with characters with whom they can identify. This enjoyment can be enhanced by encouraging children to read and allowing them to become immersed in historical fiction, providing opportunities for them to listen to historical fiction, encouraging dramatic presentations of short scenes, and using historical fiction in pleasant ways to bring new meaning and excitement to social studies.

Children can experience colonial times by reading and listening to books about colonial children, taking a penetrating look at a historical

Suggested Activities for Children's Appreciation of Historical Fiction

☐ Historical fiction provides a means of translating the information found in sterile textbooks into vivid spectacles of human drama. Choose a social studies or history text appropriate for children of a certain age, list the content and time periods covered in the text, and identify historical fiction that could be used to stimulate children's interest and understanding of that content or time period.

☐ With a group of children or a peer group, compare the information found in the textbook (see first activity) with the background information discovered in the books of historical fiction. Do the two sources agree? If they do not, research other sources in order to discover which are correct. If they do agree, discuss which sources more vividly describe history and what makes those sources more meaningful.

☐ One value of reading historical fiction is the development of an understanding that certain human qualities persist through each century and tie the past to the present. Use Chart 10-1, "Eras and Themes in Historical Fiction," (see p. 453 and the theme summaries at the end of each section of the first part of this chapter and share literature from several periods with children. Lead a discussion that helps them identify the human values expressed in those time periods. Allow them to discuss whether these values are still accepted by people today and if they think the values will still be important in the next century. Why or why not?

☐ Discussions of controversial issues have been identified as one method of creating a "springboard" strategy that allows children to become involved in stimulating debates. Historical fiction has numerous characters who took stands on controversial issues. The plots of many historical fiction stories are based on issues considered controversial during a time period. Identify several books from a time period and find paragraphs that state these issues. Develop a list of provocative questions that could be used when sharing this material with children. For example, in the Revolutionary War period, some literary characters believed that freedom was worth fighting for no matter what the consequences, others believed that the colonies should stay loyal to England, and still others felt that all killing was wrong.

☐ Encourage children to select one controversial issue found in historical fiction, pretend to be on the side of one group or another in the story, do additional research on the issue, and take part in a debate.

☐ In order to discover how vividly the setting can be presented in historical fiction, allow children to draw detailed pictures after they have read or listened to a story. To increase their appreciation of the settings described in some books, ask them to draw the setting described in an excellent historical book as well as an inadequately described setting. Discuss the differences for the reader and for the writer. Which one is more meaningful to the reader? Which one is more demanding on the author? Why?

☐ Select a scene from historical fiction that has both memorable characters and an exciting plot. With a group of children or peers, develop the scene into a creative dramatization.

These children recapture the feeling of pioneer America by singing the folk songs that were common during the time.

☐ Select the folk songs that were popular during a specific period in history. Listen to and read the words and sing the songs. What conflicts, problems, or values do the lyrics present? Are the same themes found in historical fiction of that time period?

References

1 Aiken, Joan. "Interpreting the Past." *Children's Literature in Education*. Vol. 16 (Summer 1985): 67–83.

2 Armstrong, O. K. "The British are Coming! Great Moments in U.S. History." *Reader's Digest* 106 (April 1975): 187–98.

3 Browne, C. A. *The Story of Our National Ballads*. Edited by Willard Heaps. New York: Crowell, 1960.

4 Ford, Paul Leicester. *The New-England Primer*. New York: Columbia University, Teachers College, 1962.

5 Fowke, Edith, and Glazer, Joe. *Songs of Work and Protest*. New York: Dover, 1973.

6 Gay, Carol. "Children's Literature and the Bicentennial." *Language Arts* 53 (January 1976): 11–16.

7 Glazer, Tom. *A New Treasury of Folk Songs*. New York: Bantam Books, 1961.

8 Grant, Bruce. *Famous American Trails*. Chicago: Rand McNally, 1971.

9 Sandburg, Carl. *The American Songbag*. New York: Harcourt Brace Jovanovich, 1927.

10 *Sears, Roebuck and Co., Consumers Guide*. 1900. Reprint. Northfield, Ill.: DBI Books, 1970.

11 Toothaker, Roy E. "A Conversation with Alberta Wilson Constant." *Language Arts* 53 (January 1976): 23–26.

12 Trease, Geoffrey. "The Historical Story: Is It Relevant Today?" *The Horn Book* (February 1977): 21–28.

13 Troy, Anne. "Literature for Content Area Learning." *The Reading Teacher* 30 (February 1977): 470–74.

14 Wibberly, Leonard. *John Treegate's Musket*. New York: Farrar, Straus & Giroux, 1959.

15 Wibberly, Leonard. *Peter Treegate's War*. New York: Farrar, Straus & Giroux, 1960.

16 Wibberly, Leonard. *Sea Captain from Salem*. New York: Farrar, Straus & Giroux, 1961.

17 Wibberly, Leonard. *Treegate's Raiders*. New York: Farrar, Straus & Giroux, 1962.

18 Wigginton, Eliot. *The Foxfire Book*. Doubleday, 1975.

19 Wolfe, Louis. *Let's Go with Paul Revere*. Putnam, 1964.

20 Wright, Jone P., and Allen, Elizabeth G. "Sixth-Graders Ride with Paul Revere." *Language Arts* 53 (January 1976): 46–50.

CHILDREN'S LITERATURE

Aiken, Joan. *Bridle the Wind*. Delacorte, 1983 (I:9 R:4). A thirteen-year-old boy in the 1820s rescues another boy from hanging and then helps him escape into Spain.

Armstrong, William H. *Sounder*. Illustrated by James Barkley. Harper & Row, 1969 (I:10+ R:6). A black sharecropper's family experiences prejudice.

Bauer, Marian. *Rain of Fire*. Clarion, 1983 (I:10+ R:7). A twelve-year-old boy discovers the complexity and the cruel reality of war.

Beatty, Patricia. *Eight Mules from Monterey*. Morrow, 1982 (I:10+ R:6). The Ashmores cross the California mountains in 1916.

———. *Wait for Me, Watch for Me, Eula Bee*. Morrow, 1978 (I:12+ R:7). Two white children are taken captive by Indians and the girl grows to trust an Indian brave.

Blos, Joan W. *A Gathering of Days: A New England Girl's Journal, 1830–32*. Scribner's, 1979 (I:8–14 R:6). A thirteen-year-old girl's experience on a farm.

Brenner, Barbara. *Wagon Wheels*. Illustrated by Don Bolognese. Harper & Row, 1978 (I:6–9 R:1). An easy-to-read story about a real pioneer family.

Brink, Carol Ryrie. *Caddie Woodlawn*. Illustrated by Trina Schart Hyman. Macmillan, 1935, 1963, 1973. (I:8–12 R:6). Twelve-year-old Caddie lives with her family on the Wisconsin frontier in 1864.

Carrick, Carol. *Stay Away from Simon!* Illustrated by Donald Carrick, Clarion, 1985 (I:7–10 R:3). A mentally retarded boy and a snow storm help two children realize that disabled people can have great worth.

Clapp, Patricia. *Constance: A Story of Early Plymouth*. Lothrop, Lee & Shepard, 1968 (I:12+ R:7). The story of the first few years of the Plymouth Colony.

———. *I'm Deborah Sampson: A Soldier in the War of the Revolution*. Lothrop, Lee & Shepard, 1977 (I:9+ R:6). Deborah disguises herself as a male and joins the army.

———. *Witches' Children: A Story of Salem*. Lothrop, Lee & Shepard, 1982 (I:10+ R:7). A bound girl tells about the hysteria that takes over Salem in 1692.

I = Interest by age range;
R = Readability by grade level.

Clark, Ann Nolan. *Year Walk*. Viking, 1975 (I:10+ R:7). A Spanish Basque sheepherder takes his sheep across the desert into the high country.

Collier, James, and Collier, Christopher. *Jump Ship to Freedom*. Delacorte, 1981 (I:10+ R:7). A slave obtains his and his mother's freedom.

Crofford, Emily. *A Matter of Pride*. Illustrated by Jim La Marche. Carolrhoda, 1981 (I:9–12 R:6). A ten-year-old girl tells about the Depression on an Arkansas cotton plantation.

Dalgliesh, Alice. *The Courage of Sarah Noble*. Illustrated by Leonard Weisgard. Scribner's, 1954 (I:6–9 R:3). In 1707 Sarah keeps up her courage as she and her father go through the wilderness.

DeAngeli, Marguerite. *The Door in the Wall*. Doubleday, 1949 (I:8–12 R:6). Robin overcomes a mysterious ailment in England during the time of Edward III.

Ellison, Lucile Watkins. *A Window to Look Through*. Illustrated by Judith Gwyn Brown. Scribner's, 1982 (I:7–9 R:4). Two years of a family's life in Mississippi during the early 1900s.

Fife, Dale. *Destination Unknown*. Dutton, 1981 (I:10+ R:6). A twelve-year-old boy stows away on a Norwegian fishing boat in 1940 and sails to safety in America.

Forbes, Esther. *Johnny Tremain*. Illustrated by Lynd Ward. Houghton Mifflin, 1943 (I:10–14 R:6). A silversmith's apprentice lives through prerevolutionary days and early wartime in Boston.

Fox, Paula. *The Slave Dancer*. Illustrated by Eros Keith. Bradbury, 1973 (I:12+ R:7). In 1840 a fife player experiences the misery of the slave trade.

Gray, Elizabeth Janet. *Adam of the Road*. Illustrated by Robert Lawson. Viking, 1942, 1970 (I:8–12 R:6). A young minstrel has many adventures in the England of 1294.

Greene, Constance C. *Dotty's Suitcase*. Viking Press, 1980 (I:8–12 R:4). During the Depression, a twelve-year-old girl longs to acquire a suitcase and travel to exotic places.

Haley, Gail E. *Jack Jouett's Ride*. Viking, 1973, 1976 (I:6–10 R:4). A picture storybook tells the tale of Jack Jouett as he rides to warn patriots that the British are coming.

Hancock, Sibyl. *Old Blue*. Illustrated by Erick Ingraham. Putnam, 1980 (I:7–9 R:3). Based on historical information about a lead steer on a trail drive in 1878.

Haugaard, Erik Christian. *Cromwell's Boy*. Houghton Mifflin, 1978 (I:11+ R:5). Oliver is a messenger for Oliver Cromwell and Parliament.

———. *Hakon of Rogen's Saga*. Illustrated by Leo and Diane Dillon. Houghton Mifflin, 1963 (I:9–12 R:6). A viking flees from his wicked uncle before his loyal followers help him regain his birthright.

———. *A Messenger for Parliament*. Houghton Mifflin, 1976 (I:11+ R:7). In 1641, a boy follows the Parliamentary army and is responsible for sending an important message to Cromwell.

———. *A Slave's Tale*. Illustrated by Leo and Diane Dillon. Houghton Mifflin, 1965 (I:8–12 R:4). In this Viking story, a slave tells her side of the story.

Hautzig, Esther. *The Endless Steppe: A Girl in Exile*. Cromwell, 1968 (I:12+ R:7). A true story of a Jewish girl and her parents who are exiled to Siberia during World War II.

Hickman, Janet. *Zoar Blue*. Macmillan, 1978 (I:9–14 R:4). The young men of a nonviolent Zoar, Ohio, religious group fight in the Civil War.

Hoguet, Susan Ramsay. *Solomon Grundy*. Dutton, 1986 (I:6+). A nursery rhyme forms the structure for a highly illustrated story about a nineteenth-century family.

Holman, Felice. *The Wild Children*. Scribner's, 1983 (I:10+ R:4). A group of homeless children strive to survive during the Bolshevik Revolution.

Hooks, William H. *Circle of Fire*. Atheneum, 1983. (I:10+ R:6). A boy and his friends try to prevent a Ku Klux Klan attack.

Hudson, Jan. *Sweetgrass*. Tree Frog, 1984 (I:10+ R:4). A young Blackfeet girl grows up during the winter of a smallpox epidemic in 1837.

Hunt, Irene. *Across Five Aprils*. Follett, 1964 (I:10+ R:7). Jethro Creighton must become the man of the family when his brothers go to war and his father has a heart attack.

Keith, Harold. *The Obstinate Land*. Crowell, 1977 (I:12+ R:7). In 1893, thirteen-year-old Fritz Romberg and his family move to the Oklahoma prairie.

———. *Rifles for Watie*. Crowell, 1957 (I:12+ R:7). A Civil War story involving a Cherokee raider.

Kerr, Judith. *When Hitler Stole Pink Rabbit*. Coward-McCann, 1972 (I:8–12 R:3). Anna and her family escape from Hitler's Germany.

Kullman, Harry. *The Battle Horse*. Bradbury, 1981 (I:10+ R:8). In 1930s Stockholm children play a game between rich and poor.

Lampman, Evelyn Sibley *White Captives*. Atheneum, 1975 (I:11+ R:7). The Native American viewpoint in a story about two captives of the Apache.

Lasky, Kathryn. *Beyond the Divide*. Macmillan, 1983 (I:9+ R:6). In 1849 a fourteen-year-old girl accompanies her father across the continent.

———. *The Night Journey*. Illustrated by Trina Schart Hyman. Warne, 1981 (I:10+ R:6). A nine-year-old girl learns about her great-grandmother's escape from Czarist Russia in 1900.

Lenski, Lois. *Indian Captive: The Story of Mary Jemison*. Lippincott, 1941 (I:10+ R:7). A captive white girl decides to stay with the Senecas.

Levitin, Sonia. *Journey to America*. Illustrated by Charles Robinson. Atheneum, 1970 (I:12+ R:6). A Jewish family escapes from Nazi Germany.

Lobel, Arnold. *On the Day Peter Stuyvesant Sailed into Town*. Harper & Row, 1971 (I:4–8 R:3). A picture storybook about the New Netherland Colony.

MacLachlan, Patricia. *Sarah, Plain and Tall*. Harper & Row, 1985 (I:7–10 R:3). A frontier family longs for a new mother.

McSwigan, Marie. *Snow Treasure*. Illustrated by Mary Reardon. Dutton, 1942 (I:8–12 R:4). A retelling of a real adventure against the Nazis in World War II Norway.

Moeri, Louise. *Save Queen of Sheba*. Dutton, 1981 (I:10+ R:5). A twelve-year-old boy and his young sister cross the prairie alone after their wagon train is attacked.

Monjo, F.N. *The Drinking Gourd*. Illustrated by Fred Brenner. Harper & Row, 1970 (I:7–9 R:2). An "I can read" history book about the Underground Railroad.

Morrow, Honore, *On To Oregon!* Illustrated by Edward Shenton. Morrow, 1926, 1948, 1954 (I:10+ R:6). Children travel alone to Oregon in 1844.

O'Dell, Scott. *The Amethyst Ring*. Houghton Mifflin, 1983 (I:10+ R6). The final story of Julián Escobar.

——— *The Captive*. Houghton Mifflin, 1979 (I:10+ R:6). A young Spanish

seminarian witnesses the exploitation of the Mayas during the 1500s.

———. *Carlota*. Houghton Mifflin, 1977 (I:9+ R:4). A Spanish girl fights beside her father during the Mexican War.

———. *The Feathered Serpent*. Houghton Mifflin, 1981 (I:10+ R:6). A sequel to *The Captive*.

———. *Sing Down the Moon*. Houghton Mifflin, 1970 (I:10+ R:6) The forced march of the Navajo from a young girl's perspective.

Orlev, Uri. *The Island on Bird Street*. Translated by Hillel Halkin. Houghton Mifflin, 1984 (I:10+ R:6). A twelve-year-old Jewish boy survives in the Warsaw ghetto.

Pelgrom, Els. *The Winter When Time Was Frozen*. Rudnik, Maryka, and Rudnik, 1980. (I:8–12 R:5). A World War II story set in Holland.

Pellowski, Anne. *Winding Valley Farm: Annie's Story*. Illustrated by Wendy Watson. Philomel, 1982 (I:9–12 R:6). A Polish community in rural Wisconsin during the early 1900s.

Petry, Ann. *Tituba of Salem Village*. Crowell, 1964 (I:11+ R:6). A talented, slave becomes part of the famous Salem witch trials.

Phelan, Mary Kay. *The Story of the Louisiana Purchase*. Illustrated by Frank Aloise. Crowell, 1979 (I:12+ R:7). In 1803 the territory of a young nation was doubled.

Reiss, Johanna. *The Upstairs Room*. Crowell, 1972 (I:11+ R:4). The true story of a Jewish girl's experience hiding from the Nazis.

Rylant, Cynthia. *When I Was Young in the Mountains*. Dutton, 1982 (I:4–9 R:3). Memories of Appalachia.

Sandin, Joan. *The Long Way to a New Land*. Harper & Row, 1981 (I:7–9 R:3). A Swedish family emigrates to America in 1868.

Schlee, Ann. *Ask Me No Questions*. Holt, Rinehart & Winston, 1982 (I:10+ R:6). Laura faces moral issues related to feeding hungry children in 1848 London.

Siegal, Aranka. *Upon the Head of the Goat: A Childhood in Hungary 1939–1944*. Farrar, Straus & Giroux, 1981 (I:10+ R:7). Nine-year-old Piri's experiences during the Holocaust.

Skurzynski, Gloria. *Manwolf*. Houghton Mifflin, 1981 (I:10+ R:7). A rare disease causes people in medieval Poland to believe a boy is a werewolf.

Speare, Elizabeth George. *The Bronze Bow*. Houghton Mifflin, 1961 (I:10+

R:6). A boy's hatred of the Romans is affected after he meets Jesus.

———. *Calico Captive*. Illustrated by W. T. Mars. Houghton Mifflin, 1957 (I:10+ R:6). White people are forced to march north to Indian territories in Canada.

———. *The Sign of the Beaver*. Houghton Mifflin, 1983 (I:8–12 R:5). A boy survives in a frontier cabin after an Indian friend teaches him survival techniques.

———. *The Witch of Blackbird Pond*. Houghton Mifflin, 1958 (I:9–14 R:4). A flamboyant girl is accused of witchcraft in colonial New England.

Stevens, Carla. *Anna, Grandpa, and the Big Storm*. Illustrated by Margot Tomes. Houghton Mifflin, 1982 (I:6–9 R:3). Seven-year-old Anna experiences a blizzard in New York City in 1888.

Sutcliff, Rosemary. *Blood Feud*. Dutton, 1976. An English boy is carried away in a Viking raid and sold into slavery.

———. *The Eagle of the Ninth*. Illustrated by C. Walter Hodges. Walck, 1954 (I:11+ R:8). A Roman officer's son discovers the mystery of his father's legion.

———. *Frontier Wolf*. Dutton, 1981 (I:10+ R:8). A Roman centurion leads a band of British warriors.

———. *The Lantern Bearers*. Illustrated by Charles Keeping. Walck, 1959 (I:11+ R:7). The Saxons invade Roman Britain.

———. *The Silver Branch*. Illustrated by Charles Keeping. Walck, 1958 (I:10+ R:8). Two Romans uncover a plot to overthrow the emperor.

———. *Song for a Dark Queen*. Crowell, 1978 (I:10+ R:6). The queen of a tribe of Britains leads the fight against the Roman armies.

———. *Sun Horse, Moon Horse*. Illustrated by Shirley Felts. Dutton, 1978 (I:10+ R:6). A boy saves his people from slavery in pre-Roman Britain.

Taylor, Mildred D. *Let The Circle Be Unbroken*. Dial, 1981 (I:10 R:6). A sequal to *Roll of Thunder, Hear My Cry*.

———. *Roll of Thunder, Hear My Cry*. Illustrated by Jerry Pickney. Dial, 1976 (I:10+ R:6). A black family suffers prejudice in rural Mississippi.

Tene, Benjamin. *In the Shade of the Chestnut Tree*. Translated from Hebrew by Reuben Ben-Joseph. Illustrated by Richard Sigberman. Jewish Publication Society of America, 1981 (I:10+ R:6). Growing up in Warsaw during the years prior to World War II.

Thrasher, Crystal. *A Taste of Daylight*. Atheneum, 1984 (I:10+ R:7). During the Depression, a girl and her family move from the country to the city.

Trease, Geoffrey. *Saraband for Shadows*. Macmillan, 1982 (I:10+ R:7). In the time of Charles I, the hero uncovers a plot to murder his friend.

Treece, Henry. *Viking's Dawn*. Illustrated by Christine Price. Criterion, 1956 (I:10–14 R:7). Harold joins the crew of the Viking ship *Nameless*.

Uchida, Yoshiko. *Journey Home*. Illustrated by Charles Robinson. Atheneum, 1978 (I:10+ R:5). In a sequel to *Journey to Topaz*, twelve-year-old Yuki and her parents return to California and try to adjust.

———. *Journey to Topaz*. Illustrated by Donald Carrick. Scribner's, 1971 (I:10+ R:5). A Japanese-American family is held in an internment camp in Utah during World War II.

Wilder, Laura Ingalls. *By the Shores of Silver Lake*. Illustrated by Garth Williams. Harper & Row, 1939, 1953 (I:8–12 R:6). The Ingalls move again to the Dakota Territory.

———. *The First Four Years*. Illustrated by Garth Williams. Harper & Row, 1971 (I:8–12 R:6). Laura and Almanzo spend their first four years of marriage on a South Dakota homestead.

———. *Little House in the Big Woods*. Illustrated by Garth Williams. Harper & Row, 1932, 1953 (I:8–12 R:6). The first in a series of books about a loving pioneer family.

———. *Little House on the Prairie*. Illustrated by Garth Williams, Harper & Row, 1935, 1953 (I:8–12 R:8). The Ingalls move to Kansas.

———. *Little Town on the Prairie*. Illustrated by Garth Williams, Harper & Row, 1941, 1953. (I:8–12 R:8). Laura has her first job.

———. *The Long Winter*. Illustrated by Garth Williams, Harper & Row, 1940, 1953 (I:8–12 R:6). A blizzard causes the Ingalls family great discomfort.

———. *On the Banks of Plum Creek*. Illustrated by Garth Williams. Harper & Row, 1937, 1953 (I:8–12 R:6). The Ingalls move to Minnesota.

———. *These Happy Golden Years*. Illustrated by Garth Williams, Harper & Row, 1943, 1953 (I:8–12 R:6). Laura becomes a teacher and meets her future husband.

Yates, Elizabeth. *Amos Fortune, Free Man*. Illustrated by Nora S. Unwin. Dutton, 1950 (I:10+ R:6). An African enslaved by white traders is educated by his Quaker owner in Boston.

———. *We, The People* Illustrated by Nora Unwin. Regional Center for Educational Training, 1974 (I:8–12 R:4). A family survives the Revolutionary War.

11

Multiethnic Literature

☐

OUR RICH MOSAIC

☐

INVOLVING CHILDREN IN MULTIETHNIC
LITERATURE

Our Rich Mosaic

A HEIGHTENED SENSITIVITY TO THE needs of all people in American society has led to the realization that reading programs for children should include literature by and about members of all cultural groups. Literature is an appropriate means of building respect across cultures, sharpening sensitivity toward the ways in which all individuals have much in common, and improving the self-esteem of people who are members of racial and ethnic minority groups. Laura Fisher (11) is among the many educators and critics of children's literature who maintain that children should be exposed to multiethnic literature that heightens all people's respect for the individuals, the contributions, and the values of cultural minorities.

Many of the successful multiethnic literature programs that have met these goals have accomplished them through either preservice or in-service education of teachers and librarians that stressed evaluating, selecting, and sharing multiethnic literature (20). The tasks related to developing such programs are enormous. Universities are beginning to require courses in multiethnic education that often include selecting and using multiethnic literature. Until all educators have been trained in this way, school districts must provide in-service instruction so that teachers and librarians can select and use materials that will create an atmosphere in which all children can respect one another. One of the most formidable tasks is becoming familiar with the available literature and other teaching materials. Library selection committees, teachers, and administrators must all become involved in this process.

For these reasons, this text contains a separate chapter on multiethnic literature. The chapter is not intended to isolate the literature and contributions of racial and ethnic minorities from other literature discussed in this book, but to place multiethnic literature in a context helpful to librarians, teachers, and parents who wish to select and share these materials with children or develop multiethnic literature programs.

WHAT IS MULTIETHNIC LITERATURE?

Multiethnic literature, according to Ruth Kearney Carlson (6), is literature about a racial or ethnic minority group that is culturally and socially different from the white Anglo-Saxon majority in the United States, whose largely middle-class values and customs are most represented in all American literature. Although, of course, ethnic diversity in the United States is extremely great, multiethnic literature is usually viewed as literature about Black Americans; Native Americans*; Hispanic Americans, including Mexican Americans, Puerto Ricans, Cuban Americans and others of Spanish descent or cultural heritage; and Asian Americans, including Chinese Americans, Japanese Americans, Korean Americans, Vietnamese Americans and others.

VALUES OF MULTIETHNIC LITERATURE FOR CHILDREN

Well-written multiethnic literature, like other high-quality literature, provides enjoyment for the reader or the listener. In addition, it offers the following important values—summarized by Ruth Kearney Carlson (6) and Esther C. Jenkins (16)—for both children who are members of a racial or ethnic minority and children who are not:

1   Through multiethnic literature, children who are members of racial or ethnic minority groups realize that they have a cultural heritage of which they can be proud, and that their own culture has made important contributions to the United States and to the world.

2   Pride in their heritage helps children who are members of minority groups improve their self-concepts and develop a strong sense of cultural identity.

3   Learning about other cultures allows all children to understand that people who belong to racial or ethnic groups other than theirs are real people with feelings, emotions, and needs similar to their own—individual human beings, not stereotypes.

4   Reading about other cultures helps children realize that all people have philosophies, spiritual beliefs, and creative imaginations that contribute to American and world culture.

5   Through multiethnic literature children discover that, while all people may not share

their own personal beliefs and values, individuals can and must learn to live in harmony.

6   Through multiethnic literature, children of the majority culture learn to respect the values and contributions of minority groups in the United States and the values and contributions of people in other parts of the world.

7   Children broaden their understanding of history, geography, and natural history as they read about cultural groups living in various regions of their country and the world.

8   The wide range of multiethnic themes helps children develop an understanding of social change.

9   Reading about members of minority groups who have successfully solved their own problems and made notable achievements helps raise the aspirations of children who belong to a minority group.

IMAGES OF RACIAL AND ETHNIC MINORITIES IN AMERICAN LITERATURE OF THE PAST

Only recently have Americans begun to realize that certain books—because of their illustrations, themes, characterizations, and language—can perpetuate stereotypes and result in psychological damage or discomfort to children. According to Barbara Bader (1), only as late as the 1940s did Americans begin to express publicly their growing objections to the use of certain stereotypes in literature. Many changes have occurred since that time in both American social life and American literature, but further improvements are still needed.

Some educators, through their selection of books and instructional materials, continue to communicate negative messages about minorities to children. Bettye I. Latimer (18) makes a very strong criticism of this continuing tendency in education: "If your bulletin boards, your models, and your authority lines are White, and I am Black, Latino or Native American, then you have telegraphed me messages which I will reject" (p. 156). Latimer maintains that white children are taught a distorted image of American society and are not prepared to value American society's multiracial character because they are surrounded with literature and other instructional materials that either present minorities stereotypically or make minorities invisible by omitting them entirely. Latimer also stresses that because of the

*This book primarily uses the term *Native Americans* to denote the people historically referred to as *American Indians*. The term *Indian* is sometimes used interchangeably with *Native American* and in some contexts is used to name certain tribes of Native Americans.

FLASHBACK

''Why are they always *white* children?''

The question came from a five-year-old Negro girl who was looking at a picturebook at the Manhattanville Nursery School in New York. With a child's uncanny wisdom, she singled out one of the most critical issues in American education today: the almost complete omission of Negroes from books for children. Integration may be the law of the land, but most of the books children see are all white.

But the impact of all-white books upon 39,600,000 white children is probably even worse. Although his light skin makes him one of the world's minorities, the white child learns from his books that he is the kingfish. There seems little chance of developing the humility so urgently needed for world cooperation, instead of world conflict, as long as our children are brought up on gentle doses of racism through their books.

THIS EXCERPT FROM THE SEPTEMBER 11, 1965, issue of *Saturday Review* (p. 63) is from one of the early and often-quoted articles that criticized the omission of black characters in books for children. Nancy Larrick's "The All-White World of Children's Books" reported the results of a study that analyzed trade books for children published over a three-year period in the 1960s. Most books published during that time showed blacks outside the continental United States or before World War II—only four-fifths of 1 percent of the books told stories about contemporary Black Americans. Most books that included black characters depicted them as slaves, sharecroppers, or other types of menial workers. Larrick's article in a prestigious publication may have had considerable impact on future publications for children.

comparatively small number of books written about members of racial and ethnic minorities, well-meaning librarians, teachers, and other adults are likely to accept any book that describes and/or pictures members of minority groups, without carefully evaluating the stories and the stereotypes they might be fostering. She believes that adults who work with children and literature should reeducate themselves to the social values that books pass on to children. To do this, adults must learn to evaluate and assess books written about children from all ethnic backgrounds.

Black Americans in Literature of the Past

Several researchers have investigated images of Black Americans in children's literature, focusing on stereotypes, attitudes white characters express toward black characters, and the importance of black characters in the literature. Dorothy May Broderick (3), for example, analyzed American

children's literature published between 1827 and 1967. She reported that the personal characteristics of black people portrayed in these books suggested that black people (1) were not physically attractive, (2) were musical, (3) combined religious fervor with superstitious beliefs, (4) were required to select life goals that would benefit black people, and (5) were dependent upon white people for whatever good things they could hope to acquire. Broderick concluded that in the 140-year period she studied, black children would find little in literature to enhance pride in their heritage, and that if these books were white children's only contacts with black people, white children would develop a sense of superiority.

In investigating whether or not changes in attitudes toward black people had occurred in more recent times, Julia Ann Carlson (5) compared American children's literature of the 1930s with that of the 1960s. She discovered that considerable changes in the depiction of black characters had occurred between the two time periods. Although 15 percent of the books from the earlier period mentioned black characters, these characters tended to be stereotyped. Only 10 percent of the books in the later period mentioned black characters at all, but, when they did, they tended to present black people as individuals with either a racial problem or a universal problem. In 1973, Betty M. Morgan (19) reported that the number of books with black people as the main characters had increased markedly in recent years.

Although the percentage of children's books with black main characters is increasing, Bettye I. Latimer (18) is concerned about the fact that so few children's books deal in any way with black people. She cites a three-year survey showing that only about 1 percent of all trade books for children published during the mid-1960s by sixty-three publishers dealt with black people. In the 1970s, still only about 1 percent of the estimated 2,000 to 3,000 children's books published annually involved black characters. Latimer believes that this low statistical probability of black people appearing in children's books is "frightening": "It means that the average child, White or Black, will have only one out of 100 chances to read a book that is integrated. It means that only one out of every 100 books in a classroom or library will represent Blacks." (p. 154) The likelihood that the "one book out of a hundred" reflects racial stereotypes further decreases the chances of children reading books that would raise their expectations or develop positive attitudes. Consequently, carefully evaluating and selecting books about the black experience becomes very important.

Native Americans in Literature of the Past

Native Americans fared no better than Black Americans in the literature of the past and still suffer from stereotyping in children's books. According to Mary Gloyne Byler (4):

There are too many books featuring painted, whooping, befeathered Indians closing in on too many forts, maliciously attacking "peaceful" settlers or simply leering menacingly from the background; too many books in which white benevolence is the only thing that saves the day for the incompetent childlike Indian; too many stories setting forth what is "best" for American Indians. (p. 28)

Researchers analyzing the images of Native Americans in children's literature have identified many negative stereotypes in a large percentage of the literature. Three of the most common stereotypes, according to Laura Herbst (15) characterize Native Americans as (1) savage, depraved, and cruel; (2) noble, proud, silent, and close to nature; and/or (3) inferior, childlike, and helpless. Terms and comparisons suggesting negative and derogatory images often reinforce such stereotypes. A white family, for example, may be said to consist of a husband, a wife, and a child; members of Native American families, in contrast, may be called bucks, squaws, and papooses. White authors often dehumanize Native Americans by comparing them to animals. Even Native American language is often described as "snarling," "grunting," or "yelping." *The Matchlock Gun*, by Walter Edmonds, compares the nameless Indians to trotting dogs, sniffing the scent of food. Often Native American characters are depersonalized by not being given names, which implies that they are not individuals, or even full-fledged human beings.

In addition to stereotypes about Native American people, Laura Herbst (15) also identifies three stereotypical ways in which Native American culture has been portrayed in children's literature: (1) The culture may be depicted as inferior to the white culture. The author may treat the abandonment of the Native American way of life as an improvement. Native American characters are often depicted making this gain by going to white schools or taking on the values of the white culture, leaving their own culture and even their own people behind. A common theme in such literature is that white people must be responsible for remaking Native Americans into an image acceptable to European immigrants to North America. (2) The culture may be depicted as valueless, and thus not worthy of respect. The rich diversity of spiritual beliefs and ceremonies, moral values, artistic skills, and the life-styles in Native American cultures may be ignored in favor of depicting violence as the chief Native American value. Authors may be ignorant of the fact that the cultures of the many different Native American peoples often differ from one another. (3) The culture may be depicted as quaint or superficial, without depth or warmth. White characters in children's literature of the past commonly ridicule or scorn customs that have great spiritual significance to Native Americans. They disparage sacred ceremonies, medicine men, ancient artifacts, and traditional legends as belonging to "heathen savages." Any of these three stereotypical portrayals of a culture is offensive and would not elevate Native American children's self-esteem or develop favorable attitudes in non-Native American children. More current books, however, especially those written by Native American authors or other authorities on Native American culture, are sensitive to the heritage and individuality of the native peoples of North America.

Hispanic Americans in Literature of the Past

Betty M. Morgan (19) concluded that the number of children's books with members of minority groups as main characters has increased since World War II, but she also found that this was true only for books about either Black Americans or Native Americans. Far fewer children's books have Hispanic Americans or Asian Americans as the main characters.

Both the lack of children's literature about people of Hispanic descent and/or cultural heritage and the negative stereotypes found in some of the literature have been criticized. At one children's literature conference, Mauricio Charpenel (7), consultant to the Mexican Ministry of Education, reported that very few stories are written for or about Mexican or Mexican American children. He was especially concerned about poetry: while Latin American writers publish beautiful poetry, the poems are not shared with Mexican American children in the United States. Both teachers and librarians at the conference expressed concern about the need for literature that would appeal to Hispanic American children and create positive images of their heritage.

The Council on Interracial Books for Children (8) has been very critical of children's literature that depicts Mexican Americans. After analyzing 200 books, the council concluded that little in the stories would enable children to recognize a culture, a history, or a set of life circumstances. The council criticized the theme of poverty that tediously recurs as if it is a "natural facet of the Chicano condition" (p. 57), and the tendency for Mexican American problems to be solved not by the efforts of Mexican Americans but by the intervention of Anglo Americans. The council also felt that Mexican Americans' problems had been treated superficially in the books it studied: for example, many books suggest that if children learn English all their problems will be solved.

Even fewer books are being written about Puerto Rican Americans, Cuban Americans and the many new Americans from Central American countries. The majority of books about Puerto Ricans, for example, lack literary merit and overuse a New York City ghetto setting.

Asian Americans in Literature of the Past

Since few books about Asian Americans have been published for children, researchers who have tried to evaluate books about Asian Americans have had little to study. In 1976, the Asian American Children's Book Project (9) identified sixty-six books with Asian American central characters; most of these books were about Chinese Americans. The members of the project concluded that, with only a few exceptions, the books were grossly misleading. They presented stereotypes of Asian Americans suggesting that all Asian Americans look alike, choose to live in "quaint" communities in the midst of large cities, and cling to "outworn, alien" customs. The project also criticized the books because they tended to measure success by the extent to which Asian Americans have assimilated white middle-class values and because they implied that hard work, learning to speak English, and keeping a low profile would enable Asian Americans to overcome adversity and be successful.

EVALUATING MULTIETHNIC LITERATURE

If children's literature is to help children develop positive attitudes about and respect for individuals in all cultures, children need many opportunities to read and listen to high-quality literature that presents accurate and respectful images of everyone. Because few children's books in the United States are written from the perspective of racial and ethnic minorities, and because many stories portray negative stereotypes, adults should carefully evaluate books containing non-white characters. Outstanding multiethnic literature meets the literary criteria applied to any fine book, as discussed in chapter three, but other criteria apply specifically to the treatment of ethnic and racial minorities in all books and in books that focus on the experiences of nonwhite Americans. The following criteria related to literature that represents Black Americans, Native Americans, Hispanic Americans, and Asian Americans reflect the recommendations of the Children's Literature Review Board (17), Anna Lee Stensland (21), and the Council on Interracial Books for Children (8, 9):

1　Are Black, Native, Hispanic, and Asian Americans portrayed as unique individuals, with their own thoughts, emotions, and philosophies, rather than as representatives of particular racial or ethnic groups?

2　Does a book transcend stereotypes in the appearance, behavior, and character traits of its nonwhite characters? Does the depiction of nonwhite characters and lifestyles lack any implication of stigma? Does a book suggest that all members of an ethnic or racial group live in poverty? Are the characters from a variety of socioeconomic backgrounds, educational levels, and occupations? Does the author avoid depicting Asian Americans as workers in restaurants and laundries, Hispanic Americans as illegal aliens or unskilled laborers, Native Americans as bloodthirsty warriors, Black Americans as menial service employees, and so forth? Does the author avoid the "model minority" and "bad minority" syndrome? Are nonwhite characters respected for being themselves, or must they display outstanding abilities to gain approval from white characters?

3　Is the physical diversity within a particular racial or ethnic minority group authentically portrayed in the text and the illustrations? Do nonwhite characters have stereotypically exaggerated facial features or physiques that make them "all look alike?"

4　Will children be able to identify the characters in the text and the illustrations as recognizably Black, Hispanic, Asian, or Native American and not mistake them for white? Are people of color shown as "gray"—that is, as simply darker versions of Caucasian-featured people?

5　Is the culture of a racial or ethnic minority group accurately portrayed? Is it treated with respect, or depicted as inferior to majority white culture? Does the author believe the culture worthy of preservation, rather than advocating its abandonment? Is the cultural diversity within Black American, Asian American, Hispanic American, and Native American life clearly demonstrated? Are the customs and values of those diverse cultural groups accurately portrayed? Must nonwhite characters fit into a cultural image acceptable to white characters? Is a nonwhite culture shown in an overly "exotic" or romanticized way, instead of being placed within the context of everyday activities familiar to all people?

6　Are social issues and problems related to minority group status depicted frankly and accurately without oversimplification? Must characters who are members of racial and ethnic minority groups exercise all the understanding and forgiveness?

7　Do nonwhite characters handle their problems individually, through their own efforts and/or with the assistance of close family and friends, or are problems solved through the intervention of whites?

8　Are nonwhite characters shown as the equals of white characters? Are some characters placed in a submissive or inferior position? Are white people always the benefactors?

9　Is a nonwhite character glamorized or glorified, especially in biography? (Both excessive praise and excessive deprecation of nonwhite characters result in unreal and unbalanced characterizations.) If the book is a biography, are both the personality and the accomplishments of the main character shown in accurate detail and not oversimplified?

10　Is the setting of a story authentic, whether past, present, or future? Will children be able to recognize the setting as urban, rural, or fantasy?

11　If a story deals with factual information or historical events, are the details accurate?

12　If the setting is contemporary, does the author accurately describe the life situations of nonwhite people in the United States and elsewhere today?

13　Does a book rectify historical distortions and omissions?

14　If dialect is used, does it have a legitimate purpose? Does it ring true and blend in naturally with the story in a nonstereotypical way, or is it simply used as an example of "substandard English"? If non-English words are used, are they spelled and used correctly?

15 Is offensive or degrading vocabulary used to describe the characters, their actions, their customs, or their life-styles?

16 Are the illustrations authentic and nonstereotypical in every detail?

17 Does a book reflect an awareness of the changing status of females in all racial and ethnic groups today? Does the author provide role models for girls other than subservient females?

BLACK AMERICAN LITERATURE

Many fine books of traditional literature, contemporary realistic fiction, and nonfiction reflect the heritage and modern-day experiences of Black Americans. Reading these enjoyable and well-written books will help children from all racial and ethnic backgrounds identify with and appreciate the dreams, problems, and cultural contributions of black people on this continent.

Traditional Black Literature

Traditional folk literature, the tales originally handed down through centuries of oral storytelling, includes many of the stories children most enjoy. Through reading African and Black American traditional tales, children discover a rich literary heritage, gain a respect for the creativity of the people who originated the stories, develop an understanding of the values of these originators, and share an enjoyable experience that has entertained others in centuries past. Modern writers of contemporary realistic fiction about black people often have their characters tell an African tale in order to develop a closer relationship to and understanding of the African heritage. The black children in the stories may ask older family members or friends to tell stories so that they can feel closer to their roots. In Virginia Hamilton's *The Time-Ago Tales of Jahdu*, for example, Mama Luka, sitting in her little room in a "good place called Harlem," tells young Lee Edward several delightful tales about a proud and powerful being whose favorite color is black and who undertakes many adventures from his perch high atop the only gum tupelo tree in the pine forest. Such beautiful folktales have much value for children of all backgrounds.

Ruth Kearney Carlson (6) identifies three types of traditional tales from Black Americans' cultural heritage that can be shared with children: (1) African folktales that are indigenous to various countries on the African continent; (2) African folk literature that was transported to one of the Caribbean islands and then altered in the new setting; and (3) folk literature that originated in the plantation areas of the American South. This section focuses on traditional tales that originated in Africa and those that originated in the plantation areas of the early United States.

Traditional African Tales. Many traditional African tales crossed the Atlantic with the ancestors of contemporary Black Americans. Traditional values reflected in the folklore of several African cultures are found in Harold Courlander's *The Crest and the Hide: And Other African Stories of Heroes, Chiefs, Bards, Hunters, Sorcerers, and Common People*. This collection of twenty tales from cultures such as the Ashanti, the Yoruba, the Swahili, and the Zulu emphasizes the human values of wisdom, friendship, love, and heroism, as well as some behaviors that are not respected, such as foolishness and disloyalty.

Several beautifully illustrated books contain single African folktales retold for children of all ages. Jan Carew's *The Third Gift* suggests the traditional values respected by the Jubas as they acquire the most important gifts that can be given. According to this lovely legend, "in long-time-past days" the Jubas were threatened with extinction when the prophet Amakosa gathered his people and led them to the base of a tall mountain. He told them that when he was gone the young men should climb the Nameless Mountain and the one who could climb the highest and bring back a gift of wonders would be the new leader. One young man reached the top and returned with the gift of work; he ruled for a long time and his people prospered. When it was time for that ruler to die, the young men again went to the mountain top to seek a gift, and the one destined to rule returned with the gift of beauty. During his reign, the Juba country became very beautiful. When young men climbed the mountain for the third time, the gifts brought back were the most important of all, fantasy, imagination, and faith: "So, with the gifts of Work and Beauty and Imagination, the Jubas became poets and bards and creators, and they live at the foot of Nameless Mountain to this day" (p. 32).

Carew's *Children of the Sun*, tells a tale about the birth of the sun's twin boys, one rebellious

Peace and harmony are two values emphasized in this African tale. (From *Children of the Sun*, by Jan Carew. Illustrations Copyright © 1980 by Leo and Diane Dillon. Reprinted by permission of Little, Brown and Company.)

and haughty, the other obedient and gentle. The first son attempts greatness, disobeys his father and is destroyed. The second chooses to be a good man rather than a great one and eventually brings peace and harmony, the most respected social values, to human beings.

Rosa Guy's retelling of *Mother Crocodile*, a folktale from Senegal, also stresses that the knowledge and advice of elders is important and should be taken seriously.

African folktales provide explanations for both natural and social phenomena. Verna Aardema's *Why Mosquitoes Buzz in People's Ears* explains why mosquitoes are constantly noisy. Written as a cumulative tale, it is excellent for sharing orally with children. It suggests a rich language heritage and a respect for storytelling. (See page 166 for a discussion of the language in this folktale and page 128 for a discussion of Leo and Diane

Dillon's outstanding illustrations.) Ann Grifalconi's *The Village of Round and Square Houses* reveals why the men in a Cameroon village live in square houses while the women live in round houses. The storyteller concludes that this arrangement is peaceful because people need a time to be apart as much as time to be together.

Aardema's *Who's in Rabbit's House?* is an unusual and humorous Masai tale about tricky animals, written in the form of a play performed by villagers for their fellow townsfolk. Repetition of words adds to the vivid descriptions, and the dialogue suggests the richness of African language. The jackal trots off *kpata, kpata*, the leopard jumps *pa, pa, pa*, and the frog laughs *dgung, dgung, dgung*. This is an excellent tale to stimulate creative dramatizations by children, who enjoy repeating the sound effects and dialogues out loud and creating masks of the various animals.

Another folktale rich in the language of the African storyteller is Gail E. Haley's *A Story, a Story*. This tale about Ananse, the spider man, repeats key words to make them stronger, as Ananse's wit helps him overcome serious difficulties. Ananse seeks stories from the powerful sky god, and the god laughs: "How can a weak old man like you, so small, so small, so small, pay my price?" (p. 6 unnumbered). Ananse fools the god and is able to capture the leopard-of-the-terrible-teeth; Mmboro the hornet who stings like fire; and Mmoatia, the fairy whom people never see. As a reward for these gifts, the sky god gives Ananse the stories that previously belonged only to the god. From this tale, children can understand the importance of storytelling on the African continent.

Joyce Cooper Arkhurst, says that Spider is a favorite character in West African stories, and retells six Spider stories in *The Adventures of Spider: West African Folktales*. These stories, excellent for sharing orally with children, explain how the spider acquired his thin waist, why he lives in ceilings, how he came to have a bald head, why he lives in dark corners, and how the world received wisdom.

All these beautifully expressed and illustrated traditional African tales represent some of the strongest and most noble values attributed to humanity: love of beauty, humor, work, and imagination; perseverance in attaining peace and harmony. Children discover that there is both pride and hope in being a strong black child, as well as pleasure in the richness of their cultural heritage.

Traditional African folklore elements are found in Mildred Pitt Walter's original tale *Brother to the Wind*. The story, set in Africa, reflects a boy's quest as he searches for Good Snake, the mythical being who is able to grant wishes; as he carefully follows Good Snake's directions; and as he astounds doubting villagers with his ability to fly. (Comparisons may be made between *Brother to the Wind* and the Native American contemporary tale, *Hawk, I'm Your Brother* by Byrd Baylor. Although one tale is fantasy and one tale is realistic, both tales emphasize similar themes, develop comparable quests, and portray characters whose strong desires control their actions.)

Black American Tales. New folktales developed when Africans became slaves in North America, as Virginia Hamilton (13) points out in her introduction to *The People Could Fly: American Black Folktales*: "Out of the contacts the plantation slaves made in their new world, combined with memories and habits from the old world of Africa, came a body of folk expression about the slaves and their experiences. The slaves created

tales in which various animals . . . took on characteristics of the people found in the new environment of the plantation" (p. x). For example, the favorite Brer Rabbit, who was small and apparently helpless when compared with the more powerful bear and fox, was smart, tricky, and clever, and usually won out over larger and stronger animals. The slaves, who identified with the rabbit, told many tales about his exploits. Hamilton's collection of tales is divided into four parts: animal tales, extravagant and fanciful experiences, supernatural tales, and slave tales of freedom. The collection provides sources for listening, discussing, and comparing. For example, readers can compare the folklore elements, plot development, and themes in Hamilton's "The Beautiful Girl of the Moon Tower," a folktale from the Cape Verde Islands, and Elizabeth Isele's retelling of the Russian tale "The Frog Princess."

Another group of tales that incorporate characters and language from a new environment into the stories recalled from the African homeland are found in Priscilla Jaquith's *Bo Rabbit Smart for True: Folktales from the Gullah*. The text con-

ISSUE

❈ ⟩⟩❈⟨⟨ ❈

Controversy Surrounding One Book About Black People

CONTROVERSY SURrounds Margot Zemach's 1982 book, *Jake and Honeybunch Go to Heaven*, a traditional tale with a "green pastures" depiction of heaven and black characters. The *New York Times Book Review* found literary merit in the story. Public school library selection committees in Chicago, San Francisco, and Milwaukee, however, rejected the book as lacking literary merit and/or containing racial stereotyping. The March 1983 issue of *American Libraries*[1] focused on this controversy, presenting both positive and negative points of view. After reading the book, students of children's literature may decide which of the following viewpoints reflect their own beliefs and opinions:

1 "The book is offensive and degrading, wholly inappropriate for children whether they be black or white" (p. 130).
2 "I regret that a discussion between a library and a publisher on the merits of a book has become a library selection issue debated in the public press" (p. 131).
3 "The prejudice in this book is against portraying blacks in children's books in any but the most positive way; it is appropriate, too, to portray blacks in a realistic way using valid sources" (p. 131).
4 "Do some librarians seriously assert they will not purchase such material for children at least because that time in history is viewed as repellent? If so, isn't that

tains four stories collected from black people living on islands off the coasts of Georgia and South Carolina. The storytellers, whose ancestors came from Angola and the Bahamas, still speak with a lilt similar to calypso, using words from Africa and Elizabethan England and dialect from the British provinces. Language and subject matter in these tales reflect the changes in folktales as people added elements of their current life-style while retaining important elements from the past.

The most famous collection of Black American folktales originating in the southern United States are the stories originally collected and retold by Joel Chandler Harris's "Uncle Remus" in the late nineteenth century. Here again we meet that "monstrous clever beast," Brer Rabbit, who always survives by using his cunning against stronger enemies. William J. Faulkner's *The Days When the Animals Talked* (10) presents background information on Black American folktales about animals, how they were created, and their significance in American history.

John Henry, a real person and the great black hero of American folklore, is characterized as a "steel-driving" man. Ezra Jack Keats has written and illustrated an attractive edition of John Henry's story, *John Henry: An American Legend*. "Born with a hammer in his hand," the folklore version of John Henry accomplishes seemingly impossible tasks, such as turning a huge broken paddle wheel and saving a ship from sinking, laying more railroad track than many men combined, hammering out a dangerous dynamite fuse and saving the men from a cave-in, and challenging and beating a steam drill in a race until he finally dies "with his hammer in his hand." The large, colorful illustrations in this book suggest the power and heroism of this American legend.

Fiction about Black People

Books for Young Children. Realistic fictional stories about Black Americans written for young children mainly depict black children facing situations and problems common to all young children: overcoming jealousy, adjusting to a new baby, expressing a need for attention, experienc-

like saying we have no past?" (p. 131).
5 "The shallow treatment of the story, the illustrations, the demeaning style of the writing brought a terrible sense of deja vu" (p. 131).
6 "Any library or any children's department of a library has the right to select or reject materials based on that library's selection policy. The operative question here is one raised in a news program on the Public Broadcasting Service (PBS): What do you think of the notion that the publisher is charg-

ing censorship in order to sell books over librarians' protests?" (p. 132).

Secondary controversies surrounding this book were identified by Denise Wilms:[2] "While the book's art and story are sound, its depiction of a certain segment of black culture will stir controversy. . . . In addition, its lighthearted view of heaven may be an affront to some groups who see heaven in a more somber light" (p. 619).

Symbolic misrepresentations and distortions in *Jake and Honeybunch Go to Heaven* were identified and criticized by

Beryle Banfield and Geraldine L. Wilson.[3] Banfield and Wilson state, "Significantly the book misrepresents the unique, culturally distinctive view of spiritual life held by people of African descent. . . . Zemach has not used one culturally authentic clue about heaven as understood by generations of black people" (pp. 197–198). Banfield and Wilson conclude their article with a comparison of the cultural symbols as represented in *Jake and Honeybunch Go to Heaven* with the African American perspective of those same symbols.

[1]Brandehoff, Susan E. "Jake and Honeybunch Go to Heaven: Children's Book Fans Smoldering Debate," *American Libraries* 14 (March 1983): 130–132.
[2]Wilms, Denise. "Focus: Jake and Honeybunch Go to Heaven." *Booklist* 79 (January 1, 1983): p. 619.
[3]Banfield, Beryle and Wilson, Geraldine L. "The Black Experience Through White Eyes—The Same Old Story Again." In *The Black American in Books for Children: Readings in Racism.* Edited by Donnarae MacCann and Gloria Woodard. Metuchen, NJ: The Scarecrow Press, 1985: 192–207.

ing rivalry with siblings, developing personal relationships, and overcoming family problems. Children from all ethnic backgrounds can realize from these books that black children have the same needs, desires, and problems that other children have and solve their problems in similar ways.

John Steptoe's *Stevie* tells about Robert, a happy young boy who is the center of his mother's attention until his mother begins to care for another child whose mother works. Steptoe's illustrations and text portray the increasing tension: toys are broken, and the younger child insists on having his own way. After Stevie moves away, however, Robert remembers the good times they had together and decides that Stevie was "a nice little guy," just like a little brother.

Love and respect are essential human emotions in a story that develops love between two generations. (From *THE PATCHWORK QUILT*, by Valerie Flournoy, pictures copyright © 1985 by Jerry Pinkney. Reproduced by permission of the publisher, Dial Books for Young Readers.

This warm story demonstrates a common universal emotion.

The varying interactions between a father and his two sons are featured in Steptoe's *Daddy Is a Monster . . . Sometimes*. While the father is nice most of the time, he can turn into a monster with "teeth comin' out his mouth" when his sons fight over the teddy bear, play with their food at a restaurant, are extra messy or noisy, or have an accident in the house. Daddy concludes that "I'm probably a monster daddy when I got monster kids." This book has been praised for the strong father-son relationships it develops; too often literature about black families shows children who have no father.

John Steptoe's subjects in his books for young children could be any children who have problems at home, are jealous of another child, or have a father who is sometimes unhappy with their behavior. The language and the illustrations make it a black experience. According to Karen Johnson (12), "The thing about *Stevie* that makes it black is the language. There is a cadence to the way this language is written" (p. 102). The dialect in Steptoe's books meets the criteria for multiethnic literature because it rings true and blends in naturally with the story.

Warm relationships between young children and elderly people are depicted in Sharon Bell Mathis's *The Hundred Penny Box*, in which Michael makes friends with his Great-great-Aunt Dew and the box in which she keeps a penny for every year of her life, and in Valerie Flournoy's *The Patchwork Quilt*, the story of a grandmother and granddaughter's developing relationship. Both books develop strong themes about intergenerational love and respect and the importance of shared memories, which both the hundred penny box and the patchwork quilt contain. "It's my old cracked-up, wacky-dacky box with the top broken," says Michael's Aunt Dew. "Them's my years in that box . . .That's me in that box" (p. 19).

Hugh Lewin's *Jafta* and three other books about a black South African boy bring warm crosscultural experiences to young American children. Lewin's use of figurative language is especially good for aiding children's language development. He describes Jafta's feelings and characteristics by comparing them to those animals in his world. When Jafta is happy he purrs like a lion or laughs like a hyena; when he is cross he stamps like an elephant or grumbles like a dog.

Chapters four and five discussed several other picture storybooks about black people for young readers—including Ezra Jack Keats's stories about inner-city children and Arnold Adoff's story about an interracial family, *Black is Brown is Tan*.

Books for Children in the Middle-Elementary Grades. Many stories about black people for children in the middle-elementary grades are written by authors—black and white—who are sensitive to the black experience. Some themes—such as the discovery of oneself, the need to give and receive love, the problems experienced when children realize that the parents they love are getting a divorce, and the fears associated with non-achievement in school—are universal and suggest that all children may have similar needs, fears, and problems. Other themes, such as the searching for one's own roots in the African past, speak of a special need by black children to know about their ancestry.

Virginia Hamilton's *Zeely* is a warm, sensitive story about an imaginative girl who makes an important discovery about herself and others when she and her brother spend the summer on their Uncle Ross's farm. Elizabeth is not satisfied with the status quo; she calls herself Geeder, renames her younger brother Toeboy, renames her uncle's town Crystal, and calls the asphalt highway Leadback. The plot is enhanced as the imaginative Geeder sees her uncle's neighbor, Miss Zeely Tayber. The author describes her appearance in detail: she is a thin and stately woman over six feet tall, with a calm and proud expression, skin the color of rich Ceylon ebony, and the most beautiful face Geeder has ever seen. When Geeder discovers a photograph of a Watusi queen who looks exactly like Zeely, she decides that Zeely must have royal blood. Geeder is swept up in this fantasy and shares her beliefs with the village children. Then Zeely helps Geeder make her greatest discovery. As they talk, Geeder realizes that dreaming is fine, but being yourself is even better. This realization causes her to see everything in a new way. She realizes that Zeely is indeed a queen, but not like the ones in books, with their servants, kingdoms, and wealth: Zeely is queen because she is a self-loving person who always does her work better than anybody else. Geeder realizes that what a person is inside is more important than how a person looks or what a person owns. When Hamilton shares Geeder's final thoughts about her wonderful summer and her

discovery that even stars resemble people, readers understand just how much wisdom she has gained:

Some stars were no more than bright arcs in the sky as they burned out. But others lived on and on. There was a blue star in the sky south of Hesperus, the evening star. She thought of naming it Miss Zeely Tayber. There it would be in Uncle Ross' sky forever. (p. 121)

Like Geeder, ten-year-old James in Paula Fox's *How Many Miles to Babylon?* dreams of African royalty. James, however, believes that he himself must be a long-lost prince whose ancestors had been chained and marched across the land to boats that took them to slavery in a new country. James even fantasizes that, instead of being ill and taken to the hospital, his mother has traveled to Africa to plan for his celebrated return. He goes to the basement of a dilapidated house to dress and dance like the African princes in photographs, but instead encounters a harsh reality. He learns and accepts the truth about himself when a gang of boys kidnaps him and forces him to help in stealing valuable dogs to earn reward money. When the gang takes him to a deserted amusement park, James sees the Atlantic Ocean for the first time and realizes that his gravely ill mother could not have crossed such a fearsome body of water. The author encourages readers to understand the strength of James's character and his ability to face reality by describing James's thoughts and actions when he plots his escape. James does not merely look out for his own safety; instead, he feels obligated to take the dogs with him and return them to their owners. When James returns home, he knows he is not a prince, but he also knows that he is a strong person in his own right, a person who can solve his own problems.

Another book that explores a character's personal discovery and strength of character is *Sister*, by Eloise Greenfield. (Eloise Greenfield has won several awards for her contributions to children's literature, including the Irma Simonton Black Award and a citation from the Council on Interracial Books for Children.) Sister, whose real name is Doretha, keeps a journal in which she records the hard times—and the good times that "rainbowed" their way through those harder times. Doretha's memory book helps her realize "I'm me." The words of the school song sung in *Sister* are characteristic of the themes found in this and other of Greenfield's books:

We strong black brothers and sisters
Working in unity,
We strong black brothers and sisters,
Building our community,
We all work together, learn together
Live in harmony
We strong black brothers and sisters
Building for you and for me. (p. 69)

Difficulties in school cause emotional problems for all children. In *Nellie Cameron*, Michele Murray portrays the unhappiness of nine-year-old Nellie when she has trouble learning to read. Nellie can do numbers and is better than her school-mates at athletics, but she feels horrible in reading classes and is sure that teachers think she is stupid. She wants Sunday never to end because after it comes "Monday morning like a slap at the beginning of the week" (p. 17). Although she is wistfully determined to succeed, she considers reading a mountain that she cannot climb. She can see that the mountaintop is beautiful, but does not know how to reach it. Eventually, an understanding teacher helps her climb her mountain. Nellie's problems are not all solved by her improving reading skills; she still must overcome jealousy of her gifted brother and the respect he

THROUGH THE EYES OF AN AUTHOR

Tapping One's Own Experiences

Recipient of the Edgar Allen Poe award for best juvenile mystery and the Newbery Medal, VIRGINIA HAMILTON discusses why she writes for young people.

I AM A WRITER FOR young people. Before that, I am a writer for myself. I enjoy what I do, which I call "puzzling out" ideas. Solving is as natural for me as eating or sleeping. I tend to think through problem situations of living and the process of life itself in terms of stories.

I write especially for young people, because I have come to cherish particularly fond memories from my own childhood. My rural childhood was wonderfully free and exciting, often mysterious, which is the way I will always remember it. And through acts of imagination, I am able to transpose the sense of my somewhat isolated early life experiences into books for the young.

I write also because creating is what I do easily and what I care to do best of all. I believe I have something unique to show and tell, that I can put words together in a way that is new and different from the way anyone else would put them together. It would be wonderful if people would think of me simply as a writer, for I believe adults can enjoy my books as well as children. I wish we would dispense of categories that tend to separate us.

The reading young people that I know show as much intelligence, as much imagination as many of the adults I know, and perhaps a good deal more readiness to enter into something that is imagined or made up, and to live a story. Young people are not just teenagers—another category—but individuals who will read books they like and have heard about. They will read them when they feel like it and when they are ready to read—if and when books are made available to them. This last is so important. For we can't expect our young people to become sophisticated readers, able to judge the good from the not so good book if they do not have open and free access to all kinds of books for their age. Thus, the child in the all-white suburb or the child in the all-black neighborhood should not be limited in reading because of their social and racial environment. One nice thing about America is its library system and the accessibility of all kinds of books

receives from their parents. Although she wants that kind of attention for herself, she decides that she has accomplished an important goal. This story carries a strong message for educators and parents who work with children.

Books for Older Children. Outstanding realistic fiction about Black Americans written for older children is characterized by both strong characters and strong themes. The themes in these stories include searching for human freedom and dignity, learning to live together for the benefit of humanity, tackling problems personally rather

than waiting for someone else to do so, survival of the physical body and the human spirit, and the more humorous problems involved in living through a first crush.

Virginia Hamilton has written several fine novels that older children find engrossing. In her suspenseful contemporary story *The House of Dies Drear*, she skillfully presents historical information about slavery and the Underground Railroad through the conversations of a black history professor and his son who are interested in the history of the pre–Civil War mansion they are about to rent. (Compare Hamilton's presentation of in-

---

to the young people who cannot afford to buy them.

In my childhood, comic books were what my brothers and sisters and friends, all country children, had to read. Who had books? Only the public libraries. Occasionally, we were given books for Christmas. I recall a glorious, huge book of Cinderella with marvelous, full color illustrations. But comic books were what we read after school (and during school, hidden behind our primers!), before bed and under the covers. And yet, it wasn't *what* we read that was important. It was the growing, developing habit of reading that would turn us into literate adults.

Therein lies the key to literacy and reading well. No substantial gains can be made on the problem of literacy in this country until we understand that young people must learn the *habit* of reading. Reading has to become as fundamental to young lives as television has become, and as essential as eating or sleeping.

Young people read for entertainment. A book of fiction en-

tertains by offering solace, excitement, relaxation, encouragement and escape. That escape allows the young person to find the strength and new ways to cope with her own reality when she returns to it. In so-called *realistic* fiction, the escape and encouragement come from a sense of parallel in finding a true, recognizable portraiture of real life. The reader watches as the fictional person copes with the real life situation there. When the ending is happy or resolved, the reader feels reassured.

An image occurs to me. A book follows. Something puzzles me in terms of the image and I begin writing it down. Puzzling out the plot of a book from one or two vague images is something I find extremely pleasant to do. Not only must I solve, but I am interested in having others investigate my solutions, my books. Communications is as important to me as puzzle-solving. It is an integral part of the whole puzzle. It is necessary that I write and offer books outward to the public. The response of readers, young people, to my books

makes my calling worthwhile. The hundreds of wonderful letters, sweet and silly, critical and sad, closes the circle.

Writing for the young is as rigorous as I imagine teaching the young would be. My books are full, sometimes complex, because I believe young people are equally full, growing toward complexity. What I attempt to bring them is life's range of possibilities, in situations and in terms of language that most of the time, they will find comprehensible. In my fictions, fictional people become real as they live as best they can. Through living, they learn to change and to grow. Learning to live to the utmost, living in harmony, learning that life is ultimately what each of us is given, and what we do with our lives is what I am concerned with in my stories.

The challenge for me, the writer, is to deal with all that I consider to be the real world by creating a youth literature that beyond entertaining, shows compassion, hope and humor. I try to provide ways of thinking, ways of opening young minds to possibilities.

formation about slavery with Belinda Hurmence's time travel fantasy about slavery in *A Girl Called Boy*.) Hamilton provides details for a setting that seems perfect for the mysterious occurences that begin soon after the family arrives:

The house of Dies Drear loomed out of mist and murky sky, not only gray and formless, but huge and unnatural. It seemed to crouch on the side of a high hill above the highway. And it had a dark, isolated look about it that set it at odds with all that was living. (p. 26)

Thomas's father tells him about the wealthy abolitionist Dies Drear who built the house and helped many slaves on their way toward freedom. Hamilton hints at the suspense to follow as Thomas learns that Dies Drear and two escaped slaves were murdered and that rumors say the abolitionist and the slaves haunt the old house and the hidden tunnels below. Mystery fans will enjoy this fast-paced book.

In *Junius Over Far*, Hamilton combines a search for a lost heritage with a sense of mystery. Hamilton reveals the close relationship between fourteen-year-old Junius and his grandfather Jackaro through Junius' actions. Fantasy, folklore, and American history are interwoven in Hamilton's *The Magical Adventures of Pretty Pearl*. After Pearl arrives on earth from Mount Highness in Africa, she and a spirit travel among the slaves in colonial Georgia and, following the Civil War, help former slaves journey from Georgia to Ohio. Through her interactions with the human characters, Pearl discovers both human sorrow and human joy. Hamilton's rich language and style add to the enjoyment. For example, she uses these words to express Pearl's feelings:

Oh, life is a toil and love is a trouble,
And beauty will fade and riches will flee.
Oh, pleasures they dwindle and prices they double.
And nothing is as I could wish it to be (p. 26).

Hamilton writes about the black experience with a universal appeal that speaks to readers of any ethnic heritage. Her strong characterizations in *The Planet of Junior Brown* were discussed in chapter nine. Another of Hamilton's strong characters learns that choice and action lie within his power in *M. C. Higgins, the Great*, in which the enemy is the spoil heap remaining from strip mining of the mountains, an oozing pile that threatens to swallow a boy's home and even his mother's beloved sunflower.

One rural story for older children is much lighter in tone than the previously discussed books. Bette Greene's humorous *Philip Hall Likes Me. I Reckon Maybe* is set in Arkansas. The eleven-year-old main characters are Philip Hall, the smartest boy in the class, and Beth Lambert, the girl who has her first crush. Greene creates considerable humor as Beth tries to maneuver herself and Philip into shared experiences. She is a little suspicious that he may not be the smartest child in the class: she may be letting him win. The two work together to solve the mystery of her father's missing turkeys, but are in direct competition when each of them raises a calf to show at the annual county fair. When Beth's calf wins, Philip's first reaction is shame; then he feels the unfamiliar emotions related to losing. Beth solves their problem when she invites him to be her partner in the square-dancing contest; as friends and partners, they can win or lose together. Philip finally admits what Beth has been longing to hear: "Sometimes I reckon I likes you, Beth Lambert," he said as we touched hands and together ran toward the lights, the music, and the microphone-amplified voice of Skinny Baker" (p. 135).

Chapter ten discussed other stories about Black Americans for older children, including Mildred D. Taylor's *Roll of Thunder, Hear My Cry* and James and Christopher Collier's *Jump Ship to Freedom*. The characters in all these stories meet the criteria for outstanding characterization in literature: they are memorable individuals; they are real people who face the best and the worst that life offers and who are portrayed with dignity and without stereotype. As in the literature for young readers, the stories reflect varied settings and socioeconomic levels. The main character may be the child of a highly educated college professor or the child of a destitute sharecropper. The realistic stories for older readers do, however, reflect a harsh realism in the Black American experience, whether in the past or in contemporary life. Some of these stories—such as Virginia Hamilton's *The Planet of Junior Brown* and Paula Fox's *How Many Miles to Babylon?*—portray an economically disadvantaged inner-city existence and problems of survival very different from middle-class experience. But children in the stories reflect pride in their individuality and in their decisions to be themselves. The characters' courage and determination are inspirational to all.

Nonfiction Books about the Black American Experience

Because two of the strongest purposes for sharing literature by and about Black Americans with children are to raise the aspirations of black children and to encourage nonblack children's understanding of Black American experience, biographies should play an important role in a multiethnic literature program. Biographies of black leaders and artists tell children about the contributions they have made to American society and the problems they have had to overcome.

Several biographies for children portray the life of nineteenth-century freedom fighter Frederick Douglass. For example, Lillie Patterson's *Frederick Douglass: Freedom Fighter* is a dramatic encounter with Douglass's life in slavery, protest against slavery, escape from the slave owners and then slave hunters, work on the Underground Railroad, and championing the rights of not only black people but also Chinese, Irish, and female people.

James T. DeKay's *Meet Martin Luther King, Jr.* stresses the magnitude of King's work and his reasons for fighting against injustice. Arnold Adoff's *Malcolm X* stresses how and why Malcolm X urged Black Americans to be proud of their heritage and themselves. Chapter 12 and its bibliography contain other biographies of Black Americans.

Three books reflect the contributions of Black Americans to the fine arts. Ashley Bryan's *I'm Going to Sing: Black American Spirituals, Volume Two* includes words and music that help children understand the importance of the spiritual to American heritage. The contributions of black people to the American theater are stressed in James Haskins's *Black Theater in America*. Haskins traces the American theater from minstrel shows through contemporary protest plays and drama, highlighting black writers, actors, and musicians. Ossie Davis effectively uses the poetry of Langston Hughes to create a play about the well-known black poet in *Langston: A Play*.

Several picture books for children of all ages show different aspects of the African heritage. Nonny Hogrogian's illustrations let children share the beautiful and varied sights seen by an African child in Leila Ward's *I Am Eyes, Ni Macho*. The title of the book means "I am awake"; it also means "I am eyes." Long-necked giraffes amble through tall grass; elands and elephants stroll across the land; camels rest in a desert oasis; birds soar above Mt. Kilimanjaro; colorful flamingos stand in a pond; and butterflies flutter through the air.

Leo and Diane Dillon's beautiful illustrations and Margaret Musgrove's text in *Ashanti to Zulu* portray the customs of twenty-six African peoples. This unusual alphabet book reinforces the understanding that the African continent has a rich heritage of culture and tradition. (See page 120 for a discussion of the illustrations in this book.)

The books discussed in this chapter have broad appeal for children and a wide range of content. The emergence of outstanding authors who write about the black experience with sensitivity and honesty has provided more excellent books about Black Americans than are available about other minorities in the United States. When shared with children, such books contribute toward positive self-images and respect for individuals across cultures, and do much to lessen the negative stereotypes of black people common in American literature of the past.

NATIVE AMERICAN LITERATURE

The copyright dates listed in the annotated bibliography at the end of this chapter show that the majority of recommended books about Native Americans have been published quite recently. Few copyright dates precede the 1970s, which indicates a recent increase in the number of books written from a Native American perspective. Many of these books are beautifully illustrated traditional tales, and several have won the Caldecott Medal. Some are written by Native Americans themselves; others have been written by non–Native American writers, such as anthropologist Joyce Rockwood, who have used their knowledge of native cultures to create authentic portrayals of the Native American past. The lovely poetry written by Byrd Baylor and the tales she has collected increase understanding of Native American values and heritage. There are still too few stories with contemporary settings and Native American main characters, however. Consequently, most children have few opportunities to read about Native American children facing problems in today's world.

Traditional Native American Tales

In his collection of traditional Native American tales, *Anpao: An American Indian Odyssey*, Jamake Hightower compares the teller of Native American folktales to a weaver whose designs are the threads of his or her personal saga, as well as the history of his or her people. These stories of the Native American oral tradition have been passed from one generation to the next and often mingled with tales from other tribes. Says Highwater:

They exist as the river of memory of a people, surging with their images and their rich meanings from one place to another, from one generation to the next—the tellers and the told so intermingled in time and space that no one can separate them. (p. 239)

Highwater recounts the task of preserving and transmitting traditional stories described by the Santee Dakota, Charles Eastman. Writing of his own boyhood, Eastman said that very early in life Indian boys assumed the task of preserving and transmitting their legends. In the evening, a boy would listen as one of his parents or grandparents told a tale. Often, the boy would be required to repeat the story the following evening. The household became his audience and either criticized or applauded his endeavors.

In the introduction to a collection of traditional Native American tales, *And It Is Still That Way: Legends Told by Arizona Indian Children*, Byrd Baylor says that Native Americans traditionally have had a high regard for storytellers. No one was supposed to go to sleep while the storyteller was speaking. Consequently, when the storyteller paused, the audience signaled that it was listening. The Papagos repeated the last word they had heard; the Hopis answered with a soft sound. Today, the stories are told with a feeling that they are not out of the past and finished; rather, the storyteller frequently ends with a phrase such as "It can happen like that now," "We still know such things," or "And it is still that way." Native American storytellers still express respect for everything that went before and still touches people today.

Native North Americans, like people everywhere, evolved a mythology that explained the origins of the universe and other natural phenomena. According to Virginia Haviland (14), they believed in "supernatural forces and their legends told of culture heroes and shape-shifters who used magic. Animals had power to turn into people and people into animals. The animal stories, like animal folklore of many other countries, are often humorous, and the characters are accomplished tricksters" (p. 13). Native Americans, Native Canadians, and the Inuit peoples developed a rich heritage of traditional myths and legends. John Bierhorst (2) identifies the following four categories found in Native American mythology: (1) myths that emphasize "setting the world in order," in which the world is created out of or fashioned from the chaos of nature; (2) myths that emphasize "family drama" by centering on various conflicts and affinities rising out of the kinship unit; (3) myths that emphasize "fair and foul," such as the trickster cycle tales in which the hero progresses from a character of utter worthlessness to one that displays a gradual understanding of social virtue; and (4) myths that emphasize "crossing the threshold" by depicting the passage from unconsciousness to consciousness, the ordeal of puberty, the passage into and out of the animal world, the passage into and out of death, and the transition from nature to culture. In a book for adults, *Red Swan: Myths and Tales of the American Indians*, Bierhorst presents and discusses examples of these various categories of myths.

The traditional tales of Native North Americans are available in both volumes that contain a single story and anthologies that collect several tales passed down in tribes across the North American continent.

Books Containing One Traditional Tale. John Bierhorst's *The Ring in the Prairie: A Shawnee Legend* reflects both the characteristics outlined above and Native American values. It has elements related to fair and foul tricksters, to crossing thresholds, and to family drama. First the Shawnee hunter plays the trickster as he turns himself into a mouse and creeps close to a beautiful young woman who descends from the sky; then he returns to his human form and captures his heart's desire. The tale contains several crossing-the-threshold experiences as the hunter passes into and out of the animal world before he and his family are permanently transformed into animals. His captured bride crosses from the world of the star people to the world of humans and back to the world of the star people before she is permanently transformed into a white hawk. The story reflects strong family ties as the hunter mourns the loss of his wife and son and then goes on a difficult quest so that he can be reunited with his family.

Transformations from animal to human and from human to animal are important in Elizabeth Cleaver's *The Enchanted Caribou* and Paul Goble's *Buffalo Woman*. In a retelling of Inuit tales, Cleaver emphasizes the bond between the Inuit and the white caribou. Goble's retelling of a tale from the Great Plains reflects a strong bond between humans and the buffalo herds, a bond that was essential if both the people and the buffalo were to prosper. Olaf Baker's *Where the Buffaloes Begin* also emphasizes the importance of the buffalo to the Great Plains Indians. Stephen Gammell's marvelous black-and-white drawings capture the mythical lake where the buffalo, after their birth, surge out of the water, rampage across the prairie, and eventually save Little Wolf's people from their enemies.

Selfishly taking from the land is punished, while unselfishly giving of a prized possession is rewarded, in Tomie dePaola's retelling of the Comanche tale, *The Legend of the Bluebonnet*. DePaola's text and illustrations evoke a strong feeling for the importance of living in harmony with nature.

Paula Underwood Spencer's *Who Speaks for Wolf* is a "Native American Learning Story" told to the author by her Oneida father, Sharp-eyed Hawk. The story chronicles the experience of the Oneida as they move to a new location only to discover that they have failed to consider the rights of the animals. Spencer's text concludes with information about how the oral history of the Oneida people was preserved and how this learning story was passed down through the generations of her own family.

In the days of the "long-ago time," when people and animals could talk together, but before fire was brought to their tribes, lived a Paiute boy who, according to legend, had Coyote as his friend and counselor. In Margaret Hodges's *The Fire Bringer: A Paiute Indian Legend*, Coyote helps the boy find and return fire from the Burning Mountain. This tale is an excellent example of a "why" tale that explains an animal's characteristics. The conclusion shows how many Native American storytellers suggested that their stories were true:

She ran to the place on the hill
where the Great Spirits had spoken to the shaman.
Stars filled the sky, but there was no moon.
"O Great Spirits," She-Who-Is-Alone said,
"here is my warrior doll. It is the only thing I have
from my family who died in this famine.
It is my most valued possession. Please accept it."

Living in harmony with nature is important in this Comanche tale. (Illustration reprinted by permission of G. P. Putnam's Sons from *The Legend of the Bluebonnet*, retold and illustrated by Tomie dePaola, copyright © 1983 by Tomie dePaola.

And this is the sign that the tale is true. All along the Coyote's thin sides the fur is singed and yellow to this day, as it was by the flames that blew backward from the brand when he brought it down from the Burning Mountain. (p. 31)

Repetitive language in the form of a cumulative folktale provides an enjoyable tale for listening and encouraging oral language in Betty Baker's *Rat Is Dead and Ant Is Sad*. In addition, this Pueblo tale stresses the likely consequences of reaching the wrong conclusion about something.

Collections of Traditional Tales. The legendary heroes in the traditional literature of Native Americans have many of the same characteristics found in heroic tales from other cultures. For example, like Beowulf in the Norse legend, an Inuit hero shows bravery, honor, and a willingness to avenge wrongs. Muriel Whitaker, in her introduction to one of the tales included in *Stories from the Canadian North*, states that "in order to understand fully the ending of 'The Blind Boy and the Loon,' one must realize that the Eskimo hero was predominantly an avenger. Just as the spirits of weather, thunder, lightning, and the sea took vengeance on those who mistreated them, so too was the mortal here expected to have the will and the power to exact retribution for evil" (p. 20).

Heroic legends from the Northwest coasts of the United States and Canada emphasize heroes who venture onto the unpredictable sea and overcome perils associated with the ocean wilderness. Christie Harris's *The Trouble with Adventurers* includes tales with representative themes. For example, "The Bird of Good Luck" shows that fame can arouse envy; "How Raven Gets the Oolikan" suggests that the deeds of heroes are not always to be admired; "Revenge of the Wolf Prince" suggests that heroes do not always survive to enjoy a happy-ever-after future; and "Ghost Canoe People" shows that heroes often need supernatural help, but that supernatural beings may not be inclined to offer assistance. Harris's *Mouse Woman and the Vanished Princesses* is a collection of tales about how the supernatural Mouse Woman helps daughters of chiefs who find themselves tricked by evil supernatural beings. Additional tales from British Columbia are found in *Kwakiutl Legends*, retold by Chief James Wallas.

Traditional Native American tales collected by George Grinnell in the 1870s include tales of the Pawnee, the Blackfeet, and the Cheyenne. Grinnell's *The Whistling Skeleton: American Indian Tales of the Supernatural* is an anthology of tales dealing with ghosts and other supernatural beings. Edward S. Curtis's *The Girl Who Married a Ghost and Other Tales from the North American Indian* includes a creation myth as well as trickster and ghost stories. The origins of the tales range from the Great Plains to Alaska. The tales are enhanced by Curtis's original photographs taken in the early 1900s.

Highwater has combined a number of traditional Indian tales in *Anpao: An American Indian Odyssey*. The tale begins "In the days before the people fled into the water . . . [when] there was no war and the people were at peace" (p. 15). During this time, Anpao travels across the great prairies, through deep canyons, and along wooded ridges in search of his destiny. Along the way, he observes the diverse cultures and customs of many different tribes. His odyssey illustrates the diversity of land, life styles, and folk history found within the Indian culture of North America.

The Adventures of Nanabush: Ojibway Indian Stories contains sixteen tales compiled by Emerson and David Coatsworth. Nanabush, a very powerful spirit of the Ojibway world, can turn himself into an animal, a tree stump, or a leaf; he has both supernatural abilities and human frailties. The tales in this collection include the story of how Nanabush created the world. In this flood and creation story, the Serpent People cause the water to rise in retaliation for Nanabush's destruction of two of their people. Anticipating their reactions, Nanabush builds a large raft, places it on top of a mountain, and invites the animals to join him as the water rises. After they float on the raft for a month without sighting land, Nanabush realizes that the old world has been submerged forever. In order to get substance out of which he can create a new world, he first sends animals to the old world to retrieve mud. The muskrat returns with a few particles of sand out of which Nanabush forms a tiny globe. After he breathes life into the globe, he places it on the water next to the raft and commands it to grow. The globe revolves until it is large enough to contain Nanabush and all the animals. That, according to the Ojibway tale, is how the world of today was created.

An interesting anthology of Navaho, Hopi, Papago, Pima, Apache, Quechan, and Cocopah stories to share with children is Byrd Baylor's *And It Is Still That Way: Legends Told by Arizona Indian Children*. This collection is especially meaningful to children because Native American children told the stories to Baylor, and the book is illustrated with their drawings. Baylor asked children at reservation schools to choose their favorite story, the best story they had ever heard told to them by someone in their tribe. Baylor's *God on Every Mountain* is a collection of Southwest Indian tales about the sacred mountains.

These tales, in both single editions and collections, highlight Native American storytellers' magic with beautiful illustrations. They show that the North American continent had traditional tales that were centuries old before European settlers arrived. They comprise a heritage that all North Americans should take pride in and pass on to future generations.

Native American Experience in Song and Poetry

Songs, chants, and poems are very important in the various Native American cultures. Many poems express reverence for creation, nature, and beauty. According to Ruth Kearney Carlson (6), the Native Americans created poetry for a purpose; they considered a song or a poem important because they believed there was power in the word. Songs were often part of ceremonial ritual, with their symbolism portrayed through dance.

The beauty of both ancient Native American poetry and contemporary poetry about Native American experiences are found in literature that can be shared with children. An interesting resource book that shares the music of Native Americans with children of many cultures is John Bierhorst's *A Cry from the Earth: Music of the North American Indians*. According to Bierhorst, native peoples throughout North America shared a belief in the supernatural power of music to cure disease, bring rain, win a lover, or defeat an enemy. Many Native Americans today sing the songs for pleasure and to express pride in their heritage. Bierhorst's book contains words and music for many songs, including songs of prayer, magic, and dreams, songs to control the weather, and music to accompany various dances. There are greeting songs, love songs, a Hopi flute song, a Hopi sleep song, a Cherokee lullaby, and a Kwakiutl cradlesong. Music, words, and dance steps are included so that children can recreate, experience, and respect this musical heritage. The wide range of subjects around which songs were created suggests a Native American heritage that is richly various. Bierhorst's anthology *The Sacred Path: Spells, Prayers and Power Songs of the American Indians* is organized according to themes. An introduction, a glossary, and a list of notes and sources add authenticity and additional information.

Byrd Baylor has expressed her love and concern for the Native American peoples and the land of the Southwest in a series of books written in poetic form. Two of them ponder the secrets of prehistoric peoples as seen through their drawings on canyon walls and pottery. Through Baylor's poetry and Tom Bahti's illustrations, based on rock drawings found in Arizona, New Mexico, and western Texas, *Before You Came This Way* communicates the spiritual beliefs and customs of ancient cliff dwellers, wanderers, and hunters who left their messages on canyon walls. Across these canyon walls, birds fly, coyotes howl, battles rage, and people dance. Although the pictures have been battered and dimmed by exposure to rain, winds, and age, they are still visible and inspire feelings of awe and respect for an ancient culture. The same writer-illustrator team collaborated on *When Clay Sings*, in which the designs on ancient shards of pottery created by the Anasazi, Mogollon, Hohokam, and Mimbres cultures of the Southwest are the models for Bahti's illustrations and suggest the inspiration for Baylor's poetry. According to Baylor, "Indians who find this pottery today say that everything has its own spirit—even a broken pot. . . . They say that every piece of clay is a piece of someone's life. They even say it has its own small voice and sings in its own way" (cover summary).

In both *The Other Way to Listen* and *The Desert Is Theirs*, Baylor communicates to young readers the Native American closeness to nature, and Peter Parnall's illustrations suggest the majesty of the desert and the Papago Indians' respect for it. (See pages 345–46 for a discussion of Baylor's poems.)

Masks from various tribes of native North Americans are the source for illustrations and text in Baylor's *They Put on Masks*. Ancient Native Americans believed that there was great power in a mask; it could change them into the spirit of anything. Masks allowed them to speak with the fierce gods of sun, rain, thunder, and lightning. Jerry Ingram's colorful, authentic illustrations depict, among others, the masks of the Northwestern Coastal Indians, carved in wood and decorated with hammered copper and fur; the twisted "False Face" masks of the Iroquois, carved to break the ancient spell against evil spirits and cure illness; and the Apache masks, painted with the colors of the four sacred directions—north designated by white, east by black, south by blue, and west by yellow. The book ends with an enticing challenge to children reading the book: what kind of mask would their mask be, what kind of songs would their mask bring out of them, and what dances would their bones remember?

All these books reinforce the desirable understanding that Native American peoples have diverse cultures and great artistic traditions.

Historical Fiction about Native Americans

Themes and conflicts in historical fiction about Native Americans often emphasize the survival of the physical body and/or the human spirit. Authors may emphasize periods in history in which contact with white settlers or cavalry resulted in catastrophic changes. Other books emphasize growing interpersonal relationships between Native American and white characters. Four award-winning books provide examples for these two types of historical fiction.

Scott O'Dell's Newbery honor book, *Sing Down the Moon*, focuses on the mid-1860s when the U.S. Cavalry forced the Navaho to make the three-hundred-mile Long Walk from their beautiful and productive home in Canyon de Chelly to stark Fort Sumner. O'Dell effectively develops setting and the resulting conflict through descriptions of the contrasting settings. He creates visual images by providing detailed descriptions of the Canyon de Chelly where life seems promising, a place of miracles. This idealistic setting does not last. It is followed by horror as Colonel Kit Carson's soldiers first destroy the Navaho's crops and livestock in the canyon, then force the Navahos to walk through desolate country to a setting that is unconducive to physical or spiritual survival. Fifteen hundred Navaho die, and many others lose their will to live. O'Dell's protagonist, a Navaho woman named Bright Morning, retains and further develops an inner strength based on hope for the future. While she is a captive, she hoards food and plans for the day when she and her husband will return to their canyon. This book was discussed in chapter ten, as was Jan Hudson's *Sweetgrass*, the story of a Blackfeet girl during a smallpox epidemic in the 1830s, which won the Canadian Library Associations Book of the Year Award.

Farley Mowat's Canadian Library Associations Book of the Year, *Lost in the Barrens*, takes place in the twentieth century in the remote Arctic wilderness hundreds of miles from the nearest town.

The two main characters are Awasin, a Woodland Cree, and Jamie, a white Canadian orphan who moves north to live with his uncle. The setting becomes an antagonist for both boys when they accompany the Crees on a hunting expedition and then become separated from the hunters. Mowat provides vivid descriptions of foaming rapids, searching for food, and preparing for the rapidly approaching winter. Through long periods of isolation, the boys develop a close relationship and an understanding of each other. Elizabeth George Speare's Newbery Honor Book, *The Sign of the Beaver*, which focuses on the friendship between a Native American boy and a white boy in the Maine wilderness of the 1700s, was discussed in chapter ten.

Joyce Rockwood, an anthropologist, uses her knowledge of Cherokee culture to write a lighter, more humorous story about a young Cherokee boy in 1750. In *Groundhog's Horse*, Creek Indians steal Groundhog's horse and leave a message signifying that they have taken it to Rabbit-town. Even worse the Cherokee warriors do not consider Groundhog's horse important enough to retrieve. Instead of being able to go on the trail after his horse with a loud whoop, Groundhog decides he must "sneak away like a weasel" and find his horse himself. He stealthily plans his trip and "with bravery fluttering faintly in his heart," approaches the sleeping Rabbit-town and the house in front of which his horse Midnight is hobbled. Surprisingly, he finds not only the horse, but also another young Cherokee boy captured by the Creeks and adopted into a family to replace their own son. After a series of adventures, Groundhog's horse finds the way home, and the boys are reunited with their anxious families. Rockwood weaves tradition and history naturally into the story, but the overwhelming feeling is one of human relationships and the personalities of the characters. Unlike many Native American characters in children's literature of the past, these Indians laugh and have distinctly individual personality traits and desires. Children can learn a great deal about Cherokees, as well as enjoy a humorous adventure.

Through all these stories, children can experience Native American characters who have personal thoughts and emotions and live within a family as well as within a tribe. Children will also begin to understand the impact of white people on the Native American way of life. (Additional historical stories about the Native American interactions with the white settlers are discussed in chapter ten.)

Contemporary Realistic Fiction about Native Americans

As mentioned earlier, little contemporary realistic fiction for children focuses on Native Americans. In the books that are available, Native Americans often express conflict between the old and the new ways. Characters must decide whether to preserve their heritage or abandon it. Many of these stories allow Native Americans to honor the old ways but live with the new ones. Some stories show life on modern reservations; others depict families who have left the reservation to live in cities. The universal needs of all individuals are shown as characters search for their identities or express a desire for love. The Native American characters often express hostility toward white characters who have been unfair to them, but some stories develop strong friendships between people from two different backgrounds.

Virginia Driving Hawk Sneve has written several books for young readers about modern Indian boys and their families who live on reservations in western South Dakota. She writes of this setting with knowledge, because she spent her own childhood on the Rosebud Sioux reservation in South Dakota. Her first book, *Jimmy Yellow Hawk*, was awarded first prize in its category by the Council on Interracial Books for Children. Jimmy Henry Yellow Hawk, whose nickname is Little Jim, attends the reservation school where Miss Red Owl is the teacher. Little Jim considers her special because she is one of the first Sioux from the reservation to graduate from college and return to work with her people. She is also special because she understands and respects the Native American ways. The author recreates the everyday experiences of a Native American boy as he helps his father on their ranch, takes part in a rodeo, searches for a horse on Red Butte, and attends the annual Dakota Reservation Pow Wow. Children also discover that, like themselves, Little Jim can have a personal goal in life: he wants his classmates and his family to stop calling him "Little" Jim. He plans his strategy, accomplishes his goal, and earns the name Jimmy. His classmates no longer tease him about his name, and more important, he feels grown-up.

Two other books by Sneve have settings in western South Dakota. *High Elk's Treasure* ties the past to the present with a flashback to the year 1876 when the Sioux are brought to the reservation following the defeat of General Custer at the Battle of the Little Big Horn. One hundred years later High Elk's descendants excitedly discover a pictograph of the Battle of the Little Big Horn that is later authenticated by an expert from the university. Sneve develops a strong feeling for the past and pride in Native American heritage throughout this book. In *When Thunder Spoke*, Sneve also links the past with the present, through an ancient Sioux coup stick recovered from its burial place on the sacred butte. Norman's grandfather treats the stick reverently, considering it a sacred object; his mother rejects it as a heathen symbol; and his father warns that no one should make fun of grandfather or the old ways. In order to help Norman overcome his confusion, his grandfather tells him that it is possible to be selective, to honor the old ways and to live with what he values in the new ways: "When you find something good in the white man's road, pick it up. When you find something bad, or something that turns out bad, drop it and leave it alone" (p. 76).

Nanabah Chee Dodge writes about the tender relationship between a revered grandmother and a child in *Morning Arrow*. A ten-year-old Navaho boy lives in Monument Valley, Utah, with his partially blind grandmother. Their home is a *hogan* ("house everlasting") with the door facing east toward the rising sun. Both Morning Arrow and his almost blind grandmother revere the beauty of the valley, as grandmother's description shows:

Soon the days will turn warm and the sunrises will please my eyes—such beauty I can't miss. And there will be sunsets to paint the buttes dusty red. Each bush will cast a giant shadow and all the shadows will march into the valley. (p. 12)

Dodge suggests the devotion between the boy and his grandmother as Morning Arrow longs to replace his grandmother's shawl, which is tattered with holes. His solution produces a sensitive story about a boy growing up and making major decisions. The white man who runs the reservation trading post enters into the solution to Morning Arrow's problem; unlike the trader in Virginia Driving Hawk Sneve's *When Thunder Spoke*, he is honest and does not try to cheat the boy and his grandmother. This story was awarded

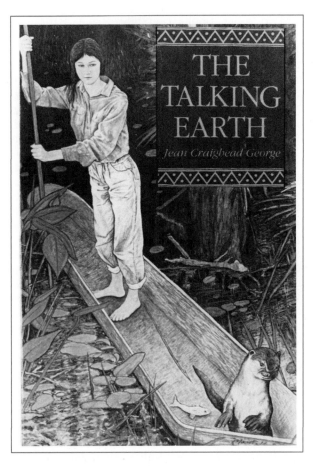

A contemporary Seminole girl searches for her legendary heritage. (Jacket art by Bob Marstall from *The Talking Earth* by Jean Craighead George. Jacket art copyright © 1983 by Bob Marstall. Reprinted by permission of Harper & Row, Publishers, Inc.)

first prize by the Council on Interracial Books for Children.

Symbolism, ancient traditions, and person-against-self conflicts are important elements in three recently published books written for children of different ages. In *The Scared One*, a book for young children, Dennis Haseley develops a personal survival story about a boy whose ancient heritage helps him face and overcome fear and ridicule. In Jean Craighead George's *The Talking Earth*, a book for middle-elementary readers, a Seminole girl who lives on the Big Cypress Reservation questions the traditions of her people. Jamake Highwater's *Legend Days*, a book for older readers, may require several readings before stu-

dents appreciate the author's use of symbolism, traditional values, and tribal customs. Children's literature students may discuss possible meanings of the book's title and trace the "legend days" motif throughout the story. Omens, powers, visions, and close relationships with animals and nature are important in this book's plot and character development. For example, Highwater compares Amana's physical development with the rhythms of nature: "Like the springtime berries, she felt ripe and whole. Like the little rivers, her blood flowed rich and warm from its winter's sleep" (p. 22). Many of Amana's inner conflicts result because she is both a warrior and a woman. She wants to be a warrior and not a woman. Through her story, readers discover the impact of both a dream and European civilization on her life. (Amana's story continues into the present time in *The Ceremony of Innocence* and *I Wear the Morning Star*, parts two and three of Highwater's Ghost Horse Cycle.)

These realistic fictional stories portray some conflicts in contemporary Native American children's lives, as well as some resolutions that reflect strong self-esteem and respect for an ancient heritage.

Nonfiction about Native Americans

Authors of informational books about Native Americans for young children often use highly illustrated texts to encourage identification with a traditional way of life and the cultural contributions made by Native Americans. Authors of informational books for older readers often stress history, the struggle for survival, and various contemporary conflicts.

In *Before Columbus*, a book for young children, Muriel Batherman uses information revealed by archaeological explorations to present and discuss the daily life of native North Americans in pre-European times. The text and illustrations depict dwellings, clothes, tools, and customs.

Native peoples of the Western Hemisphere gave the world a very important food product. Aliki's *Corn Is Maize: The Gift of the Indians* traces the history of corn in text and illustrations, from five-thousand-years-old tiny ears of corn recently discovered in a cave in Mexico, through corn's improvement into the large ears grown today. Children discover how corn is planted, cultivated, harvested, and manufactured into many different products. Illustrations show how native peoples of Mexico and North America cultivated and used corn and how they introduced it to Christopher Columbus and the Pilgrims.

Alice Hermina Poatgieter's *Indian Legacy: Native American Influences on World Life and Culture* explores broader contributions of North and South American native peoples to modern life, including agriculture, art, and democratic attitudes.

Current books of nonfiction for older children commonly emphasize Native American struggles for survival against overwhelming odds when Europeans began claiming this continent. The turbulent years between 1866 and 1895 are the focus of historian Albert Marrin's *War Clouds in the West: Indians & Cavalrymen, 1860–1890*. The text discusses various Native American peoples and their struggles to retain their way of life. Maps, early photographs, archive illustrations, and references provide additional source materials.

Brent Ashabranner's *Morning Star, Black Sun: The Northern Cheyenne Indians and America's Energy Crisis* traces the history of the Northern Cheyenne through their early migrations into Montana to their recent conflicts with power and mining companies. Through the depiction of a century-old struggle, Ashabranner characterizes the Northern Cheyenne as a people who have strong traditional values, such as respect for the land and animals, regard for bravery and wisdom, and reverence for religious principles.

In *To Live in Two Worlds: American Indian Youth Today*, Ashabranner's interviews with Native American young people, both on reservations and in urban environments, show that some young Native Americans experience confusion and conflict as they try to adjust to the dominant white culture, while others experience cultural security as they develop confidence in their own heritage. The final chapter focuses on René Cochise, the great-great-great granddaughter of the famous Apache leader Cochise. She grew up on a reservation and now works in Washington, D.C.:

I don't know yet what the Washington experience will mean to me. I've met Indians here, ones who have worked here a long time, who don't seem like Indians, not like the ones in New Mexico. I don't think that would happen to me, no matter how long I stayed away. I have the language of my tribe. I have the religion. I have the years of growing up on the land inside me. I have lived the customs of my people. I know who I am. No matter where I am, I am an Apache. (p. 145)

Biographies of Native Americans

Biographies are important reading for children because they encourage high aspirations and respect for the social contributions of outstanding people. Here again, there are fewer biographies about Native Americans than there are about Black Americans.

Maria Tallchief, by Tobi Tobias, is the biography of a world-renowned prima ballerina born in Fairfax, Oklahoma. Her grandfather, Peter Big Heart, had been chief of the Osage Indian tribe. Tobias stresses that Maria Tallchief was always proud of her Indian heritage, as illustrated by her refusal to use a stage name. The Osage celebrated her success and honored her by elevating her to the role of Indian Princess.

Thomas Fall has written a biography for young children about the life of the great athlete and Olympic hero, *Jim Thorpe*. The book chronicles the life of this Fox Indian from the time he was a young child living on a ranch in the Oklahoma Territory until he became a famous athlete. The story describes his unhappiness in school after his twin brother died, his discovery of football at the Haskell Institute in Kansas, his experiences at the Native American school at Carlisle Pennsylvania, his success on the United States Olympic Team of 1912, the loss of his medals because he had played professional baseball, and his success as a professional football and baseball player. The author stresses both the problems he overcame and the hard work required of him before he became a champion athlete. Thorpe's Olympic medals were awarded him posthumously in 1982.

Several biographies focus on famous Native Americans who interacted with white settlers of this continent. For example, *Squanto: The Indian Who Saved the Pilgrims*, by Matthew G. Grant, is an illustrated biography of the Wampamoag who played an important role in the lives of early settlers of New England. *Sacajawea, Wilderness Guide*, by Kate Jassem, is the biography of the Shoshone woman who guided the Lewis and Clark Expedition across the Rocky Mountains to the Pacific Ocean. Both these books are appropriate for young readers. Conflicts between two worlds provide numerous opportunities for characterization and plot development in Jean Fritz's *The Double Life of Pocahontas*. Fritz effectively develops a character who is torn between loyalty to her father's tribe and to her new friends in the

Jamestown colony. As in her other biographies, Fritz documents her historical interpretations. Notes, bibliography, index, and a map add to the authenticity.

Marion Marsh Brown's *Homeward the Arrow's Flight* is the biography of Susan LaFlesche, the first female Native American to become a doctor of Western medicine. Betsy Lee's *Charles Eastman: The Story of an American Indian* is the biography of a Sioux physician and crusader for Native American rights. Both books are discussed in chapter twelve.

Additional literature about Native Americans may be found in Anna Lee Stensland's *Literature by and about the American Indian* (21). (Additional Native American biographies are discussed in chapter 12.)

HISPANIC AMERICAN LITERATURE

Most children's books about Hispanic Americans depict people of Mexican or Puerto Rican heritage, although the United States population contains numerous other Hispanic groups. People of Hispanic descent are the largest minority group in the United States, but relatively few children's books have been written about them. There is also an imbalance in the types of stories available. Award-winning picture storybooks about Hispanic Americans tend to focus on Christmas celebrations. Award-winning novels are about a small segment of the Hispanic American population, the sheepherders of Spanish Basque heritage, whose ancestors emigrated to North America before they became part of the United States. Although folktales and poetry are available for adults, a shortage of children's literature exists.

Many books for children about Hispanic Americans develop strong connections between the people and their religious faith. Celebrations such as La Posada suggest this cultural heritage, while the respect for freedom is stressed through the celebration of Cinco de Mayo. Spanish vocabulary is also interspersed throughout many stories, allowing children to associate with a rich language heritage. (Misspelled and incorrectly used Spanish words have appeared all too often in this type of book, however. These errors have, understandably, caused criticism.) Several books are more factual, presenting the Spanish heritage that existed on the North American continent long before the United States became a nation. These stories suggest that Americans with a Spanish an-

cestry have a heritage worthy of respect and of sharing with others.

Hispanic Folktales

Folktales from Mexico, South and Central America, and Hispanic cultures in the United States are found in collections and in a few highly illustrated single editions. Many of the tales reflect a blending of cultures, as stated in the introduction to José Griego y Maestas's and Rudolfo A. Anaya's *Cuentos: Tales from the Hispanic Southwest:* "The stories also reflect a history of thirteen centuries of cultural infusing and blending in the Hispano mestizaje, from the Moors and Jews in Spain, to the Orientals in the Philippines, Africans in the Caribbean, and the Indians in America—be they Aztec, Apache or Pueblo" (p. 4).

M. A. Jagendorf and R. S. Boggs's *The King of the Mountains: A Treasury of Latin American Folk Stories* presents stories from twenty-six countries. Stories such as the Mexican "The Sacred Drum of Tepozteco" show that wisdom, understanding, and virtuous living are respected values that lead to rewards. In contrast, attacking a revered king and displaying an outward show for appearance's sake only are despised actions that lead to punishment.

Additional collections of tales include John Bierhorst's *The Hungry Woman: Myths and Legends of the Aztecs*, Pura Belpré's *Once in Puerto Rico*, and Francisco Hinojosa's *The Old Lady Who Ate People*, a collection of frightening stories from Mexico. Mexican *pourqui* tales collected in Marcos Kurtycz and Ana Garciá Kobeh's *Tigers and Opossums* tell why the hummingbird is richly dressed, how the opossum got his tail, and how the tiger got his stripes.

Single folktales in highly illustrated picture-book formats reflect universal folklore elements, as well as various aspects of the Hispanic heritage. For example, Pura Belpré's *The Rainbow-Colored Horse*, a Puerto Rican tale, includes motifs found in tales from other cultures: two "superior" sons cannot solve a problem (the fields are mysteriously trampled); the quietest and gentlest son solves the problem (a rainbow horse is in the field); the youngest son is granted three wishes if he will not capture the horse; a king offers his daughter's hand in marriage to anyone who can meet a challenge (while riding a horse at full gallop, the winner must toss balls into the princess's lap); the supernatural horse makes it possible for the hero to pass the test. The tale

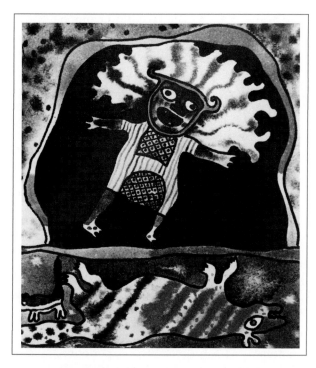

The illustrations enhance the frightening quality of these folktales. (From *The Old Lady Who Ate People,* illustrated by Leonel Maciel. Copyright © 1981 by Organización Editorial Novro, S. A.)

suggests a universality in folktales and the people who tell them and enjoy them. The Spanish names and the inclusion of Spanish phrases evoke a strong Spanish heritage.

Tomie de Paola's retelling of *The Lady of Guadalupe,* a Mexican tale, develops a strong connection between the people and their religious faith. According to legend, the Lady of Guadalupe, now the patron saint of Mexico, appeared to a poor Mexican Indian on a December morning in 1531. Juan Diego, "He-who-speaks-like-an-eagle," was walking toward the Church of Santiago when he saw a hill covered with a brilliant white cloud. Out of the cloud came a gentle voice calling Juan's name and telling him that a church should be built on that site so that the Virgin Mary could show her love for Juan's people, the Indians of Mexico. On Juan's third visit to the bishop, he was believed because he brought with him a visual sign from the Lady of Guadalupe: his rough cape had been changed into a painting of the lady. The church was built on the location, and the cape

with its miraculous change was placed inside the structure. De Paola says that he has had a life-long interest in the legend of the Lady of Guadalupe. His drawings, based on careful research, depict the dress and architecture of sixteenth-century Mexico. John Bierhorst's *Spirit Child: A Story of the Nativity* develops another strong connection between the people and their religious faith. Barbara Cooney's illustrations depict an Aztec adaptation and setting for the birth of the Christ child.

Verna Aardema's *The Riddle of the Drum: A Tale From Tizapán, Mexico* translates a folktale with universal motifs: a king with a marriageable daughter challenges suitors to a task; on the way to the palace, the suitor meets four people with exceptional skills; the king adds additional tasks

Spanish architecture enriches the illustration of a Mexican folktale. (From *The Riddle of the Drum: A Tale from Tizapán, Mexico,* by Verna Aardema. Illustrated by Tony Chen. Illustrations copyright © 1979 by Tony Chen. Reprinted by permission of Four Winds Press, a division of Scholastic Book Services.)

after the first is completed; and the suitor's extraordinary abilities allow him to win the princess. The tale also reflects a strong Spanish heritage, respect for the language, and beauty in architecture and costumes. The names are Spanish, counting is in Spanish, the foods are Mexican, and Tony Chen's illustrations depict early Mexican culture. Aardema includes a pronunciation guide for Spanish words and a glossary of their meanings.

Picture Storybooks about Hispanic Peoples

Listening to and saying rhymes from various cultures encourage children to interact with language as well as to discover the joy in language and in word play. Margot Griego's *Tortillitas Para Mama and Other Spanish Nursery Rhymes* and Isabel Schon's *Doña Blanca and Other Hispanic Nursery Rhymes and Games* are written in both English and Spanish. These texts provide a source for sharing literature in either language.

Leo Politi has written and illustrated a number of award-winning picture storybooks about Mexican American children living in southern California. His *Song of the Swallows* tells the story of a young boy whose dear friend is the gardener and bell ringer at the Mission of San Juan Capistrano. Politi shares Mexican American history with the reader as the gardener tells Juan the story of the mission and of *las golondrinas*, the swallows who always return to the mission in the spring, on Saint Joseph's Day, and remain there until late summer. Politi's illustrations recreate the Spanish architecture of the mission and demonstrate a young boy's love for plants and birds.

The Christmas season's La Posada celebration is one of the most important holidays in the Hispanic American tradition. Two other picture storybooks by Politi center around this important occasion. *Pedro, the Angel of Olvera Street* is the story of a boy in Los Angeles who loves his street, with its red-tiled pavement and old adobe houses, the *puestos* ("shops") with their colorful wares, the smell of his favorite foods, the Mexican songs played on his grandfather's violin, and best of all, the friendly people who live there. In *The Nicest Gift* Carlitos lives with his family and his dog, Blanco, in the barrio of East Los Angeles. He accompanies his mother as she goes to the *mercado* (the "marketplace") to buy foods and other goods for the holiday. Unhappily, Blanco is

lost at the market. The best gift occurs on Christmas Eve when Blanco finds Carlitos. This book is filled with Spanish terms associated with the La Posada.

Marie Hall Ets and Aurora Labastida's *Nine Days to Christmas: A Story of Mexico*, tells of a kindergarten child who is excited because she is going to have her own special Christmas party, complete with a piñata. In the midst of numerous other everyday activities, Ceci chooses her piñata at the market, fills it with toys and candy, and joins the La Posada procession. When Ceci sees her beautiful piñata being broken at the party, she is unhappy until she sees a star in the sky that resembles her piñata. Children relate to the girl's feelings and learn about the Mexican celebration of Christmas when they read this book. This story depicts a middle-class family that lives in an attractive city home. Children can see that poverty is not the natural condition of all people with a Spanish heritage.

Realistic fictional stories about Puerto Rican families, for both young children and older readers, often focus on children's experiences as they adjust to living in a big city or try to make new friends who appreciate Puerto Rico. For example, Pura Belpre's *Santiago* is the story of a young boy's experiences and feelings as he tries to share pictures of his favorite pet with his friends in New York City. His teacher and his mother help Santiago's friends appreciate Puerto Rico by sharing happy experiences with them.

Historical and Contemporary Realistic Fiction about Hispanic Americans

Only a few books of historical and contemporary realistic fiction for children portray Hispanic Americans in a suitably positive way and/or as the main characters. Marian L. Martinello and Samuel P. Nesmith's *With Domingo Leal in San Antonio 1734* takes a documentary approach to Hispanic American history and life in the United States. Published by the University of Texas Institute of Texas Cultures at San Antonio, this carefully researched book depicts a day in the life of a young Spanish boy who traveled with his family from the Canary Islands through Mexico to the Villa de San Fernando on the banks of the Rio San Antonio de Padua in present-day Texas. This historical novel can strengthen children's understanding of a lengthy Hispanic heritage in the southwestern United States. It also demonstrates that people of Spanish ancestry were living on the North American frontier before English-speaking settlers tried to claim it.

Another book of historical fiction depicting the early Spanish presence in western North America is Scott O'Dell's *Carlota*. In this story set in Spanish California in the mid-1800s, O'Dell explores the conflicts that occur between people who expect females to play a traditionally feminine role and others who encourage a different type of behavior. Carlota is the strong and independent daughter of Don Saturnino, a native Californian whose ancestors came from Spain. Her father supports her brave and adventurous inclinations. Even though her grandmother deplores such behavior, Carlota rides a black stallion around the ranchero at top speed, races horses with neighbors, brands cattle, and eventually joins her father and other men in ambushing Americans who are trying to annex California for the United States. When she wounds a young American soldier, her feelings of compassion overcome her sense of obedience to her father, and she nurses the wounded man back to health on the ranchero. Her strength of character is ultimately demonstrated when she manages the ranchero after her father's death. Like other memorable heroes in all literature, Carlota grows in self-understanding and inner strength.

The setting for Ann Nolan Clark's *Year Walk* is the sheep-ranching region of Idaho in the early 1900s. After researching the history, traditions, culture, and language of Basque families living in the Pyrenees, Clark made several visits to a sheep ranch in the area of Idaho where the Basques settled. She saw lambing and shearing and joined the sheepherders on the trails with their dogs, mules, and sheep. Her research, along with her knowledge of the western mountains, creates a story with a strong respect for the contributions of Hispanic Americans.

Joseph Krumgold's . . . *And Now Miguel*, based on a full-length documentary film feature, is the story of the Chavez family, which has been raising sheep in New Mexico since the days before their region became part of the United States. Their ancestors raised sheep in Spain. Krumgold tells the story from the viewpoint of the middle child, Miguel, who, unlike his older brother, is too young to get everything he wants and, unlike his younger brother, is too old to be happy with everything he has. Miguel has a secret wish to accompany the older family members when they herd the sheep to the summer grazing land in the Sangre de Cristo Mountains. With the help of San Ysidro, the patron saint of farmers, Miguel strives to make everyone see that he is ready for this responsibility. When he is allowed to accompany his elders on the drive and reaches the summer camp, he feels the greatest of pride in his family's traditions and in his own accomplishments:

In this place many men named Chavez had come. Those I could remember, and then my grandfather as well. And my father, Blas and my uncles, Eli and Bonifacio. And my brothers, Blasito and Gabriel. And now, watching the shining world as I knew it would look when I came to this place, I stood, Miguel. (p. 244)

Krumgold visited the real Miguel and his family when the film was produced; he celebrated saints' day with them and observed all the important functions of a sheep ranch. He grew to know a closely knit family with a proud heritage going back to ancient Spain.

The eight-year-old in Nicholasa Mohr's *Felita* has lived in her Puerto Rican neighborhood of New York City for as long as she can remember. Mohr depicts the reasons for Felita's great love of her neighborhood: when she walks down the street, she can greet everyone by name; her dearest friends live in the apartments on the block; and her grandmother, Abuelita, lives nearby. Conflict results when her father decides that the family must move to a neighborhood where the schools are better and the threats of gang violence are fewer. In the new neighborhood Anglo children call Felita names, tear her clothes, and tell her to move away. Felita's mother is shocked by the children's attitudes and tells Felita that she must not hate, because that could make her as mean inside as the people who are attacking her:

Instead you must learn to love yourself. This is more important. To love yourself and feel worthy, despite anything they might say against you and your family! That is the real victory. It will make you strong inside. (p. 39)

When violence against the family continues and no neighbors offer help, Felita's family moves back to the old neighborhood. Felita experiences anger, sorrow, and humiliation, but finally regains her feelings of self-worth. With her grandmother's help, Felita returns to her happy, lively self, secure in the surroundings of her warm, loving family and friends. Perhaps the neighborhood and the people in *Felita* seem so real because

Mohr herself was born and grew up in a similar neighborhood in New York City.

Readers may compare *Felita*'s New York City setting with the setting in *Danza!*. Lynn Hall's story takes place on a farm in Puerto Rico and emphasizes the interaction between Paulo, a Puerto Rican boy, and Danza, a Paso Fino stallion. Hall develops strong characters with believable emotions and actions.

Nonfiction about Hispanic Americans

High-quality informational books about Hispanic Americans include books on history, geography, culture, and people. For example, several recently published books focus on the discoveries about and the accomplishments of the ancient native cultures of the Western Hemisphere. Carolyn Meyer and Charles Gallenkamp's *The Mystery of the Ancient Maya* provides a thoroughly documented presentation of Mayan history and accomplishments. The authors' writing style creates interest in the subject and early photographs and drawings add to the authenticity. Likewise, Elizabeth Gemming's *Lost City in the Clouds: The Discovery of Machu Picchu* and Anne Millard's *The Incas* emphasize the achievements of these an-

ISSUE

Are Children's Books Still Perpetuating Negative Stereotypes of Hispanic Americans?

THE LACK OF CHILdren's literature about Hispanic Americans and Hispanic cultures and the negative stereotypes found in the available literature are often criticized. In a 1981 issue of *Top of the News,* Isabel Schon contends that the "overwhelming majority of recent books incessantly repeat the same stereotypes, misconceptions, and insensibilities that were prevalent in the books published in the 1960s and the early 1970s" (1, p. 79). Schon supports this contention by reviewing books published in 1980 and 1981 that develop the stereotypes of poverty, children's embarrassment about their backgrounds, distorted and negative narratives about pre-Columbian history, and simplistic discussions of serious Latin American problems.

In this review Schon contrasts two books about pre-

Columbian cultures. The first, Brenda Ralph Lewis's *Growing Up in Aztec Times*[2] is cited as a book that perpetuates a lack of appreciation for a culture and uses stereotypic phrases such as "savage," "behaved like barbarians," "ferocious nature," and "superstitious." In contrast, Elizabeth Gemming's *Lost City in the Clouds: The Discovery of Machu Picchu*[3] describes Hiram Bingham's discovery of the spectatcular monuments and achievements of the Incas. This book is recommended as one that portrays both the achievements of a people and accurate historical incidents.

Schon ends her article with a plea that young readers in the United States be exposed to more distinguished books about Hispanic peoples and cultures rather than to books that perpetuate misconceptions and negative impressions.

[1]Schon, Isabel. "Recent Detrimental and Distinguished Books about Hispanic People and Cultures." *Top of the News* 38 (Fall 1981): 79–85.

[2]Lewis, Brenda Ralph. *Growing Up in Aztec Times.* North Pomfret, Vermont: Batsford, 1981.

[3]Gemming, Elizabeth. *Lost City in the Clouds: The Discovery of Machu Picchu.* New York: Coward, 1980.

cient civilizations through carefully documented texts.

Books such as R. Conrad Stein's *Enchantment of the World: Mexico* use color photographs to enhance information about geography, history, culture, and people. In addition to labeled photographs, the text includes a map, a mini-facts section that provides statistics, a listing of important dates in chronological order, a listing of important people, and an index. Information about other geographic locations in Hispanic America are available in Pat Hargreaves's *The Caribbean and Gulf of Mexico*, Patricia Maloney Markun's *Central America and Panama*, and Edmund Lindop's *Cuba*.

While the majority of books about Spanish American celebrations for young children concentrate on the Christmas holidays, Cinco de Mayo, the commemoration of the Mexican army's defeat of the French army on May 5, 1862, is also a major holiday for Mexican Americans. June Behrens's *Fiesta!* is an informational book describing the modern-day celebration of this holiday. Photographs show a Mexican American festival where music is played by a mariachi band, costumed dancers perform traditional Mexican dances, and young and old enjoy the celebration. Photographs also illustrate children at school as they learn about and participate in the Cinco de Mayo activities. The book closes with a message from the author suggesting that Americans of all heritages have shared an experience and become good amigos.

Information on the history and contributions of Puerto Ricans, Mexican Americans, and Cubans is discussed in Milton Meltzer's *The Hispanic Americans*. Meltzer explores Spanish influences resulting from exploration and colonization. Then he considers the development of the political, economic, and cultural status of Hispanic Americans. Meltzer's chapter on the harmful influences of racism provides thought-provoking discussion material for older children.

ASIAN AMERICAN LITERATURE

Few highly recommended books for children represent an Asian American perspective. Folktales from several Asian countries discussed in chapter six, "Traditional Literature," can help Asian American children and children from other ethnic backgrounds appreciate the traditional values and creative imagination of Asian peoples. The widest range of Asian American experiences in current children's literature is found in the works of Laurence Yep, who writes with sensitivity about Chinese Americans who, like himself, have lived in San Francisco, California. His characters overcome the stereotypes associated with literature about Asian Americans, and his stories integrate information about Chinese cultural heritage into the everyday lives of the people involved. Yep has received the International Reading Association's 1976 Children's Book Award and a Newbery Honor Book award.

Yep's *Dragonwings*, set in 1903 San Francisco, is based on a true incident in which a Chinese-American built and flew an airplane. The characters are strong people who retain their values and respect for their heritage while adjusting to a new country. The "town of the Tang people" is eight-year-old Moon Shadow's destination when he leaves his mother in the Middle Kingdom (China). He is filled with conflicting emotions when he first meets his father in the country some call the "Land of the Demons," and others call the "Land of the Golden Mountain." The Tang men in San Francisco give Moon Shadow clothing and things for the body, but his father gives him a marvelous, shimmering kite shaped like a butterfly, a gift designed to stir the soul. Moon Shadow joins his father in his dream to build a flying machine. Motivated by the work of Orville and Wilbur Wright, Moon Shadow's father builds an airplane, names it *Dragonwings*, and soars off the cliffs overlooking San Francisco Bay. Having achieved his dream, he decides to return to work so his wife can join him in America.

In the process of the story, Moon Shadow learns that his stereotype of the white demons is not always accurate. When he and his father move away from the Tang men's protection, Moon Shadow meets and talks to his first demon. Instead of being ten feet tall, with blue skin, and a face covered with warts, she is a petite woman who is very friendly and considerate. As Moon Shadow and his father get to know this Anglo-Saxon woman and her family, they all gain respect for each other. When they share knowledge, the father concludes: "We see the same thing and yet find different truths."

Readers also discover that stereotypes about Chinese Americans are incorrect. This book is especially strong in its coverage of Chinese traditions and beliefs. For example, readers learn about the great respect Chinese Americans feel for the aged and the dead; family obligations do not end when a family member has retired or died. As Moon Shadow seeks to educate his white friend about the nature of dragons, readers discover traditional Chinese tales about a benevolent and wise dragon who is king among reptiles, emperor of animals. Readers realize the strong value of honor as they join the doubting Tang men who come to pull *Dragonwings* up the hill for its maiden voyage. They do not come to laugh at or applaud a heroic venture, but to share in their friend's perceived folly; if the Tang men laugh at Moon Shadow's father, they will laugh at a strong body of people who stand beside each other through times of adversity and honor. Children who read this story learn about the contributions and struggles of the Chinese Americans and the prejudice they still experience.

Other excellent books by Yep include *The Serpent's Children*, a story set in a time when China was battling both Manchu and British domination; *Child of the Owl*, in which young Casey discovers that she knows more about racehorses than about her own Chinese heritage; and *Sea Glass*, in which a boy deals with the unhappy experience of leaving Chinatown and learning to live in a non-Chinese community. The protagonists in all these books are distinct and believable individuals far from the conventional stereotypes about Asian people.

Betty Bao Lord, the author of *In the Year of the Boar and Jackie Robinson*, created a story that reflects her own experiences and beliefs. Like her protagonist Shirley Temple Wong, Lord was a Chinese immigrant to America. "Many feel that loss of one's native culture is the price one must pay for becoming an American," says Lord. "I do not feel this way. I think we hyphenated Americans are doubly blessed. We can choose the best of both" (unnumbered). In 1947, Shirley discovers that she can adore baseball, the Brooklyn Dodgers, and Jackie Robinson and still maintain the bond of family and the bond of culture.

In *Chin Chiang and the Dragon's Dance*, Ian Wallace creates a satisfactory conclusion to a person-against-self conflict. Young readers can understand Chin Chiang's conflict. He has practiced for and dreamed of dancing the dragon's dance on the first day of the Year of the Dragon. The time arrives and he runs away because he fears he will not dance well enough to make his grandfather proud. With the help of a new friend, Chin Chiang discovers that his dream can come true. Full-page watercolor paintings capture the beauty of the celebration and depict Asian influences on the city of Vancouver.

The setting of Ann Nolan Clark's *To Stand against the Wind* is wartime Vietnam. As the story begins, eleven-year-old Elm, a refugee living in America, is helping his grandmother, older sister, and uncle prepare for the traditional Day of the Ancestors when those who have recently died are honored and remembered. As the head of the household, Elm must record the family history and tell his descendants about a country they may never know. His thoughts go back, and he remembers the beautiful countryside of the Mekong River delta that had been his ancestors' home for uncounted centuries. Clark describes Elm's memories and compares them with the last time he saw his village with its buildings burned, its ground bulldozed, and its dikes destroyed. Elm remembers his father who loved the land and the American reporter who often visited them to learn about the Vietnamese. As the war progresses in Elm's memories, he recalls the male members of his family going off to fight, the reporter's description of the fall of Saigon, and the terrible day when his village was accidentally bombed by American planes. Now his mother, his father, his grandfather, his brother, and his friend the reporter are dead. Elm and his remaining family travel to America, where they are sponsored by a church group. This realistic story about a sad chapter in the life of a people concludes as Elm tries to express his memories. The only words that seem appropriate, however, are from a proverb that his father had taught him: "It takes a strong man to stand against the wind" (p. 132). Huynh Quang Nhuong's *The Land I Lost: Adventures of a Boy in Vietnam* is also a story of pre-war Vietnam in which the author takes readers back to a time of family and village experiences. Traditions and beliefs are important elements in both Clark's and Nhuong's stories.

Adjusting to a new culture and developing understanding of self and understanding of others are common problems faced by many new Americans. Two books about Vietnamese children may help children who are adjusting to new situations and new cultures. Michele Surat's *Angel Child, Dragon Child* is a contemporary realistic story about a young Vietnamese girl's difficulties developing associations with her classmates after her family moves to the United States. In Marylois Dunn's *The Absolutely Perfect Horse*, both the adoption of a Vietnamese boy and the arrival of a new baby create family difficulties. The characters, plots, and themes in these books may encourage discussion and promote understanding.

The importance of even small cultural artifacts such as eating utensils stimulates humorous plot developments in Ina R. Friedman's *How My Parents Learned to Eat*. Friedman suggests the solution to a problem on the first page of this picture storybook: "In our house, some days we eat with chopsticks and some days we eat with knives and forks. For me, it's natural" (p. 1, unnumbered). The remainder of the story tells how an American sailor courts a Japanese girl, and each secretly tries to learn the other's way of eating. The couple reaches a satisfactory compromise with each person still respecting the other's culture.

The harsh consequences of war for Japanese Americans provide the subject of Daniel Davis's *Behind Barbed Wire: The Imprisonment of Japa-*

Cultural differences may provide humorous situations in contemporary stories. (From *How My Parents Learned to Eat* by Ina R. Friedman and illustrated by Allen Say. Text copyright © 1984 by Ina R. Friedman. Illustrations copyright © 1984 by Allen Say. Reprinted by permission of Houghton Mifflin Company.)

nese Americans during World War II. In this informational book, Davis explores U.S. government actions against Japanese Americans during World War II. Davis focuses upon the denial of civil rights to an American minority and questions whether similar action could happen today. Readers may compare Davis's treatment of the subject with Yoshiko Uchida's *Journey to Topaz* and *Journey Home* discussed in chapter ten.

If children are to learn about the cultural heritage and the contributions of the Asian American people, as well as discover the similarities between Asian and non-Asian Americans, more high-quality literature about Asian Americans is needed. Because biographies and autobiographies are especially good for both raising children's aspirations and enhancing understanding about the contributions and problems of individuals, multiethnic literature programs need biographies of Asian Americans.

SUMMARY

Multiethnic literature helps children who are members of racial and ethnic minority groups in the United States realize that they have roots in a cultural heritage of which they can be proud. Through literature about Black Americans, Hispanic Americans, Native Americans, and Asian Americans, children of other backgrounds can discover that all cultural groups have made important contributions to our society and that all people have similar feelings and experiences. In the past and present, some children's literature has been criticized for presenting negative stereotypes of minority groups in the United States. Criteria for evaluating books for children assist adults in selecting books that depict all people accurately and with respect.

Multiethnic literature presents the strong traditional values of racial and ethnic minorities, such as respect for elders, love of beauty, respect for imagination, and a longing for peace and harmony. Many of the stories also provide considerable other information about certain cultures and languages. Multiethnic contemporary realistic fiction emphasizes similarities as well as differences among people. Stories with historical settings provide insights into values, behaviors, and social contributions. Children need more, and more various, multiethnic literature.

Suggested Activities for Adult Understanding of Multiethnic Literature

☐ Collect several examples of children's literature written before 1960 that contain black characters; compare these books with books written after 1975. Using the evaluative criteria on pages 507–508, compare the image of black people reflected in literature of the two time periods.

☐ Bettye I. Latimer (18) surveyed trade books published in the mid-1960s and the 1970s and concluded that about 1 percent of the books involved black characters. Choose a recent publication date; select books that have been chosen as the best books of the year by the School Library Journal Book Review Editors or some other group that selects outstanding books; then tabulate the number of books that are about Black Americans, Native Americans, Hispanic Americans, or Asian Americans. What percentage of the books selected as outstanding literature include characters who are members of minority groups?

☐ Many African tales have characteristics, such as repetition of words, that make them appealing for oral storytelling. Select several traditional African tales and identify the characteristics that make them appropriate for storytelling or oral reading.

☐ Choose an outstanding author such as Virginia Hamilton or Laurence Yep and read several of that author's books. What quality in the literature makes the plot and the characters memorable? What themes can be identified in the writer's work? Is there a common theme throughout all the writing?

☐ With a group of your peers, choose an area of ethnic literature discussed in the chapter. Select five books that develop the nine values of multiethnic literature discussed on page 503. Also select five books that do not develop the same values. Share the books and rationale for selecting them with the rest of the class.

☐ Compare the characterizations of Native Americans in children's literature published before 1960 with the characterizations of Native Americans in books published after 1975. How would readers describe Native Americans, as either individuals or a group of people, if this literature were their only contact with Native Americans? Has there been a change in characterizations between the literature of the two periods?

☐ Several books listed in Betty I. Latimer's *Starting Out Right: Choosing Books about People for Young Children* (17) the Children's Literature Review Board does not recommend because of stereotypes, unacceptable values, or terms used in relationship to the characters. Read one of these books, such as David Arkin's *Black and White*, Florine Robinson's *Ed and Ted*, Shirley Burden's *I Wonder Why*, Anco Surany's *Monsieur Jolicoeur's Umbrella*, May Justus's *New Boy in School*, or William Pappas's *No Mules*. Are the review board's recommendations accurate in your opinion? Why or why not?

☐ Several classics, or old standards, in children's literature have been praised by some, but criticized by others. In the area of literature referring to black experiences, Marguerite De Angeli's *Bright April* has been criticized because of the way April is subjected to prejudice and because of the prescribed formula for success the story implies. Likewise, Ingrid and Edgar D'Aulaire's *Abraham Lincoln* has been criticized for overromanticizing Lincoln's life and depicting both Black and Native American people as "white man's burden." Read one of these books. Discuss your reactions with your peers.

References

1 Bader, Barbara. *American Picturebooks from Noah's Ark to the Beast Within*. New York: Macmillan, 1976.

2 Bierhorst, John, ed. *The Red Swan: Myths and Tales of the American Indians*. New York: Farrar, Straus and Giroux, 1976.

3 Broderick, Dorothy May. "The Image of the Black in Popular and Recommended American Juvenile Fiction, 1827–1967." University Microfilm No. 71–4090. New York: Columbia University, 1971.

4 Byler, Mary Gloyne. "American Indian Authors for Young Readers." In *Cultural Conformity in Books for Children*, edited by Donnarae MacCann and Gloria Woodard. Metuchen, N.J.: Scarecrow, 1977.

5 Carlson, Julia Ann. "A Comparison of the Treatment of the Negro in Children's Literature in the Periods 1929–1938 and 1959–1968, University Mi-

crofilm No. 70–1245. Storrs, Conn.: University of Connecticut, 1969.

6 Carlson, Ruth Kearney. *Emerging Humanity: Multi-Ethnic Literature for Children and Adolescents*. Dubuque, Ia.: Brown, 1972.

7 Charpenel, Mauricio. "Literature about Mexican American Children." College Station, Tex.: Texas A&M University, Children's Literature Conference, 1980.

8 Council on Interracial Books for Children. "Chicano Culture in Children's Literature: Stereotypes, Distortions and Omissions." In *Cultural Conformity in Books for Children*, edited by Donnarae MacCann and Gloria Woodard. Metuchen, N.J.: Scarecrow, 1977.

9 Council on Interracial Books for Children. "Criteria for Analyzing Books on Asian Americans." In *Cultural Conformity in Books for Children*, edited by Donnarae MacCann and Gloria Woodard. Metuchen, N.J.: Scarecrow, 1977.

10 Faulkner, William J. *The Days When the Animals Talked*. Illustrated by Troy Howell. Chicago: Follett, 1977.

11 Fisher, Laura. "All Chiefs, No Indians: What Children's Books Say about American Indians." *Elementary English* 51 (February 1974): 185–89.

12 Granstrom, Jane, and Silvey, Anita. "A Call for Help: Exploring the Black Experience in Children's Books." In *Cultural Conformity in Books for Children*, edited by Donnarae MacCann and Gloria Woodard. Metuchen, N.J.: Scarecrow, 1977.

13 Hamilton, Virginia. *The People Could Fly: American Black Folktales*. New York: Knopf, 1985.

14 Haviland, Virginia. *North American Legends*. New York: Collins, 1979.

15 Herbst, Laura. "That's One Good Indian: Unacceptable Images in Children's Novels." In *Cultural Conformity in Books for Children*, edited by Donnarae MacCann and Gloria Woodard. Metuchen, N.J.: Scarecrow, 1977.

16 Jenkins, Esther C. "Multi-Ethnic Literature: Promise and Problems." *Elementary English* 50 (May 1973): 693–99.

17 Latimer, Bettye I. *Starting Out Right: Choosing Books about Black People for Young Children*. Bulletin No. 2314. Madison, Wis.: Wisconsin Department of Public Instruction, 1972.

18 Latimer, Bettye I. "Telegraphing Messages to Children about Minorities." *The Reading Teacher* 30 (November 1976): 151–56.

19 Morgan, Betty M. "An Investigation of Children's Books Containing Characters from Selected Minority Groups Based on Specified Criteria." University Microfilm No. 74–6232. Carbondale, Ill.: Southern Illinois University, 1973, .

20 Norton, Donna E. "The Expansion and Evaluation of a Multi-Ethnic Reading/Language Arts Program Designed for 5th, 6th, 7th, and 8th Grade Children." Meadows Foundation Grant, No. 55614, A Three Year Longitudinal Study, Texas A&M University, 1984–1987.

21 Stensland, Anna Lee. *Literature by and about the American Indian*. Urbana Ill.: National Council of Teachers of English, 1979.

Involving Children in Multiethnic Literature

☐

**PROVIDING BALANCED
LITERATURE OFFERINGS**

☐

**DEVELOPING MULTIETHNIC
LEARNING EXPERIENCES WITH
CHILDREN**

☐

**DEVELOPING AN APPRECIATION
FOR BLACK AMERICAN CULTURE**

☐

**DEVELOPING AN APPRECIATION
FOR NATIVE AMERICAN CULTURE**

☐

**DEVELOPING AN APPRECIATION
FOR HISPANIC AMERICAN
CULTURE**

☐

**DEVELOPING AN APPRECIATION
FOR ASIAN AMERICAN CULTURE**

☐

**PEOPLE FROM ALL ETHNIC
BACKGROUNDS HAVE SIMILAR
FEELINGS, EMOTIONS, AND NEEDS**

E DUCATORS ARE CONCERNED ABOUT both the quality and the quantity of multiethnic materials available for sharing with children. They are also concerned about the teaching strategies used in developing positive attitudes toward ethnic minorities. Geneva Gay (9) says that the major ethnic minorities in the United States, including Hispanic Americans, Black Americans, and Native Americans, "are the students most directly involved in and affected by dilemmas of cultural conflict in the classroom. Academically, they are the ones served most unsuccessfully by educational institutions" (p. 47). Authorities in multiethnic studies are very critical of the role schools play in transmitting cultural values. Gwendolyn Baker (3), for example, says that little planning has been given to the process of multicultural education. She maintains that both college students and teachers require training in the concepts to be developed, the objectives to be achieved, the knowledge about various cultures, and the integration of multicultural concepts at all levels of education.

Following a study that attempted to change the attitudes of children toward Hispanic Americans, Shirley Koeller (14) concluded that "Evidence of these negative attitudes by children suggests a need for inter-group education, a need for curricula dealing with recognition and respect for our multicultural society, and a need for teachers trained in dealing with inter-group education. The crucial role of the teacher in influencing attitudes is widely acknowledged; adequate training of teachers is vital." (p. 334)

The research also supports developing a multiethnic program that has a strong literature component. Frank Fisher (7), for example, asked fifth graders to read children's literature that developed favorable images of Native Americans. One group read the stories without discussion, a second group read the stories and then took part in discussions led by an adult, and a third group did not use the literature in any way. The greatest change in positive attitudes resulted in the group that both read and discussed the literature. Herbert Frankel (8) and Carol S. Schwartz (26) report similar findings. Results of these studies seem to imply that while reading literature is somewhat helpful for changing attitudes, it is more beneficial when combined with subsequent activities.

This section considers many types of activities that can heighten the positive value of excellent multiethnic literature. Many of the suggestions are a result of multiethnic research conducted by Donna E. Norton and research associates Blanche Lawson and Sue Mohrmann (17, 18) in both university and elementary classrooms. The results of this five-year research project indicate that college students, classroom teachers, and elementary children can improve their attitudes toward Black Americans, Native Americans, and Hispanic Americans if multiethnic literature and literature-related activities are encouraged by placing them in the curriculum and if teachers are provided instruction in selecting this literature and in developing teaching strategies that can be used to accompany it. In contrast, this research also indicates that merely placing the literature in the classroom, without subsequent interaction, does not change children's attitudes.

PROVIDING BALANCED LITERATURE OFFERINGS

One of the greatest values of all good literature is a momentary glimpse of the glow of humanity when one experiences the problems and purposes, the hates and the hurts, and the values, dignities, and human worth of another human being who is both similar to and different from oneself. (p. 3)

This value expressed by Ruth Kearney Carlson (5) can be encouraged by the literature program if children have an opportunity to read a wide range of multiethnic and nonethnic books. (Although many educators are critical of the lack of multiethnic literature in the classroom, a well-balanced program should not consist exclusively of multiethnic literature any more than it should consist totally of fantasy or nonfiction. Children need experiences with many types of literature.)

A well-balanced literature program includes literature about all ethnic minorities as well as literature that shows a variety of aspirations, socioeconomic levels, occupations, and human characteristics. This literature should avoid negative stereotypes, allow children to see similarities and differences among people, and develop an understanding that children live in a culturally heterogeneous nation.

DEVELOPING MULTIETHNIC LEARNING EXPERIENCES WITH CHILDREN

Donna E. Norton's research (17,18) has identified a series of steps that help preservice and in-service teachers create effective multiethnic learning experiences that bring about positive attitudes in the adults developing the materials and in the children using them:

1 Identify values that children can gain from multiethnic literature.
2 Investigate methods for determining and improving children's attitudes toward contributions of all people.
3 Identify traditional cultural values that may be highly valued in the literature and in the children's heritage.
4 Develop criteria for evaluating multiethnic literature.
5 Evaluate multiethnic literature available in libraries.
6 Select children's literature that provides positive multiethnic viewpoints.
7 Develop ethnic cultural webs that illustrate the varied subjects to be covered in the multiethnic literature study.
8 Develop instructional strategies and activities that encourage appreciation for multiethnic contributions to society and an understanding of the similarities and differences between ethnic groups.

DEVELOPING AN APPRECIATION FOR BLACK AMERICAN CULTURE

Using Traditional African Tales: Adding Authenticity to Storytelling

The marvelous traditional tales of Africa are natural sources of materials for storytelling; they can appear more authentic, however, and increase children's understanding of this cultural heritage if adults use African storytelling techniques discovered by folklore researchers.

Story Selections. Descriptions of storytellers from West Africa provide ideas for selecting a story from a number of possibilities. During her travels through Africa in the nineteenth century, Mary Kingsley (13) discovered story minstrels who carried nets resembling fishing nets that

CHART 11–1

Introducing traditional tales with objects

	Object	Association	Traditional Tales
1	A flower	Receiving the gift of beauty.	Jan Carew, *The Third Gift*
2	A cardboard rainbow	Pia is trying to bring harmony to human world, while his mother weaves curtains from rainbows.	Jan Carew, *Children of the Sun*
3	A rabbit and a hut	Someone has taken possession of rabbit's house.	Verna Aardema, *Who's in Rabbit's House?*
4	The mosquito	The mosquito was not always noisy.	Verna Aardema, *Why Mosquitoes Buzz in People's Ears*
5	A large spider	How did spider get a thin waist?	Joyce Arkhurst, *The Adventures of Spider: West African Folktales*
6	A box containing stories	How stories came to earth.	Gail Haley, *A Story, A Story*

contained objects such as bones, feathers, and china bits. When the listener chose an object, the storyteller would tell a story about it. Another interesting technique required the storyteller to wear a hat with articles suspended from the brim. A listener again would select an intriguing item, and the story would begin.

Teachers and librarians can easily use these techniques to help children select the story or stories they want to hear and to stimulate their interest. Cardboard cutouts, miniature objects, or real things that suggest a character or animal in a story can be chosen. Chart 11–1 gives examples of objects and the stories they represent.

Story Openings. Storytellers from several African countries introduce stories by calling out a sentence that elicits a response by the audience. For example, Philip Noss (19) relates that the following is a common story starter from Cameroon:

Storyteller: Listen to a tale! Listen to a tale!
Audience: A tale for fun, for fun.
              Your throat is a gong, your body a locust;
              bring it here for me to roast!
Storyteller: Children, listen to a tale,
              a tale for fun, for fun.

If an adult or a child prefers to use an opening statement and response in an African language, this Hausa opening from Nigeria, identified by A. J. Tremearne (29), can be used:

Storyteller: Ga ta, ga ta nan.
              (See it, see it here.)

Audience: Ta zo, muii.
              (Let it come, for us to hear.)

If the stories are from the West Indies, one of these introductions identified by Elsie Clews Parsons (21) would be appropriate:

(1) Once upon a time, a very good time
     Not my time, nor your time, old people's time
(2) Once upon a time, a very good time
     Monkey chew tobacco and spit white lime

These openings can be used with any of the traditional African tales previously described, or they can be used to introduce a series of folktales. For example, Verna Aardema's humorous *Who's in Rabbit's House* seems particularly appropriate for an introduction stressing a tale for fun. An enjoyable series of folktales might include "why" tales such as Aardema's *Why Mosquitoes Buzz in People's Ears* and Joyce Cooper Arkhurst's "How Spider Got a Thin Waist," from *The Adventures of Spider: West African Folktales*. Another series might include hero or trickster tales.

Styles of African Storytellers. The style of the traditional African storyteller, still found in many African countries today, can be characterized as a lively mixture of mimicking dialogue, body action, audience participation, and rhythm. Storytellers mimic the sounds of animals, change their voices to characterize both animal and human characters, develop dialogue, and encourage their listeners to interact with the story. They may also add musical accompaniment with drums or other rhythm and string instruments such as thumb pianos. Anne Pellowski (23) says that music and rhythm are important additions to African storytellers:

Taken as a whole, all storytelling in Africa, whether folk, religious, or bardic, whether in prose or poetry, seems to be strongly influenced by music and rhythm. It is rare to find stories that do not have some rhythmical or musical interlude or accompaniment, using either the voice, body parts, or special instruments. (p. 116)

Because children enjoy interacting with a storyteller and interpreting tempos with drums or other musical instruments, this is a natural addition to storytelling that can increase appreciation and understanding of traditional African tales. Stories such as Aardema's *Why Mosquitoes Buzz in People's Ears* and *Who's in Rabbit's House?*, with their strong oral language patterns and varied animal characterizations, can effectively introduce this traditional African style.

Ending the Story Time. Just as African storytellers use interesting story beginnings, they also often use certain types of story endings. If the story was dramatic, it could end with the Hausa *Suka zona* ("they remained") or the Angolan *Mahezu* ("finished"). If the story was an obvious exaggeration from the West Indies, the storyteller might choose this ending:

> Chase the rooster and catch the hen
> I'll never tell a lie like that again.

Storytellers from the West Indies also provided an appropriate ending for humorous folktales:

> They lived in peace, they died in peace
> And they were buried in a pot of candle grease.

Children enjoy recreating the atmosphere of traditional African tales. Black American children take special pride in the stories and the exciting ways they can be presented to an audience. Both adults and children can tell them and then discuss the traditional African approaches to storytelling and how these approaches enhanced the enjoyment for both storyteller and listeners. After the stories are told, students may read them constantly. Sue Mohrmann (18), who used folktales with eighth graders with low reading ability, indicated that the children had never enjoyed reading materials as much as they enjoyed these African folktales. In working with children, Norton found that elementary children enjoy the folktales and their enrichment through traditional means of storytelling.

An Ananse the Spider Festival. Many folktales from West Africa include a character called Ananse, the spider, or Kwaku (Uncle) Ananse. He is the main hero in a series of stories from the Ashanti people in which animals speak and act as humans. These stories usually teach a moral or account for the origin of things. According to Harold Courlander (6), Ananse is also a cultural hero, often a buffoon, who is endlessly preoccupied with outwitting the creatures of the field and forest, people, and even the deities. He is an adversary in endless contests with his community. He is shown with a range of personalities: sympathetic, wise, cunning, predatory, greedy, gluttonous, and unscrupulous. There are moral teachings in many of his defeats that suggest he was humiliated or punished because of unacceptable behavior. As a cultural hero, some of his escapades result in creating a natural phenomenon such as the moon or beginning institutions, traditions, or customs. He has frequent encounters with the Sky God, Nyame, and the earth deity, Aberewa.

The Ashanti people, according to Gerald McDermott, in his introduction to *Anansi the Spider: A Tale from the Ashanti*, have a long, established culture:

The Ashanti have had a federation, a highly organized society, for over four hundred years. Still, today as long ago, the Ashanti are superb artisans. They excel as makers of fine metal work and as weavers of beautiful silk fabric. Into this fabric they weave the rich symbols of their art and folklore—Sun, Moon, Creation, Universe, the Web of the Cosmos, and Anansi, the Spider. (p. i)*

Because the Ananse tales and Ashanti proverbs incorporate many traditional African values—wit, strength, verbal ability, achievement, and the attainment of a distinctive personality—they are excellent means of stimulating discussions and enjoyment. The following ideas were developed with fourth-grade students who enjoyed the An-

---

*Variant spellings (*Ananse* or *Anansi*) exist for this character.

anse stories so much they created a festival and shared some of the exciting activities they had experienced, art work they had created, creative writing of their own Ananse stories, knowledge of the Ashanti culture, and how the roots of present-day Black Americans may go back to the Ashanti culture:

1   The first Ananse tale shared with the group was Gail E. Haley's *A Story, A Story* (the book that created the interest in reading additional Ananse stories) that tells how the "Spider Stories" of Africa were created. After reading the story, children talked about the importance of storytelling, the beauty of the repetitive language that allowed them to visualize an Ananse who was "so small, so small, so small" and a leopard so powerful that he had to be tied "by his foot, by his foot, by his foot, by his foot." The teacher shared the fact that African storytellers often repeated words to make them stronger. The class also discussed the descriptive language connected with animals' names, such as the leopard "of-the-terrible-teeth." Finally, they discussed the wit, verbal ability, and trickery suggested by Ananse's actions in trapping the animals and acquiring the box of stories from Nyame, the Sun God.

2   The next series of stories shared were those in Joyce Cooper Arkhurst's *The Adventures of Spider: West African Folktales.* The book was introduced in this way: "In the book, *A Story, A Story*, you learned how Ananse was given all the stories by the Sky God. This book contains some of the stories that are said to have been stories of Ananse the spider. In this book, however, he is just called Spider."

☐   The titles of the Ananse stories found in the book were then written on the chalkboard:

"How Spider Got a Thin Waist"
"Why Spiders Live in Ceilings"
"How Spider Got a Bald Head"
"How Spider Helped a Fisherman"
"Why Spiders Live in Dark Corners"
"How the World Got Wisdom"

☐   The class was divided into five groups of five children after the children discussed the probable contents of the listed stories and decided which story they wanted to share through dramatization or other visual approach. (If there are not enough children, or if some stories are

not selected, the stories can be read aloud to the class or made available during free reading time.) Various methods of dramatizing their stories included pantomime, a puppet show, a play, reader's theater, a flannelboard story, and a box movie theater. The children in each group read their stories (each group read the stories orally because there were not enough books for each child to have a copy) and decided how they would share their stories with their audience. Activities for the next few class sessions revolved around the children preparing puppets, flannelboard characters, and so forth, and practicing their stories. The teacher went from group to group, giving assistance when required.

☐   Each group presented its story to the rest of the class. After each presentation, the teacher led a discussion in which the children considered the characters, the moral suggested, and the traditional values found in the story.

3   Gerald McDermott's *Anansi the Spider: A Tale from the Ashanti* stimulated the creation of a mural that depicted the six wondrous deeds performed by Ananse's sons—See Trouble, Road Builder, River Drinker, Game Skinner, Stone Thrower, and Cushion—as they tried to save their father from a terrible danger.

4   In order to show where the Ananse tales originated, the children made a large map of Africa and identified the areas in West Africa where the Ashanti live. They also showed the movement of the tales from Africa to America. During the discussion of the movement of Ashanti traditions to the United States, several children showed an interest in tracing cultural roots and learning more about these people.

5   Margaret Musgrove's *Ashanti to Zulu: African Traditions* was shared in order to observe the cultures of the various African peoples and compare them with the Ashanti culture. The children described what they saw in each picture: beautiful designs in fabrics, intricate jewelry, clothing, animals, artifacts, and characteristics of geography. Pictures from other sources were also shared.

6   Ashanti proverbs were chosen from Harold Courlander's *A Treasury of African Folklore* (6). The teacher led a discussion, and the children talked about the fact that many cultures have wise sayings that have been passed down from generation to generation. They

listed some of the proverbs they knew, and discussed the meaning of each. Then the teacher introduced some Ashanti proverbs, had the children discuss their meanings, and had the children list similar proverbs in their own families.

Only birds of the same kind gather together.
Regrets are useless.
A man with no friends has no one to help him up.

7 Children wrote their own Ananse stories.
8 They compared contemporary writings about animal characters that are given human characterizations with the Ananse characters. Examples include Snoopy and Woodstock in the "Peanuts" cartoon, Heathcliff, in the cartoon of the same name, and Winnie-the-Pooh.
9 On the day of the festival, the children invited their parents into a room decorated with their Ashanti projects. Their parents observed their creative dramatizations, read their writings, saw their art work, and listened to other information they had discovered about the Ashanti culture and Ananse the Spider.

Other Creative Dramatizations Using Traditional African Folktales. The Ananse tales suggest the types of creative dramatizations that can result from sharing folktales with children. Because Verna Aardema's Masai tale *Who's in Rabbit's House?* is written and illustrated in play form, it is easily adapted to the classroom. The story's strong animal characters shown behind large masks, the lively repetitive words describing their actions and the series of short scenes that build up to an exciting but humorous climax create a story that children enjoy reenacting. A second-grade teacher read the story to children and then discussed how it could be performed as a play. The children identified the characters and made large paper-sack masks to represent each animal: Rabbit, Jackal, Leopard, Elephant, Rhinocerous, Frog, and Caterpillar. The children made simple props, including a cardboard box (large enough to hold a crouching child) made to look like a hut with a door that opened and closed, sticks for Jackal to build a fire, and a large leaf that Frog could turn into a horn.

The children discussed how the animals would act in each scene. The teacher reminded the children that African storytellers are very good mimics of animal sounds and movements; consequently, they should try to create realistic

animals through their voices and body movements. Next the teacher read each scene, and the children acted the part of each animal character. They were leopards attacking the hut with their claws, elephants showing how easily they could trample the hut, or intelligent frogs using their wits to trick the intruder into leaving the hut. Finally, they took turns being players and audience as they created the play with each player's interpretation of the animal characters.

Other teachers and librarians have used different ways to present this story through dramatizations. For example:

1 An adult read the dialogue, and children pantomimed the actions.
2 Children combined choral reading with the creative dramatizations; as the audience, they spoke the part of the feared Long One each time he refused to leave the hut and continued to threaten Rabbit. This was very successful because children could react as players and audience, both highly involved in the presentation.
3 Students became human puppets by drawing large cardboard shapes that covered their bodies so that only their faces were visible through an opening, or they turned large boxes into animals and placed them over their bodies. The production was put on as a puppet show, but without the puppet theater.

Sharing and Discussing a Black American Folktale: John Henry

The tall tale of the steel-driving man, John Henry—as a poem, a song, or a longer narrative—can stimulate many creative activities. Teachers have used the tale in its various forms with children in all elementary grades. In the lower grades, children listen to the story and discuss the large illustrations in the picture book *John Henry*, by Ezra Jack Keats. The language of the book makes pleasant listening while children discover that American folklore heroes are from different ethnic backgrounds. Through the story and pictures, they can gain an understanding of a tall tale and the kinds of actions a hero is supposed to perform. They can discuss other folk heroes such as Davy Crockett and Paul Bunyan; they can compare the remarkable feats of each hero and decide how much of each hero's story is exaggerated.

"John Henry" in poetic form makes a good choral presentation. Classes have tried the poem as a refrain arrangement in which a leader reads the opening lines of each verse while the class enters in on each of the repetitive lines, such as "He laid down his hammer and he died." Each verse can also be read in a cumulative arrangement (see pages 359–61 for descriptions of different types of choral arrangements) in which one group begins the first verse, the second joins in on the second verse, and a third joins in on the third verse. This arrangement continues until the poem is complete.

Older children may want to learn more about the history of the railroad, how tracks were laid by work gangs, and how the steam drill changed railroad construction. One group, for example, investigated the purposes of work songs and identified songs sung by railroaders and other types of workers. These work songs or chants were done as choral readings while the group pantomimed the actions of a work gang. One such chant, used by Black Americans laying track, has a line chanted by the leader while the crew rests. It is followed by a response while the crew works in unison. The "shack-a-lack-a" response is an imitation of the sound made by the pieces of track as they are pushed into line with long metal poles:

Leader:	Oh boys, can't you line her?
Gang:	shack-a-lack-a
Leader:	Oh boys, can't you line her?
Gang:	shack-a-lack-a
Leader:	Oh boys, can't you line her?
Gang:	shack-a-lack-a
Leader:	Every day of the week we go linin' track (16, p. 19.)

(Work songs from different periods in American history are also excellent sources of information about our country's history and its people. See page 492 for a selection of songs and the historical periods when they were used.)

Because there are several versions of the John Henry tale, the books, poem, and song can be compared. Is the story the same in each version? Are the illustrations alike or different? Which version is the most effective? Why?

Teachers can encourage creative writing as children write their own work chants and tall tales. One class pretended that John Henry was a contemporary hero and wrote about the heroic deeds he could do if he lived in their lifetime.

Stories described him saving the nuclear reactor at Three Mile Island, rescuing people from the upper floors during a hotel fire, and completing work on a superhighway or a skyscraper. Illustrations accompanying the stories showed John Henry as a strong man who was also concerned with the lives of the people around him.

Other classes have used tales about John Henry to stimulate creative drama. Scenes from John Henry's life that are good for this purpose include the following:

1 John Henry's birth when the moon stood still and went backward, the stars stood still and went backward, and a mighty river flowed uphill.
2 John Henry's early life. (One class speculated about what extraordinary things he might have done as a child.)
3 John Henry's job on a riverboat when he saved the ship from sinking.
4 John Henry's work on the railroads, the tunnel cave-in, and his saving of men's lives.
5 The race between John Henry and the steam drill.

Additional Strengths Found in Black American Folktales and Ways in Which They Can Be Shared with Children

The following activities have been very effective in elementary classrooms and during library story time:

1 The strong sequential development of the cumulative tale in Verna Aardema's *Why Mosquitoes Buzz in People's Ears* makes this story appropriate for a feltboard presentation. The story can be told by an adult using the felt characters and then retold by children. The cumulative language with its considerable repetition also makes the story appropriate for choral speaking. The teacher or librarian can read the beginning of the story and encourage children to join in as the repetition begins.
2 The Swahili alphabet, words, and numbers in two books by Muriel Feelings provide stimulation for children to learn some African words and more about African culture. While these books are not folktales, they can be used effectively either with a folktale presentation or for learning more about the culture. Although these books are picture-alphabet and picture-number books, an eighth-grade

teacher reported that the students thoroughly enjoyed learning to count and say other words in Swahili. *Jambo Means Hello: Swahili Alphabet Book* presents the alphabet plus appropriate words and pictures depicting the culture; *Moja Means One: Swahili Counting Book* allows children to count up through ten. Children enjoy counting culturally related objects in the pictures and then using Swahili numbers in other situations.

Appreciation Study of Famous Black Americans

Increasing aspirations of black children and increasing respect for the contributions of black people in American history are both values suggested by multiethnic studies. The Multiethnic Research Advisory Council that worked with Donna E. Norton (18) on the development of multiethnic studies stated that one of its chief concerns was the inclusion of ethnic contributions throughout the years, not only during Black Awareness Week or other ethnic units. This advisory council, made up of educators and community leaders who themselves were members of racial and ethnic minority groups, stressed the desirability of literature that allowed children to investigate and share contributions made by Americans from all ethnic backgrounds. Nonfictional books and biographies about Black Americans discussed in this chapter and chapter twelve suggest a few of the many contributions of Black Americans to politics, medicine, science, literature, music, art, and sports. The following learning experiences were developed by children's literature students or research project members and then either incorporated into a school curriculum or shared with classroom teachers and librarians for use with history, science, literature, art, music, or sports lessons.

1   Have children search the literature and develop a time line illustrating the contributions of famous Black Americans in history. Develop a bulletin board that illustrates the time line and displays literature selections that tell about the people.
2   Ask children to share their reactions after reading a biography about Martin Luther King, Jr. Have them interview parents and other adults about the goals of the late civil rights leader.

3   When studying the Civil War, read literature about Harriet Tubman and Frederick Douglass. Re-enact scenes from the literature.
4   After reading a biography about George Washington Carver, have students prepare a presentation to be given to the U.S. Patent Office requesting a patent.
5   After reading a biography, perform "A Day in the Life of ———."
6   Share literature written by black authors. Discuss the contributions and styles of authors such as John Steptoe, Sharon Mathis, Eloise Greenfield, and Virginia Hamilton.
7   After reading biographies or stories about black musicians, share and discuss their music.
8   Read biographies of black athletes and discuss records set or other contributions.
9   After reading literature about the contributions and lives of Black Americans, create a "What's My Line" game in which a panel of children asks questions while another group answers.
10 Using a "Meet the Press" format, ask children to take roles of famous Black Americans or reporters who interview them. Prepare for the session by reading literature.

Similar activities can be developed highlighting the contributions of Native Americans, Hispanics, and Asian Americans.

DEVELOPING AN APPRECIATION FOR NATIVE AMERICAN CULTURE

Using Traditional Native American Tales: Adding Authenticity to Storytelling

Native American storytellers, like African storytellers, developed definite styles in their storytelling over centuries of oral tradition. Storytelling was an important part of early Indian life, and stories were carefully passed down from one generation to the next. It was quite common for Indians to gather around a fire or sit around their homes while listening to stories. The storyteller sessions often continued for long periods of time as each person told a story. Children have opportunities to empathize with members of Native American culture when they take part in storytelling activities that closely resemble the original experience.

Story Openings. Several collectors of Native American tales and observers of Native American storytellers have identified characteristic opening sentences that may be used when presenting Native American stories to children. Franc Newcomb (16), for example, found that many Navaho storytellers opened their stories with one of these tributes to the past:

(1) In the beginning, when the world was new
(2) At the time when men and animals were all the same and spoke the same language

A popular beginning with the White Mountain Apache was

> "long, long ago, they say."

Children can also search through stories from many Native American tribes and discover how interpreters and translators of traditional Indian folktales introduced their stories. They can investigate further and find the exact story openers a certain tribe would be likely to use. Then they can use those openings when telling stories from that tribe.

Storytelling Styles. The storytelling style used by various Indians of North America was quite different from the style described earlier for African storytellers. Melville Jacobs (12) describes the storytelling style of Northwest Indians as being terse, staccato, and rapid. It was usually compact, with little description, although the storytellers might use pantomime and gestures to develop the story. Gladys Reichard (24) found that the Coeur d'Alene Indians used dramatic movements to increase the drama of their tales.

The listening styles of the Native American audiences were also quite different from the participation encouraged by African storytellers. Native American children were expected to be very attentive and not interrupt the storyteller. Their only response might be the Hopi's repetition of the last word in a sentence, or the Crow's responsive *E!* ("yes") following every few sentences. This response, according to Byrd Baylor (4), was a sign that the audience was attentive and appreciative. Children in classroom and library story times may also enjoy using these signs to show that they are listening.

Morris Opler (20) discovered an interesting detail about Jicarilla Apache storytellers that can be used to add authenticity and cultural under-standing to Native American storytelling. Storytellers gave kernels of corn to children during story time. Because corn was very important, it was believed that if children ate the corn during the storytelling they would remember the content and the importance of the stories.

Ending the Story Time. Melville Jacobs (12) says that Clackama Indians ended many stories by telling an epilogue about an Indian's metamorphosis into an animal, bird, or fish. Most of the stories also had a final ending that meant "myth, myth" or "story, story." Jicarilla Apache storytellers sometimes ended their stories by giving gifts to the listeners because they had stolen a night from their audience.

Teachers and librarians have found that adding authentic storytelling techniques is an excellent way to increase understanding and respect for a cultural heritage and to stimulate discussions about traditional values. After children have taken part in both Native American and African traditional story times, they can also compare the oral traditions of both groups and discuss the beauty and style of each form.

Stimulating Creative Writing through Native American Literature

The imagery found in Native American folktales is closely related to nature. The wind may suggest a ghost; the sky, a bowl of ice; the moon, a man smoking a pipe; sun rays, the earth maker's eyelashes; twinkling stars, a bird flying slowly; shooting stars, a bird darting swiftly; or the sun, a yellow-tipped porcupine. These marvelous images may be found in Indian lore collected throughout the United States; they are excellent sources for stimulating children to look at nature in a different way and then write their own stories using verbal imagery and illustrations. Teachers have shared various collections of Native American lore from many different tribes, discussed with children the images suggested, had the children look at the illustrations depicting the images, and then taken the children outside to observe nature for themselves. Children have been encouraged to look at their environment in new ways, to try to picture relationships between the unknown and the known, to sketch their interpretations, and to take notes about what they experience. When they return to the classroom, they have turned their observations and sketches into creative, imaginative stories.

Byrd Baylor's *Hawk, I'm Your Brother* is an excellent reference for helping children recognize differences in literature depending on the author's point of view and for motivating the writing of a story from another point of view. In preparing the instructional sequence use the following procedures:

1 Introduce the story and tell the students that they will be listening to a story in which the author describes and develops the hero's aspirations so that the reader can understand them. Ask them to consider how they would feel as Rudy Soto and what they would feel if they were in his place. Ask them to consider the feelings and desires of the hawk.

2 After reading *Hawk, I'm Your Brother* aloud, lead a discussion in which the students identify Baylor's characterization of Rudy and the hawk and identify the major sequence of events leading up to Rudy's decision to release the hawk.

3 Ask the students to consider the significance of the book's title. Why did Baylor choose *Hawk, I'm Your Brother*? Is it an accurate description of Rudy Soto's relationship to the hawk? How are Rudy and the hawk alike? How are they different? Why did Rudy release the hawk? How do you think Rudy felt after releasing the hawk? How do you think the hawk felt after being released? What would you have done if you were Rudy Soto? How would you react if you were the hawk?

4 Tell the students that an incident may be described in different ways by several people who have the same experience. The details that characters describe, the feelings they experience, and their beliefs in the right or wrong of an incident may vary depending on who the author chooses to tell the story. Consequently, the same story could change drastically depending on the point of view of the storyteller. For example, Beatrix Potter tells her popular story of a rabbit who invades a garden through the point of view of Peter Rabbit. The story would be very different if it were told through the point of view of Mr. McGregor. (Ask the students to tell you how the story might change if it were written from a gardener's point of view.) Next, ask the students to tell you whose point of view Baylor develops in *Hawk, I'm Your Brother*. How did they know that the story was told from Rudy Soto's point of view? Then ask them to consider how the story might be written if the author chose the hawk's point of view.

5 Ask the students to imagine that they are the hawk that Rudy captured. Have them write a story about what happened to them, beginning from the time that Rudy captured the hawk from the nest high on Santos Mountain.

Two other Native American folktales that have been very successful in stimulating creative writing are William Toye's *The Loon's Necklace* and Byrd Baylor's *And It Is Still That Way: Legends Told by Arizona Indian Children*. After sharing *The Loon's Necklace*, which explains how the loon was transformed from a common black and white bird to one with beautiful markings that resemble a shell necklace, children have considered many other birds and animals that have beautiful markings and written stories suggesting how they might have been rewarded with their beautiful plumage or coats. Examples include how the monarch butterfly acquired its beautiful black and orange markings, how the raccoons acquired their masklike appearance, and how the pheasant acquired its beautiful, colorful plumage. Baylor's book has been used by teachers who are encouraging children from many different cultures to interview older adults or write down stories they themselves have been told. This book includes favorite stories told to Arizona Indian children by their families and other members of their community. It has been used in many classrooms to interest children in becoming recorders of stories that have been handed down in their own families. One teacher asked a class to record their favorite stories told by their grandparents or other older adults who came from a specific culture. The stories were divided according to culture and printed into a multiethnic folktale book for the class. Another teacher of older children asked students to interview older residents of the community and write down any stories they remembered that had been handed down from generation to generation in their own families. These stories were then recorded and made into a book. Children discovered the enjoyment in storytelling and the importance of handing down a cultural heritage.

Sharing and Discussing One Book: *Sing Down the Moon,* by Scott O'Dell

Scott O'Dell's *Sing Down the Moon* is based on a tragic time in Navaho history spanning 1863 to 1865. The story begins during a beautiful spring in Canyon de Chelly when life seems promising. Then the U.S. government sends Colonel Kit Carson to the canyon to bring the Navahos to Fort Sumner, New Mexico. In order to force the Indians' surrender, the troops destroy the crops and livestock, then drive the Navahos to the fort. This three-hundred-mile journey is known as *The Long Walk.* While at Fort Sumner, more than fifteen hundred Indians died, and many others lost their will to live.

1 *Discussion:* The creation stories of the Navahos refer to creating the mountains as "singing up the mountains." What is the significance of Scott O'Dell's title *Sing Down the Moon?* What happened to the Navaho way of life during the years depicted in the story? Why did the government force the Indians to leave their home? If people today were Navahos living at that time, how might they feel? How might a soldier feel?

2 *Ceremonies:* When it was time for Bright Morning to become a woman, the tribe prepared for the Womanhood Ceremony.

   Investigate the ceremonies celebrated by Navaho Indians. In groups, demonstrate one ceremony to the rest of the class. Explain its purpose.

3 *Folk Medicine Beliefs:* When Tall Boy was wounded, Bright Morning rode to the village to get the Medicine Man. The Medicine Man used the juice of mottled berries to treat his wound. Many medicine men effectively used herbs and berries to cure the sick.

   Using resource materials such as Joe Graham's *Grandmother's Tea, Mexican Herbal Remedies* (10), research the various plants that might cure illness. Many of these herbs and plants have significant pharmacological value. Identify the plants that have the greatest value and the illnesses they can cure. Discuss the importance of medicine men, the reasons they were respected within the tribe, and what knowledge was required.

4 *Weapons and Tools:* Tall Boy made a lance to use against the Long Knives. The only mate-

Children enjoy listening to a Native American storyteller.

rials he had to work with were those available in nature.

> Find other weapons and tools Native Americans used. Review how they made them and draw a picture of each. Choose an Indian weapon or tool and write instructions about how people would make this tool or weapon if they were Indians. Explain its purpose to the class. Bright Morning steps on a spear and breaks it when her son reaches out toward a young lamb. Discuss the symbolic meaning of this action.

5 *Setting:* Many clues in *Sing Down the Moon* suggest the environment in which Bright Morning and her tribe live. For example, O'-Dell develops a visual image as he describes the canyons:

The stone walls of the canyons stand so close together that you can touch them with your outstretched hand. (p. 1)

He describes the rain through Bright Morning's thoughts:

> At first it was a whisper, like a wind among the dry corn stalks of our cornfield. (p. 2)

Even the streams are suggested to have a voice of their own:

> The stream sounded like men's voices speaking. (p. 53)

These descriptions of the environment also suggest the Navaho's respect for nature, characteristics of their environment, and whether they were a hunting or a farming tribe. Discuss the significance of the descriptions in O'-Dell's language. How does the author feel about the Navaho? Search for other examples of visual language in the book that describe the various environments experienced by the Navaho as they leave their canyon and go to Fort Sumner. Compare the canyon environment with that at Fort Sumner. Draw a picture illustrating both locations.

> Describe two environments, one that is lovely and enjoyable to live in and one that is not. Draw a picture illustrating each; describe the pictures using language that will allow someone else to visualize them.

Artwork Stimulated by Native American Literature

The traditional Indian folktales and realistic literature provide many opportunities for artwork.

The books have vivid language and visual interpretations of cave paintings, pottery designs, ceremonial masks, sand painting, jewelry, dolls, descriptions of dwellings or clothing, woven rugs, basket weaving, and totem poles. All these contributions to our artistic heritage may be developed with class projects, scouting groups, or individual children. The following ideas are examples of artistic interpretations used effectively with children in elementary classrooms.

The designs found in cave paintings and on shards of ancient Indian pottery not only stimulate children to chronicle events in ways similar to those used by early Native American tribes, but also suggest that the Native Americans' ancient cultures existed long before the Europeans arrived. Teachers have used Baylor's *Before You Came This Way* for discussions about the animals common to the ancient Indians, plants used by them, and events that were important in their lives. They have encouraged children to carve, paint, and draw pictures resembling those found on cave walls on stone or rough paper. Murals have been made filling bulletin boards with the ancient happenings of people who lived in an area during ancient times. Children have also designed a pictorial story of their own lives for others to see. One teacher presented this problem to the class:

Our class is trying to discover a way to make people who may come to our land thousands of years from now understand what we look like, what we respect, what we do. They probably will not be able to read our writing, but we can leave them a message through carvings and paintings. (The group discussed how this could be done and considered the Indian drawings they had seen and talked about.) Pick out the most important things you want to tell these visitors from another time and draw your own story.

Teachers have used another of Baylor's books, *When Clay Sings*, to motivate the creation of clay pottery and the drawing of designs on the pottery. In another classroom, after reading and discussing this book, the teacher provided the following background information and had the children do a clay project:

The Indians dug their clay for pottery from pits and added fine white sand and crushed pieces from old pots to the clay. This clay was then mixed, water was added, and the clay was kneaded by hand until it was smooth as dough. For the base of the pot, a lump of clay was patted into the bottom of a broken bowl. Long ropes of clay were rolled out and then coiled around the base. The walls inside and outside of the pots were rubbed carefully to make them smooth. The pots were then placed in the sun to dry. After they were dry, fine red clay was rubbed over the pots. When they were dried again, they were put in a fire and baked until ready to use.

The class then made pottery from clay provided by the teacher. The designs suggested by the illustrations in *When Clay Sings* were used to carve decorations into the pottery.

The beautifully illustrated masks found in Baylor's *They Put on Masks* have been used to learn more information about the masks' significance, learn about the songs and ceremonial dances that accompanied many masks, and make masks that resemble those illustrated or that express something important to the children. An upper-elementary class investigated the masks and found additional sources that described how masks could be made from paper, cardboard, and papier-mâché. The children used the directions found in Chester Jay Alkema's *Masks* (1), Kari Hunt and Bernice Carlson's *Masks and Mask Makers* (11), G. C. Payne's *Adventures in Paper Modeling* (22), and Laura Ross's *Mask-Making with Pantomime and Stories from American History* (25) in order to make masks characteristic of those created by different Native American tribes. Activities similar to those suggested for developing an appreciation for famous Black Americans are also appropriate for encouraging children to respect the contributions of Native Americans.

DEVELOPING AN APPRECIATION FOR HISPANIC AMERICAN CULTURE

Hispanic Customs

Children's literature written about Mexican, Mexican-American, or Spanish customs stresses two customs in particular: La Posada, celebrated at Christmas, and celebrations connected with weddings. Christmas celebrations are found in Marie Hall Ets's *Nine Days to Christmas: A Story of Mexico*, Politi's *The Nicest Gift*, and Ann Nolan Clark's *Paco's Miracle*. Teachers report that young children find La Posada, with its traditional piñatas, to be especially enjoyable.

A book such as Ets's *Nine Days to Christmas* is usually used to stimulate an interest in the holiday and its related customs. After sharing the book with children, teachers and librarians have asked Mexican American children to describe their own Christmas celebrations and to decide if they are anything like the one described in the book.

Librarians and teachers have shared background information about La Posada with the children. The word *posada* means "inn" or "lodging house"; La Posada refers to Mary and Joseph's pilgrimage to Bethlehem. The celebration, which originated in Spain, is still celebrated in Mexico and in parts of the United States. The traditional celebration begins on December 16 and ends on the evening of December 24 (the nine days to Christmas). Nine community families usually entertain each other on the first eight evenings of

Children learn about Hispanic customs and traditional celebrations by taking part in dramatizations.

the celebration. During this celebration, eight families form a procession leading to the home of the ninth family. The participants, carrying lighted candles and singing, beg for admittance; but, as Mary and Joseph were refused at the inn, they are refused entrance. After this symbolic refusal, the families are invited inside for a celebration. The home may be decorated with a nativity scene, and a piñata is usually found on the patio. The piñata, which contains a clay pot filled with candy, is made out of papier-mâché. Children are blindfolded, turned in circles, given a stick, and given turns hitting the piñata until it is broken and the candy falls out.

On Christmas Eve, the most important ceremony takes place: a young girl dressed as Mary and a young boy dressed as Joseph lead the procession. On this last evening of the celebration, the pilgrims are not refused admittance to the inn, but are welcomed into the home or other community building. In addition to the piñata, fireworks, flowers, and lanterns often enhance the celebrations. This is a happy occasion, filled with singing, dancing, and laughter.

Adults usually follow this discussion of the Christmas celebration with other stories that describe the holiday and then help children have their own celebration with a piñata the children make and other decorations such as lanterns and tissue paper or crepé paper flowers that are illustrated or mentioned in the stories. In public schools, teachers usually stress the piñata, the singing, the dancing, and the food, not the religious reenactment of the Christmas Eve procession.

A star piñata, for example, can be made by inflating a balloon that expands to about eleven inches and then covering it with four layers of newspaper strips that have been dipped into starch or paste. A three-inch circular area is left uncovered at the stem end of the balloon for the piñata opening. Five star points are made by cutting and forming cones from three thicknesses of newspaper. The cones are made by overlapping

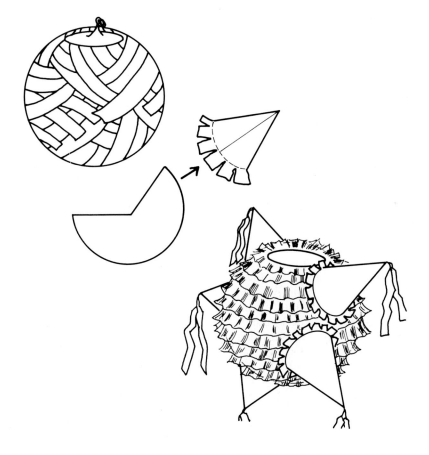

the straight edges and cementing or taping them together. Around the bottom edges of the cones one-inch cuts are made, and the cones are pasted to the piñata form. After the form has dried, the balloon is deflated, and the shape is decorated with rows of colored, ruffled crepé paper. Tassels can be cut from colored paper and added as decorations to the cone tips. The opening is filled with individually wrapped candy and unbreakable toys and is tied by a rope to a tree branch or beam. Then the children have their own piñata party.

Children can compare their piñata party with the ones described in the children's literature selections and with different Christmas celebrations observed in the United States and in other parts of the world.

Paco's Miracle, by Ann Nolan Clark, describes not only the Christmas celebration but also the traditions centered around the wedding ceremony that originated in Spain. As Paco attends a fiesta when the family accepts the new husband, he also discovers the traditional value placed on objects that have been handed down from generation to generation and the various customs related to the wedding celebration. Clark discusses customs that began in Spain, accompanied Spaniards to Mexico, and then traveled with settlers as they journeyed up the Royal Road to the mountains of New Mexico. These traditional customs can lead to lively discussions and dramatizations that enhance an understanding of traditional customs, customs that are still carried on in much the same way as in earlier times. Children can compare present-day observances with those of the past.

According to Magdalena Benavides Sumpter (28), "weddings have always been an important part of a culture, signaling, as they do, one of the most significant events in a person's life. Special rituals and ceremonies surround the acts of courtship and matrimony, and although wedding customs may vary from country to country—and change through the years—their meaningfulness and sentimental value to the participants remains as constant as human nature" (p. 19). Sumpter describes various wedding traditions and suggests activities that may be used with children in *Discovering Folklore through Community Resources*.

Following dramatizations or discussions of the traditional ceremony, children can compare the traditional Mexican wedding ceremony to a con-

temporary Mexican American wedding ceremony. Are there any similarities? They can also compare this traditional ceremony with wedding customs in other cultures. What are the similarities and differences? Children can interview their parents, their grandparents, and other older people living in their community to learn about wedding customs these persons have experienced or heard about. Children enjoy making some of the traditional Mexican foods discussed in the various books and mentioned in the wedding celebration.

Sharing And Discussing One Book: . . . *And Now Miguel* by Joseph Krumgold

1 *Motivation:* Ask students if there has ever been anything they wanted to do very badly but were told by their parents they couldn't do until they were older. Talk about some of the things the children mention. Discuss the possible reasons why they would have to be older to do those things. Then explain that this book is about a twelve-year-old boy who wants something; the story is about how he goes about getting what he wants.

2 *Procedure:* Because it will take several days to read the book, the activities listed can be used following the appropriate reading selection. The book can be read aloud to children or individually by children, if there are enough copies. If each child has a copy, the beginning of a chapter could be read aloud and the remainder of the chapter could be read silently.

3 *Setting:* Chapter one describes the setting of the story in detail. Prepare a map of New Mexico showing the Sangre de Cristo Mountain Range, the Rio Grande River, the city of Taos, and the San Juan Mountain Range. Show the cliffs of the San Juan Range going down to the Rio Grande. Have the children locate and label each detail on the map. Then have them trace the migration of the sheep as described by Miguel in chapter one. The beginning chapters also mention the following landforms: cliff, mountain, mesa, plain, canyon, and arroyo. Collect pictures to show examples of each type of landform. Discuss characteristics of each picture and how the characteristics relate to the section in the story.

☐ In chapter two, Miguel says that he must take his winter clothes to wear in the mountains even though it will be summer. Have the children speculate about the reasons for the differences between the temperature on the plain and in the mountains. Using reference books, have a group of children find the temperature ranges for New Mexico. Have them check other areas where there is a plain and nearby mountains, so they can check differences in temperature according to elevation. Lead them into a generalization on the effect of elevation on temperature and on Miguel's plans.

4 *Characters:* Miguel comes from a large, multigenerational family. Starting with Grandfather Chavez, have children make a genealogical chart of the Chavez family. Then have them make charts of their own families.

☐ The life of the Chavez family revolves around the life cycle of the sheep. Review the cycle with the children: winter on the mesa, back to the ranch in early spring for the birth of the lambs and the shearing, and into the mountains for the summer. Discuss the importance of sheep to the Chavez family and how sheep influence the life-style and desires of each family member.

☐ Ask the children to imagine they are Miguel and are planning their trip into the mountains. They will be gone all summer; they must take everything with them. Have them list everything they will need and defend why they would use valuable space on the pack mule to take each item.

☐ Ask the children to pretend they are Miguel and use a dairy format to write their feelings and experiences as they try to convince the family that they are old enough to accompany the men to the summer pasture.

5 *Values:* Mutual cooperation and dependence within the family are important values stressed in the book. Discuss how each family member contributes to its welfare.

☐ Another value developed is the strong integration of religious beliefs into daily life. There are references to this value throughout the book, but it is particularly strong beginning with chapter eight, in which Miguel explains about San Ysidro to the reader. Grandfather Chavez is the embodiment of the values, whereas Eil has seemingly rejected the religious values.

DEVELOPING AN APPRECIATION FOR ASIAN AMERICAN CULTURE

Using Asian Traditional Tales: Adding Authenticity to Storytelling

A Japanese style of storytelling that is especially interesting to children is the *kamishibai*—an outdoor form of storytelling with pictures. Although it is not as old as the African and Native American techniques discussed earlier, it is different from either the African or the Native American traditions.

Story Opening. Keigo Seki (27) identifies an opening sentence that is often used in Japanese storytelling and that can add an authentic flavor to storytelling in classrooms, especially if the storyteller begins the story in Japanese:

> Mukashi, mukash
> (Long, long ago)
> Aro tokoro ni
> (In a certain place)

Storytelling Style. Kamishibai was performed by men who had a collection of about four stories that were illustrated on cards and shown in a wooden boxholder resembling a miniature stage. The stories were illustrated on a series of picture cards and then placed in a wooden holder about one foot high and eighteen inches wide. The front of the theater had flaps that opened to reveal the stage. The cards fit into a slot in the side of the box; the storyteller pulled the sequentially placed cards out of the box; the text was written on the back of the card that preceded the picture that was currently showing on the stage. (The title was the first card removed and placed in the back of the box, the text that accompanied the next picture was on the back of the title card. This procedure continued with each card as the story unfolded in pictures and words.)

Anne Pellowski (23) describes how influential kamishibai storytelling has been in Japan:

Considering the impact that the kamishibai had on children's literature and the fact that the same publishers who produced the cards were also later producing children's books, it is no wonder that one of the most popular formats for children's picture books in Japan is the horizontal style reminiscent of the kamishibai" (p. 145).

Developing a Japanese Kamishibai Presentation. A kamishibai storytelling experience with its boxholder and picture cards is an enjoyable way for children to illustrate a story, retell the story, and also experience how Japanese children enjoy folktales. One group of children created a kamishibai theater out of a heavy cardboard box. They first cut a viewing opening in the front of the box. Next they cut flaps that could open and close across the front of the stage and attached them to the front sides of the box so the flaps could be in either an open or a closed position. Then they cut openings in the sides of the box so that the cards could be placed inside. Identical openings were placed on either side so that the

openings would provide support for the pictures viewed on the stage. The side openings were made a little taller than the front openings so that each card would be framed by the center stage.

Next they cut tagboard cards to fit inside the theater. The cards were a few inches wider than the theater so the storyteller could grasp them easily and remove them at the proper time. They were also slightly shorter than the side opening so they would go in and out easily.

The group chose a Japanese folktale, Arlene Mosel's *The Funny Little Woman*, to illustrate on the kamishibai picture cards. The group liked the story and wanted to illustrate the characters, including the wicked Oni (demons who live in un-

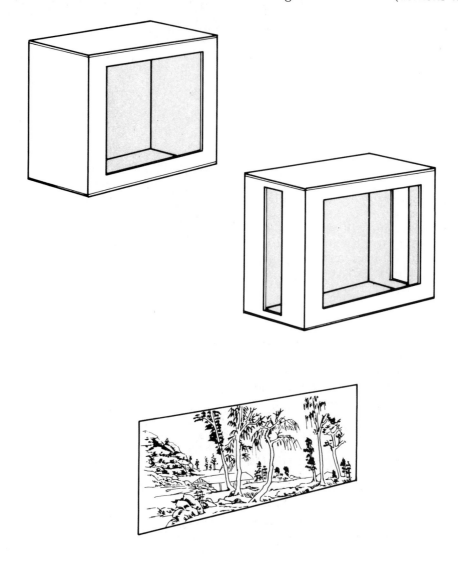

A child learns to value the contributions of a culture different from his own.

derground caverns) and the old woman they kidnap and force to cook for them. The children selected the scenes they wanted to illustrate, selected from this list the scene or scenes each one would draw (the original kamishibai presentations usually ranged from six to twenty scenes), and completed the drawings. They put the cards in sequence, including a title card for an introduction. Then, like authentic *kamishibai* storytellers, they wrote the dialogue for each card on the back of the card preceding it. They placed the cards in the theater and told the story to an appreciative audience. (As each card was removed, it was placed at the back of the box, so the storytellers would have their cues in front of them.)

This activity is especially appropriate for small groups, because each group can select a particular Japanese tale, prepare it for presentation, and present the story to the other groups. In that way, children can be both storyteller and audience. Sumiko Yagawa's *The Crane Wife* is another excellent story suitable for kamishibai presentations.

PEOPLE FROM ALL ETHNIC BACKGROUNDS HAVE SIMILAR FEELINGS, EMOTIONS, AND NEEDS

One value of sharing multiethnic literature with children is to increase their understanding that those who belong to ethnic groups other than their own are real people with feelings, emotions,

and needs similar to theirs. Elaine M. Aoki (2) says that literature can contribute to children's development of values. Consequently, she feels that adults must lead children in active discussions about those values. She says that this discussion should not be a didactic lesson, but should help children gain positive attitudes toward all people. She identifies two steps that should be included in such discussion. First, the discussion should help children focus on understanding others by having them take the viewpoint of a character in a story. When they are that character, they can consider what they would have done under similar circumstances and how they would have felt. Second, they can search for elements within the story that are related to their own experiences. They can identify times when they had feelings or needs like those the characters in the story express.

Many multiethnic books, especially those written for young children, have themes suggesting that children everywhere have more similarities than differences. These books can stimulate discussions in which children relate similar experiences they may have had, tell how they handled similar problems, suggest how they would feel if they had a similar experience, and relate ways they might respond to similar circumstances. For example, after reading John Steptoe's *Stevie*, children can talk about how they would feel if a younger child came to their room and broke their toys, how they would solve this problem if they were Stevie, and the feelings they might experience if the child were no longer there. They can discover from discussing Valerie Flournoy's *The Patchwork Quilt* that feelings of love between grandparents and grandchildren are universal.

Many books for older readers also suggest universal needs and emotions. The following books can be used to stimulate discussions around the topics suggested:

1 Experiencing prejudice creates strong emotions:
   Laurence Yep's *Dragonwings* (Chinese American)
   Nicholasa Mohr's *Felita* (Puerto Rican)
   Scott O'Dell. *Sing Down the Moon* (Native American)
   Mildred Taylor's *Roll of Thunder, Hear My Cry* (Black American)

2 People all have dreams that influence their lives:
   Laurence Yep's *Dragonwings* and *Sea Glass* (Chinese Americans)
   Joseph Krumgold's *. . . And Now Miguel* (Spanish American–Basque)
   Virginia Driving Hawk Sneve's *High Elk's Treasure* (Native American)
   Michele Murray's *Nellie Cameron* (Black American)
   Paula Fox's *How Many Miles to Babylon?* (Black American)

3 Discovering one's own heritage brings pride to the individual:
   Laurence Yep's *Child of the Owl* (Chinese American)
   Brent Ashabranner's *To Live in Two Worlds: American Indian Youth Today* (Native American)
   Virginia Hamilton's *Zeely* (Black American)

4 People can have strong feelings of love toward older family members:
   Ann Nolan Clark's *To Stand Against the Wind* (Vietnamese)
   Miska Miles's *Annie and the Old One* (Native American)
   Sharon Bell Mathis's *The Hundred Penny Box* (Black American)
   Valerie Flournoy's *The Patchwork Quilt* (Black American)

SUMMARY

Educators are concerned about the teaching strategies used in classrooms to develop positive attitudes toward ethnic minorities, as well as about the quality and quantity of multiethnic literature available for sharing with children. Research indicates that reading literature is somewhat helpful for changing attitudes, but it is more beneficial to combine the reading with subsequent activities such as discussions, creative dramatizations, and other activities that stress the values and contributions of the culture. A well-balanced multiethnic literature program includes literature that shows people with a variety of aspirations, from different socioeconomic levels, with different occupations, and a wide range of human characteristics. The literature should avoid stereotypes, allow children to see similarities as well as differences among people, and develop an understanding that children live in a culturally heterogeneous nation.

Suggested Activities for Children's Appreciation of Multiethnic Literature

☐ Choose African, Native American, or Asian traditional tales. Prepare an appropriate story opening, storytelling style, and story ending that reflects the authentic traditional presentation of the tales. Share the stories with a group of children or a peer group.

☐ Choose an African people other than the Ashanti. Suggest stories and other learning experiences that would allow children to develop an appreciation for its culture.

☐ Search a social studies or history curriculum and identify Black Americans, Native Americans, Hispanic Americans, or Asian Americans who have made contributions during the time periods or subjects being studied. Identify literature selections that include additional information about those individuals and their contributions.

☐ Develop a time line showing the chronology of famous Black Americans, Native Americans, Hispanic Americans, and Asian Americans. Identify literature that may be used with the time line.

☐ Develop a "What's My Line," a round-table discussion, or a "Meet the Press" activity that stresses the contributions of famous Black Americans, Native Americans, Hispanic Americans, or Asian Americans.

☐ Choose a Native American story and develop a series of discussion questions that would allow children to gain insights into the Indian culture portrayed in the book.

☐ Develop a lesson that encourages children to appreciate the Native American artistic heritage; suggestions include creating masks, pottery, sand painting, and weaving.

☐ Prepare the directions for a Native American dance; present the dance to a group of children or a peer group. Include the purpose for the dance and identify the particular Native Americans who created the dance.

☐ Research one of the Mexican American, Puerto Rican, Latin American, or Asian American customs described in the literature. Plan an activity, such as a creative dramatization, that would allow children to experience the custom.

References

1 Alkema, Chester Jay. *Masks*. New York: Sterling, 1971.

2 Aoki, M. Elaine. "Are You Chinese? Are You Japanese? Or Are You Just a Mixed-Up Kid?"—Using Asian American Children's Literature." *The Reading Teacher* 34 (January 1981):382–85.

3 Baker, Gwendolyn C. "The Role of the School in Transmitting the Culture of All Learners in a Free and Democratic Society." *Educational Leadership* 36 (November 1978): 134–38.

4 Baylor, Byrd. *And It Is Still That Way*. New York: Scribner's, 1976.

5 Carlson, Ruth Kearney. *Emerging Humanity, Multi-Ethnic Literature for Children and Adolescents*. Dubuque, Ia.: Brown, 1972.

6 Courlander, Harold. *A Treasury of African Folklore*. New York: Crown, 1975.

7 Fisher, Frank L. "The Influences of Reading and Discussion on Attitudes of Fifth Graders toward American Indians." University Microfilm. Berkeley, Calif.: University of California, 1965.

8 Frankel, Herbert Lewis. "The Effects of Reading the Adventures of Huckleberry Finn on the Racial Attitudes of Selected Ninth Grade Boys," University Microfilm. Philadelphia: Temple University, 1972.

9 Gay, Geneva. "Viewing the Pluralistic Classroom as a Cultural Microcosm." *Educational Research Quarterly* (Winter 1978): 45–49.

10 Graham, Joe. *Grandmother's Tea: Mexican Herbal Remedies*. San Antonio: Institute of Texan Cultures, 1979.

11 Hunt, Kari, and Carlson, Bernice W. *Masks and Mask Makers*. Nashville, Tenn.: Abingdon, 1961.

12 Jacobs, Melville. *The Content and Style of an Oral Literature: Clackamas Chinook Myths and Tales*. Chicago: University of Chicago Press, 1959.

13 Kingsley, Mary. *West African Studies*. 3d ed. New York: Barnes and Noble, 1964.

14 Koeller, Shirley. "The Effect of Listening to Excerpts from Children's Stories about Mexican Americans on the Attitudes of Sixth Graders." *Journal of Educational Research* 70 (July 1977): 329–34.

15 Metcalfe, Ralph E. "The Western African Roots of Afro-American Music." *The Black Scholar* 1 (June, 1970): 16–25.

16 Newcomb, Franc J. *Navajo Folk Tales*. Santa Fe: Museum of Navajo Ceremonial Art, 1967. p. xvi.

17 Norton, Donna E., Lawson, Blanche, and Mohrmann, Sue. "The Development, Dissemination, and Evaluation of a Multi-Ethnic Curricular Model for Preservice Teachers, Inservice Teachers, and Elementary Children." New Orleans International Reading Association, April 1981.

18 Norton, Donna. "The Expansion and Evaluation of a Multiethnic Reading/Language Arts Program Designed for 5th, 6th, 7th, and 8th Grade Children." Meadows Foundation Grant, No. 55614, A Three Year Longitudinal Study, Texas A&M University, 1984–1987.

19 Noss, Philip A. "Description in Gbaya Literary Art." In *African Folklore*, edited by Richard Dorse. Bloomington, Ind.: Indiana University Press, 1972.

20 Opler, Morris Edward. *Myths and Tales of the Jicarilla Apache Indians*. Memoirs 31. New York: American Folklore Society, 1938.

21 Parsons, Elsie Clews. *Folktales of Andros Island, Bahamas*. New York: American Folklore Society, 1918.

22 Payne, G. C. *Adventures in Paper Modeling*. New York: Warne, 1966.

23 Pellowski, Anne. *The World of Storytelling*. New York: Bowker, 1977.

24 Reichard, Gladys A. *An Analysis of Coeur d'Alene Indian Myths*. Philadelphia: American Folklore Society, 1974.

25 Ross, Laura. *Mask-Making with Pantomime and Stories from American History*. New York: Lothrop, Lee & Shepard, 1975.

26 Schwartz, Carol S. "The Effect of Selected Black Poetry on Expressed Attitudes toward Blacks of Fifth and Sixth Grade White Suburban Children." *Dissertation Abstracts International* 33 (1973): 6077-A.

27 Seki, Keigo, ed. *Folktales of Japan*. Translated by Robert J. Adams. Chicago: University of Chicago, 1963. p. xv.

28 Sumpter, Magdalena Benavides. *Discovering Folklore through Community Resources*. Austin, Tex.: Dissemination and Assessment Center for Bilingual Education, Education Service Center, Region XII, 1978.

29 Tremearne, A. J. *Hausa Superstitions and Customs: An Introduction to the Folklore and the Folk*. London: Frank Cass, 1970.

CHILDREN'S LITERATURE

Asian American Literature

Asian Culture Centre for UNESCO. *Folktales from Asia for Children Everywhere*. Three vols. Weatherhill, 1977, 1976 (I:8–12 R:6). Folktales from many Asian countries.

Clark, Ann Nolan. *To Stand Against the Wind*. Viking, 1978 (I:11+ R:4). An eleven-year-old Vietnamese boy's memories return to the beautiful land of his birth before it is destroyed by war.

Davis, Daniel. *Behind Barbed Wire: The Imprisonment of Japanese Americans during World War II*. Dutton, 1982 (I:10+ R:7). Actions taken against Japanese Americans.

Dunn, Marylois, and Mayhar, Ardath. *The Absolutely Perfect Horse*. Harper, 1983 (I:9+ R:6). A horse helps family members, including an adopted Vietnamese boy, understand their values.

Friedman, Ina R. *How My Parents Learned to Eat*. Illustrated by Allen Say. Houghton Mifflin, 1984 (I:6–8 R:3). A humorous story about trying to eat with chopsticks or with knives and forks.

Lord, Bette Bao. *In the Year of the Boar and Jackie Robinson*. Illustrated by Marc Simont. Harper, 1984 (I:8–12 R:4). Developing a love for baseball helps a Chinese girl make friends in America.

Mosel, Arlene. *The Funny Little Woman*. Illustrated by Blair Lent. Dutton, 1972 (I:6–8 R:6). A Japanese folktale in which a woman steals a magic paddle.

Nhuong, Huynh Quang. *The Land I Lost: Adventures of a Boy in Vietnam*. Illustrated by Vo-Dinh Mai. Harper, 1982 (I:8–12 R:6). The author tells about his boyhood experiences in Vietnam.

Surat, Michele Maria. *Angel Child, Dragon Child*. Illustrated by Vo-Dinh Mai. Carnival/Raintree, 1983 (I:6–8 R:4). A young Vietnamese child learns to adjust to her American home.

Wallace, Ian. *Chin Chiang and the Dragon's Dance*. Atheneum, 1984 (I:6–9 R:6). A boy dreams of dancing on the first day of the Year of the Dragon.

Yagawa, Sumiko. *The Crane Wife*. Illustrated by Suekichi Akabas. Morrow, 1981 (I:all R:6). A traditional Japanese tale depicting the consequences of greed.

Yep, Lawrence. *Child of the Owl*. Harper & Row, 1977 (I:10+ R:7). Casey learns to respect her heritage and, most important, how to look deep inside herself.

———. *Dragonwings*. Harper & Row, 1975 (I:10+ R:6). In 1903 eight-year-old Moon Shadow helps his father build a flying machine.

———. *Sea Glass*. Harper & Row, 1979 (I:10+ R:6). Craig faces problems as he tries to make his father understand his desires.

———. *The Serpent's Children*. Harper, 1984 (I:10+ R:6). Set in 19th Century China. A girl finds she has strength to protect her family.

Black American Literature

Aardema, Verna. *Bringing the Rain to Kapiti Plain: A Nandi Tale*. Illustrated by Beatriz Vidal. Dial, 1981 (I:5–8). A cumulative tale from Kenya tells how a herdsman pierces a cloud with his arrow and brings rain to the parched land.

———. *Who's in Rabbit's House?* Illustrated by Leo and Diane Dillon. Dial, 1977 (I:7+ R:3). A Masai folktale illustrated as a play performed by villagers wearing masks.

———. *Why Mosquitoes Buzz in People's Ears*. Illustrated by Leo and Diane Dillon. Dial, 1975 (I:5–9 R:6). An African folktale explaining that buzz.

Adoff, Arnold. *Black Is Brown Is Tan*. Harper & Row, 1973 (I:5–7). A story in poetic form about an integrated family.

———. *Malcolm X*. Crowell, 1970 (I:7–12 R:5). A biography of the black leader.

Arkhurst, Joyce Cooper. *The Adventures of Spider: West African Folktales*. Illustrated by Jerry Pinkney. Little, Brown, 1964 (I:7–12 R:6). A collection of West African folk tales.

Bryan, Ashley. *I'm Going to Sing: Black American Spirituals*, Vol. 2. Atheneum, 1982 (I:all). Words, music, and illustrations present a black experience.

Campbell, Barbara. *A Girl Called Bob and A Horse Called Yoki*. Dial, 1982 (I:9–12 R:5). An eight-year-old girl saves a horse from the glue factory.

Carew, Jan. *Children of the Sun*. Illustrated by Leo and Diane Dillon. Little, Brown, 1980 (I:8+ R:6). Twin boys, the children of the sun, search the world to discover the values they wish to live by.

———. *The Third Gift*. Illustrated by Leo and Diane Dillon. Little, Brown, 1974 (I:7+ R:7). A beautifully illustrated tale of how the Jubas gained the gifts

I = Interest by age level;
R = Readability by grade level.

of work, beauty, imagination and faith.

Clifton, Lucille. *Everett Anderson's Goodbye*. Illustrated by Ann Grifalconi. Holt, Rinehart and Winston, 1983 (I:6–9). Written in poetic form, the story describes a boy's pain after his father's death.

Courlander, Harold. *The Crest and the Hide: And Other African Stories of Heroes, Chiefs, Bards, Hunters, Sorcerers, and Common People*. Illustrated by Monica Vachula. Coward-McCann, 1982 (I:8+ R:5). Twenty tales from the Ashanti, Swahili, Lega, Tswana, and Yoruba cultures of Africa.

Davis, Ossie. *Langston: A Play*. Delacorte, 1982 (I:10+). Scenes from Langston Hughes's life are presented in play format.

DeKay, James T. *Meet Martin Luther King, Jr*. Illustrated by Ted Burwell. Random House, 1969 (I:7–12 R:4). Stresses the magnitude of Martin Luther King's work and the reasons he fought against injustice.

Desbarats, Peter. *Gabrielle and Selena*. Illustrated by Nancy Grossman. Harcourt Brace Jovanovich, 1968 (I:5–8). A black girl and a white girl share a close friendship.

De Trevino, Elizabeth Borton. *I, Juan de Pareja*. Farrar, Straus & Giroux, 1965 (I:11+ R:7). Story is based on the true characters of the seventeenth-century Spanish painter Velazquez and his black African slave, Juan de Pareja.

Feelings, Muriel. *Jambo Means Hello: Swahili Alphabet Book*. Dial, 1974 (I:all). A beautiful book using the Swahili alphabet.

———. *Moja Means One: Swahali Counting Book*. Illustrated by Tom Feelings. Dial, 1971 (I:all). A beautiful book using Swahili numbers.

Flournoy, Valerie. *The Patchwork Quilt*. Illustrated by Jerry Pinkney. Dial, 1985 (I:5–8 R:4). Constructing a quilt brings a family together.

Fox, Paula. *How Many Miles to Babylon?* Illustrated by Paul Giovanopoulos. White, 1967 (I:8+ R:3). Ten-year-old James discovers the truth about who he really is when he is abducted by a gang of boys.

Fufuka, Karama. *My Daddy Is a Cool Dude*. Illustrated by Mahiri Fufuka. Dial, 1975. (I:7–9). An inner-city story.

Greene, Bette. *Philip Hall Likes Me. I Reckon Maybe*. Illustrated by Charles Lilly, Dial, 1974 (I:10+ R:4). Beth Lambert experiences her first crush.

Greenfield, Eloise. *Sister*. Illustrated by Moneta Barnett. Crowell, 1974 (I:8–12 R:5). Thirteen-year-old Doretha

reviews the memories written in her journal.

Grifalconi, Ann. *The Village of Round and Square Houses*. Little, Brown, 1986 (I:4–9 R:6). A why story from Cameroon.

Guy, Rosa. *Mother Crocodile*. Illustrated by John Steptoe. Delacorte, 1981 (I:5–9 R:6). A folktale from Senegal, West Africa stresses that elders' advice should be heeded.

Haley, Gail E. *A Story, A Story*. Atheneum, 1970 (I:6–10 R:6). An African tale about a spider man's bargain with Sky God.

Hamilton, Virginia. *The House of Dies Drear*. Illustrated by Eros Keith. Macmillan, 1968 (I:11+ R:4). A contemporary, suspenseful story about a family living in a home that was a station on the Underground Railroad.

———. *Junius Over Far*. Harper, 1985 (I:10+ R:5). A boy discovers his heritage when he goes to a Caribbean island looking for his grandfather.

———. *M. C. Higgins, the Great*. Macmillan, 1974 (I:12+ R:4). M.C. dreams of fleeing from the danger of a strip mining spoil heap, but decides to stay and build a wall to protect his home.

———. *The Magical Adventures of Pretty Pearl*. Harper & Row, 1983 (I:10+ R:5). A god-child disguises herself as a human and helps poor black people.

——— Retold By. *The People Could Fly: American Black Folktales*. Illustrated by Leo and Diane Dillon. Knopf, 1985 (I:9 R:6). A collection of tales told by or adapted by Black Americans.

———. *The Planet of Junior Brown*. Macmillan, 1971 (I:12+ R:6). Three outcasts from society create their own world in a secret basement room in a schoolhouse.

———. *The Time-Ago Tales of Jahdu*. Illustrated by Nonny Hogrogian. Macmillan, 1969 (I:6–11 R:3). Four stories about a powerful, mischievous being.

———. *Zeely*. Illustrated by Symeon Shimin. Macmillan, 1967 (I:8–12 R:4). Geeder is convinced that her tall, stately neighbor is a Watusi queen.

Harris, Joel Chandler. *The Adventures of Brer Rabbit*. Illustrated by Frank Baber. Rand McNally, 1980 (I:8+ R:6). A standard English version of thirty-one stories from Harris's collection.

Haskins, James. *Black Theater in America*. Crowell, 1982 (I:10+ R:7). Stresses contributions of black people to the theater.

Hurmence, Belinda. *A Girl Called Boy*. Houghton Mifflin, 1982 (I:10+ R:6).

A black girl goes back in time to 1853 and experiences slavery.

Jaquith, Priscilla. *Bo Rabbit Smart for True: Folktales from the Gullah*. Illustrated by Ed Young. Philomel, 1981 (I:all R:6). Four tales from the islands off the Georgia coast.

Keats, Ezra Jack. *John Henry: An American Legend*. Pantheon, 1965 (I:6–9 R:4). A picture storybook of the tall tale about the baby who grew up to be a steel-driving man.

Lewin, Hugh. *Jafta*. Illustrated by Lisa Kopper. Carolrhoda, 1983 (I:3–7 R:6). A young South African boy is compared to the animals in his environment.

———. *Jafta and the Wedding*. Illustrated by Lisa Kopper. Carolrhoda, 1983 (I:3–7 R:6). Pictures show a village wedding celebration.

———. *Jafta's Father*. Illustrated by Lisa Kopper. Carolrhoda, 1983 (I:3–7 R:6). Jafta's father plays with him when he returns to the village.

———. *Jafta's Mother*. Illustrated by Lisa Kopper. Carolrhoda, 1983 (I:3–7 R:6). Jafta's mother is compared to the South African environment.

McDermott, Gerald. *Anansi the Spider: A Tale from the Ashanti*. Holt, Rinehart & Winston, 1972 (I:7–9). A colorfully illustrated African folktale.

Mathis, Sharon Bell. *The Hundred Penny Box*. Illustrated by Leo and Diane Dillon. Viking, 1975 (I:6–9 R:3). Young Michael loved to hear his elderly aunt tell the story of each penny that stood for her 100 years.

Murray, Michele. *Nellie Cameron*. Illustrated by Leonora E. Prince. Seabury, 1971 (I:8–12 R:3). Nellie Cameron's desire is to learn to read.

Musgrove, Margaret. *Ashanti to Zulu: African Traditions*. Illustrated by Leo and Diane Dillon. Dial, 1976 (I:7–12). Traditions of twenty-six African peoples in alphabetical order.

Patterson, Lillie. *Frederick Douglass: Freedom Fighter*. Garrard, 1965 (I:6–9 R:3). The biography of the great Black American leader.

Steptoe, John. *Daddy Is a Monster . . . Sometimes*. Lippincott, 1980 (I:4–7 R:3). Two children remember the times when their daddy gets angry and takes on his monster image.

———. *Stevie*. Harper & Row, 1969 (I:3–7 R:3). Robert is unhappy when Stevie plays with his toys and wants his own way.

Taylor, Mildred D. *Roll of Thunder, Hear My Cry*. Dial, 1976 (I:10+ R:6). A black Mississippi family in 1933 experiences humiliating and frightening situations, but retains its pride.

Tobias, Tobi. *Arthur Mitchell*. Illustrated by Carol Byard. Crowell, 1975 (I:7–9 R:5). A biography of the founder of Dance Theatre of Harlem.

Wagner, Jane. *J. T.* Photographs by Gordon Parks, Jr. Dell, 1969 (I:7–11 R:6). Ten-year-old J. T. discovers himself as he cares for a battered cat and interacts with people in his inner-city neighborhood.

Walter, Mildred Pitt. *Brother to the Wind*. Illustrated by Diane and Leo Dillon, Lothrop, Lee & Shepard, 1985 (I:all R:3). An African boy wishes to fly.

Ward, Leila. *I Am Eyes, Ni Macho*. Illustrated by Nonny Hogrogian. Greenwillow, 1978 (I:3–7 R:1). An African child wakes to the marvelous sights of her land.

Weik, Mary Hays. *The Jazz Man*. Illustrated by Ann Grifalconi. Atheneum, 1966 (I:7–10 R:6). When the Jazz Man moves into the apartment with the wonderful yellow walls, life seems to change for a crippled boy living in Harlem.

Yates, Elizabeth. *Amos Fortune, Free Man*. Illustrated by Nora S. Unwin. Dutton, 1950 (I:10+ R:6). An African becomes a slave in Boston.

Hispanic American Literature

Aardema, Verna. *The Riddle of the Drum: A Tale from Tizapán, Mexico*. Illustrated by Tony Chen. Four Winds, 1979 (I:6–10 R:3). The man who marries the king's daughter must guess the kind of leather in a drum.

Behrens, June. *Fiesta!* Photographs by Scott Taylor. Children's, 1978 (I:5–8 R:4). Photographs of the Cinco de Mayo fiesta.

Belpré, Pura. *Once in Puerto Rico*. Illustrated by Christine Price. Warne, 1973 (I:8–12 R:5). A collection of Puerto Rican tales.

———. *The Rainbow-Colored Horse*. Illustrated by Antonio Martorell. Warne, 1978 (I:6–10). Three favors granted by a horse allow Pio to win the hand of the Don Nicanor's daughter.

———. *Santiago*. Illustrated by Symeon Shimin. Warne, 1969 (I:5–8 R:5). A young boy, his mother, and teacher share information about Puerto Rico.

Bierhorst, John, ed. *Black Rainbow: Legends of the Incas and Myths of Ancient Peru*. Farrar, Straus and Giroux, 1976

(I:10+ R:7). Twenty traditional tales.

———, ed. *The Hungry Woman: Myths and Legends of the Aztecs*. Morrow, 1984 (I:12+ R:6). Tales include creation myths and legends about the conquest.

———, trans. *Spirit Child: A Story of the Nativity*. Illustrated by Barbara Cooney. Morrow, 1984 (I:8–12 R:6). Pre-Columbian illustrations accompany an Aztec story.

Clark, Ann Nolan. *Paco's Miracle*. Illustrated by Agnes Tait. Farrar, Straus & Giroux, 1962 O.P. (I:8–12 R:3). Paco learns to love a family in nearby Santa Fe.

———. *Year Walk*. Viking, 1975 (I:10+ R:7). A Spanish Basque sheepherder faces loneliness as he takes his 2,500 sheep across the desert into the high country.

DeMessieres, Nicole. *Reina the Galgo*. Dutton, 1981 (I:10+ R:6). An eleven-year old girl describes her experiences living in Peru.

de Paola, Tomie. *The Lady of Guadalupe*. Holiday, 1980 (I:8+ R:6). A traditional Mexican tale.

Dewey, Ariane. *The Thunder God's Son: A Peruvian Folktale*. Greenwillow, 1981 (I:5–7 R:5). Acuri is sent down to earth to learn about the people.

Ets, Marie Hall, and Labastida, Aurora. *Nine Days to Christmas: A Story of Mexico*. Illustrated by Marie Hall Ets. Viking, 1959 (I:5–8 R:3). Ceci is going to have her first Posada with her own piñata.

Gemming, Elizabeth. *Lost City in the Clouds: The Discovery of Machu Picchu*. Illustrated by Mike Eagle. Putnam, 1980 (I:10+ R:6). The story of Hiram Bingham's discovery of the Inca city.

Griego y Maestas, José, and Anaya, Rudolfo A. *Cuentos: Tales from the Hispanic Southwest*. Illustrated by Jaime Valdez. Museum of New Mexico, 1980 (I:9+ R:5). A collection of tales.

Griego, Margot C. *Tortillitas Para Mama and Other Spanish Nursery Rhymes*. Illustrated by Barbara Cooney. Holt, 1981 (I:3–7). Nursery rhymes in Spanish and English.

Hall, Lynn. *Danza!* Scribner, 1981 (I:10+ R:6). A boy and his horse share life on a farm in Puerto Rico.

Hargreaves, Pat. *The Caribbean and Gulf of Mexico*. Silver Burdett, 1980 (I:10+ R:6). Informational photographs and text.

Hinojosa, Francisco, Adapted By. *The Old Lady Who Ate People*. Illustrated by Leonel Maciel. Little, Brown, 1984

(I:all R:6). Four frightening folktales from Mexico.

Jagendorf, M. A. and Boggs, R. S. *The King of the Mountains: A Treasury of Latin American Folk Stories*. Vanguard, 1960 (I:9+ R:6). A collection of tales from twenty-six countries.

Krumgold, Joseph. *. . . And Now Miguel*. Illustrated by Jean Charlot. Crowell, 1953 (I:10+ R:3). Miguel Chavez is a member of a proud sheep-raising family.

Kurtycz, Marcos and Kobeh, Ana Gariá. *Tigers and Opossums*. Little, Brown, 1984 (I:all R:8). Animal tales from Mexico.

Lindop, Edmund. *Cuba*. Watts, 1980 (I:10+ R:6). History, geography, and current information.

Mangurian, David. *Children of the Incas*. Macmillan, 1979 (I:7–12 R:3). Photographs and text about a boy in Peru.

Markun, Patricia Maloney. *Central America and Panama*. Watts, 1983 (I:10+ R:6). Geography, history, economics, and politics of the area.

———. *The Panama Canal*. Watts, 1979 (I:8–12 R:5). History of and current information about shipping through the canal.

Martinello, Marian L., and Nesmith, Samuel P. *With Domingo Leal in San Antonio 1734*. The University of Texas, Institute of Texas Cultures at San Antonio, 1979 (I:8+ R:4). Results of research investigating the lives of Spanish settlers who arrived in Texas in the 1730s.

Meltzer, Milton. *The Hispanic Americans*. Photography by Morrie Camhi and Catherine Noren. Crowell, 1982 (I:9–12 R:6). The influence in America of Puerto Ricans, Chicanos, and Cubans.

Meyer, Carolyn and Gallenkamp, Charles. *The Mystery of the Ancient Maya*. Atheneum, 1985 (I:10 R:8). Early explorers and discoveries.

Millard, Anne. *The Incas*. Illustrated by Richard Hook. Warwick, 1980 (I:10+ R:6). Text and illustrations show the accomplishments of the Incas.

Mohr, Nicholasa. *Felita*. Illustrated by Ray Cruz. Dial, 1979 (I:9–12 R:2). Felita is unhappy when her family moves to a new neighborhood.

O'Dell, Scott. *Carlota*. Houghton Mifflin, 1981 (I:10+ R:6). A high-spirited Spanish-American girl fights beside her father during the days of the Mexican War in early California.

Politi, Leo. *The Nicest Gift*. Scribner's, 1973 (I:5–8 R:6). Carbitos lives in the barrio of East Los Angeles with his family and his dog Blanco.

———. *Pedro, the Angel of Olvera Street*. Scribner's, 1946 (I:4–8 R:4). Pedro lives on Olvera Street in Los Angeles.

———. *Song of the Swallows*. Scribner's, 1949 (I:5–8 R:4). Juan lives in Capistrano, California. Excellent illustrations of Spanish architecture.

Rutland, Jonathan. *Take a Trip to Spain*. Watts, 1980 (I:6–10 R: 3). Color photographs of Spain.

Schon, Isabel, ed. *Doña Blanca and Other Hispanic Nursery Rhymes and Games*. Denison, 1983 (I:4–8). Bilingual presentation of rhymes.

Singer, Julia. *We All Come from Puerto Rico*. Atheneum, 1977 (I:9–12 R:5). A photo-essay describes the people of Puerto Rico.

Stein, R. Conrad. *Enchantment of the World: Mexico*. Children's Press, 1984 (I:9+ R:5). Colored photographs and text describe geography, history, economy, culture, and people.

Native American Literature

Aliki. *Corn Is Maize: The Gift of the Indians*. Crowell, 1976 (I:6–8 R:2). A history of corn, how it grows, and how it was first used.

Ashabranner, Brent. *To Live in Two Worlds: American Indian Youth Today*. Photographs by Paul Conklin. Dodd, Mead, 1984 (I:10+ R:7). Indian youth tell about their own lives.

———. *Morning Star, Black Sun: The Northern Cheyenne Indians and America's Energy Crisis*. Photographs by Paul Conklin. Dodd, Mead, 1982 (I:10+ R:7). Traces history of the Northern Cheyenne and discusses fight to save their lands.

Baker, Betty. *Rat Is Dead and Ant Is Sad*. Illustrated by Mamoru Funai. Harper & Row, 1981 (I:6–8 R:2). A cumulative Pueblo Indian tale.

Baker, Olaf. *Where the Buffaloes Begin*. Illustrated by Stephen Gammell. Warne, 1981 (I:all R:6). A story about the lake where the buffaloes were created.

Batherman, Muriel. *Before Columbus*. Houghton Mifflin, 1981 (I:6–9 R:5). Illustrations and text present information about North American inhabitants revealed from archaeological explorations.

Baylor, Byrd. *And It Is Still That Way: Legends Told by Arizona Indian Children*. Scribner's, 1976 (I:all R:3). A collection of tales told by Native American children.

———. *Before You Came This Way*. Illustrated by Tom Bahti. Dutton, 1969 (I:all). Poetry describes the Native American petroglyphs on the canyon walls of the Southwest.

———. *The Desert Is Theirs*. Illustrated by Peter Parnall. Scribner's, 1975. (I:all). The life of the Papago Indians is captured in illustrations and text.

———. *God on Every Mountain*. Illustrated by Carol Brown, Scribner's, 1981 (I:6–10 R:5). Southwest Indian folktales about the sacred mountains.

———. *Hawk, I'm Your Brother*. Illustrated by Peter Parnall. Scribner's, 1976 (I:all). Rudy Soto would like to glide through the air like a hawk, wrapped up in the wind.

———. *Moonsong*. Illustrated by Ronald Himler. Scribner's, 1982 (I:all). Written in poetic style, this Pima Indian tale tells how coyote was born of the moon.

———. *The Other Way to Listen*. Illustrated by Peter Parnall. Scribner's, 1978. (I:all). If one listens carefully, nature is heard.

———. *They Put on Masks*. Illustrated by Jerry Ingram. Scribner's, 1974. (I:all). The masks of the Eskimo, Northwest Coast, Iroquois, Apache, Hopi, Zuni, and Yaqui are presented in verse and illustrations.

———. *When Clay Sings*. Illustrated by Tom Bahti. Scribner's, 1972. (I:all). A poetic telling of the ancient way of life stimulated by designs on prehistoric Indian pottery found in the Southwest desert.

Belting, Natalia. *Whirlwind Is a Ghost Dancing*. Illustrated by Leo and Diane Dillon. Dutton, 1974 o.p. (I:all R:3). A poetic text depicting the lore of many Native American tribes.

Bierhorst, John. *A Cry from The Earth: Music of the North American Indians*. Four Winds, 1979 (I:all). A collection of Indian songs of North America.

———. *The Ring in the Prairie, A Shawnee Legend*. Illustrated by Leo and Diane Dillon. Dial, 1970 (I:all R:6). One of the most skilled Indian hunters discovers a mysterious circle in an opening in the forest.

———. ed. *The Sacred Path: Spells, Prayers, and Power Songs of the American Indians*. Morrow, 1983 (I:8+). A collection of poems, prayers, and songs.

Brown, Marion Marsh. *Homeward the Arrow's Flight*. Abingdon, 1980 (I:10 R:6). The story of the first female Native American to become a doctor of Western medicine.

Bulla, Clyde Robert, and Syson, Michael. *Conquista!* Illustrated by Ronald Himler. Crowell, 1978 (I:6–10 R:2). A story about how a young Native American boy might have experienced his first horse at the time of Coronado.

Cleaver, Elizabeth. *The Enchanted Caribou*. Atheneum, 1985 (I:6–10 R:6). An Inuit tale of transformation.

Coatsworth, Emerson, and Coatsworth, David, comps. *The Adventures of Nanabush: Ojibway Indian Stories*. Illustrated by Francis Kagige. Atheneum, 1980 (I:8+ R:6). Sixteen tales told by Ojibway tribal elders.

Curtis, Edward S. *The Girl Who Married a Ghost and Other Tales from the North American Indian*. Edited by John Bierhorst. Four Winds, 1978 (I:9+ R:5). Tales from the Plains, California, the Northwest, the Southwest, and Alaska.

de Paola, Tomie. *The Legend of the Bluebonnet*. Putnam's, 1983 (I:all R:6). A Comanche tale in which unselfish actions are rewarded.

Dodge, Nanabah Chee. *Morning Arrow*. Illustrated by Jeffrey Lunge. Lothrop, Lee & Shepard, 1975 (I:7–10 R:3). Morning Arrow is a ten-year-old Navaho boy who is devoted to his partially blind grandmother.

Fall, Thomas. *Jim Thorpe*. Illustrated by John Gretzer. Crowell, 1970 (I:7–9 R:2). An illustrated biography of the great Native American athlete.

Fritz, Jean. *The Double Life of Pocahontas*. Illustrated by Ed Young. Putnam, 1983 (I:8–10 R:7). A biography of Pocahontas focuses on her involvement with two cultures.

George, Jean Craighead. *The Talking Earth*. Harper & Row, 1983 (I:10+ R:6). An Indian girl tries to discover her heritage.

Goble, Paul. *Buffalo Woman*. Bradbury, 1984 (I:all R:6). A bond between animals and humans is developed in a tale from the Great Plains.

———. *The Gift of the Sacred Dog*. Bradbury, 1980 (I:all R:6). The Sioux tale about how the horse was given to the people.

———. *The Girl Who Loved Wild Horses*. Bradbury, 1978. (I:6–10 R:5). A picture storybook about an Indian girl's attachment to horses.

Grant, Matthew G. *Squanto: The Indian Who Saved the Pilgrims*. Illustrated by John Nelson and Harold Henriksen. Publications Associates, 1974 (I:6–9 R:3). A simple biography of the Wampamoag Indian who helped the settlers at Plymouth Colony.

Grinnell, George Bird. *The Whistling Skeleton: American Indian Tales of the*

Supernatural. Edited by John Bierhorst. Illustrated by Robert Andrew Parker. Four Winds, 1982 (I:10+ R:6). Nine mystery tales told by nineteenth century storytellers.

Harris, Christie. *Mouse Woman and the Vanished Princesses*. Illustrated by Douglas Tait. Atheneum, 1976 (I:10+ R:6). Six tales from the northwestern coast of North America.

————. *The Trouble with Adventurers*. Illustrated by Douglas Tait. Atheneum, 1982 (I:10+ R:6). A collection of stories drawn from the Northwest Coast tribes.

Haseley, Dennis. *The Scared One*. Illustrated by Deborah Howland, Warne, 1983 (I:5–8 R:6). A Native American boy faces and overcomes fear and ridicule.

Highwater, Jamake. *Anpao: An American Indian Odyssey*. Illustrated by Fritz Scholder. Lippincott, 1977 (I:12+ R:5). Anpao journeys across the history of Native American traditional tales in order to search for his destiny.

————. *The Ceremony of Innocence*. Harper & Row, 1985 (I:12+ R:6). Part two of the Ghost Horse Cycle.

————. *I Wear the Morning Star*. Harper & Row, 1986 (I:12+ R:6). Part three of the Ghost Horse Cycle.

————. *Legend Days*. Harper & Row, 1984 (I:12+ R:6). A Northern Plains Indian is the focus of this part one of the Ghost Horse Cycle.

————. *Moonsong Lullaby*. Photographs by Marcia Keegan. Lothrop, Lee & Shepard, 1981 (I:all). Color photographs show the animals and other activities as the moon shines.

Hodges, Margaret. *The Fire Bringer: A Paiute Indian Legend*. Illustrated by Peter Parnall. Little, Brown, 1972 (I:7–10 R:6). Coyote leads the Paiutes on a dangerous quest for fire.

Hudson, Jan. *Sweetgrass*. Tree Frog, 1984 (I:10+ R:4). A Blackfeet girl grows up during the winter of a smallpox epidemic in 1837.

Jassem, Kate. *Sacajawea, Wilderness Guide*. Illustrated by Jan Palmer. Troll Associates, 1979 (I:6–9 R:2). An illustrated biography of the Shoshone woman who guided the Lewis and Clark Expedition.

Lee, Betsy. *Charles Eastman: The Story of an American Indian*. Dillon, 1979 (I:8 R:5). A biography of a famous doctor, writer, and worker for Native American rights.

Marrin, Albert. *War Clouds in the West: Indians & Cavalrymen, 1860–1890*. Atheneum, 1984 (I:10+ R:6). A history of the conflict.

Miles, Miska. *Annie and the Old One*. Illustrated by Peter Parnall. Little, Brown, 1971 (I:6–8 R:3). Annie's love for her Navaho grandmother causes her to prevent the completion of a rug that she associates with the probable death of her grandmother.

Mowat, Farley. *Lost in the Barrens*. Illustrated by Charles Geer. McClelland and Stewart, 1966, 1984 (I:9+ R:6). A Cree Indian boy and his friend are lost in Northern Canada.

O'Dell, Scott. *Sing Down the Moon*. Houghton Mifflin, 1970 (I:10+ R:6). A young Navaho girl tells of the 1864 forced march of her people.

Poatgieter, Alice Hermina. *Indian Legacy: Native American Influences on World Life and Culture*. Messner, 1981 (I:10+ R:7). Native North and South American contributions to democratic attitudes, agriculture, and culture.

Robbins, Ruth. *How the First Rainbow Was Made*. Parnassus, 1980 (I:6–9 R:6). A California Indian tale tells how Coyote got the Old Man Above to make the first rainbow.

Robinson, Gail. *Raven the Trickster: Legends of the North American Indians*. Illustrated by Joanna Troughton. Atheneum, 1982 (I:8–12 R:6). Nine tales from the Northwest Indian tribes.

Rockwood, Joyce. *Groundhog's Horse*. Illustrated by Victor Kalin. Holt, Rinehart & Winston, 1978 (I:7–12 R:4). A young Cherokee boy's horse is stolen by the Creeks in 1750.

Schweitzer, Byrd Baylor. *One Small Blue Bead*. Illustrated by Symeon Shimin. Macmillan, 1965 (I:all). An old man sitting at a prehistoric campfire ponders the possibility of other humans besides his people.

Sneve, Virginia Driving Hawk. *High Elk's Treasure*. Illustrated by Oren Lyons. Holiday, 1972 (I:8–12 R:6). A dream beginning in the autumn of 1876 is renewed in the 1970s when Joe High Elk's family expands the herd of palomino horses.

————. *Jimmy Yellow Hawk*. Illustrated by Oren Lyons. Holiday, 1972 (I:6–10 R:5). Awarded first prize in its category by the Council on Interracial Books for Children, this story is about a contemporary Sioux boy who lives on an Indian reservation in South Dakota.

————. *When Thunder Spoke*. Illustrated by Oren Lyons. Holiday, 1974 (I:8–12 R:4). A fifteen-year-old Sioux boy experiences conflict between the old ways and the new.

Speare, Elizabeth George. *The Sign of the Beaver*. Houghton, 1983 (I:8–12 R:5). A white boy survives through the help of a Native American friend.

Spencer, Paula Underwood. *Who Speaks for Wolf*. Illustrated by Frank Howell, Tribe of Two Press, 1983 (I:all). A Native American learning story.

Steptoe, John. *The Story of Jumping Mouse*. Lothrop, Lee & Shepard, 1984 (I:all R:4). A Great Plains Indian legend.

Tobias, Tobi. *Maria Tallchief*. Illustrated by Michael Hampshire. Crowell, 1970 (I:7–12 R:4). A biography of the great prima ballerina who was also an Osage Indian.

Toye, William. *The Loon's Necklace*. Illustrated by Elizabeth Cleaver. Oxford, 1977 (I:all R:5). This tale explains how the loon received the lovely shell markings around its neck and across its wings.

Wallas, James. *Kwakiutl Legends*. Recorded by Pamela Whitaker, Hancock House, 1981 (I:all R:4). Tales from British Columbia told by Chief Wallas of the Quatsino tribe.

Whitaker, Muriel, ed. *Stories from the Canadian North*. Illustrated by Vlasta Van Kampen. Hartwig, 1980 (I:10+ R:6). Anthology includes tales of native peoples as well as other northern authors.

12

Nonfiction: Biographies and Informational Books

☐
FROM WHO'S-WHO TO HOW-TO
☐
INVOLVING CHILDREN IN NONFICTIONAL
LITERATURE

From Who's-Who to How-To

☐
BIOGRAPHIES

☐
INFORMATIONAL BOOKS

CURIOSITY AND THE DESIRE TO MAKE discoveries about their ever-expanding world strongly motivate children to read. Books of nonfiction encourage and satisfy children's desire to seek answers, to look at the world in a new way, to discover laws of nature and society, and to identify with people different from themselves.

BIOGRAPHIES

Many children who enjoy reading well-written biographies about believable people feel as if the biographical subjects become their own personal friends. Often these children carry with them into adulthood a love of nonfiction that portrays the lives of interesting people with whom they can identify and from whom they can continue to learn more about our fascinating world. Biography offers children the high adventure and engrossing human drama that fiction also supplies, but with the special satisfaction of knowing that, in the best biographies, the people and events described are "really really real."

Writers of biographies have a vast pool of real people from which to choose. There are brave men and women who conquer seas, discover new continents, and explore space. There are equally brave and intelligent women and men who fight discrimination, change lives through their ministering or inventions, and overcome handicaps in their efforts to achieve. The way writers of children's literature choose to portray these figures, however, changes with historical time periods.

Changing Ideas about the Value and Content of Biographies for Children

A brief review of biographies for children in recent centuries shows that the authors of biographies have been influenced by prevalent social attitudes toward children, beliefs about the purposes for writing and for sharing children's biographies, beliefs about children's moral education, and attitudes about what is appropriate content.

Children's biographies written in the seventeenth through the nineteenth centuries in Europe and North America were affected by the didactic themes of the Puritan era, by the Victorian emphasis on duty to God and parents, by values associated with the American frontier, and by the belief that children should be educated in a highly structured environment in which the teacher molds the student, the student follows rules, and the adult authority provides punishment for any disobedience. In addition, early biographers believed that children's biographies should be teaching tools for religious, political, or social education. Consequently, emulation of biographical heroes was considered desirable (16). Many pre–twentieth century biographies reflected the belief that literature should save children's souls. Jon Stott (19) concludes that this time produced numerous "biographies of good little children who died early and went to Heaven and of bad little children who died early and went to Hell" (p. 177). For example, in 1671, leading Puritan writer James Janeway published a series of stories about children who died at an early age after leading saintly lives.

In the mid-1800s, the religious zeal of many early Americans was replaced by concern for a new nation and the acquisition of the "American dream." Salvation was no longer the primary goal; the supreme achievements were the acquisition of power, fame, and wealth. Consequently, biography changed from a religious tool to a political tool.

The early twentieth century brought new insights into child development. The developing science of psychology emphasized the vulnerability of youth and the need for protective legislation. Religious training placed less emphasis on sinfulness and more emphasis on the importance of moral development and responsibility toward others. In keeping with these ideas, biographers also protected children from the indiscretions of biographical subjects. Because idealized heroes were still believed to be desirable and necessary role models, biographers avoided sensitive areas concerning political beliefs and private lives. Taboos imposed by society included infamous people, unsavory or undistinguishing actions, and controversial subjects. Furthermore, in the early 1900s, as in earlier periods of American history, the contributions of both female and nonwhite Americans were either not highly regarded or were considered too controversial. Traditional social patterns also kept most women and members of minority groups out of the positions of power and fame that produced what American society considered the most appropriate subjects of biography. Consequently, few biographies dealt with women, Black Americans, Native Americans, and other members of ethnic and racial minorities.

Biographies of most political leaders published through the 1960s continued to emulate the role model required for political or social instruction. Omissions and distortions allowed biographers to stress important contributions, to emphasize accomplishments, and to highlight dates of the accomplishments rather than to explore human motives. Literary critic Margery Fisher (7) maintains that such biographies were carefully controlled by the establishment that exercises a powerful, invisible influence on the field of biography for children.

In an effort to increase children's ability to empathize with political heroes, mostly white and male, biographers writing for young readers often focused on the boyhood years of their characters. Even these stories, however, tended to glorify later accomplishments. The titles of several biographies for children published by Bobbs-Merril before 1970 reflect the biographers' knowledge of accomplishments these boy heroes would achieve: *Thomas Paine: Common Sense Boy* and *John D. Rockefeller: Boy Financier*.

Prior to the 1970s, most biographies written for children adhered to the philosophy that emulation of favorably depicted people provided necessary role models. During the late 1960s and the 1970s, traditional social, family, and personal values were changing. The new openness was reflected in children's fiction. Hence, the previous instructional uses of, and role models in, children's biography were challenged. Some literary critics, educators, and authors of children's biographies maintained that emulation not only distorted history, but also distorted human development. According to this argument, if men and women were shown only in a favorable light, children would gain an inaccurate impression of human development; and, since such an approach implied that the great people were all gone, children would assume that because they themselves make human errors, they themselves could never be great. In an effort to overcome past shortcomings in children's biographies, Marilyn Jurich (13) advocated a greater variety in the choice of subjects—including great people who were not famous, ordinary people, and antiheroes—as well as a fuller and more honest treatment of all subjects.

As with realistic fiction, educators, authors, publishers, and parents today have different opinions about what the content of children's biographies should be. Several authors have criticized biographies that avoid controversial facts about people's backgrounds, including sensitive areas about their political beliefs or their private lives. William Anderson and Patrick Groff (1) discuss the taboos imposed by society upon biographies written for children. Often these taboos are against writing about infamous people or showing the "dark, unsavory, or undistinguished side" of a great person's life. Jean Fritz (10), a well-known author of historical biographies for young children, says:

Biographies have for the most part lagged behind other types of children's literature, bogged down, for one thing, by didacticism. Famous men and women must be shown in their best colors so children can emulate them. The idea of emulation has been a powerful factor in determining the nature of biography for children; you see the word over and over again in textbooks and courses of study. And I think it has done great harm in distorting history and breeding cynicism; the great men are all gone, the implication is. Because history is old, educators are often guilty of simply repeating it instead of taking a fresh look at it. Because it is complicated, they tend to simplify by watering down material for children, whereas children need more meat rather than less, but selected for their own interests. This, of course, involves original research, a great deal of it, which twenty years ago, I think was rather rare in children's biographies. (p. 125)

Students of children's literature now find more biographies that develop many sides of a person's character—as well as more biographies about people who are female and nonwhite, like many young readers themselves. Readers may discover, through the work of authors such as Jean Fritz, that the heroes of biography were real people who, like other humans, often demonstrated negative qualities. In fact, a biographical subject who is a believable human being may be easier for children to emulate than a subject who is not.

Gertrude B. Herman (11) relates children's changing understanding of biography to their own stages of personal development. She maintains that until children are about eight years old, they have difficulty stepping out of their own time and space to explore the lives of real people whom they most likely can never meet. Herman believes that children in the fourth through sixth grades read biographies with increasing understanding and self-identification, as long as the books are about people they are interested in and the author has written in a lively style that holds children's interest. Then in adolescence, says Herman, children are—

finally ready for causes . . . and for all those fascinating persons who are not necessarily models of perfection, but who are human beings through whose doubts and triumphs, courage or villainy, victories or defeats, young people may try on personalities, life styles, and modes of thought and commitment. It is in investigating, in shifting and winnowing facts and ideas, in empathizing with the deeds and sufferings of others that growth is helped along—intellectual, emotional, and spiritual growth. It is through this integrative function that biography and autobiography, honesty presented with literary and artistic merit, can make important contributions to self-integration and social realization. The testimony of many individuals over many years supports a conviction that young people have much to gain from reading about real human beings in all their complexity, with all their sometimes troubled lives. (p. 88)

Evaluating Biographies for Children

Like other literature, biographies should be evaluated according to the criteria for good literature discussed in chapter three and should carefully avoid negative stereotypes based on gender, race, ethnicity, and physical ability. Additional concerns relate specifically to this genre of literature. With regard to literary elements, the development of characterization is of primary concern, and authors of biography must of course place special emphasis on accuracy of detail and sound research methods. Likewise, adults who select biographies for children should be concerned with the accuracy of the information, the worthiness of the subject, and the balance between fact and story line.

Characterization. Margaret Fleming and Jo McGinnis (8) compare the writing of a good biography to the artistry required in painting a portrait in which the "style and setting only enhance the portrayal of the subject. The development of character is the primary focus" (p. xi). Biographers, like other authors, have a responsibility to develop multifaceted, three-dimensional portrayals of their subjects. Biographers, unlike fictional authors, are restricted from inventing characters and indicating unsupported thoughts and actions. Elizabeth Robertson and Jo McGinnis (17) warn against unsupported characterization and provide several guidelines for evaluating characterization: "In biography, the writer can only infer from the actions of the subject and other characters what might be going on in the person's head. Look for evidence that the biographer is overstepping the bounds of scholarly writing in this respect" (p. 19).

Robertson and McGinnis recommend that readers analyze the supporting characters in a biography and their influence on the main character by answering the following questions: "Who are the people who most influenced the life of the subject? How important were these people in the development of the subject's character? Were they positive or negative influences? How are they developed as characters? What differences are there between a fictional development of character and this non-fictional work? How would life for the subject have been different if these influences had not been present?" (p. 19)

Another revealing way to analyze the characterization in a biography, according to Robertson and McGinnis, is to examine the self-revelations of the biographical subject by analyzing the sub-

THROUGH THE EYES OF AN AUTHOR

On Writing Biography

JEAN FRITZ, biographer of early American patriots, creates believable characters by admitting their foibles as well as their strengths.

THE REASON FOR WRITing biography for children is the same as for writing biography for adults: to explore human behavior; to come to grips with specific characters interrelating with their specific times. This is not as obvious as it sounds. It was once a commonly held assumption (one that still persists in some quarters) that biographies written for children should portray idealized heroes and heroines, models held up by the adult world to inspire children to attain virtue and, by implication, its concomitant rewards. Furthermore, according to some educators, the motivation of characters should not be examined, only their deeds.

Such an approach, it seems to me, is dull, unrealistic, and unfair. Children look for clues to life. They want the truth, they need the truth, and they deserve it. So I try to present characters honestly with their paradoxes and their complexities, their strengths and their weaknesses. To do this, I involve myself in as much research as I would if I were writing a biography for adults.

Contrary to what I call "old-fashioned" biography for children, I do not invent dialogue. I use dialogue only when I can document it. If the text is meaty enough, I do not think that children need facts dressed up in fictional trimmings. Indeed, children welcome hard, specific facts that bring characters to life—not only the important facts but those small vivid details that have a way of lighting up an event or a personality. Had I been present, for instance, to hear Patrick Henry give his famous "liberty or death" speech, I would certainly have been impressed by his dramatic oratory, but I would also have remembered the man in the balcony who became so excited, he spit a wad of tobacco into the audience below. The trivial and the significant generally travel hand in hand and indeed I suspect that most people find that memory of trivial off-the-record detail serves to nail down memory itself. I think of history and biography as *story* and am convinced that the best stories are the true ones.

ject's own thoughts about himself or herself as reflected in autobiographies, journals, essays, speeches, and/or letters. Does the subject perceive himself or herself in a different way from that developed by the biographer? What might account for any differences in characterization?

Factual Accuracy. Comparisons between biographies for children and reputable biographies for adults, between one biography for children and another on the same subject, and between a biography and reference books often reveal differences in basic facts. Ann W. Moore (14) reports that "errors in contemporary children's biographies fall into one of the following three categories: (1) inaccuracies in numbers, dates, and names, items easily checked in reference books or authorized and/or reputable adult titles; (2) incomplete, unclear, or misleading statements caused by attempts at simplification; and (3) patently false, incorrect information" (p. 34). Moore emphasizes the need for writers and publishers to improve the accuracy of biographies for children and for reviewers to check the facts against reputable sources. Biographies have a special responsibility to be accurate and authentic as they depict person and setting. This task is so important and demanding that May Hill Arbuthnot and Dorothy M. Broderick (2) say that biographers "should be prepared to spend months, and probably longer, in study and research before touching the typewriter" (p. 225). Their extensive research should include study of recent scholarly works and what their subjects and others of the time actually said and wrote.

According to biographer Olivia Coolidge (5), authors of biographical literature must also distinguish a fact from a judgment because "a good biography is also concerned with the effect its hero has on other people, with environment and background, with the nature of . . . achievements, and their value. I find that I examine facts in all these and many other spheres before I form judgments and that it needs great care to do what sounds quite easy, namely to distinguish a fact from a judgment" (p. 146). Coolidge concludes her concern over fact and judgment by saying:

It simply seems that I need to know everything possible—because knowledge may affect judgment or because I am not yet really certain what I shall use or omit. In other words, I find it necessary to have a habit of worrying about facts, small or large, because my

buildings are made up of these bricks, stones, or even pebbles. (p. 148)

An author's search for accuracy should include a wide range of sources, and it is helpful if the biographer includes a bibliography in the book. For example, Leonard Wibberley's bibliography for *Time of the Harvest: Thomas Jefferson, the Years 1801–1826* includes numerous books about Jefferson, a book written by Jefferson's great-granddaughter, and sources of information about figures around Jefferson, including Aaron Burr, John Marshall, and James Madison. Other authors often mention research in historical societies, newspaper records, diaries, and letters. Often they visit the actual locations. Even simple biographies for young children must be authentic in the illustrations, as well as in the text, because young children acquire considerable knowledge about a time or a setting from the illustrations rather than from detailed descriptions.

A Worthy Subject and a Believable Human. The subject of a biography should be worth reading about, just as she or he should be worthy of the author's meticulous research and time spent in writing. Has the subject made a significant impact on the world—for good or for ill—that children should be aware of? Will children have a better understanding of the complexities of human nature, both good and bad, after they have read the biography? Will they discover that history is made up of real people when they read the book? Will they appreciate the contributions of their ancestors or their heritage through the life of the person in the biography?

The subjects of biography and autobiography need not be famous, infamous, or outstanding achievers in a worldly sense in order for their lives to communicate to children important lessons about people and society. The subjects should be portrayed in a believable way, however. Whether a notable personage or an unsung hero of everyday life, the person upon whom a biographer focuses should have a many-faceted character, just like the people children know. Subjects of biography may have good and bad character traits, be liked and disliked. Jean Fritz, for example, has written a series of historical biographies suggesting that leaders of the American Revolution were very human. Fritz portrays Patrick Henry as a practical joker who did not appreciate school in his youth, and Samuel Adams as a man who was not afraid to speak out against the British but who refused to ride a horse.

Whereas Fritz's biographies emphasize the lives of well-known people, biographies such as John Jakes's *Susanna of the Alamo* develop story lines around unsung heroes. Jakes's characterization develops a brave woman whose life is spared by Santa Anna, the Mexican general, so that she can take a message to Sam Houston.

Balancing Fact and Story Line. Writers of biographies for children must balance the requirement for accuracy with the requirement of a narrative that appeals to children. Authors may emphasize humorous facts, for example, as they develop plots and characters that present information in a story format. This balance between fact and story line may cause problems for young readers. Children have difficulty evaluating differences between fiction and nonfiction. Jean Fritz's (9) foreword to her own fictionalized autobiography, *Homesick: My Own Story*, clarifies differences between fiction and biography:

Since my childhood feels like a story, I decided to tell it that way, letting the events fall as they would into the shape of a story, lacing them together with fictional bits, adding a piece here and there when memory didn't give me all I needed. I would use conversation freely, for I cannot think of my childhood without hearing voices. So although this book takes place within two years from October 1925 to September 1927, the events are drawn from the entire period of my childhood, but they are all, except in minor details, basically true. The people are real people; the places are dear to me. But most important, the form I have used has given me the freedom to recreate the emotions that I remember so vividly. Strictly speaking, I have to call this book fiction, but it does not feel like fiction to me. It is my story, told as truly as I can tell it. (unnumbered foreword)

Writers of biographies for older children usually include considerable factual detail. For example, in a note to *Under a Strong Wind: The Adventures of Jessie Benton Frémont* Dorothy N. Morrison states that whenever she uses quotation marks "the enclosed words are taken exactly from some primary source. As with my other biographies, I have not made up anything—conversations, characters, or incidents" (unnumbered author's note). Morrison effectively uses facts from books, manuscripts, and periodicals. In addition, she portrays lively, believable characters who almost come to life. The facts are presented

in such a way that the facts do not overshadow the author's style and characterizations.

Biographical Subjects

As discussed in this chapter, the subjects of biographies and autobiographies for children range from early European explorers and rulers to American space travelers and ordinary folk of today. Political leaders rise to eminence in times of need, and social activists speak out against oppression. Great achievers make contributions in science, art, literature, and sports. Common people express uncommon courage in their daily struggle for survival.

Explorers of Earth and Outer Space. People who question existing boundaries and explore the unknown fascinate children and adults alike and are the subjects of numerous biographies. The Italian Marco Polo, for example, was a marvel of his time because he crossed thousands of miles of desert and mountain to reach imperial China, the rich and fabled kingdom of "Cathay" that few, if any, other fourteenth-century Europeans had ever seen. Gian Paolo Ceserani's text and Piero Ventura's illustrations for *Marco Polo* trace Polo's travels from Venice, to China, and back to Europe, recreating the bustle of ports and the wonders of the Chinese court and other kingdoms along Polo's route, rich in the spices and silks that Europeans so valued.

By Marco Polo's time, a few Europeans had begun to believe that the world is round, rather than flat. A little over a hundred years after Polo's travels, another Italian, Christopher Columbus, sailed off to prove his contention that China and India could be reached by going due west, as well as by traveling overland in an eastward direction. The consequences of Columbus's quest are familiar to every schoolchild and are portrayed in many biographies of the discoverer of America. These biographies differ in literary style, focus, amount of detail, and development of Columbus's character. Consequently they are good for evaluation and comparison.

Alice Dalgliesh's simple, highly illustrated picture book, *The Columbus Story*, is characterized by short sentences and repetitive language. For example, Dalgliesh uses these words to introduce readers to Columbus's growing desire to go to sea:

Mystery, danger, adventure—what exciting words! Christopher wanted more than ever to be a sailor. The wind that ruffled his red hair seemed to call to him, "Come, come, come!" The waves that lapped the wharves said it over and over. (p. 3 unnumbered)

The author focuses on three incidents in Columbus's life: his unsuccessful pleas to the king of Portugal, his successful pleas to the queen of Spain, and his first voyage to America. This simpler version does not develop the problems and disappointments that later plague Columbus's life.

Ingri and Edgar Parin D'Aulaire's *Columbus*, written for slightly older children, includes details that develop quite a different character from the Columbus in the Dalgliesh version. Additional information enables children to visualize an explorer who did not recognize the magnitude of his discovery and who considered himself a failure because he had not reached the Far East: "Old and tired, Columbus returned to Spain from his fourth and last voyage. While he was searching in vain, the Portuguese had found the seaway to the East by sailing south around Africa. Now Columbus stood in the shadow" (p. 54).

The focus of Piero Ventura's *Christopher Columbus*, based on the text by Gian Paolo Ceserani, is a pictorial account of Columbus's version of his adventures. Detailed drawings depict the city of Genoa, the fleet sailing from Palos, the interior of the Santa Maria, typical clothing worn by each crew member, the Bahamas as they looked in 1492, an Indian village on the coast of Cuba, the plants discovered in the new world, and the fort built by the crew. David Goodnough's *Christopher Columbus* emphasizes Columbus's early seafaring years and his efforts to persuade Portuguese and Spanish royalty to back his exploration and first voyage.

Jean Fritz's *Where Do You Think You Are Going, Christopher Columbus?* is written in a light style that appeals to many children. Through use of detailed background information, Fritz creates a lively history inhabited by realistic people. For example, Columbus's sponsor, Queen Isabella of Spain, "was so religious that if she even found Christians who were not sincere Christians, she had them burned at the stake. (Choir boys sang during the burning so Isabella wouldn't have to hear the screams.)" (p.17). Fritz ends her book with additional historical notes and an index of people and locations discussed in the book.

This highly illustrated book captures the setting for a biography of Christopher Columbus. (From *Christopher Columbus*, by Piero Ventura, based on the text by Gian Paolo Ceserani. Copyright 1978 by Random House. Reprinted by permission of the publisher.)

The life of another explorer who took to the sea to prove his theories—this time in the twentieth century—is portrayed in *Thor Heyerdahl: Viking Scientist* by Wyatt Blassingame. Heyerdahl believed strongly that islands in the Pacific Ocean had been populated by pre-Columbian native peoples of South America. His critics maintained that the balsa rafts used by the traditional pre-Columbians would have become waterlogged and sunk long before they could have reached their destination. Heyerdahl built a balsa raft, *Kon Tiki* (named after an ancient Polynesian god), and with five friends successfully sailed 4,000 miles from Peru to the Polynesian islands of the South Pacific. Blassingame portrays a believable person through background information about what caused Heyerdahl to become interested in the origins of the early inhabitants of the Polynesian islands and why he believed they came from South America: trade winds and currents move from east to west; words like *Tiki* are common to both natives of Peru and native Polynesians; similar stone terraces are found in both locations; and the skulls of Polynesians are long, similar to those of the South Americans, rather than round like those of Asian people. Children can vicariously accompany the crew of the *Kon Tiki* on the perilous voyage through storms and pounding waves before they reach their destination.

Christopher Columbus's belief that the world is round was shared and proven by European astronomers of the fifteenth and sixteenth centuries, such as Nicolaus Copernicus and Galileo Galilei. Through their explorations of the stars—by means of mathematical equations, naked-eye observations, and the earliest telescopes—such early explorers of outer space further shook the

A twentieth-century explorer searches for the origins of the Polynesian culture. (Jacket art by Linda Lenkowski from *Thor Heyerdahl: Viking Scientist*, by Wyatt Blassingame. Reproduced by permission of the publisher, Elsevier/Nelson, a Division of Elsevier-Dutton Publishing Co., Inc.)

foundations of European world views: the earth is not only round, but is one of numerous planets rotating around the sun; the sun itself is only one of many astral bodies moving through the universe. The radicalness of these beliefs, in a time when the church itself insisted that the earth was the stationary center of the one solar system created by God, is portrayed in Sidney Rosen's *Galileo and the Magic Numbers*. Rosen suggests the reasons for Galileo's questioning of established "truth" by describing the influence of Galileo's father, who taught him: "Do not be afraid to challenge authority at any time, if a search for truth is in question. This is not the easy path in life, but it is the most rewarding" (p. 50). Because of Rosen's detailed descriptions, children are able to share Galileo's first look at the craters of the moon through the improved telescope he invented, Galileo's elation when he confirms Copernicus's theories, and Galileo's bitterness when he is charged with heresy, forced to recant his position, and imprisoned. Children are encouraged to believe in Galileo's strong will when he swears that "in spite of what they forced me to say, the earth will continue to move on its path about the sun" (p. 205).

The work of Galileo and other astronomers of his time and later centuries helped make today's space exploration possible. Helen L. Morgan's *Maria Mitchell: First Lady of American Astronomy* is a biography of one of the foremost astronomers in American history. Mitchell explored the stars, but her refusal to accept existing boundaries also extended into everyday social life. Mitchell felt strongly about the right to question and the right of women to have equality with men. By becoming an astronomer in the nineteenth century, when females were expected to confine themselves to wifehood and motherhood, Mitchell was an oddity and a social trail-blazer. Morgan presents not only a person on a quest for knowledge about the universe, but a person who had to overcome extreme prejudice against females in higher education and particularly in the sciences. Both Mitchell's love of astronomy and her strength of character in confronting obstacles are revealed in her reaction to visiting in Rome the site of Galileo's trial by the Inquisition:

Maria could imagine it all and knew how much it must have hurt Galileo to recant his belief after seeing proofs of it in the heavens. The petty restrictions of his later life, when he was ill and blind, were unpleasant but could not equal the despair he must have known in publicly denying his belief. She felt that she was on sacred ground when she walked near the place where he had suffered. (p. 104)

Morgan describes in detail the criticism Mitchell receives when she upholds Charles Darwin's theory of evolution, the discriminatory treatment of female faculty members at schools where Mitchell teaches astronomy, and the bigotry Mitchell confronts when she fights for equal rights for women. Still, Mitchell manages to become and remain both an outstanding scientist, discoverer of a new comet, and a firm advocate of her most cherished values: "I have so long believed in woman's right to a share in the government that it is like the first axiom I learned in geometry— a straight line is the shortest distance between two points" (p. 123).

Mitchell's legacy to both American science and American women is evident in Mary Virginia Fox's *Women Astronauts: Aboard the Shuttle*. This book describes the 1983 flight of Sally Ride, the first female American astronaut, and presents brief biographies of eight other female astronauts, along with numerous photographs. Michael Collins's *Flying to the Moon and Other Strange Places* is the autobiography of another contemporary space explorer, an astronaut who journeyed aboard Gemini and Apollo. Collins provides photographs of early jets, fighting planes, astronauts in training, and the moon, which should interest children who enjoy reading about space exploration.

Political Leaders and Social Activists. Men and women who have achieved noteworthy positions of political power or who have attempted to bring about social change are common subjects of biography. Often these public figures are controversial—adored by some, deplored by others. As a result, biographers sometimes create imbalanced portraits of their subjects. Because biographers usually, but not always, choose to write about people they admire, hagiography (literally, "the biography of saints"), rather than objective biography, may result. Even authors who create well-rounded portrayals of political leaders and social activists inevitably express their own individual perspectives. For example, after reading three books about a certain political leader, one student of children's literature commented that she could have been reading about three different

people. Because each author had a specific purpose in writing a biography, each author's characterization of the person, choice of events to discuss, style, and tone created a different bias in the reader. Students of children's literature would do well, if possible, to read several biographies of the same person and draw their own conclusions.

The biographer of the following book uses many techniques that make the book an excellent example of biography. Strong characterizations and vivid settings capture the people and the times in Polly Schoyer Brooks's *Queen Eleanor: Independent Spirit of the Medieval World*. Brooks portrays Eleanor of Aquitaine as she develops from a frivolous, immature girl who acts to satisfy her whims, to a mature queen who has a shrewd talent for politics. The author uses a variety of techniques to develop colorful characterization, including the use of comparisons and inclusion of verses written by poets of the time. Consider, for example, the picture that the author paints of Eleanor and her husband, Henry II, through the following comparisons:

Eleanor gradually restored some measure of peace and order to her duchy, using persuasion where Henry had used force. (p. 100)

While Eleanor had become serene, Henry had become more irascible. (p. 126)

From a queen of the troubadours, who had inspired romance and poetry, she became a queen with as much authority as a king. . . . Henry had been admired and feared; Eleanor was admired and loved. (p. 132)

The author includes verses composed about Eleanor that describe the attitudes expressed toward the Queen and reinforce the mood of medieval chivalry. The following lyrics were written by troubadour Bernard de Ventadour and were included as an integral part of the text:

Lady, I'm yours and yours shall be
Vowed to your service constantly
This is the oath of fealty
I pledged to you this long time past,
As my first joy was all in you,
So shall my last be found there too,
So long as life in me shall last. (p. 107)

Founding Fathers and Mothers of America. Some very exciting biographies for young children are Jean Fritz's stories about Revolutionary War heroes. Patrick Henry, Samuel Adams, John Hancock, Benjamin Franklin, and Sam Houston seem to come alive through Fritz's inclusion of little-known information that makes these famous personages real and down-to-earth in children's eyes. Through these books children discover that heroes, like themselves, have fears, display good and bad characteristics, and may be liked by some and disliked by others. For example, Fritz adds humor to *Where Was Patrick Henry on the 29th of May?* by developing the theory that unusual things always seemed to happen to Henry on the date of his birth. She characterizes Henry not only as a great patriot, but also as a practical joker and a person filled with "passion for fiddling, dancing, and pleasantry." Similar insights enliven Fritz's biographies of other beloved figures from the revolutionary period. Fritz doesn't only write about supporters of American independence from Great Britain, however. In *Traitor: The Case of Benedict Arnold* Fritz develops a well-rounded characterization of a man who wanted to be a success and a hero, but who, in the eyes of most American colonists, was a dastardly betrayer of the cause. Fritz attracts the reader's interest in Arnold and prepares the reader for the apparently dramatic changes in a man who chose to support the British: "Benedict Arnold succeeded beyond anyone's wildest expectations—'the bravest of the brave,' George Washington called him in 1777. Yet three years later he was described as 'the veriest villain of centuries past,' and no one would have argued with that" (p. 7). The incidents Fritz chooses to include develop many sides of Arnold's character and encourage readers to understand why he chose to join forces against his country.

In *Make Way for Sam Houston* Fritz uses Houston's belief in destiny to emphasize interactions with other characters, characterization, and plot development. For example, Houston accepted Andrew Jackson's vision of America because "now he had a picture and words for what he'd call Destiny" (p. 20). Fritz reinforces Houston's belief in destiny by describing Houston's responses each time he saw an eagle, the medicine bird that influenced major decisions in Houston's life.

Fiery words and bold actions are not the only forms of patriotism and leadership. Elizabeth Yates's *Amos Fortune, Free Man* depicts a man who advanced his country's freedom, and his own, by quiet, everyday strength of character and loving actions. Fortune was an African who was brought to slavery in Boston, learned a trade, and eventually acquired freedom. He represents

thousands of unsung heroes of the American Revolution—black and white, male and female. The words on his tombstone, erected in 1801, suggest the fundamental American values Fortune exemplified: ". . . born free in Africa, a slave in America, he purchased liberty, professed Christianity, lived reputably, and died hopefully" (p. 181).

Because of traditional social patterns that kept women out of public life in the eighteenth century, most female Americans of the times were "taking care of the homefront" and have remained anonymous in history. The prominence of male figures of the period has also cast something of a shadow over female Americans who were making important public contributions to a developing nation. Selma R. Williams's *Demeter's Daughters: The Women Who Founded America 1587–1787* attempts to rectify the oversights of standard American history and biography by providing biographical sketches of several great women of colonial and revolutionary America. This book is appropriate for older children, although it may be too complex and lengthy to appeal to many. It is a valuable source of material about the role of women in the founding of the United States.

Leaders of a Growing America. As the United States became more confident of itself as a nation, it began to expand its interests overseas. Rhoda Blumberg's *Commodore Perry in the Land of the Shogun* depicts the attempts of the American naval officer Matthew Perry to open Japanese harbors to American trade in 1853. This book, an excellent choice for multiethnic studies, strongly emphasizes the dramatic human interactions between Perry and the Japanese. Reproductions of the original drawings that recorded the expedition, Japanese scrolls and handbills, and photographs provide careful documentation, as well as enhancing children's understanding of the setting and Japanese culture.

The best-known biographer of Abraham Lincoln is probably Carl Sandburg. His *Abraham Lincoln: The Prairie Years* was the basis for his biography for children, *Abe Lincoln Grows Up*. Through this book, children vicariously share the youth of a great American leader. They discover an impoverished young man of the backwoods who is starved for books, hungry for knowledge, eager to have fun, and ambitious to test himself and his principles in a wider world:

It seemed that Abe made the books tell him more than they told other people. . . . Abe picked out questions. . . such as "Who has the most right to complain, the Indian or the Negro?" and Abe would talk about it, up one way and down the other, while they were in the cornfield pulling fodder for the winter. (p. 135)

Charles Eastman, the most famous Native American of his time, was a Sioux of the Great Plains, born in 1858, who overcame poverty and racial prejudice to become a physician and a crusader for Native American rights. Betsy Lee's *Charles Eastman: The Story of an American Indian* focuses on the influences that combined to make Eastman a spokesperson for his people, including the forced migration of the Sioux from Minnesota, his medical education, and his efforts to provide medical treatment and better living conditions for the Sioux. Eastman worked to restore broken treaties and to encourage Indians and whites to respect Native American culture. Eventually, says Lee, Eastman's decades of effort bore fruit:

Charles's message was finally heard, at long last his people would have a voice of their own. Charles Eastman, perhaps more than anyone else, kept Sioux culture and tradition alive during the silent years from 1890 to 1934. Much of what we know today about the American Indian we owe to him. (p. 62)

A desire to improve the lives of her people led Susan LaFlesche to become the first female Native American doctor of Western medicine. In *Homeward the Arrow's Flight* Marion Marsh Brown emphasizes the challenges, the hardships, and the joys LaFlesche experienced while acquiring her medical education—as well as the sense of mission that kept her going: " 'LaFlesche, arrow of the future, shot from the bow of the past.' A future worthy of the past, she hoped: a better day for her people, helped by her work . . . . This continuity—past, present, future—was what made you one with the earth" (p. 174). The biographies of Susan LaFlesche and Charles Eastman make excellent additions to a multiethnic literature program.

Like Susan LaFlesche, Lillian Wald felt a powerful commitment to social change in the late 1800s and defied traditional roles for women by entering the medical profession. In *Lillian Wald of Henry Street* Beatrice Siegel portrays the strength of Wald's commitment by contrasting the affluent life of Wald's Jewish American family

Photographs from an earlier time period add authenticity to this biography. (From *Lillian Wald of Henry Street*, by Beatrice Siegel. Copyright © 1983 by Beatrice Siegel. Photo courtesy of Visiting Nurse Service of New York.)

with the squalor of New York City's Lower East Side, where immigrants from many lands were living in disease and poverty. Siegel describes the experiences that caused Wald to develop a strong social conscience, defy her family's wishes, train for the nursing profession, and establish the Henry Street Settlement House in order to help impoverished citizens of New York.

Another excellent book about a nineteenth-century American with a strong social conscience is Anne E. Neimark's *A Deaf Child Listened: Thomas Gallaudet, Pioneer in American Education*. For centuries, deaf children had been placed in asylums for the retarded and the insane. Gallaudet, founder of American education specifically for the deaf, helped bring deaf Americans out of their "silent prison."

Twentieth-Century Leaders in America and Abroad. Biographies written for young children and for older children differ in tone, focus, choice of content, amount of detail, and development of character. Because of the range in intended audiences, biographies about political leaders and social activists in the twentieth century provide an opportunity to compare authors' techniques and content.

First, consider several "Crowell Biographies" written for young children: Jane Goodsell's *Eleanor Roosevelt*, Ophelia Settle Egypt's *James Weldon Johnson*, and Ruth Franchere's *Cesar Chavez*. The books share several features: readability levels that range from second to fourth grades, indicating that the books are meant for children's independent reading; numerous illustrations; and an emphasis on very positive characteristics and situations.

Jane Goodsell's *Eleanor Roosevelt* focuses on Roosevelt's personality development and the changes that allowed her to overcome internal conflicts and eventually become a confident individual and a great contributor to American social life. Goodsell characterizes the young Roosevelt as shy, lonely, and often bored but shows her as an adult gradually becoming an assistant to her husband in his political career, then a crusader for her own beliefs in social justice and world peace as a worker for the United Nations. Goodsell does not include any materials that hint at the personal unhappiness portrayed in biographies of Eleanor Roosevelt for adults.

Ophelia Settle Egypt forthrightly declares her admiration and affection for the Civil Rights leader, author, and educator in *James Weldon Johnson*. As a child, she says, she felt pride when singing Johnson's "Lift Every Voice and Sing," and she was also "his most ardent fan" when she was a young instructor at Fisk University, where Johnson was a professor. The author's choice of words is a good example of author's tone (the author's attitude toward the character). Egypt's choice of content and descriptions of Johnson create a similar feeling of admiration and affection in the reader.

Ruth Franchere's *Cesar Chavez* focuses on the Mexican American political leader's struggles to develop the National Farm Workers Association and gain political and economic power for Mexican Americans. Franchere arouses sympathy for Chavez's undertakings by showing pictures of the poor living conditions of a migrant farming family and providing details related to Chavez's schooling: his family moved so often that he attended thirty-six schools while acquiring an eighth-grade education. Franchere's choice of factual content directs the reader's attention to Chavez's concerns and values: he tries to organize classes where Mexican Americans can learn to read and write English; he works for Mexican American voter registration; and he organizes the 1968 grape boycott in order to demand better pay and living conditions for migrant workers.

Next, consider the biographies of Franklin Roosevelt, Adolf Hitler, Golda Meir, and Andrew Young that have been written for older children. The longer format allows authors to include more details and develop more information about the historical period.

Appropriately enough for an older audience, Barbara Silberdick's *Franklin D. Roosevelt, Gallant President* focuses in some detail upon Franklin Roosevelt's abilty to overcome physical disabilities during his rise to power and upon his political accomplishments. As the book's title suggests, Silberdick presents Roosevelt in a positive light. She includes no viewpoints that might be considered critical and gives no in-depth look at his private life.

Edward F. Dolan, Jr.'s biography for older readers, *Adolf Hitler: A Portrait in Tyranny*, exemplifies the belief that children should read about the villains in history as well as the heroes. As reflected in the title, the author's tone is not affectionate, praiseworthy, or noncritical. Instead he refers to a "frightening period in the past" that should be shared with children so they will be able to recognize "dangers" in the present and the future. Dolan's characterization includes Hitler's shrewdness in analyzing the German people and his ability to select followers who advocated his viewpoint. Dolan depicts times during Hitler's life when his rise to power might have been prevented. The details about the Holocaust and Hitler's suicide provide a look at a terrifying period of world history.

Margaret Davidson creates a well-rounded characterization of one of the memorable prime ministers of Israel in *The Golda Meir Story*. For example, she relates experiences in Meir's childhood to her achievements as an adult. She does not imply that Meir's private life was always happy; she discusses Meir's marital problems. The nuances of Meir's forceful personality are evident as Meir faces both the problems and the rewards of leading her country during the Yom Kippur war.

James Haskins's *Andrew Young: Man with a Mission* portrays the achievements of this first Black American to represent the United States at the United Nations. It also depicts Young's personal setbacks, his problems overcoming prejudice, and his struggles for civil rights as he became a minister, legislator, and ambassador.

Other sources provide information about many of the political leaders and social activists discussed in this section. Children can verify factual information presented in the biographies or extend an interest by reading more about a particular person. When children do library research, they discover some of the techniques that biographers use. Such investigations may also lead them to other outstanding, recently published biographies of social leaders, such as Lillie Patterson's *Sure Hands, Strong Heart: The Life of Daniel Hale Williams*, a Black American physician who worked for interracial hospitals.

Artists, Scientists, and Sports Figures. Barbara Brenner's *On the Frontier with Mr. Audubon* is based, according to the author, on a diary the naturalist and artist John James Audubon kept in 1820 and 1821 when he and a young assistant, Joseph Mason, traveled down the Mississippi and Ohio Rivers to find and draw birds. Brenner also used information from Alice Ford's *John James Audubon* and Audubon's other writings. The resulting biography is in the form of a journal that could have been written by the assistant. Brenner says that almost every incident in the book actually happened, but that the conversations are fictional, based on the facts found in the research. The book is illustrated with black-and-white drawings of Audubon's work and photographs from original sources showing flatboats on the river and people and places discussed in the book.

In 1891, it was unheard of for a woman to attend France's Sorbonne University for the purpose of earning a doctorate in physical science. This did not deter Marie Curie. Nancy Veglahn's *The Mysterious Rays: Marie Curie's World* tells about the long years of laboratory work during which Marie and Pierre Curie conducted experiments with pitchblende in their efforts to isolate a new element, radium. Veglahn concludes her biography with added information about the two Nobel Prizes awarded Marie Curie, the beneficial uses of radium, and the tragedy related to the damage done to the Curies by the unsuspected radiation from the radium.

Margery Facklam's *Wild Animals, Gentle Women* is a collection of short biographical sketches of eleven women who have spent their lives as ethologists studying animal behavior. The book includes Belle Benchley, former director of the San Diego Zoo; Jane Goodall, the scientist who became famous because of her work with chimpanzees; and Karen Pryor, a research scientist who specializes in behavioral studies with porpoises. The last chapter discusses ethology as a profession and makes suggestions about appropriate education, developing writing skills, learning photography, learning first aid, and becoming involved with Outward Bound or similar programs. Children and adults can make interesting comparisons between this book for older children and Mary Virginia Fox's highly illustrated biography for young children *Jane Goodall: Living Chimp Style*.

Autobiographies give children insights into the illustrators and authors of children's books. In *Self-Portrait: Erik Blegvad*, the artist reveals the motivational forces behind his career. A love of the sea inherited from his father inspired his early drawings. In *Self-Portrait: Margot Zemach*, another award-winning illustrator tells how as a child during the Depression she drew pictures to make herself and others laugh. Elizabeth Yates's *My Diary, My World* and *My Widening World*, written in journal format, express her love for books and writing during a time when females did not have careers. The entries in the books, according to the author's notes, were actually written during her growing-up years.

Keith Ferrell's *H.G. Wells: First Citizen of the Future* exemplifies books, especially those written for older children, in which the author develops a many-sided character with both strengths and weaknesses. Ferrell incorporates the strong social and political views that influenced Wells's life and writing.

The fine arts also include music and dance. *The Boy Who Loved Music*, by Joe and David Lasker, covers an incident in Joseph Haydn's life that led to the composition of a symphony with a surprise ending. Joe Lasker's illustrations create the

An elegant eighteenth-century setting provides a background for a biography about Joseph Haydn. (From *The Boy Who Loved Music*, by Joe Lasker and David Lasker. Illustrations copyright © by Joe Lasker. Reprinted by permission of Viking Penguin, Inc.)

mood and setting of an elegant eighteenth-century Europe at the court of Prince Miklos Esterhazy.

Tobi Tobias's *Arthur Mitchell* is a highly illustrated biography of a famous dancer. This book for young readers describes the experiences of a young black dancer as he tries to enter the world of classical ballet, a field in which few blacks had found acceptance. The author portrays Mitchell's numerous struggles by describing his problems in meeting the demands of ballet at the High School of Performing Arts, the audience prejudice he had to overcome while a dancer with the New York City Ballet, his dancing in a lead role developed especially for him, and his desire to form an all-black classical ballet company where young black dancers could practice and perform. Mitchell's Dance Theatre of Harlem, which began in an empty garage, is now internationally known and provides training for hundreds of black dancers.

Children who are sports enthusiasts enjoy reading about the people they see on television or those whose records they would like to duplicate. Vernon Pizer's *Glorious Triumphs: Athletes Who Conquered Adversity* is a collection of short biographies about athletes who had to overcome physical disabilities, reversals, and social obsta-

cles. The book discusses athletes such as Barney Rose, 1933 lightweight boxing champion of the world; Ben Hogan, professional golfer; Carole Heiss, Olympic gold medalist; Jerry Kramer, football player for the Green Bay Packers; and Althea Gibson, tennis professional. Howard Liss's *Bobby Orr: Lightning on Ice* presents the life story of an ice hockey great, enhanced with photographs of the hockey players and their teammates. Biographies about sports stars may quickly become dated because of rapidly changing stardom and changing team memberships. Many children who are sports enthusiasts, however, enjoy reading almost everything about their favorite sports heroes—outdated or not. Additional biographies of sports figures are found in chapter eleven, "Multiethnic Literature." Sports stories are discussed in chapter nine, "Contemporary Realistic Fiction."

People Who Have Persevered. Biographies are not always written about famous people or people of great material success. Some excellent biographies and autobiographies portray the courage and perseverance of ordinary people. One such book is David Kheridan's *The Road from Home: The Story of an Armenian Girl*. This story about the author's mother, Vernon Dumehjian, is one of courage, hope, and survival when in 1915 the Turkish government decides to eliminate its Armenian people by deporting them to the Mesopotamian desert or killing them. Vernon spends days in a caravan on the march, days of weakening physical condition, days of not knowing her destination, and days of sadness when family members die from cholera. Days of hope result when Vernon meets kind people who provide her with an education while she waits to return to her home. The security of home does not last long, however, as fighting resumes between Turkey and Greece. When Vernon's aunt is approached by a family whose Armenian American son wants a wife to join him in the United States, Vernon finally finds a means of becoming safe. Children can compare this book with other stories on similar subjects in the historical fiction chapter.

Another author who develops a theme related to the joy and sorrow of being human is Bernard Wolf. His *In This Proud Land: The Story of a Mexican American Family* is the biography of a family rather than an individual—a photographic essay about Texas farmers at home, at work, at play, and traveling to Minnesota to supplement their income by working in the sugar beet fields. The photographs and text portray warm relationships in the Hernandez family and children who work at part-time jobs to help their family financially. This story about a poor family striving to earn a living is also a story about proud people attempting to educate their children and create a better life for them in the midst of difficult circumstances. Wolf ends his story with these words:

In this proud land there are many Americas. There is an America of inequality and racial prejudice. There is an America of grave poverty, despair, and tragic human waste. And yet because of people like the Hernandez family, there is also an America of simple courage, strength, and hope. (p. 95)

Another book that traces a family's experiences is Eloise Greenfield and Lessie Jones Little's *Childtimes: A Three-Generation Memoir*. In the book's three parts, a Black American grandmother, mother, and daughter tell about their growing-up experiences in time periods ranging from the late 1800s through the 1940s. Both Greenfield and Little are well-known authors of children's books. This book concludes poignantly:

It's been good, stopping for a while to catch up to the past. It has filled me with both great sadness and great joy. Sadness to look back at suffering, joy to feel the unbreakable threads of strength. Now, it's time for us to look forward again, to see where it is that we're going. Maybe years from now, our descendants will want to stop and tell the story of their time and their place in this procession of children. A childtime is a mighty thing. (p. 175)

These words provide a fitting conclusion to this discussion of biographies written for children. What better purpose is there for sharing biographies with children than allowing them to feel good, to "catch up to the past," and to experience the sadness and great joy of other people's lives?

INFORMATIONAL BOOKS

Values of Informational Books

"I am curious." "It is easier to find the answer from reading than it is to ask my teacher." "I want to learn to take better pictures." "I want to learn about a career I might enjoy." "I like reading the books." All these reasons were given to this author by children who were asked why they read informational books. The range of answers also reflects the many values of informational books for children. Thousands of nonfiction books pro-

vide information about hobbies, experiments, the way things work, the characteristics of plants and animals, and many other phenomena in our world.

Gaining knowledge about the world is a powerful reason for reading informational books. Glenn O. Blough (3), a professor of science education and an author of science books for children, maintains that "the fact that information grows and ideas change is no excuse for not expecting children and young people to learn from science. While the great supply of information may be somewhat discouraging, and the fluctuation of ideas disconcerting, neither is an excuse for remaining ignorant of the world we live in, or not understanding the methods by which knowledge grows" (p. 420). Many recently published books contain information on timely subjects that children hear about on television or radio or read about in newspapers. For example, children excited by NASA's space explorations can consult Seymour Simon's *Jupiter* and *Saturn* for color photographs and information obtained during NASA's Pioneer and Voyager space explorations, or extend their knowledge about satellites, space shuttles, and possible space colonies by reading Franklyn M. Branley's *Mysteries of Outer Space*.

Informational books *stimulate children's curiosity* by providing opportunities for children to experience the excitement of new discoveries. Children open new doors of self-discovery as well when they follow step-by-step directions for experiments that reinforce a scientific principle. For example, they may make discoveries about the life cycle of the popcorn plant and learn about basic principles of botany when they read and do the experiments in Millicent E. Selsam's *Popcorn*; or they can discover the importance of fibers and how to spin cotton or wool by hand when they read and follow Vicki Cobb's directions in *Fuzz Does It!*; or they may make discoveries about surface tension when they follow Seymour Simon's instructions in *Soap Bubble Magic*.

Such experiments expose children to another value of informational books: *introduction to the scientific method*. Through firsthand experience and reading about the work of scientists, children discover how scientists observe, compare, formulate and test hypotheses, and draw conclusions or withhold them until more evidence is uncovered (3). They also become familiar with the instruments used by scientists. As children learn about and become comfortable with the sci-

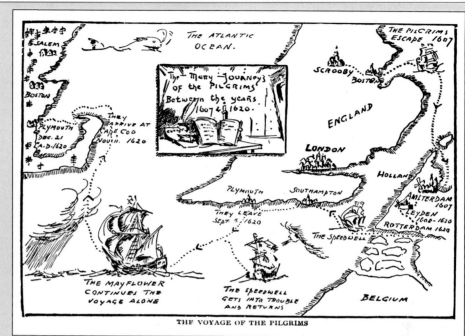

THE VOYAGE OF THE PILGRIMS

THE FIRST Newbery Medal was awarded in 1922 to an informational book that traced the steps in the development of the human race from prehistoric times to the early twentieth century. Hendrik Willem Van Loon's *The Story of Mankind* is also noteworthy because the author dealt with ideas and acts that greatly influenced the human race, rather than focusing primarily on dates and picturesque incidents. At the time of its publication the book was praised for its comprehensiveness, taste, and humor. The book was credited with changing the writing of informational books; authors were encouraged to write books that presented learning as an exciting process.

entific method, they gain an appreciation for the attitudes of people who use this method. They discover the importance of careful observation over long periods of time, the need for gathering data from many sources, and the requirement that scientists, whatever their field, make no conclusions before all the data have been collected. For example, Seymour Simon's *The Secret Clocks, Time Senses of Living Things* describes the varied experiments and the many hours of patient observation German scientist Gustav Kramer logged as he investigated the ability of birds to pinpoint their destinations when they migrate thousands of miles to the south or the north. Children may also learn that a person's achievement is not always his or hers alone; success often depends upon work completed earlier by others.

By arousing children's curiosity, informational books also *encourage self-reliance* in children's learning process, as one enjoyable discovery mo-

tivates them to make further investigations. Parents and educators need to provide books and materials that pique children's interest and then help them explore their environment. A high school student who likes to read informational books emphasizes the satisfaction in following his curiosity into broader and deeper exploration:

I enjoy reading to answer my own curiosity. Fictional books don't have the information that I want. I am more interested in real things. When I was in first grade, astronomy was the first science that interested me; the more I read, the more I learned I didn't know. As I became older I read a lot of books about the stars, space exploration, and theories about the black hole. I discovered that reality is stranger and more exciting than any fiction could be. I could not take fiction and transfer it into the real world; factual books help me learn about the real world.

Informational books can also encourage children to *develop critical reading and thinking abil-*

ities as they learn to evaluate what they read. While reading books on the same subject written by different authors, they may compare and evaluate the objectivity, truthfulness, and perspective of various authors; they may determine the qualifications of the authors to write about a particular subject; and they may check copyright dates to see if the information is current. For example, children can consider various views on using chimpanzees as experimental subjects in captivity by reading Anna Michel's *The Story of Nim: The Chimp Who Learned Language*, Joan Hewett's *Watching Them Grow: Inside a Zoo Nursery*, and Linda Koebner's *From Cage to Freedom: A New Beginning for Laboratory Chimpanzees*.

Of course all the values mentioned so far also encourage children *to stretch their minds, enlarge their vocabularies, and stimulate their imaginations*. New thoughts and ways of looking at the world are possible when children become involved in an in-depth study of a subject. When they read Caroline Arnold's *Saving the Peregrine Falcon* or David Cook's *Environment*, they may discover the perilous balance between animals, the environment, and humans and begin to think of ways their own generation could conserve animal and plant life and other natural resources. Informational books inform children about values, beliefs, lifestyles, and behaviors different from their own. Many well-written informational books expand children's vocabularies by introducing the meanings of new words, including technical terms. Meanings of technical terms are often enriched through photographs or detailed illustrations. For example, *Glaciers: Nature's Frozen Rivers* by Hershell H. and Joan Lowery Nixon introduces terms such as *crevasses* in the text: "The cracks that are found in the ice are called crevasses. They can be very deep and wide and dangerous, or very shallow" (p. 23). One of the deep crevasses is then shown in a photograph on the same page. The definition is followed by a detailed discussion of crevasses. Books also stimulate children's imagination by allowing them to think of new possibilities and creative ways to use or look at the world. Anyone who has observed young children playing with a box has seen the creative and imaginative toys they can develop. Flo Ann Hedley Norvell's *The Great Big Box Book* suggests many fascinating toys that can be created out of large boxes and then encourages children to extend their imaginations even more by thinking of yet more uses for a box.

Finally, educators and parents must not forget that one of the greatest values in informational books is *enjoyment*. Many children who make new discoveries, become involved in the scientific process, or read because of curiosity are also reading for enjoyment. In fact, enjoyment is often the primary reason children read informational literature such as histories of the ancient world or photographic essays about animal life.

Evaluating Informational Books

Guidelines suggested by several science associations concerned with the education of elementary-school children provide valuable information for the librarian, teacher, or parent responsible for selecting informational books for children. These guidelines are specifically tailored to science books but are equally valid for all types of informational books. The following guidelines are taken from recommendations made by the National Science Teachers Association (15) and the American Association for the Advancement of Science (20). The books mentioned will be discussed in detail later in the chapter.

1. All Facts Should Be Accurate.

Does the author have the scientific qualifications to write a book on the particular subject? Franklyn M. Branley, author of *Mysteries of Outer Space* and over one hundred other scientific books, has a doctorate, is an astronomer emeritus, and is the former chairman of the American Museum-Hayden Planetarium. Many books, however, provide little or no helpful information by which to evaluate authors' qualifications.

Are facts and theory clearly distinguished? Children should know if something is a fact, if it is a theory that has not been substantiated, or if it is a theory that is impossible to prove because of limited information. For example, Jack Denton Scott clearly differentiates between fact and theory in *The Book of the Goat*. During his discussion of the ancestry of the goat, he says, "One fact is certain: the goat has been with us a long time" (p. 8). He then traces the known historical record of the goat and compares this record with that of the dog. He carefully separates fact from controversial conjecture: "Despite the combined knowledge of archaeologists (who study materials from past civilizations), osteologists (who study ancient bones), and historians, controversy exists regarding which is the oldest of our friends, the goat or the dog" (p. 10). Scott then presents the evidence compiled by osteologists and archaeologists.

Are significant facts omitted? The above example shows how an author should present enough significant facts so that the text is accurate. Specialized books that give complete histories of certain animals are valuable because they help children understand the evolution of a species, its characteristics, and the need, if any, for its protection. Again, Jack Denton Scott's several books do this: they begin with the ancient history of the species, then describe its behavior, and, if the species is endangered, provide information about human efforts to preserve it.

Are differing views on controversial subjects presented? Subjects such as ecology often have proponents on both sides of an issue. In *Natural Fire: Its Ecology in Forests*, Laurence Pringle presents viewpoints supporting the benefits of forest fires and the viewpoints of those who consider forest fires detrimental. In *Africa's Flamingo Lake*, Francine Jacobs presents arguments of a group that desires uncontrolled human expansion and those of a group that fights for the protection of the environment. While both authors have definite viewpoints, they do more than present one side of the issue. If there is author bias, the author should identify that a personal point of view is not necessarily a universally held position. Sometimes, just one sentence will interject author bias into what otherwise is a factual presentation of controversial views. For example, Ann E. Sigford, in *Eight Words for Thirsty*, discusses the problems of farmers who need water for irrigation and the need of townspeople for water, but then makes this statement: "Someone has to pay the high cost of desert water, and that someone is the American people. The CAP was born in a time when farming seemed to be the only way a state could be developed. Today, however, farming contributes only about 7 percent of Arizona's income. It does not seem smart to spend so much to earn so little" (p. 77).

Is the information presented without relying on anthropomorphism? While it is perfectly acceptable for authors of fantasy to write about animals that think, talk, act, and dress like people, authors of informational books should not ascribe human thoughts, motives, or emotions to animals or to plants and other inanimate things (a practice called *anthropomorphism*). Doing so makes a book inaccurate. A writer of animal in-

formation books should describe the animals in terms that can be substantiated through careful observation. For example, in *The Book of the Pig* Jack Denton Scott describes an incident in which a boar consistently unlatched a gate and took the endangered runt of a litter out into a meadow until it was no longer a runt. Instead of giving human reasons for the pig's actions, Scott states: "Was the boar Andy exhibiting pig instinct or pig intellect when he 'adopted' Sawyer? We don't know, but a five-year research program at the University of Kentucky found that pigs not only are the smartest of all farm animals but are also more intelligent than dogs, mastering any trick or feat accomplished by canines in much shorter time" (p. 31). Scott continues to describe pigs in terms of information gained from observation and research.

Is the information as up-to-date as possible? Because knowledge in some areas is changing rapidly, copyright dates for certain types of informational books become very important. Human attitudes and values also change, as chapters on the history of literature and realistic fiction in this book show. Comparing older factual books with more recent ones is one way to illustrate how attitudes and biases change. No educator or publisher today would condone the untrue and highly offensive descriptions of Native Americans presented in *Carpenter's Geographical Reader, North America* (4) published by Frank G. Carpenter in 1898. For example, Carpenter introduces Native Americans as follows: "What queer people they are, and how sober they look as they squat or stand about the depots, with their merchandise in their hands!" (p. 290). This is Carpenter's depiction of the historical background of Native Americans: "The savage Indians were in former times dangerous and cruel foes. They took delight in killing women and children. They hid behind rocks and bushes to fight. . . . They used tomahawks to brain their victims, and delighted in torturing their captives and in burning them at the stake" (p. 293). Information about Australian native people is just as biased in Charles Redway Dryer's *Geography, Physical, Economic and Regional* (6), published in 1911, while V. M. Hillyer's 1929 text, *A Child's Geography of the World* (12), says that the most curious animals in Africa are not the animals but the people. Students of children's literature may not realize how outdated, misinformed, and biased informational books can be until they discover books such as these that influenced the thinking of school children earlier in this century.

2. Stereotypes Should Be Eliminated.

Does the book violate basic principles against racism and sexism? As the above examples make clear, informational books, like all books, should lack demeaning racist or sexist stereotypes. Brent Ashabranner's *Morning Star, Black Sun: The Northern Cheyenne Indians and America's Energy Crisis*, for example, meets this criterion. It portrays the Northern Cheyenne as a people with a culture worth preserving, who are striving to overcome their own problems. Compare Ashabranner's description of the Cheyenne Indians and their culture with quotes from the previously discussed *Carpenter's Geographical Reader*. "Although the Cheyenne did not have books, a system of writing, or schools, they had a tribal organization, codes of conduct, and ways of teaching their people that could rival those of any society anywhere" (p. 13). Later, the author describes the criteria for selecting Cheyenne leaders. "Chiefs were chosen for their wisdom, good judgment, and bravery, though they did not necessarily have to be great warriors. They did have to be good-hearted men who were concerned about their people" (p. 14). Some contemporary books reflect stereotypes through inclusion or exclusion of certain types of people in certain professions. For example, are people of both sexes and various racial and ethnic groups shown in illustrations depicting interest in science or science professions? The illustrations in Judy Cutchins and Ginny Johnston's *Are These Animals Real? How Museums Prepare Wildlife Exhibits* show that both men and women can be interested in the natural sciences.

3. Illustrations Should Clarify the Text.

Are the illustrations accurate? Illustrations should be as accurate as the text and add to its clarity. Photographs and drawings should be accompanied by explanatory legends keyed directly to the text, to allow children to expand their understanding of the principles or terminology presented. Millicent E. Selsam and Jerome Wexler's *The Amazing Dandelion*, for example, contains photographs of cross sections of a dandelion that identify the ovary, pappus, petal, anther tube, style, pollen, and stigma. As children read the technical terms in the text, they can easily locate

the corresponding parts of the dandelion in the photographs. Well-illustrated texts are very important in books that encourage experimentation. For example, Irwin Math's *Morse, Marconi, and You: Understanding and Building Telegraph, Telephone and Radio Sets* provides the young experimenter with detailed drawings of each experiment described in the book.

4. Analytical Thinking Should Be Encouraged.

Do children have an opportunity to become involved in solving problems logically? Many informational books, particularly scientific ones, should encourage children to observe, gather data, experiment, compare, and formulate hypotheses. They should encourage children to withhold judgment until enough data have been gathered or enough facts have been explored. Books that demonstrate scientific facts and principles should encourage children to do more experiments on their own and stress the value of additional background reading. Seymour Simon's *The Secret Clocks, Time Senses of Living Things* encourages readers to become involved with the principles of biological time clocks by providing step-by-step directions for experiments with bees, animals, plants, and the readers themselves. The book concludes with a list of books and magazine articles appropriate for additional reading.

5. Organization Should Aid Understanding.

Is the organization logical? Ideas in informational books should be broken down into easily understood component parts. Authors often use an organization that progresses from the simple to the more complex, or from the familiar to the unfamiliar, or from early to later development. In *Pack, Band, and Colony: The World of Social Animals*, Judith and Herbert Kohl introduce readers to the world of social animals by first telling a story about a boy's experiences with ravens and then describing how his experiences resulted in observations, informal experiments, and library research. Diagrams and recommended experiments increase comprehension of several difficult concepts. Diagrams of blocks and suggestions for manipulation by readers illustrate concepts related to dependence and independence in social animals.

Are organizational aids included? Reference aids such as table of contents, index, glossary, bibliography, and list of suggested readings can encourage children to understand the need for, and use of, organized reference skills. While books for very young children do not include all these aids, they are helpful for older children. For example, in *Farming Today Yesterday's Way* Cheryl Walsh Bellville uses boldface words in the text to identify the words that are defined in the glossary. Ruth Karen's *Feathered Serpent: The Rise and Fall of the Aztecs* has a table of contents at the beginning of the book as well as a detailed map showing the archaeological sites. At the end of the book are guides to Aztec Mexico, a pronunciation guide, a glossary, and a detailed index including cross-references.

6. *Style Should Stimulate Interest.*

Is the writing style lively and not too difficult for children of a certain age to understand? Kathryn Lasky's *Sugaring Time* is an excellent example of both stimulating literary style and careful documentation. Students of children's literature will enjoy discovering how the author uses language to depict setting. For example, she describes corn snow, large and granular snow crystals, as follows: "When Jonathan skis it sounds as if he is skimming across the thick frosting of a wedding cake" (p. 7). The maple sap "runs like streams of Christmas tinsel" (p. 19). The environment in the sugarhouse is "like sitting in a maple cloud surrounded by the muffled roar of the fire and the bubbling tumble of boiling sap" (p. 34). The photographs reinforce the language, following the family during all aspects of collecting and processing maple syrup.

Comparisons can also help clarify complex ideas or startling facts. In *Dinosaurs and Their World*, Laurence Pringle develops comparisons between known objects or animals and unknown animals when he describes dinosaurs: "Imagine a seventy-foot-long animal weighing more than a dozen elephants. . . . However, not all dinosaurs were huge. Some were only as big as automobiles. Others were as small as rabbits. . . .There were skinny dinosaurs that looked like ostriches. There were armored dinosaurs, built like army tanks" (p. 9).

Authors of credible informational books meet many of these guidelines. Consider in the following section how authors of books on history and geography, laws of nature, experiments and discoveries, and occupations and hobbies develop credible books that may stimulate and inform readers.

History and Culture

The Ancient World. Authors who write about the ancient world may develop credible books by citing the latest information gained from their own or others' research and by describing details in such a way that readers can visualize an ancient world. Because readers cannot verify facts about the ancient world through their own experiences, authors may compare known facts from ancient times with known facts from the contemporary world, include drawings that clarify information, and/or use photographs of museum objects or archaeological sites.

Ancient Mayan and Aztec civilizations in Central America are the subjects of several books. Carolyn Meyer and Charles Gallenkamp create a hint of mystery and excitement in their introduction to *The Mystery of the Ancient Maya*. Consider the development of vivid setting, the motivation of the two explorers, and the sense of discovery and anticipation in the following:

Two travelers—one American, one English—struggled through the jungle, hacking away the tangled vines with their machetes. New York City, which they had left that fall of 1839, seemed impossibly far away. Since their arrival in Central America the trip had been grueling. In the past few weeks they had endured hunger and had been thrown into a makeshift prison. They had hung on as their mules picked their way along the edges of cliffs. But now, standing on a river bank in Honduras, they felt hopeful again. On the opposite shore they could make out a stone wall, perhaps a hundred feet high but nearly hidden by the thick growth of trees. Maybe this was what they had been searching for—the lost city of Copan. (p. 3)

The organization of the book proceeds from a history of the early explorers, to the revelations made about the civilization, to the disclosures made about the people, and to the unanswered questions that are under investigation. Drawings, photographs, and excerpts from early journals add to the sense of time and place.

Malcolm E. Weiss's *Sky Watchers of Ages Past* discusses the scientific contributions of the ancient Maya and other early civilizations. Weiss introduces readers to the sophisticated astronomy developed by the Anasazi Indians, the Mayan calendar makers of the Yucatan, and Polynesian navigators.

Archaeologists in North America have investigated many of the roughly 10,000 Aztec ruins scattered from Guatemala northward to the

United States border. Ruth Karen, in *Feathered Serpent: The Rise and Fall of the Aztecs*, develops the thesis that a great civilization also flourished in North America. Her text, written for older children, is divided into three parts: a history of the Aztec civilization; a fictionalized story, "The Life of a Girl Called Windflower and the Death of a Boy Named Hungry Coyote," based on Aztec history; and a documentation of recent archaeological discoveries, including the summer palace of Cortez and a major Aztec temple site "with pyramids so ambitious in scale they match the pyramids in Egypt" (p. 169). One of the strengths of this book is its description of six vantage points that can be visited in order to gain firsthand knowledge of the Aztec people. By tying the past to the present, children may envision the possibility of making significant archaeological discoveries in the twentieth century. In addition, texts such as these provide positive materials for multiethnic studies. Children may discover that the Mayan and the Aztec civilizations are part of a strong North American heritage. They can also compare Karen's history of Aztec civilization with the settings and cultural details presented in Scott O'Dell's historical fiction *The Captive*, *The Feathered Serpent*, and *The Amethyst Ring*, discussed in chapter ten.

Archaeological investigations in Europe provide the sources for information in Susan Woodford's *The Parthenon* and Katherine East's *A King's Treasure: The Sutton Hoo Ship Burial*. Woodford's book, part of the Cambridge History Library, presents a detailed account of the building of the Greek Parthenon. The text follows a chronological order beginning in 490 B.C. and extending through current problems resulting from air pollution. Labeled drawings, captioned photographs, and detailed descriptions of ancient Greek life and religious practices could expand a study of Greek culture and Greek mythology. East's book, published in association with the British Museum, is based on an archaeological investigation that uncovered the burial site of an Anglo-Saxon king who lived in seventh-century England. East uses information and artifacts discovered at the site to reconstruct that period in history.

Readers who enjoy traditional literature and historical fiction set in medieval times and adults who would like to help children recreate medieval festivals should find Madeleine Pelner Cosman's *Medieval Holidays and Festivals: A Calendar of Celebrations* and Aliki Brandenberg's *A Medieval Feast* rewarding. Cosman's chapters are organized according to festivals characteristic of each month. Her detailed directions for costumes, games, settings, and recipes are easily followed and not too difficult to reproduce. Brandenberg's detailed illustrations follow a chronological order as the manor house is prepared, provisions are gathered, food is prepared, and the feast is presented. Sheila Sancha's *The Luttrell Village: Country Life in the Middle Ages* is good for comparative purposes. The full-page illustrations and accompanying text describe a year in the lives of people who lived in a fourteenth-century Lincolnshire village. The glossary adds to the understanding of the time period. Huck Scarry's pop-up book *Looking into the Middle Ages* will also provoke interest in the subject. These books should be helpful for librarians, teachers, and other adults who are interested in giving children a feeling for earlier times and cultures.

Authors may trace the history of a common item to show its importance in diverse cultures and across different time periods. Chris and Janie Filstrup's *Beadazzled: The Story of Beads*, for example, traces the history of beads from ancient times to the present. The authors describe and illustrate the use of beads for varied purposes such as calculating, counting prayers, money, and ornamentation. Color illustrations highlight the beauty of beadwork. Because the illustrations show beadwork from different time periods, they reinforce the authors' thesis that many cultures have created works of art and useful objects from beads. The Filstrups encourage readers to experiment with beadwork by including detailed directions for bead craft projects and sources where beads can be obtained.

History also includes religious traditions. Miriam Chaikin, the author of several books on Jewish holidays, retells the biblical story of Queen Esther and describes the celebration of Purim in *Make Noise, Make Merry: The Story and Meaning of Purim*. A glossary, an index, and a list of additional readings are excellent additions.

Piero Ventura's illustrations for Gian Paolo Ceserani's *Grand Constructions* create an architectural bridge between ancient and modern times. This large-format text includes forty-two great architectural wonders, beginning with Stonehenge and concluding with skyscrapers. The large, detailed drawings present a visual history of architectural highlights. A glossary of architectural terms provides helpful information.

The Modern World. The factual data in informational books about the modern world may be made credible by citing research, quoting authorities, quoting original sources, and providing detailed descriptions of the setting, circumstances, or situations. Photographs are often used to add authenticity.

Many informational books about the modern world help children develop an understanding of the varied people on earth, their struggles and achievements, and their impact on history. For example, Suzanne Hilton focuses on the early years of American history in *We the People: The Way We Were 1783–1793*. Hilton creates an authentic and lively history of America by incorporating quotations from primary sources such as letters, newspapers, and diaries, which clarify the attitudes of the people and the issues of the times. Consequently, this book communicates the fact that history is people rather than dates.

The cry of "Gold!" in 1898 created a great change in a land that previously had been peace-

ISSUE

···→≫◦≪←···

Content Bias in Informational Books: Creationism versus Evolutionism

A STUDY REPORTED IN *Publishers Weekly* found that the increasing controversy about the content of children's literature was most prevalent in contemporary fiction.[1] The content of textbooks and of informational library selections, however, was the second and third most often challenged. Over 95 percent of the reported challenges sought to limit rather than expand the information and points of view expressed in the literature. Objections to content focused on broad ideological questions such as evolution, creationism, and secular humanism.

Creationism versus evolutionism is receiving renewed interest as creationists claim materials centering on evolution deny students their religious beliefs. In contrast, evolutionists claim that creationism is a religious subject without scientific support. This debate extended into state legislatures and courts as states such as Arkansas and Louisiana passed laws specifying that creationism must be taught in conjunction with evolution. These laws, however, were challenged in the courts and overruled. The issue remains a topic of concern.

The religious debate broadened in 1986 when a U.S. district court ruled that "the Hawkins County, Tenn., School District must allow children of seven fundamentalist Christian families to 'opt out' of classes that have textbooks their parents consider objectionable on religious grounds" (p. 21).[2] In addition to materials on evolution, the parents in the Hawkins County lawsuit objected to readings that promoted secular humanism, feminism, the occult, pacifism, one-world government, tolerance for Eastern religions, and rebellious attitudes toward parents.

This debate will probably increase as higher courts, librarians, educators, parents, and publishers consider issues surrounding purchases for libraries and the need for, or restrictions against, a variety of viewpoints in informational literature.

[1]Mutter, John. "Study on School Censorship Finds Cases on Rise." *Publishers Weekly*, 7 August 1981, p. 12.

[2]Houston Chronicle News Service. "A 'Disaster:' Fundamentalists Bask in Educational Victory." *Houston Chronicle*, 26 October 1986, section 1, p. 21.

ful and isolated, populated by Native Americans, white trappers, and wild animals. Margaret Poynter's *Gold Rush! The Yukon Stampede of 1898* describes the people who abandoned their jobs and businesses in the United States to travel to rugged Alaska. The author, whose parents and maternal grandparents were Alaskan pioneers, uses her knowledge of the period to describe those frantic, adventuresome days. Old photographs add authenticity by showing prospectors hitting the trail, panning for gold, sluicing the gold, climbing the Chilkoot Pass in winter, and walking through downtown Skagway in 1898.

An author's style of writing may entice readers to explore the past. For example, David Weitzman's introduction to *Windmills, Bridges, and Old Machines: Discovering Our Industrial Past* encourages interest and exploration by sounding as if the author is talking to the reader:

We're about to take a walk in time, back through the years when America was growing. Along the way we'll be looking for the work of some of America's first builders and engineers, two centuries of canals, windmills, and waterwheels, steam engines and bridges, furnaces and foundries and locomotives, all kinds of wondrous things. . . . The search needn't take us very far. We're sure to find something close by . . . just around the corner, downtown, or just a little farther along a bike trail.(unnumbered introduction)

Other books exploring the industrial past of the United States include E. Boyd Smith's *The Railroad Book*, first published in 1913, and David Macaulay's *Mill*, describing and illustrating mills as they would have appeared in nineteenth-century New England.

Highly emotional periods in history are difficult to present objectively. Seymour Rossel, however, approaches *The Holocaust* with a historian's detachment. He traces Adolf Hitler's rise to power; describes the harassment, internment, and extermination of many Jewish people; and discusses the Nuremburg trials of the Nazis. Rossel effectively quotes from original sources, such as diaries and letters, to allow readers to visualize the human drama and draw their own conclusions.

Robert Goldston's *Sinister Touches: The Secret War Against Hitler* focuses upon people and organizations that struggled against the Nazis between 1939 and 1945. A chronological diary of events preceding each chapter, numerous quotations from documents and historical figures, a bibliography, and additional suggested reading

enhance the book's authenticity. The concluding chapter, "Apocalypse Now," begins with a hypothetical scenario, a description of what might have happened if Hitler had won the race for atomic weapons, dropped the atomic bomb on London, and made his demands upon the world.

Readers may compare Robert Goldston's description of atomic warfare with the highly visual and personalized description in Toshi Maruki's *Hiroshima No Pika* (The Flash of Hiroshima), and with Laurence Pringle's scientific observations in *Nuclear War: Fom Hiroshima to Nuclear Winter*. Through a picture-storybook format, Maruki relates the experiences of seven-year-old Mii on August 6, 1945, as mother and child pass by fire, death, and destruction. Maruki, who actively campaigns for nuclear disarmament and world peace, concludes her book on a hopeful note: "It can't happen again if no one drops the bomb" (p. 43, unnumbered). Pringle's text covers the history of nuclear weapons and suggests probable consequences of using them.

Daniel S. Davis's *Behind Barbed Wire: The Imprisonment of Japanese Americans during World War II* presents another emotional period in history. This book, discussed in chapter eleven, effectively explores attitudes toward Japanese Americans before and after the attack on Pearl Harbor and the effects of internment on the later lives of Japanese Americans.

All these informational books about World War II provide background for historical fiction about the period, as discussed in chapter ten.

Some authors explore various cultures by studying one person or family in depth. Investigative reporter, photographer, and author David Mangurian creates a detailed and accurate view of Indian life in Latin America in his *Children of the Incas*. He adds authenticity to his book by describing his travels through Latin America and his experiences with the people. Mangurian's colloquial, first-person narrative makes his experiences very accessible to children. He creates additional authenticity by telling part of the story from the viewpoint of a thirteen-year-old boy. Exceptional photographs document the lives of the Tasaday, a Stone Age Philippino people, in John Nance's *Lobo of the Tasaday*. Once again, by focusing on a child, an author vividly depicts social organization, living conditions, and beliefs.

Books about people from various cultures and about people who have different occupations encourage children to expand their interests and understandings. Sabra Holbrook's *Canada's Kids* relates information about the families, schools, hobbies, and expectations of Canadian children— both rural and urban, white and Native Canadian.

Lila Perl's *Red Star and Green Dragon: Looking at New China* combines a concise history of China with a description of contemporary China. The photographs of ordinary people heighten the

ISSUE

⋯⁓⧓⧓❃⧓⧓⁓⋯

Sharing Books about the Nuclear Age

TWO BOOKS THAT either depict nuclear holocaust or provide allegorical interpretations of the arms race are receiving both praise and criticism. Toshi Maruki's *Hiroshima No Pika*[1] is a highly illustrated, picture-storybook depiction of the bombing of Hiroshima. Seuss's *The Butter Battle Book*[2] is a highly illustrated, allegorical fantasy depicting the consequences when opposing forces increase the destructive powers of their weapons.

Praise for these books that actively champion nuclear disarmament is exemplified in reviews in *The New Republic*[3]; and in *Social Education*.[4] For example, Joan Ganz Cooney (3) states that *The Butter Battle Book* "brilliantly dramatized for children the number one issue of the age." The book review subcommittee for the National Council for the Social Studies Book Council identified *Hiroshima No Pika* as an excellent basis for discussions of modern war and nuclear holocaust with children who have intermediate and advanced reading ability. It was selected as a 1983 Notable Children's Trade Book in the Field of Social Studies and was awarded the Ehon Nippon Prize for the most excellent picture book published in Japan.

In contrast to these positive reviews, Richard Elias[5] voices strong concern about sharing such books with elementary-school children. Elias discusses the controversy generated by the nuclear-education movement and asks that librarians consider whether or not a book can help children cope with fear and whether or not children will benefit from the information in the books. Elias argues that both *The Butter Battle Book* and *Hiroshima No Pika* are actually adult books "in masquerade."

Students of children's literature should read the two books, read the reviews of the books, share the books with librarians and other adults, and discuss the positive and/or the negative attributes of the books. Consider Elias's charges. If you believe these books are actually books for adults masquerading as children's books, suggest some reasons why the authors would present their messages in children's-book format. Is this appropriate or inappropriate?

[1]Maruki, Toshi. *Hiroshima No Pika.* Lothrop, 1982.

[2]Seuss. *The Butter Battle Book.* Random House, 1984.

[3]Cooney, Joan Ganz. *The New Republic.* March 26, 1984.

[4]"Notable Children's Trade Books in the Field of Social Studies." *Social Education,* April 1983, pp. 241–252.

[5]Elias, Richard. "Facts of Life in the Nuclear Age." *School Library Journal* 31 (April 1985): 42–43.

Photographs illustrate the nonmechanized farming techniques described in the text. (From *Farming Today Yesterday's Way*, by Cheryl Walsh Bellville. Copyright © 1984 by Cheryl Walsh Bellville. By permission of Carolrhoda Books, Inc.)

readers' understanding. Excellent supporting information includes a list of important dates, a bibliography, and an index.

Books about rural life in the United States, illustrated with interesting photographs, include Patricia Demuth's *Joel: Growing Up a Farm Man*, which portrays the responsibilities involved in being a farmer in the Midwest, and Cheryl Walsh Bellville's *Farming Today Yesterday's Way*, which shows a twentieth-century farmer using horses and other nonmechanized farming techniques. Both books supply considerable detail and may help young readers gain a clearer understanding of farm life in America.

Roger Englander, an award-winning producer of opera, effectively uses his extensive opera background in *Opera, What's All the Screaming About?* This "guide for the curious listener" traces the development of opera from its beginnings in the European Renaissance to the contemporary musical theater. Of special interest to the novice is Englander's method of depicting the plots of famous operas through newspaper-style headlines:

LOVERS BURIED ALIVE IN TOMB
AS JILTED PRINCESS MOURNS
Aida
Music: Giuseppe Verdi
Libretto: Antonio Ghislanzoni, in Italian
First Performed: Cairo, December 24, 1871 (p. 25)

Englander's text includes extensive reference materials; lists of leading composers, librettists, and opera companies; a glossary; a discography; and an index.

Laws of Nature

Effective informational books about the laws of nature encourage children to understand their own bodies, observe nature, explore the life cycles of animals, consider the impact of endangered species, experiment with plants, understand the balance of the smallest ecosystem, and explore the earth's geology. In order to create effective and credible books, authors must blend fact into narrative; facts about animals, for example, need to be gained from observation and research. Close-up photography is especially effective in clarifying information and stimulating interest; for example, photographs may illustrate what happens inside an egg or a nest or follow the life cycle of an animal or a plant. Labeled diagrams may clarify understanding. Maps may show natural habitats of animals, migration patterns of birds, or locations of earthquakes. If authors present new vocabulary or concepts, they should define the terms, illustrate them with diagrams or photographs, and proceed from known to unknown information. Clearly developed activities that encourage children to observe and experiment add to the useful potential of a book. A bibliography, index, and list of additional readings are helpful.

The Human Body. Informational books about the human body are especially interesting to readers who are curious about their own bodies and how they function. Books for children about the human body range from overviews to detailed discussions of one aspect of the body, such as the brain or vision. Some books also discuss body-related issues such as the right to live or to die, genetic engineering, and human origins.

Two books on the human body illustrate the importance of labeled diagrams when studying anatomy. Jonathan Miller's *The Human Body* is a fascinating, twelve-page pop-up book. Each double-page spread, along with tabs that simulate functions, explains some part of the human body. Body parts are labeled with numbers and then explained in the captions for the pop-up illustrations. Ruth and Bertel Bruun clarify their longer text, *The Human Body*, with diagrams and drawings that show the interiors of various body regions and the relationships of these regions to each other.

In-depth presentations of specific body parts and functions are subjects in numerous informational books. For example, Hilda Simon focuses on the miracle of sight in *Sight and Seeing: A World of Light and Color*. Simon clarifies a complex topic through the extensive use of color-coded drawings. Color comparisons clarify corresponding parts of an eye and a camera and differences between human and animal sight. For example, in the chapter on color perception, Simon compares colors of wildflowers as humans see them and as bees might perceive them. Simon's extensive text includes a discussion of special visual adaptations that are unique to some animals. In *The Story of Your Hand*, Alvin and Virginia B. Silverstein use drawings and experiments to focus on the structure and functions of hands.

Alan Nourse's *Your Immune System* discusses the body's immune system and illustrates it with photographs and diagrams. Nourse's writing style heightens interest and understanding; for example, he compares the body's immune system to an army whose soldiers protect the body against alien invaders. Clearly written information about the body's ability to heal various injuries is found in Joanna Cole's *Cuts, Breaks, Bruises and Burns: How Your Body Heals*.

Anecdotes from real case histories increase the reader's interest in Margery and Howard Facklam's *The Brain: Magnificent Mind Machine*. Information gained by studying people who have lost various brain functions provides the background information in this text.

Two books on child birth illustrate the different perspectives found in books on this sensitive subject. Stephen Parker and John Bavosi's *Life Before Birth: The Story of the First Nine Months* is a straightforward discussion of the facts related to the fertilization of the egg, the development and growth of the fetus, and the birth of the baby. The book, which is enhanced with colored illustrations adapted from a slide program at the British Museum, concludes with a photograph of a newborn baby. Camilla Jessel develops a broader scope of coverage in *The Joy of Birth: A Book for Parents and Children*. As in the previous book, Jessel's presentation of facts is straightforward. Unlike the previous text, this book emphasizes the mother's physical changes, the birth process itself, and the care of newborn babies. Black-and-white photographs follow the sequence of an actual birth, show the breast feeding of a baby, and show babies with their families.

Several informational books for older children provide detailed information about the human species and may encourage further reading and discussion about controversial subjects. In *Human Origins*, anthropologist Richard E. Leakey traces the evolution of humans from early ape-like creatures to farmers. Maps, photographs, drawings, and recommendations for further reading clarify this informative text. Contemporary issues related to humanity are the focus in Ann E. Weiss's *Bioethics: Dilemmas in Modern Medicine*. Weiss uses case histories of people such as Karen Ann Quinlan to discuss the moral issues related to concerns such as the right to live or to die, conflicts between medicine and religion, organ transplants, and human experimentation. A bibliography of additional readings provides sources for library research and additional discussion.

Animals. Authors who write effectively about prehistoric animals or about modern-day reptiles and amphibians, birds, land invertebrates (earthworms), insects, and mammals must present their facts clearly without giving their animals human qualities and emotions. Because books about animals are popular with many different age groups, authors must consider the experiential backgrounds of their readers as they develop new concepts.

Ancient Reptiles. With scientists as detectives and fossils as clues, twentieth-century children can experience the thrill of investigating the earth's pre-human past and ancient animals. Children often become enthusiastic amateur paleontologists as they learn about dinosaurs in books, study about them in museums, search for fossilized footprints or bones, and make dinosaur models. Books on dinosaurs range from highly illustrated texts for younger children, such as Russell Freedman's *Dinosaurs and Their Young*, to texts for older children that provide extensive scientific details, such as Helen Roney Sattler's *Dinosaurs of North America*. Freedman's book explores the significance of the 1978 discovery that raised questions about how these reptiles raised their young. Drawings of both dinosaurs and excavation sites clarify the text. In contrast, Sattler's book is arranged by geologic time periods, and describes the characteristics and habitats of more than eighty types of dinosaurs. Further readings and an index add to the usefulness. Other books that explore the subject of dinosaurs are Laurence Pringle's *Dinosaurs and People: Fossils, Facts, and Fantasies*, which traces research associated with dinosaurs, David C. Knight's *"Dinosaurs" that Swam and Flew*, which discusses lesser-known reptiles, and William Mannetti's *Dinosaurs in Your Backyard*, which challenges some previous theories about dinosaurs and provides new interpretations suggesting that birds are feathered dinosaurs, dinosaurs may have been warm blooded, and some dinosaurs previously believed to be water inhabitants spent most of the time on land. Mannetti, however, implies that the theories he presents are accepted by all authorities and does not refer to opposing viewpoints or discuss how others have interpreted the same evidence. Young readers may compare these various books and critically evaluate the information they present.

THROUGH THE EYES OF AN AUTHOR

Writing Natural History for Young Readers

Naturalist, former war correspondent, spokesman for endangered species, and recipient of numerous awards for outstanding science trade books for children, author JACK DENTON SCOTT discusses his beliefs about writing children's nonfictional books.

DEMANDS ARE PRECISE: Be accurate. Be relaxed; write fluently; never write down to your readers; never try to write up either. Know your audience; also know your subject; but even if you do know it, research it so that you will know perhaps more than you or anyone else will want to know. Put these all together and they may be an axiom for writing nonfiction for your readers.

But there is more: There can be no cloudy language; writing must be simple, crisp, clear. This, in fact, should be a primer for all writing. Children demand the best from a writer. If young readers become bored, confused, puzzled by style, or showered with a writer's self-important, complicated words you've lost readers. Young readers instinctively shy away from the pretentious and the phony.

In the dozen photo-essays that photographer Ozzie Sweet and I have produced for Putnam and our brilliant editor, Margaret Frith, we have worked with one object in mind: Entertain and inform. We believe that children want to learn; and everyone knows that they want to be entertained. We have tried to do this with clarity in words and with dramatic but thoughtfully conceived photographs by perhaps the most talented man with the camera in the U.S.

We have also introduced our series of books to children with a new technique. Action, constant movement, words flowing

Worms, Insects, Spiders, and Snakes. In *Twist, Wiggle, and Squirm: A Book About Earthworms*, a book for young children, Laurence Pringle encourages children to discover and explore the different kinds of earthworms by identifying the worms' body segments, feeding habits, and value to plants. He gives readers step-by-step directions for capturing an earthworm, discovering its sensitivity to light, and locating the bristles, or setae, on each segment. The simplified text and activities appeal to many young readers.

Oxford Scientific Films effectively uses large color photographs with short captions to follow life cycles of the *Mosquito*. Julie Brinckloe's *Fireflies!* shares a young boy's fascination with the insects as he watches them, captures them in a jar, and then realizes that he must release them or they will die.

Authors of informational books may entice children's interest by presenting challenges or comparisons. In *A Spider Might*, Tom Walther encourages children to understand the remarkable capabilities of spiders by asking readers to try jumping twenty times their own length, as does the zebra spider he describes and illustrates. In *Someone Saw a Spider: Spider Facts and Folktales*, Shirley Climo compares factual information and spider folklore from various cultures.

Snakes fascinate just about everybody. In Joanna Cole's *A Snake's Body*, Jerome Wexler's series of photographs shows the functions of a python's body as it captures and swallows a chick. Seymour Simon, who has had over twenty books selected as outstanding Science Trade Books for Children, effectively presents straightforward facts about snakes and dispels some myths about them in *Poisonous Snakes* and *Meet the Giant Snakes*. In the latter book, Simon makes clarifying comparisons: the boa constrictor is as long as a sedan automobile, the African python is as long as a station wagon, and both the anaconda and the reticulated python are as long as a school bus.

Mammals. Jack Denton Scott and photographer Ozzie Sweet have collaborated to give children

into photographs, photographs flowing into words, no labored captions, no slowing of pace. Almost a cinematic technique. This is difficult, demanding that photographer and writer work closely together.

I, personally, also have the belief that too much weird way-out fiction is pushed at children. (I have nothing against fiction; in fact I also write adult fiction.) But children have their own vivid and creative imaginations that they bring to their reading. One 10-year-old boy wrote me that while he was reading our book, *Canada Geese,* he actually flew south with the geese. I bet he did. I *hope* he did.

Ozzie Sweet and I also object to violence in children's literature; it's boring, it's burdensome, and it's unwanted by children. I write of the free, wild creatures and try to give children straight information that will interest them and educate them, staying away from cuteness or giving animals or birds human traits which, of course, they don't have. There is an entire essay on our shrinking world and what wildlife means to children, wildlife that may not even be around when our readers become adults.

Finally, we believe that children who are forming habits and outlooks that will serve them forever are more important than adult readers and we feel fortunate that we have the opportunity to give them worthwhile subjects to think about. Thus we choose those subjects carefully for our intelligent and demanding audience. Ask any librarian or teacher. They know children's standards better than anyone. And thank God for librarians and teachers! Without them the darkness of ignorance would close in much more quickly than it is doing at present, pushed by television which creates non-readers and a growing careless attitude toward the written word—by adults, of course. Not children. They still are excited about good books and receptive to the well-writtten word. Ozzie Sweet and I shall continue to try to give them the best we have.

several outstanding books about mammals. Because their work exemplifies many of the characteristics of outstanding informational books for children, we will consider several of the techniques Scott uses in *The Book of the Pig*. First, he skillfully blends facts acquired from animal experts and naturalists and the observations of a pig farmer into the narrative. Consider, for example, his support of pigs' intelligence, cooperativeness, and cleanliness: he provides examples of pigs' adaptability, research demonstrating the intelligence of pigs and the meaning of the sounds pigs utter, photographs of pigs walking or playing with people, and proof that young pigs try to keep their farrowing pen clean. He uses frequent comparisons to help readers understand pigs' nature and development. For example, a family that raise pigs "romp with their piglets as they would with puppies" (p. 9). Later he cites research that claims that a newborn "piglet's mobility is equivalent to that of a 2½-year-old child" (p. 20). He clarifies the meaning of new vocabulary: "the mother, or sow," (p. 15), "giving birth to, or farrowing," (p. 19). Sweet's photographs enhance the text and frequently add warmth and humor. When the text indicates that "pigs really are in clover" (p. 7), a photograph shows piglets in a flower-dappled meadow.

Several books on animals are especially appropriate for young readers because the subjects are familiar. Joanna Cole's *A Cat's Body* explores characteristic cat behaviors such as pouncing, reacting to moving objects, and purring. The text and photographs may encourage children to observe their own pets. In *My Puppy Is Born*, Cole presents the birth of miniature dachshund puppies. Jerome Wexler's photographs show the pregnant dog going into her box, the emergence of the first puppy, born inside a sac, and the mother tearing the sac and licking the puppy. The book follows the growth of the puppies during their first eight weeks as they are unable to see or hear, as they nurse, and then as they open their eyes and take their first steps.

Other illustrated books about familiar animals that enhance younger children's observational and descriptive abilities include Lilo Hess's *Diary of a Rabbit*; David McPhail's *Farm Morning*, which accompanies a young girl and her father as they take care of the barnyard animals; zoologist Dorothy Hinshaw Patent's *Farm Animals*, *The Sheep Book*, and *Thoroughbred Horses*; and Tana Hoban's *A Children's Zoo*.

Millicent Selsam's *How to Be a Nature Detective*, illustrated by Ezra Jack Keats, encourages children to look for and identify animal tracks. In Seymour Simon's *Animal Fact/Animal Fiction*, children can decide whether humorously illustrated animals are real or creatures of fantasy. Children guess the identity of an animal silhouette in Beau Gardner's *Guess What?*, then turn the page to reveal the animal.

Wild mammals, their contributions, and their survival are common topics in informational books. Authors may describe the contributions of animals, argue for their control and protection by means of responsible population control, and use statistics to develop points on survival and to demonstrate the plight of the animal.

In *The Kingdom of the Wolves*, Scott Barry pleas for protection of the wolf, which he depicts as a powerful, intelligent, social animal that does not deserve the reputation suggested in fairy tales. His argument seems credible because he describes seven years of working with and observing wolves. (Children who have read Jean Craighead George's *Julie of the Wolves* may enjoy reading Barry's description of wolf body language and the wolves' lives on the Alaskan tundra.)

In *Whales, Giants of the Deep*, Dorothy Hinshaw Patent concludes her in-depth discussion of whales with a history of whaling and the consequences of an unregulated industry. While Patent states the arguments against a moratorium on whaling presented by Japan, Norway, and the USSR, she concludes with a strong statement in favor of the moratorium:

While the whaling nations argue that some whale species are not diminishing and will not become extinct even with continued whaling, conservationists believe that without a ban on commercial whaling, whales will disappear from the Earth. Unfortunately, all nations that kill whales do not belong to the IWC. So even if Norway, Japan, and the U.S.S.R. decide to abide by the IWC moratorium, some whaling may continue. We can only hope that it is not enough to further endanger these magnificent animals. (p. 82)

Other excellent books about wild animals and protection of species include Kay McDearmon's *Rocky Mountain Bighorns*, Barbara Ford's *Alligators, Raccoons, and Other Survivors: The Wildlife of the Future*, and Laurence Pringle's *Feral: Tame Animals Gone Wild*.

Depending upon their purposes and points of view, authors may approach the subject of monkeys, apes, and chimpanzees quite differently.

Photographs show Nim and a researcher identifying parts of the body. (Photograph copyright © 1980 by Herbert S. Terrace. Reprinted from *The Story of Nim*, by Anna Michel, photographs by Susan Kuklin and Herbert S. Terrace, by permission of Alfred A. Knopf, Inc.)

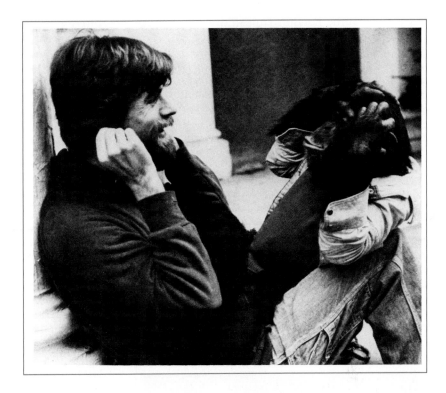

For example, Nina Leen's purpose in *Monkeys* is to provide general information and some consideration of the possible extinction of monkeys. Consequently she includes a short description of each primate's habitat, use of prehensile tail, preferred foods, vocalization, sleeping habits, grooming, family relationships, and any danger of extinction. In *Watching Them Grow: Inside a Zoo Nursery*, Joan Hewett uses photographs to depict the life of a young chimpanzee living in the nursery of the San Diego Zoo. Photographs and text inform children how the primates are cared for, how they need and respond to affection, and how they move from crib to cage, emphasizing the important work done by zoo employees. Anna Michel's *The Story of Nim: The Chimp Who Learned Language* reports Herbert Terrace's research as he tried to teach a chimpanzee to recognize and use words in sign language. Linda Koebner's *From Cage to Freedom: A New Beginning for Laboratory Chimpanzees* presents a more cautious and skeptical view of using chimpanzees for experimental purposes. Her book reports results from a research project that investigated whether formerly caged chimps can learn to survive without humans and eventually breed in their natural environment.

Birds. The topics of informational books about birds range from common barnyard fowl to exotic tropical birds. Through these books students of children's literature can observe various techniques that authors use to create interest for young children and how they present and clarify concepts new to older children.

In *A First Look at Bird Nests*, a simply written book for young readers, Millicent Selsam and Joyce Hunt describe the nests of common American birds and tell how the nests are built. The authors stimulate the development of children's observational skills by asking questions and providing puzzles. The answers to the questions are located in the accompanying illustrations. In *Window into a Nest*, a book for older children, Geraldine Lux Flanagan uses and describes more sophisticated observational techniques to reveal the stages in chickadee nesting and hatching behavior. The text describes the placement of a concealed camera into an opening in a wooden birdhouse. The photographs clarify behavioral patterns, such as floor hammering before nest building, reactions of alarm when an intruder peers into the house, struggles with straw brought into the home, and the feeding ceremony between male and female. Flanagan's text, the winner of the London Times Educational Supplement Senior Information Book Award for 1975, shows the careful research that should go into scientific investigation. The need for accuracy and observational techniques are also emphasized in Ada Graham's *Six Little Chickadees: A Scientist and Her Work with Birds*. In *A Bird's Body*, Joanna Cole relies on diagrams and photographs of parakeets and cockatiels to help readers understand flying ability and behavioral characteristics.

Close-up photography is especially effective in books written about evolving embryos. Several books clarify this development by allowing readers to see what happens inside an egg—for example, Oxford Scientific Films' *The Chicken and the Egg*, an excellent book for young children, and Hans-Heinrich Isenbart's *A Duckling Is Born*.

Powerful flying birds and exotic water birds have interested a number of eminent researchers, writers, and photographers. Because the

Carefully sequenced photographs show how an endangered species is helped by science. (From *Saving the Peregrine Falcon*, by Caroline Arnold. Photographs copyright © 1985 by Richard R. Hewett. By permission of Carolrhoda Books, Inc.)

birds and their environments may be new to young readers, many books for young children present most information through photographs. For example, in Caroline Arnold's *Saving the Peregrine Falcon* the large photographs alone are sufficient to show scientists raising the endangered birds in captivity, encouraging them to identify with falcons rather than humans, and releasing them into the environment. In contrast, Francine Jacobs's *Africa's Flamingo Lake*, written for older children, emphasizes more abstract concepts, such as the conservationist's struggle to preserve Nakuru Lake, the support for four hundred kinds of birds and for the greatest flamingo population in the world. Jacobs encourages readers to ponder the issues involved by contrasting the viewpoints and efforts of conservationists with the viewpoints and interests of people who want to develop the area. Children who enjoy reading Jean Craighead George's ecological mystery novel *Who Killed Cock Robin?* can discover that the people of Kenya are having to investigate and solve many of the same problems that are found in the northeastern United States. Like the robin in the fictional account, the flamingo is an ecological weather vane in this book depicting the realities of wildlife.

The efforts to save endangered birds or birds that are harmed through human cruelty are also effectively presented in Paula Hendrich's *Saving America's Birds* and in several books written by Jack Denton Scott and illustrated with photographs by Ozzie Sweet, including *Orphans from the Sea*, a compelling book about attempts by the Florida Suncoast Seabird Sanctuary to save the brown pelican. Because Scott includes various theories about birds and describes research, older children may discover the importance of distinguishing between fact and theory in informational books. For example, Scott presents various theories about the migrating habits of geese in *Canada Geese*. He reinforces his factual information by describing studies such as the Stellar-Orientation System that tested the star-map theory of how the geese are able to find exact locations and follow exact routes year after year.

The majority of the animal books discussed here were written by eminent authorities in animal studies. In the introduction to *The Daywatchers*, artist and author Peter Parnall identifies himself as a self-taught rather than a formally educated naturalist. Consequently, he employs his own feelings, memories, experiences, and observations when writing about and illustrating the birds of prey in this large text. Personal anecdotes enrich the writing as each chapter reveals Parnall's discoveries and his emerging feelings of wonder. The artist's eye, rather than the perfection of a camera, rules the illustrations. Parnall states that he tried to capture a feeling, "not every feather, but the character, the aura, of the creatures, whatever those qualities are that set them apart from the chicken and the mole. Children dream as lions and eagles. I still do" (p. 11). This book might motivate young readers to observe nature and to achieve their own sense of wonder.

Plants. Informational books about plants may be especially rewarding for children if the books develop clear details in logical order, include diagrams and photographs that illustrate terminology, and encourage children to become involved in learning. Because Millicent E. Selsam uses many of these techniques, her books provide worthwhile examples. In *The Amazing Dandelion*, Selsam effectively introduces the considerable reproductive potential of the dandelion by showing two photographs of a field: in one photograph the field contains a single dandelion plant; a few years later, the field is covered with dandelions. Then Selsam attracts readers' attention and speculation as she asks how the dandelion is able to spread so quickly. Why is it one of the most successful plants? The text and photographs answer this question by tracing the life cycle of the dandelion. Several experiments also encourage children's involvement in learning about why the dandelion is so successful in its reproduction. Other books by Selsam also contain step-by-step directions accompanied by photographs. In *Popcorn* Selsam describes how to sprout seeds in a glass, transplant them into a garden or container, pollinate the corn, and wait for it to reach maturity. In *Cotton* a dime next to the first two leaves of a cotton seedling clarifies size, close-up photographs effectively illustrate the stages in plant development, and labeled photographs and drawings clarify terminology.

Another example of an informational book that develops concepts about plants through chronological order and personal experience is Patricia Lauber's *Seeds Pop! Stick! Glide!* Lauber's text and Jerome Wexler's photographs help children understand the many different ways that seeds

travel and disperse. Consider, for example, the presentation of Queen Anne's lace: the text and photographs proceed in chronological order from a plant with many small flowers, to its dried appearance in early winter, and finally to what happens when the dried plant opens and closes its umbrella. Lauber encourages children's involvement in the discovery process by describing an experiment they can do that resembles the plant's changes in nature.

The Let's-Read-and-Find-Out Science Book series contains several books that allow children to explore the world of plants. For example, Phyllis S. Busch's *Cactus in the Desert* encourages children to learn about a variety of cacti, from the tall saguaro to the tiniest pincushion. The text emphasizes the ability of cacti to store water and survive in dry climates. In order to help children perceive height and quantity, the illustrations compare the cactus with known quantities: the height of a saguaro cactus is compared to ten people standing on each other's shoulders; the amount of water evaporating from a regular tree is illustrated as being about 320 quarts, compared with less than a glass from a cactus. The book concludes with suggestions of cacti that can be raised at home and recommendations for their care.

Anita Holmes's *Cactus: The All American Plant*, written for older readers, describes the major kinds of cacti, discusses the natural surroundings, and stresses the interdependence of life forms. Like Busch's book for younger readers, Holmes encourages readers to learn more about the cacti by following instructions for raising cacti. Unlike the simpler text, Holmes provides an extensive glossary, a bibliography, and information on classification.

Photographs and drawings often clarify books about the complex concepts related to photosynthesis. Masaharu Suzuki's photographs in Sylvia Johnson's *Potatoes* are especially interesting. Colored water produces photographs that clearly illustrate the location of the vascular system in a plant stem and the location of the vascular ring in the potato.

Illustrators of informational books may clarify size concepts by photographing common objects next to the plant or seed. Jerome Wexler uses this technique in *From Spore to Spore: Ferns and How They Grow* to clarify size and to show that the photographs are magnified. A common pin

Each spot is a sort of little package wrapped in a thin membrane. A single spot is called a sorus; more than one are called sori.

Magnified common objects clarify these size concepts. (From *From Spore to Spore: Ferns and How They Grow*, by Jerome Wexler. Copyright © 1985 by Jerome Wexler. By permission of Dodd, Mead & Company.)

placed next to fern seedlings and a penny shown next to a new leaf illustrate the diminutive sizes. Likewise, a greatly enlarged penny next to two sporangia illustrates the microscopic size of the spores. Without such visual comparisons readers would have difficulty understanding size perspective.

The Earth's Ecology. The planet earth is one ecosystem: a place in nature with interrelated living and nonliving parts. Much smaller ecosys-

tems exist within it, ecosystems that are small enough for children to observe and thereby gain new understandings about the balance of nature. Laurence Pringle is one of the excellent authors who write about both familiar and unfamiliar ecosystems. In *City and Suburb: Exploring an Ecosystem*, Pringle describes and encourages students to observe an environment that is familiar to many children. He entices older children's interest by describing how a city, which may be similar to their own, affects its surroundings: heat islands, air pollution beyond the city, dying trees, and adapting plants and animals. Pringle encourages children to discover these changes and a possible abundance of plants and animals by searching their own environments, including cemeteries, vacant lots, parks, and sidewalk cracks. Many children who read this book and then explore their own environments are amazed at the variety of plants, insects, mammals, birds, and snakes found within their city. Discussions may also make the children aware of the problems created by the urban environment.

Children may discover the forest ecosystem through Pringle's *Into the Woods: Exploring the Forest Ecosystem*, in which Pringle shows the various forest layers, the animals and plants that live in each layer, and how each is an important part of the forest's energy cycle; or they may understand and debate various viewpoints about the values and disadvantages of forest fires through Pringle's *Natural Fire: Its Ecology in Forests*. In *Death Is Natural*, Pringle shows that death is also a necessary part of life in the plant, animal, and human worlds, because it makes life possible for succeeding generations. Children discover answers to some important questions: Why is death necessary? What happens to a living thing after it dies? How does the death of one animal or plant affect others of its kind? These questions can stimulate discussions among students. Pringle's books encourage additional study as they contain many reference aids such as indexes, glossaries, and lists of related readings.

Seymour Simon's *The Secret Clocks, Time Senses of Living Things* is another good book for students of children's literature to evaluate. Simon uses several techniques to interest children and help them investigate and understand the biological or "internal clocks" (a term identified by the research of German scientist Gustav Kramer) that help plants, animals, and humans survive. First he stimulates interest in the subject by posing a series of questions: "What makes the clock of an animal or plant run so accurately? What sets these biological clocks and keeps them going? Do animals somehow learn to keep time, or do they depend upon changes in their surroundings? What factors work to keep a plant on time?" (p. 8). Then he uses the questions to develop a logical organization and to describe how scientists and nature observers have investigated these questions, made discoveries, and arrived at yet more questions resulting from the discoveries. He involves children in the learning process by discussing step-by-step directions for experiments with the biological clocks of plants, animals, and humans that children can perform and by suggesting related readings.

Morphology—the size, shape, and structure of living things and how these factors relate to daily life and evolution—is also important in nature. Dorothy Hinshaw Patent, a zoologist, discusses topics such as the significance of different kinds of skeletons, blood systems, types of structures used for moving, muscles, chewing and digestive organs, communicative organs, and reproductive organs. *Sizes and Shapes in Nature—What They Mean* includes photographs, drawings, an index, and a reference list of both books and magazine articles that will assist older children in investigating these topics.

The Earth's Geology. Because children often see the results of earthquakes on television, geology is a subject that interests many children. Seymour Simon's *Danger from Below: Earthquakes—Past, Present, and Future* provides a comprehensive coverage: a history of devastating earthquakes and ancient people's explanations for them; explanations of the Richter Scale and the Modified Mercali Intensity Scale; discussion of recent discoveries about how and why earthquakes occur and of how scientists are working to monitor their intensity and to predict where and when they will occur; and safety precautions children should know about. Photographs of actual earthquake damage show earthquakes' destructive power, and maps illustrate the plates of the earth's crust and identify places where earthquakes are likely to happen. Students of children's literature may find it interesting to compare this book written for older students with Hershell and Joan L. Nixon's book for younger students, *Earthquakes: Nature in Motion*. These books provide interesting background informa-

tion for children who also read Laurence Yep's novel *Dragonwings*, which describes the great San Francisco earthquake of 1906.

Children also see on television the results of volcanic eruptions. Since the eruption of Mount St. Helens, several books emphasizing volcanic activity in North America have appeared. In *The Mount St. Helens Disaster: What We've Learned*, Thomas and Virginia Aylesworth discuss the chronological order of seismic events that led up to the eruption and enrich the text with eyewitness accounts, photographs, diagrams, and maps. Comparisons may be made between the Aylesworth text and Kathryn Goldner and Carole Vogel's *Why Mount St. Helens Blew Its Top*. Hershell and Joan Nixon's *Volcanoes: Nature's Fireworks* provides a source for studying volcanic eruptions in other parts of the world.

Technical terms in informational books about geology may be difficult for children to understand unless authors clarify the terms with photographs and/or drawings. Written descriptions of terms such as *cirques*, *hanging valleys*, *stalactites*, and *stalagmites* may prove quite bewildering to children who have not seen these formations. In Hershell and Joan Nixon's *Glaciers: Nature's Frozen Rivers*, photographs show different classifications of glaciers and illustrate their ability to alter land formation in places children might visit, such as Yosemite National Park and Glacier National Park. The Nixons describe the work of glaciologists and give a history of the ice ages, when glaciers covered northern portions of the earth. The book concludes with the modern-day benefits of glaciers from the past and ways that people are using, or are trying to benefit from, the vast water supply contained in glaciers and icebergs.

Many books discussed in this section encourage children to observe nature, to become involved in experiments, and to become conservationists.

Discoveries and How Things Work

Some informational books answer children's questions about discoveries of the past and the present or provide explanations of how many kinds of machines work. Authors may clarify their texts through detailed step-by-step directions, carefully labeled diagrams, photographs that illustrate concepts, and content that proceeds from the simple to the complex or from the known to the unknown.

Discoveries. Books about discoveries range from those describing the basic principles of past discoveries to those describing latest space or computer technology. Some books combine information about discoveries with experiments designed to help children understand and duplicate earlier experiments. One such book for older students is Irwin Math's *Morse, Marconi and You: Understanding and Building Telegraph, Telephone and Radio Sets*. The text describes the invention of these communication devices and shows how to perform experiments that demonstrate the principles involved. Diagrams illustrate the necessary materials and procedures for the experiment. Proceeding from the simple to the complex, readers begin with a basic understanding of the nature of electricity and progress through the development of the telegraph, the first telephone, a wireless system, and the radio. Later experiments in the book are quite complex, but identifying an age level for this book is difficult because many young science enthusiasts are fascinated with building the devices described and illustrated.

The development of the revolutionary silicon chips that make possible the minicomputer, calculator, digital watch, and other microelectronic devices is described in Stanley L. Englebardt's *Miracle Chip: The Microelectronic Revolution*. Englebardt helps children understand the changes that have taken place in microelectronic technology. For example, photographs compare the sizes of early transistors and vacuum tubes with today's chip that can hold 3,000 separate transistors. Engelbardt links the present to the future by presenting some fascinating possibilities for using the miracle chip to improve life in the future: computers developed for medical care and supermarket use, individually programmed computers for each student, microprocessors to help the handicapped, and a multipurpose telephone system.

Discoveries obtained from space exploration have greatly increased human knowledge. Informational books about space and space travel should reflect this expanded knowledge. Copyright dates may therefore be a very important consideration when selecting these books.

Franklyn M. Branley, former chairman of the Hayden Planetarium in New York City, emphasizes the expanded knowledge in *Saturn: The Spectacular Planet* by pointing out that the Pioneer and Voyager space probes have provided more knowledge than had previously been gath-

ered during the more than three hundred years since Galileo first saw the planet in a telescope. Branley uses a readable style, which often challenges the reader, as seen in *Mysteries of Outer Space*, a source of current information. Branley uses a question-and-answer format that progresses from questions about the kinds of space and the characteristics of space to questions about survival in space and uses of space. Two of Branley's other books on space include *Space Colony: Frontier of the 21st Century* and *Halley: Comet 1986*. (Comparisons may be made between Branley's *Halley: Comet 1986* and Isaac Asimov's *Asimov's Guide to Halley's Comet*.)

Patricia Lauber's *Journey to the Planets* contains large black-and-white NASA photographs of the earth and the planets. They clarify an interesting discussion of the search for intelligent life on other planets and the human constructions that indicate intelligent life, even from millions of miles out in space. Seymour Simon has written several readable books that, through words and photographs, take young readers into the far reaches of outer space and explain comets and planets. Simon's *The Long View into Space*, *The Long Journey from Space*, *Saturn*, and *Jupiter* provide current information in a simple and illuminating way. For example, in *The Long View into Space*, Simon explains why space distances between earth and the planets are not measured in miles by saying that would be like "trying to measure the distance between New York and London in inches" (p. 4 unnumbered).

Ann Elwood and Linda C. Wood's *Windows in Space* contains two features that should stimulate children's interest: "Questions We Still Cannot Answer" and "Facts About . . . ." This latter feature may help improve readers' cognitive abilities, as the authors summarize important facts. Aspiring artists and scientists as well as readers who are curious about spaceships and artists' renditions of various spacecraft will enjoy Don Bolognese's *Drawing Spaceships and Other Spacecraft*. His detailed text and illustrations introduce readers to perspective, tools, and finishing touches. Ideally, informational books such as these will challenge young readers to search continually for answers and to understand that our knowledge of space is constantly changing and increasing.

How Things Work. Several informational books respond to children's curiosity about how common home appliances and bigger machines actually work. These books usually contain detailed diagrams or photographs accompanying two or three pages of descriptive text. While the readability and interest level are usually considered upper elementary and above, many much younger children ask questions about how percolators, dishwashers, or Thermos bottles work. Therefore parents may find these books helpful when answering young children's questions. (One mother said that her six-year-old son's favorite book was one containing diagrams of machines at work.) Michael Pollard's text in *How Things Work* describes the workings of large machines: helicopters, jet engines, rockets, steam engines, diesel engines, elevators, and televisions. Detailed drawings and colored photographs clarify the text. Robert Gardner's *This Is the Way It Works: A Collection of Machines* provides diagrams and explanations of many objects and machines found around the house: mechanisms related to light, appliances, electric apparatus, and machines used in medicine and recreation. Ron and Nancy Goor's *In the Driver's Seat* presents an interesting and novel introduction to various motorized vehicles. Each chapter begins with a photograph showing the driver's seat and the instruments the driver would use. The text then tells readers what they would do if they were in that driver's seat. The idea of driving large and complex machines such as combines, tanks, jets, eighteen-wheel trucks, and trains appeals to many children. *Cars and How They Go* by Joanna Cole explains how pistons, crankshaft, drive shaft, and axle work interdependently to motorize the car. Gail Gibbon's illustrations and Cole's text clarify a subject that otherwise might be too complex for many elementary children.

Where is the longest, the highest, or the most expensive bridge? What did the first bridge probably look like? Who were the first great bridge builders? What changes have taken place in bridge construction? These are some of the questions answered in Scott Corbett's *Bridges*. Drawings help clarify the terminology and illustrate kinds of bridges, from the early suspension bridges, to Roman arches, to medieval fortified bridges, to covered New England bridges, to railroad trestles, and finally, to the great twentieth-century bridges.

Proceeding from the simple to the complex, an important technique in books that explain concepts, Anne and Scott MacGregor develop concepts related to physical stress and the construction of domes in *Domes: A Project Book*. They begin with simple igloos and proceed to cathedrals. Models for domes and directions for building them encourage children to experiment.

Peter Schaaf's *An Apartment House Close Up* shows photographs of architectural features, typical rooms, elevators, and heating facilities in an apartment house. Photographs in Elinor Horwitz's *How to Wreck a Building* follow the demolition of an elementary school from the time the crane operator's wrecking ball strikes the building until the debris is loaded into dump trucks. Byron Barton's *Airport*, an excellent picture book for young children, answers many questions about airports and airline travel as it follows passengers from their arrival at the airport to boarding the plane.

Authors of informational books often use photographs and text to document—as in Bernard Wolf's *Firehouse*, which documents the work of New York City firefighters, and William Jaspersohn's *Magazine: Behind the Scenes at Sports Illustrated*, which follows the production staff, reporters, and photographers as they prepare a typical weekly issue of *Sports Illustrated*.

Hobbies, Crafts, and How-To Books

One of the main reasons older elementary-school children give for reading is learning more about their hobbies and interests. Children told one educator who asked them how teachers could improve children's enjoyment of reading that teachers should ask them about their hobbies and help them find books about them (18). Informational books cover almost every hobby and craft. The more useful books contain clearly understood directions, provide guidelines for choosing equipment or other materials, or give interesting background information.

Physical Activities. In addition to a history of tennis, Robert J. Antonacci and Barbara D. Lockhart's *Tennis for Young Champions* provides step-by-step directions and extensive advice for all aspects of the game. Detailed illustrations clarify terms such as *right hand forehand grip* and *back hand grip*. Both authors are professors of physical education and former tennis champions.

The humorous illustrations in Barbara Isenberg and Marjorie Jaffe's *Albert the Running Bear's Exercise Book* provide detailed directions for exercises that are appropriate for children between the ages of five and nine. Frank and Jan Asch's

Running with Rachel presents a personalized approach to running by describing how a young girl takes up running after meeting a woman jogging on the road. The book discusses warm-up and warm-down exercises and the importance of wearing the right shoes and eating proper food. Photographs of a young runner illustrate the exercises.

Jim Arnosky, an illustrator for *Rod and Reel* magazine, uses his considerable knowledge of fishing to create a credible and useful book for young people who like to fish. *Freshwater Fish and Fishing* includes clear directions for tying a fly and making lures, detailed illustrations showing types of fish, and advice on how to catch fish.

Jill Krementz, a documentary photographer, has included photographs in several books she has written about young people who have chosen hobbies they hope to extend into professional or competitive status sports. The rigorous schedule and dedication needed for success in a sport is shown in *A Very Young Skater* and *A Very Young Rider*. Krementz has also done photo essays on dancers, gymnasts, and circus performers. The pictures effectively present the joys, as well as the day-to-day struggles, of such aspiring athletes and performers.Comparisons may be made between Krementz's *A Very Young Rider* and Lynn

Hall's *Tazo and Me*, a documentary of a rider showing a horse.

Creative Arts. Young photographers stimulated by Jill Krementz's beautiful black-and-white photographs can find instructions for photography in Edward E. Davis's *Into the Dark: A Beginner's Guide to Developing and Printing Black and White Negatives*. This book includes information on setting up a home darkroom and step-by-step directions for developing negatives, making contact prints, and printing enlargements.

Clear, detailed drawings that illustrate the points made in the text are an important criterion for evaluating informational books. Jim Arnosky's *Drawing from Nature* not only provides directions for drawing water, land forms, plants, and animals, but also stimulates children's interest in carefully observing nature and increases children's understanding of science concepts. The step-by-step pencil sketches illustrate techniques that let artists accurately interpret nature. A careful reading and viewing of this text may encourage children to answer Arnosky's invitation:

Drawing from nature is discovering the upside down scene through a water drop. It is noticing how much of a fox is tail. Drawing from nature is learning how a tree

Detailed directions and photographs of finished projects help children create objects and structures out of boxes. (Photograph by Richard W. Mitchell from *The Great Big Box Book*, by Flo Ann Hedley Norvell. Photographs copyright © 1979 by Richard Warren Mitchell. By permission of Thomas Y. Crowell, Publishers.)

grows and a flower blooms. It is sketching in the mountains and breathing air bears breathe. . . . I invite you to sharpen your pencils, your eyesight, and your sense of wonder. Turn to a fresh leaf in your drawing pad and come outdoors. (unnumbered foreword)

Arnosky uses a similar technique to illustrate step-by-step drawing techniques in *Drawing Life in Motion*.

One large box and some imagination can result in a horse, a castle, or even a supermarket when young children follow the step-by-step instructions in Flo Ann Hedley Norvell's *The Great Big Box Book*. Each step in seventeen projects is numbered and illustrated with an accompanying drawing or photograph. Of interest to the slightly older child is Paul Berman's *Make-Believe Empire: A How-to Book*. Simple instructions and accompanying drawings show young construction workers how to build a city from cans, boxes, and wood; how to construct a navy; and how to create their own laws and documents.

Food. Children who read frontier stories and survival stories may be interested in discovering more about the foods eaten by the characters.

Barbara M. Walker's *The Little House Cookbook: Frontier Foods from Laura Ingalls Wilder's Classic Stories* presents frontier foods Wilder wrote about in her "Little House" stories. Walker searched for authentic recipes by reading the writings of Wilder and her daughter Rose, pioneer diaries, and local recipe collections. Her hope in sharing this collection is that children will rediscover basic connections between the food on the table and the grain in the field and the cow in the pasture, as well as between people in the past and today. Walker uses liberal excerpts from the "Little House" books and the original Garth Williams illustrations in discussing the foods and their preparation.

Readers often ask how the characters in Jean Craighead George's *My Side of the Mountain* and *River Rats, Inc.* could identify and live off the wild foods discussed in the two books. Laurence Pringle's *Wild Foods: A Beginner's Guide to Identifying, Harvesting and Cooking Safe and Tasty Plants from the Outdoors* shows how. Pringle studied wildlife conservation at Cornell University and has been the editor of *Nature and Science*, a children's science magazine published by the American Museum of Natural History. His book discusses common, edible wild plants that are easily

identified, presenting them in the seasonal order in which they appear in nature, spring to winter. Pringle describes the plants and their locations and gives instructions on how to harvest and prepare them. The drawings by Paul Breeden, an artist whose illustrations have appeared in *National Geographic*, *Audubon*, and *Smithsonian* magazines, are especially effective and clarify differences between edible plants and poisonous plants that resemble them.

Pets. Pets usually interest children. Books such as Rosmarie Hausherr's *My First Kitten* present information about caring for a common pet. *Care of Uncommon Pets*, written by veterinarian William J. Weber, answers questions about handling, housing, feeding, breeding, and caring for more unusual pets. This book should provide valuable information for children who want uncommon pets or for teachers who have small animals in their classrooms. Harriet Rubins's *Guinea Pigs: An Owner's Guide to Choosing, Raising, Breeding, and Showing* is an in-depth coverage of one pet. Written for older readers, it focuses on breeding, showing, recordkeeping, and experimenting with guinea pigs and gives guidelines for selection and care. A glossary, bibliography, and index increase the usefulness of the book. Colleen Stanley Bare's *Guinea Pigs Don't Read Books* is a simpler, highly illustrated book written for younger children.

These books encourage children to consider new hobbies or to learn more about existing ones. Children discover that some hobbies may even lead to a career.

SUMMARY

There are many values for children who read nonfictional materials. They gain knowledge about the world they live in, they are stimulated in their search for discovery, and they are introduced to the scientific method and gain an appreciation for people who use it. They are also encouraged to develop critical thinking abilities, increase their own aspirations, and have fun.

Biographies, in addition to meeting the criteria for all good literature, should be worthy of authors' meticulous research and of the time children spend in reading and should be written so that the characters are believable.

Informational books for children should be factually accurate and lacking in stereotypes; accurate illustrations should clarify the text. The text should encourage analytical thinking, its organization should be logical and helpful, and the style should be lively and not too difficult for the age of the children.

Informational books discussed in the chapter cover history, culture, and geography; the human body, animals, plants, earth's ecology, and earth's geology; experiments, discoveries, and how things work; and hobbies, crafts, and how-to books.

Suggested Activities for Adult Understanding of Biographies and Informational Books

☐ In order to provide accurate information and differentiate fact from opinion, biographers must research many sources. Select a writer of biographies for children and identify the sources the writer used in doing research for a book. Do you believe these sources were sufficient? Why or why not?

☐ Choose someone who has had several biographies written about him or her. Read several interpretations of that person's life. Compare the biographies in terms of content, accuracy of information, sources of references indicated by the author, balance of facts with story line for young readers, intended audience for the biography, and author's style.

☐ Select a well-known author who has written several biographies for older children, such as Beatrice Siegel, and another biographer who has written several biographies for younger children, such as Jean Fritz. What techniques does each author use in order to write a biography that will appeal to a specific age group?

☐ Select a content area, such as science or social studies, that is taught in an elementary- or middle-school grade. Identify from the curriculum names of men and women who are discussed in that content area. Develop an annotated bibliography of literature on a subject such as biology that could be used to stimulate interest in the subject and provide additional information about the contributors.

☐ Select the work of an outstanding author of informational books for children, such as Mil-

licent E. Selsam, Seymour Simon, or Laurence Pringle. Evaluate the books according to the criteria listed on pages 580–83. Share with the class the characteristics of the books that make them highly recommended.

☐ Select several informational books that include many illustrations. Evaluate the illustrations according to the value of the explanatory legends presented next to the illustrations, the accuracy of the illustrations, and the possibility that they will stimulate children's interest in the subject.

☐ Choose several informational books that exemplify the encouragement of logical problem solving. Share the books with a peer group and present a rationale for the belief that these books will encourage logical problem solving.

☐ Search the elementary social studies of science curriculum for a given grade level. With a peer group, develop an annotated bibliography of informational books that would reinforce the curriculum and stimulate the acquisition of additional information.

References

1 Anderson, William, and Groff, Patrick. *A New Look at Children's Literature*. Belmont, Calif.: Wadsworth, 1972.
2 Arbuthnot, May Hill, and Broderick, Dorothy M. *Time for Biography*. Glenview, Ill.: Scott, Foresman, 1969.
3 Blough, Glenn O. "The Author and the Science Book." *Library Trends* 22 (April 1974): 419–24.
4 Carpenter, Frank G. *Carpenter's Geographical Reader, North America*. New York: American Book, 1898.
5 Coolidge, Olivia. "My Struggle with Facts." *Wilson Library Bulletin* 49 (October 1974): 146–51.
6 Dryer, Charles Redway. *Geography, Physical, Economic, and Regional*. New York: American Book, 1911.
7 Fisher, Margery. "Life Course or Screaming Farce?" *Children's Literature in Education*. Vol. 7 (Autumn 1976): 108–115.
8 Fleming, Margaret, and McGinnis, Jo, eds. *Portraits: Biography and Autobiography in the Secondary School*. Urbana, Ill.: National Council of Teachers of English, 1985.
9 Fritz, Jean. *Homesick: My Own Story*. New York: Putnam's, 1982.
10 Fritz, Jean. "Making It Real." *Children's Literature in Education* 22 (Autumn 1976): 125–27.

11 Herman, Gertrude B. " 'Footprints on the Sands of Time' : Biography for Children." *Children's Literature in Education* 9 (Summer 1977): 85–94.

12 Hillyer, V. M. *A Child's Geography of the World*. Illustrated by Mary Sherwood Wright Jones. New York: Century, 1929.

13 Jurich, Marilyn. "What's Left Out of Biography for Children?" *Children's Literature: The Great Excluded* 1 (1972): 143–151.

14 Moore, Ann W. "A Question of Accuracy: Errors in Children's Biographies." *School Library Journal* 31 (Feb. 1985): 34–35.

15 National Science Teachers Association. "Outstanding Science Trade Books for Children in 1985." *Science and Children* (March 1986): 26.

16 Norton, Donna E. "Centuries of Biographies for Childhood," *Vitae Scholasticae* 3 (Spring 1984): 113–129.

17 Robertson, Elizabeth, and McGinnis, Jo. "Biography As Art: A Formal Approach." In *Portraits: Biography and Autobiography in the Secondary School*, edited by Margaret Fleming and Jo McGinnis. Urbana, Ill.: National Council of Teachers of English, 1985.

18 Roettger, Doris. "Reading Attitudes and the Estes Scale." Paper presented at the 23rd Annual Convention, International Reading Association, Houston, Texas, 1978.

19 Stott, Jon C. "Biographies of Sports Heroes and the American Dream." *Children's Literature in Education* 10 (Winter 1979): 174–85.

20 Wolff, Kathryn. "AAAS Science Books: A Selection Tool." *Library Trends* 22 (April 1974): 453–56.

Involving Children in Nonfictional Literature

☐

USING BIOGRAPHIES IN CREATIVE DRAMA

☐

COMPARING ATTITUDES AND CHECKING FACTS IN BIOGRAPHIES

☐

INVESTIGATING THE QUALITIES OF WRITERS

☐

LITERATURE IN THE SCIENCE CURRICULUM

S TIMULATING LEARNING EXPERIENCES can result from biographies and informational books that contain factual, authentic interpretations written in a style often more exciting than textbooks. Because many of the informational books discussed in this chapter relate to the science curriculum, they can be used to increase children's enjoyment and understanding of science-related topics. This section presents ways to help children acquire abilities related to content areas—such as using parts of the book, locating sources of information, understanding science vocabulary, reading for exact meaning, evaluating science literature, and applying learnings to practical problems.

The lively dialogue, confrontations between people and ideas, and the joys and sorrows connected with discovery and achievement found in many biographies are natural sources for creative dramatizations and discussions. Activities developed around biographies will suggest ways that people of the past and present can be made to seem realistic to contemporary children.

USING BIOGRAPHIES IN CREATIVE DRAMA

The biographies of significant people of the past and present are filled with lively dialogue, confrontations between new ideas and society, and the joys connected with discovery. Consequently, the plots suggest many opportunities for creative drama, as children relive the momentous experiences in people's lives. Children can pretend to be various characters in history and pantomime their actions and responses, they can create "You Are There" dramas based on scenes of historical significance, and they can devise sequence games based on the most significant incidents in a person's life. They can also create imaginary conversations between two people from the past or present or from different time periods who had some common traits but were never able to communicate because of time or distance. The following ideas are only samples of the types of creative drama that can result from using biographies in the classroom.

Pantomiming Actions

Jean Fritz's stories of Revolutionary War heroes, with their portrayal of the humorous and human side of the characters, are excellent sources for pantomime. For example, an adult can read *Where Was Patrick Henry on the 29th of May?* and ask children how Patrick Henry acted and how they would act if they were Patrick Henry. The story can then be read a second time as children pantomime all of the actions. There is another way to approach this dramatization: after listening to or reading the book, children can identify and discuss scenes they would like to depict and then pantomime each one. Children have identified the following scenes as being of special interest in Patrick Henry's life:

Scenes from Patrick Henry's Life

1 Going fishing with a pole over his shoulder.
2 Going hunting for deer or possum, with a rifle in his hands, accompanied by a dog at his heels.
3 Walking barefoot through the woods, then lying down while listening to the rippling of a creek or the sounds of birds singing and imitating their songs.
4 Listening to rain on the roof, his father's fox horn, and music of flutes and fiddles.
5 Teaching himself to play the flute when he is recovering from a broken collarbone.
6 Listening to his Uncle Langloo Winston making speeches.
7 Waiting for the school day to end.
8 Playing practical jokes on his friends, including upsetting a canoe.
9 Trying to be a storekeeper without success.
10 Attempting to be a tobacco farmer.
11 Attending court and discovering that he likes to watch and listen to lawyers.
12 Beginning his law practice and not finding many clients.
13 Defending his first big case in court and winning.
14 Arguing against taxation without representation as a member of Virginia's House of Burgesses.
15 Delivering his "give me liberty or give me death" speech at St. John's Church.
16 Governing Virginia.
17 Hearing the news that the Continental army has defeated the English troops at Saratoga, New York.
18 Speaking against the enactment of the Constitution of the United States and for individual and states' rights after the war is over.
19 Retiring on his estate in western Virginia.

These nineteen scenes may also be developed into what Ruth Beall Heinig and Lyda Stillwell (3) describe as a "sequence pantomime game." This game involves careful observation by all players, who must see and interpret what someone else is doing and at the correct time, according to directions written on their cue cards, stand and perform the next action. (Players must be able to read to do this pantomime activity.) Cue cards for the nineteen scenes from Patrick Henry's life would need to be developed. The first cue card would look approximately like this:

> *You* begin the game.
> Pretend that you are a young, barefoot Patrick Henry happily going fishing with a pole over your shoulder.
> When you are finished, sit down in your seat.

The second card would read:

> Cue: Someone pretends to be a young Patrick Henry going fishing with a pole over his shoulder.
> You are a young Patrick Henry happily going hunting for deer or possum, with a rifle in your hands and accompanied by a dog running at your heels.
> When you are finished, go back to your seat.

The rest of the scenes, written in a similar manner, would also be placed on cards. It is helpful if the cue and the directions for the pantomime are written in different colors. The cards are mixed and distributed randomly. There should be at least one cue card for each player, but more scenes may be added if a whole class is doing the activity. If there are fewer players, either the number of scenes can be reduced, or each player can receive more than one cue card. Children should be asked to watch carefully and wait for each player to complete the pantomime. It is helpful if the adult or leader has a master cue sheet containing all the cues in correct sequential order so that cueing can be accomplished if a pantomime is misinterpreted, children seem uncertain, or the group loses its direction. Heinig and Stillwell suggest that in order to involve as many children as possible, large groups may be divided into three small groups. Each small group pantomimes a set of identical cue cards independently. A child might act as leader of each group and follow the master sheet.

Incidents in the lives of other Fritz heroes—described in *Why Don't You Get a Horse, Sam Adams?* and *What's the Big Idea, Ben Franklin?*—also make enjoyable pantomime dramas. All the scenes described may also encourage oral interpretations, as children may add dialogue to their impersonations.

Children can pantomime the actions of dancers, as in *Arthur Mitchell* by Tobi Tobias; the actions of musicians, as in *The Boy Who Loved Music* by David Lasker; and the actions of a skater, as in *A Very Young Skater* by Jill Krementz.

"You Are There" Creative Dramatizations

Biographies allow children to experience some very exciting moments in history through the emotions, words, and contributions of the people who created those moments. Consequently, reenactments of those scenes can allow children to experience the excitement and realize that history is made up of real people and actual incidents.

A group of seventh graders chose to return in time to Rome in 1632, during the cruel days of the Inquisition. Their "You Are There" drama, based on Sidney Rosen's *Galileo and the Magic Numbers*, began after Galileo had published his *A Dialogue on the Two Great Systems of the World* and was facing an angry Pope Urban. The following scenes illustrate the outline of events depicted by the group:

1 The announcer prepares the audience: "You are there; the year is 1632; Galileo is facing an angry Pope Urban. The pope's face is reddened in anger, his eyes are flashing venom. He is pounding his fists on the arms of the papal throne. Shouting, he declares: 'That scoundrel! That ingrate! We try to befriend him. And how does he repay us? By doing all this behind our back! Well this time he has gone too far! Let him take care! It is out of our hands now. This is a matter for the Holy Office!' (p. 192).
With these words, the slow process of the Inquisition begins. Galileo's enemies are winning, and he is to be charged with heresy."

2 Next, the announcer, the action, and the dialogue take the audience back to Florence: Galileo waits anxiously with his health failing, his fever returning, and his eyesight failing.

3 A scene in October is described and enacted as the inquisitor of Florence appears at Galileo's door with a summons; Galileo has thirty days in which to appear before the Holy Office in Rome.

4 The scene shifts to April 12, 1633, when Galileo is summoned to the Inquisition chambers. Galileo is exhaustively questioned and threatened with torture for many days until he finally signs a document confessing his wrongdoing; he then feels shame and guilt for his weakness.

5 On June 21, Galileo discovers that signing the document is not sufficient; he is to be tried for heresy before ten cardinals who will be his judges. The scene shows a bent, graying Galileo in front of the men dressed in red cloaks and hats, sitting about a great semicircular table. The questioning begins as the judges ask Galileo whether he does, indeed, believe that the earth moves about the sun. Silence hangs over the hall as the judges await Galileo's response.

6 The scene for June 22, 1633, shows Galileo dressed in the shirt of penitence, awaiting the verdict of the Inquisition. A hush falls over the hall; Galileo, kneeling before the cardinals, listens to the long document of charges read against him. At last, he hears the words that crush all hope: "But in order that your terrible error may not go altogether unpunished, and that you may be an example and a warning to others to abstain from such opinions, we decree that your book, *Dialogue on the Two Great Systems of the World*, be banned publicly; also, we condemn you to the formal prison of this Holy Office for an indefinite period convenient to our pleasure. So we, the subscribing and presiding cardinals pronounce!" (p. 202).

Galileo and the Magic Numbers contains vividly described settings and characters and enough dialogue that children can develop a realistic

"You Are There" drama. This can be done informally with an announcer only setting the stage and the actors developing the dialogue as they proceed, or children may choose some actual dialogue from the book. The seventh-grade group chose a combination of these two approaches; they felt that their "You Are There" production was more authentic when some of the author's words were included.

Other "You Are There" episodes could be created around Christopher Columbus's meeting with Queen Isabella, his discovery of America, or his return to the Spanish court. The April 30, 1860, confrontation of scientists who wished to discredit Charles Darwin with Thomas Huxley and Robert Chambers, who supported Darwin's theory, is another dramatic moment in history (found in Irwin Shapiro's *Darwin and the Enchanted Isles*).

Imaginary Conversations between People of Two Time Periods

Children enjoy contemplating what historic personalities who have similar viewpoints or opposite beliefs might say to each other if they had the opportunity to meet. Because this is impossible except through imagination, children can be motivated to read biographies in order to enter into such conversations. For example, an exciting conversation could result if Maria Mitchell (Helen S. Morgan's *Maria Mitchell, First Lady of American Astronomy*) and Galileo (Rosen's *Galileo and the Magic Numbers*) could meet. Children can consider what questions each person might ask the other, what interests and viewpoints the two would probably share, and what differences of opinion they might express. After the children have discussed these points, they can role-play a meeting between these figures. What advice could Galileo have given Mitchell when she knew she must defend her teaching before the Vassar Board of Trustees? Galileo worried about how history would view him; how would he feel about nineteenth-century scientists' views about his work? Different children can present their views through the role-playing format; the class or group can then discuss what they believe the most likely responses would be and why they believe these responses would occur.

Other historical biographical characters might have stimulating conversations if they could meet with world figures of the 1980s. What views would emerge if Patrick Henry could share his opinions on states' rights and the rights of the individual with the current president of the United States?

When children read in order to role-play a character's actions, express a character's feelings, or state dialogue that a character might express, they interact with the character on a human level and will often read until they feel empathy with that character and the historic time period.

COMPARING ATTITUDES AND CHECKING FACTS IN BIOGRAPHIES

Elizabeth Robertson and Jo McGinnis (7) recommend that students compare the tone and attitude of a biographer, as reflected in a biography about a specific person, with the tone and attitude expressed by the biographical subject in his or her own writing. Ann W. Moore (5) recommends that reviewers check the accuracy of facts in juvenile biographies by referring to reputable adult titles and other reference books. Biographies about Eleanor Roosevelt are excellent sources for such an activity in the classroom. There are numerous children's biographies, including one written by Elliott Roosevelt, reputable adult biographies, and autobiographies written by Eleanor Roosevelt herself. The following books will provide sources for such a comparison:

Biographies for children:
Jane Goodsell's *Eleanor Roosevelt* and Sharon Whitney's *Eleanor Roosevelt*.
Biography for children written by Eleanor Roosevelt's son:
Elliott Roosevelt's *Eleanor Roosevelt, With Love*.
Biographies for adults:
Joseph P. Lash's *Eleanor and Franklin* and *Eleanor: The Years Alone* (Norton); Elliott Roosevelt and James Brough's *An Untold Story: The Roosevelts of Hyde Park* and *Mother R: Eleanor Roosevelt's Untold Story* (Putnam); and Lorena Hickok's *Eleanor Roosevelt: Reluctant First Lady* (Dodd, Mead).
Autobiographies:
Eleanor Roosevelt's *The Autobiography of Eleanor Roosevelt* (Harper); *On My Own* (Harper); *This I Remember* (Greenwood); *This Is My Story* (Harper); *Tomorrow Is Now* (Harper); and *You Learn by Living* (Harper).

INVESTIGATING THE QUALITIES OF WRITERS

What are the qualities that characterize successful writers of children's literature? Is there any way that students can discover these qualities? Are these qualities important in the lives of school children? Patricia J. Cianciolo (1) believes that the words of authors, as expressed in their autobiographies, journals, and interviews, are an excellent means of discovering the abilities, attitudes, and character traits of competent writers. Cianciolo analyzed the comments about writing expressed by children's authors Rosemary Sutcliff, Donald Hall, Katherine Paterson, M.E. Kerr, Mollie Hunter, Lois Duncan, Alan Garner, Julia Cunningham, Vera and Bill Cleaver, and Barbara Wersba.

Teachers may have students read some of the sources identified by Cianciolo and read other autobiographies by children's authors, such as Elizabeth Yates's *My Diary, My World* and *My Widening World*. The students should search for comments that reflect the authors' attitudes about writing. For example, they may find some of the same important abilities, attitudes, and character traits as those found by Cianciolo:

1 A good writer must be a good reader.
2 A good writer cares intensely about language and is sensitive to it.
3 A good writer is well educated.
4 A good writer is an alert observer.
5 A good writer is a storyteller and enjoys stories told by others.
6 A good writer is a compulsive writer.

After identifying these characteristics of a good writer, the teacher may lead a discussion in which the students identify the importance of each quality and discuss how these qualities might be used to improve their own writing and reading.

LITERATURE IN THE SCIENCE CURRICULUM

Several values of informational books identified earlier relate to the science curriculum. Interesting books—such as those by Seymour Simon, Millicent Selsam, and Laurence Pringle—allow children to experience the excitement of discovery; through experiments stimulated by books such as Selsam's *Popcorn* and Simon's *The Secret*

Clocks, Time Senses of Living Things, they can observe, experiment, compare, formulate hypotheses, test hypotheses, draw conclusions, and evaluate their evidence. Children can become directly involved in the scientific method. Through the experiments and information found in books, children learn about the world of nature. Because many informational books that deal with science subjects have greater depth of coverage than science textbooks, these materials are valuable for extending children's knowledge and understanding.

Illa Podendorf (6) maintains that communication abilities such as graphing, illustrating, recording, and reporting are especially important to science. She believes that an author of science information books should use these communication abilities often when writing science materials. She also says:

At an early age children are able to read and interpret graphs and can present their own ideas and findings in graphic form. A trade book which provides such experiences is a valuable addition to their literature. Any opportunity to help children get experience in interpreting data and making predictions from recorded data should not be overlooked. Such experiences often result in activities in which children can become actively involved. (p. 428)

However, the nature of science materials—with their heavier concentration of facts and details, new scientific principles to be understood, and new technical vocabulary—may cause reading problems for children who are accustomed to the narrative writing style. David L. Shepherd (8) identifies the following three types of reading that students face in the content area of science: (1) science textbooks that tend to be technical and require a careful, slow, and analytical reading; (2) assigned readings in scientific journals, popular science magazines, and books on scientific research that may contain many small but important interrelated details that require analytical reading; and (3) nontechnical scientific materials found in biographies of scientists, newspapers, and popular magazines reporting scientific findings that are easier to read and understand. The majority of the science-related informational books discussed in this chapter conform to the second and third of these categories.

The excellent informational materials on science-related topics may be used to encourage children's development of both the reading abilities needed for science-related materials and understanding of science-related concepts. Teachers, parents, and librarians may use science-related informational books in numerous ways to stimulate children's minds and increase vital abilities needed for science. For the object of this text, we will consider those purposes that relate to the study of both literature and the content areas: using parts of the book, locating sources of information, understanding science vocabulary, reading for exact meaning, seeing author's organization, and evaluating science materials. Specific books are mentioned, but they are only examples of the numerous books that can be used in the classroom. Students of children's literature may wish to add other informational books.

Using Parts of a Book

Both librarians and teachers provide instruction in how to use the valuable aids provided by many authors of informational books. Science informational books reinforce the ability to use parts of a book, because many books contain a table of contents, a glossary, a bibliography of further readings, and an index. Children can use the table of contents to locate a specific chapter in an informational book. They can discover the type of information provided in the index, locate a chapter, and search through it to discover if the subject is covered there. For example:

1 Find the chapter describing how to make a walkie-talkie space helmet in Flo Ann Norvell's *The Great Big Box Book* (chapter 7, p. 36).
2 Find the chapter about "Survival in Space" in Franklyn M. Blanley's *Mysteries of Outer Space* (chapter 5, p. 36).
3 Find the chapter on "People and Whales" in Dorothy Hinshaw Patent's *Whales: Giants of the Deep* (chapter 5, p. 73).
4 Find the chapter "Bridges" in David Weitzman's *Windmills, Bridges, & Old Machines: Discovering Our Industrial Past* (chapter 11, p. 77).
5 Find the chapter "Seven Helpless Chicks" in Geraldine Lux Flanagan's *Window into a Nest* (chapter 8, p. 62).

Laurence Pringle's books usually have a glossary of technical terms, an index, and a list of further readings that can provide additional information about a subject. These books can be used to reinforce the importance of each part of the book, the kind of information that is available, and the use of each locational aid. As children read Pringle's *City and Suburb: Exploring an Ecosystem; The Gentle Desert: Exploring an Ecosystem;* or *Natural Fire: Its Ecology in Forests*, they can use the glossaries that provide definitions for the technical terminology in each book, including words such as *climate, ecosystem, environment*, and *habitat*. In these books, children can find subjects in the index and then find the information on the correct page in the text. These indexes are especially useful, because an asterisk beside a page number indicates that a photograph or drawing is on that page. Children may see how rapidly they can find subjects in the index and then find them in the text. For example, find the page number for magpies in *City and Suburb: Exploring an Ecosystem*. Is it a picture or text? Find magpies in the book. In the list of further readings in each book asterisks indicate materials that are fairly simple. The easier references include magazines such as *Ranger Rick's Nature Magazine* and *Natural History* as well as other children's books on the topic. The more difficult books provide information for a highly motivated child or one in an accelerated program.

Locating and Using Sources of Information

The lists of references at the back of many informational books provide a logical source of materials to show children how to use a library card catalog for more information. The sources can be found in the library card catalog under an author card, a title card, and a subject card. For example, one additional source listed in Laurence Pringle's *City and Suburb: Exploring an Ecosystem* is Pringle's *Into the Woods: Exploring the Forest Ecosystem*. Children learn and reinforce library location skills by learning how to find this book or other informational books under three types of cards, as shown in Figure 12–1. Children can also discover related reading materials while looking for a particular reference in the card catalog.

Using Science Vocabulary

The glossary in many informational books is also a source of additional information about the meaning of technical terminology found in the book. Authors such as Caroline Arnold, in *Saving the Peregrine Falcon*, use boldface type to identify

AUTHOR CARD

```
QH
541.5     Pringle, Laurence P.
.F6          Into the woods: exploring the forest
P74       ecosystem [by] Laurence Pringle. New
          York, Macmillan [1973]
             54 p. illus. 23 cm.
             SUMMARY: Explains the interdependency
          of plants and animals and examines
          man's role in protecting this
          ecological balance.
             Bibliography: p. 51.


             1. Forest ecology--Juvenile
          literature.  I. Title
```

TITLE CARD

```
             Into the woods: exploring the forest
                ecosystem
QH
541.5     Pringle, Laurence P.
.F6          Into the woods: exploring the forest
P74       ecosystem [by] Laurence Pringle. New
          York, Macmillan [1973]
             54 p. illus. 23 cm.
             SUMMARY: Explains the interdependency
          of plants and animals and examines
          man's role in protecting this
          ecological balance.
             Bibliography: p. 51.


             1. Forest ecology--Juvenile
          literature.  I. Title
```

SUBJECT CARD

```
             FOREST ECOLOGY--JUVENILE LITERATURE.
QH
541.5     Pringle, Laurence P.
.F6          Into the woods: exploring the forest
P74       ecosystem [by] Laurence Pringle. New
          York, Macmillan [1973]
             54 p. illus. 23 cm.
             SUMMARY: Explains the interdependency
          of plants and animals and examines
          man's role in protecting this
          ecological balance.
             Bibliography: p. 51.


             1. Forest ecology--Juvenile
          literature.  I. Title
```

FIGURE 12–1

terms that are defined in the glossary. Authors of informational books for children often present the meaning of new words through their context in the text. This technique should be demonstrated to children, and they should try to understand the meaning of the word. Hilda Simon, in *Sight and Seeing: A World of Light and Color*, uses contextual clues to suggest the meaning of scientific terms. Throughout the book, Simon places new words in italics and defines the words in context. For example, "Birds of prey are further aided by

their unusual powers of *accommodation*. In optical terms, that means an extremely rapid focus adjustment of the lens to different distances" (p. 55).

Authors also clarify the meanings of technical terminology through photographs, diagrams, and charts. Even books written for young children often clarify meanings of technical terminology by including labeled drawings. An illustration by Aliki, in Judy Hawes's *Bees and Beelines*, a Let's-Read-and-Find-Out Science Book, shows the directions a bee moves when flying a "round dance" and a "waggle." This illustration is followed by four pages of drawings that resemble a map of a bee's flying actions when it leaves the hive to search for nectar. Arrows are included in the drawings so that children can follow the bee's movement. When parents or teachers share the book with children, they should help them to follow the directions of the arrows and tell what is occurring in the drawings.

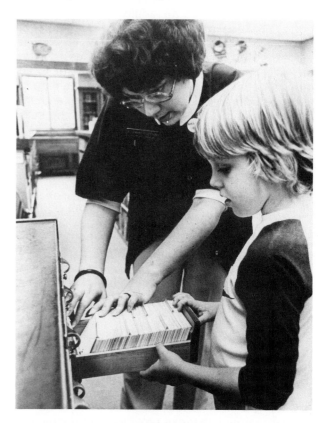

A librarian helps a child locate informational books listed in a book's reference list.

Another Let's-Read-and-Find-Out Science Book for young children that includes labeled diagrams clarifying technical terminology is Judy Hawes's *Ladybug, Ladybug, Fly Away Home*. Ed Emberley's illustrations not only appeal to young children, but also include large drawings of ladybugs with various labeled parts, such as *body, shield, head, eye, jaws, palps, feelers, claws*, and *sticky pads*. These drawings are especially effective with young children because the author indicates that the drawings are magnified by showing an actual ladybug on a human finger on the same page that introduces an enlarged drawing. Parents and teachers may use the book to encourage children to look through a magnifying glass and identify the same body parts that are shown in the enlarged, labeled drawings. Children often want to draw and label their own illustrations.

Tomie de Paola's *The Cloud Book* presents the technical names for clouds through text description and humorous illustrations. Drawings show

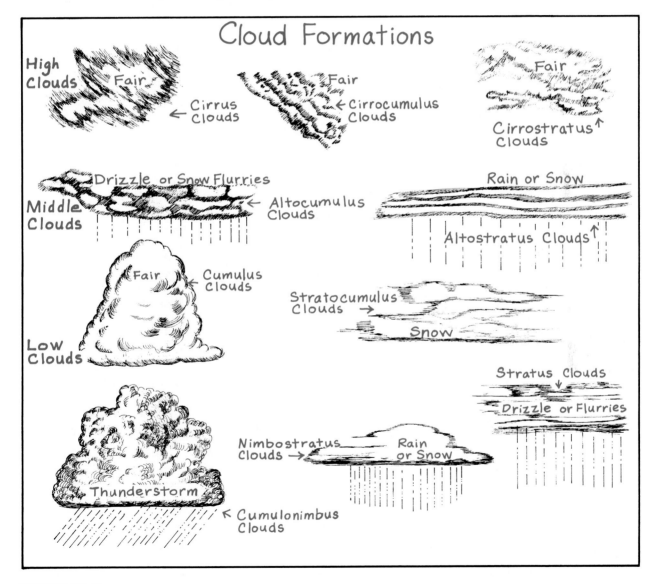

FIGURE 12–2

cirrus, cumulus, and *stratus* clouds; *cirrocumulus* and *cirrostratus* clouds; *altostratus* and *altocumulus* clouds; and *nimbostratus, stratocumulus,* and *cumulonimbus* clouds. Because many children are curious about the changing cloud formations they see in the sky, this book can be used to introduce the technical terms for the clouds observed. Drawings and bulletin boards on which different types of clouds are labeled are excellent extensions of this knowledge. A bulletin board created to extend the vocabulary in the book might look like one made by a group of fifth-grade children (see Figure 12–2, p. 611).

Reading for Exact Meaning

A major reason that many students give for reading scientific informational books is to acquire facts; therefore, comprehending the author's exact meaning is important. Unlike writings that stress make-believe, scientific informational books are based on accuracy. Children often need encouragement to note main ideas and supporting details and to see organization. Reading-methods books usually include several chapters on these comprehension abilities, but a few approaches considered here allow content-area teachers and parents to reinforce and encourage these abilities through informational books.

Noting Main Ideas. Short, fact-filled paragraphs, as well as paragraph and chapter organization, provide considerable materials for the content-area teacher who is trying to enhance children's ability to find the main idea. Because many informational books written for children have the main idea as a topic sentence at the beginning of the paragraph, one technique that has been helpful to many teachers is to have children read a paragraph or a series of short paragraphs and then visualize the author's organization of the material according to the main idea and important details. (This technique may also help them evaluate whether the author uses a logical organization.) A typical paragraph may follow this organization:

Main Idea
    Supporting Details
    Supporting Details
    Supporting Details

Seymour Simon's writing tends to follow this structure. Consider how to use this diagram with material from *Meet the Giant Snakes* to help children identify the main idea and supporting details and evaluate whether or not the organization is logical. On page 13 of Simon's book is a paragraph that describes how the python, unlike other snakes, cares for its young. If this paragraph were arranged like the above diagram, it would look something like this:

A giant python is unusual because the female cares for her young.
    She pushes her eggs into a pile.
    She coils her body around the eggs.
    She stays on the nest until the eggs are hatched in about ten weeks.
    She leaves her nest only for water.

Children can discover that each of the important details supports the idea that the giant python takes care of her young. This main idea can also be turned into a question. Children can decide if the rest of the paragraph answers these questions: Does the female giant python take care of her young? How does the female giant python take care of her young?

The same book introduces a series of paragraphs by asking the question "How does a giant snake find food to eat?" (p. 15). Each of the succeeding paragraphs answers some question about the giant python's eating habits. Children find that they will get the main idea from the three following pages if they read to answer the introductory question. This should be demonstrated to children so that they can use this important comprehension aid.

Other activities using informational books also stress the main idea:

1. If the informational material contains subheadings, ask children to turn each subheading into a question and read to answer the question. For example, in Martha Brenner's *Fireworks Tonight!*, the author uses subheadings to divide the contents of each chapter. Children could turn each of the following subheadings into questions and then read to answer those questions:

    An American Tradition (Chapter 1)
    Triumph and Tragedy on the Fourth
    Protective Regulation
    Mischief and Misuse
    How Safe Are Fireworks

2. The results of an experiment may be the main idea. After children have read the results of an

experiment or finished their own experiments, ask them to relate the purpose and the findings of the experiment in one or two brief sentences. Literature sources could include the following:

a. Dr. Frank Brown's experiments with fiddler crabs, oysters, and potatoes, described on pages 37–41 in Seymour Simon's *The Secret Clocks, Time Senses of Living Things.*

b. Gustav Kramer's experiments with migration of birds described on pages 24–29 in Seymour Simon's *The Secret Clocks, Time Senses of Living Things.* Graphic aids may be incorporated with these experiments by having children illustrate the steps taken during the completion of these experiments.

Noting Supporting Details. The outlines discussed earlier stressed the main idea and important details. When the main idea was turned into a question(s), each of the items listed provided an important detail that supported the main idea. Many important details in a science informational book may refer to characteristics of animals or plants: size, color, number, location, or texture. Have the children listen to or read a description from a science informational book and draw a picture that shows the important details. This activity also provides them with graphic aids. The following descriptions are examples of sources that could be used:

1 The description of *Kon Tiki* found on pages 44–45 in Wyatt Blassingame's *Thor Heyerdahl: Viking Scientist.*

2 The description of leaves found in Laurence Pringle's *Wild Foods: A Beginner's Guide to Identifying, Harvesting and Cooking Safe and Tasty Plants from the Outdoors*—maple leaves (p. 24), cattails (pp. 63–64), and milkweed (pp. 103–4).

3 Descriptions of city and suburb ecosystems in Laurence Pringle's *City and Suburb: Exploring an Ecosystem*—the city made by people (p. 3),

Children discuss the purposes and findings of an experiment motivated by an informational book about seeds.

how the automobile changed open land (p. 7), weeds growing in vacant lots (p. 34).

Seeing the Author's Organization. The sequence of events and the author's organization of information are often critical in science content areas. When evaluating informational books, a logical organization is also critical. Many books emphasize the life cycle of plants or animals, the correct steps to use in following an experiment, or the chain of events that occurs. These books can be used to help children increase their ability to note scientific organization and to evaluate the author's ability to develop logical organization. The following activities could be used with informational materials:

1   Number of steps identified in the butterfly's life cycle. Read Oxford Scientific Films' *The Butterfly Cycle*. Identify, draw, or list and then number the four stages in the life cycle of the butterfly.
    a.   the egg (drawing)
    b.   the caterpillar or larva (drawing)
    c.   the chrysalis or pupa (drawing)
    d.   the adult butterfly (drawing)
2   Number of steps identified in the life cycle of the frog. Read Oxford Scientific Films' *Common Frogs*. Identify, draw, or list and number the stages in the frog's cycle.
    a.   eggs at bottom of pond (drawing)
    b.   eggs rise to surface for about two weeks (drawing)
    c.   eggs hatch into tadpoles with tails (drawing)
    d.   legs develop on tadpole (drawing)
    e.   tadpole's tail has vanished and tadpole is transformed into frog (drawing)

Evaluating Scientific Materials

The ability to evaluate requires critical thinking abilities. Critical reading and thinking go beyond factual comprehension; they require weighing the validity of facts, identifying the problem, making judgments, interpreting implied ideas, distinguishing fact from opinion, drawing conclusions, determining the adequacy of a source of information, and suspending judgment until all the facts have been accumulated.

Helen Huus's (4) list of questions that students should ask about the author and the content of the material can help children evaluate both the author and the content of scientific informational books. For example, students should ask the following questions about the authors:

A Guide for Critical Evaluation of an Author

1   Why did the author write this book?
        Was it to present information?
        Was it to promote a point of view?
        Was it to advertise?
        Was it to propagandize?
        Was it to entertain?
2   How competent is the author to write an article on this topic for this purpose?
        What is the author's background?
        What is the author's reputation?
        Does the author have any vested interests in this topic?
        What is the author's professional position?

In order to critically evaluate authors of informational books (this list and activity are excellent for all informational books, not just those related to science), children should have access to many books by different authors and biographical information about the authors. One teacher of upper elementary students divided the class into five research groups according to a category of interest each group chose to investigate. The categories included botany, birds, earth and geology, land mammals, and insects.

Next, each group used John T. Gillespie and Christine B. Gilbert's *Best Books for Children, Preschool through the Middle Grades* (2) in order to identify authors who had written at least three books in their chosen category. For example, under botany, the group chose the following authors:

Anne Dowden—Three books
Rose E. Hutchins—Three books
Joan Elma Rahn—Three books
Millicent E. Selsam—Five books

Similarly, the group working with birds selected these authors:

Olive L. Earle—Three books
Roma Gans—Four books
John Kaufman—Four books
Jack Scott—Four books

The group working with earth and geology specified the following authors:

Roma Gans—Four books
Delia Goetz—Five books
Laurence Pringle—Three books

The group working with land mammals chose the following authors:

Gladys Conklin—Four books
Irmengarge Eberle—Four books
Michael Fox—Three books
Russell Freedman—Three books
Alice L. Hopf—Five books
Sylvia Johnson—Three books
Laurence Pringle—Three books
Jack Scott—Three books
Millicent E. Selsam—Five books
Alvin Silverstein—Five books
Seymour Simon—Three books

The group working with insects named these authors:

Gladys Conklin—Eight books
Rose E. Hutchins—Eight books
Robert McClung—Four books

Next, they found as many of the books as possible in the library. These books included each author's most recent publications on the subject. They read the information about the author on the dust jacket or elsewhere in the book and searched for biographical data and magazine or journal articles written by the author. Then they evaluated the author's background and read and reread the books, searching for each author's point of view and purpose for writing the book.

After the children had carefully read the books, they evaluated the content of the materials. For this evaluation, they referred to a list of content suggestions recommended by Helen Huus (4) and developed an evaluative guide.

A Guide for Critical Evaluation of Content

1 Does the author include all the necessary facts?
2 Are all the facts presented accurately?
3 Is the information recent?
4 Are the facts presented logically and in perspective?

In addition to reading the books, the children read background information in science text-books, encyclopedias, and magazine or journal articles. They checked the copyright dates of the materials; scrutinized the photographs, graphs, charts, and diagrams; and tried to evaluate whether the author had differentiated fact from opinion. If they found that there was more than one viewpoint on the subject, they tried to discover if the author had presented both.

Finally, the groups presented their information on the authors and their books to the rest of the class. Children not only learned how to critically evaluate informational books and authors but also learned much about the content area and the procedures that writers of informational books should go through as they research their subjects.

Several authors of science informational books develop themes related to endangered species and ecology. These books can provide stimulating sources for topics of debate and independent research. The criteria for evaluating author and content that were given earlier should also be used here. In addition, students should test the validity of an argument presented in written materials. Willavene Wolf (9) lists the following steps:

1 Strip the argument of any excess words or sentences.
2 Be sure students have access to all the premises upon which the author's conclusion may rest.
3 Determine whether the author is referring to all of a group, some of a group, or none of a group.
4 After students have stripped the argument to its basic framework, identified all of the premises (both stated and assumed), and transformed the premises, they are then in a better position to determine whether the conclusion logically follows from the premises.

Children can independently evaluate whether the author's conclusion is logical and supported by facts. They can also enter into debates: they can choose to take different sides of an issue presented by an author, research outside sources, and develop the contrasting viewpoints. For example, Jack Denton Scott's *Little Dogs of the Prairie* can be used for a debate on the plight of prairie dogs. One upper-elementary class used information in Scott's book to provide the framework for their debate. They chose sides in the issue, completed additional research, and presented their positions in debate format. They included this basic information from Scott's book:

Debate Subject: Protection of Prairie Dogs
Versus Total Extermination

Points for Protection:

1   At the end of the nineteenth century, there were 600,000 square miles of prairie dog towns occupied by 5 billion prairie dogs. In the 1980s, the prairie dog is vanishing.
2   Naturalists claim prairie dog burrows benefit groundwater accumulation; water can penetrate the hard soil of prairies through the tunnels.
3   Naturalists claim soil carried to the surface by prairie dogs breaks down into helpful soluble forms.
4   Naturalists claim poisoning prairie dogs sets off a chain reaction in which many other animals die.
5   Scott claims people gain an immeasurable aesthetic value from observing prairie dogs.
6   Naturalists claim that prairie dogs come to an area after it has been overgrazed by cattle, horses, or sheep.

Points for Extermination:

1   Cowboys and ranchers consider the prairie dog burrows dangerous to horses and riders.
2   Ranchers claim prairie dogs destroy grazing land, making it unfit for cattle, horses, and sheep.
3   Ranchers claim prairie dogs eat grasses that should be reserved for livestock.

Other books about animals that have been endangered because of human hunting include Dorothy Hinshaw Patent's *Whales: Giants of the Deep*, Scott Barry's *The Kingdom of Wolves*, and Dorothy Hinshaw Patent's *Where the Bald Eagles Gather*.

Some animals are not endangered because people hunt or poison them; instead, it is human pollution or land development that has endangered their survival. Books on this subject can spark debates as children consider whether the interests of people are in opposition to the interests of animals or whether the protective measures designed for animals also protect human life. Books that can be used for this purpose in-

clude Caroline Arnold's *Saving the Peregrine Falcon*, Francine Jacob's *Africa's Flamingo Lake*, Robert M. McClung's *America's Endangered Birds: Programs and People Working to Save Them*, and the biography *Thor Heyerdahl: Viking Scientist* by Wyatt Blassingame.

Applying Data from Reading to Practical Problems

After children have critically evaluated the subjects of water, land, and air pollution discussed in informational books, they may be interested in evaluating the extent of pollution in their own environment. An informational book that can spark this kind of critical evaluation through experimentation and observation is Betty Miles's *Save the Earth! An Ecology Handbook for Kids*. Several projects that appeal to third and fourth graders include planning a new town to make the best possible use of land, recording air pollution by placing several cards covered with a thin layer of

Children apply knowledge gained from informational books during an environmental project.

petroleum jelly outside in different locations and noting after twenty-four hours the pollution that has collected on the cards, and tracking water pollution in their own neighborhood, town, or city.

This last project reinforced observation, critical evaluation, and graphic interpretation abilities when a fourth-grade class identified various waterways in their town and made notes about pollution they found as they walked beside several creeks, a lake, a river, and a pond. When they returned to school, they used their notes to draw a large map of the waterways and marked on the map any pollution they found. Next, they filled in the type of building or human activity that was near the pollution. They could now more closely evaluate possible causes of water pollution in their own town. When the students discovered a definite problem, they took pictures of the evidence, wrote letters to the newspaper, made "clean up the waterways" posters, and asked people to make pledges to clean up their waterways.

Adults can encourage children to relate their reading to experiences and observations in their daily lives. In addition, children can link new applications of science principles to their previous knowledge. Helen Huus (4) emphasizes the desirability of encouraging children to place new learning into a personal context. A reader, according to Huus,

fails to obtain the greatest pleasure, enjoyment, and even knowledge from his efforts unless, in the doing he gives something of himself. He must amalgamate the total into his own background of information, what the psychologists call his "apperceptive mass," and reorganize his ideas to accommodate his new learnings, his attitudes, or his feelings. In this reorganization, he gains new insights—sees the same things from a different point of view, sees aspects hitherto not noticed, savors the color and texture of a word or phrase, stores away a new visual image, or feels empathy with characters he has previously ignored or misunderstood. (p. 164)

Deciding whether information about animals is fact or fantasy is another way for children to apply data from reading to a practical problem. Several informational books discussed previously refer to animal facts versus fables, legends, or people's erroneous opinions. These books can stimulate children's investigations into other people's perceptions of truth about animal behavior and into literature to discover other animal fa-

bles. A second-grade teacher, for example, read Seymour Simon's *Animal Fact/Animal Fable* to her students and interested them in interviewing people to discover what they believed about animal characteristics or behaviors. Because the students had often incorrectly identified a statement as fact or fable, they wondered whether other children or even their parents would know the correct interpretation of statements such as "blind as a bat," which are often stated as truths. This led to a discussion during which the teacher wrote on the chalkboard the questions the children developed from the statements in Simon's book. (See Figure 12–3).

The teacher typed and duplicated the questionnaire so that all children had their own copies. They talked about how to ask questions and how to tally responses in the yes or no column. They questioned other classes, parents, and other adults. The next day they counted the number of tallies and put their totals on a big chart. In addition to enjoying the activity, the children used oral communication skills and discovered how opinion polls are conducted.

Discussions can also be developed with children that encourage children to observe and analyze differences in behavior of real animals, behavior of real animals depicted in informational books, and behavior of the same animals depicted in folktales and modern fantasy. For example, a caged chicken might be brought into the classroom for observational purposes. Children could observe the eating, sleeping, movement, and clucking behavior of the chicken. They could also observe the chicken's appearance. This factual observation could then be compared with the presentation of chickens in an informational book such as *The Chicken and the Egg* by Oxford Scientific Films. Finally, children could consider the behavior of chickens in folktales such as Paul Galdone's *The Little Red Hen*. They might discuss the differences in behavior and identify different purposes for writing and reading the two types of literature. Children can write their own books similar to Seymour Simon's *Animal Fact/Animal Fable* but illustrate and describe characteristics of real animals instead of fantasy animals. Other observations and discussions might be stimulated by comparing a caged mouse to the informational book *Harvest Mouse* by Oxford Scientific Films and either of Beverly Cleary's fantasies *The Mouse and the Motorcycle* or *Runaway Ralph*.

		Yes	No
1	Are bats blind?		
2	Do bees sting only once?	///	//
3	Are owls wise?		
4	Does the archer fish shoot food?		
5	Can a turtle leave its shell?		
6	Does a wolf live alone?		
7	Can some fish climb trees?		
8	Does a cricket tell the temperature with its chirp?		
9	Are elephants afraid of mice?		
10	Do cats have nine lives?		
11	Can a porcupine shoots its quills?		
12	Can a dog talk with its tail?		
13	Do ostriches hide their heads in the sand?		
14	Will goats eat just about anything?		
15	Do bulls become angry when they see red?		
16	Do snakes charm their prey?		
17	Do camels store water in their humps?		
18	Do snakes bite with their tongues?		
19	Will rats leave a sinking ship?		
20	Do raccoons wash their food before they eat?		

FIGURE 12–3

SUMMARY

Most children find the writing style of informational books and biographies far more interesting than that of content area textbooks. Such books can provide many opportunities for stimulating children's learning experiences.

Biographies often include lively dialogue, confrontations between new ideas and society, and the joys and sorrows connected with discovery. Activities are suggested that allow children to interact with literature and the biographical characters through creative drama. Pantomime, "You Are There" dramatizations, and imaginary conversations between people of two time periods are suggested for creative thinking, empathizing with people in history, and developing the understanding that biographies are written about real people.

Many informational books relate to the science curriculum and provide valuable materials for helping children acquire abilities important for science education. Two types of informational materials relate specifically to the science curriculum: books on scientific topics and research that contain many small but interrelated details requiring analytical reading; and nontechnical materials, such as biographies of scientists and literature reporting scientific principles and findings, written in a style that is easy to read and understand.

In this chapter, activities are suggested so that parents, teachers, and librarians can assist children in increasing their ability to understand and enjoy science-related literature.

Suggested Activities for Children's Understanding of Biographies and Informational Books

☐ Prepare a pantomime-sequencing game that identifies both the cue and the directions for the pantomimed activity. Share the game with a peer group or a group of children.

☐ Select a biographical incident that you believe would make an excellent "You Are There" creative dramatization. Identify the introductory scene and circumstances, the consecutive scenes to be used, the characters to be involved, and the questions to be asked of children while they discuss and develop the drama.

☐ Select several biographies written about the same person. Plan a discussion that encourages children to consider the strengths and weaknesses of each biography.

☐ Identify the parts of a book that are necessary if children are to use informational materials effectively at a particular grade level. Choose a specific part of a book, such as table of contents, index, glossary, or bibliography of further readings; select several informational books that can be used to encourage the development and use of these book aids. Prepare an activity that increases children's understanding of that part of the book.

☐ Visit a public or school library. What reference aids are available to assist children in their search for nonfictional materials Explore the relationship between the author card, the title card, and the subject card in the library card catalog. Is the information on cards or computerized? Ask librarians how they help children find information.

☐ Choose several books by authors who have effectively presented the meaning of new technical terminology through the text or photographs, diagrams, and charts. Share the books with a peer group and make suggestions as to how you would use the books with children.

☐ Search through a science or social studies curriculum to identify the graphic aids that children at a particular grade level are expected to use, understand, or develop themselves. Develop an annotated bibliography of informational books by authors who have included accurate, clearly understandable graphic aids. Include page numbers for each aid you identify.

☐ Choose a reading-for-exact-meaning requirement for science-related materials (pp. 612–14). Using a science-related book not discussed in this chapter, develop a lesson that would encourage children to note the main idea of a selection, identify supporting details, or note the author's organization.

☐ Select an informational book that encourages children to perform an experiment in order to develop an understanding of a scientific principle. Perform the experiment as directed. Are the directions clearly stated? Should they be modified or clarified for use with children? Make any necessary modifications and encourage a child to perform the experiment. Follow each step of the experiment and discuss the scientific principle with the child.

☐ Develop a lesson that encourages children to critically evaluate what they read, including the author's purpose for writing the book, the author's competency, and the adequacy and accuracy of the content.

References

1 Cianciolo, Patricia J. "Reading Literature, and Writing from Writers' Perspectives." *English Journal* 74 (Dec. 1985): 65–69.

2 Gillespie, John T., and Gilbert, Christine B. *Best Books for Children, Preschool through the Middle Grades.* New York: Bowker, 1978, 1981.

3 Heinig, Ruth Beall, and Stillwell, Lyda. *Creative Dramatics for the Classroom Teacher.* Englewood Cliffs, N.J.: Prentice-Hall, 1974.

4 Huus, Helen. "Critical and Creative Reading." In *Developing Comprehension Including Critical Reading*, edited by Mildred A. Dawson. Newark, Del.: International Reading Association, 1968.

5 Moore, Ann W. "A Question of Accuracy: Errors in Children's Biographies." *School Library Journal* 31 (Feb. 1985): 34–35.

6 Podendorf, Illa. "Characteristics of Good Science Materials for Young Readers." *Library Trends* 22 (April 1974): 425–31.

7 Robertson, Elizabeth, and McGinnis, Jo. "Biography as Art: A Formal Approach." In *Portraits: Biography and Autobiography in the Secondary School*, edited by Margaret Fleming and Jo McGinnis. Urbana, Ill.: National Council of Teachers of English, 1985.

8 Shepherd, David L. *Comprehensive High School Reading Methods*, 3rd ed. Columbus, Ohio: Merrill, 1982.

9 Wolf, Willavene. "The Logical Dimension of Critical Reading." In *Developing Critical Reading*, edited by Mildred A. Dawson. Newark, Del.: International Reading Association, 1968.

CHILDREN'S LITERATURE

Biographies

Adolf, Arnold. *Malcolm X*. Crowell, 1970 (I:7–12 R:5). A biography of the Black American leader.

Aldis, Dorothy. *Nothing Is Impossible: The Story of Beatrix Potter*. Drawings by Richard Cuffari. Atheneum, 1969 (I:10+ R:6). The biography of the creator of *Peter Rabbit*.

Bains, Rae. *Harriet Tubman: The Road to Freedom*. Illustrated by Larry Johnson. Troll, 1982 (I:8–12 R:4). An illustrated version of Tubman's experiences with the Underground Railroad.

Blassingame, Wyatt. *Thor Heyerdahl: Viking Scientist*. Elsevier-Dutton, 1979 (I:8+ R:5). The story of the scientist who built and sailed the *Kon Tiki*.

Blegvad, Erik. *Self-Portrait: Erik Blegvad*. Addison-Wesley, 1979 (I:all R:5). A short autobiography written and illustrated by an artist of children's books.

Blumberg, Rhoda. *Commodore Perry in the Land of the Shogun*. Lothrop, 1985 (I:10+ R:6). In 1853 Perry leads an expedition to open trade with Japan.

Brenner, Barbara. *On the Frontier with Mr. Audubon*. Coward-McCann, 1977 (I:8–12 R:3). A trip down the Ohio and Mississippi Rivers with John James Audubon and his assistant, sketching birds.

Brooks, Polly Schoyer. *Queen Eleanor: Independent Spirit of the Medieval World*. Lippincott, 1983 (I:10+ R:8). A biography of the twelfth-century queen.

Brown, Marion Marsh. *Homeward the Arrow's Flight*. Abingdon, 1980 (I:10+ R:6). The story of the first female Native American doctor.

Collins, Michael. *Flying to the Moon and Other Strange Places*. Farrar, Straus & Giroux, 1976 (I:10+ R:6). An autobiography about travel to the moon.

Cooper, Irene. *Susan B. Anthony*. Watts, 1984 (I:10+ R:6). A biography of a leader in women's rights.

Dalgliesh, Alice. *The Columbus Story*. Illustrated by Leo Politi. Scribner, 1955 (I:5–8 R:3). A picture book version of Columbus's first voyage to America.

Dank, Milton. *Albert Einstein*. Watts, 1983 (I:10+ R:7). Biography emphasizes both Einstein's life and discoveries.

D'Aulaire, Ingri, and D'Aulaire, Edgar Parin. *Abraham Lincoln*. Doubleday, 1939, 1957 (I:8–11 R:5). A book for young children.

————. *Benjamin Franklin*. Doubleday, 1950 (I:8–12 R:6). A colorfully illustrated biography.

————. *Columbus*. Doubleday, 1955 (I:7–10 R:5). A colorfully illustrated biography.

Davidson, Margaret. *The Golda Meir Story*. Scribner, 1981 (I:9–12 R:6). Traces Meir's life through the Yom Kippur war and her tenure as prime minister.

DeKay, James T. *Meet Martin Luther King, Jr*. Illustrated by Ted Burwell. Random House, 1969 (I:7 R:4). Stresses the magnitude of King's work and his reasons for fighting injustice.

Dolan, Edward F. *Adolf Hitler: A Portrait in Tyranny*. Dodd, Mead, 1981 (I:10+ R:7). Hitler's rise to power, the days of World War II, the facts of the Holocaust, and Hitler's suicide.

Egypt, Ophelia Settle. *James Weldon Johnson*. Illustrated by Moneta Barnet. Crowell, 1974 (I:5–9 R:3). A Black-American author, educator, lawyer, and diplomat who started the first black newspaper in the United States.

Facklam, Margery. *Wild Animals, Gentle Women*. Illustrated by Paul Facklam. Harcourt Brace Jovanovich, 1978 (I:10+ R:6). Information on the lives of eleven women who have studied animal behavior.

Ferrell, Keith. *H.G. Wells: First Citizen of the Future*. Evans, 1983 (I:12+ R:7). A biography of the science fiction writer.

Fox, Mary Virginia. *Jane Goodall: Living Chimp Style*. Illustrated by Nona Hengen. Dillon, 1981 (I:6–9 R:5). A highly illustrated version of Goodall's life.

————. *Women Astronauts: Aboard the Shuttle*. Messner, 1984 (I:10+ R:8). Emphasizes Sally Ride's 1983 flight and includes brief biographies of eight women.

Franchere, Ruth. *Cesar Chavez*. Illustrated by Earl Thollander. Crowell, 1970 (I:7–9 R:4). Illustrated biography of Chavez's struggles to improve the pay and living conditions of migrant workers.

Fritz, Jean. *Make Way for Sam Houston*. Illustrated by Elise Primavera. Putnam, 1986 (I:9 R:6). The biography of a nineteenth-century hero.

————. *The Man Who Loved Books*. Illustrated by Trina Schart Hyman. Putnam, 1981 (I:6–9 R: 5). A highly illustrated biography of Saint Columba, A. D. 521–597.

I = Interest by age range;
R = Readability by grade level.

————. *Stonewall*. Illustrated by Stephen Gammell. Putnam, 1979 (I:10+ R:6). A biography of a famous Civil War general, Thomas Jackson.

————. *Traitor: The Case of Benedict Arnold*. Putnam, 1981 (I:8+ R:5). The life of the man who chose the British cause in the Revolutionary War.

————. *What's the Big Idea, Ben Franklin?* Illustrated by Margot Tomes. Coward-McCann, 1978 (I:7–10 R:5). A biography of the inventor, ambassador, and co-author of the Declaration of Independence.

————. *Where Do You Think You're Going, Christopher Columbus?* Illustrated by Margot Tomes. Putnam, 1980 (I:7–12 R:5). Fritz's style creates a believable background for Columbus's four voyages.

————. *Where Was Patrick Henry on the 29th of May?* Illustrated by Margot Tomes. Coward-McCann, 1975 (I:7–10 R:5). A humorous telling of incidents in Patrick Henry's youth and political career.

————. *Why Don't You Get a Horse, Sam Adams?* Illustrated by Trina Schart Hyman. Coward-McCann, 1974 (I:7–10 R:5). A humorous story about Samuel Adams, his refusal to ride a horse, and his final decision to ride.

————. *Will You Sign Here, John Hancock?* Illustrated by Trina Schart Hyman. Coward-McCann, 1976 (I:7–10 R:5). The rise to fame of a charming Revolutionary War hero.

Goodnough, David. *Christopher Columbus*. Illustrated by Burt Dodson. Troll Associates, 1979 (I:8–12 R:6). An illustrated life story of Columbus.

Goodsell, Jane. *Daniel Inouye*. Crowell, 1977. The life of the first Japanese-American member of Congress.

————. *Eleanor Roosevelt*. Illustrated by Wendell Minor. Crowell, 1970 (I:7–10 R:2). Eleanor's life as a shy child, as well as her years in the White House and her work after her husband's death.

Greenfield, Eloise, and Little, Lessie Jones. *Childtimes: A Three-Generation Memoir*. Crowell, 1979 (I:10+ R:5). Three black women tell about their childhood experiences.

Gutman, Bill. *The Picture Life of Reggie Jackson*. Watts, 1978 (I:5–9 R:2). A picture story of the experiences of the baseball player.

Haskins, James. *Andrew Young: Man with a Mission*. Lothrop, Lee & Shepard, 1979 (I:12+ R:7). The story of the first Black American ambassador to the United Nations.

Hyman, Trina Schart. *Self-Portrait: Trina Schart Hyman*. Addison-Wesley, 1981 (I:9–12 R:5). The autobiography of an artist.

Itsen, D. C. *Isaac Newton: Reluctant Genius*. Enslow, 1985 (I:10 R:6). Emphasizes accomplishments such as the theory of gravity.

Jakes, John. *Susanna of the Alamo*. Illustrated by Paul Bacon. Harcourt Brace Jovanovich, 1986 (I:7–12 R:6). A survivor of the Alamo retells the story of the battle.

Kheridan, David. *The Road from Home: The Story of an Armenian Girl*. Greenwillow, 1979 (I:12+ R:6). In 1915, an Armenian girl experiences the horrors of the Turkish persecution of Christian minorities.

Lasker, Joe. *The Great Alexander the Great*. Viking, 1983 (I:6–9 R:6). A highly illustrated version of the life of the conqueror.

Lasker, Joe, and Lasker, David. *The Boy Who Loved Music*. Illustrated by Joe Lasker. Viking, 1979 (I:all R:6). A story of Joseph Haydn and a new symphony.

Lawson, Don. *The Picture Life of Ronald Reagan*. Watts, 1984 (I:6–10 R:5). A brief version of Reagan's life from childhood to president.

Lee, Betsy. *Charles Eastman, The Story of an American Indian*. Dillon, 1979 (I:8–12 R:5). A biography of a famous doctor, writer, and worker for Indian rights.

Lipman, Jean, and Aspinwall, Margaret. *Alexander Calder and His Magical Mobiles*. Hudson Hills, 1981 (I:9+ R:6). The text begins with the artist's early work and illustrates work in wood, bronze, wire, and mobiles.

Liss, Howard. *Bobby Orr: Lightning on Ice*. Illustrated by Victor Mays. Garrard, 1975 (I:8–12 R:4). The hockey star's story begins when he is a young player in Canada and follows him into professional hockey.

Manes, Stephen. *Pictures of Motion and Pictures That Move: Eadweard Muybridge and the Photography of Motion*. Coward-McCann, 1982 (I:9+ R:6). A photographer in the late 1800s invents the zoopraxiscope, a machine that projects moving images.

Meltzer, Milton. *Dorothea Lange, Life Through the Camera*. Viking, 1985 (I:10+ R:5). Lange's photographs increase understanding of the photographer's biography.

Morgan, Helen L. *Maria Mitchell: First Lady of American Astronomy*. Westminster, 1977 (I:12+ R:7). Covers the years from childhood when she learns astronomy from her father through her years as first woman astronomy professor at Vassar College.

Morrison, Dorothy N. *Under a Strong Wind: The Adventures of Jessie Benton Frémont*. Atheneum, 1983 (I:10+ R:6). A biography of the wife of John Charles Frémont.

Neimark, Anne E. *A Deaf Child Listened: Thomas Gallaudet, Pioneer in American Education.* Morrow, 1983 (I:10+ R: 7). Traces the life of the founder of American education for the deaf.

Patterson, Lillie. *Frederick Douglass: Freedom Fighter*. Garrard, 1965 (I:6–9 R:3). The biography of the great Black American leader.

————. *Sure Hands, Strong Heart: The Life of Daniel Hale Williams*. Illustrated by David Scott Brown. Abingdon, 1981 (I:10+ R:5). Biography of a black physician who worked for interracial hospitals.

Pizer, Vernon. *Glorious Triumphs: Athletes Who Conquered Adversity*. Dodd, Mead, 1966, 1968, 1980 (I:12+ R:8). Includes a collection of brief biographies about sports personalities who have overcome some problem.

Provensen, Alice, and Provensen, Martin. *The Glorious Flight across the Channel with Louis Bleriot, July 25, 1909*. Viking, 1983 (I:all R:4). A highly illustrated account of the first flight across the English Channel.

Quackenbush, Robert. *Mark Twain? What Kind of a Name Is That? A Story of Samuel Langhorne Clemens*. Prentice-Hall, 1984 (I:7–10 R:5). Humorous illustrations appeal to younger readers.

Roosevelt, Elliott. *Eleanor Roosevelt, With Love*. Dutton, 1984 (I:10+ R:7). Eleanor's life from the viewpoint of her son.

Rosen, Sidney. *Galileo and the Magic Numbers*. Illustrated by Harie Stein. Little, Brown, 1958 (I:10+ R:6). A story about the astronomer and mathematician who invented the first telescope.

Sandburg, Carl. *Abe Lincoln Grows Up*. Illustrated by James Daugherty. Harcourt Brace Jovanovich, 1926, 1928, 1954 (I:10+ R:6). The first nineteen years of Lincoln's life.

Shapiro, Irwin. *Darwin and the Enchanted Isles*. Illustrated by Christopher Spollen. Coward-McCann, 1977

(I:8+ R:6). Born in England in 1809, Charles Darwin later visited the Galapagos Islands, where he discovered life forms that substantiated his theory on the evolution of animals.

Siegel, Beatrice. *An Eye on the World: Margaret Bourke-White, Photographer*. Warne, 1980 (I:10+ R:5). A biography of a famous photographer.

———. *Lillian Wald of Henry Street*. Macmillan, 1983 (I:12+ R:7). The founder of the Henry Street Settlement.

Silberdick, Barbara. *Franklin D. Roosevelt, Gallant President*. Feinberg, 1981 (I:9–12 R:6). This biography focuses upon Roosevelt's accomplishments.

Tobias, Tobi. *Arthur Mitchell*. Illustrated by Carol Byard. Crowell, 1975 (I:7–9 R:5). Describes the founder of the Dance Theatre of Harlem.

———. *Maria Tallchief*. Illustrated by Michael Hampshire. Crowell, 1970 (I:7–12 R:4). A biography of a world-renowned prima ballerina, an Osage Indian.

Veglahn, Nancy. *The Mysterious Rays: Marie Curie's World*. Illustrated by Victor Jahasz. Coward-McCann, 1977 (I:10+ R:6). Long years of dedicated experimentation provide the foundation for the Curies' discovery of radium.

Ventura, Piero. Based on text by Gian Paolo Ceserani. *Christopher Columbus*. Random House, 1978 (I:all R:6). A picture biography of Columbus's voyage to America.

———. Based on text by Gian Paolo Ceserani. *Marco Polo*. Illustrated by Piero Ventura. Putnam, 1982 (I:all R:6). A picture biography of Marco Polo's travels.

Whitney, Sharon. *Eleanor Roosevelt*. Watts, 1982 (I:10+ R:5). Follows life of Roosevelt from childhood through work with the United Nations.

Wibberley, Leonard. *Time of Harvest: Thomas Jefferson, the Years 1801 to 1826*. Farrar, Straus and Giroux, 1966 (I:12+ R:6). The final volume in a four-part biography.

Williams, Selma R. *Demeter's Daughters: The Women Who Founded America, 1587–1787*. Atheneum, 1976 (I:12+ R:7). Biographical sketches of women whose contributions made the settlement of America possible.

Wolf, Bernard. *In This Proud Land: The Story of a Mexican American Family*. Lippincott, 1978 (I:all R:4). Photographs and text follow a family from the Rio Grand Valley to Minnesota for summer employment.

Yates, Elizabeth. *Amos Fortune, Free Man*. Illustrated by Nora S. Unwin. Dutton, 1950 (I:10+ R:6). The life of a man who is captured by slave traders in Africa and brought to Boston.

———. *My Diary, My World*. Westminster, 1981 (I:10+ R:5). Journal format covers ages from 12–20.

———. *My Widening World*. Westminster, 1983 (I:10+ R:5). Journal format describes beginning writing career.

Zemach, Margot. *Self-Portrait, Margot Zemach*. Addison-Wesley, 1978 (I:all R:8). An autobiography of an illustrator of children's books.

Informational Books

Ancona, George. *Dancing Is*. Dutton, 1981 (I:6–12 R:5). Photographs and text describe different dances such as the Highland Fling.

Anderson, Joan. *The First Thanksgiving Feast*. Photographs by George Ancona. Clarion, 1984 (I:6–9 R:6). Photographs from the Plimoth Plantation in Plymouth, Massachusetts, accompany story of first Thanksgiving.

Anderson, Madelyn Klein. *Oil in Troubled Waters*. Vanguard, 1983 (I:10+ R:6). The effects of oil on marine life.

Antonacci, Robert J., and Lockhart, Barbara D. *Tennis for Young Champions*. Illustrated by Robert Handville. McGraw-Hill, 1982 (I:10+ R:6). History of tennis and step-by-step instructions for playing.

Arnold, Caroline. *Saving the Peregrine Falcon*. Photographs by Richard R. Hewett. Carolrhoda, 1985 (I:8–12 R:7). Various ways that people are trying to save the falcon from extinction.

Arnosky, Jim. *Drawing from Nature*. Lothrop, Lee & Shepard, 1982 (I:all R:6). Directions for drawing water, land, plants, and animals.

———. *Drawing Life in Motion*. Lothrop, Lee & Shepard, 1984 (I:all R:6). Directions for drawing action in nature.

———. *Freshwater Fish and Fishing*. Four Winds, 1982 (I:8–12 R:5). Information about trout, perch, and pike and how to catch them.

Asch, Frank, and Asch, Jan. *Running with Rachel*. Photographs by Jan Asch and Robert M. Buscow. Dial, 1979 (I:7–10 R:3). A young girl explains how she became interested in running.

Ashabranner, Brent. *Morning Star, Black Sun: The Northern Cheyenne Indians and America's Energy Crisis*. Photographs by Paul Conklin. Dodd, Mead, 1982 (I:10+ R:7). History of a tribe and its conflict with mining interests.

Asimov, Isaac. *Asimov's Guide to Halley's Comet*. Walker, 1985 (I:10+ R:6). Detailed information on history, formation, and anecdotes.

Aylesworth, Thomas G., and Aylesworth, Virginia. *The Mount St. Helens Disaster: What We've Learned*. Watts, 1983 (I:10+ R:6). The environmental effects resulting from the volcanic eruption.

Bare, Colleen Stanley. *Guinea Pigs Don't Read Books*. Dodd, Mead, 1985 (I:6–9 R:3). Photographs accompany a simple book on characteristics of guinea pigs.

Barry, Scott. *The Kingdom of Wolves*. Putnam, 1979 (I:9+ R:6). The author pleads for the protection of wolves.

Barton, Byron. *Airport*. Crowell, 1982 (I:3–8). Large illustrations follow passengers as they get ready to board the plane.

Bellville, Cheryl Walsh. *Farming Today Yesterday's Way*. Carolrhoda, 1984 (I:all R:7). Photographs and text describe a farm that uses early methods of farming.

Berger, Melvin. *Germs Make Me Sick!* Illustrated by Marylin Hafner. Crowell, 1985 (I:5–8 R:6). How viruses affect people.

Berman, Paul. *Make-Believe Empire: A How-to Book*. Atheneum, 1982 (I:8–12 R:6). Directions for creating a city, a navy, and other objects needed for one's own kingdom.

Bester, Roger. *Fireman Jim*. Crown, 1981 (I:5–10 R:4). Photographs and text follow a twenty-four-hour day in the life of a New York City firefighter.

Billings, Charlene. *Scorpions*. Dodd, Mead, 1983 (I:10+ R:7). The physiology, life cycle, and behavior of scorpions.

Bitter, Gary G. *Exploring with Computers*. Messner, 1981 (I:4–6 R:5). Explains the use of computers and encourages readers to do activities such as reading a punch card.

Bluestone, Naomi. *"So You Want to Be a Doctor?": The Realities of Pursuing Medicine As a Career*. Lothrop, Lee & Shepard, 1981 (I:10+ R:6). A doctor discusses what it means to be a medical student, an intern, and a resident.

Bolognese, Don. *Drawing Spaceships and Other Spacecraft*. Watts, 1982 (I:8+ R:6). Detailed illustrations introduce readers to various stages of drawing spaceships.

Brandenberg, Aliki. *A Medieval Feast.* Crowell, 1983 (I:8–12 R:4). Full-page illustrations depict the preparation for a feast in 1400.

Branley, Franklyn M. *Halley: Comet 1986.* Illustrated by Sally J. Bensusen. Dutton, 1983 (I:9+ R:6). Explains history, composition, and sighting information.

———. *Mysteries of Outer Space.* Illustrated by Sally J. Bensusen. Dutton, 1985 (I:9+ R:7). A question-and-answer format explores major questions about space.

———. *Saturn: The Spectacular Planet.* Illustrated by Leonard Kessler. Harper & Row, 1983 (I:9+ R:6). Author uses information from Pioneer and Voyager space explorations.

———. *Space Colony: Frontier of the 21st Century.* Illustrated by Leonard D. Dank. Dutton, 1982 (I:10+ R:6). The author explores possibilities of space colonies, their functions, and hazards of living in space.

Brenner, Martha. *Fireworks Tonight!* Hastings, 1983 (I:9+ R:6). Traces history of fireworks and discusses types and regulations.

Brinckloe, Julie. *Fireflies!* Macmillan, 1985 (I:5–8 R:3). A young boy catches, watches, and then releases fireflies.

Brown, Marc. *Your First Garden Book.* Atlantic-Little, 1981 (I:5–9 R:4). Over thirty simple projects that introduce children to gardening.

———, and Krensky, Stephen. *Dinosaurs, Beware!: A Safety Guide.* Little, Brown, 1982 (I:2–5 R:2). Safety rules presented through humorous pictures.

Bruun, Ruth Dowling, and Brunn, Bertel. *The Human Body.* Illustrated by Patricia J. Wynne. Random, 1982 (I:9+ R:6). An overview of the body systems.

Busch, Phyllis S. *Cactus in the Desert.* Illustrated by Harriet Barton. Crowell, 1979 (I:7–9 R:3). Discusses a variety of cacti.

———. *The Seven Sleepers: The Story of Hibernation.* Illustrated by Wayne Trimm. Macmillan, 1985 (I:7–9 R:3). What some northern animals do in winter.

Cajacob, Thomas, and Burton, Teresa. *Close to the Wild: Siberian Tigers in a Zoo.* Photographs by Thomas Cajacob. Carolrhoda, 1986 (I:6–10 R:6). Large color photographs depict life in a natural-habitat zoo.

Carrick, Donald. *Milk.* Greenwillow, 1985 (I:4–8). Large illustrations trace milk from dairy farm to grocery store.

Catchpole, Clive. *Desert.* Illustrated by Brian McIntyre. Dial, 1984 (I:6–9 R:3). A highly illustrated book about deserts.

———. *Jungles.* Illustrated by Denise Finney. Dial/Dutton, 1984 (I:6–9 R:3). The environment of the jungle is presented in colorful illustrations.

Ceserani, Gian Paolo. *Grand Constructions.* Illustrated by Piero Ventura. Putnam, 1983 (I:all). This history of architecture begins with Stonehenge and concludes with skyscrapers.

Chaikin, Miriam. *Make Noise, Make Merry: The Story of the Meaning of Purim.* Illustrated by Demi. Houghton Mifflin, 1983 (I:10+ R:7). The history and symbols related to the Jewish holiday.

Climo, Shirley. *Someone Saw a Spider: Spider Facts and Folktales.* Illustrated by Dirk Zimmer. Crowell, 1985 (I:10+ R:6). Author retells spider folktales and discusses facts about spiders.

Cobb, Vicki. *Fuzz Does It!* Illustrated by Brian Schatell. Lippincott, 1982 (I:6–12 R:6). Various fibers, their sources, and uses.

Cole, Joanna. *A Bird's Body.* Photographs by Jerome Wexler. Morrow, 1983 (I:8–12 R:4). Photographs and diagrams show birds' anatomy.

———. *Cars and How They Go.* Illustrated by Gail Gibbons. Harper & Row, 1983 (I:6–10 R:4). A simplified explanation of how parts of the car function.

———. *A Cat's Body.* Photographs by Jerome Wexler. Morrow, 1982 (I:6–12 R:4). Photographs and text show how a cat responds physically in different moods and activities.

———. *Cuts, Breaks, Bruises and Burns: How Your Body Heals.* Illustrated by True Kelley. Crowell, 1985 (I:8–10 R:4). How the body heals various injuries.

———. *A Horse's Body.* Photographs by Jerome Wexler. Morrow, 1981 (I:2–6 R:5). Text and photographs explain the horse's anatomy.

———. *An Insect's Body.* Photographs by Jerome Wexler and Raymond A. Mendez. Morrow, 1984 (I:8–12 R:4). The anatomy of a cricket is explained in text and photographs.

———. *My Puppy Is Born.* Photographs by Jerome Wexler. Morrow, 1973 (I:7–9 R:2). Text and photographs follow the birth of puppies through their first eight weeks of life.

———. *A Snake's Body.* Photographs by Jerome Wexler. Morrow, 1981 (I:8–10 R:4). Photographs and text describe the anatomy of a python.

Cone, Ferne Geller. *Crazy Crocheting.* Illustrated by Rachel Osterlof. Photographs by J. Morton Cone. Atheneum, 1981 (I:9–12 R:5). Instructions for a range of projects, including finger puppets.

Cook, David. *Environment.* Crown, 1985 (I:9+ R:6). Discusses several ecological systems and endangered species.

Corbett, Scott. *Bridges.* Illustrated by Richard Rosenblum. Four Winds, 1978 (I:10+ R:6). A history of bridges and the people who built them.

Cosman, Madeleine Pelner. *Medieval Holidays and Festivals: A Calendar of Celebrations.* Scribner, 1981 (I:9+ R:6). Medieval holidays for each month.

Costabel, Eva Deutsch. *A New England Village.* Atheneum, 1983 (I:6–10 R:4). The illustrations and text depict rural life in a nineteenth-century New England village.

Cutchins, Judy, and Johnston, Ginny. *Are Those Animals Real? How Museums Prepare Wildlife Exhibits.* Morrow, 1984 (I:9–12 R:4). Text and photographs describe steps in taxidermy.

Davis, Daniel S. *Behind Barbed Wire: The Imprisonment of Japanese Americans during World War II.* Dutton, 1982 (I:10+ R:7). The internment of Japanese Americans and how their lives were altered.

Davis, Edward E. *Into the Dark: A Beginner's Guide to Developing and Printing Black and White Negatives.* Atheneum, 1979 (I:10+ R:7). An extensive coverage of beginning photography.

Demuth, Patricia. *Joel: Growing Up a Farm Man.* Photographs by Jack Demuth. Dodd, Mead, 1982 (I:9+ R:6). Photographs and text reveal how a thirteen-year-old learns to be a farmer.

de Paola, Tomie. *The Cloud Book.* Holiday, 1975 (I:6–9 R:4). Ten clouds, their shapes, and how they forecast weather.

———. *The Popcorn Book.* Holiday, 1978 (I:3–8 R:5). Illustrations and story present facts about popcorn.

East, Katherine. *A King's Treasure: The Sutton Hoo Ship Burial.* Illustrated by Dinah Cohen. Kestrel, 1982 (I:9+ R:8). The text and illustrations describe the excavation of the burial ground of a seventh-century king.

Elwood, Ann, and Wood, Linda C. *Windows in Space.* Walker, 1982 (I:10+ R:6). A history of astronomy and the relationship with space exploration.

Englander, Roger. *Opera, What's All the Screaming About?* Walker, 1983 (I:10+ R:7). A listener's guide to opera.

Englebardt, Stanley L. *Miracle Chip: The Microelectronic Revolution.* Lothrop, Lee & Shepard, 1979 (I:10+ R:8). The development of the miracle chip used in minicomputers.

Facklam, Margery, and Facklam, Howard. *The Brain: Magnificent Mind Machine.* Harcourt Brace Jovanovich, 1982 (I:10+ R:7). Brain functions and how they were discovered.

Fenner, Carol. *Gorilla, Gorilla.* Illustrated by Symeon Shimin. Random House, 1973 (I:7–10 R:4). The early life of a gorilla and his capture and confinement in a zoo.

Filstrup, Chris, and Filstrup, Janie. *Beadazzled: The Story of Beads.* Illustrated by Loren Bloom. Warne, 1982 (I:10+ R:6). The history of beads from ancient civilizations through contemporary times.

Fischer-Nagel, Heiderose, and Fischer-Nagel, Andraes. *Life of the Honey Bee.* Carolrhoda, 1986 (I:6–10 R:6). Close-up photographs show various stages in the honey bee's life cycle.

Flanagan, Geraldine Lux, and Morris, Sean. *Window into a Nest.* Houghton Mifflin, 1975 (I:9+ R:8). Excellent, detailed account of the life of a pair of chickadees.

Ford, Barbara. *Alligators, Raccoons, and Other Survivors: The Wildlife of the Future.* Morrow, 1981 (I:9+ R:6). How animals have survived in spite of human encroachment.

Freedman, Russell. *Dinosaurs and Their Young.* Illustrated by Leslie Morrill. Holiday, 1983 (I:6–9 R:4). A picture book version of discoveries about the duck-billed dinosaurs.

———. *Sharks.* Holiday, 1985 (I:6–10 R:5). Characteristics, evolution, and types of sharks.

Gardner, Beau. *Guess What?* Lothrop, Lee & Shepard, 1985 (I:5–8). Silhouettes encourage children to observe and to predict.

Gardner, Robert. *This Is the Way It Works: A Collection of Machines.* Illustrated by Jeffrey Brown. Doubleday, 1980 (I:10+ R:7). Diagrams and text describe how various tools and machines work.

Goldner, Kathryn, and Vogel, Carole. *Why Mount St. Helens Blew Its Top.* Illustrated by Roberta Aggarwal. Dillon, 1981 (I:9+ R:6). Emphasis is on North American volcanoes.

Goldston, Robert. *Sinister Touches: The Secret War against Hitler.* Dial, 1982 (I:10+ R:9). Covers the war years from 1939 to 1945.

Goor, Ron, and Goor, Nancy. *In the Driver's Seat.* Crowell, 1982 (I:6–10 R:6). A driver's view of large vehicles.

———. *Shadows: Here, There, and Everywhere.* Photographs by Ron Goor. Crowell, 1981 (I:6–10 R:4). Experiments with shadows.

Graham, Ada. *Six Little Chickadees: A Scientist and Her Work with Birds.* Photographs by Cordelia Stanwood. Four Winds, 1982 (I:8–12 R:6). A story about Cordelia Stanwood's studies of bird life.

———, and Graham, Frank. *The Changing Desert.* Illustrated by Robert B. Shetterly. Scribner, 1981 (I:9–12 R:6). Text explores problems in the desert, including vehicles, water, overgrazing.

Hall, Lynn. *Tazo and Me.* Photographed by Jan Hall. Scribner, 1985 (I:10+ R:6). A photo documentary shows a rider caring for and showing a horse.

Hausherr, Rosmarie. *My First Kitten.* Four Winds, 1985 (I:6–9 R:3). Selecting and caring for a kitten.

Hawes, Judy. *Bees and Beelines.* Illustrated by Aliki. Crowell, 1964 (I:4–8 R:3). A Let's-Read-and-Find-Out Science Book explores flight of bees.

———. *Ladybug, Ladybug, Fly Away Home.* Illustrated by Ed Emberley. Crowell, 1967 (I:4–8 R:3). A Let's-Read-and-Find-Out Science Book encourages children to view the ladybug.

Heilman, Joan Rattner. *Bluebird Rescue.* Lothrop, Lee & Shepard, 1982 (I:9–12 R:6). Reasons for decline of the bluebird and suggestions for conservation groups.

Hendrich, Paula. *Saving America's Birds.* Lothrop, Lee & Shepard, 1982 (I:10+ R:6). The varied circumstances that result in endangered birds.

Herbst, Judith. *Sky Above and Worlds Beyond.* Atheneum, 1983 (I:9+ R:7). An enthusiastic guided tour of space.

Hess, Lilo. *Diary of a Rabbit.* Scribner, 1982 (I:9–12 R:6). Information on different breeds and the care of rabbits, as well as a five-month diary about one rabbit.

Hewett, Joan. *Watching Them Grow: Inside a Zoo Nursery.* Photographs by Richard Hewitt. Little, Brown, 1979 (I:7–12 R:6). Photographs and text show what happens in the nursery at the San Diego Zoo.

Hilton, Suzanne. *We the People: The Way We Were 1783–1793.* Westminster, 1981 (I:10+ R:7). Explores subjects such as education, living conditions, and culture.

Hoban, Tana. *A Children's Zoo.* Greenwillow, 1985 (I:2–6). Each photograph is accompanied by a list of three words that describe the animal.

Holbrook, Sabra. *Canada's Kids.* Atheneum, 1983 (I:10+ R:6). Reflects varied backgrounds of Canadian youth.

Holmes, Anita. *Cactus: The All-American Plant.* Illustrated by Joyce Ann Powzyk. Four Winds, 1982 (I:10+ R:6). Environment, interdependence of life forms, and major cactus types.

Hopf, Alice L. *Bats.* Photographs by Merlin D. Tuttle. Dodd, 1985 (I:8–12 R:6). The text includes the dangers of pesticides and loss of habitats.

Horwitz, Elinor Lander. *How to Wreck a Building.* Photographs by Joshua Horwitz. Pantheon, 1982 (I:9–12 R:5). A former student describes the procedures used to demolish an elementary school.

Hunt, Patricia. *Koalas.* Dodd, Mead, 1980 (I:8–10). Photographs depict the life of the koalas.

———. *Tigers.* Dodd, Mead, 1981 (I:8–10 R:4). The Bengal and Siberian tigers are described.

Huntington, Harriet E. *Let's Look at Cats.* Doubleday, 1981 (I:9–12 R:5). Photographs show various members of the cat family.

Isenbart, Hans-Heinrich. *A Duckling Is Born.* Translated by Catherine Edwards Sadler. Photographs by Othmar Baumli. Putnam, 1981 (I:4–8 R:3). Describes the life cycle of ducks.

Isenberg, Barbara, and Jaffe, Marjorie. *Albert the Running Bear's Exercise Book.* Illustrated by Diane de Groat. Houghton Mifflin, 1984 (I:5–9 R:6). Step-by-step directions for exercises.

Jacobs, Francine. *Africa's Flamingo Lake.* Photographs by Jerome Jacobs. Morrow, 1979 (I:9+ R:7). Author visits Lake Nakuru in Kenya, home of the largest number of flamingos in the world.

Jaspersohn, William. *Magazine: Behind the Scenes at Sports Illustrated.* Little, Brown, 1983 (I:10+ R:10). The work associated with publishing a weekly issue is shown in photographs and text.

Jessel, Camilla. *The Joy of Birth: A Book for Parents and Children.* Dutton, 1983 (I:9+ R:6). Provides an introduction to pregnancy and birth.

————. *The Puppy Book.* Metheun, 1980 (I:8–12). Follows the birth, in photographs, of nine Labrador puppies.

Johnson, Sylvia. *Potatoes.* Photographs by Masaharu Suzuki. Lerner, 1984 (I:10+ R:9). Traces the development of a potato.

Johnston, Ginny, and Cutchins, Judy. *Andy Bear: A Polar Cub Grows Up at the Zoo.* Photographs by Constance Noble. Morrow, 1985 (I:9–12 R:6). A young cub is raised by the zoo keeper.

Kalb, Jonah, and Kalb, Laura. *The Easy Ice Skating Book.* Illustrated by Sandy Kossin. Houghton Mifflin, 1981 (I:7–12 R:5). Beginning ice skating skills such as stopping, gliding, and spinning.

Karen, Ruth. *Feathered Serpent: The Rise and Fall of the Aztecs.* Four Winds, 1979 (I:10+ R:9). The history of the Aztec civilization and a description of where the best Aztec archaeological sites may be viewed.

Knight, David C. *"Dinosaurs" That Swam and Flew.* Illustrated by Lee J. Ames. Prentice-Hall, 1985 (I:8–12 R:5). Numerous drawings and lists of museums add to the text.

Koebner, Linda. *From Cage to Freedom: A New Beginning for Laboratory Chimpanzees.* Dutton, 1981 (I:9+ R:5). Scientists follow laboratory chimps after they are released on a Florida island.

Kohl, Herbert. *A Book of Puzzlements: Play and Invention with Language.* Schocken, 1981 (I:10+ R:7). A large collection of word games, including anagrams, hieroglyphics, and crossword puzzles.

Kohl, Judith, and Kohl, Herbert. *Pack, Band and Colony: The World of Social Animals.* Illustrated by Margaret La Farge. Farrar, Straus & Giroux, 1983 (I:10+ R:9). Includes wolves, lemurs, and termites.

Krementz, Jill. *A Very Young Rider.* Knopf, 1977 (I:7–12 R:3). Photographs and text describe the preparation of an Olympic hopeful.

————. *A Very Young Skater.* Knopf, 1979 (I:7–12 R:4). Ten-year-old Katherine spends several hours every day preparing for her desired goal of being an accomplished skater.

Lasky, Kathryn. *Dollmaker: The Eyelight and the Shadow.* Photographs by Christopher G. Knight. Scribner, 1981 (I:9+ R:5). A doll that will be a collector's item is described in text and photographs.

————. *Sugaring Time.* Photographs by Christopher Knight. Macmillan, 1983 (I:all R:6). Photographs and text describe collecting and processing maple sap.

Lauber, Patricia. *Journey to the Planets.* Crown, 1982 (I:8–12 R:4). Photographs and text highlight the prominent features of each planet in our solar system.

————. *Seeds Pop! Stick! Glide!* Photography by Jerome Wexler. Crown, 1981 (I:8–10 R:4). Discusses the many ways that seeds travel.

Leakey, Richard E. *Human Origins.* Dutton, 1982 (I:10+ R:7). Text traces human evolution from man-apes to early farmers.

Leen, Nina. *Monkeys.* Holt, Rinehart & Winston, 1978 (I:7–12 R:5). Photographs showing monkeys, apes, and great apes.

Linsley, Leslie. *Air Crafts: Playthings to Make and Fly.* Photographs by Jon Aron. Lodestar, 1982 (I:9–12 R:6). Six how-to activities for objects such as a boomerang and a skate sail that can be made to move through air.

Macaulay, David. *Mill.* Houghton, 1983 (I:9+ R:5). The mills of nineteenth-century New England.

MacGregor, Anne, and MacGregor, Scott. *Domes: A Project Book.* Lothrop, Lee & Shepard, 1982 (I:9+ R:7). History of domes and models for building one.

Malnig, Anita. *Where the Waves Break: Life at the Edge of the Sea.* Photographs by Jeff Rotman, Alex Kerstitch, and Franklin H. Barnwell. Carolrhoda, 1985 (I:9+ R:6). Color photography enhances a study of marine life.

Mangurian, David. *Children of the Incas.* Four Winds, 1979 (I:7–12 R:3). Photographs and text illustrate the life of a thirteen-year-old boy who lives in the highlands of Peru.

Mannetti, William. *Dinosaurs in Your Back Yard.* Atheneum, 1982 (I:9+ R:6). Some new theories about dinosaurs.

Marcus, Rebecca. *Being Blind.* Hastings, 1981 (I:9–12 R:6). Many aspects of blindness, such as inventions to help blind people, problems, and solutions.

Marrin, Albert. *Aztecs and Spaniards: Cortez and the Conquest of Mexico.* Atheneum, 1986 (I:12+ R:7). A history of the Aztecs and the influences of Cortez.

Maruki, Toshi. *Hiroshima No Pika.* Lothrop, Lee & Shepard, 1982 (I:8–12 R:4). A powerfully illustrated picture book about the after-effects of the first atomic bomb.

Math, Irwin. *Morse, Marconi and You: Understanding and Building Telegraph, Telephone and Radio Sets.* Scribner, 1979 (I:10+ R:10). The discovery of telegraph, telephone, and radio sets and detailed directions for building each one.

————. *Wires and Watts: Understanding and Using Electricity.* Illustrated by Hal Keith. Scribner, 1981 (I:10+ R:10). Experiments with electricity.

McClung, Robert M. *America's Endangered Birds: Programs and People Working to Save Them.* Illustrated by George Founds. Morrow, 1979 (I:9+ R:6). Six endangered types of birds.

McDearmon, Kay. *Rocky Mountain Bighorns.* Photos by Valerius Geist. Dodd, Mead, 1980 (I: 9+ R:6). Pictures and text describe the bighorn sheep, their habitat and behavior, and the need to protect them.

McPhail, David. *Farm Morning.* Harcourt Brace Jovanovich, 1985 (I:2–5). A young girl and her father explore the barnyard.

Meyer, Carolyn, and Gallenkamp, Charles. *The Mystery of the Ancient Maya.* Atheneum, 1985 (I:10+ R:8). Early explorers and discoveries.

Michel, Anna. *The Story of Nim: The Chimp Who Learned Language.* Photographs by Susan Kuklin and Herbert S. Terrace. Knopf, 1980 (I:8+ R:6). The story of the research study that resulted in a chimpanzee learning to identify and use 125 signs in sign language.

Miles, Betty. *Save the Earth! An Ecology Handbook for Kids.* Illustrated by Claire A. Nivola. Knopf, 1974 (I:8+ R:5). Activities designed to help children explore their environment.

Millard, Anne. *Ancient Egypt.* Illustrated by Angus McBride, Brian and Constance Dear, and Nigel Chamberlain. Warwick, 1979 (I:9+ R:6). Background information about the Egyptian civilization that lasted from 3118 B.C. to 31 B.C.

Miller, Jonathan. *The Human Body.* Viking, 1983 (I:9+). A pop-up book illustrates the human body.

Milton, Joyce. *Here Come the Robots.* Hastings, 1981 (I:8–10 R:4). A collection of stories about robots in space and in other exploration.

Murphy, Jim. *Tractors: From Yesterday's Steam Wagons to Today's Turbocharged Giants*. Lippincott, 1984 (I:9+ R:6). A history of tractors.

Nance, John. *Lobo of the Tasaday*. Pantheon, 1982 (I:9–12 R:5). Photographs and text follow a Filipino boy whose people lived in the Stone Age.

Nixon, Hershell, and Nixon, Joan Lowery. *Earthquakes: Nature in Motion*. Dodd, Mead, 1981 (I:8–10 R:5). Describes the what, how, and why of earthquakes.

————. *Glaciers: Nature's Frozen Rivers*. Dodd, Mead, 1980 (I:9+ R:6). Text and photographs describe glacier formation, different types of glaciers, results of glaciers, and use of glaciers for water supplies and electric power.

————. *Volcanoes: Nature's Fireworks*. Dodd, Mead, 1978 (I:7–10 R:5). Discusses causes of volcanoes.

Norvell, Flo Ann Hedley. *The Chicken and the Egg*. Photographs by George Bernard and Peter Parks. Putnam, 1979 (I:all R:4). Photographs show changes in the chick embryo.

————. *The Great Big Box Book*. Photographs by Richard W. Mitchell. Crowell, 1979 (I:5–9 R:5). Directions for making playthings out of large boxes.

Nourse, Alan E. *Your Immune System*. Watts, 1982 (I:10+ R:7). Information about lymphatic systems, inoculation, allergic reactions, and research.

Oxford Scientific Films. *The Butterfly Cycle*. Photographs by John Cooke. Putnam, 1977 (I:all R:5). Life cycle of the cabbage white butterfly.

————. *The Chicken and the Egg*. Photographs by George Bernard and Peter Parker. Putnam, 1979 (I:all R:4). Photographs show changes in a chick embryo growing inside the egg.

————. *Common Frog*. Photographs by George Bernard. Putnam, 1979 (I:all R:5). Beautiful photographs depict the life cycle of the frog.

————. *Harvest Mouse*. Photographs by George Bernard, Sean Morris, and David Thompson. Putnam, 1982 (I:all). Photographs show habits of the European mouse.

————. *Mosquito*. Photographs by George Bernard and John Cooke. Putnam, 1982 (I:all R:5). Large colored photographs explore the life of the mosquito.

Parker, Stephen, and Bavosi, John. *Life Before Birth: The Story of the First Nine Months*. Cambridge, 1979 (I:9+ R:6). Illustrations are from a British Museum program.

Parnall, Peter. *The Daywatchers*. Macmillan, 1984 (I:9+ R:7). The author uses his own experiences to introduce different birds of prey.

Patent, Dorothy Hinshaw. *Farm Animals*. Photographs by William Munoz. Holiday, 1984 (I:8–12 R:6). Different categories of farm animals.

————. *A Picture Book of Cows*. Photographs by William Munoz. Holiday, 1982 (I:5–8 R:3). How cows develop and are raised.

————. *The Sheep Book*. Illustrated by William Munoz. Dodd, 1985 (I:9–12 R:6). Text describes raising of and behavior of sheep.

————. *Sizes and Shapes in Nature—What They Mean*. Holiday House, 1979 (I:10+ R:8). Explores the significance of the structure of living things in their ability to relate to daily life and evolution.

————. *Thoroughbred Horses*. Holiday House, 1985 (I:9–12 R:6). Covers all aspects of raising and training thoroughbreds.

————. *Whales: Giants of the Deep*. Holiday, 1984 (I:8–12 R:6). Discusses baleen whales, toothed whales, whale mysteries, and human influences on whales.

————. *Where the Bald Eagles Gather*. Photographs by William Munoz. Clarion, 1984 (I:9–12 R:5). Describes the habits of America's endangered species.

Perl, Lila. *Red Star and Green Dragon: Looking at New China*. Morrow, 1983 (I:10+ R:6). Political, social, and economic influences on China.

Petersen, Gwenn Boardman. *Careers in the United States Merchant Marine*. Lodestar, 1983 (I:9+ R:7). Career information and facts about life at sea.

Pettit, Florence H. *The Stamp-Pad Printing Book*. Photographs by Robert M. Pettit. Crowell, 1979 (I:10+ R:6). Directions for carving, printing, and then using a stamp pad to create several projects.

Pollard, Michael. *How Things Work*. Larousse, 1978 (I:10+ R:7). Facts, diagrams, and photographs detailing how large machines work.

Powzyk, Joyce. *Wallaby Creek*. Lothrop, Lee & Shepard, 1985 (I:9+ R:6). Illustrations show Australian animals.

Poynter, Margaret. *Gold Rush! The Yukon Stampede of 1898*. Atheneum, 1979 (I:9+ R:6). The lure of the Yukon gold rush and the people who searched for gold as reported by a descendant of Alaskan pioneers.

Pringle, Laurence. *Animals at Play*. Harcourt Brace Jovanovich, 1985 (I:9–12 R:7). An introduction to animal behavior.

————. *City and Suburb: Exploring an Ecosystem*. Macmillan, 1975 (I:9–12 R:7). Suggested explorations in a city and how a city affects its surroundings.

————. *Death Is Natural*. Four Winds, 1977 (I:9–12 R:6). Death in nature is an essential part of life.

————. *Dinosaurs and People: Fossils, Facts and Fantasies*. Harcourt Brace Jovanovich, 1978 (I:9+ R:6). Describes dinosaurs and traces research.

————. *Dinosaurs and Their World*. Harcourt Brace Jovanovich, 1968 (I:8–12 R:6). How scientists over the previous fifteen years discovered what life was like millions of years ago.

————. *Feral: Tame Animals Gone Wild*. Macmillan, 1983 (I:9+ R:7). Problems related to wild birds, pigs, dogs, cats, burros, and horses.

————. *The Gentle Desert: Exploring An Ecosystem*. Macmillan, 1977 (I:9–12 R:6). Land forms, climates, soils, and life found in the North American desert.

————. *Into the Woods: Exploring the Forest Ecosystem*. Macmillan, 1973 (I:8–12 R:4). Explores the forest's energy cycle and encourages readers to respect the valuable ecosystem.

————. *Natural Fire: Its Ecology in Forests*. Morrow, 1979 (I:9–12 R:7). Develops the position that fire in the forest is not now considered as detrimental as was formerly believed.

————. *Nuclear War: From Hiroshima to Nuclear Winter*. Enslow, 1985 (I:12+ R:7). The history and consequences of nuclear weapons.

————. *Twist, Wiggle, and Squirm: A Book about Earthworms*. Illustrated by Peter Parnall. Crowell, 1973 (I:6–9 R:2). How earthworms live, how they mate, and what they eat.

————. *Vampire Bats*. Morrow, 1982 (I:9–12 R:6). Bats that feed on blood rather than insects.

————. *Wild Foods: A Beginner's Guide to Identifying, Harvesting and Cooking Safe and Tasty Plants from the Outdoors*. Illustrated by Paul Breeden. Four Winds, 1978 (I:10+ R:7). Information on identifying safe wild foods and recipes that may be used in their preparation.

Rossel, Seymour. *The Holocaust*. Watts, 1981 (I:9+ R:6). Examines Germany in the 1930s, Hitler's dictatorship, the Nuremberg trials.

Rubins, Harriet. *Guinea Pigs: An Owner's Guide to Choosing, Raising, Breeding and Showing.* Illustrated by Pamela Carroll. Lothrop, Lee & Shepard, 1982 (I:9+ R:6). Guidelines for selecting and caring for guinea pigs.

Ryden, Hope. *America's Bald Eagle.* Putnam, 1985 (I:9+ R:6). Numerous photographs illustrate the life cycle of the eagle.

Sancha, Sheila. *The Castle Story.* Crowell, 1982 (I:10+ R:7). A reference that includes considerable information about types of castles.

———. *The Luttrell Village: Country Life in the Middle Ages.* Crowell, 1983 (I:10+ R:6). Illustrations and text provide information on fourteenth-century England.

Sattler, Helen Roney. *Dinosaurs of North America.* Illustrated by Anthony Rao. Lothrop, Lee & Shepard, 1981 (I:9+ R:6). In addition to discussions about various dinosaurs, the text includes theories about their extinction.

———. *Train Whistles.* Illustrated by Giulio Maestro. Lothrop, Lee & Shepard, 1985 (I:5–8 R:4). A picture book guide to the meaning of train whistles.

Scarry, Huck. *Life on a Fishing Boat: A Sketchbook.* Prentice-Hall, 1983 (I:8+ R:6). Equipment, daily life, and types of boats related to commercial fishing.

———. *Looking into the Middle Ages.* Harper & Row, 1985 (I:8–12). A pop-up book shows castles, cathedrals, and villages.

Schaaf, Peter. *An Apartment House Close Up.* Four Winds, 1980 (I:all). Black-and-white photographs showing the various parts of an apartment house.

Scott, Jack Denton. *The Book of the Goat.* Photographs by Ozzie Sweet. Putnam, 1979 (I:9 R:5). The goat is presented as an intelligent and useful animal.

———. *The Book of the Pig.* Photographs by Ozzie Sweet. Putnam, 1981 (I:8–10 R:4). The characteristics and history of the pig.

———. *Canada Geese.* Photographs by Ozzie Sweet. Putnam, 1976 (I:9+ R:6). The migration habits of Canada geese as they fly from Canada to their southern feeding area in the Mississippi Valley.

———. *Discovering the American Stork.* Photographs by Ozzie Sweet. Harcourt Brace Jovanovich, 1976 (I:9+ R:7). Photographs and text describe the habits, habitats, and unique qualities of the American stork.

———. *Discovering the Mysterious Egret.* Photographs by Ozzie Sweet. Harcourt Brace Jovanovich, 1978 (I:9+ R:7). The background history and details of mating, nesting, and feeding are developed through photographs and text.

———. *Little Dogs of the Prairie.* Photographs by Ozzie Sweet. Putnam, 1977 (I:9+ R:6). Pictures and text present the life of the prairie dog and the contributions it makes to the prairie.

———. *Moose.* Photographs by Ozzie Sweet. Putnam, 1981 (I:8–10 R:5). Discusses physical characteristics and behavior of moose.

———. *Orphans from the Sea.* Photographs by Ozzie Sweet. Putnam, 1982 (I:8+ R:6). The work of the Florida Suncoast Seabird Sanctuary.

———. *Return of the Buffalo.* Photographs by Ozzie Sweet. Putnam, 1976 (I:9+ R:6). Photographs and text report the return of the buffalo that became almost extinct in the 1800s.

Selsam, Millicent E. *Cotton.* Photographs by Jerome Wexler. Morrow, 1982 (I:7–10 R:5). History, stages in development, and uses of cotton.

———. *How to Be a Nature Detective.* Pictures by Ezra Jack Keats. Harper & Row, 1958, 1963 (I:5–8 R:4). Encourages children to identify animals by observing their tracks.

———. *Mushrooms.* Photographs by Jerome Wexler. Morrow, 1986 (I:7–10 R:6). The history and life cycle of the common edible mushroom.

———. *Plants We Eat.* Photographs by Jerome Wexler. Morrow, 1981 (I:10+ R:5). The history and development of plants as food.

———. *Popcorn.* Photographs by Jerome Wexler. Morrow, 1976 (I:7–10 R:4). The history of popcorn and the life cycle of the plant.

———. *Where Do They Go? Insects in Winter.* Illustrated by Arabelle Wheatley. Four Winds, 1982 (I:5–10 R:3). Discusses flies, grasshoppers, and bees.

———, and Hunt, Joyce. *A First Look at Bird Nests.* Illustrated by Harriet Springer. Walker, 1985 (I:5–8 R:3). Describes nests of common American birds.

———, and Wexler, Jerome. *The Amazing Dandelion.* Morrow, 1977 (I:7–10 R:4). The life cycle of the dandelion in text and photographs.

Shapiro, Mary. *How They Built the Statue of Liberty.* Illustrated by Huck Scarry. Random House, 1985 (I:all). Detailed drawings show development of the statue.

Silverstein, Alvin and Virginia B. *The Story of Your Hand.* Illustrated by Greg Wenzel. Putnam, 1985 (I:10+ R:6). Discusses structures, functions, and experiments.

Simon, Hilda. *Sight and Seeing: A World of Light and Color.* Philomel, 1983 (I:10+ R:9). How human and animal eyes function.

Simon, Seymour. *Animal Fact/Animal Fable.* Illustrated by Diane de Groat. Crown, 1979 (I:5– R:3). A humorous presentation of beliefs about animals that are not always true: bats are blind, an owl is wise, wolves live alone.

———. *Danger from Below: Earthquakes—Past, Present, and Future.* Four Winds, 1979 (I:10+ R:6). Information developed through text, photographs, diagrams, and maps tells where earthquakes occur, why they occur, and how they are measured.

———. *Jupiter.* Morrow, 1985 (I:5–8 R:5). Color photographs from NASA reveal latest knowledge.

———. *Little Giants.* Illustrated by Pamela Carroll. Morrow, 1983 (I:7–12 R:4). Animals that are giants are compared to others of their kind.

———. *The Long Journey from Space.* Crown, 1982 (I:9+ R:6). Old and new photographs trace history and changes in comets.

———. *The Long View into Space.* Crown, 1979 (I:all R:5). A photographic essay depicting the moon, the sun, planets, stars, nebulas, and galaxies.

———. *Meet the Giant Snakes.* Illustrated by Harriet Springer. Walker, 1979 (I:7–10 R:5). Characteristics of pythons and boa constrictors.

———. *Poisonous Snakes.* Illustrated by William R. Downey. Four Winds, 1981 (I:7–10 R:5). Discusses the important role of poisonous snakes, where they live, and their behavior.

———. *Saturn.* Morrow, 1985 (I:5–8 R:5). Color photographs from NASA add to the information.

———. *The Secret Clocks, Time Senses of Living Things.* Illustrated by Jan Brett. Viking, 1979 (I:9+ R:6). The biological time clocks of plants, animals, and humans. Step-by-step experiments involve students in research.

———. *The Smallest Dinosaurs.* Illustrated by Anthony Rao. Crown, 1982 (I:5–9 R:6). Seven small members of the Coelurosauria, or hollow, lizard family.

————. *Soap Bubble Magic*. Illustrated by Stella Ormai. Lothrop, Lee & Shepard, 1985 (I:6–9 R:3). Observation and experimentation with soap bubbles.

————. *Strange Creatures*. Illustrated by Pamela Carroll. Four Winds, 1981 (I:7–10 R:5). Presents twenty-two animals who act or look strange or have extraordinary abilities.

Smith, E. Boyd. *The Railroad Book*. Houghton, 1983 (I:all). A new edition of a book first published in 1913 presents a view of railroads in the early 1900s.

Smith, Howard E. *Balance It!* Photographs by George Ancona. Four Winds, 1982 (I:9–12 R:6). How to make a mobile, a letter scale, and other things that balance.

Tinkelman, Murray. *Rodeo: The Great American Sport*. Greenwillow, 1982 (I:8–12 R:5). Black-and-white photographs illustrate each event in a rodeo.

Walker, Barbara M. *The Little House Cookbook: Frontier Foods from Laura Ingalls Wilder's Classic Stories*. Illustrated by Garth Williams. Harper & Row, 1979 (I:8–12 R:7). Authentic pioneer recipes.

Walther, Tom. *A Spider Might*. Sierra Club/Scribner, 1978 (I:all R:5). The natural histories, habits, and characteristics of spiders.

Weber, William J. *Care of Uncommon Pets*. Holt, Rinehart & Winston, 1979 (I:all R:5). A veterinarian shares information about caring for rabbits, guinea pigs, hamsters, mice, rats, gerbils, frogs, turtles, snakes, and parakeets.

Weiss, Ann E. *Bioethics: Dilemmas in Modern Medicine*. Enslow, 1985 (I:10+ R:7). Case histories reflect issues such as the right to live or die.

Weiss, Malcolm E. *Sky Watchers of Ages Past*. Illustrated by Eliza McFadden. Houghton Mifflin, 1982 (I:10+ R:6). A history of the ancient scientists.

Weitzman, David. *Windmills, Bridges, and Old Machines: Discovering Our Industrial Past*. Scribner, 1982 (I:10+ R:7). Traces America's industrial past.

Wexler, Jerome. *From Spore to Spore: Ferns and How They Grow*. Dodd, Mead, 1985 (I:9+ R:5). Follows the two phases of the fern plant.

White, Jack R. *The Invisible World of the Infrared*. Dodd, Mead, 1984 (I:10+ R:6). Defines and discusses infrared as used in pictures, cameras, missiles, and lasers.

————. *Satellites of Today and Tomorrow*. Dodd, Mead, 1985 (I:10+ R:6). History, types, and uses of satellites.

Wolf, Bernard. *Firehouse*. Morrow, 1983 (I:8+ R:7). Photographs show the demanding and dangerous job of New York firefighters.

Woodford, Susan. *The Parthenon*. Cambridge/Lerner, 1983 (I:10+ R:7). Drawings, photographs, and text describe the design, building, and destruction of the Parthenon.

Zomberg, Paul G. *A Look Inside Computers*. Raintree, 1985 (I:10+ R:6). Diagrams and photographs help clarify definitions.

Zubrowski, Bernie. *Messing Around with Water Pumps and Siphons*. Illustrated by Steve Lindblom. Little, Brown, 1981 (I:5–8 R:3). A Children's museum activity book that encourages children to experiment.

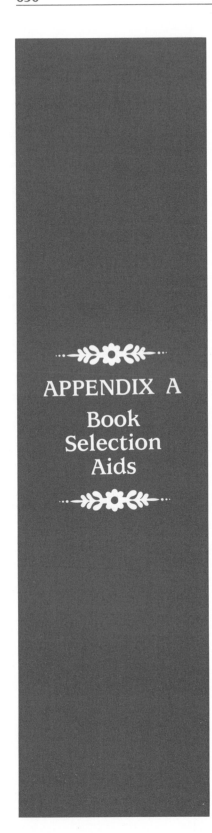

APPENDIX A

Book Selection Aids

Books

A to Zoo: A Subject Access to Children's Picture Books. 2nd ed. Bowker, 1985.

Adventuring with Books: A Booklist for Pre-K–Grade 6, ed. by Diane L. Monson and the Committee on the Elementary School Booklist of the National Council of Teachers of English. NCTE, 1985.

American Indian Stereotypes in the World of Children: A Reader and Bibliography, by Arlene B. Hirschfelder. Scarecrow Press, 1982.

Best Books for Children: Preschool Through the Middle Grades, 3rd ed., ed. by John T. Gillespie and Christine B. Gilbert. Bowker, 1985.

The Best in Children's Books: The University of Chicago Guide to Children's Literature 1966–1972, ed. by Zena Sutherland. The University of Chicago Press, 1973.

The Best in Children's Books: The University of Chicago Guide to Children's Literature 1973–1978, ed. by Zena Sutherland. The University of Chicago Press, 1980.

The Best of Children's Books: 1964–1978: with 1979 Addenda, ed. by Virginia Haviland. Library of Congress, 1980.

Bibliography on Disabled Children, Canadian Assoc. of Children's Librarians' Committee on Library Service to Disabled Children. Canadian Library Assoc., 1982.

The Black Experience in Children's Books, Barbara Rollock. New York Public Library, 1984.

The Bookfinder: A Guide to Children's Literature About the Needs and Problems of Youth Aged 2–15, Sharon Spredemann Dreyer. American Guidance Service, 1981.

Books and the Teenage Reader: A Guide for Teachers, Librarians and Parents, 2nd, rev. ed., G. Robert Carlsen. Harper & Row, 1980.

Books for the Gifted Child, ed. by Barbara Holland Baskin and Karen H. Harris. Bowker, 1980, 1981.

Books for the Teen Age, 1985 Annual. New York Public Library, 1985.

Books for Today's Young Readers: An Annotated Bibliography of Recommended Fiction for Ages 10–14, comp. by Jeanne Bracken et al. Feminist Press, 1981.

Books in American History: A Basic List for High Schools and Junior Colleges, 2nd ed., ed. by John E. Wiltz and Nancy C. Cridland. Indiana University Press, 1981.

Caldecott Medal Books: 1938–1957, ed. by Bertha Mahony Miller and Elinor Whitney Field. The Horn Book Inc., 1957.

Canadian Books for Young People, 3rd ed., comp. by Irma McDonough. University of Toronto Press, 1980.

Children's Authors and Illustrators: An Index to Biographical Dictionaries, 3rd, rev. ed., ed. by Adele Sarkissian. Gale, 1981.

Children's Books: Awards and Prizes, comp. by the Children's Book Council (revised periodically).

Children's Books in Print. Bowker (annual).

Children's Books in the Rare Book Division of the Library of Congress: Author-Title and Chronological Catalogs. Rowman and Littlefield, 1975.

Children's Books of International Interest, 3rd ed., ed. by Barbara Elleman. American Library Assoc., 1985.

Children's Books of the Year 1981, Barbara S. Smith. Watts, 1982.

Children's Books of the Year 1982. The Child Study Children's Book Committee. Bank Street College, 1982.

Children's Books Too Good to Miss: Revised Edition 1979, May Hill Arbuthnot, et al. University Press Books, 1980.

Children's Catalog, 14th ed., ed. by Richard H. Isaacson and Gary L. Bogart. Wilson, 1981.

A Comprehensive Guide to Children's Literature with a Jewish Theme, Enid Davis. Schocken, 1981.

Easy Reading: Book Series and Periodicals for Less Able Readers, Michael F. Graves, Judith A. Boettcher, and Randall A. Ryder.

International Reading Assoc. 1979.

The Elementary School Library Collection, 14th ed., ed. by Louis Winkel. Brodart, 1984.

Folklore: An Annotated Bibliography and Index to Single Editions, comp. by Elsie B. Ziegler. Faxon, 1973.

Fun for Kids: An Index to Children's Craft Books, Marion F. Gallivan. Scarecrow Press, 1981.

The Great Lakes Region in Children's Books: A Selected Annotated Bibliography, ed. by Donna Taylor. Green Oak Press, 1980.

Guide to Reference Books, 9th ed., ed. by Eugene P. Sheehy. American Library Assoc., 1976.

Guide to Reference Books for School Media Centers, 2nd ed., ed. by Christine Gehr Wynar. Littleton, CO.: Libraries Unlimited, 1981.

Guide to Reference Books: Supplement, 9th ed., ed. by Eugene P. Sheehy. American Library Assoc. 1980.

A Hispanic Heritage: A Guide to Juvenile Books About Hispanic People and Cultures, Isabel Schon. Scarecrow Press, 1980.

Hispanic Heritage: Series II, Isabel Schon. Scarecrow Press, 1985.

Index to Fairy Tales, 1949–1972, Including Folklore, Legends and Myths in Collections, comp. by Norma Olen Irland. Faxon, 1973.

Index to Poetry for Children and Young People: 1970–1975, ed. by John E. Brewton, G. Meredith Blackburn, and Lorraine A. Blackburn. Wilson, 1978.

Index to Poetry for Children and Young People: 1976–1981, comp. by John E. Brewton et al. Wilson, 1983.

Indian Children's Books, Hap Gilliland. Billings, Mont.: Montana Council for Indian Education, 1980.

Junior High School Library Catalog, 4th ed., Wilson, 1980 (annual supplements).

Learning About Aging. The National Retired Teachers Assoc. and the American Assoc. of Retired Persons. American Library Assoc., 1981.

Let's Read Together: Books for Family Enjoyment, 4th ed., comp. by Assoc. for Library Service to Children, Let's Read Together Revision Committee. American Library Assoc., 1981.

Literature by and about the American Indian: An Annotated Bibliography, 2nd ed. Anna Lee Stensland. National Council of Teachers of English, 1979.

More Juniorplots: A Guide for Teachers and Librarians, ed. by John T. Gillespie. Bowker, 1977.

A Multimedia Approach to Children's Literature: A Selective List of Films, Filmstrips, and Recordings Based on Children's Books., 3rd ed., ed. by Mary Alice Hunt. American Library Assoc., 1983.

Multimedia Library: Materials Selection and Use, James Cabeceiras. Academic Press, 1982.

Newbery Medal Books: 1922–1955, ed. by Bertha Mahony Miller and Elinor Whitney Field. The Horn Book Inc., 1955.

Newbery and Caldecott Medal Books: 1956–1965, ed. by Lee Kingman. The Horn Book Inc., 1965.

Newbery and Caldecott Medal Books: 1966–1975, ed. by Lee Kingman. The Horn Book Inc., 1975.

Notable Children's Books, 1940–1970, comp. by Children's Service Division. American Library Assoc., 1977.

Notable Children's Books, 1971–1975, comp. by 1971–75 Notable Children's Books Re-evaluation Committee, Assoc. for Library Service to Children. American Library Assoc., 1981.

Notes from a Different Drummer: A Guide to Juvenile Fiction Portraying the Handicapped, comp. by Barbara Baskin and Karen Harris. Bowker, 1977.

A Parents' Guide to Children's Reading, 5th ed., by Nancy Larrick. Westminster Press, 1982.

Periodicals for School Media Programs: A Guide to Magazines, Newspapers, Periodical Indexes, rev. ed., comp. by Selma Richardson. American Library Assoc., 1978.

Reading for Young People: The Great Plains, ed. by Mildred Laughlin. American Library Assoc., 1979.

Reading for Young People: Kentucky, Tennessee, West Virginia, ed. by Barbara Mertins. American Library Assoc., 1985.

Reading for Young People: The Middle Atlantic, ed. by Arabelle Pennypacker. American Library Assoc., 1980.

Reading for Young People: The Midwest, ed. by Dorothy Hinman and Ruth Zimmerman. American Library Assoc., 1979.

Reading for Young People: The Mississippi Delta, ed. by Cora Matheny Dorsett. American Library Assoc., 1984.

Reading for Young People: The Northwest, ed. by Mary Meacham. American Library Association, 1981.

Reading for Young People: The Rocky Mountains, ed. by Mildred Laughlin. American Library Assoc., 1980.

Reading for Young People: The Southeast, ed. by Dorothy Heald. American Library Assoc., 1980.

Reading for Young People: The Southwest, ed. by Elva Harmon and Anna L. Milligan. American Library Assoc., 1982.

Reading for Young People: The Upper Midwest, ed. by Marion F. Archer. American Library Assoc., 1981.

Reference Books for Children, comp. by Carolyn S. Peterson and Ann D. Fenton. Scarecrow Press, 1981.

A Reference Guide to Modern Fantasy for Children, by Pat Pflieger. Greenwood Press, 1984.

Science Books for Children: Selections from Booklist, 1976–1983, selected by Denise M. Wilms. American Library Assoc., 1985.

Special Collections in Children's Literature, ed. by Carolyn W. Field. American Library Assoc., 1982.

Subject Guide to Children's Books in Print. Bowker (annual).

Periodicals Containing Information on Children's Books

Appraisal: Science Books for Young People. Boston University School of Education.

Book Review Digest. Wilson.

Bookbird. International Board on Books for Young People, International Institute for Children's Literature.

The Booklist. American Library Association.

The Bulletin of the Center for Children's Books. Graduate Library School, University of Chicago Press.

Canadian Children's Literature: A Journal of Criticism and Review. Canadian Children's Literature Assoc., Canadian Children's Press.

Childhood Education. Assoc. for Childhood Education International.

Children's Literature Association Quarterly. Children's Literature Association, Purdue University Press.

Children's Literature in Education. Agathon Press, Inc.

The Horn Book Magazine. Horn Book.

Interracial Books for Children. Council on Interracial Books for Children.

Language Arts. National Council of Teachers of English.

The Lion and the Unicorn. Department of English, Brooklyn College.

Media and Methods. North American Publishing.

The New York Times Book Review. New York Times.

Parents' Choice: A Review of Children's Media—Books, Television, Movies, Music, Story Records, Toys and Games. Parents' Choice Foundation.

Phaedrus: An International Journal of Children's Literature Research. Fairleigh Dickinson University.

Previews: Non-Print Software & Hardware News & Reviews. Bowker.

Publishers Weekly. Bowker.

School Library Journal. Bowker.

School Media Quarterly. American Assoc. of School Librarians, American Library Assoc.

Science Books and Films. American Assoc. for the Advancement of Science.

Science and Children. National Science Teachers Assoc.

Teacher. Macmillan Professional Magazines.

Top of the News. Assoc. for Library Service to Children and the Young Adult Services Division, American Library Assoc.

The Web. Center for Language, Literature, and Reading, The Ohio State University.

Wilson Library Bulletin. Wilson.

···❀❀❀❀···

APPENDIX B
Professional Reading

···❀❀❀❀···

Additional References*

Aaron, Shirley L. *A Study of Combined School-Public Libraries.* Chicago: American Library Assoc., 1980. The author discusses the feasibility of combining public and school libraries.

Boner, Charles, trans. *Kate Greenaway's Original Drawings for The Snow Queen.* New York: Schocken, 1981.

Bratton, J. S. *The Impact of Victorian Children's Fiction.* Barnes & Noble Imports, 1981. The author explores Victorian literature written for moral instruction.

Butler, Dorothy. *Babies Need Books: How Books Can Help Your Child Become a Happy and Involved Human Being.* New York: Atheneum, 1985. Characteristics of children age one through five are discussed and stories that will stimulate their development are presented.

———. *Cushla and Her Books.* Boston: Horn Book, 1980. The life of a handicapped child is changed through literature.

———, and Clay, Marie. *Reading Begins at Home: Preparing Children for Reading Before They Go to School.* Exeter, N.H.: Heinemann Educational, 1982. Includes suggestions for parents and a list of recommended books.

Butler, Francelia, and Rees, Compton, eds. *Children's Literature.* Vol. 12. New Haven, Conn.: Yale University Press. 1984. Essays on children's literature.

Carpenter, Humphrey and Prichard, Mari. *The Oxford Companion to Children's Literature.* New York: Oxford University Press, 1984. Descriptions of authors, books, characters, and literary terms.

Carr, Jo, comp. *Beyond Fact: Nonfiction for Children and Young People.* Chicago: American Library Assoc., 1982. A collection of previously published essays on nonfiction, science, history, and biography.

Chambers, Nancy, ed. *The Signal Approach to Children's Books.* Metuchen, N.J.: Scarecrow Press, 1981. A collection of articles from the British literature journal are included.

Colwell, Eileen. *The Magic Umbrella and other Stories for Telling.* Lawrence, Mass.: Chatto, Bodley Head & Jonathan Cape, 1981. Includes information on how to tell stories to children.

Committee on Literature in the Elementary Language Arts, & Lamme, Linda Leonard. *Learning to Love Literature: Preschool through Grade Three.* Urbana, Ill.: National Council of Teachers of English, 1981. Guidelines for developing a literature-based curriculum.

Cope, Dawn, and Cope, Peter. *Humpty Dumpty's Favorite Nursery Rhymes.* New York: Holt, Rinehart & Winston, 1981. Reproductions of nursery rhyme postcards that were popular in the early 20th century.

Coplan, Kate. *Poster Ideas and Bulletin Board Techniques: For Libraries and Schools,* 2nd ed. Dobbs Ferry, N.Y.: Oceana, 1981. Illustrations and directions for developing bulletin boards are developed in school and library settings.

Crane, Walter, *An Alphabet of Old Friends and the Absurd ABC.* New York: Thames & Hudson, 1981. Reproductions of two of Walter Crane's toy books.

Davies, Ruth Ann. *The School Library Media Program: Instructional Force for Excellence,* 3rd ed. New York: Bowker, 1979. Discusses the future of the school media program.

Egoff, Shelia. *Thursday's Child: Trends and Patterns in Contemporary Children's Literature.* Chicago: American Library Assoc., 1981. Includes a series of essays about fantasy, picture books, realistic fiction, and poetry.

*These references provide additional adult sources. They are not referenced at the end of the preceding chapters.

Emmens, Carol A., ed. *Children's Media Market Place,* 2nd ed. New York: Neal–Schuman, 1982. This reference includes information about publishers, periodicals, and bookstores.

Engen, Rodney. *Kate Greenaway: A Biography.* New York: Schocken, 1981. A biography of the English artist.

Franklin, Linda Campbell. *Library Display Ideas.* Jefferson, N.C.: McFarland, 1980. Bulletin board and book display ideas are developed around monthly and other themes.

Goldstein, Ruth M., and Zornow, Edith. *Movies for Kids: A Guide for Parents and Teachers on the Entertainment Film for Children,* rev. ed. New York: Ungar, 1980. Recommends 430 films suitable for children.

Hart, Thomas L. *Instruction in School Library Media Center Use [K–12],* 2nd ed. Chicago: American Library Association, 1985.

Hearne, Betsy, and Kaye, Marilyn, eds. *Celebrating Children's Books: Essays on Children's Literature.* New York: Lothrop, Lee & Shepard, 1981. Text contains twenty-three essays.

Hicks, Warren B. *Managing the Building-Level School Library Media Program; School Media Centers: Focus on Trends and Issues, No. 7.* Chicago: American Library Assoc., 1981. Discusses trends and the management system in the media center.

Jacobs, Joseph, comp. *English Fairy Tales: Being the Two Collections, English Fairy Tales and More English Fairy Tales.* Lawrence, Mass.: Chatto, Bodley Head & Jonathan Cape, 1980. Versions of Jacobs's tales published in the 1890s.

Jenkins, Peggy Davison. *The Magic of Puppetry: A Guide for Those Working with Young Children.* Englewood Cliffs, N.J.: Prentice-Hall, 1980. Illustrations and text present the instructions for making more than forty puppets.

Jenkinson, Edward B. *Censors in the Classroom: The Mind Benders.* Carbondale, Ill.: Southern Illinois University Press, 1979. Reviews censorship cases and discusses factors contributing to censorship.

Keightley, Moy. *Investigating Art: A Practical Guide for Young People.* New York: Facts on File Publications, 1984. A practical guide to art techniques.

Kellman, Amy. *Guide to Children's Libraries & Literature Outside the United States.* Chicago: American Library Assoc., 1982. A helpful location reference for libraries.

Kelly, R. Gordon, ed. *Children's Periodicals of the United States.* Westport, Conn.: Greenwood Press, 1984. A historical guide to periodicals and newspapers.

Kingman, Lee, ed. *The Illustrator's Notebook.* Boston: The Horn Book Inc., 1985. Children's book artists discuss their philosophies of illustration.

Kingman, Lee; Foster, Joanna; and Lontoft, Ruth Giles; comp. *Illustrators of Children's Books: 1957–1966.* Boston: The Horn Book Inc., 1968. Articles by children's book illustrators of the period.

Kingman, Lee; Hogarth, Grace Allen; and Quimby, Harriet; comp. *Illustrators of Children's Books: 1967–1976.* Boston: The Horn Book Inc., 1978.

Klemin, Diana. *The Art of Art for Children's Books: A Contemporary Survey.* Greenwich, CT: The Murton Press, 1966. A contemporary survey of the work of 64 children's book artists.

———. *The Illustrated Book: Its Art and Craft.* Greenwich, CT: The Murton Press, 1970. A contemporary survey of the work of 74 children's book artists.

Knox, Rawle, ed. *The Work of E. H. Shepard.* New York: Schocken, 1980. Samples of Shepard's work and an outline of his life are published to celebrate the hundredth anniversary of his birth.

Kohn, Rita T., and Tepper, Krysta A. *Have You Got What They Want? Public Relations Strategies for the School Librarian–Media Specialist.* Metuchen, N.J.: Scarecrow Press, 1982. Discusses various public relations strategies that may be useful to the librarian.

Lacy, Lyn Ellen. *Art and Design in Children's Picture Books.* Chicago: American Library Association, 1986. An analysis of Caldecott-award-winning illustrations.

Lanes, Selma G. *The Art of Maurice Sendak.* New York: Harry N. Abrams, 1980. In an illustrated text, the author discusses Sendak's books, recurring themes, and early influences on his work.

Leach, Maria, ed. *Funk and Wagnall's Standard Dictionary of Folklore, Mythology, and Legend.* New York: Harper & Row, 1972.

Leland, Nita. *Exploring Color: How to Use and Control Color in Your Paintings.* Cincinnati: North Light (Writer's Digest Books), 1985.

Leonard, Charlotte. *Tied Together: Topics and Thoughts for Introducing Children's Books.* Metuchen, N.J.: Scarecrow Press, 1980. Presents ideas for book discussions, displays, and program planning.

Linder, Enid and Leslie. *The Art of Beatrix Potter.* New York: Frederick Warren and Co., 1980. Examples of the art of Beatrix Potter.

Lystad, Mary. *From Dr. Mather to Dr. Seuss: 200 Years of American Books for Children.* Cambridge. Mass.: Schenkman, 1980. The author examines the changing values expressed in children's literature.

Mahony, Bertha E.; Latimer, Louise; and Folmsbee, Beulah; comp. *Illustrations of Children's Books: 1744–1945.* Boston: The Horn Book Inc., 1947. A history of illustration.

Manguel, Alberto and Guadalupi, Gianni. *The Dictionary of Imaginary Places.* New York: Macmillan Publishing Co., 1980.

Meggendorfer, Lothar. *The Doll's House: A Reproduction of the Antique Pop-Up Book.* New York: Viking, 1979. A reproduction of a nineteenth-century mechanical picture book.

Moore, Vardine. *The Pleasure of Poetry with and by Children: A Handbook*. Metuchen, N.J.: Scarecrow Press, 1981. Includes poems and suggestions for sharing them with children.

Nickel, Mildred. *Steps to Service: A Handbook of Procedures for the School Library Media Center*. Chicago. American Library Association, 1984.

Nilsen, Alleen Pace and Donelson, Kenneth L. *Literature for Today's Young Adults,* 2nd ed. Glenview, Ill.: Scott, Foresman, 1985. Authors discuss literature written for students between twelve and twenty.

Opie, Iona Archibald, and Opie, Peter. *A Nursery Companion*. New York: Oxford University Press, 1980. A reproduction of a collection of nineteenth-century alphabets, verses, and grammars.

Paterson, Katherine. *Gates of Excellence: On Reading and Writing Books for Children,* New York: Lodestar Books, 1981. Includes speeches and book reviews by the Newbery author.

Paulin, Mary Ann. *Creative Uses of Children's Literature*. Hamden, CT; Shoestring Press 1982. Ideas for using books in the library.

Peterson, Carolyn Sue, and Hall, Brenny. *Story Programs: A Source Book of Materials*. Metuchen, N.J.: Scarecrow Press, 1980. Develops suggestions for library programs for preschool and primary children.

Polette, Nancy, and Hamlin, Marjorie. *Exploring Books with Gifted Children*. Littleton, Colo.: Libraries Unlimited, 1980. Units are developed around style, theme, character, and setting in books by L'Engle, Konigsburg, Paterson, Alexander, Lenski, and the Cleavers.

Preiss, Byron, ed. *The Art of Leo & Diane Dillon*. New York: Ballantine Books, 1981. Text and illustrations provide a review of the Dillons' works from the 1950s to the present.

Prostano, Emanuel T., and Prostano, Joyce S. *The School Library Media Center,* 3rd ed. Littleton, Colo.: Libraries Unlimited, 1982.

Rees, David. *The Marble in the Water: Essays on Contemporary Writers of Fiction for Children and Young Adults*. Boston: Horn Book, 1980. Explores similarities and differences in British and American children's literature and includes essays for well-known authors.

Schwarcz, Joseph H. *Ways of the Illustrator: Visual Communication in Children's Literature*. Chicago: American Library Assoc., 1982. Discusses illustrations in children's books.

Scott, Dorothea Hayward. *Chinese Popular Literature and the Child*. Chicago: American Library Assoc., 1980. Author discusses oral and literary heritage of the Chinese people.

Shulevitz, Uri. *Writing with Pictures: How to Write and Illustrate Children's Books*. New York: Watson-Guptill Publishers, 1985. A well-known illustrator provides a guide for aspiring children's book artists.

Silverman, Eleanor. *101 Media Center Ideas*. Metuchen, N.J.: Scarecrow Press, 1980. The ideas in the text are from the Demonstration Media Center for New Jersey.

———. *Trash into Treasure: Recycling Ideas for Library Media Centers*. Metuchen, N.J.: Scarecrow Press, 1981. Inexpensive ideas for the library.

Spiegel, Dixie Lee. *Reading for Pleasure: Guidelines*. Newark, Del.: International Reading Assoc., 1981. Discusses the development of a recreational reading program.

Taylor, Mary M., ed. *School Library and Media Center Acquisitions Policies and Procedures*. Phoenix, Ariz.: Oryx Press, 1981. Examines the selection process in media centers and presents the rationale for comprehensive selection policies.

Thomason, Nevada Wallis, ed. *The Library Media Specialist in Curriculum Development*. Metuchen, N.J.: Scarecrow Press, 1981. A collection of articles about the role of the media specialist.

Trelease, James. *The Read-Aloud Handbook*. New York: Penguin, 1982. Presents practical suggestions for sharing books orally with children.

Vandergrift, Kay E. *Child and Story: The Literary Connection*. Edited by Jane Anne Hannigan. New York: Neal-Schuman, 1981. Explores literary form, elements of the story, and practical suggestions for using literature.

Van Orden, Phyllis. *The Collection Program in Elementary and Middle Schools: Concepts, Practices, and Information Sources*. Illustrated by William R. Harper. Littleton, Colo.: Libraries Unlimited, 1982. A guide for elementary and middle school libraries.

White, Gabriel. *Edward Ardizzone: Artist and Illustrator*. New York: Schocken, 1980. Text includes samples of Ardizzone's work, discussion of his style, and information about his personal life.

Yolen, Jane. *Touch Magic: Fantasy, Faerie and Folklore in the Literature of Childhood*. New York: Putnam/Philomel, 1981. Yolen stresses the importance of folklore in stimulating children's emotional and intellectual growth.

The Association for Library Service to Children (ALSC) Film, Filmstrip, and Recording committees have identified the following films and filmstrips as demonstrating especially commendable quality, reflecting respect for children's intelligence and imagination, and encouraging children's interests. Lists of notable films and filmstrips are published in *The Booklist* (Chicago: American Library Association) and are recommended for children through age 14. Dates indicate the year in which the films and filmstrips were recognized as notable.

1984

Films

Ballet Robotique. Producer and director: Bob Rogers. Pyramid.

Clown of God. Producer: Ball and Chain Studios for Weston Woods. Director: Gary McGivney. Weston Woods.

Crac. Producer and director: Frédéric Back for Société Radio-Canada. Pyramid.

Dudh Kosi: Relentless River of Everest. Producer: Guild Sound and Vision. Indiana University Audio Visual Center.

Itzhak Perlman: In My Case Music. Producer and director: Tony DeNonno. DeNonno Pix.

Katura and the Cat. Producers and directors: Lillian Moats and J. P. Somersaulter. Perspective films.

Morris's Disappearing Bag. Producer: Morton Schindel. Director: Michael Sporn. Weston Woods.

The Snowman. Producer: John Coates. Director: Diane Jackson. Weston Woods.

The Sound Collector. Producers: Lynn Smith, Ishu Patel, and David Verall. Director: Lynn Smith. National Film Board of Canada.

Split Cherry Tree. Producer: Jan Saunders. Director: Andrei Konchalovsky. Learning Corp. of America.

What Energy Means. National Geographic.

Zea. Producer: Robert Forget. Directors: André Leduc and Jean-Jacques Leduc. National Film Board of Canada.

Filmstrips

A Dark, Dark Tale. Weston Woods.

The Loch Ness Monster and the Abominable Snowman; Atlantic and UFOs. (Mysteries Old and New) National Geographic. Two filmstrips.

Story of a Book, Second Edition: With Marguerite Henry. (First choice: Authors and Books, #19) Pied Piper Productions.

A Visit to William Blake's Inn: Poems for Innocent and Experienced Travelers. (Newbery/Caldecott series) Random House/Miller Brody.

1985

Films

Bamboo Brush. (Live and Learn Series) Beacon Films.

Bearskin. Davenport Films.

Burt Dow, Deep Water Man. Weston Woods.

Castle. PBS Video.

Curious George Goes to the Hospital. Churchill Films.

Miracle of Life. Time-Life Video.

Pigbird. National Film Board of Canada.

The Plant. Producer: National Film Board of Canada. Lucerne Films.

Please Take Care of Your Teeth. Pyramid.

Revenge of the Nerd (edited version). Learning Corp. of America.

Sound of Sunshine, Sound of Rain. FilmFair.

A Swamp Ecosystem. National Geographic.

Filmstrips

A Chair for My Mother. Random House/Miller Brody.

Doctor De Soto. Weston Woods.

The Legend of the Bluebonnet: An Old Tale of Texas. Listening Library.

Shadow. Weston Woods.

Sweet Whispers, Brother Rush. (Newbery Award Series) Random House/Miller Brody.

When I Was Young in the Mountains. (Caldecott Series) Random House/Miller Brody.

1986

Films

Booker. Walt Disney Educational Media.

The Cap. Producer: Atlantis/National Film Board of Canada. Beacon Films.

Corduroy. Producers: Joe Mantegna and Gary Templeton for Evergreen/Firehouse Productions in association with Weston Woods. Director: Gary Templeton. Weston Woods.

Cornet at Night. (Live and Learn) Producers: Michael MacMillan, Seaton McLean, and Janice Platt for Atlantis Films. Beacon Films.

Curious George. Director: John Matthews. Churchill Films.

He Makes Me Feel Like Dancin'. Producers: Judy Kinberg and Emile Andolino for Edgar J. Scherick Assoc. Director: Emile Andolino. Direct Cinema.

The Lilith Summer. A film by Bernard Wilets. Director: Dianne Haak. AIMS Media.

Memorial Day. A film by Michael Ackerman Ulick. Producer: Frank Stiefel. Direct Cinema.

Up. Producer and director: Mike Hoover. Pyramid Film & Video.

Filmstrips

Dear Mr. Henshaw. Random House. Two filmstrips.

Grant Wood: His Life and Paintings. International Film Bureau. Four filmstrips.

The Nightgown of the Sullen Moon. Random House.

Simon's Book. Random House.

Sugaring Time. Random House.

Ten, Nine, Eight. Random House.

We Can't Sleep. Random House.

Awards for outstanding children's books are presented yearly by organizations, publishers, and other interested groups. These awards have multiplied since the instigation of the Newbery Award in 1922. The following lists include the books, authors, and illustrators who have received the Caldecott Medal and honor awards, the Newbery Medal and honor awards, the Children's Book Award, the Hans Christian Andersen International Medal, or the Laura Ingalls Wilder Medal. Following this list are examples of additional awards presented in the United States, Canada, and the United Kingdom. Complete lists of book award winners, including United States, British Commonwealth, and international awards, are found in *Children's Books: Awards and Prizes,* compiled and edited by the Children's Book Council. An annotated bibliography of Newbery and Caldecott books is available in *Newbery and Caldecott Medal and Honor Books,* compiled by Linda Kauffman Peterson and Marilyn Leathers Solt, 1982.

Caldecott Medal and Honor Awards

The Caldecott awards, named after a British illustrator of children's books, Randolph Caldecott, are granted by the Children's Services Division of the American Library Association. The medal and honor awards are presented annually to the illustrators of the most distinguished picture books published in the United States. The first Caldecott Medal and honor awards were presented in 1938.

1938 *Animals of the Bible* by Helen Dean Fish, ill. by Dorothy P. Lathrop, Stokes

Honor Books: *Seven Simeon: A Russian Tale* by Boris Artzybasheff, Viking; *Four and Twenty Blackbirds: Nursery Rhymes of Yesterday Recalled for Children of To-Day* by Helen Dean Fish, ill. by Robert Lawson, Stokes

1939 *Mei Li* by Thomas Handforth, Doubleday

Honor Books: *The Forest Pool* by Laura Adams Armer, Longmans; *Wee Gillis* by Munro Leaf, ill. by Robert Lawson, Viking; *Snow White and the Seven Dwarfs* by Wanda Gág, Coward; *Barkis* by Clare Newberry, Harper; *Andy and the Lion: A Tale of Kindness Remembered or the Power of Gratitude* by James Daugherty, Viking

1940 *Abraham Lincoln* by Ingri and Edgar Parin d'Aulaire, Doubleday

Honor Books: *Cock-a-Doodle Doo: The Story of a Little Red Rooster* by Berta and Elmer Hader, Macmillan; *Madeline* by Ludwig Bemelmans, Simon & Schuster; *The Ageless Story,* by Lauren Ford, Dodd

1941 *They Were Strong and Good* by Robert Lawson, Viking

Honor Book: *April's Kittens* by Clare Newberry, Harper

1942 *Make Way for Ducklings* by Robert McCloskey, Viking

Honor Books: *An American ABC* by Maud and Miska Petersham, Macmillan; *In my Mother's House* by Ann Nolan Clark, ill. by Velino Herrera, Viking; *Paddle-to-the-Sea* by Holling C. Holling, Houghton; *Nothing at All* by Wanda Gág, Coward

1943 *The Little House* by Virginia Lee Burton, Houghton

Honor Books: *Dash and Dart* by Mary and Conrad Buff, Viking; *Marshmallow* by Clare Newberry, Harper

1944 *Many Moons* by James Thurber, ill. by Louis Slobodkin, Harcourt Brace Jovanovich

Honor Books: *Small Rain: Verses from the Bible* selected by Jessie Orton Jones, ill. by Elizabeth Orton Jones, Viking; *Pierre Pigeon* by Lee Kingman, ill. by Arnold E. Bare, Houghton; *The Mighty Hunter* by Berta and Elmer Hader, Macmillan; *A Child's Good Night Book* by Margaret Wise Brown, ill. by Jean Charlot, W. R. Scott; *Good Luck Horse* by Chih-Yi Chan, ill. by Plato Chan, Whittlesey

1945 *Prayer for a Child* by Rachel Field, ill. by Elizabeth Orton Jones, Macmillan

Honor Books: *Mother Goose: Seventy-Seven Verses with Pictures* ill. by Tasha Tudor, Walck; *In the Forest* by Marie Hall Ets, Viking; *Yonie Wondernose* by Marguerite de Angeli, Doubleday; *The Christmas Anna Angel* by Ruth Sawyer, ill. by Kate Seredy, Viking

1946 *The Rooster Crows . . .* ill. by Maud and Miska Petersham, Macmillan

Honor Books: *Little Lost Lamb* by Golden MacDonald, ill. by Leonard Weisgard, Doubleday; *Sing Mother Goose* by Opal Wheeler, ill. by Marjorie Torrey, Dutton; *My Mother Is the Most Beautiful Woman in the World* by Becky Reyher, ill. by Ruth Gannett, Lothrop; *You Can Write Chinese* by Kurt Wiese, Viking

1947 *The Little Island* by Golden MacDonald, ill. by Leonard Weisgard, Doubleday

Honor Books: *Rain Drop Splash* by Alvin Tresselt, ill. by Leonard Weisgard, Lothrop; *Boats on the River* by Marjorie Flack, ill. by Jay Hyde Barnum, Viking; *Timothy Turtle* by Al Graham, ill. by Tony Palazzo, Viking; *Pedro, the Angel of Olvera Street* by Leo Politi, Scribner's; *Sing in Praise: A Collection of the Best Loved Hymns* by Opal Wheeler, ill. by Marjorie Torrey, Dutton

1948 *White Snow, Bright Snow* by Alvin Tresselt, ill. by Roger Duvoisin, Lothrop

Honor Books: *Stone Soup: An Old Tale* by Marcia Brown, Scribner's; *McElligot's Pool* by Dr. Seuss, Random; *Bambino the Clown* by George Schreiber, Viking; *Roger and the Fox* by Lavinia Davis, ill. by Hildegard Woodward, Doubleday; *Song of Robin Hood* ed. by Anne Malcolmson, ill. by Virginia Lee Burton, Houghton

1949 *The Big Snow* by Berta and Elmer Hader, Macmillan

Honor Books: *Blueberries for Sal* by Robert McCloskey, Viking; *All Around the Town* by Phyllis McGinley, ill. by Helen Stone, Lippincott; *Juanita* by Leo Politi, Scribner's; *Fish in the Air* by Kurt Wiese, Viking

1950 *Song of the Swallows* by Leo Politi, Scribner's

Honor Books: *America's Ethan Allen* by Stewart Holbrook, ill. by Lynd Ward, Houghton; *The Wild Birthday Cake* by Lavinia Davis, ill. by Hildegard Woodward, Doubleday; *The Happy Day* by Ruth Krauss, ill. by Marc Simont, Harper; *Bartholomew and the Oobleck* by Dr. Seuss, Random; *Henry Fisherman* by Marcia Brown, Scribner's

1951 *The Egg Tree* by Katherine Milhous, Scribner's

Honor Books: *Dick Whittington and His Cat* by Marcia Brown, Scribner's; *The Two Reds* by William Lipkind, ill. by Nicholas Mordvinoff, Harcourt Brace Jovanovich; *If I Ran the Zoo* by Dr. Seuss, Random; *The Most Wonderful Doll in the World* by Phyllis McGinley, ill. by Helen Stone, Lippincott; *T-Bone, the Baby Sitter* by Clare Newberry, Harper

1952 *Finders Keepers* by William Lipkind, ill. by Nicholas Mordvinoff, Harcourt Brace Jovanovich

Honor Books: *Mr. T. W. Anthony Wood: The Story of a Cat and a Dog and Mouse* by Marie Hall Ets, Viking; *Skipper John's Cook* by Marcia Brown, Scribner's; *All Falling Down* by Gene Zion, ill. by Margaret Bloy Graham, Harper; *Bear Party* by William Pène du Bois, Viking; *Feather Mountain* by Elizabeth Olds, Houghton

1953 *The Biggest Bear* by Lynd Ward, Houghton

Honor Books: *Puss in Boots* by Charles Perrault, ill. and tr. by Marcia Brown, Scribner's; *One Morning in Maine* by Robert McCloskey, Viking; *Ape in a Cape: An Alphabet of Odd Animals* by Fritz Eichenberg, Harcourt Brace Jovanovich; *The Storm Book* by Charlotte Zolotow, ill. by Margaret Bloy Graham, Harper; *Five Little Monkeys* by Juliet Kepes, Houghton

1954 *Madeline's Rescue* by Ludwig Bemelmans, Viking

Honor Books: *Journey Cake, Ho!* by Ruth Sawyer, ill. by Robert McCloskey, Viking; *When Will the World Be Mine?* by Miriam Schlein, ill. by Jean Charlot, W. R. Scott; *The Steadfast Tin Soldier* by Hans Christian Andersen, ill. by Marcia Brown, Scribner's; *A Very Special House* by Ruth Krauss, ill. by Maurice Sendak, Harper; *Green Eyes* by A. Birnbaum, Capitol

1955 *Cinderella, or the Little Glass Slipper* by Charles Perrault, tr. and ill. by Marcia Brown, Scribner's

Honor Books: *Book of Nursery and Mother Goose Rhymes,* ill. by Marguerite de Angeli, Doubleday; *Wheel on the Chimney* by Margaret Wise Brown, ill. by Tibor Gergely, Lippincott; *The Thanksgiving Story* by Alice Dalgliesh, ill. by Helen Sewell, Scribner's

1956 *Frog Went A-Courtin'* ed. by John Langstaff, ill. by Feodor Rojankovsky, Harcourt Brace Jovanovich

Honor Books: *Play with Me* by Marie Hall Ets, Viking; *Crow Boy* by Taro Yashima, Viking

1957 *A Tree Is Nice* by Janice May Udry, ill. by Marc Simont, Harper

Honor Books: *Mr. Penny's Race Horse* by Marie Hall Ets, Viking; *1 Is One* by Tasha Tudor, Walck; *Anatole* by Eve Titus, ill. by Paul Galdone, McGraw; *Gillespie and the Guards* by Benjamin Elkin, ill. by James Daugherty, Viking; *Lion* by William Pène du Bois, Viking

1958 *Time of Wonder* by Robert McCloskey, Viking

Honor Books: *Fly High, Fly Low* by Don Freeman, Viking; *Anatole and the Cat* by Eve Titus, ill. by Paul Galdone, McGraw

1959 *Chanticleer and the Fox* adapted from Chaucer and ill. by Barbara Cooney, Crowell

Honor Books: *The House That Jack Built: A Picture Book in Two Languages* by Antonio Frasconi, Harcourt Brace Jovanovich; *What Do You Say, Dear?* by Sesyle Joslin, ill. by Maurice Sendak, W. R. Scott; *Umbrella* by Taro Yashima, Viking

1960 *Nine Days to Christmas* by Marie Hall Ets and Aurora Labastida, ill. by Marie Hall Ets, Viking

Honor Books: *Houses from the Sea* by Alice E. Goudey, ill. by Adrienne Adams, Scribner's; *The Moon Jumpers* by Janice May Udry, ill. by Maurice Sendak, Harper

1961 *Baboushka and the Three Kings* by Ruth Robbins, ill. by Nicolas Sidjakov, Parnassus

Honor Book: *Inch by Inch* by Leo Lionni, Obolensky

1962 *Once a Mouse. . .* by Marcia Brown, Scribner's

Honor Books: *The Fox Went Out on a Chilly Night: An Old Song* by Peter Spier, Doubleday; *Little Bear's Visit* by Else Holmelund Minarik, ill. by Maurice Sendak, Harper; *The Day We Saw the Sun Come Up* by Alice E. Goudey, ill. by Adrienne Adams, Scribner's

1963 *The Snowy Day* by Ezra Jack Keats, Viking

Honor Books: *The Sun Is a Golden Earring* by Natalia M. Belting, ill. by Bernarda Bryson, Holt; *Mr. Rabbit and the Lovely Present* by Charlotte Zolotow, ill. by Maurice Sendak, Harper

1964 *Where the Wild Things Are* by Maurice Sendak, Harper

Honor Books: *Swimmy* by Leo Lionni, Pantheon; *All in the Morning Early* by Sorche Nic Leodhas, ill. by Evaline Ness, Holt; *Mother Goose and Nursery Rhymes* ill. by Philip Reed, Atheneum

1965 *May I Bring a Friend?* by Beatrice Schenk de Regniers, ill. by Beni Montresor, Atheneum

Honor Books: *Rain Makes Applesauce* by Julian Scheer, ill. by Marvin Bileck, Holiday; *The Wave* by Margaret Hodges, ill. by Blair Lent, Houghton; *A Pocketful of Cricket* by Rebecca Caudill, ill. by Evaline Ness, Holt

1966 *Always Room for One More* by Sorche Nic Leodhas, ill. by Nonny Hogrogian, Holt

Honor Books: *Hide and Seek Fog* by Alvin Tresselt, ill. by Roger Duvoisin, Lothrop; *Just Me* by Marie Hall Ets, Viking; *Tom Tit Tot* by Evaline Ness, Scribner's

1967 *Sam, Bangs & Moonshine* by Evaline Ness, Holt

Honor Book: *One Wide River to Cross* by Barbara Emberley, ill. by Ed Emberley, Prentice

1968 *Drummer Hoff* by Barbara Emberley, ill. by Ed Emberley, Prentice

Honor Books: *Frederick* by Leo Lionni, Pantheon; *Seashore Story* by Taro Yashima, Viking; *The Emperor and the Kite* by Jane Yolen, ill. by Ed Young, World

1969 *The Fool of the World and the Flying Ship* by Arthur Ransome, ill. by Uri Shulevitz, Farrar

Honor Book: *Why the Sun and the Moon Live in the Sky: An African Folktale* by Elphinstone Dayrell, ill. by Blair Lent, Houghton

1970 *Sylvester and the Magic Pebble* by William Steig, Windmill

Honor Books: *Goggles!* by Ezra Jack Keats, Macmillan; *Alexander and the Wind-Up Mouse* by Leo Lionni, Pantheon; *Pop Corn and Ma Goodness* by Edna Mitchell Preston, ill. by Robert Andrew Parker, Viking; *Thy Friend, Obadiah* by Brinton Turkle, Viking; *The Judge: An Untrue Tale* by Harve Zemach, ill. by Margot Zemach, Farrar

1971 *A Story—A Story: An African Tale* by Gail E. Haley, Atheneum

Honor Books: *The Angry Moon* by William Sleator, ill. by Blair Lent, Atlantic-Little; *Frog and Toad Are Friends* by Arnold Lobel, Harper; *In the Night Kitchen* by Maurice Sendak, Harper

1972 *One Fine Day* by Nonny Hogrogian, Macmillan

Honor Books: *If All the Seas Were One Sea* by Janina Domanska, Macmillan; *Moja Means One: Swahili Counting Book* by Muriel Feelings, ill. by Tom Feelings, Dial; *Hildilid's Night* by Cheli Duran Ryan, ill. by Arnold Lobel, Macmillan

1973 *The Funny Little Woman* retold by Arlene Mosel, ill. by Blair Lent, Dutton

Honor Books: *Anansi the Spider: A Tale from the Ashanti* adapted and ill. by Gerald McDermott, Holt; *Hosie's Alphabet* by Hosea Tobias and Lisa Baskin, ill. by Leonard Baskin, Viking; *Snow White and the Seven Dwarfs* translated by Randall Jarrell, ill. by Nancy Ekholm Burkert, Farrar; *When Clay Sings* by Byrd Baylor, ill. by Tom Bahti, Scribner's

1974 *Duffy and the Devil* by Harve Zemach, ill. by Margot Zemach, Farrar

Honor Books: *Three Jovial Huntsmen* by Susan Jeffers, Bradbury; *Cathedral: The Story of Its Construction* by David Macaulay, Houghton

1975 *Arrow to the Sun* adapted and ill. by Gerald McDermott, Viking

Honor Book: *Jambo Means Hello: A Swahili Alphabet Book* by Muriel Feelings, ill. by Tom Feelings, Dial

1976 *Why Mosquitoes Buzz in People's Ears* retold by Verna Aardema, ill. by Leo and Diane Dillon, Dial

Honor Books: *The Desert Is Theirs* by Byrd Baylor, ill. by Peter Parnall, Scribner's; *Strega Nona* retold and ill. by Tomie de Paola, Prentice

1977 *Ashanti to Zulu: African Traditions* by Margaret Musgrove, ill. by Leo and Diane Dillon, Dial

Honor Books: *The Amazing Bone* by William Steig, Farrar; *The Contest* retold and ill. by Nony Hogrogian, Greenwillow; *Fish for Supper* by M. B. Goffstein, Dial; *The Golem: A Jewish Legend* by Beverly Brodsky McDermott, Lippincott; *Hawk, I'm Your Brother* by Byrd Baylor, ill. by Peter Parnall, Scribner's

1978 *Noah's Ark* by Peter Spier, Doubleday

Honor Books: *Castle* by David Macaulay, Houghton; *It Could Always Be Worse* retold and ill. by Margot Zemach, Farrar

1979 *The Girl Who Loved Wild Horses* by Paul Goble, Bradbury

Honor Books: *Freight Train* by Donald Crews, Greenwillow; *The Way to Start a Day* by Byrd Baylor, ill. by Peter Parnall, Scribner's

1980 *Ox-Cart Man* by Donald Hall, ill. by Barbara Cooney, Viking

Honor Books: *Ben's Trumpet* by Rachel Isadora, Greenwillow; *The Treasure* by Uri Shulevitz, Farrar; *The Garden of Abdul Gasazi* by Chris Van Allsburg, Houghton

1981 *Fables* by Arnold Lobel, Harper

Honor Books: *The Bremen-Town Musicians* by Ilse Plume, Doubleday; *The Grey Lady and the Strawberry Snatcher* by Molly Bang, Four Winds; *Mice Twice* by Joseph Low, Atheneum; *Truck* by Donald Crews, Greenwillow

1982 *Jumanji* by Christ Van Allsburg, Houghton

Honor Books: *A Visit to William Blake's Inn: Poems for Innocent and Experienced Travelers* by Nancy Willard, ill. by Alice and Martin Provensen, Harcourt Brace Jovanovich; *Where the Buffaloes Begin* by Olaf Baker, ill. by Stephen Gammell, Warner; *On Market Street* by Arnold Lobel, ill. by Anita Lobel, Greenwillow; *Outside Over There* by Maurice Sendak, Harper

1983 *Shadow* by Blaise Cendrars, ill. by Marcia Brown, Scribner's

Honor Books: *When I Was Young in the Mountains* by Cynthia Rylant, ill. by Diane Goode, Dutton; *Chair for My Mother* by Vera B. Williams, Morrow

1984 *The Glorious Flight: Across the Channel with Louis Bleriot* by Alice and Martin Provensen, Viking

Honor Books: *Ten, Nine, Eight* by Molly Bang, Greenwillow; *Little Red Riding Hood* retold and ill. by Trina Schart Hyman, Holiday House

1985 *St. George and the Dragon* retold by Margaret Hodges, ill. by Trina Schart Hyman, Little, Brown

Honor Books: *Hansel and Gretel* retold by Rika Lesser, ill. by Paul O. Zelinsky, Dodd; *Have You Seen My Duckling?* by Nancy Tafuri, Greenwillow; *The Story of Jumping Mouse* by John Steptoe, Lothrop

1986 *The Polar Express* by Chris Van Allsburg, Houghton

Honor Books: *King Bidgood's in the Bathtub* by Audrey Wood, ill. by Don Wood, Harcourt; *The Relative Came* by Cynthia Rylant, ill. by Stephen Gammell, Bradbury

The Newbery Medal and Honor Awards

The Newbery award, named after the first English publisher of books for children, John Newbery, is granted by the Children's Services Division of the American Library Association. The medal and honor awards are presented annually for the most distinguished contributions to children's literature published in the United States. The first Newbery Medal and honor awards were presented in 1922.

1922 *The Story of Mankind* by Hendrik Willem van Loon, Liveright

Honor Books: *The Great Quest* by Charles Hawes, Little; *Cedric the Forester* by Bernard Marshall, Appleton; *The Old Tobacco Shop: A True Account of What Befell a Little Boy in Search of Adventure* by William Bowen, Macmillan; *The Golden Fleece and the Heroes Who Lived before Achilles* by Padriac Colum, Macmillan; *Windy Hill* by Cornelia Meigs, Macmillan

1923 *The Voyages of Doctor Dolittle* by Hugh Lofting, Lippincott

Honor Books: No record

1924 *The Dark Frigate* by Charles Hawes, Atlantic/Little

Honor Books: No record

1925 *Tales from Silver Lands* by Charles Finger, Doubleday

Honor Books: *Nicholas: A Manhattan Christmas Story* by Anne Carroll Moore, Putnam; *Dream Coach* by Anne Parrish, Macmillan

1926 *Shen of the Sea* by Arthur Bowie Chrisman, Dutton

Honor Book: *Voyagers: Being Legends and Romances of Atlantic Discovery* by Padraic Colum, Macmillan

1927 *Smoky, the Cowhorse* by Will James, Scribner's

Honor Books: No record

1928 *Gayneck, The Story of a Pigeon* by Dhan Gopal Mukerji, Dutton

Honor Books: *The Wonder Smith and His Son: A Tale from the Golden Childhood of the World* by Ella Young, Longmans; *Downright Dencey* by Caroline Snedeker, Doubleday

1929 *The Trumpeter of Krakow* by Eric P. Kelly, Macmillan

Honor Books: *Pigtail of Ah Lee Ben Loo* by John Bennett, Longmans; *Millions of Cats* by Wanda Gág, Coward; *The Boy Who Was* by Grace Hallock, Dutton; *Clearing Weather* by Cornelia Meigs, Little; *Runaway Papoose* by Grace Moon, Doubleday; *Tod of the Fens* by Elinor Whitney, Macmillan

1930 *Hitty, Her First Hundred Years* by Rachel Field, Macmillan

Honor Books: *Daughter of the Seine: The Life of Madame Roland* by Jeanette Eaton, Harper; *Pran of Albania* by Elizabeth Miller, Doubleday; *Jumping-off Place* by Marian Hurd McNeely, Longmans; *Tangle-coated Horse and Other Tales: Episodes from the Fionn Saga* by Ella Young, Longmans; *Vaino: A Boy of New England* by Julia Davis Adams, Dutton; *Little Blacknose* by Hildegarde Swift, Harcourt Brace Jovanovich

1931 *The Cat Who Went to Heaven* by Elizabeth Coatsworth, Macmillan

Honor Books: *Floating Island* by Anne Parrish, Harper; *The Dark Star of Itza: The Story of a Pagan Princess* by Alida Malkus, Harcourt Brace Jovanovich; *Queer Person* by Ralph Hubbard, Doubleday; *Mountains Are Free* by Julia Davis Adams, Dutton; *Spice and the Devil's Cave* by Agnes Hewes, Knopf; *Meggy Macintosh* by Elizabeth Janet Gray, Doubleday; *Garram the Hunter: A Boy of the Hill Tribes* by Herbert Best, Doubleday; *Ood-Le-Uk the Wanderer* by Alice Lide and Margaret Johansen, Little

1932 *Waterless Mountain* by Laura Adams Armer, Longmans

Honor Books: *The Fairy Circus* by Dorothy P. Lathrop, Macmillan; *Calico Bush by Rachel Field, Macmillan; *Boy of the South Seas* by

Eunice Tietjens, Coward; *Out of the Flame* by Eloise Lownsbery, Longmans; *Jane's Island* by Marjorie Allee, Houghton; *Truce of the Wolf and Other Tales of Old Italy* by Mary Gould Davis, Harcourt Brace Jovanovich

1933 *Young Fu of the Upper Yangtze* by Elizabeth Foreman Lewis, Winston

Honor Books: *Swift Rivers* by Cornelia Meigs, Little; *The Railroad to Freedom: A Story of the Civil War* by Hildegarde Swift, Harcourt Brace Jovanovich; *Children of the Soil: A Story of Scandinavia* by Nora Burglon, Doubleday

1934 *Invincible Louisa: The Story of the Author of 'Little Women'* by Cornelia Meigs, Little

Honor Books: *The Forgotten Daughter* by Caroline Snedeker, Doubleday; *Swords of Steel* by Elsie Singmaster, Houghton; *ABC Bunny* by Wanda Gág, Coward; *Winged Girl of Knossos* by Erik Berry, Appleton; *New Land* by Sarah Schmidt, McBride; *Big Tree of Bunlahy: Stories of My Own Countryside* by Padraic Colum, Macmillan; *Glory of the Seas* by Agnes Hewes, Knopf; *Apprentice of Florence* by Ann Kyle, Houghton

1935 *Dobry* by Monica Shannon, Viking

Honor Books: *Pageant of Chinese History* by Elizabeth Seeger, Longmans; *Davy Crockett* by Constance Rourke, Harcourt Brace Jovanovich; *Day on Skates: The Story of a Dutch Picnic* by Hilda Van Stockum, Harper

1936 *Caddie Woodlawn* by Carol Ryrie Brink, Macmillan

Honor Books: *Honk, the Moose* by Phil Stong, Dodd; *The Good Master* by Kate Seredy, Viking; *Young Walter Scott* by Elizabeth Janet Gray, Viking; *All Sail Set: A Romance of the Flying Cloud* by Armstrong Sperry, Winston

1937 *Roller Skates* by Ruth Sawyer, Viking

Honor Books: *Phoebe Fairchild: Her Book* by Lois Lenski, Stokes; *Whistler's Van* by Idwal Jones, Vi-

king; *Golden Basket* by Ludwig Bemelmans, Viking; *Winterbound* by Margery Bianco, Viking; *Audubon* by Constance Rourke, Harcourt Brace Jovanovich; *The Codfish Musket* by Agnes Hewes, Doubleday

1938 *The White Stag* by Kate Seredy, Viking

Honor Books: *Pecos Bill* by James Cloyd Bowman, Little; *Bright Island* by Mabel Robinson, Random; *On the Banks of Plum Creek* by Laura Ingalls Wilder, Harper

1939 *Thimble Summer* by Elizabeth Enright, Rinehart

Honor Books: *Nino* by Valenti Angelo, Viking; *Mr. Popper's Penguins* by Richard and Florence Atwater, Little; *"Hello the Boat!"* by Phyllis Crawford, Holt; *Leader by Destiny: George Washington, Man and Patriot* by Jeanette Eaton, Harcourt Brace Jovanovich; *Penn* by Elizabeth Janet Gray, Viking

1940 *Daniel Boone* by James Daugherty, Viking

Honor Books: *The Singing Tree* by Kate Seredy, Viking; *Runner of the Mountain Tops: The Life of Louis Agassiz* by Mabel Robinson, Random; *By the Shores of Silver Lake* by Laura Ingalls Wilder, Harper; *Boy with a Pack* by Stephen W. Meader, Harcourt Brace Jovanovich

1941 *Call It Courage* by Armstrong Sperry, Macmillan

Honor Books: *Blue Willow* by Doris Gates, Viking; *Young Mac of Fort Vancouver* by Mary Jane Carr, Crowell; *The Long Winter* by Laura Ingalls Wilder, Harper; *Nansen* by Anna Gertrude Hall, Viking

1942 *The Matchlock Gun* by Walter D. Edmonds, Dodd

Honor Books: *Little Town on the Prairie* by Laura Ingalls Wilder, Harper; *George Washington's World* by Genevieve Foster, Scribner's; *Indian Captive: The Story of Mary Jemison* by Lois Lenski, Lippincott; *Down Ryton Water* by Eva Roe Gaggin, Viking

1943 *Adam of the Road* by Elizabeth Janet Gray, Viking

Honor Books: *The Middle Moffat* by Eleanor Estes, Harcourt Brace Jovanovich; *Have You Seen Tom Thumb?* by Mabel Leigh Hunt, Lippincott

1944 *Johnny Tremain* by Esther Forbes, Houghton

Honor Books: *The Happy Golden Years* by Laura Ingalls Wilder, Harper; *Fog Magic* by Julia Sauer, Viking; *Rufus M.* by Eleanor Estes, Harcourt Brace Jovanovich; *Mountain Born* by Elizabeth Yates, Coward

1945 *Rabbit Hill* by Robert Lawson, Viking

Honor Books: *The Hundred Dresses* by Eleanor Estes, Harcourt Brace Jovanovich; *The Silver Pencil* by Alice Dalgliesh, Scribner's; *Abraham Lincoln's World* by Genevieve Foster, Scribner's; *Lone Journey: The Life of Roger Williams* by Jeanette Eaton, Harcourt Brace Jovanovich

1946 *Strawberry Girl* by Lois Lenski, Lippincott

Honor Books: *Justin Morgan Had a Horse* by Marguerite Henry, Rand; *The Moved-Outers* by Florence Crannell Means, Houghton; *Bhimsa, the Dancing Bear* by Christine Weston, Scribner's; *New Found World* by Katherine Shippen, Viking

1947 *Miss Hickory* by Carolyn Sherwin Bailey, Viking

Honor Books: *Wonderful Year* by Nancy Barnes, Messner; *Big Tree* by Mary and Conrad Buff, Viking; *The Heavenly Tenants* by William Maxwell, Harper; *The Avion My Uncle Flew* by Cyrus Fisher, Appleton; *The Hidden Treasure of Glaston* by Eleanore Jewett, Viking

1948 *The Twenty-One Balloons* by William Pène du Bois, Viking

Honor Books: *Pancakes-Paris* by Claire Huchet Bishop, Viking; *Le Lun, Lad of Courage* by Carolyn Treffinger, Abingdon; *The Quaint and Curious Quest of Johnny Longfoot, The Shoe-King's Son* by Catherine Besterman, Bobbs; *The Cow-tail Switch, and Other West African Stories* by Harold Courlander, Holt; *Misty of Chincoteague* by Marguerite Henry, Rand

1949 *King of the Wind* by Marguerite Henry, Rand

Honor Books: *Seabird* by Holling C. Holling, Houghton; *Daughter of the Mountains* by Louise Rankin, Viking; *My Father's Dragon* by Ruth S. Gannett, Random; *Story of the Negro* by Arna Bontemps, Knopf

1950 *The Door in the Wall* by Marguerite de Angeli, Doubleday

Honor Books: *Tree of Freedom* by Rebecca Caudill, Viking; *The Blue Cat of Castle Town* by Catherine Coblentz, Longmans; *Kildee House* by Rutherford Montgomery, Doubleday; *George Washington* by Genevieve Foster, Scribner's; *Song of the Pines: A Story of Norwegian Lumbering in Wisconsin* by Walter and Marion Havighurst, Winston

1951 *Amos Fortune, Free Man* by Elizabeth Yates, Aladdin

Honor Books: *Better Known as Johnny Appleseed* by Mabel Leigh Hunt, Lippincott; *Gandhi, Fighter Without a Sword* by Jeanette Eaton, Morrow; *Abraham Lincoln, Friend of the People* by Clara Ingram Judson, Follett; *The Story of Appleby Capple* by Anne Parrish, Harper

1952 *Ginger Pye* by Eleanor Estes, Harcourt Brace Jovanovich

Honor Books: *Americans Before Columbus* by Elizabeth Baity, Viking; *Minn of the Mississippi* by Holling C. Holling, Houghton; *The Defender* by Nicholas Kalashnikoff, Scribner's; *The Light at Tern Rock* by Julia Sauer, Viking; *The Apple and the Arrow* by Mary and Conrad Buff, Houghton

1953 *Secret of the Andes* by Ann Nolan Clark, Viking

Honor Books: *Charlotte's Web* by E. B. White, Harper; *Moccasin Trail* by Eloise McGraw, Coward; *Red Sails to Capri* by Ann Weil, Viking; *The Bears on Hemlock Mountain* by Alice Dalgliesh, Scribner's; *Birthdays of Freedom,* Vol. 1, by Genevieve Foster, Scribner's

1954 *. . . and now Miguel* by Joseph Krumgold, Crowell

Honor Books: *All Alone* by Claire Huchet Bishop, Viking; *Shadrach* by Meindert DeJong, Harper; *Hurry Home Candy* by Meindert DeJong, Harper; *Theodore Roosevelt, Fighting Patriot* by Clara Ingram Judson, Follett; *Magic Maize* by Mary and Conrad Buff, Houghton

1955 *The Wheel on the School* by Meindert DeJong, Harper

Honor Books: *The Courage of Sarah Noble* by Alice Dalgliesh, Scribner's; *Banner in the Sky* by James Ullman, Lippincott

1956 *Carry on, Mr. Bowditch* by Jean Lee Latham, Houghton

Honor Books: *The Secret River* by Marjorie Kinnan Rawlings, Scribner's; *The Golden Name Day* by Jennie Linquist, Harper; *Men, Microscopes, and Living Things* by Katherine Shippen, Viking

1957 *Miracles on Maple Hill* by Virginia Sorensen, Harcourt Brace Jovanovich

Honor Books: *Old Yeller* by Fred Gipson, Harper; *The House of Sixty Fathers* by Meindert DeJong, Harper; *Mr. Justice Holmes* by Clara Ingram Judson, Follett; *The Corn Grows Ripe* by Dorothy Rhoads, Viking; *Black Fox of Lorne* by Marguerite de Angeli, Doubleday

1958 *Rifles for Watie* by Harold Keith, Crowell

Honor Books: *The Horsecatcher* by Mari Sandoz, Westminster; *Goneaway Lake* by Elizabeth Enright, Harcourt Brace Jovanovich; *The Great Wheel* by Robert Lawson, Viking; *Tom Paine, Freedom's Apostle* by Leo Gurko, Crowell

1959 *The Witch of Blackbird Pond* by Elizabeth George Speare, Houghton

Honor Books: *The Family Under the Bridge* by Natalie Savage Carlson, Harper; *Along Came a Dog* by Meindert DeJong, Harper; *Chucaro: Wild Pony of the Pampa* by Francis Kalnay, Harcourt Brace Jovanovich; *The Perilous Road* by William O. Steele, Harcourt Brace Jovanovich

1960 *Onion John* by Joseph Krumgold, Crowell

Honor Books: *My Side of the Mountain* by Jean George, Dutton; *America is Born* by Gerald W. Johnson, Morrow; *The Gammage Cup* by Carol Kendall, Harcourt Brace Jovanovich

1961 *Island of the Blue Dolphins* by Scott O'Dell, Houghton

Honor Books: *America Moves Forward* by Gerald W. Johnson, Morrow; *Old Ramon* by Jack Schaefer, Houghton; *The Cricket in Times Square* by George Selden, Farrar

1962 *The Bronze Bow* by Elizabeth George Speare, Houghton

Honor Books: *Frontier Living* by Edwin Tunis, World; *The Golden Goblet* by Eloise McCraw, Coward; *Belling the Tiger* by Mary Stolz, Harper

1963 *A Wrinkle in Time* by Madeleine L'Engle, Farrar

Honor Books: *Thistle and Thyme: Tales and Legends from Scotland* by Sorche Nic Leodhas, Holt; *Men of Athens* by Olivia Coolidge, Houghton

1964 *It's Like This, Cat* by Emily Cheney Neville, Harper

Honor Books: *Rascal* by Sterling North, Dutton; *The Loner* by Ester Wier, McKay

1965 *Shadow of a Bull* by Maia Wojciechowska, Atheneum

Honor Books: *Across Five Aprils* by Irene Hunt, Follett

1966 *I, Juan de Pareja* by Elizabeth Borten de Treviño, Farrar

Honor Books: *The Black Cauldron* by Lloyd Alexander, Holt; *The Animal Family* by Randall Jarrell, Pantheon; *The Noonday Friends* by Mary Stolz, Harper

1967 *Up a Road Slowly* by Irene Hunt, Follet

Honor Books: *The King's Fifth* by Scott O'Dell, Houghton; *Zlateh the Goat and Other Stories* by Isaac Bashevis Singer, Harper; *The Jazz Man* by Mary H. Weik, Atheneum

1968 *From the Mixed-Up Files of Mrs. Basil E. Frankweiler* by E. L. Konigsburg, Atheneum

Honor Books: *Jennifer, Hecate, Macbeth, William McKinley, and Me, Elizabeth* by E. L. Konigsburg,

Atheneum; *The Black Pearl* by Scott O'Dell, Houghton; *The Fearsome Inn* by Isaac Bashevis Singer, Scribner's; *The Egypt Game* by Zilpha Keatley Snyder, Atheneum

1969 *The High King* by Lloyd Alexander, Holt

Honor Books: *To Be a Slave* by Julius Lester, Dial; *When Shlemiel Went to Warsaw and Other Stories* by Isaac Bashevis Singer, Farrar

1970 *Sounder* by William H. Armstrong, Harper

Honor Books: *Our Eddie* by Sulamith Ish-Kishor, Pantheon; *The Many Ways of Seeing: An Introduction to the Pleasures of Art* by Janet Gaylord Moore, World; *Journey Outside* by Mary Q. Steele, Viking

1971 *Summer of the Swans* by Betsy Byars, Viking

Honor Books: *Kneeknock Rise* by Natalie Babbitt, Farrar; *Enchantress from the Stars* by Sylvia Louise Engdahl, Atheneum; *Sing Down the Moon* by Scott O'Dell, Houghton

1972 *Mrs. Frisby and the Rats of NIMH* by Robert C. O'Brien, Atheneum

Honor Books: *Incident at Hawk's Hill* by Allan W. Eckert, Little; *The Planet of Junior Brown* by Virginia Hamilton, Macmillan; *The Tombs of Atuan* by Ursula K. Le Guin, Atheneum; *Annie and the Old One* by Miska Miles, Atlantic-Little; *The Headless Cupid* by Zilpha Keatley Sunder, Atheneum

1973 *Julie of the Wolves* by Jean Craighead George, Harper

Honor Books: *Frog and Toad Together* by Arnold Lobel, Harper; *The Upstairs Room* by Johanna Reiss, Crowell; *The Witches of Worm* by Zilpha Keatley Snyder, Atheneum

1974 *The Slave Dancer* by Paula Fox, Bradbury

Honor Book: *The Dark Is Rising* by Susan Cooper, Atheneum

1975 *M.C. Higgins, the Great* by Virginia Hamilton, Macmillan

Honor Books: *Figgs & Phantoms* by Ellen Raskin, Dutton; *My Brother Sam Is Dead* by James Lincoln Collier & Christopher Collier, Four Winds; *The Perilous Gard* by Elizabeth Marie Pope, Houghton; *Philip Hall Likes Me. I Reckon Maybe* by Bette Greene, Dial

1976 *The Grey King* by Susan Cooper, Atheneum

Honor Books: *The Hundred Penny Box* by Sharon Bell Mathis, Viking; *Dragonwings* by Lawrence Yep, Harper

1977 *Roll of Thunder, Hear My Cry* by Mildred D. Taylor, Dial

Honor Books: *Abel's Island* by William Steig, Farrar; *A String in the Harp* by Nancy Bond, Atheneum

1978 *Bridge to Terabithia* by Katherine Paterson, Crowell

Honor Books: *Ramona and Her Father* by Beverly Cleary, Morrow; *Anpao: An American Indian Odyssey* by Jamake Highwater, Lippincott

1979 *The Westing Game* by Ellen Raskin, Dutton

Honor Book: *The Great Gilly Hopkins* by Katherine Paterson, Crowell

1980 *A Gathering of Days: A New England Girl's Journal 1830–32* by Joan Blos, Scribner's

Honor Book: *The Road from Home: The Story of an Armenian Girl* by David Kherdian, Greenwillow

1981 *Jacob Have I Loved* by Katherine Paterson, Crowell

Honor Books: *The Fledgling* by Jane Langton, Harper; *A Ring of Endless Light* by Madeleine L'Engle, Farrar

1982 *A Visit to William Blake's Inn: Poems for Innocent and Experienced Travelers* by Nancy Willard, Harcourt Brace Jovanovich

Honor Books: *Ramona Quimby, Age 8* by Beverly Cleary, Morrow; *Upon the Head of the Goat: A Childhood in Hungary, 1939–1944* by Aranka Siegal, Farrar

1983 *Dicey's Song* by Cynthia Voigt, Atheneum

Honor Books: *Blue Sword* by Robin McKinley, Morrow; *Dr. DeSoto* by William Steig. Farrar; *Graven Images* by Paul Fleischman, Harper;

Homesick: My Own Story by Jean Fritz, Putnam's; *Sweet Whisper, Brother Rush,* by Virginia Hamilton, Philomel.

1984 *Dear Mr. Henshaw* by Beverly Cleary, Morrow

Honor Books: *The Sign of the Beaver* by Elizabeth George Speare, Houghton; *A Solitary Blue* by Cynthia Voigt, Atheneum; *The Wish Giver* by Bill Brittain, Harper

1985 *The Hero and the Crown* by Robin McKinley, Greenwillow

Honor Books: *Like Jake and Me* by Mavis Jukes, Knopf; *The Moves Make the Man* by Bruce Brooks, Harper; *One-Eyed Cat* by Paula Fox, Bradbury

1986 *Sarah, Plain and Tall* by Patricia MacLachlan, Harper

Honor Books: *Commodore Perry in the Land of the Shogun* by Rhoda Blumberg, Lothrop; *Dogsong* by Gary Paulsen, Bradbury

Children's Book Award

The Children's Book Award is presented annually by the International Reading Association to a children's author whose work shows unusual promise. The award was established in 1975.

1975 *Transport 7-41-R* by T. Degens, Viking

1976 *Dragonwings* by Lawrence Yep, Harper

1977 *A String in the Harp* by Nancy Bond, Atheneum

1978 *A Summer to Die* by Lois Lowry, Houghton

1979 *Reserved for Mark Anthony Crowder* by Alison Smith, Dutton

1980 *Words by Heart* by Ouida Sebestyen, Little

1981 *My Own Private Sky* by Delores Beckman, Dutton

1982 *Good Night, Mr. Tom* by Michelle Magorian, Harper

1983 *The Darkangel* by Meredith Ann Pierce, Atlantic/Little

1984 *Ratha's Creature* by Clare Bell, Atheneum

1985 *Badger on the Barge* by Janni Howker, Greenwillow

1986 *Prairie Songs* by Pam Conrad, Harper

Hans Christian Andersen International Medal

This international award was established in 1956 by the International Board on Books for Young People. It is presented every two years to a living author and a living artist whose total works have made an outstanding contribution to children's literature. A committee of five members, each from a different country, judges the selections.

1956 Eleanor Farjeon (Great Britain)

1958 Astrid Lindgren (Sweden)

1960 Erich Kästner (Germany)

1962 Meindert DeJong (United States)

1964 René Guillot (France)

1966 Author: Tove Jansson (Finland); Illustrator: Alois Carigiet (Switzerland)

1968 Authors: James Krüss (Germany); Jose Maria Sanchez-Silva (Spain); Illustrator: Jiri Trnka (Czechoslovakia)

1970 Author: Gianni Rodari (Italy); Illustrator: Maurice Sendak (United States)

1972 Author: Scott O'Dell (United States); Illustrator: Ib Spang Olsen (Denmark)

1974 Author: Maria Gripe (Sweden); Illustrator: Farshid Mesghali (Iran)

1976 Author: Cecil Bodker (Denmark); Illustrator: Tatjana Mawrina (Union of Soviet Socialist Republics)

1978 Author: Paula Fox (United States); Illustrator: Svend Otto S. (Denmark)

1980 Author: Bohumil Riha (Czechoslovakia); Illustrator: Suekichi Akaba (Japan)

1982 Author: Lygia Bojunga Nunes (Brazil) Illustrator: Zbigniew Rychlicki (Poland)

1984 Author: Christine Nostlinger (Austria) Illustrator: Mitsumasa Anno (Japan)

1986 Author: Patricia Wrightson (Australia) Illustrator: Robert Ingpen (Australia)

Laura Ingalls Wilder Medal

The Laura Ingalls Wilder award, named after the author of the "Little House" series, is presented every five years by the American Library Association, Children's Book Division, to an author or illustrator whose books have made a lasting contribution to children's literature. The award was established in 1954 and is restricted to books published in the United States.

1954 Laura Ingalls Wilder

1960 Clara Ingram Judson

1965 Ruth Sawyer

1970 E. B. White

1975 Beverly Cleary

1980 Theodor Geisel (Dr. Seuss)

1983 Maurice Sendak

1986 Jean Fritz

Examples of Additional Book Awards for Children's Literature

Amelia Frances Howard–Gibbon Medal, Canadian Library Association, is awarded annually to a Canadian illustrator for outstanding illustrations in a children's book published in Canada. First presented in 1971.

Boston Globe/Horn Book Awards, Boston Globe, Boston, Mass., are awarded annually, since 1967, to an author of fiction, an author of nonfiction, and an illustrator.

The Canadian Library Awards, Canadian Library Association, are given annually to a children's book of literary merit written by a Canadian citizen and to a book of literary merit published in French. First presented in 1947 (Canadian citizen) and 1954 (French publication).

The Carnegie Medal, British Library Association, is awarded annually, since 1936, to an outstanding book first published in the United Kingdom.

Charles and Bertie G. Schwartz Award, National Jewish Welfare Board, New York, is awarded annually to a book that combines literary merit with an affirmative expression of Jewish thought. Established in 1952.

CIBC Award for Unpublished Writers, Council on Interracial Books for Children, New York, awards the United States writer from a racial minority whose manuscript best challenges stereotypes, supplies role models, and portrays distinctive aspects of a culture. Given for the first time in 1969.

Coretta Scott King Award is made to one black author and one black illustrator for outstandingly inspirational contributions to children's literature. The award was first given in 1970.

Jane Addams Children's Book Award, Jane Addams Peace Association and the Women's International League for Peace and Freedom, New York, is given annually, since 1953, to honor the book that most effectively promotes peace, world community, and social justice.

The Kate Greenaway Medal, British Library Association, is awarded each year to the most distinguished work in illustration first published in the United Kingdom. Established in 1956.

Mildred L. Batchelder Award, American Library Association, Children's Services Division, Chicago, is given annually to the publisher of the most outstanding book originally issued in a foreign language. First awarded in 1968.

National Book Awards, Association of American Publishers, New York, are given annually to United States authors whose books have contributed most significantly to human awareness, national culture, and the spirit of excellence. Established in 1969 (Children's Literature Division).

William Allen White Children's Book Award, William Allen White Library, Kansas State Teachers College, Emporia, Kansas, is given annually, since 1953, to an outstanding children's book selected by Kansas children.

APPENDIX E
Readability

The books in the annotated bibliographies have been evaluated according to approximate reading levels. This information is important for teachers, librarians, and parents who are interested in selecting or recommending books that children can read independently. Several readability formulas may be used to determine readability levels. The books in this text were evaluated according to the Fry Readability Graph (opposite), which calculates a book's reading level by the following method:

1 Select three 100-word passages, one each from the beginning, middle, and end of the book. Count proper nouns, initializations, and numerals in these 100-word selections. For example, "We went to the circus in Sarasota, Florida" counts as 8 words.

2 Count the total number of sentences in each 100-word passage. Estimate the number of sentences to the nearest tenth of a sentence. Average the total number of sentences in the beginning, middle, and ending passages so that you have one number to represent the number of sentences per 100 words.

3 Count the total number of syllables in each of the three 100-word passages. You will find it faster to count syllables if you tabulate every syllable over one in each word, then add this number to 100 at the end of the passage. For example:

$$\overset{1}{\text{Jim was plan}}\overset{}{\text{ning to take a camping va}}\overset{1\quad2}{\text{cation in the high coun}}\overset{1}{\text{try.}}$$
(17 syllables)

Now, find the average total number of syllables for the three 100-word passages.

4 Plot on the graph the average number of sentences per 100 words, and the average number of syllables per 100 words. The example shown below places the reading level of *Stuart Little* at fourth grade, with 9.2 average number of sentences per 100 words and 127 average number of syllables per 100 words.

Source *Stuart Little* (E. B. White)	Sentences per 100 words	Syllables per 100 words
100-word sample page 6	6.3	116
100-word sample page 72	10.5	136
100-word sample page 125	10.7	129
Total	27.5	381
Average	9.2	127

Readability formulas assume that shorter sentences and fewer syllables in words result in easier reading materials. In contrast, long sentences and numerous multisyllabic words are thought to be more difficult to read. While this is often true, the adult should be aware that readability formulas do not take into consideration such factors as the difficulty of the concepts presented, or the child's interest in a particular subject. Although readability formulas are useful, they should not be used without examining a book for difficult conceptual content, difficult figurative language, and stylistic or organizational peculiarities that might cause comprehension problems. In addition, the adult should note a book's content and interest value, since a child may be able to read a book that would otherwise be at his frustration level if he is interested in the subject.

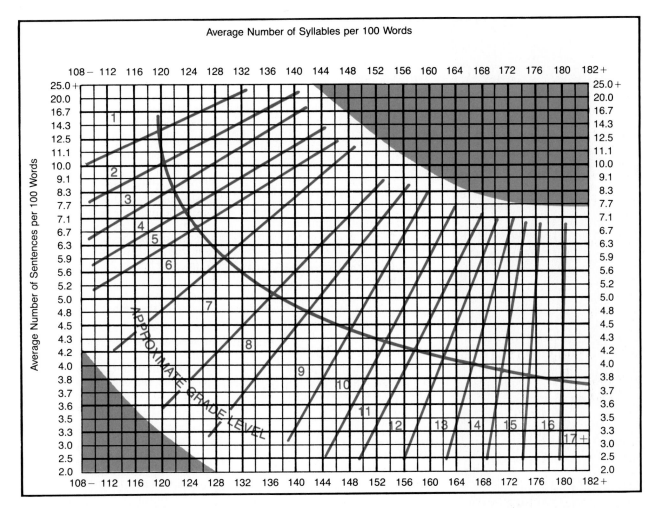

Average Number of Syllables per 100 Words

From Edward Fry, "Fry's Readability Graph: Clarifications, Validity, and Extension." *Journal of Reading* 21 (Dec. 1977): 249. The journal is published by the International Reading Association.

Abelard-Schuman Junior Books
Div. of Harper & Row Pubs., Inc.
10 E. 53rd St.
New York, N.Y. 10022

Abingdon Press
Div. of United Methodist Publishing
House
201 Eighth Ave. S.
Nashville, Tenn. 37202

Addison-Wesley Publishing
Co., Inc.
One Jacob Way
Reading, Mass. 01867

Aladdin Books
Div. of Atheneum Publishers
115 Fifth Ave.
New York, N.Y. 10003

American Library Association (ALA)
50 E. Huron St.
Chicago, Ill. 60611

Atheneum Publishers
Subs. of Scribner Book Cos., Inc.
115 Fifth Ave.
New York, N.Y. 10003

The Atlantic Monthly Press
Div. of The Atlantic Monthly Co.
8 Arlington St.
Boston, Mass. 02116

Avon Books
Div. of The Hearst Corp.
1790 Broadway
New York, N.Y. 10019

Bantam Books Inc.
666 Fifth Ave.
New York, N.Y. 10103

Beginner Books
Div. of Random House, Inc.
201 E. 50th St.
New York, N.Y. 10022

Behrman House Inc.
1261 Broadway
New York, N.Y. 10001

Bobbs-Merrill Co., Inc.
4300 W. 62nd St.
Indianapolis, Ind. 46268

Bradbury Press
Affil. of Macmillan Inc.
866 Third Avenue
New York, N.Y. 10022

Cambridge University Press
32 E. 57th St.
New York, N.Y. 10022

Carolrhoda Books, Inc.
241 First Ave. N.
Minneapolis, Minn. 55401

CBS Educational & Professional
Publishing
Div. of CBS Inc.
383 Madison Ave.
New York, N.Y. 10017

Celestial Arts
Subs. of Ten Speed Press
Box 7327
Berkeley, Calif. 94707

Chelsea House Publishers
Div. of Chelsea House Educational
Communications Inc.
133 Christopher St.
New York, N.Y. 10014

Child Welfare League of America
Inc. (CWLA)
67 Irving Place
New York, N.Y. 10003

Childrens Press
Div. of Regensteiner Publishing
Enterprises, Inc.
1224 W. Van Buren St.
Chicago, Ill. 60607

Clarion Books
Juvenile Div. of Ticknor & Fields
52 Vanderbilt Ave.
New York, N.Y. 10017

William Collins Pubs.
Collins Wm, Sons & Co.
(Canada) Ltd.
100 Lesmill Rd.
Don Mills, Ont. M3B 2T5 Canada

Copp Clark Pitman
495 Wellington St. W.
Toronto, Ont. M5V 1E9 Canada

Coward, McCann & Geog-
hegan, Inc.
Member of the Putnam Publishing
Group
200 Madison Ave.
New York, N.Y. 10016

Creative Education Inc.
Box 227
123 S. Broad St.
Mankato, Minn. 56001

Crowell-Collier Press
Macmillan Publishing Co., Inc.
Div. of Macmillan, Inc.
866 Third Ave.
New York, N.Y. 10022

Crowell Junior Books
10 E. 53rd St.
New York, N.Y. 10022

Thomas Y. Crowell Co.
Div. of Harper & Row Pub, Inc.
10 E. 53rd St.
New York, N.Y. 10022

Crown Publishers, Inc.
225 Park Ave. S.
New York, N.Y. 10003

Delacorte Press
One Dag Hammarskjold Plaza
New York, N.Y. 10017

Dell Publishing Co., Inc.
Subs. of Doubleday & Co., Inc.
One Dag Hammarskjold Plaza
New York, N.Y. 10017

Deutsch, Andre
E. P. Dutton, Inc.
2 Park Ave.
New York, N.Y. 10016

Dial Books for Young Readers
Div. of E. P. Dutton
2 Park Ave.
New York, N.Y. 10016

Dillon Press, Inc.
242 Portland Ave. S.
Minneapolis, Minn. 55415

Dodd, Mead & Co.
Subs. of Thomas Nelson
79 Madison Ave.
New York, N.Y. 10016

Douglas & McIntyre Ltd.
1615 Venables Street
Vancouver, British Columbia
V5L 2H1 Canada

Doubleday & Co., Inc.
245 Park Ave.
New York, N.Y. 10167

E. P. Dutton
Div. of New American Library
2 Park Ave.
New York, N.Y. 10016

Wm B. Eerdmans Publishing Co.
255 Jefferson Ave SE
Grand Rapids, Mich. 49503

Elsevier-Dutton
Div. of E. P. Dutton, Inc.
2 Park Ave.
New York, N.Y. 10016

Elsevier/Nelson Books
52 Vanderbilt Ave.
New York, N.Y. 10017

M. Evans & Co. Inc.
216 E. 49 St.
New York, N.Y. 10017

Faber & Faber, Inc.
Div. of Faber & Faber
Publishers Ltd.
50 Cross Street
Winchester, Mass. 01890

Farrar, Straus & Giroux, Inc.
19 Union Sq. W.
New York, N.Y. 10003

The Feminist Press
Box 311
New York, N.Y. 10128

Follet Publishing Co.
Div. of Follett Corp.
1010 W. Washington Blvd.
Chicago, Ill. 60607

Four Winds Press
50 W. 44th St.
New York, N.Y. 10036

Funk & Wagnalls, Inc.
53 E. 77th St.
New York, N.Y. 10021

Garland Publishing, Inc.
136 Madison Ave.
New York, N.Y. 10016

Garrard Publishing Co.
1607 N. Market St.
Champaign, Ill. 61820

David R. Godine, Publisher, Inc.
306 Dartmouth St.
Boston, Mass. 02116

Golden Books
Div. of Western Publishing Co.
850 Third Ave.
New York, N.Y. 10022

The Golden Quill Press
Subs. of Audio Amateur
Publications
Avery Rd
Francestown, N.H. 03043

Greenwillow Books
Div. of William Morrow & Co., Inc.
105 Madison Ave.
New York, N.Y. 10016

Grosset & Dunlap
Member of The Putnam Publishing
Group
200 Madison Ave.
New York, N.Y. 10016

Harcourt Brace Jovanovich, Inc.
1250 Sixth Ave.
San Diego, Calif. 92101

Harmony Books
Div. of Crown Publishers, Inc.
225 Park Ave. S.
New York, N.Y. 10003

Harper & Row Publishers, Inc.
10 E. 53rd St.
New York, N.Y. 10022

Hastings House, Publishers, Inc.
10 E. 40th St.
New York, N.Y. 10016

Hawthorn Books, Inc.
Div. of E. P. Dutton
2 Park Ave.
New York, N.Y. 10016

Hill & Wang
Div. of Farrar, Straus & Giroux, Inc.
19 Union Sq., W.
New York, N.Y. 10003

Holiday House, Inc.
18 E. 53rd St.
New York, N.Y. 10022

Holt, Rinehart & Winston
A Unit of CBS Educational and
Professional Publishing
521 Fifth Ave., 6th fl.
New York, N.Y. 10175

The Horn Book Inc.
31 St. James Ave.
Boston, Mass. 02116

Houghton Mifflin Co.
One Beacon St.
Boston, Mass. 02108

Houghton Mifflin/Clarion Books
Houghton Mifflin Co.
One Beacon St.
Boston, Mass. 02108

Hudson Hills Press, Inc.
220 Fifth Ave.
Suite 301
New York, N.Y. 10001

Human Sciences Press, Inc.
72 Fifth Ave.
New York, N.Y. 10011

International Reading Association
(IRA)
800 Barksdale Rd.
Newark, Del. 19714

Jalmar Press Inc.
Subs of B L Winch & Associates
45 Hitching Post Dr., Bldg. 2
Rolling Hills Estates, Calif. 90274

Jewish Publication Society
1930 Chestnut Street
Philadelphia, Pa. 19103

Alfred A. Knopf, Inc.
Subs. of Random House, Inc.
201 E. 50th St.
New York, N.Y. 10022

Larousse & Co., Inc.
Affiliate of Librairie Larousse
    USA, Inc.
572 Fifth Ave.
New York, N.Y. 10036

Lerner Publications Co.
241 First Ave. N.
Minneapolis, Minn. 55401

J. B. Lippincott Co.
Subs. of Harper & Row,
    Publishers, Inc.
E. Washington Sq.
Philadelphia, Pa. 19105

Little, Brown & Co. Inc.
34 Beacon St.
Boston, Mass. 02106

Lodestar Publishing
Div. of E. P. Dutton
2 Park Ave.
New York, N.Y. 10016

Lothrop, Lee & Shepard Books
Div. of William Morrow & Co., Inc.
105 Madison Ave.
New York, N.Y. 10016

McClelland & Stewart Ltd.
25 Hollinger Rd.
Toronto, Ont. M4B 3G2 Canada

McGraw-Hill Book Co.
Div. of McGraw-Hill, Inc.
1221 Avenue of the Americas
New York, N.Y. 10020

Macmillan Publishing Co.
Div. of Macmillan, Inc.
866 Third Ave.
New York, N.Y. 10022

Mayflower Books
W. H. Smith Publishers, Inc.
Subs. of W. H. Smith & Son, Ltd.
112 Madison Ave.
New York, N.Y. 10016

Julian Messner, Inc.
Div. of Simon & Schuster
Simon & Schuster Bldg.
1230 Avenue of the Americas
New York, N.Y. 10020

Methuen, Inc.
Subs. of Associated Book
    Publishers Ltd. (UK)
29 W 35th St.
New York, N.Y. 10001

William Morrow & Co., Inc.
Subs. of the Hearst Corp.
105 Madison Ave.
New York, N.Y. 10016

Thomas Nelson Inc.
Nelson Place at Elm Hill Pike
Nashville, Tenn. 37214

The New American Library, Inc.
1633 Broadway
New York, N.Y. 10019

Oxford University Press, Inc.
200 Madison Ave.
New York, N.Y. 10016

Pantheon Books, Inc.
Div. of Random House, Inc.
201 E. 50th St.
New York, N.Y. 10022

Parents Magazine Press
Div. of Gruner & Jahr USA,
    Publishing
685 Third Ave.
New York, N.Y. 10017

Parnassus Press
Div. of Houghton Mifflin Co.
One Beacon St.
Boston, Mass. 02108

Penguin Books
Div. of Viking Penguin, Inc.
40 W. 23 St.
New York, N.Y. 10010

S. G. Phillips, Inc.
P.O. Box 83
Chatham, N.Y. 12037

Philomel Books
Member of The Putnam Publishing
    Group
51 Madison Ave.
New York, N.Y. 10010

Platt & Munk Publishers
Div. of Grosset & Dunlap
200 Madison Ave.
New York, N.Y. 10016

Plays, Inc.
120 Boylston St.
Boston, Mass. 02116

Prentice-Hall, Inc.
Englewood Cliffs, N.J. 07632

Price/Stern/Sloan Publishers, Inc.
410 N. LaCienega Blvd.
Los Angeles, Calif. 90048

G. P. Putnam's Sons
Member of The Putnam Publishing
    Group
51 Madison Ave.
New York, N.Y. 10010

Raintree Publishers Inc.
330 E. Kilbourn Ave.
Milwaukee, Wis. 53202

Rand McNally & Co.
8255 Central Park Ave.
Skokie, Ill. 60076

Random House, Inc.
201 E. 50th St.
New York, N.Y. 10022

Schocken Books, Inc.
62 Cooper Sq.
New York, N.Y. 10003

Scholastic Inc.
730 Broadway
New York, N.Y. 10003

Charles Scribner's Sons
Div. of The Scribner Book
    Cos., Inc.
115 Fifth Ave.
New York, N.Y. 10003

The Seabury Press, Inc.
Div. of Winston Press, Inc.
600 First Ave.
Minneapolis, Minn. 55403

Simon & Schuster
The Simon & Schuster Bldg.
1230 Avenue of the Americas
New York, N.Y. 10020

Stemmer House Publishers, Inc.
2627 Caves Rd.
Owings Mills, Md. 21117

Time-Life Books, Inc.
Subs. of Time, Inc.
Alexandria, Va. 22314

Totem Books
Div. of Collins Publishers
100 Lesmill Rd.
Don Mills, Ont. M3B 2T5 Canada

Tree Frog Press
10144 89 St.
Edmonton, Alberta T5H 1P7
    Canada

Troll Associates
320 Route 17
Mahwah, N.J. 07430

Charles E. Tuttle Co. Inc.
28 S. Main St.
Rutland, Vt. 05701

Unicorn Books
Div. of E. P. Dutton
2 Park Ave.
New York, N.Y. 10016

Vanguard Press, Inc.
424 Madison Ave.
New York, N.Y. 10017

Viking Penguin, Inc.
40 W 23rd St.
New York, N.Y. 10010

Walck, Henry Z., Inc.
Div. of David McKay Co., Inc.
2 Park Ave.
New York, N.Y. 10016

Walker & Co.
Div. of Walker Publishing Co., Inc.
720 Fifth Ave.
New York, N.Y. 10019

Wanderer Books
Div. of Simon & Schuster
The Simon & Schuster Bldg.
1230 Avenue of the Americas
New York, N.Y. 10020

Frederick Warne & Co., Inc.
40 W 23rd St.
New York, N.Y. 10010

Franklin Watts, Inc.
Subs. of Grolier, Inc.
387 Park Ave. S.
New York, N.Y. 10016

Western Publishing Co., Inc.
1220 Mound Ave
Racine, Wis. 53404

The Westminster Press
Publications Unit of The
   Presbyterian Church (U.S.A.)
925 Chestnut St.
Philadelphia, Pa. 19107

Albert Whitman & Co.
5747 W. Howard St.
Niles, Ill. 60648

Windmill Books, Inc.
Div. Simon & Schuster
The Simon & Schuster Bldg.
1230 Avenue of the Americas
New York, N.Y. 10020

Winston Press Inc.
A Unit of CBS Educational &
   Professional Publishing
600 First Ave.
Minneapolis, Minn. 55403

Alan Wofsy Fine Arts
401 China Basin St.
San Francisco, Calif., 94107

AUTHOR, ILLUSTRATOR, TITLE INDEX

Illustrations are indicated by italic. The color insert appears between pages 120–121.

1850–
1890
	Childhood Seen as an Adventure, Not a Training Ground for Adulthood
	Fantasy and Nonsense
	    Edward Lear's *A Book of Nonsense* (1846)
	    Lewis Carroll's *Alice's Adventures in Wonderland* (1865)
	Adventure
	    Jules Verne's *Twenty-Thousand Leagues Under the Sea* (1869)
	    Robert Louis Stevenson's *Treasure Island* (1883)
	    Howard Pyle's *The Merry Adventures of Robin Hood* (1883)
	Real People
	    Margaret Sidney's *The Five Little Peppers and How They Grew* (1880)
	    Louisa May Alcott's *Little Women* (1868)
	    Johanna Spyri's *Heidi* (1884)
	    Mark Twain's *The Adventures of Huckleberry Finn* (1884)

1900	**Great Animal Fantasy** Beatrix Potter's *The Tale of Peter Rabbit* (1901) Rudyard Kipling's *The Just So Stories* (1902) Kenneth Grahame's *The Wind in the Willows* (1908)

1922	**The Newbery Medal First Awarded to an Outstanding Author of Children's Literature**
	Willem Van Loon's *The Story of Mankind*
	Honor Books:
	    Charles Hawes's *The Great Quest*
	    Bernard Marshall's *Cedric the Forester*
	    William Bowen's *The Old Tobacco Shop*
	    Padraic Colum's *The Golden Fleece and the Heroes Who Lived Before Achilles*
	    Cornelia Meigs's *Windy Hill*

1924	**The *Horn Book Magazine* First Published**

1938	**The first Caldecott Medal was presented to the illustrator of the most distinguished picture book published in the United States**
	Animals of the Bible by Helen Dean Fish, ill. by Dorothy P. Lathrop
	Honor Books:
	    Seven Simeon: A Russian Tale by Boris Artzybasheff
	    Four and Twenty Blackbirds: Nursery Rhymes of Yesterday Recalled for Children of To-Day by Helen Dean Fish, ill. by Robert Lawson